MA

THE
DICT
OF LAW

Visit *The Longman Dictionary of Law,*
Seventh Edition Companion Website at
www.pearsoned.co.uk/curzon to
find regular updates including new
definitions and references

We work with leading authors to develop the
strongest educational materials in law,
bringing cutting-edge thinking and best learning
practice to a global market

Under a range of well-known imprints, including
Longman, we craft high quality print and
electronic publications which help readers to
understand and apply their content,
whether studying or at work

To find out more about the complete range of our
publishing, please visit us on the World Wide Web at:
www.pearsoned.co.uk

THE LONGMAN

DICTIONARY OF LAW

Seventh Edition

L. B. Curzon

Barrister

P. H. Richards

Head of Law School, University of Huddersfield

PEARSON
Longman

Harlow, England • London • New York • Boston • San Francisco • Toronto
Sydney • Tokyo • Singapore • Hong Kong • Seoul • Taipei • New Delhi
Cape Town • Madrid • Mexico City • Amsterdam • Munich • Paris • Milan

Pearson Education Limited
Edinburgh Gate
Harlow
Essex CM20 2JE
England

and Associated Companies throughout the world

Visit us on the World Wide Web at:
www.pearsoned.co.uk

First published 1979
Seventh edition published 2007

© MacDonald Evans 1979, 1983
© Longman Group UK Limited 1988, 1993
© Financial Times Professional Limited 1998
© Pearson Education Limited 2002, 2007

The rights of L. B. Curzon and Paul H. Richards to be identified as
authors of this work has been asserted by them in accordance
with the Copyright, Designs and Patents Act 1988.

ISBN 978-0-582-89426-6

British Library Cataloguing-in-Publication Data
A catalogue record for this book is available from the British Library

Library of Congress Cataloging-in-Publication Data
Curzon, L. B. (Leslie Basil)
  Longman dictionary of law / L. B. Curzon, P. Richards.
    p. cm.
  Rev. ed. of: Dictionary of law / L. B. Curzon. 6th ed. 2002.
  ISBN 978-0- ⌐ ¬
    1. Law—   ⌐ nology.
  I. Richards, P   **MIDDLESBROUGH LIBRARIES**
  III. Title.   **AND INFORMATION**

  KD313.C87 2
  349.4103—d⌐
)53256

            0081459416

      Bertrams   **25.11.07**

      349.4203   **£11.99**
  The publish   *ts.*

Dedication

In Memory of Leslie B. Curzon

I have known Leslie Curzon since 1983, when he became my mentor after I completed my PCLL at the University of Hong Kong and was called to the Bar. Over the years I was amazed by the breadth and depth of Leslie's knowledge of the law. He not only had expertise in the law but also an extensive understanding of so many other fields and was both generous with his time and knowledge – he was a true polymath. I made use of his Dictionary of Law throughout my years in practice in Hong Kong. When I returned to the UK and was employed by the Chancellor's department as an Immigration Judge, Leslie again became my mentor and we often discussed particular terms in the dictionary as they applied to Immigration Law. He enjoyed the opportunity to explain the terms in the pragmatic manner which underlies the success of his dictionary. Leslie was greatly interested in the developing area of Immigration Law and how it was influencing other areas of the law. He was always able to adapt to those changing circumstances in the law and his Dictionary of Law is a testimony to this.

Margaret Austin
Immigration Judge

Preface

In 2005 I was approached by Rebekah Taylor of Pearson Longman about taking on the writing of a dictionary of law. She explained to me that the book was already in publication but a new edition was required. My immediate reaction was one of misgiving since a dictionary can take one into all sorts of unfamiliar places as far as the law is concerned and I was not convinced that I wanted to venture into such dark and hazardous places. My anxiety rose by a factor of ten when, on asking who had written the original work, Rebekah replied, 'Leslie Curzon'. I heard of and used Leslie's books when I first started studying Law in 1970 and no doubt many law students had also thanked their lucky stars for his excellent texts as a means of passing their examinations. Leslie's knowledge of the law was encyclopaedic as evidenced by the subjects he has published in, ranging from Criminal Law to Jurisprudence and Equity and Trusts to Roman Law and many others in between. His books were no means confined to law and he also wrote on Economics and the theory and practice of teaching itself. It was therefore with some trepidation I agreed to take on the work and spent some weeks looking over the *Dictionary of Law*. My anxiety did not diminish!

During the negotiations regarding the many matters that arise with authorship contracts with publishers I heard that Leslie had died. Leslie's death is a great loss, not just to his family and friends, but also to the legal publishing world and law students alike. His knowledge, clarity of thought and ability to make complex principles and theories of law accessible to students and general readers alike will be sadly missed. His legacy is not just the books that he had written, but also a genre of legal books that were pioneering in that they were orientated towards the student. I hope that I have been able to do justice to this, his *Dictionary of Law*.

In writing this edition I have also taken the liberty of treating some legislative measures that have been delayed by the parliamentary commencement provisions as being enacted and fully in force. Not least amongst these has been the inclusion of the Charities Bill which at the time of writing was in its final stages in the House of Lords. I have therefore been presumptuous and have referred to this as the Charities Act 2006. I have included many of the additions and modifications to the legal vocabulary by various judicial decisions and statutes such as the

Mental Capacity Act 2005, Civil Partnership Act 2004, Carers (Equal Opportunities) Act 2004, Land Registration Act 2002, Child Protection Act 2004, Children Act 2004, Commonhold and Household Reform Act 2002, Proceeds of Crime Act 2002, Consumer Credit Act 2006, Adoption and Children Act 2002, Criminal Justice and Police Act 2001, Social Security Fraud Act 2001 amongst others. I have no doubt that there may be omissions but in the traditional manner of authors I accept full responsibility for these and any errors that may become apparent.

I have debts to pay in the writing of this book, not least to Nisreen Ahmed, who acted as my research assistant in the writing of this work. Without her able help and diligence I doubt whether the book would have been completed. My thanks also go to the staff at Pearson, particularly Rebekah Taylor and Cheryl Cheasley, who have been very patient and understanding in their waiting for the manuscript. I also have to say a big 'thank you' to my two sons Phillip and William. All too often they have to put up with an absentee father due to the pressures that come with managing a busy department and attempting to meet publisher's deadlines. Needless to say I love them both dearly and I wish them both 'old memories and young hopes'.

Paul Richards
March 2007

How to Use the Dictionary

Order of entries

The entries in this dictionary are arranged in *strict alphabetical order.* This may be illustrated by the following example of a series of entries:

privilege
privilege, absolute
privilege, claim of
privileged communication
privileged nature of judicial statements
privileged will
privilege, legal profession
privilege of witness
privilege, parliamentary
privilege, public policy
privilege, qualified

Abbreviations

The following abbreviations are used throughout the text:

art	article
arts	articles
CA	Court of Appeal
CCR	County of Appeal
Chancery D	Chancery Division
chap	chapter
CPR	Civil Procedure Rules
Family D	Family Division
HL	House of Lords
JCPC	Judicial Committee of the Privy Council
JP	Justice of the Peace
LRR	Land Registry Rules
O	Order (as in orders of the Supreme Court)
OED	Oxford English Dictionary

para	paragraph
PD	Practice Directions
QBD	Queen's Bench Division
q.v / qq.v	see
r	rule
rr	rules
RSC	Rules of the Supreme Court
s	section
Sch	Schedule
SI	Statutory Instrument
ss	sections

Abbreviations for Acts of Parliament

The titles of some Acts which are referred to repeatedly are abbreviated in accordance with the list below. In every case the abbreviation is followed by the appropriate date of the Act, thus: Th.A. 1968; E.R.A. 1996.

A.C.A	Adoption and Children Act
Acc J.A.	Access to Justice Act
A.E.A	Administration of Estates Act
A.J.A	Administration of Justice Act
B.Ex.A.	Bills of Exchange Act
B.N.A.	British Nationality Act
C.C.A.	Consumer Credit Act
C.D.A.	Crime and Disorder Act
Ch.A.	Children Act
C.J.A.	Criminal Justice Act
C.J.C.S.A.	Criminal Justice and Court Services Act
C.J.P.A.	Criminal Justice and Police Act
C.J.P.O.A.	Criminal Justice and Public Order Act
C.L.A.	Criminal Law Act
C.L.R.A.	Commonhold and Leasehold Reform Act
C.L.S.A.	Courts and Legal Services Act
Cos.A.	Companies Act
County C.A.	County Courts Act
C.P.A.	Consumer Protection Act
C.P.I.A.	Criminal Procedure and Investigations Act
C.R.W.A.	Countryside and Rights of Way Act
C.S.P.S.S.A.	Child Support, Pensions and Social Services Act
C. & Y.P.A.	Children and Young Persons Act

E.P.A.	Employment Protection Act
E.P.(C.)A.	Employment Protection (Consolidation) Act
En.P.A.	Environmental Protection Act
E.R.A.	Employment Rights Act
F.I.A.	Freedom of Information Act
F.L.A.	Family Law Act
F.L.R.A.	Family Law Reform Act
F.S.A.	Financial Services Act
F.S.M.A.	Financial Services and Markets Act
G.L.A.A.	Greater London Authority Act
H.A.	Housing Act
H. & P.A.	Housing and Planning Act
H.S.W.A.	Health and Safety at Work, etc. Act
I.A.	Interpretation Act
I.C.T.A.	Income and Corporations Taxes Act
Ins.A.	Insolvency Act
J.A.	Judicature Act
L.C.A.	Land Charges Act
L.G.A.	Local Government Act
L.G.H.A.	Local Government Housing Act
L.G.P.L.A.	Local Government Planning and Land Act
Lim.A.	Limitation Act
L.P.A.	Law of Property Act
L.R.A.	Land Registration Act
Mat.C.A.	Matrimonial Causes Act
M.C.A.	Magistrates' Courts Act
M.H.A.	Mental Health Act
O.P.A.	Offences Against the Person Act
P. & A.A.	Perpetuities and Accumulations Act
P.C.C.(S.)A.	Powers of Criminal Courts (Sentencing) Act
P. & C.E.A.	Police and Criminal Evidence Act
P.O.A.	Public Order Act
P.S.I.A.	Private Security Industry Act
R.I.P.A.	Regulation and Investigatory Powers Act
S.C.A.	Supreme Court Act
S.G.A.	Sale of Goods Act
S.L.A.	Settled Land Act
S.O.A.	Sexual Offences Act
S.S.A.	Social Security Act
S.S.F.A.	Social Security Fraud Act
T.C.G.A.	Taxation of Chargeable Gains Act

T.C.P.A.	Town and Country Planning Act
Th.A.	Theft Act
Tr.A.	Trustee Act
T.U.L.R.A.	Trade Union and Labour Relations Act
T.U.L.R.(C.)A.	Trade Union and Labour Relations Consolidation Act
T.U.R.E.R.A.	Trade Union Reform and Employment Rights Act
V.(C.)A.	Vehicles (Crime) Act
W.A.	Wills Act
W.R.P.A.	Welfare Reform and Pensions Act
Y.J.C.E.A.	Youth Justice and Criminal Evidence Act

Cross references

Cross reference is achieved by the use of the abbreviation q.v., which appears in brackets following words that are explained elsewhere, and by words in small capital letters which stand at the conclusion of the particular entry. Thus, consider the following entry:

> **life estate.** An estate for the life of the tenant (e.g., by express limitation, such as a grant 'to X for life' or by operation of law, or *autre vie* (q.v.)). See ESTATE.

After studying the entry above, further reference ought to be made to *autre vie* and, finally, estate.

Legal references

Many entries contain references to cases, statutes, statutory instruments, Law Commission Reports, etc. They have been included for those who wish to make an intensive study of the subject matter of the entries.

Abbreviated titles of law reports and journals

Abbreviation	Reports/journal title	Date
Abr Ca Eq	Equity Cases Abridged	1667–1744
AC	Appeal Cases	1891 to present
Ad & E	Adolphus & Ellis	1834–40
A & E	Adolphus & Ellis	1834–40
ALJ	Australian Law Journal	1927 to present
All ER	All England Law Reports	1936 to present

Abbreviation	*Reports/journal title*	*Date*
App Cas	Appeal Cases	1875–90
Atk	Atkyns	1736–55
B	Beavan	1838–66
B & A	Barnewall & Alderson	1817–22
B & Ad	Barnewall & Adolphus	1830–4
Bank LR	Banking Law Reports	1991 to present
Barn	Barnardiston	1726–34
Barn & Adol	Barnewall & Adolphus	1830–4
Barn & Ald	Barnewall & Alderson	1817–22
Barnard	Barnardiston	1726–34
Barn & Cress	Barnewall & Cresswell	1822–30
BC	British Columbia Law Reports	1867–1947
B & C	Barnewall & Cresswell	1822–30
BCC	Brown's Chancery Cases	1778–94
BCLC	Butterworth's Company Law Cases	1978 to present
B & CR	Bankruptcy and Companies Cases	1918–41
Beav	Beavan	1838–66
Bell	Bell	1842–50
Benl	Benloe	1530–1627
Bing	Bingham	1822–34
Bing NC	Bingham, New Cases	1834–40
Blackst	Blackstone	1746–80
Bli	Bligh	1819–21
Bli NS	Bligh, New Series	1826–37
B NC	Bingham, New Cases	1834–40
BPC	Brown's Parliamentary Cases	1702–1801
BPIC	Bankruptcy and Personal Insolvency Cases	1955 to present
BPIR	Bankruptcy and Personal Insolvency Reports	1996 to present
Brac	Bracton's Note Book	1217–40
Brod & B	Broderip & Bingham	1819–22
B & S	Best & Smith	1861–70
BTR	British Tax Review	1956 to present
Bulstr	Bulstrode	1610–38
Burr	Burrow	1756–72
BWCC	Butterworth's Workmen's Compensation Cases	1908–50
Can LR	Canadian Law Review	1901–7

Abbreviation	*Reports/journal title*	*Date*
Car & P	Carrington & Payne	1823–41
Cas Eq Abr	Equity Cases Abridged	1667–1744
CB	Common Bench	1845–56
CB NS	Common Bench, New Series	1856–65
CCC	Cox's Criminal Cases	1844–1941
CC Chron	County Courts Chronicle	1848–59
CCC Sess Pap	Central Criminal Court Session Papers	1834–1913
CCR	Crown Cases Reserved	1865–75
C & F	Clark & Finnelly	1831–46
Ch	Chancery	1891 to present
Ch App	Chancery Appeal Cases	1865–75
Ch D	Chancery Division	1875–90
C & K	Carrington & Kirwan	1843–53
Cl & F	Clark & Finnelly	1831–46
CLC	Commercial Law Cases	1952 to present
CLJ	Cambridge Law Journal	1921 to present
CLR	Commonwealth Law Reports	1903 to present
CLY	Current Law Year Book	1947 to present
C & M	Crompton & Meeson	1832–4
CMLR	Common Market Law Reports	1962 to present
Co	Coke	1572–1616
COD	Crown Office Digest	1988 to present
Com	Comyns	1695–1740
Com Cas	Commercial Cases	1895–1941
Com LR	Common Law Reports	1853–5
Const LJ	Construction Law Journal	1971 to present
Conv NS	Conveyancer & Property Law, New Series	1936 to present
Co Rep	Coke	1572–1616
Cox CC	Cox's Criminal Cases	1843–1941
Cox Cty CC	Cox's County Court Cases	1860–1919
C & P	Carrington & Payne	1823–41
C & R	Clifford & Rickards	1873–84
Cr App R	Criminal Appeal Reports	1908 to present
Crim LR	Criminal Law Review	1954 to present
Cro Car	Croke	1625–41
Cro Eliz	Croke	1582–1603
Cro Jac	Croke	1603–25

Abbreviation	*Reports/journal title*	*Date*
Cromp & M	Crompton & Meeson	1832–4
Curt	Curteis	1834–44
D & B	Dearsly & Bell	1856–8
D & Ch	Deacon & Chitty	1832–5
D & E	Durnford & East's Reports	1785–1800
DLR	Dominion Law Reports	1912 to present
DM & J	De Gex, MacNaghten & Gordon	1851–7
Doug	Douglas	1778–85
Dunn	Dunning	1753–4
Durn & E	Durnford & East's Reports	1785–1800
E	East's Term Reports	1800–12
EAT	Employment Appeals Tribunal Reports	1975 to present
E & B	Ellis & Blackburn	1851–8
E & E	Ellis & Ellis	1858–61
Ed CR	Education Case Reports	1998 to present
EG	Estates Gazette	1858 to present
EGCS	Estates Gazette Case Summaries	1998 to present
EGLR	Estates Gazette Law Reports	1994 to present
EMLR	Entertainment and Media Law Reports	1993 to present
Env LR	Environmental Law Reports	1999 to present
Eq	Equity Cases	1866–75
Eq Cas	Equity Modern Reports	1722–55
Esp	Espinasse	1793–1807
Eu LR	European Law Reports	1997 to present
Ex	Exchequer Reports	1847–56
Ex	Exchequer Cases	1865–75
Exch Rep	Exchequer Reports	1847–56
Ex D	Exchequer Division	1875–80
Fam	Family Division	1972 to present
Fam Law	Family Law	1971 to present
F & F	Foster & Finlayson	1856–67
FCR	Family Court Reports	1985 to present
FLR	Family Law Reports	1977 to present
For	Forrester's Chancery Reports	1735–8
Fost & Fin	Foster & Finlayson	1856–67
FSR	Fleet Street Patent Law Reports	1963 to present
Gal & Dav	Gale & Davison	1841–3

Abbreviation	Reports/journal title	Date
Giff	Gifford	1857–65
Gl & J	Glyn & Jameson	1819–28
Godb	Godbolt	1575–1638
H	Hare	1841–53
Hale Prec	Hale's Precedents	1475–1640
Hare	Hare	1841–53
H & C	Hurlstone & Coltman	1862–6
HL	House of Lords Appeals	1866–75
HL Cas	House of Lords Cases	1847–66
H & M	Hemming & Miller	1862–5
H & N	Hurlstone & Norman	1856–62
Hodg	Hodges	1835–7
Ho Lords C	House of Lords Cases	1847–66
Horn & H	Horn & Hurlstone	1838–9
Hurl and Nor	Hurlstone & Norman	1856–62
H & W	Harrison & Wollaston	1835–6
ICR	Industrial Cases Reports	1972 to present
IJ	Irish Jurist	1935 to present
ILJ	Industrial Law Journal	1972 to present
ILPR	Insolvency Law and Practice Reports	1985 to present
ILR	International Law Reports	1950 to present
Imm AR	Immigration Appeals Report	1970 to present
IR	Irish Reports	1838 to present
IRLR	Industrial Relations Law Reports	1972 to present
Ir LT	Irish Law Times	1867 to present
ITCLR	IT and Communications Law Reports	1997 to present
ITR	Industrial Tribunal Reports	1966 to present
Jac & W	Jacob & Walker	1819–20
Jenk Cent	Jenkins' Reports	1220–1623
JPN	Justice of the Peace & Local Government Reports	1837 to present
JPL	Journal of Planning Law	1948 to present
Jur	Jurist Reports	1837–54
Jur NS	Jurist Reports, New Series	1855–66
K	Kenyon	1753–9
KB (or QB)	King's or Queen's Bench	1841 to present
Keb	Keble	1661–79

Abbreviation	*Reports/journal title*	*Date*
Keny	Kenyon	1753–9
K & J	Kay & Johnson	1854–8
Ld Ken	Kenyon	1753–9
Ld Ray	Raymond	1694–1732
Lew	Lewin	1822–38
LGR	Local Government Reports	1903 to present
LJ Adm	Law Journal Reports, Admiralty	1866–75
LJ Bk	Law Journal Reports, Bankruptcy	1832–80
LJ Ch	Law Journal Reports, Chancery	1822–1946
LJ CP	Law Journal Reports, Common Pleas	1822–80
LJ Ecc	Law Journal Reports, Ecclesiastical	1865–75
LJ KB (QB)	Law Journal Reports, King's (Queen's) Bench	1831–1946
LJ OS	Law Journal Reports, Old Series	1822–31
LJ PC	Law Journal Reports, Privy Council	1865–1946
LJ PD & A	Law Journal Reports, Probate Divorce & Admiralty	1876–1946
LJ P & M	Law Journal Reports Probate & Matrimonial	1858–75
Ll LR	Lloyd's List Law Reports	1919–50
Lloyd's Rep	Lloyd's List Law Reports	1951 to present
Lofft	Lofft's Reports	1772–4
LQR	Law Quarterly Review	1885 to present
LR	Law Reports	1865 to present
LR A & E	Law Reports, Admiralty & Ecclesiastical Cases	1865–75
LR CCR	Law Reports, Crown Cases Reserved	1865–75
LR Ch App	Law Reports, Chancery Appeal Cases	1865–75
LR CP	Law Reports, Common Pleas Cases	1865–75
LR Eq	Law Reports, Equity Cases	1865–75
LR Ex	Law Reports, Exchequer Cases	1865–75
LR HL	Law Reports, House of Lords	1865–75
LR PC	Law Reports, Privy Council Appeals	1865–75
LR P & D	Law Reports, Probate & Divorce Cases	1865–75

Abbreviation	Reports/journal title	Date
LR QB	Law Reports, Queen's Bench	1865–75
LR RP	Law Reports, Restrictive Practices Cases	1958 to present
LS Gaz	Law Society Gazette	1903 to present
LT	Law Times Reports	1859–1947
Lush	Lushington	1859–62
Madd	Maddock	1815–22
Mau & S	Maule & Selwyn	1813–17
Med LR	Medical Law Reports	1989 to present
M & C	Mylne & Craig	1835–41
M & G	Manning & Granger	1840–4
M & K	Mylne & Keen	1832–5
MLR	Modern Law Review	1937 to present
Mod Cas	Modern Cases	1702–45
Mod Rep	Modern Reports	1669–1755
Moo	Moody	1824–44
Moo	Moore	1817–27
Moo CC	Moody	1824–44
Moo & P	Moody & Payne	1827–31
Moo PC	Moore	1836–62
Morr	Morrell	1884–93
M & P	Moore & Payne	1827–31
M & S	Maule & Selwyn	1813–17
M & W	Meeson & Welsby	1836–47
Myl & Cr	Mylne & Craig	1835–41
Myl & K	Mylne & Keen	1832–5
Nev & M	Neville & Manning	1832–6
New Rep	New Reports	1862–5
NLJ	New Law Journal	1965 to present
N & McN	Neville & MacNamara	1855–1928
Not Cas	Thornton's Notes of Cases	1841–50
NPC	New Property Cases	1986 to present
NR	New Reports	1862–5
NSWLR	New South Wales Law Reports	1880–1900
NSWSR	New South Wales State Reports	1901 to present
NZLR	New Zealand Law Reports	1883 to present
P	Probate	1891–1971
P & CR	Planning & Compensation Reports	1949 to present
PD	Probate Division	1875–90

Abbreviation	*Reports/journal title*	*Date*
P D & A	Probate, Divorce & Admiralty	1875–90
Pea	Peake	1790–4
Per & D	Perry & Davison	1838–41
Phil Ecc R	Phillimore's Reports	1809–21
PIQR	Personal Injuries and Quantum Reports	1992 to present
Pl	Plowden's Commentaries	1550–80
PLR	Planning Law Reports	1988 to present
Pr	Price	1814–24
QB (or KB)	Queen's or King's Bench	1841 to present
QBD	Queen's Bench Division	1875–90
Qd R	Queensland Law Reports	1958 to present
Rep	Coke	1572–1616
RHC	Road Haulage Cases	1950 to present
R & IT	Rating & Income Tax Reports	1924–60
Rom	Romilly's Notes on Cases	1767–87
RPC	Reports of Patents Cases	1884 to present
RTR	Road Traffic Reports	1970 to present
Russ	Russell	1823–9
Russ & M	Russell & Mylne	1829–31
Russ & R	Russell & Ryan	1799–1824
R & VR	Rating & Valuation Reports	1960 to present
Ry & M	Ryan & Moody	1823–6
Salk	Salkeld	1689–1712
SALR	South African Law Reports	1948 to present
SASR	South Australian State Reports	1921 to present
SC	Session Cases	1906 to present
Sc	Scott	1834–40
SCC	Select Cases in Chancery	1724–33
Scot Jur	Scottish Jurist	1829–73
Sim	Simons	1826–52
SJ	Solicitor's Journal	1857 to present
SLT	Scots Law Times	1893 to present
Sol	The Solicitor	1934 to present
S & S	Simons & Stuart	1822–6
STC	Simons' Tax Cases	1972 to present
St Tr	State Trials	1163–1820
St Tr NS	State Trials, New Series	1820–58
Swan	Swanston	1818–19

Abbreviation	*Reports/journal title*	*Date*
Tal	Talbot's Cases in Equity	1733–8
Taun	Taunton	1807–19
TC	Tax Cases	1875 to present
TLR	Times Law Reports	1884 to present
Tot	Tothill	1559–1646
TR	Taxation Reports	1939 to present
TR	Term Reports	1785–1800
Tyr	Tyrwhitt	1830–5
UKCLR	UK Competition Law Reports	1980 to present
VATTR	Value Added Tax Tribunal Reports	1973 to present
Ves & B	Vesey & Beames	1812–14
Ves Jr	Vesey Junior	1789–1817
Ves Sen	Vesey Senior	1747–56
VLR	Victoria Law Reports	1875 to present
W Bl	Blackstone	1746–80
Wilm	Wilmot's Case Notes	1757–70
WLR	Weekly Law Reports	1953 to present
Wm Bl	Blackstone	1746–80
WN	Weekly Notes	1866–1952
WR	Weekly Reporter	1853–1906
W & W	Wyatt & Webb	1861–3
Y & C	Younge & Collyer	1834–43

A

Aarhus Convention. Convention on Access to Information, Public Participation in Decision-Making and Access to Justice in Environmental Matters, signed at Aarhus on 25 June 1998. See F.I.A. 2000, s 74(1).

abandonment. 1. Surrender or relinquishing of a chattel, right or claim, with the intention of not reclaiming it. 2. A claim (q.v.) is considered abandoned when a notice of discontinuance is served: see CPR, r 38.1(2). 3. In the case of a constructive total loss (q.v.) in marine insurance, the assured may abandon the subject matter to the insurer and treat the loss as if it were an actual total loss, after giving notice of abandonment. See Marine Insurance Act 1906, s 61. 4. Abandonment of a child means leaving it to its fate: *Watson* v *Nikolaisen* [1955] 2 QB 286. 5. Cessation of activities concerning use of land with no intention of their being resumed at any particular time: see *Pioneer Aggregates* v *Secretary of State for the Environment* [1984] 2 All ER 731; *Hughes* v *Secretary of State for the Environment* (2000) *The Times*, 18 February (objective test); T.C.P.A. 1971, s 33(1).

abatement. 1. Termination, decline, reduction. 2. Abatement of debts refers to proportionate reduction of payments where a fund cannot meet claims. 3. Abatement of legacies (q.v.) refers to receipt by legatees of only a fraction, or none, of their legacies when assets are insufficient to pay legacies in full. Pecuniary or general legacies abate proportionately before specific legacies. 4. Abatement of nuisances (q.v.) refers to their removal. Abatement notices may be served by a local authority in respect of a statutory nuisance: En.P.A. 1990, s 80(1); *Lowe* v *S. Somerset DC* [1997] EGCS 113; *R* v *Knightsbridge Crown Court ex p Cataldi* [1999] Env LR 62; *Hewlings* v *McLean Homes Ltd* (2000) *The Times*, 31 August (service of notice under s 160).

abdication. Voluntary renunciation of an office. See Declaration of Abdication Act 1936 (concerning Edward VIII).

abduction. Wrongful leading away of a person, usually involving fraud or force. It is an offence under S.O.A. 1956, s 20, to abduct an unmarried girl under 16 from her parent or guardian. See *R* v *Tegerdine* (1982) 75 Cr App R 298.

abduction, child. It is an offence for a person 'connected with a child under 16' (e.g., parent or guardian) to take or send the child out of the UK 'without the appropriate consent': Child Abduction Act 1984, s 1, as amended by Family Law Act 1986, s 65; *R* v *Dean* [2000] 2 Cr App R(S) 253; *R* v *Nelmes* (2001) *The Times*, 6 February (attempted abduction sentence). For the offence of abduction of a child by other persons, see s 2. See also Child Abduction and Custody Act 1985, as amended by Family Law Act 1986, s 67 (providing a civil procedure for securing the return of children taken abroad without permission); Ch.A. 1989, s 49 (abduction of child in care). See *Re W (Abduction: Father's Rights)* [1999] Fam 1; *Re M (Abduction)* [2000] 1 FLR 930; *Foster* v *DPP* (2005) *The Times*, 5 January.

abduction, child, Hague Convention and. Under Hague Convention 1980, contracting states must seek to secure prompt return of children wrongfully removed to, or retained in, any of those states. For refusal to order return (see art 13(b)), see *Re T (Minors) (Abduction: Custody Rights)* (2000) *The Times*, 24 April (matters to be considered after child's objection to return included: why child objected; child's age and degree of maturity; whether it was appropriate to take account of child's views, in light of their strength and validity).

abet. To encourage or assist in the commission of an offence when one is present actively or constructively. *See* ACCESSORY; ACCOMPLICE; AID OR ABET.

abeyance. Inactivity; state of suspension. An estate is in abeyance when there exists no person in whom it can vest.

ab initio. From the beginning. 1. A trespasser *ab initio* is one who, being entitled by law to perform an act, abuses his authority, so that his act becomes wrongful from the very beginning. See *The Six Carpenters' Case* (1610) 8 Rep 146a; *Chic Fashions Ltd v Jones* [1968] 2 QB 299 (in which continuing existence of the doctrine was doubted). 2. A marriage is void *ab initio* if, e.g., either party was under 16 at date of marriage ceremony. See, e.g., *Re Spence* [1990] Ch 652.

ab intestato. From an intestate. 'Succession *ab intestato*' refers to succession to the property of one who has not disposed of it by will. *See* INTESTACY.

abode. A fixed place of residence (q.v.). Usually a question of fact rather than law: *Courtis v Blight* (1862) 31 LJCP 48. 'A man's residence, where he lives with his family and sleeps at night, is always his place of abode in the full sense of that expression': *R v Hammond* (1852) 17 QB 772. See *R v Barnet LBC ex p Shah* [1983] 2 AC 309.

abode in UK, right of. A person has such a right if he is a British citizen or a Commonwealth citizen who immediately before the commencement of B.N.A. 1981 was a Commonwealth citizen having the right of abode in the UK by virtue of Immigration Act 1971, s 2(1)(*d*) and has not ceased to be a Commonwealth citizen in the meanwhile: Immigration Act 1971, s 2, as substituted by B.N.A. 1981, s 39. See Immigration Act 1988, ss 2, 3.

abortion. Separation of a non-viable human foetus (q.v.) from its mother. Under Abortion Act 1967, as amended by Human Fertilisation and Embryology Act 1990, s 37, there is no offence (see O.P.A. 1861, ss 58, 59, Infant Life (Preservation) Act 1929, s 5(1), substituted by 1990 Act, s 37(4)) where a pregnancy is terminated by a registered medical practitioner if two practitioners are of the opinion that the pregnancy has not exceeded its 24th week and that its continuance would involve risk, greater than if the pregnancy were terminated, of injury to the physical or mental health of the pregnant woman or any existing children of the family; or the termination is necessary to prevent grave permanent injury to her physical or mental health; or that the continued pregnancy would involve risk to her life greater than if the pregnancy were terminated; or that there is a substantial risk that if the child were born it would suffer from such physical or mental abnormalities as to be seriously handicapped. For abortion and multiple pregnancies, see 1967 Act, s 5(2), amended by 1990 Act. See *Rance v Mid-Downs HA* [1991] 2 WLR 159; Abortion Regulations 91/499.

abortion, mental incapacity. In *NHS Trust v D* [2004] 1 FLR 1110, it was held that an application to the court was not necessary where there was no doubt as to issues of capacity and best interest; but, where there is doubt, immediate application is essential.

abrogate. To repeal, annul, cancel, abolish (generally by formal action).

abscond. To depart secretly or to hide oneself from the jurisdiction of the court so as to avoid legal process. See Ins.A. 1986, s 358. For hearing of appeal by absconder, see *R v Gooch* [1998] 1 WLR 1100.

absconding by person released on bail. Failure, without reasonable cause, by one who has been released on bail in criminal proceedings, to surrender to custody. An offence under Bail Act 1976, s 6(1). A warrant (q.v.) for his arrest may be issued: s 7(1). See *R v Lubega* (1999) 163 JP 221.

absence. 1. Non-appearance by a party to the hearing of an application: see r 23.11; *Riverpath Properties* v *Brammall* (2000) *The Times*, 16 February. 2. Continuous absence of a spouse for seven years may be a defence to a charge of bigamy. See *R* v *Curgerwen* (1865) 29 JP 820. 3. Absence 'beyond the seas' (q.v.) refers to absence from the UK and those adjacent islands belonging to the Sovereign.

absolute. Without conditions or restrictions, complete, as in 'decree absolute' (q.v.).

absolute assignment. Assignment of the entire interest of a chose in action (q.v.) so that it is transferred unconditionally to the assignee. It includes an assignment by way of mortgage: *Hughes* v *Pump House Hotel Co* [1902] 2 KB 190. See L.P.A. 1925, s 136.

absolute, conditional discharges. 1. Where a court by or before which a person is convicted of an offence (not being an offence the sentence for which is fixed by law or falls to be imposed under ss 109(2), 110(2), 111(2)), is of the opinion, having regard to the circumstances including the nature of the offence and the character of the offender, that it is inexpedient to inflict punishment, the court may make an order discharging him absolutely or, if it thinks fit, discharging him subject to the condition that he commits no offence during a specified period not exceeding three years: P.C.C.(S).A. 2000, s 12. 2. The House of Lords held in *R* v *Longworth* (2006) *The Times*, 1 February, a defendant is not subject to the notification requirements of the Sexual Offenders Act 1997, where conditional discharge order has been made in respect of a conviction for offences contrary to s 1(1)(a) of the Protection of Children Act 1978 and s 160(1) of the Criminal Justice Act 1988. The effect of s 14(1) of the Powers of Criminal Courts (Sentencing) Act 2000 deems there to be no conviction for the purposes of s 1(1)(a) of the Protection of Children Act 1978.

absolute decree. *See* DECREE.

absolute duties. Duties to which there are no corresponding rights (e.g., according to Austin, a subject's duties to the Crown).

absolute liability. *See* STRICT LIABILITY IN CRIMINAL LAW.

absolute privilege. *See* PRIVILEGE, ABSOLUTE.

absolute title. In the case of a freehold (q.v.) registered with absolute title, the registered proprietor has a guaranteed title subject only to, e.g., entries on the register. In the case of a leasehold (q.v.), absolute title guarantees that the registered proprietor is the owner of the lease and that it was validly granted. *See* LAND REGISTRATION.

absolve. To release from some responsibility or obligation.

abstract and epitome of title. Narrative summary, which must be supplied by a landowner to a purchaser under contract of sale, of documents and events affecting title. The abstract states the history of title; the epitome is a schedule of documents going back to the root of title (q.v.). See L.P.A. 1925, s 10.

abstracting electricity. *See* ELECTRICITY, DISHONEST ABSTRACTION OF.

abuse. 1. Words of vituperation, insult, invective. It does not generally amount to defamation (q.v.); *Thorley* v *Kerry* (1812) 4 Taunt 355. See, however, *Lane* v *Holloway* [1968] 1 QB 379. 2. Maltreatment of a person, physically or mentally.

abuse, incorrectly diagnosed, remedy. CA held in *D* v *E Berks Community NHS Trust* [2003] EWCA Civ 1151, that parents and carers of children who had been incorrectly diagnosed as having been subjected to abuse were not owed a common-law duty of care by the professionals responsible for the diagnosis, so that no remedy was available.

abuse of process. Improper use of a legal process for some purpose other than that for which it was designed. For abuse of process in relation to a murder trial, see *Hui Chi-ming* v *R* [1991] 3 WLR 495. See *Grovit* v *Doctor* [1997] 1 WLR 640 (commencing and continuing an action without any intention of bringing it to a conclusion could constitute an abuse of process); *Re Norris* (2000) *The Times*, 25 February (to allow a third party to re-litigate an issue already decided could be an abuse of process); *PD (Crown Court: Abuse of Process)* (2000) *The Times*, 30 May.

ACAS. Advisory, Conciliation and Arbitration Service (q.v.).

acceleration clause. Provision in an agreement for repayment of a loan by instalments whereby if a stated number of instalments is not paid, all outstanding payments become due at once.

acceleration, doctrine of. Where inter-ests in property have been conferred by a testator in succession, e.g., 'to X for life, remainder to Y' and the gift to X is determined before the time envisaged by the testator, Y's interest is accelerated. If it is discovered that, e.g., X cannot take under the will (because he witnessed it), Y's interest becomes immediate. The doctrine does not apply to a contingent gift: *Re Scott* [1975] 2 All ER 1033. See *Re Davies* [1957] 1 WLR 922. For 'accelerated possession' procedure in relation to H.A. 1988, s 19A, see CCR, O 49, rr 6, 6A.

acceptance. 1. Acceptance of an offer to create a contract (i.e., an assent to all the terms of the offer) must be unqualified, and may be by words or conduct. It must generally be communicated to the offeror and must conform with the prescribed or indicated terms of the offer. See *Hyde* v *Wrench* (1840) 3 Beav 334; *Carlill* v *Carbolic Smoke Ball Co* [1893] 1 QB 256; *Bowerman* v *ABTA* (1995) *The Times*, 25 November. Acceptance 'subject to contract' means that the parties intend to be bound only when a formal contract is prepared and signed: *Chillingworth* v *Esche* [1924] 1 Ch 97. 2. Acceptance of goods under S.G.A. 1979, s 35, substituted by Sale and Supply of Goods Act 1994, s 2, is deemed to have taken place when a person indicates to the seller that he has accepted them, or when they have been delivered to him and he does an act in rela-tion to them which is inconsistent with the

seller's ownership, or when he retains them without informing the seller after a reasonable time (involving a reasonable opportunity of examining the goods) that he has rejected them. 3. 'Acceptance' in Th.A. 1968, s 20(2) is a term of art to be defined in the same way as in B.Ex.A. 1882: *R* v *Nanayakkara* [1987] 1 WLR 265. *See* OFFER.

acceptance, conditional. 1. Acceptance of offeror's offer by offeree, subject to a stipulation being met. 2. In relation to a bill of exchange (q.v.), where pay-ment by the acceptor is made subject to a condition. See B.Ex.A. 1882, s 19; *Society of Lloyd's* v *Twinn* (2000) *The Times*, 4 April (acceptance of offer while seeking some indulgence).

acceptance of a bill. Written signature by the drawee of a bill of exchange and the word 'accepted' across the bill: B.Ex.A. 1882, ss 17–19. He thereby undertakes to pay the bill when due. Acceptance *supra protest* (or 'acceptance for honour') is acceptance of a bill when it has been dis-honoured by one who has no interest in the bill so as to safeguard the drawee's good name: B.Ex.A. 1882, ss 65–68. Acceptance may be general or qualified (q.v.). *See* BILL OF EXCHANGE.

acceptance, special. *See* SPECIAL ACCEPTANCE.

access. 1. The existence of opportunity of sexual intercourse between husband and wife. Evidence of impossibility of access may be given to rebut the presumption of legitimacy (q.v.). See Mat.C.A. 1973, s 48. 2. Access orders may be granted to enable persons who desire to carry out work to any land which is reasonably necessary for the preservation of that land to obtain access to neighbouring land to do so: Access to Neighbouring Land Act 1992, s 1. Application for an access order must be made by the issue of a claim to be filed in the court for the district in which the dominant land is situated: CPR, Sch 2; CCR, O 49, r 1(2). The benefit of an access order is treated as personal to the applicant for that order. See *Williams* v *Edwards* [1997] CLYB 561. 3. The owner of adjoining land has right of access to a highway: *Rowley v Tottenham UDC* [1914] AC 95. See *R v Secretary of State for the Environment ex p Stevens* [1998] NPC 51. 4. An access order may be issued by a circuit judge under P. & C.E.A. 1984, s 9, Sch 1, allowing the police to obtain access to special procedure material (q.v.) which is of importance to an investigation. See *R v Manchester Stipendiary Magistrate ex p Granada TV* [1999] QB 1202.

access authority. In relation to land in a National Park, means the National Park authority; in relation to other land, means the local highway authority in whose area the land is situated: C.R.W.A. 2000, s 1(2).

access forums, local. Bodies appointed under C.R.W.A. 2000, s 94, to advise access authorities on matters relating to access to land, with reference to needs of land management, and conservation of an area's natural beauty.

accession. 1. Succeeding to the throne. 2. Procedure whereby property belonging to X becomes property of Y because it has been affixed to or annexed with that which belongs to Y. 3. Agreement of a state to a wide, international treaty. The so-called 'Treaties of Accession' signify the entry of applicant states into the European Union (q.v.): see Maastricht Treaty 1992, article O. *See* FIXTURES.

access land. Defined under C.R.W.A. 2000, s 1(1), as any land which: is shown as open country on a map in conclusive form; is shown as registered common land on such a map; is registered common land in any area outside Inner London for which no such map relating to common land registration has been issued; is situated more than 600 metres above sea level in any area for which no such map relating to open country has been issued; or is dedicated under s 16, but does not include excepted land or land treated by s 15(1) as being accessible to the public apart from this Act.

access land, dedication of land as. A person who, in respect of any land, holds the fee simple absolute in possession, or a legal term of years absolute of which not less than 90 years remain unexpired, may dedicate the land for purposes of access to the countryside, whether or not it would be access land (q.v.) apart from this section: C.R.W.A. 2000, s 16.

access land, rights of public in relation to. Any person is entitled to enter and remain on access land for purposes of open air recreation, if and so long as he does so without breaking or damaging any wall, fence, hedge, stile or gate, and he observes the restrictions under Sch 2 and other restrictions imposed under Chapter II: C.R.W.A. 2000, s 2(1). Sch 2 restrictions include, e.g., driving of vehicles on the land, committing any criminal offence, possessing a metal detector, feeding of livestock, engaging in hunting, shooting, fishing, camping, organised games.

accessory. One who is concerned in the commission of an offence otherwise than as principal. An accessory *before* the fact was one who 'being absent at the time of the felony committed doth yet procure, counsel, command or abet to commit [it]': 1 Hale PC 615. An accessory *after* the fact was one who, knowing that a felony had been committed, subsequently harboured or relieved the felon or in any way secured or attempted to secure his escape. See Accessories and Abettors Act 1861; *Johnson v Youden* [1950] 1 KB 544; *R v Fisher* [1969] 1 WLR 8; *R v Powell* [1999] 1 AC 1; *R v Gilmour* (2000) *The Times*, 21 June. *See* PRINCIPAL.

access, rights of public under enactments. See L.P.A. 1925, s 193; Commons Act 1899, Part I; National Parks and Access to the Countryside Act 1949, Part V; Ancient Monuments and Archaeological Areas Act 1979: C.R.W.A. 2000, s 15(1).

accident. 'Not a technical legal term with a clearly defined meaning. Speaking generally, but with reference to legal liabilities, an accident means any unintended and unexpected occurrence which produces hurt or loss': *per* Lord Linley in *Fenton v Thorley* [1903] AC 443. The term implies a specific incident: *Chief Adjudication Officer v Faulds* (2000) *The Times*, 16 May. *See* INEVITABLE ACCIDENT.

accident and non-event. CA held in *Re Deep Vein Thrombosis Group Litigation* (2003) *The Times*, 14 July, that a non-event does not constitute an accident, so that for purposes of claims under the Warsaw Convention 1929, art 17, failure to act in the circumstances does not constitute 'an unexpected or unusual event or happening that is external to an (air) passenger.' See *Air France v Saks* (1985) 470 US 302, 405.

accommodation, adequate. CA held in *M and Another (Children) v Secretary of State for Home Department* (2003) *The Times*, 7 February, that the phrase 'adequately accommodated by a parent' in Immigration Rules 1994, r 297(iv), ought to be interpreted purposively so as to refer to physical and welfare matters relating to children.

accommodation bill. A bill of exchange (q.v.) to which a person who has not received value for it (the 'accommodation party') has given his name, thus accepting liability and becoming, in effect, a surety for the person accommodated. See B.Ex.A. 1882, s 28.

accommodation, priority need for. Category of persons requiring special consideration by a local authority and comprising: pregnant women; persons with whom dependent children reside; persons homeless as the result of an emergency; persons vulnerable as the result of old age, mental illness or physical disability: H.A. 1985, s 59(1). See *R v Westminster CC ex p Bishop* (1997) 29 HLR 546.

accomplice. One person associated with another, whether as principal or accessory (qq.v.), in the commission of an offence.

accord and satisfaction. Occurs where, following the conclusion of a contract, one party obtains his release from his obligation by promising or giving consideration (q.v.) other than that which the other party has to accept under the contract. The new agreement is the 'accord'; the consideration is the satisfaction. See *Ferguson v Davies* [1997] 1 All ER 315; *Morris v Molesworth* (1998) 148 NLJ 1551.

accounting, false. An offence under Th.A. 1968, s 17(1) 'where a person dishonestly, with a view to gain for himself or another or with intent to cause loss to another, (*a*) destroys, defaces, conceals or falsifies any account or any record or document made or required for any accounting purpose; or (*b*) in furnishing information for any purpose produces or makes use of any account, or any such record or document as aforesaid, which to his knowledge is or may be misleading, false or deceptive in a material particular.' See *R v Oyediran* [1997] 2 Cr App R(S) 277; *R v Clark* (1999) *The Times*, 27 January.

accounting records. Records kept in accordance with Cos.A. 1985, s 221, as amended by Cos.A. 1989, Part I, containing details of company's liabilities and assets and entries from day to day of receipts and expenditure and matters in respect of which the receipts and expenditure take place. See also s 722. For 'accounting standards', see Cos.A. 1989, s 19.

accounting reference period. Company directors must prepare accounts by reference to an 'accounting reference date', notice of which must be given to the Registrar of Companies. The reference date should be such that a company's first accounting reference period, ending on the reference date, will be at least six, but no more than 18, months in length, and, thereafter, 12 months: Cos.A. 1985, s 224; Cos.A. 1989, s 3. For alteration of period, see ss 225, 226, and Cos.A. 1989, s 3.

account, order for. Order made by the court so that sums due from one party to another resulting from transactions between parties may be investigated, e.g., as between principal and agent. See S.C.A. 1981, s 61(1); *Codex Corp v Racal-Milgo Ltd* [1984] FSR 87; *A-G v Blake* [2000] 4 All ER 385.

accounts, company. *See* COMPANY ACCOUNTS; COMPANY ACCOUNTS, PUBLICATION OF.

account, settled. Statement of accounts between parties, in writing, agreed and accepted by them as correct. A defence to a claim for an account. See *Re Webb* [1894] 1 Ch 83.

account stated. An admission of a sum of money due from one person to another where neither is under a duty to account to the other.

accretion. Growth of land resulting from gradual and imperceptible accumulation by natural causes. See *Southern Centre of Theosophy* v *State of S Australia* [1982] AC 706. See AVULSION.

accrue. To increase, to fall due, to be added as an increase, to come into existence. A right 'accrues' when it vests in some person.

accumulation. Process whereby interest is invested as it accrues. Under L.P.A. 1925, s 164(1), no person may direct accumulation of income for any longer period than the grantor's or settlor's life, or a term of 21 years from the death of the grantor, settlor or testator, or duration of minority of a person living or *en ventre sa mère* (q.v.) at the death of the grantor, settlor or testator, or duration of minority of person(s) who under limitations of the instrument directing accumulation would, for the time being, if of full age, be entitled to income directed to be accumulated. Under P.&A.A. 1964, s 13(1), additional periods are: 21 years from the date disposition was made; duration of minority of any person in being at that date. The rule does not extend to accumulation of produce of timber or wood, provisions for payment of debts and raising of portions (q.v.). *See* PERPETUITIES, RULE AGAINST.

accumulation and maintenance settlement. Settlement (q.v.) in which there is no interest in possession, but one or more beneficiaries will become entitled to an interest in possession on attaining a specified age not exceeding 25 years. See *Fuller* v *Evans* (1999) 149 NLJ 1561.

accusatorial procedure. *See* ADVERSARIAL PROCEDURE.

accused. One charged with an offence. See *Re Ismail* [1998] 3 WLR 495.

accused, non-appearance of. If the prosecutor appears, but the accused does not, the court may proceed in his absence: M.C.A. 1980, s 11(1). See also s 13, amended by C.P.I.A. 1996, s 48. Where a summons has been issued, the court must be satisfied that it was served on the accused a reasonable time before the trial: s 11(2). A person may not be sentenced to imprisonment in his absence: s 11(3); C.D.A. 1998, Sch 8, para 39. *See* POST, PLEA OF GUILTY BY; PROSECUTOR, NON-APPEARANCE OF.

accused, self-incrimination of. *See* SELF-INCRIMINATION.

accused, trial of absent. In *R* v *Jones* (2002) *The Times*, 21 February, HL held that a trial judge had the discretion to begin a trial (for robbery) in the absence of an absconding defendant, and this did not breach the provisions of the Human Rights Convention.

acknowledgment. Avowal or assent to. 1. Acknowledgment of debt. Where right of action has accrued to recover a debt and the person liable acknowledges claim, the right is deemed to have accrued on and not before the date of acknowledgment: Lim.A. 1980, s 29(5). 2. Acknowledgment of signature to will (q.v.). Testator's signature must be made or acknowledged in the presence of two witnesses. See W.A. 1837, s 9 (as substituted by A.J.A. 1982, s 17); *Re White* [1990] 3 WLR 187.

ACP states. Those 71 African, Caribbean and Pacific states associated with EU member states under the Lomé Convention 1975, and allowed to benefit from the facilities of the European Investment Bank.

acquiescence. Consent which is expressed or implied from conduct, e.g., inactivity or silence. 'Quiescence under such circumstances as that assent may be reasonably inferred from it': *De Bussche* v *Alt* (1880) 8 Ch D 314. See *A* [1992] CLY 3036 (acquiescence may require informed acceptance of infringement of rights); *Schuldenfrei* v *Hilton* [1998] STC 404. *See* LACHES.

acquis communautaire. The body of general obligations of the European Union which must be accepted by individual member states. (Translated as

'Community patrimony' in Cases 80, 81/ 77.) Comprises: *normative acquis*, e.g., founding treaties; *political acquis*, e.g., principles, declarations, adopted by EU and Council of Ministers; *judicial acquis*, e.g., case law of Court of Justice. EU has as one of its objectives, 'to maintain in full and build upon the *acquis communautaire*'. *See* EUROPEAN UNION.

acquittal. Discharge from prosecution following verdict of not guilty or successful plea in bar (q.v.), etc. There is generally no appeal against acquittal unless under the appropriate statutory authority. For deemed acquittals see Prosecution of Offences Act 1985, s 22(4).

acquittal, early. A jury has the right to acquit the defendant after the end of the prosecution case and before the opening of the defence case, but such a right is subject to the invitation of the trial judge. See *R* v *Speechley* (2004) *The Times*, 1 December.

acquittal, tainted. Power allowing for a retrial in cases involving a tainted acquittal is introduced by C.P.I.A. 1996, s 54. The section applies where a person has been acquitted of an offence, and a person has been convicted of an administration of justice offence (e.g., under C.J.P.O.A. 1994, s 51(1)) involving interference with or intimidation of a juror or witness or potential witness in any proceeding which led to the acquittal: s 54(1). The court must be satisfied that, but for the interference or intimidation, the acquitted person would not have been acquitted, and that it is not contrary to the interests of justice to take proceedings against the acquitted person for the offence of which he was acquitted: s 54(2), (5). Application may be made to the High Court for an order quashing the acquittal: ss 53(3), 55 (conditions for making the order).

acquittance. 'A discharge in writing of a sum of money or other duty which ought to be paid or done': *Termes de la Ley.*

act. 1. Act of Parliament (q.v.). 2. That which is done by a person, generally consequent on volition. It may include a deliberate omission.

acte clair. Doctrine of EU law whereby a national court which considers that a point of Community law raised before it is 'sufficiently clear' may apply it without reference to the European Court (q.v.). See Treaty of Rome 1957, art 177; *R* v *Sec of State ex p Schering* [1987] 1 CMLR 277.

action. Procedures relating to the exercise of a right of suing for that which is considered due. Known now, under CPR, as a 'claim'. Usually commences with issue of claim form (q.v.). *See* CPR 1998.

action, cause of. 'A factual situation the existence of which entitles one person to obtain a remedy against another person': *Letang* v *Cooper* [1965] 1 QB 232.

action, collusive. *See* COLLUSIVE ACTION.

action, derivative. *See* DERIVATIVE CLAIM.

action plan order. A community sentence (q.v.) given where a child or young person (under 18) is convicted of an offence, and which requires the offender to comply with a three-month plan relating to his actions and whereabouts, places him under supervision for that period and requires him to comply with the directions of a responsible officer, i.e., probation officer, social worker, member of youth offending team (q.v.): P.C.C.(S.)A. 2000, s 69. For requirements of order, see s 70.

actions, real and personal. *Real* actions (*res* = thing) were brought at common law by a freeholder for the recovery of his land. See Real Property Limitation Act 1833 by which they were, in general, abolished. *Personal* actions, e.g., actions on contracts, derive from those relating to the enforcement of remedies against persons, in contrast to the recovery of things in real actions. Actions are now known as 'claims'. *See* PROPERTY.

actio personalis moritur cum persona. A personal action dies with a party to the cause of the action. The rule was reversed by Law Reform (Misc. Provs.) Act 1934: 'On the death of any person . . . all causes of action . . . vested in him shall survive for the benefit of his estate'. Thus, all claims in tort, save for defamation (q.v.) and the claim for damages for bereavement (q.v.), survive the deceased.

active trust. A trust (q.v.) which requires the trustee, known as an 'active trustee', to perform active duties, e.g., to collect rent and profits and transfer proceeds to the beneficiary (q.v.). *See* BARE TRUST.

activity offence. An offence which can relate to a single incident or a number of separate incidents comprising an activity, either of which can be charged in one count. See *R v Martin* [1998] 2 Cr App R 285 (involving Customs and Excise Management Act 1979, s 170(2)); *R v Masood* [1997] 2 Cr App R (S) 137 (involving C.J.A. 1991, s 44).

Act of God. 'An extraordinary circumstance which could not be foreseen, and which could not be guarded against': *Pandorf* v *Hamilton* (1886) 17 QBD 675. See *Nichols* v *Marsland* (1875) LR 10 Ex 255 (extraordinary rainfall); *Nugent* v *Smith* (1876) 1 CPD 423 (unusually bad weather at sea); *Southern Water Authority* v *Pegrum* [1989] Crim LR 10 (overflow of water). *See* VIS MAJOR.

Act of indemnity. An Act legalising certain activities which were illegal at the time they were carried out, or exempting certain persons from particular penalties following on breaches of the law. See, e.g., 4 Hen VIII c. 8; Indemnity Act 1920. *See* INDEMNITY.

Act of Parliament. The will of the legislature, i.e., law made by the Queen in Parliament (i.e., Queen, Lords and Commons). Concurrence of the Lords may be dispensed with under certain circumstances: see Parliament Acts 1911 and 1949. An Act comes into force on the day it receives the Royal Assent (q.v.), unless otherwise stated. Acts may be public or private, local, general or personal. In construing an Act, the intention of the legislature predominates: *A-G for Canada* v *Hallett & Carey Ltd* [1952] AC 427. 'An Act of Parliament is the exercise of the highest authority that this kingdom acknowledges upon earth': Blackstone, *Commentaries* (1765). *See* BILL, PASSAGE THROUGH PARLIAMENT; INTERPRETATION OF STATUTES; STATUTE; SECTIONS OF AN ACT.

Act of Parliament, citation of. *See* STATUTE, CITATION OF.

Act of Parliament, validity of. This cannot be questioned in court. 'The court can only look at the Parliamentary roll': *per* Nourse J in *Martin* v *O'Sullivan* [1982] STC 416 (basis of the 'enrolled Act rule'). See, e.g., *Pickin* v *British Railways Board* [1974] AC 765; *Manuel* v *A-G* [1983] Ch 77.

Act of Settlement. Passed in 1700. Provided *inter alia* for the line of succession to the throne, for the independence of judges, for the exclusion of Catholics from the throne and for the necessity of a monarch to join in communion with the Church of England. The Act affirmed that the laws of England were 'the birthright of the people'.

act of state. An act of the executive, i.e., the sovereign power of a country, that 'cannot be challenged, controlled or interfered with by municipal courts. Its sanction is not that of Law, but that of Sovereign power and, whatever it may be, municipal courts must accept it as it is, without question': *Salaman* v *Sec of State for India* [1906] 1 KB 639. *See* PREROGATIVE, ROYAL.

act, premature use of. CA held in *R v D (Video Testimony)* (2002) *The Times*, 21 May, that a judge was entitled to use an Act which was not, at the time, in force (Youth Justice and Criminal Evidence Act 1999, s 53(3)) in reaching a decision whether admission of video testimony of a witness whose competence was under challenge was in the interests of justice.

Act, structure of. Constituent elements of a statute, including: long title; preamble; enacting words; short title; principal, subsidiary, administrative and transitional provisions; interpretation and definitions; repealing clause; date of coming into operation; area of operation clause (e.g., 'This Act shall not extend to Scotland'); schedules.

actual military service. Phrase referring to a privileged will (q.v.) which allows, e.g., a soldier or airman 'in actual military service' to make an informal will. It has been given a wide meaning so as to include, e.g., an airman undergoing training in Canada (*Re Wingham* [1943] P 187), a minor serving in the army of occupation nine years after the end of the war (*Re Colman* [1958] 2 All ER 35).

actual notice. *See* NOTICE.

actus non facit reum nisi mens sit rea. An act does not itself constitute guilt unless the mind is guilty. The maxim embodies a cardinal doctrine of English criminal law. See *Fowler* v *Padget* (1798) 7 TR 509; *Younghusband* v *Luftig* [1949] 2 KB 354.

actus reus. A phrase referring to elements of the definition of an offence (save those which concern the condition of the mind of the accused), e.g., his outward conduct, its results and surrounding circumstances. Thus, the *actus reus* of false imprisonment (q.v.) is X's unlawful restraint of Y. May be merely a specified state of affairs, e.g., a 'situation' offence: see, e.g., Road Traffic Act 1988, s 4(2). Should any element of the *actus reus* not be present, the offence has not been committed. See, e.g., *Haughton* v *Smith* [1975] AC 476 ('It is not the *actus* which is *reus*, but the man and his mind respectively': *per* Lord Hailsham). *R* v *Runting* (1989) 89 Cr App R 243. *See* CRIME; MENS REA.

ad colligenda bona. To collect the goods. Grant of administration made to preserve property when no next of kin, creditor or other person applies for administration and the property is in danger of perishing. See *Re Clore* [1982] Ch 456. See GRANT.

addiction. Compulsive psychological or physiological need for, e.g., a drug. *See* DRUG ADDICT.

address. In relation to an individual, his usual residential or business address. In relation to a company, its registered or principal office in Great Britain: Cos.A. 1989, s 53(1). For 'last known address', see *Robertson* v *Banham & Co* [1997] 1 WLR 446.

ademption. A specific legacy is said to be adeemed when, as a result of implied revocation by testator, it is withheld or extinguished, wholly or in part. There is ademption in the following cases: 1. Testator makes a gift of 'my gold watch' but sells it before his death: *Re Dowsett*

[1901] 1 Ch 398. 2. Father or person *in loco parentis* (q.v.) may bequeath a legacy to a child and later make other provisions which, in effect, constitute a portion (q.v.): *Earl of Durham* v *Wharton* (1836) 10 Bli NS 526. See *R* v *Sweeting* [1988] 1 All ER 1016. *See* LEGACY.

ad hoc. For this special purpose.

ad hoc **settlements.** *See* SETTLEMENTS, AD HOC.

ad hoc **trust of land.** An obsolescent mode of land transfer. Where trustees of land are either two or more persons approved or appointed by the Court, or their successors in office, or a trust corporation (q.v.), a sale overreaches certain prior interests: L.P.A. 1925, s 2(2). The sale is known as an *ad hoc*, or special, trust of land. See Trusts of Land and Appointment of Trustees Act 1996, Sch 3, para 4(2)(*c*).

ad idem. Of the same mind; similar in essential matters. A binding contract, for example, requires *consensus ad idem* (agreement as to the same thing) by both parties. See *Raffles* v *Wichelhaus* (1864) 2 H & C 906.

adjacent. 'Close to or nearby or lying by: its significance or application in point of distance depends on the circumstances in which the word is used': *English China Clays* v *Plymouth Corporation* [1974] 2 All ER 239.

adjective law. That portion of the law dealing with procedure and practice in the courts. *See* SUBSTANTIVE LAW.

adjoining. Touching. Includes 'abutting on': Highways Act 1980, s 329(1). See *Bucks CC* v *Trigg* [1963] 1 WLR 155; G.L.A.A. 1999, s 262.

adjourn. To postpone or suspend the hearing of a case until a further date. An adjournment *sine die* (without day) is for an indefinite time. 'Adjournment of the House' refers to the suspension of a sitting of the Lords or Commons until the following or a later day.

adjournment of trial. The postponing of a trial of action by a judge who thinks it expedient 'in the interest of justice' to adjourn for such time, and to such place, and upon such terms, if any, as he thinks fit. See *Re Yates' ST* [1954] 1 WLR 564. For adjournment of a preliminary enquiry or a summary trial, see M.C.A. 1980, ss 5, 10; *R v Dudley Magistrates Court ex p Hollis* [1999] 1 WLR 642.

adjudication. Formal judgment or decision given by the court. In proceedings for bankruptcy an adjudication order declares the debtor bankrupt, so that he becomes subject to disabilities attaching to that status.

adjudicators, immigration. Appointed under Immigration and Asylum Act 1999, s 57, Sch 3. Appeal to adjudicator must be allowed where relevant decision or action was not in accordance with the law or relevant rules, or where the discretion of the Secretary of State should have been exercised differently; otherwise appeal must be dismissed: Sch 3, para 21. Appeals must be dismissed if appellant is an illegal immigrant or a deportation order is in force: para 24.

adjustment. Determining or settling of an amount entitled to be received by the assured under a policy of marine insurance. *See* AVERAGE.

ad litem. For the suit. 1. A *guardian ad litem* may be appointed by the court to represent the interests of a child in certain proceedings: Ch.A. 1989, s 41. See C.J.C.S.A. 2000, Sch 7, para 92. See *R v Cornwall CC ex p Cornwall Guardians* [1992] 1 WLR 427; *Re K (Supervision Orders)* [1999] 2 FLR 303. 2. A *grant ad litem* may be made where representatives will not act and the estate must be represented in proceedings: *Re Simpson* [1936] P 40. See LITIGATION FRIEND.

administer. Under Medicines Act 1968, s 130(9), to give to a person or animal, orally, by injection or by introduction into the body in any other way, or by external application, whether by direct contact with the body or not. See also O.P.A. 1861, s 24; *R v Gillard* (1988) 87 Cr App R 64 (s 24 covered the spraying of CS gas at a distance); *R v Nasar* [2000] 1 Cr App R (S) 333. *See* POISON.

administering a substance with intent. It is an offence for a person to intentionally administer a substance to, or cause a substance to be taken by another person, knowing that the other person does not consent, and with the intention of stupefying or overpowering that other person (B), so as to enable any person to engage in a sexual activity that involves B: Sexual Offences Act 2003, s 61(1).

administration. 1. Process of managing affairs of a bankrupt by a trustee, or those of an absent person by an attorney or agent. 2. Process of collecting the assets of a deceased person, paying debts and distributing any surplus to those entitled. See A.E.A. 1925, s 34 and Sch 1.

administration action. Claim to obtain administration of the estate of a deceased person, under the direction of the court or for the execution under the direction of the court of a trust (q.v.): CPR, Sch 1; O 85, r 1. Personal representative or any other person interested in the estate may bring proceedings by claim. See S.C.A. 1981, s 117.

administration bond. As a condition of granting administration to a person, the court may require one or two sureties to guarantee that they will make good any loss suffered by a person interested in the estate, following the breach of duties by administrator. See S.C.A. 1981, s 120.

administration, limited. *See* LIMITED ADMINISTRATION.

administration of assets. *See* ESTATES, ADMINISTRATION OF.

administration of estates. *See* ADMINISTRATION; ESTATES, ADMINISTRATION OF.

administration order, county court. Order made by a county court where a debtor is unable to pay a debt, on application of the debtor, or creditor under a judgment obtained against the debtor or of the court's own motion during the course of any enforcement or other proceedings: C.L.S.A. 1990, s 13, replacing County C.A. 1984, s 112(1).

administration order relating to companies. An order directing that, while it is in force, the affairs, business and property of a company (q.v.) shall be managed by an administrator (q.v.) appointed by the court: Ins.A. 1986, s 8(2). Its purposes include the survival of the company as a going concern, an advantageous realisation of assets, etc: s 8(3). An application is by petition presented by the company, directors or creditors: s 9(1), amended by C.J.A. 1988, s 62. For requirement for leave of court to bring criminal proceedings against a company in administration, see 1986 Act, ss 10, 11; *Clark* v *Environment Agency* (2000) 150 NLJ 227. While in force, no resolution may be passed or order for a winding-up made: s 11(3). See *Astor Chemicals Ltd* v *Synthetic Technology Ltd* [1990] BCLC 1. For discharge, see s 18. *See* BANKRUPTCY.

administration, special. *See* LIMITED ADMINISTRATION.

administration suit. A claim brought to commence administration of the estate of a deceased person.

administration, summary. Where it appears to the court that, if a bankruptcy order (q.v.) were made, the aggregate amount of the bankruptcy debts so far as secured would be less than the prescribed small bankruptcies level, and that within the period of five years ending with the presentation of the petition the debtor has neither been adjudged bankrupt nor made a composition with his creditors or a scheme of arrangement, a certificate for summary administration of the bankrupt's estate may be issued: Ins.A. 1986, s 275(1). *See* BANKRUPTCY.

administrative actions, remedies for control of. These are discretionary and comprise: prerogative orders (quashing, mandatory, prohibiting); *habeas corpus*; non-statutory remedies (e.g., injunctions, declarations); statutory remedies (e.g., rights of appeal); and collateral challenge (e.g., in claims for damages). Control of such actions does not involve an appeal in disguise; see *Healey* v *Minister of Health* [1955] 1 QB 221.

Administrative Court. Set up in 2000 to replace Crown Office List, as a specialist court, which is part of the High Court (q.v.), to deal with public and administrative law cases. It issues mandatory, prohibiting, and quashing orders. The former Crown Office is now known as the Administrative Court Office. See *Practice*

Direction (Administrative Court: Establishment) [2000] 1 WLR 1654.

administrative tribunals. Tribunals outside the hierarchy of courts exercising jurisdiction conferred by Parliament, e.g., Rent Tribunals. Chairmen are generally selected from a panel and are appointed by the Lord Chancellor. The Council on Tribunals reviews their working. They are controlled generally by the issue of quashing, mandatory and prohibiting orders. See Tribunals and Inquiries Act 1992.

administrator. (Fem: administratrix.) One appointed by the court to manage the property of a deceased person in the absence of an executor (q.v.). *See* GRANT.

administrator of a company. Appointed by the Court (see Ins.A. 1986, s 8(2)) to 'do all such things as may be necessary for the arrangement of the affairs, business and property' of the company: s 14(1). He may summon a creditors' meeting if requested to do so by one-tenth in value of the company's creditors, or if so directed by the court: s 17(3). See, e.g., *Re Atlantic Computer Systems plc* [1990] BCLC 859. See also G.L.A.A. 1999, Sch 14.

administrator of an estate, duties of. To collect, get in and administer real and personal estate of the deceased; to exhibit on oath a full inventory of the estate and render an account of its administration to the court; to deliver up to the High Court, when required to do so, the grant of probate or administration: A.E.A. 1925, s 25, as substituted by A.E.A. 1971.

Admiralty Court. A part of QBD (q.v.) consisting of puisne judges (q.v.) of the High Court, assisted by nautical assessors (the Elder Brethren of Trinity House). See S.C.A. 1981, ss 6, 20–24; PD 49F (Practice Direction – Admiralty) (replacing O 75); CPR, Part 49; C.J.J.A. 1982, s 26. It has jurisdiction (concerning civil cases arising, e.g., out of collisions); prize jurisdiction (concerning seizure of enemy ships and cargoes); salvage claims; applications under the Merchant Shipping Act 1995. For the combined Admiralty and Commercial Court Registry, see SI 87/1423; Practice Direction [1987] 1

WLR 1459; *Bain Clarkson* v *Owners of Sea Friends* [1991] 2 Lloyd's Rep 323. All Admiralty proceedings will be allocated to the multi-track: PD 49F, para 1.14. All orders made in Admiralty proceedings will be drawn up by the parties unless otherwise ordered by the court: para 19.

admissibility, conditional. *See* CONDITIONAL ADMISSIBILITY.

admissibility, multiple. *See* MULTIPLE ADMISSIBILITY.

admissibility of evidence. Evidence is receivable by the court only if both relevant and admissible. In general, all evidence relevant to an issue is admissible; all that is irrelevant or insufficiently relevant ought to be excluded. See, e.g., *Hollington* v *Hewthorn & Co Ltd* [1943] KB 587. Must be distinguished from relevance (q.v.), which is based on that which is logically probative whereas admissibility refers to that which is legally receivable whether logically probative or not. '[The terms relevance and admissibility] are frequently, and in many circumstances legitimately, used interchangeably; but I think it makes for clarity if they are kept separate, since some relevant evidence is inadmissible and some admissible evidence is irrelevant': *per* Lord Simon in *DPP* v *Kilbourne* [1973] AC 729. See M.C.A. 1980, s 5, as amended by C.P.I.A. 1996, Sch 1, para 3. *See* EVIDENCE.

admission order and mental illness. Order made for admission to hospital by Crown Court under Criminal Procedure (Insanity) Act 1964, s 5, or Court of Appeal under Criminal Appeal Act 1968, ss 6, 14, 14A. See Criminal Procedure (Insanity and Unfitness to Plead) Act 1991, Sch 1. *See* HOSPITAL ORDER; UNFITNESS TO PLEAD.

admissions. 1. In civil proceedings, those facts (or part of a case) admitted, or taken to be admitted by parties to a claim. A party may admit, by giving notice in writing, the truth of the whole or any part of another party's case: r 14.1(1), (2). Where defendant makes an admission, claimant has a right to enter judgment except where defendant is a child or patient; or where claimant is a child or patient and the admission relates to part of a claim for a specified amount of money or an unspecified amount of money where defendant offers a sum in satisfaction of the claim: r 14.1(4). See PD 14. 2. In criminal proceedings, statements made voluntarily by the accused, which are adverse to his case, e.g., by admitting the offence, plea of guilty or confession. See C.J.A. 1967, s 10 (provision for formal admission at or before trial) and SI 97/173. 3. 'Admissions by conduct' may be implied from a party's conduct. See, e.g., *R* v *Cramp* (1880) 14 Cox CC 390. See P.&C.E.A. 1984, s 82. *See* CONFESSION.

adopted children register. A register maintained by the Registrar-General at the General Register Office in which entries relating to adoption orders (q.v.) are made. Any person is entitled to search an index of the register: Adoption Act 1976, s 50. See *Re W (Adoption Details: Disclosure)* [1998] 2 FLR 625. See Police Act 1997, s 113, amended by Care Standards Act 2000, s 104 (criminal record checks).

adopters and duty of care. CA held in *A* v *Essex CC* (2004) *The Times*, 22 January, that there is, in general, no duty of care owed by an adoption agency or its employees to decide on the nature of what information ought to be conveyed to prospective adopters.

adoption. 1. Incorporation of international law into municipal law, e.g., by custom. 2. Process, effected by a court order, whereby parental responsibility (q.v.) for a child is given to the adopter(s). Recognised only after the Adoption of Children Act 1926. Regulated by Adoption Act 1976 and Ch.A. 1989. A person other than an adoption agency shall not make arrangements for the adoption of a child or place a child for adoption unless the proposed adopter is a relative of the child or he is acting in pursuance of a High Court order: 1976 Act, s 11(1). For Adoption Contact Register, see Ch.A. 1989, Sch 10, para 21. See also Adoption Rules 1984, amended by SI 91/1880; SI 97/649, 2308; Adoption (Intercountry Aspects) Act 1999, giving effect to the Convention on Protection of Children and Co-operation in respect of Intercountry Adoption (adopted at The Hague on 29 May 1993); Care Standards Act 2000, Sch 4, para 7(8), amending Adoption Act 1976, s 32, conferring status of 'protected child' on a child whom some person hopes to adopt and who is supervised by an adoption agency.

adoption agencies, regulation of. Under A.C.A. 2002, s 9, local authorities would make provision as to fitness of agency premises, their management and control, training of personnel, fitness of persons employed by them.

adoption and assessment. Under A.C.A. 2002, s 4, a local authority would have to carry out an assessment of the needs for adoption support services in relation to an adopted child, or his parents, and would be able to request the help of a registered adoption society. An assessment would be followed by the preparation of an appropriate plan.

adoption arrangements, restrictions on making. Under A.C.A. 2002, a person will not be allowed to make arrangements for a child's adoption unless the person was an adoption agency or the arrangement was made with such an agency, the person was acting in pursuance of a High Court order, or the prospective adopter was a step-parent or relative of the child. Advertising in relation to an adoption would be an offence: ss 128 and 124.

adoption by married couple or one person. Under A.C.A. 2002, s 50, an adoption order can be made on the application of a married couple where both spouses had attained the age of 21; or where one spouse was the father or mother of the person to be adopted and had attained the age of 18, and the other had attained the age of 21. Under s 51, an order would be made on the application of one person who had attained the age of 21 and was not married.

adoption, considerations affecting. Under A.C.A. 2002, s 1, paramount consideration of the court or adoption agency must be the child's welfare throughout his life; child's ascertainable wishes and feelings, particular needs, age, sex, background, any harm he has suffered; religious persuasion, racial origin, cultural and linguistic background, would be taken into account.

adoption, freeing child for. Where on the application by an adoption agency, an authorised court is satisfied in the case of each parent or guardian of the child that he freely and with full understanding of what is involved, agrees generally and unconditionally to the making of an adoption order, or his agreement to the making of the order can be dispensed with, the court may make an order declaring the child free for adoption: Adoption Act 1976, s 18(1). See also 1976 Act, s 18(2A); Ch.A. 1989, s 88, Sch 10; *Re F (Minors) (Adoption: Freeing Order)* (2000) *The Times*, 6 July.

adoption order. Defined under A.C.A. 2002, s 46, as an order made by the court on an application under ss 50 or 51, giving parental responsibility for a child to the adopter(s). The order would not be made unless the court was satisfied that the parent or guardian consented or that such consent ought to be dispensed with: s 47(2).

adoption order, status conferred by. An adopted child is treated in law, where the adopters are a married couple, as if he had been born as a child of the marriage and, in any other case, as if he had been born to the adopter in wedlock, and as if he were not the child of any person other than the adopter(s): Adoption Act 1976, s 39. For property rights of adopted children, see *Staffordshire CC v B* [1998] Fam Law 8.

adoption placement. Under A.C.A. 2002, s 18, an adoption agency would be able to place a child for adoption with prospective adopters or, where it had placed a child with persons, leave him with them as prospective adopters, but only under a placement order, or where the agency was satisfied that each parent or guardian had consented to the child being placed for adoption with identified prospective adopters.

adoption, placement order. Under A.C.A. 2002, s 21, a placement order will be made by the court authorising an adoption agency to place a child for adoption with any prospective adopters chosen by the agency. The order would continue in force until revoked, or adoption order was made, or child married or attained the age of 18. While a child was placed with prospective adopters, parental responsibility would be given to them: s 22(3).

adoption preliminaries. Under A.C.A. 2002, s 42, application for adoption order will not be made, in a case where a child was placed for adoption with applicant(s) by an agency or following a High Court order, unless at all times during the preceding ten weeks, his home had been with applicant(s), or, in the case of an application by a married couple, one or both of them. In any other case, application for adoption order would not be made unless at all times during the preceding six months, the child's home was with the applicant(s), or, in the case of a married couple, both of them: s 42(2).

adoption registers. A.C.A. 2002, ss 77 and 80, requires the Registrar General to maintain the Adopted Children Register and an Adoption Contact Register, expressing the wishes of persons included to make, or not make, contact with all or any of their relatives. A National Adoption Register would contain information about children suitable for adoption and prospective adopters suitable to adopt a child: s 80.

adoption society. A body whose functions consist of or include making arrangements for the adoption of children. See Adoption and Children Act 2002 s 2(5).

adoption, unmarried couple and. Under the Adoption Act 1976, s 14, no adoption order will be made on the application of more than one person, except where they are husband and wife. (Under s 15, however, a single person may adopt.) See *Re AB (Adoption: Joint Residence)* [1996] 1 FLR 27 (discussion of whether one partner of an unmarried couple should be allowed to adopt).

adoption with a foreign element. Under A.C.A. 2002, s 83(7) it is . . . an offence where a person habitually resident in the British Islands brings a child into the UK for adoption purposes where that child is habitually resident outside the British Islands.

adoptive Acts. Acts which become effective in a local authority's area only after formal adoption by that authority. See, e.g., the provisions relating to licensing systems in the L.G. (Misc. Provs.) Act 1982, s 1.

adoptive parents, council's duty to. A local authority has a duty to inform adoptive parents of the hypersensitive constitution of a child, rendering him impossible to control, and liable to damage the parents' home and family life. See *A v Essex CC* (2003) 153 NLJ 22.

adoptive relationship. Relationship existing by virtue of the Adoption Act 1976, s 39. An adoptive parent must be at least 18: Ch.A. 1989, Sch 10. A male adopter is known as the 'adoptive father', a female adopter as the 'adoptive mother': 1976 Act, s 41.

ADR. Alternative Dispute Resolution (q.v.).

adult. Person of full age (18). *See* MAJORITY.

adulteration. The adding of a substance to food which debases it and renders it dangerous to health, if done with the intention that it should be sold in that state for human consumption. See, e.g., Food Act 1984, s 36, repealed by Food Safety Act 1990. *See* FOOD, OFFENCES IN RELATION TO.

adultery. An act of voluntary sexual intercourse (which need not be completed) between two persons not married to each other, but one or both of whom are married at the time of the act to a third person. If the respondent has committed adultery and the petitioner finds it intolerable to live with the respondent, it may be evidence of irretrievable breakdown of a marriage, which is now the sole ground for the presentation of a divorce petition: Mat.C.A. 1973, s 1. The onus of proof is on the petitioner. For effect of cohabitation after discovery of adultery, see Mat.C.A. 1973, s 2(1).

adultery, proof of. Modes of proof include: confessions; respondent's previous convictions (see Civil Evidence Act 1968, s 11); finding of adultery and paternity in earlier civil proceedings (see Civil Evidence Act 1968, s 12(1), (2), amended by F.L.R.A. 1987, s 29); results of blood tests concerning paternity (see F.L.R.A. 1969, s 20(1), as amended by Ch.A. 1989, s 89). The standard of proof for adultery seems to be the balance of probabilities: see *Blyth* v *Blyth* [1966] AC 643; *Serio* v *Serio* (1983) 4 FLR 756.

ad valorem. In proportion to the value. In the case of an *ad valorem* tax, the amount paid is proportionate to the value of the article taxed.

advance decisions, to refuse treatment. Means a decision made by a person ('P'), after he has reached the age of 18 and when he has capacity to do so, that if (a) at a later time and in such circumstances as he may specify, a specified treatment is proposed to be carried out or continued by a person providing health care for him, and (b) at that time he lacks capacity to consent to the carrying out or continuation of the treatment, the specified treatment is not to be carried out or continued. See Mental Capacity Act 2005 s 24.

advancement. 1. Power of advancement allows a trustee (q.v.) to apply capital for the advancement or benefit of any person entitled to capital of the trust property or any share in it: Tr.A. 1925, s 32. 2. Presumption of advancement, i.e., that a gift was intended, arises where a voluntary conveyance has been made to the wife or child of the donor or to a person to whom he stands *in loco parentis* (q.v.). See *Calverley* v *Green* (1984) 56 ALR 483; *Tribe* v *Tribe* [1995] 3 WLR 913. *See* PORTION.

advancement and benefit. Means, in relation to a trustee's powers of advancement: 'any use of the money which will improve the material situation of the beneficiary': *per* Lord Radcliffe in *Pilkington* v *IRC* [1964] AC 612. See *Re Clore's ST* [1966] 1 WLR 955.

adversarial procedure. System in most common law countries whereby parties to a dispute and their representatives have the primary responsibility for finding and presenting evidence. The independent judge does not investigate the facts. See *Air Canada* v *Secretary of State for Trade (No. 2)* [1983] 1 All ER 910. ('Truth is best discovered by powerful statements on both sides of the question': Lord Eldon in *Ex p Lloyd* [1822] Mont 70.) *See* INQUISITORIAL PROCEDURE.

adverse inferences. CA held in *R* v *Knight* [2003] EWCA Crim 1977, that, in the case of a suspect who had refused to answer police questions after being cautioned but had prepared a written statement subsequently given in evidence, the jury was not entitled to draw any adverse inference from the failure to answer the police questioning. In *R* v *Becouarn* [2005] *The Times*, 1 August, however the HL held that where a defendant gives evidence, he is expected to be cross-examined as to his previous convictions. A judge has to direct the jury that adverse inferences might be drawn if the defendant fails to give evidence.

adverse occupation of residential premises. It is an offence for a person who is on premises as a trespasser, after having entered as such, to fail to leave on being required to do so by or on behalf of a displaced residential occupier of premises or a protected intending occupier (i.e., one who has in those premises a freehold interest or leasehold interest with not less than 21 years still to run who acquired the interest for money or money's worth, who requires the premises for his own occupation as a residence and is excluded by the trespasser): C.L.A. 1977, s 7(1), (2). For defences available to the accused, see s 7(6)–(8). See C.J.P.O.A. 1994, Part V.

adverse possession. Refers to one person's occupation of land which is inconsistent with the right of another who claims to be the true owner. Minor acts of trespass do not constitute adverse possession. There must be factual possession, accompanied by intent to possess; possession must be adverse to the owner, must not have been given by permission and involves an appropriate degree of physical control. See *Bucks CC v Moran* [1990] Ch 623; *Browne v Perry* [1991] 1 WLR 1297; *Central London Commercial Estates Ltd v Kato Kagaku Ltd* [1998] 4 All ER 948 (squatter acquiring rights of leaseholder); *Earnshaw v Hartley* [1999] 3 WLR 709 (adverse possession and intestacy); *Pye Ltd v Graham* (2001) *The Times*, 13 February (adverse possession and *animus possidendi*); Limitation Act 1980, ss 15(1), 32 (12-year period for action to recover land). Land Registration Act 2002, Part 9, provides a new scheme for adverse possession in relation to a registered estate in land. The essence of the scheme is that a squatter can apply to become registered after ten years' adverse possession but registered proprietor's title will not be lost merely through lapse of time: onus will be on squatter to act if he wishes to acquire title. Registered proprietor will be notified by Land Registry of a squatter's application, and if he makes an objection, application is rejected. Proprietor must then seek to evict squatter, but if squatter remains in adverse possession after two years, he has right to be registered as proprietor. *See* LIMITATION OF ACTIONS; SQUATTER.

adverse witnesses. Witnesses who disappoint the party calling them, i.e., they are unfavourable and hostile witnesses (q.v.).

advertent and inadvertent negligence. *See* NEGLIGENCE, ADVERTENT.

advertisement. Public announcement or notice. Includes, under C.C.A. 1974, s 189(1) 'every form of advertising, whether in a publication, by television or radio, by display of notices, signs, labels, showcards or goods, by distribution of samples, circulars, catalogues, price lists or other material, by exhibition of pictures, models or films, or in any other way'. See T.C.P.A. 1990, ss 220, 336(1) as amended; *R v O'Brien and Hertsmere BC* (1997) 74 P & CR 264; *R v Advertising Standards Authority ex p Robertson Ltd* (1999) *The Times*, 26 November; Broadcasting Act 1990, s 9. Public advertisement of a reward for the return of stolen or lost goods 'to the effect that no questions will be asked' is an offence under Th.A. 1968, s 23. See *Denham v Scott* (1984) 77 Cr App R 210; C.P.A. 1987, s 24(6); SI 88/915; *Torridge DC v Jarrad* [1998] 2 PLR 81.

advertiser. In relation to an advertisement, this means any person indicated by the advertisement as willing to enter into transactions to which the advertisement relates: C.C.A. 1974, s 189(1). See *O'Brien v Croydon LBC* (1999) 77 P & CR 126.

advice at door of court. HL held in *Moy v Pettman Smith* (2005) *The Times*, 4 February, that advice given by an advocate at the court door does not oblige the advocate to explain in detail all these factors likely to effect the decision.

Advisory, Conciliation and Arbitration Service. A body set up under E.P.A. 1975, s 1, charged with a general duty of promoting the improvement of industrial relations. It is controlled by a council, comprising a chairman and six members, nominated by CBI, TUC, and three independent members. See T.U.L.R.(C.)A. 1992, s 247; T.U.R.E.R.A. 1993, s 43; Employment Relations Act 1999, ss 26, 27.

advocacy and litigation services. Any services which it would be reasonable to expect a person who is exercising, or contemplating exercising, a right of audience, or a right to conduct litigation, in relation to proceedings, or contemplated proceedings, to provide: C.L.S.A. 1990, s 119, amended by Tribunals and Inquiries Act 1992, Sch 3, para 35.

advocate. Any person exercising a right of audience (q.v.) as a representative of, or on behalf of, any party to legal proceedings: see C.L.S.A. 1990, s 27(9). An 'authorised advocate' is a person who has a right of audience granted by an authorised body, e.g., General Council of the Bar, Law Society: s 119(1). Advocates no longer enjoy immunity from suit for negligence in relation to civil or criminal litigation: *Hall & Co v Simons* (2000) 150 NLJ 1147.

Advocate General. An assistant to a judge of the European Court of Justice. He is not a member of the Court, but advises, in the form of 'opinions', rather like an *amicus curiae* (q.v.), making 'reasoned submissions' on matters referred to it. Submissions are given orally before judgment is given. It is not open to parties to submit written observations in response to his opinions: *Emesa Sugar v Aruba* (2000) *The Times*, 29 February. His submissions are printed with the Court's final judgment. See Treaty of Rome 1957, arts 166, 167. *See* COURT OF JUSTICE OF THE EUROPEAN COMMUNITIES.

advocate, restraint of representation by. CA held in *Skjevesland v Geveran Trading Co* (2002) 152 NLJ 1686, that the court possesses an inherent power to act so as to prevent a likely abuse of its procedure: it can restrain an advocate from continuing to represent a party if there exists a real risk that such representation will result in an order made at the trial being set aside on appeal. It is not necessary for the party objecting to the advocate to establish that unfairness will result from his activities.

advowson. Incorporeal hereditament (q.v.) to which the law of real property applies, consisting of the perpetual right to present to an ecclesiastical living. The owner of the right is known as the 'patron'. See Lim.A. 1980, s 25; Patronage (Benefices) Measure 1986, s 6(2), amending L.R.A. 1925, s 3 (*viii*).

aedificatum solo, solo cedit. That which is built upon land becomes part of the land. *See* FIXTURES.

aerodrome. Area of land or water designed, equipped, set apart or commonly used for affording facilities for the landing and departure of aircraft: see Civil Aviation Act 1982, s 105(1). For offence of endangering safety at aerodromes by intentional acts of violence, see Aviation and Maritime Security Act 1990, s 1; SI 97/2989. For purposes of Warsaw Convention 1929, relating to

carriage of goods by air, 'aerodrome' is synonymous with 'airport': *Rolls Royce Ltd v Heavylift Ltd* (2000) *The Times*, 26 April.

aerodromes, noise restrictions. Under SI 03/1742, regulations are now in force, applying to civil airports in the UK having more than 50,000 take-offs or landings of subsonic jets annually. An 'environmental objective' for each airport must be published.

affidavit. Sworn, written statement used in evidence: see CPR, Part 32; PD 32. Should be in deponent's own words, if practicable. Only the following may take affidavits (see PD 32, para 9.1): commissioners for oaths, solicitors, circuit judges, district judges, JPs, others specified by statute. Where an affidavit is to be filed, it should be held at the court in which proceedings are taking place: PD 32, para 10.1.

affiliation order. An order of the magistrates' court adjudging, finding or declaring a person to be the father of a child and (usually) providing for the maintenance of the child. See Affiliation Proceedings Act 1957, which was superseded by F.L.R.A. 1987, Part II, abolishing affiliation proceedings.

affinity. Relationship resulting from marriage, e.g., between a wife and her husband's blood relations, as opposed to consanguinity, i.e., relationship by blood.

affirm. 1. To confirm a judgment, as where an appellate court confirms the judgment of a court below it. 2. To make a solemn declaration instead of taking an oath (if one has no religious belief, or the taking of an oath is contrary to a religious belief). The usual form is 'I . . . do solemnly, sincerely and truly declare and affirm that the evidence which I shall give shall be the truth, the whole truth, and nothing but the truth.' See Oaths Act 1978, s 6. 3. To declare expressly or impliedly with full knowledge of the facts an intention to proceed with a contract. Lapse of time may be evidence of affirmation. See *Leaf v International Galleries* [1950] 2 KB 86.

affray. A person is guilty of affray if he uses or threatens unlawful violence towards another and his conduct is such as would cause a person of reasonable firmness present at the scene to fear for his personal safety: P.O.A. 1986, s 3(1). Where two or more persons use or threaten the unlawful violence, it is the conduct of them taken together that must be considered: s 3(2). The offence may be committed in private as well as in public places: s 3(5). See *R v Rogers-Hinks and Others* (1989) 11 Cr App R (S) 234; *R v Sanchez* [1996] Crim LR 572; *R v Pollinger* [1999] 1 Cr App R (S) 128; *R v West London Youth Court ex p M* [2000] 1 Cr App R 251 (affray does not require the presence of a person threatened). In *R v W London Youth Court. ex p M* [2001] 2 WLR 765, the HL decided that the offence of affray does require threat of unlawful violence to be directed against another person present at the scene which would cause fear to a notional bystander of reasonable firmness. See Public Order Act 1986, s 3(1).

affreightment. A contract of affreightment, in the form of a bill of lading (q.v.) or charterparty (q.v.), is an undertaking by a ship owner to carry goods for a person, known as the *freighter*, in his ship for reward. *See* FREIGHT.

aforethought. Premeditated; deliberate. *See* MALICE AFORETHOUGHT.

after-acquired property. A husband was entitled at common law absolutely on his marriage to the property belonging to his wife, including that which she acquired after marriage. The separate treatment of a married woman's property was introduced by L.P.A. 1925, s 170. For accountability concerning after-acquired assets, see *Schuller v Schuller* [1990] 2 FLR 193.

after care condition. Phrase used in relation to planning permission, referring to steps to be taken, after working of minerals, to bring land to the required standard for use in agriculture, forestry, or for amenity: see T.C.P.A. 1971, s 30A (inserted by T.C.P. (Minerals) A. 1981,

s 5); T.C.P.A. 1990, Sch 5. *See* RESTORATION CONDITION.

A-G. Attorney-General (q.v.).

A-G's References, purpose of. CA gave a reminder of the purpose of A-G's References as: the prevention of gross error; allaying of concern at apparently lenient sentences; preservation of public confidence: *A-G's Reference (No 132 of 2001)* [2002] EWCA Crim 1418.

age. 'A person: is over or under a particular age if he has, or as the case may be has not, attained that age: is between two particular ages if he has attained the first but not the second': S.S.A. 1975, Sch 20. Proof of age is by direct evidence (e.g., testimony of persons present at the birth: M.C.A., s 150(4)) or hearsay (production of birth certificate). *See* FULL AGE.

agency. 'A consensual relationship in which one (the agent) holds in trust for and subject to the control of another (the principal) a power to effect certain legal relations of that other': Seavey, *Cases on the Law of Agency* (1925).

agency by estoppel. Requirements are: a representation, a reliance on that representation, alteration of a party's position as a result of that reliance: *per* Slade J in *Rama Corporation v Proved Tin Ltd* [1952] 2 QB 147; *Armagas Ltd v Mundogas SA* [1985] 2 All ER 385.

agency workers. CA held in *Brook St Bureau Ltd v Dacas* [2004] EWCA Civ 217 that it would be erroneous for an employment tribunal to fail to investigate whether an implied contract of employment existed between a worker and a company with which he was placed, in the absence of any written contract between the parties.

agent. Generally one who is employed so as to bring his principal into contractual relationships with other persons. An agency can be created: by express agreement, verbally or in writing; by implication or conduct (see *Summers v Solomon* (1857) 7 E & B 879); by estoppel (q.v.); by necessity, as when a person has been entrusted with another's property, the preservation of which requires certain actions, e.g., feeding and stabling an animal (see *GN Rwy* v *Swaffield* (1874) LR 6 Ex 132; *Eagle Recovery Services* v *Parr* [1998] CLY 3379). ('In considering what is reasonably necessary any material circumstances must be taken into account, e.g., danger, distance, accommodation, expense, time and so forth': *per* Lord Lindley in *Phelps & Co* v *Hill* [1891] 1 QB 605.) An agency may be terminated by operation of law or action of parties. See *Page* v *Combined Shipping Ltd* [1997] 3 All ER 656; *Moore* v *Piretta Ltd* [1999] 1 All ER 174. *See* RATIFICATION.

agent and principal, duties of. A principal's duties are generally: to pay the agent his agreed remuneration; to indemnify the agent against expenses, liabilities and claims incurred in discharging the agency. An agent's duties are: to respect his principal's title; to exercise his duties with appropriate care and skill (see *Chaudry* v *Prabhakar* [1988] 3 All ER 718); to perform those duties personally; to avoid conflict between his personal interests and those of the principal; to account for and hand over to the principal all money due. One who bribes an agent can be required to account for profits: *Fyffes Group* v *Templeman* (2000) *The Times*, 13 June.

agent and principal, remedies of. Agent's remedies include: claim for breach of contract, set-off, lien on goods, stoppage *in transitu*, action for taking of an account. Principal's remedies include: dismissal, claims for conversion or breach of contract, prosecution under Prevention of Corruption Acts 1906, 1916.

agent, commercial. A self-employed intermediary who has continuing authority to negotiate the sale or purchase of goods on behalf of another person (the principal), or to negotiate and conclude the sale or purchase of goods on behalf of and in the name of that principal: SI 93/3053, 98/2818. See EC Council Directive 86/653/EEC; *Page* v *Combined Shipping Ltd* [1997] 3 All ER 656; *Parks* v *Esso Ltd* [2000] Eu LR 25.

agent provocateur. 'A person who entices another to commit an express breach of the law which he would not otherwise have committed and then proceeds to inform against him in respect of such an offence': *Royal Commission on Police Powers* 1928 (Cmd 3297), cited in *R* v *Mealey and Sheridan* (1975) 60 Cr App R 59. If a crime is procured by an *agent provocateur*, that is in itself no defence, but it may result in a lighter sentence. See *R* v *Smurthwaite* [1994] 1 All ER 898. *See* ENTRAPMENT.

agent, special. An agent employed to transact particular business only.

agent's signature. A *descriptive signature* shows that the agent has contracted personally, e.g., 'as charterer'; see *Universal Steam Navigation Co* v *McKelvie & Co* [1923] AC 492. A *representative signature* indicates the representative nature of the signatory and does not result in the agent's personal liability; e.g., 'on account of my principal, P'. See *Lester* v *Balfour Williamson Ltd* [1953] 2 QB 168.

agent, universal. An agent appointed, usually by power of attorney (q.v.), with unlimited authority to act for his principal.

age of consent. *See* CONSENT, AGE OF.

age of victim, relevance of. CA held in *R* v *Bollom* (1993) *The Times*, 15 December, that, where the court considered whether injuries constituted grievous bodily harm, it was essential that an assessment be made of the effect of the injuries on a victim, taking into account his age and health.

age, proof of. Procedure whereby a person's age is proved by: production of a birth certificate and evidence of identity; declaration of a deceased person against interest or in the course of duty; someone present at the birth. In some cases (see, e.g., S.O.A. 1956, s 28(3)), there may be an 'inference of age' from appearance.

aggravated assault. An assault (q.v.), such as that committed upon a woman, meriting a more severe punishment than that following a common assault; or assault with intent to resist arrest; or assault on constable (see Police Act 1964, s 51). See O.P.A. 1861, ss 38, 43; Th.A. 1968, s 8 (under which a person guilty of assault with intent to rob is liable to life imprisonment); *R v Fernandez* [1997] 1 Cr App R 123. *See* ASSAULT, RACIALLY-AGGRAVATED.

aggravated burglary. *See* BURGLARY.

aggravated damages. *See* DAMAGES.

aggravated offences, religious. Anti-terrorism, Crime and Security Act 2001, s 39, amends Crime and Disorder Act 1998, s 28, so as to refer to religious as well as racial aggravation. 'Religious belief' is not defined. Religiously-aggravated offences are included in definition under Police and Criminal Evidence Act 1984, s 24(2) of 'arrestable offences': s 39(8).

aggravated trespass. *See* TRESPASS, AGGRAVATED.

aggravated vehicle-taking. *See* VEHICLE-TAKING, AGGRAVATED.

aggrieved person. 'A man who has suffered a legal grievance, a man against whom a decision has been pronounced which has wrongly deprived him of something, or wrongly refused him something, or wrongly affected his title to something': *per* James LJ in *Ex p Sidebotham* (1880) 14 Ch D 458. See *Cook v Southend BC* [1990] 2 WLR 61. *See* LOCUS STANDI.

agistment. Allowing another's animals to graze on one's pastures for reward. See Agricultural Holdings Act 1986, s 18(5): 'agisted livestock' means 'livestock belonging to another person which has been taken in by the tenant of an agricultural holding to be fed at a fair price.' See *Re Southern Livestock Producers* [1964] 1 WLR 34.

agnates. Relations by the father's side, e.g., one's son, brother, sister. *See* COGNATES.

agreement. A consensus of minds, or evidence of such consensus, in spoken or written form relating to anything done or to be done. 'A declared concurrence of will of two or more persons whereby a change in their legal spheres is intended': Gareis, *Encyclopaedia of Legal Theory* (1905). *See* CONTRACT.

agreement, conditional. An agreement, the operation of which is dependent on the occurrence of an uncertain event.

See *Hargreaves Transport Ltd v Lynch* [1969] 1 WLR 215.

agreement, inferred. *See* INFERRED AGREEMENT.

agreement, modifying. An agreement varying or supplementing an earlier agreement: C.C.A. 1974, s 82(2).

agreement, multiple. A term used under C.C.A. 1974, s 18, to refer to an agreement, the terms of which place a part of it within one category of agreement mentioned in the Act, and another part of it within a different category of agreement so mentioned, or within a category of agreement not so mentioned, or which place it or a part of it within two or more categories of agreement so mentioned.

agreement, non-commercial. A consumer credit agreement (q.v.) or a consumer hire agreement not made by the creditor or owner in the course of a business carried on by him: C.C.A. 1974, s 189(1).

agreements, regulated. *See* REGULATED AGREEMENTS.

agricultural holding. 'The aggregate of the land (whether agricultural land or not) comprised in a contract of tenancy which is a contract for an agricultural tenancy, not being a contract under which the land is let to the tenant during his continuance in any office, appointment or employment held under the landlord': Agricultural Holdings Act 1986, s 1(1). 'Agricultural land' is land used for agricultural purposes in relation to a trade or business. Security of tenure is conferred. Notice period is generally one year and is operative only if, e.g., consent is given by the Agricultural Land Tribunal and land is required for non-agricultural use. Rent may be fixed, in absence of agreement, by an arbitrator appointed under the 1986 Act, s 6. See CPR, Sch 2: CCR O44. See Agricultural Holdings (Am.) Act 1990; Agricultural Tenancies Act 1995; *Crawford v Elliott* [1991] 13 EG 163; *EWP v Moore* [1992] 2 WLR 184; *Barrett v Morgan* (2000) *The Times*, 28 January. *See* FARM BUSINESS TENANCY.

agricultural occupancies, assured. Tenancies or licences granted to agricultural workers and governed by H.A. 1988, Part I, chap III. An occupancy must fulfil 'the occupation condition' (e.g., it must be under an assured, but not an assured shorthold, tenancy) and 'the employment condition' (based on the Rent (Agriculture) Act 1976, Sch 3, defining 'qualifying worker'). See H.A. 1988, Sch 1, para 7, substituted by Agricultural Tenancies Act 1995, Sch 8, para 34. (For 'protected tenancies' in relation to agricultural holdings, see Rent Act 1977, s 10, substituted by Agricultural Tenancies Act 1995, Sch 8, para 27.)

agricultural property. Means 'agricultural land or pasture and includes woodland and any building used in connection with the intensive rearing of livestock or fish if the woodland or building is occupied with agricultural land or pasture and the occupation is ancillary to that of the agricultural land or pasture; and also includes such cottages, farm buildings and farmhouses, together with the land occupied with them, as are of a character appropriate to the property': Capital Transfer Tax Act 1984, s 115(2). See *Starke* v *IRC* [1996] 1 All ER 622.

agricultural tenancy, variation of. CA held in *Secretary of State for Defence* v *Spencer* (2003) *The Times*, 9 June, that where the rent of an agricultural tenancy had been varied following the addition of a small piece of land to the holding, that variation reflected no more then the value of that additional land, and it did not provide any basis for the entitlement to a three-yearly review by an arbitrator under Agricultural Holdings Act 1986, Sch 2, para 4(1).

agriculture. 'Includes horticulture, fruit growing, seed growing, dairy farming, livestock breeding and keeping, the use of land as grazing land, meadow land, osier land, market gardens and nursery grounds, and the use of land for woodlands where that use is ancillary to the farming of land for other agricultural purposes': Agricultural Tenancies Act 1995, s 38(1).

AID. Artificial insemination by donor (q.v.).

aid. To help, promote, encourage, assist. See *Anyanwu* v *South Bank Students' Union* (1998) *The Times*, 4 November (narrow meaning of 'knowingly aided' in Race Relations Act 1976, s 33).

aid or abet. Knowingly assisting the perpetrator of a crime. 'Aiding and abetting almost inevitably involves a situation in which the secondary party and the main offender are together at some stage discussing the plans which they may be making in respect of the alleged offence, and are in contact so that each knows what is passing through the mind of the other': *A-G's Reference (No. 1 of 1975)* [1975] 2 All ER 684. 'Whosoever shall aid, abet, counsel or procure the commission of any misdemeanour at common law or by virtue of any Act passed or to be passed, shall be liable to be tried, indicted and punished as a principal offender': Accessories and Abettors Act 1861, s 8. See also M.C.A. 1980, s 44; *Wilcox* v *Jeffrey* [1951] 1 All ER 464; *Hui Chi-ming* v *R* [1991] 3 All ER 897; *R* v *Alford Transport* (1997) 94 LSG 26. For 'passive assistance' in the commission of an offence, see *R* v *Bland* [1988] Crim LR 41. *See* ABET; ACCESSORY; ACCOMPLICE; PROCURING AN OFFENCE.

AIDS. Acquired immune deficiency syndrome, characterised by a failure of function of the human body's immune system. *See* AIDS (Control) Act 1987, requiring periodical reports on matters relating to AIDS to be made to the Secretary of State by Regional and District Health Authorities: see s 1, as amended by NHS and Community Care Act 1990, Sch 9, and Health Authorities Act 1995, Sch 1. For HIV (human immune deficiency virus, thought to cause AIDS), see *Re HIV Haemophiliac Litigation* (1990) *The Guardian*, 28 September; *R* v *Stark* [1992] Crim LR 384; *Re C (Child: HIV Test)* [1999] 2 FLR 1004.

air navigation, directions concerning. Secretary of State may give directions to Civil Air Authority imposing duties concerning air navigation in a managed area (i.e., UK, or an area outside UK in respect of which UK has international duties): Transport Act 2000, ss 66(1), 72(3). CAA must act in manner best calculated to secure most efficient use of airspace consistent with safety and expeditious flow of aircraft, to satisfy operators' requirements, to take account of national security interests: s 70(2). A high standard of safety has priority: s 70(1).

air pollution. A local authority may require the occupier of any premises (except private dwellings) in its area to furnish information concerning the emission of pollutants and other substances into the air from those premises: Control of Pollution Act 1974, s 80(1), as amended by En.P.A. 1990, Sch 15, and Pollution Prevention and Control Act 1999. See also Clean Air Acts 1956–93, which imposed fines for the emission of dark smoke from buildings in certain areas; *Camden LBC* v *Gunby* [2000] 1 WLR 465. *See* ENVIRONMENTAL PROTECTION; POLLUTION, ENVIRONMENTAL.

air, right to flow of. The right can subsist as an easement (q.v.) if claimed in respect of some defined channel, e.g., a ventilator. See *Cable* v *Bryant* [1908] 1 Ch 259.

airspace, interference with. A possible trespass created by an intrusion into another's airspace. See *Woollerton & Wilson Ltd* v *Richard Costain Ltd* [1970] 1 WLR 411. 'In none of [the cases] is there an authoritative pronouncement that [in the phrase "trespass to land"] "land" means the whole of space from the centre of the earth to the heavens': *Commissioner for Rwys* v *Valuer-General* [1974] AC 328. See *Bernstein* v *Skyviews* [1977] 2 All ER 902 (no right of privacy in airspace). See Civil Aviation Act 1982, s 77. *See* CUJUS EST SOLUM (etc.).

air traffic, CAA's general duty. Civil Air Authority must maintain a high standard of safety and act so as to facilitate interests of aircraft operators and owners, and passengers, to promote efficiency and economy on part of licence holders, and take account of UK's international obligations: Transport Act 2000, s 2.

air traffic, restrictions on providing services. A person commits an offence if he provides air services in respect of a managed area: Transport Act 2000, s 3(1). Exemptions may be granted to a particular person or to persons of a specified description, in respect of services of one or more specified descriptions: s 4(2).

air traffic services. These include, under Transport Act 2000, s 98, the providing of information and advice concerned with prevention of aircraft collisions, the providing of instructions to secure safe and efficient flying, the managing of air traffic flow to secure most efficient use of airspace, the providing of facilities for communicating with aircraft. See Schs 1–9.

air travel, offences relating to. SI 99/2059, amending SI 95/1970, creates new offences of acting in a disruptive manner in an aircraft, using threatening language, or behaving in a disorderly manner, towards a crew member, wilfully interfering with the performance by a member of crew of his duties. See *R* v *Ayodeji* (2000) *The Times*, 20 October.

air weapons, lethal nature of. It was held, in *DPP* v *Street* (2004) *The Times*, 23 January, that there was no necessity for an object to fall into the category of lethal weapons for it to breach the prohibition on carrying a loaded weapon in a public place. See Firearms Act 1968, s 19.

alcohol. Defined under Licensing Act 2003, s 191, as meaning spirits, wine, beer, cider or any other fermented, distilled or spirituous liquor, but not including, for example, alcohol which is of a strength not exceeding 0.5% at the time of the sale or supply in question, perfume, alcohol included in a medicinal product, denatured alcohol, or alcohol contained in liqueur confectionery.

alcohol ban. Privy Council held that European Convention, art 8 (interference with private life), had no application to a ban on alcohol imposed as a condition on the right of a doctor to practise, for reasons of his physical and mental health. See *Whitefield* v *GMC* [2002] UKPC 62.

alcoholism. Addiction to excessive consumption of alcoholic liquor. An alcoholic state induced by voluntary drinking does not constitute a defence. It could be treated as a duress (q.v.) for purposes of defence of diminished responsibility (q.v.) if defendant's intellectual or emotional impairment was caused by damage resulting from the alcoholism or by drinking which had been rendered involuntary by the alcoholism. See *R* v *Tandy* [1989] 1 All ER 267; *R* v *Inseal* [1992] Crim LR 35.

alcohol on coaches and trains. It is an offence to permit intoxicating liquor to be carried on a public service or railway passenger vehicle to or from a designated sporting event, or to have intoxicating liquor in one's possession during the period of such an event when in any area of a designated sports ground from which the event may be directly viewed: Sporting Events (Control of Alcohol etc.) Act 1985, ss 1, 2, as amended.

alcohol, prescribed limits in driving. *See* PRESCRIBED LIMITS OF ALCOHOL IN BLOOD, ETC.

aleatory contract. (*Alea* = dice.) Contract in which a party's duty of performance depends upon some uncertain event, e.g., a wagering contract, a contract of insurance. See *Ellesmere* v *Wallace* [1929] 2 Ch 1. *See* BET.

alias. (*Alias dictus* = otherwise called.) Second, or assumed, name.

alibi, evidence in support of. (*Alibi* = elsewhere). Under C.P.I.A. 1996, s 5(8), this is evidence tending to show that by reason of the presence of the accused at a particular place or in a particular area at a particular time, he was not, or was unlikely to have been, at the place where the offence is alleged to have been committed at the time of the alleged commission. (C.J.A. 1967, s 11 (notice of alibi), is repealed: C.P.I.A. 1996, s 74.) If the defence statement discloses an alibi, the accused must give particulars of that alibi in the statement; this must include the name and address of any witness the accused believes is able to give evidence in support of the alibi: s 5(7). See *R* v *Popat (No. 2)* [2000] 1 Cr App R 387.

alien. At common law, one who was 'born out of the allegiance of our sovereign Lord the King': Littleton, *Tenures* (1481). Under B.N.A. 1981, s 51(1), it means a person who is neither a Commonwealth citizen, nor a British protected person, nor a citizen of the Republic of Ireland. An *alien enemy* is a subject of a state with which this country is at war, or who resides voluntarily or carries on business in enemy, or enemy-occupied, territory. See *Sooracht's Case* [1943] AC 203; *Milltronics* v *Hycontrol* [1990] FSR 273. *See* NATURALISATION.

alienable. Capable of being transferred.

alienate. To exercise the power of disposing of or transferring property.

alienation. Power of disposing of or transferring an interest in property; the exercise of that power by an *alienor* in relation to an *alienee*.

alienation, restraint on. Conditions attempting to fetter the right to dispose of or transfer freely an interest in possession in property. Generally void. See, e.g., *Re Dugdale* (1888) 38 Ch D 176; *Caldy Manor Estate Ltd* v *Farrell* [1974] 3 All ER 753; Inheritance (Provision for Family and Dependants) Act 1975 (example of limitation of the right to alienate).

alieni juris. Of another's right. Term used to refer (in contrast to *sui juris* (q.v.)) to persons subject to the authority of another, e.g., minors.

alimentary trust. A protective trust (q.v.).

alimony. (*Alimonia* = nourishment.) 'That allowance which a married woman sues for on separation from her husband': Cowell, *Institutes of English Law* (1605). Maintenance pending suit (q.v.) has replaced alimony pending suit; financial provision for a spouse has replaced an order for permanent alimony: see Mat.C.A. 1973, Part II, as amended.

aliter. Otherwise.

aliunde. From elsewhere.

allegation. A statement of fact in proceedings made by a party who undertakes to prove it.

allegiance. 'Such natural or legal obedience which every subject owes to his prince': *Termes de la Ley*. Allegiance may be due not only from subjects (wherever they may be), but also from aliens resident in British territory or elsewhere if they retain British passports: *Joyce v DPP* [1946] AC 347. Breach of allegiance may amount to treason (q.v.). *See* LOYALTY.

allegiance, oath of. *See* OATH OF ALLEGIANCE.

all endeavours clause. Clause in contract obliging a purchaser to use 'all reasonable endeavours' to obtain certain rights for the benefit of the seller. Held enforceable in *Lambert v HTY Cymru Ltd* [1998] EMLR 629.

allocation procedure, questionnaire. Questionnaire served on each party by the court when defendant files a defence, unless the court dispenses with the need for it, or unless claimant states that money claimed has been paid (CPR, r 15.10), or defendant admits part of a specified money claim (r 14.5). It asks, e.g., whether appropriate pre-action protocols (q.v.) have been observed, whether a stay to allow for settlement is sought (r 1.4(2)(f)). If no party files the questionnaire, the claim may be struck out: PD 26, para 2.5. Allocation hearing may be held if court thinks it necessary: r 26.5(4). *See* CASE MANAGEMENT.

allocation to tracks, CPR. Fundamental rule for track allocation derives from monetary value of claim: r 26.8(2); PD 26, para 7.4. Additionally, court may consider: nature of remedy sought; complexity of facts; number of likely parties and counterclaims; views and circumstances of parties. Allocation of claim may be made to: small claims track; fast track; multi-track (qq.v.). A claim will not be allocated to a track if its financial value exceeds limit for that track, unless all parties agree: r 26.7(3). Notice of allocation is served on all parties: r 26.9. Claims with no monetary value are allocated to track considered by the procedural judge to be the most suitable. Allocation may be challenged: PD 26, para 11.

allocutus. Demand by court of a convicted person, asking whether he has cause to show why judgment should not be pronounced against him.

allodial land. Land owned outright, i.e., owned absolutely and not held of any lord or superior. All land is held, directly or indirectly, of the Crown, i.e., no subject of the Crown in England may hold land allodially; he can hold only an estate (q.v.) in land; see *Minister of State for the Army v Dalziel* (1943) 68 CLR 261.

allonge. Slip of paper securely attached to a negotiable instrument, e.g., a bill of exchange (q.v.), on which endorsements may be made. See B.Ex.A. 1882, s 32.

allotment, letter of. Notification to an applicant that shares in a company have been appropriated to him, usually by resolution of the board of directors. Generally, allotment signifies acceptance of an offer to take shares. There is no binding contract until an allotment is made and a letter has been posted, or has reached the allottee in another way. The allottee acquires an unconditional right to be included in the company's register of members: Cos.A. 1985, s 738(1). See *Household Fire Insurance Co v Grant* (1879) 4 Ex D 216. *See* SHARE.

allow. Permit (q.v.). 'A man cannot be said to allow that of which he is unaware, or that which he cannot prevent': *per* Darling J in *Crabtree v Fern Spinning Co* (1901) 85 LT 549. See *Greener v DPP* [1996] COD 200.

all risks policy. Insurance policy requiring the person insured to take all reasonable steps to prevent loss. 'All the insured has to do is to prove that there was a loss due to a fortuitous happening of some sort': *per* Hodgson J in *Port-Rose v Phoenix Assurance plc* (1986) 136 NLJ 333.

alteration. A material change (e.g., of a date), which alters the sense or effect of an instrument, generally invalidates it. An alteration in a deed (q.v.) is presumed to have been made before or at the time of execution; an alteration in a will (q.v.) is presumed to have been made after the time of execution. See W.A. 1837, s 21;

Re Adams [1990] 2 WLR 924; *Raiffeisen Zentralbank* v *Cross-seas Shipping Ltd* [2000] 1 All ER (Comm) 76 (unilateral alteration nullifies a deed only when the parties' rights and obligations are affected).

alteration of share capital. A company may alter its capital if authorised by its articles of association (q.v.): Cos.A. 1985, s 121. A resolution in a general meeting is needed and notice must be given to the Registrar: s 123. Shares may be *consolidated*, e.g., by the amalgamation of smaller into larger, and *subdivided*, or converted to stock. Nominal or authorised capital (q.v.) may be increased and unissued nominal capital cancelled. See ss 135–141. *See* SHARE.

alternative counts. *See* COUNTS, ALTERNATIVE.

alternative danger, principle of. Common law principle relating to tort, arising where the plaintiff has not necessarily contributed by negligence (q.v.) to his injuries if, as the result of the defendant's negligence, the plaintiff was placed in a dilemma and, 'in the agony of the moment', chose a wrong alternative. See, e.g., *Jones* v *Boyce* (1816) 1 Stark 493.

alternative dispute resolution. Often abbreviated to ADR: modes of resolving an issue without resort to the normally applicable trial process, e.g., mediation (q.v.), formalised settlement conferences, conciliation (q.v.). See, e.g., Practice Direction No. 49/1977 (Medical/Clinical Negligence) (1998) 148 NLJ 59, para 5(c); *Resolving Disputes Without Going to Court* (Lord Chancellor's Department, 1995).

alternative dispute resolution under CPR. Under CPR, the duty of the court 'to actively manage cases' involves 'encouraging the parties to use an alternative dispute resolution procedure if the court considers that appropriate, and facilitating the use of such procedure': r14(2)(e). When filing completed allocation questionnaire, a party may make a written request for proceedings to be stayed while parties try to settle the case by ADR or other means: r 26.4(1).

alternative verdict. *See* VERDICT, ALTERNATIVE.

amalgamation. The combination of two or more companies into one company or into a unit controlled by one company. See Cos.A. 1985, ss 425, 427, as amended; and Ins.A. 1986, ss 110, 111; *Re Savoy Hotel* [1981] Ch 351.

ambiguity. Uncertain meaning or equivocation. 1. *Patent ambiguity* (e.g., a blank space in a deed) is one apparent on the face of the instrument. It cannot generally be resolved by parol evidence (q.v.). See *Watcham* v *A-G for E Africa* [1919] AC 533. 2. *Latent ambiguity* (e.g., 'My horse I leave to my nephew, John', where the testator had two nephews of that name) is one not apparent on the face of the instrument. It may generally be resolved by parol evidence (q.v.). For the rectification, etc. of wills (q.v.) see A.J.A. 1982, ss 20–22; *Walker* v *Medlicott & Son* [1999] 1 WLR 727. *See* EQUIVOCATION.

ambulatory. (Literally, able to walk.) Capable of being revoked. Thus, a man's will is ambulatory until the moment of his death. See *Vynior's Case* (1609) 8 Co Rep 81b.

ambush defence. Means a defence which is introduced at a late stage so that it effectively hampers the prosecution, which is given no time to prepare an appropriate response. See Criminal Justice Act 2003, Part 5, and *R* v *Brizzalari* [2004] EWCA Crim 310.

ameliorating waste. Alterations which, in fact, improve leased land: *Doherty* v *Allman* (1877) 3 App Cas 709 – injunction refused where tenant was converting dilapidated store houses into dwellings. *See* WASTE.

amendment. Correction of a defect in a statement of case (q.v.), or in criminal proceedings. 'I know of no kind of error or mistake which, if not fraudulent or intended to overreach, the court ought not to correct, if it can be done without injustice to the other party': *Cropper* v *Smith* (1884) 26 Ch D 700.

amendments to statements of case. A party may amend his statement of case (q.v.) at any time before it has been served on any other party; but, after service, amendment may be made only with permission of the court or with written consent of all other parties: CPR, r 17.1. Amendments made where permission of the court was not required may be disallowed: r 17.2(1). A party applying for an amendment will usually be liable for costs arising.

amends, tender of. An offer of money tendered in satisfaction of the alleged committing of a wrong. Where used as a defence, money tendered must be brought to court. See Defamation Act 1996, s 2, under which a person who has made a statement alleged to be defamatory may offer to make amends; the offer must be in writing, may be general or qualified, must involve publication of correction, apology and payment of compensation. *See* DEFAMATION.

amenity. That which is conducive to comfort or convenience. 'In relation to any place includes any view of or from that place': Petroleum (Consolidation) Act 1928, s 23.

amenity, loss of. Also referred to as 'loss of faculty' and 'loss of enjoyment of life'. Result of injuries depriving the plaintiff of some enjoyment. See *Povey* v *Governors of Rydal School* [1970] 1 All ER 841; *Chequepoint Ltd* v *Secretary for the Environment* (1996) 72 P & CR 415.

amenity, preservation of. Basis of provisions relating to buildings of special interest, trees, caravan sites, etc. See, e.g., T.C.P.A. 1971, s 65 (substituted by H.&P.A. 1986, s 46); En.P.A. 1990, s 3. *See* PRESERVATION ORDER.

amercement. Procedure, now obsolete, involving imposition of a pecuniary penalty on an offender, based on assessment of his ability to pay. See *Re Nottingham Corporation* [1897] 2 QB 502.

amicus curiae. Friend of the court. A person who is not engaged in the case, but who brings to the court's attention a point which has apparently been overlooked. See *Morelle* v *Wakeling* [1955] 2 QB 379; *Adams* v *Adams* [1970] 3 All ER 572 (right of Attorney-General to

intervene in a private action which may affect Crown prerogatives); *Sherdley* v *Sherdley* [1987] 2 WLR 1071.

ammunition. Defined in Firearms Act 1968, as ammunition for any firearm, and includes grenades, bombs and other like missiles, whether capable of use with a firearm or not, and 'prohibited ammunition' (which includes any ammunition containing, or designed or adapted to contain, any noxious liquid, gas or other things: s 5(1), (2)). See Firearms (Amendment) Acts 1988 and 1997, s 9 (prohibition of ammunition which incorporates a missile designed or adapted to expand on impact); *R* v *Stubbings* [1990] Crim LR 811.

amnesty. An act of government by which certain past offences are obliterated from legal remembrance. Generally granted to groups who have been involved in, e.g., political offences (see 1747 amnesty for those who had fought in the second Jacobite uprising). *See* PARDON.

Amsterdam, Treaty of. Treaty, signed on 2 October 1997, concerning the aims and future of the European Union (EU). (See also European Communities (Amendment) Act 1998.) It deals with, e.g., strengthening the basic notion of EU, improving its foreign policy arrangements, and developing co-operation in matters concerning justice. In defining the principles of EU, it calls for their extension so as to include principles of liberty, democracy, respect for human rights and the rule of law. *See* EUROPEAN UNION.

anatomical examination. The examination by dissection of a body for purposes of teaching or studying, or researching into, morphology: Anatomy Act 1984, s 1(1). The examination must be carried out on properly-licensed premises: ss 2(1), 3. It is an offence to carry out such an examination in contravention of the Act: s 11.

ancestor. 1. One from whom a person is descended. 2. Before L.P.A. 1925, a person from whom real property was inherited. See *Zetland* v *Lord Advocate*

(1878) 3 App Cas 505; *Knowles* v *A-G* [1951] P 4.

ancient document. A document 20 years old or more. 'Ancient documents coming out of proper custody and purporting on the face of them to show exercise of ownership . . . may be given in evidence without proof of possession or payment of rent as being in themselves acts of ownership and proof of possession': *Malcolmson* v *O'Dea* (1863) 10 HLC 593. See Evidence Act 1938, s 4; *Bristow* v *Cormican* (1878) 3 App Cas 641. *See* DOCUMENT.

ancient lights. A right which arises 'when the access and use of light . . . shall have been actually enjoyed . . . for the full period of 20 years without interruption . . . unless it shall appear that the same was enjoyed by some consent or agreement . . . by deed or writing': Prescription Act 1832, s 3. 'Lights' refers to windows, or apertures. See, e.g., *Pugh* v *Howells* (1984) 48 P & CR 298. See also Rights of Light Act 1959.

ancient monument. Any scheduled monument or other monument, which, in the opinion of the Secretary of State is of public interest by reason of the historic, architectural, traditional, artistic or archaeological interests attaching to it: Ancient Monuments and Archaeological Areas Act 1979, s 61(12) as amended, Schs 1, 2. See National Heritage Acts 1983, 1997.

ancillary credit business. Business comprising or relating to: credit brokerage; debt adjusting; debt-counselling; debt-collecting; the operation of a credit reference agency: C.C.A. 1974, s 145(1).

ancillary probate. *See* PROBATE, ANCILLARY.

ancillary relief. Phrase used, e.g., under Matrimonial Causes Rules 1977, and Family Proceedings Rules 1991 (SI 91/1247), referring to an order for maintenance pending suit, financial provision order, property adjustment order, variation order, etc. See Mat.C.A. 1973, ss 22–24, 26(1); s 31(2) for orders that can be varied; *Re T* [1990] 1 FLR 1; *Xydhias* v *Xydhias* [1999] 1 FLR 683 (the principles to be applied to the compromise of ancillary relief application). See F.L.A. 1996, s 15; *Practice Direction (Family Proceedings: Ancillary Relief Procedure)* [2000] 3 All ER 379; SI 99/3491; *White* v *White* [2000] 3 WLR 1571. In *Miller* v *Miller*; *McFarlane* v *McFarlane* [2006] *The Times*, 25 May, the HL held that when looking at divorce settlements there are three principle points for the courts to consider; (1) the needs of the parties, (2) compensation and (3) the equal sharing principle. Other factors that the court should bear in mind are the duration of the marriage relating to non-matrimonial property and the conduct of the parties with regards to what consists of matrimonial property.

See PRODUCTION APPOINTMENT.

and. Conjunction generally used to connect words, phrases, clauses intended to be read jointly. For problems in construing 'and' in relation to the purported creation of a charitable trust (q.v.), compare *Re Sutton* (1885) 28 Ch D 464 ('charitable and deserving' objects held to be exclusively charitable), and *A-G of the Bahamas* v *Royal Trust Co* [1986] 1 WLR 1001 ('education and welfare' construed disjunctively, so that the proposed gift failed). For comment on 'and/or', see *Stanton* v *Richardson* (1875) 45 LJQB 78; *New Hampshire Insurance Co* v *MGN Ltd* [1996] 2 CLY 1396. *See* OR.

animal. Term which includes (*a*) any kind of mammal, except man, (*b*) any kind of four-footed beast, which is not a mammal, (*c*) fish, reptiles, crustaceans and other cold-blooded creatures not falling within (*a*) or (*b*) above: Animal Health Act 1981, s 87; SI 99/646. 'Any creature other than a bird or fish': Food Safety Act 1990, s 53. 'Wild animals' are animals not normally domesticated in Britain: Zoo Licensing Act 1981, s 21(1). See the Animal Health and Welfare Act 1984; Protection of Animals (Am.) Acts 1988, 2000; *Isted* v *CPS* [1998] Crim LR 194; Protection of Badgers Act 1992; *Green* v *DPP* (2000) *The Times*, 29 June.

animals, classification of. Animals *domitae naturae* or *mansuetae naturae* (tame or domesticated, e.g., horses); animals *ferae naturae* (of a wild nature), e.g., monkeys. Under the Animals Act 1971, s 2(2), liability arises, in the case of an animal of a non-dangerous species if: damage is of a kind which the animal, unless restrained, was likely to cause, or which if caused by the animal, was likely to be severe; likelihood of the danger or its severity is due to the animal's characteristics not likely to be found in animals of that species; those characteristics are known to its keeper, or his servant, or a member of the household under 16 years. See *Jaundrill* v *Gillett* (1996) *The Times*, 30 January. See also Dangerous Wild Animals Act 1976; *Hunt* v *Wallis* (1991) *The Times*, 10 May; *South Kesteven DC* v *Mackie* [1999] NPC 119. *See* DANGEROUS SPECIES; DANGEROUS WILD ANIMALS.

animals, dangerous. *See* DANGEROUS WILD ANIMALS.

animals, orders for care, disposal or slaughter. Under Protection of Animals (Amendment) Act 2000, s 2, where animals have been the subject of a prosecution for cruelty or neglect, brought under the Protection of Animals Act 1911, s 1, the court may make an order authorising the prosecutor to take charge of and care for the animals, or sell them at a fair price, or dispose of them otherwise than by way of sale, or slaughter them.

animal, wild. 'Any animal (other than a bird) which is or (before it was killed or taken) was living wild': Wildlife and Countryside Act 1981, s 27(1). See *McQuaker* v *Goddard* [1940] 1 KB 687. *See* WILD MAMMALS, CRUELTY TO.

animus. Intention; disposition. 1. *animus deserendi*. Intention of deserting. 2. *animus furandi*. Intention of stealing. 3. *animus manendi*. Intention of remaining. 4. *animus non revertendi*. Intention of not returning. 5. *animus possidendi*. Intention of possessing (see, e.g., *R* v *Secretary of State for the Environment ex p Davies* (1990) 61 P & CR 487). 6. *animus quo*. Intention with which. 7. *animus revocandi*. Intention of revoking.

8. *animus testandi*. Intention of making a will.

annexation. Joining or uniting one thing to another, e.g., the acquisition of territory by conquest or subjugation. For annexation of chattels to land, see, e.g., *Deen* v *Andrews* (1986) 52 P & CR 17; *Elitstone Ltd* v *Morris* [1997] 1 WLR 687. *See* FIXTURES.

annoyance. 'The expression "annoyance" is wider than "nuisance", and a thing that reasonably troubles the mind and pleasure – not of a fanciful person or of a skilled person who knows the truth, but of the ordinary sensible English inhabitant of a house, seems to me to be an "annoyance", although it may not appear to amount to physical detriment to comfort': *Tod-Heatley* v *Benham* (1888) 40 Ch D 80. See also *Wood* v *Cooper* [1894] 3 Ch 671.

annual return. Document required under the Cos.A. 1985, s 363, as amended by Cos.A. 1989, s 139, which must be filed annually with the Registrar of Companies, made up to the company's return date (initially one year from incorporation) after the annual general meeting and must be accompanied by a copy of the auditors' report and balance sheet. It must contain particulars set out in Cos.A. 1989, s 139.

annuity. An annual payment of a sum of money as a personal obligation of the grantor or charged on personalty or a mixed fund. See *Hill* v *Gregory* [1912] 2 KB 61. An annuity, which before 1 January 1926, was capable of being registered in the register of annuities, is void against a creditor or purchaser of any interest in the land charged with the annuity, unless it is registered in the register of annuities or register of land charges: L.C.A. 1972, Sch 1, para 4. The fact that an annuity is registered does not prevent it being overreached.

annul. To declare judicial proceedings or their outcome to be no longer of legal effect.

annulment. 1. Annulment of adjudication. The court may annul (see Ins.A.

1986, s 282, amended by H.A. 1988, s 117) an adjudication in bankruptcy (q.v.) where, e.g.: in its opinion the debtor should not have been judged bankrupt, or it is proved that the debts have been paid in full, or it approves a composition (q.v.) or scheme. 2. Annulment of marriage. 3. Appeal for annulment. Under Treaty of Rome, arts 173, 174, the European Court of Justice (q.v.) may, on appeal, annul an action of the EU Council or Commission (q.v.) because of the lack of jurisdiction, or violation of an essential procedural matter, or infringement of the Treaty, or misuse of powers.

anonymity, entitlement of police to. CA held in *R(A) v Inner South London Coroner* (2004) *The Times*, 11 November, that a police officer who was to appear at a coroner's inquest was entitled to anonymity for himself and his family if he feared reasonably for his life. See *R(A) v Lord Saville of Newdigate* [2002] 1 WLR 1249.

anonymity in proceedings. In *Re W (Children (Care Proceedings; Witness Anonymity)* (2002) *The Times*, 1 November, the CA held that, in care proceedings, a social worker witness would be given the protection of anonymity only in a very exceptional case. The need for protection of witnesses' identity had to be balanced against any likely unfairness to the parties.

antecedent negotiations. Defined in relation to credit agreements, as including, e.g., negotiations with a hirer or debtor conducted by the owner or creditor in relation to the making of a regulated agreement: C.C.A. 1974, s 1.

antecedent rights. Rights existing in their own sake, prior to the commission of a wrongful act, e.g., one's right not to have reputation attacked unjustifiably. Contrasted with *remedial rights* (which arise from the infringement of a primary right), e.g., rights to damages after events of this nature.

antecedents. Term used to refer, e.g., to an offender's record and other history. Where, after the conviction of an offender, a police officer gives evidence of the offender's character and antecedents, he must confine himself to evidence of the previous convictions, home circumstances, etc. and matters in the offender's favour. See *Practice Direction (Crime: Antecedents) (No. 2)* [1997] 1 WLR 1482; *Re a Barrister (Wasted Costs Order) (No. 9 of 1999)* (2000) *The Times*, 18 April.

ante-date. Dating of a document before the date on which it was drawn up. See B.Ex.A. 1882, s 13(2).

antenatal care, time off for. Right of a pregnant employee not to be unreasonably refused time off during her working hours to receive antenatal care: E.R.A. 1996, s 55; SI 99/101.

antenuptial agreement. *See* PRE-NUPTIAL AGREEMENT.

anticipatory breach. Term referring to the repudiation (q.v.) of a contract before the time for performance. The other party may immediately treat the contract as though it were discharged and sue for damages. See *Hochster v De La Tour* (1835) 2 E & B 678; *Woodar Investments v Wimpey Ltd* [1980] 1 All ER 571. *See* BREACH OF CONTRACT.

anti-social behaviour order. Order made under C.D.A. 1998, s 1, by a magistrates' court, where the person concerned is over 10, has acted in a manner that has caused or was likely to cause harassment, alarm or distress to one or more persons not of the same household as himself, and that the order is needed to protect persons in the local government area in which the harassment, alarm or distress was caused or likely to be caused from further anti-social acts from him. A person who, without reasonable excuse, does anything which he is forbidden to do by the order, commits an offence punishable on indictment with up to five years' imprisonment, or fine, or both, or on summary conviction to imprisonment for up to six months, or fine or both: s 1(10).

anti-social behaviour order, hearings. HL held in *Clingham v Kensington and Chelsea LBC* (2002) *The Times*, 21 October, that hearings relating to an anti-social behaviour order are essentially civil in character and, therefore, hearsay evidence is admissible; but it is necessary to satisfy the criminal standard of proof that the making of such an order is appropriate. Police Reform Act 2002, s 61, amending Crime and Disorder Act 1998, s 1, extends class of applicants for an order to include registered social landlords (Housing Act 1996, s 1).

anti-social behaviour order, imposing of. CA held in *R* v *Parkin* (2004) *The Times*, 20 February, that where a substantial custodial order had been imposed on an offender, there would be few circumstances in which it might be necessary additionally for a suspended anti-social behaviour to become effective on his release.

anti-suit injunction. Injunction granted by an English court to restrain a person from pursuing proceedings in a foreign jurisdiction: see *SNIA Aérospatiale* v *Lee Kui Yak* [1987] 3 All ER 510; *Airbus Industrie GIE* v *Patel* (1998) 148 NLJ 551 ('in exercising the jurisdiction, regard must be had to comity': *per* Lord Goff).

Anton Piller order. High Court order to defendant to permit plaintiff to enter defendant's premises to inspect, remove or make copies of documents. Plaintiff must show that there is a danger of property or vital evidence being removed. See *Anton Piller KG* v *Manufacturing Processes Ltd* [1976] Ch 55. Known now as 'search order' (q.v.).

apology. In an action for libel (q.v.), an apology accompanied by payment of money into the court may be pleaded as a defence or in mitigation of damages. In a case of unintentional defamation, an offer of amends, comprising the published correction of a statement complained of and an apology, may be tendered. See Libel Acts 1843 and 1845; Defamation Acts 1952, 1996, s 2(4)(*a*).

appeal. 'The transference of a case from an inferior to a higher tribunal in the hope of reversing or modifying the decision of the former': *Edlesten* v *LCC* [1918] 1 KB 81. In general, the right of appeal must be given by statute. The whole case must be presented on the

hearing of an appeal; it cannot be conducted in discrete sections: *Commercial Acceptances Ltd* v *Townsend Investments* (2000) *The Times*, 26 April.

appeal, changing grounds of. CA held in *Shire* v *Secretary of State for Work and Pensions* (2003) *The Times*, 30 October, that where permission has been granted, allowing an appeal to CA by a litigant who later decides to put forward an appeal differing substantially from the case already presented, the court and the other party must be informed appropriately.

Appeal Committee of House of Lords. *See* HOUSE OF LORDS, JURISDICTION OF.

Appeal, Court of. *See* COURT OF APPEAL.

Appeal Courts, Summary. Courts set up under Armed Forces Discipline Act 2000, s 14, to hear appeals from a serviceman who has not elected trial by court-martial, and whose commanding officer has found the charge against him proved. He may appeal against finding, sentence, or both. Appeal involves a rehearing. For appointment of judge advocates and officers for the court, see ss 15, 16. There is a right to apply for cases stated to High Court on ground of excess of jurisdiction or error of law: s 21.

appeal, fresh evidence on. In *R* v *Hanratty (deceased)* (2002) *The Times*, 16 May, the CA held that on appeal against conviction, fresh evidence could be introduced by the Crown even though it appeared not to relate directly to ground of appeal and its intention was to weaken the appeal. CA emphasised that in case of admission of fresh evidence, its main purpose was to assist court in furtherance of general principles of justice.

appeal, frivolous. A court considering an appeal may dismiss it summarily if it is regarded as frivolous or vexatious. See C.J.A. 1988, s 157; *R* v *Taylor* [1979] Crim LR 649 (an unarguable defence which was bound to fail). *See* VEXATIOUS PROCEEDING.

appeal, in absence of appellant. In *R* v *Crisp* (2000) *The Times*, 18 June, it was held that it is possible for an appeal to proceed in the absence of an appellant who had refused to comply with a lawful requirement that he be handcuffed while in transit from prison to court.

appeal, outside limitation period. It was held in *Giltinane* v *Child Support Agency* (2006) *The Times*, 7 April, that where a case concerns a liability order in a child support matter, the only method of appeal is by way of case stated within a short non-extendable time limit. However, where there has been a miscarriage of justice, the court has the power to provide a remedy by way of judicial review.

appeal, reopening of. Following the hearing and dismissal of an appeal by the Court of Appeal, or the abandonment of a notice of appeal, a reopening is not allowed (save in the case of a procedural defect in the hearings). The applicant may petition the Home Secretary, who can refer the case to the Court. Where there are exceptional circumstances (e.g., allegation of judge's bias), CA possesses power to reopen an appeal which has already been determined: *Taylor* v *Lawrence* (2002) 152 NLJ 22i. For 'bias', see *Porter* v *Magill* [2002] 1 All ER 465.

appeals, civil. From 2 May 2000, appeals from county court (save for family proceedings) lie to High Court; from decisions of masters, registrars, judges to a High Court judge; from High Court to Court of Appeal (q.v.); from there to House of Lords. See CPR, Sch 1; O 58, rr 1, 2; O 59; A.J. (Appeals) A. 1934, s 1; S.C.A. 1981, s 54(6); SI 00/1071; Acc.J.A. 1999, s 56 (Lord Chancellor's power to prescribe alternative destination of appeals); *Commissioners of Excise* v *Eastwood Homes* (2000) *The Times*, 7 March. Rules of court may provide that any right of appeal to county court, High Court, or Court of Appeal, may be exercised only with permission: Acc.J.A. 1999, s 54(1). For purposes of s 54, a right of appeal to Court of Appeal includes right to make an application for a new trial and right to make application to set a verdict aside: s 54(6). For

detailed explanation, see *Tanfern Ltd* v *Cameron-Macdonald* (2000) *The Times*, 17 May. *See* HOUSE OF LORDS, CIVIL APPEAL, PROCEDURE.

appeals, criminal. Appeal lies: from courts of summary jurisdiction to Crown Court (M.C.A. 1980, s 108); from justices by way of case stated to High Court (s 111); in indictable cases, from Crown Court to Court of Appeal (Criminal Division) (Criminal Appeal Act 1968, s 45), from Court of Appeal to House of Lords (q.v.). For right of prosecution to appeal on a point of law following acquittal on indictment, see C.J.A. 1972, s 36(1). See *Law Commission Consultation Paper No 158 (2000): Prosecution Appeals against Judges' Rulings*. See also C.L.A. 1977, s 44, as amended; C.J.A. 1988, ss 35, 36, allowing A-G to refer certain sentences to Court of Appeal (Civil Division) if the sentences seem unduly lenient; Criminal Appeal Act 1995, s 2(1), under which Court of Appeal shall allow an appeal against conviction if they think that the conviction is *unsafe*, and shall dismiss such an appeal in any other case. See *R* v *Clinton* [1993] 1 WLR 1181 (conviction can be set aside when accused seems to have been unfairly prejudiced by flagrantly incompetent advocacy). *See* TRIAL, NEW.

appeals, second, in civil matters. Where an appeal lies to a county court or High Court, and on hearing the appeal the court makes a decision, no appeal may be made to the Court of Appeal from that decision unless the Court of Appeal considers that the appeal would raise an important point of principle or practice, or there is some other compelling reason for the Court of Appeal to hear it. See *Clark* v *Perks* [2000] 4 All ER 1.

appear, failure to. Failure of party to litigation to appear. Where an applicant or any respondent fails to attend the hearing of an application, the court may proceed in his absence: CPR, r 23.11(1).

appellant. The person making an appeal.

appellate jurisdiction. Power of a court to hear an appeal.

appendant. Annexed to a hereditament (q.v.) by operation of law, e.g., a common of pasture. Can generally be claimed by prescription (q.v.). *See* APPURTENANT.

application notice. Document in which applicant states his intention to seek a court order: CPR, r 23.1. See PD 23, para 2.1.

applications which may be dealt with without hearing. These may arise, under CPR, r 23.8, if parties agree as to terms of the order sought, if parties agree that the court should dispose of the application without a hearing, or the court does not consider that a hearing would be appropriate. Application to set aside order may be made under r 23.10. The court is empowered under r 23.11 to proceed in the absence of a party.

applications without notice. Formerly '*ex parte* applications' (q.v.). See CPR, r 23. May be made in urgent circumstances, or where secrecy is necessary for efficacy of an application (as in a freezing order (q.v.)). A resulting order must allow respondent to apply or set aside the order within 7 days of issue: r 23.9(3).

appointee. *See* APPOINTMENT, POWER OF.

appointment, excessive. Exercise of a power of appointment (q.v.) which is excessive in the circumstances, e.g., where the appointor grants an interest greater than that authorised by the power, or where he appoints to persons who are outside the class of objects of the power. See *Re Boulton's ST* [1928] Ch 703; *Re Hay's ST* [1981] 3 All ER 786.

appointment, power of. The power given to a person, usually by trust or settlement, enabling him to dispose of an interest in property which is not his. If A confers on B the right to exercise a power of appointment, and B exercises it in favour of C, A is the *donor* of the power, B is the *donee* or *appointor*, C is the *appointee*, B's exercise of the power is the *appointment*. Powers may be: *public* (conferred by statute) and *private*; *general* (enabling the appointor to appoint in favour of any person) and

special (enabling the appointment to be made only to members of a given class); *hybrid* (neither special nor general). See L.P.A. 1925, s 1(7), under which the exercise of a power creates an equitable interest. See *Re Rank's ST* [1979] 1 WLR 1242; *Breadner v Granville-Crossman* [2000] 4 All ER 705. *See* POWER.

appointor. *See* APPOINTMENT, POWER OF.

apportionment. Division into parts which are proportionate to interests and rights of parties. See Apportionment Act 1870; L.P.A. 1925, s 140. Where a duty arises to convert assets of a hazardous and wasting nature in the interests of a remainderman, trustees must apportion between capital and income ('equitable apportionment'). *See* REMAINDER.

appreciation, margin of. Doctrine formulated by European Court of Human Rights allowing member states some discretion in their manner of implementation of the standards of the European Convention on Human Rights (q.v.), taking into account specific national traditions and circumstances. See, e.g., *Autronic AG v Switzerland* (1990) 12 EHRR 485.

apprehension or prosecution, impeding. *See* IMPEDING APPREHENSION OR PROSECUTION.

apprentice. A person bound by contract to serve and learn from a master who, in turn, undertakes to instruct him in a trade or profession. The contract must be in writing or by deed, and is usually signed also by the parent or guardian. It is binding on a minor if beneficial to him. See *Dunk v George Waller & Son* [1970] 2 QB 163.

apprenticeship, dismissal under. Employment Appeal Tribunal held that a person engaged under a standard apprenticeship pact was to be considered as an apprentice, not an employee, even though that pact obliged him to act in conformity with an employer's terms and conditions of employment: *Whitely v Marton Electrical Ltd* (2003) *The Times*, 2 January.

approbate and reprobate. Phrase referring to a person who, taking a benefit under an instrument, must either accept or reject the instrument as a whole. *Qui approbat non reprobat* (q.v.). See *Express Newspapers* v *News (UK) Ltd* [1990] 3 All ER 376. *See* ELECTION.

appropriate considerations *(in charities)*. This means (a) (on the one hand) the spirit of the gift concerned, and (b) (on the other) the social and economic circumstances prevailing at the time of the proposed alteration of the original purposes. Charities Act 2006 s 15.

appropriation. 1. Allocation of a sum of money for expenditure. An 'appropriation in aid' refers to a transaction whereby a government department receives money from a source other than the Exchequer and is allowed to set it off against expenses. The annual Appropriation Act gives legal force to Parliament's decisions on the government's estimates. 2. Exercise of control over property. See *DPP* v *John* [1999] 1 WLR 1883 ('appropriation of land' was to be construed as meaning 'set aside' or 'allocated for a specific purpose').

appropriation and payment. CA held in *E* v *Briggs* (2003) *The Times*, 17 December, that where a victim has acted so that a payment is to be made in reliance on defendant's deceptive conduct, there is no appropriation by defendant which constitutes a necessary element in the offence of theft.

appropriation, dishonest. *See* DISHONEST.

appropriation of payments. *See* PAYMENTS, APPROPRIATION OF.

approval, sale on. Where goods are delivered to a buyer on approval, or sale or return, the property passes to the buyer when he adopts the transaction, e.g., by signifying approval. If he does not signify approval or acceptance to the seller, the property passes to him if he retains the goods on the expiration of a fixed time or, if no time has been fixed, on the expiration of a reasonable time: S.G.A. 1979, s 18. See *Poole* v *Smith's Car Sales Ltd* [1962] 1 WLR 744.

approvement. Common-law right of a lord of the manor to enclose waste lands over which his tenants exercised pasture

rights. Approvement of a common now requires consent of the Secretary of State for the Environment, after a local inquiry. See L.P.A. 1925, s 194, as amended.

approximation of laws of EU. Under the Treaty of Rome 1957, members of EC (now EU) agree that the activities of the Community shall include 'the approximation of laws of Member States to the extent required for the proper functioning of the Common Market': art 3(*b*). *See* EU.

appurtenant. Belonging to; necessary to the enjoyment of a thing. Annexed to a hereditament (q.v.) by an act of parties or statute, e.g., a right of way (which can generally be claimed by express grant or prescription (q.v.)). 'An appurtenant right must be related to the needs or use of the dominant tenement. For this reason an exclusive right to grazing, or taking timber, or fishing without limit, cannot exist as appurtenant to another property': *Anderson* v *Bostock* [1976] Ch 312. See also *Hill* v *Cabras* (1987) 54 P & CR 42.

arbitration. The settling of a dispute by an arbitrator. Where arbitrators cannot agree they may appoint an 'umpire'. The decision of an arbitrator is known as an 'award'. Procedure on arbitration is based on the ordinary rules of English law. For form and content of arbitration claim form, see PD 49G, para 4.2. An award may be enforced, with leave of the High Court, as an order of the court. See PD 49G, para 31.1. Where so directed by the High Court, an arbitrator or umpire must state, in the form of a special case for the opinion of the High Court, an award or question of law arising. See Arbitration Acts 1950–96; Consumer Arbitration Agreements Act 1988; *Antaios Cia Naviera SA* v *Salen Rederierna AB* [1984] 3 All ER 229; *Geogas SA* v *Trammogas Ltd* [1991] 1 WLR 776. For permission to appeal, see PD 49G, para 20.1.

arbitration agreement. An agreement to submit to arbitration present or future disputes (whether they are contractual or not). The reference in an agreement to a written form of arbitration clause or to a document containing an arbitration clause constitutes an arbitration agreement if the reference is such as to make that clause part of the agreement: Arbitration Act 1996, s 6. See *Trygg Hansa Ltd* v *Equitas Ltd* [1998] 2 Lloyd's Rep 439.

arbitration agreement, domestic. An arbitration agreement to which none of the parties is an individual who is a national of, or habitually resident in, a state other than the UK, or a body corporate which is incorporated in, or whose central control and management is exercised in, a state other than the UK, and under which the seat of arbitration is in the UK: Arbitration Act 1996, s 85(2).

arbitration and interest. Subject to the agreement of parties, the tribunal may award simple or compound interest in relation to periods before or after the making of the award, according to the justice of the case: Arbitration Act 1996, s 49. See CPR, Sch 1; O 45, r 1; PD 49G, para 32.1.

arbitration clause. 'It embodies the agreement of both parties that, if any dispute arises with regard to the obligations which one party has undertaken to the other, such dispute shall be settled by a tribunal of their own constitution': *Heyman* v *Darwins Ltd* [1942] AC 356.

arbitration convention award. An award made in pursuance of an arbitration agreement in the territory of a state, other than the UK, which is a party to the New York Convention [on the Recognition and Enforcement of Foreign Arbitral Awards 1958]. See now Arbitration Act 1996, Part III.

arbitration, seat of. The juridical seat of the arbitration designated by the parties to the arbitration agreement, or by any arbitral or other institution or person vested by the parties with powers in that regard, or by the arbitral tribunal, if so authorised by the parties, or determined in the absence of any such designation, having regard to the parties' agreement and all the relevant circumstances: Arbitration Act 1996, s 3.

arbitration, stay of proceedings. A party to arbitration proceedings against whom legal proceedings are brought (by claim or counterclaim) may apply for a stay of proceedings, and such application may be made notwithstanding that the matter is to be referred to arbitration only after the exhaustion of other procedures of dispute resolution: Arbitration Act 1996, s 9. See PD 49G, para 6.1. See *Halki Shipping Corporation* v *Sopex Oils Ltd* [1998] 2 All ER 23; *Al-Naimi* v *Islamic Press Agency* [2000] 1 Lloyd's Rep 522.

arbitrator. A disinterested person selected by agreement of contesting parties (or by the court) to hear and settle some disputed question between them. The test for apparent or unconscious bias in an arbitrator is whether there was any real danger that he was biased: see Arbitration Act 1996, s 23; *AT&CT Corporation* v *Saudi Cable Co* [2000] 1 All ER (Comm) 201.

arbitrator, quasi-. *See* QUASI-ARBITRATOR.

arbitrators, appointment of. Appointment may be by: mutual consent of the parties to an arbitration agreement; nomination by a third person, e.g., the president of a professional body; the court.

Archbishop. Head of the clergy in a province. His jurisdiction is within his diocese and throughout the province, in which he acts as superior ecclesiastical judge. The two Archbishops in England are Canterbury and York. See Ecclesiastical Jurisdiction Measure 1963; Patronage (Benefices) Measure 1986, s 39(1).

Arches, Court of. *See* COURT OF ARCHES.

armchair principle. A rule of construction (q.v.) applied to wills. 'You may place yourself, so to speak, in [the testator's] armchair, and consider the circumstances by which he was surrounded when he made his will to assist you in arriving at his intention': *Boyes* v *Cook* (1880) 14 Ch D 53.

armed. 'An ordinary English word and, ordinarily it involves either physically carrying arms or it would involve proof that to a defendant's knowledge arms were immediately available. It is not necessary to prove an intent to use those arms if the situation should require it': *per* Tucker J in *R* v *Jones* [1987] 1 WLR 692. See Firearms Acts 1968–97; *R* v *Kelt* [1977] 1 WLR 1365.

Armed Forces. Royal Navy, Royal Marines, regular army and regular air force, and any reserve or auxiliary force of those services called out on permanent service or called into actual service or embodied: Customs and Excise Management Act 1979, s 1(1). See Armed Forces Acts 1986, 1991, 1996; Armed Forces Discipline Act 2000. *See* COURTSMARTIAL; RESERVE FORCES; SPECIAL FORCES.

arms, decommissioning of. Under Northern Ireland Arms Decommissioning (Amendment) Act 2002, s 1, the amnesty period fixed by Northern Ireland Arms Decommissioning Act 1997, s 2, and providing legal immunity until 27 February 2002, is extended until midnight, 26 February 2003.

arm's length, at. 1. Out of reach of personal influence. 2. Conduct of negotiations in a strict, formal manner. See Finance Act 2000, s 94(8).

arraign. To bring the named accused to the bar of the court so that the indictment (q.v.) can be read to him and he can be asked to plead to it. Unless the defendant is mute, insane or refuses to plead, he must plead personally to the arraignment. 'It is only after arraignment, which concludes with the plea of accused to the indictment, that it is known whether there will be a trial, and, if so, what manner of trial': *R* v *Vickers* [1975] 2 All ER 945.

arrangement, deeds of. Under Deeds of Arrangement Act 1914 (as amended by Ins.A. 1986), which refers to arrangements between the debtor and assenting creditors before bankruptcy proceedings are instituted, registration is necessary, e.g., where an assignment has been made for the benefit of creditors generally. A deed which is not registered within seven days of execution is generally rendered void as against the purchaser of any land relating to it or affected by it unless

registered under L.C.A. 1972, s 7(2). See Ins.A. 2000, Sch 3.

arrangement, voluntary, company. Proposals made under Ins.A. 1986, Part I, by a company's directors to its creditors for a composition (q.v.) in satisfaction of its debts or a scheme of arrangement of its affairs: s 1. Meetings summoned under s 3 decide whether to approve the arrangement, with or without modifications: s 4. See Ins.A. 2000, Sch 2.

array. A body of jurors.

arrears. Money remaining unpaid, in relation to a debt, after the agreed time for payment. *See* RENTAL PERIOD.

arrest. To restrain and detain a person by lawful authority. 'Whether or not a person has been arrested depends not on the legality of the arrest but on whether he has been deprived of his liberty to go where he pleases': *per* Lord Dilhorne, in *Spicer* v *Holt* [1977] AC 987. See *Hart* v *Chief Constable of Kent* [1983] RTR 484; *Hough* v *Chief Constable of Staffordshire Police* (2001) *The Times*, 14 February.

arrestable offence. An offence for which the sentence is fixed by law or for which a person may be sentenced to imprisonment for five years, and, specifically, an offence under enactments such as Customs and Excise Management Act 1979, s 1(1), Official Secrets Acts 1911, 1920, Th.A. 1968, ss 12(1), 25(1); P.&C.E.A. 1984, s 24(1), (2); Offensive Weapons Act 1996, s 1; C.J.P.O.A. 1994, s 85; C.J.C.S.A. 2000, Sch 7, para 77. Any person may arrest without a warrant anyone committing such an offence or anyone whom he reasonably suspects to be committing such an offence: s 24(4).

arrestable offence, serious. An offence specified under P.&C.E.A. 1984, Sch 5, Part I (e.g., treason, murder, manslaughter, rape) or under an enactment mentioned in Part II (e.g., hostage-taking, carrying firearms with criminal intent): s 116(1). Any other arrestable offence is 'serious' only if its commission leads, or is intended to lead, to, e.g., serious harm to state security, serious injury, financial loss, interference with investigation of offences, death: s 116(3), (6).

arrest and warrant. Arrest may be made *with* a warrant (q.v.), i.e., by order for arrest. Arrest *without* warrant ('summary arrest') is permissible in the exercise of the common-law power of arrest (q.v.), in relation to arrestable offences (q.v.) or where otherwise authorised by statute, e.g., Town Police Clauses Act 1847, s 28. See P.&C.E.A. 1984, s 25, Sch 2; C.J.P.O.A. 1994, Part V; Immigration Act 1971, s 28A, inserted by Immigration and Asylum Act 1999, s 128; *R v Self* [1992] 1 WLR 657; Terrorism Act 2000, s 41.

arrest, citizen's. See ARREST, COMMON-LAW POWER OF; CITIZEN'S ARREST.

arrest, common-law power of. In order to exercise this very exceptional power, a citizen can arrest another person, X, who was not at the time acting unlawfully, only if: there was a real threat of a breach of the peace by X; and X was clearly interfering with the rights of others; and the natural consequence of X's conduct was 'not wholly unreasonable violence' from a third party; and X's conduct was unreasonable: *Bibby v Chief Constable of Essex Police* (2000) *The Times*, 24 April. See CITIZEN'S ARREST.

arrest conditions, general, and non-arrestable offences. Under P.&C.E.A. 1984, s 25, a constable may arrest a person for a 'non-arrestable' offence if it appears that service of a summons is impracticable or inappropriate and at least one of the conditions under s 25(3) applies, e.g., the person's name is unknown and cannot be readily ascertained or there are reasonable grounds for believing that arrest is necessary to prevent the person suffering or causing physical harm or causing loss or damage to property.

arrested development of mind. This may be classified as follows: 1. *Severe abnormality*, when the patient's state includes subnormality of intelligence and is of such a nature or degree that he is incapable of living an independent life or

guarding himself against serious exploitation. 2. *Subnormality*, when the patient's state is one (not amounting to severe subnormality) including subnormality of intelligence and which requires or is susceptible to medical treatment or other special care. See M.H.A. 1983.

arrest for questioning by police. See QUESTIONING BY POLICE.

arrest, malicious. Arrest (in civil cases) effected maliciously and without reasonable cause.

arrest of judgment. The move by an accused person between conviction and sentence that judgment be not given because of defects in the indictment. It forms no bar to a new indictment. See INDICTMENT.

arrest of ship. Judicial process of securing maritime claims against a ship-owner (see PD 49F, paras 1.13, 6.1–6.11). It begins with the issue of a claim form *in rem*, executed by the Admiralty Marshal, affixed to the ship's mast, following which the Marshal has custody of the arrested property. See, e.g., *The World Star* [1986] 2 Lloyd's Rep 274; *The Sea Friends* [1991] 2 Lloyd's Rep 1991.

arrest or prosecute, discretion to. See DISCRETION TO ARREST OR PROSECUTE.

arrest, reasonable grounds for. 'The circumstances of the case should be such that a reasonable man acting without passion or prejudice would fairly have suspected the person of having committed the offence': *per* Lord Devlin in *Shaaban Bin Hussein v Chang Fook Kam* [1964] 3 All ER 1626.

arrest, resisting. Refusal to submit to arrest. 'It is the corollary of the right of every citizen to be free from arrest that he should be entitled to resist arrest unless the arrest is lawful': *Christie v Leachinsky* [1947] AC 573. See also *R v Lee* (2000) *The Times*, 24 October (assault with intent to resist lawful apprehension).

arrest, search upon. Power to search a person to ascertain the property he has on him lies with the custody officer (q.v.) in a police station: see P.&C.E.A. 1984, s 54(6). See Immigration Act 1971, s 28F, inserted by Immigration and Asylum Act 1999, s 134(1).

arrived ship. 'Before a ship can be said to have arrived at a port she must, if she cannot proceed immediately to a berth, have reached the position within the port where she is at the immediate and effective disposition of the charterer': *per* Lord Reid in *The Johanna Oldendorff* [1974] AC 479 (the so-called 'Reid test'). See *Bulk Transport Ltd* v *Seacrystal Shipping Ltd* [1987] 1 WLR 1565.

arson. The common-law offence of arson (maliciously and voluntarily burning the dwelling house of another) was abolished under Criminal Damage Act 1971, s 11(1). By s 1(3), offences committed under s 1 are charged as arson. See *R* v *Aylesbury Crown Court, ex p Simmons* [1972] 3 All ER 574; *R* v *Parker* [1997] 1 Cr App R (S) 259; *R* v *Walker* [1999] 1 Cr App R (S) 121; *R* v *Akhter* [2001] 1 Cr App R(S) 3. In cases relating to reckless arson, a court must apply the test in *R* v *Caldwell* [1982] AC 341 even where defendant is a child. Further, Human Rights Convention, art 6, has no relevance to the definition of the mens rea of this offence: see *R* v *G* (2002) *The Times*, 1 August; *Z* v *UK* (2001) 34 EHRR 3.

articles. Clauses or rules in a document, e.g., articles of partnership or clerkship (binding a person to serve as an articled clerk).

articles of association. See ASSOCIATION, ARTICLES OF.

artificial insemination by donor. Known also as AID. Introduction of semen into the uterus by other than natural means. Where, as the result of the artificial insemination of a woman who at the time was a party to a marriage and was inseminated with the semen of some person other than the other party to the marriage, then, unless it is shown that the other party did not consent to the insemination, the child will be treated in law as the child of the parties to the marriage: F.L.R.A. 1987, s 27(1). For the case of unmarried couples, see Human Fertilisaton and Embryology Act 1990,

s 28. See *U* v *W (No. 2)* [1997] 3 WLR 739; *R* v *Secretary of State for Home Department ex p Mellor* (2000) *The Times*, 5 September.

artificial insemination, information relating to. It was held in *R (Rose and Another)* v *Secretary of State for Health* (2002) *The Times*, 22 August, that Human Rights Convention, art 8, was engaged, in relation to a claim by a child born by artificial insemination, for the provision of non-identifying information concerning the donor, intended to assist in the establishing of claimant's personal identity. See also *Gaskin* v *UK* (1980) 12 EHRR 36.

artificial insemination, parent of child. CA held in *J* v *C (Void marriage: Status of children)* [2006] *The Times*, 1 June, applying the Family Law Reform Act 1987 that in order to be a parent of a child who is born through the use of artificial insemination by a donor the other parent had to be the other party to a marriage with the mother.

artificial person. A body, e.g., a corporation (q.v.) recognised by law as having rights and duties. Known also as a 'juristic person'. See I.A. 1978, s 5, Sch 1; *Bumper Development Corp* v *CPM* [1991] 4 All ER 638. *See* NATURAL PERSON.

ASBOS, publicity relating to. Publicity may be necessary so as to allow the question of an antisocial behaviour order; such publicity may necessitate, if the order is to be effective, names, photographs and even partial addresses: *R (Stanley)* v *Commissioner of Police of the Metropolis* (2004) *The Times*, 22 October.

ascertained goods. Goods identified and agreed upon when a contract is made. See S.G.A. 1979, s 16; *The Elafi* [1982] 1 All ER 208. *See* UNASCERTAINED GOODS.

asportation. Carrying away with a view to stealing. An essential feature of larceny (q.v.) in which the slightest removal of things sufficed: *R* v *Walsh* (1824) 1 Moo 14.

assault. A crime and a tort resulting from an act by which any person directly, negligently, intentionally, or possibly recklessly, causes another to apprehend reasonably the immediate application to himself of unlawful physical violence: *Fagan* v *Metropolitan Police Commissioner* [1969] 1 QB 439. Example: where X advances towards Y, shakes his fist, threatening to beat Y there and then, so that Y is put in fear of immediate violence. The term is often used to include battery, in which case it is an offence under O.P.A. 1861. Common assault (and battery) are summary offences (C.J.A. 1988, s 39) and offences of basic intent. Assault and battery are separate statutory offences: *DPP* v *Little* [1992] 1 All ER 299. For assault as a tort (which is actionable *per se*, see *Stephens* v *Myers* (1830) 4 C & P 349. See also *DPP* v *Majewski* [1977] AC 443; *R* v *Gladstone Williams* [1987] 3 All ER 411; *R* v *Richardson* [1998] 3 WLR 1292. *See* AGGRAVATED ASSAULT; ASSAULT, RACIALLY-AGGRAVATED; BATTERY; BODILY HARM, GRIEVOUS; COMMON ASSAULT.

assault, actus reus of. Where defendant had given a dishonest assurance concerning the contents of his pockets, as a result of which a police officer had been exposed to a reasonably foreseeable risk of injury which, in the event, materialised, this meant that there existed an evidential basis for the actus reus of assault occasioning actual bodily harm. See *DPP* v *Santos-Bermudez* (2004) 168 JP 373.

assault by penetration. CA held in *R* v *Garvey* (2004) *The Times*, 29 October, that the introduction under The Sexual Offences Act 2003, s 2 of the offence of assault by penetration, carrying a maximum sentence of life imprisonment, means that the sentence which will be passed by the court for that offence will be higher than that considered appropriate when the offence was one of indecent assault, carrying a lower maximum. See AG's Reference (No. 104 of 2004).

assault, consent and. *See* CONSENT AND ASSAULT.

assault, indecent. *See* INDECENT ASSAULT.

assault on the police. It is an offence for a person to assault a constable in the execution of his duty or a person assisting a constable in the execution of his duty: Police Act 1996, s 89. See *R* v *Fagan* [1968] 3 All ER 442; *R* v *Ball* [1989] Crim LR 579.

assault, racially-aggravated. A person is guilty of an offence under C.D.A. 1998, s 29(1), if he commits an offence under O.P.A. 1861, s 20 (malicious wounding or grievous bodily harm), or under s 47 of the 1861 Act (actual bodily harm), or common assault, which is racially-aggravated. See P.C.C.(S.)A. 2000, s 153. *See* RACIALLY-AGGRAVATED OFFENCE.

Assembly. An institution of the EU (q.v.), known as the European Parliament (q.v.).

assembly, public. *See* PUBLIC ASSEMBLY.

assembly, trespassory. An assembly of 20 or more persons held on land to which the public has no, or merely a limited, right of access. The police may apply for an order prohibiting the holding of such an assembly where they believe reasonably that it will result in serious disruption to the life of the community, or significant damage to land or buildings of significant interest: P.O.A. 1986, ss 14A, 14B, 14C; C.J.P.O.A. 1994; *DPP* v *Jones* [1999] 2 WLR 625 (a peaceful, non-obstructive assembly is a reasonable use of a public highway).

assent. Agreement. 'The instrument or act whereby a personal representative effectuates a testamentary disposition by transferring the subject-matter of the disposition to the person entitled to it': *Re King's WT* [1964] Ch 542. Executors and administrators (qq.v.) may transfer interests in realty and leaseholds (qq.v.) by means of an assent in writing: A.E.A. 1925, s 36.

Assent, Royal. *See* ROYAL ASSENT.

assent, vesting. *See* VESTING ASSENT.

assessing costs, professional defending claims. It was held that when assessing detailed assessment costs, Part 48 of the Civil Procedure Rules did not make a distinction between a litigant who happened to be a professional other than a solicitor or other person entitled to conduct litigation and an ordinary litigant in person. Principles derived from authorities relating to costs, equally applied to the Civil Procedure Rules and the Rules of the Supreme Court when determining which expenditure could be taken into account for the purposes of detailed assessment costs. See *Sisu Capital Fund Ltd and Others* v *Tucker & Others* [2005] *The Times*, 4 November.

assessment. The act of determining or apportioning. Used in relation to damages (q.v.), liability to tax, etc.

assessment of costs, detailed. The general rule is that the costs of any proceedings are assessed by the detailed procedure only at the conclusion of proceedings: CPR, r 47.1. Detailed assessment is not stayed pending appeal unless the court so orders: r 47.2. Detailed assessment proceedings are commenced by the receiving party serving on the paying party notice of commencement, and a copy of the bill of costs: r 47.6(1). For relevant rules, see Part 47. *See* COSTS, ASSESSMENT, DETAILED AND SUMMARY.

assessment of costs, summary. In general, the court will make a summary assessment of costs at the conclusion of a fast track trial (where the order will involve costs of the whole claim) or at the conclusion of any other hearing which has lasted less than one day (where the order will deal with costs of application), unless there is good reason not to do so: PD 44, para 4.4(1). Each party intending to claim costs must prepare a written statement of costs he intends to claim, which must be filed at the court: para 4.5(1), (4). The court will specify an amount payable as a single figure, to include all sums payable in respect of profit costs, disbursement and VAT, and the amount awarded under Part 46: para 4.7. *See* COSTS, DETAILED AND SUMMARY ASSESSMENTS.

assessments of damages cases, allocation of. Once an order or judgment involving a decision by the court on the amount of money to be paid has been made (e.g.,

assessment of damages, interest, taking of accounts), the court may list the matter for a disposal hearing (at which allocation to an appropriate track is made), or may give directions, or stay the action pending a settlement by parties. See PD 26, para 12.1(1) (defining 'relevant orders'). *See* ALLOCATION TO TRACKS, CPR.

assessors. Persons with specialist knowledge appointed to assist the court, e.g., in Admiralty business. They generally do not give oral evidence and are not open to cross-examination or questioning: r 35.15; PD 35, para 6.4. See S.C.A. 1981, s 70; County C.A. 1984, s 63, as amended by C.L.S.A. 1990, s 14; *The Savina* [1976] 2 Lloyd's Rep 26.

asset-freezing order. A freezing order is not usually effective unless defendant's assets have been disclosed. Where defendant is attempting to have such an order set aside, and accepts its continuation pending a full hearing, disclosure requirements ought not to be halted pending such a hearing: *Motorola Credit Corporation* v *Uzan* (2002) *The Times*, 10 July.

asset-freezing order, change in claimant's assets. Whilst an asset-freezing order is operating, a claimant is under a continuing duty to disclose to defendant a material deterioration in his financial position: *Staines* v *Walsh* [2003] EWHC 1486 (Civ).

asset-freezing order, worldwide. CA held in *Motorola Credit* v *Uzan (No. 2)* [2003] EWCA Civ 752, that where the court is exercising its discretion as to the inexpediency of making a worldwide asset-freezing order, it should consider: possibility of interference with management of case in primary court; danger of confusion in overlapping jurisdictions; whether court was making an order it would be unable to enforce.

assets. Physical property or rights which have a value in monetary terms. 1. The assets of a business include: *current assets*, e.g., stock, cash; *fixed assets*, e.g., machinery, goodwill. Under Cos.A. 1985, Sch 4, para 77, fixed assets were defined as those intended for use on a continuing basis in the company's activities; current assets are those not intended for such use. (See I.C.T.A. 1988, s 742(9); T.C.G.A. 1992, chap II.) 2. Assets of a deceased person consist of the property available for payment of his debts and liabilities, and include, e.g., his property, subject to general power of appointment (q.v.) which he exercised by will; entailed property held by him: A.E.A. 1925, s 32.

assets, administration of. *See* ESTATES, ADMINISTRATION OF.

assets, distribution of. *See* DISTRIBUTION OF COMPANY ASSETS.

assets, marshalling of. *See* MARSHALLING.

assets, wasting. *See* WASTING ASSETS.

assign. 1. To transfer property to another by assignment (q.v.). Used specifically in relation to the transfer of a reversion or lease (qq.v.). 2. An assignee (q.v.). For covenants not to assign, see, e.g., *Field* v *Barkworth* [1986] 1 WLR 137; Landlord and Tenant Act 1988 (imposing qualified duty on landlord to consent to assignment). See *Crago* v *Julian* [1992] 1 All ER 744; *Ashworth Frazer Ltd* v *Gloucester CC* (2000) *The Times*, 3 February.

assignee. A person to whom an assignment is made.

assignment. 1. *Legal.* Under L.P.A. 1925, s 136, as amended, debts and other legal choses in action (q.v.) may be assigned: see, e.g., *Virgin Ltd* v *Bluewall Ltd* [1998] Masons CLR 83. The assignment must be absolute, in writing, followed by express notice in writing to the debtor or trustee. Assignment of contractual rights consists of the transfer from B to C of the benefit of one or more obligations that A owed to B. (The burden of a contract cannot be assigned without consent of the other contracting party; but there may be exceptions in the case of a novation or vicarious performance.) See *Linden Garden Trust Ltd* v *Lenesta Ltd* [1994] 1 AC 85. 2. *Equitable.* An assignment which does not comply with requirements of a legal assignment. It need not be in writing if intention is clear. See *Don King Productions* v *Warren* [1998] 2 All ER 608 (discussion of principles relating to assignments of contracts). 3. *By operation of law.* A contract may be assigned automatically by operation of law, e.g., on bankruptcy and on death. See Landlord and Tenant (Covenants) Act 1995. *See* NOVATION.

assignment of lease. *See* LEASE, ASSIGNMENT OF.

assignor. A person who transfers property rights or powers (e.g., the freehold interest or freehold reversion) to another by assignment.

assistance dogs. Defined under Disability Discrimination Act 1995, s 37A, inserted by Private Hire Vehicles (Carriage of Guide Dogs etc.) Act 2002, s 1, as dogs which are trained to guide the blind or assist deaf persons, are trained by prescribed charities to assist disabled persons affected by epilepsy or suffering from a disability affecting mobility, manual dexterity, ability to lift, etc.

assisting offenders. 'Where a person has committed an arrestable offence, any other person who, knowing or believing him to be guilty of the offence or of some other offence, does without lawful authority or reasonable excuse any act with intent to impede his apprehension or prosecution shall be guilty of an offence': C.L.A. 1967, s 4(1). See Criminal Evidence (Amendment) Act 1997, Sch 1, para 10.

assize. 1. A statute or ordinance, e.g., Assize of Clarendon 1166. (The term was derived from the *session* of King and Council.) 2. Assize Courts tried criminal cases under commissions of oyer and terminer (q.v.). Abolished under Courts Act 1971, s 1.

associated employers. Any two employers are treated as associated if one is a company of which the other (directly or indirectly) has control, or if both are companies of which a third person (directly or indirectly) has control: E.R.A. 1996, s 231. See *Tice* v *Cartwright* [1999] ICR 769.

associated offence. Term used in P.C.C.(S.)A. 2000 to refer to an offence associated with another if the offender is convicted of it in the proceedings in which he is convicted of the other offence or (although convicted of it in earlier proceedings) is sentenced for it at the same time as he is sentenced for that offence; or offender admits the commission of it in the proceedings in which he is sentenced for the other offence and requests the court to take it into consideration in sentencing him for that offence: s 161(1).

associated persons. Under F.L.A. 1996, Part IV (domestic violence) (now in force), a person is 'associated with' another person if: they are or have been married to each other; are cohabitants or former cohabitants; they live or have lived in the same household (save by reason of one being the other's tenant or lodger); they are relatives: s 62(3).

association, articles of. A document which regulates a company's internal affairs, consisting of regulations governing the rights of members *inter se* and the conduct of the company's business, e.g., the appointment and powers of directors. Table A (q.v.) may be used as the articles of a company limited by shares. Articles are subject to the memorandum of association (q.v.) and cannot give any power not given by the memorandum. They can be altered by special resolution at a general meeting: Cos.A. 1985, ss 7–9. See Cos.A. 1985, s 14 (articles considered as a contract); Cos.A. 1989, s 128. Any alteration must benefit the company as a whole: *Greenhalgh* v *Arderne Cinemas Ltd* [1951] Ch 286. When registered, the articles and memorandum of association form a contract binding members to the company: *Hickman* v *Kent Sheep-Breeders Association* [1951] 1 Ch 881. See *Cane* v *Jones* [1980] 1 WLR 1451. *See* COMPANY.

association clause. A clause in a company's memorandum of association (q.v.) in which the subscribers declare that they wish to be formed into a company and agree to take the number of shares recorded opposite their names.

association, memorandum of. A document (see Cos.A. 1985, s 2) which regulates a company's external activities and constitution, and which must be drawn up on the formation of a company. It states the company's name, objects, registered office, domicile, amount of company's nominal capital, number and amount of shares, etc. It will be registered by the Registrar only when he is satisfied that it complies with statutory requirements: Cos.A. 1985, s 12. It can be varied by special resolution: Cos.A. 1985, s 4, but the alteration must be confirmed by the court if a dissentient minority petitions: Cos.A. 1989, s 110. See also Cos.A. 1989, s 108 (company's capacity not limited by its memorandum), s 110. *See* COMPANY NAME.

assurance. 1. 'That which operates as a transfer of property': *Re Ray* [1896] 1 Ch 468. 2. A contract which guarantees payment of a sum on the happening of a specified event which must happen sooner or later, e.g., death. *See* LIFE ASSURANCE.

assured shorthold tenancy. An assured tenancy (q.v.) which is a fixed-term tenancy granted for a term certain of not less than six months; and in respect of which there is no power for the landlord to determine the tenancy at any time earlier than six months from the beginning of the tenancy and in respect of which an appropriate notice has been served: H.A. 1988, s 20. See *York* v *Casey* [1998] 2 EGLR 25. For assured agricultural occupancies, see 1988 Act, chap III. See H.A. 1996, chap II, Sch 8.

assured tenancy. Tenancy under which a dwelling house is let as a separate dwelling, if the tenant (or each of the joint tenants) is an individual and occupies the dwelling house as his only or principal home, and the tenancy is not excluded under s 1(1)(c): H.A. 1988, s 1. 'Dwelling house' may be a house or part of a house: s 45. Security of tenure is conferred by s 5: landlord must serve a notice seeking possession and obtain a county court order (see CPR, Sch 2; CCR, O 49, rr 6, 6A; *Manuel* v *Menon*

(2000) *The Times*, 20 April). 'Old-style' assured tenancies created under H.A. 1980 were converted under H.A. 1988 into the 'new-style' assured tenancies. See H.A. 1996; *Sanctuary Housing Association* v *Baker* (1998) 30 HLR 809. There can be one transmission of the assured tenancy to a spouse or cohabitant who resided at the date of death with the tenant: 1988 Act, s 17.

asylum. 1. A refuge, an inviolable place of retreat and relative security. See Asylum and Immigration Appeals Act 1993; UK Asylum and Immigration Act 1996; SI 96/2070; *R* v *Secretary of State for Home Department ex p Turgut* (2000) *The Times*, 15 February; Immigration and Asylum Act 1999, s 69. 2. In international law may be *territorial* (granted by a state on its own territory), or *extra-territorial* (granted in respect of, e.g., consular premises, legations). 3. An establishment for the detention and care of sufferers from mental disease: Mental Treatment Act 1930, s 20(1). Now referred to as 'mental hospital': See M.H.A. 1983, Part II.

asylum, benefits entitlement. CA held in *R (on application of T)* v *Secretary of State for Home Department* [2003] EWCA Civ 1285, that, in deciding whether an asylum seeker who has been refused benefits has, therefore, been dealt with contrary to European Convention, art 3, no one test is applicable, and each case must be considered as fact-specific.

asylum, claim for. A claim that it would be contrary to UK's obligations under the Refugee Convention, or the Human Rights Convention, art 3, for the claimant to be removed from, or required to leave, the UK: Immigration and Asylum Act 1999, s 82(1). See also ss 11, 12, 69 (appeal to adjudicator).

asylum, double. CA held in *R (Lika)* v *Secretary of State for Home Department* (2003) *The Times*, 13 January, that an asylum seeker could not make an application in Germany, and later in UK, giving as his reason his belief that Germany was not a safe country, at the time when his application was under scrutiny in Germany.

asylum, internal relocation and. Principle which comes into play in considering an application for asylum when it is established that conditions in one part of the applicant's country are such that there is a serious possibility that he would face persecution if forced back, but there are other parts of the country where the same concern would not arise. Standard of proof in assessing facts is 'a reasonable degree of likelihood', and not the conventional civil standard of proof. See *Karankaran* v *Secretary of State for Home Department* (2000) *The Times*, 16 February.

asylum policy. It was held in *R (Rashid)* v *Secretary of State for Home Department* (2004) *The Times*, 17 November, that a clear failure to apply to a claimant a policy which had been applied to other refugee claimants in a similar position, constituted an abuse of governmental power, so that the court was entitled to make a grant of refugee status, involving indefinite leave to remain in the UK.

asylum, political. *See* POLITICAL ASYLUM.

asylum powers. Asylum and Immigration (Treatment of Claimants) Act 2004, extends powers of arrest of Immigration Service so as to include immigration-related offences, such as forgery, counterfeiting, bigamy, and a new offence of human trafficking for non-sexual exploitation.

asylum-seeker. A person who is not under 18 and has made a claim for asylum which has been recorded by the Secretary of State, but which has not been determined: Immigration and Asylum Act 1990, s 94(1).

asylum-seeker, cessation of status. HL held in *R (Anufrijera)* v *Secretary of State for Home Department* [2003] 3 WLR 252, that a person will cease to be an asylum seeker only when his claim for asylum has been recorded by the Home Department as having been determined, and he has been notified of that decision.

asylum-seekers, accommodation for. HL held in *Al-Ameri* v *Kensington and Chelsea RLBC* [2004] UKHL 4, that accommodation in an urban district provided to a destitute asylum seeker by virtue of the Immigration and Asylum Act 1999, was not capable of being regarded as residence in a district of the asylum seeker's own choice for purposes of the Housing Act 1996.

asylum-seekers, dependants of. A person in UK who is the asylum-seeker's spouse, child of his or his spouse and is under 18 and dependent on him, or falls within any additionally prescribed category: Immigration and Asylum Act 1999, s 94(1).

asylum-seekers, detention of. Short-period detention of asylum seekers at Oakington Reception Centre, so as to ensure swift processing of applications, was lawful; it did not infringe European Convention, art 5(1)(f) (deprivation of liberty, save in cases relating to prevention of unauthorised entry into UK): decision of HL in *R (Saadi and Others) v Secretary of State for Home Department* (2002) *The Times*, 1 November Update No 3.

asylum-seekers, housing of. In *Al-Almeri v Kensington and Chelsea RLBC* [2004] 2 WLR 354, the HL held that where an asylum seeker is given accommodation under a compulsory dispersal scheme, he cannot be said to reside there 'of his own choice' for purposes of establishing some 'local connection' under the provisions relating to homelessness in the Housing Act 1996.

asylum-seekers, infirm. In *R (O) v Haringey LBC* (2004) *The Times*, 27 May, the CA held that although a local authority was obliged to support a disabled asylum seeker, it had no responsibility for her dependent children, and therefore they had to seek support from the National Asylum Support Service.

asylum-seekers, preferences of. Rights of a destitute asylum-seeker concerning accommodation did not extend to his requiring Home Secretary to take into account asylum-seeker's preferences concerning nature and locality of that accommodation: *R (Hetoja) v Secretary of State for Home Department* (2002) *The Times*, 11 November.

asylum-seekers, protection of. CA held in *R (Atkinson) v Secretary of State for Home Department* (2004) *The Times*, 20 July, that where an asylum-seeker had established that the state from which he had fled was willing but quite unable to give him adequate protection from ill-treatment by persons who looked upon him with hostility as a police informer, he could succeed in his claim.

asylum-seekers, state support for. The Secretary of State may provide or arrange for the provision of support for asylum-seekers or their dependants who appear destitute or likely to become so; 'destitute' refers to a person who lacks adequate accommodation or any means of obtaining it, or has accommodation, but cannot meet other essential living needs: Immigration and Asylum Act 1999, s 95. For ways of providing support, see s 96. Asylum-seekers are excluded from mainstream benefits and other social welfare provisions: s 115. Asylum Support Adjudicators hear relevant appeals: s 102, Sch 10. In *R (Lambuela) v Secretary of State for Home Department* (2004) *The Times*, 26 May, the CA held that an asylum-seeker who failed to claim asylum as soon as was reasonably practicable after arrival in UK, had no entitlement to state support unless he was able to demonstrate that he was almost destitute and had no access to any other sources of support. Also, where support for asylum-seekers under Nationality, Immigration and Asylum Act 2002, s 55, was refused, that refusal was held to be flawed when there had been an inadequate investigation of the circumstances in which entry to the country had taken place: *R (Q) v Secretary of State for Home Department* (2003) *The Times*, 20 February. In *Westminster CC v National Asylum Support Service* [2002] 1 WLR 2956, HL held that a local authority has a duty to provide housing for a destitute and infirm asylum-seeker, who was suffering from a spinal disease.

asylum tests, differences in. In *R (Yogathas) v Secretary of State for Home*

Department [2002] 3 WLR 1276, HL held that, although tests applied in Germany and UK concerning asylum qualifications differed in context, these differences were not such as to prevent removal of asylum-seekers (from Sri Lanka) from UK to Germany, where they had not initially claimed asylum to have claims assessed. Update No. 3.

at sea. Phrase used, e.g., relating to privileged wills (q.v.), by which a mariner or seaman 'being at sea' may make an informal will. 'At sea' has been given an extended meaning so as to include, e.g., a Merchant Navy apprentice on leave between voyages and due to rejoin his ship – *In b Newland* [1952] P 71. See also *In b Rapley* [1983] 1 WLR 1069.

attachment. 1. Arrest under a writ of attachment, e.g., because of disobedience relating to a court order. Generally replaced by punishment for contempt. 2. Enforcement of direction to pay money, by attachment of earnings order. See Attachment of Earnings Act 1971 (amended by A.J.A. 1982, ss 53–54 and F.L.R.A. 1987, Sch 2); Maintenance Enforcement Act 1991, Sch 2; C.P.I.A. 1996, s 53; CPR, Sch 2; CCR, O 27 (index of orders). A 'consolidated attachment order' can be made under s 17 for payment of two or more judgment debts. 3. Attachment of debts relates to procedure in garnishee proceedings (q.v.). See O 49, r 1.

attempt, common law offence of. Performance of an act which could have been regarded as a movement to the commission of an offence and which could not reasonably be interpreted as having any other objective than the commission of the offence: *R v Button* [1900] 2 QB 597. Abolished under Criminal Attempts Act 1981, s 6(1).

attempt, intention and. 'In any case where (a) apart from this subsection a person's intention would not be regarded as having amounted to an intent to commit an offence; but (b) if the facts of the case had been as he believed them to be, his intention would be so regarded, then

[for the purposes of s 1(1) of this Act] he shall be regarded as having had an intent to commit that offence': Criminal Attempts Act 1981, s 1(3). See *R v Khan* [1990] 2 All ER 783; *A-G's Reference (No. 3 of 1992)* [1994] 1 WLR 409.

attempt, statutory offence of. 'If with intent to commit an offence to which this section applies, a person does an act which is more than merely preparatory to the commission of the offence, he is guilty of attempting to commit the offence': Criminal Attempts Act 1981, s 1(1). Applies to any offence which, if completed, would be triable as an indictable offence (q.v.) except: conspiracy; aiding and abetting; assisting offenders or accepting consideration for not disclosing information about an arrestable offence: s 1(4). A person may be guilty of attempting to commit an offence even though the facts are such that the commission of the offence is impossible: s 1(2). See *R v Shivpuri* [1987] AC 1; *R v Ball* (1990) 90 Cr App R 378; *R v Jones* [1990] 1 WLR 1057 (old case law of no help in construing the 1981 Act); *R v Geddes* [1996] Crim LR 894.

attendance. In relation to a 'letting with board or attendance', which does not constitute a protected tenancy (q.v.), means 'service personal to the tenant provided by the landlord in accordance with his covenant for the benefit or convenience of the individual tenant for his use or enjoyment of the demised premises': *Palser* v *Grinling* [1948] AC 291.

attendance allowance. Non-contributory benefit payable (under S.S. Contributions and Benefits Act 1992, s 64) to those so mentally or physically disabled that they require constant attendance. For attendance allowance for terminally ill, see s 66. See W.R.P.A. 1999, s 66.

attendance centre. A place which offenders under 21 attend, to be given, under supervision, appropriate occupation or instruction, in pursuance of an order made under P.C.C.(S).A. 2000, s 60. The order is available to the court where it has power to commit a person aged at least

21 but under 25 to prison in default of payment of a sum of money, or (in the case of persons under 21) for failing to do or abstain from doing anything required to be done or left undone. Aggregate hours of attendance are, not less than 12 (where person is under 14), not more than 24 (where he is under 16), not more than 36 (where he is 16–21).

attestation. The signature of a document by one who is not a party to it, but who is the witness to the signature of another. The W.A. 1837 requires the attestation of two witnesses. See also L.P. (Misc. Provs.) A. 1989, s 1(3). See *Re Colling* [1972] 1 WLR 1440; A.J.A. 1982, s 17. *See* WILL, VALIDITY OF.

attorney. One appointed by another to act in his place. *See* POWER OF ATTORNEY.

Attorney-General. The chief law officer of the Crown and head of the English Bar. His duties include representing the Crown in legal proceedings and conducting some Crown prosecutions. He is usually a member of the House of Commons and has ministerial responsibility for the DPP, Crown Prosecution Service, Serious Fraud Office, Treasury Solicitor's Department. He may stay proceedings by *nolle prosequi* (q.v.). He may be a member of the cabinet. His consent is necessary in some cases before prosecution: see, e.g., Official Secrets Act 1911, s 8. 'As the guardian of the public interest, the Attorney-General has a special duty in regard to the enforcement of the law . . . it is his duty to represent the public interest with complete objectivity and detachment': *A-G (ex rel McWhirter) v IBA* [1973] QB 629. Any function of the Attorney-General may be exercised by the Solicitor-General (q.v.): Law Officers Act 1997, s 1(1). For right of the Attorney-General to institute civil proceedings in aid of the criminal law, see *A-G v Blake* [1998] 2 WLR 805.

Attorney-General and relator actions. Where the A-G has refused his consent to relator proceedings in the civil courts, a private citizen who asserts that the public interest is involved by threat of a breach of the criminal law has no right to go to the civil courts for a remedy either by way of injunction or a declaration: *Gouriet v Union of Post Office Workers* [1978] AC 435. 'That it is the exclusive right of the Attorney-General to represent the public interest . . . is not technical, nor procedural, not fictional. It is constitutional': *per* Lord Wilberforce. *See* RELATOR.

Attorney-General's References. The A-G may, in his discretion, refer to the Court of Appeal (Criminal Division) points of law, following an acquittal after trial in the Crown Court: see C.J.A. 1972, s 36(1). (Court of Appeal may refer the point to House of Lords if it appears that the House should consider it: s 36(3).) 'We hope to see this procedure used extensively for short but important points which require a quick ruling of this court before a potentially false decision of law has too wide a circulation in the courts': per Lord Widgery CJ (see *Re A-G's Ref (No. 1 of 1975)* [1975] QB 773).

attorney, grants to. *See* GRANTS TO ATTORNEY.

attorney, power of. *See* POWER OF ATTORNEY.

attornment. 1. The acknowledgement of one person that he holds goods on behalf of another: S.G.A. 1979, s 45(3). 2. Agreement of an estate owner to become the tenant of one who has acquired the estate next in reversion or remainder. See *Regent Oil Co v J Gregory Ltd* [1966] Ch 402.

auction. Public sale of property by an auctioneer to the highest bidder. See, e.g., Sale of Land by Auction Act 1867; S.G.A. 1979, s 57. An *auctioneer* is one who is licensed to conduct sales by auction. A contract comes into existence as the result of an auctioneer's acts, when a bid is accepted and his hammer falls (or in other customary manner) and a bidder may retract his bid until that event. See *Moore v Khan-Ghauri* [1991] 32 EG 63; *Barry v Heathcote Ball* (2000) 150 NLJ 1377; Unfair Contract Terms Act 1977, s 12(3). *See* BID; MOCK AUCTION.

auctioneers, liability of. CA held in *Marcq v Christie Manson Ltd* [2003]

EWCA Civ 731, that where an auctioneer offers goods for sale, later returning them unsold to the prospective seller, he will not be liable in conversion to the owner, always provided that he acted in good faith and had no notice of the owner's rights.

auctioneer's obligations. Stated in *Benton* v *Campbell, Parker & Co* [1925] 2 KB 410, as: warranting his authority to sell; warranting that he knows of no defect in his principal's title; undertaking to give quiet possession against the price received by him; undertaking that possession will be undisturbed by the principal or himself. See *Derbyshire CC* v *Vincent* (1990) *The Times*, 19 June.

audi alteram partem. Hear the other side. It is a principle of natural justice (q.v.) that no man should be condemned unheard. See, e.g., *Local Government Board* v *Arlidge* [1915] AC 120; *Ridge* v *Baldwin* [1964] AC 40.

audience, right of. Right to appear and conduct proceedings in court. Under C.L.S.A. 1990, s 27, it may be exercised by a person who has a right of audience granted by an appropriate authorised body (e.g., General Council of the Bar); or who has no such right but has a right of audience under statute (e.g., County C.A. 1984, ss 60, 61) or granted by the court in question. Every barrister shall be deemed to have been granted by the General Council of the Bar a right of audience before every court in relation to all proceedings (exercisable in accordance with the qualification regulations and rules of conduct of the General Council approved for purposes of s 27 in relation to the right): C.L.S.A. 1990, s 31, substituted by Acc.J.A. 1999, s 36. For rights of audience of employed advocates, see s 31A. For right of legal executives to conduct litigation, see Acc.J.A. 1999, s 40; SI 98/1077. See *Clarkson* v *Gilbert* (2000) *The Times*, 4 July. For rights of solicitors, see C.L.S.A. 1990, ss 31–33.

audit. Detailed inspection of accounts of an organisation, usually by a person not employed within the organisation.

For damages for negligent audit, see *Bank of Credit and Commerce* v *Price Waterhouse (No. 3)* (1998) *The Times*, 2 April.

Audit Commission. Set up under Local Government Finance Act 1982, s 11, to take an audit of local authority accounts. The 15–20 members are appointed by the Secretary of State: Audit Commission Act 1998, s 1(2), Sch 1. Public notice must be given of the annual audit; the accounts are open to public inspection: 1998 Act, s 15. See *Lloyd* v *McMahon* [1987] AC 625; *Bookbinder* v *Tebbit (No. 2)* [1992] 1 WLR 217; L.G.A. 1999, s 22.

auditor. A member of a recognised body of accountants who examines accounts. See Cos.A. 1985, ss 236, 237; Cos.A. 1989, ss 9, 25; F.S.A. 1986, Part I, chap XI. An auditor's report must be attached to a company's balance sheet: Cos.A. 1985, s 238(3). It must be read at the general meeting and must be available for inspection by any member: Cos.A. 1985, s 241(2). Appointment and duties of auditors must be in accordance with Cos.A. 1985, ss 384–394, and Cos.A. 1989, ss 118–123, Sch 11. An auditor's duties are to prepare reports for company members; to acquaint himself with his duties under statute; to exercise reasonable care. See F.S.M.A. 2000, Part xxii; *Secretary of State for Trade and Industry* v *Hart* [1982] 1 All ER 817; *Caparo Industries plc* v *Dickman* [1990] 2 WLR 358 (company's auditors did not owe a duty of care to shareholders or other persons who bought shares in reliance on accounts audited negligently); *Coulthard* v *Neville Russell* [1998] 1 BCLC 143.

Auditor General. *See* COMPTROLLER.

Auditors, Court of. *See* COURT OF AUDITORS.

auditor's standards. 'His vital task is to see that errors are not made, be they errors of computation, or errors of omission or commission, or downright untruths . . . To perform this task properly he must come to it with an inquiring mind – not suspicious of dishonesty . . . but suspecting that someone may have made a mistake somewhere and that a check must be made to ensure that there has been none': *per* Lord Denning in *Fomento Ltd v Selsdon Ltd* [1958] 1 WLR 45. See *Re Gerrard* [1968] Ch 455. For auditors' rights, see Cos.A. 1989, s 120.

authenticate. To make valid and effective by proof or by appropriate formalities as required by law.

author. In relation to a work, means the person who creates it: Copyright, Designs and Patents Act 1988, s 9(1). A work is of 'unknown authorship' if the identity of the author is unknown, or, in the case of a work of joint authorship, if the identity of none of the authors is known: s 9(4). A 'work of joint authorship' means a work produced by the collaboration of two or more authors in which the contribution of each author is not distinct from that of the other author(s): s 10(1): see *Fylde Microsystems Ltd v Key Radio Systems Ltd* [1998] FSR 449; *Ray v Classic FM plc* [1998] FSR 622. In general, the author of a work is the first owner of any copyright in it: s 11(1). *See* COPYRIGHT.

authorised bodies, financial, record of. Under F.S.M.A. 2000, s 347, FSA (q.v.) must maintain records of persons authorised for purposes of the Act (see s 31), authorised unit trust schemes, open-ended investment companies, recognised schemes, investment exchanges and clearing houses.

authorised capital. The total amount of capital which a company is authorised by its memorandum of association (q.v.) to issue. Known also as 'nominal' or 'registered' capital. *See* COMPANY; ISSUED CAPITAL.

authorised securities. Securities in which trustees could invest under Tr.A. 1925. *See* TRUSTEE'S POWER OF, INVESTMENT GENERAL.

authority. 1. Judicial decision or opinion expressed by an author of repute used as grounds of a statement of law. 2. Rights bestowed by one person on another allowing full performance of an act.

3. A body exercising powers, e.g., a local authority (q.v.).

automatism. 'An act done by the muscles without any control by the mind, such as a spasm, a reflex action or a convulsion, or an act done by a person who is not conscious of what he is doing, such as an act done whilst suffering from concussion or whilst sleepwalking' (q.v.): *Bratty v A-G for Northern Ireland* [1963] AC 386. Actions resulting from a state of automatism are involuntary and, as such, not generally punishable. Where automatism is due to mental disease, the defence is known as 'insane automatism' (see *R v Burgess* [1991] 2 WLR 1206) and the M'Naghten Rules (q.v.) apply; in such a case the burden of proof is on the accused. See *Roberts v Ramsbottom* [1980] 1 All ER 7 (unsuccessful defence to negligence); *R v Hennessy* [1989] 1 WLR 287.

autonomy. 1. Independence, 2. Power of self-government. 3. Power of an association which is not a state to make law for itself. 4. Principle of 'individual autonomy' (in criminal legislation), stating that individuals must be treated as responsible for their own behaviour.

autopsy. *See* POST-MORTEM.

autrefois acquit. Formerly acquitted. A plea in bar that the accused has been acquitted previously of the same offence. 'The test to establish the plea is (1) that defendant had been previously acquitted of the same offence, or (2) that he could have been convicted at the previous trial of the offence with which he is subsequently charged, or that the two offences are substantially the same . . .': *Re Wilson* [1948] 1 WLR 680. It is for the judge to decide the issue: C.J.A. 1988, s 122. See *R v G* (2001) *The Times*, 25 May; *DPP v Khan* [1997] RTR 82; *Macpherson Report (1999)*, recommendation 38. *See* DOUBLE JEOPARDY; *NEMO DEBET BIS VEXARI*.

autrefois convict. Formerly convicted. A plea in bar that the accused has been previously tried and convicted by a court of competent jurisdiction for the same offence. The offence with which he is charged must be the same, or practically the same, offence as that with which he was previously charged. See *Connelly* v *DPP* [1964] AC 1254 (in which the plea was considered extensively by the House of Lords); *R* v *Green* [1993] Crim LR 46.

autre vie. The life of another. A tenant *pur autre vie* is a tenant for the life of another, as where A grants land to B 'during the life of C'. Exists only in equity. *See* CESTUI QUE VIE.

available market. Phrase used in S.G.A. 1979, s 50(3), providing that where there is an available market for goods, the measure of damages for breach of contract is prima facie the difference between the contract price and the market price at the date of the breach. See *Shearson Lehman Hutton Ltd* v *Maclaine Watson Ltd (No. 2)* [1990] 3 All ER 723.

available on request. A reference in a written contract to its being subject to 'the general conditions available on request', suffices to incorporate into that contract the terms contained in a current edition of those conditions. See *Smith* v *S Wales Switchgear* [1978] 1 All ER 18.

average. Derived from *averia* (damage). Used in contracts for carriage of goods by sea to refer to apportionment of loss. 1. *General average loss* is caused by an act which occurs where an extraordinary sacrifice is voluntarily and reasonably made so as to preserve property, e.g., jettison of cargo (q.v.). The loss is borne rateably by all those interested: Marine Insurance Act 1906, s 66. 2. *Particular average* arises where the property is damaged by an accident not suffered for the general benefit, e.g., loss of a ship's boat. The loss remains where it falls.

avoidance. Setting aside; making null or void.

avoidance and evasion of tax. *See* TAX AVOIDANCE AND EVASION.

avulsion. Removal, by the sudden and perceptible action of water, of soil from one person's land and its deposit on another's. Ownership of such soil does not change, as is general in the case of accretion (q.v.).

B

bad advice, damages for. CA held in *Lennon* v *Commissioner of Police of the Metropolis* (2004) *The Times*, 25 February that a duty of care was owed by a police commissioner to officers within his force, so that he was vicariously liable for economic loss sustained by an officer resulting from his having acted on negligent advice.

bad debt. A debt which, seemingly, cannot be recovered.

bad faith. Characterised by dishonesty. See *Cannock Chase DC* v *Kelly* (1977) 36 P & CR 219.

bail. *Bailler* = to deliver. Release of a person arrested on his giving security or accepting specified conditions. A person arrested may be granted bail under a duty to surrender to custody (q.v.). He may be required to provide a surety to secure his surrender: Bail Act 1976, ss 3, 8; C.D.A. 1998, s 54. On withholding of bail he may apply to the Crown Court or High Court: s 5(6). A person arrested for breach of bail conditions must be brought before a magistrate within 24 hours of that arrest: s 7(4)(a). (See P.C.C.(S).A. 2000, s 151, for effect on sentencing of offending while on bail.) See also C.J.A. 1967; Courts Act 1971; M.C.A. 1980; C.J.A. 1988, s 153. Bail need not be granted if the court is satisfied that there are substantial grounds for believing that the defendant, if released, would fail to surrender to custody, or would commit an offence while on bail or interfere with witnesses. See S.C.A. 1981, s 81 (as amended by C.J.A. 1982, s 29) for High Court's powers to grant bail; C.J.A. 1988, s 154; *Murphy* v *DPP* [1990] 2 All ER 390; C.J.P.O.A. 1994 (no bail for defendants charged with or convicted of homicide or rape after previous conviction of such an offence (except where there are exceptional cases which justify bail): s 25, amended by C.D.A. 1998, s 56; no right to bail for persons accused or convicted of committing an offence while on bail: s 26; police power of arrest for failure to answer to bail: s 29. For prosecution's right of appeal against grant of bail, see Bail (Amendment) Act 1993; *R* v *Szakal* [2000] 1 Cr App R 248. For bail in relation to persons detained under Immigration Act 1971, see Immigration and Asylum Act 1999, ss 44–50. See *Caballero* v *UK* (2000) *The Times*, 29 February (automatic denial of bail held to be in breach of human rights); *R* v *Havering Magistrates ex p DPP* (2001) *The Times*, 7 February (breach of bail).

bail after arrest, date of court appearance. P. & C.E.A. 1984, s 47, allows grant of bail by police officer to a person arrested. Under s 47(3A), inserted by C.D.A. 1988, s 46, the custody officer (q.v.) must appoint for purposes of defendant's appearance, a date which is no later than the first sitting of the court after defendant has been charged, or a later date if clerk to justices confirms that defendant cannot be accommodated until that date.

bail, and right to liberty. The statutory provision stating that persons charged with homicide or rape ought to be granted bail only where the court is satisfied that exceptional matters justify this (see Bail Act 1976, s 4, as amended) does not violate European Convention, art 5 (right to liberty): *R(O)* v *Harrow Crown Court* [2003] EWHC 868.

bail blitz. A-G announced (*The Times*, 2005, 14 January) that offenders who have skipped their bail may be instantly jailed, even if the original crime was non-imprisonable.

bail condition, doorstep. Under Bail Act 1976, court may impose a condition ordering defendant to appear 'on his doorstep' during the hours of his curfew condition, should a police officer request him to do so: *R (CPS)* v *Chorley Justices* [2002] EWHC 2162. See also Criminal Justice and Public Order Act 1994, s 27(2), and Crime and Disorder Act 1998, s 54(2).

bail conditions, electrical monitoring of compliance with. Under C.J.P.A. 2001, s 132: an electronic monitoring requirement will not be imposed on a child or young person unless he was at least 12, had been charged with or convicted of a violent or sexual offence punishable in the case of an adult with imprisonment for 14 years or more, electronic monitoring arrangements were available within the relevant area, and a youth offending team agrees that the monitoring is suitable in the case of a child or young person.

bail, continuous. Direction by the magistrates' court, where the accused is remanded on bail, with or without sureties, instructing him to appear at every time and place to which the proceedings may be adjourned from time to time: Bail Act 1976.

bailee. *See* BAILMENT.

bailee, unconscious. Where a defendant becomes possessed of goods belonging to a plaintiff through a third party's mistake, and the defendant believes that the goods were his, or is not aware that they belonged to anyone but himself, he can be described properly as an 'unconscious bailee', and before dealing with the goods he has a duty to use a sufficient standard of care in all the circumstances to ascertain that they were his own: *AVX Ltd* v *EGM Solders Ltd* (1982) *The Times*, 7 July.

bail, failure to surrender to. CA held in relation to Practice Direction (Bail: Failure to Surrender and Trial in Absence) (2004) *The Times*, 26 January that it is essential that a defendant who is granted bail ought to be made aware of the significance of his undertaking to surrender to custody exactly in accordance with the terms of bail, and that appropriate action would be taken by the court should he fail to do so.

bail, granting of. Under C.J.P.A. 2001, s 129: where a magistrates' court or the Crown Court grants bail in criminal proceedings to a person to whom Bail Act 1976, s 4, applies, after hearing representations from the prosecutor in favour of withholding bail, then the court shall give reasons for a decision to grant bail.

bail, warrant endorsed for. A magistrate, on issuing a warrant for a person's arrest, may grant bail by endorsing the warrant for bail, so that it states that person arrested is to be released on bail, subject to duty to appear before magistrates' court at a specified time, and the endorsement will fix amounts in which any sureties are to be bound. See M.C.A. 1980, s 117. *See* SURETY.

bailiff. 1. Originally 'an officer that belongeth to a manor, to order the husbandry': *Termes de la Ley*. Now a person employed by a sheriff (q.v.) to serve and execute writs and processes. See Courts Act 1971, s 22; SI 92/729. 2. Judicial official in Guernsey (Royal Court Bailiff).

bailment. The delivery of goods by one person (the 'bailor') to another (the 'bailee') so that they might be used for some specified purpose, upon a condition that they shall be redelivered by the bailee to, or in accordance with the specified directions of, the bailor, or kept until he reclaims them. Examples: deposit of goods in a railway luggage office; pawning of goods. The bailee is under a duty to take reasonable care of the goods and to return them in accordance with the terms of the contract of bailment. See *Coggs* v *Barnard* (1703) 2 Ld Ray 909; *Armory* v *Delamirie* (1722) 1 Str 505; *Bacvar* v *Jarvis Norfolk Hotel* [1999] 10 CL 112.

bailor. *See* BAILMENT.

bail with sureties. Granting of bail on condition that the person provides one or more sureties for the purpose of seeing that he surrenders to custody (q.v.): Bail Act 1976. In considering the suitability of a proposed surety, regard is had to his character, financial resources, proximity to the accused: s 8(2).

balance. 'What remains after something has been taken out of a fund': *Re Burke Irwin's Trusts* (1918) 1 IR 350.

balance of probabilities. Concept in the law of evidence relating to the standard of proof whereby the party upon whom the legal burden of proof rests is entitled to a verdict in his favour if he has established some preponderance of probability (i.e., greater weight of evidence) in his favour. See *Hornal* v *Neuberger Products* [1957] 1 QB 247. Probability in the legal sense is entirely different from mathematical probability: *Re JS (A Minor)* [1981] Fam 22. In *R* v *Cannings* [2004] EWCA Crim 1, Dame Elizabeth Butler-Sloss cited the words of Lord Nicholls in *Re H* [1996] AC 563: 'The balance of probability standard means that a court is satisfied that an event occurred if the court considers that, on the evidence, the occurrence of the event was more likely than not. When assessing the probabilities, the court will have in mind as a factor – to whatever extent is appropriate in the particular case – that the more serious the allegation, the less likely it is the event occurred, and, hence, the stronger the evidence should be before the court concludes that the allegation is established on the balance of probability.' *See* STANDARDS OF PROOF.

balance sheet. A statement showing assets and liabilities of a business at a given date. A company's balance sheet must give a true and fair picture of the company at the end of the financial year. See Cos.A. 1985, s 228(2). It must comply with requirements of Cos.A. 1985, Sch 4, as amended. *See* COMPANY ACCOUNTS, PUBLICATION OF.

ballot. A system of voting involving secret votes. See, e.g., Representation of the People Act 1985; T.U.L.R.(C.)A. 1992 (right of union members to a ballot before industrial action); Employment Relations Act 1999, Sch 3; *Post Office*

v *UCW* [1990] 3 All ER 199; T.U.R.E.R.A. 1993, ss 1–7. *See* INDUSTRIAL ACTION; STRIKE.

bank. Financial institution engaged in the accepting of deposits of money, granting of credit (by loan, overdraft, etc.) and other transactions such as discounting of bills, dealing in foreign exchange, etc. See Banking Act 1987; *United Dominions Trust Ltd* v *Kirkwood* [1966] 2 QB 431. *See* BANK, AUTHORISED.

bank account, frozen without warning and explanation. It was held in *Squirrell Ltd (Applicant)* v *National Westminster Bank (Respondent)* [2005], *The Times*, 25 May, that a bank had the right to freeze an account without providing reason, if it suspected that the account contained proceeds of crime under the Proceeds of Crime Act 2002.

bank account, liability of joint holders. CA held in *Royal Bank of Scotland* v *Fielding* (2004) *The Times*, 26 February, that, where a joint bank account was held by husband and wife, they were to be considered as jointly and severally liable for an overdraft which had arisen on that account following borrowing by either of them made without any reference to the other.

bank, authorised. Institution recognised by the Bank of England as satisfying certain criteria: see Banking Act 1987, ss 8–18, as amended. See Bank of England Act 1998, Sch 5, chap I; Postal Services Act 2000, s 7(5). Criteria (see Sch 3) include: business directed by at least two individuals; directors to be fit and proper persons; business to be conducted in a prudent manner with integrity and appropriate skills; business possesses the prescribed minimum amount of net assets.

bank, duty of care. HL held in *Commissioners of Customs and Excise* v *Barclays Bank plc* [2006] *The Times*, 22 June where a bank is notified of an asset freezing injunction, the only duty owed is to the court. The bank does not owe a duty of care in tort to the claimant.

banker. One engaged in the business of banking. 'The relation between a banker and a customer who pays money into the bank is the ordinary relation between debtor and creditor, with a super-added obligation, arising out of the custom of bankers to honour the customer's drafts': *Joachimson* v *Swiss Bank Corporation* [1921] 3 KB 110. For restrictions on use of banking names, see Banking Act 1987, Part III.

bankers' books. Under Bankers' Books Evidence Act 1879, s 3, a copy of an entry in a banker's book was received as prima facie evidence of such an entry and of the transactions and accounts recorded therein. By virtue of the Act of 1879, s 9 (amended in 1979 and 1987), the expression includes ledgers, day books, cash books, account books and other records used in the ordinary business of the bank, whether in written form or kept on microfilm, magnetic tape, or other forms of retrieval mechanism. See C.P.I.A. 1996, Sch 1, para 15. See *State of Norway's Application* [1987] QB 433; *Williams* v *Summerfield* [1972] 2 QB 513 (permission granted to the police to inspect the bank accounts of an accused person). *See* BANKER'S DUTY OF SECRECY; EVIDENCE.

banker's customer. The term 'signifies a relationship in which duration is not of the essence. A person whose money has been accepted by a bank on the footing that they undertake to honour cheques up to the amount standing to his credit is . . . a customer of the bank . . . irrespective of whether his connection is of short or long standing': *Commissioners of Taxation* v *English, Scottish and Australian Bank Ltd* [1920] AC 683. See *Redmond* v *Allied Irish Banks* [1987] FLR 307.

banker's customer's duty of care. A bank's customer owes no wider duty of care to the bank in the operation of a current account beyond a duty to refrain from drawing a cheque in a manner which facilitates fraud or forgery, and a duty to inform the bank of the forgery of a cheque drawn on his account as soon as he becomes aware of it. See *Price Meats Ltd* v *Barclays Bank plc* (2000) *The Times*, 19 January (duty does not arise where customer has only constructive

knowledge of forgery). He is not under a duty to check his bank statements for unauthorised debit items. See *Tai Hing Cotton Mill Ltd* v *Liu Chong Hing Bank Ltd* [1986] AC 519; *Barclays Bank plc* v *Khaira* [1992] 1 WLR 623.

bankers' draft. *See* DRAFT.

banker's duty of secrecy. A bank has a legal obligation to keep a customer's affairs secret: see *Hardy* v *Veasey* (1868) LR 3 Exch 107; *Tournier* v *National Provincial and Union Bank of England* [1924] 1 KB 461; *Christofi* v *Barclays Bank plc* [1998] 1 WLR 1245. Disclosure may be compelled by process of law (see Bankers' Books Evidence Act 1879, s 7); e.g., on application of any party to legal proceedings; service of a *subpoena* (q.v.); where the bank's interests require disclosure. The customer may give express or implied consent to disclosure. *See* BANKERS' BOOKS.

banking instrument. Any cheque or other instrument to which Cheques Act 1957, s 4, applies; any document issued by a public officer intended to enable a person to obtain payment from a government department of a sum mentioned in the document; any bill of exchange or promissory note, postal order, money order, credit transfer, credit or debit advice. See *Honourable Society of the Middle Temple* v *Lloyds Bank* [1999] 1 All ER (Comm) 193; Postal Services Act 2000, s 7(2).

Banking Supervision, Board of. Under Bank of England Act 1998, s 28(1), Board consists of Chairman of FSA (q.v.), his nominee, and six independent directors appointed by Chancellor of the Exchequer and Chairman of FSA. The independent members elect one of their number to chair the Board: s 28(2).

bank, multilateral development. An international financial institution having as one of its objects economic development, either generally or in any region of the world: International Development Act 2002, s 11(2).

Bank of England. The central bank of the UK. Functions and duties are set out in Bank of England Acts 1946, 1998, and

Banking Act 1987. Following 1998 Act, s 11, its objectives now include, in relation to monetary policy, maintenance of price stability and support for government economic policy, relating, in particular, to growth and employment. A Court of Directors is responsible for the Bank's affairs, and comprises the Governor, two Deputy Governors and 16 Bank directors. See 1998 Act, ss 2, 13, Sch 1.

Bank of England Monetary Policy Committee. *See* MONETARY POLICY COMMITTEE, BANK OF ENGLAND.

Bank of England, suing of. The first-ever lawsuit against the Bank of England began in January 2004, when it was sued for misfeasance in public office, relating to its role and alleged activities in the downfall of the Bank of Credit and Commerce, which collapsed in 1991.

bankrupt. 'An individual who has been adjudged bankrupt and, in relation to a bankruptcy order it means the individual adjudged bankrupt by that order': Ins.A. 1986, s 381(1). Essentially, an insolvent debtor whose estate will be administered and distributed under appropriate rules, following a direction of the court, for the benefit of his creditors.

bankrupt, automatic discharge of. An ex parte interim order which effectively suspends the automatic discharge of a bankrupt can be made where the court believes that such an order is appropriate and is needed urgently: *Bagnall* v *Official Receiver* [2003] EWHC 1398 (Ch).

bankrupt, creditor in relation to. A person to whom a bankruptcy debt (q.v.) is owed and, in relation to an individual to whom a bankruptcy petition relates, a person who would be a creditor in the bankruptcy if a bankruptcy order were made on that petition: Ins.A. 1986, s 383(1).

bankruptcy. The legal processes related to insolvency. See Ins.A. 1986; Ins.A. 2000. In *Mulkerrins* v *Pricewaterhouse Coopers* (2003) *The Times*, 1 August, the HL held that a trustee in bankruptcy could have no interest in a right of action which a bankrupt wished to bring against former advisers; the bankrupt was entitled to bring such an action in his own name.

bankruptcy debt. Includes any debt or liability to which the bankrupt is subject at the commencement of the bankruptcy, any debt or liability to which he may become subject after the commencement of the bankruptcy by reason of any obligation incurred before the commencement of the bankruptcy, any amount specified in a criminal bankruptcy made against him: Ins.A. 1986, s 382(1). See also Building Societies Act 1997, Sch 6.

bankruptcy, discharge from. Discharge releases a bankrupt from all bankruptcy debts: Ins.A. 1986, s 281, as amended by Ch.A. 1989, Sch 11 and Child Support Act 1991, Sch 5. A bankrupt is discharged automatically after three years from commencement of bankruptcy (two years in the case of summary administration procedure). Where a person has previously been adjudicated bankrupt and was an undischarged bankrupt at any time in the period of 15 years ending with the commencement of bankruptcy, he must apply for discharge by order of the court (under s 280): s 279. See *Jacobs* v *Official Receiver* [1998] 3 All ER 250.

bankruptcy offences. A person guilty of any of these offences, which apply where the court has made a bankruptcy order on a bankruptcy petition, is liable to imprisonment or a fine or both: non-disclosure of all his property; concealment of any property or debt or books and papers; false statements; fraudulent disposal of property; absconding; fraudulent dealing with property obtained on credit; obtaining credit or engaging in business; failure to keep proper accounts; gambling or rash and hazardous speculation: see Ins.A. 1986. See *R* v *Mungroo* [1998] BPIA 784.

bankruptcy order. 'An order adjudicating an individual bankrupt': Ins.A. 1986, s 381(2).

bankruptcy order, annulment of. The court may annul an order if it appears that it should not have been made, or, to the extent required by the rules, the expenses of bankruptcy have been paid or secured. The order may be annulled whether or not the bankrupt has been discharged. See Ins.A. 1986, s 282, as amended.

bankruptcy petition. A request for a bankruptcy order (q.v.) to be made against an individual. It may be presented to the court by the individual himself, or a creditor, or the person bound by a voluntary arrangement approved under Ins.A. 1986, Part VIII. It may not be presented unless the debtor is domiciled in England or Wales, is personally present there on the day of presentation of the petition, or, at any time in the period of three years ending with that day he has been ordinarily resident, or has had a place of residence, in, or has carried on business in England or Wales. The petition may not be withdrawn without leave of the court. See *Smith* v *Simpson & Co* (2000) 150 NLJ 582 (conditional tender does not stop bankruptcy); F.S.M.A. 2000, s 359. *See* CREDITOR'S PETITION; DEBTOR'S PETITION.

bankruptcy, priority of debts in distribution. Preferential debts (see Ins.A. 1986, s 386) are paid in priority to other debts; they rank equally among themselves after bankruptcy expenses are paid in full, abating in equal proportions where the bankrupt's estate is insufficient to meet them. Debts which are neither preferential nor owed to a spouse rank equally between themselves and are paid, after preferential debts, in full, abating in equal proportions in the case of an estate insufficient to meet them. See Finance Act 1996, Sch 5, para 12. *See* INSOLVENCY, PREFERENTIAL DEBTS IN.

bankruptcy reforms. Following the bringing into force on 1 April 2004 of the provisions of the Enterprise Act 2002, the following reforms will be made: discharge period will be reduced to a maximum period of one year; bankruptcy restriction orders will be introduced; there will be a limitation on the period during which it will be in his home; fast-track individual voluntary possible to realise a bankrupt's interest arrangements are to be introduced.

bankruptcy, statement of affairs in relation to. In the case of a bankruptcy order (q.v.) made otherwise than on a debtor's petition (see Ins.A. 1986, s 272(2)), the bankrupt must submit to the official receiver (q.v.), within 21 days from the date of the order, particulars of creditors, debts, assets, other liabilities and such other information as may be prescribed. It is a contempt of court (q.v.) to fail to provide the statement: s 288. For a company's statement of affairs, see s 131.

bankruptcy, trustee in. Appointed by a general meeting of the bankrupt's creditors, or by the Secretary of State or the court: Ins.A. 1986 (see s 292). The bankrupt's estate vests in the trustee immediately on his appointment taking effect: s 306(1). Any property acquired by the bankrupt after the date of the bankruptcy order may be vested in the trustee: s 307(1). For his powers, see s 314, Sch 5.

bankrupt, official receiver and. Where a bankruptcy order has been made, the bankrupt is under a duty to deliver to the official receiver possession of his estate and all relevant books and papers. Failure to comply is a contempt of court (q.v.). See Ins.A. 1986, s 291.

bankrupt, public examination of. Following a bankruptcy order, the official receiver may apply to the court for a public examination of the bankrupt in relation to his affairs, dealings, property and causes of his failure. Those who may participate include the official receiver, trustee, special manager of the bankrupt's estate and creditors who have tendered a proof in bankruptcy: Ins.A. 1986, s 290. See *Official Receiver* v *Cummings-John* [2000] BPIR 320 (imprisonment of bankrupt for contempt following dishonest evidence).

bankrupt's estate. Comprises all property belonging to or vested in the bankrupt at the commencement of the bankruptcy. It does not include: tools, books, vehicles and other items of equipment necessary to him for personal use in employment, business or vocation; such clothing, bedding, furniture, household equipment necessary for his family's domestic needs; property held by the bankrupt on trust for any other person: Ins.A. 1986, s 283, amended by H.A. 1988, s 117. Any disposition of property made by a bankrupt during the period since the presentation of the petition is void, except when made with the consent of the court or subsequently ratified: s 284. For insolvent estates of deceased persons, see Ins.A. 1986, ss 421, 421A (inserted by Ins.A. 2000, s 12). See PENSION RIGHTS, EFFECT OF BANKRUPTCY ON.

bankrupt's property, seizure of. At any time after a bankruptcy order (q.v.) has been made, the court, on application of the official receiver or trustee, may issue a warrant for the seizure of property comprised in the bankrupt's estate, and to search for and seize property or documents: Ins.A. 1986, s 365. For power to order sale of property abroad, see *Pollard* v *Ashurst* (2000) *The Times*, 29 November.

banns. Proclamation in church in the form of a public notice of an intended marriage. Banns must be published on three Sundays preceding the marriage. See Marriage Act 1949, ss 5–14, amended by Marriage (Prohibited Degrees of Relationship) Act 1986; *Chard* v *Chard* [1956] p 259.

bar. 1. A legal impediment, as in bars to divorce (q.v.), or to the establishment of a claim by claimant. 2. A place in court where a prisoner is stationed, or where barristers speak for their clients. 3. The profession of barrister.

Bar Council. The General Council of the Bar of England and Wales, created in 1894. Most of its functions were taken over in 1974 by the Senate of the Inns of Court and the Bar. It was reconstituted in 1987 and is now the governing body of the Bar. It is concerned with maintaining the standards of the Bar and with improvements in its services. It may make its own bye-laws and rules (for which judicial sanction is not required).

bare licensee. One who has been given permission to enter a place for his own purposes, so as not to be a trespasser. Example: X grants a gratuitous permission to Y to walk across X's field. Known also as a 'mere licensee'. See *Berg Homes* v *Grey* (1979) 253 EG 473. *See* LICENCE.

bare trust. A trust (q.v.) which requires the trustee to act as a mere repository of the trust property, with no active duties to perform, as where X devises property to Y in trust for Z. Y's only duty is to convey the legal estate (q.v.) to Z. Y is a 'bare trustee'. See *Christie* v *Ovington* (1875) 1 Ch D 279; Banking Act 1987, s 106(1).

bargain. Agreement, contract (q.v.).

bargain, unconscionable. A catching bargain (q.v.).

bar, pleas in. When the indictment (q.v.) is put to the defendant, he can raise pleas alleging some reason why he should not be tried and maintaining that there should be an enquiry forthwith into that reason. Examples: *autrefois acquit* (q.v.); *autrefois convict* (q.v.).

barratry. 1. Common-law offence (common barratry) committed by one who frequently incited or maintained quarrels at law. Abolished under C.L.A. 1967. 2. Wrongs which prejudice a shipowner or charterer, committed wilfully by the master or crew of a ship. See *Shell International* v *Gibbs* [1983] 2 AC 375.

barring of entailed interest. Procedure whereby a tenant in tail puts an end to the limitations of a fee tail (q.v.). A tenant in tail in possession, if of full age, may execute a deed which, in effect, converts the entail into a fee simple (q.v.): Fines and Recoveries Act 1833, s 15. A tenant in tail whose interest is in remainder may, if of full age, convert the entail into a fee simple with the consent of protector of settlement (q.v.). A tenant in tail, of full age, whose interest is in remainder may, without the protector's consent, partially bar the entail (thus creating a base fee). L.P.A. 1925, s 176, allows the devise or bequest of entails under specified conditions, so that, in effect, the beneficiary takes the fee simple absolute. See also Lim.A. 1980, s 27; Trusts of Land and Appointment of Trustees Act 1996, Sch 1, para 5(1). *See* BASE FEE.

barrister. A person called to the Bar by one of the Inns of Court (q.v.). His function is primarily that of an advocate and he has exclusive right of audience in certain types of judicial proceedings. He may not sue for fees, which are deemed to be in the nature of an honorarium: *Wells* v *Wells* [1914] P 157. See C.L.S.A. 1990, s 61 (barrister's right to enter contract for provision of his services). A barrister's general immunity (q.v.) from a claim in negligence brought by a client, was abolished in relation to civil or criminal litigation, by *Hall & Co* v *Simons* [2000] 3 All ER 673. For suspension in cases of misconduct, see *Re H* [1981] 3 All ER 205; see also *Hesford* v *General Council of the Bar* (1999) *The Times*, 20 August (suspension replaced by reprimand). For discrimination by or in relation to barristers, see C.L.S.A. 1990, s 64, modifying Sex Discrimination Act 1975, s 35; Race Relations Act 1976, s 26.

barrister's cab-rank rule. A practising barrister is bound to accept any brief to appear before a court in the field in which he professes to practise at a proper professional fee, having regard to the length and difficulty of the case. Special circumstances such as a conflict of interest or the possession of relevant and confidential information may justify his refusal to accept a particular brief: see *Code of Conduct for the Bar*. For 'double booking' (i.e., acceptance of briefs in different trials beginning on the same day), see *Re A Barrister* (1989) *The Independent*, 3 March.

barrister's duty to the court. A barrister must 'assist the court in the administration of justice and must not deceive or knowingly or recklessly mislead the court': *Code of Conduct*, para 202. 'He has a duty to the court which is paramount. It is a mistake to suppose that he is the mouthpiece of his client to say what he wants: or his tool to do what he directs. He is none of these things. He owes allegiance to a higher cause . . . the cause of truth and justice . . . He must disregard the most specific instructions of his client if they conflict with his duty to the court': *per* Lord Denning in *Rondel* v *Worsley* [1969] 1 AC

191. See *Orchard* v *SE Electricity Board* [1987] 3 WLR 102.

barrister's fees. There is no contractual relationship between an instructing solicitor and a barrister, so that payment of fees is a 'matter of honour', not a legal obligation. (The barrister, however, may refer a defaulting solicitor to The Law Society.) 'A counsel can maintain no action for his fees, which are given not as a salary, but as a mere gratuity which a counsellor cannot demand without doing wrong to his reputation': Blackstone, *Commentaries* (1765). *See* HONORARIUM.

barrister's professional obligation. 'A barrister cannot pick or choose his clients. He is bound to accept a brief from any man who comes before the courts. No matter how great a rascal he may be. No matter how given to complaining. No matter how undeserving or unpopular his cause. The barrister must defend him to the end': *per* Lord Denning in *Rondel* v *Worsley* [1969] 1 AC 191. See *Connolly-Martin* v *Davis* [1999] PNLR 826 (in the absence of any special assumption of responsibility, a barrister owes no legally enforceable duty to his client's opponents).

barter. The practice of exchanging goods for goods or services: see *La Neuville* v *Nourse* (1913) 3 Camp 351. Excluded from S.G.A. 1979. For part-barter, see *Simpson* v *Connolly* [1953] 1 WLR 911.

base fee. 'That estate in fee simple into which an estate in tail is converted where the issues in tail are barred, but persons claiming estates by way of remainder or otherwise are not barred': Fines and Recoveries Act 1833, s 1. A base fee may be converted into fee simple absolute (q.v.) in the following ways: (1) Fresh disentailing deed. (2) Owner of base fee in possession may enlarge it into fee simple by will. (3) Union of base fee with remainder in fee. (4) Lapse of time: Lim.A. 1980, s 27. See Trusts of Land and Appointment of Trustees Act 1996, Sch 1, para 5(1). *See* BARRING OF ENTAILED INTEREST.

base rate of interest. 'The interest rate set by the Bank of England which is used as a basis for other banks' rates': CPR Glossary.

bastard. An illegitimate child, i.e., one born out of lawful wedlock. See now F.L.R.A. 1987, Part I.

battered wife. 'A woman who has suffered serious or repeated physical injury from the man with whom she lives': from Minutes of Evidence of Select Committee on Violence in Marriage, 1974. For 'battered woman's syndrome', see *R* v *Hobson* [1998] Cr App R 31. See F.L.A. 1996, Part IV (now in force). *See* DOMESTIC VIOLENCE; INJUNCTIONS RELATING TO DOMESTIC VIOLENCE.

battery. A crime and a tort, involving the infliction of unlawful personal violence by defendant against plaintiff: see *Haystead* v *DPP* [2000] 3 All ER 890 (offence of battery under C.J.A. 1988, s 39, established where defendant used indirect force); *Wilson* v *Pringle* [1986] 2 All ER 440. It includes even the slightest force; no actual harm need result; it is actionable *per se*. Consent, self-defence, lawful and reasonable chastisement may be defences. In common usage 'assault' (q.v.) is often a synonym for battery; in law they are distinct. See *Kenlin* v *Gardiner* [1967] 2 QB 510; *Fagan* v *Metropolitan Police Commissioner* [1969] 1 QB 439; *R* v *Notman* [1994] Crim LR 518.

battle, trial by. Norman procedure, in essence an appeal to the 'God of battles' to bring victory to the rightful party. The plaintiff and defendant, or their 'champions', fought, the outcome being considered as a divine judgment. Abolished in 1819 after an attempt to claim use of the procedure was made in *Ashford* v *Thornton* (1818) 1 B Ald 405. For a detailed account of 'trial by wager of battle', see Blackstone's *Commentaries*, Book III, chap 22.

beach. The foreshore (q.v.). It includes land above the high-water mark which is in apparent continuity with the beach at high-water mark, or which possesses a character more akin to the foreshore than the hinterland: *Tito* v *Waddell (No. 2)* [1977] Ch 106.

bearer. *See* BILL OF EXCHANGE.

bearer shares. Shares (q.v.) for which no register of ownership is kept by the issuing company. They must pass physically from seller to buyer and are usually lodged with a bank. See Tr.A. 2000, s 18. *See* SHARES, BEARER, AND DELIVERY.

beat. To batter: *Cross* v *DPP* [1995] COD 382.

Beddoe order. Leave granted to trustees by the court so as to enable them to sue or defend and to be reimbursed out of the trust estate: *Re Beddoe* [1893] 1 Ch 547; *Midland Bank Trust Co* v *Green* [1980] Ch 590; *Singh* v *Bhasin* (1998) *The Times*, 21 August.

begging. It is an offence under Vagrancy Act 1824 for a person to wander abroad or place himself in any public place, street, highway, court or passage to beg or gather alms or to cause, procure or encourage any child to do so. See also C.&Y.P.A. 1933, s 4.

begin, right to. *See* RIGHT TO BEGIN.

behaviour, breakdown of marriage and. 'Behaviour is something more than a mere state of affairs or a state of mind . . . [it is] action or conduct by the one which affects the other. Such conduct may take the form of an act or omission . . . and, in my view, it must have some reference to the marriage': *per* Baker J in *Katz* v *Katz* [1972] 3 All ER 219. See Mat.C.A. 1973, s 1(2)(*b*); *Richards* v *Richards* [1984] AC 174; *Buffery* v *Buffery* [1988] 2 FLR 365. *See* UNREASONABLE CONDUCT.

bench. Used in a collective sense to refer to the judges or magistrates in a court. A lawyer who becomes a judge is said to be 'raised to the bench'.

Benchers. The governing body of each of the Inns of Court (q.v.). They are judges or senior members of the Bar (q.v.) and have control over the admission of students and calls to the Bar. Appeal from their decisions is to the Lord Chancellor and judges of the High Court who sit as 'visitors' (q.v.).

bench warrant. Order for the immediate arrest of a person issued by a court, e.g., for failure to appear on breach of the condition of bail (q.v.). The High Court is empowered to issue a bench warrant intended for the arrest of a person who has not complied with an order issued earlier. This is not limited to a case in which the court has already found for contempt: *Zakahorov* v *White* [2003] EWHC 2463 (Ch). *See* WARRANT.

beneficial freehold owner. One who, holding the fee simple absolute (q.v.) in law and equity, is effectively the 'sole owner' of land.

beneficial interest. The equitable interest of a beneficiary (q.v.). Thus, if land is held by X in trust for Y, X has the legal estate, Y has the beneficial interest. (The word 'beneficially' is used in explanation of how property is held by a beneficiary.)

beneficiary. 1. One entitled for his own benefit, i.e., for whose benefit property is held (e.g., by a trustee). Known also as *cestui que trust* (q.v.). See Trusts of Land and Appointment of Trustees Act 1996, s 22(1); *Re B (Child: Property Transfer)* [1999] 2 FLR 418 (order transferring property 'for the benefit of the child' held to mean no more than 'for the good of the child', so that no trust in favour of the child was created). For representation of beneficiaries by trustees, see CPR, Sch 1; O 15, r 14. 2. One who receives a gift under a will.

beneficiary, remedies of. Rights of a beneficiary arising where a trustee departs from the terms of a trust (q.v.) or where he is in breach of some duty imposed on him by statute or equity, including an order for an account; injunction; damages; tracing order. *See* TRACING TRUST PROPERTY.

benefit offence. Means, under S.S.F.A. 2001, s 1(7): any criminal offence in connection with a claim for a relevant social security benefit or in connection with the receipt or payment of any amount by way of such a benefit; or any criminal offence committed for the purpose of facilitating the commission (whether or not by the same person) of a benefit offence; or any attempt or conspiracy to commit a benefit offence.

benefit offence, loss of benefit for commission of. Under S.S.F.A. 2001, ss 7(1) and 7(2), sanctionable benefits will not be payable in the offender's case for any period comprised in a disqualification period, if: the offender is convicted of one or more benefit offences in each of two separate sets of proceedings, and the benefit offence of which he is convicted in the later proceedings is committed within three years after the date on which he was convicted in the later proceedings is committed within three years after the date on which he was convicted in the earlier proceedings, and the conditions for an entitlement to a sanctionable benefit are or become satisfied at any time within the disqualification period.

benefit, wide meaning of. CA held in *Re S (A Child) (Financial Provision)* (2004) *The Times*, 15 November, that, in relation to the Children Act 1989, Sch 1, para 1, 'benefit' is to be construed widely, allowing, for example, the extension of financial provision enabling a parent to travel to Africa to see a child who was unlawfully detained by the father.

benefits, contributory. Classified under S.S. Contributions and Benefits A. 1992, s 20 as: jobseeker's allowance, sickness benefit, invalidity benefit, maternity allowance, widow's benefit, retirement pensions, child's special allowance, bereavement benefits (see W.R.P.A. 1999, Sch 8, para 3). See also S.S. Administration Act 1992; Jobseekers Act 1995.

benefits, exclusion from, and immigration control. No person subject to immigration control (q.v.) is entitled to: income-based jobseeker's allowance; attendance, severe disablement, invalid care, allowance; income support; social fund payment; child, housing, council tax benefit, under S.S. (Contributions and Benefits) A. 1992: Immigration and Asylum Act 1999, s 115(1), (3).

benefits, false representations. If a person, for the purpose of obtaining social security benefits, makes a statement or representation which he knows to be false or produces documents which are false in a material particular, or fails to notify a change of circumstances which statutory regulations require him to notify, he shall be guilty of an offence: S.S. Administration Act 1992, s 112 amended by S.S. Administration (Fraud) Act 1997. See C.S.P.S.S.A. 2000, Sch 6, para 8.

benefits, overpayment. Where, as a result of a claimant's misrepresentation, fraudulent or otherwise, an overpayment has been made, the Secretary of State is entitled to recover: S.S. Administration Act 1992, s 71. See S.S. (Recovery of Benefits) Act 1997; S.S. Administration (Fraud) Act 1997; Tax Credits Act 1999, Sch 2, para 10.

benevolent society. A society established for a benevolent or charitable purpose under Friendly Societies Acts 1974–92. *See* FRIENDLY SOCIETY.

Benjamin order. Where personal representatives (q.v.) may experience delay in winding up and distributing an estate because they are not sure whether a missing beneficiary (q.v.) is alive or not, the court may make an order authorising distribution on the assumption that, e.g., the beneficiary is dead: *Re Benjamin* [1902] 1 Ch 723. See *Re Green's WT* [1985] 3 All ER 455.

bequeath. To dispose of personal property by will.

bequest. A gift by will of personal property, known also as a 'legacy' (q.v.).

bereavement, damages for. A claim for damages for bereavement may be included in a fatal accident claim (q.v.): PD 16, para 5.2. *See* COMPENSATION.

bereavement payment. Payment available to widows and widowers who, while of working age, lose a spouse. It will not be payable to pensioners. Widowers and widows must have been legally married to the deceased person at date of death. It will not be payable if claimant was living, at that date, with another as man and wife. See W.R.P.A. 1999, s 54; s 36(1), (2).

best evidence rule. The rule required, in effect, that the best or most direct evidence of a fact should be adduced, or its absence accounted for. Example: the best evidence of the existence of the contents

of a letter is its production in court. The rule no longer applies as the court admits all relevant evidence: *Kajala v Noble* (1982) 75 Cr App R 149. *See* EVIDENCE.

bestiality. The offence of buggery (q.v.) committed with a beast. See *R v Higson* (1984) 6 Cr App R (S) 20.

best interests, persons. The person making the determination must consider all the relevant circumstances and, in particular, he must consider (a) whether it is likely that the person will at some time have capacity in relation to the matter in question, and (b) if it appears likely that he will, when that is likely to be. Mental Capacity Act 2005 s 4(2) & (3).

best value authority. Authority designated under L.G.A. 1999, s 1(1), which has the general duty to make arrangements to secure continuous improvement in the way in which its functions are exercised, having regard to a combination of economy, efficiency and effectiveness: s 3(1). Performance indicators may be specified by Secretary of State: s 4(1). For plans and audit, see ss 6, 7; SI 01/724.

bet. Something staked on the outcome of a contingency. Often used as a synonym for wager. See, e.g., Betting, Gaming and Lotteries Acts 1963–1985; Lotteries and Amusements Act 1976; Betting and Gaming Duties Act 1981; Finance Act 1987. It did not include a stake hazarded in the course of gaming: Gaming Act 1968, s 53, Sch 2; *City Index v Leslie* [1991] 3 All ER 180 (betting on stock market). *See* GAMING; LOTTERY; SWEEPSTAKE; WAGERING CONTRACT.

betterment. 1. An increase in the value of real property because of beneficial public works nearby. 2. Prospective developmental value of land.

beyond reasonable doubt. *See* PROOF BEYOND REASONABLE DOUBT.

beyond the seas. Outside the UK, Channel Islands and the Isle of Man. See *Rover International Ltd v Cannon Film Sales Ltd* [1987] 1 WLR 1597. A defendant's absence 'beyond the seas' no longer prevents time running for purposes of limitation of actions (q.v.).

bias. Lacking impartiality. 'Its proper significance is to denote a departure from the standard of even-handed justice which the law requires from those who occupy judicial office': *Franklin* v *Minister of Town and Country Planning* [1948] AC 87. See *R* v *Gough* [1993] AC 646 (bias of jury); *R* v *Romsey Justices ex p Gale* [1992] 156 JPN 202 (appearance of bias); *R* v *Browne* (1997) *The Times*, 23 August; *R* v *Bow Street Metropolitan Stipendiary Magistrate ex p Pinochet Ugarte (No. 2)* [1999] 1 WLR 272; *Laker Airways* v *FSL Aerospace* [1999] 2 Lloyd's Rep 45 (alleged bias of barrister where both parties were represented by barristers from the same chambers). *See* NEMO DEBET ESSE JUDEX.

bias, appearance of. HL held in *Lawal* v *Northern Spirit Ltd* [2003] UKHL 35 (and reversing decisions in CA and EAT), that where counsel appears before the Employment Appeal Tribunal which includes some lay members with whom he has participated in hearings as a part-time judge, there was a possibility of subconscious bias in the minds of the lay members. The practice ought to be discontinued.

bias in tribunal. The fact that a consultant acted as the medical member of a mental health tribunal where he was employed by the NHS trust responsible for claimant's detention, did not indicate that presence of bias in the work of the tribunal, contrary to the requirements of the European Convention: *R (PD)* v *W Midlands Health Review Tribunal* (2003) *The Times*, 31 October.

bias, rule against. An implied requirement of natural justice (q.v.), namely, that no man shall be a judge in his own cause. See, e.g., *DG of Fair Trading* v *Proprietary Association* (2001) 151 NLJ 17; ECHR 1950, art 6. *See* NEMO DEBET ESSE JUDEX.

bid. To make an offer for some thing which is being sold by auction (q.v.). A bid may generally be retracted before acceptance: S.G.A. 1979, s 57(2). A bidder's offer effectively lapses immediately a higher bid is made. Where a sale is

subject to a reserve price and bids fail to reach that level, the highest bid can be treated as a 'provisional bid' which may be accepted later if the seller agrees: *Willis & Son* v *British Car Auctions* [1978] 1 WLR 438.

bigamy. The offence committed by a married person who 'shall marry any other person during the life of the former husband or wife, whether the second marriage shall have taken place in England or Ireland or elsewhere': O.P.A. 1861, s 57. It is triable either way (M.C.A. 1980, Sch 1, para 5(*i*)). To prove bigamy, the prosecution must show: proof of the first marriage of the accused; its validity; its subsistence at the date of the second marriage (q.v.); proof of a second marriage by the accused with some person other than the lawful spouse. See *R* v *Tolson* (1889) 23 QBD 168; *R* v *Cairns* [1997] 1 Cr App R (S) 118.

bilateral discharge. Applies to executory contracts. Discharge may take the form of: extinction of the contract; extinction and substitution of a new agreement; partial dissolution of the contract, e.g., by modification of terms. *See* CONTRACT.

bill. 1. Bill in Parliament. A draft Act which is discussed by Parliament and is known as an Act (q.v.) when it has received the Royal Assent (q.v.). It may be *private* (e.g., referring to a particular person or town) or *public* (relating to the whole country) or *hybrid* (q.v.). A *Private Member's Bill* is introduced by an MP not acting for the government. A *personal Bill* (now rare) relates to the estates, property, status of an individual (see e.g., Marriage Enabling Bills). Presentation of Bills to Parliament is determined by the Legislation and Future Legislation Committees of the cabinet. 2. An account delivered to a debtor by a creditor. 3. Formerly, a written petition complaining of a wrong, e.g., a bill in equity, seeking redress – the forerunner of the writ (q.v.). 4. A written instrument, e.g., bill of exchange (q.v.).

Bill, closure of debate on. Under Parliamentary Standing Order 35, any

Member may move 'that the question be now put'; motion is then put unless the Speaker states that the motion constitutes an abuse of the Rules. A 'guillotine resolution' may be moved in the House of Commons (see Standing Order 81), resulting in an allocation of time order and a compulsory timetable for debate.

bill of costs. Statement of account furnished by a solicitor to his client, relating to work done on his client's behalf. See *Bartletts de Reya* v *Byrne* (1983) 127 SJ 69. *See* COSTS.

bill of exchange. An unconditional order in writing, addressed by one person to another, signed by the person giving it, requiring the person to whom it is addressed to pay on demand, or at a fixed or determinable future time, a sum certain in money to or to the order of a specified person or to bearer: B.Ex.A. 1882, s 3(1). Person who gives the order to pay is the 'drawer'; person to whom the order to pay is given is the 'drawee'; person to whom the payment is to be made is the 'payee'. See Deregulation (Bills of Exchange) Order 1996, SI 96/2993; *HSBC Ltd* v *GD Trade Co* [1998] CLC 238.

bill of exchange, defect in title. The title of a person who negotiates a bill is defective when he obtained the bill, or the acceptance thereof, by fraud, duress, or force and fear, or other unlawful means, or for an illegal consideration, or when he negotiates it in breach of faith, or under such circumstances as amounted to a fraud: B.Ex.A. 1882, s 29(2).

bill of exchange, discharge of. A bill of exchange is discharged when all the rights and liabilities attaching to it are nullified, in one of the following ways: by payment in due course; by renunciation; by cancellation; by material alteration; by delivery up. See B.Ex.A. 1882, ss 59, 61–64; *Smith* v *Lloyds TSB* [2000] 1 All ER (Comm) 53.

bill of indictment. A written accusation which charges a person with an indictable offence and is signed by an officer of the court, can become an indictment (q.v.). It may be preferred by direction or with the consent of a High Court judge, or by direction of the Court of Appeal, or where a person is committed for trial by examining magistrates. See A.J. (Misc. Provs.) A. 1933, s 2; C.P.I.A. 1996, Sch 1, para 2; C.D.A. 1998, Sch 8, para 5; Indictments (Procedure) Rules 1971, r 4; *Practice Direction* [1990] 1 WLR 1633; *R* v *Raymond* [1981] 2 All ER 246.

bill of lading. Document used in foreign trade, signed by the shipowner, master or other agent, stating that goods have been shipped on a named ship, and setting out the terms on which they have been delivered to and received by the shipowner. It acts as a document of title to the goods and is evidence of the contract for their carriage. It is not a fully negotiable instrument (q.v.). See Carriage of Goods by Sea Act 1992. For rights under shipping documents, see s 2. For meaning of 'contract of carriage', see s 5(1). See *Borealis AB* v *Stargas Ltd* [1998] 3 WLR 1353.

Bill of Rights. An Act of 1688, providing that suspension of laws was illegal, that subjects had a right to petition the King, that parliamentary elections ought to be free, that debates in Parliament ought to be free, that excessive fines ought not to be imposed 'nor cruel and unusual punishment inflicted', etc. See *Allason* v *Haines* [1996] EMLR 143; *Hamilton* v *Al Fayed (No. 1)* [1999] 3 All ER 317.

bill of sale. A document 'given with respect to transfer of chattels used in cases where possession is not intended to be given': *Johnson* v *Diprose* [1893] 1 QB 512. It must be registered within seven days of making. An *absolute bill* is governed by Bills of Sale Act 1878; a *conditional bill* (e.g., by way of security) is governed by Bills of Sale Amendment Act 1882. See also Bills of Sale Acts 1890, 1891; *NV Slavenburg's Bank* v *Intercontinental Natural Resources* [1980] 1 All ER 955; CPR, Sch 1; O 94, r 1.

Bill, passage through Parliament. Stages are generally as follows: introduction into the Commons (unless Bill commences in the Lords); first reading (purely formal, not accompanied by debate); second reading (most important stage, calling for full debate); committee stage (in which Bill is considered by a standing committee in close detail); report stage (often purely formal); third reading (often without debate on principles); consideration of Lords' amendments; Royal Assent (q.v.).

bill procedure, voluntary. Procedure whereby the prosecution applies to a High Court judge for leave to prefer a bill of indictment (q.v.) against an accused person, e.g., after refusal by the magistrates to commit. See A.J. (Misc. Provs.) A. 1933, s 3(2)(*b*); Indictments (Procedure) Rules 1971; *Practice Direction (Crime: Voluntary Bills)* (1999) *The Times*, 5 August. Should be granted only where there is good reason to depart from normal procedure, and the interests of justice demand it: *Practice Direction (Court of Appeal)* (1991) 1 Jan. See *R v Manchester Crown Court ex p Williams* (1990) 154 JP 589 (judge's decision to issue a voluntary bill may not be the subject of an application for judicial review (q.v.)).

bills in a set. Bills of exchange executed in duplicate, triplicate, etc. Payment of one part of a set discharges the other parts also: B.Ex.A. 1882, s 71.

binding-over order. It was held by the European Court of Human Rights in *Hooper v UK (Application No. 42317/98)* (2004) *The Times*, 19 November, that where there had been a failure to allow a defendant or his representative to address the magistrate prior to the imposition of a binding-over order, his right to a fair hearing under the Convention on Human Rights had been violated. See art 6.1; see *Benham v UK* (1996) 22 EHRR 293.

bind over. To require a person to enter into a bond or recognisance (q.v.) to perform or abstain from performing an act. See M.C.A. 1980, s 115; P.C.C.(S.)A. 2000, s 150 (binding over of parent or guardian where offender is a child or young person). See *DPP v Speede* [1998] 2 Cr App R 108 (binding over to keep the peace); *Steele and Others v UK* [1998]

Crim LR 893 (binding over in relation to Convention on Human Rights, art 10 (freedom of speech)); *Hashman v UK* (1999) *The Times*, 1 December (UK held by ECHR to be in breach of human right to freedom of expression by binding over hunt saboteurs).

birth. Act of commencing existence separate from one's mother. *See* ABORTION; BORN ALIVE.

birth certificate. A certified copy of an entry in the register. It is evidence of the birth stated therein: Births and Deaths Registration Act 1953, s 34(6). No alteration may be made except as provided by statute: s 29(1). *See* BIRTH, REGISTRATION OF.

birth, citizenship by. *See* CITIZENSHIP, BRITISH, ACQUISITION BY BIRTH OR ADOPTION.

birth, concealment of. 'If any woman shall be delivered of a child, every person who shall by any secret disposition of the dead body of the said child, whether such child died before, at, or after its birth, endeavour to conceal the birth thereof, shall be guilty of a misdemeanour': O.P.A. 1861, s 60. See *R v Opie* (1860) 8 Cox 332.

birth heritage, children's. Department of Health Circular LAC (98) 20, states that the 'best family' for a child will be one that reflects his/her birth heritage. This is subject to consideration of the child's welfare as paramount: no child is to be denied adoptive parents solely on grounds of different racial or cultural backgrounds.

birth, proof of. Process of proving a person's birth by: production of the birth certificate (or a copy); evidence (by affidavit) of someone present at the birth; declaration of the deceased person against interest or in the course of duty. See Civil Evidence Act 1968; Births and Deaths Registration Act 1953; Ch.A. 1975, s 93; C.J.A. 1988, Part II.

birth, registration of. Procedure, which must be completed within 42 days of birth, consisting of furnishing the following particulars: date, place of birth, name, surname and sex of child; name, surname, place of birth and occupation of father; name, surname, maiden surname, surname at marriage, place of birth of mother; mother's usual address; name, surname, qualification, address and signature of informant; registrar's signature. See Births and Deaths Registration Act 1953; National Health Service Act 1977, s 124; F.L.R.A. 1987, Part V. For re-registration, see 1987 Act, s 25; SI 91/2275. *See* BIRTH CERTIFICATE.

blacking of goods. Refusal of employees, who are taking industrial action, to handle or work on materials supplied by the employer so as to evade the effects of that action.

blackleg. One who continues, or attempts to continue, his work while his colleagues are on strike (q.v.).

blacklists relating to trade unions. Lists containing details of union members or persons who have taken part in union activities, compiled with a view to their being used by employers or employment agencies for purposes of discrimination in relation to recruitment or the treatment of workers: Employment Relations Act 1999, s 3(1). The Secretary of State is empowered under s 3(1) to make regulations prohibiting the compilation, use, sale or supply of such lists. *See* TRADE UNION.

blackmail. An offence under Th.A. 1968, s 21(1): 'A person is guilty of blackmail if, with a view to gain for himself or another or with intent to cause loss to another, he makes any unwarranted demand with menaces [q.v.] and for this purpose a demand with menaces is unwarranted unless the person making it does so in the belief (*a*) that he had reasonable grounds for making the demand *and* (*b*) that the use of menaces is a proper means of reinforcing the demand'. See *R* v *Cutbill* (1982) 4 Cr App R (S) 1; *R* v *Bevans* (1988) 87 Cr App R 64; *R* v *Lloyd* (1995) 16 Cr App R (S) 1; *R* v *Killgallon* [1998] 1 Cr App R (S) 279. See MENACES, DEMAND WITH.

bladed articles. It was held that a butter knife without a handle, cutting edge or point was capable of being a bladed article within the meaning of the Criminal Justice Act 1988 s 139. See *Brooker* v *DPP* [2005] *The Times*, May 05.

blank transfer. Transfer of shares executed without the transferee's name being filled in on the document of transfer. *See* SHARE.

blasphemy. The offence of denying, in a scandalous way, Christianity, the Bible, the Book of Common Prayer. The Blasphemy Act 1697 was repealed by C.L.A. 1967. It remains a common-law offence. See *Bowman* v *Secular Society Ltd* [1917] AC 406; *R* v *Gott* (1922) 16 Cr App R 87. An intention to blaspheme is not required; the offence is committed by an insulting, immoderate, vilifying or offensive reference to God or Christianity: *R* v *Lemon* [1979] AC 617. See *R* v *Bow St Magistrates ex p Choudhury* [1990] 3 WLR 986.

blasphemy laws, modernisation of. Chair of Commission for Racial Equality has called for abolition of current blasphemy laws. The law should protect the believer, but not the belief itself: January 2005.

blight notice. Notice served on a prospective land-acquiring authority, in the case of a proposed land development plan, stating that the owner has genuinely and unsuccessfully attempted to sell the land for a reasonable price on the open market, and requiring the authority to purchase it. The authority must serve any counter-notice within two months. See T.C.P.A. 1990, s 150; *Norman* v *Department of Transport* (1996) 72 P & CR 210; *Burns* v *Sandwell MBC* [1998] RVR 97.

block grant. Central government aid to local authorities, based on the difference between an authority's total expenditure and an assumed contribution from rates. See Local Government Finance Act 1988, s 78.

blood relationship. The connection between persons descended from one or more common ancestors. Persons are said to be of the *whole blood* to one another if descended from the same pair of ancestors (e.g., X and Y, brothers, who have the same father and mother); of the *half blood* to one another if descended from only one common ancestor (e.g., X and Y, who have the same father but different mothers).

blood tests. 1. In some civil proceedings relating to paternity, the court may direct that a blood test be made to ascertain whether a party to the proceedings is or is not thereby excluded from being the father. See F.L.R.A. 1969, Part 3 amended by C.S.P.S.S.A. 2000, s 82; F.L.R.A. 1987, Sch 2; *Re Barony of Moynihan* (1997) *The Times*, 28 March (blood tests admissible in peerage claims); *Re O (A Minor) (Blood Tests: Constraint)* [2000] 2 All ER 29 (court could not order blood tests where parent refused consent); CPR, Sch 1; O 112; P.&C.E.A. 1984, ss 62, 63. 2. A person arrested under the Road Traffic Act 1988, s 4, can be required under s 7(3) or s 8(2) to give a blood specimen to be taken by a doctor: see *DPP* v *Jackson* [1998] 3 All ER 769. *See* DNA PROFILING; PATERNITY, DECLARATION OF.

blue book. Government publication, e.g., a report of a Royal Commission. *See* PARLIAMENTARY PAPERS.

blue chip. A well-established company's shares which have a high status as investments. See *Re Kolb's Will Trusts* [1962] Ch 531.

blue pencil test. Phrase referring to severance (q.v.) of contract. 'Severance can be effected when the part severed can be removed by running a blue pencil through it' without affecting the remaining part: *Attwood* v *Lamont* [1920] 3 KB 571. For severance of part of an instrument affected by undue influence, see *Barclays Bank* v *Caplan* [1998] FLR 532.

board. As in 'board and lodging'. Within the Rent Act 1977, s 7(1), it may be constituted by the provision of any quantity of food which is not *de minimis*, and which includes the ancillary services involved in preparation, and the provision of crockery and cutlery: *Otter* v *Norman* [1989] AC 129.

board meeting. Meeting of the directors of a company (q.v.) held for the despatch

of business. Questions are decided by majority vote; the chairman has a casting vote. See Table A, art 88.

bodily harm, grievous. Formerly interpreted to mean 'some harm sufficiently serious to interfere with the victim's health or comfort': *R* v *Ashman* (1858) 1 F & F 88. See O.P.A. 1861, ss 20, 47. In *DPP* v *Smith* [1961] AC 290, it was stated that there is 'no warrant for giving the words "grievous bodily harm" a meaning other than that which the words convey in their ordinary and natural meaning. "Bodily harm" needs no explanation, and "grievous" means no more and no less than "really serious"'. (For comment on 'really', see *R* v *Janjua* [1999] 1 Cr App R 91.) See also *R* v *Mandair* [1995] 1 AC 208; *R* v *Ireland* [1997] 4 All ER 275 (malicious telephone call amounted to bodily harm); *R* v *Burstow* [1997] 1 Cr App R 144 ('stalking' constituted the infliction of harm); *R* v *McMaster* (1988) *The Times*, 29 February (group attack on victim); *A-G's Reference (No. 19 of 1998)* [1999] 1 Cr App R (S) 275; *R* v *Jones* [1999] 1 Cr App R (S) 473. CA held in *R* v *Dica* (2004) *The Times*, 11 May, that a person can inflict grievous bodily harm where he was aware that he was suffering from a serious sexual disease and he transmitted that disease recklessly to an individual who did not know of, and did not consent to, the risk of infection. *See* MALICE; WOUNDING.

bodily harm, proof of. A verdict of assault occasioning actual bodily harm on a charge under O.P.A. 1861, s 47, may be returned upon proof of an assault together with proof that actual bodily harm was occasioned by the assault. The prosecution must prove, for a charge of grievous bodily harm under s 20, that defendant either intended or foresaw that his act would cause harm: *R* v *Savage* [1991] 4 All ER 698. See *R* v *Wilson* [1997] QB 47.

bodily injury, under Warsaw Convention. HL held in relation to air travel and the Convention that bodily injury involves a physiological change in passenger's body, including his brain, sufficiently serious to be described as an injury. Peptic ulcer induced by stress following emergency landing was an injury; severe depression resulting from indecent assault on aircraft was not. See *King* v *Bristow Helicopters* [2002] UKHL 7.

body corporate. 'A succession or collection of persons having in the estimation of the law an existence and rights and duties distinct from those of the individual persons who form it from time to time': Co. Litt. 250a. Examples: a registered company; a local authority (q.v.); a body controlled by royal charter. See *Salomon* v *Salomon & Co Ltd* [1897] AC 22. *See* CORPORATION.

body parts. Organs or tissue removed from a deceased person during a post-mortem examination: Cremation (Amendment) Regulations (SI 00/58). See Home Office Circular No. 2/2000. *See* ORGAN, HUMAN.

body sample. *See* SAMPLE, INTIMATE.

body search. *See* SEARCH, INTIMATE.

Bolam test. *See* NEGLIGENCE, TORT OF, AND BOLAM TEST.

bomb hoax. It is an offence to place any article in any place or dispatch any article by post, rail or other means with the intention of inducing in some person a belief that it is likely to explode or ignite and cause personal injury or damage to property: C.L.A. 1977, s 51(1). It is an offence to communicate information which is known to be false with the intention of inducing in a person a false belief that a bomb or other thing liable to explode or ignite is present in any place or location: s 51(2). For penalties, see s 51(4), as amended by C.J.A. 1991, s 26; SI 91/2208. See *R* v *Webb* (1995) *The Times*, 19 June; *R* v *Bosworth* [1998] 1 Cr App R (S) 356.

bona fide. In good faith; honestly.

***bona fide* holder for value.** *See* HOLDER IN DUE COURSE.

***bona fide* purchaser.** *See* PURCHASER FOR VALUE WITHOUT NOTICE.

bona vacantia. Ownerless goods. 1. Goods found with no apparent owner. In general they are deemed to belong to the first finder, except in the case of shipwrecks and treasure (q.v.). 2. Under A.E.A. 1925, the residuary estate of an intestate goes, in default of any person taking an absolute interest, to the Crown, Duchy of Lancaster or Cornwall, as *bona vacantia*. The Crown or Duchy may provide for the dependants of the intestate and for other persons for whom he might reasonably have been expected to make provision. See also Inheritance (Provision for Family and Dependants) Act 1975, s 24.

bond. 1. Agreement under seal whereby a person (the 'obligor') binds himself to another (the 'obligee') to perform or refrain from an action. It may be a 'simple bond' – without condition, or a 'common money bond' – given to secure payment of money. It binds the obligor's real and personal estate: L.P.A. 1925, s 80. 2. An interest-bearing document based on a long-term debt, usually issued by corporations.

bond, performance. Bond usually given by a bank as a guarantee of satisfactory performance of a contract by a party. It is usually payable on demand without proof or condition. A 'conditional bond' requires justification of the claim for payment. See *Wahda Bank* v *Arab Bank* [1998] CLC 689; *Balfour Beatty Engineering* v *T&G Guarantee Co* [2000] CLC 252.

bondwashing. Practice whereby shares are sold with an accrued dividend and bought back as soon as the shares have gone ex dividend and before next dividend is due; hence payment of accrued dividend is treated as a capital gain, and not as income, so that tax advantages result. See I.C.T.A. 1988, s 732; SI 92/568.

bonus. That which is received over and above what is expected, e.g., a gratuity, an additional dividend.

bonus shares. A company deciding to finance expansion from reserves comprising undistributed profits may bring its issued capital (q.v.) into line with the capital it employs by issuing bonus shares to existing shareholders to the value of the additional capital. See Cos.A. 1985, s 88. *See* CAPITALISATION.

book debt. A debt arising in due course of a business and due to its proprietor which would in the ordinary course of that business be entered in 'well kept books relating to that business': *per* Buckley J in *Independent Automatic Sales* v *Knowles* [1962] 3 All ER 27. See *Northern Bank* v *Ross* [1990] BCC 883; CPR, Sch 1; O 95, r 6 (assignment of book debts).

bookmaker. Defined under Finance Act 2004, s 15, as a person who carries on the business of receiving or negotiating pool betting operations, whether as principal or agent and whether regularly or not, or holds himself out as such a person.

books of account. Documents and other records which must be prepared and kept by a company, including, e.g., a balance sheet (q.v.), profit and loss account, auditors' report, directors' report. See Cos.A. 1985, Sch 4.

books, partnership. *See* PARTNERSHIP BOOKS, INSPECTION OF.

books, statutory. *See* STATUTORY BOOKS.

born alive. A child is considered to have been born alive (for purposes of Infant Life (Preservation) Act 1929) when it exists as a live child, that is, breathing and living by reason of its breathing through its lungs alone, without deriving any of its living or power of living by or through any connection with its mother: see *R* v *Handley* (1874) Crim Law Cas 79. A foetus (q.v.) of 18–21 weeks *en ventre sa mère* (q.v.) which was incapable of breathing was not 'a child capable of being born alive' within 1929 Act, s 1: *C* v *S* [1987] 1 All ER 1230; *Rance* v *Mid-Downes HA* [1991] 2 WLR 159.

borough. In early times, a fortified town or castle. Later, a town or city incorporated by charter, with a corporation consisting of a mayor, aldermen and councillors. The title is no longer generally used. See L.G.A. 1972.

borrow. To obtain temporarily with the intention, or purpose, of returning to the lender. For borrowing and theft, see Th.A. 1968, s 6(1); *R* v *Bagshaw* [1988] Crim LR 321; *R* v *Marshall* [1998] 2 Cr App R 282.

bottomry. Obsolescent term, meaning pledge of a ship and freight so as to secure a loan which allows a ship to continue its voyage. *Respondentia* is a pledge of the freight only. *See* HYPOTHECATION.

bought as seen. Phrase suggesting that the purchaser has bought what he had seen. When used in a sale which was not a sale by description, it confirms merely that the purchaser had seen the goods he had purchased, and does not exclude implied terms as to fitness or quality in respect of defects which could not be seen: *Cavendish-Woodhouse Ltd* v *Manley* (1984) 82 LGR 376.

boundaries, offences committed on. Where an offence is committed on the boundary between areas (e.g., of counties) or within 500 yards of such a boundary, or in a harbour or river lying between such areas, the offence may be treated as having been committed in any of those areas: M.C.A. 1980, s 3(1).

boundary. That which indicates or fixes some limit, e.g., a fence, wall. See *Lee* v *Barrey* [1957] 1 All ER 191; *Woolls* v *Powling* (1999) *The Times*, 9 March; L.R.R. 1925, rr 276–278; C.R.W.A. 2000, s 19. *See* HEDGE AND DITCH PRESUMPTION.

boundary commissions. Bodies set up under the House of Commons (Redistribution of Seats) Acts 1949 and 1958 (see Parliamentary Constituencies Act 1986, Sch 1), one each for England, Scotland, N. Ireland and Wales, each chaired by the Speaker (q.v.). They report to the Home Secretary on suggested electoral boundaries. See L.G.A. 1992, setting up Local Government Commission, and abolishing Local Government Boundary Commission.

boundary disputes. CA held in *Joyce* v *Rigolli* [2004] EWCA Civ 79 that where a conveyancer is drafting a transfer of land, it is vitally important that the boundary as identified in the transfer and plan be capable of being translated without further argument and negotiation into a precise line on the ground. The decision in *Neilson* v *Poole* (1969) is of particular relevance in cases of this nature. ('A boundary agreement is an act of peace, quieting strife and averting litigation': *per* Megarry J.)

boycott. To engage in an organised refusal to deal with a person or body, e.g., a manufacturer or supplier. See *Quinn v Leathem* [1901] AC 495.

breach. The infringing or violation of a right, duty or law.

breach, anticipatory. *See* ANTICIPATORY BREACH.

breach of close. Unlawful entry on another's land.

breach of confidence. *See* CONFIDENCE, BREACH OF.

breach of contract. The refusal or failure by a party to a contract to fulfil an obligation imposed on him under that contract, resulting from, e.g., repudiation of liability before completion, or conduct preventing proper performance. The contract is discharged where the breach results in the innocent party treating it as rescinded and where it has the effect of 'depriving the party who has further undertakings still to perform of substantially the whole benefit which it was the intention of the parties as expressed in the contract as the consideration for performing those undertakings': *Hong Kong Fir Shipping Co v Kawasaki Kisen Kaisha* [1962] 2 QB 26. See *Photo Productions Ltd v Securicor Transport Ltd* [1980] AC 827 (discussion by HL of the nature of 'fundamental breach'); *Glolite Ltd v Jasper Conran Ltd* (1998) *The Times*, 28 January (discussion of whether a breach was material and irremediable); *A-G v Blake* [2000] 3 WLR 625 (court ordering seizure of benefits (unpaid royalties) from breach of contract where defendant was a fugitive spy).

breach of privilege. Actions which constitute a contempt of a parliamentary privilege (q.v.).

breach of promise of marriage. Failure to fulfil a promise to marry. Action for breach was abolished by Law Reform (Misc. Provs.) Act 1970, s 1(1). *See* ENGAGEMENT TO MARRY.

breach of statutory duty. *See* STATUTORY DUTY, BREACH OF.

breach of the peace. Offence (most commonly under P.O.A. 1936, s 5 (now repealed)) committed whenever harm is actually done, or is likely to be done to a person, or in his presence to his property, or wherever a person is in fear of being so harmed through assault, affray, riot, unlawful assembly or other disturbance: *R v How-ell* [1982] QB 416. 'The possibility of a breach must be real to justify any preventive action': *per* Skinner LJ in *Moss v Maclachlan* (1985) 149 JP 167. See *Nicol v DPP* (1995) *The Times*, 22 November; *Steel v UK* [1998] Crim LR 893 (arrest of protestor considered in context of Convention on Human Rights, art 5). P.&C.E.A. 1984, s 17(6). When it is necessary to determine whether there is compliance with the Convention on Human Rights in the case of taking measures to prevent a breach of the peace, it is essential that a senior police officer should believe honestly and reasonably that there exists a real risk of breach of the peace in close proximity in time and place, and that the necessary, preventative measures are reasonable. Detention beyond mere transitory detention cannot be justified under the Convention, art 5, unless an arrest has been made: *R (on application of Laporte) v Chief Constable of Gloucestershire Constabulary* [2004] EWHC 253. *See* FEAR OR PROVO-CATION OF VIOLENCE.

breach of trust. The result of some improper act or omission relating to the administration of a trust or the interests of the beneficiaries (q.v.) arising under it. It may arise from failure to carry out the trustee's general duties or some abuse of his powers. A trustee is generally liable for any loss caused directly or indirectly to the trust property and to the beneficiaries' interests as a result of the breach. For the court's power to relieve a trustee from the consequences of a breach of trust, see Tr.A. 1925, s 61; see also Lim.A. 1980, s 21; *R v Clark* [1998] 2 Cr App R 137. *See* TRUST.

breach of trust by bankrupt. In relation to Insolvency Act 1986, s 281 (3) (bankruptcy debt incurred through fraud or fraudulent breach of trust), bankrupt's deliberate dishonesty is fundamental ingredient: *Woodland-Ferrari* v *UCL Group* (2002) *The Times*, 17 July. The court also held that 'wilful default' (in relation to a breach of trust) was not exactly the same as 'fraudulent breach of trust'.

break clause. An option to terminate a clause in a fixed-term lease (q.v.) which may be exercised after a certain period, e.g., at the end of the tenth and twentieth years of a 30-year lease. Time is of the essence in serving notice to terminate. See *Mannai Investment Co* v *Eagle Star Life Assurance Co* [1997] 2 WLR 945; *Ballard Ltd* v *Ashworth Ltd* [1998] 46 EG 190.

breakdown of marriage. A court hearing a petition for divorce (q.v.) should not hold that the marriage has broken down irretrievably unless satisfied by the petitioner of one or more of the following facts: that the respondent has committed adultery (q.v.) and the petitioner finds it intolerable to live with the respondent; that the respondent has behaved in such a way that the petitioner cannot reasonably be expected to live with the respondent; that the respondent has deserted the petitioner for a continuous period of two years immediately prior to the presentation of the petition; that the parties to the marriage have lived apart for at least two years immediately preceding the presentation of petition and that the respondent consents to the grant of a decree; that the parties have lived apart for a continuous period of at least five years immediately preceding the petition: Mat.C.A. 1973, s 1(2). (See F.L.A. 1996, s 5 (not brought into force), for concept of 'marital breakdown' (q.v.).)

breaking and entering. Term referring to the felony of burglary committed by one who, in the night, broke and entered a dwelling house with intent to commit any felony therein: Larceny Act 1916, s 25, repealed by Th.A. 1968. *See* BURGLARY.

breathalyser. Device consisting of a measuring bag or some other device (e.g., Alcometer) used in the administration of a breath test to a motorist by a constable

who has reasonable cause to suspect him of having alcohol in his body or having committed a road traffic offence while his vehicle was in motion. See Road Traffic Act 1988, s 11(2); *DPP* v *McKeown* [1997] 1 WLR 295. For prescribed limits, see s 11(1). *See* PRESCRIBED LIMITS OF ALCOHOL.

breath, meaning of. It was held that, in relation to road traffic legislation, the precise meaning of 'breath' was not restricted to deep lung air. The word ought to be given its appropriate dictionary definition. See *Zafar* v *DPP* (2005) *The Times*, 7 January.

breath test. A constable in uniform may require a person to provide a specimen of breath for a breath test if he has reasonable cause to suspect him of having alcohol in his body while driving or attempting to drive or in charge of a motor vehicle on a road or other public place, or if the person has been driving, attempting to drive or in charge of a motor vehicle, or if he is reasonably believed to have been involved in an accident: Road Traffic Act 1988, s 6. For provision of specimens for analysis, see s 7; *DPP* v *Falzarano* (2001) 165 JP 201; *DPP* v *Baldwin* (2000) 164 JP 606. Where a driver has provided two breath specimens, but the police have reasonable cause to believe that the breathalyser was not providing reliable readings, the driver can be given the option of providing two further specimens rather than specimens of urine and blood: *Stewart* v *DPP* [2003] EWHC 1323 (Admin).

brewster sessions. Annual meeting of licensing justices to consider applications for licences, renewals, etc. relating to the sale of alcoholic liquor. Must be held within the first two weeks of February; Licensing Act 1964, Sch 1, as amended. See Licensing Act 1988, s 14. *See* LICENSING OF PREMISES.

bribery. The offence of taking, or bestowing, or promising, a price, reward or favour intended to influence the judgment or conduct of a public official. In its legal sense it implies corruption: *Gardner* v *Robertson*, 1921 SC 132. See, e.g.,

Public Bodies Corrupt Practices Act 1889; Customs and Excise Management Act 1979, s 15; Representation of the People Act 1983, s 113; *Commissioner of ICAC v Ching Poh* [1997] 1 WLR 1175. *See* CORRUPTION.

bridging loan. Generally a short-term advance made by a bank to a customer pending the receipt by the customer of funds from some other source. See C.C.A. 1974, s 58(2)(*b*).

bridleway. Way over which the public have right of way on foot, on horseback or leading a horse, with or without a right to drive animals along the highway: Horses (Protective Headgear etc.) Act 1990, s 3. See *R v Sec of State for the Environment ex p Billson* [1998] 3 WLR 1240; C.R.W.A. 2000, s 53.

brief. Written instructions to a barrister (q.v.) from a solicitor (q.v.) relating to the representing of a client in legal proceedings. Usually includes a narrative of the facts, copies of documents, etc.

British Commonwealth. *See* COMMON-WEALTH.

British dependent territories citizenship. *See* CITIZENSHIP, BRITISH, DEPENDENT TERRITORIES.

British nationality and Community law. For purposes of Community law, a 'UK national' is as so defined in a declaration made to EU by the British Government in 1982, and is understood as referring to: '(a) British citizens; (b) persons who are British subjects by virtue of B.N.A. 1981, Part IV, and have the right of abode in the UK and are therefore exempt from UK immigration control; (c) British Dependent Territories citizens who acquire their citizenship from a connection with Gibraltar'. See *R v Secretary of State for the Home Department ex p Kaur* (2001) *The Times*, 8 March.

British overseas citizen. *See* CITIZEN, BRITISH OVERSEAS.

British overseas territories citizenship. British Overseas Territories Act 2002, s 2, renames British dependent territories citizenship, 'British overseas territories citizenship'; a person having that citizenship is a 'British overseas territories citizen'. Any person who immediately before the commencement of s 3 is a British overseas territories citizen shall, on the commencement of this section, become a British citizen: s 3(1).

British possession. Any part of Her Majesty's dominions outside the UK; and where parts of such dominions are under both a central and a local legislature, all parts under the central legislature are deemed, for the purposes of this definition, to be one British possession: I.A. 1978, Sch 1.

British protected person. One who is a member of any class of persons declared to be British protected persons by an Order in Council or by virtue of the Solomon Islands Act 1978: B.N.A. 1981, s 50(1). See also s 32(1); *Motala v A-G* [1991] 3 WLR 903. Applies to former protectorates, protected states or UK trust territories. The status is not transmissible.

British protectorates. Territories which, although not colonies and not part of HM Dominions, were governed in internal and external affairs by Britain.

broadband facilitation. The Rural Broadband Facilitation Bill 2004, has as its objective the promotion of the extension of high speed broadband connectivity in rural areas; it seeks, further, to encourage the level of private investment in essential engineering in this area of endeavour.

broadcasting. The act of making public by means of radio or television transmission. See Telecommunications Act 1984, s 6(5); Copyright, Designs and Patents Act 1988, s 6(1). A broadcast programme is publication in permanent form for purposes of defamation (q.v.) under the Defamation Act 1952. For 'cable programme service', see 1988 Act, s 7. For standards, see Broadcasting Act 1996, s 106.

Broadmoor. An institution, classified as a 'special hospital' (q.v.), providing treatment for patients (formerly known as criminal lunatics (q.v.)) with dangerous, violent or criminal propensities, under conditions of special security. See M.H.A. 1983, Part III.

broker. 1. 'One who makes a bargain for another, and receives a commission for so doing': *per* Cleasby J in *Fairlie* v *Fenton* (1876) LR 5 Exch 169. 2. 'In relation to securities, means a member of the Stock Exchange who carries on his business in the UK and is not a market maker [q.v.] in securities of the kind covered': Finance Act 1986, Sch 18. Known also as 'broker-dealer'.

brokerage. Payment or commission earned by a broker. Sum paid to a person by a company (q.v.) under authority in the articles for placing shares (q.v.).

brothel. 'A place resorted to by persons of both sexes for the purpose of prostitution': *Singleton* v *Ellison* [1895] 1 QB 607. Under S.O.A. 1956, ss 33, 36, it is an offence to keep or manage a brothel or knowingly to permit the whole or part of premises to be used for the purposes of habitual prostitution. See *Stevens* v *Christy* (1987) Cr App R 249; *Jones* v *DPP* (1992) *The Times*, 4 June; S.O.A. 1967, s 6. *See* DISORDERLY HOUSE.

budget. An estimate of government expenditure and revenue for the ensuing financial year presented to Parliament by the Chancellor of the Exchequer (q.v.). Budget proposals are embodied in a Finance Bill.

budgeting loans. Interest-free loans intended to meet intermittent expenses (e.g., for household equipment) of those on income support (q.v.).

buggery. The sexual offence characterised by anal intercourse by a man with another man or woman. Under S.O.A. 1956, s 12(1), as amended by C.J.P.O.A. 1994, s 143, it is an offence for a person to commit buggery with another except where the act takes place in private and both parties have reached the age of 16 (see S.O.(Am.)A. 2000, s 1(1)). For 'in private', see S.O.A. 1956, s 12(1B). It is an offence to assault with intention to commit buggery: S.O.A. 1956, s 16(1). The offence includes intercourse with an animal: 1956 Act, s 12(1A). Non-consensual buggery is rape (q.v.). See *R* v *W* [1999] 1 Cr App R (S) 320; *R* v *Wood* (2000) *The Times*, 21 April.

bugging. Electronic surveillance. See R.I.P.A. 2000.

building. 'Its ordinary and natural meaning is, a block of brick or stone work covered in by a roof': *Moir* v *Williams* [1892] 1 QB 264. For purposes of Building Act 1984, the word means any permanent or temporary building and, unless the context otherwise requires, it includes any other structure or erection of whatever kind or nature: s 121(1). See *Measar* v *Secretary of State for the Environment* [1998] 4 PLR 93 (definition of 'building' should be considered as a matter of fact and degree in the light of factors such as permanence, size, physical attachment, composition by components; caravans used for residential purposes did not constitute buildings). See T.C.P.A. 1990, s 336. For 'building operations', see Planning and Compensation Act 1991, s 13. For 'industrial building', see Capital Allowances Act 1990, s 18; *Girobank* v *Clarke* [1996] STC 540, *Bestway Ltd* v *Luff* [1998] STC 357. *See* MESSUAGE.

building lease. 1. Lease made partly in consideration of some person erecting new or additional buildings or improving or repairing buildings: S.L.A. 1925, s 44. A building lease for 999 years may be made by a mortgagor or mortgagee in possession or tenant for life (q.v.): L.P.A. 1925, s 99; S.L.A. 1925, s 41. 2. Lease made by a landlord generally for 99 years, at a rent known as 'ground rent', the lessee covenanting to erect buildings.

building scheme. Where land is developed, as in the case of a building scheme, e.g., for a housing estate, the developer can require the purchaser of a plot to enter into a restrictive covenant (q.v.) based upon a mutually perceived common intention, so as to maintain the character of the estate. See *Gilbert* v *Spoor* [1983] Ch 27.

building society. A society which has as its purpose or principal purpose that of making loans which are secured on residential property and are funded substantially by its members, with its principal office in the UK: Building Societies Act 1997, s 1(1). See: Building Societies (Distributions) Act 1997; F.S.M.A. 2000, s 336, empowering Treasury to transfer to FSA (q.v.) functions of Building Societies Commission; Ins.A. 2000, Sch 2, para 13.

building society advances. Advances made to members secured by a mortgage (q.v.) of a legal estate, or an equitable interest in land in England, Wales or N. Ireland, or a heritable security over land in Scotland, and, for such purposes, the society may hold land with the right of foreclosure: Building Societies Act 1986, s 10(1). Advances may be made secured on land overseas: s 14.

bulk. 'A mass or collection of goods of the same kind which is contained in a defined space or area, and is such that any goods in bulk are interchangeable with any other goods therein of the same number or quantity': Sale of Goods (Amendment) Act 1995, s 2(a).

Bullock order. Where claimant joins two defendants in the alternative because he is unsure as to which one is liable, he may be able to obtain an order against the unsuccessful defendant to pay the costs (q.v.) of the successful defendant: *Bullock v London General Omnibus Co* [1907] 1 KB 264. Claimant is not entitled to such an order as of right.

burden of proof. The obligation of proving facts. Used in a number of senses, e.g.: *general, or ultimate, burden* (proving a case); *specific burden* (proving an individual issue); *evidential burden* (adducing sufficient evidence in support of a disputed fact) (see *Jayasena v R* [1970] AC 618); *provisional burden* (borne by an opponent after the proponent has discharged the evidential burden); *persuasive burden* (requirement to prove or disprove a fact in issue beyond reasonable doubt or on a balance of probabilities). In general the burden lies on the party who substantially asserts the affirmative of the issue (i.e., the claimant or prosecution). It may shift when the claimant or prosecution establishes a prima facie case. See *Woolmington v DPP* [1935] AC 462; *Morris v London Iron and Steel Co* [1988] QB 439. *See* PROOF.

burden of proof, allocation under statute. In some few cases, allocation of burden of proof may be determined by statute: explicitly (see B.Ex.A. 1882, s 30(2); E.R.A. 1996, s 98(4)(b)); implicitly (see Factories Act 1961, s 29(1); M.C.A. 1980, s 101). See *Nimmo v Cowan & Sons* [1968] AC 107; *R v Hunt* [1987] AC 352.

burden of proof, shifting of. Phrase used in the law of evidence to indicate the moving of the burden of proof (i.e., the obligation to prove facts) from one side to the other, as where, e.g., there exists a disputable presumption of law in favour of one party (so that his adversary must rebut it) or where the subject matter of one party's allegation is peculiarly within the opponent's knowledge (so that the latter must rebut the allegation). See, e.g., *Brady v Group Lotus plc* [1987] 3 All ER 674; *R v Desai* (1992) *The Times*, 3 February. *See* EVIDENCE.

burglary. Under Th.A. 1968, s 9(1), a person is guilty of burglary if 'he enters any building or part of a building as a trespasser and with intent to commit any such offence as is mentioned in sub-s (2) [stealing, inflicting grievous bodily harm, etc.]; or, having entered any building or part of a building as a trespasser he steals or attempts to steal anything in the building or part of it or inflicts or attempts to inflict on any person therein any grievous bodily harm'. 'Aggravated burglary' is committed by one who commits burglary and has with him any firearm or imitation firearm, weapon of offence or explosive: s 10(1). See *R v Stones* [1989] 1 WLR 156; *R v Klass* [1998] 1 Cr App R 453. Burglary (but not aggravated burglary) is triable either way (M.C.A. 1980, Sch 1, para 28). For penalties, see Th.A. 1968, s 7, amended by C.J.A. 1991, s 26; Crime (Sentences) Act 1997; *A-G's Ref (No. 36 of 1997)* [1998] 1 Cr App R (S) 365; *R v Henry* [1998] 1 Cr App R (S) 289 ('distraction burglary', where H distracted X's attention while Y entered X's flat and stole articles from it). For sentence of minimum of three years for third domestic burglary (i.e. committed in building or part of a building which is a dwelling), see P.C.C.(S.)A. 2000, s 111, amended by C.J.C.S.A. 2000, Sch 7, para 191.

burglary, sentencing for. CA held in *R v McInerney* [2002] All ER(D) 300 Dec, that, in a case of burglary, a custodial sentence should be imposed only where an offender's behaviour showed that punishment in the community was impracticable. More probation should be used in sentencing domestic burglars.

burial, prevention of. It is an offence against public order to prevent the proper burial (or cremation) of a human body without lawful excuse: *R v Hunter* [1974] QB 95; *R v Pedder* [2000] 2 Cr App R (S) 38.

business. Includes any trade (q.v.), profession or vocation. Under Fair Trading Act 1973, s 137(2), it includes a professional practice and any other undertaking carried on for gain or reward or which is an undertaking in the course of which goods or services are supplied otherwise than free of charge. See Landlord and Tenant Act 1954, Part II; C.P.A. 1987, s 45; *Re Ogilby* [1942] Ch 288; *Stevenson v Rogers* [1999] QB 1028 (meaning of 'in the course of' a business); *Nella v Nella* (1999) *The Independent*, 1 November (meaning of 'carrying on' a business). *See* BUSINESS TENANCY.

business liability. Term used in Unfair Contract Terms Act 1977, s 1(3) to refer to liability for breach of obligations or duties arising from things done or to be done by a person in the course of a business (whether his own business or another's) or from the occupation of premises used for the occupier's business purposes. See also Unfair Terms in Consumer Contracts Regulations 1994 (No. 3159); EC Council Directive 93/13; Occupiers' Liability Act 1984.

business name. Under Business Names Act 1985, the use of certain types of business name (suggesting, e.g., links with government departments) is prohibited in the case of a business which does not consist of the surname of a sole trader, the surnames or corporate names of all members of a partnership, or the name of a company, in the case of a corporate business: ss 1, 2. Disclosure of persons using business names may

be required on business letters, orders, invoices and receipts: s 4. See SI 92/1196; *DTI v Cedenio* (2001) *The Times*, 22 March. *See* COMPANY NAME.

business, special. *See* SPECIAL BUSINESS.

business tenancy. A tenancy comprising property occupied by a tenant for the purposes of a business carried on by him or for those and other purposes. See *Pittalis v Grant* [1989] 3 WLR 139; *Gondal v Dillon Ltd* [1998] NPC 127; *Cricket Ltd v Shaftesbury plc* [1999] 3 All ER 283 (period of more than twelve months as tenant at will gave no rights as a business tenant). For rights of protection, see Landlord and Tenant Act 1954, Part II. 'Business' is defined, under s 23 (2) as a trade, profession, or employment and includes any activity carried on by a body of persons, whether corporate or incorporate.'

business, trading. *See* TRADING BUSINESS.

business transfers, control of. Under F.S.M.A. 2000, s 104, no insurance or banking business transfer scheme is to have effect unless an order under s 111(1) has been made, or it is excluded under s 105.

bus lane. An area of road is or forms part of a bus lane if an appropriate order provides that it may be used only by buses (or a particular description of bus), or only by buses (or a particular description of bus) and some other class or classes of vehicular traffic: Transport Act 2000, s 144(5).

but-for test. Principle in tort, applied where damage has resulted from a multiplicity of causes, resulting in the question: 'Would the damage in this case have resulted but for defendant's negligence?' See, e.g., *Wilsher v Essex AHA* [1988] AC 1074; *Malec v Hutton Ltd* [1990] 64 ALJR 316.

buyer. Under S.G.A. 1979, s 61(1), is 'a person who buys or agrees to buy goods'. A buyer in good faith does not acquire title to an object stolen from its rightful owner: *National Employers Insurance Assn v Jones* [1988] 2 WLR 952.

bye-law. Also 'by-law'. 'An ordinance affecting the public or some portion of the public imposed by some authority clothed with statutory powers, ordering something to be done or not to be done and accompanied by some sanction or penalty for its non-observance . . . it has the force of law within the sphere of its legitimate operation': *Kruse* v *Johnson* [1898] 2 QB 91. It is subject to confirmation by the appropriate minister and may be declared invalid by the courts if, e.g., not made in the manner prescribed by statute, or if repugnant to the law of the land, or unreasonable. See *Bugg* v *DPP* [1993] QB 473; *Boddington* v *British Transport Police* [1999] 2 AC 143.

byway. A highway open to all traffic, but which is used by the public mainly for the purposes for which footpaths and bridleways are so used: see Wildlife and Countryside Act 1981, ss 65(2), 66(1); *Buckland* v *Secretary of State for the Environment* (2000) *The Times*, 10 February; C.R.W.A. 2001, ss 48, 50.

C

C. 1. Chancellor (q.v.). 2. One of several abbreviations used for Command Papers. *See* COMMAND PAPERS, NUMBERING OF; PARLIAMENTARY PAPERS.

CA. Court of Appeal (q.v.).

Cabinet. 'A hyphen which joins, a buckle which fastens, the legislative part of the state to the executive part': Bagehot, *The English Constitution* (1867). A group of ministers selected by and presided over by the Prime Minister (q.v.), collectively responsible for the general character and policy of legislation, consisting of the political heads of government departments and others. Cabinet ministers are also members of the Privy Council (q.v.). *See* MINISTERIAL RESPONSIBILITY.

Cabinet documents, national security and. 'No court will compel the production of cabinet papers . . . the Cabinet is at the very centre of national affairs, and must be in possession at all times of information which is secret or confidential. Secrets relating to national security may require to be preserved indefinitely': *per* Lord Widgery in *A-G* v *Times Newspapers* [1976] QB 752.

cabotage. 1. Coastal navigation and trade. 2. A country's right to control air traffic operations within its borders. *See HS Air Service Norway* v *Civil Aviation Authority* [1997] CLC 264.

CAC. Central Arbitration Committee, first established by Employment Protection Act 1975: see now T.U.L.R.(C.)A. 1992, s 260; Employment Relations Act 1999, s 24. Functions include settling of disputes involving arbitration in trade disputes referred by ACAS (q.v.).

Caesarean section. Delivery of a child by opening wall of mother's abdomen. See *Rochdale Healthcare NHS Trust* v *C*

[1997] 1 FCR 274; *DOH Guidelines to Consent for Examination or Treatment*, April 2001. In case of a competent pregnant woman, her wishes relating to delivery of a child must be respected, irrespective of consequences; in case of a long-term incompetent person, treatment must be in her best interests.

CAFCASS. Children and Family Court Advisory and Support Service (q.v.).

Calderbank letter. A procedural device allowing a party to an action to offer to settle on a 'without prejudice as to costs' basis, while reserving the right to bring the offer to settle to the attention of the court when the question of costs is dealt with. Originally named after *Calderbank* v *Calderbank* [1976] Fam 83; see now CPR, Part 36. See *Butcher* v *Wolfe* [1999] 1 FLR 334.

call. 1. As in 'call to the Bar' – the ceremony in the Inns of Court during which students who have passed the appropriate examinations and kept terms are admitted as barristers (q.v.). 2. As in 'call' made by a company (q.v.) whereby directors are empowered to ask shareholders for instalments of payment for shares. Calls cannot be made until the minimum subscription has been allotted. 3. As in 'call on contributories' whereby a company or its liquidator makes a demand on those liable to contribute to the payment of debts.

campers, unauthorised. Persons camping on land without the occupier's consent may be directed to leave. It is an offence to fail to obey such a direction or to return within a period of three months: C.J.P.O.A. 1994, s 77. See *R* v *Lincolnshire CC ex p Atkinson* [1995] EGCS 145; *Shropshire CC* v *Wynne* [1998] COD 40.

cancellation. The act of nullifying or invalidating an instrument, e.g., by striking out signatures. The act must be accompanied by the intention to cancel.

cancellation, delivery up of documents for. An equitable remedy whereby a void document is delivered up and cancelled, e.g., lest some person be deceived by it, as where a guarantee was procured by misrepresentation (see *Cooper* v *Joel* (1859) 1 De G F & J 240), or a conveyance had been forged (see *Peake* v *Highfield* (1826) 1 Russ 559).

cannabis. Hallucinogenic, controlled drug (q.v.) (Class B), obtained from hemp (*cannabis sativa*). It is an offence under Misuse of Drugs Act 1971 to import, export, have in one's possession, produce or supply (except by authorisation) the drug or to cultivate any plant of the genus *Cannabis*. See *R* v *Ronchetti* [1998] 2 Cr App R (S) 100 (sentencing guidelines).

canon. 1. Generally, a rule of *canon law*, i.e., a Roman Catholic ecclesiastical law system, first codified in 1139. See *Codex Juris Canonici*, 1983. The only official and binding version is the Latin text. *Canon law* also refers to the law of the Church of England. (Canon law does not bind the laity: *Middleton* v *Croft* (1736) 2 Atk 690.) 2. A body of writings.

canonical disability. Sexual impotence (q.v.).

canvassing. 1. Soliciting votes from, e.g., electors. 2. Where one individual visits another off trade premises in order to obtain the entry of another into a regulated agreement (q.v.): C.C.A. 1974, s 48. Canvassing for debtor-creditor agreements (q.v.) off trade premises is illegal: s 49(1).

CAP. Common Agricultural Policy. A policy created under Treaty of Rome, arts 38–47, aims at the implementation of free trade among members of the EU. Its central features are target prices, threshold prices, support ('intervention') prices, and export subsidies or refunds. The first regulations concerning CAP were enacted in 1962 and related to grain, poultry, fruit and vegetables, and wine. *See* EUROPEAN UNION.

capacity, establishing lack of. A lack of capacity cannot be established merely by reference to (a) a person's age or appearance, or (b) a condition of his, or an aspect of his behaviour, which might lead others to make unjustified assumptions about his capacity: Mental Capacity Act 2005, s 2(3).

capacity of child in criminal law. *See* DOLI CAPAX.

capacity, persons lacking capacity. A person lacks capacity in relation to a matter if at the material time he is unable to make a decision for himself in relation to the matter because of an impairment of, or a disturbance in the functioning of, the mind or brain. It does not matter whether the impairment or disturbance is permanent or temporary: Mental Capacity Act 2005, s 2(1) & (2).

capacity to contract. The legal competence, power or fitness to enter and be bound by a contract. Thus, an infant (q.v.) generally lacks contractual capacity, save where he binds himself by contract for necessaries or for other matters relating to his benefit. See *Doyle* v *White City Stadium* [1935] 1 KB 110; and *Hart* v *O'Connor* [1985] AC 1000 (mental incapacity). *See* CONTRACT; MINORS' CONTRACTS.

capax doli. *See* DOLI CAPAX.

capital. 1. In commercial usage, the capital of a business is its net worth, i.e., the value of its assets less the amount owing to its creditors. 2. In company law, it refers to, e.g., authorised, issued or paid-up capital. For 'capital distribution', see T.C.G.A. 1992, s 122.

capital allowances. Allowances available to persons carrying on a trade, profession, vocation or employment who have incurred capital expenditure on certain types of asset (including machinery and plant) (q.v.) for the purpose of their business. See, e.g., Capital Allowances Act 2001; Finance Act 1989, Part II.

capital, alteration of. *See* ALTERATION OF SHARE CAPITAL.

capital, called-up. In relation to a company (q.v.) equals the aggregate of the calls made on shares (whether or not paid) plus any share capital paid up without being called and any share capital to be paid on a specified future date: Cos.A. 1985, s 737.

capital clause. Clause in memorandum of association (q.v.) setting out company's nominal, i.e., authorised, capital (q.v.), number and denomination of shares. In the case of a public company (q.v.) the clause must state an amount not less than the authorised minimum: Cos.A. 1985; ss 11, 118. *See* TABLE B.

capital gains tax. Tax introduced by Finance Act 1965, levied on 'chargeable gains' made on the disposal of chargeable assets. See T.C.G.A. 1992, Part I, amended by Finance Act 2000, s 37. See *Aberdeen Construction Group Ltd v IRC* [1978] 1 All ER 963; *Kirkham v Williams* [1991] 1 WLR 863. In *Jerome v Kelly* (2004) *The Times* 20 May, the HL held that when a vendor disposes by sale of an asset under a contract completed at a later date, the date of disposal for purposes of capital gains tax is the date on the contract and not the date of completion.

capital interest, qualifying. Means, in relation to any body corporate, an interest in shares comprised in the equity share capital of that body corporate of a class carrying right to vote in all circumstances at general meetings of that body corporate. For 'equity share capital', see Cos.A. 1985, s 744.

capitalisation. In relation to profits of a company (q.v.), means applying profits in wholly or partly paying up unissued shares in the company to be allotted to members as fully or partly paid bonus shares (q.v.), or transferring profits to capital redemption reserve: Cos.A. 1985, s 280; Table A. For reorganisation of capital, see *Dunstan v Young, Austen & Young* [1987] STC 709.

capital, loan. Any debenture stock or funded debt issued by a corporate body or other body formed or established in the UK or any capital raised by such a body, being capital which is borrowed, or has the character of borrowed money, whether in the form of stock or any other form and stock or marketable securities

issued by the government of a Commonwealth country outside the UK: Finance Act 1986, s 78(7).

capital money. 1. Money that is paid to trustees of a settlement in the exercise of a statutory power, e.g., money raised by mortgage of land for purposes authorised by S.L.A. 1925, sale of land or heirlooms under S.L.A. 1925, s 67(2). See Trustee Delegation Act 1999, s 7(1) (the 'two-trustee rule'). For disposition of capital money, see S.L.A. 1925, s 75(5). 2. Money that should be treated as capital, e.g., that paid under a fire insurance policy which the tenant for life (q.v.) was obliged to maintain. See S.L.A. 1925, s 81. *See* SETTLEMENT.

capital movements, free. A component of the EU's internal market arrangements. Restrictions on movements of capital belonging to residents of member states are to be abolished: Treaty of Rome, art 67; Directive 88/361. Relevant domestic rules must be liberalised: art 68; Cases 203/80, 26/83. *See* EU.

capital, paid-up. The sum of the payments for shares received by a company.

capital punishment. Death by hanging (q.v.). Abolished by Murder (Abolition of Death Penalty) Act 1965, and a sentence of life imprisonment substituted. Capital punishment for high treason and piracy was abolished under C.D.A. 1998, s 36. See European Convention on Human Rights (q.v.), Sixth Protocol, art 1 (abolition of death penalty), art 2 (death penalty may be applied in time of war or imminent threat of war).

capital redemption business. Any business which is insurance business, but not life assurance business, and consists in effecting on the basis of actuarial calculations, and carrying out, contracts under which, in return for one or more fixed payments, a sum or series of sums of a specified amount become payable at a future time or over a period: I.C.T.A. 1988, s 458(3), substituted by Finance Act 1996, s 168(1).

capital redemption reserve. Made up of amounts equal to nominal value of shares cancelled as a result of the company redeeming or purchasing its own shares out of distributable profits.

capital, reduction of. *See* REDUCTION OF CAPITAL.

capital reserve. Non-distributable funds retained in a business. 'Statutory capital reserves' include share premium account and capital redemption reserve fund. See Cos.A. 1985, s 130.

capital, reserve. *See* RESERVE CAPITAL.

capital, serious loss of. When the net assets of a public company (q.v.) fall to one half or less of called-up share capital, the directors, not later than 28 days from the day at which the loss became known to a director, must call an extraordinary general meeting (q.v.): Cos.A. 1985, s 142.

capital, share. *See* SHARE CAPITAL.

capital transfer tax. Tax charged at progressive rates, cumulatively, on the value of property transferred by chargeable transfers and made by a person in his lifetime. Introduced under Finance Act 1975, Part III. See Capital Transfer Tax Act 1984 (now known (see 1986 Act, Part V, s 100) as the Inheritance Tax 1984). Abolished by Finance Act 1986. For 'potentially exempt transfers', see 1986 Act, s 101, Sch 19. See INHERITANCE TAX.

caption. 1. Arrest. 2. Heading of a legal instrument.

car. *See* MOTOR CAR.

car access over common. In *Bakewell Management* v *Brandwood* [2004] UKHL 14, the HL held that, although it was not possible to presume a lost modern grant where a grant would have been unlawful, it was possible to acquire an easement relating to car access by long uninterrupted use, which breached a statutory provision, where the owner of the land could have made a lawful grant, thus removing any criminality attached to the use of the land.

caravan. A structure capable of being moved by towing or being transported on a motor vehicle or a trailer and designed or adapted for human habitation. See Caravan Sites Act 1968, s 13; L.G.P.L.A. 1980, ss 70, 173; Mobile Homes Act 1983; I.C.T.A. 1988, s 367; *Wye Forest DC* v *Secretary of State for the Envir-*

onment [1990] 1 All ER 780; *R* v *Hillingdon LBC ex p McDonagh* (1998) 95 LSG 35. *See* BUILDING.

carding. Administrative procedure under Terrorism Act 2000, Sch 7, para 16, and SI 01/426, whereby certain persons who disembark or embark at an air or sea port in Great Britain or Northern Ireland are obliged to provide, if required to do so by an examining officer, on a card, information concerning purpose of visit, occupation, employer, address, etc.

care. The degree of attention or diligence that may fairly and properly be expected in given circumstances.

care and supervision order. On the application of a local authority or authorised person (e.g., NSPCC) the court may make an order placing the child (who must be under 17) with respect to whom the application is made in the care of a designated local authority, or putting him under the supervision of a local authority or probation officer: Ch.A. 1989, s 31(1). See *Plymouth CC* v *C* (2000) *The Times*, 21 March. The court must be satisfied that the child is suffering or is likely to suffer significant harm, and that the harm or its likelihood is attributable to the care given to the child or the fact that he is beyond parental control: s 31(2). 'Harm' means ill-treatment or the impairment of health or physical, intellectual, emotional, social or behavioural development: s 31(9). See *Lancashire CC* v *A* (2000) 150 NLJ 429; *Re D (Child: Threshold Criteria)* (2000) *The Times*, 13 October.

care, common duty towards visitors. 'A duty to take such care as in all the circumstances of the case is reasonable, to see that the visitor will be reasonably safe in using the premises for the purposes for which he is invited or permitted by the occupier to be there': Occupiers' Liability Act 1957, s 2(2). See *Bernadone* v *Pall Mall Services* [1999] IRLR 617.

care, duty of. *See* DUTY OF CARE.

care for safety, duty of. Duty of an occupier of premises ('the common duty of care') owed to all his visitors, except trespassers, under Occupiers' Liability Act 1957, s 2. Under Defective Premises

Act 1972, s 7, a landlord has a duty of taking reasonable care to see that persons who might be affected by defects in the premises he has let are reasonably safe from danger or injury. For the duty of care owed to 'non-visitors' see Occupiers' Liability Act 1984; *Revill* v *Newberry* [1996] QB 567.

care homes. Establishments providing accommodation, together with nursing or personal care, for persons who are or have been ill, persons who have or have had mental disorders, disabled, infirm persons, those who are or have been dependent on alcohol or drugs: Care Standards Act 2000, s 3(1), (2). Hospitals, children's homes are excluded: s 3(3). Must be registered under s 11. For regulations, see s 22. For failure to comply with conditions, see s 24.

care home status. In *James* v *Commission for Social Care Inspection* (2005) *The Times*, 4 January, the CA held that where a person applies to be registered as fit to manage a care home, then the relevant burden of proof rests on the applicant to make proof of his status.

careless and inconsiderate driving. See DRIVING, CARELESS AND INCONSIDERATE.

carelessness. The quality of an act which deviates materially from the standard of care which would be expected in the circumstances from a reasonable person. *See* NEGLIGENCE.

carers. Persons aged 16 or over who provide a substantial amount of care on a regular basis for another person aged 18 or over. They may ask a local authority to carry out an assessment of their ability to provide such care. See Carers and Disabled Children Act 2000, s 1. The Carers (Equal Opportunities) Act 2004 requires local authorities to inform unpaid carers of adults and disabled children of their assessment rights.

care, servant's contractual duty of. 'The servant owes a contractual duty of care to his master, and a breach of that duty founds an action for damages for breach of contract': *per* Ackner LJ in *Janata Bank* v *Ahmed* [1981] IRLR 457.

cargo. 1. Anything carried or to be

carried in a ship or other vessel: Docks and Harbours Act 1966, s 58(1), as amended. See *National Dock Labour Board* v *John Bland & Co* [1971] 2 All ER 779. 2. Goods which are, or are to be, or have been loaded in a ship, excluding a passenger's personal baggage carried on board by him, and including anything taken on board a ship from the sea or sea-bed with a view to its being discharged to shore. For 'dangerous cargo', see Hague Rules (Carriage of Goods by Sea Act 1971, Schedule), art IV, r 6; *Effort Shipping Co Ltd* v *Linden Management* (1998) NLJ 121. For meaning of 'owner of the cargo', see *The Elphis* [1999] 1 Lloyd's Rep 606.

car hijacking, sentencing for. In *R* v *Snowden* (2000) *The Times*, 11 November, the CA held that the planned hijacking of a vehicle on the highway, aggravated by the threat of personal violence, could merit imprisonment for at least 10 years.

car insurance. In *Heeley* v *Pashen* (2004) *The Times*, 17 November, the CA held that an insurer could not avoid liability arising from circumstances in which a motorist had driven with the intention of frightening pedestrians and had killed one, on the basis that the car was not being used for 'social and domestic or pleasure use'.

carriage of goods by air, liability relating to. In general, a carrier is liable without proof of breach of contract or negligence on his part. Only the actual consignor and consignee have claims in respect of damage to goods. See Warsaw Convention 1929 (amended at The Hague in 1955); Carriage by Air Act 1961; Carriage by Air (Supplementary Provs.) Act 1962; Carriage by Air and Road Act 1979; Council Regulation 2027/97 (effective from 17 October 1998); and *Rustenberg Platinum Mines* v *S African Airways* [1977] 1 Lloyd's Rep 564.

carriageway. Way constituting or comprised in a highway (q.v.), being a way (other than a cycle track) over which the public have a right of way for the passage of vehicles: Highways Act 1980, s 329(1). See G.L.A.A. 1999, s 263.

carrier, common. One who, by profession, undertakes for money payment the carrying of goods for those who employ him. His duties include the receiving and carrying of goods of the type he professes to carry; the carrying of goods by a reasonable route; delivery without unreasonable delay. He may be sued for damages if he wrongfully refuses to carry goods. See Carriers Acts 1830, 1865; Postal Services Act 2000, s 99; *Belfast Ropework Co v Bushell* [1918] 1 KB 210; *Rosenthal v LCC* (1924) 131 LT 563.

carrier, common, liability for safety of goods. Generally, liability, as an insurer of goods, for loss or damage except where caused by Act of God (q.v.), act of Queen's enemies, consignor's fault, goods' inherent vice.

carrier, private. A carrier who is not a common carrier (q.v.), i.e., who is never bound to carry. He is liable for any loss caused by his negligence. See *James Buchanan & Co v Hay's Transport Services* [1972] 2 Lloyd's Rep 535; Immigration and Asylum Act 1999, s 40, Sch 16 (repealing Immigration (Carriers Liability) Act 1987).

carrier's lien. Common-law lien under which a carrier is entitled to keep possession of goods until he is paid freight owing to him for their carriage: *Skinner v Upshaw* (1702) 2 Ld Raym 752.

case. 1. A legal action or trial. 2. Argument put forward in legal proceedings.

case management. Under CPR, r 1.4, the court must 'actively manage' cases, e.g., by encouraging parties to co-operate in the conduct of proceedings, identifying issues at an early stage, helping parties to settle whole or part of a case, giving appropriate directions, encouraging parties to use ADR (q.v.) if the court considers that appropriate. Case management decisions are generally dealt with by Masters (in case proceedings in Royal Courts of Justice), district judges in High Court district registry and county court cases: r 2.4. Transfer of cases to appropriate courses is often the initial step in case management.

case management conferences. An essential feature of 'active case manage-ment' under CPR, para 5.1, the court will, at conferences, review steps taken by parties in case preparation, give directions for further steps necessary, ensure that any agreement that can be reached by parties about matters in issue has been made. Topics likely to be included will concern: whether claimant has made his claim clear; whether amendments to claim are required; whether disclosure of documents or expert evidence may be necessary; what factual evidence has to be disclosed; whether disclosure of documents and expert evidence will be necessary; possibility of split trial. Legal representatives of parties are expected to attend.

case management directions, sanctions for non-compliance. A party may apply for an order that the non-complying party shall comply, or for a sanction, or both: PD 29, para 7.1. The non-complying party should be warned of the intention to apply for an order. Where the order is breached, the other party may request that judgment be entered and costs imposed: CPR, r 3.5. Relief from sanctions may be sought under r 3.9 if in interests of administration of justice, if failure to comply was not intentional, if there is a good explanation of failure to apply.

cases, reallocation of. A district judge has complete discretion to reallocate a case which has been allocated to the fast track but which has been amended, revising its financial value above £15,000, where, in all the circumstances, it is just to do so: see *Maguire v Molin* (2002) *The Times*, 12 August; and CPR 1998, r 26.8(1).

case stated. A statement of the facts in a case submitted, e.g., by magistrates for the opinion of a higher court (such as the Divisional Court). Application for statement can be made by the defendant, prosecutor or a 'person aggrieved' (although not a party). Application must identify the point of law on which opinion is sought. See M.C.A. 1980, s 111; S.C.A. 1981, s 28A; Acc.J.A. 1999, s 61; *Berry v Berry* [1987] Fam 1; *Maile v Manchester CC* [1998] COD 19.

case, statement of. Under CPR, r 2.3(1), means a claim form, particulars of claim (where not included in claim form), defence, Part 20 claim, reply to defence, and any further information given in relation to them, voluntarily or by court order under r 18.1. Under r 17.1(1), an amendment of case may be made before it has been served on the other party. The court's permission is required where statement has been served: r 17(1), (2)(b). See PD 17. Statement of case drafted by a legal representative should bear his signature. See also CPR, Sch 2; CCR O6, rr 3, 5, 5A, 6; *International Distillers Ltd v Hillebrand Ltd* (2000) *The Times*, 25 January; *Stewart v Engel* [2000] 3 All ER 518.

case summary. An aspect of the case conference arising in the multi-track case procedure: see PD 29, para 5.6(3). It is designed to assist the court to understand and deal with questions before it; it is prepared by claimant and agreed with other parties, if possible; it comprises claim chronology, issues of fact, evidence required, and should not normally exceed 500 words: para 7.1.

cash. Term applied to ready money of the current coin of the realm, including notes of the Bank of England. See Terrorism Act 2000, s 24(2). Under C.C.A. 1974, s 189(1), it includes money in any form. 'Cash price' is the price at which a person indicates that he is willing to sell goods to cash purchasers: *R v Baldwin's Garage* [1988] Crim LR 438.

cash, terrorist. Under Anti-terrorism, Crime and Security Act 2001, Sch 1, para 2, an authorised officer may seize any cash if he has reasonable grounds for suspecting that it is terrorist cash. Application for forfeiture may be made under para 6. 'Authorised officer' means a constable, customs officer, immigration officer: para 19(1).

casual ejector. The nominal defendant (known as 'Richard Roe') in an action of ejectment (q.v.). (This type of action was abolished by Common Law Procedure Act 1852.)

casus omissus. A case not provided for by the law. See, e.g., *Gladstone v Bower*

[1960] 2 QB 284; *Fisher v Bell* [1961] 1 QB 394.

catching bargain. An entrapping or unconscionable bargain, e.g., a loan made on extortionate terms to one who has an expectancy (e.g., an expectant heir). See C.C.A. 1974, s 137; *Cresswell v Potter* [1978] 1 WLR 255. *See* UNCONSCIONABLE TRANSACTION.

cattle. 'Bulls, cows, steers, heifers and calves': Animal Health Act 1981, s 89(1).

cattle trespass. Damage done by cattle trespassing on land of their owner's neighbour. Was actionable *per se*, without proof of damage. See Animals Act 1971, s 4, under which the owner may be liable for damage. *See* STRAYING LIVESTOCK.

causa proxima et non remota spectatur. It is the immediate, not the remote, cause that should be considered. 'It were infinite for the law to consider the causes of causes and their implications one of another; therefore it contenteth itself with the immediate cause': Bacon, *Elements of the Common Law of England* (1630). The *causa proxima* 'is the cause proximate in efficiency, not necessarily in time': *Leyland Shipping Co v Norwich Union* [1918] AC 350. *See* PROXIMITY.

causa remota. Remote cause; one operating indirectly through intervention of other causes. *See* NOVUS ACTUS INTERVENIENS.

causation. The relation of cause and effect. Where an *actus reus* (q.v.) is so defined that the occurrence of stated consequences is required (e.g., that the *actus reus* of the accused caused a death), the conduct of the accused which is alleged to have been the cause of those consequences has to be proved. See, e.g., *R v Blaue* [1975] 1 WLR 1411; *R v Malcherek* [1981] 1 WLR 690; *R v Cheshire* [1991] 3 All ER 670; *R v Marjoram* (1999) *The Times*, 3 December. *See* NOVUS ACTUS INTERVENIENS.

causation, breaking chain of. In *Knight v Vale RBC* (2003) *The Times*, 4 August, the CA held that the occupying by a tenant of premises let on the basis of a six-month assured shorthold tenancy could constitute the breaking of a chain of causation from a situation of past intentional homelessness.

cause. 1. A suit or action. 2. That which produces or contributes to some event. 'If a man intending to secure a particular result does an act which brings that about, he causes that result': *Alphacell Ltd v Woodward* [1972] 2 All ER 475. For 'originating cause', see *Axa Reinsurance Ltd v Field* [1996] 1 WLR 1026. See *Empress Car Company v Environment Agency* [1998] 2 WLR 350 (discussion by House of Lords on essence of 'cause'). 'The object of a civil inquiry into cause and consequence is to fix liability on some responsible person and to give reparation for damage done': *per* Lord Sumner in *Weld-Blundell v Stephens* [1920] AC 956.

cause of action. 'A factual situation, the existence of which entitles one person to obtain from the court a remedy against another person': *Letang v Cooper* [1960] 2 All ER 929.

causes, concurrent. *See* CONCURRENT CAUSES.

caution. 1. A warning. 2. A formal warning issued by the police to adults who admit an offence, where the police have no intention of prosecuting. See Police Act 1997, s 126; *H v L* [1998] 1 WLR 854 (private prosecution after police caution not unfair). After C.D.A. 1998, s 65 (reprimands and warnings (q.v.)) comes into force, no child or young person may be cautioned. 3. Any person interested in registered land (q.v.) may lodge a caution with the Registrar against any proposed registered dealing with that land. Entry of dealing with such land may not then be made on the register unless the cautioner has received notice – formerly LRA 1925, ss 53, 54; L.R.A. 1986; but now repealed under the LRA 2002. Cautions are now protected as 'unilateral notices' under the LRA 2002, s 35. *See* NOTICE, PROTECTION BY.

cautioning, questioning before. In *R v Senior* (2004) *The Times*, 25 March, the CA held that where persons travelling together had prohibited drugs in their possession, customs officials were empowered to question them as to the

ownership of the bag containing the drugs, prior to the administration of a caution.

caution to detained persons. Administered on arrest unless it is impracticable to do so because of the person's condition or behaviour. 'You do not have to say anything. But it may harm your defence if you do not mention anything which you later rely on in court. Anything you do say may be given in evidence.' See Code E, P.&.C.E.A. 1984. A minor modification of these words, but which embodies their sense, is not a breach of the requirement. See also C.J.P.O.A. 1994, ss 36, 37.

caveat. Warning, usually in the form of an entry in a register intended to prevent some action being taken without notice being given to person issuing the warning (the *caveator*). See, e.g., S.C.A. 1981, s 108, which allowed a caveat against a grant of probate (q.v.) or administration to be entered in the principal registry or district probate registry; L.R.A. 1925, s 30.

caveat emptor. Let the buyer beware. In general, the buyer is expected to look to his own interests. See S.G.A. 1979, ss 13, 14. *See* CONDITION; WARRANTY.

caveat venditor. Let the seller beware.

Cd. Abbreviation for Command Papers. *See* COMMAND PAPERS, NUMBERING OF; PARLIAMENTARY PAPERS.

census. An official counting of the population, first carried out in Britain in 1801. See Census Act 1920; Census (Amendment) Act 2000, enabling particulars to be required in respect of religion.

Central Criminal Court. Established by Central Criminal Court Act 1824 as an assize court, exercising criminal jurisdiction in the Greater London area. Popularly known as the 'Old Bailey'. Abolished by Courts Act 1971, but has been retained in name, so that when the Crown Court (q.v.) sits in London it is known as the Central Criminal Court: S.C.A. 1981, s 8(3). The Lord Mayor of London and any City Alderman may sit as a judge with a High Court or circuit judge, or recorder. Appeal lies to Court of Appeal (Criminal Division).

Central Office of the Supreme Court.
Departments which carry out the administrative business of the Supreme Court; they include those of the Masters' Secretary and Queen's Remembrancer, Action, Filing and Records, Crown Office and Associates, Supreme Court Taxing Office. See S.C.A. 1981, s 96.

Central Police Training and Development Authority. Established under C.J.P.A. 2001, s 87 to provide training and facilities for police authorities.

certainties, the three. The necessary conditions for the creation of a valid private trust, stated by Lord Eldon in *Wright* v *Atkyns* (1823) Turn & R 143 and by Lord Langdale in *Knight* v *Knight* (1840) 3 Beav 148 thus: '. . . the words must be imperative . . . the subject must be certain . . . the object or persons intended to have the benefit must be certain'. See *Re Kayford* [1975] 1 WLR 279: *per* Megarry J, 'The question is whether in substance a sufficient intention to create a trust has been manifested.' *See* TRUST.

certificate, land. A certificate under seal of the Land Registry given to the current registered proprietor (q.v.) as his document of title. See L.R.A. 1925, s 63(1). It records details of the registered land (q.v.), e.g., charges (q.v.), incumbrances, class of title. The certificate is retained by the Land Registry if a charge on the land is registered or protected by mortgage caution (q.v.): L.R.A. 1935, s 65.

certificate of incorporation. *See* INCORPORATION, CERTIFICATE OF.

certificate of shares. Document enabling shareholder to show good prima facie title to his shares. See Cos.A. 1985, s 186; Cos.A. 1989, s 130. The shareholder has a right to a certificate which should be prepared and ready for delivery within two months of the allotment of shares or their transfer. See also Forgery and Counterfeiting Act 1981, s 5(6). Share certificates are personal chattels and can properly be the subject of a claim in conversion (q.v.); full damages can be recovered for value of the shares at date of conversion: *MCC Proceeds* v *Lehman Bros* [1998] 4 All ER 675.

certificate to commence business. A trading certificate (q.v.).

certification officer, union. Appointed under T.U.L.R.(C.)A. 1992, s 254, with responsibility for, e.g., maintaining lists of unions and employers' associations. There is a right of appeal from his decisions to the Employment Appeal Tribunal (q.v.): 1992 Act, s 45D, inserted by Employment Relations Act 1999, Sch 6, para B. *See* TRADE UNION.

certiorari. To be fully informed of. Originally a writ from the High Court to an inferior court commanding proceedings to be removed to a superior court 'that conscionable justice may be there-inadministered': *Termes de la Ley.* Abolished under A.J. (Misc. Provs.) A. 1938, s 7, which replaced it with an order of *certiorari.* Used, e.g., to review and to quash decisions of tribunals. See CPR, Part 54; S.C.A. 1981, ss 29, 31; *R* v *Central Criminal Court ex p Raymond* [1986] 1 WLR 710. Known now as a 'quashing order'.

cessante ratione cessat ipse lex. With the reason of the law changing, the law itself ceases to exist. The so-called 'doctrine of changed circumstances', applied, e.g., to the process of distinguishing a case (q.v.). See *Miliangos* v *George Frank Ltd* [1976] AC 443.

cessate grant. When a grant limited as to time has been made and has ceased to have effect at the end of that time, a subsequent grant is known as a *cessate* or *supplemental* grant. It is, in effect, a renewal of the entire original grant. *See* GRANT.

cesser. 1. A ceasing (usually of liability), determination or (premature) end. Thus, a 'cesser clause' in a charterparty (q.v.) states that the charterer's liability ceases when the cargo has been landed. 2. 'Provision for cesser on redemption' is a clause in a mortgage (q.v.) providing for the ending of a term of years when the loan is repaid. See L.P.A. 1925, s 116. 3. 'Cesser of interest' refers to the determination of an interest which may then pass to another.

cession. Doctrine of international law, referring to transfer by treaty of territory from one state to another. See, e.g., Treaty of Peace with Japan 1951.

cestui que trust. Shortened form of *cestui à que trust* ('he for whom is the trust'). The beneficiary (q.v.), i.e. one who has equitable rights in property. Plural: *cestuis que trust. See* TRUST.

cestui que use. Shortened form of *cestui à que use le feoffment fuit fait* (one to whose use property was conveyed). Thus, X conveyed land to Y to the use of Z and his heirs. Z was known as *cestui que use.* Plural: *cestuis que use. See* TRUST; USE.

cestui que vie. Shortened form of *cestui à que vie* (he for whose life . . .). He for whose life a grant of land is made. Thus, where X is a tenant 'for the life of Y', Y is *cestui que vie.* See *Cestui Que Vie* Act 1707. *See* AUTRE VIE.

CFP. Common Fishing Policy. Established by EU in 1970, fully implemented in 1983. Creates a common organisation over fishing market, involving common external tariff, access to all EU fishing waters to all EU fishermen (involving the waters around territories of member states to 200 nautical miles offshore excluding 12-mile territorial seas); allocation of quotas to member states; conservation measures. *See* EUROPEAN UNION; QUOTA-HOPPING.

chain of representation. An executor of a sole or last surviving executor of a testator is the executor of that testator. So long as the chain is unbroken, the last executor in the chain is the executor of every preceding testator. The chain is broken by failure to obtain probate or to appoint an executor, or by an intestacy. See A.E.A. 1925, s 7. *See* EXECUTOR.

chain of title. Successive conveyances from the original source to the present owner. *See* TITLE DEEDS.

challenge to jury. Procedure whereby, before a jury is sworn, the prosecution or defence may challenge the members 'for cause' on statutory grounds (disqualification, ineligibility) or common law grounds (privilege of peerage, previous convictions, lack of qualifications, actual or presumed bias). See Juries Act 1974, s 12; C.J.A. 1988, s 118; *Practice Note* [1988]

3 All ER 1086; *R v Ford* [1989] 1 QB 868 (fact that juror is of a particular race cannot be the basis of a challenge for cause); *R v Comerford* [1998] 1 WLR 191 (withholding of jurors' names). The prosecution may require a person to 'stand by', i.e., not to sit on the jury unless there are insufficient members of the panel to constitute a full jury.

chambers. Usually, the offices of a judge in which application by way of summons may be heard; or the offices of counsel. The public has no right to attend hearings in chambers, but, if requested, permission to attend should be granted. To disclose what occurs in chambers is not a contempt unless it prejudices the administration of justice: *per* Lord Woolf in *Hodgson and Others v Imperial Tobacco Ltd* [1998] 1 WLR 1056. See also A.J.A. 1960, s 12. *See* IN CAMERA; OPEN COURT; OPEN JUSTICE.

champerty. (*Campi partitio* = dividing of land.) An offence and tort, abolished under C.L.A. 1967, ss 13, 14, resulting from a person's maintenance (q.v.) of another in an action, on condition that the subject matter of the action was to be shared by them. Abolition of criminal and civil liability does not affect 'any such rule of law as to the cases in which a contract is to be treated as contrary to public policy or otherwise illegal': s 14(2). See *Bevan Ashford v Yeandle Ltd* [1998] 3 All ER 238; *Geraghty & Co v Awwad* [1999] NPC 148; *Stocznia Gdanska SA v Latreefers Inc* (2000) *The Times*, 15 March. The CA considered in *R (Factortame) v Secretary of State for the Environment (No. 8)* (2002) *The Times*, 9 July, whether an agreement involving a contingent fee was champertuous. Champerty (and maintenance) have been abolished as crimes and torts, but champerty survives as a public policy rule capable of rendering a contract unenforceable. CA also stated that it would be very rare for the court to be prepared to consent to an expert being instructed under a contingency fee agreement.

chancel. The part of a church near the altar, generally reserved for the choir.

Liability to repair church chancel is an 'overriding interest' (q.v.) under L.R.A. 1925, s 70(1)(c). For notice to repair, see Chancel Repairs Act 1932, s 2; CPR, Sch 2; CCR, O 49, r 2; *Parochial Church Council of Aston Cantlow* v *Wallbank* (2000) *The Times*, 30 March.

Chancellor. 1. Lord High Chancellor (known as 'the Lord Chancellor'). Appointed by the Crown on the Prime Minister's advice; the principal legal dignitary, a member of the Cabinet (q.v.), the government's legal adviser, and Speaker of the House of Lords, presiding at some judicial proceedings on appeal. Under C.L.S.A. 1990 he has responsibilities for the appointment of the Legal Services Ombudsman (q.v.). For appointment of Permanent Secretary to the Lord Chancellor, see Supreme Court (Offices) Act 1997. 2. Chancellor of the Exchequer, political head of the Treasury (q.v.) and responsible for control of national revenue and expenditure. A senior member of the Cabinet (q.v.), who presents the annual budget (q.v.) to Parliament.

chancel repairs, liability of lay rectors for. In *Parochial Church Council of Aston* v *Wallbank* [2003] UKHL 37, the HL held that liability for chancel repairs in the case of rectorial land, runs with the land; it does not constitute interference with a lay rector's right to peaceful enjoyment of his land.

Chancery, Court of. *See* COURT OF CHANCERY.

Chancery Division. Division of High Court of Justice (q.v.) consisting of the Lord Chancellor (q.v.), a Vice-Chancellor, and other puisne judges (q.v.). It is a civil court, and matters over which it has jurisdiction include company affairs, administration of estates, execution of trusts, contested probate. 'Chancery business' includes any of the matters set out in S.C.A. 1981, Sch 1, para 1: PD 7, para 2.5. It sits in London and eight provincial centres. A single judge of the Division may hear some appeals, e.g., from the Commissioner of Inland Revenue. Places at which Chancery Courts sit out of London are Birmingham, Bristol, Cardiff, Leeds, Liverpool, Manchester, Newcastle, Preston.

Chancery Division Lists. There are three main lists: Trial List (for trials to be heard with witnesses); Interim Hearing List (for interim applications, including appeals from Masters); General List (for other matters, including revenue, bankruptcy and pensions appeals).

Chancery Masters. Deputies of the judges of the Chancery Division. *See* MASTERS OF THE SUPREME COURT.

character details. In *R* v *Goss* (2003) *The Times*, 27 October, the CA held that, in the case of a defendant who had a conviction for driving a vehicle without insurance, it was a matter of judicial discretion to decide whether the judge ought to give a good character direction, taking into account whether the previous offence was deliberate or no more than of a technical nature.

character evidence. Law Commission Report, *Evidence of Bad Character in Criminal Proceedings* (2001), recommends that evidence of any person's bad character could be brought before court without its permission where it concerns 'the central set of facts' in a case, i.e., alleged facts of offence charged, or misconduct connected with investigation of offence. 'Bad character evidence' is that tending to show that defendant has committed an offence, or is disposed to behave in a way of which reasonable persons might have disapproved.

character, evidence as to. Evidence as to the character of a party (i.e., reputation (see Civil Evidence Act 1995, s 7(3)), disposition) may be given in the following circumstances: 1. *In criminal cases*. Evidence of good character of the accused (and where the accused puts his character in issue, that involves putting his past record in its entirety in issue), can always be given in chief or cross-examination (q.v.). Evidence of bad character may be given with leave of the judge to rebut evidence of good character of the accused (and where the accused puts his character in issue, that involves putting his past record in its entirety in issue), or if he has attacked the character of any witness for the prosecution. Evidence of character may be given after conviction. See *R* v *Aziz* [1996] AC 41; *R* v *Wright* (2000) *The Times*, 31 May (judge should preview character evidence). See Criminal Evidence Act 1898, s 1(*f*)(*iii*) (as amended by Criminal Evidence Act 1979, s 1); Y.J.C.E.A. 1999, Sch 4, para 1. 2. *In civil cases.* Evidence of good character may not be given (except in rebuttal) so as to aggravate damages. Evidence of plaintiff's bad character is admissible, e.g., where his character is in issue (e.g., in defamation). See Civil Evidence Act 1968, s 13. *See* EVIDENCE.

charge. 1. A criminal accusation. 2. Judge's instruction to a jury. 3. Expenses. 4. An incumbrance, e.g., on land, which secures payment of money. Charges over land capable of subsisting at law are, under L.P.A. 1925, s 1(2), e.g., charges by way of legal mortgage (q.v.). Other charges take effect as equitable interests. See L.C.A. 1972. 5. A *fixed charge* is a charge on specific property. A *floating charge* may be created by a company to secure debentures. See Cos.A. 1985, s 395; *Re Curtain Dream plc* [1990] BCLC 925. The floating charge 'is ambulatory and hovers over the property until some event occurs which causes it to settle and crystallise into a specific charge': *Barker* v *Eynon* [1974] 1 All ER 900; *Trident International* v *Barlow* [1999] 2 BCLC 506. See A.J.A. 1977, s 7(1). *See* CHARGE, CRYSTALLISATION OF.

charge by way of legal mortgage. A mortgage may be created by a charge by deed expressed to be by way of legal mortgage: L.P.A. 1925, s 85(1). The mortgagee has the same protection, powers and remedies as if he had taken a lease of a fee simple (q.v.). See *Regent Oil Co* v *JA Gregory Ltd* [1966] Ch 402. *See* MORTGAGE.

charge, crystallisation of. Conversion of a floating charge to a fixed charge, e.g., as on the winding-up of a company. See Cos.A. 1985, Part XII; Cos.A. 1989, s 100.

charge, fixed or floating. In *Re Spectrum Plus Ltd* (2004) *The Times*, 4 June, the CA held that a final, rather than a floating charge, would be created over existing book debts as the result of a debenture which provided that the company's book debts ought not to be disposed of prior to collection. Further, on collection, they had to be paid into a bank account held at the chargee bank, since the charge could be considered as imposing restrictions on the use of any proceeds of the book debts. The decision as to whether a charge created by debenture is fixed or floating requires the court to consider the nature of the obligations and rights intended by the parties, the intention of the parties relating to control of the charged assets, and consistency of the intention with the description of the charge made by the parties: *Re Spectrum Ltd* [2004] EWHC 9 (Ch).

charge, general equitable. *See* EQUITABLE CHARGE, GENERAL.

charges and rates. Under Finance Act 2004, s 23, charges and rates relating to income tax are, for 2004–5: starting rate is 10%; basic rate is 22%; higher rate is 40%. Corporation tax for 2005 is 30%.

charges, joinder of. *See* JOINDER OF CHARGES.

Charges Register. *See* REGISTER AT LAND REGISTRY.

charges, specimen. *See* SPECIMEN CHARGES.

charging clause. Clause authorising a solicitor who is a trustee (q.v.) to charge for his professional services: see *Re Royce's WT* [1959] Ch 626.

charging order. A judgment creditor (q.v.) can apply for an order imposing a charge on the debtor's land, securities, or funds in court. See Charging Orders Act 1979, s 1; CPR, Sch 1; O 50; CPR, Sch 2; CCR, O 31; *Holder* v *Supperstone* [2000] 1 All ER 473. He could also apply by summons for an order charging a partnership interest: Partnership Act 1890, s 23. See C.J.A. 1988, s 78; *Harman* v *Glencross* [1986] 1 All ER 545 (ancillary relief in divorce); *Howell* v *Montey* (1991) 61 P & CR 18 (charge to be made absolute);

County C.A. 1984, s 138(9C) (allowing the holder of a charging order to apply for relief from forfeiture: see *Croydon Ltd v Wright* [1999] 4 All ER 257). *See* JUDGMENTS, ENFORCEMENT OF.

charitable appeal. An appeal to members of the public which is (i) an appeal to them to give money or other property, or (ii) an appeal falling within subsection (4), (or both) and which is made in association with a representation that the whole or any part of its proceeds is to be applied for charitable, benevolent or philanthropic purposes: Charities Act 2006 s 45(2)(b).

charitable, benevolent or philanthropic institution. This is (a) a charity, or (b) an institution (other than a charity) which is established for charitable, benevolent, or philanthropic purposes: Charities Act 2006 s 47.

charitable purposes. A purpose which falls within any of the following descriptions of purposes: (a) the prevention or relief of poverty; (b) the advancement of education; (c) the advancement of religion; (d) the advancement of health or the saving of lives; (e) the advancement of citizenship or community development; (f) the advancement of the arts, culture, heritage or science; (g) the advancement of amateur sport; (h) the advancement of human rights, conflict resolution or reconciliation or the promotion of religious or racial harmony or equality and diversity; (i) the advancement of environmental protection or improvement; (j) the relief of those in need by reason of youth, age, ill-health, disability, financial hardship or other disadvantage; (k) the advancement of animal welfare; (l) the promotion of the efficiency of the armed forces of the Crown; (m) any other purposes within subsection (4): Charities Act 2006.

charitable trust. A trust by the terms of which the income is to be applied exclusively for purposes of a charitable nature. For disqualification of trustees, see Charities Act 1993, s 72. Trusts of this kind were named in the preamble to the Statute of Charitable Uses 1601 as trusts for the relief of poverty, the advancement of education, the advancement of religion,

other purposes beneficial to the community. 'Charity is necessarily altruistic and involves the idea of aid or benefit to others': *Re Delaney* [1902] 2 Ch 642. See *Guild v IRC* [1992] 2 WLR 397; *A-G of Cayman Islands v Wahr-Hansen* [2000] 3 All ER 642. *See* CHARITY; INVESTMENT, ETHICAL, BY CHARITIES; POLITICAL OBJECTS; PUBLIC BENEFIT; TRUST.

Charities, Central Register of. Set up under Charities Act 1960, amended by Charities Act 1993, and kept by Charity Commissioners: to provide a permanent central record of property devoted to charity; to provide information to the public concerning charities; to provide an authoritative means of determining whether an organisation is charitable in law or not. Registration is generally compulsory. There are some exceptions in the case of, e.g., 'exempt charities', 'excepted charities', very small charities with no permanent endowment, places of religious worship registered under Places of Worship Registration Act 1855. See SI 92/1901.

Charities, Register of. The register shall contain (a) the name of every charity registered in accordance with section 3A below (registration); and (b) such other particulars of, and such other information relating to, every such charity as the Commission thinks fit: Charities Act 2006 s 9.

charity. For purposes of the law of England and Wales means an institution which (a) is established for charitable purposes (q.v.) only, and (b) falls to be subject to the control of the High Court in the exercise of its jurisdiction with respect to charities. Charities Act 2006 s 1.

Charity Commissioners. A statutory body (see Charities Acts 1992, 1993, 2006) which administers charities, secures the effective use of charity property and investigates abuses, removing trustees from office where necessary. See, e.g., *Mills v Winchester Diocesan Board of Finance* [1989] 2 All ER 317. By virtue of the Charities Act 2006 s 7 and Sch 1, this is a body corporate for England and

Wales and shall consist of a chairman and at least four, but not more than eight, other members, appointed by the Secretary of State. It has the general functions of: determining whether institutions are or are not charities; encouraging and facilitating the better administration of charities; identifying and investigating apparent misconduct or mismanagement in the administration of charities and taking remedial or protective action in connection with misconduct or mismanagement therein; determining whether public collections certificates should be issued, and remain in force, in respect of public charitable collections; obtaining, evaluating and disseminating information in connection with the performance of any of the Commission's functions or meeting any of its objectives and giving information or advice, or making proposals, to any Minister of the Crown on matters relating to any of the Commission's functions or meeting any of its objectives. *See* OFFICIAL CUSTODIAN FOR CHARITIES.

charity merger, relevant. (a) A merger of two or more charities in connection with which one of them ('the transferee') has transferred to it all the property of the other or others, each of which (a 'transferor') ceases to exist, or is to cease to exist, on or after the transfer of its property to the transferee, or (b) a merger of two or more charities ('transferors') in connection with which both or all of them cease to exist, or are to cease to exist, on or after the transfer of all of their property to a new charity ('the transferee'). Charities Act 2006 s 44.

charity proceedings. Proceedings in the High Court under the court's jurisdiction with respect to charities or under the court's jurisdiction with respect to trusts in relation to administration of a trust for charitable purposes: CPR, Sch 1; O 108, r 1.

Charity Tribunal. The Tribunal shall consist of the President and its other members. The Lord Chancellor shall appoint (a) a President of the Tribunal, (b) legal members of the Tribunal, and (c) ordinary members of the Tribunal.

The Tribunal shall have jurisdiction to hear and determine (a) such appeals and applications as may be made to the Tribunal in accordance with Sch 1C to this Act, or any other enactment, in respect of decisions, orders or directions of the Commission, and (b) such matters as may be referred to the Tribunal in accordance with Schedule 1D to this Act by the Commission or the Attorney General: Charities Act 2006 s 8 and Sch 3.

charter. 1. Written instrument executed between parties, e.g., a deed (q.v.). 2. Instrument from the Crown granting rights and privileges. See *Crown Estate Commissioners* v *City of London* (1992) *The Times*, 11 May (construction of old Royal charters). 3. A constitution, e.g., the Charter of the United Nations Organisation.

charterparty. A document by which a shipowner lets his ship to a charterer for the purpose of carrying a cargo, or undertakes that his ship will carry a cargo. It must be in writing, with or without seal. A charterer has no proprietary interest in the ship: *Port Line Ltd* v *Ben Line Steamers Ltd* [1958] 2 QB 146. A *charterparty by way of demise* is one by which master and crew are the charterer's servants for the duration of the charterparty: *Baumwoll* v *Furness* [1893] AC 8. See *The Fantasy* [1991] 2 Lloyd's Rep 391 (meaning of 'at charterer's risk'); *The Petre Schmidt* [1997] 1 Lloyd's Rep 284; *Whistler International* v *Kawasaki Kisen* (2000) 150 NLJ 1856.

chastisement, reasonable, of child, defence. Defence of 'reasonable chastisement' continues to be available to a parent accused of assaulting a child; but the jury is to be directed to consider: nature, context, duration of defendant's behaviour; defendant's reasons for administering the punishment; child's age and characteristics; physical and mental consequences for the child: *per* Rose LJ in *R* v *H (Reasonable Chastisement)* (2001) *The Times*, 17 May.

chattels. Generally property other than freeholds (q.v.), i.e., personal property. 1. *Chattels real.* 'Interests issuing out of or annexed to real estates, of which they have one quality, viz., immobility, which denotes them real, but want the other, viz., a sufficient, legal indeterminate duration, and this want it is that constitutes them chattels': Blackstone. Example: leaseholds (q.v.). 2. *Chattels personal*. Pure personalty, e.g., choses in possession (q.v.) and choses in action (q.v.). See A.E.A. 1925, s 55(1), amended by Trusts of Land and Appointment of Trustees Act 1996, Sch 3, para 6(5). *Re Crispin's WT* [1975] Ch 245.

cheat. 'A deceitful practice for defrauding another of his known right by means of some artful device, contrary to the plain rules of common honesty': 1 Hawk PC. 'To cheat and defraud is to act with deliberate dishonesty as to the prejudice of another person's proprietary right': *R v Sinclair* [1968] 3 All ER 241. The common law offence was abolished by Th.A. 1968, s 32, except for offences relating to public revenue (see *R v Mavji* (1987) 84 Cr App R 34). Under Th.A. 1968, s 25(5), 'cheat' means an offence under s 15, i.e., dishonestly obtaining property belonging to another with the intention of permanently depriving the other of it: *R v Rashid* [1977] 1 WLR 298; *R v Doukas* [1978] 1 WLR 372. *See* REVENUE, CHEATING.

check-off practice. Procedure whereby employers agree to deduct employees' union subscriptions directly from pay and transfer them to the union. Workers must agree to the procedure as a term of the employment contract: *Williams v Butlers Ltd* [1974] IRLR 253. Such agreements must be periodically renewed: T.U.L.R.(C.)A. 1992, s 68, substituted by T.U.R.E.R.A. 1993, s 15. See E.R.A. 1996, s 14(4).

cheque. A bill of exchange (q.v.) drawn on a banker, payable on demand: B.Ex.A. 1882, s 73. A *crossed cheque* is one crossed with two parallel lines between which is written, e.g., the name of a bank, or the words 'and company' (often abbreviated), the purpose being to provide security against fraud by ensuring the cheque is paid only into a banking account. See also s 76. See *Smith v*

Lloyds TSB (2000) 150 NLJ 1337 (cheque materially altered by third party fraud is a worthless piece of paper). For 'cheque voucher', see Finance Act 1982, s 44(5). See Cheques Act 1992 (non-transferable cheques; use of printed phrase, 'account payee', on cheques). A claim may be brought in relation to a cheque (or bill of exchange) only where consideration (q.v.) has been given. 'Past consideration, is valuable consideration in this context. See B.Ex.A 1882, s 27(1). For liability to make restitution on cheques, see *Hollicourt Ltd v Bank of England* (2000) *The Times*, 1 November.

cheque card. Card issued by a bank and presented with a cheque to a supplier of goods or services who, as a result, is assured of payment by that bank. The drawer of the cheque represents that he has authority from the bank to use the card so as to oblige the bank to honour the cheque; where he has no such authority he may be guilty of obtaining a pecuniary advantage by deception, contrary to Th.A. 1968, s 16(1): *R v Charles* [1977] AC 177. See *R v Navvabi* [1986] 1 WLR 1311; *R v Bevan* [1987] Crim LR 129.

cheque, countermand of payment. Revocation by drawer of the authority to pay a cheque. Must be written and unequivocal: see B.Ex.A. 1882, s 75; *Barclays Bank v Simms* [1979] 3 All ER 522 (there is no reason in principle why a bank cannot recover money paid under a stopped cheque).

cheque, issue of. A cheque is 'issued' at the time of its first delivery, complete in form, to the person who takes it as a holder: B.Ex.A. 1882, s 2.

cheque, overdue. Cheque which has been in circulation for an unreasonable time. Can only be negotiated subject to any defect of title; is not, therefore, a negotiable instrument. See B.Ex.A. 1882, s 36(2), (3).

cheque, post-dated. Cheque dated subsequently to actual date on which drawn, and issued before the date it bears. See B.Ex.A. 1882, s 13(2); *Royal Bank of Scotland v Tottenham* (1894) 71 LT 168.

cheque, stale. Cheque which is 'out of date', i.e., one bearing a date six months or more prior to presentation. See *London County Banking Co v Groome* (1881) 8 QBD 288.

chief constable, suspension of. Where, in the exercise of his power to require a police authority to suspend a chief constable, the Secretary of State for the Home Departments entitled to have appropriate regard to problems involving the maintenance of public confidence throughout the nation and not merely the maker of the confidence of the public in the area which is served by the authority in question.

chief executive. *See* EXECUTIVE, CHIEF.

Chief Justice, Deputy. The first-ever Deputy Chief Justice, who will assist the Lord Chief Justice with various administrative duties, has been appointed, as from 14 July 2003. He is Lord Justice Judge.

child. Under C.&Y.P.A. 1933, s 14, and P.C.C.(S.)A. 2000, s 163, a person under 14. Under Marriage Act 1949, s 78, Ch.A. 1989, s 105(1) and CPR, r 21.1(2), a person under 18. In Mat.C.A. 1973, s 52(1), it included, in relation to one or both of the parties to a marriage, an illegitimate or adopted child of that party or of both parties. See also Inheritance (Provision for Family and Dependants) Act 1975, s 25(1). *See* YOUNG PERSON.

child abduction. *See* ABDUCTION, CHILD.

child abduction, defence to. A mother who wrongfully brought her child from Israel to UK did not succeed in her attempt to establish a defence under Hague Convention on Child Abduction 1980, art 13(b), since she was unable to show, taking everything into account, that there was a 'grave risk' of harm to the child, or a return to an 'intolerable situation' if she were to be returned to Israel: *In Re S (child) (Abduction: Custody Rights)* (2002) *The Times*, 15 July.

child abuse. Behaviour towards young children, characterised by physical, or emotional, or sexual abuse, or neglect. See *Report of the Inquiry into Child Abuse in Cleveland 1987* (1987, Cm 412). 'Sexual abuse' is defined by Schechter as 'the involvement of dependent, developmentally immature children and adolescents in sexual activities they do not fully comprehend, and to which they are unable to give informed consent, and that violate social taboos of family life': *Child Abuse and Neglect* (1976). See SI 97/2308; *A-G's Reference (No. 23 of 1997)* [1998] 1 CL 42 (undue leniency in sentencing for child abuse); *R v Paget* [1998] 1 Cr App R (S) 80. *See* CRUELTY TO CHILD; PAEDOPHILE.

child assessment order. Granted by court to a local authority if an applicant has reasonable cause to believe that a child is suffering or is likely to suffer significant harm and an assessment is needed to determine whether the child is suffering or is likely to suffer such harm: Ch.A. 1989, s 43. An 'emergency protection order' is issued if the court has cause to believe that a child is likely to suffer significant harm if not removed: s 44. For removal of children by police, see s 46.

child benefit. Cash benefit payable (tax-free) to the person responsible for a child (and replacing family allowances), i.e., one under 16, or under 19 if receiving full-time education. See S.S. Contributions and Benefits Act 1992, Part IX; Social Security Administration (Fraud) Act 1997, s 13(1A), (1B), inserted by W.R.P.A. 1999, s 69 (claimants must supply a national insurance number).

child care organisation. An organisation concerned with the provision of accommodation, social services or health care to children or the supervision of children, and whose activities are regulated by prescribed enactments: Protection of Children Act 1999, s 12(1), amended by Care Standards Act 2000, Sch 6.

child care position. Phrase used in Protection of Children Act 1999, to refer to employment concerned with provision of accommodation, social services or health care services to children or the supervision of children, and is such as to enable the holder to have regular contact with children in the course of his duties:

s 12(1). A position at an independent school which is a children's home under Ch.A. 1989, Part VIII, is excluded from s 12(1): s 12(3).

child, cruelty to. *See* CRUELTY TO CHILD.

child destruction. 'Any person who, with intent to destroy the life of a child capable of being born alive, by any wilful act causes a child to die before it has an existence independent of its mother, shall be guilty of' child destruction: Infant Life (Preservation) Act 1929, s 1(1). The section does not apply where the act was done in good faith for the purpose of preserving the mother's life. See, also, Abortion Act 1967, s 5; *R* v *Virgo* (1988) 10 Cr App R (S) 427; *R* v *Johnson* (1990) 12 Cr App R (S) 219. *See* ABORTION; BORN ALIVE; UNBORN PERSONS, KILLING OF.

child, identification of. In *Re S (A Child) (Identification: restriction on publication)* [2003] EWCA Civ 963, the CA held that., in relation to the court's inherent jurisdiction to issue an order prohibiting the identification of a defendant in a criminal trial, in the interests of a child not concerned in that trial, there should be a balancing of the child's rights under the European Convention, art 8, against the right to freedom of expression.

child minding and day care. The Chief Inspector is obliged to register those who act as child minders and who provide day care for children under eight on premises (other than domestic) within an authority's area: Ch.A. 1989, s 79A, inserted by Care Standards Act 2000, s 79. For definition of 'child minder', see s 79A(2). For cancellation of registration, see s 79G. For disqualification from working with children, see C.J.C.S.A. 2000, ss 28, 29.

child, offence against. Means under C.J.C.S.A. 2000, s 26(1): an offence mentioned in Sch 4, para 1, an offence committed against a child, mentioned in Sch 4, para 2, or that the offender falls within Sch 4, para 3.

child of the family. In relation to the parties to a marriage, means, under Ch.A. 1989, s 105(1), a child of both of those parties or any other child, not boarded out with those parties, who has been treated by them as a child of their family. See *Re A (Child of the Family)* [1998] Fam Law 14. Under the Civil Partnership Act 2004 s 101(7) a 'child of the family' means a child under the age of 16 years who has been accepted by both civil partners as a child of the family, and 'family' means the civil partners in the civil partnership, together with any child so accepted by them: s 101 (7) C.P.A 2004.

child, parental responsibility for. If a child's parents were married to each other at the time of his birth, they each have parental responsibility: Ch.A. 1989, s 2; otherwise the mother only has it: s 2(2). The father is not the 'natural guardian' of his legitimate child: s 2(4). Parental responsibility means all the rights and duties, powers, responsibilities and authority which by law a parent has in relation to the child and his property: s 3(1). Rights in the exercise of parental responsibility are subordinate to the child's welfare: *Re A (Children)* (2000) 150 NLJ 1453 (lawfulness of operation to separate conjoined twins). A person with parental responsibility may not act in any way which would be incompatible with any order made under the Act: s 2(8). See *Re H (A Minor) (Parental Responsibility)* [1998] 1 FLR 855; *M* v *M (Parental Responsibility)* [1999] 2 FLR 737; *Re X (A Minor) (Care Proceedings: Parental Responsibility)* (2000) *The Times*, 19 January (right of mother to enter into a parental responsibility agreement with unmarried father).

child, parental responsibility of unmarried father. The father shall acquire parental responsibility for the child if (a) he becomes registered as the child's father under any of the enactments specified in subsection (1A Children Act 1989); (b) he and the child's mother make an agreement (a 'parental responsibility agreement') providing for him to have parental responsibility for the child; or (c) the court, on his application, orders that he shall have parental responsibility for the child: s 111 A.C.A. 2002.

child, presence at criminal trial. A child should not be present at a criminal trial except where required as a witness or otherwise for the purposes of justice or while the court consents to his presence: C.&Y.P.A. 1933, s 36, amended by Acc.J.A. 1999, s 73(1).

children. Refers, in general, to descendants of the first degree. See *Re Coley* [1901] 1 Ch 40.

Children and Family Court Advisory and Support Service. Set up in April 2001 under C.J.C.S.A. 2000, s 11, to safeguard and promote children's welfare, and to advise courts on applications in proceedings; see Sch 2. For inspection of service, see Justices of the Peace Act 1997, s 62(3A) inserted by C.J.C.S.A. 2000, s 17(1).

children and young persons, policy of courts towards. Every court in dealing with a child (i.e., a person under 14) or young person (i.e., a person who has attained the age of 14 and is under 18) who is brought before it, either as an offender or otherwise, shall have regard to the welfare of the child or young person and shall, in a proper case, take steps for removing him from undesirable surroundings and for securing that proper provision is made for his education and training: C.&Y.P.A. 1933, s 44(1) as amended.

children, freedom of publication relating to. In *Re S (A Child) (Identification)* the HL held that, given the right to private and family life, guaranteed under the European Convention, art 8, the rights of a child where mother was to be brought to trial for the murder of her son, were effectively outweighed under art 10 of the Convention in relation to press freedom to publish.

children, harm to. The ill-treatment or impairment of health or development of a child: Ch.A. 1989, s 31(9). 'Development' involves physical, intellectual, emotional, social or behavioural development; 'health' means physical or mental health; 'ill-treatment' includes sexual abuse and forms of ill-treatment which are not physical: s 31(9). See *Lancashire CC v A* [2000] 1 FCR 509.

children, indecency with. *See* GROSS INDECENCY.

children, indecent photographs of. It is an offence for a person to take, or permit to be taken, any indecent photograph of a person under the age of 16, or to distribute or show such a photograph, or to have such a photograph in his possession with a view to its being distributed or shown by himself or others, or to advertise that he distributes, shows or intends to show such a photograph: Protection of Children Act 1978, s 1(1); C.J.A. 1988, s 160; C.J.C.S.A. 2000, s 41. Applies also to pseudo-photographs: C.J.P.O.A. 1994, s 84. For defences, see s 1(4). See *R v T (Child Pornography)* [1999] Crim LR 749; *R v Bowden* [1999] 12 CL 108 (downloading indecent images of children from the internet is capable of constituting an offence under the 1978 Act, s 1); *Atkins v DPP* (2000) *The Times*, 16 March (no offence unless defendant knew he had photographs in his possession); *R v Toomer* (2000) *The Times*, 21 November (significance for sentencing of evidence of large-scale commercial distribution).

children in need, services and accommodation for. It is the general duty of every local authority to provide an appropriate range and level of services to safeguard the welfare of children in need and to promote the upbringing of such children by their families: Ch.A. 1989, s 17. For provision of accommodation, see s 20. A 'child in need' is one who is disabled or whose health or development may be significantly impaired without the provision of services by a local authority: s 17(10). Under Ch.A. 1989, Sch 2, Part II, paras 19A, 19B, 19C (inserted by Ch. (Leaving Care) A. 2000, s 1), it is a duty of the local authority looking after a child to advise, assist and befriend him with a view to promoting his welfare when they have ceased to look after him; a personal adviser for such a child is to be appointed.

children, list of those unsuitable to work with. List kept by Secretary of State under Protection of Children Act 1999, s 1. Names on the Consultancy Services Index are to be transferred to the list. Child care organisations (q.v.)

shall, and other organisations may, refer to Secretary of State, name of individual employed in child care position (q.v.) if, e.g., he has been dismissed by the organisation on grounds of misconduct which harmed a child or placed a child at risk of harm: s 2(1), (2). For appeals against inclusion, see s 4. *See* CHILDREN, HARM TO.

children, rights of. In *Moat Housing Marketing Group* v *Harris* (2005) *The Times*, 13 January, the CA held that where the court is deliberating the grant of a stay pending a possession order, the presence of children and any likely prejudice to them should be taken into consideration.

Children's Commissioner. The Commissioner has the function of promoting awareness of the views and interests of children in England. In particular to encourage persons exercising functions or engaged in activities affecting children to take account of their views and interests; advise the Secretary of State on the views and interests of children; consider or research the operation of complaints procedures so far as relating to children; consider or research any other matter relating to the interests of children and publish a report on any matter considered or researched by him under this section: Children Act 2004, s 2.

children's homes. Homes which provide care and accommodation wholly for children (i.e., persons under 18): Care Standards Act 2000, s 1(1). Schools, health service and independent hospitals, residential family centres are not included: s 1(3). Must be registered under s 11. For regulations, see s 22. For failure to comply with conditions, see s 24.

children, suitability for work with. Under Ch.A. 1989, s 79W, inserted by Care Standards Act 2000, s 79, persons who look after or provide care for children and are not required to register under 1989 Act, Part X, and spend more than five hours weekly looking after children and would be required to register if the children were under eight, must obtain certificate of suitability from the registration authority.

child safety order. Order made by magistrates' court, on application by local authority, placing child under supervision of responsible officer, where child has committed an act which would have constituted an offence had he been over 10, or where order is necessary to prevent such an act, or child has contravened curfew notice, and has acted in a manner that caused or was likely to cause harassment, alarm or distress to one or more persons not of the same household as himself.

child, sexual abuse of. *See* CHILD ABUSE; PAEDOPHILE.

child's interests, relevance of. Although the best interests of a child in relation to whom an anti-social behaviour order had been requested were a primary consideration in the making of such an order, they were not to be considered as the sole primary consideration, since the interests of the public were also a primary consideration: *R(A)* v *Leeds Magistrates Court* (2004) *The Times*, 31 March.

child's schooling. Where parents share responsibility for a child and they have asked court to settle a dispute concerning schooling, court must not neglect its primary responsibility to decide that dispute; parents had right to a judicial determination: *Re P (A Child) (Parental Dispute: Judicial Determination)* (2002) *The Times*, 5 November.

Child Support Agency. Agency empowered to obtain information required by the Secretary of State in the context of the Child Support Act 1991, and to administer that Act in relation to the assessment of maintenance liability. See also Child Support Act 1995; S.S.A. 1998, ss 40–44; W.R.P.A. 1999, s 80, inserting in 1991 Act, Sch 2, para 1A, permitting Inland Revenue to disclose to Child Support Agency earnings of self-employed absent parents; C.S.P.S.S.A. 2000. *See* MAINTAIN, LIABILITY TO.

child support claim, right to enforce. In *Regina (Kehoe)* v *Secretary of State for Work and Pensions* [2005] *The Times*, 15 July, the HL held that it was the responsibility of the child support agency to assess, collect and enforce maintenance payments, and that a caring parent had no right to enforce a claim for maintenance payment against a non-resident parent.

child support liability. In *M* v *Secretary of State for Pensions* (2004) *The Times*, 11 November, the CA held that, in relation to assessing child support liability, it would be considered discriminatory if an absent parent's household costs were estimated differently, based upon their being a homosexual or heterosexual household.

child support, maintenance calculations. See Child Support Act 1991, s 11, substituted by C.S.P.S.S.A. 2000, s 1. Fixed by reference to 2000 Act, Sch 1. Weekly rate is the basic rate unless a reduced rate, flat rate, or nil rate applies. Basic rate is the following percentage of the non-resident parent's net weekly income: 15% where he has one qualifying child; 20% where he has two; 25% where he has three or more. See Sch 1, paras 1–4. For default and interim maintenance decisions, see 2000 Act, s 4. For variation of rules, see s 5. For appeals, see s 10. For financial penalties, see 2000 Act, s 18. *See* MAINTAIN, LIABILITY TO.

child support officers. Appointed by Secretary of State, under Child Support Act 1991, s 13, with functions in relation to maintenance of 'qualifying children' (see 1991 Act, s 3(2)). *See* MAINTAIN, LIABILITY TO.

child support, payments. In *M* v *Secretary of State for Work and Pensions* [2006] *The Times*, 14 March, the HL held that the child support scheme did not discriminate when calculating child support then, against a non-resident divorced parent who was in a same sex relationship compared to the level of contribution that would have been calculated were she in a heterosexual relationship.

child's welfare. *See* WELFARE OF A CHILD.

child tax credit. Introduced under Tax Credits Act 2002, Part I, and involving imposition of an income test on claimants, in relation, generally, to children under 16. Claim may be made

jointly by members of a married or unmarried couple, both of whom are at least 16 and are in UK. 'Unmarried couple' means a man and a woman who are not a married couple but are living together as husband and wife: 2002 Act, s 3(6).

child, transfer of cases involving. Under C.J.A. 1991, s 53, amended by C.D.A. 1998, Sch 8, para 93, where a person is charged with an offence involving sexual matters and offences involving cruelty or violence, and DPP believes that evidence of the offence would suffice for committal for trial of accused and that a child is alleged to be the victim and will be called as a witness, he may give notice of transfer of the case to the Crown Court to be heard without delay.

Chiltern Hundreds. The voluntary retirement of an MP is not permitted; but he can retire, in effect, by accepting an office of profit under the Crown (which is incompatible with membership of the Commons), i.e., the nominal office of 'Steward or Bailiff of Her Majesty's three Chiltern Hundreds of Stoke, Desborough and Burnham' – a sinecure office with only nominal duties and fees. See House of Commons Disqualification Act 1975, s 4. *See* OFFICE OF PROFIT.

chinese wall. Colloquialism referring to arrangements within solicitors' and barristers' offices, seeking to ensure that confidentiality of clients' information is effectively protected where members of a firm are working on opposite sides in the same case. See *Prince Jefri Balkiah* v *KPMG* [1999] 2 AC 222; *Koch Shipping* v *Richards Butler* [2002] EWCA Civ 1280.

chirograph. A deed written on a sheet of paper which was then divided, with 'chirographum' (i.e., 'autograph') written in capital letters between the division. A part was given to each party. An indented cutting was known as an 'indenture' (q.v.).

Chivalry, Court of. *See* COURT OF CHIVALRY.

chose. A thing. 1. A *chose in action*, i.e., 'when any man hath cause, or may bring an action for some duty due to him': *Termes de la Ley*. 'All personal rights of property which can only be claimed or enforced by action, and not by taking physical possession': *per* Channell J in *Torkington* v *Magee* [1902] 2 KB 427. Examples: debts, patents, trade marks, copyrights. See *Chan Man-Sin* v *A-G of Hong Kong* [1988] 1 All ER 1 (theft of chose in action). 2. A *chose in possession* is a movable chattel, the right in which can be enforced by taking physical possession. Example: one's goods.

Church of England. The established national church of which the Sovereign, who is the supreme head, must always be a member (Act of Settlement 1700, s 3). Organised in episcopal fashion, into dioceses (43) grouped into two provinces (Canterbury and York). Dioceses are subdivided into 14,300 parishes. The central governing body is the General Synod. Doctrine is governed by the Thirty-nine Articles (see 13 Eliz. 1 c. 12). Ecclesiastical law of the Church is a part of the law of the land: *Mackonochie* v *Lord Penzance* (1881) 16 App Cas 4. For 'communicant member', see Patronage (Benefices) Measure 1986, s 39(1).

c.i.f. contract. Cost, insurance, freight. If a merchant agrees to sell goods 'at £x per unit c.i.f. Liverpool Docks', the sum includes price of the goods, insurance premium and freight payable to Liverpool Docks. Generally, property in the goods passes to the buyer on shipment. See *The Wise* [1989] 2 Lloyd's Rep 451.

circuit judges. Some 560 judges appointed by the Queen on recommendation of the Lord Chancellor from those who have a ten-year Crown Court or ten-year County Court qualification (see C.L.S.A. 1990, s 71) or hold the position of Recorder (q.v.) or who have held a full-time appointment for at least three years in one of the offices listed in the Courts Act 1971, Sch 1, Part 1A, inserted by C.L.S.A. 1990, Sch 10. See S.C.A. 1981, s 8. For each circuit there are at least two presiding judges appointed by the Lord Chancellor from among the puisne judges of the High Court: C.L.S.A. 1990,

s 72. For removal of a circuit judge from office, following his conviction, see *The Times*, 6 December 1983.

circuit system. The country is divided into circuits for the purpose of hearing criminal and civil cases: South-Eastern, Midland and Oxford, Northern, North-Eastern, Western, Wales and Chester. Circuit committees were set up in 1972, under the Courts Act 1971, s 30, to advise the Lord Chancellor on such questions 'as he may from time to time refer to them'.

circulars, government. Communications published by government departments to local authorities, etc., relating, e.g., to statements of government policy. They have been held to constitute delegated legislation: *Jackson, Stansfield & Sons* v *Butterworth* [1948] 2 All ER 558. Judicial review (q.v.) may extend to departmental 'guidance circulars' issued without specific authority: *Gillick* v *W. Norfolk HA* [1986] AC 112. See *R* v *Secretary of State for Home Department ex p Lancs Police Authority* (1991) *The Times*, 19 November (circulars should be construed in the way in which an educated person, acquainted with the factual context, would construe them, by giving to them their commonsense meaning).

circumstantial evidence. *See* EVIDENCE, CIRCUMSTANTIAL.

citation. 1. Summons giving notice to a person to appear before the court. 2. Notice issued by an executor applying for probate (q.v.) in solemn form, calling upon persons to appear and show why probate should not be granted. 3. The referring to a decided case of legal authority in support of an argument. See *Practice Note (Court of Appeal: Citation of Reports)* [1995] 3 All ER 256; *Hamblin* v *Field* (2000) *The Times*, 26 April (Court of Appeal deplored excessive citation of authorities). See *R* v *Sheffield Stipendiary Magistrate ex p Stephens* (1992) 156 JP 555 (excessive citing of cases). *See* LAW REPORTS; UNREPORTED CASES.

citation of Act. *See* STATUTE, CITATION OF.

citation of cases, neutral. *Practice Direction* [2001] 1 WLR 194 orders that, from 11 January 2001, all High Court and Court of Appeal judgments must have media citations, involving, e.g., use of paragraph numbering instead of page numbering. It was emphasised that reports in the official Law Report Series should be cited in preference to any other reports.

citation of cases, rules. *Practice Direction (Citation of Cases)* [2001] 2 All ER 510, states that in order to limit citation of previous authority to cases of relevance and use to the court, rules applying to all courts except criminal courts would ensure that, in future: judgments in certain types of application and most county court cases, could not be cited unless they indicated clearly that they purported to set out a new principle or to extend existing law; advocates would be required to state the proposition of law that an authority demonstrated and the parts of the judgment supporting that proposition; where more than one authority in support of a proposition is to be cited, reasons for so doing must be stated.

citizen, British Overseas. A citizen of the UK and Colonies who did not become a British citizen or a British Dependent Territories citizen when B.N.A. 1981 came into operation, becomes a British Overseas citizen: s 26.

citizen's arrest. An arrest (q.v.) by a person other than a police officer where a breach of the peace (q.v.) is reasonably feared, or has been committed, and there are reasonable grounds to fear its continuation or repetition. *See* ARREST, COMMON-LAW POWER OF.

citizenship, British, acquisition by birth or adoption. After commencement of B.N.A. 1981, a person born in the UK is ·a British citizen if at the time of his birth his father or mother is a British citizen, or settled in Britain, or if he is a foundling, or if he is born in the UK and one of his parents subsequently becomes settled here or if he becomes settled here or if he becomes registered as a British citizen, or

if he is adopted in the UK and the adopter is a British citizen: s 1. See Adoption (Intercountry Aspects) Act 1999, s 7.

citizenship, British, acquisition by descent. A child born overseas is a British citizen if, at his birth, one of his parents is British (though not by descent) or is employed overseas in the service of the British Government or the E.C: B.N.A. 1981, s 2. For classes of persons regarded as British citizens by descent, see s 14. See R v *Secretary of State for Home Department ex p Ullah* (2000) *The Times*, 17 October.

citizenship, British, acquisition by registration. British Dependent Territories citizens, or British Overseas citizens, or British subjects or British protected persons may apply for registration as British citizens after satisfying certain residential period and other requirements (five years' presence in the UK, etc.). See B.N.A. 1981, ss 4, 5, 7, 8 (registration by virtue of marriage), 9, 10.

citizenship, British, acquisition by registration of minor. The Secretary of State may register any minor as a British citizen on application. A minor born abroad may be registered as a British citizen, within 12 months of his birth, or, where he is stateless, and one of his parents is a British citizen by descent and a grandparent was a British citizen otherwise than by descent: B.N.A. 1981, s 3. See also s 32.

citizenship, British, automatic acquisition of. British citizenship is acquired automatically by all those citizens of the UK and Colonies who had the right of abode (see Immigration Act 1971, s 2) in the UK at the commencement of B.N.A. 1981: s 11. For exceptions, see s 11(2).

citizenship, British, Dependent Territories. Status bestowed under B.N.A. 1981, Part II, in certain circumstances on those living in the dependent territories, e.g., Bermuda, Falkland Islands, Gibraltar. See B.N.A. 1981, Sch 6; B.N. (Hong Kong) A. 1997.

citizenship, British, renunciation and resumption of. Under B.N.A. 1981, s 12, a person may renounce his citizenship if he has, or expects to acquire, another nationality or citizenship. Under s 13, he may resume citizenship (on one occasion only) if he is of full capacity and the renunciation was necessary to enable him to retain or acquire some other citizenship or nationality.

citizenship, Commonwealth. Every person who, under B.N.A. 1981, is a British citizen, or British Overseas citizen, or a British subject or a citizen of a country listed in Sch 3, has the status of Commonwealth citizen: s 37 (as amended by B.N. (Falklands) A. 1983, s 4).

citizenship, deprivation of. *See* DEPRIVATION OF CITIZENSHIP.

citizenship of European Union. *See* EUROPEAN UNION, CITIZENSHIP OF.

City of London. An area of London (including the financial centre) of 670 acres with its own administrative government consisting of a Lord Mayor (who is Head of the Corporation of London), Court of Aldermen, common councillors and the city companies.

civil. Opposite sense of, e.g., criminal (as in a civil action) or military.

Civil Appeals Offices. Administrative centre of Court of Appeal (Civil Division), directed by Head of Civil Appeals Office who, when acting in a judicial capacity, is known as a 'master': PD Court of Appeal, para 1.3.

civil case, scooping of. In *R (Mathialogan)* v *Southwark LBC* (2004) *The Times*, 2 December, the CA held that there was no general power enabling magistrates to reopen and rehear a civil case.

civil commotion. A serious riot, falling short of attempted insurrection. 'The disturbances must have sufficient cohesion to prevent them from being the work of a mindless mob': *per* Mustill J in *Spinney's Ltd* v *Royal Insurance Co* [1980] 1 Lloyd's Rep 406.

civil disobedience. 'A public, non-violent, conscientious yet political act contrary to law, usually done with the aim of bringing about a change in the law or policies of the government': Rawls, *A Theory of Justice* (1971).

civil evidence, similar fact. In *O'Brien* v *Chief Constable of S Wales Constabulary* (2003) *The Times*, 22 August, the CA held that, if similar fact evidence is to be admissible, it ought to be logically probative of some relevant matter in the case. The need to deal with the case in a just manner had to be kept in mind

civilian. 1. One who is versed in Roman, i.e., civil, law (q.v.). 2. One who is not a member of the military forces.

Civil Justice Council. Advisory body, set up under Civil Procedure Act 1997, s 6, to keep the civil justice system under review, to advise the Lord Chancellor (q.v.) and the judiciary on the development of the civil justice system and to refer proposals for change to the Lord Chancellor and the Civil Procedure Rule Committee (q.v.). It includes members of the judiciary and legal profession and persons with experience in consumer affairs and administration of the courts.

civil law. 1. 'The law each people has settled for itself, peculiar to the State itself': Justinian's *Institutes* (533). 2. The entire *corpus* of Roman Law. 3. Non-military law. 4. Non-criminal law, generally relating to the interactions of individual citizens. 5. Legal systems, often codified, based originally on Roman law.

civil legal aid and power of court. In *Re Perotti* (2003) *The Times*, 27 November, the CA held that the question of funding of legal representation in civil proceedings was for the Legal Services Commission, since the courts were not empowered to give a litigant representation of this nature.

Civil List. An annual appropriation charged on the Consolidated Fund (q.v.), received by the Crown for purposes of maintaining the royal household, etc.

civil marriage. *See* MARRIAGE, CIVIL.

civil partnership. A relationship between two people of the same sex ('civil partners'), formed by registration of each as a civil partner of the other, which will only end on dissolution, annulment or death. Civil Partnership Act 2004, s 1 (C.P.A. 2004).

Civil Procedure Rule Committee. Body set up under Civil Procedure Act

1997, s 2, including, among others, the Master of the Rolls (q.v.), the Vice-Chancellor, a judge of the Supreme Court, a Circuit judge, a district judge and a person with knowledge of consumer affairs. They must try to make rules 'which are both simple and simply expressed': s 7.

Civil Procedure Rules. See CPR 1998.

civil remedy. A remedy available to a private individual as the outcome of civil proceedings, e.g., damages, compensation, order of specific performance, injunction, declarations as to rights. See Civil Procedure Act 1997; CPR 1998.

Civil Service. The body of servants of the Crown, some 597,000 (other than, e.g., those holding political or judicial office or members of HM Forces) who serve in a civil capacity and are paid wholly and directly out of money voted annually by Parliament. The Civil Service Appeal Board is a judicial, independent public law body, established under the prerogative powers of the Crown: *R v CSAB ex p Cunningham* [1991] IRLR 297. See *Vougioukas v IKA* [1996] ICR 913.

civil wrong. A tort (q.v.).

claim. 1. The demand or assertion of a right. 2. A privilege (q.v.). 3. Under CPR 1998, replaces the term 'action'.

claim, admissions in relation to. A party may admit the whole or part of another's case at any time during proceedings: CPR, r 14.1(1). Written notice should be given: r 14.1(2). Claimant may then apply for judgment. For admission of an entire claim for a specified sum, see r 14.4; for admission of part of a claim in relation to a specific sum, see r 14.5; in relation to an unspecified sum, see r 14.6.

claimant. The party who makes a claim: see CPR, r 2.3(1). Formerly known as 'plaintiff'. Parties to applications are known also as 'applicant' and 'respondent': r 23.1.

claimant, absence in court of. A judge should not, in the exercise of his discretion, strike out a claim because of claimant's absence if he is represented in court by his legal representatives: *Rouse v Freeman* (2002) *The Times*, 8 January.

claim, defence to. Classified under CPR, r 2.3(1) as a 'statement of case' (q.v.) which must be verified by a 'statement of truth' (q.v.). Must be filed by defendant who intends to defend a claim partially or wholly; default judgment may follow on failure to file: r 15.2. Period for filing defence is 14 days after service of particulars of claim; extension of 14 days may be claimed after acknowledgement of service; defendant and claimant may agree on a 28-day extension (r 15.5). For stay of claim where no action is taken, see r 15.11. Defence must admit or deny allegations, or ask that claimant prove them (r 16.5(1)). Denial implies that defendant will disprove allegations. See PD 15.

claim, discontinuance of. See DISCONTINUANCE OF CLAIM.

claim form and particulars of claim. Form, under CPR, containing: brief details of claim (r 16.2(a)); remedy sought (r 16.2(1)(b)); statement of value where claim is for money (r 16.2(1)(c)); statement of truth (q.v.). Particulars of claim, which can be served separately from claim form, must include: concise statement of facts on which claimant is relying (r 16.4(1)(a)); details of any interest claimed; statement that provisional, aggravated or exemplary damages are being claimed; value of goods, where claim involves recovery of possession; allegations, if any, of fraud, details of misrepresentation, unlawful default, etc.; reference to points of law on which claim is based; names of witnesses claimant wishes to call. See PD 16.

claim form, Part 7, issue of. Proceedings under CPR generally commence with court issuing a claim form: r 7.2(1). Claimant takes copy of form to the court, seal is affixed, date of issue is entered on form. It must be served on defendant within four months from issue (or six months if service is out of the jurisdiction). Particulars, if served separately, must be served within 14 days of service of claim form. Application to extend time for service may be made under r 7.6: *Smith* v *Probyn* (2000) *The Times*, 29 March. Part 7 claim may be used where claim is for a specified or unspecified amount of money or for a non-monetary claim.

claim, new. An amendment constituting what is effectively a new claim may be allowed 'only if the new claim arises out of the same facts or substantially the same facts as a claim in respect of which the party applying for permission has already claimed a remedy in the proceedings': CPR, r 17.4(2). See *Paragon Finance plc v Thakerar* [1999] 1 All ER 400.

claim of privilege. See PRIVILEGE, CLAIM OF.

claim, Part 8 procedure, relating to alternative. Under CPR, Part 8, a special procedure exists where claimant seeks the court's decision on a question likely to involve a substantial dispute of fact or a rule or PD requires or permits use of that procedure. Procedure may be used, e.g., in a claim by or against a child or mental patient settled before start of proceedings and where court's approval is needed, or claim for summary possession of poverty against squatters where dispute concerning facts is not likely to be substantial. A party may apply to the court for directions immediately a Part 8 claim form is issued; the court may also give such directions on its own initiative. A multi-track procedure is likely to follow. See PD 8.

claim, service of. Service, under CPR, may be made by the court (generally) by post (PD 6, para 8.1) or by a claimant, e.g., by personal service (on defendant or solicitor), first-class post, fax, leaving document at a specified place. See r 6.2; PD 6, para 3. Where statute authorises or requires a document to be served by post, that service is deemed to be effected by properly addressing, pre-paying, and posting a letter containing the document: I.A. 1978, s 7. Acknowledgment of service may be made by defendant if he wishes to do so; or he may immediately file and serve his defence. Under r 10.3(1), any acknowledgment should be made within 14 days following service; intention to defend all or part of claim should be

stated. For service by document exchange, e-mail, fax, see PD 6. Where particulars of claim follow claim form they must be served within four months of issue of claim form or, where service is outside the jurisdiction, six months: PD 7, para 6.1(2) as amended (see CP (Amendment) R 2000 (SI 00/22)). See *Cadogan Properties v Mount Eden Land* [1999] CPLR 476; *Molins plc v GD Spa* (2000) *The Times*, 1 March (service by fax). In *Kuenyehia and Others v International Hospitals Group Ltd* [2006] *The Times*, 17 February, the CA held that service by fax is prohibited unless written consent of the person being served is first obtained. Failure to do so was no more than a minor departure from the provisions in the Practice Directions. In *Collier v Williams, Marshall and Another v Maggs, Leeson v Marsden and Another and Glass v Surrendran* [2006] *The Times*, 3 February, the CA provided guidance on the courts' approach to rules relating to service, extending time for service of a claim form and cases where a without notice application had been refused on paper.

claims, small. See SMALL CLAIMS, TRACK.

claim, starting of. Under CPR, a claim is started in High Court or county court by presenting copies of a completed claim to the court office, serving an issued claim form on defendant, together with claim particulars.

claim, statement of. See CASE, STATE-MENT OF.

claim, transfer of. Claim for unspecified amount of money may be transferred to an individual's home court: CPR, r 26.2(1). Transfer may be made on application by a party or by court acting on its own initiative: r 30(2). See County Courts Act 1984, ss 40(2), 41(1), 42(2). Court's decision to transfer reflects claim's financial value, importance of claim to public, complexity of legal issues involved: r 30(3).

clandestine entrant. One who arrives in UK concealed in a vehicle, ship or aircraft, passes or attempts to pass, through immigration control concealed in a vehicle, or arrives in UK on a ship or aircraft, having embarked concealed on a vehicle, and at a time when the ship or aircraft was outside UK, and claims, or indicates that he intends to seek, asylum in UK or evades, or attempts to evade immigration control: Immigration and Asylum Act 1999, s 32(1). For penalties for carrying clandestine entrants, see 1999 Act, Part II. For code of practice for preventing carriage of clandestine entrants, see SI 00/684.

class action. Claim brought by one person or a small group on behalf of the interests of a large group.

class closing rules. Rules of construction based on *Andrews* v *Partington* (1791) 3 Bro CC 401, relating to gifts to a class (e.g., 'the children of A and B who shall attain 21') and to perpetuities (q.v.). Thus, a class will be closed artificially when one member is entitled to be paid, having attained a vested interest. They will not be applied where there is evidence of a contrary intention: see *Re Tom's Settlement* [1987] 1 WLR 1021; *Re Drummond* [1988] 1 WLR 134.

class gift. A gift is said to be to a class of persons when it is 'to all those who shall come within a certain category or description defined by a general or collective formula, and who, if they take at all, are to take one divisible subject in certain proportionate shares': *Pearkes* v *Moseley* (1880) 5 App Cas 714. Example: 'to all my sons who shall live to the age of 30'. It is contingent until the identity of every member of the class is ascertained. See P.&A.A. 1964, s 4; *Re Clifford's ST* [1980] 1 All ER 1013; *Re Tom's Settlement* [1987] 1 WLR 1021.

class rights. Rights attached to different classes of share (q.v.), concerning, e.g., voting, dividends, as set out in a memorandum and articles of association (qq.v.) or terms of share issue. See Cos.A. 1985, ss 125–129.

clause. A subdivision of a document; an individual section of a Parliamentary Bill.

clean break, future. In *Parlour* v *Parlour* (2004) *The Times*, 9 July, the CA held that where unusual circumstances apply in a divorce case, so that the payer's

income is significantly greater than the combined outgoings of payer and payee, and where, in spite of a very large capital base available for division, a clean break could not be considered as currently practicable, the court has an obligation to consider the future possibility of a clean break.

clean break principle. Concept in family law of encouraging spouses to diminish the bitterness of family breakdown by making a clean break with the past: see *Minton* v *Minton* [1979] AC 593; *Clutton* v *Clutton* [1991] 1 All ER 340. See Mat.C.A. 1973, s 25A(1).

clean hands. He who comes into equity must come with clean hands, i.e., the claimant must have a clear conscience as regards the past. See *Quadrant Communications Ltd* v *Hutchinson Telegraph Ltd* [1993] BCLC 442; *Memory Corporation* v *Sidhu* (2000) *The Times*, 15 February (the doctrine should not be pressed too far: *per* Walker LJ).

clearance area. Term used in H.A. 1985 to refer to an area made the subject of a declaration by the local authority (q.v.) if satisfied that, e.g., houses in the area are unfit for human habitation and ought to be demolished and that alternative accommodation can be made available for those who will be displaced, and that the authority has sufficient resources for this purpose.

clear days. Generally, days reckoned exclusively of those on which anything is begun and terminated.

clergy, disqualification of. A person is no longer disqualified from being or being elected as member of the House of Commons merely because he has been ordained or is a minister of any religious denomination; but this does not apply to the Lords Spiritual: House of Commons (Removal of Clergy Disqualification) Act 2001, s 1(1), (2).

clerks, judges'. *See* JUDGES' CLERKS.

clerk to the justices. *See* MAGISTRATES' CLERK.

client. In relation to contentious business (q.v.), any person who as principal or on behalf of another person retains or employs a solicitor, and any person who is liable to pay a solicitor's costs. In relation to non-contentious business, any person who as principal or on behalf of another has express or implied power to retain or employ, and does retain or employ, a solicitor, and any person liable to pay a solicitor's costs: Solicitors Act 1974, s 87. Under CPR and PD 22, para 2.1, a client must verify every statement of case by a statement of truth (q.v.). See CPR, r 1.3: 'The parties are required to help the court to further the overriding objective.'

client, advice to under CPR. There is a requirement under CPR that clients be advised of duties, e.g., in relation to statement of truth (r 22.1(4)); in relation to duty of search concerning disclosure of documents (r 31.2); rules concerning court sanctions (r 3.4(2)(c)).

climate change levy. Tax imposed under Finance Act 2000, s 30, and charged in accordance with Sch 6, para 3(1), on specified taxable supplies of electricity, made by an electricity utility; of gas, made by a gas utility (but excluding suppliers for domestic or charity use); of petroleum gas in liquid state; of coke, semi-coke, and petroleum coke. Hydrocarbon oil, road fuel gas, are exempted: Sch 6, para 3(2).

Clinical Disputes Forum. A multi-disciplinary body, founded in 1997, which has issued a pre-action protocol (q.v.) for the resolution of clinical disputes, with the general aims of maintaining/restoring the patient/health care provider relationship, and of resolving as many disputes as possible without litigation.

clogging the equity of redemption. No agreement which clogs the equity, i.e., which makes a mortgage irredeemable, will be recognised by the courts. See *Kreglinger* v *New Patagonia Meat Co* [1914] AC 25; *Lewis* v *Frank Love Ltd* [1961] 1 WLR 261. *See* MORTGAGE.

cloning, human reproductive. It is an offence under Human Reproductive Cloning Act 2001, s 1(1), to place in a woman's womb a human embryo which has been created otherwise than by fertilisation.

close. 1. Enclosed land. 2. Termination of proceedings.

close company. A company which, for purposes of corporation tax, is considered as under the control of five or fewer participators or by any number of participators who are directors or, if on a winding-up, the larger part of the assets will ultimately be distributed to five or fewer participators (disregarding the rights of any loan creditors): I.C.T.A. 1988, ss 414–430, as amended; *Collins* v *Addies* [1991] BTC 244. The term does not apply to a company not resident in the UK. A 'participator' is, e.g., one who owns share capital and has voting rights in the company, or a loan creditor of the company (except where the loan arises in the ordinary course of banking). *See* COMPANY.

close connection principle. Principle enunciated by Canadian Supreme Court in *Bazley* v *Curry* (1999) 174 DLR (4th) 45, considering circumstances in which it might be fair for an employer who was not at fault to bear responsibility for the tortious conduct of an employee. Applied by House of Lords in *Lister* v *Hesley Hall* (2001) 151 NLJ 728 (and overturning *Trotman* v *N Yorks CC* [1999] LGR 584). In determining whether the wrongful act of an employee has been committed in the course of his employment, it is important to consider the closeness of the connection between the essence of the employment and the tort in question by examining the work on which the employee was engaged for his employer.

closed-shop agreement. An agreement, not illegal but not generally enforceable, whereby employers agree to employ only union members. It is now unlawful to refuse a person employment on grounds related to union membership: T.U.L.R.(C.)A. 1992, s 137.

closing order. An order prohibiting the use of the premises to which it relates for any purposes not approved by the local housing authority (q.v.): H.A. 1985, s 267(2). Refers also to a local authority order relating to shops' closing hours (see Shops Act 1950). See *Taggart* v *Leeds CC* [1999] EHLR 185.

closing speeches. Speeches by each side before the summing-up. Generally, prosecuting counsel speaks first; defence usually has the right to the final word to the jury: Criminal Procedure (Right of Reply) Act 1964. For restrictions on prosecuting counsel's right, see e.g. Criminal Evidence Act 1898, s 3 (repealed in part by 1964 Act); C.J.A. 1948, s 42(1); *R v Mondon* [1969] 52 Cr App R 695; *R v Pink* [1971] 1 QB 508.

clothing, touching of. In *R v H (Sexual Assault: Touching)* (2005) *The Times*, 8 February, the CA held that, in relation to Sexual Offences Act 2003, s 78(b) (Sexual touching of clothing) it was necessary to establish whether the touching might be sexual and whether, given the circumstances, it was sexual.

club. A voluntary association of persons meeting together for recreational or social purposes. Members are generally liable only to the extent of their subscriptions to a common fund. The remedy for wrongful expulsion is a declaration or injunction (q.v.). See *Lee v Showmen's Guild of Great Britain* [1952] 2 QB 329.

Cm; Cmd; Cmnd. Abbreviations for Command Papers. *See* COMMAND PAPERS, NUMBERING OF; PARLIAMENTARY PAPERS.

coastal land. The foreshore, and land adjacent to the foreshore including any cliff, bank, barrier dune or flat: C.R.W.A. 2000, s 3(3).

coastal waters. In relation to the UK, Channel Islands and Isle of Man, so much of the waters adjoining the countries respectively as is within the fishery limits of the British Isles and, in relation to any other country, so much of the waters adjoining that country as is within the distance, to which provisions of the law of that country corresponding to the provisions of the 1934 Act extend: Whaling Industry (Regulation) Act 1934, s 17; Fishery Limits Act 1964, s 3(3); Water Resources Act 1991, s 104(1).

code. A systematical collection, in comprehensive form, of laws, e.g., the Code of Hammurabi (eighteenth century BC),

produced in Mesopotamia, the *Code Napoléon* (1804).

code of practice. Rules of practical guidance with respect to the requirements of some statute, or to professional standards of behaviour. See, e.g., the Highway Code (q.v.); City Code on Takeovers and Mergers. Failure to observe a code does not generally render a person liable to proceedings, but it may be admissible in evidence. See *R v Spens* [1991] 1 WLR 625. For approved codes of practice under H.S.W.A. 1974, ss 2–7, 16, see, e.g., Control of Asbestos at Work Regulations 1987 (SI 87/2115).

codicil. 'An addition or supplement added into a will or testament after the finishing of it, for the supply of something which the testator had forgotten, or to help some defect in the will': *Termes de la Ley*. It must be executed with all the formalities appropriate to the execution of a will. *See* TESTAMENT; WILL.

codifying statute. An Act which codifies the whole of case and statute law on a particular matter, e.g., O.P.A. 1861, B.Ex.A. 1882. For interpretation of a codifying statute, see *Bank of England v Vagliano Bros* [1891] AC 107. *See* CONSOLIDATION ACT.

coercion. The use of physical or moral force in an attempt to interfere with the exercise of free choice. See *R v Ditta* [1988] Crim LR 42 (marital coercion); *R v Shortland* [1995] 1 Cr App R 116; C.J.A. 1925, s 47. *See* DURESS; UNDUE INFLUENCE.

cognates. Those related on the mother's side. *See* AGNATES.

cognisance, judicial. Judicial notice (q.v.).

cohabitants. A man and a woman who, although not married to each other, are living together as husband and wife: F.L.A. 1996, s 62(1). For test of cohabitation, see *Re Watson* (1998) *The Times*, 31 December.

cold weather payments. Payments made to certain persons in receipt of income support (q.v.) out of the Social Fund, when the average mean daily temperature remains equal to or falls below 0°C. See SI 88/1724; 99/2781.

collateral. 1. Belonging to the common ancestral stock, although not in direct line of descent. 2. Collateral security (in the case of a bank loan) means: security deposited by some person other than the customer himself; or impersonal security, e.g., life policies, as contrasted with personal security, e.g., a guarantee. 3. Collateral contracts exist where there is one contract, the consideration for which is the making of some other contract, e.g., 'If you will make this contract we discussed, then I will give you £1,000.' 4. Collateral testimony concerns secondary matter. The answers of a witness to questions in cross-examination (q.v.) relating to collateral facts are to be considered as final: *R v Burke* (1858) 8 Cox CC 44.

collective bargaining. Negotiations relating to the conditions and terms of employment carried on between trade unions and employers or their associations. A 'collective agreement' is one resulting from such bargaining. It may be written, oral, formal or informal. It is not intended to be legally enforceable unless in writing and containing a provision to that effect. See T.U.L.R.(C.)A. 1992, ss 178, 179; E.R.A. 1996; Employment Relations Act 1999, s 17 (collective agreements: detriment and dismissal). *See* TRADE UNION.

collective responsibility. Doctrine at the basis of the constitutional convention that the Cabinet (q.v.) is collectively responsible to Parliament for the conduct of the Executive. It requires that Ministers shall be loyal to government policy and that the government as a whole shall resign if defeated on a vote of no confidence. *See* MINISTERIAL RESPONSIBILITY.

collector. In relation to a public charitable collection, any person by whom the appeal in question is made (whether made by him alone or with others and whether made by him for remuneration or otherwise). Charities Act 2006, s 47.

collision. The accidental striking together of two or more objects. For collision at sea, see, e.g., *The Filitria Legacy* [1986] 2 Lloyd's Rep 257; *The Mineral Dampier* [2000] 1 Lloyd's Rep 282; *The Niase* [2000] 1 Lloyd's Rep 455 (definition of 'collision'). For 'agony of the moment' defence, see *The State of Himachal Pradesh* [1987] 2 Lloyd's Rep 97.

collision claim. Claim within S.C.A. 1981, s 20(3)(*b*), i.e., any action to enforce a claim for damages, loss of life or personal injury arising out of: a collision between ships; or the carrying out or omission to carry out any manoeuvre in the case of one or more ships; or non-compliance on the part of one or more ships with the collision regulations: PD 49F, para 1.4(d).

collusion. Agreement, usually secret, for some deceitful or unlawful purpose. Collusion in the presentation of a petition for divorce (q.v.) is no longer a bar to divorce. See Mat.C.A. 1973, s 19.

collusive action. *See* COMMON RECOVERY.

colony. 'Any part of Her Majesty's dominions outside the British Islands except: (a) countries having fully responsible status within the Commonwealth; (b) territories for whose external relations a country other than the UK is responsible; (c) associated states': I.A. 1978, s 5.

colore officii. By virtue of one's office. For 'extortion *colore officii*' (e.g. by a public official), see *Woolwich Equitable BS* v *IRC* [1993] AC 70.

combination order. Measure under P.C.C.(S.)A. 2000, s 51 (known now, under C.J.C.S.A. 2000, s 45, as 'community punishment and rehabilitation order'), consisting of community service of up to 100 hours combined with a supervision order of one to three years. See Crime (Sentences) Act 1997, Sch 4, para 15; *Fontenav* v *DPP* [2001] 1 Cr App R (S) 15.

Comitology Committees. Bodies composed of member state representatives, chaired by a Commission representative, set up to assist the European Commission in implementing its decisions. See Council Decision 87/373/EEC; *Rothmans International BV* v *European Commission* [1999] 3 CMLR 66.

comity. Willingness by the courts of one jurisdiction to give effect to the wishes or decisions of another jurisdiction, as a matter of mutual respect, and in the absence of any obligation. See *Fayed* v *Al-Tajir* [1987] 2 All ER 396; *R* v *Manning* [1999] 2 WLR 430; *Re St Mary, Hurley* (2000) *The Times*, 26 January (request for reburial in Brazil of remains of national hero buried in UK).

Command Papers. *See* PARLIAMENTARY PAPERS.

Command Papers, numbering of. The six series are as follows: 1833–69 (number, with no prefix, e.g., '3989'); 1870–99 (numbered with prefix 'C', e.g., 'C 3550'); 1900–18 (numbered with prefix 'Cd', e.g., 'Cd 9005'); 1919–56 (numbered with prefix 'Cmd', e.g., 'Cmd 8778'); 1957 to late 1986 (numbered, with prefix 'Cmnd', e.g., 'Cmnd 3456'); and the current series (numbered with the prefix 'Cm', e.g., 'Cm 145').

command theory of law. Concept, elaborated by Austin, in 1832, of law as existing when a population habitually obeys, as a duty, the general and continuing commands of a person or group enjoining acts and forbearances, within the context of sanctions for disobedience. 'Thus, law is the command of the uncommanded commanders of society': Hart, *The Concept of Law* (1994).

commercial agent. *See* AGENT, COMMERCIAL.

commercial claims. Any case arising out of trade and commerce in general, including any case relating to: a business document or contract; export or import of goods; carriage of goods by land, sea, air, pipeline; exploitation of oil or gas reserves; insurance and re-insurance; banking and financial services; operation of markets and exchanges; business agency; arbitration. 'Commercial proceedings' has a corresponding meaning: PD 49D, r 1.2(1). *See* COMMERCIAL COURT.

Commercial Court. See S.C.A. 1981, s 6. A 'Commercial List' comprises commercial claims (q.v.) which may be entered for trial in the Commercial Court: see CPR, Part 49. The judges are puisne judges of the High Court, usually of QBD with specialist commercial knowledge. Where the Commercial Court finds that there has begun within it an action raising matters of law, construction or both which are essentially within the province of the Commercial Court, given their core nature, proceedings might be considered for transfer from the Commercial Court to the Technology and Construction Court: *Lumbermens Mutual Casualty* v *Bovis Ltd* [2004] EWHC 1614.

commercial leases. Voluntary Code of Practice for Commercial Leases, introduced in March 2002, recommends, inter, alia: that parties intending to enter into leases should obtain early advice from property professionals or lawyers; that repairing obligations and costs included in service charges should be appropriate to length of term and condition of property; that basis of rent review should be open market rent.

commercial unit. Phrase in S.G.A. 1979, s 35(7), as substituted by Sale and Supply of Goods Act 1994, s 2, to refer to a unit division of goods which would materially impair the value of the goods or the character of the unit, e.g., one shoe of a pair. Where a contract is for the sale of goods making one or more commercial units, a buyer accepting any goods included in a unit is deemed to have accepted all the goods making the unit.

commission. 1. Remuneration paid to an agent. 2. Formal authority to exercise a power. 3. A body directed to perform a duty, the members of which are known as 'commissioners'. Thus, a Commission of the Peace was appointed by the Crown, consisting of persons who were to act as justices of the peace (q.v.) in certain districts. 4. A Royal Commission is set up by the government to investigate aspects of policy.

Commission areas. A 'Commission area' means an area for which there is a commission of the peace. These areas, in England and Wales, are specified by the Lord Chancellor, but a Commission area may not consist of an area partly within and partly outside Greater London: Justices of the Peace Act 1997, ss 1, 2, substituted by Acc.J.A. 1999, s 74. A magistrates' courts committee may submit proposals to the Lord Chancellor for alterations of a commission area including the whole or any part of their area: 1997 Act, s 32A, inserted by Acc.J.A. 1999, s 74.

Commission, Competition. *See* COMPETITION COMMISSION.

Commission, Disability Rights. *See* DISABILITY RIGHTS COMMISSION.

Commission, European. 'The Guardian of the Treaty', and the executive of EU. Body consisting of some 20 nationals of member states appointed for five years by common accord of their governments with the task of ensuring the proper functioning and developing of the European Union (q.v.). They operate under the guidance of the President, and are expected to be completely independent in the performance of their duties ('. . . shall neither seek nor take instructions from any government or from any other body': art 157(2)). The Commission watches over the application of EU legislation (q.v.), formulates proposals and implements policies on a day-to-day basis. Its powers are set out in art 211EC. *See* EU.

Commissioners for Oaths. Solicitors who administer oaths, e.g., to those making affidavits (q.v.). See Commissioners for Oaths Act 1889; C.L.S.A. 1990, s 113(10), under which solicitors holding practising certificates have powers of a Commissioner for Oaths.

Commission for Health Improvement. *See* HEALTH IMPROVEMENT, COMMISSION FOR.

Commission for Racial Equality. *See* RACIAL EQUALITY, COMMISSION FOR.

Commission, Legal Services. *See* LEGAL SERVICES COMMISSION.

Commission, Low Pay. *See* LOW PAY COMMISSION.

Commissions for local administration. *See* LOCAL ADMINISTRATION, COMMISSIONS FOR.

committal for contempt. Where contempt of court is committed in connection with: proceedings before a Divisional Court of QBD; or criminal proceedings, except where the contempt is committed in the face of the court or consists of disobedience to an order of the court; or proceedings in an inferior court; or is committed otherwise than in connection with any proceedings, then an order of committal may be made only by a Divisional Court of QBD: CPR, Sch 1; O 52, r 1(2). For High Court power to punish for contempt, see O 52, r 1(4).

committal for sentence. Procedure whereby magistrates, who are of the opinion that a greater punishment than they are empowered to impose should be inflicted on an offender, commit the offender to the Crown Court (q.v.) for sentence. Matters relating to sentence must be left to the Crown Court. See M.C.A. 1980, ss 37, 38, as amended by C.J.A. 1991, s 25; P.C.C.(S.)A. 2000, ss 3–7. (The stipulation in S.C.A. 1981, s 74(1) that a court considering committal for sentence sent to it by magistrates must include them and a Crown Court Judge, is now removed, so that the judge alone deals with the committal: Acc.J.A. 1999, s 79. There are no committal proceedings for indictable-only offences (q.v.) and defendant will be 'sent forthwith' to the Crown Court for trial: C.D.A. 1998, s 51; Sch 3, amended by Acc.J.A. 1999, Sch 14, para 179.)

committal for trial. The sending of a person for trial at the Crown Court, following a preliminary investigation before magistrates. *See* COMMITTAL, SHORT.

committal for trial of person under 18 by magistrates' court. Under M.C.A. 1980, s 24(1), (1A), inserted by C.D.A. 1998, s 47(6), where a magistrates' court commits a person under 18 for trial for an offence of homicide, the court may also commit him for trial for any other indictable offence with which he is charged at the same time if the charges for both offences could be joined in the same indictment.

committal in civil proceedings. Method of enforcing a judgment by committal to prison, available, e.g., in cases of disobedience of an order of the court. See A.J.A. 1970, s 11. The disobedience, which must amount to contempt of court, must be more than casual, accidental and unintentional. *See* CONTEMPT OF COURT.

committal order. In *Sierra Leone* v *Davenport (No. 2)* [2002] EWCA Civ 230, the CA held that the natural meaning of 'committal order' under CPR 1998, Part 52, r 52.3(1)(a), is 'an order committing a party to prison'.

committal proceedings. Proceedings involving the oral presentation of evidence before a magistrates' court. The function of these proceedings is to ensure that 'no one shall stand his trial unless a *prima facie* case has been made out': *per* Lord Widgery in *R* v *Epping Justices ex p Massaro* [1973] QB 433. See *R* v *Governor of Canterbury Prison ex p Craig* [1990] 2 All ER 654. See C.J.P.O.A. 1994, s 44, repealed by C.P.I.A. 1996, s 44. See modified committal proceedings introduced by C.P.I.A. 1996, s 47 and Sch 1, effectively abolishing old-style committals.

committal proceedings, reporting of. Written reporting or broadcasting of committal proceedings is generally forbidden, except in relation to, e.g., names of parties, counsel, solicitors, witnesses, etc.: see M.C.A. 1980, s 8; Acc.J.A. 1999, Sch 4, para 16. The accused may apply for the restriction to be lifted: s 2. If, in the case of two or more accused, one objects to the making of an order lifting the restriction, the court must hear representations and may make an order only if satisfied that it is in the interests of justice to do so: s 2A (inserted by C.J. (Amendment) A. 1981, s 1(2)).

committal, short. A procedure whereby magistrates, at their option, may commit for trial without consideration of the evidence; known as 'paper committal'. See M.C.A. 1980, s 6; C.P.I.A. 1996, Sch 1, para 4; Magistrates' Courts Rules 1981, rr 6, 7.

committee. A group of persons appointed or elected by a larger, parent body to carry out general or specific delegated duties. See *R* v *Secretary of State ex p Hillingdon LBC* [1986] 1 WLR 192.

Committee of the Regions. EU body comprising representatives of local and regional bodies of member states, designed to enable those bodies to influence EU legislation. Created in 1994; term of office is four years; meets in Brussels in 'five plenaries each year. Known as 'the guardian of subsidiarity' (q.v.), and works through eight standing committees, dealing with, e.g., Regional Development, Urban Policies, Spatial Planning.

Committee of the Whole House. Procedure used in the Lords or Commons whereby, following a resolution, the House resolves itself into a Committee of the Whole House under the chairmanship (in the Commons) of the Chairman of Ways and Means and (in the Lords) the Chairman of Committees. The procedure may be used, e.g., in the passage of a Bill of fundamental constitutional significance. No other business can be taken while the Committee is sitting.

committee, select. Committee appointed by a House of Parliament, to consider and take evidence on some subject and to report to the House. Committees include Committee of Privileges, Public Accounts, European Legislation. Civil servants and other persons may be called upon to give evidence. An action for slander cannot be brought for statements given in evidence before a Commons Committee: *Griffin* v *Donnelly* (1881) 6 QBD 307.

commit to custody. To commit to prison or, where any enactment authorises or requires committal to some other place of detention instead of committal to prison, to that other place.

common. Land subject to rights of common. 'Includes any land subject to be enclosed under the Inclosure Acts 1845–82, and any town or village green': T.C.P.A. 1990, s 336. See *Hampshire CC* v *Milburn* [1990] 2 WLR 1240. *See* COMMON, RIGHT OF.

common assault. An assault (q.v.) which is not of an aggravated nature. A summary offence under C.J.A. 1988, s 39. Punishable under O.P.A. 1861, s 42. See *R* v *Beasley* (1981) 73 Cr App R 44. The term should be construed so as to include battery as well as assault: *R* v

Lynsey (1995) 2 Cr App R 667. *See* AGGRAVATED ASSAULT.

common carrier. *See* CARRIER, COMMON.

common employment. At common law a master was not liable for the negligent harm resulting from the action of one of his servants towards a fellow servant engaged in a common employment at the time of the accident. See *Radcliffe v Ribble Motor Services Ltd* [1939] AC 215. The doctrine was abolished by Law Reform (Personal Injuries) Act 1948, s 1(1).

commonhold. Land, the freehold estate in which is registered as a freehold estate in commonhold, is specified in the memorandum of association of a commonhold association as the land in relation to which the association is to exercise functions, and in relation to which a commonhold community statement makes provision for rights and duties of the association and unit-holders: C.L.R.A. 2002, s 10. It may include two or more parcels of land, whether or not contiguous: s 11.

commonhold association. A private company limited by guarantee, the memorandum of which states that an object of the company is to exercise the functions of a commonhold association in relation to specified commonhold land, and specifies £1 as the amount required to be specified in pursuance of Cos.A. 1985, s 2(4): C.L.R.A. 2002, s 34.

commonhold, common parts of. Every part of the commonhold which is not for the time being a commonhold unit in accordance with the commonhold community statement: C.L.R.A. 2002, s 25. A charge cannot be created over common parts: s 28.

commonhold community statement. A document making provision in relation to specified land for the rights and duties of the commonhold association and the unit-holders: C.L.R.A. 2002, s 31.

commonhold, freehold estates. Commonhold Regulations 2004 (SI 04/1829) provide for land in England and Wales to be registered as a freehold estate in commonhold land. See Commonhold and Household Reform Act 2002.

commonhold, land which may not be. Under C.L.R.A. 2002, Sch 2: raised land (unless all the land between the ground and the raised land is the subject of the same applications); agricultural land; land, the estate in which is contingent.

commonhold unit. A unit specified in a commonhold community statement, specifying at least two parcels of land as commonhold units, and defining the extent of each unit: C.L.R.A. 2002, s 11. A 'unit-holder' is a person entitled to be registered as the proprietor of the freehold estate in the unit: ss 12 and 13.

commonhold, unit, leasing. A term of years absolute cannot be created in a residential commonhold unit unless prescribed conditions relating to length, circumstances in which term is granted, are satisfied: C.L.R.A., s 17.

common informer. *See* INFORMER.

common land. Land subject to rights of common, and wasteland of a manor not subject to such rights. See Commons Registration Act 1965, s 22(1); Common Land (Rectification of Registers) Act 1989; C.R.W.A. 2000, s 1(2). For right to graze, see *Matthews v Wicks* (1987) *The Times*, 25 May. For vehicular access, see C.R.W.A. 2000, s 68. *See* COMMON, RIGHT OF.

common law. 'The common sense of the community, crystallised and formulated by our forefathers.' Blackstone speaks of 'the chief cornerstone of the laws of England which is general and immemorial custom, or common law, from time to time declared in the decisions of the courts of justice; which decisions are preserved among our public records, explained in our reports, and digested for general use in the authoritative writings of the venerable sages of the law' *Commentaries* (1765). The phrase apparently came into use at the end of the thirteenth century, when reference is found in the Year Books (q.v.) to '*la commune ley*'. Jurists use the phrase to refer variously to: the law which was 'common' by the time of Edward I, in that it was administered in the king's courts throughout his kingdom; the rules of law created by the judges in contrast to statute law emanating from Parliament; a general system of law deriving exclusively from the courts' decisions; a family of related legal systems based on the common law (e.g., legal systems of USA).

common law, declaratory theory of. *See* DECLARATORY THEORY OF COMMON LAW.

common law, extinguishing of by statute. It is a well established principle that a statute does not extinguish a rule of common law unless that statute makes such extinguishment clear by express provision or clear implication: *per* Lord Hutton in *R* v *Commissioner of Metropolitan Police* (2002) *The Times*, 21 May.

common-law marriage. Colloquialism ('inaccurate but expressive': *per* Bridge LJ in *Dyson Holdings* v *Fox* [1975] 3 All ER 1030), generally referring to cohabitation which has not been preceded by any religious or civil ceremony. The phrase has been used to refer also to the so-called 'clandestine marriages', recognised by common law but not canon law, which were ended by Hardwicke's Marriage Act 1753, and marriages celebrated abroad under old common-law forms, as where a clergyman was unavailable. See *Penhas* v *Tan Soo Eng* [1953] AC 304; *Taczanowska* v *Taczanowska* [1957] P 301. *See* MARRIAGE.

common-law wife. Colloquialism, and misnomer ('a misleading vulgarism' *per* Lord Simon), referring to a woman living with a man to whom she is not married, as if she were his wife: see *Davis* v *Johnson* [1978] 2 WLR 182. ('She is to be distinguished from a "mistress", where the relationship may be casual, impermanent, and secret': *per* Lord Denning.)

Common Market. Term formerly used as a synonym for EEC (q.v.) which, under the Treaty of Rome 1957, art 2, has as a task the promotion of a harmonious development of economic activities throughout the Community by establish-

ing a common market and approximating the economic policies of member states. The term 'common market' was replaced by 'internal market' under Single European Act 1986: it is defined as 'an area without internal frontiers in which the free movement of goods, persons, services and capital is ensured in accordance with the provisions of the Treaty'. See EUROPEAN UNION.

common mistake, equitable doctrine of. In *Great Peace Shipping Ltd* v *Tsavliris Salvage Ltd* (2002) 152 NLJ 1616, the CA held that where a contract is valid and can be enforced on general principles of contract law, there exists no equitable jurisdiction allowing the court a discretion to set aside that contract on the ground of common mistake. See *Bell* v *Lever Bros* [1932] AC 161; *Solle* v *Butcher* [1950] 1 KB 671.

common parts of a building. They include the structure and exterior, and common facilities provided, whether in the building or elsewhere, for persons who include the occupiers of one or more flats in the building: Local Government and Housing Act 1989, s 138.

common recovery. Mode of barring estate tail (q.v.) by a collusive action, abolished by Fines and Recoveries Act 1833.

common, right of. A *profit à prendre* (q.v.), i.e., a right to take something off the land of another. Classified as: appendant, appurtenant, in gross, *pur cause de vicinage* (q.v.), or, according to the subject matter, as a common of pasture, turbary, etc. Rights of common over common land, persons who own common land, town and village greens must be registered with a local authority. See Commons Registration Act 1965; *Re Yately Common* [1977] 1 All ER 505. *See* COMMONS, REGISTRATION OF.

Common Serjeant. Formerly a judicial officer of the City of London, who sat in the Central Criminal Court (q.v.). Now a circuit judge, appointed by the Crown, and possessing a ten-year Crown Court qualification within the meaning of C.L.S.A. 1990, s 71. See City of London

(Courts) Act 1964; Courts Act 1971, Sch 2.

Commons, House of. *See* HOUSE OF COMMONS.

commons, registration of. Registration with county councils of persons claiming to be or established as owners of common land, and rights of common (q.v.) in England and Wales. See Commons Registration Act 1965; Common Land (Rectification of Registers) Act 1989 (a temporary measure, providing for the removal from the register of land on which there had been a dwelling house since 1945); *New Windsor Corporation v Mellor* [1975] Ch 380; *R v Oxfordshire CC ex p Sunningwell Parish Council* [1999] 3 WLR 160 (use of common 'as of right'); *R v Sunderland CC ex p Beresford* (2000) *The Times*, 16 January (implied licence defeated claim to registration).

common, tenancy in. A tenancy in which tenants held in undivided shares and there was no right of survivorship (q.v.); only unity of possession was required. Existed where, e.g., land was limited to two or more persons and words of severance (q.v.) were used, e.g., 'to X and Y in equal moieties'. After 1925 a legal estate may not be held under tenancy in common. Under L.P.A. 1925, s 34, where a legal estate has been limited to tenants in common it vests in them as joint tenants upon the statutory trusts for sale. The tenancy in common continues in equity 'for giving effect to the rights of persons interested in the land': L.P.A. 1925, s 35. See L.P.A. 1925, s 36(4); *City of London Building Society v Flegg* [1988] AC 54.

Commonwealth. 1. The period from the execution of Charles I (1649) to the restoration of the monarchy (1660). 2. The Commonwealth of Nations (or British Commonwealth), i.e., a group of independent nations (the UK and nations once part of the British Empire) recognising the British monarch as Head of the Commonwealth. See, e.g., Pakistan Act 1990; Commonwealth Development Corporation Acts 1978, 1999.

Commonwealth citizen. A person who is a British citizen, British Dependent Territories citizen, British Overseas citizen, or British subject, or who is a citizen of a country listed in Sch 3: B.N.A. 1981, s 37(1). See Immigration Act 1988, s 1, repealing Immigration Act 1971, s 1(5).

commorientes. Persons dying together on the same occasion at the same time. Under L.P.A. 1925, s 184, they are presumed, for purposes affecting title to property, to have died in order of seniority. See *Re Bate* [1947] 2 All ER 418. The statutory presumption does not apply in the case of intestate spouses. See A.E.A. 1925, s 46(3); Intestates' Estates Act 1952, s 1(4), Sch 1.

communication, facilitated. Process in which an assistant supports the hand or arm of a person whose motor skills are significantly impaired, while that person is using a keyboard device. Resulting communication has been held to be not reliable when tendered as evidence: *Re D (A Child) (Evidence: Facilitated Communication)* (2000) *The Times*, 26 July.

communication, privileged. *See* PRIVILEGED COMMUNICATION.

communications, interception of. *See* INTERCEPTION OF COMMUNICATIONS.

Communities, European. *See* EUROPEAN COMMUNITIES.

community care grants. Grants payable from the Social Fund (q.v.) to those who experience 'special difficulties arising from special circumstances', e.g., after hospital treatment, and who are in receipt of income support (q.v.). See Community Care (Direct Payments) Act 1996; Community Care (Residential Accommodation) Act 1998.

community charge. Known colloquially as 'poll tax', which replaced rates on domestic properties. Introduced under Local Government Finance Act 1988. Abolished by Local Government Finance Act 1992, chap I. See *R v Warrington BC ex p Barrett* [2000] RVR 208. *See* COUNCIL TAX.

Community, European Economic. *See* EEC.

community homes. Homes for the accommodation and maintenance of children in the care of local authorities: Ch.A. 1989, s 53. For 'voluntary homes', managed by voluntary organisations, see s 60. See Community Care (Residential Accommodation) Act 1998.

Community law. The directly applicable law of the European Union, based upon treaties and instruments made by the institutions of the Union. It operates as a separate system side by side with English law but, in the event of a conflict, it takes precedence over domestic law. 'No provisions of municipal law, of whatever nature they may be, prevail over Community law': *Internationale Handelgesellschaft* v *EVSt* [1972] CMLR 255. See *R* v *Secretary of State ex p Factortame Ltd* [1991] 3 All ER 769 (a national court must set aside any rule of national law which prevents directly enforceable Community law from being fully effective); F.S.M.A. 2000, s 410. In general, community law becomes part of the law of the UK if it is, in its nature, and under EU treaties, self-executing, or is the subject of a separate enactment by Act of Parliament, or is implemented, under European Communities Act 1972, s 2(2), by statutory instrument. Treaty articles have direct effect if clear, unambiguous, unconditional, and, in themselves, become effective without further action by EU or member states: *Van Gend en Loos* (case 26/62). For citation of Community treaties, see *Practice Note (ECJ Treaty Citation)* [1999] All ER (EC) 481. Adoption of discriminatory legislation in breach of Community law may give rise to liability in damages: *R* v *Secretary of State for Transport ex p Factortame Ltd (No. 5)* [1999] 3 WLR 1062. *See* COMMUNITY LAW, SOURCES OF; COURT OF JUSTICE OF THE EUROPEAN COMMUNITIES.

Community law and national sovereignty. 'The transfer by the states from their domestic legal system to the Community legal system of the rights and obligations arising under the Treaty carries with it a permanent limitation of their sovereign rights, against which a subsequent unilateral act incompatible with the concept of the Community cannot prevail': European Court of Justice in *Costa* v *ENEL* [1964] ECR 585.

Community law, sources of. Sources of EU law are: the treaties (e.g., Treaty of Rome 1957) with their annexes and protocols; conventions between member states; secondary legislation (see Treaty of Rome 1957), e.g., regulations, directives, decisions, recommendations and opinions (qq.v.); judicial decisions of the Court of Justice of the European Communities (q.v.) and the Court of First Instance (q.v.).

Community law, state liability under. The principle of state liability for damage caused to an individual by infringement of Community law committed by that state is inherent in the scheme of the EU Treaty: *Francovich* v *Italy* [1992] IRLR 84.

Community Legal Service. Body set up under Legal Services Commission (q.v.) to promote availability of information concerning legal services and their work, provision of ADR (q.v.), and the enforcement of decisions concerning dispute resolution: Acc.J.A. 1999, s 4. Services which may not be funded as part of CLS include: those concerned with provision of help in relation to, e.g., conveyancing, trusts, defamation; advocacy in any proceedings except in House of Lords, Court of Appeal, High Court, county courts; proceedings in Crown Court and magistrates' court in certain specified matters: Sch 2. Its services are funded from Community Legal Services Fund: s 5.

Community legislation, forms of. The Council and Commission of the EU (q.v.) may: (1) make *regulations*, which have a general application and are binding in their entirety and directly applicable in all member states without the need for further enactment; (2) issue *directives*, which are binding, only as to the result to be achieved, on member states to which they are addressed (an individual may rely on a precise, unconditional ('vertical') directive against a member state: *Van Duyn* v *Home Office (No. 2)* [1975] 3 All

ER 190; there are no 'horizontal' direct effects as between persons); *Gibson* v *E Riding of Yorkshire Council* (2000) *The Times*, 6 July; *Commission of EC* v *Hellenic Republic* (2000) *The Times*, 7 July (criteria for penalties for member state's failure to comply with directive); *R* v *Secretary of State for Health ex p Imperial Tobacco Ltd* (2000) *The Times*, 10 October (annulment of directive by Court of Justice); (3) take *decisions* binding in their entirety upon those to whom they are addressed; (4) make *recommendations* or deliver *opinions*, which have no binding force. See Treaty of Rome 1957, art 189. The European Court has decided that a member state may not base criminal proceedings against a person arising from the content of an unimplemented directive. See also CPR, Sch 1; O 71, Part II. *See* DIRECT EFFECT, DOCTRINE OF.

Community legislation, interpretation of. 'Beyond doubt the English courts must follow the same principles as the European Court . . . No longer must [the English courts] examine the words in meticulous detail. No longer must they argue about the precise grammatical sense. They must look to the purpose or intent . . . They must divine the spirit of the Treaty and gain inspiration from it': *H P Bulmer Ltd* v *J Bollinger SA* [1974] Ch 401. 'Any question as to the meaning and effect of any Community instrument shall be treated as a question of law and, if not referred to the European Court, be for determination as such in accordance with the principles laid down by a relevant decision of the European Court': European Communities Act 1972, s 3(1). 'The Treaty of Rome is the supreme law of the country, taking precedence over Acts of Parliament': *per* Hoffmann J in *Stoke on Trent CC* v *B & Q* [1990] 3 CMLR 867.

community orders and sentences. Under P.C.C.(S.)A. 2000, s 33(1), these include the following orders: curfew, probation, community service, combination, drug treatment and testing, attendance centre, supervision, action plan (qq.v.). A community sentence is one which includes one or more community orders: s 33(2). The orders are not available where sentence is fixed by law: s 34. A community sentence will not be passed unless the court is of the opinion that the offence is serious enough to warrant it: s 35(1). For pre-sentence reports, see s 36. For loss of social security benefits for breach of orders, see C.S.P.S.S.A. 2000, s 62.

community punishment and rehabilitation order. New name for 'combination order' (q.v.).

community service order. A community sentence (q.v.), available where a person aged 16 or over is convicted of an offence punishable with imprisonment, and requiring him to perform unpaid work, within 12 months, for 40–240 hours: P.C.C.(S.)A. 2000, s 46. Now 'community punishment order': C.J.S.A. 2000. s 44.

commutative justice. *See* JUSTICE, COMMUTATIVE, DISTRIBUTIVE AND CORRECTIVE.

commute. 1. To substitute one punishment for another. 2. To travel regularly from one's home to a place of work.

Companies Court. Collective title given to those judges of the Chancery Division (q.v.) nominated by the Lord Chancellor, who have jurisdiction in relation to certain matters derived from the operation of companies. Thus, they have jurisdiction to wind up any company (q.v.) registered in England. See *Practice Statement (Companies Court)* (2000) *The Times*, 19 January.

companies register. Register based on Cos.A. 1985, Part XII, recording charges created by companies on or after 1 January 1970, other than floating charges (q.v.). Must be registered at the Land Charges Registry if they are to bind any purchaser. See L.C.A. 1972, s 3; *Property Discount Corp* v *Lyon Group* [1981] 1 All ER 379.

company. An association of persons formed for the purposes of an undertaking or business carried on in the name of the association. May be classified as *chartered companies* (formed by the grant of a charter from the Crown), *statutory companies* (formed under an Act of Parliament), *registered companies* (formed under Cos.A.), or as *public companies* limited by shares, or by guarantee, or unlimited. See Cos.A. 1985, Part I; PD 49B (applications under Cos.A. 1985). For 'single member companies', see SI 92/1699 (relating only to private limited companies). For 'off-the-shelf' companies, see Cos.A. 1985, s 3A. *See* CORPORATE LIABILITY; LIMITED LIABILITY.

company accounts. Accounts prepared under Cos.A. 1985, s 227, as amended by Cos.A. 1989, Part I, which must be prepared in accordance with Sch 4; they include a balance sheet, and profit and loss account ('individual company accounts'): Cos.A. 1989, s 4. They should disclose with reasonable accuracy, at any time, the financial position of the company at that time: Cos.A. 1985, s 221, as amended by Cos.A. 1989, s 2. See SI 90/515.

company accounts, failure to deliver. Penalties following failure of a company to deliver its accounts on time to the Registrar, are compliant with the European Convention; *R (POW) Trust* v *Registrar of Companies* (2003) *The Times*, 2 January.

company accounts, publication of. A company (q.v.) 'shall be regarded as publishing any balance sheet or other account if it publishes, issues or circulates it or otherwise makes it available for public inspection in a manner calculated to invite members of the public generally, or any class of members of the public, to read it': Cos.A. 1985, s 742(5). See Cos.A. 1989, s 238; EU Council Directive 78/660, art 31.

company books. *See* STATUTORY BOOKS.

company, British. A company incorporated under the laws of Great Britain, over which a Commonwealth citizen has control, or two or more Commonwealth citizens are together in a position to exercise control, or over which such a company, or two or more such companies, or such a company and a Commonwealth citizen are together in a position to exercise control: National Film Finance Corporation Act 1981, s 9(3) (since repealed:

see now Cos.A. 1989). *See* COMPANY; COMPANY, CONTROL OF.

company charges, register of. *See* REGISTER OF COMPANY CHARGES.

company contracts, form of. Contracts on behalf of a company may be made in the forms stated in Cos.A. 1985, s 36, corresponding generally to those prescribed for the contracts of private individuals.

company, control of. The power of a person to secure by means of the holding of shares or possession of voting power in or in relation to that company or any other body corporate, or by virtue of powers conferred by the articles of association (q.v.), or other document, that the affairs of the company are conducted in accordance with the wishes of that person: I.C.T.A. 1988, s 840.

company director, liability for tort. In *Standard Chartered Bank* v *Pakistan National Shipping Corporation* (2002) *The Times*, 7 November, the House of Lords held that a company director could not evade personal liability for his own tort of fraud by claiming that his fraudulent acts were undertaken on behalf of the company.

company directors. *See* DIRECTOR.

company, director's loyalty to. In *Item Software Ltd* v *Fassihi* (2004) *The Times*, 21 October, the CA held that where a company director who did not disclose his misconduct to his company, sought to divert the company's business to another of his own companies, he was in breach of loyalty to the first company.

company, dormant. *See* DORMANT COMPANY.

company, family. *See* FAMILY COMPANY.

company, holding. *See* SUBSIDIARY COMPANY.

company identification. The duty of a company to ensure that its name appears outside its place of business, on its correspondence, etc. See Cos.A. 1985, ss 348–351.

company, investigation of. The Department of Trade and Industry is empowered to investigate: the affairs of a company (q.v.) (see Cos.A. 1985, s 431); the ownership of a company (see Cos.A. 1985, s 442); the share dealings of a company (see Cos.A. 1985, ss 444, 446, 447, as amended by Cos.A. 1989, s 63). See *A-G's Reference (No. 2 of 1998)* [1999] 3 WLR 961.

company, investment. *See* INVESTMENT COMPANY.

company, limited. *See* LIMITED COMPANY.

company limited by guarantee. *See* GUARANTEE, COMPANY LIMITED BY.

company manager. 'Any person who in the affairs of the company exercises a supervisory control which reflects the general policy of the company for the time being or which is related to the general administration of the company is in the sphere of management. He need not be a member of the board of directors': *per* Shaw LJ in *Re a Company* [1980] Ch 138. See F.S.M.A. 2000, s 423.

company meetings. *See* MEETINGS, COMPANY.

company, members of a. *See* MEMBERS OF A COMPANY.

company memorandum. *See* ASSOCIATION, MEMORANDUM OF.

company name. The name of a public company (chosen by the promoter) must end with 'public limited company' (plc) or the Welsh equivalent: Cos.A. 1985, s 25(1). In the case of a private company, 'limited' or 'Ltd' will suffice. Certain names will not be registered, e.g., those suggesting a connection with the government: s 26(1). See also Company and Business Names (Chamber of Commerce, etc.) Act 1999. A company may by special resolution change its name: s 28(1). It is an offence to trade under a misleading name: s 33. See *ACPA v Secretary of State for Trade and Industry* (1997) *The Times*, 12 June. *See* BUSINESS NAME.

company name, change of. In *Halifax plc v Halifax Repossessions Ltd* (2004) *The Times*, 11 February, the CA held that the court lacked any power to order a third party to change the name of a company, nor could it instruct the Companies Registrar to undertake such an activity; the statutory arrangements must be adhered to.

company, officers of a. Term which includes directors, managers and secretary. See Cos.A. 1985, s 744. Auditors and company solicitors may be included.

company, oversea. *See* OVERSEA COMPANY.

company, participator in. *See* CLOSE COMPANY.

company, partnership. *See* TABLE G.

company, private. *See* PRIVATE COMPANY.

company proceedings. Under PD 49B (replacing RSC O 102), all proceedings relating to Cos.A. 1985 must be brought under CPR, Part 8 procedure: see PD 49B, para 2(1). Exceptions to this rule are set out in PD 49B, para 4(1) (under which certain applications must be made by petition).

company, public. *See* PUBLIC COMPANY.

company, quoted. A company (q.v.) which satisfies the conditions that its shares or some class thereof are listed in the Official List of the Exchange and are dealt in on the Stock Exchange regularly from time to time. For 'unquoted company', see Cos.A. 1985, s 389(2)(*a*).

company register of members. *See* REGISTER OF MEMBERS.

company, registration of. Procedure whereby a company is registered by the Registrar of Companies on delivery of documents including a memorandum of association, printed articles of association, a statement in prescribed form of names of intended first director(s) and first secretary, statement of capital and statutory declaration by the solicitor engaged in the formation of the company, or by a named director or secretary, of compliance with the requirements of the Acts relating to registration. See Cos.A. 1985, ss 12, 13, 359 (rectification of register).

company, related. In relation to an institution or the holding company of an institution, means a body corporate (other than a subsidiary) in which the institution or holding company holds a qualifying capital interest, i.e., an interest in the relevant shares of the body corporate held on a long-term basis so as to secure a contribution to its own activities by the exercise of control or influence arising from that interest: Cos.A. 1989, Sch 10, para 37.

company's common seal. Required in the case of deeds, share certificates and warrants, contracts which would necessitate a deed if entered into by a private person. See Cos.A. 1985, s 39; Cos.A. 1989, s 130(7), Sch 17, para 3. A company's official seal is a facsimile of the common seal, with the addition on its face of the name of the territory in which it is to be used.

company secretary. Appointed, usually at a board meeting, by the directors of a company. He can act as agent for the company and is an officer of the company. A sole director must not be the secretary. See Table A, art 99.

company's future capitalisation. In *Collins Stewart Ltd* v *Financial Times Ltd* (2004) *The Times*, 25 October, it was held that where company claimants involved in a libel case had claimed that an alleged defamation had led to a fall in the company's market value, this was too uncertain to act as an acceptable valuation for purposes of damage assessment.

company's place of incorporation. In *Base Metal Trading Ltd* v *Shamurin* (2004) *The Times*, 1 November, the CA held that the law of the place of incorporation of a company has application to the duties relating to the office of director. It is of no relevance that breach of these duties was committed in another jurisdiction.

company's profits. *See* PROFITS, COMPANY'S.

company, statutory. *See* STATUTORY COMPANY.

company, subsidiary. *See* SUBSIDIARY COMPANY.

company, unlimited. *See* UNLIMITED COMPANY.

company, unregistered. *See* UNREGISTERED COMPANY.

company, winding-up of. *See* WINDING-UP.

comparative law. *See* LAW, COMPARATIVE.

compellability of witnesses. *See* WITNESSES, COMPELLABLE.

compensation. Payment for loss or injury sustained, e.g., as under Criminal Damage Act 1971, s 8 (compensation for destruction or damaging property of another). See also P.C.C.(S.)A. 2000, s 130 (under which a convicted person may be required to pay compensation for injury, loss or damage resulting from the offence or any other offence taken into consideration by the court in determining sentence or to pay for funeral expenses or bereavement in respect of a death arising from such an offence). See *Lancashire CC* v *Municipal Insurance Ltd* [1996] 3 WLR 493; *R* v *Love (Compensation Orders)* [1999] 1 Cr App R (S) 484. Planning and Compensation Act 1991. In *Lowther* v *Chatwin* (2003) *The Times*, 4 August, the CA held that, in relation to the prevention of double recovery in damages, the phrase 'compensation for earnings lost,' in Social Security (Recovery of Benefits) Act 1997, s 8, Sch 2, refers, in the context of a self-employed claimant, to turnover lost, rather than actual income or net profit lost.

competence of witnesses. *See* WITNESSES, COMPETENCE OF.

Competition Commission. Body set up under Competition Act 1998, s 45, to exercise functions under the Act (e.g., hearing of appeals), including those formerly exercised by Monopolies and Mergers Commission (q.v.). See F.S.M.A. 2000, s 306 (competition scrutiny by Commission in relation to financial services).

competition, distortion of. The Treaty of Rome 1957, art 85, prohibits as incompatible with the Common Market (q.v.) all agreements and practices which have as their object or effect the prevention, restriction or distortion of competition within the EU. Article 86 makes illegal the abuse of a dominant position by exploitative acts, e.g., unfair prices, or anti-competitive acts, e.g., mergers. See, e.g., *London European Airways* v *Sabena* [1989] 4 CMLR 662. For exemptions, see, e.g., Regulations 1983/83 (exclusive distribution), 4078/88 (franchising). *See* Competition Act 1998.

competition for prizes. A competition where, e.g., the allocation of prizes depends on the outcome of sporting events and competitors have to forecast that outcome. Generally unlawful if conducted in or through any newspaper, or in connection with any trade or business or sale of articles: Lotteries and Amusements Act 1976, s 14(1).

competition law. That part of the law dealing with matters such as those arising from monopolies and mergers, restrictive trading agreements, resale price maintenance, and agreements involving distortion of competition affected by EU rules. See Competition Act 1998; F.S.M.A. 2000, ss 159, 164 (competition scrutiny in relation to financial services).

competition, prohibition of restrictions concerning. Subject to s 3, agreements between undertakings, decisions by associations of undertakings, or concerted practices which may affect trade within the UK and have as their object or effect the prevention, restriction or distortion of competition within the UK are prohibited: Competition Act 1998, s 1(1). This applies in particular to agreements, decisions or practices which fix purchase or selling prices, limit production, share markets or sources of supply: s 1(2). For power of Director General of Fair Trading to investigate, see s 25. *See* DOMINANT POSITION.

competition, prohibitions on, excluded agreements concerning. Under Competition Act 1998, s 3(1), prohibitions on the restriction of competition do not apply in cases excluded by or as a result of Sch 1 (mergers and concentrations), Sch 2 (competition scrutiny under other enactments), Sch 3 (planning obligations and other general exclusions), Sch 4 (professional rules). Secretary of State may amend Schedules: s 3(2). Individual exemptions may be granted or cancelled: ss 4, 5.

complainant. One who makes a formal complaint (q.v.). In relation to a person accused of a rape offence or an accusation alleging a rape offence, means the person against whom the offence is alleged to have been committed. See S.O. (Amendment) A. 1992, which extends to complainants of other sexual offences the statutory anonymity which applies to rape complainants under S.O. (Amendment) A. 1976.

complaint. 1. The initiating step in civil proceedings in the magistrates' courts: see M.C.A. 1980, Part II. 2. Allegation against a person. The complaint in a sexual case must have been made at the first reasonable opportunity after the offence and must not have been made merely in answer to questions of a leading or threatening nature: *R* v *Osborne* [1905] 1 KB 551. See *R* v *H (Sexual Assault)* [1998] 2 Cr App R 161 (need for trial judge to give an appropriate direction on effect on defence of a long delay in making complaint).

complaint, hearing of. Procedure before a magistrates' court (q.v.) in which the substance of a complaint is stated to the defendant, the court hears the evidence and the parties, and makes the order for which the complaint is made or dismisses the complaint: M.C.A. 1980, s 53. For procedure in the event of non-appearance of parties, see ss 55–57.

completely constituted trust. A trust which has been perfectly created, in that the settlor has done everything in his power necessary to transfer his interest in the trust property to a trustee for the benefit of the intended beneficiaries, or has declared himself a trustee of that property. See *Letts* v *IRC* [1956] 3 All ER 588. *See* TRUST.

completion. Term used to refer to final stages in a contract for the sale of land, effected by delivery up of the land with good title, acceptance of title and payment of agreed price, in case of unregistered land; payment of agreed price and delivery of document indicating executed transfer, in case of registered title. See L.R.A. 1925, s 110(6).

composition. 1. Sum of money accepted by creditors in satisfaction, or adjustment, of debts. Can be registered under

Deeds of Arrangement Act 1914. 2. The ingredients of which a product is made, the proportions and degrees of strength, purity, etc. See Medicines Act 1968, s 132, as amended.

compos mentis. Of sound mind.

compound. 1. To settle or adjust by agreement, e.g., by accepting a composition (q.v.). See Customs and Excise Management Act 1979, s 152. 2. Compounding a felony, i.e., the offence of agreeing for consideration not to prosecute or impede a prosecution, was abolished effectively by C.L.A. 1967. 3. Compounding an arrestable offence (q.v.), i.e., accepting or agreeing to accept consideration for not disclosing information which might be of material assistance in prosecuting an offender, was made an offence under C.L.A. 1967, s 5(1).

compound settlement. The single settlement formed by a series of separate instruments. See S.L.A. 1925, s 30(3). *See* SETTLEMENT.

compromise. Settlement, by agreement of parties, of claims in dispute. See, e.g., PD 49, para 13.1; A.J.A. 1985, s 49. 'The word implies some element of accommodation on each side. It is not apt to describe total surrender. A claimant who abandons his claim is not compromising it': *Re NFU Development Trust Ltd* [1973] 1 All ER 135. See *Dattani v Trio Supermarket Ltd* [1998] ICR 872.

comptroller. Controller. One who examines accounts relating to public money. The Comptroller and Auditor-General is head of National Audit Office (see National Audit Act 1983, s 3). He carries out an audit and certification of government departments and a large range of public sector bodies; audit of nationalised industries and other public authorities is excluded. A certification audit may be followed by a 'value for money' examination: 1983 Act, s 6(1). See I.A. 1978, Sch 1.

compulsion. *See* DURESS.

compulsory purchase order. An order for the purchase of land made in accordance with statutory procedure: see, e.g., Compulsory Purchase Act 1965;

Acquisition of Land Act 1981; H.A. 1985, Part XVII, Sch 22; Planning and Compensation Act 1991; Transport and Works Act 1992; C.R.W.A. 2000, s 75. The acquiring authority makes an order in draft which is submitted to the confirming authority (usually the Minister), objections are heard by an inspector and the order is confirmed, modified or rejected. Disputes may be heard by High Court. See L.G.P.L.A. 1980, s 91, as amended; *Hughes v Doncaster MBC* [1991] 2 WLR 16. *See* MARKET VALUE.

compulsory winding-up by the court. Procedure whereby a company (q.v.) is wound up if, e.g., it has passed a special resolution to wind up, or it is unable to pay its debts or it has failed to commence operations within a year of incorporation or the court believes it equitable that it should be wound up. See Ins.A. 1986, ss 117, 122.

computer. Any device for storing and processing information: Civil Evidence Act 1968, s 5. For the use of computers, etc., for certain company records, see Cos.A. 1985, s 723. See Data Protection Act 1998; Computer Misuse Act 1990 (creating offence of unauthorised access to computer material); *Derby & Co v Weldon (No. 9)* [1991] 1 WLR 652 (computer database as 'document').

computer documents, statements in. Under Civil Evidence Act 1968, s 5, statements contained in documents produced by computers became admissible of a fact stated therein of which direct oral evidence would have been admissible if, e.g., throughout the material time the computer had been operating properly and had been supplied with information of the kind contained in the statement. Y.J.C.E.A. 1999, s 60, repealed P.&C.E.A. 1984, s 69, so that restrictions on the use of evidence from computer records concerning criminal matters are removed.

computer misuse. Under the Computer Misuse Act 1990, it is an offence: to secure unauthorised access to computer material (s 1(1)); to commit conduct sufficient to establish the previous offence with intent to commit or facilitate more serious offences (s 2); to cause an unauthorised modification of computer material (s 3). See *A-G's Reference (No. 1 of 1991)* [1993] QB 94; *Morgans v DPP* [1999] 1 WLR 968; *R v Bow Street Metropolitan Stipendiary Magistrate ex p United States* [1999] QB 847; Criminal Justice (Terrorism and Conspiracy) Act 1998, Sch 1; *R v Maxwell-King* (2001) *The Times*, 2 January (incitement to misuse). *See* HACKING, COMPUTER.

computer, seizure for evidence. An Inland Revenue Officer executing a search warrant under Taxes Management Act 1970, s 20C, was authorised to seize and remove a computer in circumstances in which he believed reasonably that its disk contained material likely to be of relevance to criminal proceedings even though it also contained irrelevant material: *R (H) v IRC* (2002) *The Times*, 8 November.

computer-use ban. In *R v Collard* (2004) *The Times*, 7 June, the CA held that a restraining order issued so as to ban defendant from using a computer which had the capability of downloading material from the internet, was based on terms which were too wide, since employment of the computer might require use of the internet at home and also at the place of work.

concealed fraud. In the case of land, this means 'designed fraud by which a party knowing to whom the right belongs, conceals the circumstances giving that right, and, by means of such concealment, enables himself to enter and hold': *Petre v Petre* (1853) 1 Drew 397. The deliberate destruction of another's title deeds is an example. In such a case time does not run until the plaintiff has discovered, or could with reasonable diligence have discovered, the fraud: Lim.A. 1980, s 32(1). See *Liverpool RC Archdiocese Trustees v Goldberg* (2000) *The Times*, 18 July.

concealment. 1. Suppression of, or neglect to communicate, a material fact. If fraudulent, it may provide grounds for rescission of contract. 2. Concealment of

a valuable security, dishonestly and with a view to gain or with intent to cause loss to another, is an offence under Th.A. 1968, s 20(1). See *R v Kanwar* [1982] 2 All ER 523 (concealing stolen goods).

concealment of birth. *See* BIRTH, CONCEALMENT OF.

concert parties. Colloquialism for groups of persons acting in concert to acquire interests in a company's shares. See Cos.A. 1985, ss 204–207. Members of such groups must keep one another informed of their existing interests, acquisitions and disposals of shares in the company: s 206. Under City Code on Takeovers, 'persons acting in concert' are defined as persons who, pursuant to an undertaking or agreement, actively co-operate in the acquisition by any of them of shares in a company, to obtain or consolidate control of that company. 'Control' refers to an aggregate holding of shares carrying 30 per cent or more of voting rights. See *Philip Morris Inc v Rothmans Ltd* (2000) *The Times*, 10 August.

conciliation. Settlement of a dispute outside the courts by reference to a third party. In domestic proceedings it is the process of assisting parties to deal with the consequences of a marriage breakdown and to resolve differences by reaching agreement. *See* ADR.

conclusive evidence. *See* EVIDENCE, CONCLUSIVE.

concurrent and consecutive sentences. Following conviction of defendant of several offences, the court may impose separate sentences to be served at the same time (concurrently) or to follow on another (consecutively). See *R v Anomo* [1998] 2 Cr App R (S) 269; *R v King* [2000] 1 Cr App R (S) 105; *R v Everleigh* (2001) *The Times*, 16 May.

concurrent causes. Two or more events which are causative in relation to a plaintiff's injury so that both are considered proximate. See *Baker v Willoughby* [1970] AC 467; *Rouse v Squires* [1973] QB 889.

concurrent interests. Interests in land held at one and the same time, by two or more persons, e.g., grant of land 'to X and Y in fee simple'. X and Y 'hold concurrently' or 'hold in co-ownership'.

concurrent lease. A lease (q.v.) created out of a reversion on an existing lease and existing concurrently with another lease of the same property. May be utilised in the creation of second mortgages. See *Adelphi Estates* v *Christie* (1983) 47 P & CR 650.

concurrent tortfeasors. Persons who, having committed a tort (q.v.), are each answerable in full for the entire damage caused to the plaintiff.

condition. The declaration of circumstances essential to the occurrence of an event, e.g., the exercise of a right. Some restriction, limitation, qualification. 1. 'Conditions in deed' are those which are actual and expressed; 'conditions in law' are implied. 2. A *condition precedent* is one which delays the vesting of a right until the occurrence of a particular event, e.g., 'to X if he graduates in law'; a *condition subsequent* is one which provides for the defeat of an interest on the occurrence or non-occurrence of a particular event, e.g., 'to X on condition that he shall never sell out of the family': *Re Macleay* (1875) LR 20 Eq 186; a *condition concurrent* is one under which performance by one party is rendered dependent on performance by the other at the same time. See, e.g., *Re Da Costa* [1912] 1 Ch 377. 3. A condition in a contract for the sale of goods is a vital stipulation, the breach of which may give rise to a right to treat the contract as repudiated: S.G.A. 1979, s 11(3). See *Bunge Corpn* v *Tradax* [1981] 1 WLR 715 ('The courts should not be too ready to interpret contractual clauses as conditions': *per* Lord Wilberforce); *Interfoto Picture Library* v *Stiletto Visual Programmes* [1989] QB 433 (need to draw attention to onerous and unusual conditions); *Petrograde* v *Stinnes Handel* [1995] 1 Lloyd's Rep 142; S.G.A. 1979, s 11(4). See WARRANTY.

conditional acceptance. See ACCEPTANCE, CONDITIONAL.

conditional admissibility. Phrase referring to evidence, the relevance of which may be conditional on the giving of later evidence. Evidence so admitted is said to have been admitted *de bene esse* (q.v.).

conditional agreement. See AGREEMENT, CONDITIONAL.

conditional discharge. See ABSOLUTE, CONDITIONAL DISCHARGES.

conditional fee. A fee simple with an attached condition which cuts it short, e.g., grant of land 'to A in fee simple on condition that he shall not marry X, Y or Z'. *See* DETERMINABLE FEE; FEE SIMPLE ABSOLUTE IN POSSESSION.

conditional fee agreement. Under C.L.S.A. 1990, s 58, substituted by Acc.J.A. 1999, s 27(1), a conditional fee agreement is an agreement with a person providing advocacy or litigation services which provides for his fees and expenses, or any part of them, to be payable only in specified circumstances; and a conditional fee agreement provides for a success fee if it provides for the amount of any fees to which it applies to be increased, in specified circumstances, above the amount which would be payable if it were not payable only in specified circumstances. A conditional fee agreement which satisfies all applicable conditions shall not be unenforceable by reason only of its being a conditional fee agreement, but any other conditional fee agreement shall be unenforceable. (See s 58(5) concerning agreements under Solicitors Act 1974, s 57.) See *Thai Trading* v *Taylor* [1998] QB 781; SI 98/1860 (specifying 100 per cent as maximum permitted percentage by which fees can be increased in relation to C.L.S.A., s 58(3)); SI 00/823. *See* CONTINGENCY FEE.

conditional fee agreement, applicable conditions. Under C.L.S.A. 1990, ss 58(3), 58A, substituted by Acc.J.A. 1999, s 27(1), a conditional fee agreement (q.v.) must be in writing, must not relate to proceedings which cannot be the subject of an enforceable fee agreement (i.e., criminal and family proceedings), must comply with requirements prescribed by

Lord Chancellor. In the case of a conditional fee agreement providing for a success fee, it must, additionally, relate to proceedings of a description specified by the Lord Chancellor, must state percentage by which amount of the fees which would be payable if it were not a conditional fee agreement is to be increased, and that percentage must not exceed that specified by the Lord Chancellor. See CPR, r 48.9; PD 48; SI 00/692.

conditional interest. An interest on condition subsequent. *See* CONDITION.

conditional order. An order requiring a party to pay a sum of money into court, or to take a specified step in relation to his claim or defence, and provides that a party's claim will be dismissed or his statement of case will be struck out if he does not comply: PD 24, para 5.2.

conditional sale agreement. Agreement for the sale of goods or land under which the whole or part of the purchase price is payable in instalments, and the property in the goods or land is to remain in the seller until the conditions of the agreement are fulfilled. See C.C.A. 1974, s 189(1); and S.G.A. 1979, s 25(2); *Lombard North Central* v *Gate* [1998] CCLR 51; *Carlyle Finance Ltd* v *Pallas Industrial Finance Ltd* [1999] 1 All ER 659.

conditional will. A will executed with the intention that it shall be rendered operative only on the occurrence of a specified event. See *Re Govier* [1950] P 237; *Corbett* v *Newey* [1996] 3 WLR 729 (testator's instructions that date of signature was to be inserted after completion of specific transfers; will held invalid because testator was under misapprehension that dating of will, and not signature, constituted execution).

condition concurrent. *See* CONDITION.

condition precedent. *See* CONDITION.

conditions of sale. Terms upon which land is to be sold. In the case of a contract by correspondence, L.P.A. 1925, s 46, provides that it shall be governed, subject to contrary intention expressed, by Statutory Form of Conditions of Sale.

condition subsequent. *See* CONDITION.

condominium. 1. The individual ownership of a dwelling unit in a multi-dwelling unit (such as a flat in an apartment building). Generally, the individual ownership is linked with common ownership of those parts of the multi-dwelling unit which are used in common. 2. A territory over which joint sovereignty is exercised by two or more states. See Anglo-Egyptian Condominium Agreement 1899, imposing a joint Anglo-Egyptian government on the Sudan (which continued until 1935).

condonation. Pardon or forgiveness. Specifically, forgiveness of a matrimonial offence. No longer an absolute bar to divorce. *See* DIVORCE, BARS TO.

conduct. Mode or standard of individual behaviour involving action or omission. See *Regal Grand Ltd* v *Dickerson* (1997) 29 HLR 620 (non-payment of rent amounted to 'conduct' in relation to H.A. 1988, s 27(7)).

conduct, criminal. Under Proceeds of Crime Act 2002, s 76(1)(2), 'criminal conduct' is conduct which constitutes an offence in England and Wales, or would constitute such an offence if it occurred in England and Wales. General criminal conduct of a defendant is all his criminal conduct, and it is immaterial whether the conduct occurred before or after the passing of the Act, or whether property constituting a benefit from conduct was obtained before or after the passing of the Act.

conduct of trial, expeditious nature of. It was held by the European Court of Human Rights in *Henworth* v *UK (Application No. 505/02) The Times*, 2004, 22 November, that it was essential for authorities to ensure that a prosecution for alleged murder was conducted with diligence so as to minimise delay, even though defendant's own delay had contributed to periods of delay in the process.

conduct, unlawful. For purposes of Proceeds of Crime Act 2002, unlawful conduct is conduct occurring in any part of the UK which is unlawful under the criminal law of that part: s 24(1). Conduct occurring in a country outside the UK which is unlawful in that country, and which, if it occurred in a part of the UK would be unlawful under the criminal law of that part, is also unlawful conduct: s 241(2).

conduct, unreasonable. *See* UNREASONABLE CONDUCT.

confession. 1. Includes any statement wholly or partly adverse to the maker, whether made to a person in authority (q.v.) or not, and whether made in words or otherwise: P.&C.E.A. 1984, s 82(1). A confession of unaccused person may be given in evidence against him: 1984 Act, s 76(1). The court may reject a confession unless it can be shown that it was not obtained by oppression (q.v.) of the maker or obtained in circumstances rendering it unreliable: s 76(2). The fact that a confession is wholly or partly excluded under s 76 does not affect the admissibility in evidence of any facts discovered as a result of the confession: s 76(4)(a). See Code of Practice for the Detention, Treatment and Questioning of Persons by Police Officers (Code C, April 1991). For confessions of mentally handicapped persons, see 1984 Act, s 77; *R v Moss* (1990) 91 Cr App R 371. See *R v Miller* [1986] 1 WLR 1191 (confession of paranoid schizophrenic); *R v O'Brien* (2000) *The Times*, 16 February (admissibility of expert evidence concerning those who make false confessions). *See* OPPRESSION LEADING TO CONFESSION. 2. Where defendant have been given appropriate and proper advice by his solicitor, such advice could not give any ground for the exclusion of a subsequent confession under Police and Criminal Evidence Act 1984, s 76(2): *R v Wahab* (2002) *The Times*, 22 July. Update Sept 2002.

confessions, oppression. In *R v Mushtaq* [2005] *The Times*, 28 April, the HL held that it is a matter for the judge to decide whether a confession made by the defendant is admissible as evidence, where a question of oppression is raised. Where the judge has ruled that the evidence was not contained by oppression by the police, the judge directed the jury that if they were

not sure that the confession was true, they must disregard it.

confidence, breach of. Equitable doctrine whereby the donee of confidential information relating, e.g., to a business, and which requires protection, is under a duty not to use that information in an unauthorised manner to the donor's detriment. See *Bullivant v Ellis* [1987] ICR 464; *Thomas v Pearce* [2000] FSR 718; *R v Department of Health ex p Source Informatics Ltd* (2000) *The Times*, 18 January; *Venables and Another v News Group Newspapers* (2001) *The Times*, 16 January.

confidential communication. A communication which is privileged as being protected from disclosure in evidence given in proceedings, e.g., a communication between a party and solicitor made during those proceedings.

confidential information. Information, generally relating to industry or trade, reasonably believed by the owner to be such that its unauthorised release would be injurious to him or advantageous to others, and to be not in the public domain: *Thomas Marshall (Exports) v Guinle* [1978] 3 WLR 116. See *R v Secretary of State for the Environment ex p Alliance Against Relief Road* [1999] Env LR 447; *Woolgar v Chief Constable of Sussex Police* [1999] 3 All ER 604; *Intelsec Systems Ltd v Grech Cini* [1999] 4 All ER 11. *See* TRADE SECRET.

confidential information, disclosure of. In *A v B (A Company)* (2002) 152 NLJ 434, CA set out guidelines relating to balancing of right to privacy and to freedom of expression, e.g., claimant's need to accept that, as a public figure, his actions would be closely scrutinised by media.

confidentiality, breach of. In *Campbell v Mirror Group* [2002] EWCA Civ 1373, the CA held that a newspaper was justified in the public interest in printing information relating to a person's attendance at a meeting of narcotics users, so as to show that the person had deceived the public when claiming that she was not a drugs user; further, such publication did not constitute a breach of that person's right to confidentiality.

confinement. 1. Imprisonment or other restraint. 2. Labour resulting in the issue of a living child, or labour after 24 weeks of pregnancy, resulting in the issue of a child, alive or dead: see, e.g., Social Security Contributions and Benefits Act 1992, as amended by Still-Birth (Definition) Act 1992, s 2.

confiscate. To deprive of property by seizure. A confiscation order against one who has benefited from his offence may be imposed by the Crown Court or a magistrates' court: C.J.A. 1988, Part VI, amended by Proceeds of Crime Act 1995, s 1. See Drug Trafficking Act 1994, s 2; Confiscation of Alcohol (Young Persons) Act 1997; C.D.A. 1998, s 83 (power to make confiscation orders on committal for sentence); *R v Harvey* [1999] 1 All ER 710 (meaning of 'realisable property' – 'the amount appearing to the court to be the amount that might be realised at the time the order is made'); *R v Malik* (2000) *The Times*, 30 May (imprisonment in default of payment of confiscation is not a breach of European Convention on Human Rights, arts 6, 7); *R v Croft* (2000) *The Times*, 6 July (court has no discretion over making of confiscation order); *USA Government v Montgomery* (2001) 151 NLJ 136 (power of High Court to enforce foreign confiscation order). It was also held by the HL in *USA v Montgomery (No. 2)* [2004] UKHL 37, that the registration of a confiscation order made in USA under USA fugitive disentitlement doctrine does not violate the rights of the subject of an order under the European Convention, art 6. *R v Olubitan* (2003) *The Times*, 14 November, the CA held that where there was an absence of evidence implying that a conspirator had received a pecuniary advantage from the conspiracy, there could be no suggestion that, on a balance of probabilities, the conspirator had benefited from criminal conduct justifying a confiscation order. *R v Sekhon* [2002] EWCA Crim 2954, the CA held that an order confiscating profits from crime ought not to be defeated merely because a procedural defect which did not constitute an injustice had occurred.

confiscation orders, drugs-related. In *R v Pisciotto* (2002) *The Times*, 19 July, Drug Trafficking Act 1994, s 3(1); the CA held that where Crown Court is considering whether to postpone determining of the question as to whether defendant has obtained a benefit from drug trafficking, it may postpone making the determination for such period as it may specify. It was held that the second 'may' created a mandatory requirement.

confiscation orders, qualifying offences. In relation to 'qualifying offences' under the Criminal Justice Act 1988, ss 71 (4), 72 AA, it is not necessary that offences of this nature should have separate origins, or that they should be based on separate allegations of offences: *R v Smith* (2002) *The Times*, 12 November.

confiscation orders, valid notice concerning. Where confiscation proceedings are in contemplation, the serving of a valid notice under the Criminal Justice Act 1988, ss 71, 72 (1), is to be viewed as a condition precedent to the entire process: *R v Palmer* (2002) *The Times*, 5 November.

confiscation orders, value of assets. Where a court assesses value of defendant's assets in relation to confiscation proceedings under Drug Trafficking Act 1994, there should have been deducted from the value of those assets any outstanding mortgage liabilities: *R v Walls* [2002] EWCA Crim 2456.

confiscation, time limits. In *R v Young* (2003) *The Times*, 8 December, the CA held that, in the absence of exceptional circumstances, proceedings in relation to confiscation were to be ended and a determination announced within the statutory period of six months.

conflict of laws. *See* PRIVATE INTERNATIONAL LAW.

congenital disabilities, civil liability relating to. Under Congenital Disabilities (Civil Liability) Act 1976 a child has a cause of action if born disabled as the result of a tortious act done to one of his parents before the child's birth or conception: s 1. 'Disabled' refers to the child being born with any deformity, disease or abnormality, including predisposition to physical or mental defect in the future: s 4(1). See Human Fertilisation and Embryology Act 1990, ss 35, 44; *McKay* v *Essex Area Health Authority* [1982] QB 1166.

connivance. Passive consent or co-operation in relation to a wrongdoing. Specifically, permission for, or acquiescence in, a respondent's adultery. An absolute bar to divorce until abolished by Divorce Reform Act 1969. See *Mudge* v *Mudge* [1950] P 173.

consanguinity. *See* AFFINITY.

conscience, interference with. In *Mohisin* v *RAF Summary Appeal Court* (2004) *The Times*, 28 October, it was held that a volunteer airman could not claim interference with his freedom of conscience or religion by the state unless he had indicated unambiguously that he had ceased to be a volunteer.

conscientious objectors as refugees. In *Krotov* v *Secretary of State for Home Department* (2004) *The Times*, 26 February, the CA held that where consideration is given to granting refugee status to a conscientious objector (to military service) in his native land, the tribunal must take into account the nature of the conflict to which he objected and whether he might be called upon to commit actions contrary to international law.

consecutive sentences. Sentences ought to be served consecutively where they reflect the serious nature of the separate criminal activities which constitute the offender's guilt: *AG's Reference (No. 6 of 2004)* (2004) *The Times*, 6 May. *See* CONCURRENT AND CONSECUTIVE SENTENCES.

consensual. Expressing, or made as the result of, the mutual consent of parties to some course of action. For 'consensual activity' in relation to crime, see *R* v *Wilson* [1996] 3 WLR 125.

consensus ad idem. *See* AD IDEM.

consent. Compliance with or deliberate approval of a course of action. It is not

generally binding if obtained by coercion, fraud or undue influence (q.v.). See *R* v *Linekar* [1995] QB 250. *See VOLENTI NON FIT INJURIA; WILLING.*

consent, age of. The age at which a person is legally competent to consent to sexual intercourse. In the case of a female, it was raised from 12 to 13 in 1875, and to 16 in 1885. In the case of a male, the age is 16: S.O. (Am.)A. 2000, s 1. *See* HOMOSEXUAL CONDUCT.

consent and assault. Consent is generally a defence to a charge of assault (q.v.), but this is subject to considerations of public policy. In the absence of some good reason, e.g., properly conducted games, assault cannot be rendered lawful by consent if it caused, or was intended to cause, actual bodily harm. See *A-G's Ref (No. 6 of 1980)* [1981] QB 715; *R* v *Brown and Others* [1993] 2 WLR 556 (consent no defence to sado-masochistic assaults).

consent, informed. The doctrine of informed consent, i.e., the duty of completely disclosing information to a patient as to medical treatment before it is undertaken, is apparently no part of English law; a doctor is bound merely to disclose in broad terms such information as is reasonable to allow a patient to make a rational choice whether or not to accept treatment; *Sidaway* v *Bethlehem Royal Hospital Governors* [1984] 1 All ER 1018. 'Consent is not a mere formality; it is an important individual right to have control over one's own body, even where medical treatment is involved': *per* Linden J in *Allan* v *New Mount Sinai Hospital* [1980] 28 Ont (2d) 356. See *Blyth* v *Bloomsbury Health Authority* (1987) *The Times*, 11 February.

consent in relation to sexual offences. For purposes of the Sexual Offences Act 2003, a person consents if he agrees by choice, and has the freedom and capacity to make that choice: s 74.

consent orders. Orders embodying parties' agreement and settlement of a dispute. See, e.g., Mat.C.A. 1973, s 33A, inserted by Matrimonial and Family Proceedings Act 1984, s 7. They comprise: 'administrative consent orders' (where neither party is a litigant in person) and include, e.g., orders for payment of money, Tomlin orders (q.v.), orders for discharge from liability of any party; and 'approved consent orders' where one or more of the parties is a litigant in person: see CPR, r 40.6; PD 40B, para 3.1.

consequential loss. *See* MEASURE OF DAMAGES IN CONTRACT.

conservation areas. Areas of special architectural or historic interest, the character or appearance of which it is desirable to preserve or enhance, and designated as conservation areas by a local planning authority: En.P.A. 1990. Demolition within the area is controlled: s 74(1). See also Planning (Listed Buildings and Conservation Areas) Act 1990 s 69; *Lakeland DC v Secretary of State for the Environment* [1992] 1 All ER 573.

consideration. That which is actually given or accepted in return for a promise. 'Some right, interest, profit or benefit accruing to one party, or some forbearance, detriment, loss, or responsibility given, suffered or undertaken by the other': *Currie v Misa* (1875) LR 10 Ex 153. Example: X receives £50 for which he promises to deliver goods to Y; the £50 is the consideration for the promise to deliver the goods. Consideration is *executed* when the act constituting the consideration is performed; it is said to be *executory* when it is in the form of promises to be performed at a future date. Consideration is required for the formation of all simple contracts. It must be legal; it must not be past; it must move from the promisee; it must be real, i.e., something of value in the eye of the law. See, e.g., *Dunlop Tyre Co v Selfridge & Co* [1915] AC 847; *Stocznia Gdanska SA v Latvian Shipping Co* [1998] 1 WLR 574. For the consideration for a bill of exchange (q.v.), see B.Ex.A. 1882, s 27.

consideration, good. *See* GOOD CONSIDERATION.

consideration, past. Consideration which is wholly executed and finished before a promise is made. Example: X does

some service for Y and, subsequently, Y promises X that, in consideration of that service, he will pay X a sum of money. There is no consideration to support Y's promise and it cannot be sued on. See *Re McArdle* [1951] Ch 669; *Pau On v Lau Yiu Long* [1980] AC 614; B.Ex.A. 1882, s 27(1).

consideration, valuable. Consideration (q.v.) must generally be something which is of some value in the eye of the law: *Thomas v Thomas* (1842) 2 QB 851. See A.E.A. 1925, s 55(1) (*xviii*). See *R v Kensington and Chelsea LBC* [1999] 4 All ER 161 (construction of 'consideration' as not limited to 'valuable consideration' in the sense applicable to contract law (for purposes of GLC (General Powers) Act 1973, s 25(2)(a)). *See* GOOD CONSIDERATION.

consistory court. A court held by a diocesan bishop and presided over by a chancellor for the trial of ecclesiastical causes arising within his diocese.

Consolidated Fund. The general account with the Bank of England, established in 1786, into which government receipts are paid and out of which payments are made in the form of standing charges, known as Consolidated Fund Services.

Consolidation Act. An Act which repeals or re-enacts or collects in a single statute previous enactments and amendments relating to a topic. Acts of this nature may be passed without customary debate in Parliament: Consolidation of Enactments (Procedure) Act 1949, allowing corrections and minor improvements to be made: see s 2. Examples: Legal Aid Act 1974; Solicitors Act 1974. Differs from codification, which systematises statutes and case law. *See* CODIFYING STATUTE.

consolidation of mortgages. Where one person creates at least two separate mortgages in favour of one mortgagee, that mortgagee has a right to require that the mortgagor, on seeking to exercise his equitable right to redeem one of the properties, shall redeem both of the properties or neither of them: *Jennings v Jordan* (1880) 6 App Cas 698. It is allowed only where the legal date for redemption (q.v.) has passed (for both mortgages) and where the right to consolidate has been reserved by at least one of the mortgages and where the equities of redemption are vested in one person and the mortgages in another, or where that position has existed at some time in the past. See L.P.A. 1925, s 93; *Pledge* v *White* [1986] AC 187. *See* MORTGAGE.

consortium. 1. A business combination. 2. Right of one spouse to companionship and affection of the other. See *Lawrence* v *Biddle* [1966] 2 QB 504; *Hodgson* v *Trapp* [1988] 18 Fam Law 60. See A.J.A. 1982, s 2, for the abolition of certain claims for loss of services.

conspiracy. The statutory offence was created by C.L.A. 1977, s 1(1) (for which a new text was substituted by Criminal Attempts Act 1981, s 5(1)): 'If a person agrees with any other person or persons that a course of conduct shall be pursued which, if the agreement is carried out in accordance with their intentions, either (a) will necessarily amount to or involve the commission of any offence or offences by one or more of the parties to the agreement, or (b) would do so but for the existence of facts which render any of the offences impossible, he is guilty of conspiracy to commit the offence or offences in question.' See *R* v *Roberts* [1998] 1 Cr App R 441; *R* v *Drew* [2000] 1 Cr App R 91. *See* CONSPIRACY TO DEFRAUD.

conspiracy at common law. 'The crime of conspiracy is the creation of the common law and peculiar to it': *DPP* v *Doot and Others* [1973] 1 All ER 940. The offence of conspiracy at common law was abolished under C.L.A. 1977, except in relation to conspiracy to defraud (q.v.) and in so far as it may be committed by entering into an agreement to engage in conduct which tends to corrupt public morals or outrages public decency but would not amount to or involve the commission of an offence if carried out by a single person otherwise than in pursuance of an agreement: s 5. See now C.J.A. 1987, s 12. *See* CONSPIRACY TO DEFRAUD.

conspiracy, exemptions from liability for. A person is not guilty of conspiracy to commit any offence if he is an intended victim of that offence: C.L.A. 1977, s 2(1). A person is not guilty of conspiracy to commit any offence(s) if the only other person or persons with whom he agrees are (both initially and at all times during the currency of the agreement) persons of any one or more of the following descriptions: his spouse; a person under the age of criminal responsibility; and an intended victim of that offence or of each of those offences: C.L.A. 1977, s 2. See *R* v *Chrastny (No. 1)* [1992] 1 All ER 189.

conspiracy, restrictions on institutions of proceedings for. Under C.L.A. 1977, s 4(1), proceedings may not be instituted except by or with the consent of DPP (q.v.) if the offence or each of the offences in question is a summary offence. Consent of A-G (q.v.) may be required under s 4(2).

conspiracy to commit offences outside the UK. Where each of the following conditions is met, in the case of an agreement, C.L.A. 1977 has effect in relation to the agreement as if it fell within s 1(1): that the intention is that the completed act is to take place outside the UK; that the act or other event would constitute an offence in the foreign country; that the conspiracy to act would constitute an offence in England and Wales were the act to have been committed there; that a party to the agreement, or his agent, performed some activity in England or Wales in pursuance of the agreement: C.L.A. 1977, s 1A, inserted by C.J. (Terrorism and Conspiracy) A. 1998, s 5. *See* CONSPIRACY.

conspiracy to defraud. If a person agrees with any other person(s) that a course of conduct shall be pursued and that course of conduct will necessarily amount to or involve the commission of any offence(s) by one or more of the parties to the agreement if it is carried out in accordance with their intentions, the fact that it will do so shall not preclude a charge of conspiracy to defraud being brought against any of them in respect of the agreement:

C.J.A. 1987, s 12(1). See, e.g., *Wai Yu Tsang* v *R* [1992] Crim LR 425 ('intention to defraud' means an intention to practise a fraud on another, or an intention to act to the prejudice of another's right); *R* v *Naini* [1999] 2 Cr App R (S) 398. *See* DEFRAUD.

conspiracy, tort of. Combination of two or more persons, without lawful justification, so as to cause wilful damage to another, or the agreement to perform an unlawful act with resulting damage. See *Lonrho Ltd* v *Shell Petroleum Ltd* [1980] AC 173; *Kuwait Oil Tanker Co* v *Al Bader* (2000) *The Times*, 30 May (proving civil conspiracy to injure).

constable. An officer of the law whose task it is to help in maintaining the peace and bringing to justice those who infringe it. The words 'constabulary' and 'police' are synonymous: *Rubin* v *DPP* [1989] 2 All ER 241. See Police Acts 1964, 1996.

constable, chief. A police officer appointed by the police authority, subject to the approval of the Secretary of State: Police Act 1996, s 11(1). His general function is the direction and control of a police force, and in discharging that function he must have regard to the local policing plan issued by the police authority for his area: s 10(1), (2). The police authority, acting with the approval of the Secretary of State, may call upon him to resign in the interests of efficiency or effectiveness: s 11(2). The term 'chief officer' is used in some legislation (e.g., Police Act 1997) to mean: a chief officer of police of a police force in England and Wales, a chief constable of a police force in Scotland, and the Chief Constable of the Royal Ulster Constabulary (see 1997 Act, s 126(1)). For Commissioner of Police of the Metropolis, see G.L.A.A. 1999, ss 314, 315. *See* POLICE FORCE.

constituency. One of the basic, separate electoral units in the UK in which eligible persons elect a Member of the Commons or the European Parliament. See Parliamentary Constituencies Act 1986, Sch 2, para 1.

constitution. 1. The manner in which a state or other body is organised. 2. The body of fundamental doctrines and rules of a nation from which stem the duties and powers of the government and the duties and rights of the people. The UK's constitution is based on statute, common law and convention. See Royal Commission on the Constitution 1973 (Cmnd 5460). 3. A document embodying a state's constitution.

construction. The process of construing (i.e., discovering and applying the meaning of) written instruments, e.g., by resolving ambiguities and other uncertainties. Often used synonymously with 'interpretation' (q.v.): *Chatenay* v *Brazilian Submarine Telegraph Co* [1891] 1 QB 79. See *Franklin* v *A-G* [1974] QB 185. *See* INTERPRETATION OF STATUTES.

construction, rules of. Decisions of the courts relating to the interpretation of documents: e.g., the meaning of a document must be sought for in the document itself (*Simpson* v *Foxon* [1907] P 54); the intention may prevail over the words used (*Lloyd* v *Lloyd* (1837) 2 My & Cr 192); words are to be taken in their literal meaning (*Wallis* v *Smith* (1882) 21 Ch D 243); a deed is to be construed as a whole (*East Ham Corporation* v *Sunley* [1965] 1 WLR 30); *G* v *F* (Non-Molestation Order: Jurisdiction) [2000] Fam Law 519 (purposive construction given for domestic order).

constructive. Not directly expressed; inferred.

constructive desertion. Conduct of a respondent equivalent to the expulsion of a petitioner from the matrimonial home with the intention of ending consortium (q.v.). It is conduct equivalent to 'driving the other spouse away': *Boyd* v *Boyd* [1938] 4 All ER 181. Examples: husband's adultery; husband's accusing wife of immorality and telling her to go; treasonable activities of wife resulting in her conviction (*Ingram* v *Ingram* [1956] P 390). It may be an indication of irretrievable breakdown of marriage and grounds for proceedings leading to, e.g.,

separation and maintenance. *See* DESER-
TION; DIVORCE.

constructive dismissal. Indirect dismissal as where, e.g., employer unilaterally
changes terms of relationship so that an
employee has virtually no choice but to
resign. See E.R.A. 1996, s 95(1)(c); *Gold
v McConnell* [1995] IRLR 516; *Holland
v Glendale Industries* [1998] ICR 493;
TSB Bank v Harris [2000] IRLR 157. *See*
DISMISSAL FROM EMPLOYMENT.

constructive fraud. Equity considers as
fraud those transactions which lead the
court to the belief 'that it is unconscientious for a person to avail himself of the
legal advantage which he has obtained':
Torrance v Bolton (1872) 8 Ch App 118.
Equity will set aside, e.g., inequitable
dealings with the weak, poor and ignorant
(see *Miller v Cook* (1870) 40 LJ Ch 11;
L.P.A. 1925, s 174); appointments made
by the exercise of a special power (q.v.)
for a corrupt or foreign purpose (see *Re
Dick* [1953] Ch 343; and L.P.A. 1925,
s 157).

constructive knowledge. Knowledge
which a person might reasonably have
been expected to acquire from facts
observable or ascertainable by him or
from facts ascertainable by him with
the help of appropriate expert advice
which it is reasonable for him to seek: see
Lim.A. 1980, s 14A(10), as inserted by
Latent Damage Act 1986, s 1. See *Saxby
v Morgan* [1997] PIQR P531. *See*
KNOWLEDGE.

constructive malice. Malice proved
indirectly from attendant circumstances
when the state of mind of the accused
cannot be proved. Abolished with reference to homicide by Homicide Act 1957,
s 1(1), the marginal note to which reads:
'Abolition of constructive malice': 'Where
a person kills another in the course or
furtherance of some other offence, the
killing shall not amount to murder unless
done with the same malice aforethought
(express or implied) as is required for a
killing to amount to murder when not
done in the course or furtherance of
another offence . . . A killing done in the
course or for the purpose of resisting or

avoiding or preventing a lawful arrest,
or of effecting or assisting an escape or
rescue from legal custody shall be treated
as a killing in the course or furtherance of
an offence.' *See* MALICE AFORETHOUGHT.

constructive manslaughter. *See* MANS-
LAUGHTER, CONSTRUCTIVE.

constructive notice. Where a purchaser
fails to make a reasonable investigation
he will be deemed to have had notice
of what would have been discovered
had he made the normal and customary
enquiries. See L.P.A. 1925, s 199; L.P.A.
1969, ss 24, 25; Cos.A. 1985, s 711A,
inserted by Cos.A. 1989, s 142(1);
Barclays Bank v Coleman [2000] 1 All ER
385. *See* UNDUE INFLUENCE.

constructive total loss. Where the
subject matter insured is reasonably
abandoned because the actual total loss
appears unavoidable, or the expenditure
to prevent actual total loss would
exceed the value of the subject matter
if it were saved. Example: sinking of
a vessel, so that cost of raising it will
be greater than its value if recovered.
See Marine Insurance Act 1906, s 60(1);
*Assicurazioni Generali v Bessie Morris
SS Co* [1892] 1 QB 571.

constructive trust. 'An important judicial means of remedying unjust enrichment': *Sorochan v Sorochan* (1986) 29
DLR (4)1. A trust (q.v.) imposed by equity,
irrespective of the express or presumed
intentions of the parties, in the interest of
conscience and justice where one person
obtains an advantage by acting uncon-
scionably, fraudulently or inequitably,
as where X, an agent acting on behalf of
his principal, Y, makes a profit directly
out of his work and X is held to be a
constructive trustee for that profit to Y.
See *Gissing v Gissing* [1971] AC 886;
Royal Brunei Airlines v Tan [1995] 2 AC
378; *Brown v Bennett* [1998] 2 BCLC 97;
Banner Homes v Luff Developments
(2000) *The Times*, 17 February.

**constructive trusts, company directors
and.** In *Harrison Properties Ltd v
Harrison* [2001] All ER(D) 160 (Oct),
CA held that a director who obtained
company's property for himself following

his misuse of powers entrusted to him as a director was a constructive trustee. See also *Paragon Finance plc v Thakerar* [1999] 1 All ER 400.

construe. To discover and apply the meaning of a written instrument. *See* CONSTRUCTION.

consultation. The seeking of information from others. 'The essence . . . is the communication of a genuine invitation to give advice and a genuine consideration of that advice': *per* Webster J in *R v Secretary of State for Social Services ex p Assn of Metropolitan Authorities* [1986] 1 WLR 1.

consumer. 'In relation to goods, means any person who might wish to be supplied with the goods for his own private use or consumption': C.P.A. 1987, s 20(6). See *MFI Furniture v Hibbert* (1995) *The Times*, 21 July. In relation to consumer credit agreements Consumer Credit Act 2006 s 5(6) makes an amendment to the Consumer Credit Act 1974, s 158(4) i.e., s 158(4A) stating that a 'consumer' means '(a) a partnership consisting of two or three persons not all of whom are bodies corporate; and (b) an unincorporated body or persons which does not consist entirely of bodies corporate and is not a partnership'.

consumer credit. It was held in *Office of Fair Trading v Lloyds TSB* [2004] EWHC 2600 (Comm) that Consumer Credit Act 1974, s 75(1) has no application to a foreign transaction where contract is made wholly outside UK and is governed by foreign law.

consumer credit agreement. A personal credit agreement (q.v.) under which the creditor provides the debtor with credit not exceeding a statutory amount: C.C.A. 1974, s 8(2) (the upper limit rose to £25,000 on 1 May 1998, under Consumer Credit (Increase of Monetary Limits) Order 1998). It is a regulated agreement (q.v.) under the Act. The agreement may be of the following types: *restricted use* (credit facilities used for stipulated purposes only); *unrestricted use* (debtor is free to use the credit in any way he wishes); *debtor–creditor–supplier*

(credit supplied by supplier himself or an independent creditor); *debtor–creditor* (credit provided with no agent between supplier and creditor). See Consumer Credit (Exempt Agreements) Order 1989, SI 89/869; *Zoan v Rovamba* (2000) 150 NLJ 99; *Dimond v Lovell* [2000] 2 All ER 897; F.S.M.A. 2000, ss 203, 204.

Consumer Credit Appeals Tribunal. Established under the CCA 2006 s 55 by way of CCA 1974, s 40A. Previously appeals against decisions by the Office of Fair Trading went to the secretary of Sate. Such appeals will now be directed to the Consumer Credit Appeals tribunal. Appeal from the tribunal lies to the Court of Appeal. The tribunal is subject to the supervision of the Council on Tribunals. *See* COUNCIL ON TRIBUNALS.

consumer credit business. A business relating to the provision of credit under consumer credit agreements (q.v.) which are regulated agreements (q.v.): C.C.A. 1974, s 189(1). Now amended by CCA 2006 s 23 whereby such a business is defined as any business being carried on by a person so far as it comprises or relates to the provision of credit by him his being a creditor under a consumer credit agreement.

consumer credit, unfair terms. In *DG of Fair Trading v First National Bank* (2001) 151 NLJ 1610, HL decided that a term in a standard form of consumer credit contract, stating that in the event of borrower's default additional interest would be charged until payment, was not necessarily unfair within meaning of Unfair Terms in Consumer Contracts Regulations 1994.

consumer, dealing as. 'A party to a contract "deals as consumer" in relation to another party if he neither makes the contract in the course of a business nor holds himself out as doing so, and the other party does make the contract in the course of a business and in the case of a contract governed by the law of sale of goods or hire-purchase, or by s 7 [of this Act], the goods passing under or in pursuance of the contract are of a type ordinarily supplied for private use or consumption': Unfair Contract Terms Act 1977, s 12(1).

consumer goods. Any goods which are ordinarily intended for private use or consumption: C.P.A. 1987, s 10(7).

consumer goods, guarantee of. In the case of goods of a type ordinarily supplied for private use or consumption, where loss or damage arises from the goods proving defective while in consumer use (i.e., while a person is using them or has them in his possession for use, otherwise than exclusively for the purposes of a business) and results from the negligence of a person concerned in the manufacture or distribution of the goods, liability for the loss or damage cannot be excluded or restricted by reference to any contract term or notice contained in or operating by reference to a guarantee of the goods: Unfair Contract Terms Act 1977, s 5. This section does not apply as between parties to a contract under which, or in pursuance of which, possession or ownership of the goods passed: s 5(3).

consumer hire agreement. Agreement based on a bailment of goods for a period of not more than three months, requiring payment of not more than a statutory amount, which is not a hire-purchase agreement: C.C.A. 1974, s 15(1).

consumer hire business. A business relating to the bailment of goods under consumer hire agreements (q.v.) which are regulated agreements (q.v.): C.C.A. 1974, s 189(1). This is now defined by CCA 2006 s 23 as a business being carried on by a person so far as it relates to the bailment of goods under a regulated consumer hire agreement. *See* BAILMENT.

consumer protection. Legislation designed to protect the economic and other interests of consumers. Examples: Trade Descriptions Act 1968; Fair Trading Act 1973; C.C.A. 1974; C.P.A. 1987; Food Standards Act 1999; General Product Safety Regulations (SI 94/2328); SI 98/3050; *Coventry CC v Padgett Bros* (1998) 162 JP 6 73; *Thomson Tour Operations v Birch* (1999) 163 JP 465; *R v Kettering Justices ex p MRB Insurance Brokers*

(2000) *The Times*, 12 May. *See* CONSUMER SAFETY.

consumer rights. Sale of Goods Act 1979 will be amended substantially by Sale and Supply of Goods to Consumers Regulations 2002, implementing Directive 1999/44/EC. Thus, s 14 is amended by requiring that a seller is to deliver goods to the consumer (defined as 'any natural person who, in the contracts covered by the Regulations, is acting for purposes which are outside his business') which conform to the contract of sale. Where an installation is part of the contract and is incorrectly carried out, this will be considered as equivalent to lack of conformity of goods.

consumer safety. A person is guilty of an offence if he supplies any consumer goods (q.v.) which fail to comply with the general safety requirement, or offers or agrees to supply any such goods, or exposes or possesses any such goods for supply (q.v.): C.P.A. 1987, s 10(1). The 'general safety requirement' involves goods being reasonably safe (q.v.) having regard to all the circumstances, including, e.g., published standards of safety, instructions or warnings given with the goods: s 10(2). For defences, see ss 4 (the 'state of the art' defence), 10(4), 39 (due diligence). The Secretary of State has power to make appropriate safety regulations, serve prohibition and suspension notices: ss 11–14. For civil proceedings, see s 41. *See* DUE CARE.

consumer sale. A sale of goods by a seller in the course of business where the goods are of a type ordinarily bought for consumption or private use and sold to a person who does not buy or hold himself out as buying them in the course of business. See Unfair Contract Terms Act 1977.

consumer trade practice. Phrase used in the Fair Trading Act 1973 to mean any practice carried on in connection with the supply of goods or services to consumers, relating, e.g., to terms and conditions of supply, promotion, methods of salesmanship, packing of goods, methods of demanding or securing payment.

consummation of a marriage. The completion of a marital union by ordinary and complete sexual intercourse. Incapacity (permanent and incurable) of either party, or wilful refusal, to consummate makes a marriage voidable. See Mat.C.A. 1973, s 12(*a*), (*b*); *W* v *W* [1967] 1 WLR 1554.

contact order. An order requiring the person with whom a child lives to allow the child to visit or stay with the person named in the order: Ch.A. 1989, s 8. For restrictions, see s 9. See *Re L (Child) (Contact: Domestic Violence)* (2000) *The Times*, 21 June (significance of domestic violence for contact orders); *Re F (Children) (Care: Termination of Contact)* [2000] 2 FCR 481 (orders and Convention on Human Rights 1950).

contact order, adoptive child. In *Re R (a child)* [2005] *The Times*, 15 September, the CA held that where a child is living with adoptive parents and there is regular contact by an elder sister and disruption is caused to the child from settling in within the adoptive family then the court should be reluctant to make a contract order where the adoptive parents are opposed to such an order.

contact, parental, with children in care. Duty of local authority, where a child is in their care, to allow the child reasonable contact with parents or guardian: Ch.A. 1987, s 34. See *Re W (A Minor) (Parental Contact: Prohibition)* (2000) *The Times*, 22 January (court has no jurisdiction to prohibit such contact).

contemnor. One who has committed contempt of court (q.v.). See *Wright* v *Jess* [1987] 1 WLR 1076 (committal of contemnor to prison in his absence); *Taylor* v *Persico* (1992) *The Times*, 12 February (contemnor to be given chance to mitigate). See *Grupo Torras SA* v *Al Sabah (No. 4)* [1999] CLC 885 (question of whether a party in contempt can be allowed to continue participation in an action until the contempt has been purged: see also *X* v *Morgan Grampian* [1991] 1 AC 1).

contemporanea expositio. Contemporaneous interpretation. The reading of a document as it would have been read at the time of making. 'In the construction of ancient deeds and grants, there is no better way of construing them than by usage: *contemporanea expositio* is the best way to go by': *A-G* v *Parker* (1747) 3 Atk 576. See *Campbell College* v *Valuation Commissioners for N Ireland* [1964] 2 All ER 705.

contempt of court and strict liability rule. The 'strict liability rule' means the rule of law whereby conduct may be treated as a contempt of court as tending to interfere with the course of justice in legal proceedings, regardless of intent to do so: see Contempt of Court Act 1981, s 1; *A-G* v *Sunday Newspapers* [1999] COD 11. It applies only to publications (e.g., by speech, writing, or broadcasts addressed to the public at large) if it creates a substantial risk that the course of justice will be seriously impeded or prejudiced, and if the proceedings in question are 'active', e.g., when a warrant for arrest has been issued: s 2, Sch 1. See *M* v *Home Office* [1992] 2 WLR 73 (contempt by minister); *A-G* v *Birmingham Post* [1999] 1 WLR 361. For principles of sentencing, see *R* v *Moran* (1985) 81 Cr App R 51. For appeals, see A.J.A. 1960, s 13(2) amended by Acc.J.A. 1999, s 64. For power of the High Court or Court of Appeal to punish for contempt of court by an order of committal, see CPR, Sch 1; O 52; PD, RSC O 52. *See* COMMITTAL FOR CONTEMPT; FALSE STATEMENTS, PROCEEDINGS IN RELATION TO.

contempt of court, defences. These include innocent publication or distribution, contemporary report published in good faith, part of discussion of public affairs: Contempt of Court Act 1981, ss 3–5. See *R* v *McDaniel* (1990) 12 Cr App R (S) 44; *Saunders* v *Punch Ltd* [1998] 1 All ER 234.

contempt of statute. A mere rule of construction, and not a crime, whereby the courts may infer a Parliamentary intent to impose liability for breach of statutory duty (i.e., to create an offence): *R* v *Horseferry Road Magistrates' Court ex p IBC* [1986] 2 All ER 666.

contempt of the House. An act or omission which brings into contempt the authority of a House of Parliament, or which directly obstructs its proceedings. In effect, a breach of Parliamentary privilege (q.v.). Examples: disorderly conduct in the presence of either House; indignities offered to either House by spoken or written words; obstructing officers of either House.

contentious business. Business before a court or arbitrator, not being business which falls within the definition of non-contentious or common form probate business in S.C.A. 1981, s 128, i.e., in general, business of a lawyer where there is a contest between the parties: Solicitors Act 1974, s 87(1), amended by Arbitration Act 1996, Sch 4. See also ss 56–75; *Re Simpson Marshall* [1959] Ch 229.

contentious probate proceedings. Comprises claims to revoke a grant previously made in solemn form, claims relating to applications for administration ('interest actions') and claims as to the validity of wills. If a probate claim is to be commenced in the High Court, the claim form must be issued out of Chancery Chambers or one of the Chancery District registries (at Birmingham, Bristol, Cardiff, Leeds, Liverpool, Manchester, Newcastle, Preston): PD 49, para 2.1. For revocation of a grant of probate, see PD 49, para 3.1. For application for summary judgment (q.v.) under CPR, Part 24, see r 24.3 as amended: SI 00/2092. *See* PROBATE; TESTAMENTARY SCRIPT.

contested case, allocation of. In *Stevens v Newey* (2005) *The Times*, 14 January, the CA held that in a case relating to presumed undue influence and contested facts, it should not be allocated to a district judge unless the civil judge had considered the nature of the case and the skills of the district judge.

context. Parts of, e.g., a document connected with a particular passage or sentence. 'The real question which we have to decide is what does the word mean in the context in which we find it here, both in the immediate context of the subsection in which the word occurs and in the general context of the Act': *Re Bidie* [1948] 2 All ER 995. See also *Abrahams v Cavey* [1968] 1 QB 479. *See* INTERPRETATION OF STATUTES.

contiguous. Touching at some point; adjoining. See *Haynes v King* [1893] 3 Ch 439.

contingency. A right, interest, obligation, related to a possible future and uncertain event.

contingency fee. An arrangement between a client and his legal representative whereby the latter agrees to represent the former (often in personal injury cases) on the understanding that the fee to be paid will be an agreed percentage of the amount recovered and that, should the client's claim fail, the representative shall not be paid. Common in USA. See *Thai Trading Co v Taylor* [1998] QB 781; *Hughes v Kingston upon Hull CC* [1999] QB 1193 (client unable to seek order for costs where contingency fee agreement existed). *See* CONDITIONAL FEE AGREEMENT.

contingency fee agreement. In *Callery v Gray* (2002) 152 NLJ 1031, HL refused to interfere with a CA decision that the cost of after-the-event insurance, covering claimant's liability under a contingency fee agreement to pay defendant's costs if claim fails, is recoverable as part of successful claimant's costs. Matters of this nature are for CA, not HL.

contingent legacy. A legacy (q.v.) bequeathed on an expressed contingency, e.g., that the legatee shall marry.

contingent remainder. A remainder is contingent if the grantee is unascertained or if the title depends on the occurrence of a designated event. Example, grant 'to X for life, remainder in tail to his first son who shall attain the age of 21'. See *Chinn v Collins* [1981] AC 533. *See* REMAINDER.

continuous bail. *See* BAIL, CONTINUOUS.

continuous employment. In general, for the purposes of employees' statutory rights of employment, employment is presumed to be continuous unless the contrary is shown. For rules of computing the employment period, see E.R.A. 1996, s 210; *Collison v BBC* [1998] ICR 669.

contraband. 1. Goods, the import or export of which is forbidden. 2. Specifically, goods which, in time of war, may not be supplied by a neutral to a belligerent without risk of seizure.

contra bonos mores. Against morals. 'Wrong rather than right in the judgment of the majority of contemporary fellow citizens': see *Hashman v UK* (1999) *The Times*, 1 December. 'Contrary to a good way of life': *Hughes v Holley* [1987] Crim LR 253. 'Whatever is *contra bonos mores et decorum*, the principles of our law prohibit, and the King's court as the general censor and guardian of the public manners, is bound to restrain and punish': *Jones v Randall* (1744) 1 Cowp 17. See also *Shaw v DPP* [1962] AC 220; *Knuller v DPP* [1973] AC 435.

contract. A legally binding agreement creating enforceable obligations. 'A promise or set of promises which the law will enforce': Pollock, *Principles of Contract* (1876). 'Contracts when entered into freely and voluntarily shall be held sacred and shall be enforced by courts of justice': *Printing and Numerical Registering Co v Sampson* (1875) LR 19 Eq 462. *Contracts under seal*, known also as *deeds or specialty contracts*, must be in writing. *Simple contracts* include oral contracts and contracts which require some writing. *Implied contracts* arise from the assumed intentions of the parties. *Contracts of record* arise from obligations imposed by a court of record (q.v.). Contract generally involves: (1) prior offer and subsequent, qualified acceptance (except in the case of a promise in a deed); (2) *consensus ad idem* (q.v.); (3) intention to create legal relations; (4) genuineness of consent; (5) contractual capacity of the parties; (6) legality of object; (7) possibility of performance; (8) certainty of terms; (9) valuable consideration. In general, parol evidence will not be admitted so as to indicate any addition to, variation or contradiction of a written contract: see *The Nile Rhapsody* [1992] 2 Lloyd's Rep 349. For inference of contract from conduct, see, e.g., *Rayner v DTI* [1990] 2 AC 413.

contract, appropriate currency of the. In relation to contract damages, unless an appropriate currency is expressly stated in the contract, the appropriate currency will be that which truly expresses the plaintiff's loss, or that in which the loss was felt. See *The Federal Huron* [1985] 3 All ER 378.

contract as realisable property. A consultancy contract is not realisable property which the court might take into account in deciding an application for a certification of inadequacy to settle an account due under an order of confiscation: In *re Adams* (2004) *The Times*, 6 December.

contract, assignment of. *See* ASSIGNMENT.

contract, bilateral. Contract in which the parties must fulfil reciprocal obligations. *See* UNILATERAL CONTRACT.

contract, breach of. *See* BREACH OF CONTRACT.

contract by correspondence. *See* CORRESPONDENCE, CONTRACT BY.

contract, custom and. 'An alleged custom can be incorporated into a contract only if there is nothing in the express or necessarily implied terms of the contract to prevent such inclusion and, further, that a custom will only be imported into a contract where it can be so imported consistently with the tenor of the document as a whole': *per* Lord Jenkinson in *London Export Corp v Jubilee Coffee Roasting Co* [1958] 2 All ER 411.

contract, discharge of. *See* DISCHARGE.

contract, divisible. *See* DIVISIBLE CONTRACT.

contract, fixed term. In *Department for Work and Pensions v Webley* (2005) *The Times*, 17 January, the CA held that an employer's decision not to renew a fixed-term contract cannot, in itself, insure less favourable treatment of an employee.

contract, formal. *See* FORMAL CONTRACT.

contract for sale of land, formalities. A contract for the sale or other disposition of an interest in land can only be made in writing and only by incorporating all the terms which the parties have expressly agreed in one document, or, where contracts are exchanged, in each: L.P. (Misc. Provs.) A. 1989, s 2. See *Firstpost Homes* v *Johnson* [1995] 1 WLR 1567. This does not apply to contracts to grant short leases (see L.P.A. 1925, s 54(2)); contracts made in the course of a public auction; contracts regulated under F.S.A. 1986, or to matters involved in the creation or operation of resulting, implied or constructive trusts (q.v.): s 2(5). See *United Bank of Kuwait* v *Sahib* [1997] Ch 107; *McCausland* v *Duncan Lawrie Ltd* [1997] 1WLR 38.

contract for sale, uncompleted. In *Bayoumi* v *Women's Total Abstinence Union* (2003) *The Times*, 11 November, the CA held that an uncompleted contract for the sale of charity land did not constitute a disposition of the land, so that, where a surveyor's report was lacking, it was not possible to validate the contract in favour of a purchaser for money's worth in good faith.

contract, freedom of. 'A basic principle of the common law of contract . . . is that the parties are free to determine for themselves what primary obligations they will accept': *per* Lord Diplock in *Photo Productions Ltd* v *Securicor Transport Ltd* [1980] AC 827. 'There is the vigilance of the common law which, while allowing freedom of contract, watches to see that it is not abused': *per* Denning J (considering exemption clauses) in *John Lee & Sons Ltd* v *Railway Executive* [1949] 2 All ER 591. See *Lombard Tricity Finance Ltd* v *Paton* [1989] 1 All ER 918 (unilateral variation). *See* CONTRACT, VARIATION OF.

contract, frustration of. *See* FRUSTRATION OF CONTRACT.

contract, frustration of by impossibility. Two students had been expelled from university and their salaried offices as union officers had been ended following the introduction of a new union constitution, so that their contracts of employment with the union had been terminated. It was held that they had not been dismissed, but their contracts had been frustrated by

impossibility of performance: *Anyanwu* v *South Bank Student Union* (No. 2) (2003) *The Times*, 5 December.

contract, frustration of, implied term theory. 'Frustration is explained in theory as a condition or term of the contract, implied by the law *ab initio*, in order to supply what the parties would have inserted had the matter occurred to them, on the basis of what is fair and reasonable, having regard to the mutual interests concerned, and of the main objects of the contract': *per* Lord Sumner in *Hirji Muljii* v *Cheong Yue SS Co* [1926] AC 497.

contract, illegal performance of. In *Colen* v *Cebrian Ltd* (2003) *The Times*, 27 November, the CA held that where, at its inception, a contract is legal, it does not become illegal and, therefore, unenforceable, by acts of illegality arising in its performance.

contract, implied terms. In *Crossley* v *Faithful & Gould Ltd* [2004] EWCA Civ 293, the CA held that the court ought not to imply into a contract of employment any general duty of the employer to take reasonable care of the employee's economic well-being. See also *Malik* v *BCCI* [1937] 3 All ER 1. It was held in *Times Newspapers Ltd* v *Weidenfeld Ltd* [2002] FSR 29, that an implied term cannot go beyond what was needed to give efficacy to the contract, nor could it be inconsistent with the effect of the express terms.

contract, incapacitation and. A party who incapacitates himself, by his own act or default, from performing his obligations under a contract, is regarded as having refused to perform them. 'To say "I would like to but cannot", negatives intent to perform as much as "I will not"': *per* Devlin J in *Universal Carriers* v *Citati* [1957] 2 QB 401.

contracting out. Removing oneself from an obligation. For contracting out of a credit agreement, see C.C.A. 1974, s 173(1). For restrictions on contracting out of operations of E.R.A. 1996, see s 203(1); Employment Relations Act 1999, s 14.

contract, measure of damages in. *See* MEASURE OF DAMAGES IN CONTRACT.

contract, naked. *See* NUDUM PACTUM.

contract of employment. A contract of service (or apprenticeship) which may arise from an agreement expressed in writing, orally or from conduct. See T.U.L.R.(C.)A. 1992, s 295(1); E.P.(C.)A. 1978, s 153; Public Interest Disclosure Act 1998, s 15(1). Under E.R.A. 1996, s 1, employers must provide a written statement within two months of the beginning of employment to employees, setting out, e.g., job description, notice requirements, terms concerning pay and hours of work. Staff engaged on a casual 'as required' basis are not employees under contracts of employment: *Carmichael* v *National Power plc* [1999] 1 WLR 2042. In *Eastwood* v *Magnox Electric plc* [2004] UKHL 35 the HL held that, where prior to the dismissal (actual or constructive) of an employee, he has acquired a cause of action at common law relating to breach of contract, that cause of action will be unimpaired by any subsequent unfair dismissal and statutory rights following as a result.

contract of record. Judgments and recognisances (qq.v.) enrolled in the records of proceedings of a court of record.

contract of sale. Includes an agreement to sell, as well as a sale: S.G.A. 1979, s 61(1). Price is generally one of the essentials of sale so that there may be no contract of sale if it remains 'to be agreed' by the parties.

contract of service. A contract, written or oral, express or implied, to execute personally any work. It usually implies a relationship of 'master and servant'. It has been held to exist where M (the master) has the power of selection of S (his servant), where M pays S wages, where M has the right to control S's method of work, where M has the right to suspend or dismiss S: *Short* v *Henderson* (1946) 62 TLR 427. Whether or not a contract is 'of services' is to be judged by an objective test: *Davis* v *New England College of Arundel* [1977] ICR 6. *See* INTEGRATION TEST.

contract, open. *See* OPEN CONTRACT.

contractor. *See* INDEPENDENT CONTRACTOR.

contract, rescission of. *See* RESCISSION.

contract, root of. *See* ROOT OF CONTRACT.

contracts, applicable law of. Contracts (Applicable Law) Act 1990 incorporates into UK law the Rome Convention 1980, under which parties to a contract are free to choose which laws shall govern it and, where the choice is not made, the contract will be governed by the law of the country 'with which the transaction has its closest and most real connection'. See *Centrax Ltd* v *Citibank NA* [1999] 1 All ER (Comm) 557.

contracts, collateral. *See* COLLATERAL.

contract, severance of. *See* SEVERANCE.

contracts, illegal. *See* ILLEGAL CONTRACTS.

contracts, mental patients'. *See* MENTAL PATIENT.

contracts, minors'. *See* MINORS' CONTRACTS.

contracts of adhesion. *See* STANDARD FORM CONTRACTS.

contract, spot. Contract for immediate delivery and payment. See *Thames Sack Co Ltd* v *Knowles* (1918) 88 LJ KB 583.

contracts required to be in writing. The group of contracts which are valid only if written, including bills of exchange, marine insurance, bills of sale, acknowledgment of statute-barred debts, certain contracts relating to hire-purchase, contracts for the sale or other disposition of certain interests in land (L.P. (Misc. Provs.) A. 1989, s 2).

contracts, standard form. *See* STANDARD FORM CONTRACTS.

contracts, successive breaches of. In *Heaton* v *AXA* (2002) *The Times*, 15 May, HL held that where claimant had linked claims against two defendants, A and B, for successive breaches of separate contracts and had concluded a compromise agreement with A in full and final settlement of all actual and potential claims between them, and the question had arisen whether he could pursue an action against B, the correct approach was to ascertain intended effect of the compromise by interpreting words used, and where the agreement had not fixed the entire measure of claimant's loss, his action against B was not precluded.

contracts, third party rights in. A person who is not a party to a contract (a 'third party') may in his own right enforce a term of the contract if the contract expressly provides that he may, or the term purports to confer a benefit on him (but not if on a proper construction of the contract it appears that the parties did not intend the term to be enforceable by the third party): Contracts (Rights of Third Parties) Act 1999, s 1(1), (2). The third party must be expressly identified in the contract by name, as a member of a class or as answering a particular description, but need not be in existence when the contract is entered into: s 1(3). A third party cannot receive a greater right than that intended by the contracting parties: s 1(4). The third party has available to him any remedy that would have been available in an action for breach had he been a party to the contract: s 1(5).

contracts, third party rights in, exceptions to. Contracts (Rights of Third Parties) Act 1999, s 1, confers no rights: in relation to bills of exchange, promissory notes or other negotiable instruments; in relation to a company's memorandum and articles of association constituting a contract binding on the company and its members; in relation to any attempt to enforce any term of employment against an employee; in relation to contracts for the carriage of goods by sea, rail or road. See 1999 Act, s 6.

contract, subject to. *See* SUBJECT TO CONTRACT.

contract terms, unfair. *See* UNFAIR CONTRACT TERMS.

contractual liability, avoidance of. As between contracting parties (where one of them deals as consumer or on the other's written standard terms of business), then, as against that party, the other cannot by reference to any contract term, when himself in breach of contract, exclude or restrict any liability of his in respect of the breach, or claim to be entitled to render a contractual performance substantially different from that which was reasonably expected of him, or, in respect of the whole or any part of his contractual obligation, to render no performance at all except in so far as the contract term satisfies the requirement of reasonableness: Unfair Contract Terms Act 1977, s 3. See *British Fermentation Products v Compair Reavell Ltd* [1999] 2 All ER (Comm) 389.

contract under seal. A contract expressed in a document to which the maker's seal was attached and which was delivered as 'his deed'. See now L.P. (Misc. Provs.) A. 1989, s 1.

contract, unenforceable. *See* UNENFORCEABLE CONTRACT.

contract, unilateral. *See* UNILATERAL CONTRACT.

contract, variation of. A modification or alteration of terms of a contract by mutual agreement. A contract under seal may be varied by parol contract: *Berry v Berry* [1929] 2 KB 316. A simple contract, whether written or unwritten, may be varied by oral or written subsequent agreement. A contract required by law to be evidenced in writing can be varied only in writing: *New Hart Builders v Brindley* [1975] Ch 342. See *Sepong Engineering v Formula One Management* [2000] 1 Lloyd's Rep 602.

contract, vicarious performance of. *See* VICARIOUS PERFORMANCE OF CONTRACT.

contract, wagering. *See* WAGERING CONTRACT.

***contra proferentem* rule.** *See* VERBA CHARTARUM (etc.).

contravention. The violation of an order. For planning contravention notices, see T.C.P.A. 1990, s 171C, inserted by Planning and Compensation Act 1991, s 1.

contribution. 1. Payment imposed on, or made by, some person. 2. Payment of the share of an individual relating to a loss for which several persons are jointly liable, e.g., joint tortfeasors (q.v.). See

Civil Liability (Contribution) Act 1978. 3. 'A right of someone to recover from a third person all or part of the amount which he himself is liable to pay': CPR Glossary. *See* PART 20 CLAIM.

contribution, assessment of. In *Brian Warwicker Partnership* v *Hok International Ltd* [2006] *The Times*, 19 September, the CA held that when considering the Civil Liability (Contribution) Act 1978, the level of contribution from the parties in respect of the same damage the courts will take in to account any material non-causative factors to determine the amount of contribution on a just and equitable basis. There would have to be a sufficient link between it and the damage in question.

contribution, test of applicability of statute. A simple test of whether the Civil Liability (Contribution) Act 1978 is applicable to a case, was propounded in *Howkins & Harrison* v *Tyler and Another* (2000) *The Times*, 8 August. If A and B are liable to C, then if A pays money to C in satisfaction of his liability, would that sum, *ipso facto*, reduce B's liability to C? If B pays money to C in satisfaction of his liability, would that reduce A's liability? Unless both questions produce affirmative answers, the 1978 Act cannot apply.

contributories, liability on winding-up. Obligation of every past and present member of a company to contribute to its assets to any amount sufficient for payment of its debts and liabilities, and the expenses of winding-up, and for the adjustment of contributories' rights among themselves: Ins.A. 1986, s 74(1). Maximum liability is limited in the case of a company limited by shares to the amount unpaid on the shares, and, in the case of a company limited by guarantee, to the amount of the guarantee: s 74(2), (3). A past member is not liable to contribute if he has ceased to be a member for one year or more before the commencement of the winding-up: s 74(2)(a).

contributory negligence. 'A man's carelessness in looking after his own safety.' A defence established where it is proved that an injured party failed to take reasonable care of himself, thus contributing materially to his own injury: *Nance* v *British Columbia Electric Rlwy* [1951] AC 601. Under Law Reform (Contributory Negligence) Act 1945 a claim in respect of damage is reduced to such extent as the court thinks just and equitable having regard to claimant's share in responsibility for damage. 'Damage' includes loss of life and personal injury. See *Tremayne* v *Hill* [1987] RTR 131 – no duty on pedestrian who is crossing a multiple road junction to keep a lookout. See Animals Act 1971, s 10; Fatal Accidents Act 1976, s 5; *Harrison* v *British Railways* [1981] 3 All ER 679. 1945 Act does not apply to contract (see *Basildon DC* v *Lesser Ltd* [1985] QB 839), or to a claim based on a breach of the duty of utmost good faith (see *Banque Keyser Ullmann* v *Skandia Ltd* [1987] 2 WLR 1300). For contributory negligence constituted by an imprudent lending policy, see *Platform Home Loans* v *Oyston Shipways Ltd* [1999] 2 WLR 518. *See* NEGLIGENCE.

controlled drugs. *See* DRUGS, CONTROLLED.

controlled trust. Means, in relation to a solicitor, a trust of which he is a sole trustee or co-trustee with one or more of his partners or employees: Solicitors Act 1974, s 87(1). *See* TRUST.

controller. A managing director, chief executive, or a person who, either alone or with associates, controls the exercise of 15 per cent or more of voting power: Banking Act 1987, s 105(3). See also C.C.A. 1974, s 189(1).

controlling director. A director of a company, the directors of which have a controlling interest therein, who is the beneficial owner of, or who is able either directly or through the medium of other companies or by any other indirect means to control more than five per cent of the ordinary share capital of the company.

Control Orders. It was held that a non-derogating control order made by the

Secretary of State under the Terrorism Act 2005 was incompatible with the individual's right to a fair hearing under the European Convention of Human Rights. See *Secretary of State for the Home Department* v *MB* [2006] *The Times*, 17 April.

convention. 1. A treaty between states. In interpreting a statute designed to enact a convention, the court may look at it in the event of an ambiguity: *The Banco* [1971] P 137; *R* v *Chief Immigration Officer ex p Bibi* [1976] 1 WLR 979. 2. Agreed usage or practice. 3. A convention of the constitution is one of the 'rules for determining the mode in which the discretionary powers of the Crown (or of ministers or servants of the Crown) ought to be exercised': Dicey, *The Law of the Constitution* (1885). Conventions are understandings, tacitly agreed, resulting from long practice by which the conduct of the Crown and Parliament is regulated in the absence of formal legal rules ('constitutional morality': Dicey). Example: party with a majority in the Commons is entitled to have its leader made Prime Minister (q.v.). The courts recognise, but do not enforce, conventions. See, e.g., *A-G* v *Jonathan Cape Ltd* [1976] QB 752. For example of convention incorporated into statute, see Statute of Westminster 1931.

convention, estoppel by. *See* ESTOPPEL.

conversion. 1. In criminal law, 'fraudulent conversion' to one's use or benefit was formerly an offence under Larceny Act 1916, s 20. See now Th.A. 1968, s 1. 2. In equity, conversion is a notional change, under certain conditions, of land into money, or money into land, which arises as soon as the duty to convert arises. Example: P gives personalty on trust to Q to purchase land and hold it for R – the personalty is notionally considered as realty. Abolished (for many purposes) under Trusts of Land and Appointment of Trustees Act 1996, s 3. See Trustee Delegation Act 1999, s 1(7). The doctrine continues to have application in the case of a will trust where the testator dies before 1 January, 1997. See

Fletcher v *Ashburner* (1779) 1 Bro CC 497; *Irani Finance Ltd* v *Singh* [1971] Ch. 59. *See* CONVERSION, TORT OF.

conversion, liability of a series of persons relating to. In *Kuwait Airways Corporation* v *Iraqi Airways Co (Nos 4 and 5)* (2002) *The Times*, 21 May, the HL held that all persons through whose hands goods had passed in a series of conversions that had wrongfully excluded an owner from possession, were liable to the owner for any loss resulting from misappropriation of those goods.

conversion of title. Rules set out in L.R.A. 1925, s 77 (as substituted by L.R.A. 1986, s 1) whereby: good leasehold title may be upgraded to absolute title at any time; possessory title may be upgraded to absolute (if freehold) or good leasehold (if leasehold); qualified title may be converted to absolute (if freehold) or good leasehold (if leasehold) at any time.

conversion, tort of. A wilful act in relation to a person's goods which constitutes a serious and unjustifiable denial of his title to them. Claimant must show possession or the right to immediate possession. See, e.g.: *BBMB* v *Eda Holdings* [1990] 1 WLR 409; *Smith* v *Lloyds TSB Group plc* (1999) *The Times*, 23 December (consideration of Bills of Exchange Act 1882, s 64). A claim lies in conversion for loss or destruction of goods which a bailee has allowed to happen in breach of his duty to his bailor (that is to say, it lies in a case which is not otherwise conversion, but would have been detinue (q.v.) before detinue was abolished): Torts (Interference with Goods) Act 1977, s 2. For right to damages for conversion of goods asserted by an equitable owner against a bona fide purchaser for value (q.v.), see *MCC Proceeds* v *Lehman Bros* [1998] 4 All ER 675. *See* BAILMENT; DELIVERY UP OF GOODS.

conveyance. 1. Transfer of ownership of property. 2. The instrument effecting the transfer. (Where the subject matter of a conveyance is stated to be 'the property known as . . .' it is permissible to use extrinsic evidence (q.v.) to identify the property in question, where that is disputed: see *Freeguard* v *Rogers* [1998] EGCS 145.) See Law Society's *National Conveyancing Protocol* 1994. 3. Under L.P.A. 1925, s 205(1), includes 'mortgage, charge, lease, asset, vesting declaration, disclaimer, release and every other assurance of property or of an interest therein by any instrument, except a will'. See also L.C.A. 1972, s 17(1). 4. Under Th.A. 1968, s 12(1), as amended by C.J.A. 1988, s 32, it is an offence to take a conveyance (i.e., one constructed or adapted for the carriage of persons by land, water or air) for one's own or another's use without having the consent of the owner or other lawful authority. See *DPP* v *Spriggs* [1994] RTR 1. *See* JOY RIDING.

conveyance, deed of. *See* DEED.

conveyancer, licensed. One who holds a licence in force under A.J.A. 1985, Part II, allowing him to provide conveyancing services (see C.L.S.A. 1990, s 119(1)), e.g., preparation of transfers, conveyances, contracts and other documents in connection with, and other services ancillary to, the disposition or acquisition of estates or interests in land: A.J.A. 1985, s 11. See *R* v *Council for Licensed Conveyancers ex p Watson* (2000) *The Times*, 16 June.

conveyance, taking without authority. V.(C.)A. 2001, s 37, proposes an extension of prosecution time limits under Th.A. 1968, s 12(4), so that proceedings for an offence shall not be commenced after the end of the period of three years beginning with the day on which the offence was committed, but, subject to that, may be commenced at any time within the period of six months beginning with the relevant day (on which sufficient knowledge to justify the proceedings came to the prosecutor's knowledge). See now V.(C.)A. 2001.

conveyance, voluntary. *See* VOLUNTARY DISPOSITION.

Conveyancing Appeal Tribunals. Established under C.L.S.A. 1990, s 41, to consider appeals from decisions of Authorised Conveyancing Practitioners

Board to refuse, or suspend applications for, authorisation under s 37: s 41. Appeal on points of law may be heard by the High Court: s 42.

conviction. Defined under Bail Act 1976, s 2(1), as: a finding of guilt; a finding that a person is not guilty by reason of insanity; a finding under M.C.A. 1980, s 30, that the person in question did the act or made the omission charged; a conviction of an offence for which an order is made placing the offender on probation or discharging him absolutely or conditionally. For 'unsafe conviction', see *R* v *Davis* (2000) *The Times*, 25 July (Court of Appeal stated that a conviction could never be safe if there was a doubt about guilt, but a conviction might be unsafe even where there was no doubt about guilt, but because of initiation of the trial process by serious unfairness, or significant legal misdirection). See *A-G Reference (No. 3 of 1999)* [1999] 2 Cr App R (S) 433.

conviction, act in relation to. In *R* v *Auguste* (2003) *The Times*, 15 December, the CA held that, in relation to the offence of permitting the smoking of cannabis on premises, it is essential to show that an appropriate activity had taken place, not merely that defendant had given permission.

conviction and role of judge. In *R* v *Wang* (2005) *The Times*, 11 February, the HL held that there exist no circumstances in which a judge is entitled to direct a jury to enter a verdict of guilty.

conviction, proof of. The establishing of the fact of a person's conviction. Certified copies of extracts from court records are admissible. See, e.g., P.&C.E.A. 1984, ss 73(1), 74. *See* CRIMINAL CONVICTION CERTIFICATE.

conviction, referral of. In *R (Westlake)* v *Criminal Cases Review Commission* (2004) *The Times*, 19 November, the CA held that the CCRC had acted correctly, within its statutory discretion, by refusing to refer to the Court of Appeal (see Criminal Appeal Act 1995, s 9) the conviction of Timothy Evans for the murder of his daughter.

convictions, evidence of previous. *See* PREVIOUS CONVICTIONS, EVIDENCE OF.

cooling-off period. Period during which a regulated agreement (q.v.) may be cancelled by a debtor or hirer: see C.C.A. 1974, ss 67–74. See Consumer Protection (Contracts Concluded away from Business Premises) Regulations (SI 87/2117, SI 98/3050) allowing a customer who contracts to buy goods or services during a trader's unsolicited visit to his home or place of work, a seven-day cooling-off period. The regulations do not apply, e.g., to the buying or leasing of land.

co-ownership of real property. Subsists, as in a joint tenancy (q.v.) and a tenancy in common (q.v.), where two or more persons simultaneously enjoy concurrent interests in the same property. *See* COPARCENARY.

coparcenary. Where two or more persons together constituted a single heir, e.g., tenant in tail (q.v.) who has died intestate and left female heirs only. The heirs (coparceners) held in undivided shares. Abolished, save in the case of a tenant in tail who dies without having barred the entail, by A.E.A. 1925, s 45(1). *See* BARRING OF ENTAILED INTEREST.

copyhold. Tenure at the will of the lord of the manor. Converted into socage tenure (q.v.) as from 1 January 1926: L.P.A. 1922, s 128. See also L.P.A. 1925; L.P. (Amendment) A. 1926.

copy of document. *See* DOCUMENT, COPY OF.

copy, official. *See* DOCUMENT, COPY OF.

copyright. A property right (which is transmissible by assignment or will as personal property) which subsists in original literary, dramatic, musical or artistic works, sound recordings, films, broadcasts or cable programmes, and the typographical arrangement of published editions: Copyright, Designs and Patents Act 1988, s 1(1). 'Original' means originating from the author, not copied: see *Interlego* v *Tyco Industries* [1989] 3 WLR 678. 'Author' means the person who creates the work: s 9(1); he is the first owner of the copyright. For meaning of 'typographical arrangement', see *News-*

paper Licensing Agency v *Marks and Spencer plc* (2000) 150 NLJ 900. Usually endures for the holder's lifetime plus 70 years (EC Directive 93/98). An author has the right to be identified as such: s 77. Remedies for infringements include damages and injunctions: s 96. See *Phonographic Performance Ltd* v *Maitra* [1998] 1 WLR 870 (grant of injunction with immediate effect and without express time limit); *Hyde Park Residence Ltd* v *Yelland* (2000) *The Times*, 16 February (inherent jurisidiction of court to refuse to enforce copyright where enforcement would offend against policy of the law); *Jones* v *Tower Hamlets LBC* (2000) *The Times*, 14 November (protection of architectural design by copyright). Given that title to property situated in England is to be determined by English law, title to English copyright may not be removed from England by any decree of a foreign government: *Peer International Corporation* v *Termidor Music Publishers* (2003) *The Times*, 2 January. *See* AUTHOR.

copyright, acts restricted by. These comprise: copying of the work (s 17); issuing copies to the public (s 18); performing, showing or playing the work in public (s 19); broadcasting the work (s 20): Copyright, Designs and Patents Act 1988, s 16(1). For permitted acts (involving, e.g., research and private study), see chap III, 1988 Act. See *Express Newspapers* v *News (UK) Ltd* [1990] 3 All ER 376; *Designer Guild* v *Russell Williams Ltd* (2000) *The Times*, 28 November. Chancery Division has exclusive jurisdiction in all copyright matters: *Apac Rowena* v *Norpol Packaging* [1991] 4 All ER 516.

copyright, assignment of. In *Novello Ltd* v *Keith Prowse Publishing Co* (2005) *The Times*, 10 January, the CA held that the Patents Act 1988 does not act so as to prohibit an author who is the first owner of a copyright in works prior to the Copyright Act 1956 from assigning any reversionary interest in the copyright during the currency of the Act.

copyright, Crown. *See* CROWN COPYRIGHT.

copyright, in relation to random access memory. It was held in *Kabushiki* v *Ball* (2004) *The Times*, 21 October, that a silicon random access memory chip was unlawful within copyright law where it carried a copy of a protected work.

copyright, internet café fees. Where the employees of an internet café charged a fee to customers for transfer to CDs of music they had downloaded from the internet, this constituted an infringement of Copyright, Designs and Patents Act 1988, ss 17(1), 18(1): *Sony Music* v *Easyinternet Café Ltd* (2003) *The Times*, 6 February.

copyright, musical composition. Where a new edition of the performing score of an existing composition is produced, copyright could vest in the editor of that new edition: *Sawkins* v *Hyperion Records* (2004), *The Times*, 26 July.

copyright works, moral rights in. Stated in Copyright, Designs and Patents Act 1988, chap IV, as the right to be identified as: author or director ('right of paternity'); right to object to derogatory treatment of work ('right of integrity'); right to object to false attribution; right to privacy of certain photographs and films.

COREPER. Committee of Permanent Representatives of EU states. *See* COUN-CIL OF THE EUROPEAN UNION.

co-respondent. Generally refers to an alleged adulterer in relation to a petition for divorce or judicial separation and made, jointly with the wife, respondent to the suit. He need not be named in the petition: Family Proceedings Rules 1991, r 2. See Mat.C.A. 1973, s 49(1). *See* DIVORCE.

coroner. A person appointed by a local authority in each coroner's district, under the Coroners Act 1988, from barristers, solicitors and registered medical practitioners of at least five years' standing. He has jurisdiction over treasure found in his district (see Treasure Act 1996, s 7), and, principally, inquests into deaths of persons dying within his district where there is, e.g., reasonable cause for suspecting violent or unnatural death: s 8. His court is essentially a fact-finding body.

There are some 158 coroners' courts; 20 are full-time. See also A.J.A. 1982, s 62; C.L.S.A. 1990, Sch 10; Acc.J.A. 1999, s 7 (adjournment of inquest in event of judicial inquiry); 1988 Act, s 27A, inserted by Acc.J.A. 1999, s 104 (indemnification of coroners against liability for costs or damages); SI 99/3325. For screening of witness from public sight at inquest, see *R* v *Newcastle Coroner ex p A* (1998) *The Times*, 19 January; Coroners Rules, No. 17 (SI 84/552). See *Report of Macpherson Inquiry* (1999) Cm 4262 (set up under Police Act 1996, s 49), recommendation 42 (advance disclosure of evidence relating to inquests), recommendation 43 (legal aid to cover representation of victims and their families at inquests). *See* POST-MORTEM.

coroner's duty to summon jury. Under Coroners Act 1988, s 8(3), a coroner has the duty to summon a jury of 7–11 persons if it appears to him that the death occurred in prison; or in police custody; or resulted from an injury caused by a police officer in the purported execution of his duty; or was caused by an accident, poisoning, or disease, notice of which was required; or that the death occurred in circumstances, the possible recurrence of which would be prejudicial to the health or safety of the public.

coroner's jury, duties. In *R (Middleton)* v *West Somerset Coroner* [2004] UKHL 10, the HL held that although the jury need not attribute civil or criminal liability, it should, in finding how the deceased person came by his death, seek to determine by what means, and also in what circumstances, he did do.

corporal punishment. *See* PUNISHMENT, CORPORAL.

corporal punishment, statutory ban on. In *R (Williamson)* v *Secretary of State for Education* (2002) *The Times*, 18 December, the CA held that a ban on corporal punishment in schools (see Education Act 1996, s 548) does not constitute an interference with the freedom of teachers or parents of children in an independent school providing a fundamentalist Christian education, to observe their interpretation of Biblical observance.

corporate and incorporate bodies, control of by FSA. FSA (q.v.) must be notified by a person who proposes to take steps which would result in his acquiring control over a body incorporated in, or an unincorporated association formed under, UK law: F.S.M.A. 2000, s 178. For details of 'acquiring control', see s 179.

corporate body. *See* BODY CORPORATE.

corporate liability. The extension of liability for the commission of offences to companies and corporations. See *Bolton Engineering Co* v *Graham & Sons* [1957] 1 QB 159 – 'In cases where the law requires a guilty mind as a condition of a criminal offence, the guilty mind of the directors or managers will render the company itself guilty': *per* Lord Denning. See Th.A. 1968, s 18; T.C.P.A. 1990, s 331; F.S.M.A. 2000, s 400; *R* v *P & O European Ferries Ltd* (1991) 93 Cr App R 72 (corporate manslaughter); *Odyssey Ltd* v *OIC Ltd* (2000) *The Times*, 17 March (company perjuring itself through a director). See MANSLAUGHTER, CORPORATE BODY AND.

corporate veil. *See* LIFTING THE CORPORATE VEIL.

corporation. A body of persons associated for some purpose and considered as having rights and duties and the capacity of succession. A *corporation aggregate* is made up of groups of persons, e.g., incorporated companies. A *corporation sole* consists of one person and his successors in some public office, e.g., a bishop. A *corporation by prescription* (e.g., The City of London) is founded on the presumption that a charter was granted but has been lost. A corporation is domiciled in its place of incorporation: *Gasque* v *IRC* [1940] 2 KB 80. *See* BODY CORPORATE.

corporation, public. *See* PUBLIC CORPORATION.

corporation, statutory. *See* PUBLIC CORPORATION.

corporation tax. Tax paid after 1966 on profits by companies and unincorpor-

ated associations other than partnerships. See I.C.T.A. 1988, ss 8, 393; *Blackpool Marton Rotary Club* v *Martin* [1990] STC 1; Corporation Tax (Instalment Payments) Regulations 1998 (SI 98/3175); Finance Act 2000, s 35 (charged at rate of 30 per cent for 2001); *MacNiven* v *Westmoreland Investments* (2001) *The Times*, 14 February.

corporeal hereditaments. Visible, tangible property, e.g., houses, goods. *See* HEREDITAMENTS.

corpse, right of property in. Under common law there is no right of property in a corpse or any part of it. Personal representatives of the deceased have a right to possession of the corpse until burial: *Williams* v *Williams* (1882) 20 Ch D 665. See *Dobson* v *N Tyneside HA* [1996] 4 All ER 47 (claim for damages for failure to preserve deceased's brain, required as evidence in negligence claim). (See *R* v *Kelly* [1999] 2 WLR 384: it was held that a corpse, or parts of it, could be 'owned' if it had been subjected to a skilled process, such as dissection.)

corpus delicti. The body of an offence, i.e., the aggregation of fundamental facts constituting the substance of an offence.

corpus juris. 1. A body of law. 2. Specifically, the *Corpus Juris Civilis*, the collective designation (used first in 1583) of Justinian's sixth-century codification of Roman law, comprising *Institutiones, Digesta, Codex, Novellae*. 3. Contemporary political and legal movement concerned with the eventual harmonisation of the legal systems of EU member states, intended to result in a 'European Judicial Area'.

corrective justice. *See* JUSTICE, COMMUTATIVE, DISTRIBUTIVE AND CORRECTIVE.

correspondence, contract by. A contract, the terms of which are set out in letters which have passed between the parties or their agents. See L.P.A. 1925, s 46; *Stearn* v *Twitchell* [1985] 1 All ER 631 (a single letter is not 'correspondence').

correspondent. 'In relation to a postal packet or other communication, means the sender or the addressee': Postal Services

Act 2000, s 125(1). The 'sender' is the person whose communication it is: s 125(1).

corroboration. Independent, admissible and credible evidence tending to confirm that the principal evidence is true. 'Perhaps the best synonym is "support" ': *DPP v Hester* [1972] 3 All ER 1056. The common law rules of corroboration were effectively abolished under C.J.P.O.A. 1994, s 32; for abolition of corroboration requirements under S.O.A. 1956, see s 33. See *R v K (Corroboration)* [1999] Crim LR 980. See Perjury Act 1911, s 13; Road Traffic Regulations 1984 (concerning speeding).

corruption. Generally refers to an inducement by means of an improper consideration to violate some duty. See Prevention of Corruption Act 1916; *R v Parker* (1985) 82 Cr App R 60; Public Bodies Corrupt Practices Act 1889; *R v Bowden* [1996] 1 WLR 98; *R v A-G ex p Rockall* [2000] 1 WLR 882; Representation of the People Act 1983, ss 106–115, 158–160; C.J.A. 1988, s 47; *Legislating the Criminal Code: Corruption* (1998) Law Com. No. 248. *See* BRIBERY.

corruption of public morals. The phrase 'suggests conduct which a jury might find to be destructive of the very fabric of society': *Knuller Ltd v DPP* [1972] 2 All ER 898.

cost benefit analysis. Term in economic theory used occasionally in statute: see, e.g., F.S.M.A. 2000, s 330(2). It is a procedure designed to estimate the social costs and benefits of projected undertakings so as to evaluate whether or not they should be undertaken.

cost capping. In *King v Telegraph Group* (2004) *The Times*, 21 May, the CA held that the High Court lacked power to oppose a cost capping exercise in cases including defamation where claimant's extravagant costs might tend to inhibit defendant's exercise of his right to freedom of expression.

costs. 'Includes fees, charges, disbursements, expenses, remuneration, reimbursements allowed to a litigant in person under CPR, r 48.6 and any fee or reward charged by a lay representative for acting on behalf of a party in proceedings allocated to the small claims track': r 43.2(1)(a).

costs, amount, factors to be taken into account. The court will have regard to: whether assessment is on the standard or indemnity basis; any orders already made; parties' conduct before and during proceedings; efforts made to resolve dispute; amount of money involved; importance of the matter to all parties; complexity of the matter; skill, effort, specialised knowledge involved; time spent on case: CPR, r 44.5.

costs, basis of assessment. Where costs are to be assessed by the court, the assessment will be made on a 'standard basis' or on an 'indemnity basis' (but no costs will be allowed which have been unreasonably incurred or are unreasonable in amount): CPR, r 44.4(1). 'Standard basis costs' will involve only costs which are proportionate to matters in issue; the court will resolve any doubt which it may have as to whether costs were reasonably incurred or reasonable and proportionate in amount in favour of the paying party: r 44.4(2). 'Indemnity costs' will involve the court resolving any doubts as to whether costs were reasonably incurred or were reasonable in favour of paying party: r 44.4(3).

costs, claimant's or defendant's, in the case. Where party in whose favour costs order is made is awarded costs at conclusion of proceedings, that party is entitled to his costs of the part of proceedings to which order relates: see PD 44, para 44.

costs, detailed and summary assessments. 'Detailed assessment' means procedure by which amount of costs is decided by a costs officer (q.v.) in accordance with CPR, Part 47 (r 43.4). 'Summary assessment' means procedure by which the court, when making an order about costs, orders payment of a sum of money instead of fixed costs or detailed assessment: r 43.3. For fixed costs (e.g., in relation to solicitor's charges), see Part 45.

costs, estimate not given to client. In *Garbutt and Another v Edwards & Another* [2005] *The Times*, 3 November, the CA held that where a winning party's solicitor does not provide an estimate of costs to his clients, the level of costs awarded could be affected.

costs follow the event. Old terminology for general rule now stated in CPR, r 44.3(2) that an unsuccessful party will be ordered to pay costs of the successful party, should court decide to make an order about costs. See also M.C.A. 1980, s 64(1); *Bradford City MDC v Booth* (2000) *The Times*, 31 May.

costs, future. In *Cooke v United Bristol Healthcare NHS Trust* [2003] EWCA Civ 1370, the CA held that a personal claimant may not adduce evidence suggesting that his future care costs will increase at a much steeper rate than the general rate of inflation.

costs, general rules under CPR. General rule is that the unsuccessful party will be ordered to pay costs of successful party (but the court is empowered to make a different order): r 44.3(2). This rule does not apply to proceedings in Court of Appeal concerning proceedings in Family Division, nor does it apply to proceedings in Court of Appeal from judgments, decisions, made or given in probate or family proceedings. Court has discretion as to whether costs are payable by one party to another, amount of those costs and when they are to be paid: r 44.3(1).

costs here and below. Party in whose favour costs order is made is entitled to his costs in relation to proceedings in which order is made and also its costs of proceedings of any lower court: PD 44, para 2.4.

costs in any event. Party in whose favour order is made is entitled to costs relating to the part of the proceedings to which order refers, whatever other orders for costs are made in the proceedings: PD 44, para 2.4. See *Practice Direction* (1999) 149 NLJ 163: whenever a costs in any event order is to be made, court is to make a summary assessment of such costs, unless there is a good reason for not doing so.

costs in criminal cases. An acquitted defendant may be awarded costs out of central funds by a magistrates' court or the Crown Court, as compensation for properly incurred expenses, where, e.g., an information has been laid but not proceeded with or the magistrates dismiss the information: Prosecution of Offences Act 1985, s 16, as amended by C.J.A. 1987, Sch 2. A successful private prosecutor (but not a public authority) may be awarded just and reasonable costs: s 17. For award of costs out of central funds against an accused person, see s 18.

costs judge. A taxing master of the Supreme Court.

costs, no order as to. Each party will pay his own costs of the part of the proceedings to which the order relates, whatever costs order is made at conclusion of proceedings: PD 44, para 2.4.

costs officer. A costs judge; a district judge; an authorised court officer (i.e., any officer of a county court, district registry, Principal Registry of Family Division, or Supreme Court Costs Office): CPR, r 43.2(1)(c), (d).

costs order, correctness of. In *Kastor Navigation v AGF* [2004] EWCA Civ 277, the CA held that a judge ought to consider the entirety of the circumstances and stand back from the mere mathematical result of his deliberations on costs. He ought to ask himself whether, in all the circumstances, he had reached a correct result, and whether he had taken into account the demands of the Civil Procedure Rules.

costs, order for security. It was held under rule 25.13 of the Civil Procedure Rules the court could order a claimant to provide security for costs, where the claimant has taken steps with regard to his assets to make it difficult to enforce an order for costs. However the court will only make such an order where it considers it just to do so. See *Harris v Wallis* [2006] *The Times*, 12 May.

costs order, publicly-funded litigants. In *Portsmouth Hospitals NHS Trust v*

Wyatt and Another [2006] *The Times*, 3 May, the CA held that where one party is publicly funded and is unsuccessful, and the successful party applies to the court for a costs order, r 44.3 of the Civil Procedure Rules provides the court with a discretion on how to exercise its discretion as to costs. The court needs to take into account but for the costs protection, would the court have made an order for costs against the unsuccessful party.

costs orders, time for complying with. A party must comply with an order for payment of costs within 14 days of date of judgment or order, or, if amount of costs is decided later in accordance with CPR, Part 47, date of certificate which states amount: r 44.8.

costs, penalty over delay. It was held that where a court has ordered a costs order and there has been a failure to start costs proceedings on time, under rule 47.8(3) of the Civil Procedure Rules the court had power to only disallow interest payable in relation to the costs order, it did not permit any disallowance of costs. See *Haji-Ioannou and Others* v *Frangos and Others* [2006] *The Times*, 7 April.

costs, power to vary parties' agreement on. In *Republic of Kazakhstan* v *Istil Group Inc* [2005] *The Times*, 17 November, the CA held that a court has discretion to vary the amount of security agreed between parties. In exercising this discretion the court has to act justly according to the overriding objective of the Civil Procedure Rules.

costs, reasons for refusal. Just as, in a civil case, reasons for an award of costs must be given, so, in a criminal case, the court must give reasons (no matter how brief) where defendant's costs were refused following a successful appeal against sentence: *R (Cummingham)* v *Exeter Crown Court* (2003) *The Times*, 30 January.

costs, recovery of. Work relating to the professional skill and time of a barrister in proceedings to which he was a party could be treated as a properly incurred expense, in respect of which he was entitled to indemnification; costs relating

to his appearance at the hearings could not be included: *Khan* v *Lord Chancellor* (2003) 15 NLJ 94.

costs, recovery of insurance premium by way of. Where a costs order is made in favour of a party who has taken out an insurance policy against risk of incurring a liability in those proceedings, costs payable to him may, subject to rules of court, include costs in respect of the premium of the policy: Acc.J.A. 1999, r 29.

costs reserved. Procedure in which decision concerning costs is deferred to a later date; but where no later order is made, costs will be 'costs in the case': PD 44, para 2.4.

costs, security for. Where on defendant's application, it appears to the court that claimant is ordinarily resident out of the jurisdiction, or is a nominal claimant and there is reason to believe that he will be unable to pay defendant's costs if ordered to do so, or claimant's address is not stated, or incorrectly stated in claim form, or that claimant has changed his address during proceedings so as to avoid consequences of litigation, the court may order claimant to give security for defendant's costs: CPR, Sch 1; O 23, r 1. (This has application to proceedings in High Court and county courts.)

costs, successful defendants deprived. In *Daniels* v *Commissioner of Police of the Metropolis* [2005] *The Times*, 28 October, the CA held that under rule 44.3 of the Civil Procedure Rules the court has discretion to deprive a successful defendant of some or all of its costs. The court needs to consider, was the defendant being a public body acting so unreasonably that he should be deprived of his costs.

costs thrown away. Where a judgment or order is set aside, the party in whose favour costs order is made is entitled to costs incurred consequentially, e.g., preparing for and attending hearing at which judgment or order was set aside, preparing for and attending any hearing resulting in adjournment of proceedings, steps taken to enforce an order or judgment later set aside.

costs, trustees', basis. *See* TRUSTEES' COSTS BASIS.

costs, wasted. Any costs incurred by a party as a result of any improper, unreasonable or negligent act or omission on the part of any legal or other representative or any employee of such a representative; or, which in the light of any such act or omission occurring after they were incurred, the court considers it is unreasonable to expect that party to pay: S.C.A. 1981, s 51, substituted by C.L.S.A. 1990, s 4. A party may make an application under CPR, Part 23; the court may make an order under r 48(2). The court must give the legal representative a reasonable opportunity to attend a hearing to give reasons why it should not make such an order: PD 48.7(2). The court may refer the matter to a costs judge or a district judge: r 48.7(7). See PD 48; *Re A Solicitor (Wasted Costs Order)* [1996] 1 FLR 40; *Medcalf* v *Mardell* (2001) *The Times*, 2 January.

council liability, ice on roads. In *Sandhar* v *Department of Transport* (2004) *The Times*, 15 November, the CA held that there is no common law duty on a highway authority to remedy road ice formation. See *Goodes* v *E. Sussex CC* [2000] 1 WLR 1356.

Council of Europe. An inter-governmental organisation of some 40 states set up in 1949, following the Congress of Europe 1948. Apart from consultative functions it issues Conventions, which can be signed by individual states, e.g., European Convention on Human Rights 1950.

Council of the European Union. Known also as 'Council of Ministers'. A development of the Council of Ministers which was created under the Treaty of Rome 1957, art 47. Under the Treaty on European Union (q.v.) the Council has the task of providing the Union 'with the necessary impetus for its development and shall define the general political guidelines thereof' (art D). It comprises a ministerial representative from each member state and acts, in general, on proposals made by the Commission (q.v.). The Council meets at least twice a year in Brussels or Luxembourg and is chaired by the Head of State or Government of the member state which holds the presidency of the Council (which rotates among the member states every six months). The Council is assisted by the Committee of Permanent Representatives, consisting of civil servants of member states, based in Brussels (see art 151). Decisions involve a unanimous vote or a qualified majority vote. See OJ [1993] L 281/18. *See* EUROPEAN UNION.

Council on Tribunals. Body of 10–15 independent persons appointed by the Lord Chancellor and Secretary of State to keep under review the constitution and working of tribunals (q.v.). The Parliamentary Ombudsman (q.v.) is an *ex officio* member. See Tribunals and Inquiries Act 1992, ss 1–3. See Council Report: *Tribunals: their organisation and independence* (1997) (Cm 3744).

councils, county. Elected bodies for defined areas within the local government system comprising councillors (elected for four years) presided over by chairman. They are responsible for, e.g., lighting, police and fire services.

councils, district. Bodies corporate set up to administer local government in the divisions of counties known as districts (q.v.).

council tax. Tax, which replaced 'community charge' (q.v.), payable in respect of chargeable dwellings: see Local Government Finance Act 1992, ss 1, 3. Dwellings are placed in one of eight valuation bands: s 5. Provision is made for discounts where there are fewer than two residents: s 11. Where there are no residents, responsibility for payment passes to the owner. The tax is set with reference to calculations relating to local authorities' budget requirements and precepts. See SI 92/550. For council tax benefit, see S.S. Contributions and Benefits Act 1992, s 131, substituted by Local Government Finance Act 1992, Sch 9, para 4.

counsel. 1. To advise. See Accessories and Abettors Act 1861, as amended; *R* v

Calhaem [1985] QB 808. 2. Term used formerly to differentiate barristers from solicitors. Refers now, in general, to all those who advise and represent litigants, so that it covers barristers and those solicitors who have appropriate rights of audience (q.v.). *See* QUEEN'S COUNSEL.

Counsellors of State. Appointed by virtue of Regency Act 1937. Royal functions are delegated to them in the event of the Sovereign's illness (but not total incapacity) or absence abroad. See also Regency Acts 1937–53. *See* REGENT.

counsel's duty in course of trial. Prosecuting counsel 'ought not to struggle for the verdict against the prisoner, but they ought to bear themselves rather in the character of ministers of justice assisting in the administration of justice': *per* Avery J in *R v Banks* [1916] 2 KB 62. 'It is not the duty of prosecuting counsel to obtain a conviction by all means at his command but rather to lay before the jury fairly and impartially the whole of the facts which comprise the case for the prosecution and to see that the jury are properly instructed in the law applicable to those facts': *Code of Conduct for the Bar*. For duty of both counsel to assist judge with directions upon the law, see *R v L* (2001) *The Times*, 9 February.

counsel's illness during trial. In *R v Hall* [2002] EWCA Crim 1881, the CA held that if it emerges after trial that counsel was seriously ill during proceedings, the only appropriate question is whether his/her conduct of the case fell – for whatever reason – below the proper standard, resulting in the defendant not receiving a fair trial.

counsel, suing of. Where a defendant has been acquitted on retrial after two appeals, he cannot sue his barrister on the conduct of the case at the first trial and subsequent appeal: *Popat v Barnes* (2004) *The Times*, 5 July.

counterclaim. 'A claim brought by a defendant in response to the claimant's claim, which is included in the same proceedings as the claimant's claim': CPR Glossary. See *Universal Cycles plc v Grangebriar Ltd* [2000] CPLR 42.

counterfeit. A thing is a counterfeit of a currency note or of a protected coin (q.v.) if it is not a currency note or protected coin, but resembles them (whether on one side only or both) to such an extent that they are reasonably capable of passing for currency notes or protected coins, or if it is a currency note or protected coin which has been so altered that it is reasonably capable of passing for a currency note or protected coin of some other description: Forgery and Counterfeiting Act 1981, s 28(1). *See* FORGERY.

counterfeiting. It is an offence for a person to make a counterfeit of a currency note or of a protected coin (q.v.) intending that he or another shall pass or tender it as genuine: Forgery and Counterfeiting Act 1981, s 14(1). It is an offence to make a counterfeit of a currency note or of a protected coin without lawful excuse or authority: s 14(2). For counterfeiting of euro, see Council Decision OJ [2000] L 140/1. *See* COUNTERFEIT.

counterfeit notes. It is an offence to have in one's custody counterfeit notes and coins intending to pass or tender them as genuine; to have in one's custody and control things intended to be used for the purpose of counterfeiting; to import or export counterfeit notes or coins without Treasury consent: Forgery and Counterfeiting Act 1981, ss 16–21. See *R v Maltman* [1995] 1 Cr App R 239.

counter-offer. *See* OFFER, COUNTER-.

counties palatine. The counties of Chester, Durham, Lancaster. Courts of these counties exercised chancery jurisdiction until their abolition by the Courts Act 1971, s 41.

counts. The sections of an indictment (q.v.) containing separate allegations and charges. 'Every count in an indictment is equivalent to a separate indictment; the prisoner can be tried on one or all of the counts': *R v Boyle* [1954] 2 QB 292.

counts, alternative. Separate clauses in an indictment (q.v.), each charging a separate offence, where the charges are based on the same facts or form part of a series of offences of the same or a similar nature. See Indictment Rules 1971.

counts, general. Counts (q.v.) which are too general and insufficient may be quashed.

counts, separate. Where more than one offence is charged in an indictment (q.v.) each must generally be stated in a separate count (i.e., section) and each must be numbered separately. A count which charges more than one offence may be void for duplicity: *R v Molloy* [1921] 2 KB 364. See *R v GMC ex p Gee* [1987] 1 WLR 564; *R v Kidd* [1997] Crim LR 766. *See* DUPLICITY.

county. Territorial division. See L.G.A. 1972. England is divided into a collection of borough councils and similar bodies for London, six metropolitan district councils (see L.G.A. 1985) and 39 counties. Wales has eight counties.

county councils. *See* COUNCILS, COUNTY.

county court registrar. *See* REGISTRAR, COUNTY COURT.

county courts. The main civil courts (some 270) established by County Courts Act 1846. Their jurisdiction is statutory and includes: claims founded on contract and tort where the amount claimed is not more than an amount stated by Order in Council (see County C.A. 1984, s 145); equity matters, e.g., trusts and mortgages where the amount does not exceed a statutory limit; claims for the recovery of land. All judges of the Supreme Court, circuit judges and recorders are empowered to sit in county courts. District judges (q.v.), formerly known as 'registrars', hear claims including those for the recovery of land, and also order periodical payments (q.v.) and lump sums (q.v.) in matrimonial law cases. Rules of procedure are made by a rule committee (appointed by the Lord Chancellor) and are printed in the current *County Court Practice*. Trial by jury may be ordered in an exceptional case. Each court sits at least once a month. Appeals on matters of law, evidence, fact, lie to the Court of Appeal or, in some few cases (involving, e.g., bankruptcy) to the High Court. See County C.A. 1984, amended by C.L.S.A. 1990, ss 2, 3; Courts Act 1971; I.A.

1978, Sch 1; County Court Rules 1981; A.J.A. 1982, Part V; Matrimonial and Family Proceedings Act 1984, ss 33, 34; *Practice Direction (QBD: County Court Order: Enforcement) (No. 2)* [1998] 1 WLR 1557 (applications for enforcement of county court orders); SI 85/1807 (Register of County Court Judgments Regulations 1985); CPR, Sch 2; CCR, O 35 (enforcement of county court judgments outside UK). For business in county court offices, see PD 2, para 3.1.

course of employment. The scope of a person's employment. Thus, a wrong committed falls within the scope of employment if expressly or impliedly authorised by the employer or if necessarily incidental to something which the person who has committed the wrong is employed to do. See *Heatons Transport Ltd v TGWU* [1973] AC 15; *Kooragang Investments v Richardson & Wrench* [1982] AC 482; *Smith v Stages* [1989] AC 928 (employee's travel and 'course of employment': 'The paramount rule is that an employee travelling on the highway will be acting in the course of his employment if, and only if, he is at the material time going about his employer's business. One ought not to confuse the duty to turn up for work with the concept of already being on duty while travelling to it': *per* Lord Lowry).

court. 1. Residence of the Sovereign. 2. Formal assembly of a Sovereign's councillors. 3. A place where justice is administered. 4. Persons assembled under the authority of the law for the purpose of administering justice, i.e., the judge or judges. Includes any tribunal or body exercising the judicial power of the state: Contempt of Court Act 1981, s 19. The right of unimpeded access to the courts is a fundamental principle of the common law: *R v Home Secretary ex p Leech* [1994] QB 198. See C.J.J.A. 1982, s 50; C.L.S.A. 1990, s 119(1); *AEWU v Devanayagam* [1986] AC 356.

Court, Administrative. *See* ADMINISTRATIVE COURT.

Court, Admiralty. *See* ADMIRALTY COURT.

court, attributes of a. Created by the state; conducts its procedure in accordance with rules of natural justice; procedure includes public hearing, reception of oral evidence, hearing of argument, oral examination and cross-examination of witnesses; has before it at least two parties, one of whom may be the Crown; and arrives at a decision concerned with legal rights which is final and binding for so long as it stands: *per* Eveleigh LJ in *A-G v BBC* [1981] AC 303.

court, commercial. See COMMERCIAL COURT.

Court, Companies. *See* COMPANIES COURT.

Court, Consistory. *See* CONSISTORY COURT.

Court, Crown. *See* CROWN COURT.

court, election. *See* ELECTION COURT.

court-house, petty sessional. A courthouse or place at which justices are accustomed to assemble for holding special or petty sessions (q.v.) (or for the time being appointed as a substitute place) or at which a district judge (magistrates' courts) (q.v.) is authorised to do alone any act authorised to be done by more than one justice of the peace: Justices of the Peace Act 1997, s 72(1). See Acc.J.A. 1999, Sch 10, para 52.

Court of Appeal. Consists of Lord Chancellor, Lord Chief Justice, Master of the Rolls, President of the Family Division, former Lord Chancellors, Lords of Appeal in Ordinary, Lords Justices of Appeal. There are two divisions: (1) *Criminal Division.* Successor of the Court of Criminal Appeal (q.v.) which was created in 1907. It exists 'to correct demonstrable errors and to develop and clarify the law', and hears, e.g., appeals by persons convicted on indictment, or against sentence from the Crown Court (q.v.). Appeal is from the Criminal Division to the House of Lords. The Court cannot make findings of fact: *R v Twitchell* [2000] 1 Cr App R 373. (2) *Civil Division.* Hears, e.g., appeals from the High Court, county courts, various tribunals. Appeal is usually by way of rehearing. The Court is duly constituted if it consists of one or more judges, but the Master of the Rolls may give directions determining the number of judges necessary for the purpose of particular proceedings: S.C.A. 1981, s 54, substituted by Acc.J.A. 1999, s 59. For the exercise of incidental jurisdiction see S.C.A. 1981, s 58, substituted by Acc.J.A. 1999, s 60. See *Practice Direction for the Court of Appeal (Civil Division)*, which consolidates the principal Practice Directions. It may be bound by decisions of the Criminal Division. It is bound by decisions of ECJ, CFI, House of Lords. Appeal is from the Civil Division to the House of Lords. See S.C.A. 1981; C.J.A. 1988, s 43; Criminal Appeal Act 1995. *See* APPEAL; CRIMINAL CASES REVIEW COMMISSION.

Court of Appeal (Civil Division), expedited hearings. The category of appeals which require that the hearing take place immediately or within days includes: appeals against committal orders; cases in which children might suffer extraordinary prejudice if decision is delayed; cases under Hague Convention 1980 on child abduction; asylum appeals where delay might jeopardise appellant; cases involving execution of possessory order which appear to have merit; cases in which publication of allegedly unlawful material is imminent.

Court of Appeal (Civil Division), permission to appeal. Permission of court below or Court of Appeal is generally required. Since 1 January 1999, permission is required for all appeals except appeals against committal orders, refusals to grant habeas corpus, and secure accommodation orders (see Ch.A. 1989, s 25). General rule applied by Court is that permission will be given unless an appeal would have no real prospect of success; but this will not apply where a matter of unusual public interest is involved. There should be a realistic prospect of the Court coming to a different conclusion on a point of law. The Court will rarely interfere on questions of fact or exercise of judicial discretion.

Court of Appeal judges. Maximum number of ordinary judges of the Court of Appeal is increased from 35 to 37: SI 02/2837.

Court of Appeal, reception of fresh evidence by. 'First, it must be shown that the evidence could not have been obtained with reasonable diligence for use at the trial; secondly, the evidence must be such that, if given, it would probably have an important influence on the result of the case, though it need not be decisive; thirdly, the evidence must be such as is presumably to be believed, or, in other words, it must be apparently credible though it need not be incontrovertible': *per* Denning LJ in *Ladd* v *Marshall* [1954] 1 WLR 1489. See Criminal Appeal Act 1995, s 4; *R* v *Sale* (2000) *The Times*, 14 June (admission of fresh evidence after conviction).

Court of Arches. Ecclesiastical court which has the jurisdiction of the former Provincial Court of Archbishop and hears appeals from the consistory court (q.v.). See, e.g., *Re St Mary's, Banbury* [1987] 1 All ER 247.

Court of Auditors. Institution of EU (q.v.) established by Second Budgetary Treaty 1975. Functions are governed by EC Treaty, arts 246–248. It comprises 15 members approved by Council; their independence must be beyond doubt; their task is to scrutinise Commission finances and ensure sound financial management by examining accounts of EU revenue and expenditure. It has no judicial functions.

Court of Chancery. Originally a court of equity consisting of Lord Chancellor, Master of the Rolls and vice-chancellors. Merged in the Supreme Court of Judicature by J.A. 1873 and became known as the Chancery Division (q.v.).

Court of Chivalry. Ancient feudal court, presided over by the Earl Marshal, which decided disputes concerning, e.g., the right to use armorial bearings. Last convened in 1955: *Manchester Corporation* v *Manchester Palace of Varieties (Ltd)* [1955] P 133.

Court of Ecclesiastical Causes Reserved. Court composed of five judges, including two who have held high judicial office and

three diocesan bishops, exercising jurisdiction over clergy in matters relating to ritual and doctrine. Petition lies to a Commission of Review.

Court of Faculties. An office administered by the Archbishop and responsible for the granting of faculties. See Public Worship Regulation Act 1874. *See* FACULTY.

court of first instance. Court in which proceedings are initiated.

Court of First Instance of EC. Inaugurated, following the Single European Act 1986, art 11, in 1988. Sits in Luxembourg in plenary session or divisions of three or five judges (appointed by member states) to hear disputes between the EC and its staff, applications for judicial review against the Council or Commission in matters concerning, e.g., levies and prices. Appeal to the Court of Justice of the EC (q.v.) from CFI lies, within a two-month period, on grounds of CFI's lack of competence, breach of procedure and infringement of Community law. See *Practice Note (CFI: Guidance in Written And Oral Proceedings)* [1999] All ER (EC) 641, CFI; *Practice Note (CFI: Constitution)* [2000] All ER (EC) 1 (criteria for hearing before single judge).

Court of Human Rights, European. *See* EUROPEAN COURT OF HUMAN RIGHTS.

Court of Justice, International. *See* INTERNATIONAL COURT OF JUSTICE.

Court of Justice of the European Communities. Known also as 'the European Court of Justice'. Institution set up under Treaty of Rome to ensure that, in interpretation and application of the Treaty, the law is observed. It consists of judges from each member state, appointed for six-year periods, assisted by nine Advocates General (q.v.); sits in Luxembourg (in chambers of three or five, or in plenary session), expressing itself in judgments when called upon to do so in proceedings initiated by member states, institutions of the EU and natural or legal persons, and is permanently in session. Procedures are generally inquisitorial, based upon a written, followed by an oral, stage:

Statute of the Court, art 18. Article 173 provides for annulment by the Court of acts of the Council or Commission based on lack of competence, misuse of powers, infringement of the Treaty or of an essential procedural requirement. Fines may be imposed on member states. The reasons for a judgment must be delivered in open court. The language used as the procedural language in a particular case is that of the defendant or member state involved. On all matters of Community law (q.v.) courts of the UK defer to relevant decisions of the Court of Justice. See Treaty of Rome 1957; *Van Duyn* v *Home Office* [1974] 3 All ER 178; O 114. *See* COMMUNITY LAW, SOURCES OF; EEC.

Court of Justice of the European Communities, references to. See O 114 (re-enacted in CPR, Sch 1 (for High Court proceedings), Sch 2 (for county court proceedings involving CCR, O 19, r 15)). The following principles relating to references from English courts were set out in *HP Bulmer Ltd* v *J Bollinger SA* [1974] Ch 401: (1) only questions of Community law may be referred; (2) questions will not be referred if a decision is not needed to enable the English court to give judgment; (3) questions will not be referred if free from doubt and generally clear; (4) points will not be referred if already decided by Court of Justice; (5) all circumstances, including, e.g., time, interests of justice, must be taken into account. See EEC Treaty, art 177. For actions heard directly by Court of Justice see arts 173, 175, 178, 215. See *Practice Direction (ECJ: References to the ECJ by Court of Appeal and High Court under art 177)* [1999] 2 CMLR 799. See, e.g., *R* v *Henn and Darby* [1980] 2 WLR 597.

court of last resort. A court from which there can be no appeal.

Court of Probate. Created 1857; transferred in 1873 to Family Division of the High Court. *See* PROBATE.

Court of Protection. Administers property of mentally disordered persons ('patients') (within the meaning of M.H.A. 1983), or, e.g., persons with learning difficulties, and consists of a master and other officers. The affairs of patients may be managed by a receiver, who may be the Public Trustee or a member of a patient's family, supervised by the Public Trust Office. Where the property is of small value, power of administration may be exercised by High Court. See Court of Protection Rules 1984; Public Trustee and Administration of Funds Act 1986, s 2; Enduring Powers of Attorney Act 1985; *Re B* [1987] 1 WLR 552; M.H.A. 1983, s 93; SI 92/1899. The court has in connection with its jurisdiction the same powers, rights, privileges and authority as the High Court. Mental Capacity Act 2005 s 47.

court of record. Phrase referring to a court, the records of which are maintained and preserved, and which may punish for contempt of court (q.v.). May be a superior court (q.v.) or an inferior court (q.v.). See, e.g., S.C.A. 1981, s 15(1).

court of summary jurisdiction. Obsolescent expression, superseded by the term 'magistrates' court' (q.v.).

Court of Swainmote. It was held in *Verderers of the New Forest* v *Young* (2004) *The Times*, 29 January, that magistrates could share a concurrent jurisdiction with the ancient Court of Swainmote to hear a summons relating to breaches of New Forest bylaws. (The Court of Swainmote is an ancient institution which sat three times yearly to consider grievances concerning the use of forests.)

Court of Tynwald. *See* TYNWALD, COURT OF.

court, party not attending. In *Estate Acquisition and Development Ltd* v *Wilshire and Another* [2006] *The Times*, 12 June, the CA held that obligations relating to litigation are covered by the Civil Procedure Rules and where parties are in a legal relationship, a party is under no obligation to attend court proceedings of which he had no notice of.

Court, Patents. *See* PATENTS COURT.

court, payment into. *See* PAYMENT INTO COURT.

court, requesting. *See* REQUESTING COURT.

Court, Rules of. *See* RULES OF COURT.

court, sale by the. *See* SALE BY THE COURT.

courts, county. *See* COUNTY COURTS.

courts' decisions, statement of reasons for. There is a general duty to state a reason for a judicial decision: see, e.g., *Davies v Price* [1958] 1 WLR 434. See also C.J.A. 1982, s 2; *Padfield v Minister of Agriculture* [1968] AC 997; *Flannery v Halifax Estate Agencies* (1999) 149 NLJ 284 (in which the Court of Appeal stated that the duty to give reasons reflected: that the duty was a function of due process, and, therefore, of justice, and farmers required that parties should know why they had won or lost; that want of reasons might be a good ground of appeal; that, in general, the judge should enter into the issues canvassed before him and explain his preference for one case over another).

Courts, Divisional. *See* DIVISIONAL COURTS.

Court Service. An executive agency of the Lord Chancellor's Department, set up in 1995, with responsibility for providing administrative support to courts and tribunals, including High Court, Crown Court, county courts, in England and Wales.

courts, inferior. *See* INFERIOR COURTS.

courts, magistrates'. *See* MAGISTRATES' COURTS.

courts-martial. Courts governed by Army and Air Force Acts 1955, Naval Discipline Act 1957, Armed Forces Acts 1971–96, Armed Forces Discipline Act 2000. Exercising jurisdiction over members of HM Forces. Murder, manslaughter, rape and treason committed within the UK are tried by the ordinary criminal courts. Trial at a court-martial is generally preceded by an inquiry and takes place before three to five officers assisted by a judge-advocate. A finding of guilt must be confirmed by a superior officer. Courts-Martial Appeal Court was created in 1951; appeal against conviction and sentence lies from it to the House of Lords: Courts-Martial (Appeals) Act 1968; A.J.A. 1977, s 5; S.C.A. 1981, s 145; A.J.A.

1982, Sch 8; Armed Forces Act 1996, Sch 1; Investigation and Summary Dealing (Army Regulations) 1997; *R v McEnhill* (1998) 148 NLJ 1879 (sentencing guidelines); *Hood v UK* (2000) 29 EHRR 365; *Jordan v UK* (2000) *The Times*, 17 March (ruling by ECHR that a commanding officer cannot be considered impartial); Armed Forces Discipline Act 2000 (setting out details of custody, creating Summary Appeal Courts (q.v.), and appointment of judicial officers by the Judge Advocate General, and the Chief Naval Judge Advocate); SI 00/2228, 2366; *R v Spencer* (2001) *The Times*, 30 January. In *R v Dundon* [2004] EWCA Crim 621, the Courts-Martial Appeal Court held that where there had been a lack of impartiality in a tribunal, in breach of Human Rights Convention, art 6, there could be no circumstances in which the conviction could be considered other than unsafe. In *R v Spear* (2002) *The Times*, 19 July, HL held that trial of civil offences by army court-martial is compatible with the right under Human Rights Convention, art 6, to a fair and public hearing by an independent, impartial tribunal established by law.

courts-martial, naval, fairness of. The European Court of Human Rights held, in *Grieves v UK (Application No 57067/00)* (2004) *The Times*, 12 January, that Royal Navy Courts-Martial were essentially unfair because they lacked independence, given the lack of a civilian in the vital role of judge advocate. The Human Rights Convention, art 6.1 was fundamentally breached.

courts martial system. In *Morris v UK (2002) (Application 38784/97)*, European Court of Human Rights stated that the British courts martial system was in breach of Human Rights Convention because trial by officers taken *ad hoc* from their duties breached requirement of impartiality set out in art 6(1).

courts, mercantile. *See* MERCANTILE COURTS.

courts of civil jurisdiction. These include county courts, Queen's Bench Division, Chancery Division, Family Division,

Court of Appeal (Civil Division) and House of Lords.

courts of criminal jurisdiction. These include magistrates' courts, Crown Court, Divisional Courts, Court of Appeal (Criminal Division) and House of Lords.

courts of special jurisdiction. Courts exercising a jurisdiction within specialised fields, e.g., courts-martial, ecclesiastical courts.

court's powers of management under CPR. Except where CPR provides otherwise, the court may: extend or shorten time for compliance with rules or orders; adjourn or bring forward a hearing; require attendance by party or his legal representative; stay whole or part of proceedings; consolidate proceedings; exclude issues from consideration; dismiss or give judgment on claim after decision on preliminary issue; take any other step or make any other order for purpose of managing the case and furthering the overriding objective: CPR, r 3.1(2). See *GKR Karate Ltd* v *Yorkshire Post* (2000) *The Times*, 9 February.

Courts, prize. *See* PRIZE COURTS.

courts, remedies and. 'Courts of justice do not act of their own motion. In our legal system it is their function to stand idly by until their aid is invoked by someone recognised by law as entitled to claim the remedy in justice that he seeks': *per* Lord Diplock in *Gouriet* v *UPW* [1978] AC 435.

courts, superior. *See* SUPERIOR COURTS.

court, suit of. *See* SUIT OF COURT.

Court, Supreme. *See* SUPREME COURT.

courts, youth. *See* YOUTH COURTS.

Court, Technology and Construction. *See* TECHNOLOGY AND CONSTRUCTION COURT.

court, ward of. *See* WARD.

covenant. A promise usually contained in a deed. See, e.g., *Hagee* v *Co-operative Insurance Society* [1991] NPC 92. No technical words are necessary to constitute a covenant: *Lant* v *Norris* (1775) 1 Burr 287. It will be implied only where it is apparently necessary to carry out the intention of the deed. An injunction for breach of covenant may be granted at the

court's discretion (or damages in lieu may be awarded): see, e.g., *Gafford* v *Graham* [1998] NPC 66. For waiver of breach of covenant, see *Cornillie* v *Soho* (1996) 28 HLR 561; for tenant's covenant to carry on a business, see *Co-operative Insurance Society* v *Argyll Stores* [1998] AC 1.

covenant, restrictive. The running of covenants with freehold land. *See* RESTRICTIVE COVENANT.

covenant running with the land. A covenant which ran with (or 'touched and concerned') land was one which had direct reference to the land, e.g., to renew a lease, to repair property, not to build on adjoining land. A covenant of this nature may be enforced if the entire interest in the land is transferred and there is privity of contract (q.v.) between the parties. See now Landlord and Tenant (Covenants) Act 1995, which provides, generally, for the automatic release of a tenant from obligations under a lease on assignment, and of a landlord, with consent of the tenant or court. See *Kumar* v *Dunning* [1987] 2 All ER 801; *Federated Homes* v *Mill Lodge Properties* [1980] 1 WLR 594; *Oceanic Villages Ltd* v *United Attractions* (2000) *The Times*, 19 January.

covenants, implied. Covenants (q.v.) which, although not stated directly, arise in certain types of conveyance. Examples: in a conveyance as beneficial owner, implied covenants include a good right to convey, quiet enjoyment, freedom from incumbrances. See L.P.A. 1925, ss 76, 77, Sch 2; L.P. (Misc. Provs.) A. 1994, Part I (certain covenants to be implied, e.g., as to charges and incumbrances, on a disposition of property).

covenants, onerous. Covenants which impose obligations on a tenant which, at common law, he would not otherwise have, e.g., to insure, or not to exercise a particular trade. See *Cosser* v *Collinge* (1832) 3 My & K 283. *See* ONEROUS.

covenants, usual. Where the phrase is contained in a lease it refers, generally, to covenants to pay rent, to pay the tenant's taxes and rates, to keep and deliver up premises in repair, to allow the lessor to enter and view the state of repairs: *Hampshire* v *Wickens* (1878) 7 Ch D 555. The list, however, is not closed: *Flexman* v *Corbett* [1930] 1 Ch 672. See *Chester* v *Buckingham Travel Ltd* [1981] 1 WLR 96; L.P.A. 1925, s 146.

cover note. Document issued by insurer to insured, covering risks pending preparation of, and until the issue of, a policy. See *Mackie* v *European Assurance Society* (1869) 21 LT 102.

covert recording. The European Court of Human Rights held, in *Lewis* v *UK (Application No. 1303/02)* (2003) *The Times*, 15 December, that, since at the material time, no statutory system existed to regulate covert recording by the police, applicant's right to respect for his private life, together with effective remedies, had not been breached.

CPR 1998. Civil Procedure Rules 1998 revoke RSC (q.v.) with effect from 26 April 1999. They constitute a new procedural code which, together with Practice Directions (PD) (q.v.), now govern proceedings in county courts, High Court and Court of Appeal (Civil Division). CPR followed on Lord Woolf's *Access to Justice: Final Report 1996*. The Rules have no application, in general, to insolvency, non-contentious or common form proceedings, proceedings in High Court when acting as a Prize Court, proceedings before a judge within meaning of M.H.A. 1983, Part VII, family and adoption proceedings: r 2.1.

CPR 1998, objectives. CPR 1998 are intended to enable the court to deal with cases justly, i.e., ensuring that parties are on an equal footing (see *R* v *Secretary of State for Home Department ex p Quaquah* (2000) *The Times*, 21 January), saving expense, dealing with cases in ways which are proportionate to, e.g., amount of money involved, parties' financial position, ensuring case is dealt with expeditiously and fairly, allotting to it an appropriate share of court's resourcers. Parties are required to help the court to further its overriding objective of dealing with cases justly: r 1.3.

cracked trials. Contested trials before a jury at the Crown Court, where, often at the last moment, defendant pleads guilty.

credit. 1. Usually an agreed period of time given by a seller to a buyer for payment for goods. As used in C.C.A. 1974, the word covers a cash loan and financial accommodation, no matter the form in which made: s 9(1). 'Running account credit' refers in the Act to facilities under a personal credit agreement, e.g., an overdraft or shop budget. 'Fixed sum credit' refers to a hire-purchase agreement, or a loan of a fixed amount. 'Credit brokerage' is used in the Act to refer to the introduction of individuals desiring to obtain credit or goods on hire to persons who carry on a consumer credit or hire business. See also S.G.A. 1979, s 61. 'Credit bargain' is any personal credit agreement (q.v.). 2. A 'witness's credit' is his credibility. CCA 1974 s 140 as amended by CCA 2006 s 21 that introduced s 140C a 'credit agreement' means any agreement between and individual (the 'debtor') and any other person (the 'creditor') by which the creditor provides the debtor with credit of any amount. *See* CREDIT UNION.

credit business, ancillary. *See* ANCILLARY CREDIT BUSINESS.

credit card. *See* CREDIT TOKEN.

credit, cross-examination as to. Cross-examination (q.v.) of a witness designed to discredit him by showing, e.g., that his character or background is such that he ought not to be believed. Generally, cross-examination *as to credit* relates to the character of the witness, cross-examination *as to credibility* may be concerned with attributes likely to affect his credibility (e.g., some physical characteristic). See, e.g., *R* v *Sweet-Escott* (1971) 55 Cr App R 316; *R* v *Funderburk* [1990] 2 All ER 482. *See* EVIDENCE.

creditor. One to whom a debt is owing. 1. A secured creditor is one who holds a mortgage (q.v.) or charge on the debtor's property. An unsecured creditor holds no such charge. 2. A judgment creditor is one in whose favour a judgment for a sum of money has been entered against a debtor. 3. Under C.C.A. 1974, s 189(1), a creditor is a person providing credit under a consumer credit agreement or the person to whom his rights and duties under the agreement have passed by assignment or operation of law.

creditors' meeting. In relation to bankruptcy (q.v.), the summoning of every person who is a creditor of the bankrupt in respect of a bankruptcy debt, and every person who would be such a creditor if the bankruptcy had commenced on the day on which notice of the meeting is given: Ins.A 1986, s 257. The meeting may approve or modify a proposed voluntary arrangement and must report its decisions to the court: ss 258, 259. The approval of a voluntary arrangement binds all persons who had notice of the meeting and are entitled to vote: s 260.

creditors' meeting, in relation to companies. Meeting of creditors summoned under Ins.A. 1986, s 23, to decide whether to approve the proposals of an administrator (q.v.): s 24(1). A creditors' committee may be established under s 26.

creditor's petition. A bankruptcy petition presented against a debtor by a creditor (or creditors) where: the amount of the debt is equal to or exceeds the bankruptcy level (set by the Secretary of State); each debt is for a liquidated sum payable to one or more of the creditors, immediately or at some certain future time, and is unsecured; each debt is one which the debtor appears unable to pay or to have no reasonable prospect of being able to pay; and there is no outstanding application to set aside a statutory demand served in respect of the debts: Ins.A. 1986, s 267. *See* BANKRUPTCY PETITION; PAY, INABILITY TO.

creditor's petition, proceedings on. The court will not make a bankruptcy order (q.v.) on such a petition unless satisfied that the debt has been neither paid nor secured or compounded for, or the debtor has no reasonable prospect of being able to pay when it falls due: Ins.A. 1986, s 271(1). See *Re Purvis* [1997] 3 All

ER 663. The petition will be dismissed if the court is satisfied that the debtor is able to pay, or has made an offer to compound, and that acceptance of the offer would have required dismissal of the petition and has been unreasonably refused: s 272(3).

creditors, transactions defrauding. Phrase used in Ins.A. 1986, Part XVI, relating to transactions entered into at an undervalue, as where a person makes a gift to another on terms that provide for him to receive no consideration, or he enters into a transaction with the other in consideration of marriage or for a consideration the value of which is significantly less than the value of the consideration provided by himself: s 423(1). The court can make an order protecting victims of the transaction if satisfied that its purpose was to put assets beyond the reach of a claimant: s 423(2), (3). See *Arbuthnot Leasing* v *Havelet Leasing (No. 2)* [1990] BCC 636; *Dora* v *Simper* [1999] BCC 836.

credit reference agency. A business set up to supply information it has collected on a consumer's financial standing. Under C.C.A. 1974 a consumer is entitled to obtain from a creditor details of any agency from which information was sought. The agency is also obliged to give the consumer a copy of any file kept about him. A consumer can ask the agency to remove any offending entry. See C.C.A. 1974, ss 145(8), 189(1).

credit, restricted-use. *See* RESTRICTED-USE CREDIT AGREEMENT.

credit sale agreement. 'An agreement for the sale of goods, under which the purchase price or part of it is payable by instalments, but which is not a conditional sale agreement': C.C.A. 1974, s 189.

credit token. Defined under C.C.A. 1974, s 14, as 'a card, cheque, voucher, coupon, stamp, form, booklet, or other document or thing' whereby a creditor undertakes, on its production, that he or a third party will supply goods, services or cash. Under s 51 it is an offence to give a person a credit token if he has not asked for it in writing. A credit token agreement is a regulated agreement (q.v.) under C.C.A. 1974, s 14(2). See I.C.T.A. 1988, s 142; *R v Lambie* [1981] 2 All ER 776; *Re Charge Card Services* [1988] 3 All ER 702.

credit, total charge for. The true cost to the debtor of credit provided or to be provided under an actual or prospective consumer credit agreement (q.v.): C.C.A. 1974, s 20(1). See *Consumer Credit Tables* (HMSO).

credit union. Financial savings and loans co-operative owned and run by its members, who share a common bond or link, e.g., residing in the same locality or being employed in a particular employment: Credit Unions Act 1979. Its objects include the promotion of thrift by savings, making loans to members: s 1(3). See SI 96/1189; F.S.M.A. 2000, s 338.

cremation. Disposal of a deceased person by burning. See Cremation Act 1902; Regulations as to Cremation SR&O 1930 No. 1016); Cremation (Amendment) Regulations (SI 00/58) (cremation of body parts (q.v.)).

Creutzfeldt-Jacob disease. Family Division held in *Simms v Simms* (2003) 153 NLJ 21, that it was lawful and in the best interests of two patients who were suffering from a rare and fatal neurodegenerative disorder to receive a new medical treatment which remains untested on human beings suffering from an advanced stage of the disorder.

crime. Any act or omission resulting from human conduct which is considered in itself or in its outcome to be harmful and which the state wishes to prevent, which renders the person responsible liable to some kind of punishment, generally of a stigmatic nature, as the result of proceedings which are usually initiated on behalf of the state and which are designed to ascertain the nature, extent and legal consequence of that person's responsibility. (There are about 8,000 offences in our criminal law.) In *Board of Trade v Owen* [1957] AC 602, the House of Lords adopted as a definition that given in Halsbury's *Laws of England*: a

crime is an unlawful act or default which is an offence against the public and renders the person guilty of the act liable to legal punishment. For 'abnormal crime', see *R v Richardson* (1994) 15 Cr App R (S) 876. For 'criminal proceedings' see, e.g., Acc.J.A. 1999, s 12(2). Under C.J.P.A. 2002, crime means: 'Any conduct which constitutes one or more criminal offences (whether under the law of a part of the UK or of a country or territory outside the UK); or is, or corresponds to, any conduct which, if it all took place in any one part of the UK, would constitute one or more criminal offences.'

crime, proceeds of. In *R v Montila* (2004) *The Times*, 26 November, the HL held that in a prosecution for money laundering founded on an allegation that reasonable grounds for suspicion that he was dealing with proceeds of drug trafficking offers or other crimes, it was necessary for the Crown to show that the property involved was of this nature.

crimes against humanity. Classified under Statute of International Criminal Court 1998 (q.v.) as comprising any of the following acts when committed systematically against civilians: murder; extermination; enslavement; deportation; imprisonment; torture; rape and sexual slavery; persecution on racial, religious grounds; apartheid.

criminal. 1. One charged with a crime (q.v.) and found guilty. 2. Pertaining to a crime, or the character of a crime.

Criminal Cases Review Commission. Body of 14 members, independent of the Crown, appointed under Criminal Appeal Act 1995, s 8, with the task of investigating and referring to the appropriate courts cases in which there might have been a wrongful conviction or sentence. See Sch 1. Under Criminal Appeal Act 1968, s 23A (inserted by Criminal Appeal Act 1995, s 5(1)), on appeal against conviction, the Court of Appeal may direct the Commission to investigate and report on any matter which needs to be resolved before the case is decided, and it cannot be resolved without an investigation. See *R v Graham* [1999] 2 Cr App

R (S) 312 (guidance to CCRC by Court of Appeal on complaints about sentencing); *R v CCRC ex p Pearson* [1999] 3 All ER 498 (allegation that CCRC had usurped functions of Court of Appeal).

criminal conviction certificate. Certificate, issued by the Criminal Records Bureau, under Police Act 1997, s 112, giving prescribed details of every conviction of the applicant which is recorded in central records, or stating that there is no such conviction. 'Conviction' means a conviction within the meaning of the Rehabilitation of Offenders Act 1974, other than a spent conviction (q.v.). *See* CRIMINAL RECORD CERTIFICATE.

criminal damage. The offence of destroying or damaging any property belonging to another, intentionally or recklessly and without lawful excuse: Criminal Damage Act 1971, s 1(1). It is also an offence to threaten without lawful excuse, to destroy or damage property, or to possess anything with intent to destroy or damage property without lawful excuse: ss 2, 3. See *R v Caldwell* [1982] AC 341; *Lloyd v DPP* [1991] Crim LR 904; *R v Bristol Magistrates' Court ex p E* [1999] 1 WLR 390. For defence of lawful excuse (under s 5(2)(*b*)), see *Chamberlain v Linden* [1998] 1 WLR 1252 (damage resulting from self-redress intended to restore rights. *See* CRIMINAL DAMAGE, RACIALLY-AGGRAVATED.

criminal damage, racially-aggravated. A person is guilty of an offence under C.D.A. 1998, s 30, if he commits an offence under Criminal Damage Act 1971, s 1(1) (destroying or damaging property belonging to another) which is racially-aggravated. *See* RACIALLY-AGGRAVATED OFFENCE.

criminal deception. *See* DECEPTION, OBTAINING PROPERTY BY.

Criminal Defence Service. Body set up in 2001, under Legal Services Commission (q.v.) for purpose of ensuring that individuals involved in criminal investigations or proceedings have access to such advice, assistance and representation as the interests of justice require: Acc.J.A. 1999, s 12(1). The Commission will fund advice and assistance as it considers appropriate for persons arrested and held in custody at a police station and other premises, and for those involved in investigations relating to offences: s 13(1).

Criminal Defence Service, funding. Acc.J.A. 1999, s 18, allows the Lord Chancellor to pay to the Legal Services Commission sums required to meet costs of advice, assistance and representation funded by the Commission as part of the Criminal Defence Service. He may determine the manner of payment and impose appropriate conditions. The Commission is required 'to obtain the best possible value for money.'

Criminal Defence Service, funding and payment. Under Acc.J.A. 1999, s 17(1), an individual for whom services are funded by the Legal Services Commission as part of the Criminal Defence Service is not generally required to make any payment for the services, except under regulations arising under s 17(2) where the judge orders payment to be made in accordance with those regulations.

Criminal Defence Service, right to representation. Right to representation for purposes of any kind of criminal proceedings before a court may be granted to an individual such as is mentioned in relation to the type of proceedings referred to in Acc.J.A. 1999, s 12(2) (e.g., trial, sentence, appeal, binding over, extradition, criminal contempt): Acc.J.A. 1999, Sch 3. The Legal Services Commission (q.v.) will fund such representation by, e.g., entering into contracts with persons or bodies for provision of representation by them, making grants or loans to persons or bodies to enable them to provide, or facilitate the provision of, such representation: Acc.J.A. 1999, s 14(1), (2).

Criminal Injuries Compensation Scheme. Set up in 1964 to consider applications for *ex gratia* payments of compensation to victims of crimes of violence. See Criminal Injuries Compensation Act 1995; *R v CIC Board ex p K* [1998] 2 FLR 1071; *R v MOD ex p Walker* [2000] 1 WLR 806; *R v CICA ex p Leatherland* (2000) *The Times*,

12 October (reasons for refusing claims must be given); *R v CICA ex p August* (2001) *The Times*, 4 January (meaning of 'crimes of violence').

criminal investigation. An investigation which police officers or other persons have a duty to conduct with a view to it being ascertained whether a person should be charged with an offence, or whether a person charged with an offence is guilty of it: C.P.I.A. 1996, s 1(4). Under s 23, the Home Secretary is required to prepare a code of practice designed to ensure that where a criminal investigation is conducted, all reasonable steps are taken for the purpose of the investigation and all reasonable lines of inquiry are pursued: s 23(1)(*a*). Further, information which is obtained in the course of the investigation and may be relevant should be recorded: s 23(1)(*b*). See C.D.A. 1998, Sch 8; Terrorism Act 2000, s 32.

criminal jurisdiction, courts of. *See* COURTS OF CRIMINAL JURISDICTION.

Criminal Justice Act 2003, commencement of. Following the introduction of the Act on 20 January 2004, there is now an extension of stop and search rules to articles for use so as to cause criminal damage; civilians are now allowed to participate in the execution of search warrants; there is an extension of the period of detention for questioning from 24 to 36 hours for all arrestable offences.

Criminal Law Revision Committee. Committee of judges and lawyers, including DPP (q.v.), established in 1959 to advise Home Secretary on aspects of criminal law and to consider revisions.

criminal libel. *See* LIBEL.

criminal life style. For purposes of Proceeds of Crime Act 2002, s 6, a defendant is considered to have a criminal life style if any one of the following conditions is satisfied: he is convicted of an offence listed under 2002 Act, Sch 2; the offence constitutes conduct forming part of a course of criminal activity; the offence has been committed over a period of at least six months and defendant has derived benefit from the conduct which constitutes the offence.

criminal litigation. *Practice Direction (Criminal: Consolidated)* [2002] 1 WLR 2870 consolidates and amends existing Practice Statements, Directions and Notes concerning proceedings in Court of Appeal (Criminal Division), Crown Court, magistrates' courts.

criminal lunatic. Phrase formerly used under Criminal Lunatics Act 1884, s 16, replaced by 'Broadmoor patient' under C.J.A. 1948, s 62(2). *See* BROADMOOR.

criminal negligence. 'A higher degree of negligence has always been demanded in order to establish a criminal offence than is sufficient to create civil liability. An obvious illustration is the difference between the degree of negligence in accident cases required to prove the crime of manslaughter and that sufficient to create civil liability': *per* Lord Porter in *Riddell v Reid* [1943] AC 1. See also *R v Bateman* (1925) 94 LJ KB 791; *Andrews v DPP* [1937] AC 576.

criminal proceedings. In *R v Bradley* [2005] *The Times*, 17 January, the CA held that 'criminal proceedings' in s 141 of the Criminal Justice Act 2003 had the same meaning as s 112 (1), 134 (1) and s 140 of the Criminal Justice Act 2003. The new provisions of admissibility of evidence should be applied to all trials and Newton hearings that began after the commencement of the relevant provisions, on 15 December 2004.

criminal proceedings, preliminary stage of. The preliminary stage does not include any stage after start of trial (within the meaning of Prosecution of Offences Act 1985, s 22(11), as amended by C.P.I.A. 1996, s 71, and C.D.A. 1998, s 43). Start of trial on indictment occurs when jury is sworn or, if court accepts plea of guilty before jury is sworn, when that plea is accepted (but note C.J.A. 1987, s 8, and C.P.I.A. 1996 (preparatory hearings)): s 11A. Summary trial begins when court begins to hear prosecution evidence or when court accepts plea of guilty: s 11B. See Prosecution of Offences (Custody Time Limits) Regulations 1987, as amended by C.P.I.A. 1996, s 71(4); C.D.A. 1998, s 44 (additional time limits for persons under 18); *R v Leeds Crown Court ex p Briggs* [1998] 2 Cr App R 424 (extending custody time limits).

criminal propensity. In *R v Randall* [2004] 1 All ER 467, the HL held that where two persons are charged jointly with a crime and each casts blame on the other for commission of the crime (the so-called 'cut-throat' defence), one defendant may rely on the other's criminal propensity so as to suggest that one version of the events was more probable. (For 'cut-throat' defence, see also *R v Jones and Jenkins* [2003] EWCA Crim 1966, and *R v Petkar and Farquhar* [2003] EWCA Crim 2663.)

criminal record certificate. Certificate, issued by The Criminal Records Bureau, under Police Act 1997, s 113, following an application which must be accompanied by a statement that it is required for the purposes of an exempted question. The certificate gives the prescribed details of every relevant matter relating to the applicant which is recorded in central records, or states that there is no such matter. 'Exempted question' means a question in relation to which Rehabilitation of Offenders Act 1974, s 4(2)(a) or (b) has been excluded under s 4(4). 'Relevant matter' means a conviction within the meaning of the 1974 Act, including a spent conviction (q.v.), and a caution (q.v.). See Protection of Children Act 1999, s 8. *See* CRIMINAL CONVICTION CERTIFICATE.

criminal record certificate, enhanced. Certificate issued, by the Criminal Records Bureau, under Police Act 1997, s 115. Application must be accompanied by a statement that the certificate is required for purposes of an exempted question (see s 113) asked in relation to the applicant's suitability for a paid or unpaid position involving care, supervision, training of children and young persons, child minding, etc. (s 115(2), (3)). The chief constable of the relevant police force may provide information which might be relevant to the applicant's suitability, in addition to the prescribed details of every relevant matter relating to the applicant,

or a statement that there is no such matter: s 115(6). See Protection of Children Act 1999, s 8. *See* CRIMINAL CONVICTION CERTIFICATE.

cross-border   surveillance. Under Regulation of Investigatory Powers Act 2000, s 76A, inserted by Crime (International Co-operation) Act 2003, s 83, relevant surveillance carried out by foreign police or customs officers in the UK is lawful if carried out only in places to which members of the public have access, and conditions specified by the Secretary of State are adhered to.

cross-examination. Examination of a witness by the opposing side, usually after examination-in-chief (q.v.). It is designed to elicit information concerning facts in issue which might favour the party on whose behalf it is conducted, and to create doubts as to the accuracy of evidence given against that party. Known also as 'cross-examination to the issue'. Counsel may ask in cross-examination leading questions (q.v.) and questions designed to test knowledge, memory or to elicit existence of bias or previous contradictory statements. See CPR, r 32.3, allowing the court to limit cross-examination;   SI   00/2987   (cross-examination in relation to sexual offences). *See* CREDIT, CROSS-EXAMINATION AS TO.

cross-examination in proceedings for sexual and other offences. Y.J.C.E.A. 1999, s 34, prohibits a person charged with a sexual offence (see s 62) from cross-examining in person the complainant, in connection with that offence or any other offence with which he is charged. Under s 35 there is a similar prohibition where a witness is a 'protected person' (i.e., under 17 and the offence relates to S.O.A. 1956, 1967, Protection of Children Act 1978), or under 14 where the offence relates to kidnapping, false imprisonment, any offence under C.Y.P.A. 1933, s 1. For a prohibition of this nature outside ss 34, 35, see ss 36, 37. For appropriate warning to jury in these circumstances, see s 39. For power of court to appoint a qualified legal representative, in the interests of justice, to cross-examine witnesses, in the interests of the accused, where he is prevented from such examination under ss 34–36, see s 38. See SI 00/2091.

cross-examination of witness by judge. A judge has a discretionary power to put questions to a child complainant in a trial of a sexual complaint where the child refuses to answer questions, provided that fairness can be preserved, and the jury is warned of the unusual nature of this process: *per* Potter LJ in *R v Cameron* (2001) *The Times*, 3 May.

cross-examination, order for. Where, at a hearing other than the trial, evidence is given in writing, any party may apply to the court for permission to cross-examine the person giving the evidence; where the person in question does not attend as required by order, his evidence may not be used unless the court gives permission: CPR, r 32. 7.

cross-holdings. Situation in which two companies own shares in each other. Lawful, unless the companies constitute a 'group', i.e., a relationship of holding company and subsidiary to each other. See Cos.A. 1985, s 23. *See* HOLDING COMPANY.

cross-offers. *See* OFFERS, CROSS-.

Crown. The monarch, or monarchy (q.v.). Held also to mean ministers and their departments: *Town Investments v Department of the Environment* [1979] 1 All ER 813. 'A corporation aggregate . . . headed by the Queen': *per* Lord Simon. Title to the Crown derives from Act of Settlement 1700 and common law rules of descent. For domicile and seat of the Crown, see C.J.J.A. 1982, s 46, as amended by C.J.J.A. 1991, Sch 2. *See* SOVEREIGN.

Crown Agents. The Crown Agents for Oversea Governments and Administrations. They provide commercial, financial and professional services for governments of independent countries, overseas public bodies and international bodies. See Crown Agents Act 1979; and Crown Agents (Amendment) Act 1986.

Crown, Commonwealth and. The Crown is not single and indivisible, but separate in respect of each self-governing territory within the Commonwealth: *R v Secretary of State ex p Indian Association of Alberta* [1982] QB 892.

Crown copyright. Where a work is made by a Crown servant in the course of his duties it is protected by copyright for a maximum period of 125 years: Copyright, Designs and Patents Act 1988, s 163. See Government of Wales Act 1998, Sch 12, para 28; Scotland Act 1998, Sch 8, para 25; Northern Ireland Act 1998, Sch 13, para 8.

Crown Court. Created by Courts Act 1971 as part of Supreme Court (see S.C.A. 1981, s 1 (1)) and a superior court of record. Its jurisdiction, in relation to criminal charges on indictment (see S.C.A. 1981, s 46), is exercised by any High Court judge, circuit judge or recorder (qq.v.), or judge of the High Court, circuit judge or recorder sitting with not more than four JPs: S.C.A. 1981, s 8. It sits regularly at some 90 centres. ('There is one Crown Court which is indivisible': *R v Slatter* [1975] 1 WLR 1084.) It may hear appeals from magistrates' courts and may sentence persons committed for sentencing by those courts. Appeal lies to Court of Appeal: see Criminal Appeal Act 1968, s 45. For power of Crown Court to vary or rescind its sentence (within 28 days), see P.C.C.(S.)A. 2000, s 155.

Crown Court, appeal to. The defendant may appeal against conviction in a magistrates' court. He may appeal only against sentence if he pleaded guilty, or against conviction and sentence if he pleaded not guilty. See M.C.A. 1980, s 108; *R v Hereford Magistrates ex p Rowlands* [1997] 2 WLR 854. Proceedings involve a complete rehearing of the case. See S.C.A. 1981, s 48.

Crown Court, distribution of business in. See S.C.A. 1981, s 75. Offences are grouped in four classes: Class 1, to be tried by a High Court judge, including murder, genocide, offences under Official Secrets Act 1911, s 1; Class 2, to be tried by a High Court judge, including manslaughter, rape, sedition; Class 3, to be tried by a

High Court judge, or circuit judge or recorder, comprising all offences triable only on indictment other than those in Classes 1, 2, 4; Class 4, to be tried by a High Court judge, circuit judge or recorder, including all offences triable either way, and a number of specific offences including, wounding, robbery (see *Practice Direction (Crown Court: Allocation of Business) (No. 3)* [2000] 1 WLR 203. See *Direction (No. 4)* (2001).

Crown disclosure. CA held in *R v Cairns* (2002) *The Times*, 2 December, that in relation to Criminal Procedure and Investigations Act 1996, s 7(2), it is for the Crown to decide whether or not to call a witness who might be shown to be unworthy of belief.

Crown employment. Employment under or for the purposes of a government department or any officer or body exercising on behalf of the Crown functions conferred by any statutory provision: see E.R.A. 1996, s 191.

Crown immunity. In *Matthews* v *Ministry of Defence* [2002] EWCA Civ 773, the CA held that the statutory immunity of the Crown from tortious liability is not incompatible with the right to a public hearing (see Human Rights Act 1998, Sch 1, Part 1, art 6 (1)).

Crown interest. An interest 'belonging to Her Majesty in right of the Crown or belonging to a government department or held in trust for Her Majesty for the purposes of a government department': T.C.P.A. 1990, s 293(1).

Crown Land. Land in which there is a Crown interest (q.v.) or an interest belonging to Her Majesty in right of the Duchy of Lancaster or belonging to the Duchy of Cornwall: T.C.P.A. 1990, s 293(1).

Crown, liabilities in tort of. 'The Crown shall be subject to all those liabilities in tort to which, if it were a private person of full age and capacity, it would be subject in respect of torts committed by its servants or agents or for any breach of those duties which a master owes to his servants or agents at common law or in respect of any breach of the duties

attaching at common law to the ownership, occupation, possession or control of property': Crown Proceedings Act 1947, s 2. A Crown servant, for whose acts the Crown is liable, is defined in s 2(5) as an officer appointed directly or indirectly by the Crown who is paid out of the Consolidated Fund (q.v.) or money provided by Parliament, or any other fund certified by the Treasury for purposes of the Act. See CPR, Sch 1; O 77; CPR, Sch 2; CCR, O 42 (proceedings by and against the Crown); Crown Proceedings (Armed Forces) Act 1987.

Crown privilege. The principle of exclusion of evidence, the disclosure of which would be prejudicial to the interest of the Crown. Even where neither party raises objections, the judge may exclude that evidence. See Crown Proceedings Act 1947, s 28 (order for disclosure may be made against Crown, subject to doctrine of public policy); *Duncan* v *Cammell Laird & Co* [1942] AC 624; *Burmah Oil Co* v *Bank of England* [1980] AC 1090. See PRIVILEGE.

Crown property. 'Includes property in the possession or under the control of the Crown and property which has been unlawfully removed from its possession or control': Ministry of Defence Police Act 1987, s 2(5).

Crown Prosecution Service. An integrated national service answerable to Parliament through A-G, and headed by DPP (q.v.), including, for each of 42 designated areas, Chief Crown Prosecutor, assisted by Crown Prosecutors (solicitors or barristers). It is independent of the police. It is the principal duty of the Service to take over the conduct of all criminal proceedings, other than those of a specified nature, instituted on behalf of a police force, and to advise police forces on matters related to criminal offences: Prosecution of Offences Act 1985, s 3(1); C.L.S.A. 1990, Sch 10. For powers of non-legal staff, see s 7A, substituted by C.D.A. 1998, s 53. See *R* v *Pawsey* [1989] Crim LR 152; Cm 3960 (1998); *Code for Crown Prosecutors* (2000); Crown Prosecution Service Inspectorate

Act 2000 (intended to ensure maintenance of quality of casework in all areas).

Crown road. 'A road other than a highway to which the public has access by permission granted by the appropriate Crown authority or otherwise granted by or on behalf of the Crown': Road Traffic Regulation Act 1984, s 131(7). *See* ROAD.

Crown servant. An individual who holds office under, or is employed by, the Crown. See, e.g., Company Securities (Insider Dealing) Act 1985, s 16(1); F.S.A. 1986, s 173; Official Secrets Act 1989, s 12(1); *R v Lord Chancellor's Department ex p Nangle* [1991] IRLR 343. For 'public servant', see F.S.A. 1986, s 173(2).

Crown servants, dismissal of. 'Any appointment as a Crown servant, however subordinate, is terminable at will unless it is expressly otherwise provided by statute': *Kodeeswaran v A-G of Ceylon* [1970] AC 1111. See, e.g., E.R.A. 1996, s 191.

Crown service. The service of the Crown, whether within HM dominions or elsewhere: B.N.A. 1981, s 50(1).

Crown, statutes affecting the. There is a presumption that the Crown is not bound by a statute unless reference is made to it in express terms or by some necessary implication. See *BBC v Johns* [1965] Ch 32.

cruelty. Behaviour which when considered in the context of the hearing of a petition for divorce indicates that the respondent has behaved in such a way that the petitioner cannot reasonably be expected to live with the respondent, i.e., that the marriage has broken down irretrievably. See Mat.C.A. 1973, s 1(2)(*b*). Cruelty has no artificial meaning in relation to proceedings for divorce, but it must be constituted by 'grave and weighty matters'. See *Le Brocq v Le Brocq* [1964] 1 WLR 1085.

cruelty to child. Offence committed by person of 16 or over with responsibility for a child or young person, involving wilful assault, ill-treatment, neglect, abandonment, exposure, in a manner likely to cause a child or young person under 16 unnecessary suffering or injury to health (including mental derangement): C.&Y.P.A. 1939, s 1.

cryptography. The solving of ciphers through the process of encryption (defined in explanatory note to Electronic Communications Bill 1999 as 'the process of turning normal text into a series of letters and/or numbers, which can only be deciphered by someone who has the correct key'). The Secretary of State is obliged to establish and maintain a register of approved providers of cryptography support services: Electronic Communications Act 2000, s 1.

crystallisation of charge. *See* CHARGE, CRYSTALLISATION OF.

CTP. Common Transport Policy (of EU). Objectives include: creation of a safe and integrated transport system; incorporation of principles of environmental protection within CTP; integration of all EU networks into a single trans-European network. *See* EUROPEAN UNION.

cujus est solum ejus est usque ad coelum et ad inferos. Whose is the soil, his it is even to the heaven and the depths of the earth. (Attributed to Accursius of Bologna, b. 1182.) Exceptions to this general presumption, as a result of which the owner of the soil has a restricted freedom, include, e.g., rights of others over his land, statutory restrictions on the use of his land, limitation of the right to the ownership of minerals. See *Bernstein v Skyviews Ltd* [1978] QB 479; *Anchor Developments v Berkley House* (1987) 38 Build R 82.

culpability and risk perception. In *R v G and R* [2003] UKHL 50, the HL held that culpability could not attach to a defendant under the law relating to an act involving risk of injury to another or damage to property if defendant genuinely did not perceive the risk. See *R v Caldwell* [1982] AC 341.

culpable. 1. Involving the breach of a legal duty. 2. Blameworthy.

cum div. 1. Reference to a quotation relating to stocks and shares showing that the price includes dividends and interest accrued to date. 2. A transfer *cum div.* refers to a transfer of shares near the time of the declaration of the dividend by which the transferor is to obtain benefit of that dividend (as contrasted with a transfer *ex div.* (q.v.)).

cum testamento annexo. *See* GRANT OF REPRESENTATION.

cumulative legacy. *See* LEGACY, CUMULATIVE.

cur. adv. vult. *Curia advisari vult.* The court wishes to be advised. An abbreviation used in law reports indicating that the court has not given judgment immediately, but has deliberated further.

curfew order. A 'community sentence' under P.C.C.(S.)A. 2000, ordering a person convicted of an offence, to remain for specified periods at a specified place. Electronic monitoring of the person's whereabouts may be ordered: s 37. For 'local child curfew schemes', see C.D.A. 1998, s 14. See *R v Cooper* (2000) *The Times*, 5 April. For curfew order for persistent petty offenders, see 2000 Act, s 59. See also P.C.C.(S.)A. 2000, Sch 2, para 7, inserted by C.J.C.S.A. 2000, s 50.

currency of damages award, determination of. In *Lesotho Development Authority v Impregilo SPA* [2003] EWCA Civ 1159, the CA held that, in the case of a contract identifying currency of account and payment, and specifying proportions of contractual debt to be apportioned in different currencies, then, under Arbitration Act 1996, s 48(4), it is unnecessary for UK arbitrators to convert substantive debt in foreign currency into English currency, so as to make an award.

current. As applied to legislation, means 'for the time being in force.'

curtain clauses. Those provisions of the land legislation of 1925 by which certain equitable interests (q.v.) are placed 'behind a legal curtain', i.e., those equities are transferred from land to the purchase money or to rents and profits where the land is leased. See S.L.A. 1925, s 110(2).

curtilage. Garden, field or yard included within an area surrounding a dwelling house. See *Barwick v Kent CC* [1992] EGCS 12; *Skerritts Ltd v Secretary of State for Environment* (2000) *The Times*, 8 March (whether land is in the curtilage of a building is a matter of fact and degree).

custodial sentence. *See* SENTENCE, CUSTODIAL.

custodian trustee. Office created by Public Trustee Act 1906. For greater security, trust property can be vested in a custodian trustee who has custody of all securities and documents of title relating to the property and who pays or receives all sums payable to or out of income or capital of the property. Among those who may act as custodian trustee are the Treasury Solicitor (q.v.) and trust corporations (q.v.). *See* TRUST.

custody. 1. Control of some thing or person (e.g., a child) and possession (actual or constructive) in accordance with a law or duty. See *Re H (Child) (Abduction: Rights of Custody)* (2000) *The Times*, 8 February. 2. Confinement or imprisonment of a person. See *R v Coroner for Inner London District ex p Linnaine* [1989] 1 WLR 395 (meaning of 'police custody'); *R v Kerawalla* [1991] Crim LR 451; *R v Home Secretary ex p Lainder* [1998] QB 994 (fugitive remanded on bail for extradition deemed to be in custody).

custody, commit to. *See* COMMIT TO CUSTODY.

custody disputes. Proceedings relating to disputes between parents of a child, a parent and a third party, persons not related to the child (e.g., local authority and foster parents). *See* WELFARE OF A CHILD.

custody officer. A police officer (sergeant or above) appointed for a designated police station whose duties relate to the charging of detained and arrested persons: see P.&C.E.A. 1984, ss 36–39, as amended by C.J.A. 1991, s 59. See *Vince v Dorset Police* [1992] 1 WLR 47. A 'prisoner custody officer', under C.J.A. 1991, ss 89(1), 92(1) means a person in respect of whom a certificate is for the time being in force certifying that he has been approved by the Secretary of State for the performance of escort functions or custodial duties, and is authorised to perform them. *See* DETENTION, POLICE; PRISON OFFICER.

custody record. Statement which must be compiled for a person brought under arrest to a police station, or arrested there, having attended voluntarily. A copy must be supplied on request, up to 12 months after release, to a detained person or his legal representative: *Code of Practice*, issued under P.&C.E.A. 1984, and revised in April 1991.

custody, surrender to. Means 'in relation to a person released on bail, surrendering himself into the custody of the court or of the constable (according to the requirements of the grant of bail) at the time and place for the time being appointed for him to do so': Bail Act 1976, s 2(2). *See* BAIL.

custom. Long established practice considered as unwritten law. In order that a practice might be considered as a valid custom it should have been exercised from time immemorial (q.v.); have been exercised continuously; have been observed as of right; be reasonable; be contrary neither to statute nor common law; be not inconsistent with other accepted customs. Existence of a custom may be proved: by direct evidence by a witness of his personal knowledge of its existence; by a witness testifying to its exercise; by evidence of a comparable custom in a similar trade or locality. See *Mills v Mayor of Colchester* (1867) LR 2 CP 567; *North and South Trust Co v Berkeley* [1971] 1 All ER 980. For local customary rights, see, e.g., *New Windsor Corporation v Mellor* [1975] Ch 380. *See* CONTRACT, CUSTOM AND.

customs duties. Taxes on imports and exports, collected and administered by Commissioners of Customs and Excise. See, e.g., Customs and Excise Management Act 1979.

Customs hearings. In *R (Mudie) v Dover Magistrates' Court* (2003) *The Times*, 7 February, the CA held that proceedings brought in a magistrates' court

relating to the condemnation of goods seized under Customs and Excise Management Act 1979, s 139, were of a civil, not a criminal, nature.

customs union. An objective of the Treaty of Rome 1957, art 9, calling on member states of EEC to form a customs union covering all trade in goods and prohibiting, as between them, customs duties and equivalent charges, and the adoption of a common customs tariff in relation to other countries. See also arts 28–29 (common customs tariff).

cybercrime. Defined by OECD as 'any illegal, unethical or unauthorised behaviour involving automatic processing and/ or transmission of data'.

cycle track. A way over which the public have a right of way on pedal cycles (other than those which are motor vehicles within Road Traffic Act 1988) with or without a right of way on foot; but does not include a way in or by the side of a highway comprising a carriageway: C.R.W.A. 2000, s 60(5).

cycling, dangerous. An offence committed by a person who rides a cycle on the road dangerously, i.e., in a way that falls far below what would be expected of a careful and competent cyclist to whom it would be obvious that riding in such a way would be dangerous to persons or property: see Road Traffic Act 1988, s 28, as substituted by Road Traffic Act 1991, s 7.

cy-près doctrine. *Si près* = so near, as near. A charitable trust (q.v.) which by its terms is impossible initially or is impracticable, or becomes so subsequently, will not necessarily fail; the court may apply the trust property cy-près by means of a scheme (q.v.) to some other charitable purpose which resembles the original purpose as nearly as possible. See Charities Act 1993, ss 13, 14; *Re Lysaght* [1966] Ch 191; *Oldham BC v A-G* [1993] 2 All ER 432; *Varsani v Jesani* [1999] Ch 219 (significance of spirit of gift in determining its purpose). *See* TRUSTS.

cy-près schemes. Where any property given for charitable purposes is applicable cy-près, the court or the Commission may make a scheme providing for the property to be applied (a) for such charitable purposes, and (b) if the scheme provides for the property to be transferred to another charity) by or on trust for such other charity, as it considers appropriate, having regard to; (a) the spirit of the original gift, (b) the desirability of securing that the property is applied for charitable purposes which are close to the original purposes, and (c) the need for the relevant charity to have purposes which are suitable and effective in the light of current social and economic circumstances. Charities Act 2006 s 18.

D

daily. Means, generally, every day including Sunday. See, e.g., *LCC v Metropolitan Gas Co* [1903] 2 Ch 532. *See* DAY.

damage. Loss or harm, physical or economic, resulting from a wrongful act or default and generally leading to the award of a measure of compensation. Includes the death of, or injury to, any person, including the impairment of physical or mental condition: Animals Act 1971, s 11. 'The word is sufficiently wide in its meaning to embrace injury, mischief or harm done to property, and that in order to constitute "damage" it is unnecessary to establish such definite or actual damage as renders property useless or prevents it from serving its normal function': *per* Walters J in *Samuels v Stubbs* [1972] 4 SASR 200.

damage arising from tree roots. In *L Jones Ltd v Portsmouth CC* (2002) *The Times*, 21 November, the CA held that in relation to a claim for damages arising from subsidence due to tree roots desiccation, defendant's liability in negligence does not necessitate ownership or occupation of the land on which the trees stand; it suffices that the defendant lawfully exercises control over the trees.

damage, criminal. *See* CRIMINAL DAMAGE.

damage feasant. Doing damage. Usually applied to animals belonging to X which were wrongfully on Y's land and were doing damage to it. Seizure by Y of X's animals was known as distress damage feasant (q.v.), which generally suspends the alternative remedy of damages: *Boden v Roscoe* [1894] 1 QB 608. Abolished in relation to animals: Animals Act 1971, s 7.

damage, latent. Damage which does not appear until some time after it has been caused. See, e.g., *Cartledge v Jopling & Sons* [1963] AC 758. Time limits for negligence claims in respect of latent damage not involving personal injuries are now: three years from the earliest date on which claimant had the knowledge required for bringing a claim, and the right to bring such a claim; 15 years ('long stop') period: Limitation Act 1980, ss 14A, 14B, inserted by Latent Damage Act 1986, s 1. The 1986 Act applies in cases of negligence only, and not to claims for breach of contract. See *Iron Trade Mutual Insurance v Buckenham Ltd* [1990] 1 All ER 808.

damages. The court's estimated compensation in money for detriment or injury sustained by claimant in contract or tort. They can be classified as: (1) *nominal*, where no actual damage has been suffered; (2) *contemptuous*, where the amount awarded is derisory (see *Dering v Uris* [1964] 2 QB 669); (3) *substantial*, representing compensation for loss actually sustained; (4) *exemplary*, or *vindictive*, or *punitive*, 'which go beyond compensating for actual loss and are awarded to show the court's disapproval of defendant's behaviour': CPR Glossary; (5) *aggravated*, 'additional damages which the court may award as compensation for defendant's objectionable behaviour': CPR Glossary; (6) *liquidated* (i.e. *specified*), based on the pre-estimate for anticipated breach of contract; (7) *un-liquidated* (i.e. *unspecified*), dependent on the circumstances of the case. See *Rookes v Barnard* [1964] AC 1129; *Cassell & Co Ltd v Broome* [1972] 1 All ER 801; S.G.A. 1979, Part VI; Damages

Act 1996. *See* GENERAL AND SPECIAL DAMAGES; MEASURE OF DAMAGES.

damage, 'same'. In *Royal Brompton NHS Trust* v *Hammond (No. 3)* [2002] 1 WLR 1397, the HL held that the words 'liable in respect of the same damage', in Civil Liability (Contribution) Act 1978, s 1(1), must be given their ordinary, natural meaning; they are not to be construed as meaning 'substantially or materially similar damage'.

damages, exemplary, justification of. 'There are certain categories of case in which an award of exemplary damages can serve a useful purpose in vindicating the strength of the law, and thus affording a practical justification for admitting into the civil law a principle which ought logically to belong to the criminal': *Rookes* v *Barnard* [1964] AC 1129. See *Riches* v *News Group Newspapers* [1985] 2 All ER 845; *Aggravated, Exemplary and Restitutionary Damages* (Law Commission Report No. 247, 1997), in which it is suggested that 'punitive' should be used in preference to 'exemplary' and should be set by a jury.

damages for distress. It was held, in *Hamilton-Jones* v *Davis & Snape* [2003] EWHC 3147 (Ch), that damages for mental distress can be recovered by a mother whose children were abducted by her estranged husband, following negligence by her solicitors.

damages, future loss. In *Seepersand* v *Persad* [2004] UKPC 19, it was held that an award for pain and suffering should not include any potential future loss in relation to medical treatment. See also *Herring* v *MOD* [2004] 1 All ER 44. Update No. 9.

damages, inflation and. 'Inflation and the high rates of interest to which it gives rise is automatically taken into account by the use of multipliers based on rates of interest related to a stable currency. It would therefore be wrong for the court to increase the award of damages by attempting to make a further specific allowance for future inflation': *per* Lord Fraser in *Cookson* v *Knowles* [1979] AC 556. See *Nykredit Mortgage Bank*

plc v *Edward Erdman Group (No. 2)* [1997] 1 WLR 1627 (court's jurisdiction to award interest on damages); *Wisley* v *Fulton Ltd* [2000] 1 WLR 820; Damages Act 1996, s 4.

damages, measure of, in contract. *See* MEASURE OF DAMAGES IN CONTRACT.

damages, measure of, in tort. *See* MEASURE OF DAMAGES IN TORT.

damages, mitigation of. *See* MITIGATION.

damages, multiple. *See* MULTIPLE DAMAGES.

damages, provisional assessment of. *See* PERSONAL INJURIES, PROVISIONAL DAMAGES FOR.

damages, return on investment of. In determining the return to be expected from the investment of a sum awarded as damages for future pecuniary loss in a claim for personal injury, the court shall take into account such rate of return as prescribed by an order made by the Lord Chancellor: Damages Act 1996, s 1(1). See, e.g., *Van Oudenhoven* v *Griffin Inns* (2000) *The Times*, 10 April; *Lawrence* v *Chief Constable of Staffordshire* (2000) *The Times*, 25 July (guideline rate of interest).

damages, supervening event. In assessing the quantum of damages, account is to be taken of the effects of a supervening, although unrelated, condition or illness: *Jobling* v *Associated Dairies* [1982] AC 794. See SUPERVENING EVENT.

damages, time limit. In *Aer Lingus* v *Gildacroft Ltd and Another* [2006] *The Times*, 13 January, the CA held that where a tortfeasor is looking to obtain a contribution from another responsible party for the same tort, then the two-year time limit starts from the date of the judgment or award which ascertained quantum not just liability.

damnum absque injuria. Also *damnum sine injuria*. Damage without wrong, i.e., damage or loss for which no claim can be maintained.

danger, alternative, principle of. *See* ALTERNATIVE DANGER, PRINCIPLE OF.

dangerous cargo. *See* CARGO.

dangerous driving. *See* DRIVING, DANGEROUS.

dangerous machinery. 'A part of machinery is dangerous if it is a possible cause of injury to anybody acting in a way in which a human being may be reasonably expected to act in circumstances which may be reasonably expected to occur': *Walker* v *Bletchley Flettons Ltd* [1937] 1 All ER 170. See Factories Act 1961, s 14 (under which such machinery must be securely fenced); *Wearing* v *Pirelli* [1977] 1 WLR 48 (employers may be liable under Factories Act 1961, s 14(1), where an injury is caused by dangerous machinery even though the injured person did not come into contact with it); H.S.W.A. 1974.

dangerous parking. *See* PARKING, DANGEROUS.

dangerous species. A species not commonly domesticated in the UK, and whose fully grown animals normally have such characteristics that they are likely, unless restrained, to cause severe damage or that any damage they may cause is likely to be severe: Animals Act 1971, s 6(2). Where damage is caused by an animal of this type, the keeper is liable: s 2(1). See Dangerous Wild Animals Act 1976; *Cummings* v *Granger* [1975] 1 WLR 1330; *Curtis* v *Betts* [1990] 1 All ER 769. *See* DANGEROUS WILD ANIMALS.

dangerous things, liability relating to. Things likely to do mischief and the resulting liability were considered in *Rylands* v *Fletcher* (1868) LR 1 Ex 265, in which it was stated that 'the person who for his own purposes brings on his lands and collects and keeps there anything likely to do mischief if it escapes, must keep it in at his peril, and, if he does not do so, is prima facie answerable for all the damage which is the natural consequence of its escape'. Exceptions to this rule of strict liability include claimant's default or consent; *vis major* (q.v.); Act of God (q.v.); and the act of a stranger. See *Rigby* v *Chief Constable of Northants* [1985] 1 WLR 1242; *Cambridge Water Co* v *E Counties Leather plc* [1994] 2 AC 264 (in which the House of Lords stated that foreseeability of harm of the relevant type by defendant was to be considered as a prerequisite of the recovery of damages in nuisance and under *Rylands* v *Fletcher*).

dangerous wild animals. Animals enumerated in Dangerous Wild Animals Act 1976, including, wild dog, wolf, baboon, crocodile, cobra, lion, tiger, leopard, panther, chimpanzee. No person may keep any dangerous wild animal except under the authority of a licence granted by a local authority: s 1. The list was revised by Dangerous Wild Animals Act 1976 (Modification) Order 1981, SI 81/1173. *See* ANIMALS, CLASSIFICATION OF.

data. 1. Organised information. 2. 'Information which is being processed by equipment operating automatically in response to instructions given for that purpose': Data Protection Act 1998, s 1(1)(a). See also F.I.A. 2000, Sch 8, Part III. See Access to Health Records Act 1990; EC Directive 95/46. 3. Data subjects are entitled to copies of the data, to a description of the purposes for which it is being processed, information concerning the source of the data and potential recipients. See 1998 Act, s 7. Personal data may be exempt from data protection principles if required for safeguarding of national security: s 28. The obtaining, procuring or disclosing of personal data without the consent of the data controller (see s 1(1)) are offences: ss 59, 60. For data protection principles, see Sch 1, Part 1. *See* DATA, PERSONAL.

database. A collection of independent works, data or other materials which are arranged in a systematic or methodical way, and are individually accessible by electronic or other means: Copyright, Designs and Patents Act 1988, s 3A (inserted by Copyright and Rights in Databases Regulations 1997, implementing European Council Directive 96/9/EC of 11 March 1996).

database right. Right to prevent extraction and/or re-utilisation of the whole or of a substantial part, evaluated qualitatively and/or quantitatively, of the contents of the database: Council Directive (EC) 96/9, art 7(1), implemented by Copyright and Rights in Databases Regulations 1997, SI 97/3032. The expression 'database' has a very wide meaning, covering virtually all collections of data in searchable form, and the database right is independent of any copyright or other intellectual property rights existing in the database or its constituent elements: *per* Laddie LJ in *British Horseracing Board* v *William Hill Organisation* (2001) 151 NLJ 271.

data communications. Means, under R.I.P.A. 2000, s 21(4), traffic data (q.v.) comprised in or attached to a communication for purposes of a postal service or telecommunication system by means of which it is being or may be transmitted. For lawful acquisition, see s 21(2), (3).

data controller. One who determines the purposes for which, and the manner in which, any personal data are, or are to be, processed: Data Protection Act 1998, s 1(1).

data personal. Data which relate to a living individual who can be identified from those data or from those data and other information in the possession of, or likely to come into the possession of the data controller (q.v.), and includes any expression of opinion about the individual: Data Protection Act 1998, s 1(1). Sensitive personal data (see s 2) include information relating to a data subject's racial or ethnic origin, political opinions, religious beliefs, physical and mental health, sexual life, commission of an offence. See Sch 3 in relation to processing of sensitive data for, e.g., administration of justice. See F.I.A. 2000, s 40. In *Durant* v *FSA* (2004) *The Times*, 2 January, that not all information which concerns an individual and is on file in a data register can be classified as 'personal' and of a nature which requires that the data controller shall disclose it to that individual.

data processor. One who, in relation to personal data, processes the data

on behalf of the data controller: Data Protection Act 1998, s 1(1).

Data Protection Tribunal. Established under Data Protection Act 1984; continues under Data Protection Act 1998 (see Sch 5) to hear appeals arising under the Act (see Sch 6). To be known as the Information Tribunal: see SI 01/1637.

data subject. An individual who is the subject of personal data: Data Protection Act 1998, s 1(1).

data, traffic. Means, in relation to a communication, any data identifying any person, apparatus or location to or from which communication is or may be transmitted, or any data comprising signals for the actuation of apparatus used in transmission: R.I.P.A. 2000, s 2(9). See also s 21(7).

day. A period of 24 hours, from midnight to midnight. See *Re Shurey* [1918] 1 Ch 266. For 'time of day', see I.A. 1978, s 9. For 'any day', see *Carey* v *DPP* [1989] Crim LR 368. For 'from day to day' see *Thames Water Utilities* v *Reynolds* [1996] IRLR 186.

day certain. Fixed or appointed day. See S.G.A. 1979, s 49(2); *Hyundai Ltd* v *Papadopoulos* [1980] 1 WLR 1129.

days, clear. *See* CLEAR DAYS.

days of grace. The days immediately following the day on which a payment becomes due, allowed for payment to be made. Usually three days in the case of a bill of exchange (q.v.). See *Salvin* v *James* (1805) 6 East 571.

day, year and waste. A right of the Crown, now abolished, to the profits of land of a person convicted of treason or felony, and the right to commit waste (q.v.).

DC. Divisional Court (q.v.).

dead rent. Rent which must be paid under a mining lease even though the mine is not worked.

dealer. 'A person carrying on a business of selling goods, whether by wholesale or by retail': Resale Prices Act 1976, s 24(1).

dealings, commercial. Transactions (q.v.) relating to business. May also include 'the communings, the negotiations, verbal and by correspondence, and other relations which occur in a business or commercial setting': *Gye* v *McIntyre* (1991) 65 ALJR 221.

death. Cessation of life processes and all vital signs. Not defined by statute. (Note, however, a widely-accepted American definition: 'A person will be considered medically and legally dead if, in the opinion of a physician, based on ordinary standards of medical practice, there is the absence of spontaneous brain function . . .': *Kansas Statutes* 1971.) See, e.g., Human Tissue Act 1961 (amended by Corneal Tissue Act 1986); *Code of Practice for Diagnosis of Brain Stem Death* (Dept of Health, 1998).

death duties. Estate duty paid on property which passed at death. Replaced by capital transfer tax (q.v.) and inheritance tax (q.v.).

death in custody, investigation of. In *R (Amin)* v *Secretary of State for Home Department* [2003] UKHL 51, the HL held that the duty of the state to investigate the death of a prisoner in custody was not discharged unless there was an appropriate level of publicity and of participation by the next of kin of the deceased.

death, investigation of, in relation to human rights. There is a violation of the guarantee of a right to life, under the Human Rights Convention, when no effective investigation into a death has been held: European Court of Human Rights, in *McShane* v *UK (Application No. 43290/98)* (2002) *The Times*, 3 June.

death penalty. *See* CAPITAL PUNISHMENT.

death, presumption of. *See* PRESUMPTION OF DEATH.

death, proof of. Procedure whereby death is established in evidence: by production of death certificate and proof of identity; by presumption of death (q.v.); by someone who has identified the corpse; by someone present at the death.

death, registration of. Procedure which must be completed within five days (or four days if the registrar has been notified in writing of the death), consisting of the furnishing of the following particulars: date and place of death;

name, surname, sex, date, place of birth, address and occupation of the deceased; cause of death; name, surname, qualifications, address and signature of informant; signature of registrar; date of registration. See Births and Deaths Registration Act 1953.

death, survival of causes of action on. In general, on the death of a person, all causes of action (i.e. claims) subsisting against or vested in him, survive against, or for the benefit of, the estate (save causes of action for defamation). Exemplary damages will not be awarded in favour of a deceased plaintiff's estate. See Law Reform (Misc. Provs.) Act 1934, s 1; Law Reform (Misc. Provs.) Act 1970.

death, unnatural. For purposes of Coroners Act 1998, s 8, a death by natural causes is an unnatural death where wholly unexpected and it would not have happened save for a culpable human failing: *R* v *HM Coroner for Inner London* (2001) *The Times*, 30 March.

de bene esse. Of well-being. Used in relation to that which is done conditionally, provisionally, subject to some possible future challenge or exception.

debenture. Document under a company's seal acknowledging indebtedness for a capital sum, undertaking to repay on an ascertainable date and to pay interest at a fixed rate. They include, under F.S.A. 1986, Sch 1, debenture stock, loan stock, bonds, certificates of deposit and other instruments creating or acknowledging indebtedness. Debentures are not part of a company's capital. They rank first for capital and interest and are usually secured by a charge (q.v.) on company assets. Debenture holders are creditors of the company. Power to issue debentures is usually stated in express terms in the memorandum of association (q.v.). *Mortgage debentures* give the holder security by way of charge on company's property; *naked debentures* are simply undertakings to repay; *bearer debentures* are made payable to bearer (see *Edelstein* v *Schuler* [1902] 2 KB 144). See Cos.A. 1985, ss 190–197, 744; Cos.A. 1989, ss 191, 419(1); CPR, Sch 1; O 87 (debenture holders' claims).

de bonis non administratis. Of goods which have not been administered. Grant made where an administrator, with or without a will annexed, dies, or where an administrator cannot be found; *Re Loveday* [1900] P 154. In effect, a grant limited to unadministered property when a previous grant has ceased prematurely. *See* GRANT.

debt. A sum that one person is bound to pay to another. 'Debt normally has one or other of two meanings: it can mean an obligation to pay money or it can mean a sum of money owed': *DPP v Turner* [1973] 3 All ER 124. A *specialty debt* is created by deed; a debt of *record* is, e.g., a judgment debt. See T.C.G.A. 1992, s 251; Late Payment of Commercial Debts (Interest) Act 1998, under which it is an implied term in contracts for the supply of goods and services (other than excepted contracts, e.g., a consumer credit agreement) that a qualifying debt carries simple interest (see ss 1–4).

debt, acknowledgement of by telex. CA held, in *The Good Challenger* (2003) *The Times*, 27 November, that the inscription of a party's name at the end of a telex message, representing the signature of a debtor's agent, sufficed for compliance under the Limitation Act 1980 for purposes of giving rise to a fresh cause of action.

debt-adjusting. Under C.C.A. 1974, ss 145(5), 189(1), the activities carried on by a person who acts as an intermediary between an individual and the creditor with a view to the discharge of a debt due.

debt administration. In the CCA 1974 s 145 as amended by the CCA 2006 s 24 'debt administration' is the taking of steps to perform duties under a consumer credit or consumer hire agreement on behalf of the creditor or owner, or to exercise or enforce rights under such an agreement on behalf of the creditor or owner. Persons carrying on a business of debt administration must be licensed under the CCA 1974 as amended under the CCA 2006.

debt-collecting. Under C.C.A. 1974, ss 145(7), 189(1), the taking of a step to procure payment of debts due under regulated and exempt consumer credit or hire agreements (qq.v.).

debt, imprisonment for. Generally abolished under Debtors Act 1869. See also A.J.A. 1970, s 11, Sch 8; *Milnes v Milnes* [1993] Fam law 469.

debtor. One who owes a debt. Under C.C.A. 1974, s 189(1), it means 'the individual receiving credit under a consumer credit agreement or the person to whom his rights and duties under the agreement have passed by assignment or operation of law, and in relation to a prospective consumer credit agreement (q.v.) includes the prospective debtor'. See also Hire Purchase Act 1964, s 27; *Keeble v Combined Lease Finance plc* [1996] CCLR 63.

debtor–creditor agreement. Under C.C.A. 1974, s 13, a regulated consumer credit agreement (q.v.) is a restricted use credit agreement falling within s 11(1)(*b*) of the Act, but not made by a creditor under pre-existing arrangements, or in contemplation of future arrangements, between himself and the supplier, or a restricted-use agreement within s 11(1)(*c*), or an unrestricted-use credit agreement, which is not made by a creditor under pre-existing arrangements between himself and a person (the 'supplier') other than the debtor in the knowledge that the credit is to be used to finance a transaction between the debtor and supplier.

debtor–creditor–supplier agreement. Agreement, under C.C.A. 1974, s 12, whereby a creditor and supplier are the same person, or who have a business link.

debt order, registrar of bankruptcy. It was held that under the Civil Procedure Rules a registrar of bankruptcy had jurisdiction to make a third party debt order in respect of a costs order against the debtor for an unsuccessful application to set aside a statutory demand. See *Lynch Hall & Thorby (a firm) v Thakerar (No. 2)* [2006] *The Times*, 9 January.

debtor, judgment. *See* JUDGMENT DEBTOR.

debtors, harassment of. *See* HARASSMENT OF DEBTORS.

debtor's petition. Exercise of the right of a debtor to petition for his adjudication as a bankrupt on the sole ground of inability to pay his debts: Ins.A. 1986, s 272(1). The petition must be accompanied by a statement of affairs. No order will be made if it appears, e.g., that if the order were made, the aggregate amount of bankruptcy debts, so far as unsecured, would be less than the prescribed small bankruptcies level: s 273(1). An insolvency practitioner (q.v.) may be appointed to prepare a report: s 273. *See* BANKRUPTCY.

debts, late payment of. Late payment of Commercial Debts Regulations 2002 (SI 02/1674) provide that a representative body is allowed to commence High Court proceedings on behalf of small and medium-sized organizations where standard terms included by a purchaser in contracts to which the Late Payment of Debts (Interest) Act 1998 applies, contain a term purporting to vary or oust the right to statutory interest arising on debts created by such contracts.

deceit. A tort arising from a false statement of existing fact made by conduct, orally or in writing, by one person, knowingly or recklessly, with the intent that it shall be acted on by another who, as a result, suffers damage. See Misrepresentation Act 1967, s 2(1); F.S.A. 1986, ss 150–152; F.S.M.A. 2000, s 397; *Derry* v *Peek* (1889) 14 App Cas 337; *East* v *Maurier* [1991] 1 WLR 461 (damages for deceit); *Credit Lyonnais Bank* v *ECGD* [1999] 2 WLR 540 (vicarious liability for tort of deceit); *Bradford BS* v *Borders* [1942] 1 All ER 205 (mere silence will not necessarily support an action for deceit); *Standard Chartered Bank* v *Parkistan Shipping Corporation (No. 2)* [2000] 1 All ER 686. *See* DECEIVE.

deceive. To induce a person to believe that a thing is true which is false, or a thing is false which is true, contrary to that which the person practising such deceit knows or believes to be the case. See *Re London & Globe Finance Corp Ltd* [1903] 1 Ch 728; *Welham* v *DPP* [1961] AC 103.

deception, evasion of liability by. Where a person by any deception dishonestly secures the remission of the whole or part of any existing liability to make a payment, whether his own liability or another's, or with intent to make permanent default in whole or part on any existing liability to make a payment, or with intent to let another do so, dishonestly induces the creditor or any person claiming payment on behalf of the creditor to wait for payment (whether or not the due date for payment is deferred) or to forgo payment; or dishonestly obtains any exemption from or abatement of liability to make a payment; he shall be guilty of an offence: Th.A. 1978, s 2. See *R* v *Attewell Hughes* [1991] 1 WLR 955.

deception, immigration and. A person who is not a British citizen is guilty of an offence if, by means which include deception by him, he obtains or seeks leave to enter or remain in the UK, or he secures or seeks to secure the avoidance or postponement or revocation of enforcement action (e.g., a deportation order) against him: Immigration Act 1971, s 24A, inserted by Immigration and Asylum Act, s 28. See also 1991 Act, s 31 (defence based on UN Refugee Convention 1951, art 31(1)).

deception, money transfer by. It was held in *Holmes* v *Governor of Brixton Prison* (2004) *The Times*, 28 October, that it is a requirement of the offence of obtaining money by deception that, in addition to a credit by a bank account, a debit has been made to an account, and that the credit resulted from the debit and vice versa. See Theft Act 1968, s 15A.

deception, obtaining a money transfer by. A person is guilty of an offence if by any deception he dishonestly obtains a money transfer for himself or another. Such a transfer occurs when a debit is made to one account, a credit is made to another, and the credit results from the debit or the debit results from the credit: Th.A. 1968, s 15A, inserted by Theft (Amendment) Act 1996, s 1. 'Account' means an account kept with a bank or a person carrying on business in which money received by way of deposit is lent to others or any other activity of that business is financed out of capital of or interest on money received by way of deposit: s 15B.

deception, obtaining of banking services by. In *R v Sofroniou* [2003] EWCA Crim 3681, the CA held that where defendant had dishonestly obtained a credit card or operation of an account over a period of time, this was to be considered as capable of constituting the dishonest obtaining of services by deception, subject to the parties having understood that payment would be made in respect of it.

deception, obtaining property by. It is an offence under Th.A. 1968 dishonestly to obtain property by deception or to obtain a pecuniary advantage by deception: ss 15, 16. Deception means, in this context, 'any deception (whether deliberate or reckless) by words or conduct as to fact or as to law, including a deception as to the present intentions of the person using the deception or any other person': s 15(4). See *R v Rai* [2000] 1 Cr App R 242 (silence constituting deception); *R v Williams* (2000) *The Times*, 25 October (difference between 'obtaining' and 'appropriation'). The question for the jury, to be answered as a question of fact by the application of commonsense, is: was the deception an operative cause of the obtaining of the property? See *R v Johl* [1994] Crim LR 552; *R v Adebayo* [1998] 1 Cr App R (S) 15. *See* PECUNIARY ADVANTAGE.

deception, obtaining services by. A person who by any deception dishonestly obtains services from another is guilty of an offence: Th.A. 1978, s 1(1). It is an obtaining of services where the other is induced to confer a benefit by doing some act, or causing or permitting some act to be done, on the understanding

that the benefit has been or will be paid for: s 1(2). (This replaces Th.A. 1968, s 16(2)(*a*).) See *R v Widdowson* [1986] RTR 124; *R v Shortland* [1995] Crim LR 893.

decision, judicial. *See* JUDICIAL DECISION, REQUISITES OF.

decision of court, power to reopen. In *Seray-Wurie v Hackney LBC* (2002) *The Times*, 4 July, the CA held that the High Court, like CA, has jurisdiction to reopen proceedings which had been concluded, 'if it was necessary to do so in the interests of justice'. It must be established clearly, however, that a significant injustice may have occurred and no appropriate remedy exists.

decision of wrong judge. In *Baldock v Webster* (2005) *The Times*, 13 January, the CA held that it is possible to turn to the common law doctrine of de facto jurisdiction so as to give validity to the decision of a county court judge who had decided on a High Court matter under the impression that he had been hearing county court business.

decisions, inability to make. A person is unable to make a decision for himself if he is unable (a) to understand the information relevant to the decision, (b) to retain that information, (c) to use or weigh that information as part of the process of making the decision, or (d) to communicate his decision (whether by talking, using sign language or any other means). Mental Capacity Act 2005 s 3.

Decisions of EU. *See* COMMUNITY LEGISLATION, FORMS OF.

declaration. 1. A statement of claims in proceedings. See, e.g., *Messler-Dowty Ltd v Sabena SA* (2000) *The Times*, 14 March (power of court to grant non-liability declaration). 2. A decision of the court. 3. A discretionary remedy declaring the position in law based on given facts: *Vine v National Dock Labour Board* [1957] AC 488. See *Imperial Tobacco v A-G* [1981] AC 718. 4. A formal statement, e.g., to assert a right. 5. A statement or testimony made by a witness not under oath. 6. A declaration of trust is an acknowledgment by a person that he holds property in trust (q.v.) for another. It may be implied from conduct. 7. A statutory declaration is one made before a Commissioner for Oaths (q.v.) in prescribed form. See Statutory Declarations Act 1835; Th.A. 1968, s 27(4).

declaration against interest. Statements of a deceased person are generally admissible as evidence if against his proprietary or pecuniary interests. See *Ward v H S Pitt & Co* [1913] 2 KB 130.

declaration concerning pedigree. An exception to the hearsay rule, whereby an oral or written statement of a deceased person relating to the pedigree (q.v.) of a relative, which is the subject of dispute, is admissible in evidence. The declarant must be a blood relation, or the spouse of a blood relation, of the person whose pedigree is in dispute, and the declaration should have been made before the dispute in question: see *Berkeley Peerage Case* (1811) 4 Comp 401. See Civil Evidence Act 1968, s 9; *Johnson v Lawson* (1824) 2 Bing 86. See now Civil Evidence Act 1995, s 7(3). *See* EVIDENCE, HEARSAY.

declaration concerning public or general rights. An exception to the hearsay rule, whereby an oral or written statement by a deceased person concerning the reputed existence of a right, public or general, was admissible in evidence provided it was made before the proceedings had commenced and the declarant had competent knowledge. See, e.g., *R v Bedfordshire (Inhabitants)* (1855) 4 E & B 535. See now Civil Evidence Act 1995, s 7(3)(*b*). *See* EVIDENCE, HEARSAY.

declaration in course of duty. An exception to the hearsay rule, whereby a written or oral statement of a deceased person made in pursuance of a duty to act and record those acts, and made contemporaneously with those acts, was admissible in evidence. See, e.g., *Price v Torrington* (1703) 1 Salk 285. *See* EVIDENCE, HEARSAY.

declaration of intention. In relation to contract, this means merely that an offer will be made or invited in the future. It does not imply that an offer is being made now. See *Harris v Nickerson* (1873) LR 8 QB 286.

declaratory judgment. A judgment which merely states the court's opinion on a question of law, or declares rights of the parties. It does not generally carry an order for enforcement. No claim is open to objection on the ground that a merely declaratory judgment is sought: CPR, Sch 1; O 15, r 16.

declaratory theory of common law. The theory 'that every case is governed by a relevant rule of law, existing somewhere and discoverable somehow, provided sufficient learning and intellectual rigour are brought to bear': *Jones v Secretary of State for Social Services* [1972] AC 944. 'A fairy tale in which no one any longer believes': *per* Lord Browne-Wilkinson (citing Lord Reid) in *Kleinwort Benson Ltd v Lincoln CC* [1998] 3 WLR 1095. *See* COMMON LAW; *JUS DICERE*.

decree. 1. A law. 2. A judgment or order of the court. 3. In relation to dissolution of marriage, *decree absolute* is the decree which finally dissolves the marriage. It may be issued after six clear weeks from the day following the grant of a *decree nisi* (*nisi* = unless) – a type of conditional decree requiring something further to be done to make it absolute. See *Cotterell v Cotterell* [1998] 3 FCR 199. The registrar must be satisfied that, e.g., no proceedings have been commenced to appeal against the decree nisi. It must be pronounced in open court: Family Proceedings Rules 1991. (The period may be shortened for some substantial reason.) See Mat.C.A. 1973, ss 1(5), 10(1), 15B, 41(2) (amended by Ch.A. 1989); Matrimonial Causes Rules 1977, rr 65–67; *Callaghan v Andrew-Hanson* [1991] 3 WLR 464 (once decree absolute is granted it may not subsequently be challenged by one of the parties); *Garcia v Garcia* [1991] 3 All ER 451 (delaying decree absolute).

dedication of access land. See ACCESS LAND, DEDICATION OF LAND AS.

dedication of way. The creation of a public right of way by 'dedication and acceptance'. It may be established at common law on proof of dedication by the owner to the public and of acceptance by the public, usually shown by user: *Cubitt* v *Lady Maxse* (1873) LR 8 CP 704. Under Highways Act 1980, s 31, the way is deemed to have been dedicated on proof of 20 years' enjoyment of way over land as of right and without physical obstruction. See *R* v *Secretary of State for the Environment ex p Dorset CC* [2000] JPL 396.

deductions from wages. An employer shall not make a deduction from the wages of a worker employed by him unless the deduction is required or authorised to be made by virtue of a statutory provision or a relevant provision of the worker's contract, or the worker has previously signified in writing his agreement or consent to the making of the deduction: E.R.A. 1996, s 13(1). For excepted deductions (e.g., reimbursement of overpaid wages), see s 14. See E.R.A. 1996, s 23, amended by E.R. (Dispute Resolution) A. 1998, Sch 1; *New Century Cleaning Co* v *Church* [2000] IRLR 27.

deed. 1. An act performed consciously. 2. Originally, and before August 1991, a sealed contract or covenant. Now an instrument which makes it clear on its face that it is intended to be a deed by the person making it or the parties to it and is validly executed as a deed: L.P. (Misc. Provs.) A. 1989, s 1(1). Sealing is no longer required. 3. A *deed poll* is a unilateral declaration of a party's intention, e.g., to alter his name. 4. A *deed of conveyance* comprises: exordium (commencement); recitals; testatum; parcels; general words; habendum; tenendum; reddendum; conditions; powers; covenants; testimonium (qq.v.).

deeds of arrangement. *See* ARRANGEMENT, DEEDS OF.

deed, valid execution of. Valid execution of a deed by an individual requires that he shall sign in the presence of a witness who attests the signature; or at his direction and in his presence and the presence of two witnesses who each attest the

signature; and it is delivered as a deed by him or a person authorised to do so on his behalf: L.P (Misc. Provs.) A. 1989, s 1(3). 'Sign' includes making one's mark on the instrument: s 1(4). See *Shah* v *Shah* (2001) *The Times*, 15 May.

deemed. Supposed. 'Sometimes the word is used to impose for the purpose of a statute an artificial construction of a word or phrase that would otherwise not prevail. Sometimes it is used to put beyond doubt a particular construction that might otherwise be uncertain. Sometimes it is used to give a comprehensive description that includes what is obvious, what is uncertain and what is, in the ordinary sense, impossible': *St Alwyn* v *A-G (No. 2)* [1952] AC 15. See *Barclays Bank* v *IRC* [1961] AC 509. For 'deemed notice' see, e.g., Cos.A. 1989, s 142.

deemed day of service. *Godwin* v *Swindon BC* [2002] 1 WLR 997, which stated that the deemed day of service of a claim form (see CPR, r 6.7) cannot be rebutted by any evidence of the defendant's actual receipt of that form, stands, and is in no way affected by Human Rights Convention, art 6 (right to a fair trial) and Human Rights Act 1998 *Anderton* v *Clwyd CC* (2002) *The Times*, 16 July.

deep vein thrombosis. An omission by an airline company to warn passengers of the risk of deep vein thrombosis and failing to provide non-cramped seating, did not constitute an 'accident' under Warsaw Convention 1929, art 17, and Carriage by Air Act 1961: *Re Deep Vein Thrombosis Group* [2002] EWHC 285.

de facto. In fact, in reality.

defalcation. Embezzlement (q.v.). 'Essentially involves the presence of fraudulent or dishonest dealing': *per* Samuels J in *Daly* v *Sydney Stock Exchange* (1982) 2 NSWLR 421.

defamation. The publishing of a statement which tends to lower a person in the estimation of right-thinking members of society. It may be actionable without proof of special damage where it involves, e.g., imputation of a criminal offence punishable with imprisonment.

Defences may be based on justification (or truth), privilege (absolute or qualified), fair comment (qq.v.). See Defamation Acts 1952, 1996; CPR, Sch 1; O 82 (defamation claims (q.v.)); F.I.A. 2000, s 79; *Youssoupoff* v *Metro-Goldwyn-Mayer* (1934) 50 TLR 58; *Khashoggi* v *IPC Ltd* [1986] 1 WLR 1412; *Godfrey* v *Demon Internet Ltd* [1999] 4 All ER 342 (consideration of internet transmission as 'publishing'). *See* INNOCENT DISSEMINATION; LIBEL; PRIVILEGE, QUALIFIED; SLANDER; STATEMENT.

defamation and website operators. An internet service provider may be entitled to an order requiring website operators to disclose the identity of the source of material of a defamatory nature posted by an anonymous contributor to a discussion: *Totalise plc* v *Motley Fool Ltd* (2001) *The Times*, 15 March.

defamation claims. See CPR, Sch 1; O 82 (rules which apply to claims for libel and slander). Before a claim form for libel is issued it must be endorsed with a statement enabling the relevant publications to be identified: O 82, r 2. Claimant must give full details in the particulars of claim of the facts on which he relies in support of his claim for damages: O 82, r 3(4). Under O 82, r 3A, parties may apply for an order determining whether or not the words complained of are capable of bearing the meaning attributed to them in the statement of case. For payment into court, see O 82, r 4. See PD 16, para 8.1.

defamation, common law presumption of damage. In a defamation case, the common law presumption of damage continues to have application to foreign corporations, following the Human Rights Act 1998: *Jameel* v *Wall Street Journal* [2003] EWHC 2945 (QB).

defamation, offer of amends. In *Nail* v *News Group Newspapers* [2004] EWCA Civ 1708, the CA held that where an unqualified offer to make amends under Defamation Act 1996 has been accepted and an agreed policy published, there ought to be large mitigation of compensation awarded.

default, judgment in. Judgment without any trial of a claim, see CPR, Part 12. Under r 12.4, default judgment may be requested in the case of a claim for: a specified sum of money; amount of money to be decided by the court; delivery of goods where claim form allows defendant alternative of paying their value. The court must be satisfied that particulars of claim have been served, that defendant has not filed acknowledgment of service, has not satisfied claim. A default may be set aside if entered wrongly (see r 13.2) or if defendant appears to have a real prospect of successfully defending claim (see r 13.1).

default notice. Term used under C.C.A. 1974, s 87, relating to a debtor's breach of agreement, whereby he must be issued with a default notice in the prescribed form if the creditor wishes to terminate the agreement, to recover possession or to enforce a security. Under s 88(1), the notice must specify: nature of alleged breach; action required to remedy it; date before which that action is to be taken; sum payable as compensation for breach.

default sum. Consumer Credit Act 1974 s 187A as amended by the Consumer Credit Act 2006 s 18(1) a 'default sum' '(1) means in relation to the debtor or hirer under a regulated agreement, a sum (other than a sum of interest) which is payable by him under the agreement in connection with a breach of the agreement by him; (2) but a sum is not a default sum in relation to the debtor ot hirer simply because as a consequence of his breach of the agreement, he is required to pay it earlier than he would otherwise have had to.'

default, wilful. *See* WILFUL DEFAULT.

defeasible. Capable of being annulled on a specified event.

defect. Irregularity or fault. 'Lack or absence of something essential to completeness': *Tate* v *Latham* (1897) 66 LJQB 351. A *patent defect* is one that ought to be discovered by ordinary vigilance. A *latent defect* is one that could not be discovered by reasonable examination. See Latent Damage Act 1986; *Ashburner* v *Sewell* [1891] 3 Ch 405;

Holbeck Hall Ltd v *Scarborough BC (No. 2)* [2000] 2 All ER 705 (latent defect in land).

defect in a product. There is a defect, for the purposes of C.P.A. 1987, 'if the safety of the product is not such as persons generally are entitled to expect': s 3(1). The circumstances to be taken into account include: the manner in which, and purposes for which, the product has been marketed; what might reasonably be expected to be done with or in relation to the product; and the time when the product was supplied by its producer (q.v.) to another: s 3(2). See EC Directive 85/374. *See* PRODUCTS, DEFECTIVE, LIABILITY FOR.

defective. One suffering from severe subnormality, arrested or incomplete development of mind so that he is incapable of living an independent life. See M.H.A. 1983, Part I.

defective dwellings. *See* DWELLINGS, DEFECTIVE.

defective equipment, liability for. Under Employers' Liability (Defective Equipment) Act 1969 an employer may be liable for defective equipment and liable in damages to an employee injured by it. See *Knowles* v *Liverpool CC* [1993] 1 WLR 1428 (discussion of 'equipment' by House of Lords).

defective premises, liability for. Under Defective Premises Act 1972 there is a duty to build premises properly and that duty is not abated by the subsequent disposal (including letting, assignment or surrender of the tenancy) of those premises by the person who owes that duty. 'Premises' in 1972 Act means the whole premises, land and buildings, unless there is clear language to restrict its meaning: *Smith* v *Bradford Metropolitan Council* (1982) 44 P & CR 171. For demolition of defective premises, see Building Act 1984, s 76. See *McAuley* v *Bristol CC* [1992] 1 All ER 749; *Pemberton* v *Southwark LBC* (2000) *The Times*, 26 April.

defective products, liability for. *See* PRODUCTS, DEFECTIVE, LIABILITY FOR.

defence. Generally, the defendant's opposing or denying the truth of the prosecutor's or claimant's case. The word 'defence' is not restricted to its general legal description; it is a convenient expression used to comprise nature of defence, matters on which issue is taken and reasons for taking issue: *per* Beldam LJ in *R* v *Tibbs* (2000) *The Times*, 28 February.

defence counsel's duty. It is contrary to the professional duty of counsel for the defence, and against defendant's interests, for advantage to be taken of a procedural error made by the prosecution by delaying drawing attention to that error until late in the proceedings: *R* v *Gleeson* (2003) *The Times*, 30 October.

defence to claim. *See* CLAIM, DEFENCE TO.

defence relating to justifiability of Iraq war. CA held in *Jones* v *Gloucestershire CPS* [2004] EWCA Crim 1981, that, in relation to a charge of criminal damage, a defence based on defendant's beliefs concerning the legality of war with Iraq, the defence of necessity and lawful excuse (see Criminal Law Act 1967, s 3), the only objective element for a jury to consider was whether defendant had caused damage so as to protect property. It was not necessary to rule on the question of justifiability.

defendant. 'A person against whom a claim is made': CPR, r 2.3. Applied also to person charged with offences. *See* CLAIM, SERVICE OF.

defendant, compelling appearance of. Appearance may be compelled by summons, warrant for arrest and arrest without warrant. See M.C.A. 1980, s 1. For waiving of defendant's right to be present at his trial, see *R* v *Hayward* (2001) *The Times*, 14 February.

defendant's absence from judgment. In *Hackney LBC* v *Driscoll* (2003) *The Times*, 29 August, the CA held that the common-law right of a defendant who had not received notice of legal proceedings, to apply for the setting aside of a judgment, had no application to a defendant who had appeared in proceedings which had been adjourned, but had not been notified of a new date of hearing.

defer. To delay; to postpone. A decision to defer is not necessarily a refusal: *R v Middlesbrough DC ex p Cameron Holdings Ltd* [1992] COD 247.

deferred debts. Debts deferred under statute until those with priority are paid in full.

deferred shares. Shares, now rarely issued, carrying a right to all, or a substantial proportion of, profits after ordinary shares have received a dividend. Known also as 'founders' shares'. The number of such shares must usually be stated in the prospectus (q.v.): see F.S.A. 1986, ss 146–148, 162–164.

deferring of sentence. Under P.C.C.(S.)A. 2000, s 1, the Crown Court (q.v.) or magistrates' court (q.v.) can defer passing sentence on an offender (with his consent and in the interests of justice) to enable the court, in determining his sentence, to consider any change in his circumstances or conduct after conviction (q.v.). The court which deferred sentence may deal with him if, before the end of the deferment period, he is convicted in England or Wales of a later offence: s 2.

defraud. 'To deprive a person dishonestly of something which is his or of something to which he is or would or might but for the perpetration of the fraud be entitled': *Scott v Metropolitan Police Commissioner* [1974] 3 All ER 1032. *See* CONSPIRACY TO DEFRAUD.

defunct company. A company (q.v.) which the Registrar of Companies has reasonable cause to believe is non-operational or not carrying on business. He may strike it off the register: Cos.A. 1985, s 652.

de jure. By right; by lawful title.

delay in litigation. *See* LACHES.

delay in relation to criminal trial. In *AG's Reference (No. 2 of 2001)* (2003) *The Times*, 12 December, the HL held that criminal proceedings can be delayed on the ground of a violation of the necessity for a hearing to be held within a reasonable time, under the Human Rights Convention, but only if a fair hearing had become impossible, or it was unfair to try

defendant on the ground of some compelling reason.

del credere agent. *Del credere* = of belief; of trust. An agent who receives a higher rate of commission than that which is usual, in return for a guarantee that his principal will receive due payment for goods sold.

delegated legislation. Legislation made by some person or body (e.g., a minister or local authority) under authority delegated by Parliament under statute. See, e.g., Planning and Compensation Act 1991, s 84(2). It may take the form of statutory instruments (q.v.) (based commonly on Orders in Council (q.v.)), departmental orders, regulations, rules, circulars, codes of practice. Known also as 'subordinate legislation'. Can be controlled by judicial review, pre-promulgation consultation, supervision by Parliament. For challenge to validity of subordinate legislation (made under Transport Act 1962, s 67), see *Boddington v British Transport Police* [1999] 2 AC 143.

delegated legislation, justification of. Stated in *Report on Ministers' Powers* 1932, to be: pressure on Parliament's time; technicality of much legislation; ease of modification in light of experience; the need for occasional arbitrary and swift action in administrative matters.

delegated legislation, sub-. A 'three-tier' process of legisation: an enabling ('parent') Act is made; regulations are made under that Act; those regulations are utilised so as to create further regulations. See Emergency Powers (Defence) Act 1939, s 1(3); European Communities Act 1972, s 2(2), Sch 2; *Jackson, Stansfield & Sons v Butterworth* [1948] 2 All ER 558.

delegation. The empowering of one person with appropriate and sufficient authority to act for another, e.g., as a representative or agent.

delegation of personal rights. In *Gregory v North Somerset Council* (2003) *The Times*, 21 February, the CA held that a person could not confer on another, through use of power of Attorney, a right to appear in court as that person's lay advocate. The right to appear in person in court could not be delegated, since it is a personal right.

delegation, principle of. An aspect of vicarious and strict liability (qq.v.). 'When an absolute offence has been created by Parliament, then the person on whom a duty is thrown is responsible, whether he has delegated or whether he has acted through a servant; he is absolutely liable regardless of any intent or knowledge or *mens rea*. The principle of delegation comes into play, and only comes into play, in cases where, though the statute uses words which import knowledge or intent such as in this case "knowingly"; or in some other cases "permitting" or "suffering" and the like, cases to which knowledge is inherent, nevertheless it has been held that a man cannot get out of the responsibilities which have been put on him by delegating those responsibilities to another': *R v Winson* [1968] 1 All ER 197. For delegation by a government minister to his officials, see *Carltona Ltd v Commrs of Works* [1943] 2 All ER 560. See also *Vane v Yiannopoulos* [1964] 3 All ER 820. *See* MENS REA.

delegatus non potest delegare. A delegate cannot delegate. See now Tr.A. 2000, Part IV. 'The law is not that trustees cannot delegate: it is that trustees cannot delegate unless they have authority to do so': *Pilkington v IRC* [1962] 3 All ER 622. Under Trustee Delegation Act 1999, s 5, a new Tr.A. 1925, s 25(1), is substituted, allowing a trustee to delegate the exercise of trustee functions by power of attorney. The donor of a power of attorney given under s 25 is liable for a donee's acts or defaults in the same manner as if they were the donor's acts or defaults: s 25(7). See TRUSTEE'S POWER OF DELEGATION.

de lege ferenda. From law to be passed. Law made for evolving circumstances.

deliverable state. *See* GOODS, DELIVERABLE STATE.

delivery. The voluntary and formal transfer of possession, i.e., the putting of property into the legal possession of another. It may be actual or constructive, e.g., by symbolic delivery (of a bill of lading). See S.G.A. 1979, s 61; *The Naxos* [1990] 1 WLR 1337; *Gerson Ltd v Wilkinson* (2000) *The Times*, 12 September.

delivery of a deed. Formerly performed by the person executing the deed placing his finger on the seal, saying at the same time: 'I deliver this as my act and deed'. Requirement of sealing is now abolished; delivery is denoted in any way by which a party indicates that he regards the deed as binding on him. See L.P. (Misc. Provs.) A. 1989, s 1; *Longman v Viscount Chelsea* (1989) 2 EGLR 242. *See* DEED.

delivery of goods. It is the duty of the seller to deliver the goods, and of the buyer to accept and pay for them, in accordance with the terms of the contract of sale: S.G.A. 1979, s 27. Whether it is for the buyer to take possession of the goods or for the seller to send them to the buyer is a question depending in each case on the contract, express or implied, between the parties: S.G.A. 1979, s 29(1). In *Computer 2000 Ltd v ICM Computer Solutions* (2004) *The Times*, 29 December, the CA held that under a contract of sale, where goods were delivered to a specified address and person, the sellers had performed that part of the contract and were entitled to be paid. *See* TIME AS ESSENCE OF A CONTRACT.

delivery up of goods. Remedy, in a case of conversion (q.v.) or trespass to goods, by which claimant recovers his goods from defendant who is interfering with them, under Torts (Interference with Goods) Act 1977. For an appropriate order, see r 25.1(e).

delivery, writ of. Writ of execution enforcing a judgment for delivery of goods by directing the sheriff (q.v.) to seize goods and deliver to the plaintiff, or for recovery of their assessed value. See CPR, Sch 1; O 45, r 4. A writ of *specific delivery* directs the seizure of goods stated in the writ, but with no alternative for payment of assessed value. *See* JUDGMENTS, ENFORCEMENT OF.

delusion. Continuing self-deception relating to some matter, in spite of evidence to the contrary. 1. In the case of a testator (q.v.), where the delusion does not result in the impairing of his understanding and where it relates to matters which do not involve his property, he may make a valid will: *Smee* v *Smee* (1879) 28 WR 703. See also *Banks* v *Goodfellow* (1870) LR 5 QBD 549. 2. For criminal acts committed under an insane delusion, see the M'Naghten Rules (q.v.).

demanding with menaces. *See* BLACKMAIL.

demesne land. Land belonging to Her Majesty in right of the Crown which is not held for an estate in fee simple absolute in possession: Land Registration Act 2002, s 132(1).

de minimis non curat lex. The law does not concern itself with trifles. The so-called *de minimis principle* refers, e.g., to some circumstances in which the police might tend to refrain from prosecuting: *Delaroy-Hall* v *Tadman* [1969] 2 QB 208; *Regent OHG* v *Francesca* [1981] 3 All ER 327 (maxim used in relation to delivery of goods).

demise. 1. Transference, on the death of a monarch, of the royal dignity. 2. Transfer by grant of a lease (q.v.) of lands as in a mortgage by a long lease (e.g., 3,000 years): see L.P.A. 1925, ss 85, 86. For meaning of 'demised premises', see *Oceanic Village Ltd* v *United Attractions Ltd* (2000) *The Times*, 19 January. 3. Death – in *Hodgeson* v *Clare* [2002] there was a home-made will in which a testator used the phrase 'should my wife demise together with me'. It was held that the words were not ambiguous in relation to Administration of Justice Act 1982, s 21 (1), and that they were clearly related to the event of the testator and wife dying together, and that extrinsic evidence intended to aid interpretation was not admissible.

demolition order. An order requiring that premises be vacated within a specified period of at least 28 days from the date on which the order becomes operative, and be demolished within six weeks after the end of that period, or within a longer period considered reasonable by the local housing authority (q.v.):

H.A. 1985, s 267(1). See T.C.P.A. 1990, s 55; Planning and Compensation Act 1991, s 13; SI 99/293.

demonstrative legacy. A gift, in its nature general, directed to be satisfied or paid out of a specified fund or specified part of the testator's property. Example: '£1,000 out of my deposit account with Barclays'. See *Re Webster* [1937] 1 All ER 602. *See* LEGACY.

demotion claims. Part 2 of Anti-Social Behaviour Act 2003 came into force on 30 June, 2004 (see SI 04/1502). Local authorities, housing action trusts and registered social landlords are now empowered to request demotion orders against anti-social tenants. As a result, such orders can remove security of tenure, temporarily, allowing a landlord to obtain possession without having to prove grounds.

demurrage. An agreed sum to be paid by the charterer to the shipowner as liquidated damages (q.v.) for any delay beyond a time stipulated in the contract. See *The Notos* [1987] 1 Lloyd's Rep 503.

de novo. Anew. *See* VENIRE DE NOVO.

Department for Constitutional Affairs. The Government published, on 25 February 2004, the first draft of the Constitutional Reform Bill and confirmed that the office of Lord Chancellor is to be abolished and replaced by a partnership of the judiciary and the Department of Constitutional Affairs. The Bill proposes a guarantee of judicial independence and makes provision for accountability to Parliament for the efficiency and effectiveness of the court system to be exercised by the Department, which will also be responsible for supporting the judiciary to enable it to carry out its functions. Judicial appointments will be the responsibility of a new, independent judicial appointments commission which will advertise vacancies and evaluate candidates; suitable candidates will be recommended to the Secretary of State for Constitutional Affairs for appointment.

departure directions. Under Child Support Act 1991, s 28A (inserted by Child Support Act 1995, s 1),

C.S.P.S.S.A. 2000, Sch 2, a person may apply for a departure direction, which will take into account, for purposes of reassessment of maintenance: special expenses, e.g., costs incurred by non-resident parent in maintaining contact with child; costs attributable to long-term illness of a relevant child.

dependant. One who relies for his support on another. Under Inheritance (Provision for Family and Dependants) Act 1975, those who may apply for reasonable financial provision from the deceased's estate (where they can show that deceased's will or the laws of intestacy, or both together, fail to make a reasonable financial provision for them) include: wife or husband, or former wife or husband who has not remarried, or child of the deceased; any person (not being a child of the deceased) who, in the case of any marriage to which the deceased was at any time a party, was treated by the deceased as a child of the family in relation to that marriage; any other person who immediately before the death of the deceased was being maintained, either wholly or partly by the deceased: s 1; any person who was living with the deceased in the same household immediately before the date of death, and had been living with him or her in the same household for at least two years before that date, and was living during the whole of that period as the deceased's husband or wife [this has reference to cohabitants (q.v.)]: s 1(1), (1A), inserted by Law Reform (Succession) Act 1995, s 2. See *Re Hancock* [1998] 2 FLR 346; CPR, Sch 1; O 99 (application under the 1975 Act must be made by issue of a claim form); *Bouette v Rose* (2000) *The Times*, 1 February (mother considered as a dependant of her daughter).

dependent relative revocation. Where the revocation of a will is relative to another will and is intended to be dependent upon the fact of that other will being valid, then unless that other will takes effect, the revocation is ineffective. Example: testator (q.v.) destroys his will with the intention of making another

one, but then fails to make another will. The original will is considered as unrevoked. See *Dixon v Solicitor to the Treasury* [1905] P 42; *Re Finnemore* [1991] 1 WLR 793. See REVOCATION OF WILL.

dependent territory. Any territory outside the British Isles for whose external relations the government of the UK is responsible.

deponent. One who gives evidence by affidavit (q.v.) or affirmation: PD 32, para 2. See also r 34.8(2). See DEPOSITION, EVIDENCE BY, UNDER CPR.

deportation. Expulsion from a country. 'The taking of the person in question from the country from which he is deported to some other place': *R v Secretary of State for Foreign Affairs ex p Greenberg* [1947] 2 All ER 550.

deportation from the UK. Persons who do not have a right of abode are liable to be removed from the UK under the following circumstances: where over 17, following conviction for an offence punishable with imprisonment where the court recommends deportation; where another person to whose family he belongs is or has been ordered to be deported; where Home Secretary deems deportation conducive to the public good; where they have remained beyond the time limit on a stay or failed to comply with a condition of admission. The court's recommendation for deportation of an offender who comes from any EU country is subject to EU restrictions on interference with free movement of workers: *R v Bouchereau* [1978] QB 732. See Immigration Act 1971, s 3, Sch 3 (as amended by C.J.A. 1982, Sch 10); Immigration and Asylum Act 1999, ss 63, 64; *R v Immigration Appeal Tribunal ex p Patel* [1988] 1 WLR 375 (deportation for deception after entry); *R v Secretary of State ex p Cheblack* [1991] 2 All ER 319 (deportation on grounds of national security).

deportation, right of appeal against. Procedure whereby the person against whom the deportation order has been made exercises the right of appeal, in the first instance, to the adjudicators appointed by the Home Secretary. Appeal to an adjudicator is confined to cases relating to 'family' and 'the public good': see Immigration and Asylum Act 1999, s 63, Sch 14, para 44. If dissatisfied with the adjudication, the appellant or Home Secretary may appeal to the Immigration Appeal Tribunal. See Immigration Act 1971, ss 12–22, as amended; *Egbale* v *Secretary of State for the Home Department* [1997] INLR 88. *See* IMMIGRATION.

depose. To make a deposition (q.v.) or a statement on oath.

deposit. 1. A sum of money paid on terms under which it will be repaid, with or without interest or a premium, and either on demand or at a time or in circumstances agreed by or on behalf of the person making the payment and the person receiving it, and which are not referable to the provision of property or the giving of security: Banking Act 1987, s 5(1). For fraudulent inducement to make a deposit, see s 35. 2. Payment made in a contract for sale of land, so as to bind a bargain. See L.P.A. 1925, s 49(2); *Barrington* v *Lee* [1971] 3 All ER 1231. 3. Use of title deeds as security for a loan (which created an equitable charge (q.v.)). 4. In a contract for sale of goods, 'a guarantee that the purchaser means business': *Soper* v *Arnold* (1889) 61 LT 702. 5. Any sum payable by a debtor or hirer by way of deposit or down payment: C.C.A. 1974, s 189(1). 6. Includes the sense of leaving, remaining or leave lying: *Craddock* v *Green* [1983] RTR 479; *Scott* v *Westminster CC* (1996) 93 LGR 370.

deposition, evidence by, under CPR. A party may apply for an order for a person to be examined before hearing takes place. Person from whom evidence is to be obtained following the order is known as a 'deponent'; his evidence is a 'deposition'. Examination is on oath before a judge, examiner of the court or some other person appointed by the court. See r 34.15. For enforcement of attendance before an examiner, see

r 34.10. Deposition may be given in evidence at a hearing: r 34.11(1). Deponent may be required to attend hearing and give evidence orally: r 34.11(4).

deposition in criminal cases. Statements made on oath before a magistrate or court official by a witness and usually reduced to writing. Depositions may be read, e.g., if the witness is insane, or too ill to attend. See, e.g., *Henriques* v *R* [1991] Crim LR 912. In the case of certain types of offences against children, the child's deposition may be read if signed by an examining magistrate or if the court is satisfied that the child's attendance would involve serious risk to health. See M.C.A. 1980, ss 80, 97A, 103; Magistrates' Courts Rules 1981, rr 7, 33; C.P.I.A. 1996, Sch 2, para 2. See also Civil Evidence Act 1972, s 1. *See* EVIDENCE.

Deposit Protection Board. Constituted under Banking Act 1987, s 50 and Sch 4, to administer the Deposit Protection Fund (established by Banking Act 1979, s 21 (now repealed)). If at any time an authorised institution becomes insolvent (see 1987 Act, s 59(1)) the Board will pay to each depositor who has a protected deposit (see s 60) three-quarters of such deposit: s 58. See Bank of England Act 1998, s 29. *See* BANK, AUTHORISED.

deposit-taking business. Business in the course of which money received by way of deposit (q.v.) is lent to others or any other activity of the business is financed out of the capital of or interest on money received by way of deposit. In general, deposit-taking is prohibited except in the case of the Bank of England, authorised banks (q.v.), licensed institutions: Banking Act 1987, ss 3–7. For the minimum criteria, see Sch 3. See I.C.T.A. 1988, s 481, as amended; *SCF Finance Co* v *Masri* [1987] QB 1028. *See* BANK, AUTHORISED.

deprave. To corrupt. 'If someone is made or kept morally bad or worse by something they are depraved by it': *R* v *Sumner* [1977] Crim LR 362. See Obscene Publications Act 1959. *See* OBSCENITY.

deprivation of citizenship. Procedure whereby the Secretary of State may remove the status of British and British Dependent Territories citizenship from those registered or naturalised as such if he is satisfied that the registration or naturalisation was obtained by fraud, false representation or concealment of a material fact, or if he is satisfied of their disloyalty, disaffection or where the person has served a year's imprisonment within five years of registration or naturalisation: B.N.A. 1981, s 40. See *R v Secretary of State for Home Department ex p Ejaz* (1993) *The Times*, 7 December.

deprivation of property, order for. Where a person is convicted of an offence and the court is satisfied that the property in his possession or control at the time of his apprehension had been used to commit or facilitate the commission of the offence or was intended by him to be used for that purpose, an order depriving him of that property may be made: P.C.C.(S.)A. 2000, s 143.

deregulation and contracting out, ministers' powers. Deregulation and Contracting Out Act 1994, s 1, empowers government ministers to reduce burdens on businesses by amending or repealing by SI any provisions made by an enactment which imposes a burden affecting persons carrying on a trade, business or profession. Similarly, under s 5, ministers are empowered to improve enforcement procedures so far as 'fairness, transparency and consistency' are concerned. Under the 1994 Act, Part II, ministers may make orders specifying local authority functions which may be contracted out.

derivative claim. A claim by one or more shareholders of a company where the cause of action is vested in the company and relief is accordingly sought on its behalf. It is an exception to the rule that the proper plaintiff in respect of a wrong alleged to be done to a company is, prima facie, the company. See *Foss v Harbottle* (1843) 2 Hare 461; *Fargo v Godfroy* [1986] 1 WLR 1134. See CPR, Sch 1; O 15, r 12A.

derivative deed. One deed of settlement or conveyance (q.v.) related to another document of settlement or conveyance, which enlarges, confirms or otherwise alters it.

derivative trust. A sub-trust (q.v.).

derogate. To annul or restrict the strength of an obligation or right by some subsequent act. 'No man may derogate from his own grant': *Wheeldon v Burrows* (1879) 12 Ch D 31. A landlord has an implied obligation not to derogate from his grant (see *Ward v Kirkland* [1967] Ch 194); derogation may occur if the property is 'rendered unfit or materially less fit to be used for the purposes for which it was demised': *per* Parker J in *Browne v Flower* [1911] 1 Ch 219. See *Yankwood Ltd v Havering LBC* [1998] EGCS 75; *Peckham v Ellison* [2000] 79 P & CR 276. See European Convention on Human Rights 1950, art 15 (derogations from Convention).

derogation, designated and Human Rights legislation. Phrase used in Human Rights Act 1998, s 14, to refer to declared derogation of the UK from the European Convention, art 5(3) (concerning the prompt bringing of a suspect before a judge). Designation orders require Parliamentary approval within 49 days (s 16(3)); designated derogations must be reconfirmed every five years (s 16(1)). See SI 01/1216.

descendant. A person descended from an ancestor (q.v.). See *Re Eyton* [1876] WN 142. Generally refers to lineal descendants only.

descent. Devolution (q.v.) of an estate by inheritance and not by will. Prior to their abolition by A.E.A. 1925, s 45, the rules were: descent was traced from the last purchaser (q.v.); priority of males, so that the eldest took to exclusion of others in the same degree; lineal descendants of purchaser represented him; lineal ancestors took after lineal descendants; paternal were preferred to maternal ancestors.

descent, citizenship by. *See* CITIZENSHIP, BRITISH, ACQUISITION BY DESCENT.

description, sale by. Refers to a specific article sold as an article which corresponds to a description, or to articles to be identified by reference to a certain description. (Description involves 'an account of an object by a recital of its characteristics and qualities': Black.) There is an implied condition (q.v.) that, where there is a sale of goods, they shall correspond with their descriptions: S.G.A. 1979, ss 13, 14. See *Harlington Enterprises* v *Christopher Hull Ltd* [1990] 1 All ER 737; *Stevenson* v *Rogers* [1999] QB 1028.

desertion. 1. Continual absence from cohabitation, which may be a ground for a decree of divorce or judicial separation (q.v.). 'Separation without consent and just cause': *Pheasant* v *Pheasant* [1972] 1 All ER 587. Characterised by the fact that the common life and common home have ceased to exist: *Walker* v *Walker* [1952] 2 All ER 138. Cessation of cohabitation and respondent's intention permanently to desert petitioner must be proved. For case of cohabitation during desertion, see Mat.C.A. 1973, s 2(5). Desertion for period of two years may be proof of irretrievable breakdown of marriage. See Mat.C.A. 1973, s 1(2)(c). 2. Improper absence from one's place of duty with HM Forces, with the intention of remaining permanently absent. See Army Act 1955, s 38; Armed Forces Acts 1976, 1996, Sch 1; Reserve Forces Act 1996, s 98.

desertion, constructive. *See* CONSTRUCTIVE DESERTION.

desertion, mutual. *See* MUTUAL DESERTION.

designated land *(in charities)*. Land held on trusts which stipulate that it is to be used for the purposes, or any particular purposes, of the charity. Charities Act 2006 s 40.

design right. A property right in an original design, i.e., the design of any aspect of the shape or configuration of the whole or part of an article: Copyright, Designs and Patents Act 1988, s 213. The designer is the first owner of the right: s 215. Maximum period of protection is 25 years: s 216. Remedies for infringement include damages, injunction: s 229. See also Registered Designs Act 1949, as amended by 1988 Act, Sch 4.

de son tort. *See* EXECUTOR *DE SON TORT*; TRUSTEE *DE SON TORT*.

destroy. Appears to imply, not necessarily demolition, but rather the rendering of property useless for its intended purpose: *Samuels* v *Stubbs* [1972] 4 SASR 200.

desuetude. Disuse, as in reference to 'practices which have fallen into desuetude'. A statute does not become inoperative merely through desuetude: *R* v *LCC* [1931] 2 KB 215.

detain. To hold or retain as though in custody. While every arrest involves a deprivation of liberty, the converse is not necessarily true in that arrest can only be effected in the exercise of an asserted authority: *R* v *Brown* [1977] RTR 160. For detention of goods, see r 25.1(1)(c). *See* ARREST.

detainer, forcible. *See* FORCIBLE DETAINER.

detention and training orders. 1. Under P.C.C.(S.)A. 2000, s 100, the court may order that an offender under 18 shall be subject, for the term specified under the order, to a period of detention and training, followed by a period of supervision. For length of period to be served in secure accommodation (e.g., secure training centre), see ss 102, 107. 2. CA held in *R* v *Slocombe* [2005] *The Times*, 6 December, where a young offender is convicted of indecent assault and a detention and training order imposed under the Powers of Criminal Courts (Sentencing) Act 2000, for the purposes of s 131 and s 82(1) of the Sexual Offenders Act 2003, the period of detention to be considered is the actual period itself and not the whole period of the detention and training order.

detention centre. A place used solely for the detention of detained persons but which is not a short-term holding facility (place used solely for detention for periods of not more than seven days), a prison or part of a prison: Immigration and Asylum Act 1999, s 147. For management and rules, see ss 148, 153.

detention, mental health. European Court of Human Rights held in *Benjamin and Wilson* v *UK (Application No. 28212/*

95) (2002) *The Times*, 9 October, that European Convention, art 5.4 (affecting speedy decision by court in relation to lawfulness of detention) was infringed where a mental health review tribunal lacked the power to order release of a detainee (since the power lay with Home Secretary).

detention, police. A person is in police detention if he has been taken to a police station after being arrested for an offence, or he is arrested at a police station after attending there voluntarily or accompanying a constable to it, and is detained there, or is detained elsewhere in charge of a constable: P.&C.E.A. 1984, s 118, as amended; Terrorism Act 2000, Sch 8, Sch 9, para 5(12); *R v Hughes* [1994] 1 WLR 876. See *Revised Code C* (1991). He must not be kept in police detention except in accordance with the provisions of Part IV of the Act: s 34(1), as amended. In general, he must not be kept in detention for more than 24 hours before being charged: s 41(1); he must be brought before a magistrates' court as soon as practicable and not later than the first sitting after he is charged: s 46(1). See C.J.P.O.A. 1994, s 29, inserting P.&C.E.A. 1984, s 46A (power of arrest for failure to answer to police bail). For compensation for detention in custody caused by wrongful conviction, see *R v Secretary of State for Home Department ex p Garner* (1999) 149 NLJ 637.

detention, sentence of in young offender institution. No court is to pass a sentence of detention in a young offender institution or a sentence of custody for life, and no court is to make a custodial order except in relation to a person aged at least 17 but under 18: C.J.C.S.A. 2000, s 61(1).

detention, terrorism and. In *Secretary of State for Home Department v M* [2004] EWCA Civ 324, the CA held that in denying the Home Secretary leave to appeal in relation to M's continued detention, it was not enough that M may have had connections with a terrorist organisation. It had to be shown specifically that such an organisation was linked

to al-Qaeda. See Anti-terrorism, Crime and Security Act 2001.

determinable fee. A fee (q.v.) which may determine by an event, stated in express terms, before completion of the period for which it could continue. Example: 'Blackacre to X in fee simple until he shall qualify as a doctor of medicine'. An instrument under which a determinable fee is created constitutes a *settlement* (q.v.): S.L.A. 1925, s 1. See *Hopper v Liverpool Corporation* (1944) 88 SJ 213; *Re Rowhook Mission Hall* [1985] Ch 82; Highways Act 1980, s 263 (statutory creation of determinable fee simple).

determinable interests. Interests which are terminable on the happening of specified contingencies. See, e.g., *Re Leach* [1912] 2 Ch 422. For determinable life interest, see Co. Litt. 420a; for determinable term of years, see L.P.A. 1925, s 149(6).

determine. To come, or to bring, to an end.

detinue. An action by which the plaintiff sought the return of an unlawfully detained chattel. Abolished under Torts (Interference with Goods) Act 1977, s 2(1).

detriment. 1. Injury, damage or loss suffered. 2. In the law of contract, means that the promisee, in return for a promise, has foregone a legal right which he might otherwise have exercised.

devastavit. He has wasted. A personal representative (q.v.) who misapplies or mismanages the assets of a deceased person is answerable for that waste, which is said to constitute a *devastavit*. Examples: acting fraudulently in paying legacies out of the correct order or conveying an estate to the personal representative's own use. See *Re Parry* [1969] 2 All ER 512.

development. Concept of planning law, defined by T.C.P.A. 1990 as 'the carrying out of building, engineering, mining or other operations (q.v.) in, on, over or under land, or the making of any material change in the use of any buildings or other land': s 55. See also Town and

Country Planning (Use Classes) Order 1987 (SI 87/764), listing 'use classes', changes within which are not classed as 'development'. For 'development order', see 1990 Act, s 59; for 'established use', see s 191; for 'certificate of lawful use or development', see Planning and Compensation Act, 1991, s 10. See *Secretary of State for the Environment* v *Cambridge CC* [1992] JPL 644 (demolition is not development); *Ramsey* v *Secretary of State for the Environment* (2001) *The Times*, 15 May; SI 91/2805. *See* PLANNING PERMISSION.

development land. 'If the Secretary of State directs an authority to do so, it shall make an assessment of land which is in its area and which is in its opinion available and suitable for development for residential purposes': L.G.P.L.A. 1980, s 116(1).

development, permitted. Categories of development (q.v.) for which individual applications for permission are not necessary, e.g., certain developments within the curtilage (q.v.) of a dwelling house: see Town and Country Planning General Development Order 1977, art 3; T.C.P.A. 1990, s 55(2). See Planning and Compensation Act 1991.

deviation. Departure from the norm, or from the method of performance agreed in a contract. See *Edwards* v *Newland* [1950] KB 534.

devilling. An arrangement whereby one barrister obtains the assistance of another in preparing the paperwork relating to a case. The first barrister retains responsibility for the case and remunerates the other for his assistance.

devise. A gift of real property by will made by a devisor to a devisee. May be *general*, e.g., 'all my realty to X', or *specific*, e.g., 'Blackacre to Y', or *residuary*, e.g., 'all the rest of my real property to Z': *Re Wilson* [1967] Ch 53. See W.A. 1837, s 37; L.P.A. 1925, s 62. For 'specific disposition', see I.C.T.A. 1988, s 701(5).

devolution. 1. The passing of property or rights from one person to another, e.g., on death. 2. The transfer, or delegation, of powers and authority held by the central government to local or regional authorities. See Government of Wales Act 1998; Northern Ireland (Elections) Act 1998; Scotland Act 1998; *Practice Direction (Sup Ct: Devolution)* [1999] 3 All ER 466.

devolution issue. 'Broadly, a devolution issue will involve a question whether a devolved body has acted or proposes to act within its powers (which includes not acting incompatibly with Convention rights [i.e., ECHR rights and freedoms] and Community Law [i.e., rights, obligations, liabilities, restrictions created or arising under EU treaties] or has failed to comply with a duty imposed on it': *Practice Direction (Devolution Issues)*. See Government of Wales Act 1998, Sch 8; Northern Ireland Act 1998, Sch 10; Scotland Act 1998, Sch 6.

dictionary in interpretation of statutes, use of. A dictionary may be used by the court to ascertain words to which no particular legal interpretation attaches. See, e.g., *R* v *Peters* (1866) 16 QBD 636 (Dr Johnson's definition of 'credit'); *Re Ripon Housing Confirmation Order* [1939] 2 KB 838 (meaning of 'park'); *Gravesham BC* v *Wilson* [1983] JPL 607 (meaning of 'commodious'). See *R* v *Wallace* [1990] Crim LR 433 (dictionary supplied to jury after retirement); *Plastus Kreativ* v *Minnesota Mining Co* [1997] RPC 741 (dictionary might provide 'a useful starting point' in a matter of interpretation).

dictum. An observation by a judge on a matter arising during the hearing of a case, but not necessarily essential to its determination. *See* OBITER DICTUM.

differences, contract for. A contract, the purpose or pretended purpose of which is to secure a profit or avoid a loss by reference to fluctuations in the value or price of property of any description or in an index or other factor designated for that purpose in the contract: F.S.A. 1986, Sch 1. See *City Index Ltd* v *Leslie* [1992] 1 QB 98 (a contract for differences involves 'related contracts for the sale and purchase of shares or commodities to be fulfilled by the payment of differences in price and not by delivery': *per* Lord Donaldson).

digest. 1. A collection of rules of law, e.g., the *Digest of Justinian*, published in AD 533. 2. A précis of cases, in the form of head-notes or main points, arranged in alphabetical order.

dilapidation. 1. Repairs needing to be made to premises at the end of a tenancy (q.v.). 2. A state of disrepair, relating to land and buildings, where legal liability is imposed on those responsible. See, e.g., *Standard Life Ltd* v *Greycast Devonshire Ltd* (2000) *The Times*, 10 April.

diligence, due. *See* DUE CARE.

diminished responsibility. Where a person kills or is party to the killing of another, he will not be convicted of murder if suffering from such abnormality of mind (whether arising from a condition of arrested or retarded development of mind or any inherent causes or induced by disease or injury) as substantially impaired his mental responsibility for his acts and omissions in doing or being a party to the killing. Such a person is liable to be convicted of manslaughter: Homicide Act 1957, s 2. See Criminal Procedure (Insanity) Act 1964; *R* v *Byrne* [1960] 2 QB 396; *R* v *Sanderson* (1994) 98 Cr App R 325 (paranoid psychosis); *R* v *Cutlan* [1998] 1 Cr App R (S) 1 (killing of non-abusive husband); *R* v *Antoine* [2000] 2 WLR 703 (defence not available to a person found unfit to plead). For effect of alcohol on defence of diminished responsibility, see *R* v *Gittens* [1984] QB 698.

diplomatic privilege. The right extended to a foreign diplomat, or to certain members of his staff, whose government does not waive privilege, not to be prosecuted in an English criminal court. See Diplomatic Privileges Act 1964; European Communities Act 1972, s 4; Vienna Convention 1961, art 31 (immunity from suit); Consular Relations Act 1968 (granting immunity to consular officers); State Immunity Act 1978, ss 16–20; Diplomatic and Consular Premises Act 1987; Arms Control and Disarmament

(Privileges and Immunities) Act 1988; Immigration and Asylum Act 1999, s 6. *See* PRIVILEGE.

direct effect, doctrine of. Principle of EU law, holding Community law directly effective and thereby creating rights and duties for EU nationals which are enforceable before national courts: see *Van Gend en Loos Case* 26/62 [1963] ECR 1. See *Marks and Spencer plc* v *Commissioners of Customs and Excise* (2000) *The Times*, 19 January (assertion of claim under the doctrine requires that the member state must have failed to transpose a directive into domestic legislation, and the relevant provisions of the directive must be unconditional and sufficiently precise). *See* COMMUNITY LEGISLATION, FORMS OF.

direct evidence. *See* EVIDENCE, DIRECT.

direct examination. Examination-in-chief (q.v.).

directions appointment. Preliminary hearing in relation to family proceedings, e.g., orders under Ch.A. 1989, before a district judge or clerk to the justices, with a view to issuing directions on the conduct of proceedings: Family Proceedings Courts Rules 1991 (SI 91/1395), r 14.

Directives of EU. *See* COMMUNITY LEGISLATION, FORMS OF.

director. An officer of a company (q.v.) who is responsible for its management. (A private company must have at least one director, a public company, two: Cos.A. 1985, s 282.) See F.S.M.A. 2000, s 417(1). Described in Cos.A. 1989, s 53(1) as, in relation to a body corporate, any person occupying in relation to it the position of director (by whatever name called) and any person in accordance with whose directions or instructions (not being advice given in a professional capacity) the directors of the body are accustomed to act. In Income Tax (Earnings and Pensions) Act 2003 s 434(1) it states that in the case of a company whose affairs are managed by a board of directors or similar body, the term means a member of that board or similar body; in the case of a company whose affairs are managed by a single director or similar person, means that director or person; in the case of a company whose affairs are managed by its members, means a member, and includes any person who is to be or has been a director: A director is a trustee (q.v.) for the company but not for individual shareholders, and an agent for the company. A *board of directors* is appointed, in accordance with the articles of association (q.v.), by shareholders to run the company. In favour of a person who deals with a company in good faith, the board's power to bind the company is deemed free of any restrictions in the company's constitution, and a person 'deals with a company' if he is a party to a transaction to which the company is a party: Cos.A. 1985, s 35A. See Cos.A. 1985; Cos.A. 1989, s 108; Table A, art 81; Banking Act 1987, s 105(2); I.C.T.A. 1988, ss 417(5), 612(1).

director, controlling. *See* CONTROLLING DIRECTOR.

director, disqualification order. An order of the court, under the Company Directors Disqualification Act 1986, prohibiting a person, without leave of the court, from being a director for a specified period. The prohibition may arise on conviction of an indictable offence (s 2), for persistent breach of companies legislation (s 3), etc. See ss 2–11; PD: Directors Disqualification Proceedings (all disqualification proceedings are allocated to the multi-track (q.v.): para 2; a disqualification application must be commenced by a claim form: para 4.1; evidence is by affidavit: para 9.1); *Re Melcast* [1991] BCLC 288; *Re Amaron Ltd* [1997] 2 BCLC 115; *R v Evans* (1999) *The Times*, 16 November (the purpose of disqualification is not merely punitive, but, primarily, the protection of the public); *Re Westminster Property Management Ltd* (2000) *The Times*, 19 January (although directors disqualification proceedings are capable of being described as penal proceedings, they are, nevertheless, civil proceedings); *Secretary of State v Collins* (2000) *The Times*, 24 January (disqualified director can take part in the management of a

company). See Y.J.C.E.A. 1999, Sch 3, para 8; Ins.A. 2000, ss 5, 6, Sch 4.

Director General of Fair Trading. Appointed under Fair Trading Act 1973. General functions are: to keep under review commercial activities in the UK relating to the supply of goods and services to the consumer; collecting and receiving information about activities and practices that may adversely affect consumers' economic and other interests; reviewing commercial activities relating to monopoly situations; making recommendations to the Secretary of State on these matters. Under C.C.A. 1974, s 1, he has the duty to administer the licensing system set up under that Act and generally to superintend the workings of the Act. *See* FAIR TRADING, PROCEEDINGS RELATING TO.

director, managing. *See* MANAGING DIRECTOR.

Director of Public Prosecutions. A lawyer (who must possess a ten-year general qualification: see C.L.S.A. 1990, s 71), who works under the general supervision of the Attorney-General (q.v.). Also heads Crown Prosecution Service (q.v.) and may appear for the Crown in a criminal appeal to the House of Lords. Some statutes require DPP's consent to a prosecution. See Prosecution of Offences Act 1985 (as amended by C.J.A. 1987, Sch 2, para 13); *R v DPP ex p Manning* (2000) *The Times*, 19 May (DPP's decision not to prosecute).

directors' duty of care. Directors have a fiduciary duty to the company (as a whole: see *Balstone v Headline Filters* [1990] FSR 385), and a duty of care, but are not liable for mere errors of judgment. See *Re City Equitable Fire Insurance Co Ltd* [1925] Ch 407. In the performance of their functions they should have regard to the interests of the company employees as well as the interests of company members: Cos.A. 1985, s 309. See *Kuwait Asia Bank v National Mutual Life Nominees* [1991] AC 187; *Fulham FC v Cabra Estates* [1994] BCLC 363. For directors' powers to bind a company, see Cos.A. 1985, s 35, Cos.A. 1989, s 108.

directors, enforcement of fair dealing by. Provisions in Cos.A. 1985, Part X, imposing restrictions on company directors taking financial advantage by, e.g., prohibition of tax-free payments (s 311), imposition of duty on directors to disclose interests in contracts (s 317), etc.

director, shadow. 'A person in accordance with whose directions or instructions the directors of a company are accustomed to act': Cos.A. 1985, s 741(2). See *Secretary of State for Trade and Industry* v *Deverell* (2000) *The Times*, 21 January (definition includes anyone, other than professional advisers, who has real influence in the corporate affairs of the company).

directors' interests, register of. Under Cos.A. 1985, s 325, a company must keep a register recording information relating to notification by a director of any matter related to listed shares or debentures. See also ss 288, 289, as amended. Substantial contracts with directors must be disclosed in accounts: Cos.A. 1985, s 232. See SI 96/943.

director's liability for company's negligence. A company director can be held personally liable for the company's negligent advice only if he or anyone on his behalf conveys to claimant, directly or indirectly, that he has assumed a personal responsibility to claimant: *Williams* v *Natural Life Health Foods Ltd* (1998) 148 NLJ 657.

directors, loans to. A company may not make a loan to its directors or the directors of its holding company or enter into a guarantee for a loan made by another person to any of its directors: Cos.A. 1985, s 330. For exceptions, see s 334.

directors, register of. A company must keep at its registered office a register of directors and must notify the registrar within 14 days of changes in its contents: see Cos.A. 1985, s 288. See SI 98/1702.

directors, removal of. A company may by ordinary resolution remove a director before the expiration of his period of office, notwithstanding anything in the articles or in any agreement between it and him: Cos.A. 1985, s 303(1). Special notice of such a resolution is required: s 303(2).

directors, remuneration of. Unless a company's articles so provide, directors may not be paid for their services. See Cos.A. 1989, s 6(3), (4), Sch 4.

directors' report. Report to be attached to a company's balance sheet (q.v.), stating, e.g., changes in fixed assets, and giving a 'fair review of the development of the business of the company and its subsidiaries', and recommending dividend. See Cos.A. 1985, Sch 7; Cos.A. 1989, s 234. *See* COMPANY.

directors, service. Directors employed by a company in some capacity. Remuneration may be governed by Table A, art 82. See Cos.A. 1985, Part IX.

disability, person under. Phrase applied to, e.g., an infant (q.v.) or mental patient (q.v.), i.e., one who lacks some legal capacity or qualification.

Disability Rights Commission. Body corporate set up under Disability Rights Commission Act 1999, s 1 (which also abolishes National Disability Council). Its duties are: to work towards elimination of discrimination against disabled persons, to promote equalisation of opportunities for the disabled, to encourage good practice in treatment of disabled: s 21. It may issue non-discrimination notices (see s 4) and prepare codes of practice (see s 9).

disabled employee, treatment of. In *Archibald* v *Fife Council* [2004] UKHL 32, the HL held that where an employee becomes disabled, and is now at risk of losing her job because of the strain of the manual tasks involved, the employer is under a duty to consider transferring her to a sedentary post without having to require her to compete with other applicants.

disabled person. One who has a physical or mental impairment which has a substantial and long-term adverse effect on his ability to carry out normal day-to-day activities: Disability Discrimination Act 1995, s 1(1). 'Mental impairment' includes an impairment resulting from or consisting of a mental illness only if the illness is clinically well-recognised: Sch 1, para 1. 'Long term' refers to an illness which has lasted at least 12 months, or is likely to last for the rest of the life of the person concerned: Sch 1, para 2. See also Transport Act 2000, s 146. For disablement allowances, see S.S. Contributions and Benefits Act 1992, ss 68–76. (Disability working allowance is now known as 'disabled person's tax credit' (q.v.): Tax Credits Act 1999, s 1(1).) The severe disablement allowance (involving 80 per cent disablement) is abolished under W.R.P.A. 1999, s 65. For 'continuing disability', see R v CICA ex p Embling (2000) *The Times*, 15 August.

disabled persons, discrimination against. It is unlawful for an employer to discriminate against a disabled person in relation to employment, e.g., terms of employment, opportunities for promotion, transfer, training, by dismissing him: Disability Discrimination Act 1995, s 4. See *O'Neill* v *Symm Ltd* (1998) *The Times*, 12 March (no discrimination through ignorance of disability); *Goodwin* v *Patent Office* [1999] IRLR 4; SI 98/2618 (exempting firms with fewer than 15 employees from the application of the 1995 Act, Part II); *Clark* v *TDG Ltd* [1999] 2 All ER 977 (the 1995 Act draws no distinction between direct and indirect discrimination); *Abbey Life Assurance* v *Tansell* (2000) 150 NLJ 651.

disabled person's tax credit. Formerly 'disability working allowance'. Benefit under S.S. Contributions and Benefits Act 1992, s 129, substituted by Tax Credits Act 1999, s 1(2). Paid to person over 16, engaged and normally engaged in remunerative work, who has a physical or mental disability which puts him at a disadvantage in finding a job, and whose income does not exceed the prescribed applicable amount.

disabling statute. A statute which deprives persons or bodies of legal rights or qualifications.

disaffection, incitement to. It is an offence, maliciously and advisedly to endeavour to seduce any member of the Forces from his duty or allegiance to the Crown: Incitement to Disaffection Act 1934. See also Police Act 1964, s 53.

disbar. To expel a barrister (q.v.) from his Inn of Court (q.v.).

discharge. Generally, a release from an obligation. 1. Discharge of contract refers to the freeing of parties from their mutual obligations by performance, express agreement, breach, or under the doctrine of frustration (qq.v.). 2. Release of a prisoner. 3. Release of a surety (q.v.) from liability. 4. Absolute or conditional discharge (q.v.), i.e., freeing of a person found guilty of an offence. See P.C.C.(S.)A. 2000, ss 12–15. 5. Freeing of a bankrupt from debts and liabilities, by order of discharge. See Ins.A. 1986, s 280. 6. Dismissal of a jury on their having given a verdict. 7. Nullifying of rights and liabilities on a bill of exchange (q.v.). 8. Expulsion of a charge from a weapon: see *Flack* v *Baldry* [1988] 1 WLR 393.

discharge and modification of restrictive covenants. See RESTRICTIVE COVENANTS, DISCHARGE AND MODIFICATION OF.

disciplinary and grievance hearing. A disciplinary hearing is a hearing which could result in: the administration of a formal warning to a worker by his employer; the taking of some other action in respect of a worker by his employer; the confirmation of a warning issued or some other action taken: Employment Relations Act 1999, s 13(4). A grievance hearing concerns the performance of a duty by an employer in relation to a worker: s 13(5). For right of worker to be accompanied by a union official to a hearing, see s 10.

disclaimer. Denial or disavowal of a claim; renunciation of title or interest. 1. A power (q.v.) may be disclaimed by deed: L.P.A. 1925, s 156. 2. Where two gifts are made by a testator (q.v.), if one is onerous and the other beneficial, the beneficiary can disclaim the former: *Re Loom* [1910] 2 Ch 230. 3. A trustee in bankruptcy may disclaim unprofitable contracts, land burdened with very onerous covenants, etc. See A.E.A. 1925, s 23; *Re Lee (A Bankrupt)* [1998] 1 FLR 1018 (disclaimer of lease by trustee in bankruptcy under Ins.A. 1986, s 315); *Re Park Air Services plc* [1999] 2 WLR 396 (disclaimer of lease by liquidators). *Smith v Smith* (2001) 151 NLJ 784 (in effectiveness of disclaimer of benefit made before testator's death).

disclosed document, proof of authenticity. A party is deemed to have admitted the authenticity of a document disclosed to him under CPR, Part 31, unless he serves notice that he wishes the document to be proved at trial. Notice to prove must be served by the latest date for serving witness statements, or within seven days of disclosure of the document, whichever is later: r 32.19.

disclosed document, right of inspection. A party to whom a document has been disclosed has a right to inspect it except where it is no longer under the control of the party who disclosed it, or the party disclosing it has a right or a duty to withhold inspection, or where a party considers that it would be disproportionate to the issues in the case to permit inspection of documents within a particular category: CPR, r 31.3.

disclosure. In *Three Rivers DC v Governor of Bank of England* [2004] UKHL 48, the HL held that presentational advice sought from lawyers by a company or individual believing itself or himself to be at risk of criticism by an inquiry, comes within policy reasons at the basis of legal advice privilege.

disclosure before proceedings start. An application for such disclosure must be supported by evidence. An order is made only where respondent and applicant are likely to be parties to subsequent proceedings, and disclosure is desirable so as to dispose fairly of anticipated proceedings, or save costs. Specific disclosure may be ordered. See CPR, r 31.16.

disclosure, claim to withhold. A person may apply without notice for an order permitting him to withhold disclosure of a document on the ground that disclosure would damage the public interest: CPR, r 31.19(1). Supporting evidence must be given: r 31.19(7). *See* PRIVILEGE.

disclosure, duty of search. In a standard disclosure (q.v.), a party must make a reasonable search for documents. The 'reasonableness' reflects the number of documents involved, nature and complexity of proceedings, ease and expense of retrieval, significance of documents likely to be located: CPR, r 31.7.

disclosure in criminal cases. Under C.P.I.A. 1996, s 3, there is a duty on the prosecution to make a *primary disclosure* of unused material which, in the prosecutor's opinion, might undermine the prosecution's case; or he must provide the accused with a written statement that there is no material of this kind. See *R v DPP ex p Lee* [1999] 2 All ER 737. He must also provide a list of unused material which is not sensitive: s 4. See also s 24(3). The defence, in a trial on indictment (q.v.), must set out the general nature of the accused's defence and which will indicate where the defence takes issue with the prosecution: s 5(6). The duty of *secondary prosecution disclosure* requires the prosecution (following the defence disclosure) to disclose any additional unused material which might assist the accused's defence: s 7(2)(*a*). 'Material' includes material of all kinds, and, in particular, references to information, and objects of all descriptions: s 2(4). For duty of disclosure in relation to suspected terrorism, see Terrorism Act 2000, ss 19–21.

disclosure, non-. Failure to perform a duty to make known relevant material information. See *Hill v Harris* [1965] 2 QB 601; and *Williams & Glyn's Bank Ltd v Boland* [1981] AC 487. *See* INSURANCE.

disclosure of document. A party discloses a document by stating it exists or has existed: CPR, r 31.2. Duty of disclosure is limited to documents which are or have been in his control, i.e., are or have been in his physical possession, and which he has or has had a right to inspect and make copies: r 31.8. Duty of disclosure continues during proceedings: r 31.11.

disclosure of information held by police. It was held in *R (on application* of X) v *Chief Constable of W. Midlands Police* [2004] EWHC 61 (Admin), that a chief constable, in considering whether or not to make disclosure of information under Police Act 1997, s 115(7), must have regard to principles of natural justice and whether there is a vital social need for disclosure, given the factual basis of the case.

disclosure of material evidence. European Court of Human Rights held in *Dowsett v UK (Application No. 39482/98)* (2003) *The Times*, 12 July, that material evidence which is of relevance to the defence must be submitted to the trial judge for decisions in relation to matters of disclosure at the time when it might serve most effectively to protect rights of the defence.

disclosure order against a person who is not a party. Application must be supported by evidence. Order will be made only where relevant documents are likely to support applicant's case or adversely affect case of one of the parties, and disclosure is necessary so as to dispose fairly of the claim to save costs. Specific disclosure may be ordered. See CPR, r 31.17. See *Re Howglen Ltd* (2000) *The Times*, 21 April.

disclosure, protected. Essence of measure of protection offered under Public Interest Disclosure Act 1998 to a worker dismissed or otherwise penalised by an employer where the worker has made a disclosure in the reasonable belief that there has occurred or is likely to occur at the place of work, a crime, breach of a legal obligation, miscarriage of justice, danger to health or safety, damage to environment, deliberate concealment relating to any of these matters.

disclosure, specific. An order for specific disclosure requires a party to do one or more of the following: disclose documents specified in the order, carry out a search to the extent specified in the order, disclose any documents located as a result of that search: CPR, r 31.12.

disclosure, standard. Type of disclosure order requiring a party to disclose only the documents on which he relies and those which adversely affect his or another party's case or which support another party's case, and documents he is required to disclose by a relevant PD: CPR, r 31.6. Each party must make and serve on every other party, in a standard disclosure a list of documents indicating those in respect of which the party claims a right and duty to withhold inspection, and documents no longer in the party's control: CPR, r 31.10. A disclosure statement (q.v.) must be made.

disclosure statement. A statement made by a party disclosing documents, and certifying that he understands the duty to disclose, and that to the best of his knowledge he has carried out the duty: CPR, r 3.10(6).

discontinuance of claim. A claimant may discontinue all or part of a claim at any time: CPR, r 38.2(1). He may discontinue against some or all of defendants: r 38.2(3). Court's permission is needed in relation to a claim where court has granted an interim injunction or any party has given an undertaking to the court: r 38.2(2). Where there is more than one claimant, a claimant may not discontinue unless every other claimant consents in writing or court gives permission: r 38.2(c). Notice of discontinuance must be filed, and a copy served on other parties: r 38.3(1). Claimant who discontinues is liable for costs which a defendant against whom he discontinues incurred on or before date on which notice of discontinuance was served on him: r 38.6(1).

discontinuance of prosecution. Where DPP (q.v.) has the conduct of proceedings, then, in relation to the preliminary stages (i.e., in the case of a summary offence, before evidence for the prosecution has been given, or, in the case of an indictable offence, before proceedings against the accused have been transferred or evidence for the prosecution has been given), he may give notice of discontinuance to the clerk of the court. The accused has the right to require that proceedings shall continue. See Prosecution of Offences Act 1985, s 23, amended by C.J.P.O.A.

1994, Sch 4, para 62; and C.D.A. 1998, Sch 8; *R v Grofton* [1992] 3 WLR 532 (judge is not entitled to refuse to permit prosecution to discontinue a case).

discount. 1. Deduction from the catalogue price often allowed, e.g., by a wholesaler to a retailer (known as a 'trade discount'). 2. Inducement offered by a creditor to a debtor to pay swiftly (known as a 'cash discount'). 3. Procedure whereby a bill of exchange (q.v.) is acquired for a sum less than its face value.

discount, issue of shares at a. Prohibited under Cos.A. 1985, s 100(1), in the case of public or private companies.

discovery. Term used formerly to refer to disclosure by a party of relevant documents in his possession or control relating to a civil action. See now 'disclosure of document' (q.v.). See CPR, r 31.2.

discretion. The right of an official, e.g., a judge, to act in certain circumstances and within given limits and principles on the basis of his judgment and conscience.

discretionary trust. A trust under which trustees are allowed discretion to pay or apply income for beneficiaries, but no beneficiary is able to claim of right that any part or all of the income is to be paid to him or applied in any way for his benefit. Example: land is conveyed to trustees upon trust to apply rent and profits 'for the benefit of X in the absolute discretion of the trustees'. See, e.g., *Gartside v IRC* [1968] 1 All ER 121; *Turner v Turner* [1983] 2 All ER 745; *Tankel v Tankel* [1999] 1 FLR 676. *See* TRUST.

discretion, judicial. The power, residing in the court, of deciding a question fairly where latitude of judgment is allowed. A discretionary remedy is, therefore, one which may or may not be granted. 'A person entrusted with a discretion must direct himself properly in law. He must call his own attention to the matters which he is bound to consider. He must exclude from his consideration matters which are irrelevant to the matter that he has to consider': *Associated Picture Houses Ltd v Wednesbury Corporation*

[1947] 2 All ER 680. See also P.&C.E.A. 1984, s 78; *R v Metropolitan Police Commissioner ex p Blackburn (No. 3)* [1973] QB 241 (relating to police discretion).

discretion, judicial, relating to admissibility of evidence. 'In every criminal case the judge has a discretion to disallow the evidence even if in law relevant, and, therefore, admissible, if admissibility would operate unfairly against the defendant': *Callis v Gunn* [1964] 1 QB 495. See Civil Evidence Act 1968, s 8; C.P.I.A. 1996, Sch 1, para 26; CPR, r 32.2; P.&C.E.A. 1984, ss 78, 82(3); *R v Khan* [1997] AC 558. *See* EXCLUSIONARY RULES OF EVIDENCE.

discretion to arrest or prosecute. 'It is for the Commissioner of Police or the Chief Constable . . . to decide in any particular case whether enquiries should be pursued, or whether an arrest should be made, or a prosecution brought': *per* Lord Denning in *R v Chief Constable of Devon and Cornwall, ex p CEGB* [1982] QB 458. *See* CROWN PROSECUTION SERVICE.

discrimination. The according of some differential treatment to persons or bodies in the same position, e.g., sex or racial discrimination. Discrimination on grounds of nationality is prohibited under Treaty of Rome 1957, art 7. For 'age discrimination', see *Age Diversity in Employment: a Code of Practice* (Department for Employment, June 1999). See *Kelly v Northern Ireland Housing Executive* [1998] 3 WLR 735 (a firm can be considered as 'a person discriminated against'); *R v Secretary of State for Social Security ex p Taylor* (2000) *The Times*, 25 January (discrimination in SI 98/2010 – winter fuel payments); European Convention on Human Rights 1950, art 14 (prohibition of discrimination).

discrimination and disability. CA held, in *Rose v Ryanair* [2004] EWCA Civ 1751 11 January, that it is statutory policy to provide disabled individuals with access to services which will approximate as nearly as possible to the levels enjoyed by the able-bodied populace.

discrimination, claim by soldier. In *Mangera v MOD* (2003) *The Times*,

12 July, the CA held that in the case of a soldier who alleged discrimination (failure to supply him with halal meat), that he had failed to comply with the Army's internal redress procedures (see Race Relations (Complaints to Employment Tribunals) (Armed Forces) Regulations (SI 97/2161)), so that the European Convention art 6 (right to fair trial) had no application to his discrimination claim under Race Relations Act 1976, s 4(2).

discrimination, ex-employees and. In *Relaxion Group plc v Rhys Harper* [2003] UKHL 33, the HL held that an employment tribunal could hear complaints of discrimination under legislation referring to sex, race, disability, by applicants employment had terminated. See Race Relations Act 1976, s 27A, inserted by Race Relations Act 1976 (Amendment) Regulations 2003.

discrimination for sexual orientation. In *Macdonald v MOD* [2003] UKHL 34, the HL held that the Sex Discrimination Act 1975 related solely to the prohibition of discrimination on the basis of gender; it did not involve discrimination based on sexual orientation (e.g., lesbianism).

discrimination, racial. Discrimination by one person against another so that, on racial grounds (colour, race, nationality, ethnic or national origins), he treats the other less favourably than he treats or would treat others, or applies to that other a requirement which he applies or would apply equally to persons not of the same racial group as that other, but which is such that the proportion of persons who can comply with it is considerably smaller than the proportion of persons not of that racial group who can comply with it, and which he cannot show to be justifiable, and which is to the detriment of that other because he cannot comply with it: Race Relations Act 1976, s 1. Unlawful in employment and other fields, under the 1976 Act. (The phrase 'on racial grounds' has to be interpreted in the context of the 1976 Act: *Weatherfields Ltd v Sargent* [1999] ICR 425.) See also L.G.A. 1988, s 18; *Martins v Marks and Spencer* plc [1998] IRLR 326; *Chief*

Constable of Greater Manchester v Hope [1999] ICR 338; *Nagarajan v London Regional Transport* [1999] 3 WLR 425 (subconscious intention to treat an employee less favourably because of his race will suffice); *Sheriff v Klyne Tugs* [1999] ICR 1170 (damages for personal injury); Race Relations (Remedies) Act 1994, as amended by E.R.A. 1996, Sch 3, Part 2.

discrimination, racial, involving police, public authorities. Under Race Relations Act 1976, s 19B(1), inserted by Race Relations (Amendment) Act 2000, s 1, it is unlawful for a public authority in carrying out any of its functions to do any act which constitutes discrimination. 'Public authority' includes 'any person certain of whose functions are functions of a public nature' (s 19B(2)), but does not include persons mentioned in s 19B(3), e.g., members of Parliament, Security Service. The section does not apply to judicial acts: s 19C(1)(a). Liability is extended to cover police officers under 1976 Act, s 76A, inserted by 2000 Act, s 4. National security procedures may be excluded under 1976 Act, s 42, amended by 2000 Act, s 7. For bodies subject to general duty, see 2000 Act, Sch 1.

discrimination, racial, role of knowledge in. In order knowingly to aid another person to discriminate unlawfully against someone because of race, the offender had to know that the other person was, was about to, or was contemplating treating someone less favourably on grounds of race and, with that knowledge, provide him with aid: *per* Judge LJ, in *Hallam v Avery* (2000) *The Times*, 8 February.

discrimination relating to transsexuals. The Court of Justice of the European Communities held in *KB v NHS Pensions Agency (Case C-117/01)* (2004) *The Times*, 15 January, that, where legal provisions prohibited the 'marriage' of transsexuals, so that a partner was not classified as a 'spouse' and was not entitled to a survivor's pension, there existed discrimination contrary to the EC principle of equal pay for men and women.

discrimination, reverse. Social and legal policies intended to correct existing patterns of discrimination against disadvantaged groups by giving preferential treatment to those groups so as to compensate for past discrimination. 'It is a call to offset the effects of past acts of bias by skewing opportunity in the opposite directions': Katzner, *Human Rights* (1990). Known also as 'positive discrimination'. See Cmnd 8427 (Lord Scarman's *Report on the Brixton Disorders 1981*), para 6.32.

discrimination, sex. Unfavourable treatment, direct, indirect, or by victimisation, of a person because of sex or marital status. (The word 'sex' is to be interpreted as including 'on grounds of sexual orientation': *MacDonald v MOD* [2000] IRLR 748.) May be unlawful under Sex Discrimination Acts 1975, 1986, e.g., when taking on staff or affording access to promotion. A person discriminates against a woman if he applies to her a provision, criterion or practice which he applies or would apply equally to a man, but (a) which is such that it would be to the detriment of a considerably larger proportion of women than men; and (b) which he cannot show to be justifiable irrespective of the sex of the person to whom it is applied; and (c) which is to her detriment: SI 2001/2660, amending Sex Discrimination Act 1975. Further, when an employee has made a complaint and a prima facie case is established, employers will have to prove that no discrimination has taken place. See, e.g., *James v Eastleigh BC* [1990] 2 All ER 607 (test for direct discrimination is objective); *Webb v EMO Air Cargo Ltd* [1994] QB 718 (dismissal on grounds of pregnancy); *Strathclyde Regional Council v Wallace* [1998] 1 WLR 259 (significance of genuine factors not tainted by sex discrimination in pay differential); *R v Secretary of State for Employment ex p Seymour-Smith (No. 2)* (2000) *The Times*, 18 February (indirect discrimination). See EQUAL PAY.

discrimination, sex, in commercial partnership. Sex Discrimination Act 1975 has application to a two-partner firm (of medical practitioners); hence, an expelled partner may bring proceedings against the remaining partner in the latter's name: *Dave v Robinska* (2003) 153 NLJ 921.

disease. Includes injury, ailment or adverse condition whether of body or mind: Medicines Act 1968, s 132(1).

disease of the mind. 'Mind' in the M'Naghten Rules (q.v.) is used in the ordinary sense of the mental faculties of reason, memory and understanding. 'If the effect of a disease is to impair these faculties so severely as to have either of the consequences referred to in the latter part of the Rules, it matters not whether the aetiology of the impairment is organic, as in epilepsy, or functional, or whether the impairment itself is permanent or is transient and intermittent, provided that it subsisted at the time of the commission of the act': *per* Lord Diplock in *R v Sullivan* [1984] AC 156.

disentailing deed. *See* BARRING OF ENTAILED INTEREST.

disentailment. Mode of barring of an entailed interest (q.v.) by deed, known as a distentailing assurance, so that the rights of the tenant's issue and of persons whose estates should take effect after the determination or in defeasance of the entailed interests are defeated. Interests ranking prior to entailed interests cannot be defeated in this way. See L.P.A. 1925, s 133.

dishonest. Intentionally lacking an element of truth, probity or integrity. The 'dishonest appropriation' of property is an essential element in the offence of theft: Th.A. 1968, s 1(1). Appropriation is not to be regarded as dishonest if, e.g., a person appropriates property in the belief that he has in law the right to deprive another of it: s 2(1). See *Anderton v Burnside* [1984] AC 320; *R v Navvabi* [1986] 3 All ER 102; *R v Gomez* [1993] 1 All ER 1. For high standard of proof of dishonesty in a claim in equity, see *Heini v Jyske Bank Ltd* [1999] Lloyd's Rep Bank 511. For difference between 'appropriation' and 'obtaining', see *R v Williams* [2001] 1 Cr

App R 362. For acceptance of a gift as 'appropriation', see *R* v *Hinks* [2000] 3 WLR 1590.

dishonest suppression of documents. *See* SUPPRESSION OF DOCUMENTS, DISHONEST.

dishonesty, proper test for. In *Twinsectra Ltd* v *Yardley* (2002) 152 NLJ 469, the HL held that a dual test is necessary to determine whether defendant has acted dishonestly: was his conduct dishonest by the ordinary standards of reasonable and honest persons; and did he realise that his conduct was dishonest in relation to those standards. Accused can be convicted only if the answer to both questions is affirmative. See also *R* v *Ghosh* [1982] QB 1053; *R* v *Morris* [1983] QB 587; *R* v *Brennen* [1990] Crim LR 118.

dishonesty relating to failure to notify changed circumstances in relation to a social benefit. S.S.F.A. 2001, s 16, suggests a modification of S.S. Administration A. 1992, so that a person shall be guilty of an offence if there has been a change of circumstances affecting his entitlement to benefit under any provision of the relevant legislation, and the change is not excluded from the changes required to be notified, and he knows that the change affects an entitlement of his to such a benefit, and he dishonestly fails to notify the change promptly to the appropriate person.

dishonesty, time limits and. In *DEG Deutsche Investitions* v *Same (No. 3)* (2003) *The Times*, 9 September, the CA held that in the case of a managing director who had acted dishonestly and breached his fiduciary duty to the company by making an unauthorised profit, there was no time limit to the Company's claim for account of profits.

dishonour of bill. Refusal by drawee of a bill of exchange (q.v.) to accept it, or failure to pay after acceptance. See B.Ex.A. 1882, s 47; A.J.A. 1977, s 4; *Rae* v *Yorkshire Bank plc* (1987) *The Times*, 12 October (damages for dishonour of cheque); *Kpohraror* v *Woolwich BS* [1996] 4 All ER 119.

dismissal, constructive. *See* CONSTRUCTIVE DISMISSAL.

dismissal, fair. *See* FAIR DISMISSAL.

dismissal from employment. An employee is dismissed by his employer if the contract under which he is employed is terminated by the employer, whether with or without notice, or he is employed under a fixed-term contract and that term expires without being renewed under the same contract; or the employee terminates the contract under which he is employed, with or without notice, by reason of the employer's conduct (so-called 'constructive dismissal' (q.v.)): E.R.A. 1996, s 95. An employee has the right not to be unfairly dismissed by his employer: E.R.A. 1996, s 94(1); *Carver* v *Saudi Airlines* [1999] 3 All ER 61.

dismissal of worker at risk. In *Coxall* v *Goodyear Ltd* (2002) *The Times*, 8 August, the CA held that an employer is obliged to dismiss an employee who runs a risk of physical danger, so as to protect him from that danger. (Employee suffered from a predisposition to asthma, unknown initially to him and the employer.) See *Whithers* v *Perry Chain Co* [1961] 1 WLR 1314.

dismissal procedures agreement. 'An agreement in writing with respect to procedures relating to dismissal made by or on behalf of one or more independent trade unions and one or more employers or employers' associations': E.R.A. 1996, s 235(1).

dismissal statement. Employees are entitled to a written statement giving particulars of the reasons for dismissal where they are dismissed with or without notice or their fixed-term contract has expired without renewal: E.R.A. 1996, s 92(1). An employee is entitled to such a statement only on request (and, in that case, must be given the statement within 14 days), and only if he has been continuously employed by his employer for not less than one year: s 92(2); SI 99/1436. An employee who is dismissed while pregnant or in circumstances in which maternity leave ends by reason of the dismissal, is entitled to the statement without having to request it and irrespective of her period of continuous employment: s 92(4).

dismissal, summary. *See* SUMMARY DISMISSAL.

dismissal, unfair. Rights relating to unfair dismissal apply where an employee has served for an appropriate period of continuous employment (one year: see SI 99/1436) and is not over 65 or past the retirement age normally applicable to his job. Where an employee is dismissed for an inadmissible reason (e.g., for his membership of a relevant union), that dismissal is unfair, no matter what his age or period of employment. An employment tribunal will decide whether the employer's reason for dismissal was within the concept of 'fair dismissal' and whether he had acted reasonably in dismissing the employee in the circumstances. See E.R.A. 1996, Part X; T.U.L.R.(C.)A. 1992, s 212A (inserted by E.R. (Dispute Resolution) A. 1998, s 7, empowering ACAS (q.v.) to construct an arbitration scheme for resolution of unfair dismissal disputes). See National Minimum Wage Act 1998, ss 23, 24, for right of worker not to suffer unfair dismissal following a claim for the minimum wage. See *Hackney LBC v Usher* [1997] ICR 705; *Haddon v Van den Burgh Foods Ltd* [1999] IRLR 672. *See* FAIR DISMISSAL; INDUSTRIAL ACTION, PROTECTED.

dismissal, unfair, and territorial limits. In *Serco Land Ltd v Lawson* [2004] EWCA Civ 12, the CA held that the right not to be dismissed unfairly applies only to the case of employment in Great Britain. See Employment Rights Act 1996, s 94(1).

disorder, alcohol-related. C.J.P.A. 2001, s 12, empowers police to require a person not to consume in a designated public place intoxicating liquor or to surrender such liquor or a container in his possession. A local authority may, for this purpose, identify any public place in their area if satisfied that nuisance to the public, or disorder, has been associated with the consumption of intoxicating liquor in that place: s 18. Licensed premises or registered clubs are not designated public places: s 14. For closure orders relating to certain licensed premises due to disorder, see s 17. For enforcement of regulations related to under-age drinking, see s 31.

disorderly behaviour. Conduct of an unruly nature involving disturbance and disruption of the public peace. See *Chambers and Edwards v DPP* [1995] Crim LR 896 (the words 'disorderly behaviour' should be given their ordinary meaning; an element of violence, present or threatened, is not required).

disorderly house. A brothel (q.v.). See S.O.A. 1956, ss 33–36; *Moores v DPP* [1991] 3 WLR 549 (persistent disorderly use has to be shown).

disorder, violent. Where three or more persons who are present together use or threaten unlawful violence and the conduct of them (taken together) is such as will cause a person of reasonable firmness present at the scene to fear for his personal safety, each of the persons using or threatening personal violence is guilty of violent disorder: P.O.A. 1986, s 2(1). See *A-G's Reference (Nos. 25, 27, 29 of 1995)* [1996] 2 Cr App R (S) 390; *R v Green* [1997] 2 Cr App R (S) 191.

disparagement of goods. *See* SLANDER OF TITLE.

display. In the context of the phrase 'the display or sale of goods', 'display' means putting an object on show or exhibiting it with the intention of attracting persons' attention to it: *Mcahan v Windsor RBC* (2002) *The Times*, 30 July.

disposal of premises. Includes a letting, assignment or surrender of a tenancy of the premises and the creation by contract of any other right to occupy the premises: Defective Premises Act 1972, s 6(1).

disposal of uncollected goods. The bailee may give the bailor written notice (by delivery to the bailor), by post, by leaving it at his proper address, specifying goods, stating that they are ready for delivery and specifying the amount payable by the bailor in respect of the goods: Torts (Interference with Goods)

Act 1977, Sch 1. If the bailee has given notice and has failed to trace the bailor, he is entitled to sell the goods: s 12(3). See *Jerry Juhan SA v Avon Tyres* [1999] CLC 702. *See* BAILMENT.

disposition. 1. The passing of property, whether by act of parties or act of the law: *Northumberland v A-G* [1905] AC 406; *Re Billson's ST* [1984] Ch 407; L.P.A. 1925, s 15(1)(*c*). Includes 'a conveyance and also a devise [q.v.], bequest or an appointment of property contained in a will': L.P.A. 1925, s 205(1)(*ii*). See *Rye v Rye* [1962] AC 496. 2. Term used in the law of evidence to indicate a person's general tendencies to think or act in a particular way. It may be proved by evidence of character, previous convictions, conduct on other occasions. See *Selvey v DPP* [1970] AC 304; *Boardman v DPP* [1974] 3 All ER 887. *See* EVIDENCE, SIMILAR FACT.

disposition, voluntary. *See* VOLUNTARY DISPOSITION.

dispossess. To oust from land. See H.A. 1985, s 389. *See* OUSTER.

dispute. A conflict of claims or rights. Whenever one party to a contract requests something from the other party under the terms of their contract and that request is not complied with, there is a dispute: *Ellerine Bros Ltd v Klinger* [1982] 2 All ER 737.

dispute, trade. *See* TRADE DISPUTE.

disqualification. Deprivation of a right, power or privilege. See, e.g., Company Directors Disqualification Act 1986; *Re Barings plc* [1998] BCC 583. Thus, where a person is convicted of certain offences, he may be ordered by the court to be disqualified from driving for a period. See Road Traffic Act 1991, ss 19, 25; Road Traffic Offenders Act 1988, ss 36–38, 42; Child Support Act 1991, s 39A, inserted by C.S.P.S.S.A. 2000, s 16.

disrepair. In *Niazi Services v Van der Loo* [2004] EWCA Civ 53, the CA held that where a tenant had alleged that a water supply to his flat was defective because of reductions in that supply, the landlord was not liable since the water installation which caused the reduction was situated in a part of the building over which the landlord exerted no control and in which he had no interest.

dissentiente. Generally abbreviated to *diss.* Delivering a dissenting judgment.

dissolution. Breaking up; bringing to an end. 1. Dissolution of Parliament means bringing the life of an existing Parliament to an end, e.g., proroguing Parliament, which is then dissolved by proclamation of the Queen. 2. Dissolution of a marriage, e.g., by divorce decree or order (see F.L.A. 1996, s 2, which is now unlikely to be brought into force). 3. Termination of existence of a company by legal process resulting from, e.g., being struck off the register.

disance selling regulations. Regulations implementing Council Directive 97/7, under SI 00/2334, which apply to contracts for goods or services to be supplied to a consumer under a 'distance contract', that is, one made exclusively by means of distance communication, such as fax, phone, internet. Supplier must confirm in writing information already given, and provide information, including provision for cooling-off period, and right to cancel. Contract must be performed within 30 days subject to agreement between parties. Excepted contracts include those relating to financial services, sale of interest in land, auction sales.

distinguishing a case. Where the court has been invited to follow a previous decision, but feels that there are important points of difference between that decision and the case on which it was based and the case it is considering, the case is said to have been 'distinguished'.

distrain. To levy a distress (q.v.).

distress. The seizing of a personal chattel (q.v.) from a debtor or wrongdoer so as to obtain payment for a debt (e.g., up to six years' arrears of rent: L.A. 1980, s 19) or satisfaction for a wrong committed. See Distress for Rent Act 1737 (see *Ballard Ltd v Ashworth Ltd* [2000] Ch 12); Rent Act 1977, s 147; M.C.A. 1980, ss 76–78; *McLeod v Butterwick* [1998] 1 WLR 1603. Chattels may be privileged from distress *absolutely* (fixtures, goods of a third party, etc.) or *conditionally* (e.g., beasts of the plough). *See* IMPOUND.

distress damage feasant. A form of self-help taking the form of the seizure by X of a chattel or animal belonging to Y which is wrongfully on X's land and damaging it. See *Burt* v *Moore* (1973) 5 TR 329. Abolished in relation to animals by Animals Act 1971, which created a general right to detain and sell, after 14 days, trespassing livestock not under control: s 7. See *Arthur* v *Anker* [1996] 2 WLR 602 (attempt to utilise the concept in relation to wheel clamping). *See* DAMAGE FEASANT.

distribution. The division of property of an intestate among the next of kin. See A.E.A. 1925, ss 33, 46, 47; Intestates' Estates Act 1952; Family Provision Act 1966; F.L.R.A. 1969; Inheritance (Provision for Family and Dependants) Act 1975 as amended; *Re Collens* [1986] 1 All ER 611.

distribution of company assets. Distribution of company assets, in cash or otherwise to members out of profits is prohibited except when made by way of issue of fully or partly paid bonus shares, redemption of preference shares from the proceeds of fresh issue, reduction of share capital by reducing or writing off members' liability in respect of unpaid share capital, distribution or winding-up: Cos.A. 1985, s 263. Only accumulated, realised profits are available for distribution, less accumulated, realisable losses. For other restrictions, see ss 263, 264. See *MacPherson* v *ESB Ltd* [1999] 2 BCLC 203.

distribution of company assets on liquidation, order of. The order is generally: secured creditors with fixed charges; liquidation costs; preferential creditors; secured creditors with floating charges; unsecured creditors; debts due to company members as members; repayment of capital to members; division of surplus assets among members. Debts in each class are treated as if on an equal footing, save for any preferential debts: see Ins.A. 1986, s 175.

distributive justice. *See* JUSTICE, COMMUTATIVE, DISTRIBUTIVE AND CORRECTIVE.

district councils. *See* COUNCILS, DISTRICT.

district judges. *See* JUDGES, DISTRICT.

district judges (magistrates' courts). Formerly known as 'stipendiaries'. Fulltime salaried judges, appointed from lawyers of at least seven years' standing by the Lord Chancellor: Justices of the Peace Act 1997, s 10A, substituted by Acc.J.A. 1999, s 78; SI 00/1920. They are justices of the peace for Commission areas (see s 10C) and sit alone, being empowered under s 10D to do any act and to exercise alone any jurisdiction which can be done or exercised by two justices, including any act or jurisdiction expressly required to be done or exercised by justices sitting or acting in petty sessions.

district registries. Registries in England and Wales which function as branch offices of the Supreme Court (q.v.) allowing proceedings to be commenced in many parts of the country. See S.C.A. 1981, s 99.

districts. The six former metropolitan counties in England were divided into 36 metropolitan districts which have been, to a large extent, continued (see L.G.A. 1985, Parts I and II); the 39 nonmetropolitan counties were divided into 296 districts; Wales had 37 districts; Scotland had 53 (based on nine regions).

disturbance. Interference with the existence or exercise of a right by, e.g., 'trespass or nuisance, or in any other substantial manner': *Fitzgerald* v *Forbank* [1897] 2 Ch 96.

divest. To deprive, dispossess. 'The taking away of the possession of a thing': *Termes de la Ley.*

dividend. 1. Amount payable to a bankrupt's creditors after payment of expenses and preferential debts. 2. A part of a company's net profit distributed by means of 'dividend warrants' among shareholders in proportion to their shareholdings. Must, generally, be paid out of profits; see Cos.A. 1985, s 263(1); *Precision Dippings* v *Precision Dippings*

Marketing [1985] 3 WLR 812. See Table A, arts 102–107. *See* PROFITS AVAILABLE FOR DISTRIBUTION.

dividend, interim. *See* INTERIM DIVIDEND.

Divine Right of Kings. 'The State of monarchy is the supremest theory upon earth; for kings are not only God's lieutenants upon earth and sit upon God's throne, but even by God himself they are called gods . . . Kings are justly called gods for that they exercise a manner or resemblance of divine power on earth . . . it is seditious in subjects to dispute what a king may do in the height of his power . . .': James I, in a speech to Parliament, March 1610.

divisible contract. A contract in which the parties intend that their promises are to be independent of each other: *Taylor* v *Webb* [1937] 2 KB 283. An *entire* (or *indivisible*) contract is one in which there is agreement, implicit or explicit, that neither party may demand performance until he is ready to fulfil, or has fulfilled, his promise. See *Inntrepreneur Pub Company Ltd* v *East Crown Ltd* (2000) *The Times*, 5 September. *See* CONTRACT.

Divisional Courts. Term applied collectively to Queen's Bench Divisional Court, Chancery Divisional Court and Family Divisional Court. Queen's Bench Divisional Court hears appeals on points of law by way of case stated from decisions of magistrates or from Crown Court, hears appeals from Tribunals, applications for habeas corpus (q.v.), and exercises supervisory jurisdiction over inferior courts and tribunals, particularly in relation to disputes in administrative law. It consists of two to three judges. Chancery Divisional Court consists of one to two judges and hears appeals from county courts concerning, e.g., land registration and bankruptcy and appeals from Commissioners of Inland Revenue. Family Divisional Court usually consists of two High Court judges and hears appeals from decisions of Crown Court, county court and magistrates in matters of domestic law. Some urgent business may be brought during a vacation before

a single judge: CPR, Sch 1; O 64, r 4. See S.C.A. 1981, s 66.

Divisions of the High Court. Chancery Division, Queen's Bench Division and Family Division (qq.v.). See S.C.A. 1981, s 5(1).

divorce. Dissolution of marriage by the court on the ground of its irretrievable breakdown (q.v.). Proceedings commence with the filing of a petition (after at least one year from the date of marriage) in the prescribed form, which sets out the facts on which the petitioner (i.e., the person seeking a decree of divorce against the respondent) relies as proof of irretrievable breakdown of marriage, and which concludes with a prayer 'that the said marriage may be dissolved'. Proceedings may take place in divorce county courts and Family Hearing Centres: see SI 91/1677. See Mat.C.A. 1973, s 1(1); Ch.A. 1989, Sch 12, para 31; Family Proceedings Rules 1991.

divorce after F.L.A. 1996. Following repeal of Mat.C.A. 1973, ss 1–7, a new divorce procedure was to have been introduced. Parties would attend an information meeting (q.v.) at least three months prior to the initiation of the divorce process by a presentation of a statement of marital breakdown (q.v.), followed by a three-month period during which the content of the information meeting would be digested. One or both parties would then present a statement of marital breakdown, followed by a 14-day break before a nine-month period for reflection and consideration. If all were in order, the court would make a divorce order which would have immediate effect. (On 18 June 1999, the Lord Chancellor announced in a parliamentary answer that the government did not intend to implement F.L.A. 1996, Part II (Divorce and Separation), in 2000.)

divorce, and dissolution of religious marriages. Under Matrimonial Causes Act 1973, s 10A, inserted by Divorce (Religious Marriages) Act 2002, s 1, the court may order that a decree of divorce is not to be made absolute until a declaration has been made by both parties that they have taken all such steps as are required to dissolve the marriage in accordance with any relevant religious usages.

divorce and judicial separation, special procedure for. Procedure whereby, if a petition is based on either adultery or desertion or two years' separation, etc., and it is undefended, the petitioner can apply to put the case in the Special Procedure List. If the registrar agrees, evidence is considered and, if he finds the facts proved, he will announce a day for the pronouncement of the decree in open court. The parties need not attend. Known also as 'postal divorce'.

divorce, bars to. The Divorce Reform Act 1969 abolished most existing bars (e.g., connivance, condonation) to divorce. The defence now available to the respondent is that no irretrievable breakdown of marriage (q.v.) has taken place. A decree nisi may be refused where the respondent would be caused grave financial hardship (see Mat.C.A. 1973, s 1(2)(e)) or other hardship. Decree absolute will not be made until the court has considered the position of the children of the family: Mat.C.A. 1973, s 41. *See* QUEEN'S PROCTOR.

divorce by mutual consent. Term applied to a decree of divorce after two years of separation immediately preceding the presentation of the petition, where the respondent consents to the grant of a decree: Mat.C.A. 1973, s 1(2)(d).

divorce, ground for. The sole ground, after 1970, is the irretrievable breakdown of marriage (q.v.): Mat.C.A. 1973, s 1(1).

divorce, petition for. Statement by the petitioner setting out the facts relating to the breakdown of marriage (q.v.) and praying for relief by way of dissolution of the marriage. No petition for divorce can be presented to the court within one year from the date of marriage. See Mat.C.A. 1973, s 3; Family Proceedings Rules 1991, r 2, App 2 (contents of petition). *See* DIVORCE AND JUDICIAL SEPARATION, SPECIAL PROCEDURE FOR.

divorce procedure, supporting documents. Together with the petition there should be filed the marriage certificate, reconciliation certificate, any previous relevant court orders and a statement of arrangements concerning the care of children of the family and to whom Mat.C.A. 1973, s 41, applies.

DNA evidence, speculation relating to. CA held in *R* v *SM* [2004] EWCA Crim 1928, that a judge ought not to raise purely speculative and theoretical considerations in matters involving DNA evidence.

DNA, negative evidence. In *R* v *Mitchell* (2004) *The Times*, 8 July, the CA held that the existence of evidence of a particular DNA profile obtained from the crime scene, but which showed no match with that of defendant, was powerful evidence which seemed to support the defendant's case and should be considered by a jury in the process of coming to a decision.

DNA profiling. Known also as 'genetic fingerprinting'. The examination of bodily samples in order to reveal and assess the composition of the human genetic coding material (based on the pattern of deoxyribonucleic acid content) allowing deductions as to whether or not two or more samples have come from the same person, or whether there is a parent–child relationship between persons from whom samples have been taken. See P.&C.E.A. 1984, s 64, amended by C.J.P.O.A. 1994, s 57 (destruction or retention of samples); *R* v *Adams (No. 2)* [1998] 1 Cr App R 377; Criminal Evidence (Amendment) Act 1997, amending P.&C.E.A. 1984, s 63; *R* v *B* (2000) *The Times*, 15 December (unlawfully retained DNA sample may be usable in court). A DNA database is compiled and administered by the Forensic Science Service.

DNA samples and fingerprints. In *R (On Application of S)* v *Chief Constable of S Yorks* [2004] 1 WLR 2196, the HL held that a wide, blanket policy of retention and use by the police of DNA samples and fingerprints following the clearing of a suspect is compatible with Human Rights Act 1998, Sch 1, Part 1, arts 8, 14.

DNA samples, retention by police. The rights of a person to privacy and not to be discriminated against, arising from European Convention, arts 8, 14, are not breached where the fingerprints and DNA samples of such a person who has been the subject of a criminal investigation, but is not subsequently convicted, are retained by the police: *R (S) v Chief Constable of S Yorks Police* [2002] EWCA Civ 1275.

dock brief. Procedure whereby a prisoner, on trial on indictment, could directly instruct from the dock and for a nominal fee any barrister sitting robed in the court. Now largely obsolete.

dock identification. Identification of witness for the first time in court. See *R v Fergus* [1992] Crim LR 363.

dock statements. Unsworn statements (q.v.) from the dock in criminal trials. See *R v Farnham Justices ex p Gibson* [1991] RTR 309 (defendant required to give evidence from dock).

doctor, registration of. In *Qureshi v GMC* (2003) *The Times*, 3 September, the PC held that where a doctor had been ordered to collaborate in the reassessment of his professional standards, the assessment need not be confined specifically to the type of work related to that from which a complaint as to his abilities had arisen.

document. Anything in which information of any description is recorded: CPR, r 31.4. 'Filing' a document means delivering it, by post or otherwise, to the court office: r 2.3. For discussion of document as 'property', see *Huddleston v Control Risks Ltd* [1987] 1 WLR 701.

document, ancient. *See* ANCIENT DOCUMENT.

document, copy of. Anything onto which information recorded in the document has been copied, by whatever means and whether directly or indirectly: CPR, r 31.4. 'A copy of an official document, supplied and marked as such by the office which issued the original is known as an "official copy"': CPR Glossary.

documentary evidence. Documents produced with the intention that they be inspected by judge and jury. See C.J.A. 1988, Part II. *See* EVIDENCE.

document, literalistic approach to. In *Sirius International Co* (2004) *The Times*, 1 December, the HL held that in accordance with a general trend, contractual documents should be interpreted in a fashion which was commercially realistic rather than literalistic.

document possession by judge. In *Lloyds Bank plc v Cassidy* (2005) *The Times*, 11 January, the CA stressed the significance of both sides having in their possession the same documents as those preserved by the judge, so that representations may be made about them.

document, private, proof of execution of. Procedure involving: proof of handwriting; or proof of attestation (q.v.); or a presumption that a document produced from proper custody, which is not less than 20 years old, is validly executed.

document, privileged. It was held in *Schering Corporation v Cipia Ltd* (2004) *The Times*, 2 December, that in considering a document headed 'without prejudice', as to whether it might be treated as such, it was necessary to determine whether it was genuinely intended to be treated as such.

document, public. *See* PUBLIC DOCUMENT.

documents, bundles of, for hearings or trial. Generally, claimant must file a trial bundle (i.e., set of documents) not more than seven days and not less than three days, before start of trial. It should contain a copy of: claim form and all statements of case, case chronology and summary, requests for further information and responses, witness statements, witness summaries, notices of intention to rely on hearsay evidence, medical reports, expert's reports, order for directions concerning conduct of trial and other necessary documents: PD 39, paras 3.1, 3.2.

documents, disclosure of. In *R (On Application of Green) v Police Complaints Authority* [2004] 1 WLR 725, the HL held that there is no general duty on the Police Complaints Authority, to disclose documents which relate to investigation of complaints into the conduct of police.

documents, dishonest suppression of. *See* SUPPRESSION OF DOCUMENTS, DISHONEST.

document, secondary evidence of. Exceptions to the general rule that the original of a document must be put in evidence include the following cases: where the original is lost or destroyed; where the original is in possession of a third party who justifiably declines to produce it; where production of the original is highly inconvenient; where the document is a public document (q.v.); where (in civil proceedings) a party has failed to comply with a notice to produce, so that the party serving notice can put a copy of the document in evidence. *See* EVIDENCE, SECONDARY.

documents of title to goods. 'Any bill of lading, dock warrant, warehousekeeper's certificate, any warrant or order for the delivery of goods, and any other document used in the ordinary course of business as proof of the possession or control of goods, or authorising or purporting to authorise, either by endorsement or by delivery, the possessor of the documents to transfer or receive goods thereby represented': Factors Act 1889, s 1(4).

documents, interpretation of. The desirability of consistency and certainty in considering the prima facie meaning of a common expression in a document necessitates care in reliance on authorities in relation to construction of expressions in documents: *Crest Nicholson Ltd* v *McAllister* (2002) *The Times*, 10 December.

documents, power to obtain. In *Re Pantmaenog Timber Ltd* (2003) *The Times*, 7 August, the HL held that the Official Receiver was empowered to ask for documents from persons who had information concerning directors of a company in liquidation where the purpose was to obtain evidence which could be used against a former director involved in disqualification proceedings.

documents, trust. *See* TRUST DOCUMENTS.

documents, verified, false statements in. Proceedings for contempt of court may be brought against a person if he makes, or causes to be made, a false statement in a document verified by a statement of truth (q.v.) without an honest belief in its truth: CPR, r 32.14.

Doe, John. Name of the fictitious plaintiff formerly used in the action of ejectment (q.v.). See comments of Donaldson LJ in *Barrett* v *French* [1981] 1 WLR 848.

dogs, dangerous. 'Dangerous' refers not only to danger to persons, but also, e.g., to cattle: see Dogs Act 1906, s 1(4); *Briscoe* v *Shattock* [1999] 1 WLR 432; *R* v *Hutton* [1999] EHLR 281. Magistrates may order a dangerous dog to be kept under control or destroyed: Dogs Act 1871, s 2, as amended by Dogs Act 1989. Dangerous Dogs Act 1991 restricts the owning of designated breeds bred for fighting: s 1. If a dog is dangerously out of control in a public place, the owner or person in charge of the dog is guilty of an offence if the dog injures any person: s 3. For seizure of stray dogs, see En.P.A. 1990, s 149. See also Animals Act 1971; Dangerous Dogs (Amendment) Act 1997.

dogs injuring livestock. *See* LIVESTOCK.

dogs, killing or injuring of. *See* LIVESTOCK, PROTECTION OF.

doli capax. Capable of fraud or deceit. Phrase used to signify that a young person is old enough, or sufficiently intelligent, to be responsible in law for the wrongful acts of which he is accused. The rebuttable presumption of the criminal law that a child aged between 10 and 13 inclusive was incapable of committing an offence (*doli incapax*) was abolished by C.D.A. 1998, s 34 (but this does not apply in relation to anything done before the commencement of the section: Sch 9).

domain. 1. Concept involving absolute right to and authority over property. 2. Territory over which authority is exercised.

domain, eminent. *See* EMINENT DOMAIN.

domestic agreements. Agreements made within the course of family life. They are considered as not normally made in contemplation of the creation of a legal relationship. See, e.g., *Balfour* v *Balfour* [1919] 2 KB 571 ('In respect of these promises each house is a domain into which the King's writ does not seek to run': *per* Aitken LJ); *Pettitt* v *Pettitt* [1970] AC 777.

domestic animal. *See* ANIMAL.

domestic arbitration agreement. *See* ARBITRATION AGREEMENT, DOMESTIC.

domestic property. Property is domestic if: used wholly for living accommodation; is a yard, garden outhouse; is a private garage used wholly or mainly for accommodation of a private motor vehicle; is private storage premises used wholly or partly for storage of articles of domestic use: Local Government Finance Act 1988, s 66(1).

domestic tribunals. Disciplinary committees exercising judicial or quasi-judicial functions, e.g., disciplinary committee of The Law Society. The High Court exercises a supervisory jurisdiction over these tribunals (q.v.).

domestic violence. 'Any violence between current or former partners in an intimate relationship, wherever and whenever the violence occurs. Such violence might include physical, sexual, emotional or financial abuse': definition adopted by HM Inspectorate of Constabulary, in 1999. See F.L.A. 1996, Part IV (in operation since October 1997); Home Office Order 60/1990. Domestic Violence, Crime and Victims Act received Royal Assent in November 2004. It created the offence of causing or allowing the death of a child or vulnerable adult. An Independent Commission for Victims was established. *See* BATTERED WIFE; INJUNCTIONS RELATING TO DOMESTIC VIOLENCE; MOLESTATION.

domicile. Generally, the country where a person has his permanent home: *Whicker* v *Hume* (1858) 7 HL Cas 124. Under C.J.J.A. 1982, s 41(1), 'an individual is domiciled in the UK if and only if he is resident in the UK and the nature and circumstances of his residence indicate that he has a substantial connection with the UK'. A person's *domicile of origin* is that

which he receives at birth (usually the domicile of his father); this is preserved until he acquires another. See *Canada Trust* v *Stolzenberg (No. 2)* (2000) 150 NLJ 1532 (date for determining domicile). A *domicile of choice* is acquired by a person of full age establishing his residence in a chosen country, intending to remain there permanently (*animus manendi*). A *domicile of dependence* is that of a child under 16, which changes with that of its parents. No person can be without a domicile or have more than one at the same time.

dominant position. Phrase used in EU decisions to refer to 'a position of economic strength enjoyed by an undertaking which enables it to prevent effective competition being maintained on the relevant market by giving it the power to behave to an appreciable extent independently of its competitors, customers and ultimately of its consumers': *United Brands* v *Commission* (Case 27/76); *Coca Cola Co* v *EC Commission* [2000] All ER (EC) 460; see Treaty of Rome, art 86 (now art 82 EC). Under Competition Act 1998, s 18, abuse of a dominant position is prohibited if it may affect trade within the UK; such conduct is exemplified by the imposition of unfair purchase or selling prices. (For excluded cases, e.g., mergers and concentrations, see s 19.)

dominant tenement. Land to which there is attached the benefit of a right. Example: X owns Blackacre and grants to Y, his neighbour, owner of Whiteacre, a right to use a footpath over Blackacre. Whiteacre is the *dominant tenement*; Blackacre is the *servient tenement*.

Dominions. Term formerly applied to the British Commonwealth countries of, e.g., Australia, Canada and New Zealand. These countries, former dependencies of the UK, had, generally, complete self-government, usually modelled on the UK. See Statute of Westminster 1931, s 1; *Manuel* v *A-G* [1983] Ch 77.

dominium. Ownership. (In its original sense, single and indivisible, absolute and exclusive.)

domitae naturae. *See* ANIMALS, CLASSI-FICATION OF.

donatio mortis causa. A gift of property by a donor in anticipation of his death. (Plural: *donationes mortis causa.*) To be effective: the property must be capable of passing by *donatio*; death in the near future must be contemplated by donor; *donatio* must have been made conditional on donor's death; delivery is essential. See *Woodard* v *Woodard* [1995] 3 All ER 980; *Sen* v *Headley* [1991] 2 All ER 636 (land may pass in this way).

donees, appointment of. A donee of a lasting power of attorney must be (a) an individual who has reached 18, or (b) if the power relates only to P's property and affairs, either such an individual or a trust corporation. An individual who is bankrupt may not be appointed as donee of a lasting power of attorney in relation to P's property and affairs: Mental Capacity Act 2005 s 10(1) & (2).

dormant company. A company is treated as dormant for any period during which it does not enter into any significant accounting transaction, i.e., which it would be obliged by law to enter in its accounting records, other than receipt of issue price for subscribers' shares. See Cos.A. 1985, s 252(5); Cos.A. 1989, s 14.

dormant partner. A 'sleeping partner', i.e., a member of a partnership (q.v.) who does not play an active part in the running of the business.

dotards. Dead or decayed trees, that cannot be used as timber. A tenant for life (q.v.) may, in general, cut dotards and all the trees which are not timber; *Re Harker's WT* [1938] Ch 323.

double effect, concept of. Doctrine which seeks to distinguish primary from secondary consequences of some action, e.g., a course of medical treatment based upon the use of a drug so as to minimise pain, notwithstanding that it hastens death. See *R* v *Bodkin Adams* [1957] Crim LR 365.

double insurance. *See* INSURANCE, DOUBLE.

double jeopardy. Possibility of repeated prosecution for the same offence. See

Secretary of State for Trade v *Baker* (1998) *The Times*, 6 July. See *Double Jeopardy* (Law Commission Consultation Paper 1999, No. 15); European Convention on Human Rights 1950, Seventh Protocol, art 4; *A-G's Reference (No. 6 of 2000)* (2000) *The Times*, 24 May. In *R* v *Commissioner of Police for the Metropolis* (2003) *The Times*, 30 January, the CA held that the double-jeopardy rule had no application where a public disciplinary board intended to hear corruption allegations against a police officer, even though he had been discharged by an examining justice at a committal hearing, under Magistrates' Courts Act 1980, s 6, in relation to an allegation of conspiracy to pervert the course of justice. See AUTREFOIS ACQUIT.

double portions, rule against. A child is generally prohibited from taking both a sum paid to him as a portion and a legacy which has been bequeathed to him as a portion. The general principle is: 'Equity leans against double portions'. See *Fowkes* v *Pascoe* (1875) 10 Ch App 343. *See* PORTION.

double probate. A grant of probate made to an executor (q.v.) to whom power has been reserved to prove at a later date, or on the happening of a specified event, and who has proved. Example: an executor who was an infant (q.v.) and who has later attained his majority. See *Re Griffin* (1910) 54 SJ 378. *See* GRANT; PROBATE.

double renvoi. *See* RENVOI.

double value, action for. Action brought under Landlord and Tenant Act 1730 by landlord for double the yearly value of premises where a tenant holds over wilfully, and not by mistake, or under a *bona fide* claim of right, and not by mistake, after notice has been given before the expiry of possession. See *French* v *Elliott* [1960] 1 WLR 40. An action for double rent may be brought under Distress for Rent Act 1737, s 18, against a tenant under a periodic tenancy who gives notice to quit and then fails to give up possession: see *Ballard Ltd* v *Ashworth Holdings Ltd* [1999] 3 WLR 57.

doubt, reasonable. *See* REASONABLE DOUBT.

downloading. A term used in computer operations to signify the transfer of information from one storage device to another. See *R* v *City of London Magistrates' Court ex p Green* [1997] 3 All ER 451. *See* COMPUTER.

downloading from internet. Voluntarily downloading an indecent internet image to a computer monitor constitutes an act of making a photograph or pseudo photograph, in relation to Protection of Children Act 1978, s 1(1)(a): *R* v *Smith* (2002) *The Times*, 23 April.

DPP. Director of Public Prosecutions (q.v.).

draft. 1. An order for the payment of a sum of money. (A 'banker's draft' is a draft drawn by a bank upon itself, e.g., by a branch or head office or on another branch. It is not a cheque or bill.) See, e.g., *Bank of Montreal* v *Dominion Gresham Guarantee Co* [1930] AC 659; *Citibank NA* v *Brown Shipley & Co* [1991] 2 All ER 690. 2. An outline copy of an agreement or treaty.

driver. One who is in charge of a vehicle and, if a separate person acts as a steersman, the term includes that person as well as any other person in charge of the vehicle or engaged in the driving of it. Driving means 'imparting motion to a vehicle and endeavouring to control it': *Rowan* v *Chief Constable of Merseyside* (1985) *The Times*, 10 December; *James* v *DPP* [1997] 5 CL 168. For driving elsewhere than on roads, see Road Traffic Act 1988, s 34, amended by C.R.W.A. 2000, Sch 7, para 5.

driving a vehicle. Whether a cessation of movement has been for so long and in such circumstances that it could not reasonably be said that the occupant of the driving seat was 'driving' within the meaning of Road Traffic Act 1988, is a question of fact and degree: *Planton* v *DPP* (2001) *The Times*, 17 August.

driving, careless and inconsiderate. It is a summary offence for a person to drive a mechanically propelled vehicle on a road or other public place without due care and attention, or without reasonable consideration for other persons using the road or place: Road Traffic Act 1991, s 2 (amending Road Traffic Act 1988, s 3).

driving, careless, influence of drink or drugs, causing death by. If a person causes the death of another by careless and inconsiderate driving (q.v.) and he is, at the time of driving unfit to drive through drink or drugs or the proportion of alcohol in his breath, blood, urine, exceeds the prescribed limits, or he fails, within 18 hours of being required to produce a specimen, to do so, he is guilty of an offence: Road Traffic Act 1988, s 3A, inserted by Road Traffic Act 1991, s 3. See *R* v *Roche* [1999] 2 Cr App R (S) 105. *See* BREATH TEST; PRESCRIBED LIMITS OF ALCOHOL; TOTTING UP.

driving, dangerous. A person is to be regarded as driving dangerously if the way he drives falls far below what would be expected of a competent and careful driver and it would be obvious to a competent and careful driver that driving in that way would be dangerous. 'Dangerous' refers to the danger of injury to a person or of serious damage to property. See Road Traffic Act 1988, s 2A, substituted by Road Traffic Act 1991, s 1. It is an offence: to drive a mechanically propelled vehicle dangerously on a road or other public place (Road Traffic Act 1988, s 2, as substituted by Road Traffic Act 1991, s 1); to cause death by dangerous driving (1988 Act, s 1, substituted by 1991 Act, s 1). See *R* v *Cusick* [2000] 1 Cr App R (S) 444. *A-G's Reference (No. 4 of 2000)* (2001) *The Times*, 27 March.

driving disqualification. Under the Crime (International Co-operation) Act 2003, ss 54, 55, there is a duty on the appropriate Minister to give the central authority of the State in which an offender is normally resident, notice of the driving disqualification of a non-UK resident.

driving licence. Authority to drive a motor vehicle. An applicant for a licence must be physically fit and pass a driving test (unless he already possesses a licence). It is an offence to drive on a road without holding a licence. See, e.g., Road Traffic Act 1988, Part III. For revocation of licence, see Road Traffic (New Drivers) Act 1995, s 3. For driving disqualification where vehicle is used for purposes of crime, in the case of a conviction for two years or more, see P.C.C.(S).A. 2000, s 147. See also C.J.C.S.A. 2000, s 71 (access to driver licensing records). Note that the presence of a person's name on the Sex Offenders Register (see Sex Offenders Act 1997) did not act as an automatic disqualification of that person from holding a driving licence (see Road Traffic Act 1988, ss 112, 121): *Secretary of State for Transport* v *Snowdon* [2002] EWHC 2394.

driving test order. An order disqualifying an offender from driving until he passes a test showing his competence to drive. See Road Traffic (New Drivers) Act 1995, s 4 (re-testing).

driving, wheel spinning as. Where a person is sitting in a car's driving seat and the car wheels are spinning although the car is not moving, this can be held to be 'driving' for purposes of the offence of driving with excess of alcohol (see Road Traffic Act 1988, s 5(1)(a)): *DPP* v *Alderton* (2003) *The Times*, 27 November.

driving with alcohol concentration above prescribed limit. If a person drives or attempts to drive a motor vehicle on a road or other public place or is in charge of a motor vehicle on a road or other public place after consuming so much alcohol that the proportion of it in his breath, blood or urine exceeds the prescribed limit (q.v.), he is guilty of an offence: Road Traffic Act 1988, s 5. See *DPP* v *Johnson* [1995] RTR 9 ('consumption' of alcohol can include other means of ingestion, e.g., injection). *See* BREATH TEST.

drug abstinence order. New community order, under P.C.C.(S.)A. 2000, s 58A, inserted by C.J.C.S.A. 2000, s 47, ordering offender who is 18 or over to abstain from misusing specified class A

drugs, and to provide, when ordered to do so, a sample relating to this matter. For pre-sentence drug testing see P.C.C.(S.)A. 2000, s 36A, inserted by C.J.C.S.A. 2000, s 48.

drug addict. 'A person shall be regarded as being addicted to a drug if, and only if, he has as a result of repeated administration become so dependent upon the drug that he has an overpowering desire for the administration of it to be continued': SI 73/799, as amended by SI 89/1909, and Misuse of Drugs (Supply to Addicts) Regulations 1997 (SI 97/1001). See also Misuse of Drugs Act 1971, s 10(2)(*i*); *R* v *Crampton* (1991) 92 Cr App R 369.

drugs, attempted destruction of, defence. The CA held that defence under Misuse of Drugs Act 1971, s 5(4)(a) (possessor, as soon as possible after taking possession took all such steps as were reasonably open to him to destroy drugs), did not apply to defendant who, after finding himself innocently in possession of cannabis, wrapped it in foil and buried it, intending that natural forces would destroy the drug. Statutory defence envisaged that act of destruction should be that of defendant: *R* v *Murphy* (2002) *The Times*, 8 July.

drugs, controlled. Drugs, classified by the Misuse of Drugs Act 1971 as: Class A (opium, etc.); Class B (amphetamine, etc.); Class C (pemoline, etc.). Classification (which is intended to indicate the degree of harm attributable to the drugs when abused) affects the maximum penalties for the offence of having possession of a controlled drug. It is an offence for one who is an occupier of premises or concerned in their management to knowingly permit the smoking of opium or cannabis (q.v.) on those premises: s 8: see *R* v *Bett* [1999] 1 All ER 600; *R* v *Brock* (2000) *The Times*, 28 December. For meaning of 'occupier', see *Read* v *DPP* [1997] 10 CL 36. For restriction of production, see s 4(2); 'production' refers to manufacture, cultivation, or any other method: s 37(1); *R* v *Russell* [1992] Crim LR 362 (conversion of drug is 'production'). For 'preparation' containing a drug, see Sch 2, Part 1, para 1. See Controlled Drugs (Penalties) Act 1985; Public Entertainment Licences (Drugs Misuse) Act 1997; *A-G's Reference (No. 16 of 1992)* [1992] Crim LR 456; C.J. (International Co-operation) (Am.) A. 1998, s 1; *R v Leeson* [2000] 1 Cr App R 233. *See* DRUG TRAFFICKING; POSSESSION, UNLAWFUL, OF DRUGS.

drugs, supply of. It is an offence under Misuse of Drugs Act 1971, s 4(1), 'to supply or offer to supply a controlled drug to anyone'. It is not a necessary element in the concept of 'supply' that the provision should be made out of the personal resources of the person who does the supplying: see *R v Maginnis* [1987] AC 303; *R v Morris* (2000) *The Times*, 4 August (purity testing of drugs). *See* POSSESSION, UNLAWFUL, OF DRUGS.

drugs, testing of persons in police detention. Under P.&C.E.A. 1984, s 63B, inserted by C.J.C.S.A. 2000, s 57, a sample of urine or other non-intimate sample may be taken from a person aged 18 or over in police detention so as to ascertain whether he has a specified Class A drug in his body. The person concerned must have been charged with a trigger offence (i.e., an offence under Misuse of Drugs Act 1971, ss 4, 5(2), (3)).

drug trafficking. Producing, supplying, transporting, storing, importing or exporting a controlled drug in contravention of Misuse of Drugs Act 1971 or some other law: Drug Trafficking Act 1994, s 1. A confiscation order, based on the Crown Court's assessment of the value of a defendant's proceeds of drug trafficking, can be imposed: s 2. See C.J. (Terrorism and Conspiracy) A. 1998, s 1. It is an offence to assist another to retain the benefits of drug trafficking: s 50. The 'proceeds' of drug trafficking are the gross receipts and not the trafficker's profits: *R v Banks* [1997] 2 Cr App R (S) 110; *R v Luton Justices ex p Abecasis* (1999) 163 JP 828. For minimum sentence of seven years for third Class A drug trafficking offence, see P.C.C.(S.)A. 2000, s 110. In *R v Meltcalfe* (2005) *The Times*, 12 January, the CA held that

where it appeared that no more than one tablet in a million consisted of a controlled drug, it was highly unlikely that the proceeds of sale of the tablets would be involved in the benefits of drug trafficking.

drug trafficking offenders, travel restriction orders. Under C.S.P.A. 2002, s 35, that a trafficker sentenced to four years or more could be subjected to an order prohibiting him from leaving the UK at any time in the period which begins with his release from custody, and continues after that time for a period of not less than two years as may be specified in the order. Delivery up to the court of a UK passport may be ordered.

drug treatment and testing order. Community sentence (q.v.), available where a person aged 16 or over is convicted of an offence and it is shown that he is dependent on or has a propensity to misuse drugs, and that his dependency or propensity may be susceptible to treatment: P.C.C.(S.)A. 2000, s 52. For testing and treatment requirements, see s 53. For breach and revocation of order, see s 56; Sch 3. In AG's Reference (No. 64 of 2003) [2003] EWCA Crim 3514, the CA held that there are guidelines to be considered before imposing a drug treatment and testing order; these include: consideration of whether there was a realistic possibility of the order reducing addiction; whether defendant has made a determined effort to free himself from drugs; whether the charge involves serious violence (in which case an order may not be appropriate).

drunkenness. *See* INTOXICATION.

dry rent. Known also as rent seck. A rent not supported by a right of distress (q.v.). Ceased to exist after Landlord and Tenant Act 1730.

dubitante. Doubting. A term found in the law reports, indicating that a judge is doubting the correctness of some proposition relating to the decision he has to take.

Dublin Convention. Convention determining the state with responsibility for examining applications for asylum lodged in one of the member states of the European Communities, signed in Dublin on 15 June 1990. It is intended to prevent asylum seekers from making multiple applications. See Immigration and Asylum Act 1990, ss 11, 12.

due. Owed, e.g., as a debt. A debt is due when it is payable.

due care. Adequate caution in all the circumstances obtaining at a given time. See *Milkins* v *Roberts* [1949] SASR 251. For the statutory defence of 'due diligence' (i.e., that the accused 'took all reasonable steps and exercised all due diligence to avoid committing the offence'), see, e.g., C.P.A. 1987, s 39; *Drummond-Rees* v *Dorset CC* (1998) 162 JP 651.

due course, payment in. *See* PAYMENT IN DUE COURSE.

due process of law. The regular and orderly course of the law through the courts.

dum bene se gesserit. So long as he shall conduct himself well. Phrase used in relation to offices, the tenure of which depends on the holder's conducting himself well, as in the case of a judge. *See DURANTE BENE PLACITO NOSTRO.*

duplicated offences. Where an act or omission constitutes an offence under two or more Acts, or both under an Act and at common law, the offender shall, unless the contrary intention appears, be liable to prosecution and punishment under either or any of those Acts or at common law, but shall not be liable to be punished more than once for the same offence: I.A. 1978, s 18. See Petroleum Act 1998, s 28(7).

duplicity. 1. Deception, fraud. 2. The fault of uniting distinct, unrelated crimes in one indictment. See, e.g., *Nelder* v *DPP* (1998) *The Times*, 11 June; *DPP* v *Dunn* (2000) *The Times*, 1 November. *See* COUNTS, SEPARATE.

durante absentia. During absence. Administration (q.v.) is granted *durante absentia* when an executor is out of the realm.

durante bene placito nostro. During our (i.e., the Crown's) good pleasure. Phrase

used to describe the tenure of offices of judges during, e.g., the reigns of James I and Charles I. Independence of judges was assured by Act of Settlement 1700.

duress. 1. Restraint by force, e.g., imprisonment. 2. Actual violence or threats of imminent, although not necessarily immediate, violence to the person. Known also as *duress per minas* (by threats). A contract obtained by duress is voidable. 'Duress, whatever form it takes, is a coercion of will so as to vitiate consent': *per* Lord Scarman in *Pao On* v *Lau Yiu Long* [1980] AC 614. 3. Duress may be made the basis of a defence in some criminal proceedings; but see, however, *R* v *Sharp* [1987] QB 853. It is not available on a charge of murder (*R* v *Howe* [1987] AC 417), or attempted murder (*R* v *Gotts* [1992] 2 WLR 284). Voluntary duress is no defence (*R* v *Heath* (1999) *The Times*, 15 October). For 'duress of circumstances', see *R* v *Pommell* [1995] 2 Cr App R 607; *R* v *Backshall* [1998] 1 WLR 1506 (defence available to charge of driving without due care and attention); *R* v *Abdul-Hussain* (1999) *The Times*, 26 January (legislation relating to defence of duress urgently needed); *R* v *Baker* [1999] 2 Cr App R 335 (the jury should be given guidance by the judge concerning limitations of the defence of duress); *R* v *Martin* [2000] Cr App R 42 (mistake in perception of duress). For duress vitiating a marriage, see *Szechter* v *Szechter* [1971] P 286. In *R* v *Safi* [2003] All ER (D) 81, the CA held that the jury is to be directed on the basis of terms emerging from authority. It is incorrect to decide there must be a threat in fact, rather than circumstances which defendant reasonably believed to constitute a threat, before a defence of this type can be put forward. Further, if the law should be changed, this is a matter for Parliamentary intervention and not for the courts. *See* NECESSITY; UNDUE INFLUENCE.

duress, economic. Recovery of money paid under duress (i.e., illegitimate pressure resulting in compulsion), other than to the person, is not limited to duress to goods; it can include economic duress where that is constituted by a threat to break a contract, even though there is good consideration for that further contract: *North Ocean Shipping Co* v *Hyundai Construction Co* [1978] 3 All ER 1170; *The Universe Sentinel* [1983] AC 366. ('The victim's silence will not assist the bully, if the lack of any practicable choice but to submit is proved': *per* Lord Scarman); *Dimskal Shipping Co* v *ITWF* [1991] 4 All ER 871.

duress of goods. Where X is in a strong bargaining position by being in possession of Y's goods by virtue of a legal right (e.g., by way of pawn), and Y is in a weak position because he needs the goods urgently, so that X demands from Y more than is justly due and Y pays. 'Such a transaction is voidable. [Y] can recover the excess': *per* Lord Denning MR in *Lloyds Bank* v *Bundy* [1975] QB 326.

during Her Majesty's pleasure. Following a verdict of 'not guilty by reason of insanity' the offender may be ordered by the court to be detained indefinitely in a specified hospital during Her Majesty's pleasure. See Criminal Procedure (Insanity) Act 1964, s 1; M.H.A. 1983, s 46. For detention at Her Majesty's pleasure of persons under 18 who commit murder, see P.C.C.(S.)A. 2000, s 90. See *R* v *Home Secretary ex p Venables and Thompson* [1997] 3 WLR 23. See also Criminal Procedure (Insanity and Unfitness to Plead) Act 1991; Criminal Cases Review (Insanity) Act 1999.

Dutch auction. An auction (q.v.) at which property is offered at a relatively high price, then at a price which is gradually lowered, until an offer is made which is accepted. See Mock Auctions Act 1961, s 3.

duties, absolute. *See* ABSOLUTE DUTIES.

duty. 1. An act that is due by legal or moral obligation. 'A man is subject to a duty when the law commands or forbids him to do an act . . . A duty is to act or not to act so as to produce certain consequences': Terry. 2. The correlative of a right. 3. Payment levied on, e.g., imports and exports.

duty of care. 'You must take reasonable care to avoid acts or omissions which you can reasonably foresee would be likely to injure your neighbour. Who, then, in law is my neighbour? The answer seems to be – persons who are so closely and directly affected by my act that I ought reasonably to have them in contemplation as being affected when I am directing my mind to the acts or omissions which are called in question': *per* Lord Atkin in *Donoghue* v *Stevenson* [1932] AC 562. See *Murphy* v *Brentwood DC* [1990] 2 All ER 908 (overriding *Anns* v *Merton LBC* [1978] AC 728) – a builder is not liable in negligence (q.v.) for pure economic loss to the occupier caused by the defective nature of the building works: *Caparo Industries* v *Dickman* [1990] 2 AC 605 (auditors owed no duty of care to potential investors. *Per* Lord Bridges: 'I think that the law has now moved in the direction of attaching greater significance to the more traditional categorisation of distinct and recognisable situations as guides to the existence, scope and the limits of the varied duties of care which the law imposes'); *Gower* v *Bromley LBC* (1999) *The Times*, 28 October (circumstances in which a school could owe a pupil a duty of care to educate him according to his needs); *Kent* v *Griffiths (No. 2)* (2000) *The Times*, 10 February (ambulance service owes a duty of care); *Lewis* v *Six Continents plc* [2005] *The Times*, 20 January, a hotel owner did not owe a duty of care to restrict the opening of a bedroom window. It was not reasonably foreseeable that an adult leaning out of a window would fall out. *See* CARE, COMMON DUTY; OCCUPIERS' LIABILITY, PRINCIPLE OF; OCCUPIER'S LIABILITY TO NON-VISITORS.

duty of care, bank. *See* BANK, DUTY OF CARE.

duty of care, directors'. *See* DIRECTORS' DUTY OF CARE.

duty of care to employees' wives. There is no duty on employers to take all reasonable care not to expose the wives of employees to a risk of injuring their health as a result of their being exposed to asbestos dust brought home regularly in the clothes of employees.

duty solicitor. A solicitor who, in accordance with Legal Aid Act 1988 and Duty Solicitor Arrangements 1997, as amended in 1999, is in attendance at a magistrates' court for the purpose of providing advice and representation or giving advice at a police station. He may give advice to a defendant in custody or make a bail application, or attend a suspect who is to be interviewed by police under P. & C.E.A. 1984, s 24, or who complains of serious maltreatment by police. See SI 01/1181. *See* SUSPECT.

dwelling. A building or part of a building occupied or intended to be occupied as a separate dwelling, together with any yard, garden, out-houses and appurtenances belonging to or usually enjoyed with it: see, e.g., Housing Associations Act 1985, s 106; SI 96/2325; *Nicholls v Wimbledon VOA* [1995] RVR 171; *Uratemp Ventures Ltd v Collins* [1999] NPC 153 (some cooking facilities were an essential attribute of a dwelling within H.A. 1988, s 1(1)); But in *Uratemp Ventures v Collins* [2001] UKHL 43, HL held that the expression 'dwelling' in Housing Act 1988, s 1(1) means a place where the occupier lives and treats as his/her home. There is no requirement that cooking facilities must be available for premises to fall within the definition. Common Land (Rectification of Registers) Act 1989, s 3. For 'new dwelling', see C.P.A. 1987, s 23(3). In *Secretary of State for Works and Pensions v Miah* [2003] EWCA Civ 1111, the CA held that two houses in the same street, both owned by the applicant, who had 12 children, and which were used to accommodate his family, constituted the dwelling which he occupied as his home.

dwellings, defective. The Secretary of State may designate as a class buildings, each of which consists of or includes one or more dwellings, if it appears to him that buildings in the proposed class are defective by reason of their design or construction and, as a result, the value of some or all of the dwellings has been substantially reduced: H.A. 1985, s 528. See also Housing Grants, Construction and Regeneration Act 1996, s 6.

dying declaration. As an exception to the rule that hearsay is not admissible, an oral or written statement of a dying person may be admissible evidence of the cause of his death in a trial for his manslaughter or murder if he would have been competent as a witness had he lived, and if he had been 'in settled hopeless expectation' of death at the time he gave the statement. 'The principle on which this species of evidence is admitted is, that they are declarations made in extremity, when the party is at the point of death, and when every hope of this world is gone; when every motive to falsehood is silenced, and the mind is induced by the most powerful considerations to speak the truth: a situation so solemn and so awful is considered by law as creating an obligation equal to that which is imposed by a positive oath administered in a court of justice': *R v Woodcock* (1789) 1 Leach 500. See *R v Andrews* [1987] AC 281 (overruling *R v Bedingfield* (1879) 14 Cox CC 341). *See* EVIDENCE.

dying without issue. Construed, when used in a will (q.v.), to mean a want or failure of issue in the lifetime or at the time of the death of the stated person, and not an indefinite failure of his issue, unless a contrary intention shall appear by the will: W.A. 1837, s 29. *See* ISSUE.

E

earned income. Income arising in respect of remuneration for any office or employment or in respect of a pension, superannuation, deferred pay, compensation for loss of office, income from property forming part of emoluments of any office or employment of profit, and income charged under Schedules A, B, D, derived from the carrying on of a trade, profession or vocation. See I.C.T.A. 1988, ss 15–20, as amended.

earner, employed. A person who is gainfully employed in Great Britain either under a contract of service, or in an office (including elective office) with emoluments chargeable to income tax under Schedule E: S.S. Contributions and Benefits Act 1992, s 2.

earning capacity, loss of. Compensation may be made to plaintiff if he would be at a disadvantage in the labour market were he to lose his job. 'It is necessarily a matter of weighing up risks and chances in all the circumstances of a particular case': *per* Lloyd LJ in *Foster v Tyne and Wear CC* [1986] 1 All ER 567.

earnings. Sums payable to a person by way of wages or salary (including fees, bonus, overtime pay, commission) and by way of pension, but not, e.g., a disablement pension: A.J.A. 1970, s 54. 'Any remuneration or profit derived from an employment': S.S.A. 1975, s 3(1). *See* ATTACHMENT; WAGES.

ear print comparisons as evidence. In *R v Dallagher* (2002) *The Times*, 21 August, the CA held that there is no objection in principle to the admissibility in evidence of ear print comparisons taken during the investigatory process; it is for the jury to establish the weight which should be placed on such evidence.

easement. An incorporeal hereditament (q.v.), involving a right capable of forming the subject matter of a grant which is appurtenant to the land of one person and exercisable over the land of another. See I.C.T.A. 1988, s 119(3). Essentially, a right to do something or to prevent some action, in relation to land. Example: A, the owner of Blackacre, grants B, owner of adjoining Whiteacre, the right to walk across Blackacre. The right of way granted to B is in the *nature of an easement*; Blackacre is the *servient tenement*; Whiteacre is the *dominant tenement*; A is the *servient owner*; B is the *dominant owner*. An easement is *affirmative* (e.g., as where A must allow B to perform a certain act); it is *negative* where the servient owner can be compelled by the dominant owner not to perform certain acts. See L.P.A. 1925, s 62 (unless a contrary intention is expressed, a conveyance of land includes and conveys all easements); *Simmons v Dobson* [1991] 1 WLR 720. See *Peckham v Ellison* [1998] EGCS 174 (common intention and implied reservation of easement); *Chaffe v Kingsley* (1999) 77 P & CR 281 (implied reservation); *Palmer v Bowman* [2000] 1 All ER 23 (natural drainage requires no easement); *Batchelor v Marlow* (2000) *The Times*, 7 June (prescriptive easement to park cars). *See* EQUITABLE EASEMENT; QUASI-EASEMENT.

easement of necessity. Where, e.g., a grantor grants the whole of a plot of land save for an area which is surrounded by the part granted, there will be implied in favour of the part retained an easement of necessity: *Pinnington v Galland* (1853) 9 Exch 1; *Nickerson v Barraclough* [1980] Ch 325.

easement, right as. A right is an easement only where it has the following qualities: there must be a dominant and servient tenement (qq.v.); the tenements must be owned by different persons; the easement must have some natural connection with the estate as being for its benefit; the right must lie in grant. See *Marchant* v *Capital and Counties Property* (1982) 263 EG 661.

easements, extinguishment of. Easements may be extinguished by: statute (see, e.g., T.C.P.A. 1990, s 236(1)); release, express or implied; unity of seisin (q.v.), i.e., where the fee simple of the dominant and servient tenements unite under one owner. See *Huckvale* v *Aegean Hotels* (1989) 58 P & CR 163.

easements, implied. Easements implied into a lease so as to enable the tenant to carry out effectively those of his purposes known to the landlord: *Wong* v *Beaumont Property Trust Ltd* [1965] 1 QB 173.

EC. The European Community (q.v.).

ecclesiastical courts. These include: consistory courts (in each diocese); the Provincial Courts (Arches Court and the Chancery Court of York). Appeal is to the Judicial Committee of the Privy Council (q.v.). *See* COURT OF ECCLESIASTICAL CAUSES RESERVED.

economic duress. *See* DURESS, ECONOMIC.

ECOSOC. Economic and Social Committee (of the EU (q.v.)). A purely consultative committee, which meets monthly in Brussels, with a membership drawn from a broad range of persons in civil society. Groups of members (employers, workers, various other interests) are asked by the Commission (q.v.) for opinions on specified legislative matters. Twice yearly it organises a Single Market Forum to review effects of single market in member states, drawing attention, in particular, to malfunctions.

Ecstacy. Colloquial name for Class A controlled drug (methylenedioxymethylamphetamine). See *R* v *Couzens* [1992] Crim LR 822; *R* v *Harris* [1997] Crim LR 526; *R* v *Ellis* [2000] 1 Cr App R (S) 38.

ecu. Currency unit of the European Monetary System created in 1979, based on the European unit of account. Its value is based on a 'basket of currencies' from ten member states. See EURO.

education. 'Education includes ... not only teaching, but the promotion or encouragement of those arts and graces of life which are, after all, perhaps the finest and best part of the human character': *per* Vaisey J in *Re Shaw* [1952] Ch 163. See also *Hopkins' WT* [1965] Ch 669. For 'public education' see Education Act 1996, s 1: the statutory system consists of three progressive stages: primary, secondary and further education. See Learning and Skills Act 2000; see *North of England Zoological Society* v *Commissioners of Customs and Excise* [1999] STC 1027 ('education' was confined to courses, classes, lessons of instruction); European Convention on Human Rights 1950, First Protocol, art 2 (right to education).

education action zones. Groups of underachieving maintained schools brought together by order of Secretary of State, in the first instance for three years: School Standards and Framework Act 1999, s 10(1). An Education Action Forum will seek to improve standards within the groups. See SI 98/3055.

educational needs, special. A child has special educational needs if he has a learning difficulty which calls for special educational provision to be made for him: Education Act 1996, s 312(1). For Special Educational Needs Tribunal, see 1996 Act, s 333. *Phelps* v *Hillingdon LBC* [2000] 3 WLR 776 (local education authority vicariously liable for psychologist's failure to diagnose dyslexic pupils); Special Educational Needs and Disability Act 2001.

education development plans. Statement of proposals by a local authority for developing provision of education by raising standards of education or improving performance of schools: School Standards and Framework Act 1998, s 6. For power of intervention by Secretary of State, see s 8.

EEA. European Economic Area. Set up in May 1992, involving partnership of EC and EFTA (European Free Trade Association). Objective was creation of large trade area and co-operation in tourism and research and development. See Immigration and Asylum Act 1999, ss 19(10), 80; F.S.M.A. 2000, s 425, Sch 3, para 8.

EEC. European Economic Community. The Treaty of Accession was signed by the original member states in January 1972. EEC was created by Treaty of Rome 1957. Its aims include the harmonious development of economic activities, an increase in stability and an accelerated raising of the standard of living: Treaty of Rome 1957, art 2. The objects of EEC are to be attained through the establishment of a common market. Renamed 'European Union', under Treaty on European Union (1992), popularly known as the Maastricht Treaty. *See* COMMON MARKET; COMMUNITY LAW; EUROPEAN COMMUNITY; EUROPEAN UNION; SINGLE EUROPEAN MARKET.

EEC, amendment of Treaty of Rome. 'The Government of any Member State or the Commission may submit to the Council proposals for the amendment of this Treaty . . . The amendments shall enter into force after being ratified by all the Member States in accordance with their respective constitutional requirements': Treaty of Rome 1957, art 236.

effectiveness, rule of. Concept used in interpretation of international law, suggesting that preference in interpretation should be given to that construction which allows a rule its widest effect and maximum practical value. See, e.g., *Commission* v *Germany* [1973] ECR 829.

effects. Generally, a person's property. See *Mitchell* v *Mitchell* (1820) 5 Madd 69.

effet utile. Concept in public international law, and prevalent in decisions of European Court, which suggests that where an international judge is confronted with two possible interpretations of a phrase or provision in a legal enactment, he will show preference for that which gives meaning to the phrase or provision rather than that which confers little or no meaning.

efficient state. In *Fytche* v *Wincanton Logistics* [2004] UKHL 31, the HL held that the words 'in an efficient state, efficient working order and in good repair', contained within Personal Protective Equipment at Work Regulations 1992 (SI 92/2966) did not constitute an absolute concept; they had to be construed in relation to what made the equipment in question 'protective'.

EFT. Electronic Funds Transfer. Payment messages transmitted either through magnetic material, e.g., tapes and cassettes, or electronic media, e.g., telex, computers. Examples include Clearing House Automated Payment System (CHAPS), Automated Teller Machines (ATM). See Banking Act 1987, s 89, amending C.C.A. 1974, s 187.

egg-shell skull principle. A defendant must take his victim as he finds him. 'If a man is negligently run over or otherwise negligently injured in his body, it is no answer to the sufferer's claim for damages that he would have suffered less injury, or no injury at all, if he had not had an unusually thin skull or an unusually weak heart': *per* Kennedy J in *Dulieu* v *White* [1901] 2 KB 669. See *Brice* v *Brown* [1984] 1 All ER 997 (psychiatric injury); *R* v *Ruby* (1988) 86 Cr App R 186 (manslaughter).

ei qui affirmat non ei qui negat incumbit probatio. The burden of proof lies upon the person who affirms, not upon the person who denies. 'An ancient rule founded on considerations of good sense and it should not be departed from without strong reasons': *Joseph Constantine Steamship Line Ltd* v *Imperial Smelting Corp* [1942] AC 154. *See* BURDEN OF PROOF.

ejectment. Remedy which was available originally to leaseholders, and later to freeholders, wrongfully dispossessed. A person claiming a freehold was held, by a fiction (q.v.) to have leased to a fictitious person, John Doe (q.v.), who was held to have been ejected by the casual ejector, the fictitious Richard Roe. The person in possession admitted to the fiction and relied on his real title as the basis of his defence. The title of the action was, e.g., *Doe d. Smith* v *Jones* (i.e., Doe, on the demise of *Smith* v *Jones*). Abolished under Common Law Procedure Act 1852.

ejusdem generis. Of the same kind or nature. Rule of construction whereby if particular words forming a genus or kind are followed by general words, the general words are construed *ejusdem generis*, i.e., are held to be intended to describe only other things of the same kind as those enumerated by the particular words. Example: 'To A, I leave my coats, suits, hats and other wearing apparel'; 'other wearing apparel' would include shirts but probably not the testator's dress watch. The rule does not apply where a contrary intention is shown, or where the particular words exhaust the genus. See *Le Cras* v *Perpetual Trustee Co* [1967] 3 All ER 915. *See* CONSTRUCTION, RULES OF.

Elder Brethren. *See* ADMIRALTY COURT.

elderly person. Means under Transport Act 2000, s 146, a person who has attained pensionable age (within the meaning given by rules in Pensions Act 1995, Sch 4, para 1).

election. 1. The act of choosing among alternatives, e.g., as to mode of trial. See, e.g., M.C.A. 1980, s 20(3), as amended by C.J.P.O.A. 1994, Sch 4, para 33; *Nicholls* v *Brentwood Justices* [1991] 3 All ER 359. 2. Procedure whereby a constituency returns a member to the House of Commons or the European Parliament. See Representation of the People Acts 1983–91. 3. The equitable doctrine whereby he who takes a benefit under an instrument must accept or reject the instrument as a whole. Example: A, under his will, gives B £50,000 and gives C Blackacre, which belongs to B. B must elect. He may either take the £50,000 and allow C to take Blackacre, or he may retain Blackacre and claim the £50,000, but in such a case he will be obliged to compensate C by paying him the value of Blackacre out of the £50,000. See *Re Gordon's WT* [1978] Ch 145; *Barclays Ltd* v *Bluff* [1981] 3 All ER 232.

election court. A special court, comprising two High Court judges, for the trial of controversial parliamentary elections. It sits without a jury and may order, e.g., a recount, a fresh election. Its decision is communicated to the Commons by the Speaker (q.v.). See Representation of the People Act 1983, ss 120, 147(7), 159, as amended.

elections, parliamentary. There are two types: (1) general elections, held following the dissolution of Parliament and the summoning of a new one by the Sovereign; and (2) by-elections, held when a vacancy occurs in the House of Commons (q.v.) following the resignation or death of a member or his elevation to the House of Lords (q.v.). See European Convention on Human Rights 1950, First Protocol, art 3 (right to free elections). *See* PARLIAMENT; PARLIAMENTARY ELECTORS.

elective resolution. An election by a private company (q.v.) for purposes such as those relating to directors' authority to allot unissued shares or to dispense with the annual appointment of auditors: Cos.A. 1985, s 379(1), inserted by Cos.A. 1989, s 116. It requires at least 21 days' written notice and must be agreed to at the meeting, in person or by proxy, by all the members entitled to attend and vote: s 379A(2).

elector. 1. One whose name is shown on the register to be used at an election, excluding those shown on that register as below voting age (18) on polling day: Representation of the People Act 1983, ss 1, 202. For postal and proxy voting, see Representation of the People Act 1985, ss 5, 6. 2. One who, taking a benefit under an instrument, either accepts or rejects the instrument as a whole.

electors, registration of. A person is entitled to be registered as an elector if he will attain voting age (i.e., 18 or over) before the end of the 12 months following the day by which the register is required to be published. See Representation of the People Act 2000, Sch 1.

electricity, dishonest abstraction of. The dishonest use without due authority or dishonestly causing to be wasted or diverted, any electricity. An offence under Th.A. 1968, s 13. See *Low* v *Blease* [1975] Crim LR 513 (electricity held not to be 'property' within Th.A. 1968, s 4); *R* v *McCreadie* (1993) 96 Cr App R 143; *R* v *Minister of Energy ex p Guildford* (1998) *The Times*, 6 March.

electricity, supply of. It is an offence for an unlicensed person to generate electricity for supply to premises, to transmit electricity for that purpose, or to supply electricity to any premises: Electricity Act 1990, s 4. For easement (q.v.) of supply, see *Duffy* v *Lamb* (1998) 75 P & CR 364.

electronic communication. A communication transmittal (whether from one device to another or from a person to a device or vice versa) by means of a telecommunication system (q.v.) or by other means but while in an electronic form: Electronic Communications Act 2000, s 15(1). A 'key' to electronic data means any code, password, algorithm or other data, use of which allows access to the data or facilitates putting the data into electronic form: s 14(3). See Finance Act 2000, s 143, Sch 38.

electronic communications network. Defined in Communications Act 2003, s 32(1) as a transmission system for the conveyance, by the use of electrical, magnetic or electro-magnetic energy, of signals of any description, the apparatus comprised in the system, switching apparatus, and software and stored data.

electronic monitoring and community orders. A community order (q.v.) may secure electronic monitoring of offender's compliance with order: P.C.C.(S.)A. 2000, s 36B, inserted by C.J.C.S.A. 2000, s 52.

eleemosynary corporation. (*Eleemosyna* = alms.) A corporation organised for charitable purposes, usually for the distribution of alms in the name of the founder. See *Re Armitage's WT* [1972] 1 All ER 78.

e-mail intercept, legality of. Where a telecommunications agency intercepted an e-mail in the course of transmission, this was not unlawful where that e-mail was the subject of an application of production of special procedure material in pending hearings: *R (NTL Group)* v *Ipswich Crown Court* (2002) *The Times*, 6 August. See Regulation of Investigatory Powers Act 2000, s 1 (5).

embezzlement. Offence committed by a clerk or servant who fraudulently appropriated to his own use property delivered to or taken into possession by him on account of his master or employer: see Larceny Act 1916, s 17. No longer a separate offence under Th.A. 1968.

emblements. (*Emblaer* = to sow a field.) The annual profits from sown lands. A lessee (q.v.) or his personal representatives may enter, after the determination of the lease, so as to reap certain cultivated crops which he has sown. See *Graves* v *Weld* (1833) 110 ER 731.

embody. A document is said to embody a provision if the provision is set out either in the document itself or in another document referred to in the document: C.C.A. 1974, s 189(1).

embracery. The obsolescent common law offence of perverting the course of justice by attempting to influence or instruct a juror by corrupt means. See *R* v *Owen* [1976] 1 WLR 840.

embryo. Under Human Fertilisation and Embryology Act 1990, s 1, refers to 'a live human embryo where fertilisation is complete', including 'an egg in the process of fertilisation'. An embryo becomes a foetus (q.v.) when the process of development ends and the organs are formed. The creation of an embryo outside the body, except in pursuance of a licence from Human Fertilisation and Embryology Authority, is prohibited: s 3. A licence cannot authorise the keeping or using of an embryo after the appearance of the primitive streak (i.e., the heaping up of cells of the inner cell mass about the 15th day): s 3(3). For licence conditions, see ss 12–22. See Human Fertilisation and Embryology (Disclosure of Information) Act 1992; *R* v *Human Fertilisation and Embryology Authority ex p Blood* [1999] Fam 151.

emergency powers. Powers conferred by statutes such as Emergency Powers Acts 1920 and 1964, allowing the Crown to issue a proclamation of a state of emergency whenever it appears, e.g., that action is threatened or has been taken, calculated to deprive the community or any substantial portion of it of the essentials of life (e.g. 'the means and distribution of food, water, fuel, light'). The proclamation is in force for one month only, but may be renewed.

emergency protection order. Available under Ch.A. 1989, s 44, limited to eight days, to ensure a child's safety where he might otherwise suffer significant harm if not removed to accommodation provided by or on behalf of the applicant. See s 46 for police powers to take a child into protection for up to 72 hours. See FLA 1996, Sch 6, para 43; Ch.A. 1989, s 79K, inserted by Care Standards Act 2000, s 79.

emigration. The voluntary act of leaving one's country with the intention of residing elsewhere.

eminent domain. Term first used by Grotius in the seventeenth century. The right and inherent power of the state (apparently unknown to the common law) to appropriate private property within its boundaries to public use (i.e., to expropriate). *See* EXPROPRIATION.

emoluments. Some profit or advantage, i.e., anything by which a person is benefited: *R v Postmaster General* (1878) 3 QBD 428. All salaries, fees, wages, perquisites and profits whatsoever: I.C.T.A. 1988, s 131(1). See *Bird v Martland* (1982) 56 TC 89. *See* FOREIGN EMOLUMENTS.

employed earner. *See* EARNER, EMPLOYED; INCOME TAX; SELF-EMPLOYED.

employee. An individual who has entered into or works under a contract of employment. Essentially a 'worker' (q.v.): E.R.A. 1996, s 230(1). The test of whether a person is or is not an employee may be answered by reference to the question: 'Was the contract a contract of services within the meaning which an ordinary person would give to these words?': *Cassidy v Minister of Health* [1951] 2 KB 348. For an extended definition, see E.R.A. 1996,

s 43K, inserted by Public Interest and Disclosure Act 1998, s 1. *See* SERVANT; WORKER.

employee and order to work. No court may compel any employee to do any work or attend at any place for the performance of any work by way of an order for specific performance (q.v.) or an injunction (q.v.): T.U.L.R.(C.)A. 1992, s 236.

employee's duties. Generally: to obey a lawful order within the terms of the contract (see *Turner v Mason* (1845) 14 M & W 112); to serve faithfully (i.e., to cooperate with his employer); to perform his duties with proper care and diligence and indemnify his employer in appropriate cases (see *Lister v Romford Ice and Cold Storage Co Ltd* [1957] AC 555). See *Proudfoot plc v Federal Insurance Co* [1997] IRLR 659. *See* SERVANT.

employees, stress. In *Barber v Somerset CC* [2004] UKHL 13, the HL held that, although, in general, an employer was correct in assuming that his employees were able to stand up to the pressures of the job, it is possible to conceive of circumstances where the employer ought to take appropriate steps to assist an employee who was finding it difficult to cope with the stresses of his work.

employer. The master of a servant. A person (corporate or incorporate) who employs the services of others whose wages and salaries he pays. See, e.g., E.R.A. 1996, s 230(4); Part IVA, s 43K(2), inserted by Public Interest and Disclosure Act 1998, s 1. *See* EMPLOYEE; MASTER AND SERVANT; SERVANT; WORKER.

employer and employee. *See* MASTER AND SERVANT.

employers, associated. *See* ASSOCIATED EMPLOYERS.

employers' association. An organisation which consists wholly or mainly of employers or individual owners of undertakings of one or more descriptions and whose principal purposes include the regulation of relations between employers of that description or those descriptions and workers or trade unions: T.U.L.R.(C.)A. 1992, s 122. See *National Federation of*

Self Employed and Small Business Ltd v *Philpott* [1997] ICR 518.

employer's duties. Generally: to provide 'a reasonable amount of work to enable [the employee] to earn that which the parties must be taken to have contemplated' (*Bauman* v *Hulton Press* [1952] 2 All ER 1121); to indemnify the employee against liabilities and losses properly incurred in the performance of his work; to provide adequate material and a proper system and effective supervision (i.e. safe place of work, safe systems, safe plant: see *Wilsons and Clyde Coal Ltd* v *English* [1938] AC 57). See *Scally* v *Southern Health and Social Services Board* [1991] 4 All ER 563 (employers' duties to explain employees' rights).

employer's liability. The liability of an employer to pay damages to employees for personal injuries sustained in the course of employment. In general, an accident arising out of the course of employment will be deemed, in the absence of evidence to the contrary, to have arisen out of that employment.

employment. Usually taken to include business, profession, vocation, trade, etc. 'Employment under a contract of employment': E.R.A. 1996, s 230. See Public Interest Disclosure Act 1998, s 15. *See* CONTRACT OF EMPLOYMENT.

employment agency. A business, whether or not carried on with a view to profit and whether or not carried on in conjunction with any other business, of providing services (whether by provision of information or otherwise) for purpose of finding workers employment with employers or of supplying employers with workers for employment by them: Employment Agencies Act 1973, s 13(2). See Employment Relations Act 1999, Sch 7, para 3(a), (b); *First Point International Ltd* v *DTI* (1999) *The Times*, 24 August.

Employment Appeal Tribunal. A superior court of record, set up under E.P.A. 1975, s 87, Sch 6, consisting of judges of the High Court and Court of Appeal, Court of Session and lay members, to hear appeals on questions of law relating to decisions of tribunals on, e.g., Redundancy Payments Act 1965, Equal Pay Act 1970, Sex Discrimination Act 1975, E.P.A. 1975 and E.R.A. 1996. Appeal on a point of law lies to Court of Appeal (q.v.), following leave of the court: E.P.(C.)A. 1978, s 136(4). *See* Employment Tribunals Act 1996, Part II.

employment, common. *See* COMMON EMPLOYMENT.

employment, continuous. Where an employee takes time off work under a child break scheme organised by his employer, and is unpaid during that period, he may be considered as being in continuous employment during the period in question: *Curr* v *Marks and Spencer plc* [2000] Emp LR 705.

employment, contract of. *See* CONTRACT OF EMPLOYMENT.

employment, course of. *See* COURSE OF EMPLOYMENT.

employment, expenses incurred in. Claim for such expenses, under I.C.T.A. 1988, s 198, amended by Finance Act 1998, s 61, must establish: expenses were incurred in performance of duties of employment; employee was necessarily obliged to incur the expenses in performing his duties; expenses must be wholly and exclusively incurred in performing the duties. See, e.g., *Smith* v *Abbott* [1991] BTC 414; *Baird* v *Williams* [1999] STC 635.

employment relations. Royal Assent to the Employment Relations Act 2004 was given on 16 September 2004. The Act amends law relating to union recognition and taking of industrial action, and makes provision about voting in ballots and amalgamation of unions.

employment, termination of, date. In general, the effective date of termination of a contract of employment, for purposes connected with hearings before an employment tribunal, is: where the dismissal is with notice, the date on which the notice expires; where the dismissal is without notice, the date on which the termination takes effect; where the dismissal results from the expiry of a fixed-term contract, the date of expiry of the contract: E.R.A. 1996, s 97.

employment tribunal, illness of applicant. A party applying to an employment tribunal for adjournment on medical grounds must satisfy the tribunal that his inability to attend is legitimate: *Teinaz* v *Wandsworth LBC* [2002] EWCA Civ 1040.

employment tribunals. Formerly 'industrial tribunals (q.v.), renamed under E.R. (Dispute Resolution) A. 1998, s 1(1).

EMS. European Monetary System. Adopted at Bremen and Brussels Summits 1978, to replace EMU (q.v.), and in force since March 1979. Principal elements are the ECU (q.v.) and ERM (Exchange Rate Mechanism) (of which UK was a member from October 1990–September 1992). It is concerned essentially with creation of a zone of monetary stability in Europe.

EMU. Economic and Monetary Union. EU doctrine and system, envisaged as essential process in European integration, requiring common currency, reduction of exchange rate fluctuations, and a central bank. Replaced by EMS (q.v.) in 1979.

enabling statute. 1. A statute which makes legal that which was illegal. 2. A statute giving obligatory or discretionary powers.

enacting words. The introductory part of a statute, stating the authority by which it was made, which runs: 'Be it enacted by the Queen's most Excellent Majesty, by and with the advice and consent of the Lords Spiritual and Temporal, in this present Parliament assembled, and by the authority of the same, as follows . . .'.

enactment. An Act of Parliament (q.v.) or part of an Act. Includes any bye-law or regulation having effect under an enactment. *See* LEGISLATIVE HISTORY OF AN ENACTMENT.

enclosure. Also 'inclosure'. The discharge of land from all rights of common. Regulated by Commons Acts 1876, 1879; requires approval of application by the Secretary for the Environment. See Highways Act 1980, s 45(12). *See* COMMONS, REGISTRATION OF.

encourage. To urge to a course of action; to incite. 'There can be no incitement of anyone whether by words or written matter unless the incitement reaches the man whom it is said is being incited': *Wilson* v *Danny Quastel Ltd* [1965] 2 All ER 541. *See* INCITEMENT.

encroachment. Unlawfully entering upon another's rights or possessions. See *Ankerson* v *Connelly* [1907] 1 Ch 678.

encumbrance. A liability or claim which burdens property, e.g., a lease, mortgage, easement, restrictive covenant, rentcharge (qq.v.). One who has the right to enforce an encumbrance is known as an 'encumbrancer'. See L.P.A. 1925, s 205(1)(*vii*); S.G.A. 1979, s 12(2); *Ocean Chemical Transport* v *Exnor Crags Ltd* [2000] 1 All ER (Comm) 519.

encumbrance, freedom from. Warranty, under S.G.A. 1979, s 12(2)(*a*), 'that the goods are free and will remain free, until the time when the property is to pass, from any charge or encumbrance not disclosed or known to the buyer before the contract is made'.

endorsement. 1. A signature, usually on the reverse side of a document, generally operating as a transfer of rights arising from the document. An *endorsement in blank* is a simple signature usually rendering a bill of exchange (q.v.) payable to bearer. A *special endorsement* specifies the name of the person to whom or to whose order the bill is to be made payable. A *conditional endorsement* transfers the property in a bill subject to the fulfilment of a stipulated condition. A *restrictive endorsement* prohibits further negotiation (e.g., 'pay X only'). See B.Ex.A. 1882, s 32. 2. Endorsement of a driving licence is a procedure whereby a person convicted of certain offences will have particulars of the conviction noted on that licence. See Road Traffic Offenders Act 1988, ss 44, 45; Road Traffic (New Drivers) Act 1995.

endowment. 1. Giving of dower (q.v.). 2. Provision for a charity (q.v.).

endowment fund, available. In relation to a charity, means (a) the whole of the charity's permanent endowment if it is all subject to the same trusts, or (b) any part of its permanent endowment which is subject to any particular trusts that are different from those to which any other part is subject, excluding (in either case) so much of that endowment or part as consists of land held on trusts which stipulate that it is to be used for the purposes, or any particular purposes, of the charity: Charities Act 2006 s 43.

enemy. States and persons engaged in armed operations against Her Majesty's Forces. See Army Act 1955, s 225. *See* WAR.

enforcement notice. Notice served, e.g., under T.C.P.A. 1990, s 172, Planning and Compensation Act 1991, ss 5–8, by a local planning authority on the owner and occupier of land on which there has been a breach of planning control, i.e., where development (q.v.) has taken place without permission, or in disregard of the limitations of such permission. The notice specifies the breach and the steps required to remedy it and states a time for compliance. Appeal is to Secretary of State.

enforcement officer, civilian. Means, in relation to a warrant, a person employed by authority of a prescribed class which performs functions in relation to any area specified in warrant, and is authorised in the prescribed manner to execute warrants: M.C.A. 1980, s 125A, inserted by Acc.J.A. 1999, s 92.

enforcement of judgments. *See* JUDG-MENTS, ENFORCEMENT OF.

enfranchise. 1. The conferring of a right to vote at an election. 2. The conferring on a constituency of a right to return a member to Parliament. 3. The conversion of copyhold land into socage (q.v.).

enfranchisement of tenancy. Process whereby a tenant is entitled to acquire a freehold or extended long lease. The tenant must hold a tenancy exceeding 21 years at a rent less than two-thirds of the rateable value of the premises: Leasehold Reform Acts 1967, 1979. See *Woodridge v Downie* (1997) 36 EG 165. See Leasehold Reform, Housing and Urban Development Act 1993, allowing a right of 'collective enfranchisement' to be exercised by 'qualifying tenants', who are empowered to allow a person or persons nominated by them to acquire on their behalf the freehold of the premises in which their flats are situated at a price calculated in accordance with the Act: s 1(1). (See also CPR, Sch 2; O 49, r 9.) 'Qualifying tenants' are required to have held a term of years certain, in excess of 21 years when granted: s 7(1). See *Crean Davidson Investments Ltd v Earl Cadogan* [1998] 2 EGLR 96. See H.A. 1996, Sch 19, Part V.

engage. 1. To engage to do something has the same force as 'to covenant' (q.v.). 2. To be engaged in an occupation is to be occupied therein. It 'connotes such a degree of employment as occupies the whole or at least a substantial part of the [employee's] time': *Buntine v Hume* [1943] WLR 123.

engagement to marry. Under common law this was considered as a contract, the breaking of which could lead to an action for breach of promise (q.v.). The action was abolished under Law Reform (Misc. Provs.) Act 1970. (The engagement ring is now rebuttably presumed to be an absolute gift: s 3(2).) See also Matrimonial Proceedings and Property Act 1970, s 37.

English Nature. New name for Nature Conservancy Council for England: C.R.W.A. 2000, s 73(1). For conservation of biological diversity, see s 74. For compulsory purchase of sites of special scientific interest, see s 75.

engross. 1. To prepare the text of a document. An engrossment is a deed prior to its execution. 2. To buy up, e.g., corn, so as to sell it at a higher price (an offence abolished in 1843).

enjoyment. The taking of the benefit of some right. 'The amenity or advantage of using': *per* Stirling J in *Smith v Baxter* [1900] 2 Ch 138.

enlarge. 1. To free. 2. To extend a period of time, e.g., in which a person may appeal. 3. A mortgagee (q.v.) who has obtained title to the land free from the mortgage by remaining in possession for 12 years may enlarge the term of years into a fee simple (q.v.) by deed: L.P.A. 1925, ss 88, 153.

enrolment. The registration or recording on an official record of an act. See S.C.A. 1981, s 133.

entailed interest. *See* FEE TAIL.

enter. 1. To record in an account. 2. To go on land so as to assert some right. 3. The entrance of any part of the offender's body or of an instrument for removing any goods, into a house, during commission of the offence of burglary (q.v.).

enterprise zones. Designated areas in which some fiscal and administrative burdens may be removed, e.g., exemption from rates of industrial buildings: see L.G.P.L.A. 1980, s 179, Sch 32; Finance Act 1980, s 74 (as amended); Capital Allowances Act 1990, s 1; T.C.P.A. 1990, ss 6, 88; SI 92/571; Finance Act 1992, Sch 13.

entire contract. *See* DIVISIBLE CONTRACT.

entireties, tenancy by. *See* TENANCY BY ENTIRETIES.

entrapment. The enticing of a person into the commission of a crime so that he may be prosecuted. English law has no such doctrine of defence: *R* v *McEvilly* (1975) 60 Cr App R 59. Offences must not be committed so as to trap criminals: see *R* v *Sang* [1980] AC 402; *Nottingham CC* v *Amin* [2000] 1 Cr App R 426. For test purchasing in relation to entrapment, see: *London Borough of Ealing* v *Woolworths* [1995] Crim LR; *Teixeira de Castro* v *Portugal* (1998) 28 EHRR 101; Home Office Circular 17/1992; *R* v *Shannon* (2000) *The Times*, 11 October.

entrapment and human rights. European Court of Human Rights held in *Edwards and Lewis* v *UK (Application No. 39647/98)* (2003) *The Times*, 29 July, that some procedures used in relation to the disclosure of evidence and the practice of entrapment failed to protect the interests of the accused and to ensure equality of arms in subsequent court proceedings, resulting in a breach of the European Convention relating to fair trial provision (art 6.1).

entry clearances. Comprise, under Immigration Rules 1990, ss 14–18, visas, letters of consent (from non-visa foreign nationals), entry certificates (for non-visa Commonwealth citizens). May have effect as leave to enter UK: Immigration Act 1971, s 3A(3), inserted by Immigration and Asylum Act 1999, s 1. *See* IMMIGRATION.

entry, forcible. *See* FORCIBLE ENTRY.

entry into possession. Right of legal mortgagee to enter into possession of mortgaged property. A claim for possession of a dwelling house can be adjourned by the court, or the possession order suspended or postponed, if it appears that the mortgagor is likely, within a reasonable period, to pay any sums due under the mortgage or to remedy a default consisting of a breach of any other obligation. See A.J.A. 1970, s 36; A.J.A. 1973, s 8; *Four Maids Ltd* v *Dudley Marshall Ltd* [1957] 2 All ER 35; *Britannia BS* v *Earl* (1989) 22 HLR 98. *See* MORTGAGE.

entry, right of. *See* RIGHT OF ENTRY.

entry, violence for securing. It is an offence for a person who unlawfully uses or threatens violence to secure entry into premises for himself or some other person, provided that there is someone present on the premises who is opposed to the entry and the person using or threatening violence knows that that is the case: C.L.A. 1977, s 6(1). For defences, see s 6(3). See also C.J.P.O.A. 1994, s 72.

entry, without warrant. *See* WARRANT, ENTRY WITHOUT.

en ventre sa mère. In his mother's womb. Refers to a conceived but unborn child. *See* FOETUS.

environment. 'The air, water and land; and the medium of air includes the air within buildings and the air within other natural or man-made structures above or below ground': En.P.A. 1990, s 1(1) (see Pollution Prevention and Control Act 1999, Sch 3). See EEC Directives 85/337, 96/61.

environmental impact assessment. Assessment of effect of public and private projects on the environment, made in accordance with Council Directive 85/337/EEC, art 20 and SI 88/1199. See *R* v *N Yorks CC ex p Brown* (2000) *The Times*, 7 July; T.C.P.A. 1990, s 288.

environmental pollution. *See* POLLU-TION, ENVIRONMENTAL.

environmental protection. Under SI 91/472 (Environmental Protection Regulations 1991) made under En.P.A. 1990 as amended by Pollution Prevention and Control Act 1999, processes which pose the highest pollution threat are subject to control by HM Inspectorate of Pollution who have overall responsibility for control of emissions to all environmental media. Processes involving emissions to the atmosphere only are subject to local authority control. See also Competition Act 1998, Sch 3. For injunctions to prevent environmental harm, see CPR, Sch 1; O 110, r 1; CPR, Sch 2; O 49, r 7. The European Environmental Agency, set up in 1994 in Copenhagen, promotes EU policies on the environment: see, e.g., Directive 96/61 (integrated pollution prevention). *See* AIR POLLUTION.

epitome of title. *See* ABSTRACT AND EPITOME OF TITLE.

equality before the law. Concept involving the equal subjection of all persons to the ordinary law of the land. *See* LAW, RULE OF.

equality clause. A provision relating to terms of a contract under which a woman is employed, having the effect that, where she is employed on like work with a man in the same employment or on work rated as equivalent with that of a man in the same employment, her contract is to be treated as modified, if necessary, so that it is no less favourable than that of the man or so that it includes any terms corresponding to those benefiting the man. See Equal Pay Act 1970, s 1; Sex Discrimination Act 1975, s 8.

Equal Opportunities Commission. Body of 8–15 persons set up under Sex Discrimination Act 1975, s 53, to work towards the elimination of discrimination and to promote equality of opportunity between men and women generally and to review working of 1975 Act and Equal Pay Act 1970. *See* DISCRIMINA-TION, SEX.

equal pay. Under Equal Pay Act 1970 (as amended) it was provided that, as from the end of 1975, women doing the same or broadly similar work to men would qualify for equal pay and conditions of employment. Treaty of Rome 1957, art 119, calls for member states to apply the principle that men and women shall receive equal pay for equal work. The principle may be invoked before national courts: *Defresne* v *Sabena* [1981] 1 All ER 122. See *Financial Times Ltd* v *Byrne (No. 2)* [1992] IRLR 163; *Barry* v *Midland Bank* [1998] 1 All ER 805; *Preston* v *Wolverhampton NHS Trust* (2001) *The Times*, 9 February (equality and pension limits). See *Code of Practice on Equal Pay* 1997.

equitable. 1. Fair and just. 2. In accordance with rules of equity (q.v.). 3. In accordance with the practice and procedure of the courts of equity.

equitable apportionment. *See* APPOR-TIONMENT.

equitable assignment. *See* ASSIGNMENT.

equitable charge, general. An equitable charge which is not secured by a deposit of documents relating to the legal estate affected, and does not arise or affect an interest arising under a trust of land or a settlement, and is not a charge given by way of indemnity against rents, and is not included in any other class of land charge: L.C.A. 1972, s 2, as amended by Trusts of Land and Appointment of Trustees Act 1996, Sch 3, para 12(2). Example: an equitable mortgage not protected by the deposit of title deeds. 'The equitable charge does not pass an absolute or special property to the creditor or any right of possession, but only a right of realisation by judicial process in case of non-payment of the debt': *London County and Westminster Bank* v *Tompkins* [1918] 1 KB 515. See *United Bank of Kuwait* v *Sahib* [1996] 3 WLR 372; L.P.A. 1925, s 53(1). Registrable under Class C as a land charge: s 2(4)(*i*). *See* LAND CHARGES.

equitable easement. 'Any easement right or privilege over or affecting land created or arising after the commencement of this Act and being merely an equitable interest': L.C.A. 1972, s 2. Registrable as a land charge under Class D. Example: an easement for the grantee's life. See *Shiloh Spinners Ltd v Harding* [1973] AC 691. *See* EASEMENT.

equitable estate or interest. An estate, interest or charge in or over land which is not a legal estate and which takes effect as an equitable interest or right. It involves a right *in personam* (q.v.). Examples: equity of redemption (q.v.), restrictive covenant (q.v.). See L.P.A. 1925, s 1(3).

equitable estoppel. *See* ESTOPPEL.

equitable execution. Procedure whereby equitable relief is obtained by the appointment of a receiver (q.v.) or by injunction (q.v.).

equitable fraud. A wider concept than common law fraud, embracing, e.g., the unfair and unconscientious exploitation of another's weakness or ignorance, the abuse of a fiduciary relationship. See *Nocton v Lord Ashburton* [1914] AC 932; *Armitage v Nurse* [1995] NPC 110.

equitable interests. Interests, the recognition and protection of which were originally within the province of the courts of equity. See, e.g., L.P.A. 1925, s 1(1)–(3), in which they are defined by exclusion; s 4(1), apparently precluding the creation of new forms of equitable interests after 1925. *See* EQUITABLE RIGHTS.

equitable lease. A lease (q.v.) which does not satisfy the necessary requirements for a legal lease but is, nevertheless, valid in equity. There must be a valid contract to create a lease and the contract must be specifically enforceable. See *Walsh v Lonsdale* (1882) 21 Ch D 9; L.P. (Misc. Provs.) A. 1989.

equitable lien. *See* LIEN.

equitable mortgage. A mortgage which transfers an equitable interest only, either because the mortgagor's interest is equitable, or because the conveyance or other mode of transfer is equitable. See L.P.A. 1925, s 53(1)(c). It may be created, e.g., by agreement to create a legal mortgage; or by creation of an equitable charge (i.e., where property is charged with payment of the debt, but there is no transfer of possession or ownership of

the property). Deposit of title deeds alone no longer suffices to create an equitable mortgage, by virtue of L.P. (Misc. Provs.) A. 1989. See *Matthews v Goodday* (1861) 31 LJ Ch 282; *Re Cosslett* [1998] Ch 495; L.R.R. 1995. The equitable mortgagee's remedies include foreclosure, appointment of a receiver and power of sale. *See* MORTGAGE.

equitable presumptions. Presumptions raised in equity in certain cases, e.g., as where a testator bequeaths two legacies to the same person under the same will (so that if the legacies are of unequal amounts, both will be payable). See *Re Davies* [1957] 1 WLR 922.

equitable remedies. Those remedies principally evolved by equity, e.g., specific performance, rescission, delivery up and cancellation of documents, injunctions, account, receivers.

equitable rights. 1. Those rights originally recognised and enforced only in the courts of equity. 2. Those rights which are good against all persons save the *bona fide* purchaser of a legal estate for value without notice, and those who claim under such a person. (In contrast, legal rights are 'good against the whole world'.)

equitable waste. The malicious or wanton destruction of property by a lessee (q.v.), e.g., stripping a house of its doors. So-called because it could be remedied before J.A. 1873 only in a court of equity. A tenant who commits waste of this nature can be restrained by an injunction and ordered to rehabilitate the premises. See *Turner v Wright* (1860) 2 De G F & J 234. *See* WASTE.

equity. *Aequus* = fair. 1. Impartiality. 2. Natural justice (q.v.). 3. 'Any body of rules existing by the side of the original civil law, founded on distinct principles and claiming incidentally to supersede the civil law in virtue of a superior sanctity inherent in those principles': Maine, *Ancient Law* (1861). 4. A system of doctrines and procedures which developed side by side with the common law and statute law, having originated in the doctrines and procedures evolved by the Court of Chancery in its attempts to remedy some of the defects of common law. 5. A right to enforce an equitable remedy. 6. The issued share capital of a company: Cos.A. 1985, s 744.

equity and law, conflict of. *See* LAW AND EQUITY, CONFLICT OF.

equity and law, fusion of. *See* LAW AND EQUITY, FUSION OF.

equity, maxims of. Aphorisms purporting to state some of the fundamental principles of equity. A collection was published by Richard Francis in *Maxims of Equity* (1725). They include: equity acts *in personam*; equity follows the law; equity acts on the conscience; equity aids the vigilant; equity looks to the intent rather than the form; he who comes to equity must come with clean hands, etc.

equity of redemption. The sum total of the mortgagor's rights in equity, i.e., his rights of ownership of the property subject to the mortgage: *Re Wells* [1933] Ch 29. The right of redemption is inviolable and may not be restricted unduly. See *Kreglinger* v *New Patagonia Meat Co Ltd* [1914] AC 25; *Knightsbridge Estates Trust Ltd* v *Byrne* [1939] Ch 441 (postponement of right to redeem); *Pye* v *Ambrose* [1994] NPC 53. *See* MORT-GAGE; REDEMPTION. In *Jones* v *Morgan* (2001) *The Times*, 24 July, the Master of the Rolls stated that the doctrine of a clog on the equity of redemption (in relation to mortgages) no longer serves a useful purpose and would be better excised.

equity of redemption, extinguishing of. Procedure commenced against mortgagor, involving sale, foreclosure, or lapse of time. Mortgagor may extinguish the equity by releasing it to the mortgagee or by redeeming. *See* MORTGAGE.

equity's darling. Maitland's description of a *bona fide* purchaser for value of the legal estate without notice (q.v.) and one who claims under him.

equity security. A relevant share in a company (other than a share shown in the memorandum to have been taken by a subscriber to the memorandum or a bonus share) or a right to subscribe for, or to convert securities into, relevant shares in a company: Cos.A. 1985, s 94(2).

equity share capital. *See* SHARE CAPITAL, EQUITY.

equivocation. An ambiguity in a document, e.g., where a person is described in terms which could apply equally to another. Example: 'Blackacre to my nephew John', where the testator has two nephews named John. Evidence of the testator's intention may be admissible in explanation. See A.J.A. 1982, ss 20–22; *Richardson* v *Watson* (1833) 4 B & Ad 787. *See* AMBIGUITY.

erga omnes. Towards all. Doctrine of international law, referring to rights and obligations having universal validity. See *Barcelona Traction Case* (1970) ICJ Rep 3.

ERM. Exchange Rate Mechanism. Element of the European Monetary System, intended to stabilise currencies by controlling the power of the central banks of member states to allow currency fluctuations outside a fixed rate. UK was a member from 1990–92.

error. 1. 'A fault in a judgment, or in the process or proceeding to judgment or in execution upon the same': *Termes de la Ley*. See *Spice Girls Ltd* v *Aprilia BV* [2001] EMLR 8 (correction of errors of fact by trial court). 2. Writ of error was used to instruct an inferior court (q.v.) to send records of proceedings for review by a superior court (q.v.). Abolished in civil cases by J.A. 1875, and in criminal cases by Criminal Appeal Act 1907.

error, duty to rectify. It was held that under rule 1.3 of the Civil Procedure Rules, parties to a claim are required to help the court further the overriding objective of the Civil Procedure Rules; this includes cooperation between the parties. Where an error had been made by the claimant's solicitor, the defendant's solicitor is bound by duty to rectify the error. See *Hertsmere Primary Care Trust and Others* v *Estate of Balasbramanium Rabindra-Anandh and Another* [2005] *The Times*, 25 April.

error, jurisdictional. *See* JURISDIC-TIONAL ERROR.

error of law on the face of the record. An error which may be ascertained without recourse to any evidence other than examination of the record of the proceedings. The record 'must contain at least the document which initiates the proceedings, the pleadings, if any, and the adjudication; but not the evidence, nor the reasons, unless the tribunal chooses to incorporate them': *R v Northumberland Compensation Appeal Tribunal ex p Shaw* [1952] 1 KB 338.

escape. The common law offence committed by one who, being lawfully confined in connection with a criminal offence, breaks out of any place in which he is confined with the intention of escaping from custody. See Prison Act 1952, s 39, as amended by C.J.A. 1961, s 22, and Prison Security Act 1992, s 2, by which it is an offence to aid the escape of a prisoner. See *R v Roberts* [1998] 2 Cr App R (S) 455.

escape from unlawful restraint. Where a defendant believes mistakenly that he is under arrest, he remains entitled, nevertheless, to exercise reasonable force to escape from what was unlawful restraint: *R v McKoy* (2002), *The Times*, 18 June.

escape of dangerous things. *See* DANGEROUS THINGS, LIABILITY RELATING TO.

escheat. Procedure, largely obsolete, whereby land reverted on extinction of a tenancy (q.v.). See A.E.A. 1925, s 45(1); *Ho v Bess* [1995] 1 WLR 350.

escrow. A deed (q.v.) or bond delivered to a person who is not a party to it, to be held by that party until a future fixed date when conditions are performed, after which it is delivered and becomes absolute. See *Longman v Viscount Chelsea* (1989) 58 P & CR 189.

espionage, industrial. The obtaining of industrial intelligence by illegal means. See *Ansell Rubber v Allied Rubber* [1972] RPC 811.

essence of a contract. The essential conditions, the very basis, of a contract, without which no agreement would have been entered into. See S.G.A. 1979, s 10. *See* CONDITION; CONTRACT.

establishment, right of. The right to take up and pursue activities as self-employed

persons and to set up and manage undertakings in the member states of EU: Treaty of Rome 1957, art 52. See Directive 75/363; *R v Southwark Crown Court ex p Watts* [1991] COD 260. *See* EU.

estate. 1. An area of land. 2. An expression in land law which applies to the period of time for which a tenant (q.v.) was entitled to hold the land. 'All estates are but times of their continuances': Bacon. Common law recognised the following estates: (1) freehold (i.e., estates whose duration is not known) – estate in fee simple, estate in fee tail, estate for life, estate *pur autre vie*; (2) less than freehold (i.e., where the duration is certain) – leaseholds for a fixed term of years, tenancies from year to year. 3. Assets of a deceased person. For proceedings against estates, see CPR, Sch 1; O 15, r 6A.

estate agency work. Things done by a person in the course of a business pursuant to the instructions of a client who wishes to dispose of or acquire an interest in land, relating to introductions of third persons to the client and the disposal or acquisition of that interest: Estate Agents Act 1979, s 1(1). The Director General of Fair Trading (q.v.) is empowered under s 3(1) to make orders prohibiting unfit persons from doing estate agency work. See *Robinson Scammel v Ansell* (1985) NLJ 752; SI 91/860/1032; *Harwood v Smith* [1998] 1 EGLR 5; *R v Docklands Estates Ltd* (2000) *The Times*, 22 September.

estate agent's duty. An estate agent has a duty to inform and advise a client of any change of significance in the property market, such as the fact that a neighbouring house was on the market at a much higher price than that of the client's property which was for sale: *John Wood Ltd v Knatchbull* (2003) *The Times*, 16 January.

estate contract. Contracts by estate owners or persons entitled at the date of contract to have a legal estate conveyed to them, to convey or create a legal estate, including a contract conferring valid options to purchase, rights of pre-emption (q.v.) or similar rights. A Class C charge under L.C.A. 1972, s 2(4). See *Barrett v Hilton Developments Ltd* [1974] Ch 237; *Phillips v Mobil Oil* [1989] 1 WLR 888.

estate duty. Tax on the value of property passing on death. Abolished under Finance Act 1975, s 49.

estate, future. *See* FUTURE INTEREST.

estate, net. *See* NET ESTATE.

estate owner. The owner of a legal estate, i.e., the person in whom there is vested the fee simple absolute in possession (q.v.) in the case of a freehold or the term of years absolute (q.v.) in the case of a leasehold.

estate, real. *See* REAL ESTATE.

estate, registered. Legal estate, or other registered interest, if any, as respects which a person is for the time being registered as proprietor: L.R.A. 2002, ss 2, 3.

estate rentcharge. *See* RENTCHARGE.

estates, administration of. Procedure relating to assets of a deceased person, whereby they are collected, debts are paid and the surplus distributed to those beneficially entitled. Order of the application of assets (in the case of a solvent estate and subject to the testator's directions) is: property undisposed of by will; property not specifically devised or bequeathed but included in residuary gift; property specifically appropriated for payment of debts; property charged with payment of debts; fund retained to meet legacies; property specifically devised or bequeathed; property appointed under will by general power. See A.E.A. 1925, s 34(1), Sch 1, Part II; SI 91/1876, amending Non-Contentious Rules 1987. Funeral, testamentary and administration expenses have priority: A.E.A. 1925, Part I, Sch 1. For appropriation of assets, see s 41.

estates, legal. Estates capable of subsisting at law (q.v.).

estates subsisting at law. Under L.P.A. 1925, s 1, the only estates in land capable of subsisting or of being conveyed or created at law, i.e., 'legal estates' are, as from January 1926: an estate in fee

simple absolute in possession (q.v.); a term of years absolute (q.v.). All other estates take effect as equitable interests (q.v.).

estoppel. A rule of evidence (and not a cause of action) preventing a person from denying the truth of a statement he has made previously, or the existence of facts in which he has led another to believe. It is intended to prevent relitigation. 1. *Estoppel in pais* (or by conduct). Thus, a tenant who has accepted a lease (q.v.) cannot dispute the lessor's title. 2. *Estoppel by deed.* A party to a deed 'is estopped in a court of law from saying that the facts stated in the deed are not truly stated': *Baker v Dewey* (1823) 1 B & C 704. 3. *Estoppel by record.* A person cannot deny the facts upon which the judgment against him has been given. 4. *Equitable estoppel.* (i) Under the doctrine of *promissory estoppel*, where X, by words or conduct, makes to Y an unambiguous representation by promise or assurance concerning his (X's) future actions, intended to affect the legal relationship between X and Y, and Y alters his position in reliance on it, X will not be allowed to act inconsistently with that representation. (ii) *Proprietary estoppel.* Essentially related to the law of evidence. X may be estopped from denying Y's rights in X's property, e.g., where Y has incurred expenditure in the property to his detriment. See *Taylor v Dickens* [1998] 1 FLR 806; *Yaxley v Gotts* [2000] Ch 162. It has been described as involving 'an assurance, a reliance and a resulting detriment'. For 'estoppel by convention', see *Troop v Gibson* (1986) 277 EG 1134. See *ER Ives Investments Ltd v High* [1967] 2 QB 379; *Gillett v Holt* [2000] 2 All ER 289. See S.G.A. 1979, s 21(1). *See RES JUDICATA.*

estoppel, agency by. *See* AGENCY BY ESTOPPEL.

estoppel, cause of action. It 'arises where the cause of action in the later proceedings is identical to that in the earlier proceedings, the latter having been between the same parties or their privies and having involved the same subject matter ... The bar is absolute in relation to all points decided unless fraud or collusion is alleged': *per* Lord Keith in *Arnold v National Westminster Bank plc* [1991] 2 WLR 1177.

estoppel in relation to patent. It is possible to utilise the principle of estoppel so as to prevent a patent owner showing that some other company applying for a patent cannot be the real owner: *Xtralite Ltd v Hartington Ltd* [2003] *The Times*, 10 October.

estoppel, issue. *See* ISSUE ESTOPPEL.

estoppel, licence by. *See* LICENCE BY ESTOPPEL.

estoppel, partnership by. *See* PARTNERSHIP BY ESTOPPEL.

estoppel, remedies in relation to. These include: grant of monetary compensation, right to occupy (see *Greasley v Cooke* [1980] 1 WLR 1306), right of occupation plus compensation, order directing transfer of freehold (see *Pascoe v Turner* [1979] 1 WLR 431).

estoppel, tenancy by. *See* TENANCY BY ESTOPPEL.

estovers. (*Estovoir* = to be necessary.) Rights of a lessee (q.v.) to woodland timber for certain necessary or immediate repairs, e.g., hay bote (or 'bot') (for repair of fences), house bote (for repair of dwelling).

estreat. 1. A true copy of a record, relating to recognizances and fines (q.q.v.). 2. The enforcement of a fine or the forfeiture of a recognizance. For estreatment of a recognizance, see CPR, Sch 1; O 79 (no recognizance acknowledged in or removed into QBD shall be estreated without the order of a judge); *R v Warwick Crown Court ex p Smalley* [1987] 1 WLR 237.

ethnic. 'In my opinion the word still retains a racial flavour but is used nowadays in an extended sense to include other characteristics which may be commonly thought of as being associated with common racial origin. For a group to constitute an *ethnic group* in the sense of the 1976 Act it must, in my opinion, regard itself and be regarded by others, as a distinct community by virtue of certain characteristics': *per* Lord Fraser in *Mandla v Lee* [1983] 2 AC 548. See Race Relations Act 1976, s 3(1).

ethnic group, characteristics of. A long shared history, cultural tradition of its own, common geographical origin, common language, common literature, and is a minority or dominant group within a larger community: *Mandla v Lee* [1983] 2 AC 548. See *Crown Suppliers v Dawkins* [1991] ICR 583.

EU. European Union (q.v.).

EU courts, jurisdiction. Brussels Convention 1968 is replaced by Brussels Regulation 44/2001, taking effect on 1 March 2002, setting out rules for deciding which EU court has jurisdiction in disputes concerning commercial contracts. In absence of express agreement, defendant can be sued only in courts of his 'home country', as determined by his domicile (i.e., where company or other legal entity has its registered office and central administration).

euro. Official single currency of EU since 1 January 1999.

Eurobonds. Bearer bonds issued by a consortium of issuing houses and banks in London, France, Germany and Italy, paid without deduction of tax on interest. For 'quoted Eurobonds', see Finance Act 2000, s 111 (2)(*b*).

Eurocontrol. European Organisation for Safety of Air Navigation, established by Brussels Convention 1960. See Transport Act 2000, s 84.

Eurojust. Body established by EU Council Decision, 14 December 2000, confirmed on 28 February 2002, to seek to ensure co-operation of national prosecuting authorities, co-ordination of investigations into cross-border crime. Comprises 15 EU prosecutors and judges nominated by member states.

European Commission. *See* COMMISSION, EUROPEAN.

European Communities. They comprise: European Economic Community (EEC) (q.v.) (set up in 1957) (see Treaty of Rome 1957); European Coal and Steel Community (set up in 1951); European Atomic Energy Authority (Euratom) (set up in 1957). See European Communities

Act 1972, s 1; European Communities (Amendment) Act 1986; European Communities (Finance) Act 1988.

European Communities, Court of Justice of the. *See* COURT OF JUSTICE OF THE EUROPEAN COMMUNITIES.

European Community. The political and economic grouping of states which grew from the EEC (q.v.), set up under the Treaty of Rome 1957. Now known, following Treaty on European Union (q.v.), signed in 1992, as the European Union (q.v.).

European Community law. *See* COMMUNITY LAW.

European Convention on Human Rights. *See* HUMAN RIGHTS, EUROPEAN CONVENTION ON.

European Council. A twice-yearly meeting ('European Summit') of heads of state (representing members of EU), their foreign ministers, and the President of the Council. It sets priorities for EU work and gives policy direction.

European Court. Name given to the Court of Justice of the European Communities (q.v.).

European Court of Human Rights. The full-time judicial body of the Council of Europe, which sits in Strasbourg, and can hear cases involving alleged breaches of basic rights and freedoms. There is no obligation binding member states to accept its jurisdiction. It consists of a number of judges equal to the number of members of the Council and sits in committees of three members, seven in Chambers, and all the judges in a Grand Chamber. The committees may unanimously reject cases; Chambers decide on the admissibility and merits of cases; the Grand Chamber considers cases involving important matters concerning, e.g., interpretation of the Convention. Judges are elected by the Parliamentary Assembly of the Council of Europe. See SI 00/1817 (Court's immunities and privileges). *See* HUMAN RIGHTS, EUROPEAN CONVENTION ON.

European Economic Community. *See* EEC.

European Parliament. Formerly 'Assembly of EC'. Comprises some 630

'representatives of the peoples' of European Union states, directly elected every five years, and meets in Brussels and Strasbourg. Exercises advisory and supervisory powers through 20 standing committees; debates and passes resolutions; may veto admission of new member states; can force the resignation of Commission members. See Single European Act 1986; European Parliament Elections Acts 1978, 1999. Under the 1999 Act a regional list method is used in the UK, allowing political parties to obtain shares of available seats in direct proportion to the share of the total votes cast in each of the nine electoral regions: see Sch 2. 87 MEPs are elected in the UK (71 for England, 8 for Scotland, 5 for Wales, 3 for Northern Ireland).

European Parliament, UK representatives. Under European Parliamentary Elections Act 2002, s 1, as substituted by European Parliament (Representation) Act 2003, s 1(1), there will be 87 members elected for the UK.

European Social Charter. Adopted by all member states of European Council (except UK) in December 1989, requiring signatory states to accept 'basic rights', e.g., right to work, right of collective bargaining. European Commission reports annually on application of the Charter.

European Union. Known as EU. The grouping of states which grew from EEC (q.v.), and which came into existence on 1 November 1993, based upon the Treaty on European Union (q.v.). Includes currently: Germany, France, Italy, UK, Spain, Belgium, Greece, The Netherlands, Portugal, Austria, Sweden, Ireland, Denmark, Finland, Luxembourg (*c.* 378 million people). It is founded upon the European Communities, supplemented by the policies and forms of co-operation established by the Treaty on European Union. 'Its task shall be to organise, in a manner demonstrating consistency and solidarity, relations between the member states and between their people' (Art A). It is expected to respect the national identities of member states, whose systems of government are founded on the principles of democracy, to respect fundamental rights, and to provide itself with the means necessary to attain its objectives and carry through its policies (Art F). The various treaties of EU apply throughout member states territories, except, e.g., the Channel Islands, Isle of Man, the Faeroes. A Council Decision 2004/649 has appointed two UK members and five UK alternate members of the Committee of the Regions. See [2004] OJL 298/20.

European Union, accession to. The European Union (Accessions) Act 2003, s 1, makes provision in English legislation for the accession to EU of Czech Republic, Estonia, Cyprus, Latvia, Lithuania, Hungary, Malta, Poland, Slovenia and Slovakia.

European Union, citizenship of. Every person holding the nationality of a member state shall be a citizen of the Union: Maastricht Treaty, amending Treaty of Rome. Under Treaty of Amsterdam 1997, citizenship of the union will complement and not replace national citizenship. Whether a person possesses the nationality of a member state, is to be settled solely by reference to the national law of the member state concerned: Declaration annexed to 1997 Treaty.

European Union, pillars of. EU has 'three pillars': the European Communities; provisions on a common foreign and security policy; provisions on police and judicial co-operation in criminal matters. For implementation of the 'third pillar', see Anti-terrorism, Crime and Security Act 2001, s 111.

European Union, Treaty on. Signed on 7 February 1992 at Maastricht (and known also as the Maastricht Treaty). It created the European Union (q.v.) and defines its objectives as: promotion of economic and social progress, in particular through creation of an area without internal frontiers, and establishment of economic and monetary union; implementation of a common foreign and security policy, including eventual framing of a common defence policy; intro-

duction of a citizenship of the Union; development of close co-operation on justice and home affairs; maintenance in full of *acquis communautaire* (q.v.): (Art B). Treaty was brought into force on 1 November 1993.

Europol Convention. European Union Convention (1995) on establishment of a European police force, ratified by UK in 1997, intended to improve co-operation in fight against serious types of international organised crime. See OJ [1995] C316/2. It will involve exchange and analysis of computerised information. Its remit includes investigation of terrorism and illegal trade in nuclear materials.

Euro-securities. Investments which: are to be underwritten and distributed by a syndicate at least two of the members of which have their registered offices in different countries or territories; are to be offered on a significant scale in one or more countries or territories, other than the country or territory in which the issuer has its registered office; and may be acquired pursuant to the offer only through a credit institution or other financial institution: F.S.M.A. 2000, Sch 11.

euthanasia. Euphemism applied to the (illegal) practice of intentionally and painlessly bringing about the death of those suffering from incurable diseases or conditions. See *A-G v Able* [1984] QB 795. *See* MERCY KILLING.

evasion of liability by deception. *See* DECEPTION, EVASION OF LIABILITY BY.

eviction. 1. Recovery of lands from possession of another by the course of law. 2. Dispossession of a tenant (q.v.) by his landlord. 3. Dispossession by virtue of paramount title.

eviction of occupier, unlawful. It is an offence to unlawfully deprive or attempt to unlawfully deprive the residential occupier (q.v.) of any premises, of his occupation of the premises or any part thereof unless the accused can show that he reasonably believed that the residential occupier has ceased to reside therein: Protection from Eviction Act 1977, s 1(2). See H.A. 1988, chap IV (measure of damages); *Tagro* v *Corfane* [1991] 1 WLR 378; *Oseibonsu* v *Wandsworth LBC* [1999] 1 All ER 265 (tenant unlawfully evicted is entitled to a single form of redress only). For meaning of 'conduct' in relation to eviction on grounds of tenant's conduct, see *Regal Grand* v *Dickerson* (1997) 29 HLR 620. See Protection from Harassment Act 1997. *See* HARASSMENT OF OCCUPIER.

evidence. Testimony and production of documents and things relating to the facts into which the court enquires and the methods and rules relating to the establishing of those facts before the court. 'That which demonstrates, makes clear, or ascertains the truth of the very fact or point in issue': Blackstone, *Commentaries* (1765). Evidence may be classified as: direct and circumstantial; primary and secondary; conclusive and inconclusive. The law of evidence is concerned with matters such as relevance, admissibility, weight, burden of proof. *See* SPOUSES, EVIDENCE OF.

evidence, accomplices. In *R* v *Hayter* (2005) *The Times*, 7 February the HL held that, in the event of a joint trial for an offence alleged to be of a joint nature, then proof of guilt of one defendant, X, was essential to prove case against Y, and sole evidence against X was his confession made out of court then X's confession was admissible against X and Y where X's guilt could be used to establish Y's guilt.

evidence, admissibility of. *See* ADMISSIBILITY OF EVIDENCE.

evidence as to character. *See* CHARACTER, EVIDENCE AS TO.

evidence, best. *See* BEST EVIDENCE RULE.

evidence, circumstantial. Evidence resting on inference, not observation or other personal knowledge. Evidence of (collateral) facts not in issue from which can be inferred a fact in issue, e.g., evidence that skid-marks made by the defendant's motorcycle were on the wrong side of the road; facts supplying a motive for an act; facts concerning capacity to do an act. 'It is no derogation of evidence to say that it is circumstantial': *R* v *Taylor*

(1928) 21 Cr App R 20. See, e.g., *Coles* v *Underwood* (1984) 148 JP 178; *Teper* v *R* [1952] AC 480 ('. . . such evidence must always be narrowly examined').

evidence, civil, admissibility of. In *Jones* v *University of Warwick* (2003) 153 NLJ 230, the CA held that where the court is determining whether evidence relating to a civil action has been obtained illegally, it should take into account not only the justice of the case, but also the effect of the decision on the general pattern of litigation. Further, conduct of a reprehensible nature by either party can be reflected in an order for costs whether or not the evidence is considered to be admissible.

evidence, competence of witnesses to give in criminal proceedings. Persons, whatever their age, are competent to give evidence at every stage in criminal proceedings: Y.J.&C.E.A. 1999, s 53(1). A person is not competent, however, if he is unable to understand questions put to him as a witness, and is unable to give understandable answers: s 53(3); nor is he competent for the prosecution if liable to be convicted of any offence in the proceedings: s 53(4), (5). Where the question of competence of a witness is raised, it is for the party calling the witness to satisfy the court of his competence on a balance of probabilities: s 54.

evidence, conclusive. Evidence which preponderates and must be taken by the court as sufficient proof of a fact, i.e., evidence which may not be disputed. Thus, a certificate of incorporation of a company (q.v.) is conclusive evidence of its registration.

evidence, destruction of. In the case of an application by claimant to strike out a defence where defendant had destroyed evidence before the action had commenced, the appropriate order would be made only where the destruction constituted a deliberate attempt to pervert the course of justice: *Douglas* v *Hello Ltd* [2003] EWHC 55 (Ch).

evidenced in writing. Some contracts are unenforceable unless evidenced in writing, e.g., contracts of guarantee (Statute of

Frauds 1677, not yet repealed in its entirety: see *Target Holdings* v *Priestley* [1999] NPC 51). The phrase means that the writing should contain, e.g., the signature of the party to be charged, names or other identification of the parties, description of the subject matter and price. See L.P. (Misc. Provs.) A. 1989 (contracts for sale of land). *See* CONTRACT.

evidence, direct. Used in two senses. (1). Testimony, as contrasted with hearsay, i.e., an assertion by a witness offered as proof of the truth of a fact he asserts. (2). Statement by a witness that he perceived, with one of his senses, a fact in issue. Example: production of a document constituting a fact in issue, when its existence is disputed.

evidence, documentary. *See* DOCU-MENTARY EVIDENCE.

evidence, exclusion of. *See* DISCRE-TION, JUDICIAL, RELATING TO ADMISS-IBILITY OF EVIDENCE; EXCLUSIONARY RULES OF EVIDENCE.

evidence, expert. *See* EXPERT WITNESS OPINION.

evidence, extrinsic. Evidence of statements of circumstances or facts not referred to in a document which may explain or vary its meaning. Not generally admissible except in the case of, e.g., parol evidence to contradict express terms of a document, parol evidence to supplement omitted terms of a private formal document, to show real nature of a transaction, to explain a latent ambiguity (q.v.). See A.J.A. 1982, s 21(1), (2).

evidence, film identification in. In a case involving alleged criminal riot, the evidence of a witness who knew defendant well enough to recognize him as an offender, depicted in a film, was admissible; further, where the image is clear, the jury would be able to compare it with defendant in the dock and make a decision: *A-G's Reference (No. 2 of 2002)* [2002] EWCA Crim 2373. See Criminal Justice Act 1972, s 16.

evidence, first-hand and second-hand hearsay. Statement made by X which is proved by producing a document wherein X made it, or by oral evidence of Y who heard X making the statement, is *first-hand evidence*. Where a witness, Y, states on oath that X told him that Z had made a statement, that hearsay statement is *second-hand evidence*. See C.J.A. 1988, s 23; C.P.I.A. 1996, Sch 1, para 28.

evidence, hearsay. Oral or written statements of one who is not called as a witness which are narrated to the court by a witness or through a document, for the purpose of establishing the truth of what was asserted. Such evidence is generally inadmissible. Exceptions to the rule included: statutory exceptions; declarations of deceased persons (in very restricted circumstances); evidence given in former trials; depositions by witnesses; informal admissions and confessions. First-hand hearsay evidence (q.v.) was made admissible in civil proceedings by Civil Evidence Act 1968, s 2(1) (see also ss 4, 5). Under Civil Evidence Act 1995, s 1, the hearsay rule in civil proceedings is substantially abolished ('hearsay' is defined as a statement made otherwise than by a person while giving oral evidence in the proceedings which is tendered as evidence of the matters stated); some few exceptions, based on common-law rules, remain under s 7 (these relate to published works concerning matters of a public nature, public documents, records of certain courts and treaties). See also Ch.A. 1989, s 96; SI 93/621; in relation to European Convention on Human Rights, art 6, *R* v *Gokal* [1997] 2 Cr App R 266; Law Com 245, *Evidence in Criminal Proceedings: Hearsay and Related Topics* (1997) Cm 3670; *R* v *Ward* (2001) *The Times*, 2 February (hearsay evidence of presence at crime inadmissible). In criminal proceedings hearsay evidence is now governed by the Criminal Justice Act 2003, which repealed ss 23 and 24 of the Criminal Justice Act 1988. There is no longer a requirement on the prosecutor to serve notice on the magistrates and the accused in relation to statements which might be admissible as evidence in a trial: *R (on the application of Crown Prosecution Service)* v *City of London Magistrates Court* (2006) *The Times*, April 17.

evidence, hearsay, and documentary statements. A documentary statement is admissible in criminal proceedings as an exception to the hearsay rule (q.v.) if direct/oral evidence would have been admissible, if the document was created or received by a person in the course of a trade, business, profession or other occupation, or as the holder of a paid or unpaid office, and the information contained in the document was supplied by a person (whether or not the maker of the statement) who had or may reasonably be supposed to have had, personal knowledge of the matters dealt with: C.J.A. 1988, s 24 (repealing P.&C.E.A. 1984, s 68). See *R v Derodra* [2000] 1 Cr App R 41.

evidence, hearsay, common law exceptions applicable to criminal cases. These include: admissions and confessions; statements concerning the maker's physical condition, emotion or state of mind; statements relating to an event in issue; statements accompanying and explaining some relevant act; statements in former proceedings; statements by deceased persons; and statements in public documents; statements as to pedigree.

evidence, hearsay, under CPR. 'Hearsay' means a statement made, otherwise than by a person while giving evidence in proceedings, which is tendered as evidence of the matters stated; and references to hearsay evidence include hearsay of whatever degree: see Civil Evidence Act 1995, s 1; CPR, r 33.1. Where a party intends to rely on hearsay evidence at trial and either that evidence is to be given by a witness giving oral evidence, or that evidence is contained in a witness statement of a person who is not being called to give evidence, that party must serve a witness statement on the other parties in accordance with court's order: r 33.2(1). See 1995 Act, s 2(1)(a). Notice need not be given in the case of evidence at hearings other than trials, or where the requirement is excluded by a PD: r 33.3. For power to call witness for cross-examination on hearsay evidence, see r 33(4).

evidence, identification and. In *R v Stanton* [2004] EWCA Crim 490, the CA held that, where it appears likely that a direction on identification might be needed, discussions should be held between judge and counsel so as to establish how important questions are to be addressed.

evidence in chief. 'The evidence given by a witness for the party who called him': CPR Glossary.

evidence in civil proceedings other than at trial. In general, evidence at hearings other than the trial is to be by witness statement (q.v.) unless the court, a PD, or any other enactment requires otherwise. At such hearings a party may, in support of his application, rely on matter set out in his statement of case or application notice (if either is verified by a statement of truth (q.v.)): CPR, r 32.6.

evidence in civil proceedings, power of court to control. Court may control evidence by giving directions as to the issues on which it requires evidence, the nature of the evidence which it requires to decide those issues, and the way in which the evidence is to be placed before the court. Evidence that would otherwise be admissible can be excluded, and cross-examination can be limited: CPR, r 32.1.

evidence in civil proceedings, witnesses', general rule. Any fact which needs to be proved by evidence of witnesses is to be proved at trial, by their oral evidence given in public, and at any other hearing, by their evidence in writing, subject to any order of the court or any provision to the contrary contained in CPR or elsewhere: r 32.2.

evidence, indirect. Hearsay or circumstantial evidence (qq.v.).

evidence in rebuttal. May be given, subject to the control of the judge, to counter what has been said in cross-examination relating to facts in issue (q.v.).

evidence, insufficient. Evidence which is so weak that a reasonable man would be unable to decide the issue in favour of the party on whose behalf it is adduced. See, e.g., *Hawkins v Powells Tillery Steam Coal Co* [1911] 1 KB 988.

evidence, intrinsic. Evidence from within a document, needing no external matter to explain it.

evidence involving use of plans, photographs, models. Where plans etc., which are not contained in a witness statement, affidavit or expert's report, to be given orally at trial, the party intending to put them in evidence must give notice to the other parties, and an opportunity to inspect must be given: CPR, r 33.6.

evidence, irrelevant. *See* IRRELEVANT EVIDENCE.

evidence, judicial. The testimony, admissible hearsay, things, facts or documents, acceptable to a court as evidence of facts in issue. Divided into testimonial, circumstantial and real evidence (qq.v.).

evidence obtained improperly. Evidence obtained by some tort or criminal act or by an infringement of rules relating to police investigation. 'It matters not how you get it, if you steal it even, it would be admissible in evidence': *R v Leathem* (1861) 8 Cox CC 498. See *R v Sang* [1980] AC 402; *R v Pick* [1995] Crim LR 805; *R v Loveridge* (2001) *The Times*, 3 May; *R v Khan* [1997] AC 558 (evidence obtained through covert listening device held admissible). P.&C.E.A. 1984, ss 76, 78.

evidence of disposition. *See* DISPOSITION.

evidence of opinion. *See* OPINIONS IN EVIDENCE.

evidence of previous convictions. *See* PREVIOUS CONVICTIONS, EVIDENCE OF.

evidence of system. *See* SYSTEM, EVIDENCE OF.

evidence, oral. That given in court by word of mouth. It may be testimony (i.e., what the witness perceived through his senses) or hearsay (q.v.).

evidence, original. May mean 'direct evidence', or proof of some fact by first-hand means. Example: the production of a letter containing a libel is evidence of the words constituting that libel.

evidence, parol. 1. Testimony given by word of mouth of witness. 2. Extrinsic evidence (q.v.). *See* PAROL EVIDENCE RULE.

evidence, power to receive fresh. Power of Court of Appeal (q.v.) to receive fresh evidence. Under Criminal Appeal Act 1995, Court of Appeal, in considering whether to receive fresh evidence, shall have particular regard to whether the evidence appears to be credible, whether it may provide ground for allowing the appeal, whether it would have been admissible in earlier proceedings and whether there is a reasonable explanation for the failure to adduce the evidence in those proceedings: s 4(*b*), amending Criminal Appeal Act 1968, s 23(2). See *R v Cairns* (2000) *The Times*, 8 March.

evidence, presumptive. Evidence taken to be true unless contradicted successfully by other evidence, e.g. prima facie evidence.

evidence, prima facie. 'In its usual sense is used to mean prima facie proof of an issue, the burden of proving which is upon the party giving that evidence. In the absence of further evidence from the other side, the prima facie proof becomes conclusive proof and the party giving it discharges his onus': *R v Jacobson and Levy* [1931] App D 466. Thus, a share certificate is prima facie evidence of a member's title.

evidence, primary. Evidence which by its nature does not suggest that better evidence might be available. Example: the original of a document. Used synonymously with 'best evidence' (q.v.).

evidence, propensity. Evidence relying on alleged striking similarities or the 'underlying unity' of facts: see *R v P* [1992] Crim LR 41. Often used synonymously with 'similar fact evidence' (q.v.).

evidence, psychiatric. Evidence concerning a defendant's state of mind, usually given by a specialist medical practitioner. 'It is for the jury and not for medical men of whatever eminence to determine the issue [relating to a defence of insanity or diminished responsibility]': *R v Rivett* (1950) 34 Cr App R 87. See Criminal Procedure (Insanity and Unfitness to Plead) Act 1991, s 6(1); *R v Weightman* (1991) 92 Cr App R 291. *See* SPECIAL VERDICT; UNFITNESS TO PLEAD.

evidence, real. Known also as 'demonstrative' and 'objective' evidence, which is afforded by production and inspection of material objects. Examples: an exhibit (q.v.) of goods alleged to have been stolen by the accused; a person's physical appearance (e.g., his wounds); a view (q.v.); a witness's demeanour; automatic recordings. See *Castle* v *Cross* [1985] 1 All ER 87. *See* INSPECTION BY JUDGE.

evidence, relevant. *See* RELEVANCE.

evidence rule, parol. *See* PAROL EVIDENCE RULE.

evidence, secondary. That evidence which suggests the existence of better evidence and which might be rejected if that better evidence is available. Example: the copy of a document. Where an original document is destroyed, secondary evidence of its contents may be given. See Civil Evidence Act 1968. *See* DOCUMENT, SECONDARY EVIDENCE OF.

evidence, second-hand. Hearsay evidence (q.v.).

evidence, similar fact. Evidence which is adduced in an attempt to suggest, through its striking similarity, that there is an underlying link between the matters with which it purports to deal – which relate essentially to occasions other than those specifically in question – and the matter before the court. It may be used to establish identity by reference to a distinguishing characteristic, to rebut defence of accident or coincidence, to suggest some propensity (i.e., inclination): see *Lanford* v *GMC* [1990] AC 13. See *R* v *P (A Father)* [1991] 3 All ER 337 (*per* Lord Mackay: Where the offender's identity is in issue, evidence of similar facts should show some kind of 'signature or other special feature'). For the effective abrogation of the general rule, see Official Secrets Act 1911, s 1(2), Theft Act 1968, s 27(3). See *R* v *Kilbourne* [1973] AC 729; *Boardman* v *DPP* [1975] AC 421; *Designers Guild* v *Williams Textiles Ltd* [1998] FSR 275 (rule relating to civil cases); *R* v *Z (Prior Acquittal)* [2000] 1 CL 24 (double jeopardy problem). *See* SIMILARITY OF FACTS.

evidence, similar fact, test of admissibility. The test is that its probative force in support of the allegation that defendant committed a crime is 'sufficiently high' to make it just to admit the evidence, even though it is prejudicial to defendant as tending to show his guilt in relation to another crime: *DPP* v *P* [1991] 2 AC 447. In *O'Brien* v *Chief Constable of South Wales Police* [2005] *The Times*, 29 April, the HL held that the test for admissibility of similar-fact evidence in civil hearings would be admissible if it was potentially probative of an issue in the action. The judge had to bear in mind the overriding objective of rule 1.2 of the Civil Procedure Rules and to deal with the case justly and in a way in which it was proportionate, expeditious and fair.

evidence, testimonial. Assertions offered as proof of the truth of that which is being asserted. It includes a testimony (i.e., an account by a witness of what he perceived with his senses) and hearsay (q.v.).

evidence, unsworn. Evidence not given on oath or by affirmation. In the case of children (under 14), their evidence in criminal proceedings shall be given unsworn: C.J.A. 1988, s 33, inserted by C.J.A. 1991, s 52(1). No witness may be sworn where he lacks a sufficient appreciation of the solemnity of the occasion and of the particular responsibility to tell the truth which is involved in taking an oath: Y.J.C.E.A. 1999, s 55(2). (For the reception of unsworn evidence, see 1999 Act, s 56; for the summary offence of giving false unsworn evidence, see 1999 Act s 57.) An accused person might formerly have made an unsworn statement (q.v.) (see Criminal Evidence Act 1898, s 1(*b*)) but, generally, he could not be cross-examined on it. The 'right' to make such a statement was abolished by C.J.A. 1982, s 72.

evidential facts. *See* FACTS, RELEVANT.

ex abundanti cautela. From an excess of caution. See, e.g., *R* v *Thompson* [1982] QB 647.

examination. Interrogation on oath.

examination-in-chief. Known also as 'direct examination'. The object of examination-in-chief is to put the witness's story before the court so as to obtain a testimony in support of the version of the facts for which the party calling the witness is contending. It is conducted by the witness's own counsel. In general, it may not be based on leading questions (q.v.), save, e.g., where the matter is merely introductory or where it has already been put in evidence by the other side, or where the judge considers the witness hostile (q.v.) and gives leave. *See* EVIDENCE.

examination of goods, buyer's right. Where goods are delivered to the buyer, and he has not previously examined them, he is not deemed to have accepted them until he has had a reasonable opportunity of examining them for the purpose of ascertaining whether they are in conformity with the contract: S.G.A. 1979, s 34(1).

examiners. Barristers and solicitors appointed by the Lord Chancellor to take evidence out of court. See, e.g., *R v Rathbone ex p Dikko* [1985] QB 630.

examining justices. Magistrates who conduct a preliminary investigation of a charge so as to determine whether there is sufficient evidence to justify a committal of the accused. The functions of examining justices may be discharged by a single justice: M.C.A. 1980, s 4(1); s 5A, inserted by C.P.I.A. 1996, Sch 1.

excepted perils. Term used in contracts of carriage to which the Hague Rules do not apply, whereby a carrier's liability is excluded for loss or damage to goods caused by: Act of God (q.v.); act of the Queen's enemies; restraint of princes and rulers; perils of the seas; fire; barratry; piracy; robbery and theft; collisions, strandings and other accidents of navigation.

exception. 1. An objection taken to an answer, or some other challenge to it. 2. A clause in a deed preventing some thing passing which might otherwise pass under the deed. See *Drake Engineering Ltd v Jarvis & Sons plc* (1997) 13 Const LJ 263 (consideration of 'except as stated below').

exchange. 1. Reciprocal transfer of ownership or possession. For the exclusion of exchange from S.G.A. 1979, see s 61. 2. A place for the business transactions of brokers, e.g., London Stock Exchange. 3. A transfer of settlement land for other

land. An exchange of settled land or any part of it or easements may be made for other land or easements: S.L.A. 1925, s 38(*iii*).

exchange contracts. Contracts, within art VIII of s 2(b), Bretton Woods Agreement Order in Council 1946, by which the currency of one country is exchanged for that of another. See *United City Merchants Ltd v Royal Bank of Canada* [1982] QB 208; *Mansouri v Singh* [1986] 2 All ER 619.

exchange, investment. *See* INVESTMENT EXCHANGE.

Exchequer. The government department which receives and has the care of the national revenues. *See* CHANCELLOR.

excisable goods, importation of. Subordinate legislation (Excise Duty (Personal Reliefs) Order, SI 92/3155 as amended) was held to be incompatible with Council Directive 92/12/EC (OJ 1992 L76/1) and EC, art 28, in relation to amount of excisable goods imported from EC by private persons. Further, procedure of Customs personnel in seizing and refusing to return vehicles in which the goods were carried was disproportionate: *R (Hoverspeed and Others) v Commissioners of Customs and Excise* (2002) *The Times*, 8 August.

excise. Tax levied on goods produced in the UK. See *R v Customs and Excise ex p Shepherd Neame Ltd* [1998] COD 237 (setting rates of excise duty is within the sole competence of EU members).

excise dealer, registered. An approved revenue trader who may import and pay excise duties on goods from other member states of EU (q.v.) without having to make customs entries for goods clearance: see Customs and Excise Management Act 1979, s 1(1), inserted by Finance Act 1991, s 11.

exclusionary rules of evidence. 'I would hold that there has now developed a general rule of practice whereby in a trial by jury, the judge has a discretion to exclude evidence which, though technically admissible, would probably have a prejudicial influence on the minds of the jury, which would be out of proportion to its true evidential value': *per* Lord Diplock in *R v Sang* [1980] AC 402. See P.&C.E.A. 1984, s 78; *Selvey v DPP* [1970] AC 304; *R v Chalkley* [1998] QB 848. *See* EVIDENCE.

exclusion clause. 'One which excludes or modifies an obligation, whether primary, general secondary or anticipatory secondary, that would otherwise arise under the contract by implication of law': *per* Lord Diplock in *Photo Productions Ltd v Securicor Transport Ltd* [1980] AC 827. See S.G.A. 1979, s 55; *George Mitchell v Finney Lock Seeds* [1983] 2 AC 803; *BHP Petroleum Ltd v British Steel plc* [1999] 2 All ER (Comm) 544.

exclusion clauses, ambiguity of. In *University of Keele v Price Waterhouse* [2004] EWCA Civ 583, the CA held that it is important to remember the principle that exclusion clauses must be drafted clearly and unambiguously. Should there be discovered any ambiguity in the clause, the courts will generally construe it against the party seeking to rely on it.

exclusion clauses, restriction of. Under the Unfair Contract Terms Act 1977: liability for death resulting from negligence cannot be excluded or restricted by contractual terms (s 2(1)); liability for loss or damage resulting from negligence cannot be excluded or restricted by a term which fails to satisfy a reasonableness test (s 2(2)); a consumer cannot, by contract, be made to indemnify another person in respect of liability that may be incurred by that other for breach of contract or negligence except where the contract satisfies the reasonableness test (s 4); liability for loss or damage from negligent manufacture of consumer goods (q.v.) cannot be restricted or excluded in a guarantee (s 5). See *Sovereign Finance Ltd v Silver Crest Furniture* [1997] CCLR 76.

exclusion of pupils. *See* PUPILS, EXCLUSION OF.

exclusion order. 1. An order under Prevention of Terrorism (Temporary Provisions) Act 1989, Part II (which ceased to have effect under Terrorism Act 2000, s 2, but was renewed temporarily in March 2000), whereby Secretary of State excludes from the UK persons whom he is satisfied are or have been concerned in the commission, preparation or instigation of acts of terrorism (q.v.) or who attempt to enter the country for such a purpose. 2. Order related to F.L.A. 1996, Part IV (now in force), instructing respondent to leave the matrimonial home and/or prohibiting him from entering it. 3. Order prohibiting a convicted person from entering licensed premises: see the Licensed Premises (Exclusion of Certain Persons) Act 1980; *R v Grady* (1990) 12 Cr App R (S) 152. 4. Order under P.C.C.(S.)A. 2000, s 40A (inserted by C.J.C.S.A. 2000, s 46) prohibiting a convicted person from entering a place specified in the order for up to two years. For breach of order, see s 40B. See also C.J.C.S.A. 2000, s 51.

exclusion zones, shipping, temporary. Where a ship, structure or other thing is in UK waters and is wrecked, damaged or in distress, and it appears to the Secretary of State that significant harm (i.e., pollution or damage to persons or property) may occur, he may by direction identify an area to which access is restricted: Merchant Shipping Act 1995, s 100A, inserted by Merchant Shipping and Maritime Security Act 1997, s 1.

exclusive possession. *See* POSSESSION, EXCLUSIVE.

excusable homicide. 1. Homicide in reasonable self-defence of person or property. See C.L.A. 1967, s 3; *Palmer v R* [1971] AC 814; *Pollard v Chief Constable of W Yorks* [1999] PIQR P219. 2. Homicide by misadventure. See *R v Bruce* (1847) 2 Cox CC 262. *See* HOMICIDE; MURDER.

ex div. Ex dividend. Stock Exchange quotation relating to stocks and shares, stating that the price does not include dividends or interest accrued to date. *See* CUM DIV.

ex dolo malo non oritur actio. A right of action cannot arise out of fraud.

executed. That which is done or completed, as in, e.g., *executed consideration* (q.v.). Thus, an *executed trust* is one in which the settlor has declared and perfected in the trust instrument the limitations of the estate of the trustees and the beneficiaries so that no further instrument is needed to define those interests: *Egerton* v *Brownlow* (1853) 4 HL Cas 1. An *executed agreement*, under C.C.A. 1974, s 189(1), is a document signed by or on behalf of the parties, embodying the terms of a regulated agreement (q.v.) or such of them as have been reduced to writing.

execution. 1. The signing of an instrument in a manner which gives it a legally valid form. 2. The carrying out of a court's sentence of death. 3. Enforcing the rights of a judgment creditor (q.v.). See Ins.A. 1986, s 183. 4. Carrying out of the terms of a trust (q.v.).

execution of valuable security. *See* PROCURING EXECUTION OF A VALUABLE SECURITY.

execution of wills. No will is valid unless in writing and signed in order to give effect to it by the testator or by some other person in his presence and by his direction; and the signature must be made or acknowledged by the testator in the presence of two or more witnesses present at the same time, and each witness must attest and subscribe the will in the presence of the testator but not necessarily in the presence of any other witness: W.A. 1837, s 9 (as substituted by A.J.A. 1982, s 17). *See* WILL.

execution, writ of. Procedure relating to the enforcing of judgments by, e.g., a writ of sequestration (q.v.). The writ will issue on its being sealed by a court officer of the appropriate office: after a *praecipe* (q.v.) is filed; after judgment upon which the writ is to issue is produced; after the officer authorised to seal the writ is satisfied that the period specified for payment has expired. The writ is generally valid for 12 months beginning with the date of issue: CPR, Sch 1; O 46, r 8(1).

executive. The branch of government which carries out the general policy determined by the Cabinet (q.v.). It includes the Government, Cabinet, government departments, local authorities and public corporations.

executive, chief. In relation to a body corporate, an employee of that body who, alone or jointly with one or more others, is responsible under the immediate authority of the directors, for the conduct of the whole business of that body: F.S.M.A. 2000, s 417(1).

executor. One appointed by a will (q.v) to administer the testator's property and to carry out provisions of that will. In general the office can be exercised only by the person so appointed: *Re Skinner* [1958] 3 All ER 273. If a minor (q.v.) is appointed, however, probate will not be issued until he reaches the age of 18. An executor (*f*: 'executrix') who is appointed by implication is known as an executor 'according to the tenor [of the will]'.

executor de son tort. Executor 'in his own wrong'. One who is not an executor, either by express or implied appointment, and who has not obtained a grant of administration, and intermeddles with the goods of the deceased or carries out an act which is characteristic of the office of executor. He may be sued by the rightful executor, administrator, creditor or beneficiary (qq.v.). *See* A.E.A. 1925, ss 28, 55(1)(*xi*); *Re Clore* [1982] Ch 456; *James* v *Williams* [1999] 3 WLR 451.

executor, duties of. Getting in the assets of the deceased; paying funeral expenses; paying legacies; accounting for residual estate: *Re Adamson* (1875) LR 3 P & D 253.

executor's year. The period of one year from the death of the deceased in which the executor (q.v.) must complete the administration of the assets. Generally, until the end of that period, he is not bound to distribute the estate of deceased: A.E.A. 1925, s 44. See *Brooke* v *Lewis* (1822) 6 Madd 358.

executory. That which remains to be done, as in executory consideration (q.v.). Thus, an executory trust is an agreement or covenant for the execution of a trust instrument, the terms of which are not defined precisely, at some future time, or directions on the basis of which the trustee is expected to prepare a final settlement at a future date. See *Miles* v *Harford* (1879) 12 Ch D 691.

executory interest. A future interest in land or personal property, except reversions (q.v.) or remainders (q.v.).

exemplary damages. *See* DAMAGES.

exemption clauses. Clauses in an agreement seeking to exempt the parties from general liability or excluding or modifying their liability in certain contingencies. *See* EXCLUSION CLAUSE.

ex gratia. As of favour. As in *ex gratia* payment – a payment not legally compelled. See *R v Secretary of State for Home Department ex p Harrison* [1988] 3 All ER 96; *Williams v BOC Gases Ltd* (2000) *The Times*, 5 April. *See* Charities Act 1993, s 27.

exhibit. Something produced to be viewed by a judge or jury, or shown to a witness who is giving evidence, or an object referred to in an affidavit (q.v.). *See* EVIDENCE, REAL.

exhumation. Disinterring of a buried corpse. Unlawful unless authorised. See Coroners Act 1988, s 23; *Re Christ Church (Alsager)* [1998] 3 WLR 1394; *R v Hanratty* (2000) *The Times*, 26 October.

exhumation, justification for. The Court of Arches held, in *Re Saint Nicholas's Sevenoaks* (2004) *The Times*, 29 October, that curiosity in relation to family anecdotes, and speculation seeking to establish a link between petitions and the Russian royal family were insufficient to justify exhumation for purposes of DNA testing.

exile, unlawful. The court does not recognise a tort of unlawful exile: *Chagos Islanders v Attorney General* (2003) *The Times*, 10 October.

ex officio. By virtue of office. *Ex officio information* is a criminal information (q.v.) filed by the Attorney-General (q.v.) on behalf of the Crown.

exonerate. 1. To clear of an accusation. 2. To relieve from a liability.

ex parte. On behalf of; from one side only. 1. An *ex parte* injunction (q.v.) may be granted after hearing only one party and in a case of great urgency. See *Bates v Lord Hailsham of Marylebone* [1972] 1 WLR 1373; *Re First Express Ltd* (1991) *The Times*, 10 October. '*Ex p Jones*' in the

title of a case indicated the name of the party on whose application the hearing had taken place. Now known, following CPR 1998, as 'applications without notice' [being given to other side] (q.v.). See CPR, Part 54.

expatriation. 1. The voluntary act of renouncing allegiance to one's own country so as to take up residence permanently in a foreign country. 2. The act of forcing a person to leave his native country, e.g., by exile.

expectancy, interest in. *See* INTEREST IN EXPECTANCY.

expectant heir. One who has a vested remainder or contingent remainder in property, or one who has a hope of succeeding to property. Catching bargains (q.v.) with expectant heirs may be set aside by the court: *Benyon v Cook* (1875) LR 10 Ch 391. *See* REMAINDER.

expectation, legitimate or reasonable. Concept developed by the courts in relation to natural justice and first used in *Schmidt v Secretary of State for Home Affairs* [1969] 2 Ch 149. The expectation may arise 'either from an express promise given on behalf of a public authority or from the existence of a regular practice which the claimant can reasonably expect to continue': *per* Lord Fraser in *CCSU v Minister for the Civil Service* [1985] AC 374. See *R v Horseferry Road Magistrates Court ex p Rugless* [2000] 1 Cr App R (S) 484. For its use in EU legislation, see Cases 2/75 and 338/85.

expectation of life, loss of. In a claim for damages for personal injuries, no damages are recoverable in respect of loss of expectation of life caused to the injured person by the injuries, but account is taken of any suffering caused by awareness of reduction in expectation of life: A.J.A. 1982, s 1.

expenses. Monetary outlay involved in the carrying out of activities. For expense allowances in relation to income tax (q.v.), as where the expense is incurred wholly, exclusively and necessarily for the purposes of one's office or employment and has been incurred in the course of the performance of one's duties, see, e.g.,

I.C.T.A. 1988, s 198, as amended by Finance Act 1997, s 62. See, e.g., *Johnson (Inspector of Taxes)* v *Prudential Assurance Co* [1998] STC 439.

expenses, court costs as. Where costs are payable following a court order made against liquidators engaged in the processes of liquidation, they are not to be classified as expenses occurring in a winding-up under Insolvency Act 1986, ss 112, 156: *Digital Equipment Ltd v Bowker* (2003) *The Times*, 29 December.

expenses, living. *See* LIVING EXPENSES.

expert evidence, revised statement of truth. 'I confirm that insofar as the facts in my report are within my own knowledge, I have made clear which they are and I believe them to be true, and that the opinions I have expressed represent my true and complete professional opinion.' Came into use on 25 March 2002. See CPR 1998, Part 35.

expert evidence under CPR, general rules. An 'expert', under CPR, Part 35, is one who has been instructed to give or prepare evidence for the purpose of court proceedings: r 35.2. Expert evidence should be restricted to that which is reasonably required to resolve proceedings: r 35.1. The expert has a duty to help the court, and this overrides any obligation to the person from whom he has received instructions or by whom he is paid: r 35.3. No party may call an expert or put his report in evidence without the court's permission, and the court may limit fees and expenses that the party who wishes to rely on the expert may recover from any other party: r 35.4(4).

expert evidence under CPR, questions to experts. A party may put to an expert written questions about his report, within 28 days of service of that report, for purposes of clarification, and his answers are treated as part of the report. Failure to answer the question may result in an order by the court that the party instructing the expert may not rely on that expert's evidence: CPR, r 35.6; PD 35, para 4.1.

expert evidence under CPR, single expert, direction on. Where two or more parties wish to submit expert evidence on a particular issue, the court may direct that the evidence on that issue is to be given by one expert only: CPR, r 35.7(1); PD 35, para 5.

expert opinions, conflict of. In *R* v *Cannings* (2004) *The Times*, 23 January, the CA held that juries ought not to be placed in a position in which they have to make a choice between conflicting opinions of expert witnesses in the absence of any cogent evidence which could support either of them.

expert's reports under CPR. Expert evidence is generally given in a written report: r 35.5(1). Under PD 35, it should be addressed to the court and give details of the expert's qualifications, state who carried out the tests, summarise range of opinions, give reasons for expert's own opinions, contain a statement that the expert understands his duty to the court and has complied with it. It must be verified by a statement of truth (q.v.). See *Stovens* v *Gullis* [2000] 1 All ER 527; *Field* v *Leeds CC* (2000) *The Times*, 18 January.

expert witness, admissibility of evidence. Where expert medical evidence is adduced so as to help a jury in giving weight to particular witnesses' evidence, it can be admitted even though it was not founded on any physical examination of a witness whose credibility is being questioned: *R* v *Pinfold* (2004) *The Times*, 9 January.

expert witness opinion. Expert opinion is admissible evidence when the subject is one 'upon which competency to form an opinion can only be acquired by a course of special study or experience': *R* v *Kusmack* (1955) 20 CR 365. The expert's duty is to 'furnish the judge or jury with the necessary scientific criteria for testing the accuracy of their conclusions so as to enable the judge or jury to form their own independent judgment by the application of these criteria to the facts proved in evidence': *Davie* v *Edinburgh Magistrates*, 1953 SC 34. See Civil Evidence Act 1972, s 3 (admissibility of expert's opinion on matter in issue in civil proceedings); P.&C.E.A. 1984, s 81; C.J.A. 1988, s 30; CPR, Part 35. 'Expert evidence presented to the court should be seen to be the independent product of the expert, uninfluenced as to form or content by the exigencies of the litigation': *per* Lord Wilberforce in *Whitehouse* v *Jordan* [1981] 1 WLR 246. See *Portman BS* v *Bond* (1998) *The Independent*, 4 May; *Stanton* v *Callaghan* [2000] QB 75 (expert witness immunity). *See* EVIDENCE.

explosion. An extremely rapid expansion of gas or vapour under pressure caused by chemical or nuclear means; it does not include centrifugal disintegration: *per* Staughton J in *Commonwealth Smelting* v *Guardian Royal Exchange Assurance* [1984] 2 Lloyd's Rep 608.

explosive. 'Any article manufactured for the purpose of producing a practical effect by explosion, or intended by the person having it with him for that purpose': Th.A. 1968, s 10(1)(*c*). See O.P.A. 1861, ss 28–30; Explosive Substances Act 1883; Aviation and Maritime Security Act 1990, s 46; *R* v *Byrne* (1975) 63 Cr App R 33; *R* v *Bouch* [1983] QB 246 (petrol bomb as 'explosive substance'); *R* v *Berry* [1985] AC 246.

export controls. Under Export Control Act 2002, Secretary of State may issue an order for the imposition of export controls in relation to goods of any description: this involves the prohibition or regulation of the exportation of goods from UK, or their shipment as stores: s 1. For relation of controls to military equipment and technology, see Schedule, para 1.

exporter. Includes, in relation to goods being sent abroad, the shipper of the goods; see, e.g., Customs and Excise Management Act 1979, s 1(1), as amended.

expose. 1. To display, e.g., food for sale. An offence if unfit for human consumption. See Food Safety Act 1990, s 8. 2. It is an offence (known as 'indecent exposure') for a person wilfully and obscenely to expose his penis with intent to insult a female: Vagrancy Act 1824, s 4. See *Evans* v *Ewels* [1971] 1 WLR 671; *Cheeseman* v *DPP* [1992] QB 83 (see Town Police Clauses Act 1847, s 28).

ex post facto. By a subsequent act. An *ex post facto* statute has a retrospective effect. See *Phillips* v *Eyre* [1870] QB 1. *See* RETROSPECTIVE LEGISLATION.

express. Distinctly stated, rather than implied.

expressio unius personae vel rei est exclusio alterius. The express mention of one person or thing is the exclusion of another. The rule does not operate where an expression is incomplete due to accident. See, e.g., *Dean* v *Wiesengrund* [1955] 2 QB 120; *D* v *NSPCC* [1977] 1 All ER 589.

express term. An express statement of undertakings and promises contained in a contract or other written instrument. A deviation from such a term may constitute a breach of contract (q.v.): see, e.g., *The Hansa Nord* [1976] QB 44; *Johnstone* v *Bloomsbury HA* [1991] 2 WLR 1362.

express trust. A trust created as the result of a settlor's expressed intention, e.g., as where A conveys property to B on trust for C. In general, an express declaration will suffice for the creation of an express trust, e.g., by will, deed, writing not under seal, spoken word. *See* TRUST.

expropriation. The act, usually of a state, in enforcing the compulsory surrender of private property for the state's purposes, without compensation. For recognition of the validity of a foreign government's expropriation, see, e.g., *A/S Tallinna Laevauhisus* v *Tallinna Shipping Co* (1946) 80Ll LR 99. *See* EMINENT DOMAIN.

ex rel. (*Ex relatione* = from a narrative.) Applied to a person's report of proceedings usually not as the result of his having been present, but compiled from information given by another.

ex rights. Term relating to the issue of new shares to shareholders (q.v.) in proportion to their existing holdings, in which the price has been adjusted by deducting the value of the right to subscribe. *See* RIGHTS ISSUE.

extortion. The obtaining of some benefit by intimidation or physical force applied to another. The unwarranted demanding of money by threats may be blackmail (q.v.).

extortionate. Oppressive. Under C.C.A. 1974, ss 137–140, as amended, a credit bargain is considered extortionate (and may be reopened by the court) if the debtor, or relatives, are required to make grossly extortionate payments or payments which contravene in gross fashion the ordinary principles of fair dealing. If a debtor alleges that a credit bargain is extortionate, the onus of proving the contrary is on the creditor: s 171(7). See *Davis* v *Direct Loans* [1986] 1 WLR 823; *Rahman* v *Sterling Credit Ltd* [2000] NPC 84. 'Extortionate credit bargains' under the CCA 1974 ss 137–140 have now been repealed and replaced by CCA 2006 ss 19–22. See UNFAIR RELATIONSHIPS.

extradition. The surrendering by one state, at the request of another, of a person accused of a crime or alleged to be unlawfully at large after conviction, under the laws of the requesting state. It is usually regulated by reciprocal extradition treaties between states. Extradition may be barred unless for an offence punishable in the surrendering state by a period of one year's imprisonment or more. See Extradition Act 1989 (as amended by Acc.J.A. 1999, Sch 11, para 31; Terrorism Act 2000, s 64); C.J.P.O.A. 1994, s 158; C.J.A. 1967, s 34, amended by C.J.C.S.A. 2000, Sch 7, para 35. 'Extradition crimes' are defined in s 2; see *R Bow Street Stipendiary Magistrate ex p Government of the USA (No. 2)* [1998] 3 WLR 1156; *R* v *Bow Street Metropolitan Stipendiary Magistrate ex p Pinochet Ugarte (No. 3)* [1999] 2 WLR 827. For procedure, see Part III. See *R* v *Governor of Brixton Prison ex p Osman (No. 4)* [1992] 1 All ER 579; *R* v *Governor of Brixton Prison ex p Levin* [1997] AC 1 (extradition proceedings are criminal, not civil, proceedings, and the rules of criminal evidence apply); *R* v *Home Secretary ex p Launder* [1997] 1 WLR 839 (whether extradition was unjust or oppressive); *Re Ismail* [1998] 3 WLR 495 (meaning of 'accused' for purposes of 1989 Act, s 1); *Handra* v *High Instance Court of Paris* (2005) The *Times*, 6 January, (a prisoner may not be extradited during his sentence in England and Wales, in relation to an offence committed abroad).

extradition and previous convictions. Where extradition of a person is under consideration, and he is seeking habeas corpus on the ground of an allegedly trivial nature of the offence at the basis of the extradition request, it is of relevance to consider his previous convictions and the fact that the instant offence had been committed while he was on licence: In *Re Togyer* (2003) The *Times*, 12 July.

extradition, powers of search, legality of. In *R* v *Commissioner of Metropolitan Police* (2002) The *Times*, 21 May, HL held that a police officer who had effected the arrest of a person on his premises in reliance on a warrant of arrest issued under Extradition Act 1989, s 8, was empowered under common law to search the premises for items which he really believed to constitute material evidence relating to extradition crime which was the basis of the warrant. He may, further, seize those items.

extraordinary general meeting. Meeting of a company (q.v.) called, e.g., before the next ordinary meeting. The holders of not less than one-tenth of paid-up capital carrying voting rights can compel the directors to call such a meeting. See Cos.A. 1985, s 368; Cos.A. 1989, s 145, Sch 19, para 9.

extraordinary resolution. Resolution (q.v.) usually passed by a three-quarters majority at a general meeting of which notice declaring an intention to propose the resolution as an extraordinary resolution has been given. It may be used, e.g., to wind up a company voluntarily. See Cos.A. 1985, s 378(1); Ins.A. 1986, s 84.

extra-territoriality. Doctrine of international law under which some persons (e.g., ambassadors) are considered to be outside the territory of the state in which they are living so as to carry out their duties. In effect, therefore, they are not within the jurisdiction of that state. *See* DIPLOMATIC PRIVILEGE.

extrinsic. Lying outside; derived from some external source.

extrinsic evidence. *See* EVIDENCE, EXTRINSIC.

ex turpi causa non oritur actio. A right of action will not arise from a base cause.

Thus, an illegal contract is generally unenforceable. See, e.g., *Tinsley* v *Milligan* [1994] 1 AC 340; *Soleimany* v *Soleimany* [1998] 3 WLR 811.

eye witness. One who has seen personally that to which he testifies.

F

fact. A circumstance or incident relating to a case which is being heard. That which can be ascertained by the testimony of a witness.

factor. *See* AGENT, COMMERCIAL.

factory. Premises in which persons are employed in manual labour in any process for or incidental to, purposes, such as, the making of any article or any part of an article, the altering, repairing, ornamenting, cleaning, demolition, adapting for sale, of any article. See Factories Act 1961, s 175, as amended; H.S.W.A. 1974.

facts, evidential. *See* FACTS, RELEVANT.

facts, inferential. *See* INFER.

facts in issue, main. Those facts which must be proved by the party making an allegation (i.e., by claimant or prosecutor) in order to succeed, and the facts that the defendant must prove in order to establish his defence. 'Whenever there is a plea of not guilty, everything is in issue': *R v Sims* [1946] 1 All ER 697. *See* EVIDENCE.

facts in issue, subordinate or collateral. Facts affecting the admissibility of evidence and the credibility of witnesses. See *R v Yacoob* (1981) 72 Cr App R 313.

facts, investitive. Facts which invest persons with particular rights, e.g., a breach of contract investing the plaintiff with the right to claim damages. 'Divestitive facts' modify or extinguish rights, as in the case of payment of a debt.

facts, notice to admit. A party may serve notice on another party requiring him to admit the facts, or the part of the case of the serving party, specified in the notice. A notice to admit facts must be served no later than 21 days before the trial: CPR, r 32.18.

facts, notorious. *See* NOTORIOUS FACTS.

facts, primary. 'Primary facts are facts which are observed by witnesses and proved by oral testimony, or facts proved by the production of a thing itself, such as original documents. Their determination is essentially a question of fact for the tribunal of fact, and the only question of law that can arise on them is whether there was any evidence to support the finding. The conclusions from the primary facts are, however, inferences deduced by a process of reasoning from them': *British Launderers' Research Association* v *Hendon Rating Authority* [1949] 1 KB 462.

facts, probative. Facts which have a natural and logical tendency to prove or disprove a fact in issue.

facts, relevant. Facts from which facts in issue (q.v.) may be inferred. Known also as 'evidential facts'. They may be proved by testimony, documents, admissible hearsay, other relevant facts.

facts which can be established by other means than proof. The following do not generally require affirmative proof: formal admissions (see e.g., C.J.A. 1967, s 10); facts judicially noted; presumptions (q.v.).

factum probandum. (Plural: *facta probanda.*) Principal fact; fact in issue. A fact which has to be proved. *See* EVIDENCE.

factum probans. (Plural: *facta probantia.*) Evidentiary fact; fact related to the issue. Fact given in evidence intended to prove those other facts which are in issue. May be proved by testimony, documents, other things, admissible hearsay, other evidentiary facts.

faculty. A term used in ecclesiastical law to denote a special licence granted to a person to do that which is not allowed by common law, e.g., to marry without publication of banns (q.v.). See also Faculty Jurisdiction Measure 1964; Faculty Jurisdiction Rules 1967, which regulate the grant of faculties for, e.g., making changes in the fabric of a church, selling certain church equipment. See *Re Durrington Cemetery* (2000) *The Times*, 5 July.

fair. 1. 'A concourse of buyers and sellers for the purchase and sale of commodities pursuant to a franchise with an optional addition of provision for amusement': *Wyld v Silver* [1963] 1 QB 169. See Fairs Act 1871. 2. Reasonable; impartial. 3. For significance of current standards of fairness in relation to appeals, see *R v Johnson* (2000) *The Times*, 21 November.

fair comment. Defence to claim for defamation (q.v.), in which defendant shows that words complained of were not actuated by malice and were comment, were fair (in the sense of 'honest') and amounted to comment on a matter of public interest. The defence will not extend to a misstatement of fact. See Defamation Act 1952, s 6; specific details in support of the defence must be given: see PD 16, r 15; CPR, Sch 1; O 82, r 3(2). See *Control Risks Ltd v New English Library Ltd* [1990] 1 WLR 183; *Telnikoff v Matusevitch* [1991] 3 WLR 952.

fair-dealing rule. A principle related to the nature of trusteeship, whereby a trustee (q.v.) may not buy from his *cestui que trust* (q.v.), unless this was intended by the latter, and there is no concealment or fraud. See, e.g., *Coles v Trecothick* (1804) 9 Ves 233. The principle applies generally to any person in a fiduciary position (e.g., solicitor and client): see *Tate v Williamson* (1866) 2 Ch App 55.

fair dismissal. Dismissal from employment on the following grounds; capability or qualifications for the job; conduct; redundancy; where continued employment of an employee results in a contravention of law; other substantial reasons: E.R.A. 1996, s 98(1), (2). 'Capability' means the employee's capability assessed by reference to skill, aptitude, health or any other physical or mental quality: s 98(3)(*a*). See *Foley v Post Office* (2000) *The Times*, 17 August. *See* DISMISSAL FROM EMPLOYMENT.

fair hearing, entitlement to. In *Stansby v Datapulse plc* [2003] EWCA Civ 1951, the CA held that a hearing by an employment tribunal during which a member appeared to have fallen asleep could be construed as being unfair.

fair rent. That fixed for the holder of a statutory or protected tenancy under the Rent Acts 1974, 1977, when regard is had 'to all the circumstances (other than personal circumstances) and in particular to the age, character, locality and state of repair of the dwelling-house, and if any furniture is provided for use under the tenancy, to [its] quantity, quality and condition'. For certificates of fair rent issued to landlords, see Rent Act 1977, s 69 (as modified by H.&P.A. 1986, s 7). See *BTE Ltd v Merseyside RAC* (1992) 16 EG 111; *R v Secretary of State for the Environment ex p Spath Holme Ltd* [2001] 2 WLR 15 (discussion by House of Lords of Rent Acts (Maximum Fair Rent) Order 1999 (SI 99/6)).

fair trading, proceedings relating to. Under Fair Trading Act 1973, where a trader fails to give an assurance to the Director General of Fair Trading (q.v.) that an unfair consumer practice or one detrimental to the interests of consumers will cease, the Director General can take proceedings against that trader in the Restrictive Practices Court (q.v.). See F.S.A. 1986, s 124, as amended by Cos.A. 1989, Sch 23; Competition Act 1998, Sch 12. *See* UNFAIR CONSUMER PRACTICES.

fair trial and principle of proportionality. In considering what the concept of a fair trial entails, in relation to the Convention on Human Rights, art 6, and whether any limitation in relation to admissibility of evidence was arbitrary and excessive, the principle of proportionality is significant. The court must ask itself whether: the legislative objective was of sufficient importance to justify limiting a fundamental right; measures intended to meet that objective were rationally connected to it; means used to limit the right or freedom were no more than what was necessary to accomplish the objective: *per* Lord Steyn in *R v A (Complainant's Sexual History)* (2001) *The Times*, 24 May.

fair wear and tear. Where a repairing covenant exempts the covenantor from liability for fair (or 'reasonable') wear and tear, 'the tenant is bound to do such repairs as may be required to prevent the consequences flowing originally from wear and tear from producing others which wear and tear would not directly produce': *Haskell* v *Marlow* [1928] 2 KB 45. *See* WEAR AND TEAR.

falsa demonstratio non nocet cum de corpore constat. A false description does not vitiate a document when the thing is described with certainty. Thus, in *Pratt* v *Mathew* (1856) 22 Beav 328, the testator (q.v.) made a gift as follows: 'to my wife, Caroline'. He had a wife, Mary, but lived with Caroline with whom he had contracted a void marriage. It was held that the word 'wife' did not affect the validity of the gift to Caroline. See also *Maxted* v *Plymouth Corporation* [1957] CLY 243.

false. Untrue, or designedly incorrect and intended to deceive. A statement, although literally true, may be false if it is used so as to convey a false impression: see, e.g., *R v Kylsant* [1932] 1 KB 442.

false accounting. *See* ACCOUNTING, FALSE.

false imprisonment. The direct, intentional (or negligent) infliction of some bodily restraint involving complete deprivation of liberty for any time no matter how short, which is neither expressly nor impliedly authorised by law. A common-law offence and also a tort of strict liability: see *R v Governor of Brockhill Prison ex p Evans (No. 2)* [2000] 3 WLR 843 (prison governor liable for prisoner's excessive detention based on calculation of date of release). See *John Lewis & Co* v *Tims* [1952] AC 676; *Weldon* v *Home Office* [1990] 3 All ER 672 (prisoner in lawful custody entitled to protection of law in respect of residual liberty). *See* RESTRAINT, BODILY.

false instrument. *See* INSTRUMENT, FALSE.

false personation. It is an offence to personate another in certain circumstances, e.g., for the purpose of voting at an election or where the other person is a juryman. See Representation of the People Act 1983, s 60; *R v Phillips* (1984) 6 Cr App R (S) 293.

false pretence. Phrase relating originally to an offence under Larceny Act 1916, s 32. Now relates to the offence of obtaining property by deception under Th.A. 1968. *See* DECEPTION, OBTAINING PROPERTY BY.

false statement. *See* PERJURY.

false statements, proceedings in relation to. Proceedings for contempt of court may be brought against a person if he makes, or causes to be made, a false statement in a document verified by a statement of truth (q.v.) without honest belief in its truth: CPR, r 32.14(1). Proceedings may be brought only by A-G or with court's permission: r 32.14(2). (No new category of contempt has been introduced by r 32: *Malgar Ltd v Leach Engineering* (2000) *The Times*, 17 February.)

false trade description. A trade description which is false or misleading to a material degree applied by a person to goods in the course of a trade or business: Trade Descriptions Act 1968. Any person who in the course of a trade or business applies a false trade description to goods or supplies or offers to supply any goods to which a false trade description is applied, is guilty of an offence: s 1(1). See *Holloway* v *Cross* [1981] 1 All ER 1012; *Olgeirsson* v *Kitching* [1986] 1 WLR 304 (conviction of private individual); *Formula One Centres* v *Birmingham CC* (1999) 163 JP 234. *See* TRADE DESCRIPTION.

falsification of accounts. *See* ACCOUNTING, FALSE.

falsify. 1. To alter a document, e.g., by obliteration, with intent to deceive.

2. To show that some matter, e.g., an item in an account, is false.

familial link, hallmarks of. 'A degree of mutual interdependence, of the sharing of lives, of caring and love, of commitment and support': *per* Lord Slynn in *Fitzpatrick v Sterling HA* [2000] 1 FLR 271.

family. Social unit, usually consisting of a male and female adult living in one household and caring for their children. For an extended definition in relation to social security, see S.S. Contributions and Benefits Act 1992, s 137(1). See also Ch.A. 1989, s 17(10); *Re Collins* [1990] 2 All ER 47; *Fitzpatrick v Sterling HA* [2000] 1 FLR 271 (the word 'family' can be construed very broadly in ordinary language, and is no longer applied solely to a legal relationship). *See* HOUSEHOLD.

family assistance order. Order requiring a probation officer or officer of a local authority to advise, assist and (where appropriate) befriend any person named therein: Ch.A. 1989, s 16(1).

family company. Means, for the purpose of claiming relief from capital gains tax (q.v.), a company in which not less than 25 per cent of the voting rights are held by the person claiming relief or ten per cent by himself and 75 per cent by his family, including himself. ('Family' means here the person's spouse, and the brother, sister, ancestor or lineal descendant of that person or spouse.)

Family Division. Formerly, Probate, Divorce and Admiralty Division, renamed under A.J.A. 1970, s 1. A division of the High Court (q.v.) consisting of a President and other judges. Its original jurisdiction includes hearing defended matrimonial cases, adoption, family proceedings; its appellate jurisdiction includes hearing appeals from magistrates' courts and county courts and the Crown Court. Under Matrimonial and Family Proceedings Act 1984, s 39, the county court may transfer family proceedings to the High Court (and, under s 38, vice versa). See now S.C.A. 1981, s 5, Sch 1; Matrimonial and Family Proceedings Act 1984; Ch.A. 1989; C.L.S.A. 1990, s 9;

Human Fertilisation and Embryology Act 1990, s 30 (parental orders concerning gamete donors).

family home. *See* HOME.

family name. *See* SURNAME.

family order, non-compliance of. In *Robinson v Murray* [2005] *The Times*, 19 August, the CA held that when considering sentencing for contempt of non-compliance of a family order, the court should take into account the approach to sentencing of the Court of Appeal, Criminal Division. It was desirable that the offender should show signs of remorse as in criminal proceedings.

family proceedings. Formerly 'domestic proceedings'. Proceedings in relation to children under the inherent jurisdiction of the High Court; see also Ch.A. 1989, Parts I, II, IV; Mat.C.A. 1973; Adoption Act 1976; Domestic Proceedings and Magistrates' Courts Act 1983. The Lord Chancellor may allocate such proceedings to specified judges or specified descriptions of judges: C.L.S.A. 1990, s 9. See also Ch.A. 1989, s 92; C.D.A. 1998, Sch 8; Acc.J.A. 1999, Sch 11, para 27; *Practice Direction (Family Proceedings: Human Rights)* (2000) *The Times*, 12 October; C.J.C.S.A. 2000, s 12(5).

family proceedings, composition of magistrates' court. The court will comprise two or three lay justices; or a District Judge (Magistrates' Courts) as chairman and one or two lay judges; or, if impracticable for such a court to be so composed, a District Judge (Magistrates' Courts) sitting alone. So far as is practicable, the court should include both a man and woman: M.C.A. 1980, s 66, substituted by Acc.J.A. 1999, Sch 11, para 26.

family provision. The provision for a family which can be ordered by the court out of the net estate of the deceased. See Inheritance (Provision for Family and Dependants) Act 1975; *Re Coventry* [1980] Ch 461. *See* DEPENDANT.

family wishes, overruling of. In *W Healthcare NHS Trust v KH* (2004) *The Times*, 9 December, the CA held that a judge was entitled to conclude that the interests of a patient who was severely disabled, but not in a permanent vegetative state, did not rest in withdrawing treatment involving the provision of nutrition, in spite of the family's views to the contrary.

farm business tenancy. A tenancy concerning land which is farmed for business or trade purposes, which has begun before 1 September 1995, and which involves notice conditions containing, e.g., a statement to the effect that the person giving that notice intends that the tenancy is to be and remain a farm business tenancy: Agricultural Tenancies Act 1995, ss 1, 2.

farming. 'Carrying on of activities appropriate to land recognisable as farm land. It must at least include the raising of beasts, the cultivation of land and the growing of crops': *Lowe v Ashmore Ltd* [1971] 1 All ER 1057. See I.C.T.A. 1988, s 832(1).

fast track. The normal track for defended claims is the £5,000–£15,000 range which can be disposed of by a trial not exceeding one day. The following will normally be allocated to the fast track: personal injuries cases with financial value of £5,000–£15,000, or with an overall value under £5,000, where damages for pain and suffering might exceed £1,000; claims by residential tenants concerning landlord's repairs where claim does not exceed £15,000; other cases where value of claim is £5,000–£15,000. See CPR, r 26.6.

fast track procedure. Under CPR, following receipt of completed questionnaire, standard directions are to be given, comprising: requests for further information, disclosure of documents, witnesses of fact, expert evidence, questions to experts, documents to be filed: PD 28, Appendix; r 28.2. Standard period between directions and trial should be no more than 30 weeks. Trial normally takes place at court where case is being managed. Judge may confirm or vary any timetable given previously, or set his own. He may dispense with an opening address. Where trial is not finished on day for which it is listed, the judge will normally sit on the next court day to complete it. See CPR, Part 28, PD 28.

fatal accident, claim relating to. 'If death is caused by any wrongful act, neglect or default which is such as would (if death had not ensued) have entitled the person injured to maintain an action and recover damages in respect thereof, the person who would have been liable if death had not ensued shall be liable to an action for damages, notwithstanding the death of the person injured': Fatal Accidents Act 1976, s 1(1) (as substituted by A.J.A. 1982, s 3). A claim must be for the benefit of, e.g., the wife or husband, certain dependants, parent or grandparent, child or grandchild, issue of a brother, sister, uncle, aunt, of the deceased: s 1(3). For particulars of claim, see PD 16, para 5.1. See also Lim.A. 1980, s 33; *Black v Yates* [1991] 3 WLR 90; *Hunter v British Coal Corporation* [1998] 2 All ER 97. In a fatal accident claim, claimant may also bring a claim under Law Reform (Misc. Provs.) Act 1934 on behalf of the estate of the deceased: PD 16, para 5.3. *See* BEREAVEMENT, DAMAGES FOR.

father. Male parent. The rule of law that a father is the natural guardian of his legitimate child was abolished by Ch.A. 1989, s 2(4). See also s 4; Human Fertilisation and Embryology Act 1990, s 28. *See* PARENTAL RESPONSIBILITY; PUTATIVE FATHER.

fax, service by. In *Kuenyehia and Others v International Hospitals Group Ltd* [2006] *The Times*, 17 February, the CA held that service by fax is prohibited unless written consent of the person being served is first obtained. Failure to do so was no more than a minor departure from the provisions in the Practice Directions.

fear, and damages. 'Fear by itself, of whatever degree, was a normal human emotion for which no damages could be awarded . . . Fear of impending death felt by the victim of a fatal injury before that injury was inflicted could not by itself give rise to a cause of action that survived for the benefit of the victim's estate': *per* Lord Bridge in *Hicks v S Yorks Police* [1992] 1 All ER 690.

fear or provocation of violence. A person is guilty of an offence if he uses towards another person threatening, abusive or insulting words or behaviour, or distributes or displays to another person any writing, sign or other visible representation which is threatening, abusive or insulting, with intent to cause that person to believe that immediate unlawful violence will be used against him or another by any person, or to provoke the immediate use of unlawful violence by that person or another, or whereby that person is likely to believe that such violence will be used or it is likely that such violence will be provoked: P.O.A. 1986, s 4(1). See *R v W London Youth Court ex p M* [2000] 1 Cr App R 251. See also C.J.P.O.A. 1994, s 154 (offence of causing intentional harassment, alarm or distress); Protection from Harassment Act 1997; C.D.A. 1998, s 31(1)(*a*) (racially-aggravated offence).

federalism. Doctrine underlying a political organisation based on a compact between two or more separate states to achieve unity under one central government while allowing each state to remain an entity.

fee. *Feodum* = a fief (q.v.). Originally a benefice granted to a man and his heirs in return for services. Used in land law to indicate that an estate (q.v.) is capable of being inherited.

feeble minded. Extremely subnormal in intelligence. See M.H.A. 1983, Part I.

fee simple absolute in possession. One of the two estates in land which, after 1925, are capable of subsisting or being conveyed or created at law. *Fee* denotes an estate of inheritance. *Simple* denotes a fee which can pass to the general heirs of the tenant. *Absolute* means that the estate is not subject to determination by an event other than that which is implied in the words of limitation. *In possession* denotes an estate that is immediate, i.e., neither in reversion nor in remainder. In effect, it is equivalent to absolute ownership of land. See L.P.A. 1925, s 1(1); L.P. (Amendment) A. 1926.

fee simple conditional. A conditional fee (q.v.).

fee tail. *Feodum talliatum* = a fee cut down. An entailed interest. Refers to land descending neither to an ancestor nor to a collateral relative, but only to the lineal descendants of the first tenant in tail, e.g., 'to X and the heirs of his body'. The estate endures for as long as the original tenant or his lineal descendants survive. Under L.P.A 1925, an entailed interest exists only as an equitable interest behind a trust. Types of fee tail include: fee tail male general; fee tail female general; special tail (where the heir may be selected only from descendants of a specified spouse). The situation *after 1996* is as follows: Where a person purports by an instrument coming into operation after the commencement of this Act to grant to another person an entailed interest in real or personal property, the instrument is not effective to grant an entailed interest, but operates instead as a declaration that the property is held in trust absolutely for the person to whom an entailed interest in the property was purportedly granted: Trusts of Land and Appointment of Trustees Act 1996, Sch 1, para 5(1).

felo de se. Felon of himself. Term which was used to refer to one who committed suicide (*felonia de se*). *See* SUICIDE.

felony. An offence which had been made such by statute or which, at common law, carried on conviction the penalties of death and forfeiture of property (abolished in 1870). All other offences were misdemeanours (q.v.). Under C.L.A. 1967, s 1, all distinctions between felony and misdemeanour were abolished; indictable offences are now regulated by those rules applying to misdemeanours.

fence. Any type of barrier, e.g., hedge, bank, wall, cattle grid: Animals Act 1971, s 11. Right to have a fence maintained by an adjoining owner may be an easement (q.v.): *Crow v Ward* [1971] 1 QB 77. See L.P.A. 1925, s 194; Highways Act 1980, s 165(1).

ferae naturae. *See* ANIMALS, CLASSIFICATION OF.

feudal system. A political, economic and social system developed in England by the Normans after 1066, based on duties and rights resting essentially on land ownership, tenure, and resultant personal and reciprocal relationships. It was characterised by a hierarchy dominated by a king and lords from whom vassals held land in fief and to whom they owed services, some of which continued until Tenures Abolition Act 1660. See Abolition of Feudal Tenure (Scotland) Act 2000.

fiat. Let it be done. A command, endorsement, sanction.

fiat justitia, ruat coelum. Let justice be done, though the heavens fall.

fiction, legal. 'Any assumption which conceals, or affects to conceal, the fact that a rule of law has undergone alteration, its letter remaining unchanged, its operation being modified': Maine, *Ancient Law* (1861). Used to extend the courts' jurisdiction and to increase the scope of available remedies. Example: former action of ejectment (q.v.). 'A legal fiction is always consistent with equity': Coke.

fidelity guarantee insurance. Insurance taken out by an employer as indemnification against misappropriation by an employee. All the material facts must be disclosed in such a case: *London General Omnibus Co* v *Holloway* [1912] 2 KB 77.

fiduciary. 1. Involving trust or confidence, e.g., as describing the relationship between a trustee (q.v.) and beneficiary (q.v.). 'The distinguishing obligation of a fiduciary is the obligation of loyalty': *per* Millett LJ in *Bristol and West BS* v *Matthew* [1998] Ch 1. In general, where a fiduciary relationship between parties to a transaction exists, undue influence (q.v.) leading to some agreements, such as contract, may be presumed. See, e.g., *Lancashire Loans Ltd* v *Black* [1934] 1 KB 380 (mother and daughter); *Allcard* v *Skinner* (1887) 36 Ch D 145 (member of religious order and her Superior); *Companhia de Seguros Imperio* v *Heath Ltd* (2000) *The Times*, 26 September (breach of fiduciary duty); *Nationwide BS* v *Various Solicitors (No. 3)* [1999]

PNLR 606 (damages for breach of fiduciary duty should be based on the need to put the beneficiary in the position he would have been in had the fiduciary carried out his duty: see *Target Holdings* v *Redferns* [1995] 3 WLR 352). 2. Fiduciary note issue is the issue of notes by the Bank of England not backed by a bullion reserve: see Currency Act 1983, s 2; SI 99/3228.

fieri facias. Abbreviated to *fi. fa.* Cause to be made. Writ directed to sheriff (q.v.) of the county in which is situated property to be seized so as to enforce a judgment for payment of money. Sheriff is commanded to cause to be made out of debtor's property a sum of money sufficient to satisfy judgment debt, plus interest and costs of execution. Goods exempted from seizure include, e.g., tools, vehicles, clothing, for the domestic needs of the person and his family. See S.C.A 1981, s 138, as amended by C.L.S.A. 1990, s 15; CPR Sch 1; O 45, O 47; *Khazanchi* v *Faircharm Investments Ltd* (1998) 148 NLJ 479. See JUDGMENTS, ENFORCEMENT OF.

fieri feci. I have caused to be made. The report of a sheriff (q.v.) after enforcement of a writ of execution.

fi. fa. *See* FIERI FACIAS.

film. Any record, however made, of a sequence of visual images, which is a record capable of being used as a means of showing that sequence as a moving picture: Films Act 1985, Sch 1. See SI 97/1319; Copyright, Designs and Patents Act 1988, s 5(1). For 'film exhibition', see Cinemas Act 1985, s 21(1), amended by Broadcasting Act 1990, Sch 20, para 40.

finality clause. Clause in a statute providing, e.g., that 'the decision of the Minister shall be final'. 'Parliament only gives the impression of finality to the decisions of a tribunal on condition that they are reached in accordance with the law': *per* Denning LJ in *R* v *Medical Appeal Tribunal ex p Gilmore* [1957] 1 QB 574.

Finance Bill. Introduced into Parliament following a budget (q.v.), so as to give effect to its proposals.

financial circumstances order. Order by court, under P.C.C.(S.)A. 2000, s 126, to an offender, demanding such statement of his financial circumstances as the court may require. See also s 136 (statement as to financial circumstances of parent or guardian).

financial provision for children of the family. The court may make orders under M.C.A. 1973, s 23, concerning lump sums, secured or unsecured periodical payments, transfer or settlement of property and variation of nuptial settlements. See *Gojkovic* v *Gojkovic* [1992] 1 All ER 267.

financial provision order during marriage. Either party to a marriage may apply for an order on the ground that the other party has failed to provide reasonable maintenance for the applicant, or has failed to provide, or to make a proper contribution towards, reasonable maintenance for any child of the family, or has behaved in such a way that the applicant cannot reasonably be expected to live with the respondent, or has deserted the applicant: Domestic Proceedings and Magistrates' Courts Act 1978, s 1. See M.C.A. 1980, ss 59–61 for basic procedures in a magistrates' court. There are comparable provisions for High Court and county courts: Mat.C.A. 1973, ss 27–36 (as modified by Matrimonial and Family Proceedings Act 1984, Part II).

financial provision, reasonable. Term used in Inheritance (Provision for Family and Dependants) Act 1975 to refer to such provision as it would be reasonable in all the circumstances of the case for a husband or wife to receive, whether or not that provision is required by his or her maintenance: s 1(2). The court is empowered to make an order for reasonable financial provision out of the deceased's estate: s 2. See also Matrimonial and Family Proceedings Act 1984, s 25 (extending the 1975 scheme to *former* spouses); *Rajabally* v *Rajabally* (1987) 17 Fam Law 314.

financial relief. Term relating to orders, e.g., for maintenance pending a suit in divorce proceedings. See Mat.C.A. 1973, ss 21–40 (as modified by Matrimonial and Family Proceedings Act 1984, Part II) and W.R.P.A. 1999, Sch 3 (pension sharing orders (q.v.)). Magistrates' courts have separate schemes: see Domestic Proceedings and Magistrates' Courts Act 1978, Part I (also modified by 1984 Act, ss 10, 11) for matrimonial cases. See Ch.A. 1989, s 15 (financial relief with respect to children). See W.R.P.A. 1999, s 22 (overseas divorces); *White* v *White* (2000) *The Times*, 30 September (division of matrimonial assets).

financial services. 'Banking, insurance, investment, trusteeship and executorship': Building Societies Act 1986, s 34(11). See F.S.A. 1986; CPR, Sch 1; O 93, r 22 (proceedings in the High Court under F.S.A. 1986 are generally assigned to the Chancery Division). For Financial Services Tribunal, see F.S.A. 1986, chap IX. For modification of 1986 Act, see Cos.A. 1989, Part VIII; Competition Act 1998, Sch 2.

Financial Services and Markets Tribunal. Set up under F.S.M.A. 2000, Part IX, Sch 13, to hear appeals concerning, e.g., permission to carry on regulated activities under Part IV (see ss 55, 57). Decisions may be taken by a majority: Sch 13, para 12(1); orders may be enforced as if county court orders: s 133(11); appeal on points of law may be made to Court of Appeal: s 137(1).

Financial Services Compensation Scheme. Arrangements under F.S.M.A. 2000, Part XV, whereby FSA (q.v.) administers a scheme for compensating persons where relevant persons cannot satisfy claims against them (s 213(1)), e.g., as where relevant insurers are in financial difficulties (s 217).

financial services, control of provision. Under F.S.M.A. 2000, s 325, FSA (q.v.) is required to keep itself informed about the way in which designated professional bodies supervise and regulate the carrying on by members of the professions of 'exempt regulated activities', i.e., those regulated activities (under the 2000 Act) which may be engaged in without breaching any general prohibition (for which see s 327).

financial year. Usually refers to the period of 12 months ending on 31 March: I.A. 1978. *See* ACCOUNTING REFERENCE PERIOD; FISCAL YEAR.

financial year, in relation to body corporate. Where Cos.A. 1985, Part VII, applies, it means a period in respect of which a profit and loss account under s 227 is made up. The first financial year begins with the first day of its first accounting reference period (q.v.) and ends with the last day of that period, or other such date, not more than seven days before or after the end of that period, as the directors (q.v.) may determine: Cos.A. 1985, s 223, as inserted by Cos.A. 1989, s 3. In relation to any other body corporate, means a period in respect of which a profit and loss account of the body placed before it in general meeting is made up (whether, in either case, that period is a year or not): Cos.A. 1985, s 742(1).

finding is keeping. Popular misconception, suggesting that the finder of chattels acquires title as against all other persons, including the rightful owner. See Th.A. 1968, ss 1, 2; *Armoury* v *Delamirie* (1721) 1 Stra 505; *Parker* v *British Airways Board* [1982] QB 1004; *Waverley BC* v *Fletcher* [1996] QB 334.

findings of fact, reversal of. In *Vijanth* v *Secretary of State for Home Department* (2004) *The Times* 19 October, the CA held that it was not open to an immigration appeal tribunal to seek to overturn any finding of facts carried out by an adjudicator in relation to the risk to the life of an asylum seeker should he return to his country of origin.

finding, theft by, immunity from. 'A person's appropriation of property belonging to another is not to be regarded as dishonest . . . if he appropriates the property in the belief that the person to whom the property belongs cannot be discovered by taking reasonable steps': Th.A. 1968, s 2(1)(c).

fine. (*Finis* = end.) 1. Monetary penalty payable on conviction. See M.C.A. 1980,

ss 34, 150(1) (see *Chief Constable of Kent* v *Mather* [1986] RTR 36); C.L.A. 1977, Sch 6. For fixing of fines, see P.C.C.(S.)A. 2000, s 128. See also C.L.A. 1997, s 38; C.J.C.S.A. 2000, Sch 7, para 55. For imprisonment in default, see C.J.A. 1988, s 60. For the relevance of means in the assessment of a fine, see P.C.C.(S.).A. 2000, s 126. See also C.J.A. 1993, s 65; Crime (Sentences) Act 1997, s 35; *R* v *Rollco Screw Co Ltd* [1999] 2 Cr App R (S) 436. 2. Process used in conveyance by entry on court rolls. A writ was issued, followed by agreement of parties (*finalis concordia*) which was recorded on the rolls. Abolished in 1833. 3. Lump sum payment, a premium for the grant or renewal of a lease: L.P.A. 1925, s 205(1)(*ii*). See *Binion* v *Evans* [1972] Ch 359. 4. Money paid in early times by a tenant to his lord when land was alienated.

fine, payment in instalments of. A magistrates' court may order payment of a fine by instalments: M.C.A. 1980, s 85. Variation of an order was allowed under s 85A (added by C.J.A. 1982, s 51(1)).

fine, remission of. Power of a court to remit whole or part of a fine imposed by a magistrates' court, after enquiry into an offender's means (see P.C.C.(S.)A. 2000, s 126) if the court thinks it just to do so, having regard to any change in his circumstances since the conviction: M.C.A. 1980, s 85. See C.J.A. 1993, Sch 3; Crime (Sentences) Act 1997, Sch 4, para 10(2); P.C.C.(S.)A. 2000, s 129.

fine, responsibility of parent or guardian. The court may order a parent or guardian to pay the financial penalties imposed on a child or young person, unless it is unreasonable, or he or she cannot be found: see P.C.C.(S.)A. 2000, s 137. A financial circumstances order (q.v.) may be called for: s 136.

fines and imprisonment. In *R* v *Baldwin* (2002) *The Times*, 22 November, the Lord Chief Justice stated that, because of the overcrowding of prisons, a fine rather than imprisonment might be advantageous, particularly where the offender was unlikely to prey upon the public again, and would be able to obtain steady employment.

fingerprinting, repeated. C.J.P.A. 2002, s 78(8): where a person convicted of a recordable offence has already been fingerprinted, that fact may be disregarded if the previously taken fingerprints do not constitute a complete set or they are of insufficient quality to allow a satisfactory analysis, comparison or matching.

fingerprints. Impressions made by ridges at the end of the thumb and fingers, used as a means of identification. Under C.J.A. 1948, s 39, proof of previous convictions in criminal proceedings by reference to fingerprints was admissible. In *R v Buckley* (1999) 163 JP 561, the Court of Appeal held that the admissibility of fingerprint evidence depended on: expertise and experience of expert witnesses; number of matching ridge characteristics (a minimum of eight is required); any dissimilar characteristics; size of print relied on; quality and clarity of print relied on. Under C.J.P.A. 2002, s 78(8) means, in relation to any person, a record (in any form and produced by any method) of the skin pattern and other physical characteristics or features of any of that person's fingers or either of his palms. See also P.&C.E.A. 1984, ss 27, 61, 64 as amended by C.J.A. 1988, s 148 (computer data concerning fingerprints); C.J.P.O.A. 1994, s 56; C.P.I.A. 1996, s 64; P.&C.E.A. 1984, s 57 (as amended by C.J.P.O.A. 1994, s 57) (retention or destruction of prints); Immigration and Asylum Act 1999, s 141. For arrest without warrant for fingerprinting, see 1984 Act, s 27. See Terrorism Act 2000, Sch 8, para 10. *See* PALM PRINTS.

fingerprints and samples, continual use of. C.J.P.A. 2002, s 82 amends P.&C.E.A. 1984, s 64 (destruction of fingerprints and samples) so that fingerprints and samples taken from a person in connection with the investigation of an offence, may be retained but shall not be used by any person except for purposes related to the prevention or detection of crime, the investigation of an offence or the conduct of a prosecution.

firearm. Defined under Firearms Act 1968 as 'a lethal barrelled weapon of any description from which any shot, bullet or other missile can be discharged, and includes any prohibited weapon, whether it is such a lethal weapon or not'. It is an offence to purchase, acquire or possess such a weapon without a certificate. An imitation firearm is any object having the appearance of a firearm whether or not it is capable of discharging a missile. See Th.A. 1968, s 10(1)(*a*); Criminal Damage Act 1971, s 3; Firearms Act 1982 (applying the provisions of the 1968 Act to imitation firearms readily convertible into firearms); C.J.A. 1988, s 44; Firearms (Amendment) Acts 1988, 1992 and 1997 (general prohibition of small firearms); *R v Nelson* (2000) *The Times*, 7 March (proving possession); *Steed v Secretary of State for Home Department* (2000) *The Times*, 26 May (compensation for surrender of guns under 1997 Act).

firearm certificate. Certificate granted following a successful application under Firearms Act 1968, s 26, substituted by Firearms (Amendment) Act 1997, s 37. Application must be made to the chief police officer for the area in which the applicant resides, accompanied by photographs of the applicant, verification of those photographs by two referees who must state that they know of no reason why the applicant should not be permitted to possess a firearm. See *R v Cambridge Crown Court ex p Buckland* (1998) 142 SJLB 206.

firearm, illegal imitation. In *R v Bentham* [2003] EWCA Crim 3751, the CA held that a jury would be entitled to find that the offence of possessing a firearm during the course of a robbery might be established where defendant pointed his fingers underneath a jacket so that there was the appearance of a firearm. See Firearms Act 1968, s 17(2).

firearms, imitation, convertible. An imitation firearm is regarded as readily convertible into a firearm to which the Firearms Act 1968, s 1, applies if it can be converted without any special skill on the part of the person converting it in the construction or adaptation of firearms of any description, and the work of conversion does not require special equipment or tools other than such as are in common use by persons carrying out construction and maintenance work in their own homes: Firearms Act 1982, s 1(6).

firearms, small, prohibition and control of. Firearms Act 1968, s 5, is extended by Firearms (Amendment) Act 1997, so as to prohibit firearms with a barrel length of less than 30 cm, or which have an overall length of 60 cm. Exemptions (see 1997 Act, ss 2–8) include slaughtering instruments, firearms used for humane killing of animals, shooting vermin, starting guns used at athletics meetings. For control of small-calibre pistols, see Firearms (Amendment) (No. 2) Act 1997, ss 1, 2. See also 1968 Act, s 19A(2) (exemptions).

fire damage, responsibility for. In general, the owner of a house in which a fire begins by accident, and not by negligence, is not responsible for damage caused to others. See *Ribee* v *Norrie* (2000) *The Times*, 22 November. See Fire Prevention (Metropolis) Act 1744, s 86; Fire Precautions Act 1971, as amended; Highways (Amendment) Act 1986, s 1; Fire Safety and Safety of Places of Sport Act 1987 (necessity for safety certificates).

fire, false alarms. It is an offence under Fire and Rescue Services Act 2004, s 49, for a person to knowingly give or cause to be given a false alarm of fire to a person acting on behalf of a fire and rescue authority (defined in s 1(1). (The Act also abolishes the Central Brigades Advisory Council. The Fire Services Act 1947 ceases to have effect: see ss 51–52).

fire insurance. Insurance of property against damage or destruction resulting from a fire which is accidental in its origin, and from extinguishment. The premium is usually based upon the value of property at risk and the attendant degree of hazard. For covenants in relation to fire insurance, see *Lambert* v *Keymood Ltd*

[1997] 2 EGLR 70. For fire started deliberately, see *Grave* v *GA Bonus plc* [1999] 2 Lloyd's Rep 716.

fire ordeal. *See* ORDEAL, TRIAL BY.

firm. A partnership (q.v.). The name under which a partnership is carried on is known as 'the firm-name': Partnership Act 1890, s 4(1).

first instance, court of. *See* COURT OF FIRST INSTANCE.

First Lord of the Treasury. *See* TREASURY.

fiscal year. The financial year, reckoned, e.g., for income tax purposes, as from 6th April in one year to 5th April in the following year.

fishery. Known also as 'piscary'. A right of fishing. 1. *A several fishery*. 'A right to take fish *in alieno solo*, and to exclude the owner of the soil from the right of taking fish himself': *per* Lord Coleridge in *Foster* v *Wright* (1878) LR 4 CPD 438. 2. *A free fishery*. Exclusive right to fish. It may be a *Royal fishery*, i.e., exclusive right of the Crown, or a right granted to a subject. 3. *A public or common fishery*. Right to fish in another's waters, in common with the owner of the soil.

fitness for purpose. Where goods are sold in the course of a business, and the buyer expressly or impliedly makes known to the seller any particular purpose for which the goods are being bought, there is an implied condition that they are fit for that purpose: S.G.A. 1979, s 14(3). See *Business Appliances Ltd* v *Nationwide Credit Ltd* [1988] RTR 332; Sale and Supply of Goods Act 1994.

fixed charge. *See* CHARGE.

fixed penalty notice. Notice (which may be affixed to a stationary vehicle) offering the opportunity of the discharge of any liability to conviction of the offence to which the notice relates by payment of a fixed penalty: introduced by Transport Act 1982, s 27, Sch 1. See Road Traffic Offenders Act 1988.

fixed sum credit. *See* CREDIT.

fixed term. Expression relating to a lease (q.v.) for a fixed period. 'In my opinion a "fixed term" is one which cannot be unfixed by notice. To be a "fixed term", the parties must be bound for the term stated in the agreement and unable to determine it on either side': *per* Lord Denning in *BBC* v *Ioannou* [1975] 2 All ER 999. For purposes of security of tenure under H.A. 1988, a fixed-term tenancy is a tenancy other than a periodic tenancy: s 45(1).

fixed-term employees. Fixed-term Employees (Prevention of Less Favourable Treatment) Regulations 2002 (SI 02/2034) implements, as from 10 October 2002, the fixed-term Work Directive (99/7/EC22): a fixed-term employee who is treated less favourably than a permanent employee of the same employer, and who is doing similar work, may apply for relief by way of complaint to an employment tribunal.

fixtures. 1. Chattels affixed to land or to a building so that they are part thereof. Generally the degree of annexation required is such that the chattel must be connected to the land or to a building on the land in some substantial way. See *Deen* v *Andrews* (1986) 1 EGLR 262; *Elitestone* v *Morris* [1997] 1 WLR 687; *Potton Developments* v *Thompson* [1998] NPC 49. For mortgagee's right to fixtures, see *Lyon and Co* v *London City and Midland Bank* [1903] 2 KB 135. For tenant's right to remove fixtures, see *Re Palmiero* [1999] 38 EG 195. See Finance Act 2000, s 78; Agricultural Tenancies Act 1995, s 8. 2; Capital Allowances Act 2001, s 173. 'Fixtures' is also used to mean hearing dates in the Court of Appeal (Civil Division) (q.v.) fixed in advance; it means that a hearing has been fixed to begin on a specified date or on the next following sitting day at the option of the Court: *Practice Direction for the Court of Appeal*, para 6.2. See QUICQUID PLANTATUR.

flagrante delicto. Literally: while the crime is flagrant. In the very act of committing an offence.

flat. A separate set of premises, whether or not on the same floor, which forms part of a building, is divided horizontally from some other part of the building, and is constructed or adapted for use for the purposes of a dwelling: Landlord and Tenant Act 1987, s 60. 'A dwelling-house which is not a house is a flat': H.A. 1985, s 183.

floating charge. *See* CHARGE.

flood. Term used in, e.g., insurance policies to mean a large and temporary movement of water having an element of violence and suddenness: *Young* v *Sun Alliance and London Insurance Ltd* [1976] 3 All ER 561. See *Bybrook Barn Garden Centre* v *Kent CC* (2001) *The Times*, 5 January (council liability). For flood defence committees, see Environment Act 1995, s 14.

flood risks. *In Marcic* v *Thames Water Utilities* [2002] 2 All ER 55, the CA held that Thames Water's refusal to take measures needed to prevent flooding of claimant's property constituted an infringement of his right to respect for his private and family life under Human Rights Convention, art 8(1) and Human Rights Act 1998, Sch 1.

flotsam. Wreckage of a cargo floating on the sea. It may go to the Crown if unclaimed.

flying freehold. 'A man may have an inheritance in an upper chamber though the lower building and soil be in another': Co.Litt. 48b. A fee simple may exist in the above-ground-level storey of a building distinct from the rest. See *Grigsby* v *Melville* [1974] 1 WLR 80. *See* COMMONHOLD.

f.o.b. contract. Free on board. Goods are to be delivered on board by the seller, free of expense to the purchaser; they are not at the purchaser's risk until actually delivered on board, when property in them generally passes. See, e.g., *Glencore Grain Rotterdam* v *Lorico* [1997] 2 Lloyd's Rep 386. For f.o.t. (free on truck) contract, see *Zenziper Grains* v *Bulk Trading Corporation* (2001) *The Times*, 23 January.

foetus. An unborn infant that has developed to the stage of being recognisably human (i.e., from the sixth to eighth week of pregnancy) with all its organs formed. See Infant Life (Preservation) Act 1929; Abortion Act 1967, s 5; *R* v *Tait* [1989] 3 WLR 391 (threat to kill a foetus); *B* v *Islington HA* [1993] QB 204; *A-G's Reference (No. 3 of 1994)* [1994] Crim LR 766 (foetus is not a part of the mother: both are distinct organisms existing symbiotically). See BORN ALIVE.

foetus, and mother's right to refuse treatment. A mother is entitled not to be forced into medical treatment involving an invasion of her body against her will even though her own life or that of a foetus depends on it. That person's right is in no way diminished merely because a decision to exercise it might seem bizarre or morally repugnant: *St George's Health NHS Trust* v *S* [1998] 3 WLR 936.

following trust property. There is a right to follow trust property, recognised by common law and equity, where that property is in the hands of some person (e.g., as the result of a disposition of trust property in breach of trust) and is in an identifiable form. Under common law, property was considered identifiable only if not mixed with other property. See TRUST.

food. 'The word must be interpreted in its primary sense – namely as something taken into the system as nourishment, and not merely as a stimulant': *Hinde* v *Allmand* (1918) LJ KB 893. See Food Act 1984, Food Safety Act 1990, s 1, in which 'food' includes drink, articles and substances of no nutritional value used for human consumption, articles used as ingredients in the preparation of food and drink. For 'sale of food', see 1990 Act, s 2. See Food Standards Act 1999. *See* FOOD STANDARDS AGENCY.

food, offences in relation to. It is an offence to add any substance to food, to use any substance as an ingredient in the preparation of food, to abstract any constituent from food or to subject food to any treatment, so as to render the food injurious to health, with intent that it shall be sold for human consumption in that state: Food Safety Act 1990, s 7. It is an offence to sell, or advertise for sale, for human consumption, any food rendered injurious to health by means of an operation described in s 7(1): s 8. See Food Labelling Regulations 1996 (SI 96/1499);

Hackney LBC v *Cedar Trading Ltd* (1999) 163 JP 749; Food Standards Act 1999.

food, preparation of. Includes, for purposes of Food Safety Act 1990, manufacture and any form of treatment. 'Preparation for sale' includes packaging: s 53(1). See *Leeds CC* v *Dewhurst* [1990] Crim LR 725; Food Standards Act 1999. See FOOD STANDARDS AGENCY.

Food Standards Agency. Body of 8–12 members, created under Food Standards Act 1999, s 1(1), with objective of protecting public health from risks which may arise in connection with consumption of food (including its production and supply) and otherwise to protect the interests of consumers in relation to food: s 1(2). For power to carry out observations and powers of entry, see ss 10, 11. For monitoring of enforcement action, see s 12.

football matches, offences by spectators. These include, under Football (Offences) Act 1991, ss 1–4, throwing of missiles, racialist or indecent chanting (q.v.), going onto the playing area without lawful authority or excuse. See also Football Spectators Act 1989; Football (Offences and Disorder) Act 1999; Football (Disorder) Act 2000 (involving banning orders, surrender of passports, powers of arrest and detention: s 1). Football (Disorder) (Amendment) Act 2002, s 1, renews for five years banning orders under Football Spectators Act 1989, and summary procedure preventing persons from leaving the country while police seek banning orders, under Football (Disorder) Act 2000.

footpath. Way over which the public have a right of way not associated with a carriageway (q.v.): Horses (Protective Headgear etc.) Act 1990, s 3. See Highways Act 1980, s 66 (footpath provision); *R* v *Norfolk CC ex p Thorpe* [1998] COD 208; C.R.W.A. 2000, s 54.

forbearance. Refraining from enforcing, e.g., a debt. Generally, a forbearance to sue may be adequate consideration (q.v.). See *Alliance Bank* v *Broom* (1864) 2 D & S 289.

force. 1. Violence, generally of an unlawful nature. 2. 'The application of any energy to the obstacle with a view to removing it': *per* Donaldson LJ in *Swales* v *Cox* [1981] QB 849.

force majeure. A superior force. An event that can generally be neither anticipated nor controlled, e.g., an industrial strike which leads to loss of profits. See *André et Cie* v *Tradax* [1983] 1 Lloyd's Rep 254; *McNicholl* v *Ministry of Agriculture* [1988] ECR (circumstances must be abnormal and unforeseeable, so that the consequences could not have been avoided through the exercise of all due care).

force, reasonable. *See* REASONABLE FORCE.

forcible detainer. 1. Refusal to restore the goods of one who has tendered amends, the remedy for which was trover (q.v.). 2. The offence of detaining land by violence or threats, after having entered peacefully. See *R* v *Mountford* [1972] 2 QB 28. Generally abolished under C.L.A. 1977, s 13.

forcible entry. The crime (and tort) of entering land in a violent manner, in order to take possession thereof. It is immaterial whether those concerned had or had not a right to enter. Generally abolished under C.L.A. 1977, s 13. See C.J.P.O.A. 1994, s 61; P.&C.E.A. 1984, ss 17, 117 (right of police to enter a home using reasonable force); *O'Loughlin* v *Chief Constable of Essex* [1998] 1 WLR 374. *See* ENTRY, VIOLENCE FOR SECURING.

foreclosure. The judicial procedure whereby a mortgagee acquires the property freed from the mortgagor's equity of redemption (q.v.). The mortgagee's right to foreclose arises after the date for redemption has passed, or on the breach of a term in the mortgage, e.g., failure to pay interest. It is carried out by order of the court and all those interested in the equity of redemption must be made parties to the action. See L.P.A. 1925, ss 88, 89, 91; Lim.A. 1980, s 29; CPR, Sch 1; O 88, r 1. *See* MORTGAGE; POWER OF SALE.

foreign acts, valid, recognition of. In *Peer International Corporation* v *Termidor Music Publishers* (2003) *The Times*, 11 September, the CA held that the act of a foreign government affecting proprietary rights is recognised in English law, without exception, if it is valid in the country in which the property right is situated.

foreign agreement. An agreement of which the proper law (q.v.) is the law of a country outside the UK: C.C.A. 1974, s 145.

foreign appellant, right of support. In *R (Kimani)* v *Lambeth LBC* (2003) *The Times*, 6 August, the CA held that there was no right of recourse to public funds in the case of a foreigner who was entitled to remain in the UK pending the hearing of an appeal concerning a claim of right of residence, when there were no barriers to her returning to her home state.

foreign bill. *See* INLAND BILL.

foreign country. A country other than the UK, a dependent territory, the Republic of Ireland, or a country mentioned in Sch 3: B.N.A. 1981, s 50(1).

foreign currency. Any currency other than sterling, including special drawing rights and any other units of account defined by reference to more than one currency: Export and Investment Guarantees Act 1991, s 6(5).

foreign emoluments. 'The emoluments of a person not domiciled in the UK from an office or employment under or with any person, body of persons or partnership resident outside the UK': I.C.T.A. 1988, s 192(1).

foreign insolvencies, stay of. Domestic insolvency law has no application to foreign insolvency proceedings, so that it does not give the court any power to stay English proceedings against a company on the basis of its being subject to insolvency proceedings in Germany.

foreign judgments, enforcement of. In the case of contract, a foreign judgment is enforceable in an English court if the foreign court is competent, judgment is for a definite sum and is final and conclusive.

'In actions *in personam* there are five cases in which the courts of this country will enforce a foreign judgment: (1) where defendant is a subject of the foreign country in which judgment has been obtained; (2) where he was resident in the foreign country when the action began; (3) where plaintiff has selected the forum in which he afterwards sues; (4) where defendant has voluntarily appeared; (5) where defendant has contracted to submit himself to the forum in which judgment was obtained': *Emanuel* v *Syman* [1908] 1 KB 302. See Foreign Judgments (Reciprocal Enforcement) Act 1933; European Communities (Enforcement of Community Judgments) Order 1972; Civil Jurisdiction and Judgments Acts 1982, 1991; CPR, Sch 1; O 71; CPR, Sch 2; CCR, O 35.

foreign law. All law except English law. Thus, the law of Scotland, of the Republic of Ireland, comes under the heading of 'foreign law'. What the rule of the particular foreign law which applies in a case states, will be determined by the judge after considering, where appropriate, the evidence of expert witnesses. See Civil Evidence Act 1972, s 4(1); r 33.7; Private International Law (Misc. Provs.) Act 1995, Part III (choice of the 'applicable law' in relation to issues of tort arising from events occurring abroad, in relation to the rules of private international law); S.C.A. 1981, s 69(5). For 'anti-suit injunction', restraining a person from pursuing proceedings in a foreign jurisdiction, see *SNI Aerospatiale* v *Lee Kui Jak* [1987] 3 All ER 510; *Airbus Industrie GIE* v *Patel* (1998) 148 NLJ 551. For refusal of English court to recognise foreign legislation which is clearly in breach of established international law, see *Kuwait Airways* v *Iraqi Airways (No. 4)* (2000) *The Times*, 21 November.

foreign law, execution of. The courts of no country execute the penal laws of another: *Huntington* v *Attrill* [1893] AC 150. For foreign revenue laws, see *Government of India* v *Taylor* [1955] AC 491; for other public laws, see *A-G of New Zealand* v *Ortiz* [1984] AC 1.

foreign law, proof of. The burden rests on the party who is basing his claim or defence on it: *Guaranty Trust Corp* v *Hannay* [1918] 2 KB 623. For judicial notice (q.v.) see *Saxby* v *Fulton* [1909] 2 KB 208.

foreign process, service of. Service on a person in England and Wales of any process in connection with civil or commercial proceedings in a foreign court or tribunal where the Senior Master receives a written request for service from the Secretary of State for Foreign and Commonwealth Affairs, or from a consular authority where the foreign court or tribunal is in a foreign country in relation to which there subsists a civil procedure convention providing for service in that country of process of the High Court: CPR, Sch 1; O 69, rr 1, 2.

foreign student's entitlement to work. In *R (Zhan)* v *Secretary of State for Home Department* (2003) *The Times*, 7 February, the CA held that a foreign national who had leave, as a student, to enter UK, could undertake part-time employment in accordance with the Immigration Rules without having to obtain permission.

foreign terrorists suspects. In *A and Others* v *Secretary of State for Home Department* [2002] EWCA Civ 1502, the CA held that the power of the Home Secretary to detain, without any charge, non-nationals suspected of terrorism who cannot be deported because of fear for their safety, was not incompatible with the UK's obligations in relation to human rights, and was objectively justifiable during a period of public emergency.

foreman of jury. Member of a jury (q.v.) who is chosen to chair its deliberations and announce its verdict. See *R* v *Williams* (1987) 84 Cr App R 274 (dissent between foreman and jurors).

forensic. 1. Relating to legal matters. Forensic medicine (known also as 'medical jurisprudence') deals with medical facts used in the interpretation of legal problems. For duties of forensic scientists, see *R* v *Ward* [1993] 1 WLR 619. 2. Rhetorical.

foreseeability test, applicability of in race discrimination. In *Essa* v *Laing Ltd* [2004] EWCA Civ 02, the CA held that, where compensation to a victim of race discrimination was assessed, it was appropriate to show the existence of a causal link between the act of unlawful discrimination and the injury; it was not necessary to show that such injury was reasonably foreseeable in the circumstances.

foreshore. Includes 'the shore and bed of the sea and of every channel, creek, bay, estuary and navigable river as far up it as the tide flows': Salmon and Freshwater Fisheries Act 1975, s 41(1). See *Baxendale* v *Instow PC* [1982] Ch 14. *See* BEACH.

foresight. Looking forward to some event. In determining whether a person has committed an offence, the court is not bound to infer that he intended or foresaw a result of his actions by reason only of it being a natural and probable consequence of those actions, but shall decide whether he did intend or foresee that result by reference to all the evidence, drawing such inferences from the evidence as appear proper in the circumstances: C.J.A. 1967, s 8. *See* NEGLIGENCE, FORESEEABILITY AND.

forestry. Includes the felling of trees and the extraction and primary conversion of trees within the wood or forest in which they were grown, and the use of land or woodlands ancillary to the use of land for other agricultural purposes: H.S.W.A. 1974, s 53(1). 'The growing of a utilisable crop of timber': T.C.P.A. 1990, Sch 5. See also, e.g., Forestry Acts 1979, 1986; T.C.P.A. 1971, s 30A (added by T.C.P. (Minerals) A. 1981, s 5).

forfeiture. 1. A punishment whereby the offender lost all his interests in his property. Thus, the goods and chattels of a felon were, prior to Forfeiture Act 1870, s 1, forfeited to the Crown. 2. P.C.C.(S.)A. 2000, s 143, empowers the court to deprive an offender of property used, or intended to be used, for purposes of crime. See also Misuse of Drugs Act 1971, s 27; Drug Trafficking Act 1994, s 43; CPR, Sch 1; O 115; Terrorism Act 2000, ss 28–30. 3. In a lease (q.v.) a forfeiture clause reserves to the lessor a right of re-entry, upon which the lease is forfeited. See L.P.A. 1925, s 146; Protection from Eviction Act 1977, s 2; H.A. 1996, s 81(1); *Fuller* v *Judy Properties* (1992) 1 EGLR 75 (object of relief against forfeiture is continuation of lease); *Billson* v *Residential Apartments Ltd* (1992) 2 WLR 15; *Ivory Gate Ltd* v *Spetale* [1998] 2 EGLR 43; *On Demand Information plc* v *Gerson plc* (2000) 150 NLJ 1300 (relief extended to forfeiture of a finance lease). *See* DRUG TRAFFICKING.

forfeiture of benefit under will. 'A man shall not slay his benefactor and thereby take the bounty.' See *Re Crippen* [1911] P 108; *Re Hall* [1914] P 1. See Forfeiture Act 1982, giving the court a discretion to modify the rule in respect of certain forfeited property rights in given circumstances in respect of one who has unlawfully killed another. Murderers are excluded from the operation of the Act: s 5. See *Re K* [1986] Ch 180; *Re H* (1990) 1 FLR 441; *Dunbar* v *Plant* [1998] Ch 412 (relief from forfeiture for survivor of suicide pact). *See* KILLING, ACQUISITION OF PROPERTY BY.

forfeiture of shares. Shares may be forfeited (i.e., taken away from company members) by resolution of the board of directors if such a power is given in the articles of association (q.v.). The object of forfeiture must be for the company's benefit. Shares may be forfeited, e.g., where a member fails to pay a call properly made on him. See *Re Esparto Trading Co* (1879) 12 Ch D 191. *See* COMPANY; SHARE.

forgery. 'A person is guilty of forgery if he makes a false instrument, with the intention that he or another shall use it to induce somebody to accept it as genuine, and by reason of so accepting it to do or not to do some act to his own or any other person's prejudice': Forgery and Counterfeiting Act 1981, s 1. See Road Traffic Act 1988, s 173; *R* v *Ondhia* [1998] 2 Cr App R 250; *R* v *Winston* (1998) 162 JP 775. *See* COUNTERFEIT; INSTRUMENT, FALSE.

forgetfulness, excuse of. In *R v Jolle* [2003] EWCA Crim 1543, the CA held that in relation to an alleged offence of having a bladed article in a public place. (See Criminal Justice Act 1988, s 139(1)), forgetfulness would not constitute a sufficient excuse, but forgetfulness together with some other reason might provide a good reason.

forgiveness of victim. This makes no difference to the seriousness of an offence; the public, not merely the victim, must be considered: *R v Gainford* (1989) *The Times*, 31 January; *A-G's Reference (No. 75 of 1995)* [1997] 1 Cr App R (S) 198; *R v Mills* [1998] 2 Cr App R (S) 252; *R v Perks* (2000) *The Times*, 5 May. *See* VICTIM IMPACT STATEMENT.

formal contract. Term applied to a contract, e.g., for the sale of land, comprising particulars (describing property); special conditions (relating to sale in question); general conditions (standardised and incorporated into contract by reference to, e.g., 'national conditions of sale'). See LPA 1925, ss 52, 54(2); C.C.A. 1974, s 61; L.P. (Misc. Provs.) A. 1989, s 2. *See* CONTRACT.

forthwith. Immediately, or, more generally, when used in a statute, within a reasonable time. See *Hillingdon LBC v Cutler* [1968] Crim LR 109.

fortune telling. It is an offence to purport to 'exercise powers of telepathy, clairvoyance or other similar powers'. See Vagrancy Act 1824, s 4 (amended by Fraudulent Mediums Act 1951, s 2(*b*)); *R v Martin* [1981] Crim LR 109 ('other similar powers' refers to the ability to see what is beyond normal human ability).

forum. 1. A judicial assembly. 2. Country in which jurisdiction is exercised. If, e.g., X is sued in England on a contract made in Italy, England is the forum, and the *lex fori* (q.v.) is the law of England.

forum non conveniens. An unsuitable court. Doctrine whereby the court refuses to exercise its right of jurisdiction because, for the convenience of parties and in the interests of justice, a claim should be brought elsewhere. The phrase means, not that the English court is 'not conveni-ent', but that some other court is more suitable: *Spiliada Maritime Corporation v Cansulex Ltd* [1987] AC 460. See *Lubbe v Cape plc* [2000] 1 WLR 1545; *Berezovsky v Forbes Inc* (2000) 150 NLJ 741.

forum rei. The court of the country in which the subject matter of a claim is situated.

foster-child. *See* PRIVATELY FOSTERED CHILDREN.

founders' shares. *See* DEFERRED SHARES.

four unities, the. *See* JOINT TENANCY.

franchise. 1. The right of voting in a parliamentary or local election. Among those who may not vote at a parliamentary election are: aliens, persons under 18 at the date of the poll, convicts, persons suffering from mental illness, life peers, excepted peers (see House of Lords Act 1999, s 3), and persons found guilty of electoral offences. 2. A privilege belonging to the Crown, or by virtue of a grant, expressed or implied, to a subject. Example: the right to hold markets. Known also as a 'liberty'. See Wild Creatures and Forest Laws Act 1971, s 1; *Iveagh v Martin* [1961] 1 QB 232. 3. Licence to a trader or distributing agency allowing them to sell a specific product or service for an agreed period. See *Paperlight Ltd v Swinton Group* [1998] CLC 1667.

fraud at common law. Intentional deceit. A false representation by the defendant of an existing fact, made knowingly, or without belief in its truth, or recklessly, careless whether it be true or false, with the intention that the claimant should act on it, and which results in damage to the claimant. See *Redgrave v Hurd* (1881) 20 Ch D 1; *Midland Bank Trust v Green* [1981] AC 513 (discussion of fraud 'unravelling everything'); *Murria v Lord Chancellor* (2000) *The Times*, 11 January (*per* Buckley J: 'There is no general offence of fraud in law, and there can be no substantive charge of "fraud"').

fraud, concealed. *See* CONCEALED FRAUD.

fraud, constructive. *See* CONSTRUCTIVE FRAUD.

fraud in equity. *See* EQUITABLE FRAUD.

fraud, lack of entitlement in. It is not necessary for the prosecution, on a charge under Theft Act 1968, s 17(1)(b) or Forgery and Counterfeiting Act 1981, s 3, where accused has used a false instrument to obtain money, to prove that he was not legally entitled to that money: *A G's Reference (No. 1 of 2001)* (2002) *The Times*, 7 August.

fraud on a power. 'The term . . . merely means that the power has been exercised for a purpose, or with an intention, beyond the scope of or not justified by the instrument creating the power': *Vatcher* v *Paull* [1915] AC 372. Example: an appointment made for a corrupt purpose (see *Lord Hinchinbroke* v *Seymour* (1789) 1 Bro CC 385). *See* APPOINTMENT, POWER OF.

fraud on minority. *See* MINORITY SHAREHOLDERS, OPPRESSION OF.

fraud, serious. *See* SERIOUS FRAUD OFFICE.

frauds, relating to theft. Under Th.A. 1968, amended by Th.(Am.)A. 1996 the following offences relating to fraud exist: obtaining property by deception, s 15; obtaining a money transfer by deception, s 15A; obtaining a pecuniary advantage by deception, s 16; false accounting, s 17; false statements by company directors, s 19; dishonest suppression of documents, s 20(1); dishonest procuring by deception of the execution of a valuable security, s 20(2); dishonestly retaining a wrongful credit, s 24A. Each is an arrestable offence (q.v.). See also under Th.A. 1978: obtaining services by deception, s 1 (amended by Th.(Am.)A. 1996, s 4); evading liability by deception, s 2. See *R* v *Hawkins* [1997] 1 Cr App R 234; *R* v *Cooke* [1997] Crim LR 436.

fraudulent conversion. *See* CONVERSION.

fraudulent conveyance. A voluntary disposition of land made with intent to defraud a subsequent purchaser is voidable at the instance of the purchaser: L.P.A. 1925, s 173. See Ins.A. 1986, s 357, for offences relating to the fraudulent disposal of property (replacing the (repealed) L.P.A. 1925, s 172).

fraudulent mediums. *See* WITCHCRAFT.

fraudulent misrepresentation. *See* MISREPRESENTATION, FRAUDULENT.

fraudulent preference. A conveyance or transfer of a debtor's property intended to give a creditor or surety any preference over other creditors and made by a person insolvent at the time.

fraudulent trading. Trading by a company (q.v.) with intent to defraud creditors or other persons. See Cos.A. 1985, s 458; Company Directors Disqualification Act 1986; Ins.A. 1986, s 213. See also *R* v *Thobani* [1998] 1 Cr App R (S) 227; *R* v *Bevis* (2001), *The Times*, 8 February.

freedom of establishment under EU principles. In *EC Commission* v *UK (Case C-466/98)* (2002) *The Times*, 8 November, EC Court of Justice held that a provision in a services agreement between UK and USA, allowing USA to restrict air traffic rights to airlines owned or controlled by UK or its nationals, and excluding other airlines in EU, violated UK obligations under EC Treaty, art 52 (now art 43).

freedom of expression and human rights. CA held in *R (on the application of Farrakhan)* v *Secretary of State for Home Department* (2002) 152 NLJ 708, that 'where a state refuses entry to an alien solely to prevent his expression of opinions within its territory, art 10 of Human Rights Convention ('freedom of expression') is engaged. In a case of this nature, art 10.2 (restriction of this freedom in interests of national security, etc.) would apply in determining whether interference with alien's freedom of expression was justified.

freedom of information. Freedom of Information Act 2000 will not come fully into force until 2005: statement of Lord Chancellor on 13 November 2001. Police, police authorities, Armed Forces, will be affected as from June 2003.

freehold. An estate of an uncertain length of duration. The fee simple absolute in possession (q.v.) is the sole surviving legal freehold estate. Originally an estate held by a 'free man'. *See* ESTATE.

freeing order. *See* ADOPTION, FREEING CHILD FOR.

free movement. Phrase used in Treaty of Rome 1957, which set up EEC (q.v.), referring to the movement of persons, services and capital within it, which is to be without limitations. See *R v Saunders* [1979] 2 All ER 267.

free trade rules. It was held by the Court of Justice of EC in *Commission of EC v Italian Republic* (Case C-14/100) (2003) *The Times*, 21 January, that a law in a member state requiring that chocolate products containing vegetable fats other than cocoa butter, could be sold in that member state only as 'chocolate substitute', constituted an infringement of EC rules relating to free trade.

freezing order. Order restraining a party from removing from the jurisdiction assets located there, or restraining a party from dealing with any assets whether located in the jurisdiction or not: CPR, r 25.1(1)(f). Known formerly as 'Mareva injunction' (q.v.). Application must be supported by affidavit evidence: PD 25, para 3.1; PD 32, para 1.4(2). Generally applied for without notice to respondents. Under r 25.1(1)(g), court may direct a party to provide information concerning location of relevant property or assets. See *Federal Bank of Middle East v Hadkinson* (2000) 150 NLJ 393 (trust assets not caught by freezing order). In *Flightwise Travel Services v Gill* (2003) *The Times*, 5 December, it was stated by the CA that the normal practice of the court was to require a sworn statement in support of an application for a freezing order and to ensure that the freezing order was framed in a manner which would result in a minimum of interference with respondent's rights. See also *Customs & Excise v Barclays Bank* [2004] EWCA 122 (Comm).

freezing order and terrorism. Under Anti-terrorism, Crime and Security Act 2001, ss 4, 5, Treasury may make order prohibiting persons from making funds available to or for benefit of persons specified in the order. Treasury must believe reasonably: that an action to detriment to economy of UK has been or is likely to be taken or that an action constituting a threat to life or property of UK residents is likely to be taken; and that one of the persons acting in this way is a government or resident of a country outside UK.

freight. A consideration paid to a carrier for the carriage of goods. *Lump sum freight* is paid by the charterer as a sum for the use of a ship for one service. *Pro rata freight* is the amount recoverable by a carrier when the owner of goods agrees to take delivery at a port short of the agreed destination, or when the carrier delivers only part of the cargo. *Advance freight* is payable before delivery of goods.

frequenting. Term used in relation to a suspected person to suggest that he has visited a place repeatedly. It involves the notion of physical presence which is to some degree continuous: *Nakhla v The Queen* [1976] AC 1. *See* SUSPICION.

friendly society. A society registered by Chief Registrar of Friendly Societies under Friendly Societies Acts 1974–92, being a society which, as part of its ordinary business, provides benefits during sickness or other infirmity, or in old age, or in widowhood, or for orphans: S.S.A. 1975, Sch 20. See F.S.A. 1986, ss 23, 140–141; Finance Act 1987 s 30; Policyholders Protection Act 1997, Sch 4; *Re Wimbledon Democratic Club Society* (1999) *The Times*, 7 January. For criteria of prudent management, see 1992 Act, s 50; for accounts and audit, see Part VI. See F.S.M.A. 2000, ss 334, 335, for power of Treasury to order transfer of functions of Chief Registrar to FSA (q.v.); see also Sch 18, paras 1, 2.

fringe benefits. Benefits granted by an employer to an employee which do not enter into his basic wage. See Finance Act 1976, ss 60–72.

frivolous action. *See* VEXATIOUS PROCEEDING.

fructus industriales. That which is the produce of 'labour and industry'. Example: corn, as compared with *fructus naturales* (crops which grow naturally).

See S.G.A. 1979, s 61; *Marshall* v *Green* (1875) 1 CPD 35. *See* EMBLEMENTS.

frustration of contract. Where there is an extraneous event or change of circumstances so fundamental as to strike at the root of a contract as a whole and beyond what was contemplated by the parties, that contract is considered to be automatically frustrated: see *The Super Servant Two* [1990] 1 Lloyd's Rep 1. Under Law Reform (Frustrated Contracts) Act 1943, all sums payable under a frustrated contract are recoverable and sums payable cease to be payable. The Act does not apply, e.g., to a contract containing a provision to meet a case of frustration, to a contract of insurance or carriage of goods by sea, or to a contract not governed by English law. See *Fibrosa Case* [1943] AC 32; *The Super Servant Two* [1990] 1 Lloyd's Rep 1. For frustration of a lease, see *National Carriers* v *Panalpina* [1981] AC 675. See also S.G.A. 1979, s 7. *See* CONTRACT.

frustration, self-induced. Frustration of a contract due to one's own conduct or to the conduct of those for whom one is responsible: *Bank Line Ltd* v *Arthur Capel & Co* [1919] AC 435. See *The Eugenia* [1964] 2 QB 226; *The Adelfa* [1988] 2 Lloyd's Rep 466.

FSA. Financial Services Authority. Set up under F.S.M.A. 2000, s 1, charged with meeting the general regulatory objectives of market confidence, public awareness, consumer protection, reduction of financial crime in financial system. See Sch 1.

fugitive criminal. Any person accused or convicted of an extradition crime committed within the jurisdiction of any foreign state who is in or is suspected of being in some part of HM dominions. 'Fugitive criminal of a foreign state' means a fugitive criminal accused or convicted of an extradition crime committed within the jurisdiction of that state: Extradition Act 1989, Sch 1, para 20. See *R* v *Sec of State for the Home Department ex p McQuire* (1998) 10 Admin LR 534. *See* EXTRADITION.

full age. Age of majority: 18 since F.L.R.A. 1969, s 1. *See* INFANT.

functus officio. Having performed one's office. Refers to one who has exercised his authority and brought it to an end in a particular case. Thus, a judge who has convicted a person charged with an offence is *functus officio*. See *Re VGM Holdings* [1941] 3 All ER 417; *R* v *Dwight* [1990] 1 NZLR 160.

fund-raising business. 'Any business carried on for gain and wholly or primarily engaged in soliciting or otherwise procuring money or other property for charitable, benevolent or philanthropic purposes': Charities Act 1992, s 58(1). For prohibitions on professional fund-raising, see s 59. See Terrorism Act 2000, s 15.

funeral expenses. Reasonable expenses involved in burying a deceased person must be paid out of his estate prior to any other duty or debt: *R* v *Wade* (1818) 5 Pr 621.

fungibles. Movable goods which are substantially identical with others of the same nature and which are ordinarily dealt with by number, measurement or weight, e.g., grain. 'Fungible assets' are assets of a company 'substantially indistinguishable one from another': see Cos.A. 1985, Sch 4, para 31.

fur farming. It is an offence to keep animals solely or primarily for slaughter for the value of their fur or for breeding progeny for such slaughter: Fur Farming (Prohibition) Act 2000, s 1(1).

furniture. 'For articles to be furniture . . . I do not think it is essential that they shall be movable, and though, of course, articles of furniture are commonly movable, I do not think they pass out of the popular meaning of furniture because they are fixed by a nail or a screw to a wall or floor': *per* Stamp J in *F Austin Ltd* v *Commissioners of Customs & Excise* [1968] 2 All ER 13.

furniture and plenishings. Any article situated in a family home of civil partners which (a) is owned or hired by either civil partner or is being acquired by either civil partner under a hire-purchase agreement or conditional sale agreement, and (b) is reasonably necessary to enable the home to be used as a family residence, but does not include any vehicle, caravan or houseboat or such other structure as is mentioned in the definition of 'family home': Civil Partnership Act 2004 s 135. *See* HOME.

further information, obtaining. The court may at any time order a party to clarify any matter which is in dispute in proceedings, or give additional information in relation to any such matter, whether or not the matter is contained or referred to in a statement of case (q.v.): CPR, r 18.1(1). Where order is made, party against whom it is made must file his response and serve it on the other parties within the time specified by the court, and such a response needs to be verified by a statement of truth (q.v.): r 18(3). See PD 18.

future goods. *See* GOODS.

future indebtedness. Financial obligations likely to arise at some future date. See *Banner Lane Realisations Ltd* v *Berisford plc* [1971] 1 CL 111 ('future indebtedness' could refer to cases where there was an obligation to pay an un-liquidated sum in the future, or on the emergence of some contingency).

future interest. An interest limited so that it confers a right to the enjoyment of property at some time in the future. Example: grant 'to A for his life and then to the first of his sons who shall attain the age of 21' – in the case of the first of A's sons, the interest takes effect in the future.

future lease. An existing lease carrying the right to possession at a specified time in the future. *See* LEASE.

futures. 'Rights under a contract for the sale of a commodity or property of any other description under which delivery is to be made at a future date and at a price agreed upon when the contract is made': F.S.A. 1986, Sch 1, para 8.

future trespass, power to ban. CA held in *Secretary of State for Environment etc* v *Drury* (2004) *The Times*, 15 March, that where a landowner who was seeking a possession order against trespassers could establish that, if they were evicted, they would then move to another part of his property, this other part of the land could be included as a term of the order. *See* TRESPASS.

G

gage. A pledge. Something given as security for some act. In the twelfth century the *vivum vadium* (living pledge) allowed a mortgagee to take possession of land rents and profits in discharge of principal and interest. The *mortuum vadium* (dead pledge) allowed him to take rents and profits in discharge of the interest only.

gain. 'The most appropriate definition to be found in a dictionary may be "increase in resources or business advantages resulting from business transactions or dealings"': *Re Riverton Sheep Dip* (1943) SASR 344.

game. Animals *ferae naturae*, hunted for sport or food, including hares, pheasants, partridges, grouse, heath or moor game, woodcock, etc. See Game Laws (Amendment) Act 1960, by which a constable may arrest a person trespassing in pursuit of game. See also Wild Creatures and Forest Laws Act 1971, under which prerogative rights of the Crown to wild creatures (except royal fish and swans) are abolished. *See* ANIMAL; POACHING.

gaming. Known also as 'gambling'. 'The playing of a game of chance for winnings in money or money's worth, whether any person playing the game is at risk of losing any money or money's worth or not': Gaming Act 1968, s 52. The 1968 Act prohibited gaming in public bars and wherever a charge is made. It also prohibits gaming involving playing or staking against a bank or where the chances are unequal. Commercial gaming may be permitted under licence. See Betting, Gaming and Lotteries Act 1963; Lotteries and Amusements Act 1976; Gaming (Amendment) Acts 1982, 1987, 1990; Bingo Act 1992; National Lottery Acts 1993, 1998; F.S.M.A. 2000, s 412. (For a definition of 'gaming machine', see Betting and Gaming Duties Act 1981, s 25, as amended by Finance Act 1982, Sch 6, Part V.) See *R* v *Burt & Adams Ltd* [1988] 2 WLR 725. *See* LOTTERY; SWEEPSTAKE.

gaming contracts. Contracts which are wagers upon a game, e.g., a horse race. They involve 'the playing of a game of chance for winnings in money or money's worth': Betting, Gaming and Lotteries Act 1963, as amended by Gaming Act 1968. Generally null and void; no claim can be brought to recover money relating to a wager. Securities given for gaming contracts are, in effect, given for an illegal consideration (q.v.) and are void as between the parties. See Gaming Act 1968; F.S.A. 1986, s 63; *CHT* v *Ward* [1963] 3 All ER 835; *Crockfords* v *Mehta* [1992] 1 WLR 355 (licensed gaming club suing on cheques).

gangmasters, licensing of. Under Gangmasters (Licensing) Act 2004, s 1, the Gangmasters Licensing Authority is responsible for carrying out inspections, reviewing activities of gangmasters, relating to agricultural work, gathering shellfish, and associated processing for activities.

garden leave. Period following an employee's notice to determine his contract, during which, under agreement with his employer, he is not required to work at his place of employment, but continues to receive all contractual benefits, including salary. See *Symbian Ltd* v *Christensen* [2000] UK CLR 879.

garnishee. One who has been warned by a court order that a debt is to be paid to some person who has obtained a garnishee order against his creditor, and not to that creditor. See *Llewellyn* v *Carrickford* [1970] 1 WLR 1124; *Crantrave Ltd* v *Lloyd's Bank plc* (2000) *The Times*, 24 April.

garnishee order. In *Société Eram Shipping* v *Compagnie Internationale de Navigation* [2003] UKHL 30, the HL held that an English court cannot issue a granishee order absolute involving a debt based in a foreign jurisdiction, which is governed by local law which would not discharge the garnishee from liability to the judgment debt, or by complying with the order.

garnishee proceedings. Proceedings enabling a judgment creditor (q.v.) to have assigned to him the benefit of any debt owed by the garnishee (q.v.) to the judgment debtor (q.v.). Example: A owes B £1,000 and C owes A £1,000. B may commence proceedings to obtain a garnishee order so that C will pay the £1,000 directly to B. Where proceedings fail, the courts have a wide discretion as to costs and may order the judgment debtor to pay them: *Wright & Son* v *Westoby* [1972] 3 All ER 1078. See A.J.A. 1985, s 52; CPR, Sch 1; O 49; CPR, Sch 2; CCR, O 30. See *Man* v *Miyazaki Commercial Agricola* [1991] 1 Lloyd's Rep 154. *See* JUDGMENTS, ENFORCEMENT OF.

Gas and Electricity Markets Authority. Established under Utilities Act 2000, s 1, by merger of gas and electricity regulators. For financing of the Authority, see Sch 1.

gazump. Colloquial term used to refer to a situation in which the vendor of a house 'subject to contract' (q.v.) withdraws from the bargain, or threatens to do so, in the expectation of receiving a higher price.

gbh. Grievous bodily harm (q.v.).

GCHQ. Government Communications Head-quarters. Organisation set up to monitor and interfere with electromagnetic, acoustic and other emissions and relevant equipment, and to provide assistance about languages and cryptography (q.v.) to the government and the armed forces: Intelligence Services Act 1994, s 3. *See* INTELLIGENCE SERVICE.

gender bias. In *Hookenjos* v *Secretary of State for Social Security (No. 2)* (2005) *The Times*, 4 January, the CA held that the operation of the jobseekers allowance and entitlement to responsibility supplement constituted indirect discrimination on grounds of sex against a parent separated from mother, but who participated in the care of his children.

gender reassignment. Procedures undergone under medical supervision, with the intention of seeking to reassign a person's sex by changing physiological or other characteristics of his/her sex. Generally involves hormonal treatment and surgery (including archidectomy and genitoplasty). English law does not recognise the concept of sex change: *Sheffield* v *UK* [1998] 2 FLR 928. See Sex Discrimination (Gender Reassignment) Regulations 1999, SI 99/1102; *R* v *NW Lancs HA ex p A* [1999] Lloyd's Rep Med 399 (Health Authority's policy of refusing to fund gender reassignment was unlawful); *W* v *W* (2000) *The Times*, 31 October (factors determining sex of individual on marriage). *See* SEX, CHANGE OF.

gender recognition certificate. Under Gender Recognition Act 2004, s 1(1), a person of either gender who is at least 18 may make an application for a gender recognition certificate on the basis of living in the other gender, or having changed gender under the law of a country or territory outside the UK. Recognition will be granted by a Panel (see s 2(1)) if satisfied that the applicant has or has had gender dysphoria, has lived in the acquired gender for two years ending with the date of application, intends to continue to live in the acquired gender until death.

general and special damages. For purpose of procedure, damages may be divided thus: 1. *General damages*, such as will be presumed to have resulted from the defendant's acts. They may include, e.g., damages for pain, inconvenience and generally need not be specifically pleaded. 2. *Special damages*, such as will not be presumed, e.g., loss of earnings, medical expenses. These must be stated specifically and proved. *See* DAMAGES.

general average. *See* AVERAGE.

General Council of the Bar. *See* BAR COUNCIL.

general devise. *See* DEVISE.

general equitable charge. *See* EQUITABLE CHARGE, GENERAL.

general legacy. A bequest which does not identify specifically the thing bequeathed. Example: 'a horse to X and a gold watch to Y'. The subject matter of a general legacy need not form part of the testator's assets at the time of his death: *Bothamley* v *Sherson* (1875) LR 20 Eq 304. *See* LEGACY.

general lien. A right to retain possession of another's goods until all claims against that other are satisfied. It exists, e.g., in relation to bankers and solicitors. See *Halesowen Presswork & Assemblies Ltd* v *Westminster Bank Ltd* [1971] 1 QB 1. *See* LIEN.

General Medical Council. Body set up to replace General Council of Medical Education and Registration of the UK. Its Disciplinary Committee has power to strike off practitioners from the Council's register. See *GMC* v *BBC* (1998) 148 NLJ 942; *R* v *GMC ex p Toth* (2000) *The Times*, 29 June (complaints to GMC should be heard in public in absence of special reasons to contrary). *See* STRIKING OFF.

general power. *See* APPOINTMENT, POWER OF.

General Social Care Council. Body corporate set up under Care Standards Act 2000 to promote high standards of conduct and practice among social care workers and high standards in their training: s 54(1), (2).

General Teaching Council. Body set up under Teaching and Higher Education Act 1998, s 1, to contribute to improvement of teaching standards and maintenance and improvement of standards of professional conduct, in interests of public: see Sch 1. It will establish and maintain a register of teachers: s 3. For dismissal of teachers, see s 15. For requirement of teachers to serve induction

period of not less than three school terms, see s 19. See SI 00/1447.

general verdict. A finding on the point in issue; e.g., a verdict of guilty, or one of not guilty. *See* SPECIAL VERDICT.

general warrant. Warrant in which neither the persons nor the premises to be searched were named. Declared illegal in *Wilkes* v *Wood* (1765) 19 St Tr 1153. 'By the law of England every invasion of private property be it ever so minute is a trespass. No man can set foot on my ground without my licence ... he is bound to show by way of justification that some positive law has empowered or excused him': *Entick* v *Carrington* (1675) 19 St Tr 1030. See *Elias* v *Pasmore* [1934] 2 KB 164. *See* WARRANT.

general words. Words which were necessary in a conveyance (q.v.) to transfer rights and easements (q.v.). Under L.P.A. 1925, s 62, such words are implied, if no contrary intention is expressed.

genetically modified organisms. *See* ORGANISMS, GENETICALLY MODIFIED.

genetic fingerprinting. *See* DNA PROFILING.

genocide. The offence committed by one who, with intent to destroy a national, ethnic, racial or religious group, kills or causes serious bodily or mental harm to members of the group, inflicts on the group conditions of life intended to physically destroy it, or forcibly transfers children of that group to another group. See Gevena Convention on Genocide, December 1948; Genocide Act 1969; Extradition Act 1989, s 23; *Prosecutor* v *Karadzic* (1996) 1 BHRC 1 (see Statute of the International Tribunal, Art 4); *Prosecutor* v *Akayesu* (1998) International Tribunal on Rwanda (case ICTR-96-4-T) (first occasion on which an international tribunal found an individual guilty of genocide); *Hipperson* v *DPP* [1996] 1 CLY 571.

gentlemen's agreement. Colloquial term used to describe an agreement resting on the honour of the parties. It is not usually enforceable at law.

gestation. The time between conception and birth (around 267 days for humans).

See *Preston-Jones* v *Preston-Jones* [1951] AC 391. *See* FOETUS.

gift. A gratuitous transfer of the ownership of property: Blackstone. 'A transaction in which the donor by parting with his property accepts some disadvantage or sacrifice': *per* Lord Scarman in *National Westminster Bank* v *Morgan* [1985] AC 486. See *Esso* v *Customs & Excise* [1976] 1 All ER 117.

gift, imperfect. A gift which has not been completely constituted. An apparently imperfect transfer may be effective: if the conditions for *donatio mortis causa* (q.v.) are satisfied; under the rule in *Strong* v *Bird* (1874) LR 18 Eq 315; by statute, e.g., L.P.A. 1925, ss 1, 19 and S.L.A. 1925, ss 4, 9, 27; under the doctrine of equitable estoppel (q.v.). See *Choithram International* v *Pagarani* (2000) *The Times*, 30 November.

gift inter vivos. A gratuitous grant or transfer of property between living persons. Validity of the gift necessitates the intention to give and appropriate acts to make the intention effective. See, e.g., *Dewar* v *Dewar* [1975] 2 All ER 728.

gift over. A gift which comes into existence when a particular preceding estate (q.v.) is determined.

Gillick child, competence of. Concept enunciated by the House of Lords in *Gillick* v *W Norfolk HA* [1986] AC 112: a child under 16 had the legal capacity to consent to medical examination and treatment if she had sufficient maturity and intelligence to understand the nature and implications of the treatment; parents' right to determine such matters ended when child achieved sufficient intelligence and understanding to make its own decision. 'It is not enough that she should understand the nature of the advice which is being given: she must also have sufficient maturity to understand what is involved': *per* Lord Scarman. See F.L.R.A. 1969, s 8; Ch.A. 1989, s 10(8); *Re R* [1991] 3 WLR 592; *Re L (Medical Treatment: Gillick Competence)* [1998] 2 FLR 810.

gilt-edged securities. Generally stock exchange securities carrying a minimum of risk regarding regular payment of interest on due date and redemption of stock (unless undated) at the stated time. For a list, see T.C.G.A. 1992, Sch 9, Part II. See Finance (No. 2) Act 1997, s 37, amended by Finance Act 1998, Sch 27. *See* SECURITIES.

glue sniffing. *See* SOLVENT ABUSE.

going concern. A business which is in continuous, uninterrupted operation. See *Gordon* v *IRC* [1991] BTC 130.

going equipped for stealing. 'A person is guilty of an offence if, when not at his place of abode, he has with him any article for use in the course of or in connection with any burglary, theft or cheat': Th.A. 1968, s 25(1). See *R* v *Doukas* [1978] 1 WLR 372; *A-G's Ref (No. 1 of 1985)* [1986] QB 491; *R* v *Ferry* [1997] 2 Cr App R (S) 42.

golden handshake. Phrase referring to payment (usually of considerable value) made *ex gratia* (q.v.) or as compensation for loss of office. See Finance Act 1986, s 45; I.C.T.A. 1988, s 148, substituted by Finance Act 1998, s 58; *Sybron Corporation* v *Rochem Ltd* [1983] 2 All ER 707; *Shilton* v *Wilms-hurst* [1990] STC 55.

golden rule of statutory interpretation. Rule for construing a statute: *Mattison* v *Hart* (1854) 14 CB 385. 'The grammatical and ordinary sense of the words is to be adhered to unless that would lead to an absurdity or some repugnancy or inconsistency with the rest of the instrument, in which case the grammatical and ordinary sense of the words may be modified so as to avoid such absurdity, repugnancy or inconsistency, but no further': *Grey* v *Pearson* (1857) 6 HLC 61. See *River Wear Commissioners* v *Adamson* [1877] 2 AC 743; *Federal Steam Navigation Co* v *Department of Trade and Industry* [1974] 2 All ER 97. *See* INTERPRETATION OF STATUTES.

good behaviour. A person may be ordered by a magistrate to keep the peace, or to be of good behaviour and may also be ordered to enter into recognizances (q.v.). If he fails to be of good behaviour for that period the recognizances may be estreated and he becomes liable to be sentenced for the original offence. See M.C.A. 1980, ss 115, 116; SI 96/674.

good character, defendant's. The Privy Council held in *Sealy* v *The State* [2002] UKPC 52 that, in cases of an exceptional nature, defence counsel's failure to raise the issue of defendant's good character may result in an unsafe conviction and a miscarriage of justice.

good consideration. Consideration founded on generosity, natural affection or normal duty. It is not regarded as 'valuable consideration' (e.g., money, money's worth) so that, e.g., a settlement merely supported by good consideration is regarded as 'voluntary'. Because equity will not assist a volunteer, should A promise B that he will create a trust and should he fail to do so, B cannot compel performance if he has not given valuable consideration. See *Midland Bank Trust Co* v *Green* [1981] AC 513. *See* CONSIDERATION.

good faith. 'The words, in my opinion, mean "honestly". A claim is not made honestly if made with the intention of committing a criminal offence, or of facilitating the commission of a future offence': *per* Phillimore LJ in *Central Estates Ltd* v *Woolgar* [1971] 3 All ER 647. See B.Ex.A. 1882, s 90; *The Lendoudis Evangelos* [1997] 1 Lloyd's Rep 404. *See* UBERRIMAE FIDEI.

good leasehold title. A title under L.R.A. 1925, whereby no guarantee as to the lessor's right to validly grant the lease is given, but in other respects the title is effectively equivalent to absolute leasehold title.

good reason. The phrase 'good reason', as used in Civil Procedure Rules 1998, r 39.3(5), is clear enough to enable the court to decide whether, in all the circumstances, there is a good reason for a party not attending hearings: *Brazil* v *Brazil* [2002] NPC 113.

good reason, defence of. In *R* v *Bown* (2003) *The Times* ,14 July, the CA held that, in relation to a charge under Criminal Justice Act 1988, s 139(1)

(having a bladed article in a public place), where a defendant seeks to use the statutory defence of 'good reason' (see s 139(4)), it is for the judge to decide whether the explanation offered can constitute in law 'a good reason'.

good repair. Such a state of repair as will satisfy a respectable occupant using the premises fairly. See *Dashwood* v *Magniac* [1891] 3 Ch 306.

goods. Under S.G.A. 1979, modified by S.G. (Amendment) A. 1995, s 2(c) all chattels personal, other than things in action and money: s 61. In effect, therefore, all things in possession, save money used as currency of the realm. 'Every description of wares and merchandise': Merchant Shipping Act 1894, s 492. 'Future goods' are those to be manufactured or acquired by the seller following the making of the contract of sale. 'Specific goods' are those 'identified and agreed upon at the time a contract of sale is made and include an undivided share, specified as a fraction or percentage, of goods identified and agreed on': 1979 Act, s 61, modified by S.G. (Amendment) A. 1995, s 2(d). See C.P.A. 1987, s 45(1). See *St Albans CDC* v *International Computers* [1995] FSR 686. *See* ASCERTAINED GOODS; SUPPLY; UNASCERTAINED GOODS.

goods, acceptance of. *See* ACCEPTANCE.

goods, consumer. *See* CONSUMER GOODS.

goods, contamination of, or interference with. It is an offence for a person to contaminate or interfere with goods with the intention of causing public anxiety or causing injury to those using or consuming the goods, or of causing economic loss: P.O.A. 1986, s 38(1). 'Goods' include 'substances whether natural or manufactured and whether or not incorporated in or mixed with other goods': s 38(4). It is an offence to threaten to do, or claim to have done, any of the offences mentioned in s 38(1) with the intention mentioned above: s 38(2).

goods, deliverable state. Goods 'in such a state that the buyer would under the contract be bound to take delivery of them': S.G.A. 1979, s 61(5).

goods, delivery of. *See* DELIVERY OF GOODS.

goods, documents of title to. *See* DOCUMENTS OF TITLE TO GOODS.

goods, duress of. *See* DURESS OF GOODS.

goods, hire of, contract for. 'A contract under which one person bails or agrees to bail goods to another by way of hire, other than an excepted contract': Supply of Goods and Services Act 1982, s 6(1). 'Excepted contract' refers to a hire-purchase agreement or a contract under which goods are bailed in exchange for trading stamps on their redemption: s 6(2). For implied terms, see ss 7–10.

goods, parting with possession of, and property in. 'If a man intends to part not only with the possession of goods but also with the property in them or the power of disposing of them, or behaves as if he had that intention by arming the recipient with all the documents necessary to that end, he is not entitled to recover them from an innocent purchaser': *per* Denning LJ in *Central Newbury Car Auctions Ltd* v *Unity Finance Ltd* [1957] 1 QB 371.

goods, protected. *See* PROTECTED GOODS.

goods, quality of. *See* QUALITY, SATISFACTORY.

goods, rejection of. *See* REJECTION OF GOODS.

goods, safe. Means that there is no risk, or minimum risk, that the death of, or any personal injury to, any person will be caused by the goods, their keeping, use or consumption, any emission or leakage from the goods, reliance on the accuracy of measurement made by the goods: C.P.A. 1987, s 29(1). *See* CONSUMER SAFETY; DEFECT IN A PRODUCT.

goods, safety of. *See* CONSUMER SAFETY.

goods, second-hand. Goods offered for sale, having had a previous owner. They are required to be of a reasonable standard, taking into account all relevant circumstances. See S.G.A. 1979, s 14(2),

(6); *Business Applications* v *Nationwide Credit Corporation* [1988] RTR 332.

goods, slander of. *See* SLANDER OF GOODS.

goods, title to, transfer of. *See* TITLE TO GOODS, TRANSFER OF.

goods, transfer of, contract for. 'A contract under which one person transfers or agrees to transfer to another the property in goods, other than an excepted contract': Supply of Goods and Services Act 1982, s 1(1). 'Excepted contract' refers to a contract of sale of goods, a hire-purchase agreement, a contract under which property is transferred on redemption of trading stamps, a contract intended to operate by way of mortgage, pledge, charge or other security: s 1(2). For implied terms and warranties, see ss 2–5.

goods, trespass to. *See* TRESPASS TO GOODS.

goods, wrongful interference with. *See* INTERFERENCE WITH GOODS, WRONGFUL.

goodwill. 'The attractive force which brings in custom': *Inland Revenue* v *Muller* [1901] AC 224. 'The whole advantage, wherever it may be, of the reputation and connection of the firm which may have been built up by years of honest work or gained by lavish expenditure of money': *Trego* v *Hunt* [1896] AC 7. It is measured by the amount by which the value of a business as a whole exceeds the value of assets less liabilities. See Cos.A. 1985, Sch 4; *Kirby* v *Thorn EMI* [1987] STC 621; *BBC* v *Talksport Ltd* (2000) *The Times*, 29 June.

go-slow. A form of industrial action by employees, taking the form of working slowly. Known also as 'working to rule', i.e., reducing output by paying exaggerated attention to rules relating to working conditions. See *Secretary of State for Employment* v *ASLEF (No. 2)* [1972] 2 QB 455.

government. 1. The exercise of authority. 2. The institutions, customs and laws through which government functions. 3. Her Majesty's Government, i.e., a body of ministers responsible for the administration of the nation's affairs.

grant. 1. Formal transfer of property under written instrument without immediate delivery. 2. The allocation of rights, etc., to persons.

grant, block. See BLOCK GRANT; AIDS.

grant in aid. See AIDS.

grant of representation. 1. Probate (q.v.). 2. *Cum testamento annexo*, made when the deceased left a valid will which has not been proved by an executor (q.v.). See S.C.A. 1981, s 119. 3. Simple administration, when deceased died wholly intestate.

grants, special and limited. 1. Grants of representation may be limited as to property, e.g., where the testator (q.v.) has expressly limited the powers of his executor; in the case of grants as to specific settled land; grants *caeterorum* (where a grant has been made to a portion of the estate and it is necessary to apply for administration of the rest of the estate); *de bonis non administratis* (q.v.). 2. Grants may be limited as to time, e.g., until the will be found; for the use of infants (q.v.); during mental incapacity; *ad litem* (q.v.); *ad colligenda bona* (q.v.).

grants to attorney. When an executor or administrator entitled to a grant resides outside England and the grant is limited until that person shall obtain a grant, it may be made to the lawfully constituted attorney of the person entitled for his use and benefit: Non-Contentious Probate Rules 1987, r 31.

gratuities. Money given in recognition of services rendered. See *Figael Ltd v Fox* [1992] STC 83 (liability for tax on tips); SI 73/334.

gratuitous. Given freely, i.e., without legal consideration (q.v.).

grave hardship. In the case of divorce (q.v.) based on five years living apart, the respondent can object to the granting of a decree by showing that dissolving the marriage would result in 'grave financial or other hardship to him': Mat.C.A. 1973, s 5(1). 'Grave' is given its ordinary meaning and 'hardship' is to be determined objectively, according to the standard of sensible people. See *Rukat v Rukat* [1975] Fam 63. See HARDSHIP.

Gray's Inn. One of the four Inns of Court (q.v.). The site of the Inn was let by the Dean of St Paul's to Reginald de Grey, chief justice of Chester, in the thirteenth century. The Inn began to function as a legal institution *c.* 1320.

Great Britain. See UNITED KINGDOM.

Greater London Authority. Established under G.L.A.A. 1999, s 1, as a body corporate, comprising the Mayor of London (q.v.), the London Assembly (25 members, of whom 14 are members for Assembly constituencies, and 11 who are members for the whole of Greater London). 'Greater London' is not defined in 1999 Act; under London Government Act 1963, term refers to 'the area comprising the areas of the London boroughs, the City and the Temples'. Some 5 million persons in London are entitled to vote. Elections are subject to a fixed term of four years: s 5(3). It receives a general annual grant from the Secretary of State: s 100.

Greater London Authority, powers of. The Authority has power to do anything which it considers will further its principal purposes: G.L.A.A. 1999, s 30(1). 'Principal purposes' involve the promotion of economic development and wealth creation, social development, and improvement of the environment in Greater London: s 30(2). It may not incur expenditure in providing housing, education, or social or health services: s 31(3). It may promote or oppose Bills in Parliament: s 77.

Green Belt land. Land intended for preservation from industrial or building development. See Green Belt (London and Home Counties) Act 1938; T.C.P.A. 1990, s 229; *Scottish and Newcastle Breweries plc v Secretary of State for the Environment* (1992) *The Times*, 6 March; *South Buckingham DC v Secretary of State for the Environment* [1999] PLCR 72. In *R v Secretary of State for the Environment ex p O'Byrne* (2002) *The Times*, 18 November, the HL held that statutory restrictions relating to the sale of green belt land by local authorities has application only where such a sale was of a voluntary nature; no such restrictions had application where statute obliged an authority to sell.

Green Paper. *See* PARLIAMENTARY PAPERS.

grievance hearing. *See* DISCIPLINARY OR GRIEVANCE HEARING.

grievous bodily harm. *See* BODILY HARM, GRIEVOUS.

grooming, sexual, of child. Under the Sexual Offences Act 2003, s 15, it is an offence if a person aged 18 or over (A), having met or communicated with another person (B) on at least two earlier occasions, intentionally meets B, or travels with the intention of meeting B in any part of the world, and, at the time, intends to do anything to or in respect of B, during or after the meeting and in any part of the world, which if done will involve the commission by A of a relevant offence, (under the Act) and B is under 16 and A does not reasonably believe that B is 16 or over.

gross. Entire, exclusive of deductions. The term 'in gross' means, when referring to a right, that it is not appendant (q.v.) or otherwise annexed to land.

gross indecency. 1. It is an offence for a man to commit an act of gross indecency (a term not defined by statute: but see Wolfenden Committee Report 1957, Cmnd 247, p. 38) with another man in public or private, to be a party to the commission of such an act or to procure its commission. See S.O.A. 1956, s 13; *Chief Constable of Hants* v *Mace* (1987) 84 Cr App R 40. The term has been generally used to refer to a sexual act, other than buggery (q.v.), between males. See also S.O.A. 1967, ss 1, 4(3); S.O.(Am.)A. 2000, s 2; C.J.P.O.A. 1994, s 145(1); *ADT* v *UK* (2000) *The Times*, 8 August (conviction under 1967 Act, s 1, involving male group sex, held to violate privacy, contrary to Convention on Human Rights, art 8). 2. It is an offence for a person to commit an act of gross indecency with or towards a child under the age of 16 or to incite such a child to do such an act with him or any other person: Indecency with Children Act 1960,

modified by C.J.C.S.A. 2000, s 39; Crime (Sentences) Act 1997, s 52; *B* v *DPP* [2000] 2 WLR 452 (for a conviction under the 1960 Act it is necessary for the prosecution to prove the absence of a general belief on the part of the accused, which did not have to be on reasonable grounds, that the victim was 14 or over).

gross negligence. Used colloquially to refer to negligence (q.v.) characterised by total indifference to the rights of others and the consequences of one's act. 'The use of the expression "gross negligence" is always misleading. Except in the one case when the law relating to manslaughter is being considered, the words "gross negligence" should never be used in connection with any matter to which the common law relates because negligence is a breach of duty, and, if there is a duty and there has been a breach of it which causes loss, it matters not whether it is a venial breach or a serious breach': *Pentecost* v *London District Auditor* [1951] 2 KB 759.

gross negligence, killing by. In a case of alleged killing by gross negligence, the facts must be such 'that in the opinion of the jury, the negligence of the accused went beyond a mere matter of compensation between subjects and showed such disregard for the life and safety of others as to amount to a crime against the State and conduct deserving of punishment': *R* v *Bateman* (1925) 133 LT 730. See *R* v *Sulman* [1993] 3 WLR 927; *R* v *Singh* [1999] Crim LR 582; *A-G's Reference (No. 2 of 1999)* [2000] 3 All ER 182. *See* NEGLIGENCE.

gross value of premises. Phrase used in Rent Acts to mean letting value of premises by the year, assuming that the cost of insurance and repairs is carried by the landlord.

gross weight. In relation to any goods, the aggregate weight of the goods and any container in or on which they are made up: Weights and Measures Act 1985, s 94(1).

ground rent. *See* BUILDING LEASE.

group accounts. Accounts laid in general meeting before a company which has subsidiaries: Cos.A. 1985, s 229. They must consist of a consolidated balance sheet and profit and loss account and must comply with requirements of the Cos.A. 1985, Sch 4.

group litigation, discontinuance of. It was held, in *Sayers* v *Smithkline Beecham plc* (2004) *The Times*, 22 October, that in a case of group litigation relating to disabled persons, where several claimants intended to discontinue, they did not need permission of the court if their discontinuance did not constitute a settlement and their claim forms did not name other claimants.

guarantee. A collateral engagement to answer for the debt, default or miscarriage of another person. To be enforceable, such a promise must be evidenced in writing: Statute of Frauds 1677, s 4. 'Miscarriage' refers here to 'that species of wrongful act for the consequences of which the law would make the party civilly responsible': *Kirkham* v *Marter* (1819) 2 B & A 613. See Cos.A. 1985, s 331(2); *Gulf Bank* v *Mitsubishi* [1994] 3 Bank LR 74; *MP Services Ltd* v *Lawyer* (1996) 72 P & CR D 49.

guarantee, company limited by. Company (q.v.) formed, e.g., for charitable or educational purposes. If it has share capital, a member is liable up to the amount unpaid on his shares and also up to the amount of guarantee; but if it has no share capital, he is liable only up to the amount of the guarantee. See Tables C and D; and Cos.A. 1985, s 30. With effect from December 1980, a company cannot be formed as, or become, a company limited by guarantee with a share capital: Cos.A. 1985, s 1(4).

guarantee payments. Where throughout a day during any part of which an employee would normally be required to work in accordance with his contract of employment, the employee is not provided with work by his employer by reason of a diminution in the requirements of the employer's business for work of the kind which the employee is employed to do, or any other occurrence affecting the normal working of the employer's

business in relation to work of the kind which the employee is employed to do, the employee is entitled to be paid by his employer an amount in respect of that day: E.R.A. 1996, s 28. For exclusions from right to guarantee payments, see s 29. For calculation of guarantee payment, see s 30. For limits on amount of and entitlement to payments, see s 31, amended by Employment Relations Act 1999, s 35.

guarantees in sale and supply of goods. Under Sale and Supply of Goods to Consumers Regulations 2002, para 7, where guarantees are offered at no extra charge to consumer, they will be legally binding. Any guarantee offered must be supplied in writing on consumer's request.

guarantor. One who promises to answer for another; a surety (q.v.). For co-guarantors, see *Stimpson* v *Smith* (1999) 149 NLJ 414. See Minors' Contracts Act 1987, s 2.

guardian. One appointed to take care of another person, his affairs and property. A guardian may be appointed if the child has no parent with parental responsibility (q.v.) for him: Ch.A. 1989, s 5(1)(a). A parent who has parental responsibility may appoint another person to be the child's guardian in the event of his death: s 5(4). For revocation and disclaimer, see s 6; F.L.A. 1996, Sch 8, para 41(2).

guardian *ad litem*. *See* AD LITEM.

guardian removal of. The court may terminate the appointment of a guardian on the application of the child concerned or any person with parental responsibility (q.v.) for him or if the court considers that it should be ended even though no application has been made: Ch.A. 1989, s 6(7). For disclaimer, see s 6(5).

guardian, special. A.C.A. 2002, s 115, proposes a new s 14A in Ch.A. 1989, creating a special guardianship order appointing a person over 18 to be a child's special guardian. Applicants must be: the child's guardian, or a person in whose favour a residence order is in force with respect to the child. The order may also give leave for the child to be known by a different surname.

guilt, certainty of. CA held, in *R v Stephens* (2002) *The Times*, 27 June, that it was unhelpful for a judge who was seeking to assist the jury in matters of burden of proof, to attempt to distinguish 'certainty of guilt' from 'being sure of guilt'. As in ordinary English usage, 'sure' and 'certain' are virtually indistinguishable.

guilty, a plea of. Confession by the defendant that he has committed the offence with which he is charged. He may plead guilty to one count in an indictment, but not guilty to another. A plea of guilty made under pressure upon counsel from the trial judge is not a proper plea, so that the ensuing trial is a nullity: *R v Inns* (1975) 60 Cr App R 231. For changing guilty plea, see *S v Recorder of Manchester* [1969] 3 All ER 1230. For a mistaken plea of guilty, see *R v Phillips* [1982] 1 All ER 245. See *R v Newton* (1983) 77 Cr App R 13; *R v Tolera* [1999] 1 Cr App R 29 (defendant, after pleading guilty, sought to be sentenced on different factual basis from that upon which the prosecution case rested); *R v Thomas* [2000] 1 Cr App R 447 (the overturning of a conviction following a plea of guilty). *See* NOT GUILTY; VERDICT.

guilty, a plea of, and sentencing. Following a plea of guilty, the court, in sentencing the offender, must take into account the stage in the proceedings at which he indicated his intention to make the plea, and the circumstances in which that indication was given: P.C.C.(S.)A. 2000, s 152.

guilty knowledge. That awareness by virtue of which a person's act or omission is rendered criminal in nature. In *Roper v Taylor's Central Garages (Exeter) Ltd* [1951] 2 TLR 284, it was categorised as: (1) actual knowledge, which could be inferred from the accused's conduct; (2) knowledge in the eye of the law, where the accused has deliberately refrained from making enquiries; (3) constructive knowledge (q.v.).

guilty mind. *See* MENS REA.

guilty, plea by post of. *See* POST, PLEA OF GUILTY BY.

guilty, plea of. CA held in *R v Mulla* [2003] All ER (D) 170, that where the prosecution has stated that they might accept a plea of guilty to a lesser offence, and then change their mind in favour of the more serious offence, it is necessary to consider whether this event constitutes an abuse of process.

gypsies. Described in Caravan Sites Act 1968 as 'persons of nomadic habit of life, whatever their race or origin'. Local authorities had the duty under the 1968 Act, Part II, to provide adequate accommodation for gypsies residing in or resorting to their area, but this was repealed by C.J.P.O.A. 1994, s 80. See *Hedges v Secretary for the Environment* (1997) 73 P & CR 534. For purposes of Race Relations Act 1976, they constitute a 'racial group': *Commission for Racial Equality v Dutton* [1989] 2 WLR 17. See *Reigate BC v Brown* (1992) 24 HLR 442; *R v Leeds CC ex p Maloney* (1999) 31 HLR 552; *Chapman v UK* (2001) *The Times*, 30 January. In *Wrexham CBC v National Assembly of Wales* (2003) *The Times*, 4 July, the CA held that where members of a gypsy family (see Caravan Sites and Control of Development Act 1950, s 24) had abandoned their way of life because of ill health, they could not be considered to fall, for planning purposes, within the definition of 'gypsies'.

gypsies, sites for. CA held in *R (Butler) v Bath and NE Somerset DC* (2003) *The Times*, 4 November, that where a local authority decides to reject recommendations to produce plans for gypsies and travellers in relation to accommodation, they must publicise their rejection and invite representations from the public.

gypsy site eviction. European Court of Human Rights held in *Connors v UK (Application No. 66746/01)* that eviction of applicant and family from a local gypsy caravan site had not involved the appropriate procedural safeguards relating to breach of right concerning family life, as guaranteed under European Convention, art 8.

H

habeas corpus. 'That you have the body'. A prerogative writ ('the great writ of liberty') used to command a person who is detaining another in custody to produce that person before the court. It is not a discretionary remedy, and will usually be made available as of right, should the detainee show good cause. 'The King is at all times entitled to have an account why the liberty of his subjects is restrained': Blackstone, *Commentaries* (1765). The writ *habeas corpus ad subjiciendum* commands a person to produce the detainee, with details of the day and cause of his caption and detention, to do, submit to and receive what shall be directed by the court. QBD has jurisdiction to issue the writ; an application takes precedence over other business. See Habeas Corpus Acts 1679 (q.v.), 1816, 1862. See A.J.A. 1960, s 14; amended by Acc.J.A. 1999, s 65; Extradition Act 1989, s 11. Application for a writ of habeas corpus must be made to a judge in court, except that: it shall be made to a Divisional Court of QBD if the court so directs; it may be made to a judge otherwise than in court at any time when no judge is sitting in court; any application on behalf of a child must be made in the first instance to a judge otherwise than in court: CPR Sch 1; O 54, r 1. See *Re D (Mental patient: Habeas Corpus)* (2000) *The Times,* 19 May; *Re Burke* [2000] 3 WLR 33.

Habeas Corpus Amendment Act 1679. 'An Act for the better securing the liberty of the subject and for prevention of imprisonment beyond the seas.' Among its provisions were: that an unconvicted prisoner could demand from a judge a writ of habeas corpus (q.v.); that no person

once delivered by habeas corpus should be recommitted for the same offence; and that no inhabitant of England should be sent to imprisonment out of England.

habendum. To have. The clause in a conveyance (q.v.) which defines the extent of the purchaser's interest or estate (e.g., 'to hold unto the purchaser in fee simple').

habit, presumption from. The fact that a person was in the habit of acting in a certain way may be relevant to the issue of whether he acted in that way in the circumstances which forms the basis of the court's enquiry. See *Joy v Phillips, Mill & Co Ltd* [1916] 1 KB 849: evidence was admitted of a boy's practice of teasing a horse, in an action resulting from his death caused by a kick from the horse. *See* EVIDENCE.

hacking, computer. The process of obtaining unauthorised access to computers. An offence under the Computer Misuse Act 1990, ss 1–3.

Hague Conventions. 1. Agreements signed at the Hague Peace Conference in 1899 and 1907 relating to, e.g., the definition of a state of belligerency. 2. Agreement relating to child abduction (q.v.), signed in 1980.

Hague Rules, application to goods of. Article I of 1924 Rules, as amended in 1968 (by Visby Protocol), defines goods to which the Rules apply, as including: 'goods, wares, merchandise and articles of every kind whatsoever, except live animals and cargo which by the contract of carriage is stated as being carried on deck and is so carried'. Carriage of goods 'covers the period from the time when the goods are loaded on to the time when they are discharged from the ship'. See *The Captain Gregos* [1990] 1 Lloyd's Rep 310.

half blood. *See* BLOOD RELATIONSHIP.

half-secret trust. Created where a will or other instrument discloses the existence of a trust, but not its terms, e.g., as where property is left to X 'on the trusts I have discussed with him'. Thus, where a sealed letter handed by the testator (q.v.) to the trustee (q.v.) is marked 'not to be opened until after my death' and the trustee knows that it contains terms of a trust which he agrees to carry out, such a communication suffices to create a half-secret trust. See *Re Keen* [1937] Ch 326; *Re Bateman's WT* [1970] 3 All ER 817.

hallmark. Mark used by assay offices for the marking of silver, platinum and gold. See Hallmarking Act 1973; SI 98/2978, 2979.

handcuffs in court. In general, a defendant should remain handcuffed in court only if the prosecution applies for this, and if there is reasonable ground for believing that he might escape or become violent: *R v Vratsides* [1988] Crim LR 251; *R v Mullen* [2000] 150 NLJ 1303.

handling. 'A person handles stolen goods if (otherwise than in the course of the stealing) knowing or believing them to be stolen goods he dishonestly receives the goods, or dishonestly undertakes or assists in their retention, removal, disposal or realisation by or for the benefit of another person, or if he arranges to do so': Th.A. 1968, s 22(1). See *A-G's Ref (No. 4 of 1979)* [1981] 1 All ER 1193; P.&C.E.A. 1984, s 74; *R v Hacker* [1995] 1 Cr App R 332; *R v Gingell* [2000] 1 Cr App R 88 ('another', in s 22(1), does not include a co-accused). For theft and handling as alternative charges, see *R v Shelton* (1986) 83 Cr App R 379.

handwriting, proof of. Types of relevant evidence include: direct evidence, e.g., testimony of the person whose writing has to be proved; opinion, e.g., by a handwriting expert; comparison (see, e.g., *Cobbett v Kilminster* (1865) 4 F & F 490). See also *R v Silverlock* [1894] 2 QB 766; *R v Ewing* [1983] QB 1039; *Fuller v Strum* (2001) *The Times*, 14 February. *See* EVIDENCE.

hanging. Execution by the gallows, abolished in relation to murder by Murder (Abolition of Death Penalty) Act 1965. *See* CAPITAL PUNISHMENT.

Hansard. Colloquial name for the *Official Report of Parliamentary Debates*, usually published daily, so-called after T.C. Hansard, printer to the Commons. *Hansard* may be referred to in construing a statute in cases where the relevant legislation is obscure, ambiguous or may lead to an absurdity, and where a clear statement made in Parliament by a Minister might resolve the obscurity or ambiguity: *Pepper v Hart* [1993] AC 593. See *Practice Direction (Hansard Extracts)* [1995] 1 WLR 192; *U v W (Admissibility of Hansard)* [1997] Eu LR 342; *R v Deegan* [1998] 2 Cr App R 121 (*Pepper v Hart* submission rejected, since the ministerial statements sought to be adduced were not sufficiently clear); *Practice Direction for the Court of Appeal (Civil Division)*, para 10.2.2; *R v Secretary of State for Environment ex p Spath Holme* (2000) 150 NLJ 1855 (constant citation from *Hansard* not acceptable). *See* INTENTION OF PARLIAMENT.

harassment. Protection from Harassment Act 1997 creates the summary offence of harassment and an indictable offence related to the creation of fear of violence: ss 2, 4. A statutory *tort* of harassment is created under s 3. 'A person whose course of conduct causes another to fear, on at least two occasions, that violence will be used against him, is guilty of an offence if he knows or ought to know that his course of conduct will cause the other so to fear on each of those occasions': s 4(1). For sentencing guidelines, see *R v Liddle* [1999] 3 All ER 816. For restraining order, see s 5; *R v Mann* (2000) *The Times*, 11 April (protected parties must be identified in order by name). See *Huntingdon Life Sciences Ltd v Curtin* (1997) *The Times*, 11 December (misuse of the Act in relation to persons who were exercising their right to protest about a matter of public interest); CPR, Sch 1; O 94, r 16. *See* HARASSMENT, RACIALLY-AGGRAVATED.

harassment, corporations and. A company may not bring a claim under the Protection from Harassment Act 1997, since it cannot be the victim of harassment. Persons who are non-corporate claimants have an entitlement to the protection of the statute: *Daiichi UK Ltd* v *Stop Huntingdon Animal Cruelty* (2003) *The Times*, 22 October; *DPP* v *Dzuirzynski* (2002) *The Times*, 8 July.

harassment of a person in his home. Under C.J.P.A. 2002, s 42, police present at the scene would be allowed to give oral directions stopping the harassment of a person in his home by another who is present, outside or in the vicinity of that home, and where the police believe that the other person is present for the purpose of persuading the victim that he should not do something he is entitled or required to do, or that he should do something that he is not under any obligation to do.

harassment of debtors. It is an offence for a person, with the object of coercing another to pay money claimed from the other as a debt due under a contract, to harass the other with demands for payments which are calculated to subject him or members of his family or household to alarm, distress or humiliation, or to falsely represent that criminal proceedings lie for failure to pay the money claimed: A.J.A. 1970, s 40. See *R* v *Bokhari* [1974] Crim LR 559.

harassment of occupier. It is an offence to do acts likely to interfere with the peace or comfort of a residential occupier or member of his household or to persistently withdraw or withhold services reasonably required for occupation with intent to cause the occupier to give up occupation or refrain from exercising any right or pursuing any remedy in respect of the premises: Protection from Eviction Act 1977, s 1(3), as amended by H.A. 1988, s 29. See *R* v *Pheeko* [1981] 1 WLR 1117 (not an absolute offence); *R* v *Burke* [1990] 2 WLR 1313; *West Wiltshire DC* v *Snelgrove* (1998) 30 HLR 57.

harassment, racially-aggravated. A person is guilty of an offence under C.D.A.

1988, s 32, if he commits an offence under Protection for Harassment Act 1997, s 2 (harassment), s 4 (putting people in fear of violence) which is racially aggravated. *See* RACIALLY-AGGRAVATED OFFENCE.

harassment, sexual. 1. 'Conduct of a sexual nature or other conduct based on sex, affecting the dignity of men and women at work': EC Official Journal C 157/2. Not specifically recognised under Sex Discrimination Acts 1975, 1986, but a resignation consequent on sexual harassment could result in a claim for constructive dismissal (q.v.). See *Cornelius* v *University College of Swansea* [1987] IRLR 141; *Reed* v *Stedman* [1999] IRLR 299 (an objective test is not appropriate in determining detriment suffered by employee). 2. Defined in EU Directive, agreed in April 2002, as taking place 'where any form of unwarranted verbal, non-verbal or physical conduct of a sexual nature occurs with the purpose or effect of violating a person's dignity, in particular when creating an intimidating, hostile, degrading, humiliating or offensive environment.'

harbour. Estuaries, navigable rivers, piers, jetties and other works in or at which ships can obtain shelter or ship and unship goods or passengers: Merchant Shipping Act 1995, s 313.

harbouring. Providing shelter, with the object of concealing. See *Nicoll* v *Catron* (1985) 81 Cr App R 339 (harbouring escaped prisoner).

hardship. 'The word "hardship" is not a word of art . . . in my judgment the ordinary sensible man would take the view that there are two aspects of "hardship" – that which the sufferor from the hardship thinks he is suffering and that which a reasonable bystander with knowledge of all the facts would think he was suffering': *per* Lawton J in *Rukat* v *Rukat* [1975] 1 All ER 343. 'Undue hardship' means excessive hardship: *per* Brandon J in *The Pegasus* [1967] 2 QB 86. *See* GRAVE HARDSHIP.

harm. Loss or detriment to a person. It may be financial or physical (see C.J.P.O.A. 1994, s 51(4)). See *R* v

Normanton [1999] Crim LR 220. *See* CHILDREN, HARM TO; POLLUTION, ENVIRONMENTAL.

harmonisation of laws. Phrase used to refer to the adjustment of legislation by member states of EU (q.v.) in a given area of social and economic policy. See Treaty of Rome 1957, art 95.

hay bote. *See* ESTOVERS.

hazardous substances. Not defined by statute. Term generally includes inherently dangerous, unstable materials. Secretary of State may make regulations specifying such substances: Planning (Hazardous Substances) Act 1990, s 5; Control of Substances Hazardous to Health Regulations 1994. Consent for the presence of such substances is required under s 4(1); for exceptions, see s 4(2), (4). See also En.P.A. 1990, Sch 13; SI 92/725; Merchant Shipping Act 1995, s 182A, inserted by Merchant Shipping and Maritime Security Act 1997, s 14.

Head of Criminal Justice. The Lord Chief Justice, or if the Lord Chief Justice appoints another person, that person: s 8 C.R.A. 2005.

Head of Division. Means any of the following: the Master of the Rolls; the President of the Queen's Bench Division; the President of the Family Division; the Chancellor of the High Court: s 122 C.R.A 2005.

Head of Family Justice. The President of the Family Division is Head of Family Justice: s 9 C.R.A. 2005.

headings. Words prefixed to sections of a statute, regarded as preambles (q.v.). Reference to headings may be made so as to assist in resolving an ambiguity. See *DPP v Schildkamp* [1971] AC 1; *Governors of John Lyon School v James* (1995) *The Times*, 7 July.

head lease. A lease (q.v.) from which lesser interests (i.e., sub-leases) have been created. See *Gratton-Storey v Lewis* (1987) 283 EG 1562. *See* SUB-LEASE.

head note. Summary of points decided in a case, placed at the head of a law report. A head note is not authoritative.

headstone and interment. The Consistory Court held in *Re St Peter's*

Churchyard, Limpsfield, that the erection of a monument in a churchyard is permitted only where it makes a grave of a person whose remains are buried there; it may not be used for the commemoration of one whose remains were interred elsewhere. See (2004) *The Times*, 8 June 2004.

health and safety at work. In *Fytche v Wincanton plc* [2004] UKHL 31, the HL held that the phrase 'in efficient state, efficient working order and in good repair' does not constitute an absolute concept, but should be considered in relation to that which makes the equipment 'protective equipment'. See Personal Protective Equipment at Work Regulations 1992 (SI 92/2966), regs 4, 7.

Health Improvement, Commission for. Body corporate set up under Health Act 1999, s 19. Functions include providing of advice or information concerning arrangements by Primary Care Trusts or NHS Trusts so as to monitor and improve quality of health care for which they have responsibility, reviewing and reporting on those arrangements, reviewing and reporting on availability of certain types of health care. See Sch 2.

health, legislation plans. Government White Paper, 'Choosing health – Making healthy choice easier' (November, 2004) suggests legislation relating to: smoking (e.g., ban for enclosed public places and work places by end of 2007); obesity (e.g., limitation of presentation to children of unhealthy foods); sexual health (e.g., chlamydia screening programme to cover all England by 2007).

Health Protection Agency. Body corporate set up under Health Protection Agency Act 2004, s 1(1) charged with functions of protecting community against infectious disease, prevention of spread of infections disease, provision of assistance to persons who exercise these functions.

health record. Record consisting of information relating to the physical or mental health of an individual who can be identified from that information, or from that and other information in the possession of the record holder, and has been made by or on behalf of a health professional in connection with the care of that individual: Access to Health Records Act 1990, s 1(1), amended by Health Authorities Act 1995, Sch 1, para 119. For right of access, see s 3, amended by Data Protection Act 1998, Sch 16.

Health Service, National. The health service established in 1948 in England and Wales and in Scotland respectively, in pursuance of s 1 of National Health Service Act 1946 (for England and Wales), and National Health Service (Scotland) Act 1947. For definition of 'health professional', see Data Protection Act 1998, s 69. See Health Services Act 1980; Health and S.S.A. 1984; Health and Medicines Act 1988; NHS and Community Care Act 1990; Health Services Commissioners Acts 1993, 1996, 2000; Health Authorities Act 1995; Health Act 1999. *See* NATIONAL HEALTH SERVICE CONTRACTS.

hearing. The trial of a cause or claim.

hearsay evidence. *See* EVIDENCE, HEARSAY.

hearsay evidence, victim's statement as. Hearsay evidence of a statement made to a witness by the victim of an attack, naming or describing the attacker, is admissible in evidence at the trial of the attacker, as part of the *res gestae* (q.v.), if the statement was made in conditions which were sufficiently spontaneous and contemporaneous with the attack to preclude the possibility of concoction or distortion. See *R v Andrews* [1987] AC 281 (overruling *R v Bedingfield* (1879) 14 Cox CC 341); *Hearsay and Related Topics* (1997) Law Com No. 245.

hedge and ditch presumption. Where there is nothing else to identify a boundary (q.v.) and there is a ditch and a bank, the presumption is that the person who dug the ditch dug it to the extremity of his land and threw the soil on his own land to make the bank: *Fisher* v *Winch* [1939] 1 KB 666. The presumption may be rebutted by production of title deeds. See *Falkingham* v *Farley* (1991) *The Times*, 22 February; *Alan Wibberley Building*

Ltd v *Insley* [1999] 1 WLR 894 (presumption not displaced by reference to Ordnance Survey map in conveyance).

heir. One who succeeds by descent (q.v.). Under L.P.A. 1925, s 132, a limitation of property in favour of the heir (special or general) which, prior to the Act, would have conferred on the heir an estate by purchase, confers a corresponding equitable interest (q.v.) on the person who would have answered the description of heir before the Act.

heir apparent. A person (e.g. the eldest son) who, if he survives his ancestor, will be his heir unless excluded by a valid will. He is not 'the heir' until after the death of the ancestor.

heirloom. 'Any piece of household stuff which, by custom of some countries, having belonged to a house for certain descents, goes with the house, after the death of the owner, unto the heir and not to the executors': *Termes de la Ley*. The tenant for life can sell heirlooms, the money arising from the sale being capital money: S.L.A. 1925, s 67.

heir presumptive. One who would be the heir (e.g. a daughter) who loses her right to inheritance on the birth of a person with a higher priority to the title of heir, e.g. one more closely related.

heirs of the body. Words of limitation in a conveyance which comprehends 'all the posterity of the donee in succession': *Re Woodward Estate* [1945] 1 WLR 722. *See* LIMITATION, WORDS OF.

Henry VIII clause. Clause in statute conferring powers, e.g., on government minister, to make some exceptions to the operation of the statute. So-called because of that monarch's habits relating to exercise of personal powers. See, e.g., Banking Act 1987, s 4(3). 'Henry VIII powers' are not confined to making minor or modest changes in legislation; thus, Parliament could delegate power to amend primary legislation, and subordinate legislation made by ministers in implementation of EU Metrication Directives, by modification of Weights and Measures Act 1985, was valid: *Thorburn* v *Sunderland CC* (2002) 152 NLJ 312.

hereditaments. 1. Real property which devolved on an heir (q.v.) on an intestacy (q.v.). Classified as: *incorporeal* (rights of property, e.g., easements); *corporeal* (physical objects, e.g., land, buildings). 2. A hereditament means property which is or may become liable to a rate, being a unit of such property which is, or would fall to be, shown as a separate item in the valuation list: General Rate Act 1967, s 115(1); Local Government Finance Act 1988, s 64. A hereditament is non-domestic if either it consists entirely of property which is not domestic, or part only consists of domestic property (q.v.): 1988 Act, s 64.

heresy. Deliberate and overt denial of some accepted dogma of the church. A capital offence until 1677. See Ecclesiastical Jurisdiction Measure 1963; *Noble* v *Voysey* (1871) LR 3 PC 357.

High Court and county courts, allocation of business among. Under CPR a claimant may start proceedings in the High Court or any county court (see PD 7, para 1). But a money claim in High Court may be issued only where claimant expects to recover at least £15,000. A personal injuries claim must not be commenced unless claimant expects to recover at least £50,000. Claims for libel or slander, applications concerning decisions of local authority auditors, must not be brought in a county court. Applications concerning habeas corpus (q.v.) and judicial review (q.v.) must be issued in QBD of High Court. Chancery business may be heard in High Court or county courts (see S.C.A. 1981, Sch 1, para 1). For transfer of business, see CPR, r 26.2(1), (3); Part 30.

High Court, appeal from. In *Westminster CC* v *O'Reilly* [2003] EWCA Civ 107, the CA held that it lacked jurisdiction to hear an appeal against a decision of the High Court on appeal by way of case stated, because the High Court's decision in this matter was final. See Magistrates' Courts Act 1980, s 111.

High Court, jurisdiction of. If an application for permission to appeal is lodged at the High Court in circumstances where there is no doubt that a High Court judge has no jurisdiction, it must be rejected unanimously; there is no requirement for a reasoned judgment in these circumstances: *Slot* v *Isaac* (2002) *The Independent*, 2 May.

High Court of Justice. A court of unlimited civil jurisdiction with appellate jurisdiction in civil and criminal matters, created by Judicature Acts 1873–5. Part of Supreme Court of England and Wales (S.C.A. 1981, s 1). Consists of the Lord Chancellor, Lord Chief Justice, President of the Family Division, Vice-Chancellor, and up to 96 puisne judges. (High Court work generally involves one judge sitting alone.) It sits at the Royal Courts of Justice in London and at 26 first-tier Crown Court centres outside London. Its divisions are Chancery Div., Queen's Bench Div. and Family Div.: S.C.A. 1981, ss 4, 5. It includes the Administrative Court (q.v.). The Patents Court is part of Chancery Div.; Admiralty Court and Commercial Court are part of Queen's Bench Div.: s 6. For general jurisdiction, see ss 19, 25–31. For distribution of business, see s 61, Sch 1. For allocation of business between High Court and county courts, see C.L.S.A. 1990, s 1; *Practice Direction* [1991] 1 WLR 695. For penalty for launching proceedings in the wrong court, see S.C.A. 1981, s 51(8), (9), substituted by C.L.S.A. 1990, s 4.

High Judicial Office. The office as a judge of any of the following courts, the Supreme Court, Court of Appeal in England and Wales, High Court in England and Wales, the Court of Session, the Court of Appeal in Northern Ireland, the High Court in Northern Ireland, or as a Lord of Appeal in Ordinary. See C.R.A 2005.

high seas. The seas lying more than 5 km beyond the coast of a country. The criminal law of England extends to all British ships upon the high seas (*Oteri* v *The Queen* [1976] 1 WLR 1272) and to acts of British subjects when passengers on foreign ships on the high seas (*R* v *Kelly* [1982] AC 665).

highway. A road or way either on land or water (e.g., path, bridge) used by the public for passing and repassing as a matter of right. It may exist by statute, dedication (q.v.) or prescription (q.v.). See Highways Act 1980; T.C.P.A. 1990, s 247, amended by G.L.A.A. 1999, Sch 22; New Roads and Street Work Act 1991, s 86; *Buckland* v *Secretary of State for the Environment* [2000] 3 All ER 205. *See* PUBLIC NUISANCE.

Highway Code. A standard of conduct for road users, issued by the Secretary of State for the Environment. Failure to observe the Code does not, in itself, render a person liable to criminal proceedings; it may, however, be taken into account in such proceedings (Road Traffic Act 1972, s 37 (as substituted by Transport Act 1981, s 60)). See Road Traffic Act 1988, s 38.

highway, nuisance in relation to. 'Any wrongful act or omission upon or near a highway, whereby the public are prevented from freely, safely and conveniently passing along the highway': *Jacobs* v *Lee* [1950] AC 361. See Highways Act 1980; *Cross* v *Kirklees* [1998] 1 All ER 564 (duty to maintain highways under the 1980 Act is absolute); *Goodes* v *E Sussex CC* [2000] 3 All ER 603 (duty to repair highway does not include ice removal).

highway, obstruction of. 1. If a person's land abuts on the highway he can bring a claim for trespass against a person who uses the highway in an unreasonable manner, e.g., by obstruction. See *Harrison* v *Duke of Rutland* [1893] 1 QB 142. 2. The wilful (i.e., intentional) obstruction of a highway is an offence. 'An obstruction is something which permanently or temporarily removes the whole or part of the highway from public use': *per* Lord Evershed in *Trevett* v *Lee* [1955] 1 All ER 406. See Highways Act 1980, ss 130A (inserted by C.R.W.A. 2000, s 63), 137; Rights of Way Act 1990; *Hereford and Worcester CC* v *Pick* (1996) 71 P & CR 231.

hijacking. Unlawfully seizing by force or threats of any kind the control of an aircraft in flight: Aviation Security Act 1982, s 1(1). For hijacking of a ship or fixed platform, see Aviation and Maritime Security Act 1990, ss 9, 10.

hire. Payment for the temporary use of something, e.g., a good, or a person's labour power. In a contract of hire there is an implied warranty (q.v.) that the goods hired are as fit for the purpose of their hiring as skill and care can make them. Under C.C.A. 1974, a hirer is the bailee of goods under a consumer hire agreement (q.v.) or the person to whom the hirer's rights and duties under the agreement have passed by assignment (q.v.) or operation of law. See *Dimond* v *Lovell* [2000] 2 WLR 1121 (hire agreement under which hire payment was deferred for a period after the end of the hire falls within C.C.A. 1974).

hire or reward, for. 'The probable explanation of the composite phrase is that the words "for hire" were used because they were the most familiar words to describe remuneration for carriage in some vehicles, and the words "or reward" were added since "reward" is a wider word and apt to cover some forms of remuneration or some arrangements for which the words "for hire" might not be appropriate': *per* Lord Pearson in *Albert* v *Motor Insurers' Bureau* [1971] 2 All ER 1345. For 'plying for hire', see Town Police Clauses Act 1847, s 38; *Eastbourne BC* v *Stirling* (2000) *The Times*, 16 November.

hire-purchase agreement. An agreement, other than a conditional sale agreement (q.v.) under which goods are bailed in return for periodical payments by the bailee and the property in the goods passes to the bailee if the terms of the agreement are not complied with and the bailee exercises his option to purchase or some other specified event occurs: C.C.A. 1974, s 189(1). See I.C.T.A. 1988, s 784(6); Hire Purchase Act 1964; *Forthright Finance Ltd* v *Carlyle Finance Ltd* [1997] 4 CL 50; SI 98/1203. For hire-purchase claims, see PD, para 7.1. See *Close Asset Co* v *Care Graphics* [2000] CCLR 43.

historic buildings. *See* LISTED BUILDINGS.

HIV. Human Immune Deficiency Virus. *See* AIDS.

HIV, deliberate transmission of. In *R* v *Dicca* (see *The Times* story, 4 November 2003, page 5), D was sentenced to eight years' imprisonment for having knowingly infected women by deliberately transmitting HIV. (Conviction and sentence are likely to be appealed.) See also *R* v *Clarence* (1888) 22 QBD 23.

HIV risk. Where an asylum seeker, a mother who was HIV positive, might breastfeed her child and pass on the condition because she lacked means to buy appropriate milk, the Home Secretary was required to consider whether additional financial support was deserved under the Immigration and Asylum Act 1999, s 96 (2): *R (T)* v *Secretary of State* (2002) *The Times*, 5 August.

HMSO. Her Majesty's Stationery Office, controlled by the Queen's Printer of Acts of Parliament and responsible for supplying official publications. Copyright of all government documents vests in the Controller of the Office. The work of the Office is now carried out by The Stationery Office Ltd.

hold and search. In *Hepburn* v *Chief Constable of Thames Valley Police* [2002] EWCA Civ 1841, the CA held that a citizen's right to freedom of person and movement is inviolable save where the police have an unequivocal right to restrict it. In this case their power to hold and search a person under Misuse of Drugs Act 1971, s 23(2)(a), was not authorized by warrant to enter and search premises for drugs.

holder. The holder of a bill is the payee or endorsee who is in possession of it, or the bearer thereof: B.Ex.A. 1882, s 2. *See* BILL OF EXCHANGE.

holder for value. Holder of a bill of exchange (q.v.) for which value has been given at some time (not necessarily by the holder himself).

holder in due course. A holder who has taken a bill which is regular and complete on the face of it under the following conditions: that he became the holder before it was overdue and without notice of its having been previously dishonoured (if that were so); that he took it in good faith and for value; that at the time the bill was negotiated he had no notice of defective title of the negotiator. See B.Ex.A. 1882, ss 29(1), 30(2), 38(2). *See* BILL OF EXCHANGE.

holding charge. A minor charge made pending the investigation of a more serious charge. See, e.g., *Christie* v *Leachinsky* [1947] AC 573; *Hussein* v *Chong Fook Kam* [1970] AC 942.

holding company. *See* SUBSIDIARY COMPANY.

holding out. A course of action which persuades others to believe in a party's possessing an authority which, in fact, does not exist. A person who acts in this way may be stopped from denying the truth of his representations if others have acted on them. 'The holding out must be to the particular individual who says he relied on it, or under such circumstances of publicity as to justify the inference that he knew of it and acted upon it': *per* Lord Lindley in *Farquharson Bros* v *King & Co* [1902] AC 325. See Partnership Act 1890, ss 3, 14; *Hudgell Yeates & Co* v *Watson* [1978] 2 All ER 363.

holding over. The continuation in possession of land by a tenant (q.v.) after the expiration of the tenancy agreement. The tenant who has received oral or written notice to quit may become liable to a claim for possession and double rent and damages. See Distress for Rent Act 1737. *See* SUFFERANCE, TENANCY AT.

holiday lettings. The letting of property for a holiday under terms allowing its recovery at the end of that period. Not a protected tenancy (q.v.): see Rent Act 1977, s 9. ('Holiday' was considered in *Buchmann* v *May* [1978] 2 All ER 993, to be 'a period of cessation from work or a period of recreation'.) See *Caradon DC* v *Paton* (2000) *The Times*, 17 May.

holiday pay, calculation of. Calculation of daily amount of pay in relation to holiday pay is to be made by considering number of working days involved, not number of calendar days in a year:

Leisure Leagues Ltd v *Maconachie* (2002) *The Times*, 3 May.

holiday pay, topping up. The Employment Appeal Tribunal held, in *Marshalls Clay Products* v *Caulfield* (2003) *The Times*, 25 August, that in the case of an agreement between employer and employee, allowing for a basic wage to be topped up by a given sum allocated to holiday pay, the agreement was valid.

holiday rights. A school pupil, aged 15, who delivered papers for six days a week was not a 'worker' under Working Time Regulations (SI 98/1833), reg 2, and, therefore, had no right to paid holidays: *Addison* v *Ashby* (2003) 153 NLJ 145.

holograph. A document, such as a will or deed, written entirely in the testator's or grantor's own hand. See *Re Kanani* (1978) 122 SJ 611.

home. One's dwelling place. See *Re Y* [1985] Fam 136: concept of 'home' considered incapable of precise definition, but it should comprise an element of regular occupation (past, present or intended for the future) with a degree of permanence, based on some right of occupation: H.A. 1985, s 81. See H.A. 1996, s 10; *Buckley* v *UK* (1996) 23 EHRR 101 (caravan constituted home). For sale of family home on bankruptcy, see *Re Citro* [1991] Ch 142; Ins.A. 1986, s 35A; Trusts of Land and Appointment of Trustees Act 1996, s 14; Human Rights Act 1998, Sch 1, art 8(1); In *Malekshad* v *Howard de Walden Estates Ltd* [2002] 3 WLR 1881, the HL held that a house and adjoining mews let under one single head lease and later divided vertically so as to form separate properties did not constitute a single home under Leasehold Reform Act 1967, s 2(1); Under the Civil Partnership Act 2004, s 135 'family home' means any house, caravan, houseboat or other structure which has been provided or has been made available by one or both of the civil partners as, or has become, a family residence and includes any garden or other ground or building attached to, and usually occupied with, or otherwise required for the amenity or convenience of, the house, caravan, houseboat or other structure but does not include a residence provided or made available by one civil partner for that civil partner to reside in, whether with any child of the family or not, separately from the other civil partner; In *Qazi* v *Harrow LBC* [2001] EWCA Civ 1834, CA held that there was no requirement, for purposes of Human Rights Convention art 8 (respect for a person's home), for occupation of the premises to be lawful or for the existence of an occupier's legal interest. See *Buckley* v *UK* (1996) 23 EHRR 101 – significance of exact circumstances, such as existence of sufficient and continuous links.

homeless caravan dweller. CA held in *Codona* v *Mid-Beds DC* (2004) *The Times*, 21 July, that in circumstances in which a local housing authority had discharged its obligation to obtain suitable accommodation for a homeless gypsy caravan dweller, when it offered her temporary bed and breakfast accommodation, that obligation had been carried out in spite of her declared aversion to having to live in conventional housing.

homelessness. A person is homeless if he has no accommodation in the UK or elsewhere which he is entitled to occupy by virtue of an interest in it or by virtue of a court order, has a licence to occupy, or occupies a residence by virtue of any enactment or rule of law giving him the right to remain in occupation or restricting the right of another to recover possession: H.A. 1996, s 175(1). He is also homeless if he has accommodation but cannot secure entry to it, or it consists of a moveable structure and there is no place where he is allowed to place it and reside in it: s 175(2). A person is 'threatened with homelessness' if it is likely that he will become homeless within 28 days: s 175(4). For duties of local housing authorities to provide advisory services, see s 179; SI 96/3205. *Nairne* v *Camden LBC* [1999] 1 WLR 384; *Lewisham LBC* v *Akinsola* (2000) 32 HLR 414.

homelessness application. It was held in *R (Griffin)* v *Southwark LBC* (2005) *The*

Times, 3 January, that where a second homelessness application is made by the same applicant, a local authority is obliged to make a reconsideration, save where the facts are precisely the same.

homelessness, intentional. A person becomes homeless intentionally if he deliberately does or fails to do anything in consequence of which he ceases to occupy accommodation which is available for his occupation and which it would have been reasonable for him to continue to occupy: H.A. 1985, s 60(1). See *R v Harrow LBC ex p Fahia* [1998] 1 WLR 1396; *Minchin v Sheffield CC* (2000) *The Times*, 26 April (prisoner held to be intentionally homeless). In *R (C) v Lewisham LBC* (2003) 153 NLJ 1064, the CA held that the discretion of a local authority to extend the period of time needed for the review of a decision that a person is intentionally homeless (see Housing Act 1996, s 202(3)) is unrestricted, save for the ordinary principles of 'reasonableness' set out in *Associated Provincial Picture Houses Ltd v Wednesbury Corporation* [1947] 2 All ER 680. See also *Tower Hamlets LBC v Chetnick Developments* [1988] 1 All ER 961. *See* HOMELESSNESS.

homelessness, priority need and. CA held in *Higgs v Brighton and Hove CC* (2003) *The Times*, 11 July, that the unexpected disappearance of a caravan used by a person as his home comes within the description of 'emergency' entitling him to priority need for accommodation. But where he was homeless at the time of the disappearance of the caravan, he would be unable to establish a case for priority need. See Housing Act 1996, s 189(1(d)).

homelessness review. A review of current and likely future homelessness levels in an authority's district; activities carried out in such a district for preventing homelessness, securing that accommodation is or will be available in such a district for people who are or may become homeless in that district; providing support for people who are or may become homeless and need support to

prevent its recurrence: Homelessness Act 2002, s 2. A local authority is expected to carry out such a review from time to time: s 1(1).

home loss. Term used in Land Compensation Act 1973, s 29, as amended by Planning and Compensation Act 1991, s 68, whereby compensation is made available for the loss of a house acquired by a local authority for demolition, and for injury sustained through the loss of a house.

home, mobile. A caravan (q.v.): Mobile Homes Act 1983, s 5(1). See *Walker v Badcock* (1998) 30 HLR 513. In *Howard v Charlton* (2002) *The Times*, 18 August, CA held that the essential character of a mobile home is not changed by the addition of a bolted-on porch extension. See Caravan Sites and Control of Development Act 1960, s 29, as modified by Caravan Sites Act 1968, s 13.

home, principal. In deciding whether a person is occupying premises as 'his only or principal home' (See Protection from Eviction Act 1977, s 3A (2), particular attention must be given as to where he sleeps, even as a temporary state of affairs: *Sumeghovo v McMahon* (2000) *The Times*, 6 November.

Home Secretary. The Secretary of State in charge of the Home Department, which deals, in general, with the domestic functions in England and Wales not specifically assigned to other departments of state. He is generally responsible for the maintenance of law and order, and, in practice, exercises some prerogative powers of the Crown, including the prerogative of mercy (q.v.). He is concerned, specifically, with the administration of justice, the prison service, treatment of offenders, community relations, immigration and naturalisation procedures, supervision of the control of firearms and dangerous drugs.

home worker. An individual who contracts with a person, for purposes of the person's business, for the execution of work to be done in a place not under the person's control or management: Employment Relations Act 1999, s 13.

homicide. The killing of a human being by a human being. May be categorised as *lawful* (e.g., committed in the execution of justice) or *unlawful*, or as *justifiable* (q.v.), *excusable* (q.v.), or *criminal* (i.e., a killing, neither justifiable nor excusable, such as murder, manslaughter, infanticide). *See* INFANTICIDE; MANSLAUGHTER; MURDER.

homosexual conduct. Sexual activity with a member of one's own sex. Buggery (q.v.) or indecency (q.v.) with another man is no longer an offence if both parties have attained the age of 16 (see S.O. (Amendment) A. 2000, s 1(2)), if both have consented and the act is done in private: S.O.A. 1967. Prosecution may require consent of DPP (q.v.). See also C.J.P.O.A. 1994, ss 144, 145(1), 146(4). Ban against homosexuals in armed services was lifted in January 2000. See *Fitzpatrick v Sterling HA* [2000] 1 FLR 271 (same-sex partner of a tenant can succeed to a tenancy on death of the other partner).

honeste vivere. Phrase used by the Roman jurist Ulpian and adopted in Justinian's *Institutes* (AD 533) in a summary of the basic precepts of the law, thus: *honeste vivere, alterum non laedere, suum cuique tribuere* (to live honestly, not to harm another and to give every man his due).

honorarium. A voluntary, or honorary, payment or reward, often given as compensation for services in circumstances in which payment cannot be enforced at law or in which tradition might not allow a payment. *See* BARRISTER'S FEES.

honour clauses. Clauses in agreements intended as express declarations that transactions between the parties to which those agreements relate are not to be binding in law: see, e.g., *Diocese of Southwark v Coker* (1997) 141 SJLB 169. The courts will generally give effect to such declarations: see, e.g., *Edwards v Skyways* [1964] 1 WLR 349 (*ex gratia* payment).

horseplay and damages. In *Blake v Galloway* [2004] EWCA Civ 814, the CA held that the victim of an accident resulting from youthful horseplay among friends would not usually be held to be able to recover damages unless he could show that the injury resulted from a failure to take care which amounted to recklessness or a very high degree of carelessness or that it resulted from intent to cause harm.

hospital. A health service hospital within the meaning of the National Health Service Act 1977, or any accommodation provided by any person pursuant to arrangements made under the 1977 Act, s 23(1), and used as a hospital. For independent hospital and clinic, see Care Standards Act 2000, s 2.

hospital order. An order by the magistrates' court (q.v.) or Crown Court (q.v.) authorising an offender's admission to, and detention in a specified hospital. See M.H.A. 1983, s 37, amended by Crime (Sentences) Act 1997, Sch 6; Courts Act 1971, ss 56, 62. Applications for discharge are heard by Area Mental Health Review Tribunals (q.v.). Under M.H.A. 1983, s 45A, inserted by Crime (Sentences) Act 1997, s 46, the court, when satisfied on the evidence of two medical practitioners that an offender is suffering from a psychopathic disorder (q.v.) which makes it appropriate for him to be detained for medical treatment which is likely to improve, or prevent a deterioration in his conditon, may issue an order directing a hospital admission.

hospital premises. Premises 'used or to be used for the prevention, diagnosis or treatment of illness or for the reception of patients': Health Services Act 1976, s 14(1). See NHS and Community Care Act 1990, Sch 10.

hospital records, privacy of. Because of the importance of the protection of integrity of hospital medical records, an order made against newspaper publishers requiring them to disclose sources of information relating to those records was justified: judgment of HL in *Ashworth Hospital for Authority v MGN Ltd* (2002) *The Times*, 1 July.

hospital, special. *See* SPECIAL HOSPITAL.

hostage. 1. Person taken by a belligerent and held as security. 2. Person seized in the UK or elsewhere in order to compel a state, international governmental organisation or person to do or abstain from doing any act. One who threatens to kill, injure or continue to detain the hostage commits an offence under Taking of Hostages Act 1982, s 1(1). See Extradition Act 1989, s 25.

hostel. A building in which is provided, for persons generally or for a class or classes of persons, residential accommodation (otherwise than in separate and self-contained sets of premises) and either board or facilities for the preparation of food adequate to the needs of those persons, or both: H.A. 1985, s 622, as amended. For 'bail hostel' and 'probation hostel', see P.C.C.(S.)A. 2000, Sch 9, para 50(3); C.J.C.S.A. 2000, s 9.

hostile witness. One who, in the opinion of the court, is hostile to the party calling him and is unwilling to tell the truth. With leave of the court that party may cross-examine him. See Criminal Procedure Act 1865, s 3; Civil Evidence Act 1968, s 3(1)(*a*); Civil Evidence Act 1995, s 10(3), (5); *R v Ugorji* (2000) *The Independent*, 5 July. See UNFAVOURABLE WITNESS.

hostilities. Acts or operations, usually connected with war (q.v.), committed by belligerents: *Spinney's Ltd v Royal Insurance Co Ltd* [1980] 1 Lloyd's Rep 406.

hotchpot. (*Hocher* = to shake together.) The bringing together of properties into a common lot so that equality of division may be assured. See A.E.A. 1925, ss 47, 49. The rule was repealed under Law Reform (Succession) Act 1995, s 1(2).

hotel. 'An establishment held out by the proprietor as offering food, drink and, if required, sleeping accommodation, without special contract, to any traveller presenting himself who appears able and willing to pay a reasonable sum for the services and facilities provided and who is in a fit state to be received': Hotel Proprietors Act 1956, s 1(3). See Capital Allowances Act 1990, s 19. *See* INN.

hours of darkness. The time between half-an-hour after sunset and half-an-

hour before sunrise: Highways Act 1980, s 329(1).

house. Includes any part of a building occupied or intended to be occupied as a separate dwelling, and any yard, garden, outhouses and appurtenances belonging to the house or usually enjoyed with it: Housing Associations Act 1985, s 106(1), as amended. See also Leasehold Reform Act 1967, s 1; *Malpas v St Ermine's Property Co* (1992) 17 EG 112 (maisonette may be a 'house'); *Dugan-Chapman v Grosvenor Estates* (1997) 10 EG 152.

houseboat. Boat constructed or altered in design so as to provide living accommodation. The meaning of the term 'residential houseboat' was to be decided by the jury as a question of fact and degree: *Sussex Investments v Secretary of State for Environment* [1997] NPC 190. It is not of the same genus as 'real property': *Chelsea Yacht Club v Pope* [2000] 22 EG 139.

house bote. *See* ESTOVERS.

housebreaking. Breaking and entering (q.v.) a dwelling house or other building. *See* BURGLARY.

housebreaking implements, possession of. 'A person shall be guilty of an offence if, when not at his place of abode, he has with him any article for use in the course of or in connection with any burglary, theft or cheat': Th.A. 1968, s 25(1). See *R v Ellames* [1974] 3 All ER 130 (it was held that s 25 was aimed at acts preparatory to a burglary, theft or cheat); *Re McAngus* [1994] Crim LR 602. *See* BURGLARY.

household. The term has been held to have 'an abstract meaning': *Santos v Santos* [1972] Fam 247. 'A family unit or something akin to a family unit – a group of persons, held together by a particular kind of tie, who normally live together, even if individual members of the group may be temporarily separated from it': *per* Lord Emslie in *McGregor v Haswell* 1983 SLT 626. See *Rogers v Islington LBC* [1999] 37 EG 178.

house in multiple occupation. *See* MULTIPLE OCCUPATION, HOUSE IN.

housekeeping allowances, savings from. 'If any question arises as to the right of a husband or wife to money derived from any allowance made by the husband for the expenses of the matrimonial home or for similar purposes, or to any property acquired out of such money, the money or property shall, in the absence of any agreement between them to the contrary, be treated as belonging to the husband and wife in equal shares': Married Women's Property Act 1964, s 1.

House, Leader of the. Member of the House of Commons (and Minister of the Crown) who is responsible for the arrangement of government business in the House. The Leader of the Lords has similar functions. See Parliamentary and Other Pensions Act 1987, s 5(1).

house, meaning of. A property which consists of one or two floors of commercial uses with extra floors of residential accommodation above and behind, whether or not it is actually used for living purposes, can be capable of being considered as a house under Housing Act 1985, s 17: *Ainsdale Investments Ltd v First Secretary of State* (2004) *The Times*, 2 June.

House of Commons. The Lower House of Parliament. A representative assembly elected by universal adult suffrage, consisting of 650 members (523 for England, 38 for Wales, 72 for Scotland, 17 for N Ireland). Its chief officer is the Speaker (q.v.). Persons disqualified for membership include: aliens; persons under 21; holders of certain judicial offices; civil servants; members of the police and regular armed forces; life and 'excepted' hereditary peers and peeresses; prisoners; persons suffering from mental illness; bankrupts, clergy (with some exceptions, e.g. nonconformist ministers); members of a legislature of a country outside the UK: House of Commons Disqualification Act 1975, s 1(1). A quorum for voting purposes is 40 members. *See* PARLIAMENT; PARLIAMENTARY ELECTORS.

House of Lords, appointment of woman judge. The first woman judge, Lady Hale, has been appointed as a Law Lord. The number of female judges is as follows: Law Lords 1/12; Heads of Division 1/5; Lord Justices of Appeal 2/38; High Court judges 6/106; Circuit judges 69/610; Recorders 175/1369); District judges 8/44.

House of Lords, before end of 1998–99 session. The Upper House of Parliament. It consisted of the *Lords Temporal* (i.e., all hereditary peers and peeresses who had not disclaimed their peerages under the Peerage Act 1963, life peers and peeresses, Lords of Appeal in Ordinary) and the *Lords Spiritual* (Archbishops of Canterbury and York, Bishops of London, Winchester and Durham and 21 other senior bishops of the Church of England). The House (which comprised 1,186 members) is presided over by the Lord Chancellor. The Lords have a restricted right (see Parliament Acts 1911, 1949) to initiate, amend and reject Bills. *See* HOUSE OF LORDS, JURISDICTION OF; HOUSE OF LORDS, TRANSITIONAL ARRANGEMENTS; LAW LORDS; PARLIAMENT; PEER.

House of Lords, civil appeal, procedure. Appellants are expected to prepare statements of fact agreed between parties, and disputed material; transcripts of any unreported judgments to be cited only when they contain authoritative statements of a relevant legal principle not found in a reported case; directions or documents to be produced must be given: *Practice Direction (HL: Civil Procedure Amendments)* [1999] 1 WLR 1833.

House of Lords, correction of its errors. '[Their Lordships] propose to modify their present practice and, while treating former decisions of this House as normally binding, to depart from a previous decision when it appears right to do so': *Practice Statement* [1966] 1 WLR 1234. See, e.g., *R v Shivpuri* [1987] AC 1. *See* PRECEDENT.

House of Lords, jurisdiction of. The right of a peer to be tried 'by his peers' was abolished by C.J.A. 1948. The House has full appellate jurisdiction. In civil cases it hears appeals from the Court of Appeal (q.v.) with leave of that court or the Appeals Committee of the House. In criminal cases it hears appeals from the Court of Appeal if that court certifies that a point of law of general public importance is involved and either the court or the House gives leave to appeal because the point is one which ought to be considered by the House. It may hear appeals from the High Court, the Court of Session, the Court of Appeal in N Ireland, the Courts-Martial Appeals Court. The judges in the Lords are Lords of Appeal in Ordinary (q.v.) and peers who have held, or hold, high judicial office. Generally, five Law Lords will sit; in an unusually important case, seven may sit (see, e.g., *Pepper* v *Hart* [1993] AC 593). Lay peers do not participate (see *O'Connell* v *R* (1844) 11 Cl & F 155). The Appellate Committee, presided over by the Lord Chancellor (q.v.) or the senior Lord of Appeal in Ordinary, reports its conclusions to the House. Judicial decisions of the House of Lords are binding on all other courts but may be overruled by a decision of the European Court of Justice and the Court of First Instance (qq.v.), or statute, may be distinguished, and may be rejected if considered to have been given *per incuriam* (q.v.). See A.J.A. 1960, s 1; Criminal Appeal Act 1968, s 33; C.P.I.A. 1996, s 36 (providing for appeals to the House of Lords against decisions of the Court of Appeal on an appeal under s 35); *R* v *Weir* (2001) *The Times*, 9 February (time to apply for leave to appeal to House).

House of Lords, petitions for appeal to. Petition for leave to appeal is referred to the Appeal Committee (three Lords of Appeal) who will consider whether it appears competent to be received by the House and, if so, whether it should be referred for an oral hearing. See House of Lords Directions as to Criminal Procedure [1999] 1 WLR 1830.

House of Lords, transitional arrangements. Following government policy moves to reform House of Lords, and House of Lords Act 1999, the House comprised, on 1 January 2000, 616 members including: life peers; excepted peers (elected by hereditary members) plus the Earl Marshal and Lord Great Chamberlain; current and retired Lords of Appeal in Ordinary; Lords Spiritual. See *Lord Gray's Motion* and *Lord Mayhew's Motion* (House of Lords Committee for Privileges) (1999) *The Times*, 12 November. *See* SECOND CHAMBER, PROPOSALS FOR.

housing accommodation, privately let. Local housing authorities may provide financial assistance for the purpose of acquisition, construction, conversion, improvement, maintenance of property intended to be privately let as housing accommodation: L.G.A. 1988, Part III. See also H.A. 1996, s 22.

housing action trust area. Area designated by order under H.A. 1988, s 60, comprising two or more parcels of land, and involving the physical state, design, management of housing accommodation, social activities, etc. The trust may secure repair, improvement, proper management and use of that accommodation. See H.A. 1996, Sch 19.

housing association. A society, body of trustees or company not trading for profit, established so as to construct, improve or manage houses: Housing Associations Act 1985, s 1; SI 96/2325.

housing association tenancy. A tenancy arising where the interest of the landlord belongs to a housing association (q.v.) or housing trust (q.v.), or to the Housing Corporation (q.v.); Rent Act 1977, s 86. For rent limits, see s 88, as amended by H.A. 1988, Sch 18. See also H.A. 1980, s 56.

housing authority, local. A district council, London borough council, the Common Council of the City of London, the Council of the Isles of Scilly: H.A. 1985, s 1. It is empowered to provide housing accommodation by erecting or acquiring houses or converting buildings into houses: s 9. It may make such reasonable charges as it may determine for the tenancy or occupation of its houses: s 24. For 'public sector housing', see H.A. 1985, s 429A (inserted by H.&P.A.

1986, s 16). See also Housing Grants, Construction and Regeneration Act 1996.

housing benefit. Benefit under S.S. Contributions and Benefits Act 1992, s 130, S.S. (Consequential Provisions) A. 1992, Sch 2, amending Rent Act 1977, s 72, paid to a claimant who is liable to make payments in respect of a house he occupies as his home and there is an appropriate maximum housing benefit in his case and he has no income or his income does not exceed the applicable amount. See S.S.A. 1998, s 69; W.R.P.A. 1999, s 79 (measures to reduce under-occupation by housing benefit claimants who are tenants in the public or social rented sector); C.S.P.S.S.A. 2000, s 71 (recovery of fraudulent benefit payments).

Housing Corporation. An authority set up under H.A. 1964, s 1, with extended powers and functions under H.A. 1974, s 1 (both Acts now repealed and re-enacted), which is concerned with, e.g., promotion and assistance of develop-ment of registered housing associations and unregistered building societies. See H.A. 1996, ss 30–38.

housing of disabled children. CA held in *R (A)* v *National Asylum Support Service* (2003) *The Times*, 31 October, that there existed an absolute duty on the part of the National Asylum Support Service to make available adequate accommodation to an asylum-seeking family with dis-abled children.

housing subsidy. Subsidy payable to local authorities, new town corpora-tions and Development Board for Rural Wales: H.A. 1985, s 421, as amended. The subsidy to local authorities is calculated by adding the base amount (see s 423) to the housing costs differential (see s 424) and subtracting the local contribution differential (see s 425): s 422. See L.G.H.A. 1989, Sch 11.

housing trust. A corporation or body of persons which is required by the terms of its constituent instrument to devote its funds to the provision of houses, and other purposes incidental thereto, or is required to devote its funds to charitable purposes and in fact devotes them to the provision of houses: Housing Associations Act 1985, s 2.

human habitation, unfitness for. A house will be regarded as unfit for human habitation if it is defective in one of the following matters so that it is not reasonably suitable for occupation in that condition: repair, stability, freedom from damp, lighting, ventilation, water supply, drainage and sanitary conveni-ences, cooking facilities. See H.A. 1985, s 604, substituted by L.G.H.A. 1989, Sch 11; *Dover DC* v *Sherred* [1997] NPC 13. *See* REPAIRING OBLIGATION.

Human Rights, European Convention on. The European Convention for the Protection of Human Rights and Funda-mental Freedoms, signed and ratified by members of the Council of Europe in November 1950 and in force since September 1953. Rights and freedoms it seeks to protect include: right to life; freedom from torture and slavery; right to liberty and fair trial; freedom of thought and religion, etc. Some of the rights are absolute (e.g. art 4(1) relating to slavery); some others may be subject to limited derogation, e.g. in time of war. Under the Convention were created the Com-mission on Human Rights (abolished in 1998), and the Court of Human Rights (q.v.). See Human Rights Act 1998, ss 1, 2, Sch 1, making the core concepts of the Convention enforceable in courts in the UK, as from 2 October 2000. For pro-cedure for bringing claims under the Act, see SI 00/2002.

Human Rights, European Convention, UK legislation concerning. Human Rights Act 1998 (in force since 2 Octo-ber 2000) gives effect in the UK to rights and freedoms guaranteed under the Convention (q.v.). Any court or tribunal determining a question which has arisen relating to a Convention right must take into account any judgment, decision, declaration or advisory opinion of the European Court of Human Rights: s 2(1). Primary and subordinate legislation, whenever enacted, must be read and given effect in a way which is compatible with human rights (so far as it is possible to do so): s 3(1). House of Lords, JCPC, High Court, Court of Appeal, must make a declaration of incompatibility in relation to primary legislation where satisfied of such incompatibility: s 4. Public authorities, e.g., courts and tribunals must not act in any way which is incompatible with a Convention right: s 6(1), (3).

Human Rights, European Court of. *See* EUROPEAN COURT OF HUMAN RIGHTS.

human rights legislation, retrospective nature of. HL held in *R v Saunders and Others* (2002) The Times, 15 November that CA was bound, whenever hearing an appeal, to accept the substantive law as it was at the time of a particular trial. The qualification in 1999 (following a judgment of the European Court) of the Companies Act 1985, s 434 (5), had no retrospective effect. In *R v Kansal (No. 2)* [2001] 3 WLR 1562, HL decided that decision in *R v Lambert* [2001] 3 WLR 206 (that although Human Rights Act 1998 is retrospective in relation to proceedings brought by or following instigation of public authority, it is not retrospective in relation to appeals in such proceedings) should be followed even though a majority of Law Lords in the present case felt that it had been decided wrongly.

Human Rights, primary and subordinate legislation in relation to. For purposes of Human Rights Act 1998, 'primary legislation' includes any public general, local and personal, private, Act, measure of Church Assembly, and Order in Council made in exercise of the Royal Prerogative. 'Subordinate legislation' includes Orders in Council (other than those made under Royal Prerogative), Acts of Scottish and N Ireland Parliaments, orders, rules and regulations made under primary legislation: s 21.

Human Rights, remedial action under Convention. Where a legislative provision (i.e., primary legislation) is declared under Human Rights Act 1998, s 4, to be incompatible with a Convention right, and a minister considers that there are compelling reasons, he may, by Order in Council, make an amendment to the legislation, necessary to remove the incompatibility: s 10(2). Where he considers that subordinate legislation is incompatible, and that it is necessary to amend the primary legislation, he may amend the primary legislation by order, should there be compelling reasons: s 10(3). For procedural requirements, see Sch 2; they include approval of remedial orders by both Houses.

Human Rights, Universal Declaration of. Adopted by the United Nations Commission on Human Rights and by the General Assembly in 1948. Relates to rights such as life, liberty, security of a person, freedom from arbitrary arrest, right to a fair hearing, freedom of thought and religion, right to social security and to work, right to education.

human tissue, removal of. Under Human Tissue Act 1961 (as amended by Corneal Tissue Act 1986 and SI 00/90), the removal of parts of the body of a deceased person by a medical practitioner for therapeutic purposes, medical education or research, is permitted if that person has so requested in writing, or orally during his last illness in the presence of two or more witnesses. See *Dobson* v *N Tyneside HA* [1994] 4 All ER 474; *R v Northumberland Coroner ex p Jacobs* (2000) 53 BMLR 21; Anatomy Act 1984. *See* BODY PARTS; ORGAN, HUMAN.

hung jury. *See* JURY, HUNG.

hunt. A body of persons who combine wholly or partly for the purpose of hunting wild mammals with dogs: Hunting Bill 2000, Sch 1. 'Wild animals' include, in particular, one which has been bred or tamed for the purpose of being hunted or for any other purpose, one which is in, or has escaped or been released from, captivity or confinement. Hunting Act 2004, s 11(1).

hunting, defences to charge. It is a defence for a person charged under the Hunting Act 2004, s 2 to prove that the conduct to which the charge relates consisted of stalking a fox, hare or rabbit or flushing it out of cover, for the purpose of protecting livestock, fowl, game birds or crops, or for the purpose of rodent control, or recapturing or rescuing animals: Sch 1.

hunting with dogs. Under Hunting Act 2004, s 1, a person commits an offence if he hunts a wild animal with a dog, or knowingly permits his dog to be used in the commission of that offence.

husband and wife. At common law they were considered as 'one person' so that, e.g., the husband was entitled on marriage to chattels and choses in possession (q.v.) belonging to his wife. Statutes have vitiated the significance of this concept: thus, e.g., under Th.A. 1968, s 30(1), husbands and wives are liable in respect of offences which they commit against one another's property as if they were not married; under Law Reform (Married Women and Tortfeasors) Act 1935, s 1, a married woman is capable of acquiring, holding and alienating property as if a single person. See also Law Reform (Husband and Wife) Act 1962; Matrimonial Proceedings and Property Act 1970; P.&C.E.A. 1984, s 80; amended by Y.J.C.E.A. 1999, Sch 4, para 13; *Royal Bank of Scotland* v *Etridge (No. 2)* [1998] 4 All ER 705 (guidelines in cases of presumption of undue influence between husband and wife).

hybrid Bill. 'A public Bill which affects a particular private interest in a manner different from the private interest of other persons or bodies of the same category or class': Speaker of the House, 1962. See, e.g., Channel Tunnel Bill 1986–87. It may be introduced by the government or a private member, and is treated like a private Bill after its second reading.

hypothecation. The right of a ship's master, in case of necessity, to assign the ship or the ship and its cargo by bottomry bond undertaking to repay the principal and interest on the safe arrival of the ship. A *letter of hypothecation* is one addressed to a bank, giving details of a shipment of goods relating to a draft. In the event of dishonour of the draft, the bank is allowed to sell the goods. *See* BOTTOMRY.

hypothetical dispute. Issues based on mere supposition. In general, the courts will not adjudicate upon disputes of this kind: *Glasgow Navigation Co* v *Iron Ore Co* [1910] AC 293. Nor will the courts pronounce on abstract questions of law: (*Ainsbury* v *Millington* [1987] 1 WLR 379) or appeals which are academic between the parties (*R* v *Secretary of State for Home Department ex p Salem* [1999] 1 AC 450).

I

identification, eye witness procedures.
Under Police and Criminal Evidence
Act 1984 (Codes of Practice) (Temporary
Modifications to Code D) Order 2002
(SI 615/2002), duty to conduct formal
identification procedures is limited to
circumstances where it is reasonably
practicable to do so. Police may exercise
discretion to decline to hold identification
parade where they believe that holding it
would serve no useful purpose relating to
proof of suspect's involvement in the
offence.

identification of suspect. CA held in
R v George [2002] EWCA Crim 1923,
that a qualified identification by a witness
of a defendant charged with a criminal
offence might be admissible in evidence
if relevant and probative.

identification   parade. Procedure
whereby persons, including an arrested suspect, are viewed by a witness for purposes
of identification. See Code of Practice
issued under P.&C.E.A. 1984; *R v Penny*
(1992) 94 Cr App R 345; *R v Kelly*
(1998) *The Times*, 23 February (failure to
comply with the code is not necessarily
fatal in every case); *R v Popat (No. 2)*
[2000] 1 Cr App R 387 (parade is not
required after proper and adequate
identification); *R v Jones and Nelson*
(1999) 143 SJLB 122 (force used to
secure compliance with organisers of
identification parade); *R v Forbes* (2000)
The Times, 19 December.

identity, evidence of. 1. *Primary
(direct) evidence*, e.g., obtained by an
identification parade (q.v.) before trial.
See also revised *Code of Practice*, under
P.&C.E.A. 1984, *Code D*, allowing
identification by video. For voice
identification, see *R v Robb* (1991) *The
Times*, 6 February. 2. *Secondary evidence*, e.g., by an identifying witness
who swears that he identified the accused
on a former occasion, and by another
witness to say that he saw this. See
R v Christie [1914] AC 545; *R v Fergus*
(1991) *The Times*, 11 November; the
Turnbull warning (q.v.). 3. *Circumstantial evidence*, e.g., the accused's fingerprints, DNA traces. For flawed evidence
of identity in a conviction which resulted
in an execution (in 1952), see *R v Mattan*
(1998) *The Times*, 5 March. For 'dock
identification', see *R v Tricoglus* (1977)
65 Cr App R 16. For 'identification by
jury', see *R v MacNamara* [1996] Crim
LR 750.

idle and disorderly person. One who
was found guilty of a relatively trivial
offence under the Vagrancy Act 1824,
e.g., begging in a public place (q.v.).

ignorantia   juris   neminem   excusat.
Ignorance of the law does not excuse.
When mistake is pleaded as a defence, the
mistake must be one of fact, not of law.
'Every man of England is, in judgment
of law, party to the making of an Act of
Parliament, being present thereat by his
representatives': Blackstone. 'Every man
must be taken to be cognisant of the
law, otherwise there is no knowing of
the extent to which the excuse of ignorance might be carried. It would be urged
in almost every case': *R v Bailey* (1800)
Russ & Ry 1. 'The rule is not that a man
is always presumed to know the law,
but that no man shall be excused for
an unlawful act' from his ignorance of
the law': *per* Talfourd J in *R v Bentley*
(1850) 4 Cox CC 406. See *R v Esop*
(1836) 7 C & P 456; *Secretary of State v
Hart* [1982] 1 WLR 481.

ILEX. Institute of Legal Executives, established 1963. Professional body of some 22,000 legal executives (q.v.) and trainee legal executives. It has responsibilities for education and training, and regulation of members' practice standards and conduct. After 1998 it became an authorised body for purposes of C.L.S.A. 1999, able to grant appropriate rights of advocacy to suitably qualified fellows.

illegal. In violation of a law or rule which has the force of law.

illegal contracts. Contracts which are forbidden by statute or are contrary to common law or public policy and are, therefore, generally void. Examples: a contract tending to injure the public service, e.g., by the attempted sale of a public office or a contract to procure a title of honour (see *Parkinson v College of Ambulance* [1925] 2 KB 1); a contract in restraint of trade (see *Nordenfelt v Maxim Nordenfelt Gun Co Ltd* [1894] AC 535); a contract to commit a criminal offence or civil wrong (see *Napier v National Business Agency* [1951] 2 All ER 263). See Law Com No. 154 (1999), *Effect of Illegality on Contracts and Trusts.* In *21st Century Logistic Solutions v Madysen* [2004] EWHC 231, it was held that not every contract entered into with the intention of committing an illegal act is itself illegal and unenforceable. It is insufficient for a defence of illegality to be made out where an individual may have merely intended that the contract should be a part of a fraudulent scheme. *See* CONTRACT.

illegal entrant. 'A person unlawfully entering [the UK] or seeking to enter in breach of a deportation order or of the immigration laws and includes a person who has so entered': Immigration Act 1971, s 33(1). His detention is lawful: Sch 2. See, e.g., *R v Secretary of State for the Home Department ex p Chan* (1992) *The Times*, 1 January; *R v Naille* [1993] 2 WLR 927 (disembarkation is not entry). See Immigration and Asylum Act 1999, s 32(1).

illegal trust. One which offends against statute or morality or public policy. In the

case of an intentional creation of a trust for an illegal purpose, a resulting trust (q.v.) may be implied in favour of the settlor if the illegal purpose has not been executed. See *Ayerst v Jenkins* (1873) LR 16 Eq 275. *See* TRUST.

illegitimate child. One born out of lawful wedlock. 'References (however expressed) to any relationship between two persons shall, unless the contrary intention appears, be construed without regard to whether or not the father and mother of either of them, or the father and mother of any person through whom the relationship is deduced, have or had been married to each other': F.L.R.A. 1987, s 1(1). For property rights, e.g., succession on intestacy, see 1987 Act, Part III. See also SI 91/1980.

illusory appointment. An appointment (q.v.), under which a merely nominal share was appointed to an object, which could be set aside: *Wilson v Piggott* (1974) 2 Ves Jun 35. Under L.P.A. 1925, s 158, no appointment is to be invalid merely on the ground that 'an unsubstantial, illusory or nominal share only is appointed to or left unappointed to devolve upon any one or more of the objects of the power'.

illusory trust. A conveyance by a debtor to trustees upon trust for creditors which can be revoked, in some circumstances, by the debtor, is an example. See *Johns v James* (1878) 8 Ch D 744. *See* TRUST.

immediate. 'It does not mean instantaneous . . . it connotes proximity in time and proximity in causation': *R v Horseferry Rd Stipendiary Magistrate ex p Siadatan* [1991] 1 All ER 324. See *Valentine v DPP* [1997] COD 339 (the word 'immediate' in P.O.A. 1986, s 4 ('immediate unlawful violence') did not necessarily mean 'instantaneous' and could mean 'within a short time').

immigration. Entering a country for purposes of permanent residence there. See Immigration Act 1971, which confers the right of abode on, e.g., citizens of the UK and colonies who are connected with Britain by birth. Power to refuse leave to enter the UK rests initially with immigration officers. The Secretary of State has power to give leave to remain in the UK: s 4. For power of Secretary of State to give or refuse leave before the person concerned arrives in UK, see 1971 Act, s 3A, inserted by Immigration and Asylum Act 1999, s 1. See also Immigration Act 1988; Asylum and Immigration Act 1996; Special Immigration Appeals Commission Act 1997 (allowing further types of appeal in relation to the 1971 Act, ss 13–15 and extending the circumstances in which a deportation order may not be made while appeal is pending (see Sch 2, para 2)); Immigration and Asylum Act 1999, Part IV, and Schs 2, 3, 4 (appeals procedures).

immigration advice. Advice given which relates to a particular individual concerning, e.g., claim for asylum, leave to enter or remain in UK, nationality and citizenship, removal or deportation from UK and is not concerned with criminal proceedings: see Immigration and Asylum Act 1999, s 82(1). Persons providing such advice must be qualified under s 84(1), (2).

immigration and deception. *See* DECEPTION, IMMIGRATION AND.

immigration and human rights. A person who alleges that a decision has been taken under the Immigration Acts relating to his entitlement to enter and remain in UK, and that the decision is in breach of his human rights, may appeal to an adjudicator: see Immigration and Asylum Act 1999, s 65(1). See Human Rights Act 1998, s 6(1).

Immigration Appeal Tribunal. See Immigration and Asylum Act 1999, s 56, Sch 2. Members are appointed by the Lord Chancellor. Appeals from decisions of adjudicators may be heard: see Sch 4, para 22. Appeal from decisions of the Tribunal may be made to the appropriate court on a question of law material to that decision: para 23(1). In *A v Secretary of State for Home Department* (2004) *The Times*, 3 August, the CA held that the general jurisdiction of the Appeal Tribunal is now restricted to decisions only where the adjudicator has made some error of law. *See* ADJUDICATORS, IMMIGRATION.

immigration control, person subject to. Means, for Immigration and Asylum Act 1999, Part VI, a person who is not a national of an EEA state and who: requires leave to enter and remain in UK, but does not have it; has leave to enter or remain in UK which is subject to a condition that he does not have recourse to public funds; has leave to enter or remain in UK given as result of a written undertaking by another person to be responsible for his maintenance and accommodation, or only as a result of a pending appeal: see s 115(9), (10).

immigration, illegal, sentencing. CA held in *R v Toor* (2003) *The Times*, 3 February, that because offences of facilitating illegal immigration were now widespread, deterrent sentences were necessary.

Immigration Services Commissioner. Appointed by Secretary of State under Immigration and Asylum Act 1999, s 83, to secure that those who provide immigration advice (q.v.) or services are competent to do so, act in their clients' best interests, do not knowingly mislead any court or tribunal and do not seek to abuse immigration procedures. For appeal from a decision of the Commissioner to Immigration Services Tribunal, see s 87. See Sch 5. 'Immigration services' means the making of representations on behalf of an individual in civil proceedings before a court or tribunal in UK, or in correspondence with a minister or government department in connection with relevant matters: s 82.

immoral contracts. Agreements founded on an immoral consideration (q.v.). In general, they are void. See *Fender v Mildmay* [1938] AC 11; *Armhouse Lee Ltd v Chappell* (1996) *The Times*, 7 August. *See EX TURPI CAUSA NON ORITUR ACTIO.*

immovables. Generally, land and property attached.

immunity. Freedom or exemption from some obligation, penalty, or power of another. Thus, e.g., an advocate has no general immunity from being sued in negligence by his client; but no claim lies against a judge in respect of words or actions arising in the exercise of his judicial office ('judicial immunity' (q.v.)); no claim lies in respect of words spoken in the course of proceedings by any witnesses or parties (see, e.g., *Roy* v *Prior* [1971] AC 470); no foreign sovereign may be impleaded in an action *in personam*, or *in rem* (see *The Cristina* [1938] AC 485). Hohfeld, *Fundamental Legal Conceptions* (1917), uses 'immunity' to signify 'the relations of A to B when B has no legal power to affect one or more of the existing legal relations of A.' For Crown immunity, see, e.g., Crown Proceedings Act 1947; *Pearce* v *Secretary of State for Defence* [1988] 2 WLR 1027. For police immunity, see *Docker* v *Chief Constable of W Midlands Police* (2000) *The Times*, 1 August.

immunity, diplomatic. Diplomatic privilege (q.v.).

immunity from jurisdiction, state, sovereign. A state is immune from the jurisdiction of the courts of the UK and courts shall give effect to that immunity, even though the state does not appear in the proceedings in question: State Immunity Act 1978, s 1. See *Holland* v *Lampen-Wolfe* (2000) *The Times*, 27 July. *See* IMMUNITY, RESTRICTIVE.

immunity, restrictive. Doctrine suggesting that, in the interests of justice, it may be necessary to allow individuals engaging in commercial transactions with states to bring such transactions before the courts. See *Trendtex Trading Corp* v *Central Bank of Nigeria* [1977] QB 529. The doctrine is accepted as part of the law of England: *I Congreso Del Partido* [1983] 1 AC 244. See State Immunity Act 1978, s 3.

immunity, vicarious. Principle that an agent performing a contract is entitled to any immunity conferred on his principal. It was enunciated in *Elder, Dempster & Co* v *Paterson, Zochonis & Co* [1929] AC 522, but rejected in *Scruttons Ltd* v *Midland Silicones Ltd* [1962] AC 446.

impeachable of waste. Liability of a person, e.g., tenant for life (q.v.), for waste. See, e.g., *Re Ridge* (1885) 31 Ch D 504. *See* WASTE.

impeachment. (Impeach = to challenge the credibility of; to accuse.) The prosecution of an offender by the House of Commons (q.v.) before the House of Lords (q.v.). The jurisdiction was last exercised in 1806 (in the case of Viscount Melville, First Lord of the Admiralty, for alleged malversation in office).

impeding apprehension or prosecution. 'Where a person has committed an arrestable offence, any other person who, knowing or believing him to be guilty of the offence or of some other arrestable offence, does without lawful authority or reasonable excuse any act with intent to impede his apprehension or prosecution shall be guilty of an offence': C.L.A. 1967, s 4. *See* ARRESTABLE OFFENCE.

imperative theory of law. Known also as the 'command theory' (q.v.).

imperfect gift. *See* GIFT, IMPERFECT.

imperfect trust. An executory trust. *See* EXECUTORY.

impersonation. False personation (q.v.) for some improper motive.

implied. Suggested or understood by implication or deduction from the circumstances.

implied condition. Where a buyer makes known to a seller, expressly or by implication, the purpose for which goods are required, in a manner showing that he relies on the seller's skill or judgment and the goods are of a description which it is in the course of the seller's business to supply, there is an implied condition that the goods are reasonably fit for the purpose: S.G.A. 1979, s 14. See: *Stevenson* v *Rogers* [1999] QB 1028 (meaning of 'in course of business'); *Viskase Ltd* v *Paul Kiefal GmbH* [1999] 1 All ER (Comm) 641.

implied contract. A contract inferred from the conduct of parties or from some relationship existing between them. *See* CONTRACT; QUASI-CONTRACTS.

implied covenants. *See* COVENANTS, IMPLIED.

implied malice. 1. An intention (in a case of homicide) to do grievous bodily harm as compared with express malice, i.e., an intention to kill. 2. Malice inferred from all the circumstances. *See* MALICE.

implied tenancy. *See* TENANCY, IMPLIED.

implied term. A term which will be implied (e.g., from statute or custom) where it is reasonable and necessary to carry out the presumed intention of the parties to a contract and is so obvious that the parties must have intended it to apply. May be known as a 'standardised term'. Such a term will not override an express term (q.v.). See Supply of Goods (Implied Terms) Act 1973; S.G.A. 1979, s 12; Unfair Contract Terms Act 1977; Supply of Goods and Services Act 1982; Sale of Goods (Amendment) Acts 1994, 1995; *Shell UK Ltd* v *Lostock Garage Ltd* [1977] 1 All ER 481; *Johnstone* v *Bloomsbury HA* [1992] 1 QB 333; *Ocean Chemical Transport* v *Exnor Craggs Ltd* [2000] 1 All ER 519.

implied trust. A trust which will be enforced by the court as a result of surrounding circumstances, or the language of the parties, so that effect is given to their implied, but unexpressed, intentions. (Considered by some jurists as synonymous with the 'resulting trust', and by others as synonymous with the 'constructive trust'.) Example: X purchases property in the name of Y; there is a presumption in equity that X intended Y to hold that property in trust for him. See *Re Howes* (1905) 21 TLR 501. *See* TRUST.

importer. Includes any owner or other person for the time being possessed of or beneficially interested in goods coming from abroad (e.g., consignor, consignee, agent, broker).

importune. To make advances to another for an immoral purpose. It is an offence for a man persistently to solicit or importune in a public place for immoral purposes: S.O.A. 1956, s 32. See *R* v *Goddard* (1991) 92 Cr App R 185. It is an offence under S.O.A. 1985, s 1, to 'kerb-crawl', i.e., to solicit from a motor vehicle while it is in a street or public place. It is an offence for a common prostitute to loiter or solicit in a street or public place for the purpose of prostitution (q.v.): Street Offences Act 1959, s 1; *Behrendt* v *Burridge* [1976] 3 All ER 285; *Darroch* v *DPP* (1990) 91 Cr App R 378. *See* LOITER.

impossibility. That which is contrary to the law of nature, to some rule of law or to the very nature of some transaction.

impossibility of performance. Impossibility does not generally excuse from performance. Where, however, an event occurs which destroys the basis of the contract and which is not the fault of the parties, the contract is terminated. See *Taylor* v *Caldwell* (1863) 3 B & S 826. (For the validity of an 'impossible term' in contract, see *Eurico* v *Philipp Bros* [1986] 2 Lloyd's Rep 387.) *See* FRUSTRATION OF CONTRACT.

impotence. The inability to have, or to permit, ordinary sexual intercourse. Impotence of either party to consummate a marriage is a ground for rendering that marriage voidable. See *S* v *S* [1956] P 1; *W* v *W* [1967] 3 All ER 178.

impound. To seize and take goods into custody, e.g., during the process of distress (q.v.). *See* WALKING POSSESSION.

imprisonment. The restraint of a person's liberty, generally by confining him within a prison. A man is said to be a prisoner 'so long as he hath not his liberty freely to go at all times to all places whither he will, without bail or mainprise or otherwise': *Termes de la Ley.*

imprisonment for life. *See* LIFE IMPRISONMENT.

imprisonment for non-violent offences. In *R* v *Kefford* [2002] All ER(D) 37, Lord Woolf LCJ called for courts to accept the realities of the upsurge in prison population, and to think carefully about imprisoning perpetrators of economic, non-violent, crimes.

imprisonment of persons under 21. No court shall pass a sentence of imprisonment on a person for an offence if he is under 21 when convicted, or commit a person under 21 to prison for any reason. This will not apply where the person is remanded in custody, committed in custody for trial or sentence, or sent in custody for trial under C.D.A. 1998, s 51.

imprisonment, tariff period. Where a murderer who had been tried and convicted in Scotland was later transferred to an English prison, he could not invoke European Convention, art 7, so as to seek to challenge a longer mandatory life sentence tariff set by the Home Secretary: *R (McFetrich)* v *Secretary of State for Home Department* (2003) *The Times*, 28 July.

improvement grants. Payments made by local housing authorities towards cost of works required for the improvement of dwellings, houses in multiple occupation: L.G.H.A. 1989, s 101.

improvement notice. Notice served on a person, e.g., under H.S.W.A. 1974, s 21, by an inspector who is of the opinion that the person is contravening a provision in circumstances that make it likely that the contravention will continue or be repeated. The notice requires that the contravention shall be remedied. *See* PROHIBITION NOTICE.

imputations. 1. 'A judgment by which someone is regarded as the originator of an action, which is then called a "deed"': Kant, *Metaphysics of Morals* (1797). 2. Statement ascribing misconduct or fault to some person. It was established in *Selvey* v *DPP* [1970] AC 304 that Criminal Evidence Act 1898, s 1(*f*)(*ii*), permits cross-examination (q.v.) of an accused person as to his character when imputations on the character of the prosecutor and witnesses are cast so as to show their unreliability as witnesses, independently of the evidence they have given, and when the casting of such imputations is essential to allow the accused to establish a defence.

imputed notice. *See* NOTICE.

inalienability, rule against. Known also as the 'rule against perpetual trusts'. The general principle is that property must not be rendered inalienable. See *Re Wightwick's WT* [1950] Ch 260; *Re Denley's Trust Deed* [1969] 1 Ch 373.

inalienable. Incapable of being transferred.

in bonis. In the goods of. Abbreviated to '*In b* Smith', and used in connection with litigation concerning the estate or goods of a deceased person.

in camera. In a chamber. In a [judge's] private room, i.e., private sittings. It refers to a case heard, not in open court, but in closed court or a judge's private room, e.g., where the case relates to aspects of the Official Secrets Act 1920, or involves hearing evidence relating to indecency involving children. See, e.g., M.C.A. 1980, s 121(4). *See* CHAMBERS; OPEN COURT; OPEN JUSTICE.

incapable of self-support. 'A person is incapable of self-support if, but only if, he is incapable of supporting himself by reason of physical or mental infirmity and is likely to remain so incapable for a prolonged period': S.S.A. 1975, Sch 20.

incapable of work. One who cannot work 'by reason of some specific disease or bodily or mental disablement, or deemed in accordance with regulations to be so incapable': S.S.A. 1973, s 99(1). See S.S.A. 1986, Sch 11.

incapacitation and contract. *See* CONTRACT, INCAPACITATION AND.

incapacity. 1. Lack of legal power, competence, because of, e.g., infancy. 2. Lack of mental or physical powers.

incapacity benefit. Replaces sickness and invalidity benefits, under S.S. (Incapacity for Work) A. 1994. Short-term incapacity benefit is paid for each day of incapacity for work, payable at a lower rate for the first 28 weeks, and at the higher rate for the 29th–52nd weeks. Long-term benefit is payable at the highest rate after 52 weeks. For those with a recent work record, their doctor provides medical evidence for the first 28 weeks; thereafter, a personal capability assessment follows (see S.S. (Contributions and Benefits) A. 1992, s 171C, substituted by W.R.P.A. 1999, s 61). See *R* v *Social Security Commissioner ex p Chamberlain* (2000) *The Times*, 1 August (tests for reviewing decisions).

incest. Sexual intercourse between persons who are within certain degrees of consanguinity. It is an offence under S.O.A. 1956 for a man to have sexual intercourse with a woman whom he knows to be his granddaughter, daughter, sister or mother and for a woman of the age of

16 or over to permit a man whom she knows to be her grandfather, father, brother, or son to have intercourse with her by her consent: ss 10, 11. See *A-G's Reference (No. 4 of 1989)* (1989) *The Times*, 11 November; *R v B* [1999] 1 Cr App R (S) 174.

incest, incitement to. It is an offence for a man to incite to have sexual intercourse with him a girl under the age of 16 whom he knows to be his granddaughter, daughter or sister: C.L.A. 1977, s 54(1).

in charge of. Having effective control of persons, things and events. See, e.g., *R v Rawlings* [1994] Crim LR 433.

inchoate. Begun, or in an early stage, but not complete. Inchoate offences (e.g., incitement, attempt), are committed even though the substantive offences with which they are connected are not committed, i.e. the prohibited harm has not occurred at that stage.

inchoate bill. A bill of exchange (q.v.) wanting in some material particular. The person in possession has prima facie authority to make good the omission as he thinks fit: B.Ex.A. 1882, s 20. The bill must be completed within a reasonable time and in accordance with the authority given. See *Griffiths v Dalton* [1940] 2 KB 264.

incidental, meaning of. CA held, in *FA Premier League v Panini UK Ltd* (2003) *The Times*, 17 July, that there is no difference in principle between 'integral' and 'incidental' (see Copyright, Design and Patents Act 1988, s 31(1)). 'Incidental' is an ordinary descriptive word: it has not been given any special meaning, and there is no reason why the courts should seek to define it.

incitement. The act of urging or provoking to a course of criminal action. It is a common law offence for one person to incite another to commit an offence. See Incitement to Mutiny Act 1797; Incitement to Disaffection Act 1934 (it is an offence, maliciously and advisedly to attempt to seduce a member of the armed forces from his duty or allegiance to the Crown); Official Secrets Act 1920,

s 7 (it is an offence for a person to incite another to commit an offence under the Act); S.O. (Conspiracy and Incitement) A. 1996; *R v Fitzmaurice* [1983] QB 1083 (incitement to do the impossible); *R v Sirat* (1986) 83 Cr App R 41; *DPP v Armstrong* (1999) 143 SJLB 279 (a person incited to commit an offence need not have the same parity of *mens rea* as possessed by the inciter).

inclosure. *See* ENCLOSURE.

include. To contain; take in; involve. See *Wiggins v Arun DC* (1997) 74 P & CR 64 (the work 'includes' is capable of two interpretations – 'means' or 'comprises').

income. The financial return from one's labour, business, land or capital. 'The term "income" means, as applied to a commercial business, the profits made in that business . . . the balance of gain over loss. It seems to me to be altogether straining the ordinary signification of the term "income" to say that it means the volume of business. That is the "turnover", not the "income"': *Yates v Yates* (1913) 33 NZLR 281.

income-related benefits. Benefits under S.S. (Contributions and Benefits) A. 1992, as subsequently amended, including: income support, working families' tax credit, disabled person's tax credit, housing benefit, council tax benefit (qq.v.).

income support. Benefit under S.S. Contributions and Benefits Act 1992, s 124, paid to persons over 18 (or, in some cases, 16) who have no income or whose income does not exceed the applicable amount, who are not engaged in remunerative work. The person must be available for employment and must not be receiving relevant education. He must not be entitled to a jobseeker's allowance. See I.C.T.A. 1988, ss 151, 617; W.R.P.A. 1999, Sch 9, para 28. For recovery of income support payments from a person who persistently refuses or neglects to maintain himself or any person he is liable to maintain, see S.S. Administration Act 1992, s 105. CA held in *Secretary of State for Work and Pensions v Hourigan* (2002) *The Times*,

28 December that where an income support claimant (see Income Support (General) Regulations (SI 87/1967)) owned one-sixth of a property, she was not to be treated as though she owned a 'half share' in that property.

income tax. An annual tax charged on all income originating in the UK and on all income arising abroad of persons resident in the UK. It is imposed for the year of assessment beginning in April. The tax is based on the following schedules (see I.C.T.A. 1988, ss 15–20): A (rents, rentcharges, other receipts from land ownership); B (occupation of commercial woodlands); C (profits from public revenue dividends); D (trade, professional profits or gains); E (salaries, wages, annuities, etc.); F (company dividends, etc.). See annual Finance Acts; Taxes Management Act 1970; and I.C.T.A. 1988. (Current rates of tax, 2001–2002 (see Finance Act 2001, s 31), are, after tax allowances have been given: 10 per cent on the first £1,880 (starting rate); 22 per cent on £1,881 to £29,400 (basic rate); 40 per cent on income over £29,400 (higher rate).) For 'self-assessment', see Finance Act 1994, s 179. Complaints may be made: to the area Inland Revenue Director; to the Adjudicator; through an MP, to the Independent Commissioner for Administration (Ombudsman). *See* TAX AVOIDANCE, TAX EVASION.

income tax allowances. The following are taken into account in calculating a personal tax code: personal allowance, married allowance, widow's bereavement allowance, blind person's allowance, maintenance payments (relating to divorced or separated spouse or child under 21), loan interest, death or superannuation payments, job expenses and professional subscriptions, retirement annuity payments, personal pension relief (for those paying higher rate of tax), charity gifts relief, starting rate tax allowance, double taxation relief.

income tax appeal tribunals. Bodies set up to hear disputes concerning the Inland Revenue relating to liability to tax, each consisting (in the case of General Commissioners of Income Tax) of local business and professional persons assisted by a qualified clerk, or (in the case of Special Commissioners) of barristers and members of the Inland Revenue Department. Appeal on a point of law lies to the High Court.

income tax, minimum wage, VAT changes. Income tax rates for 2006–7 are, after allowances: 10 per cent on first £2,150 (starting rate band); 22 per cent on £2,151–33,300 (basic rate band); 40 per cent on income over £33,300 (higher rate). Minimum wage goes up from 1 October 2006 to £5.35 per hour for workers aged 22 or over; £4.45 per hour for workers aged 18–21 inclusive. Registration level for VAT is £61,000 p.a. after 1 April 2006 (deregistration limit is £59,000 p.a.).

income tax, yearly assessment. 'Every assessment and charge to income tax shall be made for a year commencing on April 6th and ending on the following April 5th': I.C.T.A. 1988, s 2(2). For date of payment, see s 5.

incommunicado. Isolated; without a way of communicating with others. By *Code of Practice* issued under P.&C.E.A. 1984 (and revised in April 1991) a detainee has the right not to be held *incommunicado*. See *R* v *Quayson* [1989] Crim LR 218.

incompletely constituted trust. A trust which requires some further action by the settlor before it is perfectly created. See *Milroy* v *Lord* (1862) 4 De G & J 264; *Re Fry* [1946] 2 All ER 106. *See* TRUST.

in consequence. As a direct result of. See *R* v *Havant BC ex p Marten* [1995] 1 CLYB 729.

inconsiderate driving. *See* DRIVING, CARELESS AND INCONSIDERATE.

in contemplation of death. 'It is sufficient that [the donor of a gift made in contemplation of death] is suffering at the relevant time from an illness which may prove mortal; in such circumstances the gift is taken to be made "in contemplation of death" and the implication is that it is conditional on death': *Dufficy* v

Mollica [1968] 3 NSWR 751. *See* DONA-
TIO MORTIS CAUSA.

incorporate. 1. To combine into a
whole, e.g., as where one document is
taken to be part of another. 2. To admit
to membership of a corporation. 3. To
form into a corporation, e.g., by Act of
Parliament. An 'unincorporated body' is
made up of 'two or more persons bound
together for common purposes, not being
business purposes, by mutual undertakings,
each having mutual duties, in an organisation which has rules which identify in
whom control of it and its funds rests':
per Lawton LJ in *Conservative Central
Office* v *Burrell* [1982] 1 WLR 522. See
also *Worthing RFC Trustees* v *IRC* [1987]
1 WLR 1057.

incorporation by reference. 'If a testator, in a testamentary paper duly executed, refers to an existing unattested
testamentary paper, the instrument so
referred to becomes part of his will; in
other words it is incorporated into it':
In b Smart [1902] P 238. See *Re Tyler*
[1967] 1 WLR 1269. *See* WILL.

incorporation, certificate of. Issued by
the Registrar of Companies after inspection of a company's documents, e.g.,
memorandum and articles of association
(q.v.), list of those who have consented
to be directors. Issue incorporates members of the company into a *persona* at
law, and is conclusive evidence that the
requirements of the Cos.A. relating to
registration have been complied with. See
Cos.A. 1985, ss 13 (as amended), 117;
Cos.A. 1989, s 145, Sch 19, para 14. *See*
COMPANY.

incorporation, doctrine of. Doctrine
that rules of international law are incorporated automatically into English law
unless they are in conflict with an Act of
Parliament, as contrasted with the doctrine
of transformation (q.v.). The doctrine
was accepted as correct in *Trendtex
Trading Corporation* v *Central Bank of
Nigeria* [1977] QB 529.

incorporeal hereditaments. Rights of
property, such as annuities, advowsons,
easements, profits, franchises, tithes,
rentcharges (qq.v.). *See* HEREDITAMENTS.

increase in property value. In *Shalson
v Keepers of the Free Grammar School of
John Lyon* [2003] UKHL 32, the HL
held that where a tenant (T) had carried
out work so as to re-convert a house to
a single dwelling from conversion into
separate flats, made by a previous tenant,
T's work constituted an improvement
of the property, and T was entitled to a
diminution in the purchase price to the
extent to which the value of the house had
been increased. See Leasehold Reform
Act 1967, s 9(1A)(d).

incriminate. 1. To charge with a crime.
2. To involve in the possibility of a
prosecution. A person cannot generally
be compelled to answer a question the
answer to which would incriminate him.
See S.C.A. 1981, s 72; *Coca-Cola* v
Gilbey [1995] 4 All ER 711. *See* SELF-
INCRIMINATION; SILENCE, RIGHT OF
ACCUSED TO.

incumbrance. Encumbrance (q.v.).

indecency. 'Indecency is not confined
to sexual indecency; indeed it is difficult to find any limit short of saying that
it includes anything which an ordinary
decent man or woman would find to
be shocking, disgusting or revolting':
Knuller Ltd v *DPP* [1972] 2 All ER 898.
See S.O.A. 1967, s 1; S.O.(Am.)A. 2000,
s 2. *See* OBSCENITY.

indecency, gross. *See* GROSS INDECENCY.

indecency with children. *See* GROSS
INDECENCY.

indecent assault. An intentional assault
capable of being considered by right-
minded persons as indecent (or in relation
to its accompanying circumstances). See
S.O.A. 1956, ss 14, 15; *R* v *Court* [1989]
AC 28; *R* v *Brough* [1997] 2 Cr App
R (S) 202. (The offence is one of basic
intent.) 'The offence is concerned with
contravention of standards of decent
behaviour in regard to sexual modesty
or privacy': *R* v *Kowalski* (1988) 86 Cr
App R 339 (indecent assault within
marriage); *R* v *Sargeant* [1997] Crim LR
50 (touching or threat of touching is not
required to establish the offence); *R* v *C*
[2000] 1 Cr App R (S) 533 (indecent
assault on partner). For joinder of count

of bodily harm with indecent assault, see *R v S* [1998] Crim LR 576. For consent through deceit as to nature, not quality, of act, see *R v Tabassum* (2000) *The Times*, 26 May.

indecent assault on men. An offence under S.O.A. 1956, s 15. A boy under 16, or a man who is a defective, cannot in law give any consent which would prevent an act being an assault for the purposes of s 14. See *R v Sant* (1989) 11 Cr App R (S) 441 (indecent assault by woman on boy); *R v Bayfield* [1996] 2 Cr App R (S) 441 (indecent assault on severely handicapped male). *See A-G's Reference (No. 34 of 1997)* [1998] 1 FLR 515.

indecent assault on women. An offence under S.O.A. 1956, s 14. A girl under 16, or a woman who is a defective, cannot in law give any consent which would prevent an act being an assault for the purposes of s 14. See *R v K* (2000) *The Times*, 7 November.

indecent display. If indecent matter is publicly displayed (i.e., displayed in or so as to be visible from any public place), the person making the display or causing or permitting the display is guilty of an offence: Indecent Displays (Control) Act 1981, s 1(1), (2). 'Public place' includes any place to which the public have access (whether on payment or otherwise); it does not include part of a shop which the public can enter only after passing an adequate warning notice: s 1(3), (6). Certain specified matter is excluded from the Act, e.g., that included in a TV broadcast, the display of an art gallery: s 1(4). See Cinemas Act 1985, Sch 2, amended by Deregulation and Contracting Out Act 1994, Sch 17.

indecent exposure. *See* EXPOSE.

indecent photographs. *See* CHILDREN, INDECENT PHOTOGRAPHS OF.

indecent photographs, sentencing. In *R v Oliver* [2002] EWCA Crim 2766, the CA held that in relation to sentencing for offences involving indecent photographs of children, the primary factors to be taken into account were the nature of the indecent material and the extent of the offender's involvement in the making

and production of the photographs. The offence would be aggravated if the photographs had been shown to a child.

indefeasible. That cannot be annulled or made void.

indemnifying measure. *See* ACT OF INDEMNITY.

indemnity. 1. Exemption from incurred penalties. See, e.g., Indemnity Act 1920; and Charitable Trusts (Validation) Act 1954. 2. Compensation for injury or loss. See *Royal Bank of Scotland v Sandstone Property* [1998] 2 BCLC 429. 3. Indemnity insurance is based on the principle that the insured cannot recover more than his actual loss: *Darrell v Tibbitts* (1880) 5 QBD 560; *Callaghan v Dominion Insurance Co* [1997] 2 Lloyd's Rep 541. 4. 'A right of someone to recover from a third party the whole amount which he himself is liable to pay': CPR Glossary. See CPR, r 20.6. Contract of indemnity is exemplified thus: X and Y enter a shop and Y says to the shopkeeper, 'Let X have these goods, I will see you are paid' (see *Birkmyr v Darnell* (1704) 1 Salk 27). Such a contract need not be in writing, unlike a contract of guarantee. 5. Indemnity clauses contain formula providing for calculation of compensation for breach of contract: see *Jervis v Harris* [1996] Ch 195; *Total Transport v Arcadia Petroleum* [1998] 1 Lloyd's Rep 351. *See* ACT OF INDEMNITY.

indemnity basis for costs. A standard applied to the consideration whether a sum incurred in litigation should be allowed to be paid by/to a party; under it the taxing officer will allow all costs except insofar as they are unreasonable in amount or have been unreasonably incurred. See r 44.4. *See* COSTS, BASIS OF ASSESSMENT.

indemnity clauses, unreasonable. 'A person dealing as consumer cannot by reference to any contract term be made to indemnify another person (whether a party to the contract or not) in respect of liability that may be incurred by the other for negligence or breach of contract, except in so far as the contract term satisfies the requirement of reasonableness': Unfair Contract Terms Act 1977, s 4(1).

indenture. A deed (q.v.) made on paper which was cut or indented, so that its two parts ('counterparts') could be fitted together. Although a deed which purports to be an indenture is not in fact indented, it may have the same effect: L.P.A. 1925, s 56(2).

independent contractor. One who by contract agrees to perform a particular task for another and who, in the execution of his work, is not under the control of the person for whom it is performed, and who may use his discretion as to the general mode of execution. In general, an employer is not liable for the torts of an independent contractor unless he has authorised them explicitly or implicitly. (For an exception, e.g., liability where contractor has been employed to carry out an extra-hazardous task, see *Alcock* v *Wraith* (1991) *The Times*, 23 December.) See *Mersey Docks & Harbour Board* v *Coggins & Griffiths Ltd* [1947] AC 1; *D & F Estates* v *Church Commissioners* [1989] AC 177. See also I.C.T.A. 1988, s 560.

independent trade union. *See* TRADE UNION, INDEPENDENT.

indexation. The linking of incomes, rents, pensions, benefits, etc., with changes in the index of retail prices. See, e.g., S.S.A. 1986, s 63(1); C.S.P.S.S.A. 2000, s 51; *Wyndham Investments* v *Motorway Tyres* [1991] EGCS 9. For index-linked interest rates, see *Multi-Service Bookbinding* v *Marden* [1979] Ch 84. See T.C.G.A. 1992, s 53 (indexation allowance), amended by Finance Act 1994, s 93.

index map. *See* PUBLIC INDEX MAP.

index section in statute. Section in Parliamentary Acts, listing expressions and relevant defining provisions. See, e.g., Human Fertilisation and Embryology Act 1990, s 47.

indictable offence. An offence which, if committed by an adult, is triable on indictment (q.v.) whether it is exclusively so triable or triable either way: C.L.A. 1977, s 64(1)(*a*). For procedure where trial on indictment appears more suitable, see M.C.A. 1980, s 21; and S.C.A. 1981, s 46. See also C.D.A. 1998, s 51

(no committal proceedings for indictable-only offences); P.C.C.(S.)A. 2000, s 77; I.A. 1978, Sch 1. *See* OFFENCES TRIABLE EITHER WAY.

indictment. A written or printed formal accusation of a crime. 'A plain, brief and certain narrative of an offence committed': 2 Hale PC 169. Its form is determined by provisions of Indictments Act 1915 and Indictment Rules 1971. It consists of three parts: the commencement (name of case and defendant, court of trial, statement that named person is charged with offence(s) which follow(s)); the statement of offence(s); and the particulars (e.g., description of offence, date, place of offence, name of victim). See *R* v *Tyler* (1993) 96 Cr App R 332; *R* v *Roberts* [1998] 1 Cr App R 441; *R* v *Hemmings* (1999) 96 (40) LSG 42 (power of trial judge to amend indictment). *See* BILL OF INDICTMENT.

indictment, objection to. *See* OBJECTION TO INDICTMENT.

indictment, pleas to. *See* BAR, PLEAS IN.

indirect evidence. *See* EVIDENCE, INDIRECT.

individual. Includes not only a natural person but also (a) a partnership consisting of two or three persons not all of whom are bodies corporate; and (b) an unincorporated body or persons which does not consist entirely of bodies corporate and is not a partnership: Consumer Credit Act 2006 s 1 amending CCA 1974 s 189(1).

indivisible contract. *See* DIVISIBLE CONTRACT.

indorsement. Endorsement (q.v.).

inducement. 1. Persuasion by promise or threat to a course of action. 2. Inducement or procuration leading to a breach of contract involves persuading an employee to break his contract. See *Lumley* v *Gye* (1853) 2 E & B 216 ('To draw a line between advice, persuasion, enticement and procurement is practically impossible in a court of justice').

industrial action. Concerted activities by employees in pursuance of a complaint and intended to affect the outcome of a dispute. See, e.g., T.U.L.R.(C.)A. 1992, Part V; T.U.R.E.R.A. 1993, s 21;

Employment Relations Act 1999, Sch 5. Must be preceded by a secret ballot (q.v.) if organised by a union. Obligation to hold a ballot applies to employees and persons working under any contract under which one person personally does work or performs services for another: T.U.L.R.(C.)A. 1992, s 233. The constituency for the ballot is a 'place of work'. At least seven days' notice of official industrial action must be given to the employer. T.U.R.E.R.A. 1993, s 21. *See* STRIKE.

industrial action, protected. An employee takes protected industrial action if he commits an act which, or a series of acts each of which, he is induced to commit by an act which by virtue of T.U.L.R.(C.)A. 1992, s 219, is not actionable in tort: s 238A, inserted by Employment Relations Act 1999, Sch 5. An employee who is dismissed shall be regarded as unfairly dismissed if the reason, or principal reason, for the dismissal is that he took protected industrial action: s 238A(2).

industrial and provident society. A society registered under Industrial and Provident Societies Act 1965–78, which carried on an industry, business or trade specified in its rules, wholesale or retail, including dealings with land. See also I.C.T.A. 1988, s 486, amended by Finance Act 1996, Sch 14, para 30; F.S.M.A. 2000, s 338.

industrial development certificate. Certificate issued by Secretary of State for the Environment, required before applying for planning permission to erect an industrial building or to alter the use of a building for industrial purposes.

industrial diseases benefits, and compensation. Benefits payable to employees in respect of injuries and prescribed diseases arising from the nature of the employment. See, e.g., S.S.A. 1975, ss 76–78; Pneumoconiosis etc. (Workers' Compensation) Act 1979 (lump sum payments as compensation for disablement caused by noxious dust at work); *Ballantine* v *Newalls Insulation Co* (2000) *The Times*, 22 June.

industrial dispute. A dispute between workers and their employer or organisations of employers and one or more workers relating wholly or mainly to terms and conditions of work, engagement or non-engagement or suspension or termination of employment, allocation of work, etc. See T.U.L.R.(C.)A. 1992, s 244; T.U.R.E.R.A. 1993, s 21; *University College NHS Trust* v *Unison* [1999] ICR 204.

industrial injuries benefits. Benefits provided under, e.g., S.S.A. 1975, ss 50–75 (as amended by S.S.A. 1986, Sch 3 and S.S. Contributions and Benefits Act 1992, Part V) to employed earners (q.v.) suffering personal injuries caused by accidents arising out of and in the course of their employment, and to the relatives and spouses of those killed in such accidents and to employed earners suffering prescribed diseases due to the nature of their employment. 'Accidents' include mishaps arising where the employee is, at the time of the accident, in breach of orders or statutes or where the cause is misconduct or negligence on the part of some other person.

industrial premises. Premises used or designed or suitable for use for the carrying on of any such process or research (or ancillary premises used for those purposes) specified, e.g., in T.C.P.A. 1971, s 66(1). For 'industrial building or structure', see Capital Allowances Act 1990, s 18.

industrial tribunals. Renamed 'employment tribunals', under E.R. (Dispute Resolution) A. 1998, s 1(1). First established under Industrial Training Act 1964; developed, following other legislation (e.g., E.P.(C.)A. 1978, s 128), into bodies hearing complaints relating to unfair dismissal, redundancy payments, terms of employment. See Employment Tribunals Act 1996. Each tribunal consists of a legally qualified chairman (a barrister or solicitor who has been qualified for at least seven years) appointed by the Lord Chancellor, and two other persons. The tribunals sit in over 50 centres in different parts of the country as and when required and may conduct proceedings in whatever manner is considered suitable. Appeal lies on points of law to Employment Appeal Tribunal (q.v.); on other matters to QBD. For pre-hearing review of proceedings, at which a party may be required to pay a deposit if he wishes to continue to participate in the proceedings, see Employment Tribunals Act 1996, s 9. An employment tribunal is an 'inferior court' within the meaning of O 52, r 1(2)(a): *Peach Grey & Co v Sommers* [1995] 2 All ER 513. See *Sogbetun v London Borough of Hackney* [1998] IRLR 676 (matters relating to tribunal chairman sitting alone; see also E.R. (Dispute Resolution) A. 1998, s 3); *Vidler v Unison* [1999] ICR 746; *Bache v Essex CC* (2000) *The Times*, 3 February (employment tribunal has no power to stop a representative chosen by a party from acting for her). *See* TRIBUNALS, EMPLOYMENT, PROCEDURAL MATTERS.

ineffective contract. Term applied to a case in which money has been paid by one party to another on the strength of a transaction which he believes is a contract, but which, in fact, is of no effect, as where there is a total failure of consideration. See, e.g., *Rowland v Divall* [1923] 2 KB 500.

inevitable accident. An unlooked for mishap which could not have been avoided by the exercise of reasonable care or skill. See *Stanley v Powell* [1891] 1 QB 86; *Jones v LCC* (1932) 48 TLR 577.

in extenso. At length. Used with reference to the detailed, unabridged, reporting of a case, rather than a summary.

infamous conduct. 'If a medical man in the pursuit of his profession has done something with regard to it which would be reasonably regarded as disgraceful or dishonourable to his professional brethren of good repute and competency, then it is open to the General Medical Council, if that be shown, to say that he has been guilty of infamous conduct in a professional respect': *Allinson v General Medical Council* [1894] 1 QB 750. See also Medical Act 1978; Dentists Act 1984.

infant. Under F.L.R.A. 1969 a person under the age of 18. Such a person may be described also as a 'minor'. See Minors' Contracts Act 1987. *See* MINORS' CONTRACTS.

infanticide. The offence committed by a woman who by any wilful act or omission causes the death of her child, under the age of 12 months, when at the time of the act or omission the balance of her mind is disturbed by reason of her not having fully recovered from the effect of giving birth to the child or by reason of the effect of lactation consequent on the birth of the child. She is punished as if guilty of manslaughter (q.v.): Infanticide Act 1938, s 1(1). See *R v Sainsbury* (1989) 11 Cr App R (S) 533; *R v Lewis* [1990] Crim LR 348. For attempted infanticide, see *R v Smith* [1983] Crim LR 739.

infer. To reason by deducing a fact or proposition from other facts. 'Inferential facts' are those established indirectly by conclusions drawn from evidence. See *R v Doldur* (1998) *The Times*, 7 December (a jury cannot convict solely on an adverse inference); *R v Cowan* [1996] QB 373.

inferential facts. *See* INFER.

inferior courts. Those courts, e.g., county courts, magistrates' courts, with a jurisdiction limited, geographically and in relation to the value of that which is in dispute and subject to the supervision of a superior court. *See* SUPERIOR COURTS.

inferred agreement. An agreement in which the intention of the parties is a matter of inference from their conduct: see, e.g., *Wilkie v LPTB* [1947] 1 All ER 258.

inflicting bodily injury. *See* MALICIOUS WOUNDING.

influence, undue. *See* UNDUE INFLUENCE.

information. Statement by which a magistrate is informed of the offence for which a summons or warrant is required. In general, any person may lay an information, unless there is a statutory rule to the contrary. An information will suffice if it merely describes the alleged offence in ordinary, non-technical language. It is usually in writing and may be substantiated on oath and includes the name of the party charged, the offence (when and where committed). See M.C.A. 1980, s 1; *R v Scunthorpe Justices ex p M* (1998) *The Times*, 10 March. *See* LAYING AN INFORMATION.

information, amendment of. Magistrates' Courts Act 1980, s 123, allows the exercise by justices of a wide discretion to amend an information unless this could result in an injustice to defendant. Justices had erred in refusing prosecution permission to substitute 'drove a car' for 'used a car', thus bringing the information within the Road Traffic Act 1988, s 5: *DPP v Short* [2002] EWHC Admin 885.

information and consultation. Information and Consultation Directive (2002/14/EC), to be implemented by March 2005, requires EU Member States to announce detailed provisions for 'minimum requirements for the right to information and consultation of employees and undertakings or establishments within the Community'. 'Employees' will be defined in terms of national employment law and practice.

information, freedom of. Under F.I.A. 2000, s 1(1), any person making a request for information to a public authority is entitled to be informed in writing by the authority whether it holds that information, and, if that is the case, to have it communicated to him. This is subject to exemptions stated in the Act, Part II. Information is held by a public authority if held by that authority otherwise than on behalf of another person, or it is held by another person on behalf of the authority: s 3(2). There is an exemption where cost of compliance exceeds appropriate limits: s 12(1). For fees, see s 9. The authority is not obliged to comply with a request which is vexatious, or repeated, unless a reasonable interval has elapsed between compliance with the previous request and the making of the current request: s 14. *See* INFORMATION, REQUEST FOR.

information, laying an. *See* LAYING AN INFORMATION.

information, request for. Under F.I.A. 2000, s 8(1), a request for information must be in writing, stating name and address of applicant and describing information requested. A request may be treated as made in writing where the text of the request is transmitted electronically, received in legible form, and is capable of use for subsequent reference: s 8(2). Time for compliance by authority to whom request is made is up to the twentieth working day following date of receipt: s 10(1).

information, request for, refusal of. Where an authority refuses a request for information, and is relying on statutory exemptions, it must give applicant a notice stating that fact, specifying the exemption, and stating why exemption applies: F.I.A. 2000, s 17(1). For appeals, see Parts IV, V.

information, request for, statutory exemptions relating to. F.I.A. 2000, Part II, sets out circumstances in which an applicant may be refused information, and these include: where the information is accessible to applicant by other means: s 21; where information is intended for future publication: s 22; where it relates to security matters, national security, defence, or may prejudice international relations or relations within UK or the economy: ss 23–29; where it relates to investigations and proceedings conducted by public authorities, or law enforcement or Court records: ss 30–32; where it involves audit functions, Parliamentary privilege, or where it might prejudice effective conduct of public affairs: ss 33–36; where it relates to communications with Her Majesty, where it might endanger health and safety, or relates to certain environmental matters, where it is personal data, or has been provided in confidence, or relates to legal professional privilege, trade secrets, or is prohibited under any enactments: ss 37–44.

informer. 1. One who brought an action, or informed, in a court so as to recover a penalty on a conviction. 2. One who informs the police of violations of the law. The police may not use informers in such a way that crimes result: *R v Birtles* [1969] 2 All ER 1131. See *R v Vaillencourt* (1992) *The Times*, 12 June; *R v Saggar* [1997] 1 Cr App R (S) 167; *R v A (Informer: Reduction of Sentence)* [1999] 1 Cr App R (S) 52. 3. A 'common informer' was one who sued for a penalty which went to the person informing of a breach; procedure was abolished by Common Informers Act 1951.

infringement. Violation of or trespass on some right.

in gross. *See* GROSS.

ingross. Engross (q.v.).

inhabitant. One who resides, actually and permanently, in some given place and has his domicile (q.v.) there. The word refers generally to something more permanent than mere residence (q.v.). See *IRC v Duchess of Portland* [1982] Ch 314.

inherent vice. A defect inherent in goods which causes damage to them, e.g., fruit rotting because of some latent defect (see *Bradley v Fed Steam Navigation Co* (1927) 137 LT 266); couplings of a carriage breaking because of a defect in their construction (*Lister v Lancs and Yorks Rwy Co* [1903] 1 KB 878). A common carrier (q.v.) is not generally liable for damage resulting from inherent vice.

inheritance. That which descends to the heir (q.v.) on the death of the owner. The old canons of inheritance (largely abolished by A.E.A. 1925) were the rules concerning descent of land the owner of which died intestate. See Inheritance (Provision for Family and Dependants) Act 1975. *See* DEPENDANT; INTESTACY.

inheritance tax. Formerly 'capital transfer tax' (q.v.), the new scheme (see Finance Act 1986, ss 100–107) differs mainly (see Inheritance Tax Act 1984, s 101, Sch 19) in excluding lifetime transfers from liability to the tax. The tax threshold is £234,000 for tax charges arising on or after 6 April 2000. See generally Inheritance Tax Act 1984 (originally passed as the Capital Transfer

Tax Act 1984, a consolidating Act); Finance Act 1989, s 171.

inhibition. Formerly under the LRA 1925, s 57 this was an entry on the proprietorship register (q.v.) on application of any person interested, e.g., as where a proprietor's land certificate has been stolen. It prohibits the registration or entry of any dealing with registered land absolutely or until the occurrence of an event named in the prohibition. Inhibitions have now been repealed by the LRA 2002 and are now dealt with as 'restrictions' (q.v.).

in invitum. Against a person's consent or will.

injunction. An order of the court directing a person to refrain from doing or continuing to do an act complained of, or restraining him from continuing an omission. Non-compliance is a contempt of court (q.v.). Classified thus: (1) *prohibitory* (forbidding continuation or omission of a wrongful act); (2) *mandatory* (restraining continuation of omission by direct performance of a positive act); (3) *interlocutory* (q.v.) (temporary injunction, intended to maintain *status quo* until trial); (4) *perpetual* (granted after the hearing of a claim); (5) *ex parte* (q.v.); (6) *interim* (restraining defendant until some specified date); (7) *quia timet* (q.v.). See S.C.A. 1981, s 37; F.S.M.A. 2000, s 380.

injunction against person unknown. It is now permissible, following the introduction of the Civil Procedure Rules 1998, for a defendant to be joined by description rather than name, so that the court is empowered to grant an injunction against such a person: *Bloomsbury Publishing v News Group Newspapers* [2003] EWHC 1205 (Ch).

injunction applications. It was held in *Hipgrave v Jones* (2005) *The Times*, 11 January, that the civil standard of proof ought to be applied to any injunction application bought under Protection from Harassment Act 1997, s 3.

injunction, damages in lieu of. There is a discretionary power of the court to substitute damages for an injunction where, e.g., the injury to claimant's right is slight and is capable of being estimated in, and compensated by, small monetary terms. Damages should be awarded, where, e.g., an injunction would effectively 'stop a great enterprise and render it useless': *per* Lord Denning in *Allen* v *Gulf Oil Refining Ltd* [1980] QB 156. See Chancery Amendment Act 1858; S.C.A. 1981, s 50; *Leeds Industrial Co-operative Society* v *Slack* [1924] AC 851.

injunction, interlocutory, grant of. Principles were clarified in *American Cyanamid Co* v *Ethicon Ltd* [1975] AC 396. There is no rule requiring claimant to establish a prima facie case; the court must be satisfied that there is a serious, not frivolous, question for trial. Governing consideration is then the balance of convenience (although inadequacy of damages is of significance). Relative strength of the case of both parties is considered only as a last resort. See *Films Rover* v *Cannon Film Sales* [1986] 3 All ER 772; *Bankers Trust Co* v *PT Jakarta International Hotels* [1999] 1 All ER 785.

injunction, Mareva. *See* MAREVA INJUNCTION.

injunction not to publish. In *AG* v *Punch Ltd* [2002] UKHL 50, the HL held that a third party will be in contempt of court if he publishes information in breach of the terms of an injunction even though he believed that such information: (relating, in this case, to secret service procedures) would not damage national security.

injunctions, orders for, under CPR. Unless the court orders otherwise, orders must contain an undertaking by applicant to the court to pay any damages sustained by respondent which the court considers applicant should pay. Any order for an injunction must set out clearly what respondent must or must not do. See PD 25, para 25. For penal notices to be inserted in injunction orders, see PD 40B, para 9.1.

injunctions relating to domestic violence. Under F.L.A. 1996, Part IV (in force since October 1997), the court may, in cases involving threatened or actual domestic violence, grant one of a series of 'occupational orders', requiring, e.g., that respondent permit applicant to enter and remain in the dwelling house, or that respondent leave the dwelling house or a part of it (see s 33). A *'non-molestation order'* (see s 42) prohibits respondent from molesting a child and/or some other person associated with respondent. Applications for an occupation order or non-molestation order under Part IV must be dealt with in chambers unless the court otherwise directs: Family Proceedings (Amendment No. 3) Rules, r 2 (SI 97/1893). See *Banks* v *Banks* [1999] 1 FLR 726 (verbal and physical abuse); *Practice Direction (Arresting Officer: Attendance)* (2000) *The Times*, 19 January (see F.L.A. 1996, s 47(7)); *Re B-J (Power of Arrest)* [2000] FLR 443; *Hale* v *Tanner* [2000] 3 FCR 62 (penalties for breach of order). *See* BATTERED WIFE; DOMESTIC VIOLENCE; MOLESTATION.

injuria sine damno. Wrong without damage. Phrase used in the law of torts to refer to the violation of an interest which may constitute an actionable tort (q.v.) without proof of damage (i.e., pecuniary loss).

injuries, personal, claim for damages. Proceedings in which there is a claim for damages in respect of personal injuries to the claimant or any other person or in respect of a person's death; and 'personal injuries' includes any disease and any impairment of a person's physical or mental condition. See CPR, r 2.3. For particulars of claim, see PD 16, para 4.1. See also C.P.A. 1987, s 45(1); I.C.T.A. 1988, s 329; *Longden* v *British Coal Corp* [1997] 3 WLR 1336 (calculation of damages); *Norman* v *Ali* (2000) *The Times*, 25 February (wide meaning of 'personal injury' for purposes of Lim.A. 1980, s 11); *Heil* v *Rankin* (2000) *The Times*, 24 March (for awards above £10,000, there should be a tapered increase up to a maximum increase of one-third in awards for the most catastrophic injuries).

injurious affection. Land may be affected injuriously where part is taken from the owner by the state's exercise of compulsory purchasing powers and, in such a case, the owner may be entitled to compensation if, e.g., the value of the remaining land has fallen. See Compulsory Purchase Act 1965, s 10; L.G.P.L.A. 1980, ss 112, 113; Planning and Compensation Act 1991; *Wildtree Hotels Ltd* v *Harrow LBC* (2000) 150 NLJ 984.

injurious falsehood. A tort (q.v.), resulting from written or oral falsehoods, maliciously published, calculated in the ordinary course of things to produce, and, in the event, producing, actual damage: *Ratcliffe* v *Evans* [1892] 2 QB 524. Known, at one time, as 'slander of title' (q.v.) and 'slander of goods' (q.v.). Defamation Act 1952, s 3(1), refers to 'slander of title, slander of goods or other malicious falsehood'. See *Fielding* v *Variety Incorporated* [1967] 2 All ER 497.

injury. 1. The violation of one's rights, or its results. 2. An actionable wrong. 3. 'Any disease and any impairment of a person's physical or mental condition': Fatal Accidents Act 1976, s 1(6). See *Bradley* v *London Fire Authority* [1995] IRLR 46.

injury benefit. Benefit payable under, e.g., S.S.A. 1975 in respect of an injury as a result of which an employee is incapable of work. See also S.S.A. 1986, Sch 3.

injury claim. In *Hardings* v *Weslands* (2005) *The Times*, 5 January, the CA held that in the realm of private international law, the law of the country in which the tort occurred would not necessarily be considered as determinative of the question as to whether damage assessment was procedural and not substantive so that an English court could not apply them.

injury in sport. In *R* v *Barnes* (2005) *The Times*, 10 January, the CA held that criminal proceedings ought to be brought by a player who caused injury to another player during a sporting event only where the conduct is grave enough to be considered criminal.

injury, personal. Any disease and any impairment of a person's physical or mental condition: Lim.A. 1980, s 38(1). See C.P.A. 1987, s 45(1). For personal injury proceedings, see SI 00/774.

injury to feelings, damages for. In *Chief Constable of West Yorkshire Police* v *Vento* [2002] EWCA Civ 1871, the CA held that only an exceptional case involving injury to feelings would attract damages of more than £25,000. Top band of damages (£15,000–£25,000) related to the more serious cases; middle band (£5,000–£15,000) for serious cases; lower band (£500–£15,000) for less serious cases. Damages less than £500 should be avoided.

inland bill. A bill of exchange which is both drawn and payable within the British Isles or which is drawn within the British Isles upon some person resident therein. The term 'foreign bill' is applied to any other bill. See B.Ex.A. 1882, s 4. *See* BILL OF EXCHANGE.

Inland Revenue, Commissioners of. The government body which administers the laws relating to taxation and advises the Chancellor of the Exchequer on relevant matters. For power of Commissioners to prosecute an indictment without consent of A-G, see *R* v *CCRC ex p Hunt* (2000) *The Times*, 24 November.

inland waters. Waters [within Great Britain] which do not form part of the sea or of any creek, bay or estuary or of any river as far as the tide flows: T.C.P.A. 1990, s 55(4A), inserted by Planning & Compensation Act 1991, s 14. See also Water Resources Act 1991, s 222; Transport and Works Act 1992, s 67.

in lieu. In place of.

in loco parentis. In the place of a parent. Generally it refers to one who, although not the parent of a particular child, takes on himself parental offices and duties in relation to that child.

inn. At common law, a house, the owner of which holds himself out as being willing to receive travellers who are willing to pay an appropriate price for accommodation. See Hotel Proprietors Act 1956; *Williams* v *Linnit* [1951] 1 KB

565. For limitation of an innkeeper's liability, see s 2. *See* HOTEL.

Inner Temple. One of the Inns of Court (q.v.). It stands on land granted in perpetuity by James I in 1609.

inner urban area, assistance for. If the Secretary of State is satisfied that special social need exists in any inner urban area in Great Britain and that the causes could be alleviated by his exercising powers, he may by order specify a district including that area as a 'designated district', empowered to make loans for the acquisition by any person of land within that district or the carrying out by any person of works on the land, intended to benefit the district. See Planning and Compensation Act 1991, Sch 4; Environment Act 1995, Sch 2.

innocence. An absence of guilt for a specific charge, resulting from a verdict of Not Guilty.

innocence, presumption of. *See* PRE-SUMPTION OF INNOCENCE.

innocent dissemination. A common-law defence in relation to defamation (q.v.). Superseded by statutory defence under Defamation Act 1996, s 1, by which a person has a defence if he shows that he was not the author, editor or publisher of the statement complained of, that he took reasonable care in relation to its publication, and that he did not know, and had no reason to believe, that what he did caused or contributed to the publication of a defamatory statement.

innocent misrepresentation. *See* MIS-REPRESENTATION.

innominate. Neither named nor classified. Innominate terms in a contract are also known as 'intermediate terms' (q.v.): see *Hong Kong Fir Shipping Co v Kawasaki Ltd* [1962] 2 QB 26; *Union Eagle Ltd v Golden Achievement Ltd* [1997] AC 514.

in nomine. In the name of.

Inns of Chancery. Former seminaries associated with the Inns of Court (q.v.), which ceased to exist in the nineteenth century. They included Staple Inn, Lyon's Inn and Clement's Inn.

Inns of Court. Lincoln's Inn, Inner Temple, Middle Temple, and Gray's Inn (qq.v.), which have the exclusive right of call to the Bar (q.v.). Their members are benchers (q.v.), barristers (q.v.) and students. The Inns of Court and Bar Educational Trust was founded in 1997, taking over the responsibility of the Council of Legal Education (1852–1997).

innuendo. (*Innuere* = to hint.) An allegation by claimant in a claim relating to defamation (q.v.) that, although the words are not defamatory in themselves, by reason of a conjuncton of the words and some extrinsic statement, they have, in effect, a secondary defamatory meaning. See PD 16; CPR, Sch 1; O 82. See, e.g., *Grappelli v Derek Block (Holdings)* [1981] 1 WLR 822; *Polly Peck (Holdings) v Trelford* [1986] QB 1000.

in pais. (*Pays* = country.) In the country (as contrasted with 'in court'). Refers to a transaction which has taken place without legal proceedings. *Trial per pais* referred to trial by jury (i.e., trial 'by the country'). *See* ESTOPPEL.

in pari delicto **doctrine.** One who has participated in a wrongful act cannot recover damages resulting from the wrongdoing.

in pari materia. Relating to the same matter. See *Payne v Bradley* [1962] AC 343; *R v Newcastle Justices ex p Skinner* [1997] 1 All ER 349.

in personam. Against a person. Used to indicate, e.g., proceedings taken against some specific person (*actio in personam*). 'Equity acts *in personam*' refers to the old procedure of the Court of Chancery which issued an order 'upon a person' so that he was commanded to do or refrain from doing an act.

inquest. *See* CORONER.

inquest, convictions of deceased and. Where, during a coroner's inquest, any person (including the coroner) wishes to submit evidence involving previous convictions of the deceased, that person is obliged to notify all other parties in the absence of the jury: *R (Stanley) v Coroner for Inner North London* (2003) *The Times*, 12 June.

inquest, fresh. Exceptional circumstances, e.g., as where the coroner had not been given a complete account of all material circumstances in relation to a matter of real public concern, might justify an order for a fresh inquest: *Re Maddison* (2002) *The Times*, 28 November.

inquest, public funding of. In *R (Khan)* v *Secretary of State for Health* (2003) *The Times*, 15 October, the CA held that public funding for an inquiry or inquest had to be arranged for the bereaved relatives of a person whose death was the result of actions by an agent of the state.

inquest, retrospective. In *Re McKerr* (2004) *The Times*, 12 March, the HL held that the existence under Human Rights Act 1998, s 6(1), of an implied right to carry out a full investigation of the circumstances of a violent death had no application to a death which occurred before the statute came into force. No corresponding common law obligation was within the province of the court.

inquiry, preliminary. *See* PRELIMINARY INVESTIGATION.

inquiry, tribunals of. Bodies set up by Parliament to enquire into matters of urgent public importance. They may summon witnesses, take evidence on oath. Sittings are generally in public. See *R* v *Secretary of State for Health ex p Wagstaff* (2000) *The Times*, 31 August.

inquisition. 1. Enquiry by a jury (q.v.). 2. Verdict of an inquest, consisting of three sections: caption (date, place of inquest, coroner, jury); verdict (finding of identity of deceased, time, place, probable cause of death); attestation (signatures of coroner, concurring jurors). *See* CORONER.

inquisitorial procedure. System in force in some continental countries under which the judge decides the scope and range of the hearing, searches for facts, listens to witnesses, examines documents and orders that evidence be taken, after which he makes further investigations if he considers them necessary. *See* ADVERSARIAL PROCEDURE.

in re. In the matter of; concerning.

in rem. Against a thing. An expression used to indicate, e.g., an action taken against no specific person, but, rather, 'against the world', e.g., to assert a right of property against all persons (a claim *in rem*, relating to *jura in rem*). A judgment *in rem* is the judgment of 'a court of competent jurisdiction determining the status of a person or thing, or the disposition of a thing (as distinct from a particular interest in it of a party to the litigation)': *Lazarus-Barlow* v *Regent Estates* [1949] 2 KB 465. Example: a decree of nullity or divorce; see *Callaghan* v *Andrew-Hanson* [1992] 1 All ER 56.

insanity. Term used to refer to one whose state of mind prevents his knowing right from wrong so that he cannot be held responsible for his acts. See M.H.A. 1983. Every person is presumed sane until the contrary has been proved. The burden of proving insanity is generally on the accused: *Woolmington* v *DPP* [1935] AC 462. For sleepwalking and insanity, see *R* v *Burgess* [1991] 2 WLR 1206. The defence of insanity is unavailable for an offence of strict liability: see *DPP* v *Harper* [1997] 1 WLR 1406 (defence of insanity not available in the case of an offence of driving with excess alcohol contrary to Road Traffic Act 1988, s 5(1)(A)). *See* M'NAGHTEN RULES; SPECIAL VERDICT.

insanity inquiry. In *R* v *H* [2003] UKHL 1, the HL held that, in the context of Criminal Procedure (Insanity) Act 1964, s 4A, and Criminal Procedure (Insanity and Unfitness to Plead) Act 1991, s 2, the procedures intended to establish whether accused had done the act charged against him, did not constitute the determination of a criminal charge (for purposes of European Convention, art 6.2 (presumption of innocence)).

insanity, not guilty by reason of. *See* SPECIAL VERDICT.

inscribed stock. Stock for which a certificate of ownership is not issued.

insider dealing. Dealing by 'insiders' in current, listed securities of a company, using confidential information likely to affect their market value. Generally prohibited: see F.S.A. 1986, Part VII; C.J.A.

1993, s 52; Cos.A. 1989, s 74; *A-G's Reference (No. 1 of 1988)* [1989] 2 WLR 729; SI 00/1923. 'Insiders' include a person who, within the preceding six months has been knowingly connected with the company and has unpublished, price-sensitive information (q.v.) relating to the securities, and any person who has contemplated a takeover involving the company and is in possession of such information. Specified individuals (e.g., some public servants) are prohibited from abusing information obtained in their official capacity. Prohibitions apply also to off-market deals (q.v.).

in situ. In its original or natural position.

insolvency. Inability to pay one's debts, because of lack of sufficient property. (For meaning of 'unable to pay one's debts', see *Re Coney (A Bankrupt)* [1998] BPIR 333.) See Insolvency Act 1986. Includes, in relation to a company, the approval of a voluntary arrangement, the making of an administrative order, the appointment of an administrative receiver: s 247(1). See Insolvency Rules 1986 (SI 86/1925); *Practice Direction: Insolvency Proceedings*; Cos.A. 1989, ss 174, 183. For criminal liability in relation to insolvency, see 1986 Act, ss 206–211. *See* BANKRUPTCY.

insolvency practitioner. A person acts as an insolvency practitioner in relation to a company by acting as its liquidator, provisional liquidator, administrator, administrative receiver or as supervisor of a voluntary arrangement; and, in relation to an individual, by acting as his trustee in bankruptcy, or receiver, or trustee under a deed of arrangement, or supervisor of a voluntary arrangement, or, in the case of a deceased person, as administrator of his estate: Ins.A. 1986, s 388, amended by Ins.A. 2000, s 4(2). See SI 86/1995; *Re Adams* [1991] BCC 62.

insolvency practitioner, bars to acting as. An individual may not act as an insolvency practitioner (q.v.) unless he is authorised so to act by virtue of membership of a professional body, or holds an authorisation granted by a competent authority: Ins.A. 1986, ss 390, 391, 393, amended by Ins.A. 2000, Sch 4, para 16. He may not so act if he is an undischarged bankrupt or is disqualified under Company Directors Disqualification Act 1986, or is incapable because of mental disorder: s 390(4). It is an offence (of strict liability) to act in this capacity when not qualified: s 389(1). See Ins.A. 2000, s 4(3), (4).

insolvency, preferential debts in. In the case of a company or individual, these are (as listed in Ins.A. 1986, Sch 6): money owed to Inland Revenue for income tax deducted at source; VAT, car tax, betting and gaming duties; social security and pension scheme contributions; remuneration of employees: s 386(1). *See* BANKRUPTCY, PRIORITY OF DEBTS IN DISTRIBUTION.

insolvency proceedings. European Regulation on Insolvency Proceedings came into force on 31 May 2002: it applies to collective insolvency proceedings which entail the partial or total divestment of a debtor and the appointment of a liquidator; it confirms jurisdiction in the country containing the debtor's main interests. Qualifying insolvency proceedings include winding up by the court, creditor's voluntary winding up, administration, voluntary arrangements under insolvency legislations, bankruptcy.

Insolvency Services Account. Account kept by Secretary of State with the Bank of England relating to sums standing to the credit of bankrupt estates or to liquidated companies: Ins.A. 1986, s 403.

insolvency, transfer of assets. Transfer of an asset conditional on the revesting of the asset in the transferor in the event of the transferee's insolvency is, in general, ineffective: *Money Markets Stockbrokers Ltd v London Stock Exchange plc* [2001] 4 All ER 223.

inspection and investigation of a company. Procedure whereby the Department of Trade and Industry is empowered to inspect a company's papers and books, to investigate a company's affairs, membership, director's interests in its shares or debentures. See, e.g., Cos.A. 1985, Part XIV. *See* COMPANY.

inspection by judge. Provision whereby a judge may inspect a place or thing with respect to which a question has arisen in a cause or other matter. 'I think that a view is part of the evidence just as much as an exhibit. It is real evidence': *per* Denning LJ in *Goold* v *Evans & Co* [1951] 2 TLR 1189. See *Tito* v *Waddell* [1975] 3 All ER 997. *See* VIEW.

instalment. Portions into which a sum of money, or a debt, may be divided for payment at fixed intervals.

instalment deliveries. Unless otherwise agreed, the buyer of goods is not bound to accept delivery of them by instalments: S.G.A. 1979, s 31(1).

instance, court of first. A court in which proceedings are commenced, as contrasted with, e.g., the Court of Appeal (q.v.).

instant committal. Short committal. *See* COMMITTAL FOR TRIAL.

in statu quo. In the state or position in which something was or is.

instruct. To authorise an advocate to act, or to communicate information to him relating to legal proceedings.

instrument. A written document (such as a deed or will) executed formally, evidencing, e.g., rights, duties.

instrument, banking. *See* BANKING INSTRUMENT.

instrument, false. Phrase used in Forgery and Counterfeiting Act 1981, s 1. An instrument is false if, e.g., it purports to have been made in the form in which it is made by a person who did not in fact make it in that form: s 9(1). 'Instrument' includes any document, formal or informal, stamp sold by the Post Office, Inland Revenue stamp, disc, tape, soundtrack or similar device. See *R* v *Moore* [1986] Crim LR 552; *A-G's Reference (No. 1 of 2000)* (2000) *The Times*, 28 November. *See* FORGERY.

insulting behaviour. It was held in *Hammond* v *DPP* [2004] EWHC 62, that where an evangelical Christian had displayed a sign reading 'Stop Immorality and Homosexuality' in circumstances which upset and insulted viewers, it was open to magistrates to convict under the Public Order Act 1986, s 5. The magistrates' view that defendant's conduct was not reasonable within s 5(3)(c) was clearly open to them to reach.

insurable interest. An interest giving an insured person a right to enforce a contract of insurance. It exists if the insured person is liable to sustain some monetary loss, or if he may be claimed against following a loss to another. Examples: a father has not necessarily an insurable interest in his son's life (*Halford* v *Kymer* (1830) 10 B & C 724); a husband may insure his wife, and a wife her husband (*Griffiths* v *Fleming* [1909] 1 KB 805); a trustee may insure in respect of the interest of which he is trustee (*Tidswell* v *Ankerstein* (1792) Peake 151).

insurance. Generally a contract (q.v.) of indemnity against a contingency. The *insurer* assumes the risks of the contingency in consideration of payment of a *premium*, so that the *insured*, who suffers the damage, will be compensated from a common insurance fund. It is a contract necessitating full disclosure of *all* facts affecting the risk: *Black King Shipping* v *Massie* [1985] 1 Lloyd's Rep 437; *HIH Casualty Ltd Insurance Ltd* v *Chase Manhattan Bank* (2000) *The Times*, 19 September. 'Insurance' is used with reference to events which *may* happen (e.g., fire on one's property); 'assurance' (q.v.) is used to refer to events which *must* happen (e.g., death). A contract of insurance may be not only for the payment of money, but for a benefit corresponding to such payment: *Department of Trade and Industry* v *St Christopher's Motorists Association* [1974] 1 WLR 99. See Insurance Companies Act 1982; Policyholders Protection Acts 1975, 1997; F.S.A. 1986, s 133; I.C.T.A. 1988, s 431. For 'insurance warranty' (which is generally equivalent to 'a condition' in other types of contract) see *The Good Luck* [1990] 1 QB 818. See Consultation Paper of Law Commission (January 1998) proposing amendments to Third Parties (Rights Against Insurers) Act 1930, which would ease victims' insurance claims against insolvent wrongdoers' insurers. *See* COSTS, RECOVERY OF INSURANCE PREMIUM BY WAY OF.

insurance business. Divided, under Insurance Companies Act 1982, s 1(1), into 'long-term business' (meaning insurance business of the classes specified in Sch 1 – life (i.e. industrial life and ordinary life business) and annuity, tontines (q.v.), pension fund management, etc.) and 'general business' (meaning insurance business of the classes specified in Sch 2, Part I – accident, sickness, fire, damage to property, suretyship, etc.). See 1982 Act, s 95; F.S.A. 1986, ss 22, 129–139; Export and Investment Guarantees Act 1991 (insurance of overseas investments); PD 49B (applications under Insurance Companies Act 1982). For 'financial year' in relation to insurance companies, see 1982 Act, s 96. For insurer's duty of care to clients' dependants, see *Gorham v BT plc* (2000) *The Times*, 16 August. See F.S.M.A. 2000, ss 141, 142 (insurance asset identification rules). For 'general insurer', see Finance Act 2000, s 107(7).

insurance, double. Insurance by the insured of one risk on the same interest in the same property with more than one insurer. See *LGAS v Drake Insurance Co* [1992] 1 All ER 283.

insurance, fire. *See* FIRE INSURANCE.

insurance, over-. Situation in which the aggregate of all the insurance exceeds the total value of the insured's interests.

insurrection. 'An organised and violent uprising in a country with, as a main purpose, the object of trying to overthrow or supplant the government': *per* Saville J, in *National Oil Company of Zimbabwe v Sturge* (1991) *The Financial Times*, 12 March. *See* REBELLION.

intangible property. *See* TANGIBLE PROPERTY.

integration test. 'One feature, which seems to run through the instances, is that, under a contract of service (q.v.), a man is employed as part of the business, and his work is done as an integral part of the business; whereas, under a contract for services, his work, although done for the business, is not integrated into it, but

is only necessary to it': *per* Denning LJ in *Stevenson, Jordan and Harrison v Macdonald & Evans* [1952] 1 TLR 101.

intellectual property. A group of rights, e.g., patents, registered designs, copyright, trade marks, know-how (q.v.). See S.C.A. 1981, s 72(5); Atomic Energy Authority Act 1986, s 8(2); I.C.T.A. 1988, ss 520–538. For attitude of EU, see *Deutsche Grammophon v Metro 78/70* [1971] ECR 487; Treaty of Rome, art 36.

Intelligence Service. An organisation under the authority of the Secretary of State with functions exercisable only in the interests of national security, with particular reference to defence and foreign policy, in the interests of the economic well-being of the UK, and in support of the prevention or detection of serious crime: Intelligence Services Act 1994, s 1(2). For functions of Intelligence Services Commissioner, see R.I.P.A. 2000, s 59.

intent and form in equity. 'A court of equity makes a distinction between that which is a matter of substance and that which is a matter of form; should it find that by insisting on form, the substance will be defeated it holds it to be inequitable to allow a person to insist on such form, and thereby defeat the substance': *per* Romilly MR in *Parkin v Thorold* (1852) 16 Beav 59. See *Re Lovegrove* [1935] Ch 464.

intent, basic or general, crimes of. Offences in which either recklessness or intention will suffice as proof of the necessary *mens rea*. Examples: assault (common and indecent); rape (see *R v Eatch* [1980] Crim LR 650). See *R v Hardie* [1984] 3 All ER 848; *R v Hutchins* [1988] Crim LR 379.

intention. 'The most culpable form of blameworthiness.' 'A state of affairs which the party "intending" does more than merely contemplate. It connotes a state of affairs which, on the contrary, he decides, so far as in him lies, to bring about, and which, in point of possibility, he has a reasonable prospect of being able to bring about by his own act of volition': *Cunliffe v Goodman* [1950]

2 KB 237. 'The intention is the aim of the act, of which the motive is the spring': Austin, *Lectures on Jurisprudence* (1861). Intention may be inferred from foresight of consequences, but must not be equated with foresight: see *R v Moloney* [1985] 1 All ER 1025; *R v Hancock and Shankland* [1986] 1 All ER 641. *See* MENS REA; MOTIVE.

intention of Parliament. Phrase used in the interpretation of statutes (q.v.). 'We do not sit here to pull the language of Parliament to pieces and make nonsense of it . . . We sit here to find out the intention of Parliament and of ministers and carry it out, and we do this better by filling in the gaps and making sense of the enactment than by opening it up to destructive analysis': *Magor and St Mellons RDC v Newport Corporation* [1950] 2 All ER 1226. This approach was rejected later by the House of Lords. See *Hadmor Productions v Hamilton* [1983] 1 AC 191. *See* HANSARD.

intent, specific or ulterior, crimes of. Offences in which the requirement of *mens rea* is satisfied only by proof beyond reasonable doubt that the defendant had the intention of committing the *actus reus*. Proof of negligence (q.v.) or recklessness (q.v.) will not suffice. Examples: murder; unlawful wounding; stealing.

intent, wounding with. *See* WOUNDING WITH INTENT.

inter alia. Among other things.

inter alios. Among other persons.

interception of communications. It is an offence under R.I.P.A. 2000 for a person intentionally and without lawful authority to intercept in the UK any communication in the course of its transmission by means of a public postal service or public or private telecommunication system: s 1(1), (2). Interception in relation to a private system may also be a tort: s 1(3). An interception may be lawful if authorised under s 1(3), (4), or takes place in accordance with an interception warrant under s 5, or in relation to any stored communication, in the exercise of a statutory power: s 1(5). Interception of

a communication broadcast for general reception is not included: s 2(3). For functions of Interception Commissioner, see ss 57, 58. For powers of Tribunal to hear and determine complaints, see ss 65–69. See SI 00/2699.

interception of communications, use as evidence. R.I.P.A. 2000, s 17, prohibits disclosure in legal proceedings of matter from which may be inferred contents of an intercepted communication or any related communications data. But this does not apply to matter gathered lawfully under ss 1(5)(c), 3, 4: s 18(4).

interception of communications with warrant. Procedure, necessary under R.I.P.A. 2000, in interests of national security, for prevention or detection of serious crime, for safeguarding economic well-being of UK, for giving effect to international assistance agreements: s 5(3). Secretary of State will not issue a warrant unless conduct which it authorises is proportionate to what is to be achieved by that conduct: s 5(2). Application for warrant must be made by or on behalf of persons specified in s 6(2), including, e.g., Director-General of Security Service, Chief of Secret Intelligence Services, Director of GCHQ, Commissioners of Customs and Excise. For necessary contents, see s 8. For offence of unauthorised disclosure of contents, see s 19.

intercourse, sexual. *See* SEXUAL INTERCOURSE, PROOF OF.

interest. 1. A right, duty, claim, legal share in something. 2. A right in property. 'It extendeth to estates, rights and titles that a man hath of, in, to, or out of lands': Coke. 3. The return on capital invested ('the price of money'). 4. A share of control in, e.g., a company (q.v.). 5. Concern in the outcome of an event. For 'interest rate swap agreements', see *Guinness Mahon Ltd v Kensington and Chelsea RLBC* [1998] 3 WLR 829. *See* STATUTORY INTEREST ON LATE PAYMENT OF DEBTS; SWAPS TRANSACTIONS.

interest, compound, award of. In general, the courts may award compound interest only: as special damages; in relation to a specific agreement; in equity;

where a course of dealing involved the implication of compound interest. See *Westdeutsche Landesbank* v *Islington LBC* [1996] AC 669; *The Maria* [1990] 1 All ER 78; S.C.A. 1981, s 35A.

interest, declaration against. *See* DECLARATION AGAINST INTEREST.

interest, disclosure of. 1. The duty of, e.g., a member of a local authority to make known the fact that he has a direct or indirect pecuniary interest in a contract which is under discussion by the authority and to refrain from voting on it. See L.G.A. 1972, ss 94–98; *Readman* v *DPP* (1991) *The Times*, 4 March. 2. A compulsory register of interests of Members of Parliament was established following a debate on 12 June 1975. See Report of the Nolan Inquiry, May 1995. 3. A register of interests of members and co-opted members of local authorities is kept by the monitoring officer: L.G.A. 2000, s 81.

interest, future. *See* FUTURE INTEREST.

interest in expectancy. A reversionary interest. *See* REVERSION.

interest in possession. An interest which confers a right to present enjoyment of property.

interest on debts and damages. The High Court and county courts (qq.v.) are empowered in proceedings for the recovery of a debt or damages to award simple interest at such rate as is thought fit: S.C.A. 1981, s 35A (inserted by A.J.A. 1982, Sch 1). See Private International Law (Misc. Provs.) Act 1995, s 1; *All-in-One Design Ltd* v *Motocomb Estates* (2000) *The Times*, 4 April ('interest' has different meanings in different contexts: see, e.g., r 36.21). *See* JUDGMENT DEBT.

interest reipublicae ut sit finis litium. It concerns the state that litigation shall not be protracted. See *Ras Beharilal* v *King-Emperor* [1933] All ER 723. ('Finality is a good thing, but justice is a better': *per* Lord Atkin.)

interests, registrable. Those interests set out in L.R.A. 1925 as capable of substantive registration (i.e., in their own right under a specific title number). They comprise those estates capable of subsisting as legal estates. *See* LAND REGISTRATION.

interests, theory of. Theory, proposed by the American jurist, Pound (1870–1964), suggesting that the main problem for legislators and judges is the balancing of individual, public and social interests. 'Interests' are seen as demands, desires or expectations which human beings, individually or in groups, seek to satisfy.

interference with goods, wrongful. Conversion of goods (also called 'trover' (q.v.)), trespass to goods, negligence so far as it results in damage to goods or to an interest in goods, any other tort so far as it results in damage to goods or to an interest in goods: Torts (Interference with Goods) Act 1977, s 1. See also C.P.A. 1987, Sch 4. Relief given may take form of: order for delivery of the goods and payment of consequential damages; or an order for delivery, but giving the defendant the alternative of paying damages by reference to the value of the goods, together in either alternative with payment of any consequential damages; or damages: s 3(1), (2). See *Jerry Juhan SA* v *Avon Tyres Ltd* (1999) *The Times*, 25 January; *Kuwait Airways* v *Iraq Airways (No. 5)* (2000) *The Times*, 31 May.

interference with subsisting contract. Tort (q.v.) committed by X who, without lawful justification, intentionally interferes with a contract between Y and Z by persuading Y to break his contract with Z or by committing a tortious act which prevents Y's performing the contract. See *Torquay Hotel Ltd* v *Cousins* [1969] 2 Ch 106; *Merkur Island Corpn* v *Laughton* [1983] 2 AC 570.

interference with vehicles. *See* VEHICLE, INTERFERENCE WITH.

interfering with witnesses. It is an offence at common law to attempt to dissuade or prevent a witness from appearing at a hearing or giving evidence. For the statutory offence of intimidating a juror or witness, see C.J.P.O.A. 1994, s 51(1), substituted by Y.J.C.E.A. 1999, Sch 4, para 22 (a person commits an offence if: he does an act which intimidates, and is intended to intimidate, another person ('the victim'), he does the act knowing or believing that the victim is assisting in the investigation of an offence or is a witness or potential witness or a juror or potential juror in proceedings for an offence, and he does it intending thereby to cause the investigation or the course of justice to be obstructed, perverted or interfered with). See *R* v *Singh* [2000] 1 Cr App R 31. See INTIMIDATION.

interim dividend. A dividend declared at any time between two annual general meetings of a company (q.v.). It is not in the nature of a debt due from the company and cannot be sued for by a shareholder. See Table A, art 103, and Cos.A. 1985, s 272, as amended. See DIVIDEND.

interim orders and remedies under CPR. Formerly 'interlocutory orders'. Under r 25.1, the court may grant interim remedies, including interim injunctions, interim declarations, orders for inspection or detention of relevant property, freezing injunctions, orders under Torts (Interference with Goods) Act 1997, s 4, Civil Procedure Act 1997, s 7. Orders can be made before proceedings are started and after judgment has been given: r 25.2(1). Application for pre-action remedy (e.g., freezing order) is made to court where it is likely that the substantive claim will be started: r 23.2(4); such application may be made if the matter is urgent: r 25.2(2)(b). Interim injunctions cease if claim is stayed or struck out: r 25.10, 11. See APPLICATIONS WITHOUT NOTICE.

interim payment order. Order under CPR, r 25.6, for payment by defendant on account of any damages, debt, or other sum (except costs) which the court may hold defendant liable to pay. Copy of application notice must be served at least 14 days before hearing and be supported by evidence: r 25.6(3). Order will be made only if defendant against whom order is sought has admitted liability to pay damages or other sum to claimant and the court is satisfied that if the case went to trial, claimant would obtain judgment for a substantial sum of money: r 25.7. (See PD 25B.)

interim relief. Granting of an interlocutory injunction (q.v.). See S.C.A. 1981, s 32 (interim payment of damages); r 25.3; *American Cyanamid Co* v *Ethicon* [1975] AC 396 ('balance of convenience' test for interlocutory injunctions).

interim rent. When a landlord (q.v.) has given notice to terminate a tenancy, or a tenant has requested a new one, the landlord can apply to the court to determine an interim rent to be paid until commencement of new tenancy. See Landlord and Tenant Act 1954, s 24A; CPR, Sch 1; O 97, r 9A; *Follett* v *Cabtell Investment Co* (1986) 280 EG 639.

interlineation. Writing between (or on) the lines of a document. Under W.A. 1837, s 21, no interlineation in a will made after execution has effect except insofar as the words or effect of the will before interlineation shall not be apparent, unless it is executed as a will. See *In b Heath* [1892] P 253.

interlocutory. (*Interloqui* = to speak between.) Not final (i.e., during the course of legal proceedings). Examples: interlocutory injunction (q.v.) or interlocutory judgment or order (one which does not finally determine the proceedings).

interlocutory injunction. *See* INJUNCTION.

intermediate term. Term (q.v.), the breach of which will not always entitle the innocent party to consider himself as discharged. The seriousness of the breach and its effects will be decisive. See, e.g., *Bunge Corporation* v *Tradax Export SA* [1981] 1 WLR 711; *State Trading Corporation of India* v *Golodetz* [1989] 2 Lloyd's Rep 277. Known also as 'innominate term'. *See* INNOMINATE.

intermixture. The commingling of substances so that the parts can no longer be distinguished. See *Smith* v *Torr* (1862) 7 F & F 505; *Sandeman & Sons* v *Tyzack* [1913] AC 680.

Internal Market, EU. Term which replaced 'common market' in European Communities Act 1972. Defined as 'an area without internal frontiers in which the free movement of goods, persons, services and capital is ensured in accordance with the Treaty provisions.'

International Court of Justice. Principal judicial organ of the United Nations Organisation, which succeeded the Permanent Court of International Justice in 1946. Its seat is at The Hague and its function is to pass judgment on disputes between states (but not individuals). A state which has not accepted the court's jurisdiction cannot be sued without that state's consent. Disputes are decided by majority vote of the judges, in accordance with international law, customs and conventions, or (with agreement of parties) *ex aequo et bono*, i.e., on the foundation of a 'fair solution'. Its judges are elected by the Security Council and General Assembly of UNO.

International Criminal Court. Institution proposed in 1998 by 120 UNO member states, to be established at The Hague, intended to try cases involving war crimes, genocide, aggression and crimes against humanity (q.v.) from any country. See International Criminal Court Act 2001. It came into existence in The Hague in July 2002. The United States has withdrawn from the ICC Treaty; China, Israel, Russia have not ratified the treaty. Its jurisdiction is intended to be complementary to national criminal justice institutions and to relate to 'the most serious crimes' of international concern.

international law. 1. The *corpus* of legal rules applying between sovereign states, known as *public international law*. 2. The body of rights and duties of citizens of different sovereign states towards one another, known as *private international law* (q.v.) or 'conflict of laws'.

international supply contract. Phrase used in Unfair Contract Terms Act 1977, s 26, to refer to a contract made by parties whose places of business (or, if they have none, habitual residences) are in the territories of different states, if the goods to which the contract relates are, at the time of its conclusion, in the course of carriage, or will be carried from the territory of one state to that of another, or the acts constituting the offer and acceptance have been done in the territories of different states, or the contract provides for the goods to be delivered to the territory of a state other than that within whose territory those acts were done.

internet libel, forum for. In *King* v *Lewis* (2004) *The Times*, 25 October, the CA held that, in determining an appropriate forum for a libel claim trials involving the internet, the court will take into account the global nature of the medium chosen by the publisher; hence every jurisdiction where the text might be downloaded could be brought under consideration.

internment. Detention within prescribed limits, generally without formal trial, e.g., as with enemy aliens in time of war.

interpleader summons. Procedure whereby a person who is sued, or expects to be sued, by rival claimants takes out a summons which is served on the parties, calling on them to appear before a master so as to stake their claims. The court may then order that the issue between the parties be tried and will direct who shall be the claimant and defendant. A *stakeholder's interpleader* relates to, e.g., a banker holding cash and faced with opposing claims. A *sheriff's interpleader* relates to goods seized under writ of *fi.fa.* (q.v.) and a claim by a third person that they belong to him. See CPR, Sch 1; O 17, r 1; CPR, Sch 2; CCR, O 16, 33.

interpretation clause. Part of an Act which provides that certain words and phrases used in that Act shall have certain meanings. See, e.g., L.P.A. 1925, s 205; Acc. J.A. 1998, s 26. 'An interpretation clause of this kind is not meant to prevent the word receiving its ordinary, popular and natural sense whenever that would be properly applicable, but to enable the word as used in the Act, where there is nothing in the context or the subject matter to the contrary, to be applied to some things to which it would not ordinarily be applicable': *per* Lord Selborne in *Robinson* v *Barton*

Eccles Local Board (1883) 8 App Cas 198. See *Carter* v *Bradbeer* [1975] 3 All ER 158.

interpretation, legal. The seeking out of the real meaning of legal phraseology; often used as a synonym for 'legal construction' (q.v.). 'It has to do with determining the meaning of that which is in some relevant respect unclear or indeterminate': Marmor, *Interpretation and Legal Theory* (1992).

interpretation of statutes. Where a statute's words are not clear or not certain, the courts may be called upon to interpret them. ('The fundamental object of statutory construction in every case is to ascertain the legislative intention . . . The rules of interpretation are no more than the rules of common sense, designed to achieve this object': *per* Mason J in *Cooper Brookes Ltd* v *FCT* (1981) 35 ALR 151.) In this they are guided by rules, such as: (1) Literal rule (q.v.) – words of a statute in their original sense will prevail unless they would produce unintended consequences: *Corocraft* v *Pan Am Airways* [1969] 1 All ER 82. (2) Golden rule (q.v.) – manifest absurdity resulting from interpretation to be avoided: *Becke* v *Smith* (1836) 2 M & W 191. (3) Statute must be read as a whole. (4) There is a presumption against altering the law or ousting the courts' jurisdiction. (5) The court must adopt an interpretation which will correct the mischief which the statute was passed to remedy: *Heydon's Case* (1584) 3 Co Rep 7a. For conflicts between international obligations and specific statutory provisions, see *Cheney* v *Conn* [1968] 1 All ER 779. See Lord Scarman's Interpretation of Legislation Bill, introduced into the House of Lords in 1981; *Inco Europe Ltd* v *First Choice Distribution* [2000] 1 WLR 586; *Mock* v *Pensions Ombudsman* (2000) *The Times*, 7 April. That when a court is seeking to establish questions of compatibility of primary legislation with European Convention, it is entitled to consider the policy objectives of the legislation by examining ministerial statements made during progress of the bill

through Parliament: *Wilson* v *First County Trust* (No. 2) [2003] UKHL 40.

interpretation of statutes and correction of obvious drafting errors. House of Lords has stated, in *Inco Europe Ltd* v *First Choice Distribution* (2000) *The Times*, 10 March, that the court must be able to correct obvious drafting errors on a statute by adding, omitting or substituting words. The court must be quite sure of the intended purpose of the statute, that draftsman and Parliament had failed to give effect to that purpose, and (crucially important) of the substance of the provision that Parliament would have made had the error in the Bill been noted. (The House was considering S.C.A. 1981, s 18(1)(g), as amended by Arbitration Act 1996, s 107, Sch 3.)

interpretation of statutes, conflicting interpretation of. The court must strive to reconcile conflicting provisions in the same statute, and where it cannot do so it must decide which is the leading provisions and which is subordinate, so that the latter may give way to the former: *per* Lightman J in *Padmore* v *IRC (No. 2)* [2001] STC 280.

interpretation of statutes, consolidating statute. Where there are inconsistent provisions in a consolidating statute, earlier legislation may be taken into account only where the language of the statute is ambiguous, obscure, or likely to result in an absurdity: *Padmore* v *IRC (No. 2)* [2001] STC 280.

interpretation of statutes, purposive approach. 'When there is no obvious meaning to a statutory provision, the modern emphasis is on a contextual approach designed to identify the purpose of a statute and to give effect to it: *per* Lord Steyn, in *IRC* v *McGuckian* [1997] 1 WLR 991. See also *Fothergill* v *Monarch Airlines* [1980] 3 WLR 209; *Ng Ka Ling* v *Director of Immigration* [1999] 6 BHRC 447.

interpreter. One who translates the words of a witness. An accused who is unable to understand English properly is entitled to an interpreter's services: *R* v *Lee Kun* [1916] 1 KB 337. In civil proceedings the court has a discretion to allow the use of an interpreter: *Re Fuld* [1965] P 405. See *R v Attard* (1959) 43 Cr App R 90 (use of notes to refresh interpreter's memory); *R v Tower Hamlets BC, ex p Begum* [1993] AC 509 (competence of interpreter questioned). Interpreters may be selected from National Register of Public Service Interpreters. For principles governing use of double translation, see *R v West London Youth Court ex p J* [1999] COD 444.

interregnum. Period during which a throne is vacant, e.g., between the death of a monarch and accession of the successor.

interrogation. Questioning of suspects by the police. See *Averill v UK* (2000) *The Times*, 20 June (access to lawyer to be guaranteed before interrogation).

interrogatories. *See* FURTHER INFORMATION, OBTAINING.

in terrorem. By way of terror. Threat or intimidation, e.g., by way of a condition in a gift. Example: gift of personalty by X to Y, on condition that Y shall never marry Z. Conditions of this nature are usually void. See *Wilbeam v Ashton* (1807) 1 Camp 78 – penalty (q.v.) held over a party to a contract *in terrorem*; *Jenner v Turner* (1886) 16 Ch D 188.

interruption. The breaking of continuity, e.g., of enjoyment of some right. See, e.g., Prescription Act 1832, s 4.

intervener. One who intervenes in a suit (e.g., relating to divorce) in his own, or the public's interest. *See* QUEEN'S PROCTOR.

intervening cause. An independent cause coming between the original act or omission and an injury so that a result is produced which might not otherwise have occurred. 'To break the chain of causation (q.v.) it must be shown that there is something which I will call ultroneous, something unwarrantable, a new cause which disturbs the sequence of events, something which can be described as either extraneous or extrinsic': *per* Lord Wright in *The Oropesa* [1943] P 32. *See* CAUSATION; *NOVA CAUSA INTERVENIENS*.

interview. A face-to-face discussion. It should not be given a restricted meaning for purposes of P.&C.E.A. 1984. A conversation may be an interview for related purposes: *R v Matthews* [1990] Crim LR 190. See *DPP v Rouse* [1991] Crim LR 911; *R v Chief Constable of RUC ex p Begley* [1997] 1 WLR 1475. Code C, revised in 1991, issued under the 1984 Act, restricts interviews outside police stations. For records of interviews, see Code C, para 11.5. See *Batley v DPP* (1998) *The Times*, 5 March.

interview, fairness of. In the absence of reliable and relevant documentary evidence, relating to the age of an asylum seeker without means of support, a local authority can rely on appearance, behaviour and background, always provided that minimum standards of fairness are observed: *R (B) v Merton LBC* (2003) *The Times*, 18 July.

inter vivos. Between parties who are alive.

inter vivos, gift. *See* GIFT *INTER VIVOS*.

intestacy. State of dying intestate, i.e., without having made a valid will (q.v.). A partial intestacy results from a will which disposes of only part of deceased's property. On the death of a person intestate as to any real or personal estate, that estate shall be held in trust by his personal representative with the power to sell it: A.E.A. 1925, s 33(1), as amended by Trusts of Land and Appointment of Trustees Act 1996, Sch 2, para 5. For administration and devolution on intestacy see A.E.A. 1925; A.E.A. 1971; Intestates' Estates Act 1952; Law Reform (Succession) Act 1995, s 1(1) ('Where the intestate's husband or wife survived the intestate but died before the end of the period of 28 days beginning with the day on which the intestate died, [A.E.A. 1925, s 2A] shall have effect as respects the intestate as if the husband or wife had not survived the intestate').

intestacy, surviving spouse, and. Where intestate leaves a surviving spouse (S) but no issue (children, grandchildren) or specified relatives (parent, brother, sister of the whole blood or their issue), S takes entire residuary estate absolutely.

Where intestate leaves issue, S takes personal chattels absolutely, £125,000 absolutely, life interest in half residuary estate. S may require personal representatives to appropriate the matrimonial home to him/her. Where intestate leaves no issue, but specified relatives, S takes personal chattels absolutely, £200,000 absolutely, half of residuary estate absolutely. (Subject to S's rights, property is held on special statutory trusts for surviving issue in equal shares: A.E.A. 1925, ss 46, 47.) See Intestates' Estates Act 1952, as amended; SI 93/2906.

intimidation. The act of intentionally and unlawfully frightening or coercing another into a course of action. See S.O.A. 1956, s 2 (offence of procuring a woman by threats or intimidation to have sexual intercourse); *A-G v Butterworth* [1963] 1 QB 696 (intimidation of juror or witness, which is treated as a contempt (q.v.): see also C.J.P.O.A. 1994, s 54, amended by Y.J.C.E.A. 1999, Sch 4, para 22). The *tort of intimidation* arises where A threatens B so that B acts, or refrains from acting, to B's and C's detriment. See *Rookes v Barnard* [1964] AC 1129; *Godwin v Uzoigwe* [1993] Fam Law 65; *A-G's Reference (No. 1 of 1999)* [1999] 2 Cr App R (S) 398 (intimidation of a witness may arise by communication of a threat by a third party where intention is established); C.J.P.O.A. 1994, s 51, substituted by Y.J.C.E.A. 1999, Sch 4. *See* INTERFERING WITH WITNESSES; THREAT.

intoxicating liquor. Beer, cider, wine, spirits, etc. See Licensing Acts 1964 and 1988; Licensing (Low Alcoholic Drinks) Act 1990. Under 1990 Act, the level at which alcohol is classified as 'intoxicating' is 0.5 per cent. For protection of persons under 18, see 1988 Act, s 16.

intoxication. Condition of stupefaction induced by alcohol or a narcotic. Self-intoxication is no defence to any crime, the definition of which does not require a specific intent. See *R v Lipman* [1970] 1 QB 152; *R v Caldwell* [1982] AC 341; *R v Kingston* [1995] 2 AC 355; *R v Richardson* [1999] 1 Cr App R 392 (intoxication and *mens rea*). For the

basis of a 'drunken intent' direction to the jury, see *R v McKnight* (2000) *The Times*, 5 May. *See* ALCOHOLISM; DIMINISHED RESPONSIBILITY; SOLVENT ABUSE.

intoxication caused by inhalation. *See* SOLVENT ABUSE.

in transitu. During the passage. Right of stoppage *in transitu* is the right, under S.G.A. 1979, ss 44–46, to stop goods in transit, to resume and to retain possession until the price is paid. The right is available when the buyer becomes insolvent.

intra vires. Within its powers.

intrinsic. Essential to, or inherent in, something.

intrinsic evidence. *See* EVIDENCE, INTRINSIC.

inventory. An itemised list or catalogue. Under A.E.A. 1925, s 25(*a*), the personal representatives (q.v.) of a deceased person are under a duty to exhibit on oath a full inventory of the estate when required by court to do so.

investigation, criminal. *See* CRIMINAL INVESTIGATION.

investigation of a company. *See* COMPANY, INVESTIGATION OF.

investigation, preliminary. *See* PRELIMINARY INVESTIGATION.

investitive facts. *See* FACTS, INVESTITIVE.

investment. 'The verb "to invest" when used in an investment clause may safely be said to include as one of its meanings "to apply money in the purchase of some property from which interest or profit is expected and which property is purchased in order to be held for the sake of the income which it will yield" ': *Re Wragg* [1919] 2 Ch 58. Generally, the term means the laying out of money with a view to earning an income from it, by way of interest, dividend, rent, etc. Under F.S.A. 1986, Sch 1, 'investments' comprise assets, rights, interests (including shares, debentures, government and other public securities, long-term insurance policies, etc.): s 1(1). See *Larussa-Chigi v CS First Boston Ltd* [1998] CLC 277 (whether foreign exchange transactions constituted investments).

investment business. Includes dealing in, arranging deals in, managing and advising on, investments: F.S.A. 1986, s 1, Sch 1. The carrying on of such a business in the UK is restricted to authorised or exempted persons: ss 3, 207, and Part I, Chap III. For the conduct of such a business, see Part I, Chap V (prohibiting, e.g., misleading statements inducing persons to enter investment agreements). For restrictions on advertising, see ss 57, 58. For 'investment trust', see I.C.T.A. 1988, s 842; T.C.G.A. 1992, s 99.

investment business, persons authorised to carry on. 'The Secretary of State may issue statements of principle with respect to the conduct and financial standing expected of persons authorised to carry on investment business': F.S.A. 1986, s 47A, inserted by Cos.A. 1989. This power has been delegated to the Securities and Investments Board (q.v.).

investment company. Any company whose business consists wholly or mainly in the making of investments and the principal part of whose income is derived therefrom: I.C.T.A. 1988, s 130.

investment company, open-ended. Collective investment scheme (q.v.) by which the property belongs beneficially to, and is managed by, a body corporate which invests funds so as to spread investment risk and give its members the benefit of management of those funds, and a reasonable investor would be satisfied that his investment could be realised in a reasonable time on a basis calculated by reference to the value of the body's property: F.S.M.A. 2000, s 236. See also ss 262, 263.

investment, ethical, by charities. 'If trustees are satisfied that investing in a company engaged in a particular type of business would conflict with the very objects their charity is seeking to achieve, they should not so invest': *per* Nicholls V-C in *Lord Bishop of Oxford* v *Church Commissioners* [1993] 2 All ER 300.

investment exchange. An organisation which offers to deal in securities with a subscriber whose identity is not revealed to other subscribers and which records and confirms acceptance of its offers: Company Securities (Insider Dealing)

Act 1985, s 13; F.S.A. 1986, s 36, Sch 4. A 'recognised' investment exchange is one which is qualified to receive a recognition order from FSA, under F.S.M.A. 2000, s 286. For revocation of recognition, see s 297. (For similar arrangements concerning 'clearing houses', see ss 285, 288.)

investment scheme, collective. Any arrangement concerning property of any description, including money, the purpose or effect of which is to enable participants (whether by becoming owners of the property) to receive profits or income arising from the acquisition, holding, management or disposal of the property or sums paid out of such profits or income. Participants do not have day-to-day control over management; property is managed as a whole by scheme operator; participant's contributions, profits and income are pooled. See F.S.M.A. 2000, s 235. For restrictions on promotion, see s 238.

invitation to treat. An offer to receive an offer. 'According to the ordinary law of contract the display of an article with a price on it in the shop window is merely an invitation to treat. It is in no sense an offer for sale, the acceptance of which constitutes a contract': *per* Lord Parker in *Fisher* v *Bell* [1961] 1 QB 394. See *Pharmaceutical Society* v *Boots* [1953] 1 All ER 482; *Gibson* v *Manchester CC* [1979] 1 WLR 294; *Scancarriers* v *Aotearoa Ltd* [1985] 2 Lloyd's Rep 419. *See* OFFER.

invitee. One who is present on property by the express or implied invitation of the owner or occupier, e.g., a person 'invited to the premises by the owner or occupier for purposes of business or of material interest': *Fairman* v *Perpetual Investment Building Society* [1923] AC 74. See Occupiers' Liability Act 1957, s 2; *Murphy* v *Bradford MC* (1991) *The Times*, 11 February. *See* OCCUPIERS' LIABILITY, PRINCIPLE OF.

in vitro. Refers to fertilisation of an egg outside the body. See Human Fertilisation and Embryology Act 1990, s 1(2)(*a*). *See* EMBRYO.

involuntary conduct. A person's action in circumstances in which his mind was not in control of his bodily movement. Generally a defence to a charge, except, e.g., where the accused has voluntarily consumed alcohol or drugs, or in the case of strict liability in criminal law (q.v.). 'No act is punishable if it is done involuntarily': *Bratty v A-G for N Ireland* [1963] AC 386. *See* AUTOMATISM.

IOU. Abbreviation of phrase 'I owe you', used as written acknowledgment of a debt. It is not generally a negotiable instrument, merely evidence of debt. See *Brooks v Elkins* (1836) 2 M & W 74.

ipse autem rex non debet esse sub homine sed sub Deo et sub lege, quia lex facit regem. The King himself should not be subject to any man, but he should be subject to God and the law, for the law makes him King: Bracton, *On the Laws of England* (1250).

ipso facto. By the fact itself.

irrationality. 'It applies to a decision which is so outrageous in its defiance of logic or accepted moral standards that no sensible person who had applied his mind to the question to be decided could have arrived at it': *per* Lord Diplock in *CCSU v Minister for the Civil Service* [1985] AC 374. See *Hammersmith & Fulham LBC v Secretary of State for the Environment* [1990] 3 All ER 589.

irrationality in relation to Ombudsman's findings. In a case in which the financial services Ombudsman adjudicated on a matter concerning fairness in relation to the Banking Code 1988, his findings could be overruled only where it could be shown that they were legally irrational: *R (Norwich BS) v Financial Ombudsman Service Ltd* (2002) *The Times*, 13 December.

irrebuttable presumptions. Those inferences which may not be rebutted because evidence will not be admitted to contradict them. Known also as 'conclusive evidence'. Example: the presumption that everyone knows the law. *See* PRESUMPTION.

irregularity, material. Some aspect of legal proceedings based upon a violation of, or failure to observe, rules and procedures. It is not synonymous with 'illegality'. See, e.g., *R v Pitman* [1991] 1 All ER 468.

irrelevant evidence. Facts not in issue or not tending to prove facts in issue, e.g., 'similar fact evidence' (that a person has behaved in a certain way on other occasions). Generally inadmissible, since 'it fails to afford a reasonable inference as to the principal matter in dispute': *Hollingham v Head* (1858) 27 LJCP 241. See, e.g., *Makin v A-G for NS Wales* [1894] AC 57; *Harris v DPP* [1952] AC 694. *See* EVIDENCE.

irresistible impulse, defence of. The defence of a man's having committed an offence under an uncontrollable impulse is not accepted. '. . . A fantastic theory . . . which if it were to become part of our criminal law, would be merely subversive': *per* Lord Hewart in *R v Kopsch* (1925) 19 Cr App R 50.

irretrievable breakdown of marriage. *See* BREAKDOWN OF MARRIAGE.

irrevocable. Incapable of being revoked. Thus, a will (q.v.) is not irrevocable unless the testator (q.v.) ceases to be of sound mind, thus losing testamentary capacity. See *Vynior's Case* (1609) 8 Co Rep 81b; I.C.T.A. 1988, s 665.

ISA. Individual Savings Account. Designed so as to extend savings habit to wider sections of the community. See Finance Act 1998, ss 75–78. Can include up to three components: stocks and shares; cash; life assurance, but it is not necessary to hold all three types of investment. ISAs are exempt from income tax and capital gains tax.

island company. An oversea company (q.v.) incorporated in the Channel Islands or the Isle of Man. See Cos.A. 1985, s 699; SI 92/3179.

Isle of Man. A Crown dependency, not strictly a part of the UK, with its own legislative assembly, law and courts. See *Frankland v The Queen* [1987] AC 576 (appeal to JCPC from High Court of Justice of the Isle of Man). *See* TYNWALD, COURT OF.

issue. 1. Offspring. A person's issue comprises his children, grandchildren and other lineal descendants. See *Re Hammond* [1924] 2 Ch 276 (gift of personalty 'to A and his issue'); *Re Manley's WT* [1976] 1 All ER 673; *Re Drummond* [1988] 1 WLR 234. 2. The matter in dispute. 3. Total amount of banknotes in circulation.

issued capital. That part of a company's nominal capital (q.v.) which has been issued to shareholders.

issue, dying without. *See* DYING WITHOUT ISSUE.

issue estoppel. 'Issue estoppel can be said to exist when there is a judicial establishment of a proposition of law or fact between parties to earlier litigation and when the same question arises in later litigation between the same parties. In the latter litigation the established proposition is treated as conclusive between the same parties': *R v Hogan* [1974] 2 All ER 142. In *DPP v Humphrys* [1977] AC 1, the House of Lords held that issue estoppel was not part of the criminal law of England. See *Hines v Birkbeck College* [1991] 3 WLR 557.

itemised pay statement. *See* PAY STATEMENT, ITEMISED.

IVF and consent. There exists an unconditional statutory right of a party to withdraw or alter consent to the utilisation of embryos involved in vitro fertilisation at any time prior to the implanting of the fertilised embryo in the woman. The court is not empowered to override this: *Evans v Amicus Healthcare Ltd* [2003] EWHC 2101 (Fam).

IVF, withdrawal of. In *Evans v Amicus Healthcare* (2004) *The Times*, 30 June, the CA held that there was no power in the court to override the unconditional statutory right of either party to withdraw or vary consent to the use of embryos for in vitro fertilisation at any time before the fertilised embryo was implanted in the woman.

J

J. Justice. (title of High Court judge). *See*
PUISNE.

JCPC. Judicial Committee of the Privy
Council (q.v.).

jeopardy. 1. Vulnerability. 2. Risk of
conviction and punishment. *See* DOUBLE
JEOPARDY.

jetsam. Equipment or cargo of a ship
which is cast overboard and sinks.

jettison. To throw overboard a ship's
cargo or tackle so as to lighten it in an
emergency.

jobseeker's allowance. The Jobseekers
Act 1995 replaced unemployment benefit
with an allowance made to a claimant who
has entered into a jobseeker's agreement,
is actively seeking employment, is capable
of work but not engaged in remunerative
employment, is in Great Britain, and
satisfies certain other conditions under
the Act. He must be at least 18. Entitlement ceases after, in the aggregate, 182
days: s 5(1). See SI 00/239. For special
arrangements for claimants in 'employment zones', see W.R.P.A. 1999, s 60.
See JOINT-CLAIM COUPLE.

job settlement, termination of. In
Wilson v *Clayton* (2005) *The Times*,
12 January, the CA held that a single
payment which had been made by an
employer to his employee as the result
of a consent order following a negotiated
compromise of a dismissal dispute, would
not be chargeable to income tax.

John Doe. *See* DOE, JOHN.

joinder of charges. 'Charges for any
offences may be joined in the same
indictment if those charges are founded on
the same facts or form or are a part of a
series of offences of the same or a similar character': Indictment Rules 1971, r 9.
See C.J.A. 1988, s 40; Indictments Act

1915, s 5; *R* v *Simon* [1992] Crim LR 444;
R v *O'Brien* (2000) *The Times*, 23
March.

joinder of documents. Phrase referring
to the formation of, e.g., a memorandum
by two or more documents read
together. See PD 5, para 3.1.

joinder of offenders. The joint indictment
(q.v.) of two or more persons alleged to
have joined in the commission of an
offence. See *R* v *Moghal* [1977] Crim LR
373; *Lui Mei Lin* v *R* [1989] 2 WLR 175;
R v *Townsend* [1997] 2 Cr App R 540.

joinder of parties. The joining together
(as claimants or defendants) of two or
more persons in a single claim. A single
claim form may be used to start all those
claims which can be disposed of in the
same proceedings: r 7.3. All those entitled
jointly to a remedy must be joined as
joint claimants, r 19.2. See S.C.A. 1981,
s 49(2). A party may be added or removed
as party to a claim if this is desirable:
r 19.1(2),(3). *See* PARTIES, PROCEDURE
FOR ADDING AND SUBSTITUTING.

joint account clause. Statement inserted
in a joint mortgage (q.v.) where two or
more persons had lent money, declaring
that on the death of one mortgagee, the
survivor's receipt would suffice as a
discharge for the money. See L.P.A.
1925, s 111.

joint and several liability. 'Parties who
are jointly liable share a single liability
and each party can be held liable for the
whole of it. A person who is severally liable
with others may remain liable for the
whole claim even where judgment has
been obtained against the others': CPR
Glossary.

joint-claim couple. Means for purposes
of the Jobseekers Act 1995, a married or

unmarried couple who are not members of any family whose members include a person in respect of whom a member of the couple is entitled to child benefit, and are of a prescribed description: W.R.P.A. 1999, Sch 7. Provision is made under Sch 7, requiring certain couples to make joint claims for an income-based jobseeker's allowance (q.v.). Where a joint-claim couple make a claim, they may nominate one of them as the member of the couple to whom the allowance is to be payable: Jobseekers Act 1995, s 3B, inserted by W.R.P.A. 1999, Sch 7.

joint enterprise. 1. Commercial activity undertaken by a group of persons, e.g., partners. 2. Term used in criminal law to refer to the participation of two or more persons in a criminal activity. See, e.g., *R v Francom* [2001] 1 Cr App R 237; *R v Uddin* [1999] 1 Cr App R 319 (killing by single stab wound in group attack; significance of weapon); *R v Mitchell and King* (1999) 163 JP 75 (communication of a withdrawal from a joint enterprise is necessary where accused argues for his dissociation from pre-planned violent activity; but this is not so where the violence is spontaneous). *See* SECONDARY PARTY.

joint heir. Co-heir. *See* HEIR.

joint liability of employers. HL held in *Fairchild v Glenhaven Ltd* (2002) 152 NLJ 998, that where a claimant has been employed at different times by different defendants, both of whom had failed to prevent him from inhaling asbestos dust, resulting in mesothelioma, and he is unable to prove that the disease resulted from a breach of duty by either of the defendants individually, or both together, he may, nevertheless, in such circumstances, succeed in a claim for damages. See also *McGhee v NCB* [1973] 1 WLR 1 (significance of principle of causation).

joint obligation. A bond entered into jointly by two or more persons. All those persons must sue, or be sued, upon the bond together. A release given to one will release all.

joint purchase. Where X and Y purchase property in Y's name there is generally a resulting trust (q.v.) in favour of X as a proportionate beneficiary (as to the money he advanced). See *Jones v Maynard* [1951] Ch 572. In *Butler v Byford* [2004] 1 FLR 56, it was held that, where husband and wife had made a purchase, in their joint names, of a property which was to be used as their matrimonial home, neither party was entitled to take the benefit of an increase in the value of the property without making an allowance for the amount expended by the other in order to obtain it. The general principles of equitable accounting have application in a case of this nature.

joint stock company. 'A company having a permanent paid-up or nominal share capital of fixed amount divided into shares, also of fixed amount, or held and transferable as stock, or dividend and held partly in one way and partly in the other, and formed on the principle of having for its members the holders of those shares or that stock, and no other persons': Cos.A. 1985, s 683(1).

joint tenancy. Existed where land was held by two or more persons under a grant without words which indicated that they were to hold separate and distinct shares (e.g., 'to X and Y in fee simple'). Each joint tenant was possessed of the property 'by every part and by the whole'. Joint tenants each enjoy *jus accrescendi* (q.v.). Possession was based on the 'four unities' of possession, interest, time (of vesting) and title. Under L.P.A. 1925, s 36, joint tenants hold legal estate in trust (see Trusts of Land and Appointment of Trustees Act 1996, s 4). Such a tenancy may be determined by: alienation to a stranger; acquisition by one tenant of a larger estate; agreed sale; partition; mutual agreement; any course of dealing suggesting that 'the interests of all were mutually treated as constituting a tenancy in common': *Burgess v Rawnsley* [1975] Ch 429; *Hammond v Mitchell* [1991] 1 WLR 1127; *Kinch v Bullard* [1999] 1 WLR 423 (validity of delivery of notice of severance where sender destroyed notice after delivery by post). *See* SEVERANCE.

joint tortfeasors. Persons whose shares in the commission of a tort (q.v.) have resulted from concerted action in the furtherance of a common design. Examples: principal and agent; partners. Their liability is joint and several and release under seal (or by way of accord and satisfaction (q.v.)) releases all (but this is not so in the case of concurrent tortfeasors (q.v.)). See *Ronex Properties Ltd* v *John Laing Ltd* [1983] QB 398; Civil Liability (Contribution) Act 1978 (for liability of tortfeasors *inter se*).

jointure. 1. A joint interest limited to husband and wife. 2. An estate (q.v.) settled on a wife, taken by her in place of dower (q.v.).

joint venture. Business arrangement in which undertakings are jointly controlled by two or more other undertakings, allowing the sharing of skills and resources. A 'full-function' joint venture may have as its object the co-ordination of competitive aspects of independent undertakings. See EC Regulation 4064/89, art 3(2); *The Greystoke Castle* [1947] AC 265.

joint will. One document in which two or more persons incorporate their testamentary wishes. It takes effect as the separate wills of the persons who have made it. See *Re Duddell* [1932] 1 Ch 585. *See* WILL.

Journals. The authentic record of proceedings of the Lords and Commons, known as the *Journals of the House of Commons, and the Journals of the House of Lords*. They date from 1547 (Commons) and 1509 (Lords), and are published annually.

joy riding. Euphemism for a ride taken in a stolen vehicle. It is an offence to take a motor vehicle or other conveyance (q.v.) for one's own or another's use without the consent of the owner or other lawful authority, or knowing that it has been taken without authority to drive it or to allow oneself to be carried in it: Th.A. 1968, s 12(1). *See* VEHICLE-TAKING, AGGRAVATED.

JP. Justice of the Peace. *See* MAGISTRATES.

judge. One with power to decide disputes and determine appropriate penalties, etc. In the UK, judges of the High Court, circuit judges and recorders (qq.v.) are recommended for appointment by the Lord Chancellor. Lords of Appeal in Ordinary, the Lord Chief Justice and the Master of the Rolls are recommended for appointment by the Prime Minister. See S.C.A. 1981, s 10. For precedence of judges of the Supreme Court, see s 13. Judges have been generally appointed from practising barristers (q.v.) (but a solicitor can now be appointed). See C.L.S.A. 1990, s 71. Superior judges are subject to the power of removal only by the Queen on an address presented by both Houses of Parliament (which must originate in the Commons). (A judge was last removed in this way in 1830 – Sir Jonah Barrington, a judge of the Irish Admiralty Court, who had misappropriated money paid into the Court.) Their salaries and pensions are paid direct from the Consolidated Fund (q.v.). Retiring age is 70, but this can be extended to 75 where the appropriate Minister considers this desirable in the public interest: Judicial Pensions and Retirement Act 1993, s 26. A judge is not liable in tort for any judicial act performed by him within his jurisdiction, or for acts, performed in good faith, in excess of that jurisdiction. See Courts Act 1971, ss 17(4), 21(6). A holder of a UK judicial office may hold office in a court established for any purposes of the European Communities or any international court without being required to relinquish the UK judicial office: Acc.J.A. 1999, s 68(1).

judge advocate. A barrister (q.v.) appointed by the Office of the Judge Advocate-General (or, in the case of the Navy, a legally qualified serving officer appointed by the convening authority) to sit in a court-martial involving more serious cases. See *R* v *Aitken* [1992] 1 WLR 1006; Armed Forces Discipline Act 2000.

Judge Advocate-General's Department. Advises Secretary of State for Defence and Defence Council on legal matters relating to the administration of military law, and reviews proceedings of courts-martial.

judge and jury, questions of law and fact. In general, questions of law are for the judge, questions of fact are for the jury. For exceptions, see, e.g., Perjury Act 1911, s 11(6); S.C.A. 1981, s 69(5); P.&C.E.A. 1984, s 76.

judge, apparent bias of. There was no bias in the conduct of a judge who had called counsel into the judge's corridor so as to suggest that parties to a dispute concerning alleged infringement of a trade mark might consider a settlement. European Convention, art 6 (right to fair and public hearing) was not breached: *Hart* v *Relentless Records Ltd* [2002] EWHC 1984 (Ch). (For consideration by CA of apparent bias of advocate who had sat as a part-time judge, see *Lawal* v *Northern Spirit Ltd* (2002) *The Times*, 7 November).

judge, impartiality of. A judge who has refused an application of appellant for permission to appeal is to be considered a proper and impartial member of a tribunal constituted later to hear the substantive appeal: *Sengupta* v *Holmes and Others* (2002) *The Times*, 8 August.

judges' clerks. Clerks attached to the Lord Chief Justice, Master of the Rolls, President of Family Division, Vice-Chancellor, Lords Justices of Appeal and puisne judges of the High Court. Appointed by the Lord Chancellor. See S.C.A. 1981, s 98; C.L.S.A. 1990, Sch 10.

judges, district. Formerly 'district registrars'. Appointed by the Lord Chancellor for each county court district. See County C.A. 1984, ss 6–9; C.L.S.A. 1990, s 74. Their jurisdiction includes the determination of interlocutory applications, the conduct of pre-trial reviews, hearing claims where the amount involved is relatively small.

judges, judgments by. CA held, in *Cooper* v *Floor Cleaning Machines Ltd* (2003) *The Times*, 24 October, that a judge hearing an action involving negligence, is obliged, save in a highly exceptional case, to consider and interpret the evidence and decide, in the form of a judgment, which party is the more likely

to be correct, in relation to the question of liability.

judge's oath. Oath taken by a judge on his appointment: 'I do swear by Almighty God that . . . I will do right to all manner of people after the laws and usages of this Realm without fear or favour, affection or ill will.' See Promissory Oaths Act 1868; S.C.A. 1981, s 10(4); C.L.S.A. 1990, s 76.

judge's order. An order made by a judge in chambers on a summons.

judges, part-time employment. Department of Constitutional Affairs announced, in a press release, 'Broadening the Bench', that, as from 1 April 2005, all new and existing salaried judicial appointments below High Court level will be considered suitable for part-time sitting unless the needs of the office or business state otherwise.

judges, presiding. *See* PRESIDING JUDGES.

judges, senior. These are the judges of the Supreme Court, the Lord Chief Justice of England and Wales, the Master of the Rolls, the Lord President of the Court of Session, the Lord Chief Justice of Northern Ireland, the Lord Justice Clerk, the President of the Queen's Bench Division, the President of the Family Division, the Chancellor of the High Court. See C.R.A 2005 s 60.

judge, undue intervention of. 'The judge's part . . . is to hearken to the evidence, only himself asking questions of witnesses when it is necessary to clear up any point that has been overlooked or left obscure; to see that the advocates behave themselves and keep to the rules laid down by law; to exclude irrelevancies and discourage repetition; to make sure by wise intervention that he follows the points that the advocates are making and can assess their work; and at the end to make up his mind where the truth lies. If he goes beyond this, he drops the mantle of a judge and assumes the role of an advocate: and the change does not become him well': *per* Lord Denning in *Jones* v *NCB* [1957] 2 QB 55. See *R* v *Wiggan* (1999) *The Times*, 22 March (it is not generally appropriate for the judge to cross-examine witnesses); *R* v *Tuegel* [2000] 2 All ER 872.

judgment. A formal decision made and pronounced by a court of law or other tribunal. It takes effect from the day when given or made, or on a later specified date; r 40(7); see *Prudential Assurance* v *McBains Cooper* (2000) 150 NLJ 832. It may include the reasoning leading to the decision. See C.J.J.A. 1982, s 18(2). With some rare exceptions no judgment can be regarded as a secret document: *Forbes* v *Smith* [1998] 1 All ER 973. See *Stewart* v *Engel* (2000) *The Times*, 26 May (reopening of case after final judgment).

judgment creditor. *See* CREDITOR.

judgment debt. A sum payable under a judgment or order enforceable by a court (not being a magistrates' court (q.v.)); or order of a magistrates' court for payment of money recoverable summarily as a civil debt; or any order of any court which is enforceable as if it were for the payment of money so recoverable. See County C.A. 1984, s 74; Late Payment of Commercial Debts (Interest) Act 1998, s 3(1); r 40.8 (interest on costs runs from date judgment was given). In *Coulter* v *Chief Constable of Dorset Police* (2004) *The Times*, 22 October, the CA held that it did not seem to be unjust to set aside a statutory demand served by a new chief constable relating to a judgment debt in front of his predecessor, who had assigned that debt before the hearing of the application. *See* INTEREST ON DEBTS AND DAMAGES.

judgment debtor. One against whom judgment has been given for a sum of money, whose property may be taken in execution. An order for his examination to discover, e.g., whether he has the means of satisfying the judgment or order: see CPR, Sch 1; O 48, r 1(1); CPR, Sch 2; CCR, O 25.

judgment in default. *See* DEFAULT, JUDGMENT IN.

judgment, mistakes in. *See* SLIP RULE.

judgment, reversal of. *See* REVERSAL OF JUDGMENT.

judgment, revisiting of. In *R* v *Mills* (No. 2) (2003) *The Times*, 26 June, the CA held that although on a reference by the Criminal Cases Review Commission to CA, it is possible to argue any point, CA, nevertheless, is obliged to seek exceptional circumstances justifying its revisiting a previous decision, in the absence of new arguments relating to law or fact, or the adducing of new evidence.

judgments and orders, drawing up and filing of. The court may direct that a judgment or order drawn up by a party (see CPR, r 40.3(1)) must be checked by the court before it is sealed; or before a judgment or order is drawn up by the court, parties must file an agreed statement of its terms: r 40.3(2). When judgment or order is to be drawn up by a party, he must file it no later than seven days after the date on which the court ordered or permitted him to draw it up so that it can be sealed by the court: r 40.3(3). See PD 40B, paras 1.2–1.5.

judgments, enforcement of. In the case of judgments for payment of money, they may be enforced: in the High Court (q.v.) under CPR, Sch 1; O 45, r 1, by writ of *fi. fa.* (q.v.), garnishee proceedings (q.v.), charging order, appointment of receiver, order of committal, writ of sequestration (q.v.); in the county court (q.v.) by judgment summons or order for attachment of earnings. In case of judgments for possession of land, enforcement may be by writ of possession: O 45, r 3. In case of judgments for delivery of goods, enforcement may be by writ of delivery: O 45, r 4. In case of judgments relating to performance of or abstention from some act, enforcement may be by order of committal or sequestration. See also C.J.J.A. 1982, s 4; C.L.S.A. 1990, s 15.

judgment, summary. *See* SUMMARY JUDGMENT PROCEDURE.

judgment summons. Procedure for enforcing judgments of the High Court and county court. See County C.A. 1984, s 147(1).

judicial act. An act resulting from the exercise of judicial power, e.g., determination by the court of a question of rights. 'No action lies for acts done or words spoken by a judge in the exercise of his judicial office, although his motive is malicious and the acts or words are not done or spoken in the honest exercise of his office': *Anderson* v *Gorrie* [1895] 1 QB 668. *See* JUDICIAL IMMUNITY.

Judicial Appointments and Conduct Ombudsman. The Ombudsman is appointed by Her Majesty on the recommendation of the Lord Chancellor. See C.R.A 2005, s 62, Sch 13.

Judicial Appointments Commission. A corporate body, consisting of a chairman, and 14 other Commissioners, appointed by Her Majesty on the recommendation of the Lord Chancellor. See C.R.A 2005, s 61, Sch 12.

judicial bias. In *Co-operative Group* v *International Computers* (2004) *The Times*, 19 January, the CA held that where a trial judge had made an observation in the early stages of a trial suggesting that claimant had no case, this demonstrated a bias which prevented him trying the case fairly.

Judicial Committee of the Privy Council. Created by Judicial Committee Act 1833, amended by Appellate Jurisdiction Acts 1876–1947. Sits in London, and consists of the Lord Chancellor, Lord President of the Council, ex-Lord Presidents and Lords of Appeal in Ordinary but can also include members of the Privy Council (q.v.) who hold or have held high judicial office. Its jurisdiction includes: appeals from some Commonwealth courts outside the UK; appeals from ecclesiastical courts (q.v.); appeals from medical tribunals. It does not deliver a judgment, but tenders advice to the Sovereign, who acts on the report and approves an appropriate Order in Council. It is not bound by its own previous decisions (see, e.g., *Baker* v *R* [1975] AC 774). Dissenting opinions may be delivered in open court: Judicial Committee (Dissenting Opinions) Order in Council 1966. Decisions are not binding on English courts, but are treated by them as persuasive. See SI 99/1320 (Judicial Committee (Powers in Devolution Cases) Order 1999, concerning powers of JCPC: see Government of Wales Act 1998, Sch 8, para 34, Northern Ireland Act 1998, s 82, Scotland Act 1998, s 103).

See *Bainton* v *General Dental Council* (2000) *The Times*, 17 October (discretion of JCPC to extend time for appeal).

judicial control of jury. *See* JURY, JUDICIAL CONTROL OF.

judicial creativity. Apparent power of the judges to modify the scope and pattern of existing offences and to create new offences, resulting in 'judge-made law'. See, e.g., *R* v *Soul* (1980) 70 App Cas 295. 'The judges have no power to create new offences': *per* Viscount Dilhorne in *DPP* v *Withers* [1975] AC 842. For comment on criteria for judicial creativity, see Lord Lowry's statement in *C* v *DPP* [1996] AC 1. *See* JUS DICERE.

judicial decision, requisites of. A judicial decision presupposes an existing dispute between two or more parties and involves: presentation of case by parties to dispute; ascertainment of fact by means of evidence adduced by parties; submission of legal arguments; decision which disposes of the whole matter by a finding on disputed facts and an application of law of the land to facts so found, including, where necessary, ruling on any disputed question of law: Committee on Ministers' Powers 1932, Cmd 4060. See *R* v *Secretary of State for Employment ex p Equal Opportunities Commission* [1992] 1 All ER 545.

judicial decision, statement of reasons for. *See* COURTS' DECISIONS, STATEMENTS OF REASONS FOR.

judicial discretion. *See* DISCRETION, JUDICIAL.

judicial evidence. *See* EVIDENCE, JUDICIAL.

judicial function, delegation of. In general, judicial functions may not be delegated: see *R* v *Gateshead Justices ex p Tesco* [1981] QB 470.

judicial immunity. 'Every judge of the courts of this land – from the highest to the lowest – should be protected to the same degree, and liable to the same degree. . . . Each should be protected from liability to damages when he is acting judicially. Each should be able to do his work in complete independence and free from fear. . . . Nothing will make him liable except it be shown that he was not acting judicially, knowing that he had no jurisdiction to do it': *Sirros v Moore* [1975] QB 118. *See* IMMUNITY; JUDICIAL ACT.

judicial independence. Practice in the UK whereby judges are freed from outside pressures. Secured by, e.g., the charging of judges' salaries on the Consolidated Fund (q.v.), separation of judiciary from Parliament, security of tenure of office, judicial immunity (q.v.).

judicial notice. Known also as 'judicial cognisance'. Means 'those facts which a judge can be called upon to receive and to act upon either from his general knowledge of them, or from enquiries to be made by himself for his own information from sources to which it is proper for him to refer': *Commonwealth Shipping Representative v P & O Branch Services* [1923] AC 191. Examples of such facts are: territorial and geographical divisions; matters of common and certain knowledge; law and custom; professional practice (see *Davey v Harrow Corporation* [1958] 1 QB 60). The doctrine may extend also to juries in relation to matters within their everyday experience and knowledge. See I.A. 1978, s 3; European Communities Act 1972, s 3(2); *R v Olkolie* (2000) *The Times*, 16 June (foreign law cannot be the subject of judicial notice). *See* KNOWLEDGE, LOCAL AND PERSONAL.

judicial proceedings, reporting of. Publication of reports of proceedings, which have been regulated by, e.g., Judicial Proceedings (Regulation of Reports) Act 1926; or Domestic and Appellate Proceedings Act 1968. Reports of nullity cases and cases concerning children usually carry only initials of parties. See also M.C.A. 1980, s 69; *Moynihan v Moynihan* [1997] 1 FLR 59. *See* REPORTING RESTRICTIONS.

judicial review. Control exercised by courts over procedure of statutory authorities and other subordinate bodies which may result in grant of prerogative orders (q.v.), or declarations (q.v.) stating a person's rights. It is concerned not with

the decision of which review is sought but with a review of the manner of the decision-making process: *R v Chief Constable of W Wales Police ex p Evans* [1981] 1 WLR 1155; *R v Civil Service Appeal Board ex p Cunningham* [1991] IRLR 297 (duty to give reasons for decision). For judicial review of criminal proceedings, see *R v Bolton Magistrates, ex p Scally* [1991] 2 WLR 239 (granting of *certiorari* (q.v.) to quash conviction). In *S. Bucks DC v Coates* [2004] EWCA Civ 1378, the CA held that where a decision turns on a test of proportionality, the judge is under a duty to clarify to the parties the reasons leading to his decision. Update No. 11. *See* ADMINISTRATIVE ACTIONS, REMEDIES FOR CONTROL OF.

judicial review, aptness of. CA held in *R (Davis) v FAST* (2003) *The Times*, 6 October, that the process of judicial review is not appropriate where a person is attempting to challenge a warning notice served on him by FSA.

judicial review, claim for. Claim begins with issue of claim form. Documents are to be filed at Administrative Court Office. Failure to file acknowledgment of service within 21 days may preclude participation, except where court permits this. Claim for permission to proceed must be made promptly and, in any event, within three months from date when grounds arose. See CPR, Part 54; PD 54. If claimant has statutory right of appeal, permission for judicial review should only exceptionally be given: see *R v Falmouth HA* [2000] 3 All ER 306.

judicial review, claim for, description of parties. Parties to an application are described in the proceedings as 'The Queen on the application of [name of applicant], claimant, versus, the public body against whom the proceedings were brought, defendant': *PD (Administrative Court: Establishment)* (2000) *The Times*, 27 July.

judicial review, discretionary nature of remedies. Relief may not be granted where: review would serve no useful purpose; an alternative appropriate remedy is available. See *R v IRC ex p Preston*

[1985] AC 835; *R v Secretary of State for Home Department ex p Ketowoglo* (1992) *The Times*, 6 April (duty of applicant not to mislead court).

judicial review, House of Lords and. In *R v Hammersmith and Fulham LBC ex p Burkett* (2002) *The Times*, 24 May, HL held that it had jurisdiction to consider appeal from refusal of CA, on a renewed application under RSC, Order 59, r 14(3), of leave to apply for judicial review (in relation to planning appeal).

judicial review, immunity from. CA held in *R (Tucker) v National Crime Squad* (2003) *The Times*, 23 January, that the police had the right to conduct their operations and to take managerial decisions without any intervention by the courts; hence matters of this nature were not amenable to the process of judicial review.

judicial review of administrative action. Grounds of such a review were summarised by Lord Diplock as illegality, irrationality, and procedural impropriety: *Council of Civil Service Unions v Minister for the Civil Service* [1985] AC 374. 'In a system based on the rule of law, unfettered governmental discretion is a contradiction in terms': Wade (approved in *Tower Hamlets v Chetnik Developments* [1988] 1 AC 858).

judicial review of decision of mental health tribunal. Where a mental health review tribunal has decided on the discharge of a patient, and that decision appears to be unreasonable, a hospital authority may not detain him without first applying for judicial review of the decision: *R (H) v Ashworth Hospital Authority* (2002) *The Times*, 10 July.

judicial review, pre-action protocol for. A claim or judicial review lodged after 4 March 2002 must comply with the Pre-action Protocol: see *Practice Statements from Administrative Court* [2002] All ER (D) 12 (Feb). It involves requirement for a letter before claim to be sent to all concerned, and a letter of response from appropriate public body within 14 days.

judicial review, subject matter of. 'The subject matter of every judicial review is a decision made by some person (or body of persons) whom I will call "the decision maker" or else a refusal by him to make a decision. . . . The decision must have consequences which affect some person (or body of persons) other than the decision maker, although it may affect him too': *per* Lord Diplock in *CCSU v Minister for the Civil Service* [1985] AC 374. Matters of public policy, e.g., charge-capping local authorities, are not generally open to judicial review: *Hammersmith LBC v Department of Environment* [1991] 1 AC 521.

judicial separation. Remedy based on a judicial decree under which it becomes no longer necessary for the petitioner to cohabit with the respondent. See Mat.C.A. 1973, s 17. A petition may be presented by either party on grounds of, e.g., the respondent's adultery and the petitioner's finding it intolerable to live with the respondent, desertion for a period of two years by the respondent. There is no one-year time bar to presentation of the petition. Irretrievable breakdown of marriage need not be proved. For ancillary relief, see Mat.C.A. 1973, ss 24, 24A. Grant of the decree is no bar to a subsequent divorce founded on the same facts: s 4(1).

Judicial Studies Board. An independent body controlled by a Board whose members are appointed by the Lord Chancellor, set up in 1979, following the Bridge Report 1979, consisting of representatives of the judiciary, academics, Lord Chancellor's Department and Home Office. Concerned essentially with the provision of high quality training to full-time and part-time judges in relation to the exercise of their jurisdiction. It works through a main Board and six divisions: criminal, civil, family, magisterial, tribunals, equal treatment advisory Committees.

judicial trustee. 'Any fit and proper person nominated for the purpose in the application [by a settlor, beneficiary or trustee (qq.v.)] may be appointed a judicial trustee, and, in the absence of such nomination, or if the court is not satisfied of the fitness of a person so nominated, an official of the court may be appointed': Judicial Trustees Act 1896, s 1(3). See A.J.A. 1982, s 57. He must audit accounts annually, on request of a beneficiary (q.v.) or trustee, and, on appointment, exercises all the powers of any other trustee. *See* TRUST.

judiciary. The judges collectively. The 'higher judiciary' comprises: Lords of Appeal in Ordinary, Judges of the Supreme Court of England and Wales, Judges of the Court of Session and Judges of the Supreme Court of N Ireland.

judicium parium. Judgment of one's peers: see Magna Carta (q.v.) 1215, cl. 39. (Holdsworth, *History of English Law* (1903), denies that the phrase refers to trial by jury.)

junior barrister. 1. A barrister who is not a Queen's Counsel (q.v.). 2. The junior of two counsel appearing for a party.

jura in personam. Rights *in personam* (q.v.).

jura in rem. Rights *in rem* (q.v.)

jurat. *Jurare* = to swear. 1. The jurat of an affidavit is a statement set out at the end of the document which authenticates the affidavit: PD 32, 5.1. It is signed by all deponents. 2. Magistrate in the Channel Islands.

juridical. Relating to, or acting in, the administration of justice.

jurimetrics. Term introduced by the American jurist, Loevinger, 'Jurimetrics is concerned with such matters as the quantitative analysis of judical behaviour, the application of communication and information theory to legal expression, the use of mathematical logic in law, the retrieval of legal data by electronic and mechanical means, and the formulation of a calculus of legal predictability': *Law and Contemporary Problems* (1963).

jurisdiction. 1. Power of a court to hear and decide on a case. 2. Authority to legislate. 3. Territorial limits within which legal authority may be exercised. In the case of the English courts, held to comprise England, Wales, and those parts of the sea claimed as territorial waters: *R v*

Kent Justices ex p Lye [1967] 2 QB 153; see CPR, r 2.3. See *Union Transport plc v Continental Lines SA* [1992] 1 WLR 15. 4. The term 'jurisdictional act' means a legislative, administrative or judicial measure of the Sovereign.

jurisdictional error. Error committed when, e.g., an administrative agency acts beyond the jurisdiction conferred on it. See *Pearlman v Keepers and Governors of Harrow School* [1979] 1 All ER 365; *Re Racal Communications Ltd* [1980] 2 All ER 634.

jurisdiction, ouster of. *See* OUSTER OF JURISDICTION.

jurisdiction, service out of the. Serving of a claim form based on leave granted under O 11 (significantly revised in 1983 to allow a large number of cases to proceed without leave being required). For application to serve, see CPR, Sch 1; O 11, r 4. See *BP Exploration Co v Hunt* [1976] 3 All ER 879.

jurisprudence. The philosophy of law. 'Recorded thinking about the source, nature, end and efficiency of law, substantive and adjective, and of legal institutions': Reuschlein (1951).

juristic person. *See* ARTIFICIAL PERSON.

juror. A member of a jury. See Juries Act 1974, Sch 1; C.L.S.A. 1990, Sch 18. See *Bushell's Case* (1670) 6 St Tr 999. For intimidation of juror, see C.J.P.O.A. 1994, s 51, substituted by Y.J.C.E.A. 1999, Sch 4, para 22. *See* INTERFERING WITH WITNESSES; JURY.

juror's oath. 'I swear by Almighty God that I will faithfully try the defendant and give a true verdict according to the evidence': *Practice Note* [1984] 3 All ER 528.

jury. A body of persons (generally 12, but, in cases of illness or death of a juror, the number must not fall below 9) selected according to the law and sworn to give a verdict on some matter according to the evidence. Introduced in 1220. See S.C.A. 1981, s 69; County C.A. 1984, s 66. In general, all evidence must be given in presence of jury. Picked from those registered as electors, aged 18–70, who have been resident in the UK for at least five years since the age of 13: Juries Act 1974, s 1, as amended. Those ineligible include barristers and solicitors, clergy, mentally ill, persons on bail in criminal proceedings (see C.J.P.O.A. 1994, s 40(1)), members of certain religious bodies (1994 Act, s 42). For discharge of disabled persons from jury service, see Juries Act 1974, s 9B. Those disqualified include persons who, at any time in the last ten years have, in the UK, served any part of a sentence of imprisonment: Juries (Disqualification) Act 1984, s 1(1). 'Whenever a man is on trial for serious crime, or when in a civil case a man's honour or integrity is at stake, or when one or other party must be deliberately lying, then trial by jury has no equal': *Ward* v *James* [1966] 1 QB 273. For protection of juries, see *R* v *Ling* [1987] Crim LR 495. For coroner's inquest jury, see Coroners Act 1988, s 9. For trial by anonymous jury, see *R* v *Comerford* [1998] 1 WLR 191. For importance of random selection of jury, see *R* v *Tarrant* [1998] Crim LR 342. For allegation of racial bias in jury, see *Gregory* v *UK* (1998) 25 EHRR 577. For questions from jury to judge, see *Berry* v *R* [1992] 2 AC 364 (*per* Lord Lowry: 'The jury are entitled at any stage to the judge's help'); *R* v *Falls* (1998) *The Times*, 15 January. *See* CHALLENGE TO JURY; VERDICT.

jury, challenge to. *See* CHALLENGE TO JURY.

jury, communication from. The judge must state in open court in the presence of defendant and his counsel the nature and content of any note received from the jury, unless it raises a matter unconnected with the trial or contains information which should not be disclosed: *R* v *Gorman* [1987] 1 WLR 545. See *Ramstead* v *R* [1999] 2 AC 92.

jury, confidentiality of. In *R* v *O'Connor* [2004] 2 UKHL the HL held that it is essential to apply the common law rule that, following delivery of a verdict, any evidence concerning matters intrinsic to the deliberations of the jurors is inadmissible.

jury, coroner's. *See* CORONER'S DUTY TO SUMMON JURY.

jury deliberations. Despite Human Rights Act 1998, investigation into jury deliberations is not permitted: *R* v *Quereshi* (2001) *The Times*, 11 September.

jury directions, complex. CA held in *R* v *Taylor* [2003] EWCA Crim 2447, that where a criminal trial necessitated complex directions to the jury on points of law, the judge ought to allow counsel to see and comment on the intended directions before he addresses the jury.

jury, direction to. A judge's instructions to a jury, relating to burden of proof, role of judge and jury, summary of issues of fact as to which a decision is required, summary of evidence, arguments, inferences to be drawn, etc. '[It] should be custom-built to make the jury understand their task in relation to a particular case': *per* Lord Hailsham in *R* v *Lawrence* [1982] AC 510. It is impermissible to leave a question of law to the jury: *Ward* v *Chief Constable of W Midlands Police* (1997) *The Times*, 15 December. Where the evidence warrants it, a judge may direct a conviction: see *R* v *Ferguson* (1970) 54 Cr App R 410. See also *DPP* v *Stonehouse* [1978] AC 55. For defects in jury directions, see *R* v *Bentley* [1999] Crim LR 330. For a trial judge's continuing duty to provide appropriate assistance to a jury, see *R* v *Sharif* (1999) *The Times*, 8 June.

jury, discrimination in listing. The Privy Council held in *Rojas* v *Burllaque* (2003) *The Times*, 13 November, that there must be no discrimination in jury listing. A statutory provision which resulted in women rarely participating in a jury, damaged the constitutional right to a fair trial.

jury, foreman of. *See* FOREMAN OF JURY.

jury, further guidance for. CA held, in *R* v *Jones* (2003) *The Times*, 19 June, that where fresh guidance is given to a jury where each defendant denies responsibility for the alleged crime, the jury ought to consider: case for and against each defendant separately; possibility of each defendant having an interest to serve; need to decide on all the evidence) including evidence of co-defendant and defendant whose case was under consideration.

jury, hung. Jury unable to agree on any verdict.

jury, judicial control of. Ways in which a judge exercises control over a jury, as where, e.g., he rules that there is no case to answer, or that there is insufficient evidence on an issue (so that the jury does not consider it), or by his summing up (q.v.). See also Criminal Appeal Act 1968, s 2(1); *R v McKenna* [1960] 1 QB 411 (implied threat by judge to jury that they might be locked up for the night if they delayed returning a verdict. *Per* Cassels J: 'A jury shall deliberate in complete freedom, uninfluenced by any promise, unintimidated by any threat').

jury, retirement of. *See* RETIREMENT OF JURY.

jury's deliberations, confidentiality of. It is a contempt of court to obtain, disclose or solicit a jury's deliberations, arguments or votes cast: Contempt of Court Act 1981, s 8. For disclosure of jury secrets, see *A-G v Associated Newspapers* [1994] 2 WLR 277.

jury trial in civil cases. Under S.C.A. 1981, s 69, and County C.A. 1984, s 66 there is a qualified right to jury trial, e.g., where, in the case of a claim to be heard in QBD, there is in issue a charge of fraud, or a claim relating to deceit, libel, slander, malicious prosecution, false imprisonment, and the trial will not require prolonged examination of documents or accounts. There is a discretion to order jury trial in other cases. Application for jury trial is to be made within 28 days of defence: C.P.(Am.)R. 2000 (SI 00/2092), r 10. See *Ward v James* [1966] 1 QB 273; *Rothermere v Times Newspapers* [1973] 1 WLR 448.

jury, vetting. The checking of potential jurors (e.g., as to their backgrounds) so as to exclude those who might be disqualified. Held to be not unlawful: see *R v Mason* [1981] QB 881. See *R v Sheffield Crown Court ex p Brownlow* [1980] QB 530; *A-G's Guidelines* (1989) 88 Cr App R 124.

jus. A right, deriving from a rule of law – a concept of Roman Law. 1. *Jus naturale*: 'what nature has taught all living things' (an ideal to which the law should seek to conform). 2. *Jus gentium*: the law of peoples, i.e., law of universal application. 3. *Jus civile*: 'the law each people has settled for itself'. Refers also to the entire *corpus* of Roman Law.

jus accrescendi. Right of survivorship (q.v.).

jus accrescendi inter mercatores pro beneficio commercii locum non habet. For the benefit of commerce, the right of survivorship (q.v.) among merchants is not known.

jus cogens. Compelling law. Principle of public international law whereby a treaty would be invalidated if it departed from the body of principles or norms from which no derogation is generally permitted, e.g., *pacta sunt servanda* (q.v.). See Vienna Convention on Law of Treaties 1969, arts 53, 64.

jus dicere. To say what the law is. 'Judges ought to remember that their office is *jus dicere* and not *jus dare*; to interpret law, and not to make law, or give law': Bacon, *Of Judicature* (1630). 'Whoever hath an absolute authority to interpret any written or spoken laws, it is he who is truly the law-giver to all intents and purposes and not the person who first wrote or spoke them': Bishop Hoadly, in a sermon before George I in 1717. *See* JUDICIAL CREATIVITY.

jus quaesitum tertio. Right on account of third parties. *See* CONTRACTS, THIRD PARTY RIGHTS IN.

jus soli. Law of the 'place of one's birth'. Principle that nationality by birth is determined by the country in which the birth takes place. It no longer applies in English law, following B.N.A. 1981: see s 1.

jus spatiandi et manendi. The right to stray and remain. May form an easement (q.v.), as in the right to use a garden. See *Re Ellenborough Park* [1956] Ch 131.

just and equitable. Phrase used, e.g., in company law, relating to a petition to wind up a company when the court is of opinion that it is 'just and equitable' that it should be wound up. Companies have been wound up under this head because of, e.g., deadlock among members, the company's insolvency; or the company has misapplied funds. See Cos.A. 1985, s 517(1); *Re A & BC Chewing Gum Ltd* [1975] 1 WLR 579. *See* COMPANY.

jus tertii. Right of a third person. Defence set up by X who is apparently liable to Y and, on being sued by Y, asserts that the property or money claimed by Y belongs by paramount title to Z. In general, a wrongdoer may not set up *jus tertii* (but see Torts (Interference with Goods) Act 1977, s 8(1)). See *Amory* v *Delamirie* (1721) 1 Stra 505 (in relation to conversion (q.v.)); *Asher* v *Whitlock* (1865) LR 1 QB 1 (in relation to ejectment (q.v.)).

justice. 1. The basic value underlying a system of law, or the objective which that system seeks to attain. 2. The virtue which results in each person receiving his due: Justinian. 3. The impartial resolution of disputes arising from conflicting claims. 4. 'Justice is the correct application of a law, as opposed to arbitrariness': Ross, *On Law and Justice* (1958).

justice, commutative, distributive and corrective. Jurisprudential concept derived from Aristotle (384–322BC). *Commutative justice* is rendering every person the exact measure of his dues. *Distributive justice* is concerned essentially with the allocation of rights, duties and burdens among the members of a community so that equilibrium is ensured. ('It orders the equal treatment of those equal before the law': Friedmann, *Legal Theory* (1967).) *Corrective* (or 'remedial', 'emendatory') *justice* corrects disequilibrium in a community. (It 'is usually administered by a court or other organ invested with judicial or quasi-judicial powers': Bodenheimer, *Jurisprudence* (1974).) See comments of Lord Steyn in *McFarlane* v *Tayside Health Board* (1999) 149 NLJ 1868.

justice, course of. In *R* v *Cotter* (2002) *The Times*, 29 May, the CA held that a criminal investigation following a false

allegation, can be included in the concept of 'the course of public justice'.

justice, natural. 'Justice that is simple or elementary, as distinct from justice that is complex, sophisticated and technical': *John* v *Rees* [1970] Ch 345. 'There must be due inquiry. The accused person must have notice of what he is accused. He must have an opportunity of being heard, and the decision must be honestly arrived at after he has had a full opportunity of being heard': *Leeson* v *General Medical Council* (1889) 43 Ch D 366. 'It is to be implied, unless the contrary appears, that Parliament does not authorise by [an] Act the exercise of powers in breach of the principles of natural justice': *Fairmount Investments Ltd* v *Secretary of State for the Environment* [1976] 2 All ER 865. See, e.g., *R* v *Commissioner for Racial Equality ex p Cottrell* [1980] 3 All ER 265; *R* v *Secretary for the Environment ex p Slot* [1997] COD 118.

justice, natural, requirements of. 'The requirements must depend on the circumstances of the case, the nature of the inquiry, the rules under which the tribunal is acting, the subject matter that is being dealt with, and so forth': *per* Tucker LJ in *Russell* v *Duke of Norfolk* [1949] 1 All ER 109. See *R* v *Parole Board ex p Wilson* [1992] QB 740. *See* AUDI ALTERAM PARTEM; BIAS, RULE AGAINST.

justice, open. *See* OPEN JUSTICE.

justice, perverting the course of. *See* PERVERTING THE COURSE OF JUSTICE.

justice, restorative. *See* RESTORATIVE JUSTICE.

justice, retributive. Theory of punishment based on a supposed moral link between wrongdoing and justice. Offenders, it is claimed, ought to be punished under the law in proportion to their guilt and the injury inflicted on their victims. 'The instinct for retribution is part of the nature of man, and channelling that instinct in the administration of criminal justice serves an important purpose in promoting the stability of a society governed by law': *Furman* v

Georgia 408 US 238 (1972). Said to be derived from Kant's principle of retribution ('like must be matched with like'), set out in *The Philosophy of Law* (1797). *See* LEX TALIONIS.

justices' clerk. *See* MAGISTRATES' CLERK.

justices of the peace. *See* MAGISTRATES; MAGISTRATES' COURTS.

justiciability. The appropriateness of a subject matter for examination by the courts. See, e.g., *Cox* v *Green* [1966] Ch 216 (a dispute relating to the concept of professional etiquette was considered to be not justiciable); *Notts CC* v *Secretary for the Environment* [1986] AC 240 (ministerial guidance to local authorities on expenditure was not a matter for the judges or the House of Lords in its judicial capacity).

justifiable homicide. The killing of one person by another where no blame attaches to the killer, e.g., as in the carrying out of an authorised death sentence. See *A-G for N Ireland's Reference (No. 1 of 1975)* [1977] AC 105. *See* HOMICIDE.

justification. A defence which admits the claimant's allegations, but pleads that the events referred to were justifiable. Example: in libel (q.v.) the defendant admits that he published the words complained of, but pleads that they were true. The defendant must justify the precise imputation on which the claimant's allegation is founded. 'Defendant has to prove not only that the facts are truly stated but also that any comments upon them are correct': *Cooper* v *Lawson* (1838) 8 A & E 746. See Defamation Act 1952, s 5; CPR, Sch 1; O 82; *Khashoggi* v *IPC Magazines* [1986] 1 WLR 1412; *Prager* v *Times Newspapers* [1988] 1 All ER 300; *B* v *J* [1999] EMLR 490 (requirements for plea of justification as defence in libel proceedings).

justifying bail. Proof of sufficiency of bail or of sureties in relation to their ownership of property. *See* BAIL.

juvenile courts. Now renamed 'youth courts' (q.v.).

K

kangaroo court. A parody of a hearing, in which elementary and generally accepted norms of justice are not observed.

KB. King's Bench.

KC. King's Counsel.

keeping term. *See* TERM.

keeping the peace. In essence, being of good behaviour. A person can be bound over by a magistrate to keep the peace. See M.C.A. 1980, ss 115, 116.

kerb-crawling. Importuning from a motor vehicle. See S.O.A. 1985; s 1; *Paul v DPP* (1990) 90 Cr App R 173. *See* IMPORTUNE.

keyholders. Those who keep custody of, or control access to, any key or similar device for operating a lock, i.e., a mechanism for protecting premises against unauthorised entry or for securing any safe or other container specifically designed or adapted to hold valuables: P.S.I.A. 2001, Sch 2, para 6.

kidnapping. The common law offence of stealing and carrying away, or secreting, of a person of any age, by force or fraud. See *A-G's Reference (No. 19 of 1996)* [1997] 1 Cr App R (S) 313; *R v D* [1984] AC 778; *R v Walters* [1998] 2 Cr App R (S) 167; *R v Williams* [1999] 1 Cr App R (S) 105. *See* ABDUCTION, CHILD.

kidnapping, consent and. Where a passenger had given his consent to being driven in a car, the driver could, nevertheless, be guilty of kidnapping where the passenger's consent had been obtained by fraud. In offences of kidnapping involving fraud it is probably not necessary to prove the absence of consent: *R v Cort* (2003) *The Times*, 25 July. See *R v D* [1984] AC 778.

kill. To cause the death of another by some act or omission. *See* HOMICIDE; MANSLAUGHTER; MURDER.

killing, acquisition of property by. A beneficiary (q.v.) who, by some criminal act kills the testator, or next of kin who kills an intestate, will not be allowed to benefit from his crime. See *Re Crippen* [1911] P 108; *Re Giles* [1972] Ch 544; Forfeiture Act 1982. *See* FORFEITURE OF BENEFIT UNDER WILL.

kin. Relationship by blood.

King. *See* MONARCHY; SOVEREIGN.

King can do no wrong. A rule of law, part of the so-called 'prerogative of perfection', under which the Crown could not be sued at common law. The position was changed under Crown Proceedings Act 1947. Further modifications to the basic principle were contained in, e.g., National Health Service (Amendment) Act 1986, Crown Proceedings (Armed Forces) Act 1987.

Kings, Divine Right of. *See* DIVINE RIGHT OF KINGS.

knives. Instruments which have a blade or are sharply pointed: Knives Act 1997, s 10. See also C.J.A. 1988, s 139A, inserted by Offensive Weapons Act 1996, s 4; *R v Daubney* (2000) 164 JP 519. It is an offence to market a knife in a way which suggests that it is suitable for conflict or that it is likely to stimulate or encourage violent behaviour using the knife as a weapon: s 1(1). See *R v Targett* [1999] 2 Cr App R (S) (robbery involving threat of use of knife).

knives, disguised. Disguised knives are added to the list of offensive weapons contained in SI 98/2019, and specifying the descriptions of weapons to which Criminal Justice Act 1988, s 141, applies:

Criminal Justice Act 1998 (Offensive Weapons) Order 2002 (SI 02/1668).

knives in public places. It is wrong to construe 'public place' in Criminal Justice Act 1988, s 139, so that the phrase includes land adjoining areas of public access, if the harm at which the criminal act is directed could be inflicted from a place of that nature: *R v Roberts* [2003] EWCA Crimp 2753.

knock for knock. An agreement under which insurance agencies pay those they have insured (without regard as to responsibility, e.g., for an accident), and do not insist on actions being brought by one party against the other. See *Hobbs v Marlowe* [1977] 2 All ER 241.

knock-out agreement. An agreement among bidders at an auction (q.v.) that some of them shall desist from bidding. Illegal when entered into by a dealer. See Auctions (Bidding Agreements) Act 1927; *Rawlings v General Trading Co* [1920] 3 KB 30.

know-how. Knowledge of how to accomplish something. Expert skill. 'Any industrial information and techniques likely to assist in the manufacture or processing of goods or materials . . .': I.C.T.A. 1988, ss 530, 531. 'It indicates the way in which a skilled man does his job, and is an expression of his individual skill and experience': *Stevenson, Jordan and Harrison v Macdonald & Evans* [1952] 1 TLR 101.

knowingly. With knowledge of the facts in question. 'With a design': *R v Bannen* (1844) 1 Car & Kir 295. For 'knowingly', construed as 'intentionally', see *R v Dunne* (1998) 162 JP 399 (the word may connote a requirement of *mens rea*).

knowledge. Awareness of, or acquaintance with, fact or truth. 'The case of shutting the eyes is actual knowledge in the eyes of the law; . . . the legal conception of constructive knowledge (q.v.), generally speaking, has no place in the criminal law': *per* Devlin J in *Roper v Taylor's Central Garage* [1951] 2 TLR 284. See *Warner v Metropolitan Police Commissioner* [1969] 2 AC 256; *Saxby v Morgan* [1997] 8 Med LR (knowledge in relation to Lim.A. 1980, s 14). For a five-fold categorisation of 'knowledge' in relation to a constructive trust (q.v.), see *Baden Delvaux v Société Générale* [1983] BCLC 325; *BCCI v Akindele* (2000) 150 NLJ 950. See TURNING A BLIND EYE.

knowledge, local and personal. Justices may use their own knowledge of matters concerning a particular locality in arriving at a decision. The knowledge must be of a general nature. Where justices rely on personal local knowledge in a trial, they must make this known to the parties and provide them with an opportunity of commenting. See *R v Blick* (1966) 50 Cr App R 280 (juror's local knowledge); *Bowman v DPP* [1991] RTR 263; *Norbrook Laboratories v Health and Safety Executive* [1998] EHLR 207. See JUDICIAL NOTICE.

L

label, misleading. When considering whether an offence has been made out under the Trade Descriptions Act 1968, in relation to the labelling of a drink, the justices are entitled to read the label as a whole: *Northants CC* v *Purity Soft Drinks* (2004) *The Times*, 27 December.

labour, manual. *See* MANUAL LABOUR.

laches. (*Lasche* = indolent.) Negligence and unreasonable delay in the assertion of a right will defeat equities. 'A court of equity has always refused its aid to stale demands where a party has slept upon his rights and acquiesced for a great length of time. Nothing can call forth this court into activity but conscience, good faith and reasonable diligence': *Smith* v *Clay* (1767) Amb 645. See Lim.A. 1980, s 36(2); *Wroth* v *Tyler* [1974] Ch 30; *Frawley* v *Neill* (1999) 143 SJLB 98 (contemporary approach of the court is to adopt a broad view of whether delayed assertion of equitable rights would be unconscionable). For delay in matters relating to the public interests, see *R* v *Secretary of State for Trade and Industry ex p Greenpeace* [1998] Env LR 415 (*per* Laws LJ: 'Delay will be tolerated much less readily in public interest litigation').

land. 1. 'Land in the legal signification comprehendeth any ground, soil or earth whatsoever, as meadows, pastures, woods, moor, waters, marshes, furzes and heath . . . It legally includeth also all castles, houses and other buildings': Coke, *Coke on Littleton* (1628). 2. '"Land" includes land of any tenure, and mines and minerals, whether or not held apart from the surface, buildings or parts of buildings (whether the division is horizontal, vertical, or made in any other way) and other corporeal hereditaments; also a manor, an advowson, and a rent and other incorporeal hereditaments, and an easement, right, privilege, or benefit in, over, or derived from land . . .': L.P.A. 1925, s 205(1)(*x*). See I.A. 1978, Sch 1. *See* ALLODIAL LAND.

land, annual value of. Rent which might reasonably be expected to be obtained on a letting from year to year, with the tenant paying the usual rates and taxes and the landlord bearing costs of repairs, insurance and maintenance: I.C.T.A. 1988, s 837(1).

land certificate. *See* CERTIFICATE, LAND.

land charges. Those rights and interests affecting land, e.g., estate contracts (q.v.), restrictive covenants (q.v.), general equitable charges and easements (q.v.). See L.C.A. 1972; *Phillips* v *Mobil Oil* [1989] 1 WLR 888.

land charges, local. *See* LOCAL LAND CHARGES.

land charges, register of. A register kept in the Land Charges Department of the Land Registry, recording six classes of charge; registration is generally against the name of the estate owner whose estate is intended to be affected: L.C.A. 1972, s 3(1): (1) *Class A*. Rent, or annuities, or principal money payable by instalments, not created by deed, but by charge on land created pursuant to some person's application under the provisions of statute; (2) *Class B*. Statutory land charges arising automatically; (3) *Class C*. Puisne mortgages, limited owner's charges, estate contracts, general equitable charges; (4) *Class D*. Charge for inheritance tax, restrictive covenants, equitable easements; (5) *Class E*. Annuities created before 1 January 1926 and not registered as annuities; (6) *Class F*. Those affecting land by virtue of the statutory right of occupation ('matrimonial home right') under F.L.A. 1996, Part IV (now in force). See L.C.A. 1972; Local Land Charges Act 1975; SI 90/485. *See* LOCAL LAND CHARGES.

land, compulsory purchase of. The acquisition of land, freehold or leasehold by an authority under statute, commencing with a compulsory purchase order, followed, where necessary, by the hearing of objections. The expropriated owner must be compensated by the acquiring authority for the land taken, by way of purchase price, for any damage directly consequent on the taking and for depreciation of land he retains. Basis of compensation may be 'market value', i.e., the amount which the land if sold in the open market by a willing seller might be expected to realise. See, e.g., Land Compensation Acts 1961, 1973; Acquisition of Land Act 1981; Planning and Compensation Act 1991, Part III; *Procter and Gamble Ltd* v *Secretary of State for the Environment* [1991] EGCS 63. For ownership of land, in relation to planning permission, see T.C.P.A. 1990, s 65(8), substituted by 1991 Act, s 16 ('owner' is: fee simple owner; those entitled to tenancy in total exceeding ten years of which at least seven are unexpired; those entitled to an interest in a mineral prescribed by development order). *See* COMPULSORY PURCHASE ORDER.

land, contract for sale of. *See* CONTRACT FOR SALE OF LAND, FORMALITIES.

land, development. *See* DEVELOPMENT LAND.

landlord. The owner or holder of land (q.v.) leased to another. Includes under Rent Act 1977, s 152(1), 'any person from time to time deriving title under the original landlord'. See, e.g., H.A. 1988, s 27(9)(*c*); Landlord and Tenant Act 1987, s 2. For denial of landlord's title, see *W G Clarke Ltd* v *Dupre Properties* [1991] 3 WLR 579. A body may be registered as a 'social landlord', under H.A. 1996, s 2, if it is a registered charity which is a housing association (q.v.), a company or a society, registered under Industrial and Provident Societies Act 1965 or under Cos.A. 1985, which has among its objects or powers the provision and management of houses to be let and hostels.

landlord's identity. In the case of tenancies and residential accommodation, but not including an assured tenancy (q.v.), the tenant may make a written request concerning disclosure of the landlord's identity: Landlord and Tenant Act 1985, s 1. See *Morrow* v *Nadeem* [1986] 1 WLR 1381; Landlord and Tenant Act 1987, ss 47, 51.

land, meaning of. A beneficial interest under a bare trust of registered land did not constitute a registrable estate, but took effect in equity as minor interest only; hence it did not constitute 'land' within the meaning of Land Registration Act 1925, s 3(viii). See also Land Registration Act 1925, s 70(1)(g), s 3(xv): *UCB Group* v *Hedworth* (2002) *The Times*, 13 June.

land of special scientific interest. Where the organisation, English Nature, believes that the statutory criteria relating to a site of special scientific interest are satisfied, it does not possess discretion allowing it to reject an earlier confirmation because of some collateral reason: *Fisher* v *English Nature* (2003) *The Times*, 15 September. See also Wildlife and Countryside Act 1981, s 28(1).

land planning control. System administered by a central authority (Department of Environment) and local planning authorities (i.e., county, district councils (qq.v.)). The county planning authority formulates policy and general proposals which it submits to the Secretary of State, who appoints persons to examine proposals publicly. Local plans are then published. See T.C.P.A. 1971, 1984; Inquiries Procedure Rules 1974; Planning and Compensation Act 1991.

land, public, use of. In *R* v *Sunderland CC* (2003) *The Times*, 14 November, HL held that the process of grass cutting and the placing of seating on a public open space did not suffice to justify any inference of the public making use of the land merely by virtue of a licence of the authority.

land, registered disposition of. Dispositions of land by a registered proprietor, completed by registration, involving the grant or transfer of a legal estate, or the creation or reservation of a legal right over the land: see LRA 2002 which repeals LRA 1925.

land registration. System of registration of title (by any estate owner or any person entitled to call for the vesting of a legal estate in him, other than a mortgagee: L.R.A. 2002, s 3, 27 repealing LRA 1925, s 4, 8(1), as amended), which now covers the entire country, based on Land Registration Acts and Rules. The system has now been extensively re-modelled by the LRA 2002. Title (normally legal freeholds and leases with more than 3 years to run: LRA 2002, s 3) is entered on a central register, the headings of which are 'property', 'proprietorship', 'charges'. The register may be altered, see LRA 2002, s 65 and Sch 4 (formerly known as 'rectification' under L.R.A. 1925, s 82) when, e.g., there is fraud, or the court so orders, or where it is unjust not to alter the register. See as an earlier example *Hodgson* v *Marks* [1971] 1 Ch 892. *See* MINOR INTERESTS; OVERRIDING INTERESTS; REGISTER AT LAND REGISTRY.

land registration, electronic communication. SI 01/169, amending L.R.R. 1925, allows applications to register a dealing with registered land to be noted electronically, following the issue of an appropriate notice by the Registrar.

land registration, electronic conveyancing. Land Registration Act 2002, Part 8, authorises Registrar to establish and operate a network of electronic conveyancing.

land registration, essence of. Its principles have been described as 'mirror' (register mirroring actual structure of rights in the land), 'curtain' (overreaching (q.v.) of certain interests), and 'guarantee' (state guarantee of title on register). See LRA 2002 which repeals LRA. 1925–97; *Overseas Investments Ltd* v *Simcobuild Ltd* (1995) 70 P & CR 322.

land registration, failure to effect. LRA 2002, s 4 sets out the events that trigger the compulsory first registration of title. These were updated and extended by the Land Registration Act 1997, and the LRA 2002 largely replicates this. Compulsory registration is triggered by specified types of transfer of a qualifying estate, which is defined as either a legal freehold estate, or a legal lease with more than seven years to run. After two months from the date of grant or assignment, total failure to register renders the transfer void so far as regards the grant or conveyance of the legal estate: see L.R.A. 2002, s 7(1), which repeals LRA 1925, s 123A, as substituted by L.R.A. 1997, s 1. The legal estate then revests in the transferor who will hold it on trust for the transferee. Section 6 imposes a duty on the responsible estate owner to apply for registration within the period for registration if the registration requirement applies. By LRA 2002, s 4(5) the registrar may, on application by an interested person, specify a longer period for registration if there is a good reason for doing so. By s 27(1) if a disposition of a registered estate or registered charge is required to be completed by registration, it does not operate at law until the relevant registration requirements are met. Essentially s 27 sets out those dispositions of registered land that must be completed by registration if they are to operate at law. They are similar to, but not identical provisions, formerly set out in the LRA 1925, ss 18 and 21. In principle, all dispositions that create or transfer a legal estate by express grant should be subject to some form of registration, whether with their own titles or by the entry of some form of notice on the title which is subject to them. The section therefore provides that any transfer of, or the grant or reservation of any legal estate out of, registered land, is a registrable disposition.

land registration, leases and. Under Land Registration Act 2002, s 4, leases of over seven years must be registered. The Lord Chancellor is empowered to reduce this period.

Land Registry registers. Five registers are kept: pending actions; annuities; writs and orders affecting land; deeds of arrangement affecting land; land charges. See L.C.A. 1972; Local Land Charges Act 1975. *See* LAND CHARGES, REGISTER OF.

Lands Tribunal. Set up under Lands Tribunal Act 1949. Consists of a President, lawyers, surveyors and valuers who hear disputes relating, e.g., to compulsory purchase, assessment of compensation. Appeal lies to the Court of Appeal. See SI 00/941.

land, structures in relation to. In relation to Electricity Act 1989, Sch 4, para 6 (grant of wayleave), 'land' does include buildings and structures: *British Waterways Board* v *London Power Networks* (2002) *The Times*, 21 November. See also Law of Property Act 1925, s 205(1)(x).

lapse. Failure of a legacy (q.v.) or devise (q.v.) because of the death of the intended legatee or devisee before that of the testator. Doctrine of lapse does not apply to beneficiaries under a secret trust (q.v.). See W.A. 1837, s 33 (as substituted by A.J.A. 1982, s 19); Law Reform (Succession) Act 1995, s 3; Trusts of Land and Appointment of Trustees Act 1996, Sch 4.

lapse of offer. An offer is held to have lapsed: on the death either of the offeror or offeree before acceptance; where no time for acceptance is prescribed; by non-acceptance within a reasonable time; by non-acceptance within the time prescribed for acceptance by the offeror. See *Financings Ltd* v *Stimson* [1962] 3 All ER 386. *See* OFFER.

larceny. Theft, under Larceny Act 1916, s 1 (repealed by Th.A. 1968). *Petty larceny* referred to stolen property with a value not exceeding 12 pence; *grand larceny* referred to stolen property with a value exceeding 12 pence. *See* THEFT.

la reyne le veult; la reyne s'avisera. See ROYAL ASSENT.

last known address. Claimant must take all reasonable steps to discover the current place or last place at which defendant carried on business. Services will be ineffective should the claim force

be not actually delivered after posting: *Spade Lane Cool Stores* v *Kilgour* [2004] All ER (D) 303.

latent ambiguity. *See* AMBIGUITY.

latent damage. *See* DAMAGE, LATENT.

latent defect. *See* DEFECT.

laundering money. The processing through an apparently legal channel of money obtained illegally, so that its original sources cannot be traced. See, e.g., Drug Trafficking Act 1994, ss 49–51. On a charge of acquiring, using or having possession of proceeds of criminal conduct (see C.J.A. 1988, s 93B, as inserted by C.J.A. 1999, s 30), where defendant claims that he acquired or used or had possession of money 'for adequate consideration', it is for him to show on a balance of probabilities that the defence applied: *R* v *Gibson* (2000) *The Times*, 3 March. See F.S.M.A. 2000, s 146; Terrorism Act 2000, s 18. First Money Laundering Directive (Council Directive 9/308/EEC), seeking to prevent misuse of banks and other financial institutions for laundering of criminal funds, implemented by Money Laundering Regulations 1999 (SI 93/1933), is followed by Second Directive (2001/97/EC) extending regulations to solicitors (to be implemented by 28 June 2003). Money Laundering Regulations 2003 (see SI 03/3075) are effective as from 1 March 2004. See (in relation to the reporting of suspicions or knowledge related to money laundering) *P* v *P* [2003] EWHC Fam. 2260.

laundering money, proceeds of. Where a person has been charged with giving assistance to another to avoid prosecution by concealing or transferring property which he knew was the proceeds of drug trafficking or crime, the Crown is not obliged to prove that the proceeds are, in fact, criminal in nature: *R* v *Montilla* (2003) *The Times*, 12 November.

law. 1. The written and unwritten body of rules largely derived from custom and formal enactment which are recognised as binding among those persons who constitute a community or state, so that they will be imposed upon and enforced among those persons by appropriate sanctions. 'The body of rules and guidelines within which society requires its judges to administer justice': *per* Lord Scarman in *Duport Steels Ltd* v *Sirs* [1980] ICR 161. 2. Jurisprudence (q.v.). 3. The general condition of a state in which laws are accepted and observed.

law and equity, conflict of. 'Wherever there is any conflict or variance between the rules of equity and the rules of the common law . . . the rules of equity shall prevail': S.C.A. 1981, s 49(1). See *Walsh* v *Lonsdale* (1882) 21 Ch D 9.

law and equity, fusion of. 'The innate conservatism of English lawyers may have made them slow to recognise that by the Judicature Act 1873 the two systems of substantive and adjectival law formerly administered by courts of law and equity have surely mingled now': *per* Lord Diplock in *United Scientific Holdings Ltd* v *Burnley BC* [1978] AC 904.

Law Centres. Some 50 centres in England and Wales, managed by the Law Centres Federation, staffed largely by solicitors and trainees, funded by government and charitable foundations, giving individual advice on, e.g., landlord and tenant problems.

law, classification of. Arbitrary division of law into categories, e.g.: (1) *Public law* – concerned with relationships of members of the community and the state, e.g., constitutional law, criminal law; (2) *Private law* – derived from relationships of members of the community *inter se*, e.g., contract, torts. Salmond classifies law by reference to sources: enacted law; case law; customary law; conventional law.

Law Commission. Body established under Law Commissions Act 1965, consisting of a chairman and four members (usually lawyers of high standing), appointed by the Lord Chancellor on a full-time basis for up to five years in the first instance, whose duty it is to keep the law under review with a view to its systematic development and reform, including codification, elimination of anomalies, repeal of obsolete enactments, reduction

in number of separate enactments. See C.L.S.A. 1990, Sch 10, para 25.

law, comparative. The branch of legal studies which is based upon a comparison of the world's different legal systems. The term 'suggests an intellectual activity with law as its object and comparison as its process': Zweigert and Kötz, *Introduction to Comparative Law* (1998).

lawful. Warranted or authorised by, or not contrary to, nor forbidden by, the law. *See* LEGAL.

lawful homicide. Excusable or justifiable homicide (qq.v.).

Law Lords. Lord Chancellor, Lords of Appeal in Ordinary, ex-Lord Chancellors and other peers (21 in all) who have occupied high judicial office, and sit in the House of Lords (q.v.).

law merchant. That source of English law based on the settlement of disputes between merchants and their usages. 'It is neither more nor less than the usages of merchants and traders in the different departments of trade, ratified by decisions of courts of law': *Goodwin* v *Robarts* (1875) LR 10 Ex 337. *See* USAGE.

law, natural. 'It is possible to deduce from nature, that is to say from the nature of man, from the nature of society, and even from the nature of things, certain rules which provide an altogether adequate prescription for human behaviour, that by a careful examination of the facts of nature we can find the just solution of our social problems. Nature is conceived of as a legislator, the supreme legislator': Kelsen, *The Pure Theory of Law* (1934).

law officers of the Crown. The Attorney-General and Solicitor-General; the Lord Advocate and Solicitor-General for Scotland; the Attorney-General for Northern Ireland. See Law Officers Act 1997; F.I.A. 2000, s 35(5).

law, positive. The legal rules adopted and actually endorsed in formal fashion by the state. 'Law established or "*positum*" in an independent political community by the express or tacit authority of its sovereign supreme government': Austin, *The Province of Jurisprudence Determined* (1832).

law, private and public. *See* PRIVATE LAW; PUBLIC LAW.

Law Reform Committee. Consists of five judges, four practising barristers, two solicitors and three academic lawyers, appointed by the Lord Chancellor to consider changes to particular aspects of law which are desirable, having particular regard to judicial decisions.

Law Reports. Law reporting falls into three periods: (1) the Year Books (q.v.) *c.* 1270–1530; (2) the private reporters (Coke, Dyer, etc.) *c.* 1535–1865; (3) the modern semi-official reports from 1865, undertaken by the Incorporated Council of Law Reporting for England and Wales (e.g., *Weekly Notes*, up to 1952, and *Weekly Law Reports*, from 1953) and the modern private reports, including, e.g., *All England Law Reports, Lloyd's Law Reports*. In the House of Lords and Court of Appeal, the rule is that, in general, the Law Reports published by the Incorporated Council should be cited in preference to other reports where there is some choice: see *Practice Direction* by the Master of the Rolls (1990) *The Times*, 7 December; *Bray* v *Best* [1989] 1 WLR 167; *Copeland* v *Smith* (1999) 143 SJLB 276 (advocates' failure to draw attention to reported cases). Under *Practice Direction (Judgments: Neutral Citation)* (2002) *The Times*, 17 January, system of 'neutral' case citation in operation in HL and CA is extended to cover judgments delivered by High Court judges. Neutral citations should be given before the reference to series of reports in which the judgment appears. *See* CITATION; UNREPORTED CASES.

law reports, importance of. That there exists a professional obligation on all parties advising persons involved in litigation to make the court alert to the fact that there was a good chance of judicial time being wasted in preparing an appeal which had been settled or might be settled as the result of negotiation, and that appropriate and relevant cases had been reported: *Yell Ltd* v *Garton* (2004) *The Times*, 26 February.

law, rule of. 1. Government based on the general acceptance of the law. 2. A legal rule. 3. Concept outlined by Dicey, *Law of the Constitution* (1881) – the regular law of the land predominates over and excludes the arbitrary exercise of power by the government, all people are equally subject to the law administered by the ordinary courts and that law is derived from individuals' rights as declared by the courts.

law sittings. *See* SITTINGS.

Law Society. The body which controls solicitors, constituted under the Royal Charter of 1845. It is governed by an elected Council and its objects are 'promoting professional improvement and facilitating the acquisition of legal knowledge'. Under Solicitors Act 1974 it may make regulations concerning legal education and training and examinations. See Acc.J.A. 1999, s 48, Sch 7. In order to practise as a solicitor a person must have been admitted as a solicitor, must be enrolled on the Society's Roll and must have a current practising certificate: Solicitors Act 1974, s 1. *See* SOLICITOR.

Law, sources of English. Generally held to include: common law; equity; legislation; custom; law merchant; canon law; EU law.

law, sources of EU. *See* COMMUNITY LAW, SOURCES OF.

law, substantive and adjective. *Substantive law* comprises those rules which guide the courts in arriving at decisions. *Adjective law* (or rules of procedure) comprises those rules which determine the course of an action, e.g., in which court a case is to be heard.

lawyer. A professional practitioner of the law. *See* LEGAL PROFESSION.

lay days. 1. Days during which a ship is delayed in port. 2. Days allowed by a charterparty (q.v.) for loading or unloading cargo. They begin to run against the charterer from the time he has notice that the vessel is ready to load: *Fairbridge* v *Pace* (1844) 1 C & K 317; *The Point Clear* [1975] 2 Lloyd's Rep 243; *The Agamemnon* [1998] 1 Lloyd's Rep 675.

laying an information. Procedure whereby a magistrate is informed, e.g., by a police officer, of a suspected offence. See M.C.A. 1980, s 1. 'An information is ... the statement by which the magistrate is informed of the offence for which the summons or warrant is required': *R v Hughes* (1879) 4 QBD 614. 'No objection shall be allowed to any information ... for any defect in it in substance or in form, or for any variance between it and the evidence adduced on behalf of the prosecutor or complainant': M.C.A. 1980, s 123. An information is laid when received by the office of the clerk to the justices: *R v Manchester Stipendiary Magistrate ex p Hill* [1983] 1 AC 328. The procedures of laying an information at the magistrates' court were considered in *Atkinson v DPP* [2004] EWHC 1457. It was held that the 'information date' that appears on the summons is not always effective since it does not indicate with reliability when the information was laid. An information will not become informative until its validation; an information can be considered to be laid only on validation. *See* INFORMATION.

laying documents before Parliament. Procedure whereby Parliamentary control is exercised over delegated legislation (e.g., SIs (q.v.)). If the 'affirmative procedure' is followed, SIs or Orders in Council are subject to the requirement that their effect shall not continue unless one or both Houses approve the documents; the 'negative procedure' arises from a provision in the parent Act that any instruments made thereunder are subjected to annulment following resolutions of either House. *See* DELEGATED LEGISLATION.

lay magistrates. Unpaid magistrates, as compared with paid district judges (magistrates' courts), formerly known as 'stipendiaries'. *See* MAGISTRATES.

LC. Lord Chancellor (q.v.).

LCJ. Lord Chief Justice (q.v.).

Leader of HM Opposition. *See* OPPOSITION, LEADER OF HM.

Leader of the House. *See* HOUSE, LEADER OF THE.

lead evidence, to. To call or adduce evidence (q.v.).

leading questions. Questions put to a witness (q.v.) which suggest the desired answer or put the answer into his mouth or, in the case of a disputed matter, permit only the reply, 'Yes' or 'No'. Example: 'Did you see X at noon in Trafalgar Square on Saturday, 18th October last?' Answers to such questions are not generally admissible in evidence, save, e.g., in examination-in-chief (q.v.), where the matter is only introductory and not material, or in the case of matter already put in evidence by the other side, or in cross-examination. '"Leading" is a relative, not an absolute, term': Best, *Principles of Law of Evidence* (1994). *See* EVIDENCE.

leapfrog procedure. Procedure introduced by A.J.A. 1969, s 12, whereby an appeal in civil proceedings can go directly from the High Court (q.v.) or a Divisional Court (q.v.) to the House of Lords (q.v.) without prior appeal to the Court of Appeal (q.v.). A certificate must be granted by the trial judge after agreement of all parties, and the Lords must grant leave to appeal: s 13.

Learning and Skills Council for England. Body corporate, appointed under Learning and Skills Act 2000, s 1, consisting of 12–16 members, appointed by Secretary of State, with duties: to provide education (other than higher education) and training suitable to persons above compulsory school age, but who have not yet attained age of 19, and organised leisure time occupations associated with such training and education: s 2(1); to secure appropriate education and training for persons over 19: s 3; to encourage persons to undergo post-16 education and training and to encourage employers to participate: s 4. Local learning and skills councils are to be established: s 19. A National Council for Education and Training for Wales is set up under s 30. For functions of Adult Learning Inspectorate, see s 52.

lease. A term of years (q.v.) (see *Re Land and Premises at Liss* [1971] Ch

986), or leasehold (q.v.), or the document used to bring into existence a term of years, i.e., an interest in land for a fixed period of a certain maximum duration. One of the two recognised legal estates (q.v.). Where L grants a lease to T, L is known as the *lessor*, or *landlord* (q.v.) and T is known as the *lessee*, or *tenant* (q.v.). In essence, a bilateral contract. Generally involves a grant of exclusive possession (q.v.) for a term for a periodic money payment. See *Street* v *Mountford* [1985] AC 809; *Westminster CC* v *Clarke* [1992] 1 All ER 695; *Mehta* v *Royal Bank of Scotland* (1999) 78 P & CR D11 (the 'hallmarks' of *Street* v *Mountford* are not to be considered as decisive if other factors of equal significance have to be considered); *Bruton* v *Quadrant Housing Trust* [1999] 3 WLR 150 (grant of lease, generally in return for a periodic payment in money). See T.C.G.A. 1992, Sch 8, para 10.

lease, assignment of. Disposal by lessee (q.v.) of his estate in land. Assignment of a legal term must be by deed if it is to be effective at law; an assignment of an informal nature for value may be valid in equity. See L.P.A. 1925, ss 52, 146(2); *Target Holdings* v *Priestley* [1999] 1 Lloyd's Rep Bank 175. For unreasonable refusal by a landlord to consent to an assignment, see, e.g., *International Drilling Fluids Ltd* v *Louisville Investments Ltd* [1986] Ch 513. Under Landlord and Tenant Act 1988, s 1, a landlord must give consent (unless he has a good reason for withholding it) within a reasonable period. See *Moss Bros* v *CSC Properties* [1999] EGCS 47. See Landlord and Tenant (Covenants) Act 1995; *Footwear Corp Ltd* v *Amplight Properties* [1999] 1 WLR 551. In *Ashworth Frazer Ltd* v *Gloucester CC* (2001) 151 NLJ 1695, HL stated that as a matter of law it could not be said that a landlord's belief, however reasonable, that a proposed assignee intended to use leased premises for a purpose which would produce a breach of a user covenant, could not in itself be a reasonable ground for withholding consent to the assignment.

lease, concurrent. *See* CONCURRENT LEASE.

lease, contract to create. Doctrine of *Walsh* v *Lonsdale* (1882) 21 Ch D 9, converts the contract into a valid equitable lease. But the doctrine has limitations, e.g.: it does not create privity of estate (q.v.); the equitable tenant may be insecure against a third party who purchases the landlord's title, and he cannot claim the benefit of L.P.A. 1925, s 62. See L.P. (Misc. Provs.) A. 1989.

lease, delivery of. Where a local authority has effectively sealed a lease conditionally on the other party agreeing to sign the counterpart by a stated date, the sealing could not be said to have excluded the need for delivery to the other party so that the lease might be completed: *Bolton MBC* v *Torkington* (2003) *The Times*, 13 November.

lease, determination of. A lease may come to an end by: notice; expiry; surrender or merger; becoming a satisfied term (q.v.); forfeiture; enlargement; frustration.

lease, equitable. *See* EQUITABLE LEASE.

lease, forestry. A lease to the Ministry of Agriculture for any purpose for which it is authorised to acquire land. Rent may be nominal for the first ten years, or variable according to the annual value of timber cut. See also S.L.A. 1925, s 48.

lease, future. *See* FUTURE LEASE.

leasehold. The interest, i.e., term of years, created by a lease (q.v.), or agreement for lease. If created by lease it is a *legal leasehold estate*; if created by agreement for lease, it is, in effect, an *equitable lease*. See *Walsh* v *Lonsdale* (1882) 21 Ch D 9. Leasehold estates recognised at law are: term of years; periodic tenancy; tenancy at will; tenancy at sufferance. *See* ESTATE; FREEHOLD; LEASE, CONTRACT TO CREATE; TENANCY; TERM OF YEARS.

leasehold, enfranchisement of. *See* ENFRANCHISEMENT OF TENANCY.

leasehold ownership. That which exists where the tenant (or lessee) is granted exclusive possession of land by the landlord (or lessor) with the intention that he should hold it as the tenant only for a fixed period of time less than that held by the landlord.

lease, legal. *See* LEGAL LEASE.

lease, parol. *See* PAROL LEASE.

lease, perpetually renewable. *See* PERPETUALLY RENEWABLE LEASE.

lease, renewal of. Grant of a further term of years in relation to an expiring lease. A contract for renewal of a lease or sub-lease for a term exceeding 60 years from the end of the lease or sub-lease is void: L.P.A. 1922, Sch 15. See also L.P.A. 1925, s 149; Landlord and Tenant Act 1954, s 30(1); *Dolgellau Golf Club* v *Hett* (1998) 76 P & CR 526; *VCS Car Park Management* v *Regional Railways North East* (2000) *The Times*, 11 January.

leases, unfair terms. In *LB of Newham* v *Khatun* [2004] EWCA Civ 55, the CA held that the Unfair Terms in Consumer Contracts Regulations (SI 99/2083) do apply to contracts relating to land, including the grant of leases.

leave to appeal, refusal of. It was held in *Sinclair Gardens Investments Ltd* v *Lords Tribunal* (2004) *The Times*, 2 November, that a refusal by the Lords Tribunal of permission to appeal from it to a Leasehold Valuation Tribunal ought to be granted by the High Court in circumstances of an exceptional nature.

legacy. A gift of personal property by will (to a legatee). A legacy may be: (1) *specific* (gift of a specified thing, e.g., 'my gold wedding ring'); (2) *demonstrative* (q.v.); (3) *general* (q.v.); (4) *pecuniary* (sum of money, but an annuity is also included under A.E.A. 1925, s 55(1)); (5) *residuary* (i.e., residue of personal estate); (6) *contingent*, e.g., 'to X on her entering university'. A legacy may fail because of, e.g., disclaimer, lapse, ademption, uncertainty. Where an account of legacies is directed by a judgment, interest can be allowed on each legacy at the rate of 6 per cent per annum: CPR, Sch 1; O 44, r 10.

legacy, cumulative. Legacy additional to one previously given to the same legatee in the same or a subsequent instrument.

legacy, substitutional. Gift of personalty (q.v.) by a testator (q.v.) made in lieu of a previous gift where he indicates that he does not wish the legatee to take both gifts.

legal. 1. In accordance with forms of law. 2. According to common law (q.v.), but not equity (q.v.). *See* LAWFUL.

legal adviser, foreign. Prison Rules (SI 99/728), r 2, referring to representation of a prisoner by a 'legal adviser' were held to cover an Italian advocate who conformed to the domestic law relating to EU rules concerning right of lawyers to provide appropriate services: *R (Van Hoogstraten)* v *Governor of Belmarsh Prison* (2002) 152 NLJ 1531.

Legal Aid Board. Body established under Legal Aid Act 1988, s 3, and Sch 1 (repealed under Acc.J.A. 1999, Sch 14), with overall responsibility for the Legal Aid Scheme. Now replaced, under Acc.J.A. 1999, s 1, Sch 14, by Legal Services Commission (q.v.).

legal aid, essence of. The provision of a framework for advice, assistance or representation for those who, on account of their means might otherwise be unable to obtain such help. Introduced under Legal Aid and Advice Act 1949. See Legal Aid Act 1988; Acc.J.A. 1999, Parts I, II, Sch 15 (repealing much of 1988 Act). *See* COMMUNITY LEGAL SERVICE; CRIMINAL DEFENCE SERVICE; LEGAL SERVICES COMMISSION.

Legal Aid Scheme. Aid is available to an applicant who passes financial and merits tests (i.e., who can show that he may have more than a 'fifty-fifty' chance of success). It is not available where alternative forms of funding are available or where case is likely to be referred to small claims track (q.v.), or in cases involving the course of business, partnership, Lands Tribunal proceedings, inheritance and wills, administration of trusts. Everyone is entitled to free advice at a police station when first arrested; further aid depends on income and savings, but is available freely to those in receipt of income support, working families' tax credit, income-based jobseeker's allowance. In cases involving family proceedings, aid may be free for those receiving income support or income-based job-seeker's allowance.

legal assignment. *See* ASSIGNMENT.

legal easement. An easement created by statute, deed or prescription for an interest equivalent to an estate in fee simple absolute in possession (q.v.) or a term of years absolute (q.v.). Enforceable against 'all the world', unlike the equitable easement (q.v.) which cannot be enforced against the bona fide purchaser for value of the legal estate without notice. *See* EASEMENT.

legal estates. Estates (q.v.) capable of subsisting at law (q.v.). They involve rights *in rem* (q.v.). See L.P.A. 1925, s 1(1), restricting the number to two (fee simple, term of years absolute).

legal executives. Staff employed by solicitors, e.g., managing clerks, and other paralegals, i.e., non-lawyer support staff. The Institute of Legal Executives is responsible for regulations relating to qualifications, etc., see Acc.J.A. 1999, s 40 (right to conduct litigation). *See* ILEX.

legal fiction. *See* FICTION, LEGAL.

legal formalism. (1) Legal analysis involving the presentation of argument as though conclusions followed inexorably from indisputable premises. (2) Pejorative term describing very strict adherence to the rigidities of external forms of rules.

legal interests and charges. Five categories capable of existence 'at law', defined by L.P.A. 1925, s 1(2) as: easements, rights and privileges; rentcharges; mortgages; miscellaneous charges; rights of entry.

legality, presumption of. *See* OMNIA PRAESUMUNTUR.

legality, principle of. *See* NULLUM CRIMEN SINE LEGE.

legal lease. A leasehold estate for a term of years created, in general, by deed. See L.P.A. 1925, ss 1(1), 52(1), 54(2). *See* LEASE.

legal liability. *See* RESPONSIBILITY.

legal memory. *See* TIME IMMEMORIAL.

legal mortgage. Mortgage created, in the case of *freehold land* by a demise for a term of years absolute with a provision for cesser on redemption, or by charge by

deed expressed to be by way of legal mortgage; in the case of *leasehold land*, by sub-demise for a term of years absolute (q.v.) at least one day less than the mortgaged lease with a proviso for cesser on redemption, or by charge by deed expressed to be by way of legal mortgage. The legal mortgage operates so as to secure the repayment of a debt or the discharge of some other obligation. See L.P.A. 1925, s 85; *Weg Motors* v *Hales* [1962] Ch 49; *Westminster CC* v *Haymarket Publishing* [1981] 1 WLR 677. *See* EQUITABLE MORTGAGE; EQUITY OF REDEMPTION; MORTGAGE.

legal personality. *See* PERSONALITY.

legal positivism. *See* POSITIVISM, LEGAL.

legal profession. Solicitors and barristers – a division dating from the fourteenth century, unique to parts of the British Commonwealth. See C.L.S.A. 1990. *See* BARRISTER; SOLICITOR.

legal professional privilege. *See* PRIVILEGE, LEGAL PROFESSIONAL.

legal professional privilege, and Inland Revenue. In *R* v *Special Commissioners ex p Morgan Grenfell* [2002] UKHL 21, HL held that the policy of legal professional privilege extends beyond the confines of judicial and quasi-judicial proceedings. 'Clients should be secure in the knowledge that protected documents and information will not be disclosed at all': per Lord Hoffman.

legal profession, proposals for reform. Sir David Clementis' suggestions (15 December 2004) include: near regulatory framework based on Legal Services Board to promote interests of public and consumers; front-line legal bodies to separate regulatory and representative functions; Office for Legal Complaints, subject to oversight of LSB to be set up; alternative business structures may be established.

legal relations, intention to create. An essential element in the creation of a contract. Where the parties do not expressly deny the intention, it is a question of construction: *Balfour* v *Balfour* [1919] 2 KB 571. Where the parties expressly deny intention (as in the so-called gentlemen's agreement (q.v.)), the agreement will not generally be enforced: *Jones* v *Vernons Pools Ltd* [1938] 2 All ER 626. See also *Edwards Skyways* [1964] 1 WLR 349; *Orion Insurance* v *Sphere Drake Insurance* [1992] 1 Lloyd's Rep 239. *See* CONTRACT.

legal representative in civil procedure. A barrister or solicitor, solicitor's employee or other authorised litigator (as defined in C.L.S.A. 1990) who has been instructed to act for a party in relation to a claim: CPR, r 2.3(1).

legal rights. Rights *in rem* (q.v.), i.e., available 'against the world at large', as compared with equitable rights (q.v.).

legal separation. *See* JUDICIAL SEPARATION.

Legal Services Commission. Body corporate, set up under Acc.J.A. 1999, s 1, to which will be assigned the functions of the Community Legal Service and the Criminal Defence Service (qq.v.). Comprises 7–12 members, appointed by Lord Chancellor, who have knowledge of the work of the courts, consumer affairs, social conditions, management, and the provision of services to be funded as part of CLS and CDS: s 1. See Sch 1; SI 00/622.

Legal Services Commission, support funding. Legal aid scheme offering partial financial help where, e.g., an insurance scheme is available. Currently available only for certain types of personal injury claims. Involves investigating strength of claim, and litigation support. Application is to be made to the Commission; applicants must satisfy the income and capital requirements tests necessary so as to obtain a legal representation certificate.

Legal Services Complaints Commissioner. Acc.J.A. 1999, s 51, authorises the Lord Chancellor to appoint a Complaints Commissioner (who must not be a professional lawyer, and who serves for three years). Where the Lord Chancellor considers that complaints about members of a professional body are not being handled correctly, he may direct the Commissioner to exercise his powers to require that body to provide appropriate information or to submit to the

Commissioner a plan for the handling of complaints about its members, and failure to submit such a plan may involve penalties: s 52. See Sch 8.

Legal Services Consultative Panel. Body, which replaces Lord Chancellor's Advisory Committee on Legal Education, set up under C.L.S.A. 1990, s 18A, substituted by Acc.J.A. 1999, s 35. Its duties are to assist in maintenance and development of standards in education, training and conduct of persons offering legal services, and to assist the Lord Chancellor in advising on particular matters relating to any aspect of the provision of legal services: s 18A(3).

Legal Services Ombudsman. *See* OMBUDSMAN, LEGAL SERVICES.

legal tender. Money that can be offered in the final discharge of a debt and cannot be refused by the creditor. Unlimited legal tender is money that can be tendered up to any amount (e.g., Bank of England notes).

legal year. The annual period of time constituted by the four sittings of the court (Michaelmas, Hilary, Easter, Trinity). *See* SITTINGS.

legatee. One to whom a legacy is left. *See* LEGACY.

leges posteriores priores contrarias abrogant. Later laws abrogate prior contrary laws. The basis of the doctrine of 'repeal by implication', and theme of the doctrine that Parliament can never bind its successors. See, e.g., *Ellen Street Estates* v *Ministry of Health* [1934] KB 590.

legislation. 1. A body of statutes. 2. The making of laws by a competent authority. In the UK this takes three major forms: Acts of Parliament (q.v.); delegated legislation (q.v.); autonomic legislation, i.e., by bodies, such as the unions, making their internal rules and regulations.

legislation, burdensome, reform of. A ministerial order may be made so as to reform legislation which effectively imposes burdens affecting persons, so as to remove or reduce those burdens: Regulatory Reform Act 2001, s 1(1). 'Burden' includes restrictions, conditions, sanctions for failure to observe restrictions; but a burden affecting only a government department is excluded: s 2(1).

legislation, proportionality of. Doctrine which examines whether the effect of a law exceeds what is necessary to be achieved, and whether it is in proportion to a specific objective. A principle of EU law: 'Any action by the Community shall not go beyond what is necessary to achieve the objectives of this Treaty': Maastricht Treaty 1992, art 3b (see, e.g., Case 44/79, *Hauer v Land Rheinland-Pfalz* [1979] ECR 3727). See, e.g., *Brind v Secretary of State for Home Department* [1991] 2 WLR 588; *Bowman v UK* (1998) 26 EHRR 1 (consideration by Court of Human Rights of Representation of the People Act 1983, s 75).

legislation, subordinate. Delegated legislation (q.v.). (Under Human Rights Act 1998, s 3(1), primary and subordinate legislation must be read and given effect in a way which is compatible with Convention rights.)

legislative history of an enactment. Term used in statutory interpretation to refer to the general background relating to the passing of a Bill, e.g., reports of committees, drafts of the Bill, parliamentary debates. The general rule is that no reference to these matters may be made where the meaning of the statute is plain without making recourse to it. See now *Pepper v Hart* [1993] AC 593; *Three Rivers DC v Bank of England (No. 2)* [1996] 2 All ER 363.

legislature. The Queen in Council in Parliament, i.e., Crown, Lords and Commons. The supreme authority in the realm. *See* PARLIAMENT.

legitimacy. Status of a child resulting from birth in lawful wedlock. See F.L.R.A. 1987. Under F.L.A. 1986, s 55A, inserted by C.S.P.S.S.A. 2000, s 83, a person domiciled in England and Wales may apply to the High Court, a county court or a magistrates' court for a declaration as to whether or not a person named in the application is or was the parent of another person so named.

legitimacy, presumption of. *See* PRESUMPTION OF LEGITIMACY.

legitimate expectation. *See* EXPECTATION, LEGITIMATE.

legitimation. Legitimation of a child by subsequent marriage of its parents *(per subsequens matrimonium)*. See Legitimacy Acts 1926 (ss 1, 8), 1976 (ss 2, 3); F.L.A. 1986, s 56 (as substituted by F.L.R.A. 1987, s 22).

leonina societas. A partnership (q.v.) (generally illegal) in which one partner takes all the profits (i.e., has 'the lion's share') and another carries all the losses.

le roi le veult; le roi s'avisera. *See* ROYAL ASSENT.

lesbianism. Female homosexuality. Not regarded by law as a criminal offence. See *Kerr v Kennedy* [1942] 1 KB 409 (an imputation of lesbianism held to be an imputation of unchastity, in relation to an action for slander (q.v.)); *Gardner v Gardner* [1947] 1 All ER 630 (conduct of wife was ground for a divorce petition where the husband's health suffered, so that he could allege cruelty); *B v B* [1991] 1 FLR 402; *Grant v South-West Trains Ltd* [1998] 1 FLR 839 (decision of Court of Justice of the European Communities (Case C-249/96) that employer's refusal to grant rail-travel concessions to an employee's partner of the same sex did not amount to discrimination contrary to EC Treaty, art 119 or Council Directive 75/117/EEC); *Pearce v Mayfield School Governors* (2000) *The Times*, 19 April (gender-specific words of abuse held not to be sex bias).

lessee. One to whom a lease is made. Includes also those who derive title under him: L.P.A. 1925, s 205(1)(*xxiii*). Known also as 'tenant' (q.v.). *See* LEASE.

lessor. One who makes a lease to another. See *Adelphi Estates Ltd v Christie* (1983) 269 EG 221. *See* LEASE.

lethal. Causing or designed to cause death. See, e.g., Firearms Act 1968, s 57(1). The test for a 'lethal weapon' is that when misused it was capable of causing injury from which death might result: *R v Thorpe* [1987] 1 WLR 383.

letter. 'Any communication in written form on any kind of physical medium to be conveyed and delivered otherwise than electronically to the person or address indicated by the sender on the item itself or on its wrapping (excluding any book, catalogue, newspaper or periodical); and includes a postal packet (q.v.) containing any such communication': Postal Services Act 2000, s 125(1).

letter of attorney. Power of attorney (q.v.).

letter of comfort. 1. Letter in which a person or body assumes a moral but not a legal obligation to assist another person to meet liabilities. It has no contractual effect: *Kleinwort Benson Ltd* v *Malaysia Mining Corpn* [1989] 1 All ER 785. 2. Document issued by European Commission (q.v.) in the form of an opinion concerning a possible breach of Treaty of Rome, art 85(1) (relating to competition law). It does not have the legal status of a decision (q.v.). See *Stork Amsterdam* v *EC Commission* [2000] 5 CMLR 31.

letter of credit. Document provided, e.g., for the exporter by the importer, so that the exporter can draw his draft upon a bank. It usually states the period within which it can be drawn, the maximum amount, and refers to documents accompanying it. See *Power Curber Ltd* v *Nat Bank of Kuwait* [1981] 1 WLR 1233 (a letter of credit ranks as cash and must be honoured); *Seaconsar Ltd* v *Bank Marcazi* [1999] 1 Lloyd's Rep 36.

letter of hypothecation. *See* HYPOTHE-CATION.

letter of intent. Device whereby X indicates to Y that he (X) is very likely to enter into a contract with Y. May amount to a conditional contract. See *British Steel Corp* v *Cleveland Bridge Co Ltd* [1984] 1 All ER 504.

letter of request. Letter issued to a foreign court asking a judge to take the evidence of some person within that court's jurisdiction, or arrange for it to be taken: see CPR, r 34.13; PD 34, para 5.1, Annex A. See C.J.A. 1988, s 29; Criminal Justice (International Co-operation) Act 1990, s 3. Known also as a 'rogatory

letter'. See *Boeing Co* v *PPG Industries* [1988] 3 All ER 839; *First American Corp* v *Al-Nahyan* [1998] 4 All ER 439.

letters of administration. Document issued to an administrator (q.v.) granting his authority in relation to an estate.

lex causae. The law relating to the legal system governing a matter. See, e.g., *Leroux* v *Brown* (1852) 12 CB 801.

lex domicilii. Law of the place of a person's domicile (q.v.).

lex fori. Law of the place in which a case is heard.

lex loci actus. Law of the place where an act is carried out.

lex loci contractus. Law of the place where a contract is made. See *Bodley Head Ltd* v *Flegon* [1972] 1 WLR 680.

lex loci delicti commissi. Law of the place where a wrong was committed. See *Monro* v *American Cyanamid Corporation* [1944] 1 All ER 386. See also CPR, Sch 1; O 11.

lex loci situs. Law of the place where the property in question is situated.

lex loci solutionis. Law of the place where the contract is to be performed, or payment made.

lex talionis. Law of retaliation. 'Eye for eye, tooth for tooth, hand for hand, foot for foot.' See *Exodus*, xxi, 24. *See* JUSTICE, RETRIBUTIVE.

liability. 1. Legal obligation or duty. 2. Amount owed.

liability, business. *See* BUSINESS LIABILITY.

liability, concurrent. 'The common law is not antipathetic to concurrent liability ... there is no sound basis for a rule which automatically restricts the claimant to either a tortious or a contractual remedy': *per* Lord Goff in *Henderson* v *Merrett Syndicates* [1995] 2 AC 145.

liability, corporate. *See* CORPORATE LIABILITY.

liability for manufactured products. 'A manufacturer of products which he sells in such a form as to show that he intends them to reach the ultimate consumer in the form in which they left him with no reasonable possibility of intermediate examination, and with the knowledge that the absence of reasonable care in the preparation or putting up of the products will result in an injury to the consumer's life or property, owes a duty to the consumer to take that reasonable care': *Donoghue* v *Stevenson* [1932] AC 562. See also C.P.A. 1987. *See* PRODUCT LIABILITY.

liability, joint and several. *See* JOINT AND SEVERAL LIABILITY.

liability, legal. *See* RESPONSIBILITY.

liability, limited. *See* LIMITED LIABILITY.

liability, occupiers'. *See* OCCUPIERS' LIABILITY, PRINCIPLE OF.

liability, strict, in criminal law. *See* STRICT LIABILITY IN CRIMINAL LAW.

liability, vicarious. The liability which arises because of one person's relationship to another. Thus, an employer is generally liable to a third party for the torts of his employee performed in the course of his employment. See, e.g., *Harrison* v *Michelin Tyre Co* [1985] 1 All ER 918; *Heasmans* v *Clarity Cleaning Ltd* [1987] IRLR 321. In criminal law a master may sometimes be held liable for a servant's offences: see, e.g., Trade Descriptions Act 1968; *Ferguson* v *Weaving* [1951] 1 KB 814. In *Majrowski* v *Guy's and St Thomas's NHS Trust* [2005] *The Times*, 21 March, an employer could be held vicariously liable under s 1 of the Protection from Harassment Act 1979, for harassment by an employee in the course of his or her employment. The principle can also extend to partners thus in *Dubai Aluminium Co* v *Salaam* [2002] UKHL 48, the House of Lords held that a partner in a firm of solicitors was acting in the ordinary course of business, even though he had acted without the authority and knowledge of the partners, since his acts were very closely connected to the acts he was authorised to perform. The firm was vicariously liable for loss resulting from those acts. The case of *Mattis* v *Pollock* [2003] EWCA Civ 887 also demonstrates that the limits for vicarious liability can be very wide. Here the CA held that where a club doorman who stabbed a person in the immediate vicinity of the club as an act of revenge for an earlier attack on him, he had committed the stabbing in the course of his employment and the owner of the club was vicariously liable. See also *Lister* v *Hesley Hall* [2002] 1 AC 213.

libel. The publication in permanent form of a statement which tends to expose a person to hatred, ridicule or contempt. The broadcasting of words by radio is treated as publication in permanent form: Defamation Act 1952, s 1. Libel may be a crime as well as a tort if it is of a 'serious kind', and is actionable *per se* without proof of special damage. See Law of Libel (Amendment) Act 1888; A.J.A. 1985, s 57 (reducing the limitation period in libel cases); Defamation Act 1996 (involving one-year limitation period for bringing an action: Lim.A. 1980, s 4A, substituted by 1996 Act, s 5); *Goldsmith* v *Bhoyrul* [1997] 4 All ER 268 (right of political party to sue in libel); *Cruise* v *Express Newspapers plc* [1999] 1 WLR 327; *Taylor* v *Director of Serious Fraud Office* [1999] 2 AC 177 (a prosecution statement cannot be used as the basis of a libel action). *See* DEFAMATION; JUSTIFICATION.

libel, damages assessment. Privy Council held in *The Gleaner Co Ltd* v *Abrahams* (2003) *The Times*, 22 July, that in considering the comparison between awards of general damages in libel and in personal injury cases, there is some element of deterrence in an award for defamation which is not generally to be found in personal injury cases.

libel, justification rules. CA held in *Chase* v *News Group Newspapers* (2002) *The Times*, 31 December, that the Human Rights Act 1998 had not changed three vital principles relating to defamation where defendant had pleaded justification based on reasonable grounds for suspecting that claimant had committed an offence; these principles are: hearsay not permitted; defence had to focus on claimant's conduct giving rise to the suspicions; a ground post-dating publication was not to be pleaded in relation to a defence of this nature.

libelling of politicians. The Privy Council held in *Worme* v *Commissioner* of *Police of Grenada* (2004) *The Times*, 5 February, that the reputation of public figures, such as politicians, must not be debased falsely, and where a person's reputation is attacked by false accusations of misconduct in public office, it is justifiable, in the interests of a democratic society, that such attacks be subjected to criminal sanctions.

liberty. 1. Absence of restraint. 'In accordance with British jurisprudence no member of the executive can interfere with the liberty or property of a British subject except on condition that he can support the legality of his action before a court of justice': *per* Lord Atkin in *Eshugbayi Eleko* v *Government of Nigeria* [1931] AC 62. See European Convention on Human Rights 1950, art 5 (right to liberty and security). 2. The condition of government under the law. 3. A franchise (i.e. a special privilege).

licence. 1. Necessary, generally revocable, authority to act granted by a competent authority. 2. In land law, a licence is given by X to Y when X, the occupier of land, gives Y permission to perform an act which, in other circumstances, would be considered a trespass, e.g., where X allows Y to reside in X's house as a lodger. A *bare licence* is merely gratuitous permission, and can be revoked at any time. A licence may be *coupled with an interest*, as where X sells standing timber to Y on condition that Y is to sever the timber; in this case the sale implies the grant of a licence to Y to enter X's land. For *contractual licence*, granted under the terms of a contract, see *Horrocks* v *Forray* [1976] 1 WLR 230. See *Somma* v *Hazelhurst* [1978] 2 All ER 1011; *Street* v *Mountford* [1985] AC 809.

licence by estoppel. Where a licensee has been allowed by the licensor to act so that an estoppel emerges in his favour, the licensor is bound by it. See *Crabb* v *Aran DC* [1975] 3 All ER 865. *See* ESTOPPEL.

licence period, extended. In the case of a sentence incorporating an order for an extended licence period, that extension was not to be considered as a breach of European Convention, art 7, because the

order was of a preventive rather than a punitive, nature: *R* v *R (Sentencing: Extended Licences)* (2003) *The Times*, 4 August.

licence, release on. *See* PAROLE.

licence, vehicle driver's. It is an offence to drive a motor vehicle without a driver's licence: Road Traffic Act 1988, s 87. See also Road Traffic (Driver Licensing & Info Systems) Act 1989, s 3. For tests of competence to drive, see 1988 Act, s 89 as amended by 1989 Act, s 4. For requirements of physical fitness of drivers, see 1988 Act, s 92, as amended by Road Traffic Act 1991, s 18. See also 1991 Act, s 17; Road Traffic (New Drivers) Act 1995.

licensable activities. Under the Licensing Act 2003 the following are held to be licensable activities: sale by retail of alcohol; supply of alcohol by or on behalf of a club to, or to the order of, a club member; the provision of regulated entertainment, and the provision of late night refreshment: s 1(1). Under s 2, a licensable activity may take place lawfully only in accordance with a premises licence.

licensed conveyancer. *See* CON-VEYANCER, LICENSED.

licensee. 1. One who has permission, express or implied, to enter premises for his own purpose, but not for any business interest of the occupier. See H.A. 1980, s 48. 2. One granted a licence, under Licensing Acts, 1964, 1988, for the sale of intoxicating liquor on the premises. For offence of sale to person under 18, or purchase of alcohol on behalf of such a person, see 1964 Act, ss 169A–169C, substituted by Licensing (Young Persons) Act 2000, s 1.

licensees as council tenants. Homeless individuals who have been granted a sub-licence allowing them to occupy accommodation temporarily passed to a housing trust by a local authority, do not, as a result become secured tenants of the local authority: *Kay* v *Lambeth LBC* (2004) *The Times*, 26 July.

licensing authorities, general duties of. Under the Licensing Act 2003, s 4, a licensing authority must carry out its statutory functions with a view to promoting the following objectives: prevention of crime and disorder; public safety; prevention of public nuisance; protection of children from harm.

licensing committees. Each licensing authority must establish a licensing committee consisting of 10–15 members of the authority: Licensing Act 2003, s 6. Under s 7, the committee is empowered to discharge any of the functions of the licensing authority, save for the determination of general licensing policy.

licensing of premises. The granting of justices' licences at the general annual licensing meeting, enabling intoxicating liquor to be sold on the premises. See Licensing Acts 1964 (as variously amended), 1988; Acc.J.A. 1999, Sch 13. *See* BREWSTER SESSIONS.

lien. *Ligare* = to bind. A right to hold and retain another's property until a claim is satisfied. 1. *Possessory lien.* Right to retain until a claim is met. Possession must be continuous, rightful and not for a particular purpose. It may be general or particular (qq.v.); see *Re Hamlet International plc* [1998] 2 BCLC 164. 2. *Maritime lien.* Right specifically binding a ship or cargo for payment of claim arising under maritime law. It is not founded on possession. See *The Turiddu* [1999] 2 All ER 161. 3. *Equitable lien.* Charge on property conferred by law until claims have been satisfied. It is attached independently of possession and is binding on all who acquire the property with notice of the lien. 4. *Unpaid seller's lien.* Right of an unpaid seller of goods to retain possession of them until payment or tender of the price where, e.g., the buyer becomes insolvent: S.G.A. 1979, ss 41–43.

lien, banker's. 'I think we should discard the use of the word "lien" in this context and speak simply of a banker's "right to combine accounts" or a right to "set off" one account against another': *per* Lord Denning in *Halesowen Presswork Ltd* v *Westminster Bank Ltd* [1971] 1 QB 1.

lien, vendor's. *See* VENDOR'S RIGHTS.

life annuity. Annual payment which continues during a life or lives. See I.C.T.A. 1988, s 657(1). *See* ANNUITY.

life assurance. Contract (q.v.) based on agreement by the assurer to pay a given sum upon the happening of some event contingent upon the duration of life. A *whole life* policy secures a capital sum at death, whenever it may occur. An *endowment assurance policy* secures a capital sum on survival to a fixed date, or at an earlier death. A *last survivor assurance* secures a sum payable at the death of the last survivor of two or more lives. A *temporary assurance policy* secures a capital sum only if death takes place within a specified term. See *Fuji Finance Inc* v *Aetna Life Assurance* [1994] 4 All ER 1025; Finance Act 2000, s 108(1). *See* ASSURANCE; INSURANCE.

life estate. An estate for the life of the tenant (e.g., by express limitation, such as a grant 'to X for life') or by operation of law or *autre vie* (q.v.). *See* ESTATE.

life imprisonment. Fixed penalty for murder. See Murder (Abolition of Death Penalty) Act 1965. For some other offences, e.g., manslaughter, it is the maximum penalty. Where imposed for murder, the court is empowered to declare the minimum term (usually 12–35 years) which ought to be served, but this does not bind the Home Secretary (who consults the Lord Chief Justice and trial judge before ordering such a release). Recommendation for a minimum term cannot be made except in the case of murder: *R* v *Flemming* [1973] 2 All ER 401. See *R* v *Secretary of State for Home Department ex p Stafford* [1998] 3 WLR 372; *R* v *Secretary of State for Home Department ex p Hindley* [2000] 2 WLR 730; *R* v *Lichniak* (2001) *The Times*, 16 May; Crime (Sentences) Act 1997, ss 28–32; C.J.C.S.A. 2000, s 61.

life interest. An interest in property for the duration of one's life, or the life of another. Necessarily an equitable interest: see L.P.A. 1925, s 1(3). *See* INTEREST.

life or lives in being. For purpose of the rule against perpetuities (q.v.), the common law rule was that the lives in being selected by the donor could be stated expressly or by implication and there is no restriction as to the number of lives selected: *Re Villar* [1928] Ch 471. All persons alive or conceived when the instrument creating interest becomes operative are eligible lives in being. Changes introduced by P.&A.A. 1964 relate to so-called 'statutory lives in being' (q.v.).

life policy. Instrument by which a payment of money is assured on death (except death by accident only) or the happening of a contingency dependent on human life or an instrument evidencing a contract subject to the payment of premiums for a term dependent on human life: Insurance Companies Act 1982, s 96(1). See I.C.T.A. 1988, s 266.

life sentence for second serious offence. Under P.C.C.(S.)A. 2000, s 109, the court has a duty to pass a life sentence on an offender: who was 18 or over when he committed the offence for which the court is to sentence him; the offence was of a serious nature, as set out in s 109(5) (e.g., attempt to commit murder; manslaughter; rape; robbery while in possession of a firearm); he has been convicted of a serious offence before he committed the offence for which the court is to sentence him (s 109(1)). Where the court does not impose a life sentence, it shall state in open court that it is of the opinion that there are exceptional circumstances, and what they are: s 109(3). The two offences need not be the same: thus, a person convicted of wounding, and convicted at a later date of an attempt to commit rape, will fall into the category of persons to whom a mandatory life sentence might apply. See *R* v *Kelly* (1998) *The Times*, 29 December ('exceptional' in s 109(3) is not a term of art, but is to be interpreted as a familiar English adjective, meaning out of the ordinary course, unusual, special or uncommon); *R* v *Newman* (2000) *The Times*, 3 February (defendant's acute mental illness not of itself an 'exceptional circumstance'); *R* v *Buckland* [2000] 2 Cr App (S) R 217.

life tenant. *See* TENANT FOR LIFE.

life term for murder, duration of. The Lord Chief Justice announced in July 2002 that the minimum term for offenders sentenced to life imprisonment for 'normal' murders is reduced from 14 to 12 years. In a case arising out of provocation, or so-called 'mercy killing', minimum term could be 8–9 years. For most serious murders, e.g., of children, minimum term is increased from 14 to 16 years. For serial killers a minimum term of 30 years is possible.

lifting the corporate veil. Phrase describing the process whereby the court and the public may look behind the 'curtain of corporate secrecy'. Thus, although the court is bound by the principle of a company's being a separate legal person distinct from its members, it will look at the underlying economic reality, e.g., where the company has been engaged in fraudulent trading or where the company is a mere sham (q.v.). See Cos.A. 1985, ss 117, 356; Ins.A. 1986, s 213; *Ord* v *Belhaven Pubs Ltd* [1998] 2 BCLC 447; *Adams* v *Cape Industries plc* [1990] Ch 433. *See* COMPANY.

light, easement of. The right by easement that light flowing over adjoining land shall not be obstructed unreasonably. See *Allen* v *Greenwood* [1980] Ch 119; *Dance* v *Trip-low* (1992) 17 EG 103 (burden of proving right to light). There is no natural right to light – the easement exists only in relation to a window or skylight: see *Tapling* v *Jones* (1865) 11 HLC 290. See Prescription Act 1832, s 3; Rights of Light Act 1959; Local Land Charges Act 1975, s 17. *See* EASEMENT.

likely. Probably, expected. 'A word protean in character in that its meaning might vary with the context . . . the court should state what meaning the word has in its statutory context': *R* v *Whitehouse* (1999) *The Times*, 10 December (' . . . in a manner likely to endanger an aircraft' (see SI 95/1970) should be construed as meaning, 'Is there a risk, a real risk, a risk that should not be ignored?'). See *Re H (Minors)* [1996] AC 1 ('likely' as used in Ch.A. 1989, s 31 (' . . . is likely to suffer significant harm') referred to a real possibility, which could not be sensibly ignored).

limitation of action, knowledge of facts. In *Bowie v Southorns* (2002) 152 NLJ 1240, it was held that the principle of Limitation Act 1980, s 14, that a claimant is not obliged to possess knowledge of whether a duty of care was owed to her, but merely that she possessed a broad knowledge of the specific facts upon which the complaint is founded, applies with equal force to s 14A (relating to latent damage) inserted by Latent Damage Act 1986, s 1. In *Cave v Robinson-Jarvis & Rolf* (2002) 152 NLJ 671, the HL ruled that defendant in a negligence action can rely on defence of limitation even though he did not disclose a relevant fact, as long as his concealment had not been deliberate: (See Limitation Act 1980, s 32.) The construction of s 32(2) by CA in *Brocklesby v Armitage* [2001] 1 All ER 172 was wrong.

limitation of actions. Provision whereby, after a certain period of time stated by statute, claims cannot be brought. A 'limitation period' is 'the period within which a person who has a right to claim against another person must start court proceedings to establish that right': CPR Glossary. Generally: in the case of land, 12 years from the date of accrual of action; in the case of tort and simple contract, six years from the date of accrual of action (for contract under seal, 12 years from the date of accrual). See Lim.A. 1980; Latent Damage Act 1986; C.P.A. 1987, Sch 1; PD 16 para 16.1; Law Commission Consultation Paper No. 151 (1998), *Limitation of Actions*. ('The English Limitation Acts bar the remedy and not the right': *per* Donaldson LJ in *Ronex Properties v John Laing Ltd* [1983] QB 398.) See *Dale v British Coal Corporation* [1993] 1 All ER 317; *Lowsley v Forbes* [1998] 3 WLR 501; *James v East Dorset HA* (1999) *The Times*, 7 December. Law Commission has recommended repeal of Limitation Act 1980: *Limitation of Actions* (2001). A single regime of lim-

itation periods is recommended which will apply to all claims, with a primary limitation period of three years and a long-stop ten-year limitation period commencing on the date on which the relevant events take place. For discretionary exclusion of time limits for claims in cases of personal injuries or deaths, see ss 11, 33; *Long v Tolchard & Sons Ltd* (2000) *The Times*, 5 January. It was held in *Re Loftus (deceased)* [2005] *The Times*, 28 March that in relation to Limitation Act 1980, the limitation period of 12 years in respect of a claim to the personal estate of a deceased ran from the end of the executor's year and not from the date of death of the deceased. *See* EXECUTOR'S YEAR. Note that in relation to land the Land Registration Act 2002, s 96 provides that, in relation to a registered estate in land or a registered rentcharge, no period of limitation runs in relation to actions for the recovery of land except in favour of a chargee, or actions for redemption and so the title to such an estate or rentcharge cannot be extinguished. The exception in favour of chargees means that section 15 of the Limitation Act 1980 will continue to apply to an action by a chargee for possession or foreclosure, to enforce its security. As regards actions for redemption, at present, once a mortgagee has been in possession for twelve years, the mortgagor loses his or her right to redeem the mortgage and his or her title is extinguished. This will no longer be the case. *See* ADVERSE POSSESSION.

See NULLUM TEMPUS OCCURRIT REGI.

limitation of actions, and settlement agreements. Where a settlement agreement is made and then becomes part of a consent order, the time relating to limitation purposes under the Civil Liability (Contribution) Act 1978 generally runs from the date of the agreement, not the order: *Knight v Rochdale NHS Trust* [2003] EWHC 1831 (QB).

limitation periods, right of access to court. It has been held that it was not disproportionate that there was a limitation bar on the claimant's right to access to court when bringing an action against a defendant several years after the cause of action occurred. See *A v Hoare* [2005] *The Times*, October 14.

limitation, words of. In land law, those words in an instrument which delimit the estate, i.e., which indicate the size of the interest given. Example: land given 'to X and his heirs', the words of limitation are 'and his heirs', indicating X's quantum of interest, but giving nothing to the heirs by direct gift (in this case X is the 'purchaser' (q.v.)). Strict words of limitation must be used to create a fee tail (q.v.). See *Shelley's Case* (1581) 1 Co Rep 93b; and L.P.A. 1925, s 131. *See* PURCHASE, WORDS OF.

limited administration. Administration of the assets of a deceased person which is limited, e.g., in time (as where the person appointed sole executor is an infant (q.v.)), or pending legal proceedings or where the person nominated sole executor is of unsound mind. *See* ADMINISTRATION.

limited company. A public company (q.v.). It is considered to be a distinct being or *persona*: *Salomon v Salomon & Co Ltd* [1897] AC 22. Liability of each shareholder may be limited by shares of guarantee and the winding-up of the company, if insolvent, will not make members bankrupt (q.v.). Its powers are limited to those arising under the memorandum of association (q.v.). *See* COMPANY.

limited executor. One granted limited probate, e.g., where a testator (q.v.) limits his will to specific property. *See* EXECUTOR.

limited liability. Principle by which, in the case of a company limited by shares, no shareholder will be called upon to pay more than the amount remaining unpaid on his shares. See, e.g., Cos.A. 1985, ss 1(2)(*b*), 13, as amended.

limited liability partnership. A body incorporate, with legal personality separate from that of its members, formed by incorporation under Limited Liability Partnerships Act 2000. Such a partnership will be fully liable for its debts; its

members will be liable for those debts up to their separate financial interests in the partnership. In general, the law relating to partnership has no application to a limited liability partnership. Name must end with abbreviation 'llp': see Schedule.

limited owner. One who owns an interest in property which is less than the fee simple (q.v.).

limited owner's charge. An equitable charge acquired under statute by a tenant for life or a statutory owner. A registrable Class C land charge (q.v.). See L.C.A. 1972, s 2(4)(*ii*), amended by Inheritance Act, Sch 8, para 8. *See* LAND CHARGES, REGISTER OF.

limited partnership. Consists of general partners (liable for the firm's debts and obligations) and limited partners (who, at the time of entry, contribute a sum as capital or property which is valued at a stated amount). It is not a legal entity distinct from the persons who compose the firm. See, e.g., Limited Partnerships Act 1907; Cos.A. 1985, s 716(2), (3); I.C.T.A. 1988, s 117(2). *See* PARTNERSHIP.

Lincoln's Inn. One of the Inns of Court (q.v.). Its records commence in 1422, the Inn having been sited originally in Shoe Lane. Its name is derived from that of the Earl of Lincoln who, in the reign of Edward II, arranged for professors of law to teach there.

lineal consanguinity. Relationship between ascendants and descendants, e.g., grandfather and grandson.

linked transaction. Term used in C.C.A. 1974, s 19(1), to refer to the debtor's entry into one transaction linked with another (e.g., purchase of a deep freezer on credit and a later agreement to buy food for stocking purposes). Generally treated as a 'regulated agreement' (q.v.).

lip-reading warning. Evidence taken from a video by lip reading, was, like the technique of facial mapping, which might meet tests of evidence and reliability, but which required a special warning from the judge as to risks of error, etc: *R v Lutrell* (2004) *The Times*, 9 June.

liquidated damages. *See* DAMAGES.

liquidation. 1. Settling of an obligation by legal proceedings or agreement. 2. The winding-up of the affairs of a business by identifying and converting assets into cash and paying off liabilities. See, generally, Ins.A. 1986, ss 100, 101, 143–146.

liquidation, fraud relating to. Relevant offences include: falsification of a company's books; false representations to creditors; material omissions from statements relating to company affairs; transactions in fraud of creditors; fraud in anticipation of winding-up: Ins.A. 1986, ss 206–211.

liquidation, voluntary. *See* VOLUNTARY WINDING-UP.

liquidator, company. One who is appointed in the case of a company which is being wound up by the court, 'to secure that the assets are got in, realised and distributed to creditors and, if there is a surplus, to those entitled to it': Ins.A. 1986, s 143(1). He is empowered to summon a final meeting of creditors: s 146. See, generally, ss 163–174.

liquidators, removal of. Insolvency Act 1986, s 108(2), allowing the court, on cause shown, to remove a liquidator, suggests: that the court has a discretion to do so; that it would do so on the good grounds; that these grounds must be established by the person seeking the order; that whether good grounds have been established depends on the specific facts of the case. Removal would not necessarily follow on it being shown that the liquidator's conduct has failed to live up to the ideal in one or two aspects: *AMP Enterprises* v *Hoffman* (2002) *The Times*, 13 August. See also *In Re Keypak Homecare* [1987] BCLC 409.

lis. Action; suit; dispute; claim.

lis alibi pendens. Suit pending elsewhere. Such a situation may provide grounds for staying a claim. See, e.g., *McHenry* v *Lewis* (1882) 22 Ch D 397.

lis pendens. See PENDENS LIS.

listed buildings. Buildings of special architectural or historic interest listed by the Secretary of State: Planning (Listed Buildings and Conservation Areas) Act 1990, s 1(1). Their alteration, extension, demolition, require consent: ss 7, 8, 17. For exceptions, see ss 9, 60. See also T.C.P.A. 1990; Planning and Compensation Act 1991, s 29.

listed securities. In relation to a company, means any securities of a public company listed on a recognised stock exchange (q.v.): Company Securities (Insider Dealing) Act 1985, s 12(*b*). See F.S.A. 1986, Part IV, Sch 16, para 28. Stock Exchange listing conditions include: that the securities are freely transferable; that offer documents have been approved by DTI. See F.S.M.A. 2000, Part VI for official listing rules.

listening devices. European Court of Human Rights held that where there is no statutory system for the regulation of covert listening devices used by the police, there is a violation of human rights under the European Convention, art 8 (respect for private life): *Hewitson* v *UK (Application No. 50015/99)* (2003) *The Times*, 10 June.

lite pendente. See PENDENTE LITE.

literal rule. A method for the construction (i.e. interpretation) of a statute by the courts. Its basis is: that words are to be taken prima facie in their ordinary, literal or grammatical meaning; that they are to be taken to be used in the same sense they had when the statute was passed; that the same words carry the same meaning. But 'the literal meaning of the words is never allowed to prevail where it would produce manifest absurdity or consequences which can never have been intended by the legislature': *Corocraft* v *Pan Am Airways* [1969] 1 QB 616. See *Duport Steels* v *Sirs* [1980] 1 WLR 142; *Lees* v *Secretary of State for Social Services* [1985] 2 All ER 203. *See* INTERPRETATION OF STATUTES.

literary work. 'Any work, other than a dramatic or musical work, which is written, spoken or sung, and accordingly includes a table or compilation and a computer program': Copyright, Designs and Patents Act 1988, s 3(1). See *Anacon Corp* v *Environmental Research Technology* [1994] FSR 659; *Narowzian*

v *Arks Ltd (No. 2)* [1999] FSR 79; SI 97/3032.

literary work, original. 'The originality . . . relates to the expression of the thought': *per* Peterson J in *University of London Press* v *University Tutorial Press* [1916] 2 Ch 601. See Copyrights, Designs and Patents Act 1988, s 3(1). *See* PLAGIARISM.

litigant. *See* LITIGATION.

litigant in person, costs of. Costs awarded to the litigant in person. He may recover for work reasonably done in his leisure time, and earnings lost through taking time off from work, to prepare or conduct the case. He may charge only for work which would have been done by a solicitor had he been legally represented.

litigants in person, curbing of. In *Bhamjee* v *Forsdick* (2003) *The Times*, 31 July, the CA held that the abuse of court procedures by vexatious litigants ought to be restrained under the courts' inherent jurisdiction. A set of rules for the courts' guidance was considered, including reference to the duty of a judge at any level to consider restraining a litigant from making further application proceedings without permission of the court.

litigation. The taking of legal action by a party, who is known as a 'litigant'.

litigation friend. A person who conducts proceedings on behalf of mental patients or children (under 18) involved in those proceedings. See CPR, r 21.1(2); PD 21, para 2.1. Will generally be a parent or other relative, guardian, receiver appointed under M.H.A. 1983, or Official Solicitor. A child may conduct proceedings without a litigation friend at the court's discretion: r 21.2(3), (4).

litigation funding agreement. Agreement under which a person ('the funder') agrees to fund (in whole or part) the provision of advocacy or litigation services (by someone other than the funder) to another person ('the litigant'), and the litigant agrees to pay a sum to the funder in specific circumstances: C.L.S.A. 1990, s 58B(2), added by Acc.J.A. 1999, s 28.

litigation funding agreement, applicable conditions. Under C.L.S.A. 1990, s 58B, added by Acc.J.A. 1999, s 28, a litigation funding agreement (q.v.) must be in writing, must not relate to proceedings which cannot be the subject of an enforceable conditional fee agreement (q.v.); the funder must be a person of a description prescribed by the Lord Chancellor.

litigator, authorised. Any person (including a solicitor) who has a right to conduct litigation granted by an authorised body in accordance with provisions of C.L.S.A. 1990: C.L.S.A 1990, s 119(1).

litter, offences in relation to. It is an offence to throw down, drop or otherwise deposit and leave litter in circumstances as to cause, or contribute to, or tend to lead to, the defacement by litter of any public open space and other places such as special roads. The term 'litter' should be given its natural meaning of 'miscellaneous rubbish left lying about'; it included commercial waste left on the highway: *Westminster CC* v *Riding* (1995) *The Times*, 31 July. See En.P.A. 1990, s 87; *Felix* v *DPP* [1998] Crim LR 657. See also Litter Act 1983; SI 99/672.

lives in being, statutory. *See* STATUTORY LIVES IN BEING.

livestock. Any creature kept for the production of food, wool, skins or fur, or for the purpose of its use in the farming of land or the carrying on of any agricultural activity: Agricultural Tenancies Act 1995, s 38(1). 'Cattle, horses, asses, mules, hinnies, sheep, pigs, goats and poultry, and also deer not in the wild state': Animals Act 1971, s 11. See *Hunt* v *Wallis* [1994] PIQR 128. 1971 Act, s 4, imposes liability on a person in possession of livestock which stray on to another's land and damage it or any property on it. Under s 3, the keeper of a dog which causes damage by killing or injuring livestock is liable for the damage.

livestock, protection of. It is a defence to an action for injuring or killing a dog to prove that it was done by a person entitled so to act for the protection of livestock and that notice was given at a

police station within 48 hours: Animals Act 1971, s 9.

living apart. In relation to divorce proceedings, this does not necessarily mean mere physical separation, but it involves a spouse's ceasing to recognise the marriage as subsisting: *Santos* v *Santos* [1972] 2 All ER 246.

living expenses. The term is to be construed as meaning 'expenses of living'; it is not limited to living expenses solely attributable to an individual person's expenditure. It includes expenses representing costs incurred for housing, food, clothing, necessary travelling and the like, and encompasses all the usual costs associated with any individual's particular life style: *Nutbrown* v *Rosier* (1982) *The Times*, 1 March.

living together. A man and his wife are not deemed to be living otherwise than together unless they are permanently living in separation either by agreement or under an order of the court, or one has deserted the other and the separation incident to the desertion has not come to an end.

living will. Colloquialism, known also as an 'advance directive'. Usually takes the form of a written statement setting out in advance what types of medical treatment the maker of the will does or does not desire to receive in specific circumstances, should he be incapable of giving or refusing consent. Law Commission Report No. 231 (1995), *Mental Incapacity*, recommends the creation of a statutory framework which would allow persons to consent to treatment or to refuse it.

LJ. Lord Justice of Appeal (q.v.).

LL.B. *Legum baccalaureus* (Bachelor of Laws). See also LL.M. (*Legum magister* – Master of Laws); LL.D. (*Legum doctor* – Doctor of Laws).

Lloyd's. An insurance market place constituted by syndicates of London underwriters, incorporated by statute in 1871. Controlled by Lloyd's Act 1982 and Insurance (Lloyd's) Regulations 1983, issued under Insurance Companies Act 1982. Under F.S.M.A. 2000, s 315,

The Society of Lloyd's is permitted to carry on regulated activities concerning the arranging of deals in contracts of insurance written at Lloyd's, and deals in participation in Lloyd's syndicates, and other activities related to these matters. FSA has a duty to keep itself informed of Lloyd's regulated activities: s 314.

loan capital. *See* CAPITAL, LOAN.

loan, quasi-. *See* QUASI-LOAN.

local administration, commissions for. Bodies, for England and Wales, set up under L.G.A. 1974, s 23(1), amended by Government of Wales Act 1998, Sch 12, para 12, each including the Parliamentary Commissioner (q.v.), to investigate complaints of injustice in consequence of maladministration in local government. Each commission submits an annual report to its representative body, comprising representatives of authorities subject to the commissions' jurisdiction. *See also* OMBUDSMAN, LOCAL ADMINISTRATION.

local authority. Defined under Finance Act 1974, s 52(2), as '(*a*) any authority having power to make or determine a rate; (*b*) any authority having power to issue a precept, requisition or other demand for the payment of money to be raised out of a rate'. Includes: county councils, district councils, London Borough Council, Common Council of City of London, Council of Isles of Scilly: L.G.A. 2000, s 1. In Charities Act 2006 s 47 'local authority' means a unitary authority, the council of a district so far as it is not a unitary authority, the council of a London borough or of a Welsh county or county borough, the Common Council of the City of London or the Council of the Isles of Scilly. A person is disqualified from membership of a local authority if he holds a 'politically restricted' post, e.g., statutory chief officer: L.G.H.A. 1989, s 1. See Local Government and Rating Act 1997; Local Government (Contracts) Act 1997; Representation of the People Act 2000, s 1. For power to promote 'well-being', see L.G.A. 2000, s 2. For appointment of overview and scrutiny committees, see L.G.A. 2000, s 21. For standard of conduct of members, see L.G.A. 2000, Part III. *See* PRECEPT.

local authority, performance standards of. Under L.G.A. 1992, s 1, the Audit Commission (q.v.) may direct the publication by relevant bodies of information concerning their activities in a financial year, facilitating the making of appropriate comparisons, by reference to criteria of costs, efficiency, etc., between standards of performance achieved by different relevant bodies. See L.G.A. 1999. *See* BEST VALUE AUTHORITY.

local government. Government on a local basis by elected committees, forming part of the UK's administrative system, based on pattern of elected bodies for defined areas with responsibility for the provision of services within those areas. See L.G.A. 1972–92; *Hazell* v *Hammersmith and Fulham LBC* [1991] 2 WLR 372; *R* v *Lewis* [1998] 1 Cr App R (S) 13 (allegation that candidate had forged details of proxy voters). For elections, see L.G.A. 2000, Part IV.

Local Government Commission for England. Body of 5–15 members established under L.G.A. 1992, s 12, to conduct a review of areas in England and recommend structural, boundary or electoral changes. See Sch 2.

local government, wilful misconduct. HL stated that the policy of selling council houses in marginal wards for purpose of increasing number of voters who agreed with a particular political party's policies constituted wilful misconduct: *Magill* v *Weeks* (2001) 151 NLJ 1886; Local Government Finance Act 1982, s 20.

local land charges. Any charge acquired by a local authority which is binding on successive owners of the land affected; any prohibition or restriction on the use of land imposed by a local authority or minister or government department which is binding on successive owners of the land affected; any positive obligation affecting land enforceable by a minister, government department or local authority binding on successive owners of the land affected: Local Land Charges Act 1975, s 1. Registers of local land charges are kept in London by London boroughs and the City of London, and in other areas by district councils. See Local Land Charges Rules 1977, as amended; En.P.A. 1990, s 143.

local land charges register. Consists of 12 parts: part 1 includes general financial charges; part 2 includes specific financial charges; part 3 includes planning charges; part 4 is reserved for charges not registrable in the other parts; part 5 includes fenland ways maintenance charges; part 6 relates to land compensation charges; part 7 refers to New Towns charges; part 8 includes civil aviation charges; part 9 refers to open-cast coal charges; part 10 is reserved for listed buildings charges; part 11 is for light obstruction notices; part 12 is for drainage scheme charges. Failure to register does not affect enforceability of the charge: Local Land Charges Act 1975, s 10. See I.A. 1978, Sch 1.

lock-out. The closing by an employer of a place of employment, or the suspension of work, or the refusal by an employer to continue to employ any number of persons employed by him, in consequence of a dispute, done by him with a view to compelling persons employed by him, or to aid another employer in compelling persons employed by him, to accept terms or conditions of or affecting employment: E.R.A. 1996, s 235(4).

lock-out agreement. Described in *Walford* v *Miles* [1992] 2 AC 128, as an agreement for valuable consideration between a vendor of property (V) and a potential purchaser (P) that for a short fixed period V will negotiate exclusively with P with a view to achieving at the end of the negotiation a binding contract for the sale of that property to P and will not deal with any other prospective purchaser. It may be unenforceable as a contract because of lack of certainty. See *Moroney* v *Isofam* [1997] EGCS 178.

loco parentis. See IN LOCO PARENTIS.

locum tenens. Holding an office. One who acts as a lawful substitute or deputy.

locus in quo. Place in which. Scene of the event. See *R* v *Hunter* [1985] 1 WLR 613.

locus poenitentiae. A 'place for repentance'. An opportunity of changing one's mind, e.g., by withdrawing from a planned criminal enterprise. See *R v Whitefield* [1984] Crim LR 97; *Tribe v Tribe* [1995] 3 WLR 913.

locus regit actum. The place governs the act, i.e., an act is governed by the law of the place where it is performed. See, e.g., *R v Bham* [1966] 1 QB 159.

locus sigilli. Place of the seal. 'LS' may be used in a document to show where the seal should be. See *First National Securities Ltd v Jones* [1978] 2 All ER 221. *See* SEALING.

locus standi. Place to stand. A right to be heard, a sufficient interest, or the legal capacity to challenge some decision. See, e.g., *R v North Somerset DC ex p Garnett* [1998] Env LR 91; *Pemberton v Southwark LBC* [2000] 21 EG 135. *See* AGGRIEVED PERSON.

lodger. One who occupies part of a house, but whose occupation is under control of a landlord or his representative who resides in or retains possession of or dominion over that house: *Thompson v Ward* [1906] 1 KB 60. ('The occupier is a lodger if the landlord provides attendance or services which require the landlord or his servants to exercise unrestricted access to and use of the premises. A lodger is entitled to live in the premises but cannot call the place his own': *per* Lord Templeman in *Street v Mountford* [1985] AC 809.) See *Brooker Settled Estates Ltd v Ayers* (1987) 19 LR 246.

lodging house, common. A house (other than a public assistance institution) provided for the purpose of accommodating by night poor persons, not being members of the same family, who resort to it and are allowed to occupy one common room for the purpose of sleeping or eating, and includes, where part only of a house is so used, the part so used: H.A. 1985, s 401. Such houses must be registered: s 402.

loiter. To act in a way which suggests that a person is idling in the street for an unlawful purpose. Loitering for purposes of prostitution is an offence: Street Offences Act 1959, s 1. See *DPP v Bull* [1995] QB 88. *See* IMPORTUNE.

London Assembly, general function of. The Assembly keeps under review the exercise by the Mayor of his statutory functions. Members may prepare reports concerning the actions and decisions of the Mayor and members of staff of the Greater London Authority, and may submit proposals to the Mayor: G.L.A.A. 1999, ss 58, 59. *See* GREATER LONDON AUTHORITY.

London, City of. *See* CITY OF LONDON.

London Development Agency. Created under Regional Development Agencies Act 1998, amended by G.L.A.A. 1999, s 304. The Mayor is responsible for appointment of members. Its principal task is to formulate and submit to the Mayor a draft strategy in relation to its purposes: see 1998 Act, s 7A, inserted by G.L.A.A. 1999, s 306(2).

London, Mayor of. A member of the Greater London Authority (q.v.), elected under G.L.A.A. 1999. Must be a citizen of the Commonwealth, or the Republic of Ireland, or the EU: s 20. For disqualifications, see s 21. He is responsible for formulation of the Authority's capital spending plans and the preparation and publication of strategies relating to transport, spatial development, biodiversity action, municipal waste management, air quality, ambient noise, culture: ss 41, 122. He may resign at any time by giving notice (s 12) and will cease to be Mayor if he fails on six successive occasions to attend Assembly meetings (s 13).

London, Transport for. The highway authority for all Greater London Authority roads: Highways Act 1980, s 1(2), inserted by G.L.A.A. 1999, s 259(2). Also the traffic authority for all Greater London Authority roads: Road Traffic Regulation Act 1984, s 121A(1A), inserted by G.L.A.A. 1999, s 271. The London Traffic Control system is transferred to Transport for London under G.L.A.A. 1999, s 275.

lone parent. *See* PARENT, LONE.

long tenancy. 'A tenancy granted for a term of years certain exceeding 21 years, whether or not subsequently extended by act of the parties or by any enactment, but excluding any tenancy which is, or may become, terminable before the end of the term by notice given to the tenant': L.G.H.A. 1989, Sch 10, para 2(3). See SIs 97/3005/3007/3008.

long title. *See* TITLE, LONG.

looting. 1. Sacking; plundering; robbing. 2. Stealing from any person killed, injured or detained during military operations or taking otherwise than for the public service any vehicle, equipment or stores abandoned by the enemy: Armed Forces Act 1971. See *R v Bailey* (1982) 4 Cr App R (S) 15.

lord. 1. Peer of the realm. 2. One of whom land is held by a tenant (q.v.). *See* PEER.

Lord Advocate. The Crown's principal law officer in Scotland. He represents the Crown in legal proceedings and conducts Crown prosecutions.

Lord Chancellor. *See* CHANCELLOR.

Lord Chief Justice. Presides over QBD and Court of Appeal (Criminal Division) and ranks next to the Lord Chancellor in the legal hierarchy. Appointed by the Sovereign upon recommendation of the Prime Minister. See S.C.A. 1981, s 10(2)(*a*).

Lord-Lieutenant of the County. Office first created in the sixteenth century when the holder was commander of county militia and chief among county justices. Now appointed by the Crown for each county in England and each area in Scotland, on the advice of the Prime Minister. See Lieutenancies Act 1997.

Lords, House of. *See* HOUSE OF LORDS.

Lords Justices of Appeal. Judges who sit in the Court of Appeal (q.v.), appointed by the Queen from High Court judges or persons with a ten-year High Court qualification (see C.L.S.A. 1990, s 71): S.C.A. 1981, s 10, as amended.

Lords of Appeal in Ordinary. Senior members of the judiciary, usually appointed from the Court of Appeal (q.v.), who hear appeals in the House of Lords (q.v.). They have held other high judicial office for two years, or have held a Supreme Court qualification, within the

meaning of C.L.S.A. 1990, s 71, for 15 years. See Appellate Jurisdiction Acts 1876–1947; C.L.S.A. 1990, Sch 10.

Lords Spiritual. *See* HOUSE OF LORDS.

Lords Temporal. *See* HOUSE OF LORDS.

lorry park. Where aggregate was being excavated from a lorry park being constructed together with a warehouse, it was considered to have been exempt from an aggregated levy, since its excavation was in connection with the erection of a building: *Commissioners of Customs and Excise v E Midlands Aggregates Ltd* (2004) *The Times*, 24 May.

loss leaders. Goods sold not primarily to make a profit but to attract customers so that they might also buy other goods, or to advertise the business: see Resale Prices Act 1976, s 13(2); *JJB (Sports) Ltd v Milbro Sports Ltd* [1975] ICR 73.

loss, liability in marine insurance for. An insurer will be liable for losses proximately caused by a peril which has been insured against. A *partial loss* is a loss other than a total loss. A *total loss* may be *actual* or *constructive*; *actual total loss* is where the subject matter insured is destroyed or so damaged that it has ceased to be a thing of the kind insured against; *constructive total loss* is where the subject matter insured has been abandoned because its actual total loss seems unavoidable.

lost modern grant. Doctrine based on fiction (q.v.) whereby the court can presume from long user (i.e., 20 years) that a grant of easements and profits has been made at some time after 1189, but that it has now been lost. User as of right must be shown, right claimed must be capable of being acquired by grant. Claim may be made only where a presumption at common law is not possible in the circumstances: *Tehidy Minerals v Norman* [1971] 2 QB 528. See *Bridle v Ruby* [1988] 3 WLR 191 (presumption of lost modern grant was not rebutted by mistaken belief as to right of way).

lottery. A game of chance. Generally unlawful: Lotteries and Amusements Act 1976, s 1. Exceptions: small lotteries incidental to 'exempt entertainments' (e.g., bazaars, sales of work, dances); private lotteries (e.g., those in which the sale of tickets is restricted to members of one society); societies' lotteries (i.e., promoted on behalf of a society concerned with athletics, charitable purposes, etc.). A lottery ticket 'includes any document evidencing the claim of a person to participate in the chances of the lottery': 1976 Act, s 23(1). See *Re Vanilla Accumulation Ltd* (1998) *The Times*, 24 February (lottery constituted by a marketing scheme, leading to the winding-up of a company); National Lottery Acts 1993, 1998; *R v Secretary of State for Home Department ex p International Lottery in Leichtenstein Foundation* [1999] 3 CMLR 304 (right of UK to prohibit all large lotteries except National Lottery). *See* GAMING; SWEEPSTAKE.

Low Pay Commission. Appointed under National Minimum Wage Act 1998, s 8(9), consisting of a chairman and eight other members appointed by Secretary of State: Sch 1. It has advised on, e.g., base hourly rates, periods over which the entitlement to a minimum wage is to be calculated, exemption of particular groups: see s 5(2).

loyalty. Faithfulness and allegiance (q.v.) to one's sovereign or government.

l.s. *Locus sigilli* (q.v.).

lucid interval. A temporary period of rational thought and behaviour between periods of insanity. A will (q.v.) made during such a period may be admitted to probate (q.v.). See *Chambers and Yatman* v *Queen's Proctor* (1840) 2 Curt 415, in which the deceased made a will during a lucid interval and killed himself, while insane, on the following day, and the will was admitted to probate.

lucrum cessans. Ceasing gain. The element of compensation in an award of damages intended to reflect anticipated lost profits as compared with *damnum emergens* (the actual loss).

lump sum award. A once-for-all award of damages, comprising pecuniary loss incurred up to the trial and a final estimate of future pecuniary and non-pecuniary loss. For lump sum order under Mat.C.A. 1973, see s 24A. See *Duxbury* v *Duxbury* [1987] 1 FLR 7; *Purba* v *Purba* [2000] Fam Law 86; *Cowan* v *Cowan* (2001) *The Times*, 17 May.

lump sum contract. Contract (q.v.) by which it is intended that complete performance shall take place before payment may be demanded. Failure to complete performance prevents any payment being recovered. See *Sumpter* v *Hedges* [1898] 1 QB 673; *Hoenig* v *Isaacs* [1952] 1 All ER 176 (recovery of sum relating to faulty workmanship).

lump sum freight. *See* FREIGHT.

lunatic. An idiot or person of unsound mind: Lunacy Act 1890, s 341. This term has been replaced by 'patient'. See M.H.A. 1983, s 145(1).

lunatic, criminal. *See* CRIMINAL LUNATIC.

lying in relation to proof of guilt. Although lying might demonstrate to a jury that defendant might be concealing guilt, they should be reminded that an innocent defendant might lie, and an inference of guilt that might be drawn does not follow automatically. The question for the jury is: 'Why did defendant tell that lie?' See *R* v *Lucas* [1981] 3 WLR 120; *R* v *Middleton* (2000) *The Times*, 12 April.

M

Maastricht Treaty. *See* EUROPEAN UNION, TREATY ON.

machinery and plant. Expression relating to capital allowances, used in the Finance Acts in relation to a deduction against income tax, based on expenditure on machinery and plant purchased for the purpose of one's trade. See Capital Allowances Act 1990, Part II. *See* PLANT.

machinery, dangerous. *See* DANGEROUS MACHINERY.

magistrates. There are some 30,000 honorary (or lay) magistrates (as contrasted with 92 district judges (magistrates' courts) (q.v.)) who are part-time justices of the peace (q.v.) appointed by the Crown on the advice of the Lord Chancellor and Advisory Committees. The office of justice of the peace originated in the late twelfth century royal proclamation creating 'knights of the peace' to aid the sheriff (q.v.) in the enforcement of the law. Known later as *custodes pacis* (keepers of the peace) and, from *c.* 1360, as 'justices of the peace'. See (for schemes for appointment, retirement, etc.) Justices of the Peace Act 1997. They may be removed by the Lord Chancellor without showing cause. For disqualification in case of bankruptcy and in case of justices who are members of local authorities, see 1997 Act, ss 65, 66. At the age of 70 they are placed on the supplemental list and cease to be entitled to exercise any judicial function (see 1997 Act, s 7). Functions include: committing offenders for trial by judge and jury; trying offences summarily; sitting with judges of the Crown Court to hear appeals from magistrates' courts; licensing of premises selling intoxicating liquor; etc. For immunity for acts within and beyond the

jurisdiction, see 1997 Act, ss 51, 52. See M.C.A. 1980; S.C.A. 1980; Acc.J.A. 1999, Sch 13. See *R v Doncaster Justices ex p Jack* (1999) 163 JPN 1026 (costs awarded against magistrates who had failed repeatedly to comply with correct principles).

magistrates, appropriate qualities for appointment as. Lord Chancellor's Direction to Advisory Committees (July 1998) suggests six key qualities in relation to personal suitability of candidates for appointment as magistrates: good character, powers of understanding and communication, social awareness, maturity, sound judgment, commitment and reliability.

magistrates' clerk. He must be a person who has a five-year magistrates' courts qualification (within C.L.S.A. 1990, s 71) or a lawyer who has served for at least five years as assistant to a magistrates' clerk: see Justices of the Peace Act 1997, s 43. His functions include: giving advice to magistrates, at their request, about law, practice or procedure; this includes questions arising when the clerk is not personally attending on them: s 45(4); assisting unrepresented parties; helping to ensure a fair trial. He must not go with magistrates when they retire to consider their verdict (see *R v E Kerrier Justices ex p Mundy* [1952] 2 QB 719). For immunities, see ss 51, 52. See *R v Corby Justices ex p Mort* (1998) 162 JP 310 (clerk entitled to question fines defaulter). See C.D.A. 1998, s 49(2); Justices of the Peace Act 1997, s 48, substituted by Acc.J.A. 1999, s 89 (independence of clerks); 1997 Act, s 53A, inserted by Acc.J.A. 1999, s 98 (immunity from costs): SI 99/2784; *Practice Direction*

(Justices: Clerk to court) [2000] 1 WLR 1886 (responsibilities of clerk for effective delivery of case management and reduction of unnecessary delays).

magistrates' courts. Some 700 courts, each constituted by any justice or justices of the peace acting under common law or any enactment or by virtue of a commission: M.C.A. 1980, s 148. Consists generally of two to seven part-time, unpaid JPs who hear complaints and try certain cases summarily. A single justice may conduct a preliminary investigation. See, e.g., M.C.A. 1980, s 121(1), as amended. Jurisdiction, which is local, is civil and criminal, largely comprising matters relating to: summary offences; indictable offences triable summarily; indictable offences triable only on indictment; offences triable either way; some domestic proceedings (see Domestic Proceedings and Magistrates' Courts Act 1978, Ch.A. 1989). See Justices of the Peace Act 1997; Magistrates' Courts (Procedure) Act 1998; P.C.C.(S.)A. 2000, s 135 (limits on fines on young offenders).

magistrates' courts committees. Appointed under Justices of the Peace Act 1997, s 27, substituted by Acc.J.A. 1999, s 81, composed of up to 12 magistrates for the area to which the committee relates. The 96 committees are responsible for the efficient and effective administration of the magistrates' courts for their areas (s 31(1)). They appoint a justices' chief executive (who acts as clerk to each committee); for role of chief executives, see 1997 Act, s 41, substituted by Acc.J.A. 1999, s 88. See also 1997 Act, s 30A, inserted by Acc.J.A. 1999, s 30A (the Greater London Magistrates' Court Authority); Acc.J.A. 1999, Sch 13; SI 00/2148.

magistrates' courts' powers exercisable by a single justice. A single JP may exercise powers of a magistrates' court, under C.D.A. 1998, s 49(1), including extension of bail conditions, dismissing an information where prosecution offers no defence, requesting a medical report, remitting an offender to another court for sentence, extending (with consent of accused) a custody time limit or overall time limit.

magistrates' courts, sittings of. A magistrates' court may sit on any day of the year, and (if the court thinks fit) on Christmas Day, Good Friday or any Sunday: M.C.A. 1980, s 153.

magistrates, ex-officio. Those who became magistrates by virtue of holding another office, e.g., that of mayor. Generally abolished under Justices of the Peace Act 1968 and A.J.A. 1973, save for High Court judges and the Lord Mayor and some aldermen in the City of London.

magistrates, restrictions on imprisonment by. In general, a magistrates' court has no power to impose imprisonment or detention in a young offender institution for less than five days, or more than six months in respect of any one offence: M.C.A. 1980, s 132; P.C.C.(S.)A. 2000, s 78. The aggregate of consecutive terms of imprisonment may not generally exceed six months: s 133(1). (For exceptional cases involving 12 months, see s 133(2).)

magistrates, stipendiary. *See* STIPENDIARY MAGISTRATES.

Magna Carta. The Great Charter (of Liberties), dated 15 June 1215. A statement in 37 chapters by King John of concessions to church and freemen, comprising a preamble and 63 clauses. It enunciated a number of fundamental principles, e.g., 'to none will we sell, to none will we deny or delay right or justice'. For a modern reference to the Charter, see *A-G's Reference (No. 1 of 1990)* (1992) 142 NLJ 563.

mail, interfering with. It is an offence for a person to intentionally delay or open a postal packet in the course of its transmission by post or to intentionally open a mail-bag, without reasonable excuse: Postal Services Act 2000, s 84.

maim. To injure a person so that he is rendered less capable of defending himself.

main purpose rule. *See* REPUGNANCY.

main residence. A tenant who occupied more than one residence could exercise his rights under Leasehold Reform Act 1967 only in relation to the house he occupied as his main residence: s 1. Thus, one who owned a main residence abroad and the lease of a house in the UK would have no rights under the Act. Which of two houses is the main residence is a matter of fact and degree. See also Capital Gains Tax Act 1979, s 101; *Goodwin* v *Curtis* [1998] STC 475.

maintain, failure to. Either party to a marriage may apply to the court for an order that the other party has failed to provide reasonable maintenance for the applicant or for any child of the family: Mat.C.A. 1973, s 27, as amended by Domestic Proceedings and Magistrates' Courts Act 1978, s 63.

maintain, liability to. A man is liable to maintain his wife and children, and a woman is liable to maintain her husband and children: see, e.g., S.S.A. 1975, s 17. Each parent of a 'qualifying child' is responsible for maintaining him: Child Support Act 1991, s 1(1). A child is a 'qualifying child' if one or both of his parents is, or are, not living in the same household with him, or he has his home with a person 'with care' (e.g., one who usually provides day to day care for him): s 3. For details of child support maintenance, see s 4. For failure to maintain and income support (q.v.), see S.S. Administration Act 1992, s 105. See also Child Support Act 1995; C.S.P.S.S.A. 2000, Sch 1.

maintenance. 1. Intermeddling in an action. 'A taking in hand, bearing up or upholding of quarrels and sides, to the disturbance of the common right': Coke, *Institutes* (1641). Criminal and tortious liability for maintenance was abolished by C.L.A. 1967, ss 13–14 (but this has no application to the case of a contract which is contrary to public policy). See *Giles* v *Thompson* [1994] 1 AC 142. 2. The supply of necessaries, e.g., food, clothing. Trustees (q.v.) may be empowered by provisions in a settlement or under Tr.A. 1925, to apply income of a trust fund towards the maintenance of a beneficiary (q.v.). See Tr.A. 1925, s 31; *Fuller* v *Evans* (1999) 149 NLJ 1561.

3. Financial arrangements embodied in a maintenance agreement (q.v.).

maintenance after termination of marriage. The court may make orders under Mat.C.A. 1973, ss 23, 24, known as 'financial provision orders' (for lump sums or secured or unsecured periodical payments) and 'property adjustment orders' (for settlement or transfer of property, variation of ante- or post-nuptial settlements or reduction of interest in such settlements). See W.R.P.A. 1999, Sch 3, paras 3, 4.

maintenance agreement. A written agreement made in respect of a child, between its father and mother and containing provision in respect of the making or securing of payments, or the disposition or use of any property, for the maintenance or education of the child: F.L.R.A. 1987, s 15(1). See Ch.A. 1989, Sch 1, paras 10, 11.

maintenance agreement by deceased person. Under Inheritance (Provision for Family and Dependants) Act 1975, s 17(4), means: any agreement made, in writing or not, and whether before or after the commencement of the Act, by the deceased with any person with whom he entered into a marriage, being an agreement containing provisions governing rights and liabilities towards one another when living separately of the parties to that marriage (whether dissolved or annulled) in respect of the making or securing of payments or the disposition or use of any property, including any rights and liabilities with respect to maintenance or education of any child, whether or not a child of the deceased or a person treated by the deceased as a child of the family in relation to that marriage.

maintenance order. An order, which provides for the periodical payment of sums of money towards the maintenance of any person, being a person whom the person liable to make payments under the order is liable to maintain: Maintenance Orders (Reciprocal Enforcement) Act 1972, s 21(1). See Child Support Acts 1991, 1995; Acc.J.A. 1999, Sch 13.

maintenance pending suit. Replaced 'alimony (q.v.) pending suit'. On petition for divorce, nullity or separation, the court may order either party to the marriage to make to the other periodical payments for his or her maintenance beginning not earlier than the date of the presentation of the petition and ending with the date of determination of the suit: Mat.C.A. 1973, s 22.

majority. 1. Full age, 18, under F.L.R.A. 1969. 2. The greater number of those present, or voting, at an assembly or other meeting.

majority rule. 1. Basic principle of democratic organisation. 2. Principle whereby a company's shareholders exercise control of the company through the general meeting. Minority shareholders are protected by common law (see *Foss v Harbottle* (1843) 2 Hare 461) and provisions of Cos.A. 1985.

majority verdict. *See* VERDICT, MAJORITY.

making off without payment. Offence under Th.A. 1978, s 3, committed where a person who, knowing that payment on the spot for any goods supplied or service done is required or expected from him, dishonestly makes off without having paid as required or expected and with intent to avoid payment of the amount. 'Payment on the spot' includes payment at the time of collecting goods on which work has been done or in respect of which service has been provided. Does not apply where supply of goods or provision of service is contrary to law or where service done is such that payment is not legally enforceable. Any person may arrest without warrant anyone who is, or whom he, with reasonable cause, suspects to be, committing or attempting to commit this offence: s 3(4). See *R v McDavitt* [1981] Crim LR 843 (upheld in *R v Brooks* (1983) 76 Cr App R 66); *R v Allen* [1985] AC 1029 (there must be an intent permanently to avoid payment); *R v Vincent* (2001) *The Times*, 13 March.

maladministration. Insufficient, weak or dishonest administration. See, e.g., *R v Local Commissioner ex p Bradford MCC* [1979] QB 287. There is no general right to damages for maladministration: *R v Knowsley MBC ex p Maguire* [1992] COD 499. For power of a local authority to compensate, see L.G.A. 2000, s 92. *See* OMBUDSMAN, LOCAL ADMINISTRATION.

male issue. Male descendants in the male line only (unlike 'male descendants' which may refer to male descendants of the *propositus* (q.v.) through males or females). See *Re Du Cros' ST* [1961] 3 All ER 193.

malfeasance. The commission of an unlawful act. *See* MISFEASANCE.

malice. 1. Generally refers to an attitude inherent in 'a wrongful act done intentionally without just cause or excuse': *Bromage v Prosser* (1825) 4 B & C 247. 2. In relation to *mens rea* (q.v.) of murder, categorised as: (1) *express* (an intention to kill); (2) *implied* (q.v.) (an intention to do only grievous bodily harm (q.v.)); (3) *universal* (e.g., where X fires a gun into a crowd, not caring who is killed, and killing Y); (4) *transferred* (as where X, intending to kill Y, shoots at him, but kills Z, who, unknown to X, was standing near Y, so that X's malice is considered as having been 'transferred' to Z: *R v Salisbury* (1553) 1 Plowd 100; *R v Monger* [1973] Crim LR 301); *R v Slimmings* [1999] Crim LR 69; *A-G's Reference (No. 3 of 1994)* [1996] 1 Cr App R 351; (5) *constructive* (q.v.). *R v Farrell* [1989] Crim LR 126; *Sooklal v Trinidad and Tobago* [2000] 1 WLR 2011. 3. A constituent of defamation (q.v.). The plaintiff must prove that words complained of were published maliciously, e.g., in abuse of fair comment. See Defamation Act 1996. *See* RECKLESSNESS, CATEGORIES OF.

malice aforethought. The requisite mental element for the offence of murder (q.v.). The prosecution must prove malice aforethought solely by proof that defendant either intended to kill another person or that he intended to cause that person really serious harm. ('Foresight' is not to be equated with 'intention'.) See C.J.A. 1967, s 8; *DPP v Smith* [1961]

AC 290; *Hyam* v *DPP* [1975] AC 55; *R* v *Cunningham* [1982] AC 566; *R* v *Hancock and Shankland* [1986] AC 455; *Frankland* v *R* [1987] AC 576.

malice prepense. Malice aforethought (q.v.).

malicious arrest. *See* ARREST, MALICIOUS.

malicious communications. It is an offence, intending to cause distress, to send letters conveying threats, indecent or grossly offensive messages or information known to be false by the sender: Malicious Communications Act 1988, s 1(1). For defences, see s 1(2). See *Chappell* v *DPP* (1988) 89 Cr App R 82 (comments of Divisional Court in relation to s 1(1)).

malicious damage. An offence involving damage to property caused by acts done unlawfully and maliciously under Malicious Damage Act 1861, replaced by Criminal Damage Act 1971. See *R* v *Gittins* [1982] RTR 363. *See* CRIMINAL DAMAGE.

malicious falsehood. A false and malicious statement concerning a person, made to someone other than that person, relating to his property or business interests which damages his general material interests. 'Malicious' involves some dishonest or other improper motive (but not carelessness). Known also as 'slander of title' (q.v.). See Defamation Act 1952, s 3(1); Defamation Act 1996, s 5, amending Limitation Act 1980, s 4A, relating to time limit for actions for defamation or malicious falsehood (one-year); *Joyce* v *Sengupta* [1993] 1 WLR 337; *Schulke & Mayr UK Ltd* v *Alkapharm UK Ltd* [1999] FSR 161; *Khodaparast* v *Shad* (1999) *The Times*, 1 December (award of aggravated damages).

malicious prosecution. A tort (q.v.) in which the plaintiff proves: that he has sustained damage; that the defendant prosecuted him; that the prosecution ended in the plaintiff's favour; that the prosecution lacked any reasonable and probable cause; that the defendant acted maliciously (i.e., with some other motive than desire to bring to justice a person whom

the accuser believes to be guilty): *Brown* v *Hawkes* [1891] 2 QB 718. See *Oliver* v *Calderdale MBC* (1999) *The Times*, 7 July (no automatic right to jury trial in a case of malicious prosecution); *Gregory* v *Portsmouth CC* (2000) *The Times*, 2 February (House of Lords held that the malicious institution of internal disciplinary proceedings could not give rise to a claim for damages for malicious prosecution); *Sallows* v *Griffiths* (2000) 23(4) IPD 23035.

malicious prosecution, reasonable and probable cause in relation to. Definition approved by House of Lords in *Herniman* v *Smith* [1938] AC 305 is: 'An honest belief in the guilt of accused based upon full conviction, founded upon reasonable grounds, of the existence of a state of circumstances, which, assuming them to be true, would reasonably lead any ordinarily prudent and cautious man, placed in the position of the accuser, to the conclusion that the person charged was probably guilty of the crime imputed.'

malicious wounding. Offence committed under O.P.A. 1861, s 20, by a person who unlawfully and maliciously wounds or inflicts any grievous bodily harm (q.v.) upon another either with or without any weapon or instrument. Known also as 'unlawful wounding'. For 'inflict', see *R* v *Burstow* [1996] Crim LR 331. *See* WOUNDING; WOUNDING WITH INTENT.

malicious wounding, proof of. The prosecution must prove either that defendant (D) intended or actually foresaw that his act would cause harm; it is not sufficient to show that D ought to have foreseen that his act would cause harm. It is unnecessary to show that D intended or foresaw the gravity of the harm that his acts would cause, as long as he foresaw some physical harm, even of a minor nature: *R* v *Savage* [1992] 1 AC 699.

malingerer. One who falsely pretends to be suffering from sickness or disability; or who injures himself so as to render himself unfit for service, or causes himself to be injured by another with that intent, or who prolongs or aggravates any sickness or disability. See Army Act

1955, s 42(1); *Burgess* v *British Steel* (2000) *The Times*, 29 February (malingering claim and normal costs rule).

malitia supplet aetatem. Malice supplements age. *See* DOLI CAPAX.

malversation. Misbehaviour or corruption in an office of public trust.

man. A male adult person. In Sex Discrimination Act 1975, s 82(1) it includes a male 'of any age'.

manager, appointment of. Equitable remedy allowing the court to appoint a manager who is empowered to continue a business. Often the same person is appointed as receiver and manager. 'Nothing is better settled than that this court does not assume the management of a business or undertaking except with a view to the winding-up and sale of the business or undertaking': *Gardner* v *London Chatham and Dover Rwy* (1887) 2 Ch App 201.

manager, company. *See* COMPANY MANAGER.

manager, special. *See* SPECIAL MANAGER.

managing director. A director (q.v.) who has charge of the management of the company. See Table A, arts 72, 84.

mandamus. We command. Originally a writ from the High Court (q.v.) ordering performance of a public duty. Replaced by an order, under A.J.A. 1938, s 7. Used, e.g., to direct the holding of municipal elections (*Re Barnes Corporation* [1933] 1 KB 668); to compel hearing of an appeal by an inferior tribunal. See now S.C.A. 1981, ss 29, 31; CPR, Part 54; PD 54. Known now as 'mandatory order'.

mandate. 1. A direction from a superior to an inferior court. 2. A contract of agency to perform a task for another person. 3. An order or injunction. 4. A commission granted by former League of Nations to a member state relating to the establishment of government over conquered territory, e.g., former German territories in Africa after First World War.

mandatory injunction. *See* INJUNCTION.

manned guarding. Activities involved in: guarding premises against unauthorised access or occupation against outbreaks of disorder or against damage; guarding property against destruction or damage, against being stolen or against being otherwise dishonestly taken or obtained; guarding individuals against assault or against injuries that might be suffered in consequence of the unlawful activities of others: P.S.I.A. 2001, Sch 2, para 2.

man of straw. 1. One who is used to shield another, e.g., in a claim. 2. One of little means and, hence, not worth suing.

manor. A feudal unit of land, usually comprising the lord's manor house and the land he occupied and cultivated, together with land held by tenants and waste used for pasture. See L.P.A. 1925, s 205(1)(*ix*). 'Manorial rights' include the lord's sporting rights, rights to mines and minerals, right to hold fairs and markets: L.P.A. 1922, Sch 12.

mansion house, principal. Phrase used in S.L.A. 1925, s 65, to refer to a house occupied as a main residence, except if usually occupied as a farmhouse, which, together with its grounds, exceeds 25 acres in extent (in which case it could be disposed of by a tenant for life (q.v.) without trustees' consent). See *Re Feversham Settled Estates* [1938] 2 All ER 210.

manslaughter. Generally, unlawful homicide which cannot be classified as murder (q.v.), e.g., as X kills Y as a result of grossly negligent conduct. May be classified as (1) *voluntary*, i.e., intentional, as in the case of a killing which would have been murder, but is considered as manslaughter because the accused successfully pleads diminished responsibility (q.v.) or provocation; (2) *involuntary*, i.e., as where the *actus reus* (q.v.) of homicide is unaccompanied by malice aforethought (q.v.), resulting from an act performed with criminal negligence. See *R* v *Seymour* [1983] 2 AC 493; *R* v *Arobieke* [1988] Crim LR 314; *R* v *Lebrun* [1991] 3 WLR 653 (problem of coincidence in time of *mens rea* and *actus reus*); *R* v *Khan* [1998] Crim LR 830 (discussion of duty required in a case of manslaughter by omission); *R* v *Kennedy* [1999] 1 Cr App R 54; *R* v *Antoine* [2000] 2 WLR 703.

manslaughter, aiding and abetting. Following the joint purchase of heroin by X and Y, X handed the preparation to Y who injected himself and died as a result. X was charged with manslaughter; injecting oneself with heroin was considered unlawful, and aiding and abetting such an act rendered X liable for Y's death. CA held that it was not an offence under Misuse of Drugs Act 1971 or at common law for a person to inject himself with a prohibited drug; X was not guilty of manslaughter resulting from his acts leading to Y's self-injection: *R v Dias* [2002] 2 Cr App R 5.

manslaughter, constructive. Type of manslaughter (q.v.) limited to death resulting from an offence likely to cause some harm. See *R v Dawson* (1985) 81 Cr App R 150 – the requisite 'harm' was caused if the unlawful act so shocked the victim as to cause him physical injury. See *R v Watson* [1989] 1 WLR 684.

manslaughter, corporate body and. A corporate body is capable of being found guilty of manslaughter but only if the *mens rea* and the *actus reus* of the offence can be established against those that were identified as the embodiment of the corporate body (the so-called 'identification test'): *R v HM Coroner for E Kent ex p Spooner* (1987) 3 BCC 638; *R v P&O European Ferries Ltd* (1991) 93 Cr App R 72; *A-G's Reference (No. 2 of 1999)* [2000] 3 All ER 182. See Law Commission Report No. 237, *Legislating the Criminal Code: Involuntary Manslaughter* (1996), in which there is a recommendation for recognition of a new offence of 'corporate killing'. *See* CORPORATE LIABILITY.

manslaughter, joint illegality as defence. It is in the interests of public policy that the criminal law shall not refuse to find that one person is criminally responsible for the death of another merely on the ground that both were undertaking an unlawful joint activity at the time: *R v Wacker* [2002] EWCA Crim 1944.

mansuetae naturae. Tame by nature. Term applied to animals, such as horses, dogs. *See* ANIMALS, CLASSIFICATION OF.

manual labour. Includes work done with the hands, even though it is highly skilled and technical: *Stone Lighting & Radio Ltd v Haygarth* [1968] AC 157.

Mareva injunction. Procedure based on an interlocutory prohibitory injunction, whereby the court comes to a creditor's aid when the debtor (resident or non-resident) has absconded or is overseas but has assets in this country. The assets required to satisfy a judgment or expected judgment are temporarily frozen. See *Mareva Compania Naviera SA v International Bulk-Carriers SA* [1975] 2 Lloyd's Rep 509. Known now as a 'freezing order' (q.v.). See C.J.J.A. 1982, s 25; *Ryan v Friction Dynamics Ltd* (2000) *The Times*, 14 June.

marginal notes. Notes printed in margins of Acts of Parliament, explanatory of the clauses. They do not form part of an Act (except in the case of certain private Acts). They may be considered by the court in a case of ambiguity. See *Chandler v DPP* [1964] AC 763; *DPP v Schildkamp* [1971] AC 1.

marine adventure. The exposure of a ship, goods or other movables to maritime perils (i.e., perils consequent on, or incidental to, the navigation of the sea): Marine Insurance Act 1906, s 3.

marine insurance contract. Contract (q.v.) whereby an insurer engages to indemnify the assured against those losses incident to a marine adventure (q.v.). See Marine Insurance Act 1906; *The Good Luck* [1991] 2 WLR 1279; *Mander v Commercial Union plc* [1998] Lloyd's Rep IR 93.

marine waters. Waters, other than inland waters (q.v.) within the seaward limits of the territorial sea adjacent to Great Britain: Diseases of Fish Act 1983, s 7(8).

maritime lien. *See* LIEN.

maritime perils. Perils arising from navigation of the sea, e.g., fire, war, pirates, restraints of princes (q.v.), jettisons and other perils which may be designated by the insurance policy: see Marine Insurance Act 1906, s 3. The term 'perils of the seas' does not include the ordinary action of wind and waves: see *Samuel & Co v Dumas* (1922) 13 Ll LR 503. For 'maritime claim', see C.J.J.A. 1982, Sch 3.

market. 1. Trading area in which activities are held under common law, by which 'everyone was entitled to come into the market place to sell and buy without let or hindrance, moving about or walking to and fro': *R v Barnsley Metropolitan BC ex p Hook* [1976] 3 All ER 452. 2. 'A place to which sellers who have not found buyers take their goods in the hope of finding buyers, and to which buyers resort in the hope of finding the goods they want': *Scottish CWS Ltd v Ulster Farmers' Mart Co Ltd* [1959] 2 All ER 486. See *Birmingham CC v Anvil Fairs* [1989] 1 WLR 312.

market abuse. Behaviour relating to specified investments traded on designated markets likely to be regarded as below standard, if such behaviour is likely to be considered as distorting the market in those investments or giving false information as to supply and demand in that market, or based on significant information not generally available in the market: F.S.M.A. 2000, s 118. For penalties, see s 123.

market, available. *See* AVAILABLE MARKET.

Market, Common. *See* COMMON MARKET.

market contract. Contract connected with a recognised investment exchange or recognised clearing house: Cos.A. 1989, s 155(1).

market maker. A person (individual, partnership or company) who holds himself out in compliance with the rules of a recognised stock exchange as willing to buy and sell securities at prices specified by him, and is recognised as doing so by that exchange: Company Securities (Insider Dealing) Act 1985, s 3(1) (inserted by F.S.A. 1986, s 174(2)).

market overt. An 'open public and legally constituted market', held on days prescribed by charter, custom or statute. It meant, in relation to the City of London (q.v.), every shop in which goods usually sold in that shop were exposed for sale. Where goods were sold in market overt, the buyer obtained title provided they were bought in good faith and without notice of any defect or lack of title on part of the seller: S.G.A. 1979, s 22(1). Abolished under S.G. (Amendment) A. 1994.

market price. 1. 'The value of marketable goods which a trader holds in stock either for sale or consumption in his business': *BSC Footwear v Ridgway* [1971] 2 All ER 534. 2. Price at which buyers and sellers are ready and willing to buy and sell in the ordinary course of trade.

market, statutory. In *R (Corporation of London) v Secretary of State for Environment* (2004) *The Times*, 27 December, the CA held that he lacks the power to consent to the Covent Garden Market Authority to grant leases at the market for the trade of fish and meat.

market value. 1. 'The price of the commodity in the market as between the manufacturer and an ordinary purchaser': *Orchard v Simpson* (1857) 2 CBNS 299. See I.C.T.A. 1988, s 146; Capital Allowances Act 2001, s 577. 2. In the case of compulsory purchase of land, the basis of compensation is the amount which the land if sold in the open market by a willing seller might be expected to realise. See Land Compensation Act 1961, s 5; Planning and Compensation Act 1991; *Palatine Graphic Art Co v Liverpool CC* [1986] QB 335; *Halstead v Manchester CC* [1998] 1 All ER 33. For the essence of 'true market value', see *Singer and Friedlander v Wood* (1977) 243 EG 212. 3. In relation to shares, means the amount that might reasonably be expected to be obtained from a sale of the interest in the open market: Income Tax (Pensions and Earnings) Act 2003, s 208.

marriage. The act or rite based on a consensual union creating the legal and social status of husband and wife. 'The voluntary union for life of one man and one woman to the exclusion of all others': Mat.C.A. 1857. Minimum age of parties is 16: Marriage Act 1949, s 2. (For parental consent, see Sch 2 (modified by F.L.R.A. 1987, s 9).) Marriages in England must be registered. See, e.g., Marriage Acts 1949–94; Marriage (Enabling) Act 1960; Marriage (Registrar General's Licence) Act 1970; Marriage (Prohibited Degrees of Relationship) Act 1986, Sch 1; Foreign Marriage (Amendment) Act 1988; European Convention on Human Rights 1950, art 12 (right to marry and found a family).

marriage articles. Contract setting out terms upon which a marriage settlement (q.v.) is to be executed.

marriage, breakdown of. *See* BREAKDOWN OF MARRIAGE.

marriage, capacity for. Family Division held in *Sheffield City Council v E* (2005) *The Times*, 20 January, that the question of capacity to marry should be treated as distinct from the problem of whether it was wise to marry any specific person, or at all, in the circumstances.

marriage ceremony, categories of. In English law, the principal categories are: civil marriage; marriage according to Anglican rites; marriage according to non-Anglican religious rites; Jewish and Quaker marriages.

marriage, Church of England. Under Marriage Act 1949, s 5, amended by Immigration and Asylum Act 1999, Sch 14, para 3, a Church of England marriage is solemnised only after publication of banns or by authority of a common or special licence or superintendent registrar's certificate. It must be celebrated by a clergyman in the presence of two or more witnesses: s 47.

marriage, civil. Marriage which takes place in a register office in the presence of a registrar, and involving a secular ceremony. See Marriage Act 1949, ss 45, 46, modified by Marriage Ceremony (Prescribed Words) Act 1996; Marriage Act 1994, enabling civil marriages to take place on premises approved by local authorities.

marriage, common-law. *See* COMMON-LAW MARRIAGE.

marriage, common licence for. Licence, issued under the authority of the bishop of a diocese, enabling the parties to marry in the Church of England without waiting for the publication of banns (q.v.). See Marriage Act 1949.

marriage consideration. Marriage is 'the most valuable consideration imaginable': *A-G v Jacobs-Smith* [1895] 2 QB 341. Persons within the consideration are husband, wife, issue of the marriage and grandchildren. See *Re Plumptre's Settlement* [1910] 1 Ch 609; *Re Cook's ST* [1965] Ch 902. *See* CONSIDERATION.

marriage, consummation of. *See* CONSUMMATION OF A MARRIAGE.

marriage, defects invalidating. Under Marriage Act 1949, a marriage is void if the parties have knowingly and wilfully disregarded certain requirements, e.g., as in the case of a ceremony in the absence of a registrar, where that is required, or marriage by a person not in Holy Orders: see ss 25, 49; *CAO v Bath* [2000] 1 FLR 8. Failure to obtain parental consent does not invalidate a marriage: s 48(1). See Marriage Act 1994, Schedule, para 3; Immigration and Asylum Act 1999, Sch 14, para 7.

marriage, mistake in. *See* MISTAKE AND MARRIAGE.

marriage, notice of. Both parties to a proposed marriage must give notice to the registrar; he is required to ask for names and surnames, marital status, occupations, places of residence and nationality: Marriage Act 1949, s 27, amended by Immigration and Asylum Act 1999, s 161. Under 1949 Act, s 28A, inserted by 1999 Act, s 162, the registrar is empowered to require appropriate evidence of name, age, marital status and nationality to be given. Where registrar refuses to issue a marriage certificate because he is not satisfied that there is no lawful impediment to a marriage, appeal may be made to the Registrar General: 1949 Act, s 31A, inserted by 1999 Act, s 163.

marriage, nullity of. *See* NULLITY OF MARRIAGE.

marriage of housebound and detained persons. Under Marriage Act 1983, marriages may be solemnised at the place of residence if one of the parties is housebound, i.e, unable to leave the home because of illness or disability, or one of the parties is detained in prison, and notice has been given under Marriage Act 1949, s 27. See Immigration and Asylum Act 1999, ss 160, 161.

marriage of prisoner and prosecution witness. In *R (CPS)* v *Registrar-General of Births, Deaths and Marriages* (2002) *The Times*, 14 November, CA held that a proposed marriage between a prisoner on remand and his long-term partner could not be prevented by the court on public policy grounds even though the marriage would render the partner a non-compellable witness for the prosecution in the prisoner's trial for murder. This did not constitute a perversion to the course of justice. See also European Convention, art 12 (right to marry).

marriage, polygamous. A person is party to a polygamous marriage if he is a party to a marriage entered into under a law which permits polygamy, and either party to the marriage has a spouse additional to the other party: Tax Credits Act 2002, s 43(2).

marriage, presumption of. See PRESUMPTION OF MARRIAGE VALIDITY.

marriage, proof of. Procedure whereby a valid marriage is proved by the production of the marriage certificate and proof of identity; by declaration of a deceased person against interest or in the course of duty; by records (see Civil Evidence Act 1968); by evidence of the ceremony given by one who was present; by presumption from cohabitation (see *Re Taylor* [1961] 1 WLR 9).

marriage, Registrar General's licence relating to. Under Marriage (Registrar General's Licence) Act 1970, the Registrar General is empowered to license a marriage to be solemnised elsewhere than in a registered building or register office. Used where Registrar General is satisfied that one of the persons to be married is not expected to recover from an illness and cannot be moved to a place where a normal marriage would be solemnised. See Immigration and Asylum Act 1999, Sch 14, para 38.

marriage, registration of. Procedure whereby the following particulars of a marriage are officially recorded: date; surname; residence of parties; surname and profession of male parents; church where marriage takes place (in the case of a Church of England marriage).

marriage settlement. Arrangement made prior to and in consideration of a marriage, resulting in the settlement (q.v.) of property for the benefit of spouses and children.

marriage, sham. See SHAM MARRIAGE.

marriage, special licence for. Special dispensation granted by the discretion of the Archbishop of Canterbury, enabling a marriage to be solemnised under Church of England rites at any convenient place and time. See Marriage Act 1949, s 79(9).

marriage, Superintendent-Registrar's certificate relating to. Certificate issued by the Superintendent-Registrar of the district in which the parties have lived for the preceding seven days. Notice is issued in a document open to public inspection. If no caveat is entered, the certificate is issued for production to the person before whom the marriage is solemnised. See Marriage Act 1949; Deregulation (Validity of Civil Preliminaries to Marriage) Order 1997, SI 97/986; Immigration and Asylum Act 1999, Part IX.

marriage, void and voidable. See NULLITY OF MARRIAGE.

marriage, will in contemplation of. In general, a will is revoked automatically by a testator's marriage, but where it appears from the will that at the time it was made the testator was expecting to be married to a particular person and that he intended that the will should not be revoked by his marriage, the will is not revoked by his marriage to that person: W.A. 1837, s 18(1), (3) (as substituted by A.J.A. 1982, s 18(1)). (Where a testator dies after 1995, then, in the absence of a contrary intention stated in the will, any gift in the will to his former spouse (given a dissolution of the marriage) will pass, and any provision in the will which appoints her as an executor has effect as if she had died on the termination of the marriage: W.A. 1837, s 18A(1), inserted by Law Reform (Succession) Act 1995, s 3(1).)

married couple. A man and woman who are married to each other and are members of the same household: S.S.A. 1986, s 20(11). (An 'unmarried couple' means a man and a woman who are not married to each other but are living together as husband and wife.)

marshalling. Equitable principle under which, where there are two creditors of one debtor, and one creditor is entitled to resort to one fund only for payment of the debt, while the other creditor is entitled to resort to two funds, the funds will be marshalled by the court so that both creditors may be satisfied, as far as possible. Example: X mortgages Blackacre and Whiteacre to Y. Later X mortgages Blackacre to Z. If Y takes out of Blackacre money owing to him which he could have taken out of Whiteacre, then, to that extent, equity will give Z a charge on Whiteacre. Doctrine applies only where the mortgagor of both properties is the same person. See *Trimmer* v *Bayne (No. 2)* (1803) 9 Ves 209.

martial law. Rule by military authorities during an emergency when the civil authority cannot function. See *Ex p Marais* [1902] AC 109.

masks, removal of. A constable may require any person to remove any item which he reasonably believes is being worn wholly or mainly for the purpose of concealing identity: C.J.P.O.A. 1994, s 60(4A), inserted by C.D.A. 1998, s 25.

master and servant. Relationship, known now as 'employer and employee', subsisting between one person and another who controls his work. Distinguished from 'independent contractor' (q.v.). 'The ultimate question is . . . who is entitled to give the orders as to how the work shall be done': *Mersey Docks and Harbour Board* v *Coggins & Griffiths Ltd* [1947] 1 AC 1. Indicia of the relationship were held in *Short* v *Henderson Ltd* (1946) 62 TLR 427 to be: master's

power of selection of his servant; payment of wages or other remuneration; master's right to control the method of doing the work; master's right of suspension or dismissal. In a relationship of this kind a master's implied duties are to retain the servant for an agreed period, to pay agreed remuneration and to take reasonable care for servant's safety. See, e.g., E.R.A. 1996; *Clifford* v *UDM* [1991] IRLR 518. *See* EMPLOYEE; EMPLOYER; SERVANT.

Master of the Bench. Full title of a Bencher (q.v.).

Master of the Rolls. Formerly a keeper of the records of Chancery, later, a judge of the Court of Chancery. Now a member of the High Court (q.v.) and *ex-officio* member of the Court of Appeal (q.v.). Presides over the Civil Division of the Court of Appeal: see S.C.A. 1981, s 10. For delegation of his functions, see C.L.S.A. 1990, s 73.

Masters of the Supreme Court. Masters in the Chancery Division, Masters of the QBD and Masters who are involved in taxation of costs, and cases in the Chancery and QBD. A master has the general jurisdiction of a judge in chambers. See S.C.A. 1981, s 89.

material fact. 'Every fact is material which would, if known, reasonably affect the minds of prudent, experienced insurers in deciding whether they will accept the risk': *Stroshein* v *Wawanesa Mutual Insurance Co* [1943] 3 WLR 509. See *St Paul Fire Insurance Co* v *McConnell* [1996] 1 All ER 96.

maternity allowance, state. Under S.S. (Contributions and Benefits) A. 1992, s 35(1), substituted by W.R.P.A. 1999, s 53, a woman is entitled to a maternity allowance at an appropriate rate, determined under s 35A, if she has become pregnant and has reached, or been confined before reaching, the commencement of the 11th week before the expected week of confinement, and has been engaged in employment as an employed or self-employed earner for any part of the week in the case of at least 26 of the 66 weeks immediately preceding the expected week of confinement, and her average weekly earnings are not less than the maternity allowance threshold, and she is not entitled to statutory maternity pay for the same week in respect of the same pregnancy.

maternity leave. Under E.R.A. 1996, s 71, substituted by Employment Relations Act 1999, ss 7–9, Sch 4, an employee may, provided that she satisfies prescribed conditions, be absent from work at any time during an ordinary maternity leave period. She is entitled to return from leave to the job in which she was employed before her absence on terms and conditions no less favourable than those which would have applied if she had not been absent. See SI 99/3312, referring to period of maternity leave of 18 weeks, additional maternity leave for 28 weeks from beginning of week of childbirth, right to leave for women employed for at least one year.

matrimonial home. The domicile of a husband and wife who live, or have lived together. Where one spouse is not a co-owner of the home, certain matrimonial home rights, e.g., the right, if in occupation, not to be evicted or excluded from the home by the other spouse, except by leave of the court, and, if not in occupation, the right, by leave of the court, to enter and occupy the home: see F.L.A. 1996, Part IV (now in force). A right of this type is registrable as a Class F land charge in the register of land charges (q.v.). See *Bull v Bull* [1995] 1 QB 234; *Baroden v Dhillon* [1998] 1 FLR 524; Land Registration (Matrimonial Home Rights) Rules 1997 (SI 97/1964); L.R.R. 2001.

matrimonial home, equitable interest in. In *Mountney v Treharne* (2002) *The Times*, 9 September, the CA held that where a property adjustment order is made, under which a husband transfers his interest in the matrimonial home to his wife, this effectively grants her an equitable interest at the time when the order takes effect; further, the husband's trustee in bankruptcy takes subject to the order.

matrimonial home, order restricting occupation of. Order available under F.L.A. 1996, Part IV (now in force) restricting right of occupation of the home in cases of domestic violence (q.v.). *See* INJUNCTIONS RELATING TO DOMESTIC VIOLENCE.

matrimonial property, financial provision. In *Lambert v Lambert* (2002) 152 NLJ 1751, the CA held that, in relation to a division of matrimonial property, there should be an end to the 'sterile assertion' that the contribution of the breadwinner weighs heavier than that of the homemaker; there was no justification for an unequal division of family property on the basis of such an assertion.

maturity. Time at which a bill of exchange (q.v.) becomes due.

mayor. Chairman of a city council elected by councillors. See L.G.A. 1972, ss 3–5, 245. For election by electors for a local authority area, see L.G.A. 2000, s 39.

Mayor of London. *See* GREATER LONDON AUTHORITY: LONDON, MAYOR OF.

Mayor's and City of London Court. London court formally abolished under Courts Act 1971. The Act provides, however, that the county court for the City of London county court district is to be known as the Mayor's and City of London Court: s 42.

McKenzie friend. One who, while not participating in proceedings, and having no *locus standi* (q.v.), may 'sit, advise and quietly offer help' to a participant. See C.L.S.A. 1990, s 27; *Re H (Chambers Proceedings: McKenzie Friend)* [1997] 2 FLR 423; *R v Bow County Court ex p Pelling* [1999] 3 FCR 97 (right of a litigant in person to have the assistance of a McKenzie friend unless the judge is satisfied that the interests of justice do not require this); *Bache v Essex CC* [2000] EAT 251.

measure. Legislation concerning matters relating to the Church of England, intended to have effect as statutes in accordance with the provisions of Church of England (Assembly) Powers Act 1919, as amended by Synodical

Government Measure 1969. See, e.g., Cathedrals Measure 1999 (No. 1).

measure of damages by reason of death. 'The actual pecuniary loss of each individual entitled to sue can only be ascertained by balancing, on the one hand, the loss to him of the future pecuniary benefit, and on the other, any pecuniary advantage which from whatever source comes to him by reason of the death': *Davies v Powell Duffryn Associated Collieries Ltd* [1942] AC 601. The claim is brought in the name of the executor or administrator of the deceased. It lies for the benefit of the wife, husband, children, grandchildren, father, mother, step-parents, grandparents, etc. See, e.g., *Taylor v O'Connor* [1971] AC 115; A.J.A. 1982, s 1.

measure of damages in contract. The principle upon which assessment of actual monetary compensation is to be paid for damage. In general, in the case of contract, there must be *restitutio in integrum* (q.v.), i.e., compensation in full must be paid for the proximate damage suffered by the plaintiff. See *Hadley v Baxendale* (1854) 9 Exch 341; *Victoria Laundry Ltd v Newman Industries Ltd* [1949] 2 KB 528, 'Where a party sustains a loss by reason of a breach of contract he is, as far as money can do it, to be placed in the same situation with respect to damages as if the contract had been performed': *per* Parke B in *Robinson v Harman* (1848) 1 Exch 850. See *Roxley Electronics v Forsyth* [1995] 3 WLR 118 (damages for partial failure of contract). The contractual term, 'consequential loss', is to be interpreted as meaning the loss proved by plaintiff in excess of that which was a direct result of the breach, based upon the rule in *Hadley v Baxendale (supra)*: *British Sugar plc v NEI Power Projects Ltd* (1997) *The Times*, 21 February. *See* DAMAGES.

measure of damages in contract, non-physical distress and annoyance. A contract breaker is not generally liable for distress, anxiety caused by the breach; but, exceptionally, where the object of the contract is to provide pleasure, relax-ation, damages may be awarded if the fruit of the contract is not provided. In cases not falling within this exception, damages are recoverable for physical inconvenience and discomfort caused by the breach: see *Watts v Morrow* [1991] 1 WLR 1421; *Farley v Skinner* (2000) *The Times*, 14 April (aircraft noise damages not recoverable).

measure of damages in tort. 'That sum of money which will put the party who has been injured, or who has suffered, in the same position as he would have been if he had not sustained the wrong for which he is now getting his compensation or reparation': *per* Lord Blackburn in *Livingstone v Rawyards Coal Co* (1880) 5 App Cas 25. See *Hicks v S Yorks Police* [1992] 1 All ER 690.

mediation. The act of a neutral third party relating to the settling of a dispute between two contending parties. See F.L.A. 1996, Part III (repealed by Acc.J.A. 1999, Sch 15).

mediation, supervision and. In *Al-Khatib v Masry* (2004) *The Times*, 21 October, the CA held that it is important for there to be an appropriate element of judicial supervision in the processes attached to mediation.

mediation, willingness of parties. It was held in *Shirayama v Danovo* [2004] BLR 207 that the court possesses jurisdiction to order mediation even where one party shows no willingness to participate in the process.

medical complaints. It was held in *David v General Medical Council* (2005) *The Times*, 12 January, that particular caution was needed by the court in deciding whether to quash decisions of the GMC Preliminary Proceedings Committee against any complaints referred to the Committee's Professional Conduct Committee.

medical examination, remand for. A magistrates' court may remand accused for medical examination if, on his trial for an offence punishable on summary conviction with imprisonment, the court is satisfied that he did the act or made the omission charged but is of the opinion that an inquiry is necessary into his physical or mental condition before the method of dealing with him is ascertained: P.C.C.(S.)A. 2000, s 11(1). The adjournment may be for 3–11 weeks: s 11(2).

medical practitioner. One who holds one or more primary UK qualifications and has passed a qualifying examination and satisfied the requirements of the Medical Act 1983, Part II, as to experience; or being a national of any member state of the Communities, holds one or more primary European qualifications: 1983 Act, s 3. See also Medical Qualifications (Amendment) Act 1991; National Health Service Act 1977, s 46, substituted by Health Act 1999, s 40 (disqualification of practitioners because of fraud or conduct prejudicial to the efficiency of the health services).

medical treatment. Medical, surgical or rehabilitative treatment: S.S.A. 1975, s 20. May include nursing: M.H.A. 1983, s 145(1). See also S.S. Contributions and Benefits Act 1992, s 122(1). For refusal of court to order a doctor to adopt a course of treatment, see *Re J* [1992] 3 WLR 507; *SW Herts HA v KB* [1994] 2 FCR 1051. For guidelines to be followed where there are severe doubts as to a patient's capacity to accept or refuse treatment, see *St George's Healthcare NHS Trust v S (Guidelines)* [1999] Fam 26. Patient's interests are paramount: *A NHS Trust v D* (2000) *The Times*, 19 July.

medical treatment, refusal of. It was held in *B v An NHS Hospital Trust* (2002) 152 NLJ 470 that there was a presumption that a patient possesses the mental capacity to decide whether to accept or refuse medical treatment in circumstances where a refusal will almost certainly lead to the patient's death. If mental capacity is not in issue and the patient has chosen to refuse treatment, the decision must be respected by the doctors. Questions as to the 'best interests of the patient' are irrelevant. (B later died after asking doctors to switch off her life-support machine: *The Times*, 30 April 2002, p. 7.)

medicine. 'Everything which is to be applied for the purpose of healing, whether externally or internally': *per* Lush J in *Berry v Henderson* (1870) LR 5 QB 296.

mediums, fraudulent. *See* WITCHCRAFT.

meeting, board. *See* BOARD MEETING.

meetings, company. Meetings of a company (q.v.) attended by shareholders. (1) Annual general meetings (see Cos.A. 1985, s 366) held each calendar year, with not more than 15 months between meetings. (2) Extraordinary general meetings, held whenever the directors wish (see Table A, art 37) or on requisition by members holding at least one-tenth of the paid-up capital carrying right to vote. (3) Class meetings, called for a particular class of shareholder to discuss, e.g., variation of class rights. See Cos.A. 1985, s 371; *Cane v Jones* [1981] 1 All ER 533. *See* RESOLUTION; VOTING AT MEETINGS.

Member of Parliament. One elected by a constituency to sit in the House of Commons (q.v.) Persons disqualified from membership of the Commons include, e.g., most peers, judges, mental patients, certain classes of prisoner. See House of Commons Disqualification Act 1975, Representation of the People Acts 1983, 1985. *See* PARLIAMENT.

Members' oath. A Member of Parliament may not sit and vote unless he has taken the oath (or has made a solemn affirmation under Oaths Act 1978, s 5). The oath (see Promissory Oaths Act 1868) is: 'I do swear that I will be faithful and bear true allegiance to Her Majesty Queen Elizabeth, her heirs and successors, according to law. So help me God.'

members of a company. Those who have subscribed to a company's memorandum of association (q.v.), or have agreed to become members by applying for an allotment of shares or by taking a transfer from an existing member. Persons cease to be members by, e.g., forfeiture, surrender, transfer, death. Capacity to become a member is that of the ordinary rules of contract.

A company may not be 'a member of itself': *Kirby* v *Wilkins* [1929] 2 Ch 444. See Cos.A. 1985, s 22; Ins.A. 1986, s 250; Commonwealth Development Corporation Act 1999, Sch 2, para 7. *See* COMPANY.

members, register of. *See* REGISTER OF MEMBERS.

memorandum. A note recording the particulars of an event, e.g., a commercial transaction.

memorandum of association. *See* ASSOCIATION, MEMORANDUM OF.

menaces, demand with. For the *actus reus* of blackmail see Th.A. 1968, s 21. 'If the circumstances of the case were such that an ordinary reasonable man would understand that a demand for money was being made upon him and that the demand was accompanied by menaces – not perhaps direct, but veiled menaces – so that his ordinary balance of mind was upset, then you would be justified in coming to the conclusion that a demand with menaces had been made': *R* v *Collister* (1955) 39 Cr App R 100; *R* v *Garwood* [1987] 1 WLR 319. *See* BLACKMAIL.

men, indecent assault on. *See* INDECENT ASSAULT ON MEN.

mens rea. Translated as 'guilty mind' or 'wicked mind'. More accurately, 'criminal intention, or an intention to do the act which is made penal by statute or by the common law': *Allard* v *Selfridge Ltd* [1925] 1 KB 129. The so-called 'fault element' of an offence. May include also recklessness relating to the circumstances and consequences of an act which comprise the *actus reus* (q.v.). See *R* v *Tolson* (1889) 23 QBD 168; *Sweet* v *Parsley* [1970] AC 132. It does not involve blameworthiness: *R* v *Dodman* [1998] 2 Cr App R 338. In general, there must be a coincidence of time of *actus reus* and *mens rea*: see, e.g., *Fagan* v *MPC* [1969] 1 QB 439 (*actus reus* as a continuing act). *See* ACTUS NON FACIT REUM NISI MENS SIT REA; INTENTION; MOTIVE.

Mental Capacity Bill 2004. The Bill seeks to establish a system of advanced decisions, lasting powers of attorney, and court-appointed deputies authorised to refuse treatment on behalf of patients.

mental disorder. 'Mental illness, arrested or incomplete development of mind, psychopathic disorder, and any other disorder or disability of mind': M.H.A. 1983, s 1(2). A person may not be classified as mentally disordered by reason only of 'promiscuity or other immoral conduct, sexual deviancy [q.v.] or dependence on alcohol or drugs': M.H.A. 1983, s 1(3). Categories include mental illness, severe mental impairment, mental impairment and psychopathic disorder (q.v.). 'Severe mental impairment' is 'a state of arrested or incomplete development of mind which includes severe impairment of intelligence and social functioning and is associated with abnormally aggressive or seriously irresponsible conduct': M.H.A. 1983, s 1(2). ('Mental impairment' is defined similarly – see s 1(2) – but includes 'significant impairment of intelligence'.) See M.H.A. 1983, Part I; Protection of Children Act 1999, s 12(1). For confessions by a mentally handicapped person, see P.&C.E.A. 1984, s 77 (jury must be warned of the special need for caution where case against such a person depends wholly or substantially on his confession made not in the presence of an independent witness). See *Botchett* v *CAO* (1996) 32 BMLR 153.

mental distress. Generally involves worry, anxiety, grief, despair, etc. Should be differentiated from nervous shock (q.v.). Damages for mental distress are rarely awarded in a claim for breach of contract (see *Addis* v *Gramophone* Co [1909] AC 488; *Jarvis* v *Swans Tours* [1973] QB 233); they may be awarded in tort where the cause is, e.g., nuisance or assault or battery (see *Bone* v *Seale* [1975] 1 WLR 797).

Mental Health Commission. Authority set up under M.H.A. 1983, s 121, with a general protective function over detained patients. May visit and interview patients and investigate complaints.

Mental Health Review Tribunals, Area. Bodies set up under M.H.A. 1959, consisting of doctors, lawyers and others,

substituted by G.L.A.A. 1999, s 23. See SIs 00/1474/1549.

metropolitan stipendiary magistrates. Full-time, professional magistrates who sit as sole justices in Metropolitan Stipendiary Courts, i.e., petty sessional courts in London. See Justices of the Peace Act 1997, ss 16–20. To be known as District Judges (Magistrates' Courts): see 1997 Act, s 10A, substituted by Acc.J.A. 1999, s 78(1). See STIPENDIARY MAGISTRATES.

Middle Temple. One of the Inns of Court (q.v.). It was granted its premises in perpetuity by James I in 1609.

military prison, death in. It was held in *R (Al-Skeini)* v *Secretary of State for Defence* (2004) *The Times*, 20 December, that the European Convention on Human Rights obligated the UK authorities to hold an investigation into a death at the hands of soldiers serving in Iraq.

military testament. A privileged will (q.v.) made by a soldier on active service.

mine. 'An excavation or system of excavations made for the purpose of, or in connection with, the getting, wholly or substantially by means involving the employment of persons below ground, of minerals . . . or products of minerals': Mines and Quarries Act 1954, s 180(1).

minerals. 'All substances in, on or under the land, obtainable by underground or surface working': S.L.A. 1925, s 117(1)(*xiv*). See also I.C.T.A. 1988, s 122(6); T.C.P.A. 1990, s 336; Capital Allowances Act 1990, s 161 (for 'mineral deposits'); Planning and Compensation Act 1991, Sch 1, para 7; T.C.G.A. 1992, s 201 (mineral royalties).

minimum subscription. Minimum amount of capital, decided on by directors or promoters of a company (q.v.) which will allow them to provide for preliminary expenses, underwriting commissions, price of property to be paid from proceeds of issue, working capital. Must be stated in the prospectus (q.v.): Cos.A. 1985, s 83.

minimum term. In *Practice Statement Life Sentences* [2002] 1 WLR 1789, replacing *Practice Statement (Juveniles:*

Murder Tariff) [2002] 1 WLR 1655, the Lord Chief Justice announced the term 'tariff' is no longer to be used, because of misunderstanding. It is to be replaced by 'minimum term', to make clear that, even when released, an offender has not served his sentence, which continues for the remainder of his life. When announcing a minimum term, the judge should make it clear how that term has been calculated. In exceptionally grave cases, the judge, rather than setting a whole life minimum term, can state that there is no minimum period which is appropriate in that particular case.

minimum wage, enforcement. Under National Minimum Wage (Enforcement Notices) Act 2003, s 1, enforcement officers are empowered to issue enforcement notices relating to past pay periods where some or all of past or present workers are concerned. This restores the position before *Inland Revenue* v *Bebb Travel* [2003] EWCA Civ 563. Any period that is more than six years before the date on which the notice is served will not be covered. The Act came into force on 8 July, 2003.

minimum wages. See WAGE, NATIONAL MINIMUM.

mining lease. A tenant for life (q.v.) may lease the whole or part of the land for 100 years in the case of a mining lease: S.L.A. 1925, s 41. If the tenant is impeachable for waste (q.v.) relating to minerals (q.v.), three-quarters of the rent becomes capital. For a definition of 'mining operation', see T.C.P.A. 1990, s 55. See Mineral Workings Act 1985; I.C.T.A. 1988, s 122(6); Capital Allowances Act 1990, s 121.

ministerial responsibility. Doctrine (based on convention) that ministers of the government are responsible to Parliament (q.v.) for the exercise of the powers and duties of their departments, whether personally authorised by ministers or not. See COLLECTIVE RESPONSIBILITY.

Minister of the Crown. 'The holder of any office in Her Majesty's Government in the UK, and includes the Treasury': Ministers of the Crown Act 1975, s 8(1);

Government Trading Act 1990, s 1. Appointed by the Crown on the Prime Minister's advice. Ministers are ranked as: Cabinet Ministers, Ministers of State, Parliamentary Under-Secretaries of State, Parliamentary Secretaries, Parliamentary Private Secretaries. For 'ministerial communications', see F.I.A. 2000, s 35(5).

Ministry. 1. The government, headed by the Prime Minister (q.v.). 2. A department of government.

minor. A person under the age of 18. *See* INFANT.

minor, conveyance of legal estate to. Where, after the commencement of this Act a person purports to convey a legal estate to a minor, the conveyance cannot pass that estate, but operates as a declaration that the land is held in trust for the minor, or if that person purports to convey it to the minor in trust for any persons, for those persons: Trusts of Land and Appointment of Trustees Act 1996, Sch 1, para 1(1).

minor interests. Term formerly used in land registration under the LRA 1925 where they were defined as 'the interests not capable of being disposed of or created by registered dispositions and capable of being overridden (whether or not a purchaser has notice thereof) by the proprietors unless protected as provided by this Act, and all rights and interests which are not registered or protected on the register and are not overriding interests': L.R.A. 1925, s 3(*xv*). Originally they were protected by notice, inhibition, restriction or caution (qq.v.). See *Peffer* v *Rigg* [1977] 1 WLR 285; *Lyus* v *Prowsa Developments Ltd* [1982] 1 WLR 1044. Under the LRA 2002 the term has supposedly been abandoned, though it continues to be used colloquially. The LRA 2002 has reduced the categories whereby such interests can be protected to two, cautions and notices. *See* OVERRIDING INTERESTS.

minority. 1. The smaller group in number of those present at an assembly or other meeting. 2. Below 18 years of age: F.L.R.A. 1969.

minority, fraud on. *See* FRAUD ON MINORITY.

minority shareholders, oppression of. Conduct of a company (q.v.) unfairly prejudicial to the interests of some of its shareholders. See, e.g., *Foss* v *Harbottle* (1843) 2 Hare 461; *Re Sam Weller Ltd* [1990] BCLC 80 (test of oppression is objective); *Re Regional Airports* [1999] 2 BCLC 30; *O'Neill* v *Phillips* (1999) 149 NLJ 805 (the court must have regard to equitable considerations in determining whether the majority's reliance upon their strict legal powers is unfair). See Cos.A. 1985, s 459, as amended by Cos.A. 1989, s 145, Sch 19, para 11. *See* SHAREHOLDERS, PROTECTION OF.

minors' contracts. A minor (q.v.) is bound by contracts: for the sale of necessary goods sold and actually delivered to him; for necessary services; for beneficial contracts of service, apprenticeship. See *Nash* v *Inman* [1908] 2 KB 1; *Doyle* v *White City Stadium* [1935] 1 KB 110. Minors' Contracts Act 1987, s 1, repealed Infants Relief Act 1874 (which invalidated certain contracts made by minors and prohibited actions to enforce contracts ratified after majority) and Betting and Loans (Infants) Act 1892 (invalidating contracts to repay loans advanced during minority). The 1987 Act gives the court a discretionary power to order restoration to a seller where a minor has acquired property on credit and fails to pay for it: s 3. *See* NECESSARIES.

minutes. Notes providing a record of proceedings. A company must keep minutes of its meetings. See Cos.A. 1985, ss 382, 722; Cos.A. 1989, s 143. Minutes signed by a chairman are usually prima facie evidence of proceedings.

misadministration. CA held in *N British Housing Association* v *Matthews* (2005) *The Times*, 11 January, that where access in relation to a reduction in rent, an attribution of these arrears to a housing benefit authority's misadministration is not to be considered as an exceptional circumstance rendering application of the schemes of severity.

misadventure. An accident which is not the result of a criminal or negligent act.

There is no valid distinction between a coroner's verdicts of 'death by misadventure' and 'accidental death': *R v Coroner for City of Portsmouth ex p Anderson* [1987] 1 WLR 1640.

misappropriation. Dishonest appropriation (q.v.) of another's property. See Th.A. 1968, ss 1, 3(1) (assumption of another's rights); *R v Gomez* [1991] 3 All ER 394.

miscarriage. 1. Failure in the administration of justice. For compensation, see C.J.A. 1988, s 133; *R v Secretary of State for Home Department ex p Atlantic Commercial Ltd* [1997] BCC 692 (compensation not payable to company). 2. Synonym for abortion (q.v.). For attempting to procure a miscarriage, see O.P.A. 1861, s 58. 3. Term used in Statute of Frauds 1677, s 4, relating to 'that species of wrongful act for the consequences of which the law would make the party civilly responsible': *Kirkham v Marter* (1819) 2 B & Ald 613. 4. Meaning of the term (which refers, generally, to a non-induced, spontaneous abortion) was considered by Munby J in *R (Smeaton) v Secretary of State for Health* (2002) *The Times*, 2 May. The word is an ordinary English word of flexible meaning which Parliament chose not to define in Offences against the Person Act 1861, ss 58, 59. It should be interpreted as currently understood and in the light of current medical knowledge. It is the termination of pregnancy which begins once the blastocyst is implanted in the endometrium, and this clearly excludes results brought about by use of the 'morning-after' pill. (See Prescription Only Medicines (Human Use) Amendment (No. 3) Order 2000).

miscarriage of justice. In *R (Mullen) v Secretary of State for Home Department* [2004] UKHL 18, the HL held that the term 'miscarriage of justice' when used in the process of calculating and awarding statutory compensation, could refer to a case in which a person was clearly innocent, and it might be extended further to a case in which, as a result of some failure in the trial process, the person should not have been convicted, whether guilty or innocent. 'Wrongful conviction' is not a legal term of art and does not have a fixed meaning. In ordinary parlance it is extended to those who ought clearly not to have been convicted. The common factor in cases of this nature was that something had gone seriously wrong during the actual investigation of the offence or in the conduct of the trial.

mischief. 1. Harm resulting from intentional conduct. 2. The 'mischief of a statute' is the wrong for which it is intended to provide a remedy.

mischief rule. Method of construing a statute which necessitates asking: what was the common law before the statute; what was the mischief (q.v.) for which common law did not provide; what remedy has Parliament resolved so as to cure it; what is the true reason of that remedy? See *Heydon's Case* (1584) 3 Co Rep 7a; *Maunsell v Olins* [1975] AC 373; *Royal College of Nursing v DHSS* [1981] 2 WLR 279. *See* CONSTRUCTION; INTERPRETATION OF STATUTES.

misconduct. 'It means no more than incorrect or erroneous conduct of any kind of a serious nature, and does not necessarily connote moral censure': *per* Webster J in *R v Pharmaceutical Society ex p Sokoh* (1986) *The Times*, 4 December.

misconduct in public office. It was held in AG's Reference (No. 3 of 2004) [2004] EWCA Crim 868 that the offence of misconduct in a public office involves a clear breach of duty by the officer, based upon an act of commission or omission, which was not only negligent but which constituted an abuse of the trust of the public in the office holder and which lacked any excuse or justification. Conduct of a wilful nature was generally involved.

misconduct, professional. *See* PROFESSIONAL MISCONDUCT.

misconduct, wilful. *See* WILFUL MISCONDUCT.

misdemeanours. Offences not amounting to felonies (q.v.). Under C.L.A. 1967, s 1, all distinctions between felony and misdemeanour are abolished.

misdescription. Usually refers to a description of the subject matter of a contract which is false or misleading in some substantial way. In such a case the contract may be voidable at the option of the party who is misled.

misdescription of property. *See* PROPERTY, MISDESCRIPTION OF.

misdirection. Failure by the judge to direct the jury adequately as to the issues requiring a decision, or the law applicable, or the legal effect of evidence, or total failure to direct: *Hobbs* v *Tinling* [1929] 2 KB 1. A conviction may be quashed on this ground: see, e.g., *R* v *Trigg* [1963] 1 WLR 305. See O 59, r 11.

misfeasance. Improper performance of some essentially lawful act. See, e.g., Highways Act 1980, s 58. For common law crime of misbehaviour in public office, see *R* v *Bowden* [1996] 1 WLR 98. For test for misfeasance in public office, see *Three Rivers DC* v *Bank of England (No. 3)* (2000) 150 NLJ 769 (defendant must have acted in the knowledge that the act was beyond his powers, and that the act would probably injure the claimant or a class of persons of which claimant was a member).

misinformation and public judgment. Family Division held in *Blunkett* v *Quinn* (2004) *The Times*, 7 December, that the court could deliver in open court a judgment relating to a family appeal which had been heard in private, in order that false information in the public domain could be corrected.

misleading price. *See* PRICE, MISLEADING.

misprision. (*Mesprendre* = to make a mistake.) Misprision of felony was failure to report a felony (q.v.) committed by another: *Sykes* v *DPP* [1962] AC 528. See C.L.A. 1967, s 5(1), by which the offence no longer exists generally. Misprision of treason remains as a common-law offence committed when a person knows, or has reasonable cause to believe that another has committed treason and fails within a reasonable time to inform an appropriate authority. *See* TREASON.

misrepresentation. A false statement which misrepresents an existing material fact: which is made before the conclusion of a contract with a view to inducing another to enter that contract; which is made with the intention that the person to whom it is addressed shall act on it; which is acted on, having induced the contract; which is not merely extravagant advertising. 'In my opinion any behaviour, by words or conduct, is sufficient to be a misrepresentation if it is such as to mislead the other party. If it conveys a false impression, that is enough': *per* Denning LJ in *Curtis* v *Chemical Cleaning and Dyeing Co Ltd* [1951] 1 KB 805. See Misrepresentation Act 1967 (which, under s 2(1) creates statutory liability for misrepresentation, unless the person making the misrepresentation had reasonable ground to believe and did believe up to the moment of making the contract that the facts represented were true); *Hedley Byrne & Co* v *Heller & Partners* [1964] AC 465; *Spice Girls Ltd* v *Aprilia World Service* [2001] EMLR 8.

misrepresentation, fraudulent. A false representation made knowingly or without belief in its truth or recklessly, careless whether it be true or false: *Derry* v *Peek* (1889) 14 App Cas 337. See Misrepresentation Act 1967; F.S.M.A. 2000, s 397; *Clef Aquitaine* v *Laporte Materials* [2000] 3 All ER 493.

misrepresentation, innocent. A misrepresentation in which there is no element of fault, i.e., fraud or negligence. Remedies include avoidance and action for indemnity against any obligation created by the contract. See, e.g., *Lamare* v *Dixon* (1873) LR 6 HL 414.

misrepresentation, negligent. A false statement made by a person who has no reasonable grounds for believing that statement to be true. Remedies include avoidance, damages and rescission (qq.v.). See *Box* v *Midland Bank* [1979] 2 Lloyd's Rep 391; *Hussey* v *Eels* [1990] 1 All ER 449.

misstatements of fact, common law approach in defamation matters. See *Reynolds* v *Times Newspapers Ltd* [1999] 3 WLR 1010, *per* Lord Steyn: matters to be taken into account in giving weight to importance of freedom of expression in libel proceedings: nature, source of information and its significance as a matter of public concern; seriousness of allegation; steps taken to verify information; status of information; urgency of matter; whether comment had been sought from claimant; presence of claimant's side of the story; tone of article; time of publication. *See* PRIVILEGE, QUALIFIED.

mistake. *Common mistake* – both parties make the same error relating to a fundamental fact. *Mutual mistake* – both parties fail to understand each other. *Unilateral mistake* – only one party is mistaken. 'If mistake operates at all, it operates so as to negative or in some cases to nullify consent': *Bell* v *Lever Bros Ltd* [1932] AC 161. Mistake is, generally, no defence to an intentional tort (q.v.). See Lim.A. 1980, s 32 (as amended by Latent Damage Act 1986, s 4); *Raffles* v *Wichelhaus* (1864) 2 H & C 906; *Geest plc* v *Fyffes plc* [1999] 1 All ER 672. For 'mistake in equity', see *Laurence* v *Lexcourt Holdings* [1978] 2 All ER 810. For equitable relief and assertion of mistake in contract, see *Clarion Ltd* v *NPI* [2000] 2 All ER 265. For mistaken receipt of property, see Th.A. 1968, s 5(4). See also S.G.A. 1979, s 6. *See* IGNORANTIA JURIS.

mistake and marriage. A mistake is operative if it relates to the fundamental nature of the ceremony or the identity of the other party. See *Valier* v *Valier* (1925) 133 LT 830; *C* v *C* [1942] NZLR 356.

mistake of law. Error as to the law and its effects. Rarely a defence, since every person is presumed to know the law. Where money is paid under a mistake of law it is *prima facie* recoverable, if the mistake is the belief of the payer that he will be entitled to recover the amount paid provided that the mistake is related directly to the payment or it is involved directly in the payer–payee relationship and, save for the mistake, there would have been no payment: *Nurdin & Peacock* v *Ramsden & Co (No. 2)* [1999] 1 WLR 1249. *See* IGNORANTIA JURIS NEMINEM EXCUSAT.

mistake of law, compromise. In *Brennan* v *Bolt Burden* [2004] EWCA Civ 1017, the CA held that a compromise, like other types of contract, may be vitiated by a common mistake of law or fact only if the mistake renders the performance of the compromise impossible.

mistake, operative. A mistake which operates so as to avoid a contract, e.g., mistake as to the identity or existence of the subject matter, or as to the nature of the document signed. See *Hector* v *Lyons* (1989) 58 P & CR 156. *See* CONTRACT.

mistake, rectification in magistrates' court of. Power under statute enabling magistrates to vary or rescind a sentence or other defective order imposed by them in criminal proceedings: see M.C.A. 1980, s 142; *R* v *Thames Magistrates Court ex p Ramadan* [1999] 1 Cr App R 386.

mistress. Obsolescent term for a woman who, without marriage, lives as a wife. See *Spindlow* v *Spindlow* [1979] 1 All ER 169; *Layton* v *Martin* (1986) 16 Fam Law 212. *See* COMMON-LAW WIFE.

mistrial. An abortive trial, resulting from error or misconduct. 'To constitute a mistrial the proceedings must have been abortive from beginning to end': *R* v *Middlesex Judges ex p DPP* [1952] 2 QB 758.

mitigation. 1. Diminution, e.g., of some penalty. Plea in mitigation of sentence (i.e., statement of 'mitigating circumstances') may be heard at the end of the trial. Nothing may be urged in mitigation which could have constituted a defence to the offence charged. See *R* v *Bernard* [1996] Crim LR 673; *R* v *Jones* [1980] Crim LR 58 (counsel's duty to make plea in mitigation); C.P.I.A. 1996, s 58 (empowering the court to restrict reports of derogatory assertions made in speeches in mitigation); P.C.C.(S.)A. 2000, s 158. 2. Mitigation of damages: it is the duty of the plaintiff to take all reasonable steps to mitigate the loss caused by a breach of contract (q.v.). 3. Mitigation of tax involves taking advantage of the law so as to minimise the incidence of tax: see *Ensign Tankers Ltd* v *Stokes* [1992] 2 WLR 469.

mixed fund. A fund comprising the proceeds of the sale of real and personal property.

mixed property. Property compounded of realty and personalty and having some of the legal attributes of both. For 'mixed goods', see *Indian Oil Corporation* v *Greenstone Shipping Co* [1987] 3 WLR 869.

M'Naghten Rules. Answers of the House of Lords relating to questions concerning criminal responsibility, arising from the verdict in *R* v *M'Naghten* (1843) 10 C & F 200, where the accused, acting under insane delusion, killed the secretary of Sir Robert Peel and was found not guilty on the ground of insanity. The Rules remain legal criteria when insanity is pleaded as a defence. They state: (1) A person is presumed sane until the contrary is proved. (2) To establish a defence on the ground of insanity, it must be clearly proved that at the time of committing the offence, the accused was labouring under such a defect of reason, from disease of the mind (q.v.), as not to know the nature and quality of his act, or, if he did know it, that he did not know what he was doing was wrong. If the accused was conscious that the act was one he ought not to do and if that act was at the time contrary to law of the land, he is punishable. (3) Where a person under an insane delusion as to existing facts commits an offence in consequence thereof, and making the assumption that he labours under such partial delusion only, and is not in other respects insane, he is considered in the same situation as to responsibility as if the facts with respect to which the delusion exists were real. See *R* v *Codère* (1916) 12 Cr App R 21; *R* v *Windle* [1952] 2 QB 826; *R* v *Sullivan* [1983] 3 WLR 123. See comment of the Royal Commission on Capital Punishment (1953): 'The M'Naghten test is based on an entirely obsolete and misleading conception of the nature of insanity.'

mobile home. *See* HOME, MOBILE.

mobile phone masts. The process of considering and weighing up alternative sites is essential for the process of assessment of an application concerning the approval of the siting and construction of a telecommunications mast: *R (Phillips)* v *Secretary of State* (2003) 30 October. See Town and Country Planning Act 1990, s 288.

mobile 'phones, reprogramming of. Under Mobile Telephones (Reprogramming) Act 2002, s 1, it is an offence for a person to change a unique device identifier, or to interfere with the operation of that identifier. A 'unique device identifier' is an electronic equipment identifier which is unique to a mobile wireless communications device. The offence is not committed by the device manufacturer or by a person acting with the manufacturer's written consent. Under s 2, it is an offence to possess or supply anything for reprogramming purposes.

mobile photography in court. CA held in *R* v *D (Contempt of Court)* (2004) *The Times*, 13 May, that the use of mobile phones to make unlawful photographs during criminal proceedings had the potential to prejudice the administration of justice and might attract a sentence of immediate imprisonment.

mobility allowance. Component of disability living allowance paid to a person suffering from a physical disablement such that he is either unable to walk or is virtually unable to do so. See S.S. Contributions and Benefits A. 1992, s 73; W.R.P.A. 1999, s 67(3).

mock auction. Auction during which articles are given away or offered as gifts, or the right to bid is restricted to persons who have bought or agreed to buy an article, or any lot is sold to a bidder at a price lower than the amount of his highest bid for it, or part of the price is repaid or credited to him. An offence under Mock Auctions Act 1961. A 'lot' consists of, or includes, plate, linen, china, glass, books, furniture, jewellery, etc. See *Allen* v *Simmons* [1978] 1 WLR 79. *See* AUCTION; DUTCH AUCTION.

modifications. 'Includes additions, omissions and amendments': Disabled Persons (Services Consultation and Representation) Act 1986, s 16. See C.P.A. 1987, s 45(1).

moiety. One of two equal parts. See *Re Angus' WT* [1960] 1 WLR 1296.

molest. 'A wide plain word which . . . if I had to find one synonym for it, I should select "pester"': *per* Stephenson LJ in *Vaughan* v *Vaughan* [1973] 3 All ER 449.

molestation. 1. Activities, the tendency of which is, in general, to injure or annoy, which were intended to injure or annoy the complainant. See F.L.A. 1996, Part IV (now in force). Revelations to newspapers do not constitute molestation: C v C [1998] 2 WLR 599. 2. The following of a person in a persistent and disorderly manner, or by hiding his property, so as to compel him to do or abstain from doing an act.

molestation, non-, clause. *See* INJUNCTIONS RELATING TO DOMESTIC VIOLENCE.

monarchy. The institution of the Crown (q.v.). Dates of the reigns of England's monarchs are as shown in the following table:

House	Name	Year of accession
Normandy	William I	1066
	William II	1087
	Henry I	1100
	Stephen	1135
Plantagenet	Henry II	1154
	Richard I	1189
	John	1199
	Henry III	1216
	Edward I	1272
	Edward II	1307
	Edward III	1327
	Richard II	1377
Lancaster	Henry IV	1399
	Henry V	1413
	Henry VI	1422
York	Edward IV	1461
	Edward V	1483
	Richard III	1483
	Henry VII	1485
	Henry VIII	1509
	Edward VI	1547

House	Name	Year of accession
Tudor	Jane	1553
	Mary	1553
	Elizabeth I	1558
	James I	1603
Stuart	{Charles I	1625
	The Commonwealth	1649}
	{The Protectorate	1653}
	Charles II	1660
	James II	1685
Stuart	William & Mary	1689–94
	William III	1694–1702
	Anne	1702
	George I	1714
	George II	1727
	George III	1760
Hanover	George IV	1820
	William IV	1830
	Victoria	1837
Saxe-Coburg	Edward VII	1901
	George V	1910
Windsor	Edward VIII	1936
	George VI	1936
	Elizabeth II	1952

Monetary Policy Committee, Bank of England. Consists of Governor of the Bank, two Deputy Governors, and six other appointees. It has responsibility for formulation within the Bank of a broad approach to general monetary policy: Bank of England Act 1998, s 13.

money. That which by common consent is used as a medium of exchange, measure and store of value and standard of deferred payment. 'The word "money" at the present time has a diversity of meanings, and when it is found in a will there is no presumption that it has one meaning rather than another': *Perrin* v *Morgan* [1943] AC 399. See Currency Act 1983, s 1; *Re Gammon* [1986] CLY 3547; *Thompson* v *Hart* (2000) *The Times*, 24 April.

money Bill. A Bill (q.v.) usually introduced in the Commons which, in the opinion of the Speaker of the Commons, deals only with the imposition, repeal or alteration of taxation, the imposition of charges on the Consolidated Fund (q.v.), etc. If sent to the Lords at least one month before the end of the session and not passed by them, it is presented to the Crown and becomes an Act on the Royal Assent (q.v.) being signified: Parliament Act 1911. If the Speaker certifies a Bill to be a money Bill, this is recorded in the Journal; that certification is conclusive and may not be questioned by a court. (A 'money Bill' under the 1911 Act should not be confused with a 'Bill of aids and supplies', e.g., a Finance Bill, which may involve matters not mentioned in the definition of a 'money Bill'.) *See* PARLIAMENT.

money had and received. Claim (derived from former writ of account) for sum of money as 'had and received by defendant to his use', e.g., where defendant had received money on a failed consideration. See *Bank of America* v *Arnell* [1999] Lloyd's Rep Bank 399.

money judgment, costs of enforcing. Where a person takes steps to enforce a judgment or order of the High Court or a county court for payment of a sum due, the costs of any previous attempt to enforce that judgment are recoverable to the same extent as if they had been incurred in the taking of those steps: S.C.A. 1981, s 138, as inserted by C.L.S.A. 1990, s 15(1). See *QBD Practice Direction, No. 47*, November 1991.

money laundering. *See* LAUNDERING MONEY.

money laundering, disclosure relating to. Where a legal adviser is made aware of or has a suspicion of, some arrangement which is intended to facilitate money laundering, he must make an authorised disclosure: *P* v *P (Ancillary relief: Proceeds of crime)* [2003] EWHC 2260 (Fam).

moneylender. A person whose business is that of moneylending, or who advertises or announces himself or holds himself out in any way as carrying on that business. See Moneylenders Acts 1900, 1927 (repealed by C.C.A. 1974). He must be licensed by the Director General of Fair Trading (q.v.) in his name at a registered address.

money-lending company. A company, the ordinary business of which includes the making of loans or quasi-loans (q.v.) or the giving of guarantees in connection with them: Cos.A. 1985, s 338(1). See also Cos.A. 1989, s 138.

monitoring banking transactions. If it appears to a judicial authority in the UK, on an application made by a prosecuting authority, that the information which the applicant seeks to obtain is relevant to an investigation in the UK into criminal conduct, the judicial authority may request assistance under the Crime (International Co-operation) Act 2003, s 44. The assistance that may be requested under this section is any assistance in obtaining from a participating country details of transactions to be carried out in any period specified in the request in respect of any accounts at banks situated in that country.

Monopolies and Mergers Commission. Appointed by the Secretary of State to investigate and report on any question referred to it under Fair Trading Act 1973 with respect to: existence or possible existence of a monopoly situation (i.e., where at least one-quarter of the market is controlled by a single firm); the creation or possible creation of a merger situation (i.e., where two or more enterprises combine and the value of assets taken over exceeds a prescribed amount). It was dissolved under Competition Act 1998, s 45, and its functions were transferred to the Competition Commission (q.v.).

monopoly. 1. Market structure with only a single seller of a commodity or service. (A single buyer constitutes a 'monopsony'.) 2. Royal privilege for the buying, selling or making of a commodity, to be enjoyed by the grantee only. 3. Under Fair Trading Act 1973, 'control of one-quarter of the sales in a market'. Under EU legislation, state monopolies must not be allowed to obstruct free movement of goods and provision of services; their activities should be adjusted rather than prohibited: see Treaty of Rome 1957, art 37. For monopoly investigations, see Competition Act 1998, s 66.

month. There is a statutory presumption that in all deeds and other instruments coming into force on or after 1 January 1926, 'month' means 'calendar month' (i.e. one of the 12 time divisions of the year) unless the context otherwise provides. See L.P.A. 1925, s 61; I.A. 1978, Sch 1; and *Dodds* v *Walker* [1981] 2 All ER 609.

moot. An assembly of members of an Inn of Court (q.v.) or law school often in the form of a court, at which points of law are argued.

moratorium. An authorised period of delay in the performing of an obligation, e.g., settling a debt.

moratorium for insolvent debtor. An interim order of the court issued under Ins.A. 1986, s 252, where an individual debtor intends to make a voluntary arrangement or composition with his creditors. See Ins.A. 2000, Sch 3. The order will not be made unless the court is satisfied that, e.g., no previous application has been made by the debtor for an interim order in the year ending with the present day of application: s 255(1). *See* BANKRUPTCY.

moratorium where directors propose voluntary arrangement. Under Ins.A. 1986, amended by Ins.A. 2000, Sch 1, where directors of a company propose a voluntary arrangement and they are not excluded from being eligible (if, e.g., an administration order is in force or company is being wound up (see 1986 Act, Sch A1, para 4(1), inserted by 2000 Act, Sch 1)), they must submit to a nominee terms of arrangement and statement of company's affairs. During period of moratorium no petition for an administration order or winding-up may be presented, and obtaining of credit is limited: see Sch 1, para 12. For extension of moratorium, see Sch 1, para 32. For challenge of directors' actions during moratorium, see Sch 1, para 4.

mortgage. The disposition of a legal or equitable interest in land or other property in order to secure the payment of a debt or the discharge of some other obligation, and involving a provision for redemption (q.v.). See *Santley* v *Wilde* [1899] 2 Ch 474. Example: A borrows money from B and later conveys property to B as security for repayment of the loan; A is the *mortgagor*, B is the *mortgagee*. A mortgage may be legal (q.v.) or equitable (q.v.). It may be discharged by foreclosure (q.v.), redemption (q.v.), exercise of mortgagee's power of sale, merger (q.v.) or under L.P.A. 1925, s 115. See Law Com. No. 204 (1991); HFC Bank Act 1999, s 15(1)(*a*).

mortgage actions. Applications by mortgagees for possession of property or payment of principal, arrears, interest, etc. See O 88; Lim.A. 1980, s 29; *Royal Bank of Scotland plc* v *Etridge (No. 2)* [1998] 4 All ER 705.

mortgage and consumer credit. A mortgage comes within C.C.A. 1974 if it is in effect a regulated agreement (q.v.), i.e., a personal credit agreement under which the debtor is supplied by the creditor with a credit not above a statutorily-fixed amount (but loans made by a building society or local authority for house purchase are exempt). An improperly executed agreement can be enforced against a debtor by court order only. The court can open an agreement considered extortionate. The debtor may redeem prematurely at any time, on giving notice to the creditor: s 94. A security cannot be enforced by reason of breach of the regulated agreement without notice served on the debtor: s 87. See also ss 113, 177(2).

mortgage cases. In *Royal Bank of Scotland plc* v *Etridge (No. 2)* [2001] 3 WLR 1021, HL gave guidance as to when a bank is put on notice that a guarantor's relationship with a debtor may increase risk of undue influence. In general, this occurs whenever a wife offers to stand surety in relation to husband's debts. The bank must explain to her the risks of the secured transaction.

mortgage claims. Any claim by a mortgagee or motgagor or by any person having the right to foreclose or redeem any mortgage, being a claim in which there is a claim for any of the following remedies: payment of money secured by the mortgage; sale of mortgaged property; foreclosure; delivery of possession by mortgagor or mortgagee; redemption; reconveyance of property or its release from the security: CPR, Sch 1; O 88, r 1(1). Claim form may not be issued out of a district registry, which is not a Chancery district registry, unless mortgaged property is situated in the district of the registry: CPR, Sch 1; O 88, r 3(1).

mortgage debt, limitation on. Limitation Act 1980, s 20, affects the claim for a mortgage debt even though the mortgagee had exercised his power of sale prior to issuing proceedings to recover the debt. The mortgagee has 12 years from the date on which the cause of action accrued, to sue for principal, and 6 years to sue for interest. See *Bristol and West plc v Bartlett* (2002) *The Times*, 9 September.

mortgagee. *See* MORTGAGE.

mortgagee and right to take possession. A legal mortgage entitles the mortgagee to take possession immediately mortgage is made: *Four Maids Ltd v Dudley Marshall Ltd* [1957] Ch 317. The right is exercised where the mortgagee is entitled to enforce his security. For adjournment of proceedings, see A.J.A. 1970, s 36; A.J.A. 1973, s 8; *Ropaigealach v Barclays Bank* [1999] 3 WLR 37 (the protection given by s 36 has application only where lender has brought an action for possession).

mortgage, equitable. *See* EQUITABLE MORTGAGE.

mortgagee's rights. Generally: to take possession; to sell (in which case he has a duty to take reasonable precautions to obtain the true market value of the mortgaged property: *Cuckmere Brick Co v Mutual Finance* [1971] Ch 949); to foreclose and repossess; to lease; to hold title deeds; to appoint a receiver; to sue the mortgagor personally on covenants in the mortgage deed. See A.J.A. 1970, s 36; *Western Bank v Schindler* [1977] Ch 1;

Ropaigealach v Barclays Bank plc [1999] 2 WLR 17 (lender entitled to repossess and sell without court order). *See* FORECLOSURE; POWER OF SALE.

mortgagee's statutory right of sale. A statutory power of sale arises, where mortgage has been made by deed, under L.P.A. 1925, s 101(1) when legal date for redemption has passed (usually six months from date of mortgage) and no contrary intention appears in the deed. Power of sale may be exercised only if interest is unpaid for at least two months or notice to mortgagor has been followed by three months' default, or there has been a breach of covenant (other than covenant to pay capital and interest) in mortgage deed: s 103.

mortgage, legal. *See* LEGAL MORTGAGE.

mortgage of registered land, protection of. *See* REGISTERED LAND, PROTECTION OF MORTGAGE OF.

mortgages, consolidation of. *See* CONSOLIDATION OF MORTGAGES.

mortgage, second. A mortgage generally subject to the prior claims of a first mortgage. It may be created: in the case of freeholds, by charge by deed expressed to be by way of legal mortgage, or by demise for a term of years absolute; in the case of leaseholds, by charge by deed, or by sub-demise for term of years absolute. A second mortgagee should register the mortgage as a Class C land charge (q.v.). *See* PRIORITIES, RULES CONCERNING MORTGAGES.

mortgages, local authority. A local authority may advance money to a person for the purpose of acquiring, constructing, altering, enlarging, repairing or improving a house or converting another building into a house, or for the purpose of facilitating the repayment of an amount outstanding on a previous loan made for any of these purposes: H.A. 1985, s 435(1). The advance and interest on it must be secured by a mortgage of the land concerned: s 436(1).

mortgages, priority of. *See* PRIORITIES, RULES CONCERNING MORTGAGES.

mortgage, standing. Procedure whereby the borrower pays interest regularly on the loan and repays the capital in a single lump sum.

mortgage,   Welsh. *See*   WELSH MORTGAGE.

mortgagor. *See* MORTGAGE.

mortgagor's rights. Generally he is entitled to possession of the property, to receive income and profits, to redeem. See *Britannia BS* v *Earl* [1990] 2 All ER 469 (right of possession and application for relief under A.J.A. 1970, s 36). *See* EQUITY OF REDEMPTION.

mother. Female parent. See Human Fertilisation and Embryology Act 1990, s 27; Ch.A. 1989, s 4. 'Motherhood, although also a legal relationship, is based on fact, being proved demonstrably by parturition': *per* Lord Simon in *Ampthill Peerage Case* [1977] AC 547. *See* PARENTAL RESPONSIBILITY.

motion. 1. Formal proposal made at a meeting. 2. Oral or written application to a judge or court requesting an order directing performance of some action in the applicant's favour.

motive. That which incites to action. 'The source of power for a given act.' It should not be confused with *mens rea* (q.v.). It is usually irrelevant to the question of the determination of criminal responsibility, but may be relevant as circumstantial evidence or in deciding punishment following conviction. See *R* v *Rowley* [1991] 1 WLR 1020; *Birch* v *DPP* (2000) *The Independent*, 13 January ('motive' and 'purpose' (q.v.)). *See* INTENTION.

motor car. Mechanically propelled vehicle, not being a motor cycle or invalid carriage, constructed to carry a load or passengers with an unladen weight not in excess of that stated in Road Traffic Act 1988, s 185(1). See Capital Allowances Act 1990, s 36; 2001, s 81; *Chief Constable of Avon* v *Fleming* [1987] 1 All ER 318.

motor cycle. Mechanically propelled vehicle, not being an invalid carriage, with less than four wheels and an unladen weight not in excess of 410 kilograms: Road Traffic Act 1988, s 185(1). See *DPP* v *Saddington* (2000) *The Times*,

1 November (motorised scooter is a motor vehicle under s 185(1)).

motor cycles, crash helmets and. It was held in *DPP* v *Parker* (2004) *The Times*, 29 June, that a two-wheeled vehicle with roof, seat belts and safety bars was a motor cycle, requiring the driver to wear an appropriate crash helmet.

Motor Insurers' Bureau. Group of motor vehicle insurers which, by agreement (originally with the Ministry of Transport), undertakes to satisfy or cause to be satisfied, a judgment obtained against a motorist for a liability required to be covered by an insurance policy and which is not satisfied within seven days. The Bureau also makes payments relating to death or personal injury caused by a vehicle whose owner or driver cannot be traced. See Road Traffic Regulation Act 1984, s 136; Road Traffic Act 1988, s 143; SI 00/726 (compulsory motor insurance).

motor salvage operators. Under V.(C.)A. 2001, s 1(1), (2), motor salvage operators must be registered in a local authority area where they carry on a business in the recovery for re-use or sale of salvageable parts from motor vehicles or in the purchase of written-off vehicles and their subsequent repair and resale. Appropriate registers must be maintained by local authorities: s 2. 'Motor vehicle' refers to any vehicle whose function is or was to be used on roads as a mechanically propelled vehicle; 'written-off motor vehicle' means a motor vehicle which is in need of substantial repair but in relation to which a decision has been made not to carry out the repair: s 16.

motor vehicle, taking of. The unauthorised taking of a vehicle is an offence under Th.A. 1968, s 12, as amended by Aggravated Vehicle Taking Act 1992, s 1. See also P.&C.E.A. 1984, s 1(8)(c). *See* CONVEYANCE; VEHICLE-TAKING, AGGRAVATED.

mountain. Includes any land situated more than 600 metres above sea level: C.R.W.A. 2000, s 1(2).

movables. Term generally applied to personal, as opposed to real (or 'immovable'), property. See *R* v *Hoyles* [1911] 1 Ch 179.

MP. Member of Parliament (q.v.).

MR. Master of the Rolls (q.v.).

mugging. Colloquialism referring to robbery (q.v.) of an isolated pedestrian. See *R* v *Robinson* (1987) 9 Cr App R (S) 47; *R* v *Byfield* (1994) 15 Cr App R (S) 674.

multiple admissibility. Principle of evidence (q.v.) stating that if evidence is admissible for one purpose it may not be rejected solely because it is not admissible for some other purpose. See, e.g., *Morton* v *Morton* [1937] P 151.

multiple damages. An amount of damages (q.v.) calculated by multiplying the sum which might be truly compensatory. Under Protection of Trading Interests Act 1980, s 6, there is a right of action for a UK citizen or a person carrying on business in the UK or a body corporate incorporated in the UK to recoup payment made on account of a foreign award of multiple damages. See also C.J.J.A. 1982, s 38. *See* DOUBLE VALUE, ACTION FOR.

multiple occupation, house in. A house which is occupied by persons who do not form a single household; the word 'house' may include any part of a building which, apart from this subsection, would not be regarded as a house, and was originally constructed or subsequently adapted for occupation by a single household: H.A. 1985, s 345(1), (2), as amended by L.G.H.A. 1989, Sch 9, para 44. See H.A. 1996, Part II; *Barnes* v *Sheffield CC* (1995) 27 HLR 719 (criteria applicable to decision as to whether a group of students living in a shared house constituted a 'single household'); *Norwich CC* v *Billings* (1997) HLR 679 (consideration of Housing (Management of Houses in Multiple Occupation) Regulations 1990 (SI 90/830)); *Livingwaters Christian Centres Ltd* v *Conwy CBC* (1999) 77 P & CR 54; *Brent LBC* v *Patel* (2000) *The Times*, 30 November.

multiplicity of issues. Phrase relating to the exclusion of evidence (q.v.) which 'raises side issues upon which the court cannot decide without injustice to other parties': *A-G* v *Nottingham Corporation* [1904] 1 Ch 673.

multi-track, essence of. The usual track for claims for which the small claims track (q.v.) or the fast track (q.v.) is not the normal track (CPR, r 26.6(6)), e.g., cases involving claims exceeding £15,000, and cases less than that amount where trial is expected to last beyond one day. Cases with an estimated value of less than £50,000 are transferred from RCJ to a county court: PD 29, para 2.2 (exceptions include cases required by statute to be tried in High Court, claims for professional negligence, fraud, undue influence, defamation, contentious probate). *See* ALLOCATION TO TRACKS, CPR.

multi-track, hallmarks. 'The ability of the court to deal with cases of widely differing values and complexity, and the flexibility given to the court in the way it will manage a case in a way appropriate to its needs': PD 29, para 3.2.

multi-track procedure. Allocation to multi-track is followed by allocation directions which may involve a case management conference (q.v.), the issue of directions (e.g., disclosure, witness statements), issue of listing questionnaires, confirmation of trial date, possible pre-trial review, trial. The court should fix the trial date or period in which the trial is to take place as soon as possible: CPR, r 29(2). Once trial has begun, judge will normally sit on consecutive court days until it has been concluded: PD 29, para 10.6.

Münchausen's Syndrome by Proxy. Known also as 'fictitious injury abuse'. Basis of a type of behaviour thought to manifest itself in child abuse (q.v.), characterised by a person's invention of stories of a child's illness, or the fabrication of illness, resulting in unnecessary investigation and medical treatment. (Named after fictitious 'tall-story teller' of the eighteenth-century writer, Raspe.) See *Re DH* (1994) 1 FLR 679.

municipal law. 'A rule of civil conduct, prescribed by the supreme power in a state, commanding what is right, and prohibiting what is wrong': Blackstone, *Commentaries* (1765). The law of a nation or state, as distinguished from the law of nations (i.e., international law). May be divided into *public* and *private* law (qq.v.).

muniments of title. Title deeds and other evidence relating to title to land. *See* TITLE.

munitions. Explosives, firearms, ammunition, and anything used or capable of being used in the manufacture of an explosive, a firearm or ammunition: Terrorism Act 2000, Sch 10, para 1(3).

murder. Unlawful homicide with malice aforethought (q.v.). Described by Coke (1552–1634) as '. . . when any man of sound memory, and of the age of discretion, unlawfully killeth within any county of the realm any reasonable creature *in rerum natura* under the King's peace, with malice aforethought, either expressed by the party or implied by law, so as the party wounded, or hurt, etc., die of the wound or hurt, etc., within a year and a day [q.v.] after the same': 3 Co. Inst. 47. See *DPP v Smith* [1961] AC 290; *Hyam v DPP* [1975] AC 55; *R v Moloney* [1985] AC 905; *R v Hancock and Shankland* [1986] AC 455. For conspiracy to murder, see *R v Basra* (1989) 11 Cr App R (S) 327. For *mens rea* required to found a conviction for murder by a secondary party, see *R v Powell, R v Daniels* [1997] 3 WLR 959. *See* LIFE IMPRISONMENT; YEAR AND DAY RULE.

murder, attempted. The offence requires an intention to kill, not merely to cause grievous bodily harm: see *R v Whybrow* (1951) 36 Cr App R 141; *R v Gotts* [1992] 2 WLR 284 (duress not a defence); *R v Mortiboys* [1997] 1 Cr App R (S) 141. See Crime (Sentences) Act 1997, s 2(5)(a).

murder, body of victim. Where murder is charged, it is not necessary for a body to have been found. See *R v Onufrejczyk* [1955] 1 QB 388.

murder, definition of, proposals for reform. 'A person is guilty of murder if he causes the death of another (a) intending to cause death; or (b) intending to cause serious personal harm and being

aware that he may cause death . . .' (Law Commission Draft Criminal Code, s 54(1)): Law Com. No. 177, 1989. See *R v Woollin* [1999] AC 82.

murderer's memoirs, ban on. In *R (Nilson) v Governor of Full Sutton Prison* (2004) *The Times*, 23 November, the CA held that a prison rule prohibiting from publishing an account of his offences was lawful and did not violate his right to free expression.

murder, intention, direction to jury. Where a charge is murder, and in the unusual cases where a simple direction that it is for the jury to decide whether defendant intended to kill or do serious bodily harm, is insufficient, the jury should be directed that they are not entitled to find the necessary intention unless they feel sure that death or serious bodily harm was a virtual certainty (save for some unforeseen intervention) as a result of defendant's actions and that defendant appreciated that such was the case: *R v Woollin* [1999] AC 82. See also *R v Nedrick* [1986] 3 All ER 1.

murder, juvenile, tariffs, LCJ's suggestions. In *Practice Statement (Juveniles: Murder Tariffs)* (2000) *The Times*, 9 August, the Lord Chief Justice makes interim suggestions, pending legislation, providing for tariffs for defendants under 18 to be set by trial judge in open court, appealable by defendant or A-G, based on a period which could be increased or reduced to allow for aggravating and mitigating features: the former to include, e.g., killing of a child or police officer, gratuitous violence, killing for gain in the course of burglary and robbery; the latter to include age, mental abnormality, excessive response to personal threat. See *Re Thompson and Venables (Tariff Recommendations)* (2000) *The Times*, 27 October.

murder, life sentence. In *R v Lichniak, R v Pyrah* (2000) *The Times*, 26 November, the HL held that there is no incompatibility of a life sentence for murder passed under Murder (Abolition of the Death Penalty) Act 1965, s 1(1), and European Convention, arts 3, 5.

murder, life sentence, fixing of tariff term. In *R (Anderson)* v *Secretary of State for Home Department* (2002) *The Times*, 26 November, the HL held that where the Home Secretary had fixed a tariff term to be served (on punitive grounds) by defendant who had been sentenced under Murder (Abolition of Death Penalty) Act 1965, s 1(1), he had acted in a manner incompatible with European Convention, art 6.1. The tariff should be fixed by an independent and impartial tribunal; the Home Secretary was not such a tribunal.

murder, plans for law reform. The Law Commission, in its consultation paper 'Partial Defences to Murder', published in November 2003, suggests the development of a partial defence based upon a pre-emptive use of force in self-defence, where there is abuse, and the killing is effected in the honest belief that it is the only way to prevent future violence to the person who has applied violence or to another.

murder, soliciting to. *See* SOLICITING TO MURDER.

murder, threats to. A person who without lawful excuse makes to another a threat, intending that that other would fear it would be carried out, to kill that other or a third person is guilty of an offence: O.P.A. 1861, s 16; C.L.A. 1977, Sch 12; Criminal Evidence (Amendment) Act 1997, Sch 1. See *R* v *Cousins* [1982] QB 526; *R* v *Perry* (1986) 8 Cr App R (S) 132; *R* v *Tait* [1989] 3 WLR 891.

mute. When asked to plead, an accused person may stand mute. If considered to be mute of malice (i.e., deliberately silent) a plea of not guilty is entered for him and the trial proceeds. If considered mute 'by visitation of God' (i.e., deaf and dumb) an attempt is made to make him understand and answer the charge by some means and where this fails, a plea of not guilty is entered for him. Where there is doubt, a jury will decide. See *R* v *Paling* (1978) 67 Cr App R 229; C.L.A. 1967, s 6(1)(*c*).

mutiny. A combination between two or more persons subject to military law, or between persons, two at least of whom are subject to military law, to overthrow, or resist lawful authority in the Forces or any forces co-operating therewith, to disobey such authority so as to make the disobedience subversive of discipline, or to impede the performance of any duty or service in the Forces or in any forces co-operating therewith. 'An offence of collective insubordination, collective defiance or disregard of authority or refusal to obey authority': *per* Lord Goddard in *R* v *Grant* [1957] 1 WLR 906. See, e.g., Mutiny Acts 1689–1879; Army Act 1955, s 31(3). *See* PRISON MUTINY.

mutual dealings. Where there have been mutual (i.e., reciprocal) dealings between a debtor and one of his creditors, account must be taken of what is due from one to the other, and the balance of the account (but no more) shall be paid or claimed. See *Rolls Razor Ltd* v *Cox* [1967] 1 QB 552.

mutual desertion. Result of each spouse, independently and without just cause, leaving the other. See *Hosegood* v *Hosegood* [1950] WN 218; *Price* v *Price* [1968] 3 All ER 543.

mutual wills. Wills made by two or more persons, conferring reciprocal benefits, and based on an agreement to make such wills and not to revoke them without consent of the other. On the death of the first testator, a constructive trust (q.v.) is imposed. See *Re Dale* [1994] Ch 1; *Re Goodchild* [1996] 1 All ER 670; *Re Hobley* (1997) *The Times*, 16 June (unilateral alteration to a mutual will destroys the effect of the wills and renders them unenforceable).

N

naked contract. *See* NUDUM PACTUM.

naked trust. Bare trust (q.v.).

name and arms clause. Clause in settlement (q.v.) or will (q.v.) directing forfeiture of a beneficiary's interests unless he takes and uses a stated surname (usually that of the settlor or testator) on all occasions. See *Re Neeld* [1962] Ch 643.

name, change of. A surname may be changed by operation of law (as on marriage), by statutory declaration, by deed poll, by advertisement (in, e.g., a local newspaper). See *Dancer* v *Dancer* [1949] P 147 (change of name by repute); *Re C (A Minor) (Change of Surname)* [1998] 1 FLR 549; *Re T (Change of Surname)* [1998] 2 FLR 260; *Dawson* v *Weatmouth* [1999] 2 AC 308. For change of a Christian name (i.e., that given at baptism) see *Re Parrott* [1946] Ch 183. For change of a child's name, see Ch.A. 1989, ss 13, 33(7); for change of a child's name following parents' divorce, see M.C. Rules 1977, r 92(8), and *W* v *A* [1981] Fam 14. *See* SURNAME.

name change of company. In *Ricketts* v *Ad Valorem Ltd* [2004] 1 BCLC 1 the CA held that, a director may be held personally liable for a company's relevant debts, even where it is acknowledged that he had no intention of deceiving the public, in matters involving a change of company name.

name, family. *See* SURNAME.

National Assembly of Wales. Known as *Cynulliad Cenedlaethol Cymru*. Set up under Government of Wales Act 1998, consisting of 60 members (one for each of the 40 Assembly constituencies in Wales and four for each of the five Assembly electoral regions). Its functions are those which are transferred to, or made exercisable by, the Assembly by virtue of the 1998 Act, or conferred or imposed on the Assembly by or under the Act or any other Act: s 21.

National Audit Office. *See* COMPTROLLER.

National Care Standards Commission. Body corporate, set up under Care Standards Act 2000, s 6, responsible for informing Secretary of State about availability of provision and quality of services pertaining to the 2000 Act, Part II. See SI 01/1193.

National Crime Squad. Organisation set up under Police Act 1997, 'to prevent and detect serious crime which is of relevance to more than one police area in England and Wales': s 48(1). Its Director General must be a Chief Constable or an officer eligible for promotion to that level: s 52. See SI 99/821 (objectives of NCS).

National Criminal Intelligence Service. Maintained by NCIS Service Authority, headed by a Director General: Police Act 1997, ss 2, 6. Its functions are: the gathering and analysis of information so as to provide criminal intelligence, the provision of intelligence to police forces and acting in support of police forces carrying out criminal intelligence activities: s 2(2). (See SI 99/822 (objectives of NCIS).)

National Health Service. *See* HEALTH SERVICE, NATIONAL.

National Health Service contracts. Arrangements under which one health services body (e.g., a Health Authority) plans for the provision to it by another health service body of goods or services which it reasonably requires for the purposes of its functions: NHS and Community Care Act 1990, s 4, as amended by Health Act 1999. There is no contractual relationship between a patient and a doctor treating him under NHS arrangements: *Pfitzer Corporation* v *Ministry of Health* [1965] AC 512.

National Health Service, evasion of charges. A person is guilty of an offence if, with a view to evading a charge in relation to the provision of goods and services he knowingly makes or causes or knowingly allows another to make a false statement or representation or, in the case of a document which he knows to be false in a material particular, produces it or causes or allows another to produce it: NHS Act 1977, s 122C, inserted by Health Act 1999, s 39.

National Health Service trusts. Bodies corporate appointed by the Secretary of State to assume responsibility for the ownership and management of hospitals previously managed by Health Authorities or to provide and manage hospitals or other establishments: NHS and Community Care Act 1990, s 5. For powers of NHS trusts to enter into externally financed development agreements, see NHS (Private Finance) Act 1997, s 1.

national insurance. System of social security benefits controlled by the state. See National Insurance Acts 1946–74; Social Security Acts 1973–98; C.S.P.S.S.A. 2000, ss 74–77.

National Insurance Tribunals. *See* SOCIAL SECURITY TRIBUNALS.

nationalisation. The bringing of the ownership and management of businesses or industries under public ownership through state control. See, e.g., Coal Industry Nationalisation Act 1946 (as amended by Coal Industry Act 1987, Sch 1).

nationality. The legal relationship attaching to membership of a nation resulting from, e.g., birth, naturalisation (q.v.), marriage. Generally implies duties of allegiance and protection by state. '"Nationality" in the sense of citizenship of a certain state must not be confused with nationality as meaning membership of a certain nation in the sense of race': *London Borough of Ealing* v *Race Relations Board* [1972] 1 All ER 104. 'Dual nationality' refers to citizenship held simultaneously in two countries. See B.N.A. 1981; B.N. (Falkland Islands) A. 1983.

National Parks. Parks set up 'for the purpose of conserving and enhancing the natural beauty, wildlife and cultural heritage of certain specified areas and of promoting opportunities for the understanding and enjoyment of the special qualities of those areas by the public': National Parks and Access to the Countryside Act 1949, s 5, substituted by Environment Act 1995, s 61. See *R* v *Northumberland National Park Authority* (1999) 79 P & CR 120.

national security. 'Those who are responsible for the national security must be the sole judges of what the national security requires. It would be obviously undesirable that such matters should be made the subject of evidence in a court of law or otherwise discussed in public': *per* Lord Parker in *The Zamora* [1916] 2 AC 77. See *CCSU* v *Minister for the Civil Service* [1985] AC 374; *Secretary of State for Home Department* v *Rehman* (2000) *The Times*, 31 May. See F.I.A. 2000, s 24. *See* GCHQ; INTELLIGENCE SERVICE; SECURITY SERVICE.

nations, law of. International law (q.v.).

natural allegiance. The allegiance (q.v.) owed to his country by a subject. See *Joyce* v *DPP* [1946] AC 347.

naturalisation. Process resulting in an alien's receiving the status pertaining to a native citizen. In the UK it follows the grant of a certificate and the taking of an oath of allegiance. The alien must show that he is of good character, has a sufficient knowledge of English, Welsh or Gaelic, that his principal home will be in the UK, that he was in the UK at the beginning of the period of five years ending with the date of his application and that he has not been absent in that period from the UK for more than 450 days and has not been in breach of immigration laws: B.N.A.1981, s 6(1), Sch 1; *R* v *Secretary of State for Home Department ex p Al Fayed* (2000) *The Times*, 7 September.

natural justice. *See* JUSTICE, NATURAL.

natural law. *See* LAW, NATURAL.

natural person. A human being, as contrasted with an 'artificial person' (q.v.), e.g., a corporation (q.v.).

natural rights. 1. Rights said to be conferred upon man by the natural law (q.v.). 2. Those basic rights found commonly in the laws of civilised nations, e.g., freedom of speech. 3. Term used in land law to refer to a group of general rights attaching to the fee simple (q.v.), including, e.g., right to the support of land. *See* RIGHT.

naval court. Summoned by the commander of one of HM ships on a foreign station to investigate a complaint, or loss of a ship in the area, and consisting of naval officers. Appeal lies to Divisional Court and Court of Appeal (q.v.).

naval disciplinary courts. Naval Discipline Act 1957, s 52G, under which a disciplinary court may be ordered for the trial of an officer below the rank of commander, is abolished: Armed Forces Act 2001, s 18.

navigation, right of. Right of the public to use a river as a highway for, e.g., shipping. Rights of Way Act 1932, s 1(1), does not apply to rights of navigation on non-tidal waters: *A-G (ex rel Yorks Derwent Trust) v Brotherton* [1991] 3 WLR 1126.

navigation rights. Public rights of navigation of the Thames may be extinguished only by statute; exercise of a statutory power; destruction of the subject matter of those rights: *Rowland v Environment Agency* (2002) *The Times*, 28 December.

ne exeat regno, writ of. Where the conditions contained in the Debtors Act 1869, s 6, are satisfied, so that a tipstaff was given immediate authority to arrest a debtor, the court must have been satisfied that the order ('he shall not leave the kingdom') was both proportionate and essential for the securing of the ends of justice: *Ali v Naseem* (2003) *The Times*, 3 October.

necessaries. 1. Goods suitable to the condition in life of an infant (q.v.) or minor or other person and to his actual requirements at the time of the sale and delivery. 'A minor may bind himself to pay

for his necessary meat, drink, apparel, necessary physic, and such other necessaries, and likewise for his good teaching and instruction, whereby he may profit himself afterwards': Co. Litt. 172a. See S.G.A. 1979, s 3; *Nash v Inman* [1908] 2 KB 1. 2. In the case of husband and wife, 'things that are really necessary and suitable to the style in which the husband chooses to live, in so far as the articles fall fairly within the domestic department which is ordinarily confided to the management of the wife': *Phillipson v Hayter* (1870) LR 6 CP 38. *See* MINORS' CONTRACTS.

necessaries, contracts made by wife for. A man is not generally liable on contracts made by his wife for necessaries if: the trade has been expressly warned not to supply her with goods on credit; she has been forbidden to pledge her husband's credit; she was supplied with the means to purchase necessaries without pledging her husband's credit; the trader gave credit exclusively to her; the husband has a sufficient supply of the goods purchased. The common law rules concerning a wife's agency of necessity were abrogated by Matrimonial Proceedings and Property Act 1970, s 41.

necessity. Circumstances compelling a course of action. As a defence in criminal law, rejected in *R v Dudley and Stephens* (1884) 14 QBD 273 (shipwrecked mariners killing and eating a boy so as to survive); *London Borough of Southwark v Williams* [1971] 2 All ER 175 (squatting by homeless persons). For recognition of defence in extreme circumstances, see *R v Martin* [1989] 1 All ER 652; *R v Pommell* (1995) 2 Cr App R 607. In the law of tort (q.v.) the defence may succeed where the damage has been caused to prevent a greater evil and the act was reasonable: *Leigh v Gladstone* (1909) 26 TLR 139; *Rigby v CC of Northampton* [1985] 1 WLR 1242; *Re F* [1990] 2 AC 1 (necessity as defence to tort of trespass to the person). *See* DURESS.

necessity, agent by. *See* AGENT.

nec vi, nec clam, nec precario. Not by violence, stealth or entreaty. Phrase used in relation to, e.g., prescriptive acquisition as of right (i.e., the user must not be forcible, concealed in any way, or permissive, e.g., founded on a licence). See *AF Beckett v Lyons* [1967] Ch 449.

ne exeat regno. He shall not leave the kingdom. Writ (q.v.) restraining a person's leaving the realm, used in the case of political offenders and, later, debtors where there was probable cause to believe that they were about to leave the country. See, for a review of the law, *Felton v Callis* [1969] 2 QB 200; *Allied Arab Bank v Hajjar* [1988] 2 WLR 942.

negative clearance. Procedure in EU law, whereby parties to an agreement may seek a declaration that it does not come within the scope of, and therefore does not infringe, the Treaty of Rome 1957, art 85 (prohibiting agreements which prevent, restrict or distort competition). See EEC Council Regulation No. 17/62, art 2; Commission Decision No. 72/403/EEC [1973] CMLR 77; *Koelmar v EC Commission* [1996] EMLR 555. *See* EU.

neglect. Culpable omission to perform a duty. See, e.g., *Monarch Airlines v London Luton Airport Ltd* [1997] CLC 698 (consideration of 'neglect or default'). One who undertakes the care of another who, by reason of sickness or age, is incapable of providing necessaries for himself, is criminally responsible if his conscious neglect causes the death of that other. See *R v Instan* [1893] 1 QB 450; *R v Stone and Dobinson* [1977] QB 354 (in a case of manslaughter (q.v.) it is not necessary to prove that defendant was reckless as to whether the victim might suffer serious bodily harm or death).

neglect, wilful. *See* WILFUL NEGLECT.

negligence. 'Not a state of mind, but a falling short of an objective standard of conduct': Pollock, *The Law of Torts* (1887). 'In strict legal analysis, negligence means more than heedless or careless conduct, whether in omission or commission; it properly connotes the complex concept of duty, breach and damage thereby suffered by the person to whom the duty was owing': *per* Lord Wright in *Lochgelly Iron & Coal v*

M'Mullan [1934] AC 1. ' "Negligence" is not an affirmative word; it is a negative word; it is the absence of such care, skill and diligence as it was the duty of the person to bring to the performance of the work which he is said not to have performed': *per* Willes J in *Grill v General Iron Screw Co* (1860) 35 LJCP 330. Negligence and error are not the same: *per* Stoker LJ in *Flynn v Vange Scaffolding Ltd* (1987) *The Times*, 26 March. See also *Carroll v Fearon* [1998] PIQR. In Unfair Contract Terms Act 1977, s 1(1), means the breach of any obligation arising from the express or implied terms of a contract, to take reasonable care or exercise reasonable skill in the performance of a contract, or the breach of any common-law duty to take reasonable care or exercise reasonable skill (but not any stricter duty), or the breach of the common duty of care imposed by Occupiers' Liability Act 1957. (See also Occupiers' Liability Act 1984.) For professional negligence, see, e.g., *Nash v Kingston and Richmond HA* [1997] 8 Med LR 387; *Hyde and Associates Ltd v Williams & Co* (2000) *The Times*, 4 August (professional negligence means falling below a proper standard of competence, and where there is more than one acceptable standard, competence should be gauged by the lowest of them). *See* BOLAM TEST; DUTY OF CARE; OCCUPIERS' LIABILITY TO NON-VISITORS.

negligence, advertent. Situation in which a tortfeasor (q.v.) displays 'an attitude of mental indifference to obvious risks': *per* Eve J in *Hudston v Viney* [1921] 1 Ch 98. In *inadvertent negligence*, the tortfeasor has displayed mere carelessness.

negligence claim in relation to unwanted pregnancy. In *Rees v Darlington Memorial Hospital NHS Trust* [2003] UKHL 52, the HL held that a disabled mother who had given birth to a healthy, normal child, following an unsuccessful sterilisation operation, could not be awarded damages intended to cover the additional costs of rearing the child which would arise because of the disability. (A conventional sum would be awarded, nevertheless, in recognition of her being the victim of a legal wrong.)

negligence, clinical, proceedings. Proceedings which include a claim for damages in respect of a duty of care or trespass to the person committed in the course of the provision of clinical or medical services (including dental or nursing services): SI 00/774.

negligence, contributory. *See* CON-TRIBUTORY NEGLIGENCE.

negligence, criminal. *See* CRIMINAL NEGLIGENCE.

negligence, foreseeability and. 'It is not necessary that the precise concatenation of circumstances should be envisaged. If the consequence was one within the general range which any reasonable person might foresee (and was not of an entirely different kind which no one would anticipate) then it is within the rule that a person who is guilty of negligence is liable for the consequences': *per* Lord Denning in *Stewart* v *W African Air Terminals* (1964) 108 SJ 838. See *Etheridge* v *K (A Minor)* [1999] Ed CR; *Jolley* v *Sutton LBC* [2000] 3 All ER 409.

negligence gross. *See* GROSS NEGLIGENCE.

negligence, in failure to warn. In *Chester* v *Afshar* [2004] UK HL 41, the HL held that in a case in which a patient whose doctor did not warn her of the existence of an inherent risk when she gave her consent to treatment and who later suffered injury when that risk emerged, the test for consortium in negligence was satisfied if she were able to show that, had she been correctly informed, she would not have undergone the operation.

negligence liability, avoidance of. By Unfair Contract Terms Act 1977, s 2(1), a person cannot by reference to any contract term or notice given to persons exclude or restrict his liability for death or personal injury resulting from negligence and, in the case of other loss or damage, he cannot so exclude or restrict his liability for negligence except insofar as the term or notice satisfies the requirement of reasonableness (which will be considered by reference to, e.g., strength of bargaining position of parties relative to each other, whether goods were manufactured to the customer's special order, whether the customer knew or ought reasonably to have known of existence and extent of the term: Sch 2).

negligence, sport and. Participants in competitive sport owe a duty of care to one another to take all reasonable care, having regard to the particular circumstances in which they are placed: *Condon* v *Basi* [1985] 2 All ER 453.

negligence, tort of. The breach of a legal duty to take care, resulting in damage to claimant which was not desired by defendant. 'The omission to do something which a reasonable man, guided upon those considerations which ordinarily regulate the conduct of human affairs, would do, or doing something which a prudent and reasonable man would not do': *Blyth* v *Birmingham Waterworks Co* (1856) 11 Ex 781. Burden of proof is generally on claimant. See *Donoghue* v *Stevenson* [1932] AC 562. For negligence in performance of a service, see, e.g., *Henderson* v *Merrett Ltd* [1995] 2 AC 145. *See* DUTY OF CARE.

negligence, tort of, and Bolam test. Principle stated in *Bolam* v *Friern Hospital Management Committee* [1957] 1 WLR 582, according to which a professional person will not be guilty of negligence if he can show that he has acted in accordance with practices accepted by a substantial, responsible body of persons skilled in his field. The test applies to all who exercise or profess to exercise a particular skill, and its application does not depend on the actual possession of a relevant qualification: *per* Morritt LJ, in *Adams* v *Rhymney Valley DC* (2000) 150 NLJ 1231.

negligent misstatement. A statement carelessly made in circumstances where there is a duty to be honest and careful, resulting in loss to some person to whom that duty is owed and who has acted on the statement. Liability for such a statement may arise in tort (q.v.) and contract (q.v.). See *Hedley Byrne & Co Ltd* v *Heller and Partners* [1964] AC 793; *Esso*

Petroleum Co Ltd v *Mardon* [1976] QB 801.

negotiable. 1. In relation to an instrument, the quality of being transferable free from equities. 2. Subject to bargaining.

negotiable instrument. A written instrument with the following characteristics: (1) title to it passes by delivery; (2) holder for the time being may sue in his own name; (3) notice of assignment need not be given to person liable thereon; (4) bona fide holder for value takes free from any defect in title of predecessors; (5) instrument is of a type recognised by law as negotiable. Examples: bills of exchange; promissory notes and cheques; dividend warrants; debentures payable to bearer (see *Bechuanaland Exploration Co* v *London Trading Bank Ltd* [1898] 2 QB 658). See B.Ex.A 1882, ss 31, 32. *See* NOT NEGOTIABLE.

negotiable instruments, quasi-. Those choses in action (q.v.) which, although not completely negotiable, possess some of the characteristics of negotiable instruments. Examples: IOU; bill of lading (q.v.).

negotiable instruments, renunciation of. When the holder of a bill, at or after its maturity, absolutely and unconditionally renounces his rights against the acceptor, the bill is discharged. The renunciation must be in writing, unless the bill is delivered up to the acceptor: see B.Ex.A. 1882, s 62(1).

negotiation of a bill. The transferring of a bill of exchange (q.v.) from one person to another so that the transferee becomes the holder of the bill: B.Ex.A. 1882, s 31(1).

negotiorum gestio. The management of affairs. *Negotiorum gestor* is one who interferes in the affairs of another for that other's advantage, but without authority. Not generally recognised in English law; but see B.Ex.A. 1882, s 65. See *Falcke* v *Scottish Insurance* (1887) 34 Ch D 249.

neighbour concept in law. *See* DUTY OF CARE; NUISANCE, NEIGHBOURHOOD.

nemine contradicente. Abbreviated to *nem con.* No one saying otherwise, i.e., without dissent.

nemo dat quod non habet. No one can give that which he has not. See S.G.A. 1979, s 21(1). Thus, a person cannot give better title than he has. In some cases, however, a buyer acquires a good title, notwithstanding a defect in the seller's title. Examples: sale in market overt (q.v.); sale under an order of the court; transfer of a negotiable instrument (q.v.) to a holder in due course; under the doctrine of estoppel (q.v.). See Factors Act 1889, s 2; *Shaw* v *Commissioner of Metropolitan Police* [1987] 1 WLR 1332.

nemo debet bis puniri pro uno delicto. No man ought to be punished twice for one offence. See *R* v *Statutory Cttee of Pharmaceutical Society of Great Britain* [1981] 1 WLR 886.

nemo debet bis vexari. No man ought to be twice vexed. No person should be again prosecuted upon the same facts if he has been tried by a competent court. *See* AUTREFOIS ACQUIT; DOUBLE JEOPARDY.

nemo debet esse judex in propria causa. No person should be a judge in his own cause. The rule applies also to any cause in which that person has an interest: see, e.g., *R* v *Barnsley Metropolitan BC ex p Hook* [1976] 3 All ER 452. See *Re Pinochet Ugarte* (1999) 149 NLJ 88, in which the House of Lords set aside its order of 25 November 1998, after learning that Lord Hoffmann, one of the Law Lords who had participated in the appeal leading to the order, was chairperson of Amnesty International, which had intervened in the proceedings. The House stated that a judge was automatically disqualified from sitting as a judge in proceedings where he had a close connection to parties whose interest in those proceedings was the attainment of a particular result. Hence, any order resulting from the outcome would be set aside without need for an investigation into the likelihood or suspicion of any judicial bias. See, for guidelines, *Locabail Ltd* v *Bayfield Properties* [2000] QB 461. *See* BIAS, RULE AGAINST.

nemo tenetur seipsum accusare. No person is bound to incriminate himself. See *Commissioners of Customs and Excise* v *Ingram* [1948] 1 All ER 927. *See* INCRIMINATE.

neonate. A newborn child. For medical duty in relation to handicapped neonates, see, e.g., *Re J* [1990] 3 All ER 930.

nervous shock. Actual illness in the form of physical symptoms or psychiatric illness. Regarded as a personal, bodily hurt, constituting a tort (q.v.). 'It is now well recognised that an action will lie for injury by shock sustained through the medium of the eye or ear without direct contact': *Bourhill* v *Young* [1943] AC 92. For manslaughter arising from shock, see *R* v *Dawson* (1985) 81 Cr App R 150.

nervous shock and liability. Liability for psychiatric illness depends on foreseeability and a relationship of proximity between claimant and defendant. It is not reasonable to regard viewing a television broadcast of a disaster as giving rise to shock, in the sense of a sudden assault on the nervous system. Psychiatric claims by plaintiffs in close family relationship with the victims are recognisable as based on the rebuttable presumption of love and affection normally associated with that relationship; but such claims are not to be confined to that relationship. See *Alcock and Others* v *CC of S Yorks Police* [1991] 4 All ER 907; *Page* v *Smith* [1995] 2 WLR 644 (injury foreseeability sufficient for nervous shock liability).

NESTA. National Endowment for Science, Technology and the Arts, set up under National Lottery Act 1998, s 16, to support and promote talent, innovation and creativity in the fields of science, technology and the arts. Its 15 members are appointed by the Secretary of State.

net estate. In relation to a deceased person, it includes: property which he had power to dispose of by will, less funeral, testamentary and administration expenses; property in respect of which he held a general power of appointment (q.v.) not exercised; sums which he nominated another to receive; *donationes mortis causa* (q.v.): Inheritance (Provision for Family and Dependants) Act 1975.

new. Recent, original. Whether an article is 'new' is a question of fact or degree

in every particular case: *Raynham Farm Co Ltd* v *Symbol Motor Corp Ltd* (1987) *The Times*, 27 January.

Newton hearing. Where, although there has been a plea of guilty, a factual dispute emerges which could affect the sentencing process, the trial judge will call for evidence in order to determine the matters of fact: see *R* v *Newton* (1982) 77 Cr App R 13. See SI 89/343, Sch 3, para 1. For power of Court of Appeal to hold a Newton hearing, see *R* v *Guppy* [1994] Crim LR 614. See *R* v *Gass* [2000] 1 Cr App R (S) 475.

new trial. *See* TRIAL, NEW.

next friend. Now known as a 'litigation friend' (q.v.). An adult through whom a child (a person under 18) or patient (within the meaning of M.H.A. 1983) sues, e.g., the infant's father or person *in loco parentis*, patient's receiver, or Official Solicitor (qq.v.). For procedure of appointment, see PD 21.

next of kin. Generally, one's nearest blood relations. 'Statutory next of kin' may be construed technically, to denote next of kin who, on a person's death intestate, would have taken his personalty (q.v.) under the Statute of Distributions. See *Re Sutcliffe* [1929] 1 Ch 123.

nexus. Connection or bond. For 'familial nexus', see, e.g., *Dyson Holdings* v *Fox* [1976] QB 503.

night. The time from sunset to sunrise. See, e.g., SI 91/2125. In relation to working time regulations, means a period, the duration of which is not less than seven hours and which includes the period between midnight and 5am (where there is an agreement) or between 11pm and 6am (where there is no relevant agreement): SI 98/1833, reg 2.

night worker. 'A worker who, as a normal course, works at least three hours of his daily working time during night time; or who is likely, during night time, to work at least such proportion of his annual working time as may be specified in a collective or a workforce agreement: SI 98/1833, reg 2. His normal hours of work shall not exceed an average of eight hours for each 24 hours: reg 6.

nisi. Unless. Not final or absolute.

nisi per legale judicium parium suorum, vel per legem terrae. '[No freeman is to be taken, imprisoned or exiled] unless by the lawful judgment of his peers or [and] by the law of the land'. Provision of Magna Carta (q.v.).

nisi prius. Unless before. Trial at *nisi prius* followed after the sheriff (q.v.) was commanded to secure the attendance of a jury at Westminster 'unless before' that day the county should be visited by a judge of assize (q.v.). The term was used in recent years to refer to commission to try causes, conferred on judges of assize.

no case, ruling of. A Crown Court judge is entitled, even when the defence case is completed, to rule that there is no case to go before the jury if there is a lack of evidence on a count, or if no reasonable jury could convict on the evidence presented: *R* v *Brown* [2002] 1 Cr App R 5.

no case to answer. Submission by defendant, at the close of the prosecution's case, that a prima facie case has not been made out. The submission should be made in absence of the jury: *Crosdale* v *R* [1995] 1 WLR 864. If submission succeeds, judgment is entered for defendant. It may be based on a point of law or absence of evidence relating to essential facts. See *R* v *Barker* (1975) 65 Cr App R 287; *R* v *Galbraith* [1981] 1 WLR 1039; *R* v *Smith* [1999] 2 Cr App R 238; *Mullan* v *Birmingham* CC (1999) *The Times*, 29 July. It was held by the CA in *Benham Ltd* v *Kythira Investments Ltd* [2003] EWCA Civ 1794, that there will be very few, if any, circumstances in which a judge trying a civil action without a jury accepts a submission of no case to answer. The true test must be whether or not the evidence presented by the claimant has any real prospect of being successful.

noise. 'Sound which is undesired by the recipient': *Wilson Report*, 1963. An action may lie in some circumstances for nuisance resulting from noise: see, e.g., *Lambert Flat Management Ltd* v *Lomas* [1981] 1 WLR 898. Includes vibration: see En.P.A. 1990, s 79(*g*). See *Southwark LBC* v *Mills* [1999] 4 All ER 449 (no legal remedy for tenants of flats where noise arose from ordinary activities in neighbours' flats); G.L.A.A. 1999, s 370 (London's 'ambient noise strategy'); *Camden LBC* v *Gunby* [2000] 1 WLR 465; Noise and Statutory Nuisance Act 1993; Noise Act 1996; Council Directive 2000/14; Noise at Work Regulations 1989; Aeroplane Noise Regulations 1999 (SI 99/1452). For significance of World Health Organisation recommended level, see *Murdoch* v *Glacier Metal Co* [1998] EHLR 198.

noise, permitted level, warning. A warning notice, issued by an officer of a local authority; must state that noise is being emitted from an offending dwelling during night hours, and that the noise exceeds, or may exceed, the permitted level, as measured from within the complainant's dwelling, and must give warning that persons responsible may be guilty of an offence: Noise Act 1996, s 3.

noise pollution. It was held in *Andrews* v *Reading BC* [2004] EWHC 970 that noise emanating from public authority schemes was capable of interfering with the right to private life, but a fair balance had to be struck between an individual's interests and those of the community as a whole and the availability of reasonable measures to diminish the effects of the noise as a whole.

noise, seizure of equipment causing. Noise Act 1996, s 10, authorises the local authority's officers to enter a dwelling house from which noise is being or has been emitted, so as to seize and remove any equipment which is or has been used in the emission of noise.

nolle prosequi. Unwilling to prosecute. In a criminal case the entry of a *nolle prosequi*, which stays a prosecution on indictment (q.v.), is made by the Attorney-General (q.v.) before judgment; he need not give any reasons: see *Gouriet* v *UPOW* [1978] AC 435. Prosecution or defence may apply to the A-G for entry of a *nolle prosequi*. It is not an acquittal; fresh proceedings may be brought on the same charge at a later date. For common-law basis, see *R* v *Comptroller of Patents* [1899] 1 QB 909.

nolo contendere. I do not wish to contend. Generally, an implied confession of guilt.

nominal capital. A company's authorised capital (q.v.). See Cos.A. 1985, s 121.

nominal damages. *See* DAMAGES.

nominal partner. Known also as 'ostensible partner'. One who holds himself out as having an interest in a business.

nomination. 1. Designation or proposal by name for a vacant office. 2. A direction to a person who holds funds on behalf of another to pay them to a nominated person in the event of death. Nomination may be made by an adult or infant (q.v.) who has reached the age of 16. See *Baird v Baird* [1990] 2 All ER 301.

NOMS. The National Offender Management Service (NOMS) is a department of the Home Office responsible for the correctional services in England and Wales (separate arrangements exist in Scotland and Northern Ireland). It was created by combining parts of the headquarters of the National Probation Service and Her Majesty's Prison Service. NOMS was created on 1 June 2004 following a Home Office paper, *Reducing Crime, Changing Lives* (January, 2004).

non-attendance of party at court. *See* COURT, PARTY NOT ATTENDING.

non-commercial agreement. 'A consumer credit agreement or a consumer hire agreement (qq.v.) not made by the creditor or owner in the course of a business carried on by him': C.C.A. 1974, s 189(1). Example: agreement for a loan made between friends and not in the course of a business transaction.

non compos mentis. Not of sound mind.

non constat. It is not clear. It does not follow. It is not agreed.

non-contentious business. Business not contained within the definition of contentious business (q.v.), e.g., drafting of a will, conveyancing. Mode and amount of remuneration are governed by orders under Solicitors Act 1974, s 56. See S.C.A. 1981, s 128.

non-delivery. Failure to deliver goods, which amounts to a breach of contract, may give rise to an action for damages.

The principal rules of assessment of such damages are set out in S.G.A. 1979, s 51. See, e.g., *Tai Hing Cotton Mill Ltd v Kamsing Knitting Factory* [1979] AC 91; *The Alecos M* [1991] 1 Lloyd's Rep 120.

non-direction. Failure of a trial judge to direct the jury on a necessary point of law.

non-disclosure. *See* DISCLOSURE, NON-.

non-discrimination notice. 1. Notice under Race Relations Act 1976, s 58, after investigation by Commission for Racial Equality (q.v.), whereby a person who is committing or has committed an unlawful discriminatory act or an act contravening ss 28–31, is required not to commit such acts. Appeal against notice may be made to an employment tribunal (q.v.) or county court (q.v.). A register of such notices was established under s 61. 2. Notice issued under Sex Discrimination Act 1975, s 67, by Equal Opportunities Commission (q.v.) requiring a person not to commit an unlawful discriminatory act. There is a right of appeal under s 68. See *R v Commission for Racial Equality, ex p Westminster CC* [1985] ICR 822.

non-economic loss and unfair dismissal. The Employment Appeal Tribunal held in *Dunnachie v Kingston upon Hull CC* [2003] IRLR 384 that there can be no recovery for non-economic loss arising from a claim of unfair dismissal (resulting in injury to feelings) heard by an employment tribunal.

non est factum. It is not [his] deed. Plea which denies that an instrument is that of the defendant, e.g., where there has been a mistake as to the nature of the transaction. See *Chiswick Investments v Pevats* [1990] 1 NZLR 169; *Lloyds Bank v Waterhouse* [1991] Fam Law 23. 'A person who signs a document, and parts with it so that it may come into other hands, has a responsibility . . . to take care what he signs, which, if neglected, prevents him from denying his liability under the document': *United Dominions Trust Ltd v Western and Another* [1976] QB 513.

nonfeasance. Failure to perform an act which one is bound by law to do. 'The distinction between misfeasance and nonfeasance is valid only in the case of highways repairable by the public at large. It does not apply to any other branch of law': *Pride of Derby Ltd v British Celanese Ltd* [1953] Ch 149. See also Highways Act 1980, s 58. *See* MISFEASANCE.

non-intervention principle. Known also as 'no-order principle'. 'Where a court is considering whether or not to make one or more orders under [Ch.A. 1989] with respect to a child, it shall not make the order, or any of the orders, unless it considers that doing so would be better for the child than making no order at all': Ch.A. 1989, s 1(5). See, e.g., *B v B (Grandparent: Residence Order)* [1992] 2 FLR 327.

non-jury list. A list in the QBD of cases to be tried by a judge sitting alone, or with assessors (q.v.).

non-molestation clause. *See* INJUNCTIONS RELATING TO DOMESTIC VIOLENCE.

non obstante. Notwithstanding.

non placet. It does not please; it is not approved. Formula used by an assembly to record a negative vote.

non-suit. The renouncing by claimant of a claim before the verdict, e.g., on discovery of a defect. Refers also to the withdrawal by a judge of the case from the jury, and the direction of the verdict in defendant's favour. Non-suit in the High Court was replaced by discontinuance, which is now covered by CPR, r 38.

non-user. The apparent end of the exercise of rights. Thus, non-user may be evidence of abandonment of a private right of easement (q.v.), but in itself it will not suffice. See *Swan v Sinclair* [1925] AC 227; *Snell v Dutton Mirrors* [1995] 1 EGLR 259.

no-par-value shares. Because of the requirement that the nominal share capital of a company must be divided into shares of a fixed amount, shares of no-par-value cannot be issued. The *Jenkins Report 1962* recommended their issue.

Northern Ireland Assembly. Following Northern Ireland (Elections) Act 1998, s 1, setting up the Assembly, consisting of 108 members (six per constituency), and the granting of an Order for devolution, full legislative powers were granted to the Assembly under the Northern Ireland Act 1998. Bills become Acts when passed by the Assembly and after Royal Assent: s 5(1), (2). For entrenched enactments, see s 7. A First Minister, deputy and Presiding Officer are elected by Assembly members: ss 16(1), 39. The executive power in Northern Ireland continues to be vested in the Crown: s 23(1).

Northern Ireland, status of. Northern Ireland in its entirety remains part of the UK and shall not cease to be so without the consent of a majority of the people of Northern Ireland voting in a poll held for the purpose of this section in accordance with Sch 1: Northern Ireland Act 1998, s 1(1).

noscitur a sociis. Known from its associates. A rule of interpretation whereby the meaning of a word may be ascertained by reference to its immediate context. 'English words derive colour from those which surround them': *Bourne v Norwich Crematorium Ltd* [1967] 2 All ER 576.

notary. Known also as 'notary public'. Rights and privileges arise from Public Notaries Acts 1801–43. See also C.L.S.A. 1990, s 113; Acc.J.A. 1999, s 53. Usually a solicitor who attests deeds, or one, who, in the case of a dishonoured bill, notes or protests it.

not guilty. 1. Plea to an indictment which is, in essence, a challenge to the prosecution to establish guilt. It may be changed once the trial has started. 2. Verdict following trial, which, in effect, is an acquittal. The accused may be found not guilty of offences specifically charged in the indictment, but guilty of another offence arising from allegations therein. Where defendant pleads not guilty and the prosecution does not offer evidence, the judge may order the recording of a verdict of not guilty: C.J.A. 1967, s 17. See *R v Central Criminal Court ex p Spens* [1993] COD 194. *See* GUILTY; VERDICT.

not guilty by reason of insanity. A special verdict (q.v.) which is, in form, an acquittal.

notice. 1. Knowledge of some fact. May be (1) *actual*, as where, e.g., a purchaser is made aware during negotiations of the existence of a prior interest (see *Reeves* v *Pope* [1914] 2 KB 284); (2) *constructive* (q.v.); (3) *imputed*, as where, e.g., a purchaser employs a solicitor or other agent who obtains actual or constructive notice. See *Barclays Bank* v *Thompson* [1997] 4 All ER 816. 2. Notification of some state of affairs, required by law or some agreement. 3. Notice of a right or incumbrance entered on the charges register formerly under Land Registration Rules 1925, r 7, which acts to protect a minor interest (q.v.) but now governed by the LRA 2002, ss 32–37.

notice for possession, correct date of. In *McDonald* v *Fernandez* (2003) *The Times*, 9 October, the CA held that where a landlord issued a notice for possession, it was essential that the last date of the period of the periodic tenancy be stated. See Housing Act 1988, s 21(4)(a), and Housing Act 1996, s 98.

notice, minimum period of. Notice required to be given by an employer to terminate a contract of employment for a person who has been employed for one month or more is: not less than one week if period of employment is less than two years; not less than one week for each year of continuous employment if the period of continuous employment is two years or more but not less than 12 years; not less than 12 weeks if the period of continuous employment is 12 years or more: E.R.A. 1996, s 86(1). Notice required to be given by an employee who has been continuously employed for one week or more is not less than one week: s 86(2). A contract may be treated as terminable without notice by reason of the conduct of the other party: s 86(6).

notice of abandonment. Written or oral notice indicating that the assured (under a policy of marine insurance) abandons the subject matter insured unconditionally to the insured. If notice is not given, the loss is considered as partial. Notice must be given with reasonable diligence. *See* ABANDONMENT.

notice of dishonour. Notice that a bill of exchange (q.v.) is dishonoured must be

given to the parties whom the holder is seeking to hold liable. See B.Ex.A. 1882, s 49. *See* DISHONOUR OF BILL.

notice of hearing. An assertion by an asylum seeker that he has never received a notice of hearing necessitates his being given an opportunity to give evidence of that fact: *R (Karagoz)* v *Immigration Appeal Tribunal* (2003) *The Times*, 11 June.

notice of service. In *C Webber Ltd* v *Railtrack plc* (2003) *The Times*, 5 August, the CA held that where a postal recorded delivery notice has been sent by a landlord to a tenant at his place of work, it is deemed to have been served, and service is deemed to have been served irrebuttably, not at the date of actual delivery, but on the date the notice was sent. (It was held, further, that *Lex Services plc* v *Johns* [1990] 10 EG 67 was decided per incuriam.)

notice of title. Knowledge (actual, imputed, constructive) acquired by an intending purchaser that title is encumbered by rights or interests. *See* NOTICE; TITLE.

notice, protection by. Notices in registered land were originally classified as minor interests (q.v.) and protected by notice of an interest entered on the Charges Register (see L.R.R. 1925, rr 2, 7); they were then protected by making them binding on any third party who acquires interests thereafter in the land. See L.R.A. 1925, ss 48(1), 52(1); *Clark* v *Chief Land Registrar* [1994] Ch 370. Notices have now been subject to reform under the LRA 2002, s 32(1) where they are defined as 'an entry in the register in respect of the burden of an interest affecting a registered estate or charge'. The fact that a notice is registered does not necessarily mean that it is valid, though if it is valid it is protected against a purchaser of the registered estate for valuable consideration. Notices now exist in two forms: 'agreed notices' (LRA 2002, s 32 and 'unilateral notices' (LRA 2002, s 35) the latter protecting what were formerly cautions (q.v.).

notice to admit. Notice calling on the party served to admit the facts or the part of the case of the serving party, specified in the notice. Notice to admit facts must be served no later than 21 days before the trial. See r 32.18.

notice to quit. Notice, which must be unconditional, required to be given by a landlord or tenant or their authorised agents prior to the determination of tenancy. No notice to quit premises let as a dwelling is valid unless in writing and contains information prescribed by the Secretary of State by statutory instrument, and is given not less than four weeks before the date on which it is to take effect: Protection from Eviction Act 1977, s 5. See also L.P.A. 1925, s 196; Rent Act 1977, ss 103–106; *Rous v Mitchell* [1991] 1 WLR 469 (notice is invalid if it contains a false statement made fraudulently by the landlord, irrespective of whether the tenant is deceived); *Newlon Housing Trust v Alsulaimen* [1998] 3 WLR 451 (consideration by the House of Lords of the effect of a notice by a tenant to quit a joint periodic tenancy).

notification requirements in relation to sexual offences. A person is subject to notification requirements under the Sexual Offences Act 2003, for the appropriate notification period (set out in s 82): if he is convicted of an offence listed in Sch 3; if he is found not guilty of such an offence by reason of insanity; if he is found to be under a disability and to have done the act charged against him in respect of such an offence; if in England and Wales and Northern Ireland he is cautioned in respect of such an offence: s 80.

notification requirements where circumstances change. Under the Sexual Offences Act 2003, s 84, relevant offenders must, within a period of three days beginning with (a) his using a name which has not been notified to the police under s 83(1), this subsection, or Sex Offenders Act 1997; (b) any change of his home address; (c) his having resided or stayed for a qualifying period at any premises in the UK the address of which has not been notified to the police; (d) his release from custody pursuant to a court

order or from imprisonment, service detention or detention in a hospital, notify to the police that name, the new home address, the address of those premises, or the fact that he has been released, and other information set out in s 83(5).

noting a bill. Process of attaching a memorandum to a bill of exchange by a notary (q.v.), giving the reason for its having been dishonoured, as the first step to a protest (q.v.). See B.Ex.A. 1882, s 51. *See* BILL OF EXCHANGE.

not negotiable. Words marked on, e.g., a cheque or postal order, as a safeguard, so that the holder has no better right than the previous holder. See B.Ex.A. 1882, ss 76, 81; *Redmond v Allied Irish Banks* [1987] FLR 307. *See* NEGOTIABLE INSTRUMENT.

notorious facts. Matters of common knowledge of which, generally, judicial notice (q.v.) will be taken, e.g., that human gestation cannot be completed within 14 days (see *R v Luffe* (1807) 8 East 193).

nova causa interveniens. New intervening cause in a sequence of events. See, e.g., *Cummings v Sir William Arrol & Co Ltd* [1962] 1 All ER 623.

novation. Essentially a substituted agreement. Contract whereby a creditor at the request of a debtor agrees to take another person as debtor in place of the original debtor. The original debtor is thereby released from his obligations which fall on the new debtor. The new agreement requires consideration (q.v.). See *Customs and Excise Commissioners v Diners Club Ltd* [1989] 1 WLR 1196; *Re Datadeck Ltd* [1998] BCC 694.

novus actus interveniens. New intervening act. General defence in an action in tort (q.v.). When the act of a third person intervenes between the original act or omission and the damage, that act or omission is considered as the direct cause of the damage if the act of the third person could have been expected in the particular circumstances: *Scott v Shepherd* (1733) 2 Wm Bl 892. See *R v Pagett* (1983) 76 Cr App R 279; *The Sivand* [1998] 2 Lloyd's Rep 97. *See* CAUSA REMOTA.

no win, no fee. A conditional fee agreement (q.v.).

noxious. That which is offensive, or which causes or tends to cause injury to health. See O.P.A. 1861, ss 23, 24; *R v Marcus* [1981] 1 WLR 774 (concept of a 'noxious thing' depends not only on quality and nature of substance, but also the quantity administered); *R v Cronin-Simpson* [2000] 1 Cr App R (S) 54.

nuclear explosions, prohibition of. It is an offence for a UK national to knowingly cause a nuclear explosion in the UK or elsewhere except in the course of an armed conflict: Nuclear Explosions (Prohibition and Inspections) Act 1998, s 1 (giving effect to the Comprehensive Nuclear-Test Ban Treaty, adopted in New York in 1996). Provision for on-site inspections is made under s 5.

nuclear installations, operation of. No person other than the UK Atomic Energy Authority may use any site for purposes of nuclear plant operation unless a licence has been granted by the minister. See, e.g., Nuclear Installations Acts 1965 and 1969; Nuclear Materials (Offences) Act 1983; Energy Act 1983; Atomic Energy Act 1989; *MOD v Blue Circle Industries* [1999] 1 WLR 295; Nuclear Safeguards Act 2000 (powers of entry of inspectors of International Atomic Energy Agency); Terrorism Act 2000, s 55 (definition of nuclear weapon).

nuclear weapons, use of. Under Anti-terrorism, Crime and Security Act 2001, s 47, it is an offence to use, develop, produce, possess, participate in transferring, a nuclear weapon, subject to exceptions authorised by Secretary of State or in the course of armed conflict.

nudum pactum. A 'nude' contract, i.e., 'a bare promise of a thing without any consideration': Cowell, *Institutes of English Law* (1605). *See* CONSIDERATION.

nuisance. In law of torts, an unlawful interference with another's use of, enjoyment of, or right over or in relation to, land, or damage resulting from such interference: *Read v Lyons & Co Ltd* [1945] KB 216. Nuisance may be *public* (in which case it is also a crime), e.g.,

obstruction of a highway, or *private*, e.g., causing substantial and unreasonable personal discomfort to another. Remedies include: abatement, claim for damages, injunction (qq.v.). Defences include trivial injury only, isolated interference, result of lawful use of land (see *Bradford Corporation v Pickles* [1895] AC 587), prescriptive right. It is no defence that claimant came to the nuisance: *Miller v Jackson* [1977] QB 966. For 'statutory nuisances' in relation to pollution, see En.P.A. 1990, s 79. See also *R v Bristol CC ex p Everett* [1999] 1 WLR 92; *Griffiths v Pembrokeshire CC* (2000) *The Times*, 19 April. For nuisance by tenant as derogation from grant, see *Chartered Trust plc v Davies* (1997) 49 EG 135. For exemplary damages, see *AB and Others v SW Water Services Ltd* (1992) 142 NLJ 897. *See* ABATEMENT; PUBLIC NUISANCE; TORT.

nuisance, continuing. In *Delaware Mansions Ltd v Westminster CC* (2001) 151 NLJ 1611, HL decided that where there was a continuing nuisance (damage to property resulting from tree roots) of which defendant knew or ought to have known, the property owner may recover reasonable remedial expenditure he has incurred.

nuisance, neighbourhood. Conduct which interferes with a neighbour's quiet enjoyment of his home. See Protection from Harassment Act 1997. Under H.A. 1985, Sch 2, a protected tenancy can be forfeited where the tenant or person residing in a dwelling house has been guilty of conduct 'which is a nuisance or annoyance to neighbours'. See *Northampton BC v Lovatt* [1998] EHLR 59, in which Henry LJ stated that 'neighbours' was clearly intended to cover all persons sufficiently close to the conduct complained of to be adversely affected by that conduct, and cited GK Chesterton's observation: 'Your next door neighbour . . . is not a man; he is an environment'.

nuisance, unreasonableness causing. 'It may broadly be said that a useful test is perhaps what is reasonable according to the ordinary usages of mankind living in society, or, more correctly, in a particular society': *per* Knight-Bruce VC in *Sedleigh-Denfield* v *O'Callaghan* [1940] AC 880. 'Those acts necessary for the common and ordinary use and occupation of land and houses may be done, if conveniently done, without subjecting those who do them to an action': *Bamford* v *Turnley* (1860) 3 B & S 62.

null and void. Having no force; invalid.

nullity decree, recognition of foreign. The decree (in relation to a marriage) is recognised if: granted by a court in the parties' common domicile; although granted elsewhere, it is recognised as effective by courts of common domicile; granted by a court of the parties' common residence or a court of the country in which a void marriage was celebrated; at the time of the decree either party had a substantial connection with the country granting the decree.

nullity of marriage. Marriages may be rendered *void* (because the parties are within prohibited degrees of relationship (q.v.), or either party is under 16, or either party was lawfully married at the time of the ceremony) or *voidable* (because of, e.g., wilful refusal to consummate (q.v.), incapacity, pregnancy at time of marriage by some person other than the petitioner, lack of valid consent to the marriage). 'A void marriage is one that will be regarded by every court in any case in which the existence of the marriage is in issue as never having taken place, and can be so treated by both parties to it without the necessity of any decree annulling it; a voidable marriage is one that will be regarded by every court as a valid and subsisting marriage until a decree annulling it has been pronounced': *De Reneville* v *De Reneville* [1948] P 100. See Mat.C.A. 1973, ss 11, 12, 15B; Marriage Act 1983,

s 6; for time limits on bringing proceedings (and other bars to the decree) see Mat.C.A. 1973, s 13 (as amended by Matrimonial and Family Proceedings Act 1984, s 2); Marriage Act 1949, s 49, as amended by Marriage Act 1994, Schedule, para 3.

nullum crimen sine lege. No crime except in accordance with the law – an aspect of the so-called 'principle of legality'. Basis of the rejection of retrospective legislation (q.v.). 'The great leading rule of criminal law is that nothing is a crime unless it is plainly forbidden by law. This rule is no doubt subject to exceptions but they are rare, narrow, and to be admitted with the greatest reluctance, and only upon the strongest reasons': *per* Stephen LJ in *R* v *Price* (1884) 12 QBD 247. See European Convention on Human Rights 1950, art 7.

nullum tempus occurrit regi. Time does not run against the Crown, i.e., there is no limitation period on prosecutions unless specifically provided by statute. See Lim.A. 1980, s 37; M.C.A. 1980, s 127. See also *R* v *Lewis* [1979] 1 WLR 970; *Re Debtor (No. 647)* (2000) *The Times*, 10 April.

number and gender, rules of interpretation. In any statute, unless the contrary intention appears, words in the singular include the plural, and words in the plural include words in the singular; words importing the masculine gender include the feminine and words importing the feminine gender include the masculine: I.A. 1978, s 6. See *Re Surrey Leisure Ltd* [1999] 2 BCLC 457.

nuncupative will. (*Nuncupare* = to name, declare.) A verbal testament. Abolished under W.A. 1837, s 9, except in the case of privileged wills (q.v.) made by those on active service.

O

oath. A solemn appeal (usually to God) to witness that some statement is true or that some promise is binding. In general all evidence (q.v.) must be on oath. A witness's oath is: 'I swear by Almighty God that the evidence which I shall give shall be the truth, the whole truth and nothing but the truth'. See Oaths Act 1978; C.&Y.P.A. 1963, s 28; Ch.A. 1989, s 96(1); *R v Bellamy* (1986) 82 Cr App R 222; *R v Kemble* [1990] 1 WLR 1111. *See* AFFIRM; MEMBERS' OATH; PERJURY.

oath, judge's. *See* JUDGE'S OATH.

oath, juror's. *See* JUROR'S OATH.

oath of allegiance. Oath taken, e.g., by officers of the Crown on appointment. 'I do swear that I will be faithful and bear true allegiance to Her Majesty Queen Elizabeth II, her heirs and successors, according to law.' See Promissory Oaths Acts 1868, 1871; C.L.S.A. 1990, s 76. A somewhat similar oath is taken by an alien on obtaining a certificate of naturalisation.

Oaths, Commissioners for. *See* COMMISSIONERS FOR OATHS.

obedience to superior's orders, defence of. There is no general defence of superior orders in English criminal law: *per* Lord Slynn in *Yip Chiu Cheung v R* [1995] 1 AC 111. See also *R v Clegg* [1995] 1 AC 482.

obiter dictum. (*Pl*: *obiter dicta*.) Something said by the way. Refers to: a statement of the law by the judge based on facts which were not present, or not material, in a case (see, e.g., the judgment of Denning J in *Central London Property Trust Ltd v High Trees House Ltd* [1947] KB 30); a statement of law based on facts as found, but not forming the basis of the decision (e.g., a statement upon which a dissenting judgment is based).

It will be of persuasive authority only, and its worth will reflect the seniority of the judge and his position. See *West & Parners Ltd v Dick* [1969] 1 All ER 289. *See* RATIO DECIDENDI.

objection to indictment. Procedure whereby the accused attempts to show that the indictment (q.v.) is open to legal objection, e.g., because the court lacks jurisdiction to try that offence.

objects clause. Clause in memorandum of association (q.v.) setting out the objects which a company (q.v.) has been formed to pursue. See Cos.A. 1985, s 2(1)(c). A company may adopt a single object, namely to carry on any business or trade whatsoever: Cos.A. 1989, s 110. Objects may be altered by special resolution: Cos.A. 1989, s 110, amending Cos.A. 1985, s 4. See *Brady v Brady* [1988] 2 WLR 1308.

objects, main, rules. Where in a company's memorandum of association the objects clause sets out that company's main objects and links others, those others will be construed as incidental to the main objects: see *Stephens v Mysore Reefs Mining Ltd* [1902] 1 Ch 745; *Cotman v Brougham* [1918] AC 514.

objects of a power. Where an appointor is authorised to appoint an interest to the members of a generally restricted class (e.g., 'amongst the children of X'), those whom he may select are known as the 'objects of the power'. *See* APPOINTMENT, POWER OF.

obligation. 1. A duty, usually legal or moral and of one's choosing, to undertake or not to undertake a course of action. 'The word means, primarily, a tie. Legally it was in origin the binding tie established by what is called a "bond" as between the obligor and the obligee': *per* Scott LJ in *Watkinson v Hollington* [1943] 2 All ER 573. For 'reciprocity of obligations', see *Jamaica Mutual Life Assurance Society v Hillsborough Ltd* [1989] 1 WLR 1101. 2. A bond (q.v.) with a condition annexed, usually involving a penalty for non-fulfilment. 3. A 'planning obligation', under Planning and Compensation Act 1991, s 12, restricts the development of land in a specified way.

obligee. *See* BOND.

obligor. *See* BOND.

obliteration. That which has been made impossible to decipher, e.g., by erasure. In the case of a will (q.v.), no obliteration is valid except so far as the words of the will before the obliteration are not apparent, unless the obliteration has been properly signed and attested. A complete obliteration is usually valid, so that probate (q.v.) will be granted as though the will contained blanks. See *In b Horsford* (1874) LR 3 P & D 211.

obscenity. 'An article shall be deemed to be obscene if its effect or (where the article comprises two or more distinct items) the effect of any one of its items is, if taken as a whole, such as to tend to deprave [q.v.] and corrupt persons who are likely, having regard to all relevant circumstances, to read, see or hear the matter contained or embodied in it': Obscene Publications Act 1959, s 1(1). Obscenity is not confined to books, etc., dealing with sex: *Calder Publications Ltd v Powell* [1965] 1 QB 509. It is an offence to possess an obscene article for publication for gain (Obscene Publications Act 1964, s 1(1)); to send by post a packet containing any indecent or obscene print or article (Postal Services Act 2000, s 85(3)). For obscene phone calls, constituting a public nuisance, see *R v Norbury* [1978] Crim LR 435. See Cable and Broadcasting Act 1984, s 25; Broadcasting Act 1990, s 162; C.J.P.O.A. 1994, s 85 (power of immediate arrest of persons trading in obscene matter and child pornography); *R v Gibson* [1990] 3 WLR 595 (offence of outraging public decency at common law); *R v Fellows* [1997] 1 Cr App

R 244 (images on computer disk). *See* PUBLICATION.

obstruction of highway. *See* HIGHWAY, OBSTRUCTION OF.

obstruction of police. *See* POLICE, OBSTRUCTION OF.

obstruction of recovery of premises. *See* RECOVERY OF PREMISES, OBSTRUCTION OF.

obtaining   credit,   undischarged bankrupt. An offence if the bankrupt obtains credit to the extent of the prescribed amount or over without informing the intending creditor that he is an undischarged bankrupt, or without disclosing the name under which he was adjudged bankrupt. See Ins.A. 1986, s 20; *Re Alexander Securities Ltd* [1999] 1 BCLC 124.

obtaining further information. Where a written request for further information is served on a party, and made under CCR, Part 18, and no response or an insufficient response, is received, an application for an order can be made, and an order served on all parties to a claim: r 18.1. Objections to a response may be based on insufficient time to formulate a reply, or expense of responding which is disproportionate to claim. The court can order that the information in question be given.

obtaining pecuniary advantage. *See* DECEPTION, OBTAINING PROPERTY BY.

occasional. That which occurs casually or intermittently: *per* Hale LJ in *Shell Tankers Ltd v Jeromson* (2001) *The Times*, 2 March.

occupancy. The taking possession of, and acquiring title to, that which has no apparent owner.

occupant. 1. One who takes by occupancy. 2. One who resides in a place.

occupation. 1. A person's trade, calling. 2. The taking and controlling of enemy territory by the armed forces of the Crown. 3. Control, actual physical possession, of land, or its use. A person was held to be 'in actual occupation' only if that occupation was recognisable as such and apparent to a purchaser: *Hodgson v Marks* [1970] 3 All ER 513. 'Occupation is a matter of fact and only exists where there is sufficient measure of control to prevent strangers from interfering': *Newcastle CC v Royal Newcastle Hospital* [1959] 1 All ER 734.

occupational order. *See* INJUNCTIONS RELATING TO DOMESTIC VIOLENCE.

occupational pension scheme. 'Any scheme or arrangement which is comprised in one or more instruments or agreements and which has, or is capable of having, effect in relation to one or more descriptions or categories of employment so as to provide benefits, in the form of pensions or otherwise, payable on termination of service, or on death or retirement, to or in respect of earners with qualifying service in an employment of any such description or category': Pension Schemes Act 1993, s 1. See Finance Act 2000, Sch 13; C.S.P.S.S.A. 2000, s 43. *See* PERSONAL PENSION SCHEME.

occupational stress. A condition experienced by persons who perceive an inability to meet demands and pressures placed on them, resulting in ill-health of a psychological and/or physiological nature. See H.S.W.A. 1974, s 2(1); Management of Health and Safety at Work Regulations 1992, reg 3; SI 92/2051; SI 99/2024; *Walker v Northumberland CC* [1995] IRLR 35.

occupation rent. The court can order payment of an occupation rent where one co-owner in occupation has ousted the other, and in any other case where it is necessary to do equity between the co-owners: In *Re Byford* (2003) *The Times*, 13 June.

occupation road. *See* ROAD, OCCUPATION.

occupier. One who has possession as owner or tenant (q.v.) of land or a house and has the degree of control associated with his presence on the land or in the house. For 'multiple occupancy', see, e.g., *Hadjiloucas v Crean* [1988] 1 WLR 1006. *See* HOUSE IN MULTIPLE OCCUPATION.

occupier, residential. *See* RESIDENTIAL OCCUPIER.

occupiers' liability. HL held in *Tomlinson v Congleton BC* [2003] UKHL 47,

that where a swimmer suffered serious injury following his diving in an area in which diving was prohibited, the local council was not liable for a claim under Occupiers' Liability Act 1984, s 1.

occupiers' liability, principle of. An occupier has a common duty of care (q.v.) to all persons on his premises by his invitation or permission, express or implicit. 'Wherever a person has a sufficient degree of control over premises to realise that any failure on his part to use care may result in injury to a person coming lawfully there, then he is an "occupier"': *Wheat v Lacon & Co* [1966] AC 552. See Occupiers' Liability Acts 1957, 1984; Defective Premises Act 1972; *Jolley v Sutton LBC* (2000) *The Times*, 24 May.

occupier's liability to a visitor. In *Maquire v Sefton Metropolitan Borough Council and Another* [2006] *The Times*, 16 March, the local authority were not liable under the Occupier's Liability Act 1957 for injuries sustained by a visitor in a leisure centre where they had taken reasonable steps by entering into a maintenance contract with a third party to ensure that the equipment was safe for use.

occupiers' liability to non-visitors. An occupier of premises owes a duty to another (not being his visitor (q.v.)) if he is aware of any danger due to the state of the premises or has reasonable grounds to believe that the danger exists, and knows or has reasonable grounds to believe that the other is in the vicinity of the danger concerned and the risk is one against which, in all the circumstances, he may reasonably be expected to offer the other some protection: Occupiers' Liability Act 1984, s 1. See C.R.W.A. 2000, s 13. See *Smith v Littlewoods* [1987] AC 241; *Ratcliff v McConnell* [1999] 1 WLR 670.

occupier's liability, trespasser's activities. In *Keown v Coventry Healthcare NHS Trust* [2006] *The Times*, 10 February, the NHS Trust were not liable under s 1(1) of the Occupier's Liability Act 1984, as it was the claimant's activity that put him in danger and not the state of the premises.

occupying tenant. In relation to a dwelling, this means the person who is not an owner-occupier but who occupies or is entitled to occupy the dwelling as a lessee, or is a statutory tenant of the dwelling, or occupies the dwelling as a residence under a restricted contract (q.v.) or occupies or resides in the dwelling as part of his employment in agriculture: H.A. 1985, s 236(2).

OECD. Organisation for European Co-operation and Development, established in 1961, comprising 29 member states. Its objective is the promotion of freer trade and the stimulation of Western aid to undeveloped countries. A group of seven states (Canada, France, Germany, Italy, Japan, UK, USA) is known as the Group of Seven (G7) which steers the organisation.

OFCOM. The Office of Communications, set up under the Communications Act 2003, s 1. Its principal duties are to further the interests of citizens in relation to communications matters, and to further the interests of consumers in relevant markets, where appropriate by promoting competition: s 3.

OFCOM's Content Board. Under the Communications Act 2003, ss 12, 13, a committee is to be set up, comprising a chairman and other members, with the duty of ensuring that the interest of the public in the nature and quality of TV and radio programmes is represented within OFCOM.

OFCOM's Standards Code. Under the Communications Act 2003, s 319, OFCOM has a duty to set, review and revise programme content of TV and radio so as to secure 'standards objectives'. These include: protection of persons under 18; exclusion of material likely to encourage or incite commission of crime or lead to disorder; reporting of news with due accuracy and impartiality; exclusion of advertising which may be misleading or harmful.

offence. Generally, that which is equivalent to a crime, i.e., an act or omission punishable under criminal law: *Derbyshire CC* v *Derby* [1896] 2 QB 57; *Horsfield* v *Brown* [1932] 1 KB 355. *See* ACTIVITY OFFENCE; OFFENDER.

offence, associated. *See* ASSOCIATED OFFENCE.

offence, racially-aggravated. *See* RACIALLY-AGGRAVATED OFFENCE.

offences, duplicated. *See* DUPLICATED OFFENCES.

offences, general classification of. Division of offences for purposes of criminal procedure into: indictable offences; summary offences; offences triable either way (qq.v.): C.L.A. 1977, s 14 (repealed without needing replacement).

offences triable either way. Offences which, if committed by an adult, are triable either on indictment (q.v.) or summarily (q.v.): C.L.A. 1977, s 64(1)(*c*). See M.C.A. 1980, s 17, as amended by C.P.I.A. 1996, s 49, allowing accused to indicate an intention to plead guilty, following which the court will proceed as if the proceedings constituted from the beginning the summary trial of the information and as if accused had pleaded guilty under M.C.A. 1980, s 9. Some offences triable either way may be tried summarily if the value involved is small: M.C.A. 1980, s 22. See I.A. 1978, Sch 1; *Practice Note* [1990] 3 All ER 979.

offence, violent. *See* VIOLENCE.

offence, weapon of. 'An article made or adapted for use for causing injury to or incapacitating a person, or intended by the person having it with him for such use': Th.A. 1968, s 10(1)(*a*); C.L.A. 1977, s 8(2). For use of the head as a weapon ('head-butting'), see *R* v *Rigg* (1997) *The Times*, 4 July. *See* OFFENSIVE WEAPON.

offender. One who is guilty of an offence (q.v.). For 'persistent offender', see P.C.C.(S.)A. 2000, s 59; *R* v *C (Young Person: Persistent Offender)* (2000) *The Times*, 11 October (consideration of definition in Home Office Circular *(Tackling Delays in Youth Justice System)* 1997, 15 October, Annex C).

offender, fugitive. *See* FUGITIVE CRIMINAL.

offender-naming scheme, intrusion into family life. Proposal by police of a scheme of offender-naming, intended to reduce burglary, ought to be further considered and appraised so as to determine whether its likely benefits are proportionate to the resulting intrusion into an offender's family and personal privacy: *R (Ellis)* v *Chief Constable of Essex Police* (2003) *The Times*, 17 June.

offenders, management of. Home Secretary has announced (see *The Times*, 14 January 2005) that a contemplated Management of Offenders and Sentencing Bill will allow for maximum fines of £15,000 to be imposed by magistrates, and for lie detectors to be used on sex offenders released on licence. Offenders' fines may be linked to disposable income as well as seriousness of offence.

offender's sentence history. In *R* v *Egan* (2004) *The Times*, 9 March, the CA held that offender's history should contain details of previous sentences, dates of release, since, in the absence of information of this nature, the sentencing judge's task became difficult.

offensive weapon. 'Any article made or adapted for use for causing injury to the person, or intended by the person having it with him for such use by him or by some other person': Prevention of Crime Act 1953, s 1(4), as amended by P.O.A. 1986. It is an offence to have, without lawful authority, or reasonable excuse, such an article in any public place: s 1(1). See P.&C.E.A. 1984, s 1(9); C.J.A. 1988, ss 139, 141; Offensive Weapons Act 1996; Terrorism Act 2000, s 54 (offence of providing weapons training); *Houghton* v *Chief Constable of Manchester* (1987) 84 Cr App R 320; *R* v *Densu* [1998] 1 Cr App R 400 (defence of 'good reason'); *R* v *Glidewell* (1999) 163 JP 557 (forgetfulness may be relevant in determining a 'reasonable excuse'). *See* KNIVES.

offensive weapon, possession of, sentencing. In *R* v *Poulton* (2002) *The Times*, 1 November, the CA held that, in considering seriousness of having a weapon in a public place, attention should be given to: offender's intention (e.g., specific planned use of weapon to commit violence, any context of racial hostility); circumstances of offence (e.g.,

presence of specially vulnerable persons); nature of weapon. Mitigation might be found if, e.g., weapon was being carried only temporarily.

offer. A proposal, written or oral, to give or do something, e.g., to enter a legally binding contract on specified terms. It may be *express* or *implied* from conduct. The person making the offer is the *offeror*; the person to whom it is made is the *offeree*. General rules are: (1) an offer may be made to a definite person, definite class of persons or the world at large; (2) an offer must be communicated to the offeree before acceptance; (3) it is only made when it reaches the offeree, not when it might have reached him in ordinary course of post. Where negotiation becomes a definite offer from one party and only requires acceptance to make it into a binding contract, there is said to be a 'firm offer': see, e.g., *Dickinson* v *Dodds* (1876) 2 Ch D 463. See, e.g., *Adams* v *Lindsell* (1818) 1 B & Ald 681; *Carlill* v *Carbolic Smoke Ball Co* [1893] 1 QB 256; *Schuldenfrei* v *Hilton* [1998] STC 404. *See* ACCEPTANCE; CONTRACT; LAPSE OF OFFER; REJECTION OF OFFER.

offer, counter-. Response of an offeree which, in effect, suggests an agreement on terms which differ from those of the original offer. Example: 'You can have my car for £3,000.' 'I'll give you £2,800 for it.' It amounts to a rejection of the original offer. See *Hyde* v *Wrench* (1840) 3 Beav 334; and *Butler Machine Tool Co* v *Ex-Cell-O Corp* [1979] 1 WLR 401.

offer for sale. Document offering shares to the public, issued by an issuing house which has bought the shares outright from a public company. See Cos.A. 1985, s 58 (now repealed: F.S.A. 1986, Parts IV, V).

offers, cross-. Offers which cross, e.g., in the post. Example: A and B discuss the sale and purchase of A's motor car; A then writes to B offering to sell the car for £10,000, and, simultaneously, B writes to A offering to buy it for £10,000. See *Tinn* v *Hoffman* (1873) 29 LT 271.

office of profit. A paid office under the Crown. Except as provided by House of

Commons Disqualification Act 1975, a person shall not be disqualified from membership of the House by reason of his holding an office or place of profit under the Crown or any other office or place: 1975 Act, s 1(4), as amended.

office premises. A building or part of a building, the sole or principal use of which is an office or for office purposes: Offices, Shops and Railway Premises Act 1963, s 1. See also H.S.W.A. 1974; Workplace (Health, Safety and Welfare) Regulations 1992.

officer. One holding a position of command, authority, trust. See *Moberley* v *Alsop* [1992] COD 190 (key to meaning of the word was in the designation of an employee to perform a particular duty).

Official Custodian for Charities. Created under Charities Act 1960, s 3. Charity property may be vested in him by a court order; he does not exercise powers of management, but has, in general, the same powers as a custodian trustee (q.v.). See Charities Act 1993, s 2(1); *Muman* v *Nagasena* [1999] 4 All ER 178. *See* CHARITY.

official receiver. Appointed by Secretary of State in relation to matters concerning bankruptcy (q.v.) and winding-up (q.v.): Ins.A. 1986, s 399. He is considered an officer of the court in relation to which he exercises the function: s 400(2).

official referee. Judge appointed to consider, e.g., an arbitration agreement, trials involving substantial technical detail or documents or matters relating to accounts. See also C.L.S.A. 1990, s 11. The office was abolished under Courts Act 1971, s 25, and jurisdiction conferred upon persons nominated by the Lord Chancellor to take 'official referees' business'. Appeal was to Court of Appeal. See S.C.A. 1981, s 68 (as amended by A.J.A. 1982, s 59); *Tate and Lyle Ltd* v *Davy McKee Ltd* [1990] 1 All ER 157. The Official Referee's court is now to be known as The Technology and Construction Court (q.v.). *See* REFEREE.

official search. Search by the registrar, made on requisition (q.v.), so as to discover the existence of registrable incumbrances on land. The issue of an official certificate is conclusive in favour of a purchaser or intending purchaser, so that he is free from liability arising from rights which the official search failed to disclose.

official secrets. Matters concerning state security, covered under Official Secrets Acts 1911–1989. It is an offence for a person to approach or inspect a prohibited place for any purpose prejudicial to the safety or interests of the state, to use certain types of information for the benefit of a foreign power or in another manner prejudicial to state interests. Categories of official information, the unauthorised disclosure of which may be a crime, are set out in the 1989 Act; see also SI 90/200. See European Communities Act 1972, s 11; *R* v *Galvin* [1987] QB 862; *R* v *Blake* [1998] Ch 439.

Official Solicitor. An official who acts for those involved in High Court (q.v.) proceedings who are under a disability. He will brief counsel to appear as 'next friend' (q.v.) where there is no other person willing or competent to do so. He may also defend, e.g., a minor (q.v.) or patient as guardian *ad litem* (q.v.). He can be appointed as judicial trustee (q.v.) in proceedings relating to disputed trusts. See S.C.A. 1981, s 90.

off-market deals. Defined in Company Securities (Insider Dealing) Act 1985, s 13 (as modified by F.S.A. 1986, s 174), as dealings otherwise than on a recognised investment exchange (q.v.) in a company's advertised securities through an off-market dealer (i.e., one who is authorised under, e.g., Cos.A. 1985, s 164). See Cos.A. 1985, s 163 (as amended by F.S.A. 1986, Sch 16, para 17). *See* INSIDER DEALING.

offshore fund. Defined under Finance Act 2004, Sch 26, para 3, as a collective investment scheme constituted by a company that is resident outside the UK, or a unit trust scheme the trustees of which are not resident in the UK.

offshore fund, material interest in. An interest in any collective investment scheme which is constituted by (a) a company which is resident outside the UK; (b) a unit trust scheme the trustees of which are not resident in the UK; or (c) any arrangements which do not fall within para (a) or (b) above, which take effect by virtue of the law of a territory outside the UK and which, under that law, create rights in the nature of co-ownership (without restricting that expression to its meaning in the law of any part of the UK): I.C.T.A. 1988, s 759, as amended by Finance Act 1995, s 134(2). For 'collective investment scheme', see F.S.A. 1986, s 75. See T.C.G.A. 1992, Sch 10, para 14(5); SI 97/213.

offshore installation. Defined under Finance Act 2004, Sch 27, as a structure which is to be or has been put to a specified use while standing in any waters, stationed by whatever means in any waters or standing on the foreshore or other land intermittently covered with water. 'Use' includes, e.g., for exploitation of mineral resources by means of a wall, for storage of gas, for conveyance of things by means of a pipe.

Ogden Tables. Actuarial tables for use in personal injury and fatal accident cases, issued by the Government Actuary's Department. They are admissible in evidence for the purpose of assessing in an action for personal injury, the sum to be awarded as general damages for future pecuniary loss: Civil Evidence Act 1995, s 10(1). They may be proved by the production of a copy published by HMSO: s 10(2). 'Personal injury' includes, for the purposes of s 10, any disease and any impairment of a person's physical or mental condition; 'action for personal injury' includes an action brought by virtue of Law Reform (Misc. Provs.) Act 1934, or Fatal Accidents Act 1976: s 10(3). See *Worrall* v *Powergen plc* [1999] Lloyd's Rep Med 177. A new edition of the Tables (relating to the calculation of future losses) was published in November 2004.

OJ. Official Journal. The official daily publication of the European Union containing, e.g., details of Community legislation, proceedings of the European Court and proposals made by the Commissioners. Published in all official languages of EU, and in three series: 'L' (Legislation), including text of EU legislative acts; 'C' (Communications), including legislative proposals from commission, and extracts from Court judgments; 'S' (Supplement), including invitations to tender for public works contracts.

old-age pension. Colloquialism for social security benefit, known as 'state retirement pension'. *See* PENSION, STATE RETIREMENT.

Old Bailey. Central Criminal Court (q.v.).

Ombudsman. Swedish term for 'representative'. See, e.g., L.G.A. 1974, s 23; F.I.A. 2000, Sch 7, paras 1, 2, 12.

Ombudsman, Conveyancing. Appointed under C.L.S.A. 1990, s 43, to consider and report on any breach of the regulations concerning the conduct of authorised conveyancing practitioners. See Sch 7.

Ombudsman, European Community. Appointed by European Parliament under Treaty of Rome 1957, art 138e. He may receive complaints relating to maladministration by Community institutions (except the Courts of Justice and First Instance) made directly or through an MEP. He has no sanctions at his disposal.

Ombudsman, Legal Services. Appointed under C.L.S.A. 1990, s 21 and Legal Services Ombudsman (Jurisdiction) Order 1990, by the Lord Chancellor to investigate the way in which a complaint has been handled by legal professional bodies. He is also empowered to investigate the original complaint: s 22(2). He may recommend reconsideration of the complaint and payment of compensation for loss or distress suffered by the complainant, or order a person or body to take appropriate action following his investigation: s 23 amended by Acc.J.A. 1999, s 49. For funding by professional bodies, see C.L.S.A. 1990, Sch 3, para 7(1), (1A), substituted by Acc.J.A. 1999, s 50. The powers of the Ombudsman have no application where the Legal Services Complaints Commissioner (q.v.) is involved in an investigation: s 50(6). For discharge of functions, see Sch 3.

Ombudsman, Local Administration.
Commissioner appointed under L.G.A.
1974, s 23, with jurisdiction involving, e.g.,
the investigation of complaints against
local councils, involving, e.g., maladministration (q.v.). See *Croydon LBC* v
Commissioner for Local Administration
[1989] 1 All ER 1033.

Ombudsman,   Pensions. Appointed
under Social Security Pensions Act 1975,
as amended by S.S.A. 1990, s 12, Sch 3,
Pensions Scheme Act 1993, Part X, and
C.S.P.S.S.A. 2000, ss 53, 54, to investigate
and determine written complaints in connection with any act or omission of the
trustees or managers of an occupational
or personal pension scheme. See *Edge* v
Pensions Ombudsman [1999] 4 All ER
546 (persons who will be affected by the
Ombudsman's decisions must have a fair
opportunity to make representations to
him); *Wakelin* v *Read* (2000) *The Times*,
10 April (Ombudsman can act only in
accordance with legal principles). *See*
OCCUPATIONAL PENSION SCHEME.

omission. A blank in a document.
The general presumption (q.v.), where
blanks are found to have been filled in a
will by the testator, is that they were
filled before the execution of the will. See
Birch v *Birch* (1848) Not Cas 581; *Re
Shearn* (1880) 50 LJP 15.

omission to act. Failure to execute a
duty to act may constitute an element of
an *actus reus* (q.v.). Examples include the
duty to act imposed by: statute (see, e.g.,
Road Traffic Act 1988, s 170; Prisoners
(Return to Custody) Act 1995, s 1);
contract (see, e.g., *R* v *Pittwood* (1902)
19 TLR 37); relationship (see, e.g., *R* v
Smith [1979] Crim LR 251); office (see
R v *Dytham* [1979] QB 722). See *Smith* v
Littlewoods Ltd [1987] AC 241 (discussion of acts and omissions); *Greener* v
DPP [1996] COD 200.

***omnia praesumuntur rite et solemniter
esse acta.*** All things are presumed to
be done correctly and solemnly (i.e., until
the contrary shall be proved). The so-
called 'presumption of legality'. See, e.g.,
Dillon v *R* [1982] AC 484; *R* v *IRC ex
p Coombs* [1991] STC 97.

onerous. Unreasonably burdensome. For
the power of a trustee in bankruptcy to
disclaim onerous property (e.g., unprofitable contracts, unsaleable property),
see Ins.A. 1986, ss 178(3), 315.

**one-stop procedure and immigration
appeals.** Where a person is an illegal
entrant, is liable to be removed under
Immigration and Asylum Act 1999, s 10,
or has arrived in UK without leave to enter
or an entry clearance or work permit,
and makes an asylum claim, the person
responsible for determining the claim
must serve on claimant a notice requiring
him to state any additional grounds he has
for wishing to enter or remain in UK: 1999
Act, s 75. See SI 00/2244.

onus probandi. Burden of proof (q.v.).

open contract. In the case of a contract
for sale of land it refers to one which
merely contains, e.g., names of parties,
price, description of property. Certain
conditions are implied by law, e.g., that
the vendor shall show good title. See
Bigg v *Boyd Gibbins Ltd* [1971] 1 WLR
913. *See* FORMAL CONTRACT.

open country. Land which appears to the
appropriate countryside body to consist
wholly or predominantly of mountain,
moor, heath or down, and is not registered common land: C.R.W.A. 2000,
s 1(2).

open court. Court to which public has
unrestricted access. See *R* v *Denbigh
Justices* [1974] QB 759, *per* Lord Widgery:
'The injunction to the presiding judge or
magistrate is: do your best to enable the
public to come in and see what is happening, having a proper commonsense
regard for the facilities available and the
facility for keeping order, security and
the like.' See M.C.A. 1980, s 121(4).
Under CPR, hearings shall be held in
public (r 39.2(1)) except where: publicity
would defeat the object of the hearing, or
national security is involved, or confidentiality might be destroyed, or the interests
of a child or mental patient require protection, or the interests of justice necessitate a private hearing: r 39.2(3). Under O
52, r 6 (see CPR, Sch 1) an application
for an order of committal may be heard

by a court sitting in private, where, e.g., secret processes or matters of national security are involved. See PD 39, para 1.5; European Convention on Human Rights, art 6(1); *B* v *UK (Hearing In Private)* [2000] 2 FCR 97. *See* IN CAMERA.

open court, proceeding in. In *R (CPS)* v *Bolton Magistrates' Court* [2004] 168 JP 10, it was held that the taking of a deposition from a witness who refuses to make a statement voluntarily (see Crime and Disorder Act 1998, Sch 3, para 9) is to be considered as a proceeding in open court.

opening speech. Speech made by prosecuting counsel comprising allegations against the defendant (in outline) and the evidence it is proposed to call. Defending counsel may make an opening speech where he is calling witnesses as to fact in addition to the defendant.

open justice. 'It is not merely of some importance but is of fundamental importance that justice should not only be done, but should manifestly and undoubtedly be seen to be done': *per* Lord Hewart CJ in *R* v *Sussex Justices ex p McCarthy* [1924] 1 KB 256. See Official Secrets Act 1920, s 8; M.C.A 1980, s 121(4); C.J.A. 1988, s 159; C.P.I.A. 1996, s 61; *Re Crook* [1992] 2 All ER 687.

open space. Any land, enclosed or not, on which there are no buildings or of which not more than one-twentieth part is covered with buildings, and the whole or remainder of which is laid out as a garden or is used for recreational purposes, or lies waste and unoccupied: see Open Spaces Act 1906, s 20. See also T.C.P.A. 1990, s 336(1); *Ward* v *Secretary of State for the Environment* (1989) *The Times*, 5 October; *Re West Norwood Cemetery (No. 2)* [1998] Fam 84.

open verdict. Verdict of coroner's jury leaving open the question of how a person met his death.

operations in land development. Work which changes the physical characteristics of the land, or of what is below it, or of the air above it: *per* Lord Parker in *Cheshire CC* v *Woodward* [1962] 2 QB 126. *See* DEVELOPMENT.

operative part. That part of a deed (q.v.) in which the principal object is effected (e.g., actual conveyance of property) as contrasted with recitals (q.v.).

operative words. The precise words through which the purpose of some document is attained, e.g., the words which can create or transfer an estate (q.v.). *See* LIMITATION, WORDS OF.

opinion. 1. Term applied to a judgment delivered by the Law Lords in the House of Lords (q.v.). 2. Advice by counsel on a particular point. 3. Inference based upon observations.

opinion, expert. *See* EXPERT WITNESS OPINION.

opinions, EU. *See* COMMUNITY LEGISLATION, FORMS OF.

opinions in evidence. Opinions (i.e. thoughts, beliefs, inferences) of ordinary (non-expert) persons are generally irrelevant and inadmissible as evidence. Exceptions include: matters of identity; age; speed of a car; handwriting (where the witness has seen the accused person writing); proof that the witness understood a libel to refer to the plaintiff. Under Civil Evidence Act 1972, s 3, in civil proceedings a non-expert witness may give his opinions on an ultimate issue in the form of a statement made as a way of conveying relevant facts personally perceived by him. See Civil Evidence Act 1995, Sch 2; *R* v *Robb* (1991) 93 Cr App R 161. *See* EXPERT WITNESS OPINION.

Opposition, Leader of HM. 'That member of the House [of Commons] who is for the time being the Leader in that House of the party in opposition to HM Government having the greatest numerical strength in the House of Commons': Ministerial and other Salaries Act 1975, s 2(1).

oppression. 'A disregard of the essentials of justice and the infliction of a penalty which is not properly related to the crime of which the party stands convicted, but is either to be regarded as merely vindictive or having proceeded upon some improper or irregular consideration': *Stewart* v *Cormack* 1941 SC(J) 73.

415

oppression leading to confession. 'The exercise of authority or power in a burdensome, harsh or wrongful manner, unjust or cruel treatment of subjects, inferiors; the imposition of unreasonable or unjust burdens': OED definition adopted in *R* v *Fulling* [1987] QB 426. '"Oppression" includes torture, inhuman or degrading treatment, and the use or threat of violence (whether or not amounting to torture)': P.&C.E.A. 1984, s 76(8); C.P.I.A. 1996, Sch 1, para 25. See *R* v *Ismail* [1990] Crim LR 109; *R* v *Souter* [1995] Crim LR 729. *See* CONFESSION; TORTURE.

oppressive questioning. CA held in *Shierson* v *Rastogi* (2002) *The Times*, 20 November, that questioning of a defendant (in liquidation proceedings) who was alleged to have been responsible for serious wrongdoing, so as to provide a pretrial deposition which could have proved the case against himself, was oppressive; such oppression, nevertheless, could be balanced and outweighed by the liquidator's lawful needs, e.g., for information to be obtained quickly.

OPRA. Occupational Pensions Regulatory Authority. See W.R.P.A. 1999, s 2 (duty of Authority to keep a register of stakeholder pensions schemes).

option. A right which may be acquired by contract to accept or reject a present offer within a given period of time. Under S.L.A. 1925, s 51, a tenant for life (q.v.) may grant an option to purchase or take a lease of the settled land within ten years. Provision that a mortgagee shall have an option to purchase the property is generally inconsistent with a mortgage and, therefore, void, but this may not be so if the option is part of an independent transaction: *Reeve* v *Lisle* [1902] AC 461. 'Under an option, only one step is normally needed to accept a contract, namely the exercise of the option. Under a right of pre-emption two steps will usually be necessary, the making of the offer in accordance with the right of pre-emption, and the acceptance of that offer': *Brown* v *Gould* [1972] Ch 53. See *Pritchard* v *Briggs* [1980] Ch 338 (option

to purchase may be an 'estate contract' within L.C.A. 1972, s 2(4)(*iv*)). For 'share options' see *IRC* v *Burton Group plc* [1990] STC 242. See *Close Asset Finance Ltd* v *Care Graphics* (2000) *The Times*, 21 March (option to buy not creating legal obligation).

or. Used generally in a disjunctive sense to connect words, phrases, clauses representing alternatives. For its interpretation as 'and', see *Federal Steam Navigation Ltd* v *Department of Trade and Industry* [1974] 2 All ER 97. See also *Ormerod* v *Blaslov* (1990) 52 SASR 263. *See* AND.

oral agreement, modification of contract by. Following a written contract, the parties are free, by a later oral agreement, to 'either altogether waive, dissolve or annul the former agreement, or in any manner to add to, or subtract from, or vary or qualify the terms of it, and thus to make a new contract; which is to be proved, partly by the subsequent verbal terms engrafted upon what will be thus left of the written agreement': *Goss* v *Nugent* (1833) 5 B & Ald 58. *See* CONTRACT.

oral deal relating to land. In *Nweze* v *Nwoko* (2004) *The Times*, 6 May, the CA held that an oral compromise relating to a dispute and containing a term affecting the price of the property, could not be construed as a contract for the sale of land, and, as a result, could not be enforced.

oral evidence. *See* EVIDENCE, ORAL.

orality, principle of. The oral examination of witnesses, which is a fundamental feature of trial under English law. See, however, evidence given on affidavit (q.v.).

oral will. *See* NUNCUPATIVE WILL.

ordeal, trial by. Ancient procedure whereby an appeal was made to God to make manifest the guilt or innocence of the accused. It was considered as *judicium Dei* (q.v.). It could involve, e.g., ordeal *by fire* (in which guilt was established if the wounds of the accused sustained during the carrying of a heated iron for nine steps were not healed after three days), or *by water* (in which the accused was bound with a rope and let down into the water, innocence being established if he sank to a knot tied in the rope). Abolished in 1215 when Fourth Lateran Council prohibited clerical participation in the ordeal.

order, hospital. In *R (SW Yorks Mental Health NHS Trust)* v *Bradford Crown Court* (2004) *The Times*, 23 January, the CA held that all orders made in the crown court, including custodial orders in the absence of a conviction relating to judicial review, were to be considered as criminal matters, so that they cannot be heard by the Civil Division of the Court of Appeal.

order, revocation of. A rule giving the court which is making an order the power to make a variation or a relocation of that order is not retrospective, and has no application to any order made before it came into force: *DEG* v *Korshy (No. 4)* (2005) *The Times*, 7 January.

orders. 1. Directions of the court. 2. Constituents of the procedural codes of the Supreme Court and of the county courts.

Orders in Council. Orders made by the Sovereign and Privy Council (qq.v.) or by the government (which are sanctioned by the Privy Council). They may be used, e.g., to bring Acts into force. See I.A. 1978, s 13; Northern Ireland Act 2000, Schedule, paras 1, 2. *See* DELEGATED LEGISLATION; STATUTORY INSTRUMENTS.

Orders of Council. Orders made by the Privy Council (q.v.) in the absence of the Sovereign.

ordinance. Decree promulgated by Parliament (q.v.) without the consent of a constituent element (e.g., Lords), or a declaration by the Sovereign made without Parliament's consent.

ordinarily resident. *See* RESIDENT IN UK.

ordinary meetings. *See* MEETINGS, COMPANY.

ordinary resolution. A resolution (q.v.) passed by a simple majority of those present at the general meeting of a company (q.v.). See, e.g., Cos.A. 1985, ss 303, 386. *See* EXTRAORDINARY RESOLUTION.

ordinary shares. Those which carry the greatest risk and rank for repayment of capital and payment of dividends after

debenture-holders and preference share-holders. Preferred ordinary shares are a type of participating preference shares (q.v.) without priority for repayment of capital. *See* SHARE.

organ, human. Any part of a human body consisting of a structured arrangement of tissues which, if wholly removed, cannot be replicated by the body: Human Organ Transplants Act 1989, s 7(1). The Act prohibits any commercial dealing in human organs (s 1) and restricts transplants between persons not genetically related (s 2). SI 91/408 (concerning UKTSSA (q.v.)) defines 'organ' as 'any part of a human body or any product derived from the human body'. For organ donation, see Human Tissue Act 1961, amended by Corneal Tissue Act 1986. *See* BODY PARTS; TRANSPLANT CENTRE; UKTSSA.

organisms, genetically modified. Organisms in which any of the genes or other genetic material have been modified by artificial techniques prescribed in authorised regulations, or are inherited from genes or other genetic material so modified: En.P.A. 1990, s 106. For control, see 1990 Act, Part VI. See *R* v *Secretary of State for the Environment ex p Watson* (1998) *The Times*, 31 August; *Monsanto plc* v *Tilly and Others* [1999] EGCS 143 (damage to genetically modified crops; the defences of necessity and public interest not accepted in action for trespass); SI 00/768; Directive 01/81. Under s 110, prohibition notices may be served on persons proposing to import, acquire, release or market genetically modified organisms where there is a risk of damage to the environment.

orse. Otherwise.

OSS. Office for the Supervision of Solicitors. New title (1996) for the Solicitors Complaints Bureau. Set up by the Law Society to deal with complaints about solicitors and to regulate their work. It monitors how solicitors deal with complaints, and examines complaints about the quality of solicitors' service. It may act as a conciliator, and can reduce bills and discipline solicitors.

ostensible authority. Apparent authority. See, e.g., *Freeman and Lockyer* v *Buckhurst Properties* [1964] 1 All ER 630; *The Ocean Frost* [1986] AC 717.

ostensible partner. Nominal partner (q.v.).

ought, meaning of. The word generally involves duty or obligation. In *White* v *white* [2001] 1 WLR 481, Lord Nicholls, construing 'knew or ought to have known', said that 'ought' imported a standard by reference to which conduct was measured, and that the meaning of the phrase depended on context.

oust. To eject, disposses, exclude, bar. See *Richards* v *Richards* [1984] AC 174.

ouster. An act which wrongfully deprives a person of his freehold (q.v.) or other inheritance.

ouster clause. A clause in a statute which excludes the jurisdiction of the courts (e.g., 'This shall not be questioned in any legal proceedings whatsoever'). See, e.g., *Anisminic* v *Foreign Compensation Commission* [1969] 2 AC 147.

ouster of jurisdiction. Removal from the court of its power to hear and determine an action. There is a presumption against a statute's ousting the jurisdiction of the courts: *Pyx Granite Co Ltd* v *Minister of Housing* [1960] AC 260.

ouster order. Order under Ch.A. 1989, s 38A (inserted by F.L.A. 1996, Sch 6) giving the court power to include exclusion requirements in an interim care order; see also Ch.A 1989, s 44A. The order has the effect of prohibiting, suspending or restricting the exercise by a spouse of the right to occupy the matrimonial home.

outer Bar. Known also as 'utter Bar'. Term used to refer to junior barristers who were said to plead 'outside the bar' and were known as 'utter barristers'. See BARRISTER.

outlawry. Procedure whereby an offender was placed outside the protection of the law. His property was forfeited and he lost all civil rights, being stigmatised as 'an animal to be hunted and struck down if encountered'. Criminal outlawry was abolished in 1838; outlawry in civil proceedings, in 1879.

outstanding offences. Those offences which are outstanding may be taken into account when the court is considering sentence. They must not be dissimilar offences, or offences in respect of which the court has no jurisdiction.

outstanding term. A term of years (q.v.) which has not ended although the purpose for which it came into existence has been fulfilled. See SATISFIED TERM.

overcrowding. A dwelling is overcrowded when the number of persons sleeping there is such as to contravene the room standard (q.v.) or the space standard (q.v.): H.A. 1985, s 324. A notice to abate overcrowding within 14 days of date of service may be issued by a local housing authority (q.v.) to the occupier: s 338(1). For penalties for landlords causing or permitting overcrowding, see s 327, as amended by L.G.H.A. 1989, Sch 11. See ROOM STANDARD.

overdraft. Bank loan allowing a customer's current account to go into debit. See C.C.A. 1974, s 74(3), (3A) (inserted by Banking Act 1979, s 38(1)). 'A payment by a bank under an arrangement by which the customer may overdraw is a lending by the bank to the customer of the money'; *per* Harman J in *Re Hone* [1951] Ch 58.

overdue bill. A bill which remains in circulation after the due date. A bill payable on demand is deemed overdue, for purposes of negotiation, if it appears to have been in circulation for an unreasonable length of time. 'Unreasonable' is a question of fact: B.Ex.A. 1882, s 36(3). See BILL OF EXCHANGE.

overdue cheque. See CHEQUE, OVERDUE.

over-insurance. See INSURANCE, OVER-.

overpaid bonus. In *Price-Jones* v *Commerzbank AG* (2003) *The Times*, 26 November, the CA held that where a city banker, rather than moving to another bank, had remained in his job, this could not be seen as a sufficient 'change or position' entitling him to keep an overpayment of £25,000, paid to him by his employer, in error.

overreaching. 'A conveyance to a purchaser of a legal estate in land shall overreach any equitable interest or power affecting that estate, whether or not he has notice thereof . . .': L.P.A. 1925, s 2.

overreaching and land held subject to trust. Procedure whereby land held subject to trust is sold to a purchaser free from the trust, even though he has notice of it. An equitable interest overreached is transferred from the land to the purchase money in the trustees' hands. Example: *ad hoc* trust of land (q.v.). See, e.g., *Shiloh Spinners Ltd* v *Harding* [1973] AC 80; S.L.A. 1925, s 72; *State Bank of India* v *Sood* [1997] Ch 276.

overriding interests. Those encumbrances, interests, rights and powers that were originally stated in L.R.A. 1925, s 70(1) as not entered on the register but subject to which registered dispositions of land take effect. Hence, a registered proprietor is bound by such rights, irrespective of registration and notice. Such interests were always regarded as a defect in the system of land registration because they bound a purchaser but did not appear on the register. Examples: legal easements (q.v.), profits, local land charges, rights of persons in occupation (q.v.). An overridden interest cannot be enforced against anyone, whereas an overreached interest is transferred from land to money. See L.R.A. 1986, s 4; *Williams & Glyn's Bank* v *Boland* [1981] AC 487; *Abbey National BS* v *Cann* [1990] 2 WLR 832; *Hypo-Mortgage Services* v *Robinson* [1997] 2 FLR 71; *Ferrishurst Ltd* v *Wallcite Ltd* [1998] EGCS 175; Law Com. Report (1987), No. 158. See L.R.A. 1925, s 70. Overriding interests are now dealt with by the Land Registration Act 2002 which has reduced the number of potential overriding interests and has attempted to limit their effect so that the registers reflect the original concept behind the land registration system in that all incumbrances should be capable of being detected from the registers. There are now two lists of overriding interests to be found in Sch 1 and 3 of the LRA 2002. *See* LAND REGISTRATION; MINOR INTERESTS.

overriding interests, rights of people in occupation as. A claimant must prove that the right subsisted in reference to land, that the owner of the right was in actual occupation (or in receipt of rents or profits), and that no enquiry has been made of that person. 'Actual occupation' is a question of fact. See L.R.A. 1925, s 70(1)(*g*); *Strand Securities* v *Caswell* [1965] Ch 958; *Kingsnorth Finance Ltd* v *Tizard* [1986] 1 WLR 783; *Collings* v *Lee* (2000) *The Times*, 26 October.

overrule. To set aside. Thus, a decision may be overruled by statute, or a higher court in a later case. Overruling by the latter operates retrospectively; by the former, from the date on which the statute comes into operation. See, e.g., *Button* v *DPP* [1966] AC 591. Should be distinguished from reversal of judgment (q.v.). For 'prospective overruling', see *Kleinwort Benson Ltd* v *Lincoln CC* [1998] 4 All ER 513 (idea overruled); *R* v *Governor of Brockhill Prison ex p Evans* [1999] 11 Admin LR 6.

oversea company. A company incorporated outside Britain which has established a place of business in Britain. See Cos.A. 1985, ss 691, 694, 744; Banking Act 1987, s 74(1). For 'offshore funds', see I.C.T.A. 1988, s 759. *See* OFFSHORE FUND, MATERIAL INTEREST IN.

oversea company, name of. The Secretary of State may, if of the opinion that it is or would be undesirable for an oversea company to carry on the business in Great Britain under its corporate name, cause a notice to that effect to be served on the company by the registrar of companies: Cos.A. 1985, s 694.

overseas branch register. A company having a share capital whose objects comprise the transaction of business in any of the countries or territories specified in Cos.A. 1985, Sch 14, Part I, should keep in any such country or territory a branch register of members resident there: Cos.A. 1985, s 362.

overstayer. 'A person who, having only limited leave to enter or remain in the UK, remains beyond the time limited by the leave': Immigration and Asylum Act

1999, s 9(6). For application by over-stayer to remain in UK, see s 9(1)–(4). See SI 00/265.

overstayer's family fare. CA held in *R (Grant)* v *Lambeth LBC* (2005) *The Times*, 5 January, that, as an alternative to primary subsistence for an overstaying illegal immigrant, a local authority was empowered to provide her and her family with a single-way ticket for her and her family to their country of origin.

overt. Open, as in overt act, market overt (q.v.).

overtime pay. In *Bamsey* v *Albon Engineering plc* (2004) *The Times*, 15 April, the CA held that although an employee worked overtime on a regular basis, this ought not to be taken into account when calculating his holiday pay which was based solely on his hours as fixed by his contract of employment.

owner, in relation to premises. A person other than a mortgagee not in possession who is for the time being entitled to dispose of the fee simple (q.v.) in the premises, whether in possession or reversion, and a person holding or entitled to the rents and profits of the premises under a lease (q.v.) of which the unexpired term exceeds three years: H.A. 1985, s 56.

owner-occupier of a dwelling. 'The person who, as owner or as lessee under a long tenancy, occupies or is entitled to occupy the dwelling': H.A. 1985, s 237. 'The person who occupies the whole or a substantial part of the hereditament in right of an owner's interest in it': T.C.P.A. 1990, s 168(1).

ownership. The aggregation of rights to the exclusive enjoyment of some thing based on rightful title. 'The entirety of the powers of use and disposal allowed by law': Pollock, *Possession in the Common Law* (1888). 'A right, indefinite in point of user, unrestricted in point of disposition, and unlimited in point of duration, over a determinate thing': Austin, *Lectures on Jurisprudence* (1861). It may be *absolute* or *restricted, corporeal* (relating to, e.g., a book, a car) or *incorporeal* (relating to, e.g., the right to recover a debt), *legal* (as where A has fee simple absolute in possession (q.v.)) or *equitable* (as where A has a life interest), *vested* or *contingent*. In essence, it is based on a relationship *de jure* (q.v.), so that possession of the thing is not necessary. *See* POSSESSION.

ownership, acquisition of. Ownership may be acquired *originally* (e.g., by asserting ownership over something not previously owned by anyone), *derivatively* (e.g., by purchase), or by *succession* (e.g., by inheritance).

ownership, legal and equitable. Term used in land law to distinguish estates in land capable of being conveyed or created at law (fee simple absolute in possession (q.v.) in case of freeholds, and term of years absolute (q.v.) in case of lease-holds) and all other ownership interests. See L.P.A. 1925, s 1.

ownership, proof of. Establishment of ownership of property by, e.g., production of authenticated documents of title; proof of possession; proof of ownership of connected property (in the case of land) indicating a probability that its owner also owned the property in dispute.

P

P. President of the Family Division (q.v.), as in, e.g., Sir Stephen Brown P. See S.C.A. 1981, s 10.

packaging. Products used for the containment, protection, handling, delivery and presentation of goods from producer to user or consumer: Producer Responsibility Obligations (Packaging Waste) Regulations 1997, reg 2(1); Council Directive 94/62.

pact. A contract, promise, covenant, treaty between states.

pacta sunt servanda. Contracts are to be kept. This maxim is at the core of contract law and international treaties.

paedophile. A person for whom young children constitute the preferred partners in sexual activity. A child under 16 may not give a valid consent to his or her participation in a sexual act: see, e.g., S.O.A. 1956. See also Indecency with Children Act 1960. Under Sex Offenders Act 1997, s 7, Sch 2, it is an offence for a British citizen or resident to commit a sexual act against children abroad. See *R v A* [1999] 2 Cr App R (S) 92 (determinate sentence on lifelong paedophile).

paedophiles, controls on. Persons convicted of, or cautioned by the police in relation to, certain specified sexual offences, must notify the police of their names, addresses and any changes in that information: Sex Offenders Act 1997, ss 1, 2. For release of information obtained under 1997 Act, see Home Office Guidelines (1 September 1997); HOC 39/1997; *R v Chief Constable of N Wales Police ex p AB* [1997] 4 All ER 969. See Sex Offenders Act 1997, Part I; C.D.A. 1998, s 20; C.J.C.S.A. 2000, ss 66–69, Sch 5.

paedophiles, sentencing of. CA held, in Attorney General's Reference (No. 42 of 2003) that in a case in which a man who was much older than a teenager had established contact through the internet with young girls, resulting in a series of sexual offences against those girls, the appropriate sentences should be at the top end of the range. The courts might be enabled to take a more punitive attitude following Parliament's reconsideration of the relevant law.

pager intercept, and privacy. The interception of a pager message by police, and use of the contents during a trial, constituted an unjustified interference with a person's life and correspondence, thus violating European Convention, art 8: European Court of Human Rights, in *Taylor-Sabori v UK (Application No. 47114/99)* (2002) *The Times*, 31 October.

palm prints. Impressions of the palm used for identification purposes. See *R v Tottenham Justices ex p ML* (1986) 82 Cr App R 277. *See* FINGERPRINTS.

papers, confidential, use of in another case. In *Smithkline Beecham plc v Generics (UK) Ltd* (2003) *The Times*, 25 August, the CA held that in a case in which a judge had examined confidential documents and concluded that their use ought to be restricted, this would not prevent any use of the documents in a different group of proceedings.

Parades Commission. Body set up under Public Processions (N Ireland) Act 1998, to make recommendations to Secretary of State concerning public processions in N Ireland and to issue determinations in respect of particular proposed processions: s 2(2)(b).

parallel disciplinary and civil proceedings. The Administrative Court held, in *R v Executive Council of Accountants' Joint*

Disciplinary Scheme (2002) 152 NLJ 1617, that there was no element of unfairness inherent in the bringing of disciplinary proceedings by a professional body at a time when civil proceedings emerging from the same subject matter are being heard. See also *R v Panel on Takeovers ex p Fayed* [1992] BCLC 938.

paramount. Superior. *Title paramount* is superior title. Example: where X held land in fee of Y, and Y held that land in fee of Z, so that Z was lord paramount. A *paramount clause* in a charterparty or bill of lading (qq.v.) is a clause incorporating all the Hague Rules: *Nea Agrex SA v Baltic Shipping Co Ltd* [1976] QB 933. For use of 'paramount' in relation to a child's welfare (q.v.), see Ch.A. 1989, s 1; *F v Leeds CC* [1994] 2 FLR 60; *R v Secretary of State for Home Department ex p Gangadeen* [1998] Imm AR 106.

parcels. 1. Plots of land. 2. Term used in a conveyance (q.v.) to indicate the clause giving a physical description of property conveyed, e.g., 'all that dwelling-house known as . . .'. See *Scarfe v Adams* [1981] 1 All ER 843.

parceners. *See* COPARCENARY.

pardon. The excusing of an offence or remission of a punishment by the Sovereign (on the advice of the Home Secretary) or by Act of Parliament (q.v.). Some offences cannot be pardoned, e.g., committing a person to prison beyond the seas (see Habeas Corpus Act 1679), or an unabated public nuisance. 'A free pardon does not quash a conviction in the same way that the Court of Appeal can quash a conviction . . . it is, however, generally accepted that [it] has the effect of wiping out the conviction and all its consequences': Secretary of State for the Home Department (*Hansard*, 13 January 1977). There is a statutory right to compensation where a person has been pardoned on the ground that a new or newly discovered fact has shown beyond reasonable doubt that there has been a miscarriage of justice: C.J.A. 1988, s 133, Sch 12. *Ex gratia* payments may be made by the Home Secretary where the miscarriage of justice is not within the statutory scheme. See *R v Secretary of State for Home Department ex p Atlantic Commercial Ltd* [1997] BCC 692 (compensation is not payable to a company). *See* MERCY, PREROGATIVE OF.

parent. Father or mother. Used, e.g., in Ch.A. 1989, Sch 1, para 16(2) to include 'any party to a marriage (whether or not subsisting) in relation to whom the child concerned is a child of the family'. See *J v J (A Minor)* [1993] 2 FLR 56; *Re C (A Minor)* [1995] 2 FLR 483 ('parent' means one who has parental responsibility (q.v.) for a child). For presumption of parentage in child support cases, see Child Support Act 1991, s 26(2), amended by C.S.P.S.S.A. 2000, s 15. *See* CHILD, PARENTAL RESPONSIBILITY FOR; LEGITIMACY.

parent, absent. Term used in Child Support Act 1991, s 3(2) to indicate, in relation to a child, a parent who is not living in the same household with the child, and the child has his home with a person who is, in relation to him, 'a person with care' (q.v.): s 3(2). Known now as 'non-resident parent': C.S.P.S.S.A. 2000, Sch 3, para 11(2).

parentage, declaration of. *See* LEGITIMACY.

parental leave. See Employment Relations Act 1999, s 7, Sch 4, Part I, substituted for E.R.A. 1996, Part VIII; SI 99/3312. All employees with 12 months' continuous service with the employer are eligible to take up to 13 weeks' unpaid leave before a child's fifth birthday. Twenty-one days' notice should be given to the employer. No more than four weeks in any particular 12-month period in respect of an individual child may be taken. The leave may be postponed if the employer considers that his business would be unduly disrupted. The Maternity and Parental Leave Amendment Regulations 2001 (SI 2001/4010) give all parents of children born or adopted by them between December 1994–December 1999 the right until 31 March 2005 to take parental leave.

parental preferences concerning education. Local education authorities have duties to arrange for children's parents to express a preference for schools at which they wish their children to be educated: School Standards and Framework Act 1998, s 86. See *R v Sheffield City Council ex p H* [1999] ELR 242.

parental responsibility. *See* CHILD, PARENTAL RESPONSIBILITY FOR.

parenting order. Order under C.D.A. 1998, s 4, available where, in any court proceedings, a child safety order, anti-social behaviour or sex offender order is made in respect of a child or young person convicted of an offence (see also offences under Education Act 1996 in relation to failure to comply with school attendance order). The order may require the parent to comply, for a period not exceeding 12 months, with requirements specified in it, and to attend counselling or guidance sessions specified in it.

parent, lone. 'A parent who has no spouse or is not living with his spouse; and is not living with any other person as his spouse': S.S.A. 1998, s 72(2). See SI 00/1926 (lone parents and requirements for work-focused interviews (q.v.)).

parents' liability for children's torts. Parents are not generally liable for their child's torts, save, e.g., where the child is employed by a parent and commits a tort in the course of his employment and where torts are due to a parent's negligence, or if a parent had authorised the commission of the tort. See *Bebee v Sales* (1916) 32 TLR 413.

parish. Originally an ecclesiastical area (see Ecclesiastical Fees Measure 1986, s 10); later a local government unit. Parish councils in England are constituted in a way similar to district and county councils (qq.v.). There must be a minimum of five members. Functions include responsibility for recreational facilities. In Wales, parishes are replaced by communities (q.v.). For crime prevention powers, see Local Government and Rating Act 1997, s 31. See L.G.A. 1972, Sch 1; Local Government Rating Act 1997.

parking, dangerous. Under Road Traffic Act 1988, s 22, it is an offence for a person in charge of a vehicle to remain at rest on a road in such a position or circumstances as to be likely to cause damage to other persons using the road.

parking rights. In some circumstances an easement of parking on a neighbour's land for the benefit of the dominant tenement might exist, but the right to park an unlimited number of cars on such land could not be capable of being an easement, since it would render the residual ownership of the land illusory: *Central Midland Estates Ltd v Leicester Dyers Ltd* (2003) *The Times*, 18 February.

Parks, National. *See* NATIONAL PARKS.

Parliament. The supreme legislature of the United Kingdom of Great Britain and Northern Ireland, consisting of the Queen, House of Lords and House of Commons. Its life is fixed for five years, divided into sessions (one or more each year). Its functions are: to pass laws; to vote taxes; to scrutinise government policy and administration; to debate current political issues of great importance. It can legislate as it pleases, since it is sovereign, for the whole of the UK or any constituent part. Legislation usually necessitates the concurrence of the Sovereign, Lords and Commons. *See* SOVEREIGNTY OF PARLIAMENT.

Parliament Act 1949. It was held, in *R (Jackson) v AG* (2005) *The Times*, 31 January, that the Hunting Act 2004 was valid since the Parliament Act 1949 which was relied upon to ensure its passage through Parliament was valid.

Parliamentary Commissioner for Administration. The 'Ombudsman'. Office created by Parliamentary Commissioner Act 1967. The Commissioner, who is appointed by the Crown, investigates complaints by members of the public who believe they have suffered injustice as the result of maladministration arising from the functioning of government departments and public authorities. A written complaint is forwarded to an MP who sends it to the Commissioner; he then exercises his discretion whether or not to investigate. See Parliamentary and Health Service Commissioners Act 1987.

Parliamentary control. Control of government is based on power exercised by the House of Commons which is able to force its resignation or to reject votes of confidence. Other aspects of control include, e.g., question time, motions for adjournment.

Parliamentary Counsel. Some 30 lawyers who are civil servants engaged in drafting government Bills, amendments by the government to those Bills, etc. The Office of Parliamentary Counsel is headed by the First Parliamentary Counsel.

Parliamentary electors. A person is entitled to vote in a constituency if, on the date of the poll, he: is registered in the constituency register; is either a Commonwealth citizen or citizen of the Republic of Ireland; is not under a legal incapacity to vote (e.g., he is a hereditary peer, or a convicted person, or mentally ill). He may not vote in more than one constituency at any parliamentary election. See Representation of the People Act 1983, s 1(1), (2), substituted by Representation of the People Act 2000, s 1; Peerage Act 1963, s 5, repealed by House of Lords Act 1999, Sch 2.

parliamentary immunity and margin of appreciation. European Court of Human Rights held that the rule relating to absolute parliamentary immunity did not exceed the margin of appreciation granted to states concerning the limitation of rights of access to the courts: *A v K (Application No. 353373/87)* (2002) *The Times*, 28 December. ('Margin of appreciation' allows states a discretion in applying the standards of the European Convention, taking into account specific natural traditions and circumstances.)

Parliamentary Papers. 1. Command Papers published by the government for Parliament's consideration (in theory, presented by Her Majesty's Command; in practice, by a Minister). They may be: '*White Papers*' (introduced in 1967), i.e., statements of government policy or principles of a Bill to be introduced (see *A-*

G's Reference (No. 1 of 1988) (1989) 89 Cr App R 60 (reference to White Paper for interpretation of criminal statute)); '*Blue Books*', i.e., reports of committees, commissions; '*Green Papers*', i.e., government plans and formative proposals intended for discussion. 2. Bills (q.v.). 3. House of Commons or House of Lords papers, published by order of the House, as reports of the Houses' own committees.

Parliamentary privilege. The aggregate of the particular rights and immunities enjoyed by each House of Parliament, designed to allow members to carry out their duties unhindered. They apply collectively and individually to every MP. Questions of privilege may be referred to the Committee of Privileges. Privileges include: freedom of speech in debate (evidence of what is said and done in Parliament is not generally used in legal proceedings: *Church of Scientology v Johnson-Smith* [1972] 1 QB 522); the right to control proceedings; right to penalise those who commit breach of privilege; the right to expel members whom Parliament considers unfit to serve; freedom of access to the Sovereign; freedom from arrest or molestation. The absence of precedent does not prevent an act being considered a breach of privilege. See *Prebble v Television New Zealand* [1995] 1 AC 321. (A Select Committee of Standards and Privileges has been established and oversees the work of the Parliamentary Commissioner for Standards. See *Hamilton v Al-Fayed (No. 1)* [2000] 2 WLR 609 (effect of waiver of privilege on defamation proceedings).) See F.I.A. 2000, s 34.

Parliament, European. *See* EUROPEAN PARLIAMENT.

Parliament, intention of. *See* INTENTION OF PARLIAMENT.

Parliament, legislative supremacy of. Parliament alone can, by statute, make or unmake any law. 'The very keystone of the constitution': Dicey, *The Law of the Constitution* (1885). Parliament can pass Acts of indemnity (q.v.) and retrospective legislation. No other body in the state can declare any Act invalid: see, e.g., *Pitkin v*

British Rlwys Board [1974] AC 765. It cannot, however, bind its successors. 'A sovereign power cannot, while retaining its sovereign character, restrict its own powers by any parliamentary enactment': Dicey, *The Law of the Constitution* (1885). See Treaty of Rome 1957, arts 177, 189; European Communities Act 1972; *Manuel* v *A-G* [1983] Ch 77; *R* v *Secretary of State ex p Factortame Ltd* [1991] 3 All ER 1026. See SOVEREIGNTY OF PARLIAMENT.

Parliament, primacy of. In *R* v *Saunders and Others* (2002) *The Times*, 1 February, the CA held that the Human Rights Act 1998 preserved Parliamentary sovereignty; even if convictions resulted from procedures characterised by Court of Human Rights as unfair, those convictions could not be declared unsafe by CA, because the stigmatised procedures had been permitted expressly by Parliament.

Parliament, registration of Members' interests. Following a report of the Select Committee on Members' Interests (Declaration), endorsed by the Commons, June 1975, Members are required to register, e.g., remunerated directorships of companies, remunerated trades, professions, vocations, financial sponsorships, payments or material benefits received from or on behalf of foreign governments. The rules were made much stricter in 1996.

Parliament, Scottish. *See* SCOTTISH PARLIAMENT.

Parliament, summons and dissolution of. A new Parliament is summoned following a proclamation issued by the Queen on advice from the Privy Council (q.v.); that proclamation dissolves the old Parliament, commands the issue of writs by the Lord Chancellor, and states the date for the meeting of the new Parliament. Dissolution arises by proclamation or the passage of time (five years under the Parliament Act 1911, s 7).

parol. Verbal, oral. Formerly applied to a contract not under seal: *Rann* v *Hughes* (1788) 7 TR 350.

parol contract. Simple contract (q.v.).

parole. Early release of prisoners by Parole Board: see C.J.P.O.A. 1994, s 149; Crime (Sentences) Act 1997. For power to release short-term prisoners on licence, see C.J.A. 1991, s 34A, inserted by C.D.A. 1998, s 99. For inclusion of curfew order in licence, see C.D.A. 1998, s 100. For recall to prison of short-term prisoners, see C.D.A. 1998, s 103, Sch 8. See C.J.C.S.A. 2000, ss 62–65.

Parole Board. A body set up to advise the Secretary of State with respect to any matter referred to it by him which is connected with the early release of prisoners. See *Daniels* v *Griffiths* [1998] EMLR 489 (the proceedings of the Board are not part of the proceedings of a court of law and confidential communications to it are not protected from disclosure by absolute privilege). See C.J.A. 1991, s 32, Sch 5. See *R* v *Secretary of State for Home Department ex p Francois* [1998] 2 WLR 530 (jail terms to be added for calculating release date: C.J.A. 1991, s 51(2)); *Oldham* v *UK* (2000) *The Times*, 24 October. In relation to European Convention, art 5 (right to liberty), the Parole Board had to be satisfied that, in the general interests of public security, a prisoner who had been recalled to complete an extended sentence should be confined because of the risk that he would reoffend by committing further offences of either a violent or sexual nature with which his sentence was intended to deal. Further, hearsay evidence was admissible by the Board in arriving at its decision. See *R (Sim)* v *Secretary of State for Home Department* (2003) *The Times*, 21 February.

Parole Board and fairness. HL held in *R (West)* v *Parole Board* (2005) *The Times*, 28 January, that the Board's duty should reflect the service at stake for the prison and society. Hence, an oral hearing might be involved.

parole for life prisoners. Where a prisoner was under 18 when he committed the offence for which he was sentenced, and that sentence was not one fixed by law, and the court had ordered that this section should apply to him as soon as he had served a specified part of the sentence, the Secretary of State, on recommendation of the Parole Board, may release him on licence: Crime (Sentences) Act 1997, s 28. See also C.D.A. 1998, Sch 8, para 130; P.C.C.(S.)A. 2000, s 116; C.J.C.S.A. 2000, Sch 7, para 136 (relating to life prisoner serving two or more life sentences). If recommended to do so by the Parole Board, the Secretary of State may, after consultation with the Lord Chief Justice together with the trial judge, if available, release on licence a life prisoner who is one to whom s 28 does not apply: s 29(1). See also Northern Ireland (Sentences) Act 1998, s 6; *R* v *S (A Juvenile)* [1999] 2 Cr App R (S) 31.

parole, ministerial acts. In *R (Clift)* v *Secretary of State for Home Department* (2004) *The Times*, 13 May, the CA held that the powers of the Home Secretary to reject a Parole Board recommendation for release on licence of prisoners serving determinate sentences of 15 years or more was reasonable and was not a contravention of prisoners' human rights under the terms of the European Convention.

parole on compassionate grounds. The Secretary of State may at any time release a prisoner on licence if satisfied that exceptional circumstances exist which justify his release on compassionate grounds. See Crime (Sentences) Act 1997, s 30; SI 99/1748.

parol evidence rule. Where the record of a transaction is embodied in a document, extrinsic evidence (q.v.) is not generally admissible to vary, qualify or interpret the document or as a substitute for it. See *Bank of Australasia* v *Palmer* [1898] AC 540. Abolition of the rule was recommended in *Law Commission Working Paper* 1976, No. 70. *See* EVIDENCE, PAROL.

parol lease. Lease (q.v.) taking effect in possession for a term not exceeding three years at the best rent which can be reasonably obtained without taking a fine: L.P.A. 1925, s 54(2).

Part 20 claim. A claim other than a claim by a claimant against a defendant, e.g., a counterclaim, is known under CPR as a 'Part 20 claim', and is covered by CPR, Part 20 and PD 20. Defendant may counterclaim by filing particulars under r 20.4(1); where filed with defence, the court's permission to make the counterclaim is not required; permission is required where defendant wishes to file counterclaim after service of defence (r 20.4(2)(b)). It must be set out as a claim, and verified by a statement of truth (q.v.). For defence to counterclaim, see r 15(4). For procedure where defence claims that a money claim has been paid, see r 15.10(1).

Part 36 matters. CPR, Part 36, is concerned with offers to settle and payments into court, and the consequences where an offer to settle or payments into court are made in accordance with this Part: r 36.1(1).

Part 36 offers. In *Garratt* v *Saxby* [2004] 148 SJLB 237, the CA held that there are circumstances in which the inadvertent disclosure to a judge of an offer under CPR, Part 36, breaches the provisions of r.52.12. The judge may, however, in the general interests of justice order a new trial before another judge or decide to continue with the case himself.

Part 36 offers and payments and interest. Unless a claimant's Part 36 offer which offers to accept a sum of money or a Part 36 payment notice indicates to the contrary, any such offer or payment will be treated as inclusive of all interest until the last date on which it could be accepted without needing the court's permission: CPR, r 36.22(1).

Part 36 offers to settle and payments into court. An offer made in accordance with CPR, Part 36, is called, if made by way of payment into court, 'a Part 36 payment', otherwise 'a Part 36 offer'. They may be made at any time after proceedings have started, and in appeal proceedings. A Part 36 offer must be in writing and may relate to the whole or part of a claim (and this must be stated in the offer). Where made not less than 21 days before start of trial, offer must be expressed to remain open for acceptance for 21 days from date it is made: r 36.5.

The offer is treated as 'without prejudice except as to costs': r 36.19(1). A Part 36 offer is made when received by offeree; a Part 36 payment is made when written notice of payment into court is served on offeree: r 36.8.

Part 36 offer to settle, made before proceedings commence. Where a person makes an offer to settle before proceedings are begun which complies with provisions of this rule, the court will take that offer into account when making any order as to costs: CPR, r 36.10(1). Offer must be expressed to be open for at least 21 days after date it was made: r 36.10(2)(a). See *Greening v Williams* (1999) *The Times*, 10 December.

Part 36 payment, claim for provisional damages. Defendant may make a Part 36 payment in respect of a claim which includes a claim for provisional damages. Payment notice must state that the sum paid into court is in satisfaction of the claim for damages on the assumption that the injured person will not develop the disease or suffer the type of deterioration specified in the claim: CPR, r 36.7(3).

Part 36 payment in foreign currency. Money must be paid into court in a foreign currency where it is a Part 36 payment and the claim is in a foreign currency, or under court order: PD 36, para 9.1. The court may direct that the money be placed in an interest bearing account in the currency of the claim or any other currency: para 9.2.

partial loss. *See* LOSS, LIABILITY IN MARINE INSURANCE FOR.

particular average. *See* AVERAGE.

particular lien. Right to retain goods until all charges incurred in respect of them have been paid. Example: lien in respect of goods carried by common carriers. See *Bowmaker v Wycombe Motors Ltd* [1946] KB 505. *See* LIEN.

particulars. Matters concerning statements of case in a claim, needed by the other party so that he shall understand the case to be made. Replaced under CPR by 'order for further information'. *See* FURTHER INFORMATION, OBTAINING.

particular tenant. The owner of a particular estate (q.v.).

parties. 1. 'They that make a deed and they to whom it is made are called parties to the deed': *Terms de la Ley*. 2. Those persons who sue or are sued. Their names must be set out at the head of a claim form (q.v.) and they form the title of the claim. No one can appear on the record as both claimant and defendant: *Re Phillips* (1931) 101 LJ Ch 338. See CPR, r 23.1.

parties, procedure for adding and substituting. An application for permission to add, remove, substitute a party may be made by an existing party or a person who wishes to become a party. An application for an order substituting a new party where existing party's interest or liability has passed to the new party may be made without notice and must be supported by evidence. Nobody may be added or substituted as claimant unless he has given his written consent, filed with the court. See CPR, r 19.3; PD 19. See *International Distillers Ltd v Hillebrand Ltd* (2000) *The Times*, 24 January. *See* JOINDER OF PARTIES.

partition. 1. Distribution, division. 2. Division of a governmental unit into two or more areas, each under a separate administration. 3. Term used in land law to refer to the disuniting of joint possession (q.v.) so that former co-tenants become separate owners. See *Biggs v Peacock* (1882) 22 Ch D 284. Now voluntary only, since compulsory partition was abolished by repeal of Partition Acts in 1925. See L.P.A. 1925, s 28(3).

partition of chattels. Where chattels belong to persons in undivided shares, the persons interested may apply to the court for an order for the division of all or any of them: L.P.A. 1925, s 188.

partition of land by trustees. Where beneficiaries are of full age and absolutely entitled in undivided shares to land subject to a trust, the trustees may partition the land, or any part of it, and provide by way of mortgage or otherwise for the payment of equality money: Trusts of Land and Appointment of Trustees Act 1996, s 7(1).

partner, salaried. A partner 'who receives a salary as remuneration, rather than a share of the profits, although he may, in addition to his salary, receive some bonus or other sum of money dependent on the profits': *per* Megarry J in *Stekel* v *Ellice* [1973] 1 All ER 463.

partners, duties of. To render true accounts and full information; to account for benefits derived from transactions concerning the partnership; to account for profits derived from a competing business; see Partnership Act 1890, ss 28, 30. See *Law* v *Law* [1905] 1 Ch 40; *Pathirana* v *Pathirana* [1967] 1 AC 233.

partners, expulsion of. 'No majority of the partners can expel any partner unless a power to do so has been conferred by express agreement between the partners': Partnership Act 1890, s 25. See, e.g., *Hitchman* v *Crouch Butler Savage Associates* (1983) 127 SJ 441.

partnership. The relationship which subsists between persons carrying on a business in common with a view of profit: Partnership Act 1890, s 1. See SI 94/2421; *Keith Spicer Ltd* v *Mansell* [1970] 1 All ER 462; *Strathearn Gordon Associates* v *Commissioner of Customs and Excise* (1985) VATTR 79. It cannot consist, in general, of more than 20 persons. See Cos.A. 1985, s 716. (Exempt from this limit are partnerships of solicitors, multinational partnerships of lawyers accountants, stockbrokers (see SIs 91/2729, 00/2711).) The liability of each partner in respect of the partnership's contracts is joint; in respect of the partnership's wrongs, the liability is joint and several. For liability of firm for partner's wrongful acts, see 1890 Act, s 10; *Dubal Aluminium Ltd* v *Salaam* (2000), *The Times*, 21 April. A partnership may be dissolved by order of court, by the parties themselves, or by death; see *Chandroutie* v *Gajadhar* [1987] AC 147. See also *Khan* v *Miah* (2000) 150 NLJ 1658 (partnership commences on venture, not on trade). See Partnership Act 1890, s 32; I.C.T.A. 1988, chap VII. See Limited Liability Partnership Act 2000. For

'limited partner', see I.C.T.A. 1988, s 117(2). For the enforcing of a judgment or order in actions between partners, and attachment of debts owed by a partnership, see CPR, Sch 1; O 81, rr 6, 7. See SI 92/1028. *See* FIRM; LIMITED PARTNERSHIP.

partnership, agency and. 'Every partner is an agent of the firm and his other partners for the purpose of the business of the partnership': Partnership Act 1890, s 5. See *Hirst* v *Etherington* (1999) 149 NLJ 1110. *See* AGENT.

partnership agreement. The doctrine of repudiatory breach has no application to a partnership agreement: *Mullins* v *Laughton* [2002] EWHC 2761.

partnership at will. A partnership determinable at will of either of the parties. See Partnership Act 1890, s 26; *Abbott* v *Abbott* [1936] 3 All ER 823.

partnership books, inspection of. Right given by Partnership Act 1890, s 24(9), to a partner to inspect and copy the partnership books. It can be exercised by an agent of the parties.

partnership by estoppel. Any person who by spoken or written words or conduct represents himself, or allows himself to be represented as a partner in a particular firm, is liable as a partner to anyone who has on the faith of any such representation given credit to that firm: Partnership Act 1890, s 14(1). See *Tower Cabinet Co Ltd* v *Ingram* [1949] 2 KB 397; *Bass Brewers Ltd* v *Appleby* (1997) 73 P & CR 165.

partnership, dissolution of. A partnership may be dissolved by: expiration of the period for which it is to last, or notice of dissolution; illegality (see *Hudgell Yentes* v *Watson* [1978] QB 451); order of the court or an arbitrator; death or bankruptcy of a partner; force of a clause giving right to claim dissolution on the occurrence of a specified event. See Partnership Act 1890, ss 32–35; *Hurst* v *Bryk* [2000] 2 All ER 193 (continuing liability of innocent partner after breach by another, leading to dissolution). Following dissolution, assets are distributed to: paying debts and liabilities to non-partners;

repaying partnership loans and capital (residue to be divided among partners. See s 44(b); Ins.A. 1986, s 420(1) (dissolution of insolvent partnership); SIs 86/2142, 94/2421.

partnership, limited. *See* LIMITED PARTNERSHIP.

partnership property. Property held by partners and applied only for partnership purposes under partnership agreement: Partnership Act 1890, s 20. Where land is included it is held under Trusts of Land and Appointment of Trustees Act 1996, on a trust for land. See *King Productions* v *Warren* [1999] 2 All ER 218.

part payment rule. Payment of a lesser sum on the due day cannot be satisfaction for the whole debt. See *Pinnel's Case* (1602) 5 Co Rep 117; *Foakes* v *Beer* (1884) 9 App Cas 605; Lim.A. 1980, s 29.

part performance. Equitable doctrine, whereby defendant (q.v.) who had acquiesced in claimant's performance of a contract (q.v.) was barred from pleading absence of writing. See L.P. (Misc. Provs.) A. 1989 (doctrine no longer applies to contracts covered by s 2).

part-time worker. Defined under SI 00/1551 as one 'who is paid wholly or in part by reference to the time he works and, having regard to the custom and practice of the employer in relation to workers employed by the worker's employer under the same type of contract, is not identifiable as a full-time worker'. See Employment Relations Act 1999, ss 19, 20; Council Directive 97/81 OJ [1998] L 1419. Under SI 00/1551, part-time workers have the right not to be treated less favourably than full-time workers of the same employer who work under the same type of employment contract. See *Davies* v *Neath Port Talbot CBC* [1999] ICR 1132.

party wall. (a) A wall which forms part of a building and stands on lands of different owners to a greater extent than the projection of any artificially formed support on which the wall rests; and (b) so much of a wall not being a wall referred to in (a) as separates buildings belonging to different owners: Party Wall etc. Act 1996, s 20. See L.P.A. 1925, s 38; *Prudential Assurance* v *Waterloo Real Estate* [1999] 2 EGLR 85 (party wall will cease being regarded as such where a co-owner does nothing in relation to it for more than 12 years so that the other owner is enabled to assume intentional and exclusive possession of it for that period of time).

passenger. One who is carried in a conveyance for compensation.

passing off. A tort (q.v.) committed by one person who, in a manner calculated to deceive, and in the course of trade, passes off his goods or business as those of another, e.g., by imitating their appearance or selling them under a similar name or trade mark. Essence is deceit practised on the public: *Reckitt & Coleman Products* v *Borden* [1990] 1 All ER 873. For elements of a successful claim, see *Mont Blanc* v *Sepia Products Inc* (2000) *The Times*, 2 February. Claimant's remedies include damages, injunction (qq.v.), account. See *Bollinger* v *Costa Brava Wine Co* [1960] Ch 262; *Harrods Ltd* v *Harrodian School* [1996] RPC 697; *Matthew Gloag & Son* v *Welsh Distillers (No. 2)* [1998] FSR 718; *HFC Bank plc* v *HSBC Bank plc* (1999) 22 (12) IPD 22119 (customers' confusion concerning brand names is insufficient to constitute the tort).

passing of property in a sale of goods. Where there is a contract for the sale of specific or ascertained goods, the property in them is transferred to the buyer at such time as the parties intended. The intention of the parties is ascertained by reference to the terms of the contract, the parties' conduct and the circumstances of the case. See S.G.A. 1979, s 17.

passive trust. A bare trust (q.v.).

passport. Document issued by the Foreign Office to citizens of the UK and British protected persons which is intended to ensure their safe passage from one country to another and their safe protection in that other country: see *R* v *Brailsford* (1905) 2 KB 730. (The so-called 'European passport' is merely a passport produced in a style and pattern agreed by member states of the EU; those states are the issuing authorities.) In *Joyce* v *DPP* [1946] AC 347, it was held that the holder of a British passport owes allegiance to the Crown and that it is immaterial that he has no intention of availing himself of the Crown's protection. See *R* v *Wardenier* [1999] 1 Cr App R(S) 244 (obtaining passport by deception); Schengen Agreement, in force since March 1995, abolishing internal border controls by most members of EU (but not UK).

passports, false, sentencing. In *R* v *Kolawole* (2004) *The Times*, 16 November, the CA held that an appropriate sentence for using or holding, intending to use, a false passport, even where there is a guilty plea, should be within the range of 12–18 months' imprisonment.

past consideration. *See* CONSIDERATION, PAST.

pasture, common of. The right of feeding one's cattle on another's land. See *Tyrringham's Case* (1584) 4 Co Rep 36b.

patent. An exclusive right conferred on one who invents or discovers some process, machine, etc. to make, use, sell or assign it for a certain period of time (usually 20 years) which may be extended. See Patents Acts 1949–77; PD 49E, para 1.3; Copyright, Designs and Patents Act 1988; Treaty of Rome 1957, art 85(1); *Merck Ltd* v *Primecrown Ltd* [1997] FSR 237.

patent agent. An individual registered as a patent agent in the register, a company lawfully practising as a patent agent in the UK or a person who satisfies the conditions in Copyright, Designs and Patents Act 1988, ss 274, 275. For 'trade mark agents', see s 282.

patent ambiguity. *See* AMBIGUITY.

patent defect. *See* DEFECT.

patentee. A person registered as grantee or proprietor of a patent (q.v.).

patent, grant of. A patent may be granted only for an invention in respect of which the following conditions are satisfied: it must be new; it must involve an inventive step; it must be capable of industrial application; it must not be an invention which will encourage offensive, immoral or antisocial action; it must not consist of a scientific theory, computer program, aesthetic creation, etc.: Patents Act 1977, s 1(1)–(3). (For refusal of patent based on a claim considered as too broad, in relation to genetic engineering, see *Biogen Inc* v *Medeva plc* [1996] TLR 607.) It may be granted to the inventor, joint inventors, persons who by virtue of any enactment or treaty or agreement with the inventor were entitled to the whole of the property in it (other than equitable interests (q.v.)) in the UK, or successors in title of those persons: s 7(2). The term of a patent is 20 years beginning with the date of filing of the application: s 25. See *PCME Ltd* v *Goyen Controls Co* (1999) 22(5) 1PD 22043 (patent invalid for obviousness). See also Design Rights (Semiconductor Topographies) Regulations 1989 (computer chip design protection).

patent, infringement of. A patent is infringed where a person does one of the following without the consent of the patent's proprietor: where the invention is a product and he makes, disposes of, offers to dispose of, uses or imports the product or keeps it for disposal or otherwise; where the invention is a process and he uses, or offers it for use in the UK when he knows this is an infringement; where the invention is a process and he disposes of, offers to dispose of, uses or imports any product obtained directly by means of the process or keeps it for disposal or otherwise: Patents Act 1977, s 60(1). Remedies include injunction, damages, account of profits, delivery-up of infringing materials.

patent, revocation of. The court may revoke a patent on any one of the following grounds: that it is not a patentable invention; that the patent was granted to a person who was not entitled to the grant; that the specification does not disclose the invention clearly and competently enough for it to be performed by a person skilled in the art; that the matter disclosed in the specification extends beyond that disclosed in the application for the patent; that the protection conferred by the patent has been extended by an amendment which should not have been allowed: Patents Act 1977, s 72(1), as amended by Copyright, Design and Patents Act 1988, Sch 5.

patent right. The right to do, or authorise the doing of, anything which, but for that right, would be an infringement of a patent.

Patents Court. Includes the Patents Court of the High Court and the Patents County Court. Constituted in 1978 as part of the Chancery Division 'to take such proceedings relating to patents and other matters as may be prescribed by rules of court'. Under PD 49E, para 1.3, Patents Court business includes any claim under Patents Acts 1949–61, 1977, Registered Designs Acts 1949–61, Defence Contracts Act 1958, matters relating to patents under the inherent jurisdiction of the High Court. Judges include puisne judges (q.v.) of the High Court nominated by the Lord Chancellor. Scientific advisers may be appointed to assist the Court: Patents Act 1977 s 96(4). See S.C.A. 1981, ss 6, 70; PD 49E (replacing RSC O 104). Patents county courts may be designated by the Lord Chancellor: Copyright, Design and Patents Act 1988, s 277. For rectification of Register of Patents or Designs, see PD 49E, para 18.1.

paternity, declaration of. Declaration that a stated person is the father of a stated child. See *Re JS* [1980] 1 All ER 1061. See Civil Evidence Act 1968, s 12 (amended by F.L.R.A. 1987, s 29; Ch. A. 1989, Sch 13). For paternity tests, see F.L.R.A. 1969, Ch.A. 1989, s 89; CPR, Sch 1; O 112. See *T v Child Support Agency* [1997] 4 All ER 27. *See* BLOOD TESTS.

paternity leave. Paternity and Adoption Leave (Amendment) Regulations 2004 (SI 04/923) came into force on 6 April 2004. On the employee's return to work, all terms and conditions must be no less favourable than if he had continued to work.

paternity, legal. In *Re R (Parental Responsibility: IVF baby)* (2003) *The Times*, 20 February, the CA held that for purposes of Human Fertilisation and Embryology Act 1990, s 28, legal paternity was created on the date on which the embryo or sperm and eggs from which the birth of the child resulted were implanted.

pathological grief reaction. In *North Glamorgan NHS Trust v Walters* (2003) *The Times*, 13 February, the CA held that the fact that the precipitating event in a claim for a pathological grief reaction lasted 36 hours (i.e., from the time of a ten-month old child suffering a fit to its death in claimant's arms) did not defeat that claim.

patient confidentiality, patient under sixteen. It was held in *Regina (Axon) v Secretary of State for Health* [2006] *The Times*, 26 January, a young person aged under 16 has a right to confidentiality when wishing to seek advice and treatment on contraception, sexually transmitted diseases and abortion and that this does not infringe a parent's right under article 8 of the European Convention on Human Rights.

patient, recall of. In *R (L) v Secretary of State for Home Department* (2005) *The Times*, 27 January, the CA held that in the case of a defendant, acquitted of murder on ground of insanity and subject to detention in secure hospital, he could be recalled from a later conditional charge into the community.

patient, restricted, detention of. In *R(H) v Secretary of State for Home Department* (2003) *The Times*, 14 November, the HL held that where a mental health review tribunal had ordered the conditional discharge of a restricted patient, provided that arrangements for his treatment in the community could be made, and had then deferred the discharge until completion of those arrangements, the tribunal could, in the event of unsuccessful arrangements, order a continuation of the patient's detention.

patients, discharged, rights of. In *R v Richmond LBC ex p Watson* (2002) *The Times*, 29 August, the HL held that local social services authorities had no right to charge for after-care services provided under Mental Health Act 1982, s 117, to individuals residing in their areas who had been discharged from compulsory detention under s 3.

patients, incompetent. In *R (MH) v Secretary of State for Health* (2004) *The Times*, 8 December, the CA held that there was an obligation on the government to make provision for referring to the court persons detained under the Health Act 1983 who were incapable of exercising their rights to apply to a mental health review tribunal under their own initiative.

patrial. The former term for a person who had a right of abode under Immigration Act 1971, s 3. See B.N.A. 1981, s 39.

pawn. 1. An article subject to a pledge (q.v.): C.C.A. 1974, s 189. 2. The delivery of a chattel (q.v.) by the pawnor to the pawnee as security for a loan. The chattel remains the property of the pawnor who has the right to redeem. See C.C.A. 1974, ss 114–122. The pawnee may retain possession until the debt is paid and can sell the chattel if the debt is not paid on the date fixed: s 121.

pawnbroker. One who is engaged in the business of taking goods and chattels in pawn. A licence is required from the Director General of Fair Trading (q.v.). See C.C.A. 1974, ss 114–122; SI 98/998.

payable at sight. *See* SIGHT, PAYABLE AT.

pay as you earn. System (known generally as PAYE) introduced in 1943, whereby wage and salary earners pay their income tax. Tax is deducted from earnings at source and accounted for to the Inland Revenue by the employer. See I.C.T.A. 1988, s 203; Finance Act 1998, s 67.

payee. One to whom a bill of exchange (q.v.) is made payable. The term 'fictitious payee' is used where a cheque is drawn in favour of a fictitious, or non-existent payee. The cheque may then be treated as a bearer cheque: see B.Ex.A 1882, s 7(3); *Clutton v Attenborough* [1897] AC 90.

pay, inability to. In relation to a bankruptcy petition, it is the debtor's apparent inability to pay a debt payable immediately, and either the petitioning creditor has served a statutory demand in prescribed form, and three weeks have elapsed and the debt has not been paid, or execution issued in respect of the debt has been returned unsatisfied: Ins.A. 1986, s 268(1). A company's inability to pay its debts is shown by proof that the value of its assets is less than the amount of its liabilities, taking into account contingent and prospective liabilities: s 123(2). See also s 123(1). *See* BANKRUPTCY.

payment. The passing of money from payer to payee in satisfaction of some debt or obligation. For 'payment under reserve', see *Banque de L'Indochine v JH Rayner Ltd* [1983] 1 All ER 1137.

payment in due course. Discharge of a bill of exchange (q.v.) by payment made at or after the maturity of bill by the acceptor to the holder thereof in good faith and without notice that his title is defective (if that is so): B.Ex.A. 1882, s 59(1).

payment of money wages. For purposes of Wages Act 1986, means a payment in cash, by cheque, money or postal order, or by a payment (however effected) into any account kept with a bank or other institutions: s 17(7). *See* WAGES.

payments, appropriation of. Where a debtor owes several debts to one creditor and payment is made, the debtor can appropriate the payment to a debt, expressly or by implication, at the time of payment. In absence of such appropriation, the creditor may appropriate at any time. See *Clayton's Case* (1816) 1 Mer 572; *Siebe Gormand Co v Barclays Bank* [1979] 2 Lloyd's Rep 142. For appropriation of payments under a hire-purchase contract, see C.C.A. 1974, s 81.

payment-in, delays costs order. In *HSS Hire Services Group plc v BMB Building Merchants Ltd and Another* [2005] *The Times*, 31 May, the CA held that where there is a trial of a preliminary issue and there is a Part 36 offer or payment-in, the correct approach but for exceptional circumstances would be to adjourn the matter of costs. To deal with all issues including damages and then deal with the quantum of costs, where the amount of the Part 36 offer or payment-in can be revealed to the judge and the discretion in relation to costs exercised in the knowledge of it.

pay statement, itemised. Under E.R.A. 1996, s 8, at or before the time when the payment of wages or salary takes place, every employee is entitled to receive from his employer a statement showing: gross amount of wages or salary; net amount of wages or salary; amounts of fixed and variable deductions and purposes for which made.

pay when paid clauses. Conditional payment clauses, providing that a principal contractor shall not become liable to pay a subcontractor until the principal contractor has been paid for the work done by the subcontractor. For a prohibition on the use of such clauses, see Housing Grants, Construction and Regeneration Act 1996, s 113(1).

PC. Privy Council (q.v.). Privy Councillor.

PD. Practice Direction relating to civil procedure under CPR (q.v.).

peace, breach of. *See* BREACH OF THE PEACE.

peace-keeping and combat. It was held in *Bici* v *Ministry of Defence* (2004) *The Times*, 11 June, that in the absence of any imminent attack or threat of attack, no defence of combat immunity was available where the British Army had negligently caused injury while peace-keeping.

peculiar. A parish (q.v.) exempt from the jurisdiction of the bishop.

pecuniary advantage. The cases in which a pecuniary advantage within the meaning of Th.A. 1968, s 16 (obtaining pecuniary advantage by deception) arises are where: any debt or charge for which a person makes himself liable (including one not legally enforceable) is reduced or in whole or in part evaded or deferred; a person is allowed to borrow by way of overdraft or to take out any policy of insurance or annuity contract, or obtains an improvement of the terms on which he is allowed to do so; a person is given the opportunity to earn remuneration or greater remuneration in an office or

employment, or to win money by betting. See, e.g., *R* v *Melwani* [1989] Crim LR 565; *R* v *Callender* [1993] QB 303. *See* DECEPTION, OBTAINING SERVICES BY.

pecuniary legacy. *See* LEGACY.

pedigree. A line of ancestors. *See* DECLARATION CONCERNING PEDIGREE.

pedlar. An itinerant person who sells wares carried on foot from place to place and who regularly earns a part of his living from this activity. See Pedlars Act 1871; *Watson* v *Malloy* [1988] 1 WLR 1026; *R* v *Westminster CC ex p Elmagsoglu* [1996] COD 357.

peer. The holder of a dignity carrying the title 'Lord', or a peer of the realm. A *peeress* is a woman who has the dignity of peerage as a result of marriage or in her own right. Grades, in ascending order, are baron, viscount, earl, marquess and duke. *Hereditary peers and peeresses* may be created by the Crown, on advice of the Prime Minister, by issue of a writ of summons or by letters patent. The title of one who succeeded to a hereditary peerage could be disclaimed for life, within 12 months of succession (or one month in the case of members of, and candidates for, the Commons). See Peerage Act 1963, as amended by House of Lords Act 1999, Sch 2. *Life peers and peeresses* are appointed by the Crown on advice of the Prime Minister, under the Life Peerages Act 1958. No one shall be a member of the House of Lords by virtue of a hereditary peerage: House of Lords Act 1999, s 1. Under s 2, some 92 'excepted peers' (90 elected by the hereditary peers) are allowed to sit, as part of the transitional arrangements. Under s 3, hereditary (but not life or excepted) peers may vote at, or stand for, election to, the Commons. *See* HOUSE OF LORDS, TRANSITIONAL ARRANGEMENTS.

peers, temporal. *See* HOUSE OF LORDS.

peers, trial by. Under Magna Carta (q.v.) a man was entitled to the judgment of his peers (i.e., those of the same rank). ('Peer' was apparently misinterpreted as referring to the barons.) A peer could be tried before the House of Lords (q.v.). (Thus, Lord De Clifford was tried and acquitted of manslaughter in 1935.) Trial by peers in cases of treason and felony was abolished under C.J.A. 1948, s 30.

penal statutes. 1. Statutes creating offences. 2. Statutes providing for the recovery of penalties in civil proceedings. There is a presumption in favour of the strict construction of a penal statute. See, e.g., *Salesmatic Ltd v Hinchcliffe* [1959] 3 All ER 401.

penalties on the spot. C.J.P.A. 2002, s 2, provides for on the spot penalties for certain types of disorderly behaviour, e.g., being drunk in a public place, unlawful damage to property, use of threatening, abusive or insulting words likely to cause alarm or distress. The penalties may be administered by a constable to a person who appears to be aged 18 or over: s 2. A penalty notice must be in the prescribed form and should state the alleged offence and amount of penalty: s 3. The person concerned may be tried for the alleged offence: s 4. Penalty must be paid to justices' chief executive: s 7.

penalty. 1. A punishment. 'Unless penalties are imposed in clear terms they are not enforceable': *A-G v Till* [1910] AC 50. 2. A threat, held over a party to a contract *in terrorem* (q.v.). The plaintiff who brings an action to enforce a penalty can generally recover only the damage suffered. Whether a sum is or is not a penalty is to be decided 'upon the terms and inherent circumstances of each particular contract, judged of as at the time of making the contract, not as at the time of the breach': *Dunlop Pneumatic Tyre Co Ltd v New Garage & Motor Co Ltd* [1915] AC 79. See also *ECGD v Universal Oil Products Co* [1983] 1 WLR 399.

penalty, fixed, notice. A constable may issue a driver with a fixed penalty notice on the spot, where the offence appears to the constable to be one listed under the Road Traffic Offenders Act 1988, Sch 3, as amended by Road Traffic Act 1988, Sch 8: 1988 Act, s 51. For payment of penalty, see s 69.

penalty points. *See* TOTTING UP.

pendens lis. A pending action (q.v.).

pendente lite. While an action is pending.

pendente lite, **administration.** The court has power to appoint an administrator (q.v.) where there is a dispute as to the validity of a will (q.v.) or the right of administration. See S.C.A. 1981, s 117. The appointment will be made only where it can be shown to be necessary. The administrator *pendente lite* is entitled to remuneration.

pending action. Claims or proceedings pending in court relating to land or any interest in or charge on land, which must be registered on the register of pending actions: L.C.A. 1972, s 17(1). Claims of this type do not bind a purchaser without express notice of them, unless registered: s 5(7). See *Arab Monetary Fund v Hashim* [1992] 1 All ER 645. See CPR, Sch 1; O 15, r 7(1).

pension. Payments made periodically to a person on retirement from service. Generally taxable as earned income. See *Preston v Wolverhampton Healthcare* [1998] 1 WLR 280 (meaning of 'employment' for pensions); Pension Schemes Act 1993.

pension, annual uprating. In *R (Carson) v Secretary of State for Work and Pensions* (2002) *The Times*, 24 May, it was held that the exclusion of pensioners resident abroad from the annual uprating of state retirement pensions was not in breach of Human Rights Convention. The matter involved a political decision, not a judicial one, and had to be made by Parliament.

Pension calculations. A payment for con-contractual overtime does not constitute remuneration for purposes of pension calculations under Local Government Pension Scheme Regulations 1995, 1997 (SI 97/1612): *Newman BC v Skingle* (2002) 152 NLJ 917.

pension credit benefit. Means, in relation to a scheme, the benefits payable under the scheme to or in respect of a person by virtue of rights under the scheme attributable (directly or indirectly) to a pension credit: Pensions Schemes Act 1993, s 101B, inserted by W.R.P.A. 1999, s 37. *See* PENSION SHARING RIGHTS.

pension credit rights. Rights to future benefits under a scheme which are attributable (directly or indirectly) to a pension credit: Pension Schemes Act 1993, s 101B, inserted by W.R.P.A. 1999, s 37. *See* PENSION SHARING RIGHTS.

pension earmarking. In divorce proceedings, Mat.C.A. 1973, s 25B(1), inserted by the Pensions Act 1996, s 166, states that the court may take into account benefits which a spouse has, or may have, under an occupational or personal pension arrangement, and those benefits which a spouse may lose under a pensions scheme. See W.R.P.A. 1999, Sch 4. See *T* v *T (Financial Relief: Pensions)* [1998] 1 FLR 1072.

pensioners outside the jurisdiction. In *R (Carson)* v *Secretary of State for Work and Pensions* (2003) *The Times*, 28 June, the CA held that the UK was not in breach of European Convention by its exclusion of pensioners resident in other jurisdictions from the effects of the annual upgrading of state retirement pensions.

pension rights, effect of bankruptcy on. Where a bankruptcy order is made against a person on a petition presented after the coming into force of this section, any rights of his under an approved pension arrangement are excluded from his estate: W.R.P.A. 1999, s 11. See *Dennison* v *Krasner* [2000] 3 All ER 234.

pension scheme. Under Finance Act 2004, s 150, means a scheme or other arrangement comprised in one or more instruments or agreements, having or capable of having effect so as to provide benefits to or in respect of persons: on retirement; on death; not having reached a particular age; on the onset of serious ill health or incapacity; or in similar circumstances.

pension scheme, occupational. *See* OCCUPATIONAL PENSION SCHEME.

pension scheme, personal. *See* PERSONAL PENSION SCHEME.

pension scheme, registration of. Under Finance Act 2004, s 153, application may be made to Inland Revenue for registration of a pension scheme. The application must contain information reasonably required by Inland Revenue and must be accompanied by a declaration that the application is made by the scheme administrator.

pension scheme, stakeholder. Scheme registered as such under W.R.P.A. 1999, s 2, and established as a trust or in some other prescribed way, and fulfilling the following conditions: appropriate compliance with instruments establishing the scheme; benefits provided by the scheme are money purchase benefits (see Pension Schemes Act 1993); scheme complies with requirements relating to defraying of its administrative expenses and to disclosure of information to members under 1993 Act, s 113; members of the scheme may make such contributions as they think appropriate; scheme accepts transfer payments: 1999 Act, s 1. OPRA (q.v.) keeps a register of such schemes: s 2.

pension sharing order. An order which provides that one party's shareable rights under a specified pension arrrangement, or shareable state scheme rights, be subject to pension sharing for the benefit of the other party, and specifies the percentage value to be transferred: Mat.C.A. 1973, s 21A, inserted by W.R.P.A. 1999, Sch 3. On granting a decree of divorce or nullity of marriage or at any time thereafter, the court may make one or more pension sharing orders in relation to the marriage: s 24B.

pension sharing rights. Under W.R.P.A. 1999, Part IV, pension sharing is available in relation to a person's shareable rights under any pension arrangement other than an expected public service pension scheme: s 27(1). The transferor's shareable rights become subject to a debit of the appropriate amount; the transferee becomes entitled to a credit of that amount as against the person responsible for that arrangement: s 29(1). See SI 00/1116.

pension, state retirement. A social security benefit, paid, after claim is made and accepted, to men of 65 and women of 60, who meet National Insurance contribution conditions. (The age is likely to be equalised to 65 for men and women after 2010.) The pension is made up of a basic component ('basic pension'), additional, graduated and over-80s pensions, age-related and invalidity additions, with, in some cases, an extra pension for dependants (i.e., where husband or wife is dependent on claimant). All components of the total pension are taxable. See, e.g., S.S. (Contributions and Benefits) A. 1992, ss 43–57; C.S.P.S.S.A. 2000, ss 30–39.

peppercorn rent. A nominal, usually insignificant, rent paid to keep alive a title. See L.P.A. 1925, s 99; S.L.A. 1925, s 44.

per capita. By heads. Individually, as in distribution *per capita*, where property is divided among those entitled to it, each receiving a share.

per curiam. Abbreviated to *per cur.* By the court. Refers to a decision of the court as a whole, in contrast to the opinion of a single judge.

peremptory challenge. *See* CHALLENGE TO JURY.

peremptory pleas. Pleas in bar (q.v.).

perfect and imperfect rights. A *perfect* right is one recognised and enforced by a legal system; an *imperfect* right is one recognised, but not enforced directly, by the law. (Example: although a statute-barred debt cannot be recovered generally in a court, if the debtor pays, he cannot subsequently sue for recovery of the money as having been paid without consideration.) *See* RIGHT.

perfection of gift. *See* GIFT, IMPERFECT.

perfect trust. An executed trust (q.v.).

performance. 1. The completion of an act. 2. An act which, in precise and exact accordance with the terms of a contract, discharges it, e.g., by tender (q.v.), payment. For 'partial performance', see S.G.A. 1979, s 30(1). For 'place of performance' of contract, see S.G.A. 1979, s 14; *Viskase* v *Paul Kiefol* [1999] 1 All ER (Comm) 641.

performance bond. *See* BOND, PERFORMANCE.

performance, tender of. *See* TENDER OF PERFORMANCE.

perils, excepted. *See* EXCEPTED PERILS.

perils of the seas. An accident on the seas beyond the normal action of winds and waves. It includes damage caused by violent winds or storms, or striking a submerged rock. It does not include direct damage done to cargo by rats or bad stowage. See Marine Insurance Act 1906, Sch 1.

per incuriam. Through want of care; inadvertently. A mistaken decision of a court. It was held in *Young* v *Bristol Aeroplane Co Ltd* [1946] 1 All ER 98 that the Court of Appeal (q.v.) was not bound to follow one of its earlier decisions if satisfied that it was reached *per incuriam*. Application of the doctrine should be made only in the case of 'decisions given in ignorance or forgetfulness of some inconsistent statutory provision or of some authority binding on the court concerned': *Morelle* v *Wakeling* [1955] 2 QB 379. See *Duke* v *Reliance Systems* [1987] 2 All ER 858; *Rakhit* v *Carty* [1990] 2 QB 315.

per infortunium. By mischance.

periodical payments. A court may order a husband to make regular payments, e.g., to his wife for such a term as the court may direct (e.g., until remarriage of the payee or death of either party). See Mat.C.A. 1973, ss 23(1), 25A(3). See also F.L.R.A. 1969, s 6(3) (as modified by F.L.R.A. 1987, Sch 1); Ch.A. 1989, s 15, Sch 1; *Twiname* v *Twiname* [1992] 1 FLR 29; *Jones* v *Jones* (2000) *The Times*, 11 April (power to extend order after its expiry).

periodic tenancy. A tenancy (q.v.) which continues for an original period and then automatically for subsequent similar periods until determined by notice given by either party, e.g., a tenancy from year to year. It may be created expressly or by implication. See L.P.A. 1925, s 54(2) (periodic tenancy as legal lease); *Centaploy Ltd* v *Matlodge Ltd* [1974] Ch 1. For 'assured periodic tenancy', see H.A. 1988, s 5(1). See Lim.A. 1980, Sch 1.

perished goods. In a contract for the sale of specific goods the contract is void if, unknown to the seller, the goods have perished at the time of the making of the contract: S.G.A. 1979, s 6. See *Couturier v Hastie* (1856) 5 HL Cas 673; *Barrow, Lane Ltd v Phillips & Co* [1929] 1 KB 574.

perjury. Offence committed by a person lawfully sworn as a witness or interpreter in a judicial proceeding who wilfully makes a statement, material in that proceeding, which he knows to be false or does not believe to be true. See Perjury Act 1911; Prosecution of Offences Act 1985, s 28; *R v Rider* (1986) 83 Cr App R 207; *R v Peach* [1990] 2 All ER 966; *R v Sood* [1998] 2 Cr App R 355 (motive is irrelevant in establishing perjury: 'the vice is the abuse of the occasion'); *Kuwait Airways v Iraqi Airways* (2001) *The Times*, 14 February.

perjury and perverting course of justice, sentencing for. In principle there is no difference between civil and criminal proceedings in relation to sentencing for perjury; it might be kept in mind, however, as factor to be considered alongside matters such as: number of offences involved; period over which offences were committed; whether offences were planned or spontaneous; whether the lies did have an impact on the proceedings: *R v Archer* (2002) *The Times*, 2 August.

perjury, subornation of. *See* SUBORNATION.

permanently depriving, intention of. Essential element in the *mens rea* of theft (q.v.), existing, e.g., where defendant intends to treat the property as his own to dispose of regardless of another's rights. See Th.A. 1968, s 6; *R v Lloyd* [1985] QB 829; *R v Coffey* [1987] Crim LR 498; *R v Marshall* [1998] 2 Cr App R 282 (theft in sale of unexpired rail ticket).

per minas. By menaces.

permission to drive. Permission to drive a motor vehicle belonging to another can be given validly for purposes for insurance where there is a genuine and mistaken belief as to the exact circumstances of the person to whom permission was given. See *Lloyd-Wolper v Moore* (2004) *The Times*, 6 August.

permissive waste. That which arises from an omission by a tenant to do that which should be done, e.g., failing to repair a building. A tenant for life (q.v.) is not liable for permissible waste unless the agreement indicates otherwise: *Re Cartwright* (1889) 41 Ch D 532. *See* WASTE.

permit. 'If a man permits a thing to be done, it means that he gives permission for it to be done, and if a man gives permission for a thing to be done, he knows what is to be done or is being done': *Lomas v Peek* [1947] 2 All ER 574. See *Vehicle Inspectorate v Nuttall* [1999] 1 WLR 629 (discussion of 'permitted', in Transport Act 1968, s 96(11A)).

per my et per tout. By the half and by all. Applied to a joint tenancy (q.v.) under which each joint tenant is possessed of the property *per my et per tout*. See L.P.A. 1925, s 36.

per pais. See IN PAIS.

perpetual injunction. *See* INJUNCTION.

perpetually renewable lease. Lease (q.v.), the holder of which was entitled to enforce the perpetual renewal thereof. Abolished under L.P.A. 1922, as from 1926. Those existing on that date were converted into leases for 2000 years from the date of commencement of the existing term. See *Marjorie Burnett Ltd v Barclay* (1981) 125 SJ 199.

perpetual trusts, rule against. *See* INALIENABILITY, RULE AGAINST.

perpetuating testimony. Procedure whereby evidence (q.v.) can be recorded where there is a danger of its loss and where it may be required for some future action. See O 39, r 15.

perpetuities, rule against. Where there is a possibility that a future interest (q.v.) in property might vest after expiration of the perpetuity period, such an interest is generally void. The common-law period is lives in being (q.v.) at the time the instrument creating the interest becomes effective, plus 21 years and any gestation period. Under P.&A.A. 1964, s 1, the perpetuity period may be a fixed period of years not exceeding 80. See *Re Green's Will Trusts* [1985] 3 All ER 455;

Re Drummond [1988] 1 WLR 234; *Air Jamaica Ltd* v *Charlton* [1999] 1 WLR 1399; *The Rule Against Perpetuities and Excessive Accumulations (1998)* (Law Com. 251). *See* ACCUMULATION; WAIT AND SEE PRINCIPLE.

perpetuities rule, exceptions to. The rule does not apply to: interests following an entailed interest; a gift to charity followed by a gift over to another charity on a certain event; covenants for renewal contained in a lease; postponement of the mortgagor's right to redeem; the right of the lessor to enter on a breach of covenant.

per pro. (*Per procurationem* = by proxy.) Abbreviated to *p.p.* On behalf of. See *Charles* v *Blackwell* (1977) 2 CPD 151.

per se. By itself; taken on its own.

persecution. Ill-treatment, based upon hostility to individuals or groups, arising generally from political or religious extremism. See *Kagema* v *Home Secretary* [1997] Imm AR 137 (discussion of meaning of the term); *R* v *Secretary of State for Home Department ex p Adan* (2000) *The Times*, 20 December; *Horvath* v *Secretary of State for Home Department* [2000] 3 WLR 379 (adequacy of state protection is highly relevant to fear of persecution). *See* POLITICAL ASYLUM; REFUGEE.

persecution, past, and refugee status. Where a person is continuing to suffer from the effects of persecution in the past, he cannot thereby show a currently well-founded fear of persecution so as to enable him to qualify as a refugee under Convention Relating to Status of Refugees 1951, art 1A (2): *R (Hoxha)* v *Special Adjudicator* (2002) *The Times*, 31 October.

persistent vegetative state. *See* PVS.

person. A *natural person* is a human being, capable of attracting rights and duties. An *artificial person* (known also as 'juristic', 'legal', 'fictitious') is, e.g., a corporation to which the law attributes personality (q.v.). See I.A. 1978, Sch 1. See *Harford* v *Swiftrim* [1987] ICR 439; *Worthing RFC Trustees* v *IRC* [1987] 1 WLR 1057.

personal action. *See* ACTIONS, REAL AND PERSONAL.

personal Bill. A private Bill concerning the property or status of an individual. *See* BILL.

personal chattel. *See* CHATTELS.

personal credit agreement. An agreement between a debtor and creditor by which the creditor provides the debtor with credit of any amount: C.C.A. 1974, s 8(1). See *Humberclyde Finance Ltd* v *Thompson* [1997] CCLR 23.

personal data. *See* DATA, PERSONAL.

personal injuries. *See* INJURIES, PERSONAL, CLAIM FOR DAMAGES.

personal injuries, damages for. Purpose of awarding lump sum for damages for costs of future care and loss of future earnings is to put claimant in the same financial position as if the injury had not happened. 'Multipliers' should be calculated by reference to returns available from index-linked government bonds: *Wells* v *Wells* [1998] 3 WLR 329. (For 'multipliers', see *Hodgson* v *Trapp* [1989] AC 807; *Barry* v *Ablerex Ltd* (2000) *The Times*, 30 March.) See *Heil* v *Rankin* [2000] 3 All ER 138. *Provisional damages* may be awarded if there is proved or admitted to be a chance that at some definite or indefinite time in the future the injured person will, as a result of the act or omission which gave rise to the cause of action, develop some serious deterioration in his physical or mental condition: S.C.A. 1981, s 32A (inserted by A.J.A. 1982, s 6(1)), and if the particulars of claim include a claim for provisional damages (see r 41.2). 'Chance' involves a possibility that had to be measurable rather than fanciful; 'serious deterioration' means a clear risk of deterioration beyond the norm that could be expected: *Willson* v *Ministry of Defence* [1991] 1 All ER 638. The order must specify the disease or type of deterioration in respect of which an application may be made at a future date: CPR, r 41.2(2)(a).

personality. *Legal personality* is the sum total of a person's legal rights, powers, capacities, and duties ('his advantages and disadvantages'). *Corporate personal-*

ity is the sum of rights and duties borne by a corporate body: see, e.g., Cos.A. 1985, s 13(3); *Salomon* v *Salomon* [1897] AC 22. *See* PERSON.

personal pension scheme. Any scheme or arrangement which is comprised in one or more instruments or agreements and which has, or is capable of having, effect so as to provide benefits, in the form of pensions or otherwise, payable on death or retirement to or in respect of employed earners who have made arrangements with the trustees or managers of the scheme for them to become members of it: Pension Schemes Act 1996, s 1. See Finance Act 2000, Sch 13; C.S.P.S.S.A. 2000, s 43. *See* OCCUPATIONAL PENSION SCHEME.

personal property. Property other than land, e.g., goods and chattels. Leasehold interests are classed as personal property. Divided into *choses in possession* and *choses in action* (q.v.). *See* PROPERTY.

personal representative. 'The executor, original or by representation, or administrator for the time being of a deceased person': A.E.A. 1925, s 55(1). See S.C.A. 1981, s 114; I.C.T.A. 1988, s 701(4); *Re Radley-Kane (Deceased)* [1998] 3 WLR 617. *See* ADMINISTRATOR; EXECUTOR.

personalty. Personal property (q.v.).

persona non grata. An 'unacceptable person', e.g., a diplomatic official not acceptable to the government of the country to which he is accredited.

person in authority. For purposes of a 'confession' (q.v.), 'persons in authority' have been held to include: prosecutor; prosecutor's spouse; police officer; magistrate; magistrate's clerk; but not a police officer's wife or a fellow prisoner or a prison chaplain. See P.&C.E.A. 1984, s 82(1); *R* v *Platt* [1981] Crim LR 332.

person in charge of car. Where a person is supervising a learner-driver, and has no intention of driving the car, he is, nevertheless, in charge of that car for purposes of the Road Traffic Act 1988, s 5 (consumption of alcohol): *DPP* v *Janman* [2004] EWHC 101.

person of unsound mind. One suffering from a mental disorder (q.v.).

person with care. A person is a 'person with care', in relation to any child, if he is a person with whom the child has his home, who usually provides day-to-day care for the child (whether exclusively or in conjunction with another person): Child Support Act 1991, s 3(3). See also Child Support Act 1995, Sch 3, para 16.

per stirpes. According to stock. Refers to the distribution of property of an intestate divided among those entitled according to the stocks of descent.

persuasive authorities. Precedents (q.v.) which are not technically binding; decisions of inferior courts, decisions of Irish, Scottish, Commonwealth and foreign courts; some very few textbooks, e.g., Bracton; Coke. See *Cordell* v *Second Classified Properties* [1969] 2 Ch 9.

perverse verdict. A verdict altogether against the evidence, or one given by a jury which refuses to follow a judge's direction relating to a matter of law. See, e.g., *R* v *Ponting* [1985] Crim LR 318 (verdict of not guilty in trial involving Official Secrets Act 1911, after clear statement by judge that defendant was guilty of offence charged). Such a verdict is not, in itself, ground for appeal against acquittal. See *Grobbelaar* v *News Group Newspapers* (2001) 151 NLJ 102 (Court of Appeal overturned a verdict that, given all the evidence, was not properly or reasonably open to the jury). *See* VERDICT.

perverse verdicts. In *Grobbelaar* v *News Group Newspapers* [2002] UKHL 40, HL held that a CA decision to quash as perverse a jury libel verdict, could not stand: the jury had fallen into serious error, and its award of high damages could not be supported, but this did not constitute a perverse error. (The award of £85,000 damages was reduced to £1 nominal damages.)

perverting the course of justice. Acting in a way which has a tendency and is intended to pervert the administration of public justice. See, e.g., *R* v *Bailey* [1956] NI 15 (false confession); *R* v *Murray* [1982] 1 WLR 475 (fabricating evidence); *R* v *Williams* (1991) 92 Cr

App R 158 (attempting to pervert the course of justice is a substantive offence); *R* v *Firetto* [1991] Crim LR 208 (bogus sample of blood); *R* v *Lalani* [1999] 1 Cr App R 481 (need for prosecution to prove requisite intent); C.J.P.O.A. 1994, s 51. *See* INTERFERING WITH WITNESSES.

petition. A written application praying for relief or remedy, as in a petition for divorce, petition of right (q.v.). Available only where statute or rules of procedure specifically prescribe it as a mode of procedure. Thus, a petition is necessary for applications for administration orders, winding-up and bankruptcy orders: see, e.g., Ins.A. 1986, ss 9(1), 124(1), 126(1).

petition of right. 1. Declaration of the liberties of the people, made in 1628. 2. Procedure of obtaining restitution from the Crown or compensation in damages. See Crown Proceedings Act 1947; *Franklin* v *R* [1974] QB 202 (in which the form of the petition is set out).

petitions to Parliament. It is 'the inherent right of every commoner in England to prepare and present petitions to the House of Commons in case of grievance, and the House of Commons to receive the same': Resolution of the Commons 1699. The petition should present a case in which the House has jurisdiction to interfere and should ask, in conclusion, for such relief as is within the power of the House to grant. It should be presented by a Member (but he cannot be compelled to present it: see *Chaffers* v *Goldsmid* [1894] 1 QB 186).

petroleum. Includes any mineral oil or relative hydrocarbon and petrol gas existing in its natural condition in strata, but not including coal or bituminous shales or other stratified deposits from which oil can be extracted by destructive distillation: Petroleum Act 1998, s 1. Property in petroleum in strata is vested in the Crown: see Petroleum (Production) Act 1934, s 1(1); 1998 Act, Sch 3, para 3. Rights of searching and boring are vested in the Crown: s 2. For licences to search and bore, see s 3.

petrol, unleaded. Defined under Hydrocarbon Oil Duties Act 1979 s 1, as substituted by Finance Act 2004, s 7, as 'petrol that contains not more than 0.013 grams of lead per litre of petrol. 'Petrol is "leaded petrol" if it is not unleaded petrol.'

petty sessions. Court of summary jurisdiction, based initially on a statute of 1946. Known as 'magistrates' court' (q.v.). See M.C.A. 1980; Justices of the Peace Act 1997, ss 4, 72. 'Petty sessions areas' are specified by the Lord Chancellor, under Justices of the Peace Act 1997, s 4, substituted by Acc.J.A. 1999, s 75.

PFI. Private Finance Initiative. Government policy aimed at involving the private sector in the provision of public general services, with the object of improving the national industrial infrastructure and public services without increasing the burden of taxation.

PGO. Public Guardianship Office, set up in April 2001, to replace Public Trust Office and to act as administrative office of the Court of Protection to protect and manage the funds of persons lacking mental capacity.

philanthropic purposes. Gifts for 'philanthropic' or similar purposes have been held to be wider than gifts for 'charitable purposes', so that they do not necessarily constitute a charity. 'It seems to me that "philanthropic" is wide enough to comprise purposes not technically charitable': *per* Stirling J in *Re Macduff* [1896] 2 Ch 451. *See* CHARITABLE TRUST.

photographs, indecent. *See* CHILDREN, INDECENT PHOTOGRAPHS OF.

photographs, right to take. 'In my judgment no one possesses a right of preventing another person photographing him any more than he has a right of preventing another person giving a description of him, provided the description is not libellous or otherwise wrongful': *per* Horridge J in *Sports and General Press Agency* v *'Our Dogs' Publishing Co* [1916] 2 KB 880. For breach of copyright in photograph, see *Williams* v *Settle* [1960] 1 WLR 1072.

photographs, use of in identification. Photographs of suspects must not be shown to witnesses for the purpose of identification if circumstances allow of a personal identification. Photographs used must be available for production in court. See *R* v *Cook* [1987] QB 417 (the rule against hearsay (q.v.) does not apply to photofit pictures).

picketing, peaceful. It is lawful for a person, in contemplation or furtherance of a trade dispute, to attend at or near his own place of work, or, if he is a union official, at or near the place of work of a member of the union whom he is accompanying and whom he represents, for the purpose only of peacefully obtaining or communicating information, or peacefully persuading any person to work or abstain from working: T.U.L.R.(C.)A. 1992, s 220. Those who picket another's place of work may lose their immunity in tort. See *Dupont Steels* v *Sirs* [1980] 1 WLR 142; *Rayware Ltd* v *TGWU* [1989] 1 WLR 675; SI 92/476 (Code of Practice (Picketing)). *See* SECONDARY ACTION; STRIKE.

pickpocket. One who steals money or property, usually secretly, from the person of another. See, e.g., *R* v *Daniel* (1988) 10 Cr App R (S) 341.

piracy. 1. Piracy *jure gentium* (piracy at common law) involves an act of armed violence committed upon the high seas within the jurisdiction of the Admiralty, and not being an act of war. See Geneva Convention on the High Seas 1958, arts 15–17. (Term may include mutiny of passengers: *Naylor* v *Palmer* (1854) 10 Exch 382.) Piracy may also be committed against an aircraft: see Aviation Security Act 1982, s 5. See Merchant Shipping and Maritime Security Act 1997, s 26; *Athens Maritime Enterprises* v *Hellenic Mutual War Risks Assn* [1982] Com LR 188. For abolition of death penalty for piracy, see C.D.A. 1998, s 36. 2. Infringement of a copyright: see Copyrights, Designs and Patents Act 1988, s 107; *R* v *Carter* (1992) *The Times*, 31 January (distribution of pirated tapes akin to theft); *R* v *Blake* [1997] 1 WLR 1167.

piscary, common of. Right to catch fish in waters belonging to another. See *Lovett* v *Fairclough* (1990) 61 P & CR 385. *See* FISHERY.

placement order. This is an order made by the court authorising a local authority to place a child for adoption with any prospective adopters who may be chosen by the authority. The court may not make a placement order in respect of a child unless the child is subject to a care order, the court is satisfied that the conditions in section 31(2) of the 1989 Act (conditions for making a care order) are met, or the child has no parent or guardian: s 21 A.C.A. 2002.

places open to public, removal of articles from. 'Where the public have access to a building in order to view the building or part of it, or a collection or part of a collection housed in it, any person who without lawful authority removes from the building or its grounds the whole or any part of any article displayed or kept for display to the public in the building or that part of it or in its grounds shall be guilty of an offence': Th.A. 1968, s 11(1). See *R* v *Durkin* [1973] 2 All ER 872.

placing of shares. *See* SHARES, PLACING OF.

plagiarism. The unauthorised appropriating and utilising of another's ideas, works or compositions and presenting them as one's own. See *R* v *Cambridge University ex p Beg* (1999) 11 Admin LR 505. It may amount to the tort of passing off (q.v.) or a breach of copyright under the Copyright, Designs and Patents Act 1988, as amended. For 'infringing copy', see s 27.

plaintiff. One who brings a claim (q.v.) into court. Known now, under CPR, r 2.3.(1), as 'claimant' (q.v.).

planning control, breach of. Development of land (q.v.) without appropriate planning permission, or failure to comply with conditions attached to a permission. It can lead to a local planning authority serving an enforcement notice or stop notice (qq.v.) prohibiting specified operations on the land. See T.C.P.A. 1990, Part VII; Planning and Compensation Act 1991, ss 2, 3. For limitation periods concerning enforcement, see 1991 Act, s 4. For planning contravention order, see 1990 Act, s 171C, inserted by 1991 Act, s 1.

planning permission. Formal consent of a local planning authority which must be sought by one who wishes to develop land. For 'planning authorities', see T.C.P.A. 1990, Part I. Permission may be granted unconditionally or subject to such conditions as the authority thinks fit, or may be refused. See *Arfon BC ex p Walton Commercial Group* [1997] JPL 237. See generally, T.C.P.A. 1990; Planning and Compensation Act 1991, s 10 (certificates of lawful use and development); SI 95/418; *Dyason v Secretary of State for the Environment* [1998] EGCS 11 (danger of informal hearings leading to error); *Secretary of State for the Environment* v *Fletcher Estates* (2000) *The Times*, 23 February. Planning inquiries should be held in public, subject to certain exemptions: see 1990 Act, ss 320, 321, Sch 8. For powers to revoke or modify planning permission, see 1990 Act, s 97. For compensation, see ss 120, 144; see also 1991 Act. See *R v Secretary of State for the Environment* (2001) 151 NLJ 727 (compatibility of planning procedure and right to fair hearing). See DEVELOPMENT.

planning policy, disregard of. In *T-Mobile Ltd v First Secretary of State* (2004) *The Times*, 16 November, the CA held that where government policy has been set out clearly in guideline form, any departure from that policy by an inspector requires a statement by the inspector of the unusual circumstances behind his decision.

planning zones, simplified. See ZONES, SIMPLIFIED PLANNING.

plant. 'It includes whatever apparatus is used by a businessman for carrying on a business. Not his stock in trade which he buys or makes for sale, but all goods and chattels, fixed or movable, which he keeps for permanent employment in his business': *Yarmouth* v *France* (1887) 18 QBD 647. See Capital Allowances Act 1968; Finance Act 1971, ss 41, 44; *IRC*

v *Scottish & Newcastle Breweries Ltd* [1982] 1 WLR 322; *Attwood* v *Anduff Car Wash Ltd* [1996] STC 110. In *Shove* v *Lingfield Park Ltd* (2004) *The Times*, 26 April, the CA held that the track surface of a racecourse artificial all-weather installation was not to be considered as 'plant' for purposes of Capital Allowances Act 1990, s 24. The track was no more than a part of the premises within which the business was carried on. See MACHINERY AND PLANT.

plant, essence of. Expenditure relating to the installation of an artificial race track was not to be considered as having been incurred on 'plant and machinery' for purposes under Capital Allowances Act 1990, s 24: *Shore* v *Lingfield Park Ltd* (2003) *The Times*, 11 August.

plc. Abbreviation for 'public limited company' (q.v.). See COMPANY NAME.

plea. A formal answer by defendant to a charge brought against him.

plea, ambiguous. A plea which, in response to an indictment, is equivocal or not clear. Example: 'Guilty, but I wasn't sure that the goods did not belong to me.' If a plea remains ambiguous, a plea of not guilty is entered on behalf of accused: C.L.A. 1967, s 6(1). See *R v Plymouth Justices ex p Hart* [1986] QB 950.

plea bargaining. Informal procedure usually in chambers, whereby the defendant could agree to plead guilty as an exchange for the prosecution's dropping other charges (or a sentence concession, i.e., 'sentence bargaining'). See *R v Turner* [1970] 2 QB 321. *A-G's Guidelines on the Acceptance of Pleas* (issued 7 December, 2000) (2000) 150 NLJ 1860, state: 'Jurisprudence in this jurisdiction, save in the most exceptional circumstances, is conducted in public. This includes the acceptance of pleas by the prosecution and sentencing ... Only in the most exceptional of circumstances should plea and sentence be discussed in chambers.' Where there is such a discussion, the prosecution advocate should make a full note, which should be made available to prosecuting authority. Where there is to be a discussion on plea and sentence and the prosecution advocate takes the view that the circumstances are not exceptional, he must dissociate himself/herself from involvement in any discussion on sentence, and remind the judge of relevant decisions of the Court of Appeal.

plea, change of. Change of plea by the accused at any stage of the trial. It must come from the accused personally. See *R v Drew* [1985] 1 WLR 914. It was held in *R v P* [2002] 2 Cr App R 13, that where defendant changes a plea of not guilty to guilty during the course of a trial, it is not necessary for the judge to ask the jury for a formal verdict of guilty. The judge may, if he wishes, discharge the jury and pass sentence.

plead. To put forward a plea (q.v.).

pleading guilty by post. *See* POST, PLEA OF GUILTY BY.

pleadings. Formal written statements in a civil action, usually drafted by counsel, served by a party on his opponents, stating allegations of fact upon which the party pleading was claiming relief, but not the evidence by which the facts were to be proved. Replaced under CPR by 'statement of case' (q.v.).

plea in bar. Plea by defendant in a trial on indictment, e.g., *autrefois acquit, autrefois convict* (qq.v.).

pleas, discount on. In *R v Barber* [2001] All ER (D) 335 (Oct), CA held that, in relation to an offence triable only on indictment, an appropriate discount for a prompt plea was around one-third. A higher discount might be appropriate in the case of offences triable either way, where the plea was entered at plea-before-venue stage.

pledge. 1. A surety. 2. Transfer of a chattel (q.v.) (or documents of title thereto) by the pledgor to the pledgee, as security for the payment of a debt incurred by the transferor, or performance of some engagement. See Factors Act 1889, ss 1–5. 3. Pawnee's rights over an article taken in pawn: C.C.A. 1974, s 189(1).

plene administravit. He has fully administered. Defence by an executor (q.v.) or administrator (q.v.) who is sued upon the testator's debts, claiming that he has administered the estate fully and has nothing left with which to satisfy claimant's demands.

plenipotentiary. One invested with full powers, e.g., as the Sovereign's representative.

poaching. Illegal taking of game or fish, and trespassing for that purpose. See Night Poaching Act 1828; Game Act 1831, s 30 (covers poaching in daytime, i.e., one hour before sunrise, and ends one hour after sunset); Game Laws (Amendment) Act 1960; Th.A. 1968, Sch 1; Wild Creatures and Forest Laws Act 1971; Deer Act 1991, s 1(1); *R v King* (1991) *The Times*, 4 July.

points, unargued. It was held in *Adams v Bullock* (2005) *The Times*, 6 January, that where points in a witness statement are not argued at a hearing, they will generally be regarded as having been abandoned.

poison. Substance which when administered is injurious to health or life. It is an offence under O.P.A. 1861, ss 23, 24, unlawfully to administer to a person any poison or noxious thing so as to endanger life or inflict grievous bodily harm. See also O.P.A. 1861, s 59 (procuring a poison: *R v Mills* [1963] 1 QB 522); Poisons Act 1972, which regulates the sale of poisons. See *R v Marcus* [1981] 1 WLR 774. For sentencing principles, see *R v Jones* (1990) 12 Cr App R (S) 323. *See* ADMINISTER; NOXIOUS.

police. The state's civil force which is responsible for the maintenance of public order. 'Individuals given the general right to use coercive force by the state within the state's domestic territory': Klockars. Members of the police force are neither servants nor agents of the Crown. For powers of the police, see, e.g., P.&C.E.A. 1984; C.J.P.O.A. 1994; Police Acts 1996, 1997; Codes of Practice; Police (Property) Acts 1897, 1997. See also Police (Health and Safety) Act 1997; SI 98/1542; *R v DPP ex p Duckenfield* [2000] 1 WLR 55. Police representation is effected through Association of Chief Police Officers, Superintendents' Association, Police

Federation. *See* TORT, OFF DUTY POLICE OFFICER.

police anonymity at inquest. A police officer who was considered to be a potential witness at a coroner's inquest, could claim anonymity for himself and his family where he was in fear of his life and such fear was based on reasonable grounds in the objective sense: *A v Inner South London Coroner* (2004) *The Times*, 12 July.

police areas. England and Wales are divided into police areas: 41 areas, as listed in the Police Act 1996, Sch 1, amended by Police Act 1997, s 129, the metropolitan police district and the City of London Police Area: Police Act 1996, s 1. A police force is to be maintained in every police area: s 2. Each area has a police authority which is charged under s 6 with the maintenance of an efficient and effective service; for justification of allocation of resources, see *R v Chief Constable of Sussex ex p International Traders' Ferry Ltd* [1998] 3 WLR 1260. For definition of 'police authorities', see I.A. 1978, s 5; *R v HM Treasury ex p National Crime Squad Service Authority* [2000] STC 638. A police authority comprises 17 members: s 4(1).

police, assaults on. *See* ASSAULT ON THE POLICE.

police complaints. Under Police Reform Act 2002, s 9, an Independent Police Complaints Commission is set up, comprising a chairman and ten other members, none of whom may have held office as a constable in any part of the UK.

Police Complaints Authority. Established under P.&C.E.A. 1984. See now Police Act 1996, s 66, Sch 5. It consists of a chairman and not less than eight other members; no member shall be a person who is or has been a constable in any part of the UK. On receiving a complaint, the chief officer must determine that it concerns the conduct of an officer and is not about operational issues.

police court. Magistrates' court (q.v.).

police detention. *See* CUSTODY; DETENTION, POLICE.

police force. Defined under R.I.P.A. 2000, s 81, as any of the following: any police force maintained under Police Act 1996 (police forces in England and Wales outside London); metropolitan police force; City of London police force; and police force maintained under or by virtue of Police (Scotland) Act 1967; Royal Ulster Constabulary; Ministry of Defence Police; Royal Navy Regulating Branch; Royal Military Police; Royal Air Force Police; British Transport Police.

police, obstruction of. It is an offence to resist or wilfully obstruct a constable in the execution of his duty or a person assisting a constable in the execution of his duty: Police Act 1996, s 89(2). See *Rice v Connolly* [1966] 2 QB 414; *Plowden v DPP* [1991] Crim LR 850; *Redmond-Bate v DPP* [1999] Crim LR 998.

police records. Under new regulations (see SI 03/2823), made under Police and Criminal Evidence Act 1984, s 27, and in force as from 1 December 2003, the offences of begging and persistent begging contrary to the Vagrancy Act 1824, ss 3, 4, and touting for hire car services, contrary to the Criminal Justice and Public Order Act 1994, s 167, become recordable offences.

police right to question. *See* QUESTIONING BY POLICE.

policy of insurance. The instrument containing the contract made by the insurer with the insured. See Insurance Companies Act 1982, s 96; Policyholders Protection Act 1997. *See* INSURANCE.

policy tribunal, immunity of. CA held in *Heath v Commissioner of Police of the Metropolis* (2004) *The Times*, 22 July, that a police disciplinary board was to be considered as a judicial or quasi-judicial body, the members of which enjoyed immunity from suit in the exercise of their functions.

political asylum. Refuge and safety offered to one escaping from political oppression overseas. See Fugitive Offenders Act 1967; Asylum and Immigration Act 1996; *Danian v Secretary of State for Home Department* [1999] INLR 533; *Ahmed v Secretary of State for Home Department* (1999) *The Times*, 8 December; Immigration and Asylum

Act 1999, Part VI. *See* ASYLUM; PER-SECUTION; REFUGEE.

political fund. That part of a union's total funds used exclusively in the furtherance of political objects (q.v.). See T.U.L.R.(C.)A. 1992, ss 71, 86, 87 (amended by E.R. (Dispute Resolution) A. 1998, s 6); T.U.R.E.R.A. 1993, Sch 1.

political objects. 1. In reference to a charity (q.v.): 'Equity has always refused to recognise [political] objects as charitable': *Bowman* v *Secular Society Ltd* [1917] AC 406. These objects include, e.g., advancing the interests of a political party, opposing changes in the law, party political education. See *Southwood* v *A-G* (2000) 150 NLJ 1017. 2. For political objects on which trade unions may not expend money by using their political funds, see T.U.L.R.(C.)A. 1992, ss 72, 72A, inserted by Employment Relations Act 1999, Sch 6, para 13. *See* CHARITA-BLE TRUSTS.

political offence. Term used in relation to extradition (q.v.), which will not normally take place on the basis of a political offence. 'In my opinion the idea that lies behind the phrase is that the fugitive is at odds with the state that applies for his extradition on some issue connected with the political control or government of the country': *per* Viscount Radcliffe in *Schtraks* v *Government of Israel* [1964] AC 556. For 'non-political offence', see *T* v *Home Secretary* [1995] Imm AR 142. See *R* v *Secretary of State for Home Department ex p Kerrouche* [1997] Imm AR 610.

political offence, exclusion of cases from. Under Suppression of Terrorism Act 1978, certain offences are not to be regarded as of a political character. They include: murder, manslaughter or culpable homicide, rape, kidnapping, false imprisonment, assault occasioning actual bodily harm or causing injury and wilful fire-raising; offences under O.P.A. 1861, ss 18, 20–24, 28–30, 48, 55; offences under Explosive Substances Act 1883, ss 2, 3; offences under Aviation Security Act 1982 and Aviation and Maritime Security Act 1990, s 1; attempts to commit any of these offences. See 1978

Act, Sch 1, as amended; Terrorism Act 2000, Sch 15, para 3.

political office. The office of member of Parliament, member of the European Parliament, or member of a local authority, or any position within a political party: T.U.L.R.(C.)A. 1992, s 72.

political parties, register of. *See* REGISTER OF POLITICAL PARTIES.

political party, membership of. The Association of Chief Police Officers of England, Wales and Northern Ireland, have stated in their press release 'Chief Officers prohibit membership of BNP' (October, 2004) that they have adopted a policy of prohibiting police officers from membership of the British National Party.

political uniforms. It is an offence to wear in any public place or public meeting a uniform 'signifying association with any political organisation or the promotion of any political purpose': P.O.A. 1936, s 1(1). See *O'Moran* v *DPP* [1975] QB 864. For wearing uniforms of proscribed organisations, see Terrorism Act 2000, s 13.

poll. Procedure involved in taking, registering, counting votes and declaring the result in an election. See, e.g., Representation of the People Act 1983, Sch 1; Cos.A. 1985, s 373.

poll, deed. *See* DEED.

poll tax. Tax per person or head. *See* COMMUNITY CHARGE.

pollution, environmental. Pollution of the air, water or land which may give rise to any harm. 'Pollution' includes pollution caused by noise, heat or vibrations or any other kind of release of energy, and 'air' includes air within buildings and air within other natural or man-made structures above or below ground. 'Harm' means harm to the health of human beings or other living organisms; harm to the quality of the environment taken as a whole; harm to the quality of the air, water or land, and other impairment of or interference with the ecological systems of which any living organisms form part; offence to human beings' senses; damage to property; impairment of or interference with amenities or other legitimate uses of the environment: Pollution Prevention and Control Act 1999, s 1: Council Directive 96/61/EC.

polygamy. Practice under which a person has several spouses. See Matrimonial Proceedings (Polygamous Marriages) Act 1972; Mat.C.A. 1973, ss 11, 47; Matrimonial Causes Rules 1977, r 108; Private International Law (Misc. Provs.) Act 1995, s 5. Immigration Act 1988, s 2, restricts the exercise of right of abode in the UK in cases of polygamy. See also S.S. Contributions and Benefits Act 1992, s 133; *Bibi* v *Chief Adjudication Officer* [1997] Fam Law 793.

pornography. Obscene material (books, films, etc.). See *R* v *Elliot* [1996] 1 Cr App R 432; *R* v *Travell* [1997] 1 Cr App R (S) 52. For computer pornography, see C.J.P.O.A. 1994, s 84. *See* OBSCENITY.

pornography, dismissal relating to. Employment Appeal Tribunal held, in *Thomas* v *Hillingdon LBC* (2002) *The Times*, 4 October, that the dismissal of an employee for gross misconduct for using an office computer during working hours to access pornographic material, was a reasonable response by the employer; it was not for an employment tribunal to act on its own view that the employee's behaviour in these circumstances was no more than misconduct.

port. Includes harbours, rivers, estuaries, havens, docks, canals or other places where persons are empowered under statute to make charges in respect of ships entering and using the facilities: S.C.A. 1981, s 22(2). See Ports Act 1991. *See* SAFE PORT.

portion. Gift of money or other property made to a child by a father or one *in loco parentis* (q.v.) so as to establish that child in life or to make a permanent provision for him. A 'portion-debt' arises from a convenant to give a portion.

position, change of, as defence to restitution claim. The defence is available to a person whose position has so changed that it would be inequitable in all the circumstances to require him to make restitution, or alternatively to make restitution in full: *per* Lord Goff, in *Lipkin Gorman* v *Karpnale Ltd* [1991] AC 548.

positive discrimination. *See* DISCRIMINATION, REVERSE.

positive law. *See* LAW, POSITIVE.

positivism, legal. Doctrine in legal theory based on the examination of man-made law, which is set down (i.e., posited) by man for man. It is concerned, essentially, with law as it is, rather than as it ought to be. Hence: propositions of law are 'true' only when describing correctly the rules of law or the content of laws; investigation of such matters must be 'value-free'.

possession. Concept based on a degree of physical control and involving: *corpus* (that which is possessed) and *animus possidendi* (q.v.). May be prima facie evidence of ownership. 'Possession gives defendant a right against every man who cannot show a good title': *per* Lord Mansfield in *Haldane* v *Harvey* (1769) 4 Burr 2484. Defined variously as, e.g., 'physical detention coupled with intention to use the thing detained as one's own': Maine, *Ancient Law* (1861); 'continuing exercise of a claim to the exclusive use of some material object': Salmond, *Jurisprudence* (1902); 'the present control of a thing, on one's own behalf and to the exclusion of all others': Tay, *Possession in the Common Law* (1964). See *Lockyer* v *Gibb* [1967] 2 QB 243 (possession without mental element in relation to crime); Terrorism Act 2000, s 57 ('possession' for terrorist purposes). *See* OWNERSHIP.

possession action, fast. Provided by RSC O 113, or CCR, O 24 (both re-enacted in CPR, Schs 1, 2), allowing the court to make an order for possession by a landlord dispossessed by squatters or trespassers, five days after service of a summons. A master, rather than a judge, may hear proceedings in case of an emergency. See *Dutton* v *Manchester Airport plc* (1999) 149 NLJ 333 (licensee not in occupation can claim possession against a trespasser where that remedy has become necessary to give effect to rights of occupation enjoyed under contract with the licensor).

possession, exclusive. Concept of particular importance in relation to leases (q.v.) and licences (q.v.). ('Exclusive possession, de jure or de facto, now or in the future is the bedrock of English land law': per Lord Hoffmann in Hunter v Canary Wharf Ltd [1997] AC 655.) A lease gives the grantee the right to exclusive possession of the demised premises, i.e., a degree of territorial control including the ability to keep out strangers (and the landlord, except, e.g., to view or repair). Not to be confused with 'exclusive occupation'. See Street v Mountford [1985] AC 809; Brillouet v Landless (1995) 28 HLR 836; Huwyler v Ruddy (1996) 72 P & CR D3; Pemberton v Southwark BC [2000] 21 EG 135 (concept of 'the tolerated trespasser' who is allowed to stay on after the making of a conditional order for possession against him).

possession, interest in. See INTEREST IN POSSESSION.

possession order, no avoidance. CA held, in Harlow District Council v Hall [2006] The Times, 15 March, where a possession order has been granted against a secure tenant to give up possession and he subsequently becomes bankrupt, the possession cannot be avoided.

possession, quiet. See QUIET POSSESSION.

possession, recent. See RECENT POSSESSION.

possession, unity of. See UNITY OF POSSESSION.

possession, unlawful, of drugs. It is an offence under Misuse of Drugs Act 1971: to have a controlled drug in one's possession (s 5(1)); to have a controlled drug in one's possession whether lawfully or not, with the intention to supply it to another in contravention of s 4. 'Possession' involves more than mere control; the person in control should know that the thing is in his control. For defences, see ss 7(1), 28. See Warner v Metropolitan Police Commissioner [1969] AC 256; R v Yeardley [2000] 1 QB 374. See DRUGS, CONTROLLED; DRUGS, SUPPLY OF.

possession, writ of. Writ directing a sheriff (q.v.) to enter upon land so as to give vacant possession to the plaintiff. Used for direct enforcement of order or judgment for possession of land. See

H.A. 1985, Sch 2. For orders for possession, see H.A. 1985, s 83 (possession of dwelling house let under secure tenancy), s 84 (suspended possession order); Tower Hamlets LBC v Azad (1998) 30 HLR 241; CPR, Sch 1; O 10, r 4; Jephson Homes Ltd v Moisejevs (2001) The Times, 2 January.

possessory lien. See LIEN.

possessory title. Title based on the possession of land where the applicant is, for the time being, unable to establish title in the usual way, e.g., by title deeds. First registration of such title has the effect of registering land with absolute title, but that title will not affect any rights or interests subsisting or capable of arising at the time of registration. See L.R.A. 1925, ss 4, 6, 11; L.R.A. 1986, s 1. Possessory title to leasehold land may be granted to an applicant in possession or in receipt of rents and profits. See Jessamine Investment Co v Schwartz [1976] 3 All ER 521. See TITLE.

possibility. Term used in land law (e.g., as in 'double possibility') to describe an interest in land which will arise on some uncertain event. 'Bare possibility' described the expectation of an eldest son to succeed to his father's lands; 'possibility coupled with an interest' refers to, e.g., a contingent remainder (q.v.).

postal packet. A letter (q.v.), parcel, packet or other article transmissible by post: Postal Services Act 2000, s 125(1). See SI 01/878.

Postal Services Commission. Body corporate, set up under Postal Services Act 2000, s 1, to ensure provision of a universal postal service, including the promotion of effective competition between postal operators (i.e., persons who provide the service of conveying postal packets from one place to another by post or any of the incidental services of receiving, collecting, sorting and delivering such packets), and the provision of advice to the Secretary of State (see s 42) concerning the number, location and accessibility of public post offices.

Postal Services, Consumer Council for. Body corporate, set up under Postal Services Act 2000, s 2, to represent interests of users of postal services and to make proposals to the Secretary of State and the Postal Services Commission about postal services. See s 52 for functions of Council.

postal services, restriction on provision of. No person shall convey a letter from one place to another unless he holds a licence authorising him to do so, or he is acting as an employee or agent of a person who is authorised by a licence to do so: Postal Services Act 2000, s 6(1). For exceptions, see s 7. For penalties for contravention of a licence, see s 30.

post, contracts by. Contracts made, e.g., by letter or telegram. In general, an offer by post must be accepted by post unless the offer has indicated anything to the contrary. Acceptance is complete as soon as the letter is properly addressed, prepaid and posted, whether it reaches the offeror or not. See *Adams* v *Lindsell* (1818) 1 B & Ald 681.

post-dated cheque. *See* CHEQUE, POST-DATED.

post-mortem. After death. Term used to refer to the examination of a body after death so as to determine, e.g., the cause of death. Known also as an 'autopsy'. See Coroners Rules 1984; Coroners Act 1988, ss 19–23; Human Tissue Act 1961, s 2; Anatomy Act 1984. It was held in *AB* v *Leeds Teaching Hospital NHS Trust* [2004] EWHC 644, that no claim for the tort of wrongful interference with a corpse could be established where a post-mortem had been carried out in lawful circumstances. *See* ANATOMICAL EXAMINATION; CORONER.

post-mortem, psychological, standing of. Psychological evidence concerning the state of mind of a defendant or victim, falling short of mental illness, might be admissible as evidence, where based on medical records; but the present academic status of psychological autopsies is insufficient to allow them to be admitted as expert evidence: *R* v *Gilfoyle* (2001) *The Times*, 13 February. See also *R* v *Strudwick* [1995] CLY 1205.

Post Office Company. The re-formed Post Office, set up under Postal Services Act 2000, s 62, to enable the Post Office

to function and compete commercially, while remaining in public ownership. For dissolution of Post Office, see s 75.

post, payment by. Generally not good payment where the letter is lost in the post, unless the creditor requested payment by post. Such a request does not absolve the debtor from paying in a reasonable manner and in accordance with the accepted business practice. See *Pennington* v *Crossley & Son* (1897) 77 LT 43.

post, plea of guilty by. Procedure under M.C.A. 1980, s 12, amended by C.J.P.O.A. 1994, Sch 5, and Magistrates' Courts (Procedure) Act 1998, s 1, often used in motoring cases, and where the offence is summary and punishable by not more than three months' imprisonment. The prosecutor serves the summons and statement of facts to be placed before the court. The defendant must then inform the clerk that he wishes to plead guilty without appearance. (He may change his mind and appear.) The statement of facts read out in court must be exactly the same as that served on the defendant. The hearing is adjourned if the possibility of imprisonment or disqualification (motoring cases) arises. (Under the 1998 Act, the police are allowed to prepare witness statements which can be served with the summons; where defendant fails to plead guilty by post and is tried in his absence, the prosecution case can be based on those statements.)

post, service by. Where statute authorises or requires a document to be served by post, that service is deemed to be effected by properly addressing, pre-paying, and posting a letter containing the document: I.A. 1978, s 7.

post-traumatic stress disorder. Neurasthenia, i.e., anxiety disorder, brought about as a reaction to the shock of some painful event outside normal human experience. It may result in personality change, depression, inability to carry out normal activities. See *Alcock* v *Chief Constable of S Yorks* [1992] 1 AC 310; *Greatorex* v *Greatorex* [2000] 1 WLR 1970. *See* PSYCHIATRIC HARM, DAMAGES FOR.

poverty. 'It is quite clearly established that poverty does not mean destitution; it is a word of wide and somewhat indefinite import; it may not unfairly be paraphrased as meaning persons who have to "go short" in the ordinary acceptation of that term, due regard being had to their status in life, and so forth': *Re Coulthurst* [1951] Ch 661.

power. Authority vested in the donee (of the power) to modify a legal relationship, as where one disposes of property for his own or another's benefit. May be: simply collateral (q.v.) (where the donee has no interest in the property); in gross (q.v.); appendant or appurtenant (qq.v.). For 'legal' and 'equitable powers', see L.P.A. 1925, s 205(1). *See* APPOINTMENT, POWER OF.

power, capricious. A power which is void because 'it negatives a sensible consideration by the trustees of the exercise of the power': *Re Manisty's Settlement* [1974] Ch 17.

power coupled with interest. Power to perform some act, together with an interest (united in the same person) in the subject matter of that act.

power of appointment. *See* APPOINTMENT, POWER OF.

power of attorney. Instrument authorising one person to act for another during the absence of that other. Under Tr.A. 1925, s 25, as amended by Powers of Attorney Act 1971, a trustee (q.v.) has the power to delegate the exercise of his powers and discretions to an attorney. Under Enduring Powers of Attorney Act 1985, a person may appoint an attorney whose authority will not be revoked by that person's subsequent incapacity (defined in s 13(1)). The donee of a power of attorney is not prevented from doing an act in relation to land, capital proceeds of a conveyance of land, or income from land, by reason only that the act involves the exercise of a trustee function of the donor if, at the time when the act is done, the donor has a beneficial interest in the land, proceeds or income: Trustee Delegation Act 1999, s 1(1). (This subsection applies only if and

so far as a contrary intention is not expressed in the instrument creating the power of attorney: s 1(3)(*a*).) See *Re W* [2000] 1 All ER 175; L.P. (Misc. Provs.) A. 1989, Sch 1, 2. It was held in *Re F (Enduring Powers of Attorney)* [2004] EWHC 725, that in order for the court to refuse registration under Enduring Powers of Attorney Act 1985, s 6(5)(e), it is essential that the court be satisfied that the choice of a person shall not be rejected because of matters such as hostility to that person from a sibling or other relative.

power of sale. 1. Power of a tenant for life (q.v.) to sell settled land (q.v.) or any part thereof, or any easement, right or privilege over the land: S.L.A. 1925, s 38. Sale must be made for the best consideration in money that can be obtained. 2. Power of trustee (q.v.), under Tr.A. 1925, to sell or concur with any other person in selling all or part of the trust property. 3. Power of a mortgagee (q.v.), under L.P.A. 1925, s 101(1), to sell when the legal date for redemption (q.v.) has passed. Proceeds are used: in discharge of prior incumbrances, expenses of sale, discharge of money due to mortgagee under the mortgage; balance to mortgagor: L.P.A. 1925, s 105.

power of search. *See* SEARCH, POWER OF.

powers of attorney, lasting. A lasting power of attorney is a power of attorney under which the donor ('P') confers on the donee (or donees) authority to make decisions about all or any of the following: (a) P's personal welfare or specified matters concerning P's personal welfare, and (b) P's property and affairs or specified matters concerning P's property and affairs, and which includes authority to make such decisions in circumstances where P no longer has capacity. Mental Capacity Act 2005 s 9(1).

p.p. *See* PER PRO.

PPP agreements. Public-private partnership agreements under G.L.A.A. 1999, s 210, intended primarily to provide funding for the London underground system. At least one of the parties to the contract must be London Regional

Transport, Transport for London, or their subsidiaries, and the contract must involve the provision, construction, renewal, or improvement and maintenance of a railway or proposed railway belonging to London Regional Transport or Transport for London: s 210(2), (3), (4). The PPP Arbiter is a corporation sole appointed under s 225 to give directions on matters referred to him by parties to a PPP agreement.

practice. Formal procedures relating to proceedings in a court. Governed generally (in the Supreme Court) by Rules of the Supreme Court (q.v.), and Civil Procedure Rules 1998, as amended.

Practice Directions. Directions and notes, generally published in the law reports, indicating the views of the judges of the Court of Appeal or the judges, masters, registrars of the High Court, relating to matters of practice and procedure of the courts. They do not have any statutory authority.

practice form. 'Form to be used for a particular purpose in proceedings, the form and purpose being specified by a practice direction': CPR Glossary.

practice, general and approved. Practice taken into account in determining standard of care in actions for negligence. 'A defendant . . . can clear [himself] if he shows that he acted in accordance with general and approved practice': *per* Lord Alness in *Vancouver General Hospital* v *McDaniel* (1935) 152 LT 56.

practising certificate. Solicitors require a certificate issued by the Law Society, which entitles them to practise: see Solicitors Act 1974, ss 9–18; C.L.S.A. 1990, Sch 18; *Hudgell Yeates & Co* v *Weston* [1978] 2 All ER 363. Barristers are granted a practice certificate by the Bar Council after they have successfully completed a twelve-months' pupillage and have attended further education courses as required by the Bar Council. For fees, see Acc.J.A. 1999, ss 46, 47.

preamble. Introduction to a statute or Bill, explaining the facts and assumptions behind it. Where an operative part of a statute is ambiguous, the preamble

may be resorted to so as to show, e.g., the intention of the Act. 'It is only when it conveys a clear and definite meaning in comparison with relatively obscure or indefinite enacting words that a preamble may legitimately prevail': *A-G* v *Prince Ernest Augustus of Hanover* [1957] AC 436. See also *The Norwhale* [1975] QB 589.

pre- and post-nuptial settlements, variation of. The court may make an order under Mat.C.A. 1973, s 24(1)(c),(d), varying, for the benefit of parties to a marriage and of the children, any pre- or post-nuptial settlement (including a settlement made by will) made on the parties to the marriage. See *E* v *E* [1990] 2 FLR 233; *F* v *F (Ancillary Relief: Substantial Assets)* [1995] 2 FLR 45.

precarious possession. Possession simply at will. 'What is "precarious"? – that which depends not on right, but on the will of another person': *Burrows* v *Lang* [1901] 2 Ch 511.

precatory trust. Trust arising as a result of the use of precatory words (q.v.) and their construction. *See* TRUST.

precatory words. (*Precari* = to entreat.) Words of an entreaty, prayer, desire, etc., which, when they accompany a transfer or bequest of property, suggest that the transferor had in mind the creation of a trust (q.v.), e.g., 'I most heartily beseech . . .'; 'I will and desire that . . .' The court is guided by the intention of the testator (q.v.) apparent in the will (q.v.), and not by any particular words in which the wishes of the testator are expressed: *Re Williams* [1897] 2 Ch 12. See also *Re Adams and Kensington Vestry* (1884) 27 Ch D 394; *Re Diggles* (1888) 39 Ch D 253.

precedent. 1. Judgment or decision cited so as to justify a decision in a later, apparently similar, case. 'The process by which forms of conduct are stamped in the judicial mint as law, and thereafter circulate freely as part of the coinage of the realm': Cardozo CJ, *The Growth of Law* (1924). An *authoritative precedent* is generally binding and must be followed. A *persuasive precedent* (based, e.g., on *obiter dicta*) need not necessarily be followed. A *declaratory precedent* merely applies an existing rule of law. An *original precedent* creates and applies a new rule of law. Decisions on questions of fact must not be cited as precedents: *Qualcast Ltd* v *Haynes* [1959] AC 743. 2. Precedent as applied to the hierarchy of courts (the so-called 'vertical dimension of precedent') is as follows: *House of Lords* – generally bound by previous decisions (see *London Street Tramways Co* v *LCC* [1898] AC 375) but will depart from such decisions where it appears right to do so (see *R* v *Shivpuri* [1987] AC 1); *Court of Appeal (Civil Division)* – bound by previous decisions, except where given *per incuriam* (q.v.) or where inconsistent with a subsequent House of Lords decision; *Court of Appeal (Criminal Division)* – apparently bound by previous decisions; *High Court and Crown Court* – bound by decisions of superior courts; *county courts and magistrates' courts* – bound by decisions of superior courts. See *Young* v *Bristol Aeroplane Co Ltd* [1944] KB 718; *Davis* v *Johnson* [1978] 1 All ER 1132. See also Human Rights Act 1998, s 2, under which, in determining questions concerning a right under the Convention, a court is obliged to 'take into account' judgments, decisions, declarations of the European Court of Human Rights (q.v.) and decisions of the European Commission of Human Rights. UK courts must treat rulings of the European Court of Justice concerning the interpretation of EU Treaties and the validity of acts of EU institutions as binding: European Communities Act 1972, s 3(1). *See* HOUSE OF LORDS, CORRECTION OF ITS ERRORS; STARE DECISIS.

precedent, condition. *See* CONDITION.

precedent, departure from. Any exception to or modification of the rule of precedent is to be applied only in the most obvious cases and must be limited very carefully. The proposition in question must have been assumed by the previous court, but not necessarily decided by it: *Kadhim* v *Brent LBC* (2001) *The Times*, 27 March. See also *Re Hetherington* [1990] Ch 1.

precedent, significance of. 'Precedents should be stepping-stones and not halting-places': *per* Lord Macmillan in *Birch* v *Brown* [1931] AC 630. 'The only proper use of precedents is to establish principles': Allen, *Law in The Making* (1958).

precept. 1. Command. 2. Written order. 3. Order referring specifically to the payment of rates: L.G.A. 1972, s 149. See L.G.A. 1988, Part IV. (For the limitation of precepting powers see, e.g., Local Government Finance Act 1992, chap V.)

pre-contract negotiations, relevance of. CA held, in *P and S Platt Ltd* v *Crouch* [2003] EWCA Civ 1110, that negotiations which had taken place prior to the contract between the parties were of no relevance in the determination of a question as to whether particular rights had been transferred on the sale of real property. See *Birmingham, Dudley and District Banking Co* v *Ross* (1888) 38 Ch D 295.

predecessor. One (e.g., a settlor; testator (qq.v.)) from whom benefit is derived of succession to property. A 'predecessor in title' is one through whom another is able to trace a title in property.

pre-emption. Right to purchase before others, i.e. a 'right of first refusal'. See L.P.A. 1925, s 186; L.C.A. 1972, s 2(4) (whereby it is registrable as an estate contract (q.v.)); *First National Securities* v *Chiltern DC* [1975] 2 All ER 786; *Tuck* v *Baker* (1990) 32 EG 46; *Ground-premium Property Ltd* v *Longmint Ltd* [1998] 1 EGLR 131. For pre-emption rights of shareholders, see Cos.A. 1985, ss 89–96; *Scott* v *Petch* (2001) *The Times*, 8 February. *See* OPTION.

pre-emption as property. A right of pre-emption is 'property' within the definition in Ins.A. 1986, s 436: *Dear* v *Reeves* (2001) *The Times*, 22 March.

pre-emption, rights of. Under Land Registration Act 2002, s 115, a right of pre-emption in relation to registered land has effect from time of creation as an interest capable of binding successors in title (subject to rules concerning effect of dispositions on priority). The section has effect in relation to rights of pre-emption created on or after the day on which this section comes into force.

preference, fraudulent. See FRAUDU-LENT PREFERENCE.

preference, right of. Right of a personal representative (q.v.) to pay one creditor in preference to another of the same class. Abolished in relation to deaths occurring after 1971: A.E.A. 1971, s 10.

preference shares. Shares ranking for payment after debentures (q.v.) and before ordinary shares (q.v.). 'Convertible preference shares' involve an option for holders to convert their shares into ordinary shares at a stated future date: see I.C.T.A. 1988, s 832(1). For 'fixed rate preference share capital', see 1988 Act, s 312. See SHARE.

preferential debts. After payment of the costs of bankruptcy (q.v.), certain types of liabilities must be paid in priority to others. After preferential debts, ordinary liabilities of the bankrupt rank for dividend *pari passu inter se*.

preferment. 1. Advancement or promotion within the church. See Bishops (Retirement) Measure 1986, r 10(1). 2. Bringing or laying of a charge or bill of indictment (q.v.).

pregnancy. The processes involved in the female's carrying a developing child within her body. For purposes of Human Fertilisation and Embryology Act 1990, a woman is not to be treated as carrying a child until the embryo (q.v.) has been implanted: s 2(3). See *Re MB* (1997) NLJ 600; *Goodwill* v *British Pregnancy Advisory Service* [1996] 1 WLR 1397; *McFarlane* v *Tayside Health Board* [2000] 2 AC 59 (question of recoverability of damages after negligent medical advice resulting in unwanted pregnancy); *Greenfield* v *Irwin* (2001) *The Times*, 6 February (claim over misdiagnosis). See ABORTION; FOETUS.

pregnancy, dismissal on grounds of. Dismissal from employment solely because of, or for any reason connected with, pregnancy. Treated as unfair dismissal: E.P.(C.).A. 1978, s 60, and E.R.A. 1996, s 99. See *Stockton BC* v *Brown* [1987] ICR 897; *Webb* v *EMO Air Cargo*

[1992] IRLR 116. Council Directive 76/207/EEC precludes dismissal of a female employee at any time during pregnancy because of absences arising from pregnancy-related illness. See *Brown* v *Rentokil Ltd* [1998] ICR 790. See MATERNITY LEAVE.

pregnancy per alium. Pregnancy by some other [person]. A marriage is voidable on the grounds that at the time of the marriage the respondent was pregnant by some person other than the petitioner. See Mat.C.A. 1973, s 12. See NULLITY OF MARRIAGE.

pre-hearing assessment. Procedure concerning employment tribunal (q.v.) whereby either party, or the tribunal, may ask for a pre-hearing. If it is then decided that the originating application is 'unlikely to succeed or that the submission or arguments put by either party have no reasonable prospect of success' and the application is not withdrawn, costs may be awarded. See *Mulvaney* v *London Transport Executive* [1981] ICR 351.

pre-incorporation contract. A contract made between a person acting as agent (q.v.) or trustee (q.v.) for a company about to be formed and another party. Contracts intended to bind a company on incorporation, but entered into before registration, will be personally enforceable against those who purported to act for the company and enter the contract: Cos.A. 1985, s 36(4); Cos.A. 1989, s 130(4); *Badgerhill Properties Ltd* v *Cottrell* [1991] BCLC 805.

prejudice. 1. Preconceived judgment. 'Without prejudice' is a term used so as to attempt to protect the writer of a document against the construing of its contents as an admission of liability and means, in effect, 'without prejudice to rights of writer of the statement'. See *Peterborough CC* v *Manchester Developments Ltd* [1996] EGCS 60. 2. 'Negotiations with a view to a settlement are usually conducted "without prejudice", which means that the circumstances in which the content of those negotiations may be revealed to the court are very restricted': CPR Glossary. See

Unilever plc v *Procter and Gamble plc* (1999) 149 NLJ 370 (significance of the rule against the use of 'without prejudice' negotiations); *Instance* v *Denny Ltd* (2000) *The Times*, 28 February (extension of protection to subsequent litigation).

preliminary investigation. Known also as 'preliminary enquiry'. Investigation by magistrates of a case which may go for trial to a higher court. The object is to establish whether the prosecution can show a prima facie case against the accused; if it can, the accused is committed for trial; if not, the defendant is discharged. See, e.g., M.C.A. 1980, ss 4–7; C.J.P.O.A. 1994, Sch 4, para 31.

preliminary point of law. Point of law, e.g., whether or not certain facts constitute the offence charged, considered by the judge who hears the argument on it, following a plea of not guilty and before the jury (q.v.) is empanelled. See *R* v *Vickers* [1975] 2 All ER 945.

premises. 1. Those operative parts of a deed (q.v.) which precede the habendum (q.v.) and set out, e.g., the names of parties, property to be transferred. 2. Property, e.g., land, buildings. See, e.g., Building Act 1984, s 126; *Kay Green* v *Twinsectra* [1996] 1 WLR 1587; *Pike (Butchers) Ltd* v *Independent Assurance Co* [1998] Lloyd's Rep IR 410 (meaning of 'premises' in insurance contract). 3. Propositions in an argument from which a conclusion is drawn.

premises, disposal of. *See* DISPOSAL OF PREMISES.

premises, industrial. *See* INDUSTRIAL PREMISES.

premium. 1. Periodical payment made for keeping up an insurance (q.v.). 2. Reward. 3. Sum paid over and above a fixed wage (e.g., a bonus) or price. 4. 'Any fine or other like sum and any other pecuniary consideration in addition to rent and any sum paid by way of a deposit, other than one which does not exceed one-sixth of the annual rent and is reasonable in relation to the potential liability in respect of which it is paid': Rent Act 1977, s 128 (as substituted by H.A. 1980, s 79). Premiums and loans

(secured or unsecured) on a grant of protected tenancies (q.v.) were prohibited under the 1977 Act, s 119. See H.A. 1988, s 115.

premium, issue of shares at a. Issue of shares at a price above par or nominal value. Premium must be transferred to share premium account: Cos.A. 1985, s 130.

pre-nuptial   agreement. Agreement made before the celebration of a marriage and dealing, usually, with possible financial claims, division of property, to be made by one spouse on another in the event of divorce. Not generally considered to be binding by English courts, except, perhaps, where held to fall within Mat.C.A. 1973, s 25(g). See *F* v *F (Ancillary Relief: Substantial Assets)* [1995] 2 FLR 45; *S* v *S (Divorce Staying Proceedings)* [1997] 2 FLR 100; *N* v *N (Jurisdiction: Prenuptial Agreement)* [1999] 2 FCR 583. *See* MARRIAGE SETTLEMENT.

preparatory hearings. Where it appears to a Crown Court judge that an indictment reveals a case of such complexity, or a case whose trial is likely to be of such length, that substantial benefits are likely to accrue from a hearing before the jury is sworn and for purposes such as, identifying issues likely to be material to the jury's verdict, or assisting the jury's comprehension of those issues, or expediting the proceedings, he may order a preparatory hearing: C.P.I.A. 1996, s 29(1), (2). The order may be made on the application of the prosecutor, the accused, or on the judge's own motion: s 29(4). See s 29(3) for the case of a serious and highly complex fraud, as mentioned in C.J.A. 1987, s 7(1). When a preparatory hearing is ordered, the trial starts with that hearing, and arraignment takes place at the start of that hearing: s 30. In complex, long cases, such as fraud, where it appears appropriate that a preparatory hearing should be held, the court is empowered to decide, as part of such a hearing, that questions of evidence that might arise under Police and Criminal Evidence Act 1984, s 78, should be heard. Rulings made as a result in such circumstances are subject to appeal. In *Re Kanaris* [2003]

UKHL 2, that in relation to two defendants charged in the same indictment with criminal offences, a judge in the Crown Court was entitled to hold two separate hearings. See Criminal Procedure and Investigations Act 1996, ss 29, 31.

prerogative, judicial review of. 'Whatever their source, powers which are defined, either by reference to their object or by reference to procedure for their exercise, or in some other way, and whether the definition is expressed or implied, are . . . normally subject to judicial control to ensure that they are not exceeded': *per* Lord Fraser in *CCSU v Minister for the Civil Service* [1985] AC 374. See JUDICIAL REVIEW; PREROGATIVE, ROYAL.

prerogative orders. Quashing, prohibiting and mandatory orders. See certiorari, mandamus, prohibition (qq.v.); CPR, Part 25.

prerogative, royal. 'The residue of discretionary or arbitrary authority which at any given time is legally left in the hands of the Crown': Dicey, *The Law of The Constitution* (1885). Examples: summoning and dissolving Parliament; appointing bishops and judges; exemption from most statutes. These are, today, nominal rather than substantial. See *A-G v De Keyser's Royal Hotel* [1920] AC 508; *Council for Civil Service Unions v Minister for the Civil Service* [1985] AC 374. See MERCY, PREROGATIVE OF; PREROGATIVE, JUDICIAL REVIEW OF.

prescribe. 1. To claim by prescription (q.v.). 2. To set out under a regulation.

prescribed limits of alcohol in blood, etc. Proportions of alcohol in blood, etc., prescribed in relation to driving offences. They include: 35 microgrammes of alcohol in 100 millilitres of breath; 80 milligrammes in 100 millilitres of blood; 107 milligrammes in 100 millilitres of urine: Road Traffic Act 1988, s 11(1).

prescription. Generally, acquisition or extinction of rights by lapse of time. Claim must be based on the actual and continuous user; enjoyment must be of right; the user must generally be by owner in fee simple (q.v.) against another owner in fee simple who has acquiesced in that user: see *Simmons v Dobson* [1991] 1 WLR 720. Prescription at common law required proof of: user since time immemorial (q.v.); user *nec vi, nec clam, nec precario* (q.v.); continuous user. Under Prescription Act 1832, in the case of easements (q.v.) other than light, the uninterrupted user for 60 years makes a claim to a *profit à prendre* indefeasible. See *Jones v Price* (1992) *The Independent*, 16 January. See LOST MODERN GRANT.

prescription, custom and. 'Prescription and custom are brothers, and ought to have the same age, and reason ought to be the father, and consequence the mother, and use the nurse, and time out of memory to fortify them both': *per* Coke CJ in *Rowles v Mason* (1612) 2 B & G 192.

prescription, registered land and. 'Easements, rights and privileges adversely affecting registered land may be acquired in equity by prescription in the same manner and to the same extent as if the land were not registered': LRR 1925, r 250(1).

present. To offer or tender.

pre-sentence report. Written report by an appropriate officer (e.g., probation officer) made with a view to assisting the court in determining the most appropriate method of dealing with an offender, containing information concerning matters prescribed by rules made by Secretary of State: P.C.C.(S.)A. 2000, s 162. For disclosure, see s 156. See *R v Armsarah* (2000) *The Times*, 25 October. See SENTENCE.

presentment. 1. Presenting a bill of exchange (q.v.) to an acceptor for payment or to a drawee for acceptance. See B.Ex.A. 1882, s 45. 2. Presentation to a benefice (i.e. recommendation by a patron for the filling of a vacant benefice). See Pastoral Measure 1968.

presents. As in the phrase 'these presents'. The phrase refers to the document itself in which the words are contained.

preservation order. Order issued under, e.g., T.C.P.A. 1990, in relation to work needed for the preservation of an unoccupied listed building (q.v.), or in relation to a non-listed building of special architectural or historic interest which is threatened with demolition or alteration, or in relation to trees: see ss 203, 211. 'Preserving' can mean 'not causing harm to' rather than 'making a positive contribution to': *S Lakeland DC* v *Secretary of State for the Environment* (1991) 2 PLR 97.

President of the Courts of England and Wales. The Lord Chief Justice holds the office of President of the Courts of England and Wales and is Head of the Judiciary of England and Wales. The president is entitled to sit in any of the following courts: the Court of Appeal, the High Court, the Crown Court, the county courts or the magistrates' courts. s 7 Constitutional Reform Act 2005 (C.R.A. 2005).

presiding judges. High Court judges assigned to circuits in England and Wales who have a general responsibility for a High Court and Crown Court centre.

presumption. 1. Legal assumption which must be made until the contrary is proved. 2. Conclusion that facts exist which must, or may, be drawn if other facts are proved or admitted.

presumption concerning ouster of jurisdiction. *See* OUSTER OF JURISDICTION.

presumption concerning penal statutes. *See* PENAL STATUTES.

presumption concerning vested rights. *See* VESTED RIGHTS.

presumption of accuracy. Presumption that instruments (e.g., speedometers, watches) were in order on the occasion of the incident being investigated. See *Nicholas* v *Penny* [1950] 2 All ER 89.

presumption of advancement. *See* ADVANCEMENT.

presumption of continuance. Presumption of fact suggesting that any proved state of affairs can be presumed to have continued for some time. Thus, from the fact that a person was alive at one date it may be inferred that he was alive at some subsequent date. See *Re Forster's Settlement* [1942] Ch 199.

presumption of death. 'If a person has not been heard of for seven years, there is a presumption of law that he is dead': *Lal Chand Marwari* v *Mahant Ramrup Gir* (1925) 42 TLR 159. See O.P.A. 1861, s 57; L.P.A. 1925, s 184; *Chard* v *Chard* [1956] P 259. Under Mat.C.A. 1973, s 19(1), (3), a decree of presumption of death and dissolution of marriage is available. *See* DEATH, PROOF OF.

presumption of good faith and value. The holder of a bill is prima facie presumed to be a holder in due course (q.v.): B.Ex.A. 1882, s 30(2).

presumption of innocence. An accused person is presumed innocent until the prosecution has proved the case against him beyond reasonable doubt, so that his guilt is established. See *Woolmington* v *DPP* [1935] AC 462; *R* v *Sang* [1980] AC 402 (the concept means that the court is under a duty to ensure the accused a fair trial: *per* Lord Scarman); *Vasquez* v *R* [1994] 3 All ER 674; European Convention on Human Rights 1950, art 6.2; *R* v *Lambert* (2000) *The Times*, 5 September; *R* v *Benjafield* (2000) *The Times*, 28 December. In *Davies* v *Health and Safety Executive* (2002) *The Times*, 27 December, the CA held that the requirement under Health and Safety at Work Act 1974, s 40, which imposes a legal burden of proof on a defendant, so as to breach the presumption of innocence, was necessary, justified and proportionate. (See also *R* v *S* (2002) *The Times*, 2 December in relation to defence under Trade Marks Act 1994, s 92 (5).) The Privy Council held, in *Khan* v *State of Trinidad and Tobago* (2003) *The Times*, 26 November, that the statutory reintroduction of the felony murder rule, under which a killing in the course of an arrestable offence involving violence constituted murder, irrespective of intention, did not alter the necessity for the burden of proof of guilt to remain on the prosecution throughout the trial.

presumption of innocence, reversal of. CA held, in *AG's Reference (No. 1 of 2004)* (2004) *The Times*, 30 April, that the common law and the fair trial provisions under the Convention on Human Rights, art 6, allowed a derogation from the presumption of innocence so as to allow a statutory legal burden of proof to be placed upon a defendant in certain circumstances. A reverse legal burden would be justified in general where it was necessary for the prosecution to prove the essential elements of an offence, but it was reasonable and fair concerning a particular issue, to refuse defendant the general protection ordinarily guaranteed by the presumption of innocence.

presumption of lawful origin. Persuasive presumption that he who possesses property is its owner.

presumption of legality. *See* OMNIA PRAESUMUNTUR RITE ET SOLEMNITER ESSE ACTA.

presumption of legitimacy. A child born during lawful wedlock is presumed to be legitimate: *Banbury Peerage Case* (1811) 1 Sim & St 153. The presumption may be rebutted only by strong preponderance of evidence (e.g., blood group evidence), but 'even weak evidence against legitimacy must prevail if there is not other evidence to counterbalance it': *S* v *McC* [1972] AC 24. 'Any presumption of law as to the legitimacy of any person may in civil proceedings be rebutted by evidence which shows that it is more probable than not that that person is illegitimate or legitimate, as the case may be, and it shall not be necessary to prove that fact beyond reasonable doubt in order to rebut the presumption': F.L.R.A. 1969, s 26. See *F* v *CSA* (1999) *The Times*, 9 April.

presumption of legitimacy, strength of. Justices were in error where they placed greater weight on the presumption of legitimacy in the case of a child born in wedlock than on the general inference of paternity to be inferred from a refusal to undergo appropriate DNA testing: *Secretary of State for Work and Pensions* v *Jones* (2003) *The Times*, 13 August.

presumption of marriage validity. 'Where there is evidence of a ceremony of marriage having been followed by cohabitation of the parties, the validity of the marriage will be presumed, in the absence of decisive evidence to the contrary': *Russell* v *A-G* [1949] P 391. There is a presumption also that the marriage is monogamous: *Cheni* v *Cheni* [1965] P 85. See *Chief Adjudication Officer* v *Bath* (1999) *The Times*, 28 October.

presumption of negligence. *See* RES IPSA LOQUITUR.

presumption of sanity. A presumption in criminal cases that a person is sane until the contrary is proved. For the presumption in testamentary cases, see, e.g., *Sutton* v *Sadler* (1857) 3 CBNS 87. *See* M'NAGHTEN RULES.

presumption of survivorship. *See* COMMORIENTES.

presumptions, classifications of. 1. *Traditional classification:* (*a*) *Praesumptiones juris et de jure*, i.e., drawn by law and in an obligatory manner; inference of fact which cannot be contradicted; (*b*) *Praesumptiones juris sed non jure*: inferences of fact which hold good only where there is no contradictory evidence; (*c*) *Praesumptiones facti*, i.e., inferences of fact which the court may, but need not, draw from the facts before it. 2. *Lord Denning's suggested classification* (see 61 LQR 379): (*a*) *Provisional*, i.e., presumptions of fact; (*b*) *Conclusive*, i.e., irrebuttable presumptions of law; (*c*) *Compelling*, i.e., conclusions which must be drawn when basic facts are proved 'unless the other side proves the contrary or proves some other fact which the law recognises as sufficient to rebut the presumption', e.g., the presumption of legitimacy (q.v.).

presumptions, conflicting. Two presumptions having application to the same set of facts, thereby creating conflicting results. In such a case they are effectively cancelled out. See *R* v *Willshire* (1881) 6 QBD 366.

presumptions, irrebuttable. Known also as conclusive presumptions. In effect, rules of substantive law (q.v.). Evidence to contradict them cannot be called. See, e.g., Civil Evidence Act 1968, s 13 (defamation); L.P. (Misc. Provs.) A. 1989, s 1(5) (conclusive presumption of authorisation to deliver an instrument as a deed).

presumptions, rebuttable. 1. *Of law*, which *must* be observed in the absence of evidence to the contrary, so that the burden of rebuttal is on opposing party. Example: L.P.A. 1925, s 184, regarding commorientes (q.v.). 2. *Of fact*, which *may* be observed in the absence of evidence to the contrary. Example: *omnia praesumuntur rite et solemniter esse acta* (q.v.).

presumptions relating to construction of statutes. Presumptions laid down by the courts to assist in construing Acts of Parliament, i.e., legislative intent. They include: legislature does not make mistakes (see *Fisher v Bell* [1961] 1 QB 394); legislature does not intend what is unreasonable (see *Re AB & Co* [1900] 1 QB 541); words are presumed to be used in their popular sense in statutes (see *Re Hall's Settlement* [1954] 1 WLR 1185); the Crown is unaffected by a statute unless expressly named therein (see *Lord Advocate v Dumbarton DC* [1990] 1 All ER 1); presumptions against changes in the common law, against ousting the courts' jurisdiction, against interference with vested rights, against non-compliance with international law. *See* INTERPRETATION OF STATUTES.

presumptive heir. *See* HEIR PRESUMPTIVE.

presumptive title. Title arising only from occupancy (q.v.), or mere possession.

pretence, false. *See* FALSE PRETENCE.

pre-trial review under CPR. Procedure allowing court an opportunity to establish party compliance with earlier orders and directions. It will involve determining a trial timetable, stating time limits for examination of witnesses, speeches. Specifically, it deals with directions concerning expert evidence, trial time estimate, preparation of trial bundles, trial date and place. See r 1.4(d), (g).

previous consistent statements in criminal cases, proof of. Certain previous consistent statements in criminal cases may be proved, e.g., where they form part of the *res gestae* (q.v.) (but see Civil Evidence Act 1995, s 6(2)); are complaints in charges of sexual offences (see *R v Osborne* [1905] 1 KB 551; *R v Valentine* [1996] 2 Cr App R 213); are made by the accused on arrest; are made at a date which tends to disprove the allegation that the witnesses' testimony had been recently concocted; are part of the identification of the accused by the prosecution witness; are made on recovery of recently stolen articles. See *R v Roberts* [1942] 1 All ER 187. *See* EVIDENCE.

previous convictions, evidence of. Generally excluded as irrelevant, save where they form an essential ingredient of the offence, or where relevant to prove the offence itself, or in the course of cross-examination (q.v.) of the opposing witness as to credit, etc. See *Maxwell v DPP* [1935] AC 309; *R v Britzmann* [1983] 1 WLR 350; *R v Soffe* (2000) *The Times*, 5 April (judge's duty to assist jury when previous convictions are adduced). In civil proceedings a person's previous conviction may be relevant to prove that he committed the offence for which he was convicted: Civil Evidence Act 1968, s 11. See also 1968 Act, s 12, amended by F.L.R.A. 1987, s 29. See Criminal Evidence Act 1898, s 1(*f*); Official Secrets Act 1911, s 1(2); Th.A. 1968, s 27(3); Rehabilitation of Offenders Act 1974 (relating to spent convictions (q.v.)); P.&C.E.A. 1984, s 74. For effect of previous convictions to prove guilty conduct and in sentencing, see *A-G of Hong Kong v Siu Yuk-shing* [1989] 1 WLR 236. In *R v Burns* [2006] *The Times*, March 7, the CA held that where a memoranda of conviction is submitted as prima facie evidence of the defendant's identity and previous convictions, it is a matter for the jury to consider whether such a memoranda of conviction is conclusive proof of the defendant's identity.

previous statements, inconsistent. 'When a witness is shown to have made previous statements inconsistent with the evidence given by that witness at the trial the jury should not merely be directed that the evidence given at the trial should be regarded as unreliable; they should also be directed that the previous statements whether sworn or unsworn do not constitute evidence upon which they can act': *R* v *Golder, Jones and Porritt* [1960] 3 All ER 457. See also Civil Evidence Act 1968, s 3(1)(*a*); *Baron* v *Lovell* (1999) CPLR 630 (indemnity costs award).

price. 'In relation to any goods, services, accommodation or facilities, means the aggregate of the sums required to be paid by a consumer for or otherwise in respect of the supply (q.v.) of goods or the provision of services, or accommodation or facilities': C.P.A. 1987, s 20(6). See C.J.A. 1993, s 56(3). *See* SALE.

price in contract of sale. May be fixed by the contract or left to be fixed in a manner therein agreed, or may be determined by a course of dealing between the parties: S.G.A. 1979, s 8(1). Where the price is not determined in accordance with the foregoing provision, the buyer must pay a reasonable price: s 8(2). See *Ingram* v *Little* [1961] 1 QB 31; *Baber* v *Kenwood* [1978] 1 Lloyd's Rep 175.

price, misleading. A misleading price, for the purposes of C.P.A. 1987, is one which indicates or suggests, e.g., that the price is less than in fact it is or that the price covers matters in respect of which an additional charge is in fact made, or that the applicability of the price does not depend on facts or circumstances on which its applicability does in fact depend: s 21(1). It is an offence for a person, in the course of business to give such misleading indications: s 20(1). See *Toyota Ltd* v *N Yorks CC* (1998) 162 JP 794. For defences, see ss 24, 39.

price-sensitive information. Phrase used in relation to insider dealing (q.v.) to refer to specific matters relating or of concern (directly or indirectly) to a company (i.e., information not of a general nature) and which is not generally known to those persons accustomed or likely to deal in the securities in question, but which, if it were known, would be likely materially to alter their market price.

prima facie. Of first appearance; on the face of it. Based on a first impression.

A prima facie case is one in which the evidence in favour of a party is sufficient to call for an answer from his opponent.

prima facie evidence. *See* EVIDENCE, PRIMA FACIE.

Primary Care Trusts. Bodies established under National Health Service Act 1977, s 16A, inserted by Health Act 1999, s 2(1), following abolition of GP fund-holding practices by the 1999 Act, s 1. Functions include provision of hospital-based and community services provided by GPs. See 1999 Act, Sch 1.

primary evidence. *See* EVIDENCE, PRIMARY.

primary facts. *See* FACTS, PRIMARY.

Prime Minister. Conventional title of the Head of Her Majesty's Government, appointed by the Crown. Usually the leader of the party with a majority in the House of Commons (q.v.) and, by convention, always now sits in the Commons. (By tradition he is also First Lord of the Treasury.) Duties include presiding over the Cabinet (q.v.) exercising general supervision over government departments and speaking for the government in the Commons.

principal. 1. Sum of money invested. 2. One on whose behalf an agent (q.v.) works. See *MHC Consultants* v *Tansell* (2000) *The Times*, 19 April (liability as principal in spite of lack of contract). 3. A principal in the *first degree* is the actual perpetrator of an offence; a principal in the *second degree* is one who, by being present, aids and abets. *See* ACCESSORY.

principal, undisclosed. Where an agent (q.v.) conceals the fact that he is merely a representative, and has authority at the time of the contract to act on behalf of another, either the agent or principal when discovered can be sued and can sue the other party to the contract. See *The Astyanax* [1985] 2 Lloyd's Rep 109.

priorities, rules concerning mortgages. The equitable rule by the application of which the rank of competing interests, e.g., successive mortgages (q.v.) of an equitable interest in property, will be determined. The fundamental rule is *qui* *prior est tempore potior est jure* (q.v.), i.e., priority is determined by the order of the creation of interests. The rule is qualified by: the doctrine of purchaser without notice; fraud; negligence; estoppel (q.v.); registration of rights; overreaching of interests. See L.P.A. 1925, s 97; L.R.A. 1925, s 29 (mortgages of legal interests in registered land); *Dearle v Hall* (1828) 3 Russ 1; *Cheah Theam Swee v Equiticorp Finance* [1991] 4 All ER 989 (altering priority without mortgagor's consent).

priority notice. A person who is entitled to apply for registration as the first proprietor of land may reserve priority for that application by a priority notice. See L.R.A. 1925, s 144; L.C.A. 1972, s 11. *See* LAND REGISTRATION.

priority of debts of insolvent estate. The Lord Chancellor has power to direct that relevant provisions of Ins.A. 1986 should apply in relation to the administration of the estates of deceased persons which prove to be insolvent (see Ins.A. 1986, s 421).

prison. Place of detention for those committed to custody under the law. Includes young offender institution: C.J.A. 1991, s 92(1), amended by C.J.C.S.A. 2000, Sch 7, para 115. Prison policy is administered by the Prison Department of the Home Office through a prison service headed by a Director-General. See Prison Act 1952; Prison Rules 1999 (SI 99/728), amended by SI 00/1794; Prison Security Act 1992, s 1(6); *Johnson v Leicestershire Constabulary* (2000) *The Times*, 7 October. Reports on administration are made by boards of visitors (including magistrates) appointed by the Home Secretary. See C.J.P.O.A. 1994, Part VIII. For 'directly managed' and 'contracted out' prisons, see ss 99, 106. *See* PRISON OFFICER.

prisoner. A person held in custody in a prison or kept in police detention after being charged with an offence, or who has been committed to detention in a police station under M.C.A. 1980, s 128(7), or is in the custody of the court: C.J.A. 1991, s 192(1). See C.J.O.P.A. 1994, s 93(5); Prisoners' Earnings Act 1996

(power of Secretary of State to authorise deductions and impose levies in relation to prisoners' net weekly earnings). 'Under English law, a convicted prisoner, in spite of his imprisonment retains all civil rights which are not taken away expressly or by implication': *per* Lord Wilberforce in *Raymond v Honey* [1983] AC 1. See *R v Secretary of State for Home Department ex p Wynne* [1993] 1 WLR 115 (rights of prisoner to present his own case in court); *Secretary of State for Home Department ex p Mulkerrins* [1998] COD 235 (prisoner not entitled to challenge his categorisation as 'an exceptional escape risk'); *R v Secretary of State for Home Department ex p Simms* [1999] 3 All ER 400 (imposition of blanket ban on oral interviews of prisoners by journalists was *ultra vires*).

prisoner, continued detention of. European Court of Human Rights decided, in *Stafford v UK (Application No. 46295/99* (2002) *The Times*, 31 May, that the continued detention of a prisoner, following an order from the executive based on the perceived fear of his future criminal conduct, for which evidence was lacking, and in the absence of a review procedure, breached the Human Rights Convention, arts 5.1, 5.4.

prisoner, killing of by cell-mate. In *Edwards and Another v UK (Application 46477/99)* (2002) *The Times*, 1 April, Court of Human Rights held that UK was in breach of Human Rights Convention, art 2 (right to life) when the appropriate agencies failed to warn prison staff of danger presented by a violent prisoner, who later killed his cell-mate.

prisoner on-licence, rights of. CA held, in *R (Smith) v Parole Board* (2003) *The Times*, 2 September, that where the Parole Board had made a recommendation revoking the licence of a prisoner who had been released on licence, and recalling him to prison, his right to liberty had not been infringed, because that liberty had been lost on sentence and could be revived only after his sentence had come to an end.

prisoner, recall of. CA held, in *R (Sim)* v *Parole Board* (2004) *The Times*, 2 January, that the right to liberty, guaranteed under Human Rights Convention, art 5, did apply to the case of a prisoner serving an extended sentence, who had been released on licence, followed by his recall and further detention.

prisoner, recall procedure. European Court of Human Rights held, in *Waite* v *UK (Application No. 53236/99)*, (2002) *The Times*, 31 December, that the failure to allow a released prisoner an oral hearing by the Parole Board before revoking his licence, was a breach of his rights under the European Convention art 5.4.

prisoner, records of liberty. It was held, in *R (Gleaves)* v *Secretary of State for Home Department* (2004) *The Times*, 15 November, that prison governors involved in a disciplinary inquiry must keep written details of the fundamentals of the case and, where appropriate, reasons for rejection of a defence, since the prisoner's liberty is in issue.

prisoners' disenfranchisement, European Convention, and. The law disenfranchising prisoners (see Representation of the People Act 1983, s 3(1)) is not incompatible with the First Protocol to the European Convention, art 3: see *R* v *Secretary of State for Home Department* (2001) *The Times*, 17 April. For right of persons on remand to vote, see 1983 Act, s 7A, inserted by Representation of the People Act 2000, s 5. For disenfranchisement of offenders detained in mental hospitals, see 1983 Act, s 3A, inserted by 2000 Act, s 2.

prisoners, early release of. *See* PAROLE.

prisoners' representation rights. The denial by prison governors of prisoners' rights to legal representation in disciplinary proceedings is a breach of the prisoners' human rights to a fair trial, guaranteed under Human Rights Convention, art 6.3(c): European Court of Human Rights, in *Ezeh and Connors* v *UK* (2002) *The Times*, 30 July.

prisoner's right concerning writing. The decision of a prison governor and the Secretary of State for the Home Department, resulting in a refusal to return a prisoner's written autobiography was not incompatible with his right to freedom of expression and the Secretary of State was entitled to take into account the likely effect of publication on members of the public, including survivors and the families of victims of the prisoner's serial killings.

prisoner's right to a fair hearing. The European Court of Human Rights held, in *Ezeh and Connors* v *UK* (Application Nos 39665/98 and 40086/98) (2003) *The Times*, 30 October, that a breach of a prisoner's right to a fair hearing guaranteed under the European Convention, art 6.3(c), had taken place when a prison governor had denied the right of a prisoner to be legally represented in hearings of a disciplinary nature.

prisoner's right to vote. The European Court of Human Rights has held, in *Hirst* v *UK (No. 2) (Application No. 74025/01)* (2004) *The Times*, 8 April, that the denial of the right to vote to prisoners is a disproportionate breach of art 3 of Protocol 1 to the European Convention on Human Rights.

prisoners, use of computers by. *R (Ponting)* v *Governor of Whitemoor* [2002] EWSA Civ 224, accepts the need for the prison service to deal with prisoner's requests for access to IT. Prison Service Instruction 05/2002 states that such requests (relating, e.g., to legal proceedings) must be balanced against security and safety considerations. See also *R* v *Governor of Risley ex p Cooper* [2002] EWHC 125 Admin.

prison mutiny. An offence under Prison Security Act 1992, s 1, committed where two or more prisoners, while on the premises of any prison, engage in conduct (including acts and omissions) which is intended to further a common purpose of overthrowing lawful authority in that prison. Where there is such a mutiny, a prisoner who has or who is given a reasonable opportunity of submitting to lawful authority fails, without reasonable excuse, to do so, shall be regarded as taking part in the mutiny: s 1(4). See *R* v

Mitchell (1995) 16 Cr App R (S) 924; *R v Secretary of State for Home Department ex p Quinn* (1999) 143 SJLB 136.

prison officer. One who holds any post to which he has been appointed for purposes of Prison Act 1952, s 7, or Prison Act (Northern Ireland) 1953, s 2(2), or is a custody officer (q.v.): C.J.P.O.A. 1994, s 127(4). Chaplains, assistant chaplains and medical officers do not come within s 127(4), for purposes of ss 126, 127, which restrict the right of prison officers to take industrial action.

prison rules. See Prison Act 1952, s 47; Prison Rules 1999 (SI 99/728), replacing 1964 Rules. Rules 51–61 involve offences against discipline. Under the Rules, the purpose of training and treating prisoners is 'to encourage and assist them to lead a good and useful life.' See *Prison Discipline Manual* (pub. Home Office). See SI 00/1794 introducing s 51A, relating to new disciplinary offence involving racist behaviour. 'The prison rules are regulatory in character, they provide a framework within which the prison regime operates, but they are not intended to protect prisoners against loss, injury and damage, nor to give them a right of action in respect thereof': *per* Lord Jauncey in *Weldon v Home Office* [1991] 3 WLR 340. See *R v Deputy Governor of Parkhurst ex p Hague* [1992] 1 AC 154; *R v Secretary of State for Home Department ex p Daly* [1999] 11 CL 422 (authorisation of cell searches); *R v Governor of Frankland Prison ex p Russell* (2000) *The Times*, 1 August (segregation of prisoners: see 1999 Rules, rr 45, 55(1)(e)).

privacy. Not defined by statute. 'A boundary through which information does not flow from the person who possesses it to others': Shils, *Theory of Action* (1957). English law recognises a right of personal privacy grounded in the equitable doctrine of breach of confidence (q.v.): *Douglas v Hello Ltd* (2001) *The Times*, 16 January. See Convention on Human Rights 1950, art 8; Human Rights Act 1998, s 12.

privacy, breach of. European Court of Human Rights held, in *Peck v UK*

(Application No. 44647/98) (2003) *The Times*, 3 February, that the disclosure of CCTV footage of applicant to television companies, without safeguards relating to respect for his private life, amounted to a disproportionate and unjustified invasion of his rights under European Convention, art 8.

privacy, invasion of. HL held, in *Secretary of State for Home Department v Wainwright* [2003] UKHL 53, that there existed no general common law tort of invasion of privacy. See also *Kaye v Robertson* [1991] FSR 62. The HL held, in *Campbell v Mirror Group Newspapers plc* (2004) *The Times*, 7 May, that where a newspaper had printed detailed information concerning a celebrity's treatment for drugs addition, accompanied by photographs of her leaving a treatment establishment, her right to respect for her private life had been infringed, outweighing a publisher's right to freedom of expression.

private Act of Parliament. An Act concerning private persons, or a local Act passed on behalf of a public company or municipal corporation. It must not impinge on an issue of public policy or be of general application.

private Bill. *See* BILL.

private company. A company which is not a public company: Cos.A. 1985, s 1(3). It may be limited by shares or guarantee, or may be unlimited. It may be formed by one member: s 1, SI 92/1699. It may have an unlimited number of members. It may not offer its shares or debentures directly to the public: s 81. There is no minimum nominal, issued or paid-up capital requirements, and it can convert to an unlimited company: s 49.

private defence. Where a person commits a tort (q.v.) in defence of himself or his property, he is not necessarily liable if the act has been, in the circumstances, of a reasonable nature. See *Cockcroft v Smith* (1705) 2 Salk 642; *Barnard v Evans* [1925] 1 KB 794.

private international law. That part of English law which deals with cases involving a foreign element and seeks to determine, e.g., whether English courts have jurisdiction over a case; if so, what system of law must be applied; circumstances in which English courts will recognise and enforce judgments of foreign courts. Known also as 'conflict of laws'.

private investigation. Term applied, in relation to the private security industry, to any surveillance, inquiries or investigations carried out to obtain information about a particular person or his activities or whereabouts, or about the circumstances in which or means by which property has been lost or damaged: P.S.I.A. 2001, Sch 2, para 4.

private law. Those areas of the law concerned primarily with duties and rights of individuals with which the state is not immediately and directly concerned, e.g., the law of contract. For assertion of private law rights, see *Wandsworth LBC v Winder* [1985] AC 461. See PUBLIC LAW.

privately fostered children. Children under 16, cared for and provided with accommodation by someone other than their parents or relatives: Ch.A. 1989, s 66. Their welfare is a concern of the local authority: s 67. For persons disqualified, see s 68. For inspection of homes, see s 80; Care Standards Act 2000, s 45. See SIs 91/910, 97/2308, 99/2768; *Re J (Foster Placement)* [1998] 3 FCR 579.

private Members' Bills. Bills of a public nature introduced, not by the government, but by private members of either House of Parliament. See, e.g., Abortion Act 1967, sponsored by David Steel MP. Bills of this nature may be introduced: through the ballot held each session; under Standing Order 39; under the Ten-Minute Rule Bills (Standing Order 13) (the Bail (Amendment) Act 1993 was introduced in this way).

private nuisance. *See* NUISANCE.

private prosecution. *See* PROSECUTION, PRIVATE.

privatisation. Policy of transferring enterprises from the state to the private sector. It generally involves a transfer of assets and undertakings of state or public corporations to public limited companies, with shares privately-owned. See, e.g., Public Utility Transfers and Water Charges Act 1988; Ports Act 1991.

privilege. A special right, exemption or immunity, conferred on some person or body, e.g., members of Parliament; or a rule of evidence justifying a witness's refusal to produce a document or to answer a question. 'The right of a party to refuse to disclose a document or to produce a document or to refuse to answer questions on the ground of some special interest recognised by law': CPR Glossary. See r 31.19(3); *S County Council v B* [2000] 3 WLR 53; *Brown v Bennett* (2000) *The Times*, 13 June. Some matters are protected from disclosure on the ground of privilege, e.g., affairs of state, professional confidences. See *Waple v Surrey CC* [1998] 1 WLR 860. *See* PARLIAMENTARY PRIVILEGE.

privilege, absolute. Protection attaching to certain statements, which would otherwise be defamatory, so that no action lies even though the statements might have been false and malicious. Example: statements made in the course of judicial proceedings or in debates in Parliament. See Defamation Act 1996, s 14 (a fair and accurate report of proceedings in public before any court in the UK (including any tribunal or body exercising the judicial power of the state), European Court of Justice, European Court of Human Rights, is absolutely privileged if published contemporaneously with the proceedings). For journalistic privilege, see, e.g., *John v Express Newspapers* (2000) 150 NLJ 615.

privilege, claim of. Claim entitling a person to refuse, e.g., the production of documents for inspection. It may apply to communications between solicitors and clients; opinions of counsel; incriminating documents; state papers.

privileged communication. A communication which, although containing defamatory material, is protected, or one which is generally protected from disclosure in evidence (q.v.). See, e.g., *D v NSPCC* [1978] AC 171; *Goodridge v*

Chief Constable of Hampshire [1999] 1 All ER 906.

privileged nature of judicial statements. Judges may not be compelled to give evidence relating to the cases they have tried: *Buccleuch* v *Metropolitan Board of Works* (1872) LR 5 HL 418. See also Contempt of Court Act 1981, s 8, protecting the confidentiality of a jury's deliberations: see *R* v *Young* [1995] 2 WLR 430; *R* v *Miah* [1997] 2 Cr App R 12.

privileged speech of MP. The Privy Council held (2004) *The Times*, 19 July, that although a MP who had made a defamatory statement in the House was protected from liability by absolute privilege, he could be held liable in defamation should he later affirm the statement without repeating it on some occasion, which had no protection by privilege.

privileged will. The right of a soldier being in actual military service, or a mariner or seaman being at sea to make a valid will without any formal requirements. The intention to make a will must be shown. See W.A. 1837, s 11; Wills (Soldiers and Sailors) Act, 1918, s 3(1); F.L.R.A. 1969, s 3(1)(*b*); *Re Wingham* [1949] P 187; *Re Rapley* [1983] 1 WLR 1069. *See* WILL.

privilege in relation to summaries. Where privileged material is disclosed to third parties, the privilege remains attached to it even though it is no more than a mere paraphrase or summary of the privileged information in its entirety: *USP Strategies plc* v *London General Holdings Ltd* (2004) *The Times*, 30 April.

privilege, legal professional. Right whereby communications between client and legal adviser may not generally be given in evidence without client's consent if made in relation to contemplated or pending litigation, or made to enable adviser to give, or client to receive, legal advice. Such communications are defined under P.&C.E.A. 1984, s 19(6) as 'communications between a professional legal adviser and his client or any person representing his client made in connection with the giving of legal advice to the

client . . . or in contemplation of legal proceedings'. See also s 10(1). See *Alfred Crompton Amusement Machines* v *Customs and Excise Commissioners* [1974] AC 405; *R* v *Derby Magistrates ex p B* [1996] AC 487 (explanation by House of Lords of basis of the privilege): 'a fundamental condition on which the administration of justice as a whole rests'); *Re L (A Minor)* [1997] AC 16 (exclusion of the privilege in proceedings under Part IV, Ch.A. 1989); *Nationwide BS* v *Various Solicitors* (1998) 148 NLJ 241 (overriding of the privilege); *Goodrich* v *Chief Constable of Hampshire* [1999] 1 All ER 896 (public interest immunity ought to be weighed against need for justice to be done); *R* v *Manchester Crown Court ex p R (Legal Professional Privilege)* [1999] 1 WLR 832 (principle of legal professional privilege docs not apply to records of client's appointments).

privilege of witness. 1. Rule that a witness is not bound to answer certain types of question in legal proceedings. Examples: incriminating questions; questions relating to matters, publication of which might injure the state; questions relating to communications between counsel, solicitor and client on professional matters. 2. A witness is privileged (so that no action can be brought for defamation) to the extent of what he says during examination. 'What he says before he enters or after he has left the witness box is not privileged': *Seaman* v *Netherclift* (1876) 2 CPD 56.

privilege, parliamentary. *See* PARLIAMENTARY PRIVILEGE.

privilege, public policy. Phrase used in a statement of principle excluding relevant evidence where disclosure could prejudice the public interest. Known also as 'public interest immunity'. See CPR, rr 15.10, 31.19(1). See *Conway* v *Rimmer* [1968] AC 910; *R* v *Governor of Pentonville Prison ex p Osman (No. 4)* [1991] 1 WLR 281; *Powell* v *Chief Constable of N Wales* (2000) *The Times*, 11 February (exclusion of public interest immunity evidence). For 'public immunity certificates', see Crown Proceedings Act 1947. See also C.P.I.A. 1996, s 14; F.I.A. 2000, s 42. 'If a document is relevant and material then it must be disclosed unless it is confidential and unless a breach of confidentiality will cause harm to the public interest which outweighs harm to the interests of justice caused by non-disclosure': *per* Lord Templeman in *R v Chief Constable of W Midlands Police ex p Wiley* [1994] 3 WLR 433. See *Scott Report* 1996 (arms exports to Iraq); *Re Barings plc* [1998] 1 All ER 673.

privilege, qualified. Protection afforded to the maker of a statement which may be defamatory, if made honestly, i.e., without malice. Includes: fair and accurate reports of parliamentary and judicial proceedings and reports of public meetings (see *Turkington* v *Times Newspapers* (2000) 150 NLJ 1657); statements made in pursuance of a legal, moral or social duty; statements made to procure redress of a public grievance. See Defamation Act 1952; *Reynolds* v *Times Newspapers Ltd* [1999] 3 WLR 1010 (it is not appropriate for the common law to recognise a generic qualified privilege defence to libel proceedings, requiring plaintiff to prove actual malice in the publication of a misstatement relating to political information, opinion and argument printed in a newspaper). See Defamation Act 1996, s 15, under which qualified privilege will protect publication of any report mentioned in Sch 1 (e.g., fair and accurate report of proceedings in public of a legislature or court anywhere in the world) unless the publication has been made with malice. See *Loutchansky* v *Times Newspapers* (2001) 151 NLJ 643. In relation to European Convention, art 10 (freedom of expression), a communication between persons who have an existing relationship and a common and corresponding interest in the subject matter, does, in the absence of malice, attract qualified privilege; this does not include communications between the Bar Council and barristers: *Kearns* v *General Council of the Bar* (2002) 152 NLJ 1752.

privity. Relationships arising from participation in or knowledge of some transaction or event. See *The Eurysthenes* [1976] 3 All ER 243.

privity of contract. Principle based upon relationship between parties to a contract. For recent modification, see Contracts (Rights of Third Parties) Act 1999. *See* CONTRACT, THIRD PARTY RIGHTS IN.

privity of estate. Relationship of tenure existing between persons whose estates constitute one estate in law, i.e., all those who stand in position of landlord and tenant to one another, such as lessor and lessee, tenant and sub-tenant. See *Spencer's Case* (1583) 5 Co Rep 16a; Landlord and Tenant (Covenants) Act 1995.

Privy Council. Until the eighteenth century, the chief source of executive power in the state. Now plays a much-diminished role, advising the Sovereign on Orders in Council (q.v.), issue of Royal proclamations, etc. Headed by the Lord President of the Council, it consists of Cabinet ministers, Archbishops, Lord Chief Justice, Master of the Rolls, Speaker of the Commons, etc. The whole Council (390 members in all) is called together on the death of the Sovereign. The Judicial Committee of the Privy Council (q.v.) has appellate jurisdiction.

prize competition. *See* COMPETITION FOR PRIZES.

prize courts. Courts specially set up to decide matters relating to the capture of ships or cargoes, in time of war. Appeal is to Judicial Committee of the Privy Council (q.v.). See Naval Prize Acts 1864–1916; S.C.A. 1981, s 16(2).

probate. Document issued under the seal of the court as official evidence of the authority of an executor (q.v.). If the validity of a will (q.v.) is contested, probate is granted only after the court has pronounced in favour (grant 'in solemn form'). Probate 'in common form' is granted where litigation is unnecessary. Documents required in order to obtain probate include: Inland Revenue account; executor's oath; any renunciations by executors; engrossments; affidavit of due execution. For compromise of probate action, see A.J.A. 1985, s 49; PD 49, para 13.1.

probate, ancillary. Subsidiary grant of probate relating to a grant obtained outside the UK, giving powers of administration to a foreign executor over property in the UK.

probate claim. A claim in respect of any contentious matter arising in connection with an application for grant or revocation of probate or letters of administration, and includes a claim for an order pronouncing for or against the validity of an alleged will: PD 49, para 1.2. *See* CONTENTIOUS PROBATE PROCEEDINGS.

Probate, Court of. *See* COURT OF PROBATE.

Probate, Divorce and Admiralty Division. Former division of the High Court (q.v.), renamed Family Division by A.J.A. 1970. Admiralty jurisdiction was assigned to QBD, to be exercised by Admiralty Court. Probate (other than non-contentious, common form probate business) was assigned to Chancery Division. See S.C.A. 1981, s 5(1)(c).

probate proceedings. The proceedings in which a probate claim is brought: PD 49, para 1.2.

probate, resealed. Certificate of probate sealed for a second time, e.g., in order to give an executor (q.v.) powers of administration outside the UK.

probate rules. Rules of court made by President of Family Division, concerned with regulating and prescribing the practice and procedure of the High Court with respect to non-contentious or common form probate business: S.C.A. 1981, s 127.

probation. Process designed to assist in the rehabilitation of offenders aged 16 or over requiring them to remain under the supervision of probation officers for six months to three years and to be of good behaviour; or to assist in the protection of the public from harm from them, or preventing the commission by them of other offences: P.C.C.(S.)A. 2000, s 41, amended by C.J.C.S.A. 2000, Sch 7, para

165. Local probation boards, set up as part of the National Probation Service, assist in arrangement for, e.g., accommodation for persons on probation: see C.J.C.S.A. 2000, ss 4–5, Sch 1. For work of inspectorate, see C.J.C.S.A. 2000, ss 6, 7. Failure to comply with the order may result in a sentence for the original offence.

probation centres. Premises, approved by the Secretary of State, at which non-residential facilities are provided for use in connection with the rehabilitation of offenders and are suitable for persons subject to probation orders: see C.J.A. 1991, Sch 1. See P.C.C.(S.)A. 2000, Sch 9, para 50.

probationer. A person under supervision by virtue of a probation order (to be known as a 'community rehabilitation order': see C.J.C.S.A. 2000, s 43(1)).

Probation Service, National. Set up under C.J.C.S.A. 2000, s 1, to have particular regard to protection of public, reduction of reoffending, proper punishment and rehabilitation of offenders, ensuring offenders' awareness of effect of crime on victims: s 2(2). Probation officers are now known as 'officers of a local probation board': 2000 Act, Sch 7, para 4(1).

probative facts. *See* FACTS, INVESTITIVE.

pro bono. Phrase relating to free provision of legal assistance is to be replaced by term 'law for free': announcement by Lord Woolf LCJ: see 152 NLJ 1795.

proceedings in chambers. The right to fair trial does not require that all proceedings shall be heard in open court; nor is this required by Human Rights Act 1998, Sch 1, Part 1, art 6. Family proceedings may be heard in chambers in private, under Family Proceedings Rules 1991: *Cliberry v Allan* [2002] 1 All ER 865.

proceedings, legal. The systematic conducting of business before a court. See *Savings and Investment Bank Ltd v Gasco Investments (No. 2)* [1988] 1 All ER 975. 'Any criminal or civil proceedings or inquiry in which evidence is or may be given': Bankers' Books Evidence Act

1879, s 10. For 'institution of proceedings' see *R* v *Bull* (1994) 99 Cr App R 193.

proceedings, order of criminal. Generally: arraignment; empanelling and swearing of jury; opening speech by prosecution; prosecution case; defence submissions; defence opening speech; defence case; closing speeches; summing-up; verdict; plea in mitigation; sentencing. For 'criminal proceedings', see SI 00/774.

proceedings, stay of. See STAY OF PROCEEDINGS.

proceeds. Money or other material returns derived from a transaction or other event. See Th.A. 1968, s 5(4); *R* v *Davis* (1989) 88 Cr App R 347.

proceeds, of a public charitable collection. All money or other property given (whether for consideration or otherwise) in response to the charitable appeal in question. Charities Act 2006 s 47.

process. 1. Summons and warrant compelling appearance of defendant (q.v.). Before the issue of process, a magistrate (q.v.) must be satisfied that he has appropriate jurisdiction and that there is sufficient evidence against the person named to justify the issue. See M.C.A. 1980, s 1; S.C.A. 1981, s 80; Criminal Justice (International Co-operation) Act 1990, s 1 (service of overseas process in UK). 2. Mode of operation. Signifies 'substantial uniformity or system of treatment': *Vibroplant* v *Holland* [1982] 1 All ER 792. See *Nurse* v *Morganite Crucible* [1989] 2 WLR 82.

process, abuse of. See ABUSE OF PROCESS.

procession. 'A body of persons moving along a route': *Flockart* v *Robinson* [1950] 2 KB 498. See PUBLIC PROCESSION.

process, misuse of. A claim intended not to vindicate a right (in libel case) but to result in harassment and unwarranted expense should be struck out as a misuse of process: *Wallis* v *Valentine* (2002) *The Times*, 9 August.

proclamation, royal. Formal public announcement by the Crown. No law can be made or unmade in this manner unless a proclamation is issued by the authority of an Act of Parliament (q.v.). See *Case of Proclamations* (1611) 12 Co

Rep 74; *Re Grazebrook* (1865) 4 De G J & S 662.

procreation, words of. Words which limit persons mentioned in a grant to the issue of a particular individual, e.g., 'To Z and the heirs of his body'.

procurement. It is an offence for a person to procure a woman by threats, intimidation, false pretences or false representations to have sexual intercourse in any part of the world: S.O.A. 1956, s 2, amended by C.J.P.O.A. 1994, Sch 9, para 2. See 1994 Act, s 33 (1)(*a*), (*b*) (abolition of corroboration requirements).

procuring an offence. Bringing about, instigating, a crime, i.e., 'setting out to see that it happens and taking the appropriate steps to produce that happening.' It involves producing an offence 'by some endeavour': *A-G's Reference (No. 1 of 1975)* [1975] QB 773. See, e.g., S.O.A. 1967, s 4. The common law offence of procuring materials for crime was abolished under Criminal Attempts Act 1981, s 6(1). *See* AID OR ABET.

procuring breach of contract. *See* INDUCEMENT.

procuring execution of a valuable security. It is an offence when a person dishonestly, with a view to gain for himself or another or with intent to cause loss to another, by any deception procures the execution of a valuable security: Th.A. 1968, s 20(2). For 'execution', see *R* v *Kassim* [1992] 1 AC 9; *R* v *Horsman* [1998] QB 531. For 'valuable security', see *R* v *Bolton* [1992] Crim LR 57.

producer. Means, in relation to a product, the manufacturer, the person who won or abstracted it, or the person who carried out the processes giving it its essential characteristics: see C.P.A. 1987, s 1(2).

production appointment. Hearing, in relation, e.g., to application for ancillary relief (q.v.), based on a party's application for a person to attend and produce documents which appear to the court 'to be necessary for disposing fairly of the application for ancillary relief or for saving costs': Family Proceedings Rules 1991, r 2.62(7). See also *Khanna* v *Lovell*

White Durrant [1995] 1 WLR 121; CPR, r 34.2(4) (witness summons).

production order. Order under P.&C.E.A. 1984, s 9, Sch 1, allowing police to obtain access to 'excluded material' (see s 11) (e.g., personal records) and 'special procedure material' (q.v.), where there is a reasonable suspicion that a serious arrestable offence has been committed and the material might be of significance in an investigation. See *R v Manchester Stipendiary Magistrates ex p Granada TV* [2000] 2 WLR 1; *R v Central Criminal Court ex p Bright* (2000) *The Times*, 26 July (s 9 and self-incrimination).

product liability. Generally, the liability of persons for damage caused by defective products. See: 'product liability Directive' of EEC (85/374/EEC); S.G.A. 1979, s 14(3); C.P.A. 1987, Part I. *See* DEFECT IN A PRODUCT.

products, defective, liability for. Where damage is caused wholly or partly by a defect in a product, the following are liable: the producer of the product; any person who, by using a distinguishing mark or his own name on the product, has held himself out to be the producer (q.v.); any person who, in the course of business, has imported the product into a member state of EU (q.v.) from outside EU: C.P.A. 1987, s 2(1), (2). 'Damage' means death or personal injury or any loss or damage to property: s 5(1). For defences, see s 4; *Commission of EC v UK (C300/95)* [1997] All ER (EC) 481. *See* DEFECT IN A PRODUCT.

profession. 'A "profession" in the present use of language involves the idea of an occupation requiring purely intellectual skill, or if any manual skill, as in painting and sculpture, or surgery, skill controlled by the intellectual skill of the operator': *per* Scrutton LJ in *IRC v Maxse* [1919] 1 KB 647. A 'professional body' means a body which regulates the practice of its profession: F.S.A. 1986, s 16(1). *See* BOLAM TEST.

professional disciplinary body, decision of. In *Andi v GMC* [2004] EWHC 2317 (Admin), one of the first cases involving the Administrative Court, which has removed from the JCPC the right of consideration of appeals from the GMC Committee was heard.

professional misconduct. Behaviour considered by the governing body of a profession to be unworthy of a member of that profession. May lead to removal from a professional register. See, e.g., Medical Act 1983, Part V; Dentists Act 1984, s 27; C.L.S.A. 1990, Sch 10; *Doughty v General Dental Council* [1987] 3 WLR 769; *Dad v General Dental Council* (2000) *The Times*, 19 April (suspension considered disproportionate to offences). *See* INFAMOUS CONDUCT; STRIKING OFF.

profit and loss account. Yearly account, which must be compiled up to a date not more than nine months before the date of a company's meeting, in accordance with the requirements of Cos.A. 1985, Sch 4, Part I. It must give a true and fair view of the company's profit and loss for the year: 1985 Act, s 226(2). See I.C.T.A. 1988, chap III. *See* COMPANY.

profits à prendre. Rights to enter another's land and take something off it (e.g., rights of common). May be created, e.g., by Act of Parliament or grant, and extinguished by statute, unity of seisin, release or alteration of dominant tenement (qq.v.). Cannot be claimed by custom (q.v.). They comprise profits of pasture, turbary, piscary, estovers, in the soil. See *Lady Dunsany v Bedworth* (1979) 38 P & CR 546; *Bettison v Langton* [1999] 3 WLR 39. *See* COMMON, RIGHT OF.

profits available for distribution. Under Cos.A. 1985, s 263, a company may make a distribution only of profits available for that purpose, i.e., from accumulated realised profits less accumulated realised losses. A distribution must be justified by the accounts. A public company may make a distribution only if, at the time, its net assets are not less than the aggregate of called-up share capital plus non-distributable reserves, and if the distribution does not reduce those assets to less than that aggregate: s 264(1). See also Cos.A. 1989, s 4(1), Sch 4, para 91. See RESERVES, UNDISTRIBUTABLE.

profits, company's. 'Profit for the year is regarded as any gains arising during the year which may be distributed while maintaining the amount of the shareholders' interest in the company at the beginning of the year, which is regarded as the company's capital': *Inflation Accounting 1975* (Cmnd 6225, para 105). As to 'where profits arise', see *IRC v Hang Seng Bank* [1991] 1 AC 306.

profits, with. See WITH PROFITS.

programme commissioning for TV. Under the Communications Act 2003, s 285, OFCOM is obliged to draw up a code of practice which will necessitate the setting out of principles to be observed when independent TV productions are commissioned.

prohibited article. Under P.&C.E.A. 1984, s 1(7), an offensive weapon (q.v.) which may be seized by the police if found in the course of a search. See Firearms Act 1968, s 5(1)(*b*); *Brown v DPP* (1992) *The Times*, 27 March; *R v Law* [1999] Crim LR 837.

prohibited degrees of relationship. See RELATIONSHIPS, PROHIBITED DEGREES OF.

prohibited steps order. An order under Ch.A. 1989, Part II, that no step which could be taken by a parent in meeting his parental responsibility for a child, and which is of a kind specified in the order, should be taken by any person without the consent of the court: 1989 Act, s 8(1). See *Re D (Prohibited Steps Order)* [1996] 2 FLR 273.

prohibition. An order of the High Court (q.v.) preventing or prohibiting a body from acting, which will lie against an inferior tribunal or body in relation to decisions affecting an individual's rights. Issued, e.g., to prohibit an imposition of sentence on the accused if there has been no proper trial. See *Re Godden* [1971] 2 QB 662. For applications for an order see CPR, Part 54; PD 54; S.C.A. 1981, s 29. Known now as a 'prohibiting order'.

prohibition notice. Notice served, e.g., by an inspector under H.S.W.A. 1974, s 22, stating that he is of the opinion that activities involve or will involve a risk of serious personal injury and directing that the activities shall cease unless the matters specified are remedied. See also C.P.A. 1987, s 13, Sch 2.

prohibitory injunction. See INJUNCTION.

prolonging life guidelines. Guidelines on practice relating to the withholding and withdrawing of life-prolonging treatments, published by the General Medical Council, are untenable to judicial review where they seem to have been erroneous in point of law. A claimant who has satisfied the court that the general guidance was incompatible with common law in the context of the European convention, has an entitlement to the processes of judicial review: *R (Burke) v General Medical Council* (2004) *The Times*, 6 August.

promise. An undertaking, explicit or implicit, by words or conduct, to act or to refrain from acting, in relation to a specified event. Of no legal effect generally, unless in the form of a contract (q.v.) or covenant (q.v.). A promise is made by a *promisor* to a *promisee*.

promissory estoppel. See ESTOPPEL.

promissory note. 'An unconditional promise in writing made by one person to another, signed by the maker, engaging to pay on demand or at a fixed or determinable future time, a sum certain in money, to, or to the order of, a specified person, or to bearer': B.Ex.A. 1882, s 83. The note is ineffective until delivered to the payee. See *Kwok v Commissioner of Estate Duty* [1988] 1 WLR 1035.

promoter. 1. One who begins the procedure for the passing of a local, personal, private Bill (q.v.). 2. 'One who undertakes to form a company with reference to a given project, and to set it going, and who takes the necessary steps to accomplish that purpose': *Twycross v Grant* (1877) 36 LT 812. He is neither trustee (q.v.) nor agent (q.v.) for the company, but stands in a fiduciary relationship to it. Whether a person is or is not a promoter is a question of fact in every case: *Jubilee Cotton Mills v Lewis* [1924] AC 958. See Cos.A. 1985, s 67(3) (now repealed, and term replaced by 'issuer' (see F.S.A. 1986, ss 142(7), 158(3)) and 'person responsible for prospectus' (see ss 152, 168)).

promoter, to a public charitable collection. This means (a) a person who (whether alone or with others and whether for remuneration or otherwise) organises or controls the conduct of the charitable appeal in question, or (b) where there is no person acting as mentioned in paragraph (a) any person who acts as a collector in respect of the collection, and associated expressions are to be construed accordingly. Charities Act 2006 s 47.

promptitude, significance of. CA held, in *Mamidoll Petroleum Company SA v Okta Crude Oil*, that where an application under Civil Procedure Rules, r 52.9, was made so as to set aside grant of permission to appeal, that application had to be made promptly.

proof. Method by which the existence or non-existence of a fact is established to the satisfaction of the court. Means of proof include: evidence; presumptions; judicial notice (qq.v.). 'Evidence becomes proof when the jury accept it as being sufficient for proof': Williams.

proof beyond reasonable doubt. 'Proof beyond reasonable doubt does not mean proof beyond the shadow of a doubt . . . If the evidence is so strong against a man as to leave only a remote possibility in his favour, which can be dismissed with the sentence "of course it is possible but not in the least probable" the case is proved beyond reasonable doubt, but nothing short of that will suffice': *Miller* v *Minister of Pensions* [1947] 2 All ER 372.

proof, burden of. *See* BURDEN OF PROOF.

proof, reverse onus of. HL held, in *Sheldrake* v *DPP* (2004) *The Times*, 15 October, that statutory defences available to an accused person did impose a reverse onus of proof upon defendant. See Terrorism Act 2000, s 11(2).

proof, standards of. *See* STANDARDS OF PROOF.

proper law of a contract. Phrase used in private international law (q.v.) to denote the system of law which governs a contract. Defined by Dicey as 'the law, or laws, by which the parties intended, or may be fairly presumed to have intended, the contract to be governed': *Conflict of Laws* (1896). 'It is the law which the parties intended to apply. Their intention will be ascertained by the intention expressed in the contract, if any, which will be conclusive': *R* v *International Trustee* [1937] 2 All ER 164. *See* CONTRACT.

property. 1. That which can be owned. 2. Rights to the possession and use of goods and land, etc. See S.G.A. 1979, s 61. Must be 'definable, identifiable by third parties, capable in its nature of assumption by third parties, and have some degree of permanence or stability': *National Provincial Bank* v *Ainsworth* [1965] AC 1175. 'A foundation of expectation of deriving certain advantages from the thing said to be possessed': Bentham, *Introduction to Principles of Morals and Legislation* (1843). 'English law has one single law of property made up of legal and equitable interests': *per* Lord Browne-Wilkinson in *Tinsley* v *Milligan* [1993] 3 All ER 65. 3. An aggregate of rights having money value. 4. 'Includes money and all other property, real or personal, including things in action and other intangible property': Th.A. 1968, s 4(1). Classified as *real property* (realty); *personal property* (personalty) (qq.v.). For 'domestic property' (q.v.), see Local Government Finance Act 1988, s 66. For 'property development', see I.C.T.A. 1988, s 298(5). For property and 'a particular interest in the property' (in Finance Act 1986, s 102), see *Ingram* v *IRC* [1999] 2 WLR 90. *See* OWNERSHIP.

property adjustment order. Order made under Mat.C.A. 1973, s 21, relating to the transfer or settlement, of property or variation of settlement, or the extinguishing of or reducing an interest in a settlement, on or after the grant of a decree of divorce (q.v.), nullity or judicial separation (q.v.). See *Potter* v *Potter* [1990] 2 FLR 27; *Piglowska* v *Piglowski* [1999] 1 WLR 1360. The making by the court of a property adjustment order under Matrimonial Causes Act 1973, s 24, was not out of order where that property was also subjected to proceedings brought by Customs and Excise so as to enforce an order for confiscation after a husband's conviction under Drug Trafficking Act 1994, s 29: *Commissioners for Customs and Excise v A* (2002) *The Times*, 24 July.

property and residence. CA held in *Bennett* v *Copeland BC* (2004) *The Times*, 28 May, that for all purposes of determining liability for council tax, a person could not be considered to be a resident of property in which he had never lived at any time. See Local Government Finance Act 1992, s 6(2); *R (Williams)* v *Horsham DC* [2004] 1 WLR 1137.

property in goods. May be: (1) *General*, i.e., title or ownership ('Property means the general property in goods, and not merely a special property': S.G.A. 1979, s 62(1)); (2) *Special*, e.g., that which arises under a bailment (q.v.). See Police (Property) Act 1997, s 1.

property, misdescription of. It is an offence to make false or misleading statements about any matter relating to land which is specified by an order made by the Secretary of State in the course of an estate agency business or a property development business: Property Misdescriptions Act 1991, s 1. See *Lewin* v *Barratt Homes Ltd* (2000) 164 JP 182. For defence of due diligence, see s 2.

property of unmarried couple, sharing of. CA held, in *Oxley* v *Hiscock* (2004) *The Times*, 14 July, that in circumstances in which unmarried partners had pooled resources to buy a home registered in the sole name of one of them and without specific agreement relating to extent of respective shares, the appropriate time and method of assessment of each's shares would be, not the date of acquisition, of property, but when it was sold, taking into account contributions made by each after purchase of home in money and other material terms.

property register. *See* REGISTER AT LAND REGISTRY.

property, right of. 'That sole or despotic dominion which one man claims

and exercises over the external things of the world, in total exclusion of the right of any other individual in the universe': Blackstone, *Commentaries* (1765). See European Convention on Human Rights 1950, First Protocol, art 1 (protection of property).

property, right to security of. 'The great end for which men entered into society was to secure their property. That right is preserved sacred and is incommunicable in all instances where it has not been taken away or abridged by some public law for the good of the whole . . . No man can set his foot upon my ground without my licence but he is liable to an action': *per* Lord Camden in *Entick* v *Carrington* (1765) 19 St Tr 1029. *See* CRIMINAL DAMAGE; TRESPASS.

proponent. 1. The party who must raise an issue in the first instance (e.g. the prosecutor, the claimant). 2. The party who bears the evidential burden of proof (q.v.) and, usually also, the legal burden.

proportionality. *See* LEGISLATION, PROPORTIONALITY OF.

propositus. 1. The person immediately concerned with an issue. 2. The person from whom descent is traced. 3. A testator (q.v.).

proprietary estoppel. *See* ESTOPPEL.

proprietary estoppel, and mere equities. Land Registration Act 2002, s 116 declares, for the avoidance of doubt that, in relation to registered land, each of the following: (a) an equity by estoppel, and (b) a mere equity, has effect from the time the equity arises as an interest capable of binding successors in title.

proprietary rights. Relating to private rights of ownership, i.e., rights *in rem* (q.v.). For equitable proprietary rights, see *Westdeutsche Landesbank* v *Islington LBC* [1996] AC 669 (the legal title carries with it all rights, so that unless and until there is a separation of legal and equitable estates, there is no separate equitable interest).

proprietary rights, essence of. 'Before a right or an interest can be admitted into the category of property, or of a right affecting property, it must be definable, identifiable by third parties, capable in its nature of an assumption by third parties, and have some degree of permanence or stability': *per* Lord Wilberforce in *National Provincial Bank* v *Ainsworth* [1965] AC 1175.

proprietor. One who has title to property.

proprietor in possession. Under Land Registration Act 2002, s 131(1), land is in the possession of the proprietor of a registered estate in land if it is physically in his possession, or in that of a person who is entitled to be registered as the proprietor of the registered estate; thus land in possession, or which is treated as being in possession of a tenant or licensee is treated for purposes of s 131(1) as in the possession of the landlord or licensor. A squatter who is physically in possession is not to be considered as a proprietor in possession: s 131(3).

proprietorship register. *See* REGISTER AT LAND REGISTRY.

prorogation. The ending of a session of Parliament (q.v.) by exercise of the royal prerogative. Its effect is to terminate the current business of Parliament, except appeals before the House of Lords. See Prorogation Act 1867.

proscribed organisation. An organisation, listed in Terrorism Act 2000, Sch 2, which commits or participates in acts of terrorism, prepares for, promotes, encourages, or is otherwise concerned in terrorism: s 3. For application for deproscription, and appeal to Proscribed Organisations Appeal Commission, see ss 3–7. It is an offence under s 11(1) to belong or profess to belong to a proscribed organisation.

proscribed organisation, membership of. CA held in *R* v *Hundal* (2004) *The Times*, 13 February, that a person in the UK could have committed the offence of belonging to a proscribed organisation (the International Sikh Youth Federation) contrary to the Terrorism Act 2000, s 11(1), even though he had joined or participated in the activities of the organisation in some country where there was no ban on the organisation.

prosecution. The instituting of criminal proceedings involving an accused person in the courts.

prosecution, criteria for instituting proceedings. See *Code for Crown Prosecutors* issued (in revised form in October 2000) under Prosecution of Offences Act 1985, s 10. The Crown Prosecutor must be satisfied, first, of 'evidential sufficiency', i.e., that there is admissible, substantial and reliable evidence and 'a realistic prospect of conviction'. He will consider also, the 'public interest test', i.e., whether a conviction is likely to result in a significant sentence, whether defendant used a weapon or threatened violence, whether he was in a position of trust, whether he was a ringleader, whether offence was racially motivated, whether there is evidence of premeditation, etc. See CROWN PROSECUTION SERVICE.

prosecution, private. '[It] remains a valuable constitutional safeguard against inertia or partiality on the part of authority': *per* Lord Wilberforce in *Gouriet* v *UPW* [1978] AC 435. Legal aid is not available to a private prosecutor, but costs may be awarded out of central funds (see Prosecution of Offences Act 1985, s 17) provided the case relates to an indictable offence. See *R* v *Stockport Magistrates' Court ex p Cooper* [1984] Crim LR 233. (For summary cases see s 19.) See O.P.A. 1861, s 42; Prosecution of Offences Act 1985, s 6; *R* v *DPP ex p Duckenfield* [2000] 1 WLR 55; *R* v *Lemon* [1979] AC 617 (which began as a private prosecution); *R* v *DPP ex p Camelot Group* (1997) *The Independent*, 22 April.

prosecution, time limit. HL held in *R* v *J* (2004) *The Times*, 15 October, that where more than 12 months had passed since an act of unlawful intercourse with a girl under 16 had taken place, so that no prosecution could commence under Sexual Offences Act 1956, s 5(1), it would not be permissible for the Crown to prosecute under the same facts under s 14(1).

prosecutor. One who institutes criminal proceedings, usually in the name of the Crown. *See* DIRECTOR OF PUBLIC PROSECUTIONS.

prosecutor, non-appearance of. If the accused appears for the trial of an information (q.v.) and the prosecutor fails to appear, the court may dismiss the information or, if evidence has been received on a previous occasion, proceed in the absence of the prosecutor: M.C.A. 1980, s 15; *Holmes* v *Campbell* (1998) 162 JP 655. If both parties fail to appear, the court may dismiss the information or proceed in their absence: s 16. *See* ACCUSED, NON-APPEARANCE OF.

prosecutors, near plans for. AG announced on 12 January 2005 that a formal system of bargaining for offenders, allowing them to plead guilty and turn Queen's evidence, under the protection right to grant immunity from prosecution may be introduced. The prosecution will work with a new Serious Organised Crime Agency.

prospectus. Any document containing information about securities: F.S.A. 1986, s 159(1)(*a*). See EC Directive, May 1989; SI 95/1537 (Public Offers of Securities Regulations); F.S.M.A. 2000, ss 84–87.

prospectus, untrue statements in. If a person has acquired securities to which a prospectus relates and there is any untrue or misleading statement in the prospectus (or omission from it) which resulted in a loss to that person, the person responsible for the prospectus is liable to compensate for the loss: F.S.A. 1986, s 166. For exemptions from liability see s 167; for the definition of 'person responsible' see s 168. The general duty of disclosure in the prospectus is required by s 163.

prostitution. 'Prostitution is proved if it be shown that a woman offers her body for purposes amounting to common lewdness for payment in return': *R* v *Webb* [1964] 1 QB 357. It is not limited to cases involving promiscuous sexual intercourse. It is not, in itself, an offence, but it is an offence to cause others to become prostitutes, or to live on the earnings of prostitution: S.O.A. 1956; see C.J.P.O.A. 1994, s 33 (abolition of corroboration requirements relating to S.O.A. 1956, s 22(2) (causing prostitution of women)); *IRC* v *Aken* [1990] 1 WLR 1374 (taxation within Schedule D of earnings from prostitution); *R* v *Powell* (2000) *The Times*, 15 August. For the offence of exercising control over a prostitute (S.O.A. 1956, s 31), see *A-G's Reference (No. 2 of 1995)* [1996] 3 All ER 860.

prostitution, advertisements relating to. It is an offence for a person to place on, or in the immediate vicinity of, a public telephone, an advertisement relating to prostitution with the intention that it should come to the attention of other persons: Criminal Justice and Police Act 2001, s 46(1). 'Public telephone' means any telephone located in a public place and made available for use by the public, or a section of the public: s 46(5).

prostitution, common. It is an offence to procure a woman for the purpose of common prostitution: S.O.A. 1956, s 22(1). 'Common' involves procuring a woman to act as a prostitute on more than one occasion: *R* v *Morris-Lowe* [1985] 1 WLR 29.

protected coin. A coin customarily used as money in any country or specified in an order made by the Treasury under Forgery and Counterfeiting Act 1981. See s 27(1)(*b*); SI 99/2095 (designation of euro as protected coin). *See* COUNTER-FEITING.

protected costs orders in public law cases. CA held in *Regina (Corner House Research)* v *Secretary of State for Trade and Industry* [2005] *The Times*, 7 March, the court's jurisdiction was governed by s 51 of the Supreme Court Act 1981, Parts 43 & 48 of the Civil Procedure Rules and Practice Directions. Where a case is of general public importance an applicant should not be deterred in pursuing a claim for the fear of being exposed to serious financial risk, where the court considers the case of public interest a protected costs order should be made.

protected goods. Goods which, under C.C.A. 1974, s 90, are the subject of a regulated hire-purchase or credit sale agreement (qq.v.) and in relation to which the debtor has not terminated the agreement and has paid one-third or more of the total price in the goods. They cannot be recovered except by court order, or voluntary surrender by the debtor. See *Julian Hodge Bank Ltd* v *Hall* [1998] CCLR 14.

protected industrial action. *See* INDUSTRIAL ACTION, PROTECTED.

protected person. Head of State, member of body performing functions of Head of State, Head of Government or Minister of Foreign Affairs who is outside the territory of the state in which he holds office; persons who represent a state or international organisation of an inter-governmental character; person who is a member of the family of those mentioned above: Internationally Protected Persons Act 1978, s 1(5). For offences relating to attacks and threats of attacks on them, see s 1(1)–(4).

protected person, British. *See* BRITISH PROTECTED PERSON.

protected states. Member states of the Commonwealth (q.v.) over whose external affairs the UK exerts full control, but who have a considerable measure of control over internal affairs.

protected tenancy. A contractual tenancy concerning a dwelling house let as a separate dwelling, formerly protected by the Rent Act 1977. For exclusions, see, e.g., ss 5–12. Replaced under H.A. 1988 by the 'assured tenancy' (q.v.). No tenancy granted after January 1989 can be 'protected' unless entered into in pursuance of a pre-commencement contract: see 1988 Act, s 34(1). See *Laimond Properties Ltd* v *Al Shakarchi (No. 2)* [1998] EGCS 21; *Cadogan Estates* v *McMahon* (2000) 150 NLJ 1625.

protection and indemnity associations. Known also as 'P & I Clubs'. Mutual insurance arrangement common in marine insurance, whereby shipowners contribute to the association on the basis of their tonnage, and the association agrees to meet the cost of certain liabilities not usually covered by marine hull insurance policies, e.g., quarantine

expenses. See Third Parties (Rights Against Insurers) Act 1930 (and Law Commission Consultation Paper No. 152); *Firma-C Trade SA* v *Newcastle P & I Association* [1990] 3 WLR 78; *Western Shipowners Association* v *Hellenic Industrial Bank* [1998] CLC 1431; *The Oakwell* [1999] 1 Lloyd's Rep 249.

Protection, Court of. *See* COURT OF PROTECTION.

protection order. 1. Court order, under C.C.A. 1974, s 131, made on application of creditor or owner under a regulated agreement (q.v.) to protect property from damage or depreciation pending determination of proceedings under the Act. 2. Orders made under Domestic Proceedings and Magistrates' Courts Act 1978, ss 16–18, and injunctions under Domestic Violence and Matrimonial Proceedings Act 1976, s 1 (now repealed), ordering respondent not to use or threaten to use violence against the applicant or a child of the family. See F.L.A. 1996, Part IV (now in force), ss 42–52.

protective award. Award by an industrial tribunal (q.v.) for remuneration to a dismissed employee where an employer has failed to take appropriate steps relating to consultation with union representatives in the event of redundancy: see T.U.L.R.(C.)A. 1992, s 188; SI 1991/925.

protective force, defence of. In a case involving aggravated trespass, contrary to the Criminal Justice and Public Order Act 1994, s 68(1)(3), it was held that a private defence of protective force had no application to aggravated trespass arising where protestors against the cultivation of genetically modified crops had entered a field and tied themselves to tractors. The use of protective force referred to the warding off of unlawful force, to avoid being detained unlawfully and to escape from that detention.

protective measure. Means a measure directed to the protection of the person or property of an adult; and it may deal in particular with any of the following (a) the determination of incapacity and the institution of a protective regime, (b) placing the adult under the protection of an appropriate authority, (c) guardianship, curatorship or any corresponding system, (d) the designation and functions of a person having charge of the adult's person or property, or representing or otherwise helping him, (e) placing the adult in a place where protection can be provided, (f) administering, conserving or disposing of the adult's property, (g) authorising a specific intervention for the protection of the person or property of the adult. Mental Capacity Act 2005 Sch 3 s 5.

protective trust. A trust for life, or any lesser period, determinable on the occurrence of certain events, e.g., the beneficiary's bankruptcy, upon which the trust income will be applied at the absolute discretion of trustees for the support of the beneficiary and his family. Example: 'Life interest to X until he shall become bankrupt.' Can be created expressly or by implication. See Tr.A. 1925, s 33; F.L.R.A. 1969, s 15(3). *See* TRUST.

protectorates, British. *See* BRITISH PROTECTORATES.

Protectorate, the. Era (1653–8) during which Cromwell (1599–1658) was Lord Protector of the Commonwealth of England, Scotland and Ireland. *See* COMMONWEALTH.

protector of settlement. One who could prevent a tenant in tail (q.v.) entitled only in remainder from disentailing. A tenant in tail in remainder could bar the entail (q.v.) by executing disentailing assurance with the protector's consent. Disentailment without the protector's consent created a base fee (q.v.). See *Re Darnley's WT* [1970] 1 WLR 405. See Trusts of Land and Appointment of Trustees Act 1999. *See* SETTLEMENT.

protest. 1. Document under seal made by a notary (q.v.) attesting the dishonour of a bill of exchange (q.v.). Accepted as proof that bill has been dishonoured. 2. Payment under protest is made where the payer will not agree that money is due from him.

protest, right to. 'Everyone has the right publicly to protest against anything which displeases him and publicly to proclaim his views, whatever they might be. It does not matter whether there is any reasonable basis for his protest or whether his views are sensible or silly': *per* Salmon LJ in *Morris* v *Crown Office* [1970] 1 All ER 1079.

protocol. 1. An original draft or preliminary memorandum. 2. Minutes of a meeting setting out matters of agreement. 3. Code of procedure. 4. An agreement between states which is less formal than a treaty or convention.

protocols, pre-action. 'Statements of understanding between legal practitioners and others about pre-action practice and which are approved by a relevant practice direction': CPR Glossary. Objectives of the protocols are: to encourage exchange of early and full information about the prospective legal claim; to enable parties to avoid litigation by agreeing a settlement of claim before commencement of proceedings; to support efficient management of proceedings. See CPR, r 3.1(4), (5). The court will expect all parties to have complied with approved protocols; non-compliance may involve order for costs (on an indemnity basis): see r 44.3.

Provincial Courts. Ecclesiastical courts of the Archbishops of Canterbury and York, e.g., the Court of Arches.

proving a debt. Establishing a debt due from the estate of a bankrupt (q.v.). See SI 86/1925, Part 4, chap 9, as amended.

proving a will. Obtaining probate (q.v.) of a will.

provisional bid. *See* BID.

provisional orders. Orders which normally do not take effect until confirmed by Parliament (q.v.), issued by government departments relating, e.g., to schemes of local authorities.

provision, financial. *See* FINANCIAL PROVISION, REASONABLE.

provision, transitional statutory. 'Its operation is expected to be temporary, in that it becomes spent when all the past circumstances with which it is designed to deal have been dealt with, while the primary legislation continues to deal indefinitely with the new circumstances which arise after its passage': *per* Lord Keith in *R v Secretary of State for Social Security ex p Britnell* [1991] 1 WLR 198.

proviso. 1. In a deed (q.v.), a condition upon which its general validity is based. May begin: '. . . provided always that . . .'. 2. In a statute, a clause qualifying or exempting from the enactment something which, but for the proviso, would have been included. It is construed with the preceding part of the clause to which it is attached. It never enlarges an enactment unless that is unavoidable: *Ex p Partington* (1844) 6 QB 649.

proviso, applying the. Where the Court of Appeal or House of Lords was satisfied that the point raised in an appeal should be decided in favour of the appellant, they could, nevertheless, dismiss that appeal if they considered that no miscarriage of justice had actually occurred: Criminal Appeal Act 1968, proviso to s 2(1). Exercise of this power was known as 'applying the proviso'. No longer a part of English law (see *R v Foley* (1997) *The Times*, 17 March), following its replacement by Criminal Appeal Act 1995, s 2(1), under which an appeal against conviction is allowed only if the Court thinks it unsafe. *See* APPEALS, CRIMINAL.

provocation. May be pleaded only on a charge of murder so as to reduce the charge to manslaughter (q.v.). 'Provocation is some act or series of acts done by the dead man to the accused, which would cause in any reasonable person and actually causes in the accused, a sudden and temporary loss of self-control, rendering accused so subject to passion as to make him for the moment not master of his mind': *R v Duffy* [1949] 1 All ER 932. 'The question whether the provocation was enough to make a reasonable man do as [accused] did shall be left to be determined by the jury; and in determining that question the jury shall take into account everything both done and said according to the effect which, in their opinion, it would

have on a reasonable man': Homicide Act 1957, s 3. Whether a jury should take into account the effect of defendant's depression on his powers of self-control, in relation to the question of whether his behaviour had measured up to the standard of self-control which ought reasonably to have been expected of him, was essentially a matter which was entirely for them to decide: *R v Smith* [2000] 3 WLR 654. See *Mancini v DPP* [1942] AC 1; *DPP v Camplin* [1978] AC 705; *R v Johnson* [1989] 1 WLR 740 (self-induced provocation); *R v Thornton* [1992] 1 All ER 306 (provocation in context of continuing domestic violence). Defences of lack of intent and provocation cannot be raised on behalf of a defendant found to be under a disability rendering him unfit to plead to a count of murder under Criminal Procedure (Insanity) Act 1964, s 4A: *R v Grant* (2001) *The Times*, 10 December. The CA held in *R v Miao* (2003) *The Times*, 26 November, that, in the case of a charge of murder where there was no more than a speculative possibility that defendant might have been provoked by the victim, the judge ought not to direct the jury to consider the issue of provocation as a defence.

provocation, directions to jury. CA held in *R v Rowland* [2003] EWCA Crim 3636, that in a trial on a charge of murder, where the judge intends to direct the jury concerning provocation, he is obliged, before speeches, to discuss with counsel the terms of the direction.

provocation, question of time and. The issue is 'whether there had been time for the blood to cool, and for reason to resume its seat . . . in which case the crime would amount to wilful murder': *per* Tindal CJ in *R v Hayward* (1833) 6 C & P 157. 'The question is whether such a period of time had elapsed as would be sufficient to enable the mind to recover its balance': *per* Hannen J in *R v Selten* (1871) 11 Cox C C 674. See *R v Ibrahim* (1981) 74 Cr App R 154; *R v Braille* [1995] Crim LR 739.

proximate cause. *See* CAUSA PROXIMA ET NON REMOTA SPECTATUR.

proximity. Immediate nearness in relation to time, space. In the context of tort and duty of care (q.v.), see *Caparo plc v Dickman* [1990] 2 AC 633, *per* Lord Oliver: 'Proximity is a convenient expression so long as it is realised that it is no more than a label which embraces not a definable concept but merely a description of circumstances from which, pragmatically, the courts will conclude that a duty of care exists.' 'Proximity is convenient shorthand for a relationship between two parties which makes it fair and reasonable one should owe the other a duty of care': *per* Lord Nicholls in *Stovin v Wise* [1996] AC 923.

proxy. 1. One appointed with authority or power to act for another in, e.g., attendance at meetings and elections. See Cos.A. 1985, s 372; Representation of the People Act 1985, ss 5, 6; Table A, arts 59–63. 2. Document containing such an appointment.

psychiatric harm, damages for, police claim. Police officers are not entitled to recover damages against a chief constable for psychiatric injury suffered by them resulting from the aftermath of a disaster in the course of their duties: *White and Others v Chief Constable of S Yorks Police* (1998) 148 NLJ 1844. See Law Com. Report No. 249, March 1998.

psychiatric illness, stress-induced. In *Sutherland v Hatton* [2002] EWCA Civ 76, CA set out guidelines for courts in determining negligence claims against an employer where claimant had been unable to continue work because of a stress-induced psychiatric illness. An assessment of damages would take into account any pre-existing disorder or vulnerability.

psychiatric services, high security. Hospital accommodation and services provided for persons who are liable to be detained under M.H.A. 1983, and who require treatment under conditions of high security on account of their dangerous, violent or criminal propensities: National Health Services Act 1977, s 4(1), substituted by Health Act 1999, s 41(1). See SIs 96/708; 00/267. *See* SPECIAL HOSPITAL.

psychopathic disorder. 'A persistent disorder or disability of mind (whether or not including significant impairment of intelligence) which results in abnormally aggressive or seriously irresponsible conduct on the part of the person concerned': M.H.A. 1983, s 1(2). See *Re F (A Minor)* (1999) 96 (39) LSG 38.

Public Accounts Commission. Comprises the Chairman of the House of Commons Committee of Public Accounts, Leader of the Commons, and seven other Members of Parliament (excluding Ministers). They examine the annual estimates of the National Audit Office (q.v.). See National Audit Act 1983, s 2, Sch 2.

public Act of Parliament. An Act (q.v.) which affects the public at large. Every Act passed after 1850 is a public Act unless it is expressly provided therein to the contrary: I.A. 1978, s 3.

public and private hearings. *See* OPEN JUSTICE.

public assembly. An assembly of 20 or more persons in a public place which is wholly or partly open to the air: P.O.A. 1986, s 16. For the imposition of conditions, see Part II. See European Convention on Human Rights 1950, art 11 (freedom of assembly).

publication. 1. Term applied in relation to defamation (q.v.) to refer to the communication of words complained of to at least one other person than the person defamed. See *Bata v Bata* [1948] WN 366. See also Defamation Act 1996; *Godfrey v Demon Internet Ltd* [1999] 4 All ER 342 (a defamatory article stored by an internet service provider is published each time it is accessed by a subscriber); C.J.A. 1987, s 11(15). 2. Term applied in relation to Obscene Publications Act 1959, whereby a person 'publishes' an article who distributes, circulates, sells, lets on hire, gives, or lends it, or who offers it for sale or for letting on hire, or in the case of an article containing or embodying matter to be looked at, or a record, shows, plays or projects it. See 1959 Act, s 1(3); *A-G's Reference (No. 2 of 1975)* [1975] 2 All ER 753; *R v Waddon* [1999] ITCLR 422 (obscenity published on internet). 3. In relation to Copyright, Designs and Patents Act 1988, means the issue of copies of a work to the public or making it available by electronic retrieval: s 175. *See* REPORTING RESTRICTIONS.

publication schemes, public authority. Under F.I.A. 2000, s 19, every public authority must adopt and maintain a scheme relating to the publication of information, and specifying classes of information which it intends to publish.

public barrister and membership of chambers. CA held in *1 Pump Court Chambers* v *Norton* (2004) *The Times*, 21 July, that an application made for admission to a set of barristers' chambers as a pupil barrister could not be considered as an application for membership of a trade organisation.

public benefit. A valid charitable trust must promote some public benefit, i.e., 'the benefit of the community or of an appreciably important class of the community': *Verge* v *Somerville* [1924] AC 496. A trust for the relief of poverty may be charitable, although not for the benefit of the public or even a 'section' of it: *Re Coulthurst* [1951] 1 All ER 774. See *IRC* v *Educational Grants Association Ltd* [1967] Ch 123; *Southwood* v *A-G* (2000) 150 NLJ 1017. *See* TRUST.

public Bill. *See* BILL.

public body. 'A body . . . which has public or statutory duties to perform and which performs those duties and carries out its transactions for the benefit of the public and not for private profit': Halsbury, adopted in *DPP* v *Manners* [1978] AC 43.

public charitable collections. A charitable appeal which is made (i) in any public place, or (ii) by means of visits to houses or business premises (or both). Charities Act 2006 s 45(2)(a).

public communications provider. Refers, under the Communications Act 2003, s 151, to a provider of a public electronic communications service or network, and a person who makes available facilities that are 'associated facilities' by reference to a public electronics communications network or service.

public company. Company (q.v.) either limited by shares or by guarantee with a minimum prescribed share capital, provided that its memorandum states that it is to be a public company and the statutory provisions concerning registration are complied with: Cos.A. 1985, s 1(1). It must have at least two members (s 1(1)), and at least two directors (s 282). Its shares are, in general, freely transferable. For minimum capital requirements, see Cos.A. 1985, s 118; EC Second Directive 1976.

public corporation. A business organisation created by an Act, responsible for the day-to-day operation of public enterprises. Members are appointed by the relevant minister. Annual accounts must be placed before Parliament. Known also as a 'statutory corporation'. See, e.g., Finance Act 1987, Sch 15, para 7(1).

public decency. 'I think that [the authorities] establish that it is an indictable offence to say or do or exhibit anything in public which outrages public decency, whether or not it also tends to corrupt and deprave those who see or hear it': *per* Lord Reid in *Shaw* v *DPP* [1961] 2 All ER 446. See also *Knuller Ltd* v *DPP* [1972] 2 All ER 898; *R* v *Rowley* [1991] 1 WLR 1020 (offence involves commission of an act which was, *per se*, lewd or obscene); *R* v *Walker* [1996] 1 Cr App R 111; *R* v *Gaynor* [2000] 2 Cr App R (S) 163. For powers of arrest in order to prevent the offence, see P.&C.E.A. 1984, s 25(3)(d)(iv).

public document. 'A document that is made for the purposes of the public making use of it, and being able to refer to it': *Sturla* v *Freccia* (1880) 5 App Cas 623. It is generally authenticated by a public officer. Examples: court records; public registers. Statements in a public document made by an officer in pursuance of a public duty are admissible evidence of the facts stated therein: Civil Evidence Act 1968, s 9; Civil Evidence Act 1972; Civil Evidence Act 1995, s 7(2). *See* DOCUMENT.

public duties, time off for. An employer is under a duty, under E.R.A. 1996, s 50, to give time off to certain employees in relation to their duties, e.g., those who are magistrates, members of local authorities. See SI 99/101.

public good, defence of. Defence under Obscene Publications Act 1964, s 4(1), whereby a person will not be convicted of an offence of possessing obscene articles for publication for gain if it is proved that publication was justified as being for the public good on the ground that it is in the interests of science, literature, art or learning, or of other objects of general concern. See *DPP* v *Jordan* [1976] 3 All ER 775. 'Learning' means 'a product of scholarship': *A-G's Reference (No. 3 of 1977)* [1978] 1 WLR 1123.

Public Guardian. Appointed by the Lord Chancellor, having the functions of (a) establishing and maintaining a register of lasting powers of attorney, (b) establishing and maintaining a register of orders appointing deputies, (c) supervising deputies appointed by the court, (d) directing a Court of Protection Visitor to visit: (i) a donee of a lasting power of attorney, (ii) a deputy appointed by the court, or (iii) the person granting the power of attorney or for whom the deputy is appointed ('P'), and to make a report to the Public Guardian on such matters as he may direct, (e) receiving security which the court requires a person to give for the discharge of his functions, (f) receiving reports from donees of lasting powers of attorney and deputies appointed by the court, (g) reporting to the court on such matters relating to proceedings under this Act as the court requires, (h) dealing with representations (including complaints) about the way in which a donee of a lasting power of attorney or a deputy appointed by the court is exercising his powers, and (i) publishing, in any manner the Public Guardian thinks appropriate, any information he thinks appropriate about the discharge of his functions. Mental Capacity Act 2005 s 58.

Public Guardian Board. The Board's duty is to scrutinise and review the way in which the Public Guardian discharges his functions and to make such re-

commendations to the Lord Chancellor about that matter as it thinks appropriate. Mental Capacity Act 2005 s 59.

public house. Premises licensed for the sale of intoxicating liquor for consumption on those premises where the sale of such liquor is, or is apart from any other trade or business ancillary or incidental to it, the only trade or business carried on there: L.G.A. 1966, s 17(2).

public index map. Index of separate parcels of registered land, kept at the Land Registry and open to inspection by any person: L.R.R. 1925, rr 8, 12; L.R.R. 1988; SI 92/122.

public interest, defence of. In *R* v *Shayler* (2002) *The Times*, 22 March, HL held that an ex-member of the Security Service, prosecuted under Official Secrets Act 1989, for unauthorised disclosure of documents acquired during his service, had no entitlement to rely on defence of his disclosure having been made in the public interest.

public interest immunity. *See* PRIVILEGE, PUBLIC POLICY.

publicity, prejudicial. CA held in *R (Mahfouz)* v *General Medical Council* (2004) *The Times*, 19 March, that there was no reason why knowledge of prejudicial publicity would be necessarily fatal to the general fairness of a hearing by the GMC's committee for professional conduct, but it was necessary to take into account its effect within the context of the proceedings in their entirety.

public law. Those areas of the law concerned primarily with the duties and powers of the state itself, e.g., constitutional law. See *Roy* v *Kensington and Chelsea FPC* [1992] 1 All ER 705; *Pawlowski (Collector of Taxes)* v *Dunnington* [1999] STC 550 (taxpayers may invoke a public law defence where there is no statutory right of appeal); *R* v *HM Treasury ex p University of Cambridge* (2000) *The Times*, 17 October (discussion by European Court of Justice on meaning of 'body governed by public law'). *See* PRIVATE LAW.

public lending right. Right conferred on authors by the Public Lending Right

Act 1979, s 1(1), to receive out of a central fund payment in respect of books lent out to the public by libraries in the UK.

public limited company. *See* PUBLIC COMPANY.

public meeting. Any meeting in a public place and any meeting which the public or any section thereof are permitted to attend, whether on payment or otherwise: P.O.A. 1936, s 9 (as amended by C.J.A. 1972 and P.O.A. 1986, Sch 3). For purposes of Defamation Act 1952, a meeting is 'public' if its organisers open it to the public or manifest an intention or desire that proceedings should be communicated to a wider public by issuing a general invitation to the press: *Turkington v Times Newspapers* (2000) 150 NLJ 1657.

public mischief. Formerly an offence tending to the prejudice of the community: *R v Manley* [1933] 1 KB 529 (false statements causing the police to waste their time). See C.L.A. 1967, s 5(2). In *DPP v Withers* [1974] 3 All ER 984, the House of Lords held that the law does not recognise a crime in an individual accused of conduct tending to cause a public mischief.

public morals, courts and. 'In the sphere of criminal law I entertain no doubt that there remains in the courts of law a residual power to enforce the supreme and fundamental purpose of the law, to conserve not only the safety and order but also the moral welfare of the state . . .': *per* Lord Simonds in *Shaw v DPP* [1961] 2 All ER 446.

public nuisance. 'A nuisance which is so widespread in its range or so indiscriminate in its effects that it would not be reasonable to expect one person to take proceedings on his own responsibility to put a stop to it, but that it should be taken on the responsibility of the community at large': *per* Lord Denning in *A-G v PYA Quarries Ltd* [1957] 2 QB 169. A crime triable summarily or on indictment, and a tort. See *AB v SW Water Services Ltd* [1993] QB 507 (award of exemplary damages). *See* NUISANCE.

public office. Any office under the Crown, or under the charter of a city or borough, or under the Acts relating to local government or public health or public education: Representation of the People Act 1983, s 185; SI 99/787.

public officer. 'An officer who discharges any duty in the discharge of which the public are interested, more clearly so if he is paid out of a fund provided by the public': *R v Whitaker* [1914] 2 KB 1283.

public order offences, football. CA held in *R v O'Keefe* [2004] 1 Cr App R (S) 67, that any offence of threatening behaviour under Public Order Act 1986, s 4(1)(a), committed during a period which was relevant for purposes of the Football Spectators Act 1989 was relevant in relation to the purposes of the 1989 Act.

public order offences, racially-aggravated. A person is guilty of an offence under C.D.A. 1998, s 31, if he commits an offence under P.O.A. 1986, s 4 (causing fear or provocation of violence), s 4A (intentional harassment, alarm or distress), s 5 (harassment, alarm or distress) which is racially aggravated. *See* RACIALLY-AGGRAVATED OFFENCE.

public or general rights, declaration concerning. *See* DECLARATION CONCERNING PUBLIC OR GENERAL RIGHTS.

public place. Any highway and any place to which at the material time the public or any section of the public has access, on payment or otherwise, as of right or by virtue of express, or implied permission: P.O.A. 1986, s 16. See, e.g., *DPP v Vivier* [1991] 4 All ER 18; *Felix v DPP* [1998] Crim LR 657 ('public open place'). The CA held in *R v Roberts* [2004] 1 WLR 181, that it was not appropriate to construe 'public place' in Criminal Justice Act 1988, s 139(7) as including land adjacent to areas where the public might have access, as long as the harm against which the Act was designed to provide protection in no sense be inflicted from that place.

public policy. 'That principle of law which holds that no subject can lawfully do that which has a tendency to be injurious to the public, or against the public good': *Egerton v Brownlow* (1853) 4 HL Cas 1. 'What the law recognises as contrary to public policy turns out to vary greatly from time to time': *per* Lord Haldane in *Rodriguez v Speyer Bros* [1919] AC 59.

public privilege. *See* PRIVILEGE, PUBLIC POLICY.

public procession. A procession (q.v.) in a public place (q.v.): P.O.A. 1986, s 16. For duties concerning the giving of advance notice, see s 11. *See* PARADES COMMISSION.

public prosecutor. Director of Public Prosecutions (q.v.).

public records, access to. Records in the Public Records Office are generally not available for public inspection until 30 years after the year next to that in which they were created, or other period as may be prescribed: see Public Records Acts 1958, 1967. Longer periods have been prescribed for, e.g., exceptionally sensitive papers, documents containing information supplied in confidence, disclosure of which might constitute a breach of good faith. See F.I.A. 2000, s 15; Sch 5.

public service, contracts tending to injure. Contracts (generally illegal), e.g., for the sale of public offices, for procurement of a title of honour for reward. See *Parkinson v College of Ambulance Ltd* [1925] 2 KB 1 (which led to Honours (Prevention of Abuses) Act 1925).

public service pension scheme. An occupational pension scheme (q.v.) established by or under an enactment or the Royal prerogative or Royal charter, all the particulars of which are set out in, or in a legislative instrument made under, an enactment, Royal warrant or charter, and which cannot come into force or be amended without the approval of a Minister or government department: Pension Schemes Act 1993, s 1.

public services vehicle. *See* VEHICLE, PUBLIC SERVICES.

public trust. A trust which has as its object the promotion of the public wel-

fare, as opposed to a private trust, which is for the benefit of an individual or class. *See* TRUST.

Public Trustee. Appointed under Public Trustee Act 1906; he may act on the application of a beneficiary or trustee (qq.v.). He may be appointed as an ordinary trustee, or custodian trustee (q.v.), or personal representative (q.v.). He may decline to accept a trust, but not on the sole ground of its being of small value. Powers, duties and liabilities are those of an ordinary trustee.

publish. *See* PUBLICATION.

puisne. (French: *puis* (after), *né* (born).) Junior, inferior. 1. A *puisne mortgage* is a legal mortgage (q.v.) not protected by the deposit of documents relating to the legal estate affected, and is a Class C charge under L.C.A. 1972. See L.P.A. 1969, s 30(1). 2. High Court judges are styled *puisne judges* or 'Justices of the High Court': S.C.A. 1981, s 4(2); SI 99/3138 (fixing maximum number at 106).

punctual. On the day named for payment: *Leeds Theatre Co v Broadbent* [1898] 1 Ch 343.

punctuation. The division of words in a document by stops, commas, etc. 'It is from the words and from the context, not from the punctuation, that the sense must be collected': *Sandford v Raikes* (1816) 1 Mer 646. See *DPP v Schildkamp* [1971] AC 1; *Hanlon v The Law Society* [1981] AC 124.

punishment. Penalty inflicted by a court on a convicted offender. The primary sanction of the criminal law. 'A person is said to suffer punishment whenever he is legally deprived of the normal rights of a citizen on the ground that he has violated a rule of law, the violation having been established by trial according to due process of law, provided the deprivation has been carried out by the recognised legal authorities of the state, that the rule of law clearly specifies both the offence and the attached penalty, that the courts construe statutes strictly, and that the statute was on the books prior to the offence': Rawls, *Civil Disobedience* (1969).

punishment, capital. Under Human Rights Act 1998 (Amendment) Order SI 04/1574, in force since 22 June 2004, and following UK ratification of Thirteenth Protocol to European Convention on Human Rights, the death penalty is now abolished under all circumstances. The Sixth Protocol, relating to death penalty in war time or imminent threat of war is now superseded.

punishment, components of. 'A social response which: occurs where there is a violation of a legal rule; is imposed and carried out by authorised persons on behalf of the legal order to which the violated rule belongs; involves suffering or at least other consequences normally considered unpleasant; expresses disapproval of the violator': Ross, *On Law* (1958).

punishment, corporal. Physical chastisement of a convicted offender (e.g., by flogging, whipping). See C.J.A. 1914, s 36; C.J.A. 1948, s 1 (abolishing the punishment). For abolition of corporal punishment in schools, see Education Act 1996, s 548; School Standards and Framework Act 1998, s 131 (in which corporal punishment is referred to as an action 'for the purpose of punishing a child . . . which, apart from any justification, would constitute battery').

punitive damages. It was held in *Design Progression Ltd* v *Thurloe Properties Ltd* [2004] EWHC 324 that in the case of a tenant having made written application to his landlord for permission to assign a lease, he had the right to ask for punitive damages where the landlord had breached the statutory duty to respond within a reasonable time. The sum awarded ought to cause the landlord to take serious consideration of his future conduct in this area.

pupil. 1. A person for whom education is being provided at a school, other than a person who has attained the age of 19 for whom further education is being provided, or a pupil for whom part-time education suitable to the requirements of persons of any age over compulsory school age is being provided: Education Act 1996, s 3. 2. Someone serving a

12-month internship as a barrister after call to Bar. See *Edmonds* v *Lawson* [2000] 2 WLR 1091 (a pupillage with a barrister's chambers does not constitute an apprenticeship, and a pupil barrister does not qualify for payment of the national minimum wage (q.v.)).

pupils, exclusion of. The head teacher of a school may exclude a pupil on disciplinary grounds for a fixed period or permanently: Education Act 1996, ss 156, 307; Education Act 1997, s 6; School Standards and Framework Act 1998, s 64. The fixed period is not more than 45 days in a school year: s 64(2). For appeals, see s 67. See *R* v *Northamptonshire CC ex p D* [1998] Ed CR 14; *R* v *Governors of Dunraven School ex p B* (2000) *The Times*, 3 February (pupil is entitled to know what is being said against him); SI 99/1868; *R* v *Governors of B School ex p W* (2000) *The Times*, 14 November (reinstatement of pupil is not reintegration in class).

pupils, selection of. No admission arrangements for a maintained school may make provision for selection by ability unless they make provision for a permitted form of such selection, or the school is a grammar school: School Standards and Framework Act 1998, s 99(1). For selection by aptitude, see s 99(2). For ballots of parents relating to retention of selective admission, see s 105.

pur autre vie. *See* AUTRE VIE.

purchaser. 1. One who acquires goods or land in exchange for money. 2. Under L.P.A. 1925, s 205(1), a purchaser in good faith for valuable consideration, including a lessee and mortgagee. 3. Under L.C.A. 1972, s 17(1) 'any person (including a mortgagee or lessee) who, for valuable consideration, takes any interest in land or in a charge on land'. 4. One to whom land is expressly transferred other than by descent, i.e., by the act of the parties by conveyance on sale, will, gift, etc. See *IRC* v *Gribble* [1913] 3 KB 212; *Powell* v *Cleland* [1948] 1 KB 262.

purchaser for value without notice. A *bona fide* purchaser of a legal estate for valuable consideration without notice of the equitable interests in the land. 'Good faith' is a 'separate test which may have to be passed even though absence of notice is proved': *per* Lord Wilberforce in *Midland Bank Trust Co v Green* [1981] AC 513. 'Valuable consideration' means any consideration (q.v.) in money, money's worth or future marriage. He is generally bound only by equitable interests of which he did have notice. *See* EQUITY'S DARLING.

purchaser, recommended new definition. Law Com. No. 254 (1998) suggests: 'Purchaser' should be defined to mean any person (including a mortgagee or lessee) who, for valuable consideration, takes an interest in land or in a charge on land. 'Valuable consideration' in existing definition should be defined to mean money or money's worth, but should not include marriage or a nominal consideration in money: para 3.50.

purchase, words of. Words pointing out, by name or description, the transferee, i.e., the person, who is to acquire an interest in land, e.g., 'to X and his heirs'. (X is the 'purchaser'.)

purpose. That which one seeks to accomplish. 'I have no doubt that [the meaning] is subjective. A purpose must exist in the mind. It cannot exist anywhere else. The word can be used to designate either the main object which a man wants or hopes to achieve by the contemplated act, or it can be used to designate those objects which he knows will probably be achieved by the act, whether he wants them or not. I am satisfied that in the criminal law in general . . . its ordinary sense is the latter one': *per* Lord Devlin in *Chandler v DPP* [1962] 3 All ER 142.

purpose axiom. Concept in administrative law relating to the exercise of discretion (q.v.) by a public authority. 'Parliament must have conferred the discretion with the intention that it should be used to promote the policy and objects of the Act; the policy and objects of the Act must be determined by construing the Act as a whole, and construction is always a matter of law for the court': *per* Lord Reid in *Padfield v Minister of Agriculture* [1968] AC 907.

purpose, purity of. It was held that where a lender exercises his power of sale, with a genuine purpose of recovering an amount secured by a mortgage, it was not necessary for the lender to have purity of purpose. See *Meretz Investments NV and Another v ACP Ltd and Others* [2006] *The Times*, 27 April.

purpose trust. *See* TRUST, PURPOSE.

putative father. (Putative = reputed, supposed.) The person alleged to be the father (q.v.) of an illegitimate child. See *Turner v Blunden* [1986] Fam 120; *Re L* (1990) *The Times*, 22 October; Child Support Act 1991, s 26 (disputes about parentage).

PVS. Persistent vegetative state. Defined by the Royal College of Physicians in 1996, as 'a clinical condition of unawareness of self and environment in which the patient breathes spontaneously, has a stable circulation and shows cycles of eye closure and eye opening which may stimulate sleep and waking.' See *Airedale NHS Trust v Bland* [1993] AC 789; *Re G (Persistent Vegetative State)* [1995] 2 FCR 46; *NHS Trust A v H* (2001) *The Times*, 17 May; *Withholding and Withdrawing Life-Prolonging Medical Treatment: Guidance for Decision Making* (BMA, July 1999).

pyramid selling. Scheme whereby a distributor collects franchise payments from others who are subsequently introduced, qualifying for special benefits and terms according to the number of sub-agents introduced. Under Fair Trading Act 1973, these schemes are controlled by, e.g., a cooling-off period for those who join schemes, and written contracts for participants. See Trading Schemes Regulations 1997, SI 97/30; *Re Delfin Marketing (UK) Ltd* [1999] 1 CL 71.

Q

QB. Queen's Bench.
QBD. Queen's Bench Division (q.v.).
QC. Queen's Counsel (q.v.).
qua. In the character of.
quaere. *See* SED QUAERE.
qualification shares. The number of shares or amount of stock which, under a company's articles (q.v.) must be held by a person acting as director. See Cos.A 1985, s 291(1).
qualified acceptance. Refers, e.g., to the conditional or partial acceptance of a bill of exchange (q.v.). See B.Ex.A. 1882, s 19.
qualified majority voting. Procedure used, e.g., in EU Council of Ministers, giving each member a 'weighted vote' on the basis of its population size, so that, given total weightings of 87, the votes necessary for adoption of a measure proposed by the Council total 62.
qualified privilege. *See* PRIVILEGE, QUALIFIED.
qualified property. Limited rights of property, e.g., chattel in possession of bailee.
qualified title. Title with which the applicant is registered under L.R.A. 1925, where the registrar is unable to grant absolute, good leasehold, or possessory title. See L.R.A. 1925, ss 7, 12, 77(3); L.R.A. 1986, s 1(1).
qualifying capital interest. *See* CAPITAL INTEREST, QUALIFYING.
quality partnership schemes, local. A local transport authority, or two or more such authorities acting jointly, may make a quality partnership scheme if they are satisfied that the scheme will to any extent implement the policies set out in their bus strategy or strategies. A quality partnership scheme is a scheme under which the authority or authorities provide particular facilities in the whole or part of their area or combined area, and operators of local services who wish to use the facilities must undertake to provide local services of a particular standard when using them: Transport Act 2000, s 114(1), (2).

quality, satisfactory. Where the seller sells goods in the course of a business, there is an implied term that the goods supplied under the contract are of satisfactory quality. Goods are of satisfactory quality if they meet the standard that a reasonable person would regard as satisfactory, taking account of any description of the goods, the price (if relevant) and all the other relevant circumstances. 'Quality' includes state, condition, appearance, safety, durability, fitness for purposes for which goods of the kind in question are commonly supplied. See S.G.A. 1979, s 14, substituted by Sale and Supply of Goods Act 1994, s 1. See *Stevenson* v *Rogers* [1999] QB 1028 (discussion of 'in the course of a business'). In relation to Sale of Goods Act 1979, s 14(2), as substituted by Sale and Supply of Goods Act 1994, s 1 (1), when considering whether goods are of a satisfactory quality, it is essential to ask whether a reasonable person would make such an assessment, given the circumstances of the individual purchaser and the context of the transaction in question: *Jewson Ltd* v *Kelly* (2002) *The Times*, 3 October.

quamdiu se bene gesserit. For as long as he shall behave himself. Phrase used to indicate that an office (e.g., that of a judge) will be held during good behaviour and will not be lost, therefore, save for bad behaviour. See S.C.A. 1981, s 11(3).

quangos. Quasi-autonomous, non-governmental organisations, generally carrying out regulatory and operational functions or commercial and semi-commercial activities. Some members may be appointed by the government, but they are not answerable to it.

quantity, correct. A seller must deliver the correct quantity of goods: S.G.A. 1979, s 30(1). Unless otherwise agreed, the buyer is not bound to accept delivery by instalments: s 31(1). See *Duffus SA v Berger & Co* [1984] AC 382. For unreasonable rejection, in the case of non-consumer contracts, see s 30(2A), (2B), (2C) inserted by Sale and Supply of Goods Act 1994, s 4.

quantum. How much. A quantity, amount. The amount in damages, estimated or real.

quantum meruit. As much as he has deserved (i.e., earned). On breach of contract (q.v.) the party injured may be entitled to claim for work done and services performed. See *Crown House Engineering v AMEC Projects* (1990) Const LJ 141; *Countryside Communications v ICL Pathways* [2000] CLC 324.

quantum valebat. As much as it was worth. Refers to a claim for goods supplied, where no price had been agreed on.

quarantine. Period of time (originally 40 days, but now variable), in which ships, animals and persons coming from a country in which serious infectious disease has spread are isolated. See Animal Health Act 1981, as amended.

quarry. A system of excavations for minerals which is not a mine (q.v.). See Mines and Quarries Act 1954.

quarter days. These are Lady Day (March 25), Midsummer Day (June 24), Michaelmas Day (September 29) and Christmas Day (December 25).

quash. To annul; to make void; to repress. *See CERTIORARI.*

quasi. As if; apparent; having some resemblance to, but lacking some requisites.

quasi-arbitrator. 'Where a matter is left by two parties to the judgment of a third who is to determine their rights, and the task is not merely one of arithmetic, but involving technical skill and knowledge, that person is in the position of a quasi-arbitrator': *Stevenson v Watson* (1879) 4 CPD 148. See *Palacath v Flanagan* [1985] 2 All ER 161.

quasi-contracts. Cases in which the law imposes on a person an obligation to make repayment on grounds of unjust benefit, e.g., when he has been enriched at the expense of another. See *Holt v Markham* [1923] 1 KB 504; *Shamia v Joory* [1958] 1 QB 448. *See* UNJUST ENRICHMENT.

quasi-easements. Where one person owns two or more adjoining and separate properties, rights which he may have been exercising over one or other of them are known as quasi-easements, since an owner cannot have an easement over his own land. See *Ward v Kirkland* [1967] Ch 194. *See* EASEMENT.

quasi-entail. An estate *pur autre vie* (q.v.), for the life of A granted 'to B and the heirs of his body'. See *Ex p Sterne* [1801] 6 Ves 156. *See* FEE TAIL.

quasi ex contractu. As if arising out of a contract.

quasi-indorser. One who signs a bill of exchange (q.v.) otherwise than as a drawer or acceptor, thereby incurring the liabilities of an indorser to a holder in due course (q.v.): see B.Ex.A. 1882, s 56.

quasi-judicial. Having a character which is partly-judicial, e.g., proceedings conducted by an arbitrator (q.v.).

quasi-loan. Used in Cos.A. 1985 to describe a transaction under which one party (the 'creditor') agrees to pay, or pays otherwise than in pursuance of an agreement, a sum for another (the 'borrower'), or agrees to reimburse, or reimburse otherwise than in pursuance of an agreement, expenditure incurred by another party for another (the 'borrower'), on terms that the borrower (or a person on his behalf) will reimburse the creditor, or in circumstances giving rise to a liability on the borrower to reimburse the creditor: s 331(3). In general, a non-private company may not make a quasi-loan to any of its directors: s 332.

Queen's Bench Division. Division of the High Court (q.v.), possessing civil, criminal, original, appellate and supervisory jurisdiction (including applications for *habeas corpus* (q.v.) and judicial review). It deals with, e.g., claims in tort and contract, and is presided over by the Lord Chief Justice (q.v.) with a staff of puisne judges (q.v.). A vice-president is appointed by the Lord Chancellor: Acc.J.A. 1999, s 69. It includes the Commercial Court and Admiralty Court (qq.v.). See S.C.A. 1981, ss 5, 6, Sch 1. See DIVISIONAL COURTS.

Queen's Counsel (or King's). A senior barrister (i.e., one who has practised successfully at the Bar for at least ten years) appointed on the recommendation of the Lord Chancellor. He wears a silk gown (hence the phrase 'to take silk') and takes precedence over the other barristers in court. He may appear in any case for or against the Crown. See Acc.J.A. 1999, s 45; SI 00/1876 (criteria for assignment of QCs to Crown Court cases); *Practice Direction (Crown Court Counsel)* [1995] 1 WLR 261.

Queen's evidence. Evidence for the Crown given by one co-accused who 'turns Queen's evidence', i.e., confesses guilt and acts as a competent witness against his associates.

Queen's Proctor. The solicitor (usually the Treasury Solicitor (q.v.)) representing the Crown who may intervene in the case of proceedings for a divorce order (q.v.). The court may direct papers to be sent to the Proctor who may instruct counsel to argue any question in relation to that case. Any person may give information to the Proctor on any matter relevant to the case, and the Proctor may then take such steps as are considered necessary. See Mat.C.A. 1973, s 8; Matrimonial Causes Rules 1977, rr 61–62; *Ebrahim* v *Ali* [1984] FLR 95. See DECREE.

Queen, The. 'Elizabeth the Second, by the Grace of God of the United Kingdom of Great Britain and Northern Ireland and of Her other Realms and Territories Queen, Head of the Commonwealth, Defender of the Faith': Royal Titles Act 1953. See *MacCormick* v *Lord Advocate* 1953 SC 396. Nominally, the supreme executive power; supreme head of the

church; head of defence forces. A *queen regent* or *regnant* holds the Crown in her own right; a *queen consort* is the king's wife; a *queen dowager* is the widow of a deceased king. See CROWN; MONARCHY; SOVEREIGN.

questioning by police. Following *Codes of Practice* issued under P.&C.E.A. 1984, a police officer may question any person from whom he thinks useful information can be obtained, subject to certain restrictions. The purpose of questioning is to obtain an explanation of facts, not necessarily an admission. For the questioning of juveniles by the police (in the presence of an 'appropriate adult'), see *Code C*. Oppressive questioning is forbidden and an accurate record must be made of interviews with suspects. See OPPRESSION LEADING TO CONFESSION.

qui approbat non reprobat. He who accepts cannot reject. See ELECTION.

quia timet. Because he fears. Claim for injunction (q.v.) relating to a virtually irreparable wrong merely feared or threatened, but not yet committed. Claimant must show a very strong probability of imminent grave damage accruing to him. Cost to defendant must also be considered. 'What is aimed at is justice between the parties, having regard to all the circumstances': *Hooper* v *Rogers* [1975] Ch 43.

quicquid plantatur solo, solo cedit. Whatever is affixed to the soil, belongs to the soil. See *Simmons* v *Midford* [1969] 2 Ch 415; *Royco* v *Eatonwill Construction* [1979] Ch 276; Agricultural Tenancies Act 1995, s 8. See FIXTURES.

quid pro quo. Something for something. Applied, e.g., to the concept of consideration (q.v.) in contract.

quiet enjoyment. Implied obligations of a lessor that a lessee's peaceful enjoyment of the premises shall not be interfered with by the lessor or by any person who claims under him. 'Quiet' is not restricted to an absence of noise; it has been interpreted as 'uninterrupted'. Tenant's remedies for breach are damages and injunction (qq.v.); see also H.A. 1988, ss 27, 28 (harassment of residential tenant and award of damages). See

Celsteel Ltd v *Alton House Holdings (No. 2)* [1987] 1 WLR 291; *Southwark LBC* v *Mills* [1999] 3 WLR 939; *Baxter* v *Camden LBC (No. 2)* [1999] 1 All ER 237; *Brent LBC* v *Botu* [2000] EGCS 34. *See* LEASE.

quiet possession. In a contract of sale there is an implied warranty (q.v.) that the buyer will enjoy quiet possession of the goods except so far as it may be disturbed by the owner or other person entitled to the benefit of any charge or encumbrance so disclosed or known: S.G.A. 1979, s 12(2)(*b*). See *Microbeads AG* v *Vinhurst Road Markings Ltd* [1975] 1 WLR 218.

qui facit per alium facit per se. He who does a thing through another does it himself.

qui in utero est. He who is in the womb [is held as already born, whenever a question arises for his benefit]. See *B* v *Islington HA* [1991] 2 WLR 501 (unborn child acquired a cause of action, which crystallised on its birth, for damages, resulting from a negligently performed operation on the mother). *See* FOETUS.

qui prior est tempore potior est jure. He who is before in time is the better in right (i.e., priority in time gives preference in law). See L.P.A. 1925, s 137; *Dearle* v *Hall* (1828) 3 Russ 1; *Barclays Bank* v *Bird* [1954] Ch 274.

qui sentit commodum sentire debet et onus; et e contra. He who enjoys the benefit should bear the burden; and vice versa.

quit, notice to. *See* NOTICE TO QUIT.

quit rent. Fixed rent paid by a copyholder to his lord in discharge of his obligation to perform agricultural services. See L.P.A. 1925, s 121. *See* COPYHOLD.

quorum. Of whom. Referred formerly to the commission issued to justices of the peace (q.v.). Now used to indicate the specified minimum number of members of a body, in the absence of which it cannot formally meet or act legally. See, e.g., Cos.A. 1985, s 370(4), Table A, art 40.

quota-hopping. An activity which arises under EU Common Fisheries Policy which apportions the North Sea fish stocks, when a foreign fishing vessel obtains a listing on another member state's register of vessels, thereby obtaining the right to fish under that state's allocated quota. See *R* v *Secretary of State for Transport ex p Factortame (No. 3)* [1991] 2 Lloyd's Rep 648.

quotation. 1. Term used in C.C.A. 1974, ss 152, 189(1), to refer to a document by which a person who carries on a consumer credit or hire business or business of credit brokerage or debt-adjusting gives prospective customers information about terms on which he is prepared to do business. 2. Amount of money suggested as a price. See *Scancarriers* v *Aotearoa International* (1985) 135 NLJ 799 (difference between quotation and contractual offer). 3. Listing of a share price on a stock exchange (q.v.).

quoted company. *See* COMPANY, QUOTED.

R

R. Abbreviation for *Rex* (King) or *Regina* (Queen), as in *R* v *Smith*.

racial. Pertaining to mankind's ethnic stocks. '"Racial" is not a term of art, either legal or, I surmise, scientific. I apprehend that anthropologists would dispute how far the word "race" is biologically at all relevant to the species amusingly called *homo sapiens*': *per* Lord Simon in *Ealing LBC* v *Race Relations Board* [1972] AC 342. 'Within the human race there are very few, if any, distinctions which we scientifically recognise as racial': *per* Lord Fraser in *Mandla* v *Lee* [1983] 2 AC 548. *See* ETHNIC.

racial discrimination. *See* DISCRIMINA-TION, RACIAL.

racial discrimination, aiding. In an allegation of one person 'aiding' another to commit unlawful racial discrimination under Race Relations Act 1976, s 33(1), it is immaterial which of them has instigated the relationship of collaboration: *Anyanwu* v *South Bank Student Union* (2001) 151 NLJ 501. *Per* Lord Bingham: 'Aids' in s 33(1) is a familiar word in every-day use, bearing no special meaning in that context. One person aids another whether his help is substantial and productive or whether it was not, provided that the help was not so insignificant as to be negligible. See also *Hallam* v *Avery* (2001) *The Times*, 27 March.

Racial Equality, Commission for. Body of eight to 15 individuals, set up under the Race Relations Act 1976, s 43(1), to work towards the elimination of discrimination; to promote equality of opportunity and good relations between racial groups; to review the working of the 1976 Act. It is empowered to issue non-discrimination notices (q.v.) and apply for injunctions (q.v.) to restrain persistent discrimination.

racial group. 'A group of persons defined by reference to colour, race, nationality or ethnic or national origins, and references to a person's racial group refer to any racial group within which he falls': Race Relations Act 1976, s 3(1). See *Mandla* v *Lee* [1983] 2 AC 548; *Gwynned CC* v *Jones* [1986] ICR 833. *See* ETHNIC.

racial hatred. Hatred against a group of persons in Great Britain defined by reference to colour, race, nationality (including citizenship) or ethnic (q.v.) or national origins: P.O.A. 1986, s 17.

racial hatred, offences relating to. Under P.O.A. 1986, Part III, offences may be committed where a person intends to stir up racial hatred or, having regard to all the circumstances, racial hatred is likely to be stirred up. The offences include the use of words or behaviour or display of written material of a threatening, abusive or insulting nature (s 18), publishing or distributing written material of this nature (s 19), having in one's possession racially inflammatory material (s 23). See Broadcasting Act 1990, s 164; Protection from Harassment Act 1997; *Jones* v *Tower Boot Co* [1997] 2 All ER 406.

racialist chanting. The repeated uttering of any words or sounds in concert with one or more others, consisting of or including matter which is threatening, abusive or insulting to a person by reason of his colour, race, nationality or ethnic or national origins. It is an offence to engage or take part in chanting of this nature at a designated football match: Football (Offences) Act 1991, s 3, as amended by Football (Offences and

Disorder) Act 1999, s 9. The chanting of the word 'Paki' at a football match was racialist and, hence, constituted a criminal offence within Football (Offences) Act 1991, s 3: *DPP* v *Stoke on Trent Magistrates Court* [2003] EWHC 1593 (Admin). *See* FOOTBALL MATCHES, OFFENCES BY SPECTATORS.

racially-aggravated offence. Under C.D.A. 1998, s 28, an offence is racially aggravated if at the time of committing the offence, or immediately before or after doing so, the offender demonstrates towards the victim of the offence hostility based on the victim's membership (or presumed membership) of a racial group; or the offence is motivated wholly or partly by hostility towards members of a racial group based on their membership of that group. 'Membership' in relation to a racial group includes association with that group. 'Presumed' means presumed by the offender. 'Racial group' means a group of persons defined by reference to race, colour, nationality (including citizenship) or ethnic or national origins. For increase in sentences for racial aggravation, see s 82, and P.C.C.(S.)A. 2000, s 153; *R* v *Saunders* (2000) *The Times*, 28 January.

racial segregation. 'Segregating a person from other persons on racial grounds is treating him less favourably than they are treated': Race Relations Act 1976, s 1(2).

rack rent. 1. A rent (q.v.) which is not less than two-thirds of the rent at which the premises might reasonably be expected to be let from year to year, free from all usual tenant's rates and taxes and deducting therefrom the probable average annual cost of repairs, insurance and other expenses necessary to maintain the premises in a state to command such rent: Building Act 1984, s 126. See *Newman* v *Dorrington Developments* [1975] 1 WLR 1642. 2. A rent raised to the highest level obtainable. See *Ashworth Frazer Ltd* v *Gloucester CC* [1997] EGCS 7.

radar trap. Electronic devices used by police to measure speed of a motor vehicle; must be of a type approved by Secretary of State. See Road Traffic Offenders Act 1988, s 20; Road Traffic Act 1991, s 23; SI 92/1209. *See* SPEEDING OFFENCE.

radioactive material. Any material having a specific activity in excess of 70 kilobecquerels per kilogram, or such lesser specific activity as may be specified by order of the Secretary of State: Radioactive Material (Road Transport) Act 1991, s 1(1). See Radioactive Substances Act 1993; *R* v *Environment Agency* [2001] *The Times*, 1 May.

railway. A system of transport employing parallel rails which provide support and guidance for vehicles carried on flanged wheels, and form a track which either is of a gauge of at least 350 millimetres or crosses a carriageway (whether or not on the same level), and is not a tramway: Transport and Works Act 1992, s 67. See Railways Act 1993; G.L.A.A. 1999, s 207.

Ramsar sites. Wetlands in UK designated under Ramsar Convention 1971, art 2, para 1, as of international importance. Their designation must be reported to English Nature (q.v.), Environment Agency, and internal drainage boards: Wildlife and Countryside Act 1981, s 37A, inserted by C.R.W.A. 2000, s 77.

ransom. Price paid for release from captivity. See *R* v *Pitts* (1986) 8 Cr App R (S) 84.

rape. Under S.O.A. 1956, s 1(1), (2), as substituted by C.J.P.O.A. 1994, s 142: it is an offence for a man to rape a woman or another man; a man commits rape if he has sexual intercourse (whether vaginal or anal) with a person who at the time of the intercourse does not consent to it, and at the time he knows that the person does not consent to the intercourse or is reckless as to whether that person consents to it. See *R* v *Flitter* (2001) *The Times*, 13 February. Rape is an offence of basic intent, and is a 'serious arrestable offence' under P.&C.E.A. 1984, Sch 5. Rape is also committed by a man who induces a married woman to have sexual intercourse with him by impersonating her husband: S.O.A. 1956, s 1(3), as substituted by C.J.P.O.A. 1994, s 142. For rape of sleeping woman, see *R* v *Sellars* [1998] 1 Cr App R (S) 117. For anal rape of unconscious woman, see *R* v *B (Rape)* [1999] 1 Cr App R (S) 232.

rape, acquaintance, and relationship. CA in *R* v *Millberry* (2002) *The Times*, 11 December, approved, in general, the statement of the Sentencing Advisory Panel: 'We use the term "relationship rape" to include both marital rape and cases where the offender and victim ... were or had been partners in a consensual sexual relationship at the time of the offence. We use the term "acquaintance rape" in preference to "date rape" because it covers a wider range of situations, and also because the latter is sometimes taken as belittling the seriousness of the offence.'

rape, anonymity in cases of. A complainant is given anonymity from the time of the complaint: C.J.A. 1988, s 158(2). Under s 158(5), anonymity given to defendant by S.O. (Amendment) A. 1976, s 6, is removed. S.O. (Amendment) A. 1992 extends statutory anonymity to sexual offences other than rape. See *Brown* v *DPP* (1998) 162 JP 333; Y.J.C.E.A. 1999, Sch 2, para 6.

rape, attempted. On a charge of attempted rape, it is not incumbent on the prosecution, as a matter of law, to prove that the defendant, with the requisite intent, had physically attempted penetration. It suffices that there is evidence from which the intent can be inferred, and there are proved acts which a jury could properly infer were more than merely preparatory to the commission of the offence. See *A-G's Reference (No. 1 of 1992)* [1993] 1 WLR 274; *R* v *Khan* [1990] 1 WLR 813.

rape, consent and. 'Consent' in rape covers states of mind ranging from actual desire to reluctant acquiescence; it is no longer necessary in proving rape to establish that intercourse took place as a result of fear, fraud or force, but merely that it occurred without the woman's consent: *R* v *Olugboja* [1982] QB 320. See *R* v *Linekar* [1995] QB 250; *A-G's*

Reference (No. 7 of 1989) (1990) 12 Cr App R (S) 1; *R* v *Adkins* [2000] 2 All ER 185.

rape offence. 'Rape, attempted rape, aiding, abetting, counselling and procuring rape or attempted rape, and incitement to rape': S.O. (Amendment) A. 1976, s 7(2). The Act imposes reporting restrictions in such cases: See *R* v *C* (1992) *The Times*, 11 March.

rape, retrospective conviction for. CA held in *R* v *Crooks* (2004) *The Times*, 25 March, that it might be proper to convict a husband of the rape of his wife even though the event in question occurred before the fiction of the wife's deemed consent was ended following the decision of CA in *R* v *R* [1992] 1 AC 599.

rape, sentencing guidelines. CA held in *R* v *Millberry* (2002) *The Times*, 11 December, that the gravity of a rape depended very much in relation to sentencing on the circumstances of a particular case, reflecting degree of harm to victim, level of offender's culpability, level of risk to society represented by offender.

rape within marriage. 'The supposed marital exemption in rape (see Hale 1 PC 627) forms no part of the law of England': *per* Lord Keith in *R* v *R* [1991] 3 WLR 767. See *R* v *C* (1993) 14 Cr App R (S) 642; *R* v *W* [1998] 1 Cr App R (S) 375.

rashness. The mental state of one who 'thinks of the probable mischief; but in consequence of a missupposition begotten by insufficient advertence, he assumes that a mischief will not ensue in the given instance': Austin, *Lectures on Jurisprudence* (1861).

rates. Local taxes paid by the occupiers of lands, houses, etc., so as to help to meet the cost of local services. Replaced by 'community charge' (q.v.) under Local Government Finance Act 1988. *See* COUNCIL TAX.

ratification. Confirmation; approval. In the case of ratification of a contract made by an agent (q.v.), the contract must be made on behalf of the principal; the principal must be competent at the time of the contract; there should have been an act capable of ratification. See *Firth* v *Staines* [1897] 2 QB 70. *See* CONTRACT.

rating valuation. In valuing a non-domestic property for rating, there is a fundamental assumption that it is in a reasonable state of repair except where disrepair is so extensive that a reasonable landlord would consider repairs uneconomic: Local Government Finance Act 1988, Sch 6, amended by Rating Valuation Act 1999, s 1.

ratio decidendi. The reason for a judicial decision. Usually a statement of law applied to the problems of a particular case. In essence, the principle upon which a case is decided. (Goodhart suggests that this principle is to be found by taking account of the facts treated by the judge as material, and his decision as based on them: (1930) 40 Yale LJ 161.)

rave. A gathering on land in the open air of 100 or more persons (whether or not trespassers) at which amplified music is played during the night and is such as, by reason of its loudness, duration and the time at which it is played, is likely to cause serious distress to inhabitants of the locality: C.J.P.O.A. 1994, s 63(1). See *R* v *Shorrock* [1993] CLY 3014. The police are empowered to give directions for persons to leave the land on which such a gathering is held: s 63(2).

re. In the matter of.

readings. The stages through which a Parliamentary Bill (q.v.) must pass before it becomes law.

real. 1. Relating to things (*res*), as distinct from persons. 2. Relating to land, and, specifically, freehold interests, as in 'real action'.

real action. *See* ACTIONS, REAL AND PERSONAL.

real estate. 'Chattels real, and land in possession, remainder, or reversion (qq.v.) and every interest in or over land to which a deceased person was entitled at the time of his death; and real estate held on trust (including settled land (q.v.)) or by way of mortgage or security, but not money to arise under a trust for sale of land, nor money secured or charged on land': A.E.A. 1925, s 3(1).

A gift of 'real estate' under a will does not include a leasehold, except where the testator had no freehold: *Re Holt* [1921] 2 Ch 17.

real evidence. *See* EVIDENCE, REAL.

real property. Property which could be recovered in a real action, i.e., interests in land, more specifically, freehold interests (as compared with 'personal property' (q.v.)).

real security. A security charged on land, See Tr.A. 1925, s 5. *See* TRUST.

realty. Generally, freehold interest in land.

reasonable contemplation test. Principle relating to damages awarded for breach of contract (q.v.). 'The damages . . . should be such as may fairly and reasonably be considered either arising naturally, i.e., according to the usual course of things, from such breach of contract itself, or such as may reasonably be supposed to have been in the contemplation of both parties at the time they made the contract as the probable result of the breach': *Hadley* v *Baxendale* (1854) 9 Exch 341. It is a test of remoteness, not of quantification: *Re National Coffee Palace Co* (1883) 24 Ch D 367.

reasonable doubt. 'That degree of doubt which would prevent a reasonable and just man from coming to a conclusion': *Bater* v *Bater* [1951] P 35. 'It is far better, instead of using the words "reasonable doubt" and then trying to say what is a reasonable doubt, to say to a jury: "You must not convict unless you are satisfied by the evidence given by the prosecution that the offence has been committed"': *R* v *Summers* [1952] 1 TLR 1164. 'Jurymen themselves set the standard of what is reasonable in the circumstances . . . A reasonable doubt which a jury may entertain is not to be confined to a "rational doubt" or a "doubt founded on reason"': *per* Barwick CJ in *Green* v *R* (1971) 126 CLR 28.

reasonable financial provision. *See* FINANCIAL PROVISION, REASONABLE.

reasonable force. The degree of force reasonably necessary, e.g., to effect an arrest, considering all the circumstances.

'A person may use such force as is reasonable in the circumstances in the prevention of crime, or in effecting or assisting in the lawful arrest of offenders or suspected' offenders or of persons unlawfully at large': C.L.A. 1967, s 3. See P.&C.E.A. 1984, s 117; *R* v *Barrett* (1981) 72 Cr App R 212 (belief in right to use force); *Beckford* v *R* [1988] AC 130 (right to pre-emptive use of force to confront likely attack); *R* v *Clegg* [1995] 1 AC 402; *O'Loughlin* v *Chief Constable of Essex* [1998] 1 WLR 374. *See* SELF-DEFENCE.

reasonable man. 'The fair and reasonable man who represents after all no more than the anthropomorphic conception of justice . . .': *Davis Contractors Ltd* v *Fareham UDC* [1956] AC 696. 'It is left . . . to the judge to decide what, in the circumstances of the particular case, the reasonable man would have in contemplation, and what, accordingly, the party sought to be made liable ought to have foreseen . . . The standard of foresight of the reasonable man . . . eliminates the personal equation and is independent of the idiosyncrasies of the particular person whose conduct is in question': *Glasgow Corporation* v *Muir* [1943] AC 448.

reasonable man test in provocation. *See* PROVOCATION.

reasonable time. In relation to the delivery of goods, is a question of fact: S.G.A. 1979, s 29(5). Where a contract does not refer specifically to time, there is an implication that the promised act will be carried out within a reasonable time: *Ford* v *Cotesworth* (1868) LR 4 QB 132. See *Seaconsar Far East Ltd* v *Bank Marcazi* [1997] 2 Lloyd's Rep 89 (consideration of 'expeditious means'). *See* TIME AS ESSENCE OF A CONTRACT.

reasonably practicable. Term which, when used in relation to employers' duties concerning safety at work 'is a narrower term than "physically possible" and implies that a computation must be made in which the quantum of risk is put in one scale and the sacrifice involved in measures necessary to avert the risk, in money, time, trouble, is placed in the other, and that, if it be shown that there is gross disproportion between them – the risk being insignificant in relation to the sacrifice – defendants discharge the onus upon them': *per* Asquith LJ in *Edwards* v *NCB* [1949] 1 All ER 4743. For 'practicable' (interpreted in the light of current knowledge and invention), see *Schvalb* v *Fass* (1946) 175 LT 345.

reasons, judge's duty to give. In *English* v *Emery Reimbold Ltd* (2002) *The Times*, 10 May, CA held that it was the duty of a judge to give a judgment that explained clearly why an order had been made. Such a judgment had to enable the parties and an appellate court to understand the reasons for the decision, and it should identify the vital issues and the manner of their resolution.

rebate. Refund; credit; discount. See C.C.A. 1974 s 94 (for an example of 'statutory rebate').

rebellion. Organised resistance to the ruler or government with the intention of supplanting them or at least depriving them of authority over part of their territory: *Spinney's Ltd* v *Royal Insurance Co Ltd* [1980] 1 Lloyd's Rep 406. *See* INSURRECTION.

rebus sic stantibus. Things standing in this manner. Doctrine of international law, which assumes as a condition of all treaties that they will cease to be obligatory if there is a substantial change of the facts on which they were founded.

rebut. To oppose; contradict; disprove.

recall of witness. *See* WITNESS, RECALL OF.

recaption. The lawful retaking of one's chattels from another who has wrongfully taken and detained them. See, e.g., *Blades* v *Higgs* (1861) 10 CB NS 713.

receipt. Written acknowledgment of goods or money received. It is prima facie evidence of payment of a debt (but other evidence is also acceptable: see Cheques Act 1957, s 3): *Wilson* v *Keating* (1859) 27 Beav 121.

receiver. 1. One appointed to enable a judgment creditor to obtain payment of a debt. May be known as 'receiver by way of equitable execution'. See L.P.A. 1925, s 101(1) (appointment relating to mortgage money: see *Shamji* v *Johnson Matthey* [1991] BCLC 36); S.C.A. 1981, s 37; A.J.A. 1977, s 7; CPR, Sch 1; O 30; O 51; *Bond Holdings Ltd* v *National Australia Bank Ltd* [1990] 1 ABLR 445; *Triffit Nurseries* v *Salads Ltd* (2000) *The Times*, 26 April. For default by receiver, see CPR, Sch 1; O 30, r 7. 2. One appointed to preserve property which is endangered, for the benefit of those entitled to it. 3. One who received stolen property. See now, Th.A 1968, s 22; *R* v *Gingell* [2000] 1 Cr App R 88.

receiver, administrative. A receiver or manager of a company's property appointed by or on behalf of holders of the company's debentures (q.v.) secured by a charge (q.v.) which, as created, was a floating charge, or by such a charge and one or more other securities: Ins.A. 1986, s 29(2). For details of the statement of affairs to be submitted to him, see s 47. For receivership costs, see *Mirror Group* v *Maxwell* [1998] 1 BCLC 638.

receiving. The former offence of receiving stolen goods knowing them to have been stolen: Larceny Act 1916, s 33 (now repealed). Now part of the offence of 'handling' (q.v.). See *R* v *Smythe* (1980) 72 Cr App R 8.

recent possession. 'Convenient but grammatically incorrect expression to describe the possession by someone of things which had recently been stolen': *R* v *Hobbs and Geoffrey-Smith* (1982) 132 NLJ 435. It may raise a presumption of theft or handling (q.v.). See *R* v *Wanganeen* (1989) 50 SASR 433; *R* v *Powers* [1990] Cr LR 586; *R* v *Lloyd* [1992] Crim LR 361.

reciprocity. Mutuality in relationships or actions. Refers, in international law, to relationship between two states, each of which gives the other, and its inhabitants, similar privileges. For reciprocal enforcement of judgments, see Foreign Judgments (Reciprocal Enforcement) Act 1933; CPR, Sch 1; O 71.

recitals. Part of a deed of conveyance of sale indicating the effect and purpose of that deed and stating the history of the property to be conveyed. They are not essential to the deed's validity. Recitals of particular facts may operate as an estoppel (q.v.): *Bensley* v *Burdon* (1830) 8 LJ Ch 85. See L.P.A. 1925, s 45(6).

recklessness. The state of deliberately or negligently disregarding the consequences of one's actions. Not defined by statute. Law Commission (Report No. 89, 1978) suggested two standard tests of recklessness: as to *result* ('Did the person whose conduct is in issue foresee that his conduct might produce the result, and, if so, was it unreasonable for him to take the risk of producing it?'); as to *circumstances* ('Did the person whose conduct is in issue realise that the circumstances might exist and, if so, was it unreasonable for him to take the risk of their existence?').

recklessness, categories of. Two categories of recklessness in criminal law may be discerned. 1. 'Cunningham-type' (*R* v *Cunningham* [1957] 2 QB 396): defendant knows of an unreasonable risk, is willing to take it and takes it deliberately. 2. 'Caldwell-type' (*R* v *Caldwell* [1982] AC 341), which does not apply to any crimes of specific or ulterior intent: defendant performs an act which creates an obvious risk, and, when performing the act, he has either given no thought to the possibility of such a risk arising or he recognised that some risk existed, but went on to take it. The HL held in *R* v *G* [2003] UKHL 50, that *R* v *Caldwell* [1982] AC 341 was a misinterpretation of the law and it was necessary to depart from the decision. ('Recklessness' was under discussion within the context of the Criminal Damage Act 1971.) Recklessness should be taken as referring to one who acts when he is aware that a risk exists, or will exist, and, in the circumstances of which he is aware, that it is unreasonable for him to take that risk. (There is no such offence as 'murder by recklessness': *Leung Kam Kwok* v *R* (1985) 81 Cr App R 83.) See, e.g., *R* v *Lawrence* [1982] AC 510; *R* v *Coles* [1995] Crim LR 820; *R* v *Paine* (1998) 1 Cr App R 36; *R* v *M*

(*A Juvenile*) (1999) *The Times*, 3 December. *See* INTENTION.

recognizance. Formal undertaking to pay the Crown a specified sum if an accused person fails to surrender to custody. See M.C.A. 1980, s 120 (forfeiture of recognizances); C.D.A. 1998, s 55; P.C.C.(S.)A. 2000, s 139 (powers of Crown Court concerning recognizances), amended by C.J.C.S.A. 2000, Sch 7, para 139. See *R* v *Reading Crown Court, ex p Bello* [1992] 3 All ER 353. *See* ESTREAT.

Recommendations of EU. *See* COMMUNITY LEGISLATION, FORMS OF.

reconciliation. The act of harmonising differences and settling disputes. Thus, under Mat.C.A. 1973, s 6, provision is made by rules of court to require a solicitor acting for a petitioner for divorce to certify whether he has discussed with the petitioner the possibility of a reconciliation. Proceedings may be adjourned to enable attempts at reconciliation. A period of six months, or periods of up to a total of six months, during which spouses may resume cohabitation without loss of the chance of subsequent divorce, are known as 'reconciliation periods'. Provisions of s 6 apply also to judicial separation. See also Domestic Proceedings and Magistrates' Courts Act 1978, s 28; C.J.C.S.A. 2000, Sch 7, para 57; Matrimonial Causes Rules 1977, r 12(3). *See* CONCILIATION.

reconstruction of company. The transference of a company's assets to a new company under an arrangement whereby the shareholders of the old company receive shares, or similar interests, in the new company. It can be effected by, e.g., a scheme of arrangement under Cos.A. 1985, ss 425–427. See Ins.A. 1986, ss 1–7. *See* COMPANY.

reconveyance. Procedure whereby, before 1 January 1926, the mortgagee had to revest the legal estate in the mortgagor on redemption. A receipt on the mortgage deed now suffices to extinguish the mortgage. See L.P.A. 1925, s 115. *See* MORTGAGE.

record. 1. To make a written account. 2. An authentic account, usually in documentary form, of some event(s). 3. A memorial of an action heard in a court of record (q.v.). See P.&C.E.A. 1984, s 68; *H* v *Schering Chemicals* [1983] 1 WLR 143. For computerised 'records of opinion', see Civil Evidence Act 1968, s 5. For 'personal records' (i.e., documentary and other records concerning an individual, living or dead, who can be identified from them), see P. & C.E.A. 1984, s 12. See F.I.A. 2000, s 32. *See* DATA, PERSONAL.

record, contract of. *See* CONTRACT OF RECORD.

record, court of. *See* COURT OF RECORD.

Recorders. Judges appointed by the Queen on the recommendation of the Lord Chancellor to try criminal cases in the Crown Court (q.v.).

recording. 1. The preservation of a sound or visual performance for future reproduction. See Copyright, Designs and Patents Act 1988, s 180 (recording rights of performers): *Bassey* v *Icon Entertainment plc* [1995] EMLR 596. 2. At any hearing in the High Court or a county court, the judgment (and any summing up) will be recorded unless the judge directs otherwise. Oral evidence will normally be recorded: PD 39, para 6.1. The use of unofficial recording equipment without permission constitutes a contempt of court: para 6.2.

records admissible in civil cases. Records, i.e., documents (q.v.) containing information, admissible in evidence in civil proceedings. For proof of statements contained in documents admissible in evidence in civil cases, see Civil Evidence Act 1995, s 8. *See* EVIDENCE.

records admissible in criminal cases. Records in criminal proceedings which are admissible in evidence, i.e., when the record was compiled by a person acting under a duty from information supplied by a person (whether acting under a duty or not) who had, or might reasonably be supposed to have had, personal knowledge of the matters dealt with in that information and the supplier of information (a) is dead or is mentally or physically unfit to act as a witness; (b) is abroad and cannot reasonably be called as a witness; or (c) cannot reasonably be expected to have any active recollection of the matters in question. Further requirements include taking all reasonable steps to identify the supplier of information and to locate him. Comparable requirements apply to the use of computer records. See P.&C.E.A. 1984, s 68; *R v Canale* [1990] 2 All ER 187. *See* EVIDENCE.

recovery. 1. 'A claim for the recovery of land – 'the modern equivalent of the old action of ejectment': *Bramwell v Bramwell* [1942] 1 KB 370. The claim must be brought within 12 years of accrual of the cause of action: Lim.A. 1980, s 15. A claim for the recovery of land must be brought only in the court for the district in which the land is situated: CPR, Sch 2; CCR, O 4, r 3. See also CPR, Sch 2; CCR, O 24, r 1 (summary proceedings for the recovery of land). See also C.J.P.O.A. 1994, ss 75, 76, enforcing interim possession orders by criminal sanctions. 2. A collusive action, known as common recovery (q.v.).

recovery of premises, obstruction of. Resistance to, or intentional obstruction of, court officers executing process for possession against unauthorised occupiers is an offence under C.L.A. 1977, s 10(1). For defences, see s 10(3).

recovery order. Order issued by the court under Ch.A. 1989, s 50(1), where there is reason to believe that a child has been taken away unlawfully, or has run away, or is missing. The order operates as a direction to any person who is in a position to do so to produce the child on request by any authorised person and authorises the removal of the child by any authorised person. See *Re R (Recovery Orders)* [1998] 2 FLR 401.

recreational charity. A trust for the public benefit which provides facilities for recreation or other leisure time occupation in the interests of social welfare. See Recreational Charities Act 1958; *Guild v IRC* [1992] 2 AC 310. *See* CHARITY; TRUST.

rectification. Where a written document does not accurately express an agreement

between parties, as the result of some common mistake, equity has the power to rectify that mistake: *Craddock Bros v Hunt* [1923] 2 Ch 136; *Pappadakis v Pappadakis* (2000) *The Times*, 19 January. Rectification is not of the agreement itself, merely of the instrument recording the agreement. See *Freer v Unwins Ltd* [1976] Ch 288; *Mace v Rutland House Ltd* (2000) *The Times*, 11 January. For rectification of land register, see L.R.A. 1925, s 82(1) and L.R.A. 1997, s 2 (power to award indemnity where rectification is obtained, but loss is suffered); *Norwich and Peterborough BS v Steed* [1993] 1 All ER 330; *Grains & Fourrages SA v Huyton* [1997] 1 Lloyd's Rep 628.

rectification of mistake in magistrates' court. *See* MISTAKE, RECTIFICATION IN MAGISTRATES' COURT OF.

rectification of will. If the court is satisfied that a will is so expressed that it fails to carry out the testator's intentions, in consequence of a clerical error or of a failure to understand his instructions, it may order rectification so as to carry out those intentions: A.J.A. 1982, s 20(1). A copy of every order made for the rectification of a will must be sent for filing to the principal registry of the Family Division: PD 49, para 17.2. See, e.g., *Wordingham v Royal Exchange Trust Ltd* [1992] 2 WLR 496; *Re Chittock's Estate* (2000) *The Times*, 5 April. *See* AMBIGUITY.

recusal. Disqualifying oneself as a judge in a particular hearing. See, e.g., *Weatherill v Lloyds TSB* [2000] CPLR 584; *DG of Fair Trading v Proprietary Association of Great Britain* (2001) *The Times*, 2 February.

reddendum. That which is to be paid. Clause in lease (q.v.) stating the amount of rent and when it is payable. See *King v King* (1980) 255 EG 1205.

redeemable preference shares. Preference shares (q.v.), first introduced by Cos.A. 1929, that can be redeemed out of profits or out of a fresh issue of shares. See Table A, art 3. Shares cannot be redeemed in this manner unless fully paid: Cos.A. 1985, Part V, chap VII, ss 159, 160; Cos.A. 1989, s 133.

redeem up, foreclose down. Rule relating to redemption of mortgage (q.v.). Example: M has mortgaged property to L1, L2, L3, L4, L5, in that order of priority. L4 wishes to redeem L2. L4 must redeem those mortgages between him and the prior mortgage he wishes to redeem and he must also foreclose any subsequent mortgagees and the mortgagor. L3, L5 and M must be made parties to the action. L3 must be redeemed. L5 and M must be foreclosed and allowed an opportunity to pay off the prior mortgage. *See* MORTGAGE.

redemption. The recovery (i.e., repossession) of mortgaged property on payment of the debt. Rights to redeem are: *legal* (right at law to redeem on the exact day fixed by the mortgage); *equitable* (right to redeem after that date has passed). See *Gomba Holdings* v *Minories Finance* [1993] Ch 171. *See* EQUITY OF REDEMPTION; MORTGAGE.

redemption period for a pawn. The longest of the following periods: six months after the pawn was taken; any period fixed by the parties for duration of credit secured by the pledge (q.v.) or for duration of redemption period: C.C.A. 1974, s 116. *See* PAWN.

redress. *See* RELIEF; REMEDY.

reduction into possession. Conversion of a chose in action (q.v.) into a chose in possession (q.v.). Example: a debt which is paid.

reduction of capital. A company limited by shares may, if its articles permit, reduce its capital by means of a special resolution (q.v.) to be confirmed by the court: Cos.A. 1985, s 135. It may be effected for reasons such as: loss of capital by wastage of assets and the company wishes to write off the loss; share capital issued may not be fully paid and the company has the capital it needs. See Cos.A. 1985, Part V, chap IV, s 171; *Practice Direction* [1997] 1 WLR 1. *See* COMPANY.

redundancy. 1. Irrelevant matter in statement of case (q.v.). 2. Dismissal of an employee 'by reasons of redundancy' arises where the dismissal is wholly or mainly attributable to the fact: that the employer has ceased or intends to cease to carry on the business for the purposes of which the employee was employed, or to carry on that business in the place where the employee had been employed; or the fact that the requirements of that business for employees to carry out work of a particular kind, or for employees to carry out work of a particular kind in the place where the employee was employed, have ceased or diminished or are expected to cease or diminish: E.R.A. 1996, s 139(1). See *Warner* v *Adnet Ltd* [1998] IRLR 394.

redundancy and retirement. CA held in *AGCO Ltd* v *Massey Ferguson Ltd* (2003) *The Times*, 14 July, that, in relation to a company pension scheme under which a pension could be paid before an employee's normal retirement date, where retirement followed the employer's request, the voluntary acceptance of dismissal for purposes of redundancy constituted a retirement.

redundancy payments. The amount of a redundancy payment is calculated by: determining the period, ending with the relevant date, during which the employee has been continuously employed; reckoning backward from the end of that period the number of years of employment falling within that period; allowing the appropriate amount for each of those years of employment: E.R.A. 1996, s 162(1). For 'appropriate amount', see s 162(2). See *Digital Equipment Ltd* v *Clements* [1998] ICR 258; *Secretary of State for Trade and Industry* v *Lassman* [2000] IRLR 413.

re-engagement order. Order made by a tribunal, under E.R.A. 1996, s 115(1), whereby a former employee had to be re-engaged by the employer in employment comparable to that from which he was dismissed or other suitable employment.

re-entry. Right of entry (q.v.).

re-examination. Examination of a witness (q.v.) by counsel who called him. Usually limited to matters arising from cross-examination (q.v.) by opposing side. In general, leading questions may not be asked, and questions on new matter may not be asked save by leave of the judge. See *R v Reading Stipendiary Magistrate ex p Dyas* (2000) 164 JP 117.

referee. 1. One to whom a dispute is referred for an opinion. In the case of statements by a referee: 'If a man refers another upon any particular business to a third person, he is bound by what this third person says or does concerning it, as much as if that had been done or said by him': *Williams v Innes* (1804) 1 Camp 364. 2. One who provides a character reference for another.

referee, official. *See* OFFICIAL REFEREE.

reference. 1. Referring of a matter to an arbitrator (q.v.) for his decision. 2. Decision by an arbitrator or referee (q.v.). 3. An authority relied on in legal argument. 4. Declaration to a prospective employer concerning a person's character, work record, etc. See *Bartholomew v Hackney LBC* [1999] IRLR 246 (a former employer owes a duty of care to a former employee to provide a true, fair and accurate reference); *Chief Constable of W Yorks v Khan* (2000) *The Times*, 15 March (refusal to provide reference was evidence of victimisation).

reference, incorporation by. *See* INCORPORATION BY REFERENCE.

referendum. The submission to popular vote of a question or a proposed legislative measure. See the (repealed) Referendum Act 1975; Referendums (Scotland and Wales) Act 1997; Political Parties, Elections and Referendum Act 2000.

referential settlements. *See* SETTLEMENTS, REFERENTIAL.

refer to drawer. Phrase used by a bank in dishonouring a customer's cheque. Held, in *Jayson v Midland Bank* [1968] 1 Lloyd's Rep 409, to be libellous if used incorrectly. See (for interpretation of a similar phrase 'present again') *Baker v Australia and New Zealand Bank* [1958] NZLR 907.

refreshing memory. Permission granted to a witness under examination to refer to a document so as to recall some matter, e.g., because of a lapse of time since

events took place. The document must generally have been made by the witness, or under his supervision, or checked by him, substantially at the time of occurrence of the event in question and must be handed to the opposite party or jury, for inspection, on request. A witness may refresh his memory from a note written by some other person, as long as he adopts it as his own, particularly if he does so by signing it: *Groves v Redbart* [1975] RTR 268. See also Civil Evidence Act 1968, s 3(2); Civil Evidence Act 1995, s 6(4); *R v Da Silva* [1990] 1 WLR 31; *R v Ribble MC ex p Cochrane* [1996] 2 Cr App R 544.

refugee. One who 'owing to well-founded fear of being persecuted for reasons of race, religion, nationality, membership of a particular social group or political opinion, is outside the country of his nationality and is unable or, owing to such fear, is unwilling to avail himself of the protection of that country; or who, not having a nationality and being outside the country of his former habitual residence as a result of such events, is unable or, owing to such fear, is unwilling to return to it': Convention on the Status of Refugees 1951, art 1. See *R v Home Secretary ex p Sivakumaran* [1988] 2 WLR 92 (the test of a 'well-founded fear' is objective); *Islam v Secretary of State for Home Department* (1999) 149 NLJ 528 (meaning of 'membership of a particular social group'); *R v Secretary of State for Home Department, ex p Yurekli* [1990] Imm AR 334 (harassment may not be sufficient to amount to persecution); *R v Secretary of State for Home Department ex p Adan* (2000) *The Times*, 20 December. See Immigration Rules 1990, r 75. *See* PERSECUTION; POLITICAL ASYLUM.

refugees, removal of. CA held in *R (Ullah) v Immigration Appeal Tribunal* (2002) *The Times*, 18 December that the Home Secretary's decision to return an alien to a country in which his religion was not respected, did not constitute an infringement of Human Rights Act 1998.

refusal, wilful. *See* WILFUL REFUSAL.

regent. One appointed by Act of Parliament to fulfil royal functions if the Sovereign is under 18 on accession, or incapacitated. See Regency Acts 1937 and 1953.

regional development agencies. Agencies set up under Regional Development Agencies Act 1998, s 1(a), so as to further the economic development and regeneration of an area, to promote employment, business efficiency, investment and competitiveness, to enhance the development and application of skills relevant to employment and to contribute to the achievement of suitable development in the UK: s 4(1). There are nine English regions: see Sch 1.

register at Land Registry. The register of title to land kept by the Chief Land Registrar at the Land Registry in London, and 22 District Registries (see SI 98/140), subdivided into *Property Register* (describing property and estate (q.v.) for which it is held); *Proprietorship Register* (stating name and address of proprietor class of title, e.g., absolute, qualified); *Charges Register* (containing notices of charges or incumbrances). See LRR 2002, r 2. *See* LAND REGISTRATION.

registered estate. *See* ESTATE, REGISTERED.

registered land. Land, title to which is registered under LRA 2002. *See* LAND REGISTRATION.

registered land, protection of mortgage of. LRA 2002, s 27(1) provides that 'if a disposition of a . . . registered charge is required to be completed by registration, it does not operate at law until the relevant registration requirements are met'. LRA 2002, s 27(2) provides that 'in the case of a registered estate, the following are the dispositions which are required to be completed by registration . . . (f.)) the grant of a legal charge'. Note also that under LRA, s 4(1)g the creation of a 'protected first legal mortgage' of an unregistered estate may itself trigger a requirement to register the estate charged and the mortgage or charge. *See* CAUTION; NOTICE, PROTECTION BY; MINOR INTERESTS; MORTGAGE.

registered office. A company's official address, which it must have at all times. It must be sent to the Registrar of Companies at the time the memorandum (q.v.) is submitted for registration: Cos.A. 1985, s 10(6). The Registrar must be notified of any change within 14 days: s 287. See Cos.A. 1989, s 136.

register of company charges. Every limited company must keep at its registered office a register of forms of security interest (fixed or floating) over property, other than an interest arising by operation of law: Cos.A. 1989, s 93. For details of register and delivery of particulars for registration, see ss 94–96. *See* CHARGE.

register of directors. *See* DIRECTORS, REGISTER OF.

register of interests. Register, kept under Cos.A. 1985, s 325, in which directors notify the company of interests in voting share capital. *See* INTEREST, DISCLOSURE OF.

register of interests of Members of Parliament. *See* INTEREST, DISCLOSURE OF.

register of members. A register, required under Cos.A. 1985, s 352, which must contain, e.g., names and addresses of members and shares held by them, together with the amount paid up on shares. This must be kept at the company's registered office and may be inspected by any member during business hours: ss 353, 356. For rectification, see s 359; *Keene* v *Martin* [1999] 2 BCLC 346.

register of political parties. Register maintained by Registrar of Companies, recording details of political parties in the UK, which is to be used in relation to elections for Parliament, European Parliament, Scottish Parliament, National Assembly for Wales, Northern Ireland Assembly, Local Government: Registration of Political Parties Act 1998, s 1(2). Applications for registration must include party's name, address of headquarters, names of leader and nominating officer: Sch 1. General access to register is allowed under s 11. See SI 98/2873.

registrar, county court. *See* JUDGES, DISTRICT.

registration of birth. *See* BIRTH, REGISTRATION OF.

registration of company. *See* COMPANY, REGISTRATION OF.

registration of death. *See* DEATH, REGISTRATION OF.

registration of land. *See* LAND REGISTRATION.

registration of marriage. *See* MARRIAGE, REGISTRATION OF.

registration of title. *See* LAND REGISTRATION.

registration, UK citizenship resulting from. *See* CITIZENSHIP, BRITISH, ACQUISITION BY REGISTRATION.

regularity, presumption of. *See* OMNIA PRAESUMUNTUR RITE ET SOLEMNITER ESSE ACTA.

regulated agreements. Agreements to which provisions of C.C.A. 1974 relate, i.e., consumer credit agreements; consumer hire agreements; credit token agreements (qq.v.): see s 189(1). The agreements must be in writing, must contain all express terms in legible form, must comply with appropriate regulations and be signed by the debtor personally and by the other parties. Failure to comply renders agreements 'improperly executed'. See *Sovereign Leasing Ltd v Ali* [1992] CCLR 79; *Dimond v Lovell* [2000] 2 WLR 1121; *Ketley v Gilbert* (2001) *The Times*, 17 January.

regulated position. It is an offence, under C.J.C.S.A. 2000, s 35, for an individual who is disqualified from working with children to knowingly apply for, offer to do, accept or do any work in a regulated position. Such positions, for purposes of the Act include, under s 36, a position in which the normal duties include (under s 36(1), (2)) work in an educational institution, children's home; position involving work on day care premises; position involving caring for children under 16 in the course of the children's employment.

regulated tenancy. A protected or statutory tenancy (qq.v.): Rent Act 1977, s 18(1), amended by H.A. 1980, Sch 26. Replaced by assured tenancy (q.v.).

Regulations of EU. *See* COMMUNITY LEGISLATION, FORMS OF.

rehabilitation. 1. Actions of the state or private institutions aimed at the reformation of an offender's character and behaviour. 2. 'A right to an opportunity to return to society with an improved chance of being a useful citizen and staying out of prison': Rotman, *Beyond Punishment* (1990). See Rehabilitation of Offenders Act 1974.

rehabilitation period. Periods of, e.g., five to ten years, depending on the sentence, running from conviction, during which a person may be 'rehabilitated' and his convictions considered as 'spent' under the Rehabilitation of Offenders Act 1974. There is no rehabilitation under the Act where the sentence is, e.g., life imprisonment. See Police Act 1977, s 133; C.D.A. 1998, Sch 8; C.J.C.S.A. 2000, s 38(1). *See* SPENT CONVICTIONS.

re-hearing. A second, or new, hearing of a case already adjudicated upon. Example: appeal to the Crown Court (q.v.) from conviction by a magistrates' court (q.v.), where there is a complete re-hearing and where fresh evidence may be introduced by either side without leave. See, e.g., *Griffith v Jenkins* [1992] 2 WLR 28. For re-hearing pursuant to M.C.A. 1980, s 142 (power of magistrates' court to reopen cases to rectify mistakes, etc.), see *R v Croydon Youth Court ex p DPP* [1997] 2 Cr App R 411; *R v Ealing Magistrates' Court ex p Sahota* (1998) 162 JP 73.

reinstatement. 1. Restoring of an employee to the position he occupied prior to dismissal. An order for reinstatement, stating that an employer shall treat the former employee in all respects as if he had not been dismissed may be made after hearing a complaint against unfair dismissal (q.v.) under E.R.A. 1996, s 114(1). 2. Replacement or repair of damaged property under insurance policy. See, e.g., Fires Prevention (Metropolis) Act 1774, s 83; L.P.A. 1925, ss 47, 108(2); Tr.A. 1925, s 20(4).

reinsurance. Agreement between the reinsured (known as the 'direct' or 'primary' insurer) and the reinsurer whereby the reinsured undertakes to cede, and the reinsurer undertakes to accept, a fixed share of risk. It takes the form of 'facultative reinsurance', i.e., reinsurance against liability on a stated policy, or 'treaty reinsurance', i.e., reinsurance against liabilities on policies in general. See *Baker* v *Black Sea Insurance Ltd* [1998] 1 WLR 974 (implied terms).

rejection of goods. Right of buyer, following breach of contract by seller, to repudiate contract of sale and refuse to accept the goods. See *Bernstein* v *Pamson Motors* [1987] 2 All ER 220; *Graanhandel* v *European Grain* [1989] 2 Lloyd's Rep 531; *Truk Ltd* v *Tokmakidis* [2000] 1 Lloyd's Rep 543. For loss of right, see S.G.A. 1987, s 11(4). For partial rejection, see Sale and Supply of Goods Act 1994, s 3, inserting S.G.A. 1979, s 35A(1): 'If the buyer has the right to reject the goods by reason of a breach on the part of the seller that affects some or all of them, but accepts some of the goods, including, where there are any goods unaffected by the breach, all such goods, he does not, by accepting them, lose his right to reject the rest.'

rejection of offer. An offer (q.v.) is rejected: if the offeree communicates his rejection to the offeror; if the offeree accepts subject to conditions; if the offeree makes a counter-offer. See, e.g., *Jordan* v *Newton* (1838) 4 M & W 155.

related company. *See* COMPANY, RELATED.

relation back. Principle whereby an act is referred to a prior date, from which time it is construed as being effective. Example: the rule that probate when granted relates back to the time of the testator's death: *Whitehead* v *Taylor* (1839) 10 A & E 210.

relations. Generally, the next of kin (q.v.). Those who would take under the intestacy laws: *Re Bridgen* [1938] Ch 205.

relationships, prohibited degrees of. Relationships within which a marriage celebrated after July 1971 is void: Mat.C.A. 1973, s 11(*a*)(i). They are: *for a man* – mother, daughter, grandmother, granddaughter, sister, aunt, niece, father's

or son's or grandfather's or grandson's wife, wife's mother or daughter or grandmother or granddaughter; *for a woman* – father, son, grandfather, grandson, brother, uncle, nephew, mother's or daughter's or grandmother's or granddaughter's husband, husband's father or son or grandfather or grandson. Marriage (Prohibited Degrees of Relationship) Act 1986 allows marriage between a man and a woman who is the daughter or granddaughter of a former spouse of his, if both parties are over 21 and the younger party has not, before attaining the age of 18, been a child of the family in relation to the other party.

relatives. Relations (q.v.); kinsmen. The term usually includes persons who are relatives by marriage or adoption and persons who would be relatives if some persons born illegitimate had been born legitimate: S.S.A. 1975, Sch 20. See also Adoption Act 1976, s 72(1); M.H.A. 1983, s 26; I.C.T.A. 1988, s 275. For 'dependent relatives', see 1988 Act, s 367(1).

relatives' identity, right to know. Adopted persons over 18 may be supplied by the Registrar General with names and addresses of relatives maintained on the Adopted Contact Register (which is not open to public inspection). 'Relative' means any person other than an adopted relative who is related to the adopted person by blood (including half-blood) or marriage. See Adoption Act 1976, s 51A, inserted by Ch.A. 1989, Sch 10, para 21; SI 99/672; *D* v *Registrar General* [1997] 1 FLR 715. *See* ADOPTION.

relator. A private person at whose suggestion an action is commenced by the Attorney-General (q.v.) (as in the case of a matter of public interest, such as a public nuisance). See *Gouriet* v *UPW* [1978] AC 435. For relator actions, see CPR, Sch 1; O 15, r 11. *See* ATTORNEY-GENERAL AND RELATOR ACTIONS.

release. 1. 'The giving or discharge of the right or action which any hath or claimeth against another, or his land': *Termes de la Ley*. For deed of release of tenancy, see *Burton* v *Camden*

LBC (2000) *The Times*, 23 February.
2. Abandonment of right to performance
of a contract. 3. A document which acts
as discharge of a claim. 4. Discharge
from custody.

**release, and claims of which releasor
was unaware.** Before it could be inferred that a party to a release agreement
intended to surrender rights and claims
of which he could not be aware when
he entered the agreement, clear language
to that effect would be required: *per*
Lord Bingham in *Bank of Credit and
Commerce* v *Ali* [2001] 2 WLR 725.
(Statement of Scott V-C: 'In my judgment there are no such things as rules of
equitable construction of documents',
was approved.)

release of prisoners, early. *See* PAROLE.

relevance. Known also as 'relevancy',
'logical relevancy'. Term used in the law
of evidence to refer to a connection or relationship between facts and events which
ordinarily tends to render one probable
from the very existence of the other. The
general rule of relevance in evidence is that
all facts which, though not in issue, may
be given as evidence so that the court is
enabled to reach a conclusion on facts in
issue, are relevant. When one fact logically
tends to prove a fact in issue it will be
generally admissible unless excluded by
some rule (exceptions include: hearsay
(q.v.); opinion; reputation of the accused;
conduct of the accused on other occasions).
(Relevance must be distinguished from
'admissibility'.) *See* ADMISSIBILITY OF
EVIDENCE; EVIDENCE.

relevant facts. *See* FACTS, RELEVANT.

relief. 1. Payment by a feudal tenant
who succeeded to land on the death of a
former tenant. 2. Remedial action of a
court. 2. Tax allowance. *See* REMEDY.

relief, financial. *See* FINANCIAL RELIEF.

relief, interim. *See* INTERIM RELIEF.

religion. 'The Court of Chancery makes
no distinction between one religion and
another, unless the tenets of a particular
sect inculcate doctrines adverse to the very
foundations of all religions': *Thornton* v
Howe (1862) 31 LJ Ch 767. 'As between
different religions the law stands neutral,

but it seems that any religion is at least
likely to be better than none': *Neville
Estates Ltd* v *Madden* [1962] Ch 832.
See *Re South Place Ethical Society* [1980]
1 WLR 1565; *Re Hetherington* [1989]
2 WLR 1094. For religious education in
schools, see School Standards and Framework Act 1998, s 69.

religion, advancement of. 'To advance
religion means to promote it, to spread its
message ever wider among mankind; to
take some positive steps to sustain and
increase religious belief; and these things
are done in a variety of ways which may
be comprehensively described as pastoral
and missionary': *United Grand Lodge* v
Holborn BC [1957] 1 WLR 1080.

religion, freedom of. 'The essence of
the concept of freedom of religion is the
right to entertain such religious beliefs
as a person chooses, the right to declare
religious beliefs openly and without fear
of hindrance or reprisal, and the right
to manifest belief by worship and practice, by teaching and dissemination': *per*
Dickson CJC in *Big M Drug Mart Ltd*
(1985) 18 DLR (4th) 321. See European
Convention on Human Rights 1950, art
9 (freedom of thought, conscience and
religion).

**religious law, and relevance of English
law.** CA held in *Kastner* v *Jason* (2004)
The Times, 21 December that where an
arbitration had been conducted under
substantive Jewish law, English law was
irrelevant for the purpose of discovering a remedy for which Jewish law had
no provision.

relocation, internal, principle of. *See*
ASYLUM, INTERNAL RELOCATION AND.

remainder. 'A residue of an estate in
land depending upon a particular estate
and created together with the same at
one time': Coke. Example: 'to X for life,
then to Y in fee simple' – X is entitled
to actual possession (his estate is the *particular estate*), Y's estate is a *remainder*,
and Y is the *remainderman*. A *vested
remainder* is one ready to come into possession immediately the particular estate
is determined, as contrasted with a *contingent remainder* (q.v.).

remainder, common law rules. A remainder was void: if limited after a fee simple (q.v.); if not preceded by a particular freehold estate created under the same instrument; if limited so that it took effect by defeating the particular estate; if limited so that there was abeyance of seisin (q.v.).

remainderman. *See* REMAINDER.

remand. To dispose of the person of an individual charged with a crime, e.g., on the adjournment of a hearing. Thus, magistrates may remand a defendant on bail (q.v.) or in custody when proceedings are adjourned. See, e.g., M.C.A. 1980, ss 128–131 (as amended); Bail Act 1976. The period of remand may not generally exceed eight days without the release of the accused on bail: M.C.A. 1980, s 128(6). See C.J.A. 1988, s 155, allowing a provision for remand for up to 28 days without consent of the accused, where he had been remanded in custody previously and a date had been set for the next part of the proceedings. In general a person may not be remanded in custody without being brought before the court: see, however, C.J.A. 1982, s 59, Sch 9, which introduced the now common practice of remanding a prisoner in his absence, provided he consents to the use of the procedure, for up to three successive hearings. See also C.P.I.A. 1996, s 52; *R v Governor of Haverrig Prison ex p McMahon* (1997) 147 NLJ 1458; C.&Y.P.A. 1969, s 23, amended by C.D.A. 1998, ss 97, 98 (remands and committals for children and young persons). For taking time on remand into account in sentencing, see *R v Ganley* (2000) *The Times*, 7 June. 'Remand in custody' is defined in P.C.C.(S.)A. 2000, s 88, as holding a person in police detention; remanding him in or committing him to custody by court order or to local authority accommodation; remanding him to hospital under M.H.A. 1983, ss 35, 36, 38, 48.

remand for medical examination. *See* MEDICAL EXAMINATION, REMAND FOR.

remedial rights. *See* ANTECEDENT RIGHTS.

remedial statute. A statute intended to remedy an existing defect in the law.

remedy. 1. The means provided by the law to recover rights or to obtain redress or compensation for a wrong, e.g., action for damages. 2. The relief or redress given by a court.

remission. 1. Pardoning of an offence. 2. Cancelling of the whole or part of some obligation. Remission of a prisoner's sentence for good conduct was now abolished under C.J.A. 1991.

remoteness of damage. 1. In contract (q.v.), the general rule is that damages for breach will be too remote to be recovered unless such that the defendant, as a reasonable man, would have foreseen as likely to result: *Hadley v Baxendale* (1854) 9 Exch 341; *Parsons Ltd v Uttley Ingham & Co* [1978] 1 All ER 525. 2. In tort (q.v.), the general rule is that, once negligence (q.v.) is established, the defendant is liable for all the direct consequences, even though not foreseeable by an ordinary, reasonable man in similar circumstances: *Overseas Tankship (UK) Ltd v Morts Dock & Engineering Co Ltd* [1961] AC 388; *Johnson v MOD* [2000] 1 WLR 2055. *See* MEASURE OF DAMAGES IN TORT.

remoteness, rules against. General rules affecting the period of time for which control over property may be exercised by a person. They include rules against perpetuities, inalienability, accumulations.

removal of proceedings. Transfer of proceedings, e.g., to the county court from the High Court (qq.v.) and vice versa. See, e.g., County C.A. 1984, s 42; r 30.2; PD 30.

remuneration. Consideration for services rendered, generally in the form of wages, salaries. Includes 'any benefit, facility or advantage, whether in money or otherwise, provided by the employer': Remuneration, Charges and Grants Act 1975, s 7. See *Perrott v Supplementary Benefits Commission* [1980] 3 All ER 110 (remuneration considered as arising from 'work which is paid for, and not merely work resulting in a profit'). 'Pay' under Treaty of Rome 1957, art 119, means 'the ordinary basic or minimum wage or salary or any other consideration whether in cash or kind received directly or indirectly by the worker in respect of his employment from his employer'. For 'contractual remuneration', see E.R.A. 1996, s 32.

remuneration of directors. This must be stated in a company's balance sheet and prospectus: see Cos.A. 1985, Sch 5, Part V; Table A, art 82. Directors are not entitled to remuneration except by express agreement. Where the articles (q.v.) provide for remuneration there can be no change without a special resolution.

remuneration of trustees. Not usually permitted except where authorised under the trust instrument, or by order of the court, or under statute: see Tr.A. 1925, s 42; Judicial Tr.A. 1896, s 1(5). See Tr.A. 2000, s 28, allowing payment to trust corporations and professional trustees, even where work done could have been performed by a lay trustee. For concept of 'reasonable remuneration', see Tr.A. 2000, s 29(3). See Tr.A. 2000, Part V.

rendition. Doctrine in international law whereby an offender can be returned to a state to be tried there, under special arrangements or even in the absence of an extradition treaty. See *Barton* v *Commonwealth of Australia* (1974) 48 ALJR 161.

renewal areas. Where a local authority is satisfied that living conditions in an area within their district, consisting primarily of housing accommodation, are unsatisfactory, they may declare the area a 'renewal area': Local Government and Housing Act 1989, s 89. The authority is required to carry out appropriate works, including demolition, within that area: s 93. See Housing Grants, Construction and Regeneration Act 1996, Sch 1, para 14.

renewal of lease. *See* LEASE, RENEWAL OF.

renouncing probate. Refusal of executor (q.v.) to accept office. See A.E.A. 1925, s 5; *Re Biggs* [1966] P 118. *See* PROBATE.

rent. A periodic payment made by the tenant (q.v.) or other occupier of land to the owner for its possession and use: *Ingram* v *IRC* [1995] 4 All ER 334. It is an acknowledgement of the landlord's reversionary title. Usually, but not always, it takes the form of money payment; services might be an alternative. See *Bostock* v *Bryant* (1991) 22 HLR 449; *Nurdin and Peacock plc* v *Ramsden & Co (No. 2)* [1999] 1 WLR 1249 (recovery of overpayment of rent).

rental period. 'A period in respect of which a payment of rent falls to be made': H.A. 1985, s 116. Rent is payable in arrear save where there is a contrary provision expressed clearly in the lease. See *Maryland Estates* v *Joseph* (1997) 46 EG 155 (meaning of 'all the rent in arrear').

rent assessment committees. Committees, appointed by the Secretary of State, under Rent Act 1977, s 65, Sch 10. See H.A. 1980, s 142; Landlord and Tenant Act 1987, s 31; H.A. 1988, s 14; SI 88/2199.

rent book. Document usually recording the terms of tenancy and rent payments. See Landlord and Tenant Act 1985, ss 4, 5; SIs 88/2198; 90/1067.

rentcharge. 'Any annual or other periodic sum charged on or issuing out of land except rent reserved by a lease or tenancy or any sum payable by way of interest': Rentcharges Act 1977, s 1. The creation of rentcharges is now prohibited, under s 2(1), save in the case of, e.g., the rentcharge having the effect of making land on which rent is charged settled land (q.v.) by virtue of S.L.A. 1925, s 1(1)(*v*). Rentcharges are extinguished at the expiry of 60 years beginning with the passing of the 1977 Act or the date on which the rentcharge first became payable, whichever is the later. For apportionment, see s 4. For release of charity rentcharges, see Charities Act 1993, s 40. For family charges (e.g. family arrangements), see Trusts of Land and Appointment of Trustees Act 1996, Sch 1, para 3.

rent, fair. *See* FAIR RENT.

rent, interim. *See* INTERIM RENT.

rent, non-payment, remedies. These include: distress (q.v.) on the tenant's goods; action for rent, based on express covenant in lease or agreement implied by law from parties' conduct; action for compensation for use and occupation; forfeiture of lease. See, e.g., L.P.A. 1925, s 146; L.A. 1980, s 19.

rent officers. Officers appointed under the Rent Act 1977, s 63, as amended by H.A. 1988, s 120, with powers to keep registers of rents, consider applications relating to fair rents (q.v.), etc. See SI 89/580.

rent restrictions. Statutory limitations on the amount of rent payable by a tenant (q.v.). See, e.g., Rent Acts 1974, 1977. Market rents must be paid in the case of assured, and assured shorthold, tenancies under H.A. 1988.

rent review clause. A clause in a lease (q.v.) allowing a rent to be increased at regular intervals to a 'fair market value', based on a formula for rent re-assessment. See, e.g., *British Airways v Heathrow Airport* [1991] NPC 127; *Brown v Gloucester CC* [1998] 1 EGLR 95; *Braid v Walsall MBC* (1999) 78 P & CR 94.

rent seck. Dry rent (q.v.).

rent service. 1. Periodic payment, or labour given, by a tenant (q.v.) to his landlord, deriving from tenure (q.v.), unlike a rentcharge (q.v.) which is not attributable to tenure. 2. A service charge which, under a lease, is to be treated as rent: see *Escalus Properties v Robinson* [1996] QB 231.

rent tribunals. Appointed by the Secretary of State for the Environment, each consisting of a chairman and two other members, to consider references arising from rents under restricted contracts.

renunciation. Intentional abandonment of a right or liability, e.g., under a contract: see, e.g., *Mitsubishi Ltd v Gulf Bank* [1997] 1 Lloyd's Rep 342. A statement of, or action amounting to, disclaimer (q.v.). 'There must be an absolute refusal [by one of the contracting parties] to perform his part of the contract': *per* Keating J in *Freeth v Burr* (1874) LR 208.

renunciation of negotiable instrument. *See* NEGOTIABLE INSTRUMENTS, RENUNCIATION OF.

renvoi. (*Renvoyer* = send back.) Doctrine in private international law (q.v.) involving the reference back of a question to English law. The concept of *partial renvoi* (where the court might make a reference to the whole of the foreign law and treat a remission to English law as a reference to English internal law) appears not to form a part of English law (but see *Re Johnson* [1903] 1 Ch 821). Where the court takes a reference to foreign law as meaning the law which the foreign court would, in fact, apply to the question, this is known as '*total*' or '*double*' *renvoi*. See *Re Annesley* [1926] Ch 692.

repairing obligation. In a short lease, i.e., less than seven years, in this context (see Landlord and Tenant Act 1985, ss 13, 14, as modified by L.G.H.A. 1989, Sch 11), there is an implied covenant (q.v.) by the lessor to keep in repair the structure and exterior of the dwelling house, to keep in repair and proper working order water, gas, electricity and sanitation, space and water heating installations: s 11(1). See H.A. 1988, s 116. ('Lease' does not include a mortgage term: s 16(*a*).) To 'keep in repair' means to put and keep in repair: *Liverpool CC v Irwin* [1977] AC 239. Liability to repair arises only after notice has been given or there is actual knowledge of a defect: *O'Brien v Robinson* [1973] AC 912. See *Crewe Services v Silk* [1998] 2 EGLR 1. For specific performance of tenant's repairing covenant, see *Rainbow Estates v Takenhold* [1998] 3 WLR 980 (see Landlord and Tenant Act 1985, s 17); *Eyre v McCracken* (2000) 80 P & CR 220 (repairing obligations and 'improvements').

repair notice. Notice served on the person having control of a dwelling house or house in multiple occupation by the local housing authority (q.v.) when they are satisfied that the house is unfit for human habitation, unless they are satisfied that service of the notice is the most satisfactory course of action: H.A. 1985, s 189 as modified by L.G.H.A. 1989, Sch 9. Appeal may be made to the county court within 21 days after service of the notice:

s 191(1). See also Planning (Listed Buildings etc.) Act 1990, s 48.

repair, reasonable. In determining what is 'reasonable repair' in relation to a dwelling or house, a local housing authority (q.v.) shall have regard to the age, character and locality of the dwelling or house and shall disregard the state of internal decorative repair: H.A. 1985, s 519.

repairs. Work of maintenance, decoration or restoration. '"Repair" always involves renewal; renewal of a part, of a subordinate part': *Lurcott* v *Wakely* [1911] 1 KB 905; 'the putting back into good condition of something that, having been in good condition, has fallen into bad condition': *per* Lord Evershed in *Day* v *Harland and Wolff Ltd* [1953] 2 All ER 387; *Ultraworth Ltd* v *General Accident Corporation* [2000] EGCS 19.

repairs to premises, shared. Where a roof serves claimant's and defendant's premises, in the circumstances of a flying freehold, both parties who share benefits must share the burden of repair expenses: *Abbahall* v *Smee* (2002) *The Times*, 28 December.

reparations order for young offender. The court may, where a child or young person is convicted, make an order requiring him to make specified reparations to specified persons (e.g. victims) or to the community at large: P.C.C.(S.)A. 2000, s 73, Sch 8.

repatriation. 1. The resumption of one's former nationality by leaving one country and settling in one's native land. 2. Sending back a person to his own country. See Repatriation of Prisoners Act 1984; Extradition Act 1989, s 21; Crime (Sentences) Act 1997, s 42; C.D.A. 1998, Sch 8.

repeal. To rescind or revoke. Refers, e.g., to the express or implied abrogation of one statute by a later Act. 'The test of whether there has been a repeal by implication by subsequent legislation is this: are the provisions of a later Act so inconsistent with, or repugnant to, the provisions of an earlier Act that the two cannot stand together': *West Ham*

Church Wardens v *Fourth City Montreal Building Society* [1892] 1 QB 654. See Statute Law (Repeals) Act 1998. Result of repealing a statute is that it is treated as though it had never been enacted, save for actions concluded prior to repeal: *Kay* v *Goodwin* (1836) 6 Bing 576. Where a person is charged under a repealed Act and convicted, the conviction will be quashed: *Stowers* v *Darnell* [1973] RTR 459. See also I.A. 1978, ss 15, 16. For an example of 'self-repealing statute', see Acc.J.A. 1999, Sch 15, repealing its own Sch 10, para 16(2).

replevin. (*Replevire* = to give security.) Formerly a remedy of re-delivery for one whose chattels had been wrongfully seized by way of distress (q.v.); later used in cases involving wrongful detention of chattels, and as a form of interlocutory relief. See Torts (Interference with Goods) Act 1977. See *Swaffer* v *Mulcahy* [1934] 1 KB 608.

reply. Formal reply to a defence in civil procedure; not essential, but where a reply is not made this may be construed as an admission of matters raised in the defence: CPR, r 16.7(1). See PD 16. No statement of case (q.v.) beyond a reply may be filed or served without permission of the court: r 15.9.

reporting restrictions. Restrictions on reporting of alleged offences by persons under 18 from the time of commencement of a criminal investigation to commencement of court proceedings are imposed under Y.J.C.E.A. 1999, and extend to alleged victims or witnesses: s 44. Restrictions may be imposed by any court with criminal jurisdiction, and relate in particular to names, addresses, schools, places of work and photographs of the persons: s 44(5). Restrictions may be modified or lifted if the court considers this to be in the interests of justice: s 44(7). Similar restrictions apply under s 45 to reporting of criminal proceedings involving persons under 18. See also Acc.J.A. 1999, s 72; Guidelines (Lord Chancellor's Department), September 2000.

reporting restrictions relating to adult witnesses. Where the court determines that a witness over 18 is 'eligible for protection' (i.e., where fear or distress caused by risk of public identification diminishes the quality of his evidence) a reporting direction may be given by the court, prohibiting publication of information which might identify him: Y.J.C.E.A. 1999, s 46. The interests of justice, and the public interest (see s 52) will be taken into account by the court: s 46(8). For offences arising from contraventions of ss 44–47, see s 49; for defences (e.g., lack of awareness that publication included prohibited material) see s 50.

repossession. Exercise of a mortgagee's right to take possession of the mortgaged property, which arises as soon as the mortgage is made, resulting in the entire estate vested in the mortgagor being conveyed to the mortgagee free from the mortgagor's equity of redemption (q.v.). See L.P.A. 1925, ss 88, 89, 103, 104. The right may be exercised, e.g., where interest has fallen into arrear and is unpaid for at least two months. *See* MORTGAGE.

representation. 1. Taking the place of another, e.g., as in the relationship of principal and agent (qq.v.). 2. Being represented in a legislative body (e.g., the House of Commons (q.v.)). 3. A statement made by one party to another, relating to some past event or existing fact (but not as to law), which induces a course of action, e.g., signing of a contract. It may be inferred from conduct. Includes, under C.C.A. 1974, s 189(1), any condition or warranty and any other statement or undertaking, whether oral or in writing. For representation in intestate succession, see A.E.A. 1925, Part IV.

representation, chain of. *See* CHAIN OF REPRESENTATION.

representative. One who stands in the place of another, e.g., a personal representative (q.v.).

representative action. Action brought by one or more of a number of persons having the same interest in proceedings. Judgment is binding on all those represented if (as plaintiffs) they have a common grievance and are able to benefit

from the relief claimed. See CPR, Sch 1; O 15, r 12; *Irish Shipping Ltd v Commercial Union* [1990] 2 WLR 117.

reprieve. Formal suspension of execution of a sentence.

reprimands and warnings. Procedures relating to a child or young person ('the offender') arising where a constable has evidence that the offender has committed an offence and: he considers that there is a realistic prospect of the offender's conviction; offender admits offence; offender has not previously been convicted of an offence; constable is satisfied that prosecution of offender is not in public interest: C.D.A. 1998, Sch 65(1). A *reprimand* may be given if the offender has not previously been reprimanded or warned: s 65(2). A *warning*, may be given if offender has not been previously warned, or has not been warned within the two years before commission of the offence: s 65(3). Reprimands and warnings are to be given at a police station and, where the offender is under 17, in the presence of an appropriate adult, e.g., parent, guardian, social worker: s 65(5), (7). See C.J.C.S.A. 2000, s 56.

republication of will. Where a testator (q.v.) desires that his unrevoked will should take effect as if written on a subsequent date, he may republish it with the formalities needed in the case of a will, by re-execution or by making a subsequent codicil (q.v.) showing the intention to republish. *See* WILL.

repudiation. Refusal to be bound by, e.g., a contract. It generally amounts to a breach of contract (q.v.), as where a party states that he will not carry out a promise (see *Heyman v Darwins Ltd* [1952] 1 All ER 337) or does some act which disables him from performing his promise (an implied repudiation). The test for implicit repudiation is whether the conduct 'evinces an intention not to perform': *Freeth v Burr* (1874) LR 9 CP 208. See *Tai Hing Cotton Mill Ltd v Kamsing Knitting Factory* [1979] AC 91 – date for assessing damages for repudiation; *Johnson v Agnew* [1980] AC 367; *The Santa Clara* [1996] AC 800.

repugnancy. Inconsistency of two or more provisions in a deed (q.v.) or other document. The inconsistent provisions may be struck out by the court when no other method is possible to make effective the principal intention of the parties to the document (the so-called 'main purpose' rule). If the court cannot say which of two provisions ought to be rejected, then the general rule is that, in the case of a will (q.v.), the later one remains, but in the case of a deed (q.v.), the earlier remains: *Gwynn* v *Neath Canal Co* (1865) LR 3 Ex 209. See *Evans & Son* v *Andrea Merzario* [1976] 1 WLR 1078.

reputation. The estimation in which a person is generally held. Disparagement of reputation may constitute defamation (q.v.). *See* CHARACTER, EVIDENCE AS TO.

requesting court. Court or tribunal making application to a UK court for assistance in obtaining evidence for civil proceedings in that court: see, e.g., Evidence (Proceedings in Other Jurisdictions) Act 1975, s 1; *Re Norway's Application* [1989] 2 WLR 458.

request, letter of. *See* LETTER OF REQUEST.

requisition. 1. Demand by a purchaser for the official search relating to title (q.v.). See L.P.A. 1925, s 45(1)(*b*). 2. Requests for supplies. 3. Compulsory taking of property, e.g., for military purposes.

re-registration. Procedure under Cos.A. 1985, ss 43–55, whereby a private company is converted into a public company as from the date of its registration for all purposes, or a public company is converted into a private company, or an unlimited company becomes limited, or a limited company becomes unlimited.

res. A thing.

resale, right of. Right of the seller, under S.G.A. 1979, s 48, to resell even though ownership has passed to the original buyer, if the goods are perishable or if he has given notice to the original buyer of his intention to resell and the original buyer does not make payment. See *Damon Cia Naviera* v *Hapag-Lloyd* [1985] 1 All ER 475.

rescission. Remedy for inducing a contract by innocent or fraudulent misrepresentation (q.v.), whereby the contract is abrogated. A party intending to rescind must notify the other party. A rescission *ab initio* results in the contract being treated as though it had never been. See *TSB Bank plc* v *Camfield* [1995] 1 WLR 430. Right of rescission is lost: if *restitutio in integrum* (q.v.) is impossible; if the injured party takes a benefit under the contract with the knowledge of the misrepresentation; if a third party has acquired for value rights under the contract. See Misrepresentation Act 1967; Contracts (Rights of Third Parties) Act 1999, s 2; *Lagunas Nitrate Co* v *Lagunas Syndicate* [1899] 2 Ch 392; *Stocznia Gdanska SA* v *Latvian Shipping Co* [1998] 1 WLR 574 (problem of a total failure of consideration); *Zanzibar* v *British Aerospace Ltd* (2000) *The Times*, 28 March (damages as alternative to rescission). *See* CONTRACT.

rescue cases. Cases in which the claimant is injured while intervening in a situation so as to save the life or property endangered by defendant's negligence. Generally, if claimant's intervention is reasonable in the circumstances, it does not constitute an assumption of risk, but if unreasonable, *volenti non fit injuria* (q.v.) applies. See *Haynes* v *Harwood* [1934] 2 KB 240; *Ogwo* v *Taylor* [1987] 3 All ER 961. For discussion of 'duty to rescue', see *Barrett* v *MOD* [1995] 3 All ER 87; *The Ogopogo* [1970] 1 Lloyd's Rep 257.

reservation. 1. Generally, a limiting condition. 2. Action by a vendor of land, selling part of it and wishing to reserve easements (q.v.) and profits. See L.P.A. 1925, s 65; *Wiles* v *Banks* (1985) 50 P & CR 81.

reservation, designated and human rights legislation. In the Human Rights Act 1998, the term means the UK's reservation to art 2 of the first Protocol to the Convention (relating to the provision of instruction and training), and any other reservation by the UK to an article of the European Convention, or of any protocol to the Convention, which is designated by the Secretary of State: Human Rights Act 1998, s 15. Designated reservations must be reviewed every five years: s 17.

reserve capital. That part of the uncalled capital which a limited company determines by special resolution not to call up except when the company is being wound up: Cos.A. 1985, s 124.

Reserve Forces. Royal Fleet Reserve, Royal Naval Reserve, Royal Marines Reserve, Army Reserve, Territorial Army, Air Force Reserve and Royal Auxiliary Air Force: Reserve Forces Act 1996, s 1. See ARMED FORCES.

reserves, undistributable. Included are a company's share premium account, capital redemption reserve fund, accumulated unrealised profits less accumulated realised losses, other reserves which a company may not distribute: see Cos.A. 1985, s 264 (3).

reserve, without. See WITHOUT RESERVE.

res extincta. The subject matter of an agreement which is, in fact, non-existent. In such a case no contract ensues. See, e.g., *Couturier* v *Hastie* (1856) 5 HL Cas 673.

res gestae. Things done; the events which happened. All the facts constituting, accompanying or explaining a fact in issue (the 'transaction'). See *R* v *Christie* [1914] AC 545; *R* v *Andrews* [1987] AC 281. 'As regards statements made after the event, it must be for the judge, by a preliminary ruling, to satisfy himself that the statement was so clearly made in circumstances of spontaneity or involvement in the event that the possibility of concoction can be disregarded . . . And the same must in principle be true of statements made before the event . . . The expression *res gestae* may conveniently sum up these criteria, but the reality of them must always be kept in mind': *Ratten* v *R* [1972] AC 378.

residence. Place where a person abides, i.e., where he has his home. A 'residence' in the sense of a 'dwelling house' can comprise several dwellings not physically joined: *Batey* v *Wakefield* [1982] 1 All ER 61. In the case of a corporation, the place where its management is carried on. See I.C.T.A. 1988, ss 334–336; *Reed* v *Clark* [1986] Ch 1; for 'residing with a tenant' (see Rent Act 1977, Sch 1, Part 1, para 1), see *Swanbrae Ltd* v *Elliott* (1987) 281 EG 916. 'Habitual residence' was defined, in *R* v *Barnet LBC ex p Shah* [1983] 2 WLR 16, as 'voluntary residence with a degree of settled purpose'. For 'ordinarily resident', see *Re J (A Child)* (1999) *The Times*, 1 June. See *Re S (A Minor) (Abduction: European Convention)* (1997) *The Times*, 30 July; *Nessa* v *Chief Adjudication Officer* [1998] 1 FLR 879. The CA held, in *R (Williams)* v *Horsham DC* (2004) *The Times*, 29 January, that, for purposes of deciding where a dwelling is, a council taxpayer's sole or main residence is the place where he actually lives. See ABODE; DOMICILE.

residence order. An order of the court settling the arrangements to be made as to the person with whom a child is to live: Ch.A. 1989, s 8(1). For enforcement, see s 14. See *Re F (Minors)* [1996] 7 CL 19; *Re W (Residence Order)* [1998] 1 FCR 75; *G* v *F (Contact and Shared Residence)* [1998] 2 FLR 799 (shared residence by lesbian couples criteria to be applied); *Re P (A Minor)* [1999] 3 WLR 1164 (relevance of child's religious or cultural heritage).

residential care homes. Term referring to houses for disabled, old persons and mentally disordered persons (not including hospitals, nursing or mental nursing homes). They must be registered. See Health and Social Services Adjudication Act 1983, Sch 4; Community Care (Residential Accommodation) Act 1992; Finance Act 2000, Sch 15, para 32(3). For 'residential family centres' (which must be registered), see Care Standards Act 2000, s 4(2).

residential occupier. A person occupying premises as a residence whether under a contract or by virtue of any enactment or rule of law giving him the right to remain in occupation or restricting the right of any other person to recover possession of the premises: Protection from Eviction Act 1977, s 1(1). For 'displaced residential occupier', see C.L.A. 1977, s 12(3); C.J.P.O.A. 1994, s 72.

residential premises, adverse occupation of. *See* ADVERSE OCCUPATION OF RESIDENTIAL PREMISES.

residential property loan. Any loan secured on land in the UK made to an individual in respect of the acquisition of land which is for his residential use or the residential use of a dependant of his: C.L.S.A. 1990, s 104(1). For the 'tying-in' of such a loan to the provision of conveyancing services, see ss 104, 105.

resident in UK. 'Ordinarily resident' refers to a man's abode in a particular place which he has adopted voluntarily and for settled purposes as part of the regular order of his life for the time being, whether of short or long duration: *per* Lord Scarman in *Akbarali* v *Brent London BC* [1983] 2 AC 309. 'Residence' implies lawful presence: see *R* v *Secretary of State ex p Marguerite* [1983] QB 180. A person who is resident in the UK for a period or periods totalling 183 days in any year is regarded as a resident in the UK for that year for tax purposes: I.C.T.A. 1988, s 336. See *Levene* v *IRC* [1982] AC 217; *Nessa* v *Chief Adjudication Officer* (1999) 149 NLJ 1619 (a person is not 'habitually resident' in UK unless he has taken up residence and lived here for a period: see *Shah* v *Barret LBC* [1983] 1 All ER 226).

residual negative principle. Jurisprudential concept, suggesting that everything which is not legally prohibited is deemed to be legally permitted.

residuary devise. *See* DEVISE.

residuary devisee. The devisee who takes the real property which remains after specific gifts of real property under a will (q.v.) have been satisfied. *See* DEVISE.

residuary estate. Testator's property not specifically bequeathed or devised. See A.E.A. 1925, s 33, amended by Trusts of Land and Appointment of Trustees Act 1996, Sch 2, para 5.

residuary legacy. *See* LEGACY.

residue. That which remains of an estate after payment of debts, funeral expenses, testamentary expenses, legacies, annuities, costs of administration, etc. See I.C.T.A. 1988, s 701(6).

resignation. The deliberate relinquishing of some position or office. See, e.g., *Kwik-Fit Ltd* v *Lineham* [1992] ICR 183 (resignation and repudiation of contract).

resile. To withdraw from (e.g., an agreement).

res integra. A whole, 'unopened', thing. A question on which there is no rule, and no decision has been taken in a court of law and which must be resolved upon principle.

res inter alios acta alteri nocere non debet. A transaction between strangers should not prejudice another party. A special rule of evidence. Example: an admission generally binds only the person making it. See *Beswick* v *Beswick* [1968] AC 58; *Naumann* v *Ford* (1985) 275 EG 542.

res ipsa loquitur. The thing speaks for itself. A rule of evidence in actions for injury where the mere fact of an accident occurring raises the inference of defendant's negligence, so that a prima facie case may be said to exist. 'You may presume negligence from the mere fact that it happens': *Ballard* v *N British Rwy* 1923 SC 43. See *Ward* v *Tesco Ltd* [1976] 1 WLR 810 (slipping on a supermarket floor); *Waldie* v *Cook* (1988) 91 FLR 413 (no application in criminal law); *Widdowson* v *Newgate Meat Corporation* [1998] PIQR P138 (liability in road traffic accident); *Fryer* v *Pearson* (2000) *The Times*, 4 April (judicial disapproval of use of Latin maxims such as this).

resisting arrest. *See* ARREST, RESISTING.

res judicata. A final judicial decision pronounced by a competent judicial tribunal. Known also as 'action estoppel'. 'It is a very substantial doctrine, and it is one of the most fundamental doctrines of all courts that there must be an end to all litigation, and that the parties have no right of their own accord, having tried a question between them, and obtained a decision of a court, to start that litigation over again on precisely the same question': *per* Brett MR in *Re May* (1885) 28 Ch D 516. See *Arnold* v *National Westminster Bank* [1989] 1 Ch 63 (exception where new evidence became available after first hearing); *Brillovette* v *Hachette* [1996] BPIR 522; *Dattani* v *Trio Supermarkets Ltd* [1998] IRLR 240.

res nullius. A thing belonging to no one. In international law, territory not under the sovereignty of any state. See *Clipperton Island Arbitration* (1931) 2 RIAA 1105 (obtaining title to *res nullius* by occupation).

resolution. A formal expression of opinion by an organised body, e.g., as in a meeting or assembly. In the case of companies, resolutions may be ordinary; extraordinary; special (qq.v.). See Cos.A. 1985, ss 376–381; Table A, art 53. *See* VOTING AT MEETINGS.

res perit domino. The loss falls on the owner. See S.G.A. 1979, ss 7, 20, 32.

respondeat superior. Let the principal answer. In general, a master is responsible for the acts of his servant committed in the course of employment. *See* MASTER AND SERVANT.

respondent. One against whom an order is sought, and such other person as the court may direct: r 23.1.

respondentia. *See* BOTTOMRY.

responsibility. 1. Care and consideration for the outcome of one's actions. 2. Legal liability, i.e., accountability for some state of affairs to which one's conduct has contributed, together with an obligation to repair any injury caused.

responsibility, collective. *See* COLLECTIVE RESPONSIBILITY.

responsibility, ministerial. *See* MINISTERIAL RESPONSIBILITY.

responsibility, parental. *See* CHILD, PARENTAL RESPONSIBILITY FOR.

res sua. One's own goods. Phrase used, e.g., where a person makes a contract to purchase that which, in fact, belongs to him. The contract is void. See *Bligh* v *Martin* [1968] 1 WLR 804.

restitutio in integrum. Restoration to the original position. Right to rescind a contract for misrepresentation is lost if *restitutio in integrum* is not possible. Rescission (q.v.) must put parties *in statu quo ante* and restore things 'as between them to the position in which they stood before the contract was entered into':

Abram Steamship Co v *Westville Shipping Co* [1923] AC 773. See *O'Sullivan* v *Management Agency* [1985] QB 428.

restitution. 1. Restoration to the rightful owner. Under P.C.C.(S.)A. 2000, s 148, the court may order anyone in possession or control of stolen goods to restore them to any person entitled to recover them from him. 2. The equitable doctrine of restitution refers to the case, e.g., of an infant who, having fraudulently obtained goods, is ordered to restore his ill-gotten gains. See Minors' Contracts Act 1987, s 3; *Lloyd's Bank plc* v *Independent Insurance Ltd* [1999] 2 WLR 986; *Kleinwort Benson Ltd* v *Lincoln CC* [1998] 3 WLR 1095; F.S.M.A. 2000, s 384 (power of FSA (q.v.) to require restitution).

restitution, law of. The body of law concerned with claims for the reversal of unjust enrichment (q.v.), the prevention of one who has committed a wrong from profiting from it, the restoration of a claimant's property rights adversely affected by defendant's actions, and the provision of appropriate restitutionary remedies. See *Lipkin Gorman* v *Karpnale Ltd* [1991] AC 548; *Woolwich Equitable BS* v *IRC* [1993] AC 70. Remedies, intended to effect 'a fair and just balance between rights and interests of the parties concerned', include rescission, award of interest, subrogation, equitable damages, restitutionary damages, account of profits, *quantum valebat*.

restoration condition. Phrase used in relation to planning permission, referring to restoration of a site after working of minerals, by the use of subsoil, topsoil and soilmaking material: see T.C.P.A. 1971, s 30A (inserted by T.C.P. (Minerals) A. 1981, s 5). See T.C.P.A. 1990, Sch 5. *See* AFTER CARE CONDITIONS.

restorative justice. Phrase used in explanatory notes to Y.J.C.E.A. 1999, Part I, referring to the imposition on a young offender of the principle of restorative justice, i.e., a combination of making restoration to the victim, reintegrating the offender into the community, and making the offender accept the consequences of his behaviour.

rest periods, workers'. Under SI 98/33, regs 10–12: an adult worker is entitled to a daily rest period of not less than 11 consecutive hours in each 24-hour period during which he works for his employer; a young worker is entitled to a rest period of not less than 12 consecutive hours in each 24-hour period during which he works for his employer. An adult worker is entitled to a weekly rest period of not less than 24 hours; a young worker is entitled to a weekly rest period of not less than 48 hours. Where an adult worker's daily working time is more than 6 hours, he is entitled to a rest break of at least 20 minutes away from his workstation; where a young worker's daily working time is more than 4.5 hours, he is entitled to a rest break of at least 20 minutes.

restraint, bodily. Involves a total restraint of a person's liberty in every direction. See, e.g., *Bird* v *Jones* (1845) 7 QB 742. *See* FALSE IMPRISONMENT.

restraint of marriage. An attempt to prevent a person marrying, by a condition in a contract, is void as contrary to public policy if in general restraint, but not necessarily so if in partial restraint. A condition in restraint of a second marriage may be valid: *Allen* v *Jackson* (1875) 1 Ch D 399. For restraining order in relation to S.O.A. 1997, s 5A, see C.J.C.S.A. 2000, s 6(1).

restraint of trade, contract in. 'Any contract which interferes with the free exercise of [a person's] trade or business, by restricting him in the work he may do for others, or the arrangements which he may make with others, is a contract in restraint of trade. It is invalid unless it is reasonable as between the parties and not injurious to the public interest': *Petrofina* v *Martin* [1966] Ch 146. Question of reasonableness is for the court, not for the jury: *Dowden* v *Pook* [1904] 1 KB 48. See *Watson* v *Prager* [1991] 1 WLR 726; *Rock Refrigeration* v *Jones* [1997] 1 All ER 1.

restraint on alienation. *See* ALIENATION, RESTRAINT ON.

restraint, order. Order by High Court, under C.J.A. 1988, s 77, as amended, prohibiting a person from dealing with realisable property, so as to preserve it as the basis of a confiscation order under s 71. See *Re M* [1992] 1 All ER 537.

restraints of princes. Phrase used in some insurance policies to indicate interference with or frustration of some commercial endeavour (in connection with, e.g., transport of goods by sea) as the result of activities of rulers of a country. See, e.g., *Rickards* v *Forestal Land Co* [1942] AC 50.

restricted-use credit agreement. A regulated consumer credit agreement (q.v.) to finance a transaction between a debtor and creditor, whether forming part of that agreement or not, or to finance a transaction between the debtor and a person other than the creditor, or to refinance any existing indebtedness of the debtor's whether to the creditor or another person: C.C.A. 1974, s 11(1).

restriction order. An order made by the Crown Court based, e.g., on a hospital order (q.v.) subjecting the offender to special restrictions for a specified or unlimited time. See *R* v *Merseyside MH Review Tribunal ex p K* [1990] 1 All ER 694; M.H.A. 1983, s 41; *R* v *Reynolds* (2000) *The Times*, 1 November.

restriction order, share. Where a company fails to disclose information concerning share acquisitions or disposals under Cos.A. 1985, s 216, its shares are 'frozen', i.e., they cannot be transferred and no voting rights may be exercised in respect of them. See *Re Lonrho* (1989) 5 BCC 776.

restriction, protection by. Under the LRA 1925, s 58(1) a restriction was a minor interest (q.v.) that could be protected by recording on the Proprietorship Register a limitation on the powers of disposition of the registered proprietor until he has complied with certain conditions and requirements. This has now been replaced by LRA 2002, s 41(1) which defines a restriction as 'an entry in the register regulating the circumstances in which a disposition of a registered estate . . . may be subject of an entry in the register', i.e., a restriction on dealings with the registered estate. The restriction may impose a complete ban on any dealing or could impose conditions that must be met before any dealing will be registered.

restrictions on publication. Where the Court of Appeal considers publicity could have a prejudicial effect on a retrial, it is reasonable to order a restriction on publicity order. See *R* v *D (Acquitted Person: Retrial)* [2006] *The Times,* March 6.

restrictive covenant. 1. A covenant by which use of the covenantor's land is restricted for the benefit of the covenantee's adjoining land. Known also as a 'negative covenant'. The burden of such a covenant may bind an assignee of the covenantor's tenement, i.e., it may be considered as a covenant running with the land (q.v.). See L.P.A. 1925, s 56; L.C.A. 1972, s 2(5). 2. Covenant restraining an employee from exercising his skills on the termination of his employment. See, e.g., *Thamesmead Town* v *Allotey* [1998] 3 EGLR 97; *Hollis* v *Stocks* [2000] UKCLR 658. *See* COVENANT.

restrictive covenants, discharge and modification of. Powers for discharge and modification of restrictive covenants concerning land are contained in L.P.A. 1925, s 84 (as amended by L.P.A. 1969, s 28). Application is made to the Lands Tribunal (q.v.). Each application under s 84 must be considered on its merits: *Re Willis' Application* (1998) 76 P & CR 97. 'For an application to succeed on the ground of public interest is so important and immediate as to justify the serious interference with private rights and the sanctity of contract': *Re Collins' Applications* (1975) 30 P & CR 527; *Re North's Application* (1998) 75 P & CR 117. See Planning and Compensation Act 1991, s 12.

restrictive indorsement. *See* ENDORSE-MENT.

Restrictive Practices Court. A superior court of record (q.v.) created by Restrictive Trade Practices Act 1956, and constituted under the Restrictive Practices Court Act 1976, presided over by a High Court judge. Abolished under Competition Act 1998, s 1(a).

resulting trust. A trust (q.v.) which arises in circumstances where the beneficial interest comes back ('results') to the person or his representatives who transferred the property to the trustee (q.v.) or who provided the means of obtaining the property. Example: X transfers funds to trustees to be held on the trusts of a marriage settlement; the marriage is later declared void *ab initio* (q.v.), so that the fund is held on a resulting trust for X. See L.P.A. 1925, s 60; 'Any property that a man does not effectively dispose of remains his own': *per* Megarry V-C in *Re Sick and Funeral Society of St John* [1973] Ch 51; *Winkworth* v *Edward Baron Development Co* [1986] 1 WLR 1512 (displacement of presumption of resulting trust); *Lowson* v *Coombes* (1998) *The Times,* 2 December; *Abrahams* v *Trustee in Bankruptcy of Abrahams* (1999) *The Times,* 26 July (property rights of person purchasing National Lottery tickets in name of another).

resulting use. An equitable interest arising where feoffment (q.v.) was made without declaring a use in favour of the feoffee (q.v.). See the L.P.A. 1925, s 60(3). *See* USE.

retail transaction. 'The sale or supply of goods, or the supply of services (including financial services)': E.R.A. 1996, s 17(3). See C.P.A. 1987, s 10(5).

retirement of jury. Period, following the summing-up (q.v.), in which the jury considers its verdict. No further evidence can be called once the jury has retired. 'A jury shall deliberate in complete freedom, uninfluenced by any promise, unintimidated by any threat': *R* v *McKenna and Busby* [1960] 1 QB 411.

retirement of trustees. A trustee (q.v.) can retire only under express power or statutory power conferred by Tr.A. 1925, s 39, or by the consent of all the beneficiaries, or by order of the court. *See* TRUSTEESHIP, TERMINATION OF.

retiring age, normal. The earliest age at which an employee could be required to retire; it is a matter of evidence, not depending exclusively on a contract of employment, although that provides the best evidence as to the normal retiring age: *Post Office* v *Wallser* [1981] 1 All ER 668. See E.P.(C.)A. 1978, s 64(1)(*b*), as amended by Sex Discrimination Act 1986, s 3(1); 1978 Act, s 82(1); *Doughty* v *Rolls Royce* [1992] IRLR 126; S.S. Contributions and Benefits Act 1992, ss 43–55. The CA held, in *Wall* v *British Compressed Air Society* (2004) *The Times*, 9 January, that an employee who occupied a unique position (as director-general) within an organisation, was to be considered as having a normal retiring age for purposes of the Employment Rights Act 1996, s 109(1)(*a*). See PENSION, STATE RETIREMENT.

retour sans protêt. Return without protest. Request by the drawer of a bill that if it is dishonoured it can be returned without protest (q.v.). *See* BILL OF EXCHANGE.

retrial. *See* TRIAL, NEW.

retrial, judge's lapse of memory. In *Taylor* v *Williamson* (2002) *The Times*, 9 August, CA considered a judge's memory lapse resulting in his circulating a judgment prior to opportunity of considering counsel's closing submissions. It was held that this did not justify a re-trial on ground of bias. See *Porter* v *Magill* [2002] 2 WLR 37.

retributive justice. *See* JUSTICE, RETRIBUTIVE.

retrospective legislation. Known also as 'retroactive legislation'. Laws which, expressly or by implication, operate so as to affect acts done prior to their having been passed. See, e.g., Validation of Wartime Leases Act 1944; War Damage Act 1965; War Crimes Act 1991, s 1; *Yew Bon Tew* v *Kanderaan Bas Mara* [1983] 1 AC 553. There is a presumption (q.v.) against the retrospective operation of a statute relating to substantive law (q.v.): *Re Athlumney* [1898] 2 QB 547; *Arnold* v *CEGB* [1988] AC 228. 'The court will not ascribe retrospective force to new laws affecting rights unless by express words or necessary implication it appears that such was the intention of the legislature': *per* Willes J in *Phillips* v *Eyre* (1870) LR 6 QB 1. For retrospectivity of

regulations (SI 97/786) see *Westminster CC* v *Haywood (No. 2)* (2000) *The Times*, 10 March. See Convention on Human Rights, art 7 (discussed, in relation to limited retrospectivity, in *R* v *Benjafield* (2000) *The Times*, 28 December). *See* EX POST FACTO; NULLUM CRIMEN.

return. 1. Formal statement or report, e.g., annual return (q.v.) required under Cos.A. 1985, s 363. 2. Election of a member to serve in Parliament (q.v.).

returning officer. A person (e.g., sheriff, mayor (qq.v)) who is responsible for the conduct of a parliamentary election. See Representation of the People Act 1983, s 27; *Greenway-Stanley* v *Paterson* [1977] 2 All ER 663.

return order. Court order for the return of goods to a creditor, under C.C.A. 1974, s 133(1)(*b*)(*i*). It may be made, e.g., in an action brought by a creditor under a hire-purchase agreement to recover possession of the goods to which the agreement relates.

revenge. Retaliation, reprisal. 'Revenge is a kind of wild justice, which the more man's nature runs to, the more ought law to weed it out': Bacon (1625). See *R* v *Watson* (1990) 12 Cr App R (S) (the court will not condone retaliatory violence). *See* LEX TALIONIS.

revenue. Income; yield of taxes; return on investment.

revenue, cheating the. The common law offence does exist, but a conspiracy to cheat (q.v.) may be charged as a statutory offence under C.L.A. 1977, s 1(1): *R* v *Mulligan* [1990] STC 220. See *R* v *James* [1997] 2 Cr App R (S) 294.

revenue statutes. Statutes concerned with, e.g., taxation. The general rule is that 'the subject is not to be taxed except by plain words'. Where clearly worded they must be applied no matter what their effect on persons, but 'if [a provision] is capable of two alternative meanings, courts will prefer that meaning more favourable to the subject': *IRC* v *Ross and Coulter* [1948] 1 All ER 616. Foreign revenue laws are not enforceable in UK: *QRS* v *Frandsen* [1999] 1 WLR 2169.

reversal of judgment. The altering of a judgment on appeal. Generally applied to the procedure involved in the overturning of the decision in a specific case by a higher court. *See* OVERRULE.

reversion. Known also as 'reverter'. Where X, owner of fee simple in Blackacre, grants Blackacre to Y for life, X retains reversion, i.e., an interest which remains in him, since Blackacre will revert to him on Y's death. X is known as the 'reversioner'. A 'reversionary interest' was defined in the Inheritance Tax Act 1984, s 47, as 'a future interest under a settlement, whether it is vested or contingent'. See *Fraser* v *Canterbury DBF* (2000) *The Times*, 22 February (reverter under School Sites Act 1841).

reversionary lease. A lease (q.v.) which is to become effective at some future time. Grant of such a lease is now void unless it takes effect within 21 years from the date of the instrument creating it: L.P.A. 1925, s 149(3). See *Re Strand Properties* [1960] Ch 582 (option to renew contained in lease).

reverter, possibility of. Possibility of a grantor's having an estate at some future time. It was destroyed if the determining event could not occur. Example: land is given 'to X and his heirs until Y marries', and Y dies unmarried. See Reverter of Sites Act 1987, s 1, amended by Trusts of Land and Appointment of Trustees Act 1996, Sch 2, para 6, replacing the right of reverter in some cases by a trust.

revival of will. Where a testator (q.v.) has revoked his will and wishes later to restore it to effect, he may revive it by re-execution with appropriate formalities or by a subsequent codicil (q.v.), showing the intention to revive. The revived will takes effect as though written at the date of revival. See W.A. 1837, ss 22, 34. *See* WILL.

revocation. An act by which one annuls something he has done.

revocation of offer. An offer may be revoked at any time before acceptance; after acceptance it is irrevocable. Revocation does not take effect until actually communicated to the offeree.

See *Dickinson* v *Dodds* (1876) 2 Ch D 463; *Byrne* v *Van Tienhoven* (1880) 5 CPD 349. *See* OFFER.

revocation of probate. Revocation of a grant by the court when, e.g., one of the executors has become incapable of acting, or probate has been obtained by fraud, or the testator is found to be alive. See S.C.A. 1981, s 121. *See* PROBATE.

revocation of will. A will can always be revoked by the testator before his death. Revocation may be effected by the destruction of the will (q.v.), or by the execution of another will or codicil (q.v.), or as a result of marriage. See W.A. 1837, ss 18–20 (as amended by A.J.A. 1982, s 18). (For revival of revoked will, see W.A. 1837, s 22.) *Animus revocandi* (q.v.) at the time of the destruction of the will is essential. See *Re Adams* [1990] 2 All ER 97; *Re Finnemore* [1991] 1 WLR 793. *See* MARRIAGE, WILL IN CONTEMPLATION OF; WILL; WILL, DESTRUCTION OF.

rewards for return of goods. Where a public advertisement of a reward for the return of lost or stolen goods uses words to the effect that no questions will be asked or that the person producing the goods will be safe from apprehension, an offence is committed under Th.A. 1968, s 23. See *Denham* v *Scott* (1984) 77 Cr App R 210.

Richard Roe. *See* ROE, RICHARD.

rider. 1. Clause added to a Bill, or agenda. 2. Statement, e.g., a recommendation, appended to a jury's verdict.

right. 1. That to which a person has a just or lawful claim. 2. An interest which will be recognised and protected by a rule of law, respect for which is a legal duty, violation of which is a legal wrong: Salmond, *Jurisprudence* (1902).

right, new. 'No new right in the law, fully-fledged with all the appropriate safeguards, can spring from the head of a judge deciding a particular case: only Parliament can create such a right . . . The wider and more indefinite the right claimed, the greater the undesirability of holding that such a right exists': *per* Sir Robert Megarry V-C in *Malone* v *MPC (No. 2)* [1979] Ch 344.

right of action. 1. The right to bring an action (now 'claim'). 2. Chose in action (q.v.).

right of entry. Right of resuming possession of land by entering. Proviso for re-entry in a lease indicates that a lessor (q.v.) may re-enter on a breach of covenant by the lessor. Under L.P.A. 1925, s 146, right of re-entry is not enforceable unless and until notice is served on the lessee and reasonable time is afforded to him to remedy the breach. See H.A. 1996, s 82; *Savva* v *Hussein* (1997) 73 P & CR 150. It is unlawful to enforce a right of re-entry except through court proceedings while the occupier is lawfully residing in the premises: Protection from Eviction Act 1977, s 2. See T.C.P.A. 1990, s 324. See *Khazanchi* v *Faircharm Investments Ltd* [1998] 1 WLR 1603 (forcible re-entry justified by deliberate exclusion); *Re Lomax* [1999] 3 WLR 652.

right of resale. *See* RESALE, RIGHT OF.

right of support. The natural right to have one's soil supported by the soil of one's neighbour's land. The right to the support of buildings by adjoining buildings or land may be acquired as an easement (q.v.). See *Dalton* v *Angus & Co* (1881) 6 App Cas 740; *Midland Bank* v *Baragrove Properties* (1991) 24 Con LR 98; *Holbeck Hall Hotel* v *Scarborough BC (No. 2)* [2000] 2 All ER 705.

right of way. The right to pass over another's land. A public right of way can be created by statute or by dedication and acceptance. It can be extinguished by natural causes, order under, e.g., T.C.P.A. 1990, Part X, C.R.W.A. 2000, s 53 (unrecorded right). For 'prescriptive right of way', see *Ironside and Crabb* v *Cooke and Barefoot* (1981) 41 P & CR 326. See Highways Act 1980, Part IX, as amended by Rights of Way Act 1990, s 1; T.C.P.A. 1990, s 258; Regional Development Agencies Act 1998, Sch 6; *Loder* v *Gaden* (1999) 78 P & CR 223; *Trevelyan* v *Secretary of State for the Environment* (2000) *The Times*, 22 March. CA held, in *Massey* v *Boulden* [2002] EWCA Civ 1634, that where a person drove a vehicle over a village green

without permission, he was using that land unlawfully and could not, even in a case of more than 40 years of such use, acquire prescriptive rights (but under Countryside and Rights of Way Act 2000, s 68, an easement could be considered). See also *Bakewell Management* v *Brandwood* (2003) *The Times*, 5 February. *See* DEDICATION OF WAY.

right, petition of. *See* PETITION OF RIGHT.

rights, antecedent. *See* ANTECEDENT RIGHTS.

rights issue. Issues of shares whereby existing shareholders are given a prior right to take some part of the new issue at a price below the market value of the shares. See Cos.A. 1985, s 89. *See* SHARE.

rights, natural. *See* NATURAL RIGHTS.

rights offer. An offer of shares in a company made by 'letter of rights' sent by the company to existing members in proportion to their existing holdings, e.g., two for one.

rights, perfect and imperfect. *See* PERFECT AND IMPERFECT RIGHTS.

rights, vested. *See* VESTED RIGHTS.

right-thinking members of the public, test. Concept enunciated by Lawton LJ in *R* v *Bradbourne* (1985) 7 Cr App R (S) 182, in relation to an offence which 'right-thinking members of the public, knowing all the facts, would feel that justice had not been done by the passing of any sentence other than a custodial one'. 'Right-thinking' seemed to refer to persons having sound principles. See also *R* v *Cox* [1993] 1 WLR 188; *R* v *Howells* [1999] 1 WLR 307, in which Lord Bingham CJ rejected the test as unhelpful, since there were no means of consulting such persons and ascertaining their views.

right to begin. Generally belongs to the party on whom the burden of proof (q.v.) rests. In criminal cases the prosecution begins where there is a plea of not guilty. (Defendant would begin where, e.g., a special plea of *autrefois convict* is raised.) In civil cases the claimant (q.v.) began where the onus of proving an issue was on him, and where he claims substantial and unliquidated damages. Where the onus of proving all issues was on a defendant (q.v.) he would generally begin. See now CPR, r 32.1, giving the court power to control the way in which evidence is to be placed before it.

riot. Where twelve or more persons who are present together use or threaten unlawful violence for a common purpose and the conduct of them (taken together) is such as would cause a person of reasonable firmness present at the scene to fear for his personal safety, each of the persons using unlawful violence for the common purpose is guilty of riot: P.O.A. 1986, s 1(1). A person is guilty only if he intends to use violence or is aware that his conduct may be violent: s 6(1). See *R v Keys and Sween* [1987] Crim LR 207; *R v Tyler* (1993) 96 Cr App R 332.

riot sentencing. CA held in *R v Najeeb and Others* (2003) *The Times*, 5 February, that prison sentences from 5–10 years could be expected in the case of a serious riot involving considerable damage to property and causing large numbers of police to be put in fear and suffering injury.

riparian. Relating to the bank of a river or stream. A riparian owner may, under common law, take and use water for ordinary purposes relating to tenement if the water is restored unaltered in character and substantially undiminished in value. See, e.g., *Embrey v Owen* (1851) 6 Exch 353; *Ipswich BC v Moore* (2000) *The Times*, 4 July.

risk, transfer of. Principle whereby, in performance of a contract for the sale of goods, risk generally passes with the property, unless the parties agree otherwise. See S.G.A. 1979, ss 20, 33; *Demby Hamilton v Barden* [1949] 1 All ER 435.

river. A natural stream of water flowing in a channel to the sea or another river, and including (see Salmon Act 1986, s 40(1)) tributaries and any loch from or through which any river flows. See Water Resources Act 1991. For 'main river', see 1991 Act, s 113.

road. 'Any highway or any other road to which the public has access, and includes

bridges over which a road passes': Road Traffic Regulation Act 1984, s 142. See also s 60(4); *Cutter v Eagle Star Ltd* [1997] 1 WLR 1082; *Clarke v Kato* [1998] 1 WLR 1647 (it is very rarely that a car park, the essential function of which is to enable vehicles to stand and wait, will be considered as a road, for purposes of insurance under Road Traffic Act 1988, s 145(3)(*a*)); *Sadiku v DPP* (1999) *The Times*, 3 December. *See* HIGHWAY; ROAD CHECKS.

road, and car park. A railway car park is not to be considered as a 'road' where it has no features of a road save for its use as an access to the railway staff car park: *Brewer v DPP* (2004) *The Times*, 5 March. See also *Cutter v Eagle Star Insurance Co Ltd* [1997] 1 WLR 1082.

road checks. Police are empowered to block a road (see Road Traffic Act 1972, s 159) under P. & C.E.A. 1984, s 4, so as to stop a vehicle to ascertain whether it is carrying a person unlawfully at large (q.v.), or one who intends to commit, or has committed, a serious arrestable offence (q.v.) or a witness to such an offence. See also Terrorism Act 2000, ss 33–36 (power to impose a police cordon).

road, Crown. *See* CROWN ROAD.

road, occupation. A road, the right to use which is confined to occupiers of land and premises which it serves. See Highways Act 1980, s 31(3)(*b*); *Fitch v Rawling* (1795) 2 Hy Bl 393.

road rage. Colloquialism for irrational, aggressive behaviour which is perceived by some persons as accompanying or explaining offences such as dangerous driving, assaults on drivers. See *R v Maben* [1997] Cr App R (S) 341.

road traffic casualties, payment for treatment. Under Road Traffic (NHS Charges) Act 1999, s 1, if a traffic casualty has suffered injury, or has suffered injury and died, following the use of a motor vehicle on the road, and a compensation payment has been made in respect of that injury or death, and the casualty has received NHS treatment at a health service hospital in respect of his injury, the person making that payment is liable to pay appropriate NHS charges in respect of the treatment.

road user charging schemes. 'Charging scheme' means a scheme for imposing charges in respect of the use or keeping of motor vehicles on roads: Transport Act 2000, s 163(1). Such charges are to be paid by the vehicle's registered keeper, or other persons specified in regulations: s 163(2). For enforcement of schemes, see s 173.

road-users, causing danger to. It is an offence for a person intentionally and without lawful authority or reasonable cause to cause anything to be on or over a road, or to interfere with a motor vehicle or traffic equipment in circumstances that it would be obvious to a reasonable person that to do so would be dangerous: Road Traffic Act 1988, s 22A, inserted by Road Traffic Act 1991, s 6.

robbery. Offence committed by one who steals and immediately before or at the time of doing so, and in order to do so, uses force on any person or puts or seeks to put any person in fear of being then and there subjected to force: Th.A. 1968, s 8(1). See *R* v *Guy* (1991) 93 Cr App R 108 (robbery necessarily includes theft); *R* v *Khan* (2000) *The Times*, 15 June; *A-G's Reference (No. 7 of 2000)* (2000) *The Times*, 15 June (unduly lenient sentences).

Roe, Richard. Name of a fictitious defendant (q.v.) used in an action of ejectment (q.v.).

rogatory letter. *See* LETTER OF REQUEST.

rogues and vagabonds. Persons who, under Vagrancy Act 1824, as subsequently amended, are found in a building or an enclosed area for any unlawful purpose, etc. See C.J.A. 1982, s 70; *Talbot* v *Oxford City Justices* (2000) *The Times*, 15 February (a room is not an 'enclosed area' in the context of the 1824 Act, s 4).

Romalpa clause. Stipulation in a contract of sale that the property in goods shall not leave the seller until he has received full payment. Known also as 'reserved title' or 'retention of title' clause. See *Aluminium*

Industrie Vaassen BV v *Romalpa Ltd* [1976] 2 All ER 552 (remedy of tracing allowed); *Armour* v *Thyssen AG* [1990] 3 All ER 481.

Rome, Treaty of. Founding treaty of the EEC (q.v.), signed in Rome on 25 March 1957 by founder states – Belgium, France, Federal Republic of Germany (i.e. West Germany), Italy, Luxembourg and The Netherlands.

room standard. In relation to overcrowding (q.v.), the room standard is contravened when the number of persons sleeping in a dwelling and the number of rooms available as sleeping accommodation is such that two persons of opposite sexes who are not living together as husband or wife must sleep in the same room. (Children under ten are left out of account; a room is considered to be available as sleeping accommodation if it is of a type used in the locality as a bedroom or living room.) See H.A. 1985, s 325(1), (2). *See* OVERCROWDING.

root of contract. The fundamental, essential features of a particular contract. See, e.g., *Decro-Wall International SA* v *Practitioners in Marketing Ltd* [1971] 2 All ER 216.

root of title. An instrument of disposition which describes land to be sold so that it can be identified, which relates to the ownership of the whole legal and equitable interest and which contains nothing to cast doubt on the title. Examples: voluntary conveyance, conveyance on sale. See *Re Duce* [1937] Ch 642; and *Wimpey Ltd* v *Sohn* [1967] Ch 487. *See* TITLE.

Royal Assent. This transforms a Bill into an Act of Parliament (q.v.) and takes the following forms: for ordinary bills, *la reyne (le roi) le veult* (the Queen (King) desires this); for private bills, *soit fait comme il est désiré* (let it be done as it is wished); for money bills, *la reyne remercie ses bons sujets, accepte leur benevolence, et ainsi le veult* (the Queen thanks her subjects, accepts their kindness and agrees that it be done). Refusal of the Assent (last exercised by Queen Anne in 1707) takes the form: *la Reyne s'avisera* (the Queen will take advice). See Royal

Assent Act 1967 (introducing Assent by Notification, under which the Assent is read out in both Houses, together with the Assent formula).

Royal prerogative. *See* PREROGATIVE, ROYAL.

royalties. Share of a product or profit paid to the owner of property from which it arises. Refers, in particular, to payments to an author by a publisher, usually based on a (fixed) percentage of the selling-price. See *Elton John* v *James* [1991] FSR 397; *Sterling Fluid System's Application* [1999] RPC 775.

Royal warrant. Authority issued to one who acts as a supplier of goods or services to a member of the Royal Family. See Trade Descriptions Act 1968, s 2, which makes false representations as to Royal approval an offence.

RSC. Rules of the Supreme Court (q.v.).

RSI. Repetitive Strain Injury. A form of tendinitis, occurring in arms and hands, resulting from continuous keyboard work. See *Pickford* v *ICI plc* [1998] 1 WLR 1189, in which the House of Lords stated that the term was of no diagnostic value, and that the trial judge had been correct in concluding that a typist had failed to prove that her condition was organic in its origins or that it was caused by excessive typing.

rule. 1. A regulation, principle, direction. 2. A standard by which to judge an individual's conduct.

rule, main purpose. *See* REPUGNANCY.

rule of law. *See* LAW, RULE OF.

rules of court. Rules made by the authority having for the time being power to make rules or orders regulating the practice and procedure of a court: I.A. 1978, Sch 1.

Rules of the Supreme Court. Rules relating to practice and procedure in the Supreme Court, made under S.C.A. 1981, s 84, by a Rule Committee. RSC were revoked with effect from 26 April, 1999 and are replaced by Civil Procedure Rules (CPR) 1998. See SI 98/3132. Some RSC were re-enacted in CPR, Schs 1, 2. *See* CPR.

running account credit. *See* CREDIT.

running days. Phrase referring to a charterparty (q.v.) in which days run consecutively, as contrasted with 'working days' (which exclude Sundays and public holidays).

running with the land. *See* COVENANT RUNNING WITH THE LAND.

S

s. Abbreviation for 'section' of an Act (q.v.), as in, e.g., P.C.C.(S.)A. 2000, s 2.

sabotage. Malicious destruction of or damage to property, so as to injure, e.g., a business or the military potential of the state. 'The saboteur just as much as the spy in the ordinary sense is contemplated as an offender under the Official Secrets Act': *Chandler* v *DPP* [1964] AC 763.

sacrilege. An offence consisting of breaking and entering and committing a felony in, or entering, committing a felony in and then breaking out of, any place of divine worship: Larceny Act 1916, s 24 (repealed by Th.A. 1968). See now Th.A. 1968, s 9. *See* BURGLARY.

sadistic conduct. CA held in *R* v *Sean Swindon; R* v *Michael Peart* [2006] *Attorney-General's Reference* (No. 108 & 109 of 2005) *The Times*, 22 February, for the purposes of the Criminal Justice Act 2003, Sch 21, para 5(2)(e), there need not be a sexual constituent involved for conduct to be held sadistic. What needs to be taken in to account is whether such conduct constitutes a sentence with a starting point of 30 years.

sado-masochism. A type of sexual perversion, characterised by the infliction of pain and humiliation, resulting in gratification for the parties involved. See *R* v *Brown* [1994] 1 AC 212, *per* Lord Templeman: 'I am not prepared to invent a defence of consent for sado-masochistic encounters which breed and glorify cruelty and result in offences under O.P.A. 1861, ss 20 and 47.' (European Court of Human Rights (q.v.) held that the prosecution and conviction of the applicants was a necessary intervention by the state in the safeguarding of health.) See *R* v *Emmett* (1999) *The Independent*, 19 July (risk of permanent injury outweighs consent).

safe goods. *See* GOODS, SAFE.

safe port. 'A port to which a vessel can get laden as she is and at which she can lay and discharge, always afloat': *per* Sankey J in *Hall Bros* v *Paul Ltd* (1914) 111 LT 812. It must be a port from which the vessel can return safely: *Limerick SS Co* v *Stott* [1921] 1 KB 568. See *Atkins International* v *Islamic Republic of Iran Shipping Lines* [1987] 1 FTLR 379.

safety at work. Under H.S.W.A. 1974, a general duty is placed on an employer to ensure the health and safety and welfare at work of his employees: s 2. See *McDermid* v *Nash* [1986] 2 All ER 676 (employer's duty to provide safe place of work). SI 92/2932 imposes an absolute duty on employers to maintain work equipment so as to ensure employee's safety: *Stark* v *Post Office* (2000) *The Times*, 29 March.

safety of goods. *See* CONSUMER SAFETY; GOODS, SAFE.

sale. 1. The act of selling. 2. A contract for the sale of goods whereby the seller transfers or agrees to transfer the property in goods to the buyer for a money consideration called the price: S.G.A. 1979, s 2(1). It includes 'bargain and sale' as well as 'sale and delivery': s 6(1). It does not include an agreement to sell (see s 2(4)): *Shaw* v *CMP* [1987] 1 WLR 1332. *See* PRICE.

sale, bill of. *See* BILL OF SALE.

sale by description. *See* DESCRIPTION, SALE BY.

sale by mortgagee in possession. In *Corbett* v *Halifax BS* (2002) *The Times*, 28 December, the CA held that where a mortgagee in possession had sold at an undervalue, that sale could not be set aside under Law of Property Act 1925, s 104(2), since it did not involve any improper exercise of the power of sale or an element of bad faith.

sale by the court. Sale of property following an order of the court, as in an action to enforce a mortgage. Under CPR, Sch 1; O 31, r 2, the court may give directions appointing person who will conduct the sale, fixing manner of sale, reserve or minimum price, obtaining evidence of value of property. See *Raja* v *Lloyds TSB* (2000) *The Times*, 16 May (duty of mortgagee on sale to obtain a proper price is owed in equity, not contract or tort).

sale of goods. *See* SALE.

sale of goods, passing of property in a. *See* PASSING OF PROPERTY IN A SALE OF GOODS.

sale or return. *See* APPROVAL, SALE ON.

sale, power of. *See* POWER OF SALE.

sale under voidable title. *See* VOIDABLE TITLE, SALE UNDER.

salvage. Reward to persons ('salvors') who save, or assist in saving, a ship, cargo or freight from shipwreck or similar jeopardy: *Wells* v *Owners of Whitton* [1897] AC 344. Amount payable is usually assessed by the court and apportioned among owners, crew, officers and master of the salving vessel. It must be shown that any services rendered were voluntary, skilled and beneficial. It is restricted to operations in tidal waters (q.v.): *The Goring* [1988] 2 WLR 460. See Merchant Shipping Act 1995, s 255(1). See *The Nagasaki Spirit* [1997] 2 WLR 298.

salvage claim. Includes any claim in the nature of salvage, any claim for special compensation under Merchant Shipping Act 1995, Sch 11, any claim for apportionment of salvage and any claim arising out of or connected with any contract for salvage services: PD 49F, para 1.4(e).

salvage of trust property. In a case of absolute necessity the court is able to sanction the mortgage or sale of part of an infant's beneficial interest for the

benefit of property retained: *Re Jackson* (1882) 21 Ch D 786. *See* TRUST.

same-sex survivors and tenancies. HL held in *Ghaidan* v *Godin-Mendoza* (2004) *The Times*, 24 June, that the survivor of a same-sex partnership possessed the same status as the spouse of a protected tenant entitled to succeed on the tenant's death as did a statutory tenant.

sample. Specimen presented for examination as evidence of the composition or quality of the whole. 'The office of a sample is to present to the eye the real meaning and intention of the parties . . . The sample speaks for itself': *per* Lord Macnaghten in *Drummond* v *Van Ingen* (1887) 12 App Cas 297.

sample, intimate and non-intimate. There is a power, under P.&C.E.A. 1984, s 62, amended by C.J.P.O.A. 1994, s 54, and Terrorism Act 2000, Sch 15, para 5, to take from persons in police detention, with consent, samples of blood, semen, or other tissue fluid, urine, saliva, pubic hair or swabs from a body orifice. 'Non-intimate sample' includes, e.g., footprints, samples of hair other than pubic. Consent to the taking of a non-intimate sample generally requires consent in writing: P.&C.E.A. 1984, s 63(1),(2). Consent is not required if the person concerned: is in police detention or is being held in custody by the police on the authority of a court (s 63(3)); or has been convicted of a recordable offence or has been charged with such an offence or informed that he will be reported for such an offence (s 63(3A),(3B)); or has been detained following acquittal on grounds of insanity or finding of unfitness to plead (s 62(3C)). See also 1984 Act, s 63B, inserted by C.J.C.S.A. 2000, s 57. Time allowed for requiring a person to attend a police station to have a sample taken is one month: C.J.P.O.A. 1994, as amended. For 'recordable offences', see P.&C.E.A. 1984, s 27. See Criminal Evidence (Amendment) Act 1997; *R* v *Cooke* [1995] 1 Cr App R 318; P.&C.E.A. 1984, s 64, amended by C.J.P.O.A. 1994, s 57 (retention or destruction of samples). *See* DNA PROFILING.

519

sample, sale by. Under S.G.A. 1979, s 15(2), amended by Sale and Supply of Goods Act 1994, Sch 2, para 5, it is implied in a contract of sale (q.v.) that the bulk shall correspond with the sample, that the buyer shall have a reasonable opportunity of comparing bulk and sample and that goods shall be free from any defect making their quality unsatisfactory which would not be apparent on reasonable examination of sample. See *Godley v Perry* [1960] 1 WLR 9.

sanction. 1. A solemn agreement. 2. That which authorises or confirms. 3. Measure used to punish some action. 'The appointed consequences of disobedience': Pollock, *Essays in Jurisprudence* (1882). 'It is because a rule is regarded as obligatory that a measure of coercion may be attached to it; it is not obligatory because there is coercion': Goodhart, *Law and the Moral Law* (1953). 4. Measure adopted by nations to coerce into an acceptable course of action a state offending against international law.

sanity, presumption of. *See* PRESUMPTION OF SANITY.

sans recours. Without recourse [to me]. Phrase used on a bill of exchange so that the endorser (e.g., the agent endorsing for the principal) is not personally liable. See B.Ex.A. 1882, s 16. *See* BILL OF EXCHANGE.

satisfaction. 1. Extinguishing of a claim, e.g., by performance. 2. Equitable doctrine, i.e., 'the donation of a thing with the intention that it is to be taken either wholly or in part in extinguishment of some prior claim of the donee': *Lord Chichester v Coventry* (1867) 36 LJ Ch 673. The general rule regarding satisfaction of debts by legacies (q.v.) is: 'if one, being indebted to another in a sum of money, does by his will give him a sum of money as great as, or greater than, the debt, without taking any notice at all of the debt, this shall, nevertheless, be in satisfaction of the debt, so that he shall not have both the debt and the legacy': *Talbot v Duke of Shrewsbury* (1714) Prec Ch 394.

satisfactory quality. *See* QUALITY, SATISFACTORY.

satisfied term. A term of years (q.v.) created for a purpose which is now fulfilled. See L.P.A. 1925, ss 5, 116.

savings bank. A society formed in the UK for the purpose of accepting deposits of money, accumulating the produce of the deposits at compound interest and returning the deposits and produce to the depositors after deducting necessary expenses of management but without deriving any benefit from the deposits or produce: Trustee Savings Bank Act 1981, s 1(3) (since repealed). See Trustee Savings Bank Act 1985; Banking Act 1987; *Ross v Lord Advocate* [1986] 1 WLR 1077.

schedule. 1. A formal list. 2. An appendix to a Bill or Act; it is, in every sense, a part of the Act. In the case of a contradiction between a schedule and a clause, the earlier enacted of the two prevails: *A-G v Lamplough* (1873) 3 Ex D 214. See *Buchanan & Co v Babco Ltd* [1978] AC 141.

scheme. 1. A scheme of arrangement is an agreement between a debtor and creditors allowing the debts to be paid under that agreement, rather than his being adjudged bankrupt. 2. An arrangement for the administration of a charitable trust (q.v.), e.g., so that it may be applied *cy-près* (q.v.). Whether it is ordered is in the discretion of the court: *Re Hanbey's WT* [1954] Ch 264.

school. An educational institution which is outside the further education and higher education sectors, and is an institution for providing primary, secondary, or primary and secondary education, whether or not the institution also provides part-time education suitable to the requirements of junior pupils or further education: Education Act 1997, s 51. For compulsory ages involved in schooling (currently 5–16), see Education Act 1996, s 8. Local education authorities have a duty to arrange for parents to express a preference as to the school at which they wish education to be provided for their children: School Standards and Framework Act 1998, s 86.

school, absence from. It was held in *Sutton LBC v S* (2004) *The Times*, 1 November, that a local education authority must consider carefully whether or not to appeal against an acquittal by the justices to acquit of the offence of failing, without justification, to send a child to school. The decision would be the responsibility of the chief education officer. *See SCHOOL ATTENDANCE.*

school accident, liability for. Where a school had diagnosed a potential or possible hazard in a play area, this did not did not imply that the school had a duty to take all steps so as to render use or access impossible: *Simonds v Isle of Wight Council* (2003) *The Times,* 9 October.

school attendance. Where a parent knows that his child is failing regularly to attend school and fails without reasonable justification to cause him to do so, he is guilty of an offence: Education Act 1996, s 444(1A), inserted by C.J.C.S.A. 2000, s 72.

school exclusion construction. It was held in *R (Shabina Begum) v Denbigh High School* (2004) *The Times,* 18 June that there was no exclusion, constructive or otherwise, where a school pupil had chosen not to wear school uniform, in the knowledge that the school would not be likely to allow her to attend unless she did.

schools, discipline in. The governing body of a school is obliged to ensure that policies designed to promote good behaviour and discipline on the part of its pupils are pursued at the school: School Standards and Framework Act 1998, s 61(1). The head teacher has the duty of determining measures, which may include the making of rules and provision for enforcing them, to be taken with a view to the promotion of self-discipline of pupils and proper regard for authority: s 61(4).

scienter rule. (*Sciens* = knowing.) Common law ruling that an animal must be kept securely by its owner from causing damage where he knows or is presumed to know of its mischievous disposition. See also Animals Act 1971, s 2(2); *Hunt v Wallis* (1991) *The Times,* 13 May; *Jaundrill v Gillett* (1996) *The Times,* 30 January.

scilicet. Abbreviated to *scil.,* or *sc.* That is to say.

scintilla juris. A spark or trace of a right or interest.

Scottish Executive. Created by Scotland Act 1998, s 44. Comprises First Minister (see s 46), and such other ministers as the First Minister may appoint under s 47, the Lord Advocate and the Solicitor General for Scotland. For shared powers with ministers of the Crown, see s 56.

Scottish Parliament. A unicameral body set up under Scotland Act 1998, s 1(1). One part comprises members singly representing constituencies; the other part comprises members elected by proportional representation on a regional basis: s 1(2). The Presiding Officer and two deputies are elected by the Parliament: s 19. Powers of legislation are conferred by s 28. Bills must be submitted by the President for Royal Assent (q.v.). For enactments protected from modification by the Scottish Parliament, and other reserved matters, see Schs 4, 5.

Scottish zone. *See ZONE, SCOTTISH.*

screens in court. A special measures direction may provide for a witness, while giving testimony or being sworn in court, to be prevented by means of a screen or other arrangement from seeing the accused. It must not prevent the witness from being able to see and be seen by the judge, justices, jury, legal representatives, interpreters: Y.J.C.E.A. 1999, s 23. See *R v Brown* [1998] 2 Cr App R 364.

scrip. A certificate or memorandum of shares held in a company. Generally a negotiable instrument (q.v.).

scuttling. The sinking of a ship, e.g., for the purpose of recovering insurance money. See *Probatina Shipping Co v Sun Insurance Office* [1974] QB 635.

SDLT. Stamp Duty Land Tax, imposed under the Finance Act 2003, s 42, chargeable under land transactions involving the acquisition of a chargeable interest, i.e., an estate, interest, right or power in or over land in the UK, or the benefit of an obligation, restriction or condition affecting the value of any such estate, interest, right or power other than an exempt interest (e.g., a licence to use or occupy land). From 1 December 2003, stamp duty is replaced by Stamp Duty Land Tax, save for any transactions relating to transfer of stock and marketable securities.

seal. 1. Wax impressed and attached to a document so as to authenticate it. 2. 'A seal is a mark which the court puts on a document to indicate that the document has been issued by the court': CPR Glossary.

seal, contract under. *See* CONTRACT UNDER SEAL.

sealing. Process used in the execution of some documents, e.g., deeds (q.v.), based on signifying assent. 'To constitute a sealing neither wax nor wafer nor a piece of paper, not even an impression is necessary': *Re Sandilands* (1871) LR 6 CP 411. The seal may be in the form of the word 'seal' printed in a circle on the document. See L.P. (Misc. Provs.) A. 1989, s 1(1), abolishing the requirement of sealing for the valid execution of an instrument as a deed by an individual. *See* LOCUS SIGILLI.

search and seizure cases. Cases in which police entering premises under a search warrant may seize goods which afford some evidence of a criminal offence (even though those goods are not of the description specified in that warrant). In *R (on application of Rottman)* v *Commissioner of Police of the Metropolis* [2002] 2 WLR 315, HL held that a police officer effecting an arrest under Extradition Act 1989, s 8 (1), has a common law power to search the home of the arrested person and to seize his documents and goods. See also *Anton Piller* orders (now known as search orders (q.v.)); P.&C.E.A. 1984, s 32, amended by Terrorism Act 2000, Sch 15, para 5. *R* v *Beckford* [1991] Crim LR 918.

searches. Investigations made, e.g., at the Land Charges Registry to check the existence of registrable encumbrances (q.v.). See L.R.A. 1925, s 112(1), substituted by L.R.A. 1988, s 1(1); SI 93/3276.

search, intimate. A search of a detained person, which consists of the physical examination of the body's orifices, may be authorised by a police superintendent where there are reasonable grounds for believing that an object (which might be used to cause physical injury, or is a Class A drug) cannot be found without such a search: see P.&C.E.A. 1984, ss 55(1), (2), 118(1). The court may draw such inferences 'as appear proper' from a person's refusal to submit to such a search: s 62(10). See *Brazil* v *Chief Constable of Surrey* [1983] 1 WLR 1155; Terrorism Act 2000, Sch 15, para 5. *See* SAMPLE, INTIMATE AND NON-INTIMATE.

search orders. Defined under CPR, r 25.1(h) as orders under Civil Procedure Act 1997, s 7, empowering court to make orders, in the context of proceedings, for the preservation of evidence which is or may be relevant, or the preservation of property which is or may be the subject matter of proceedings. The orders permit persons to enter premises in England and Wales so as to carry out a search for or inspection of anything described in the orders, or the retention for safe-keeping of anything described in the orders. Known formerly as 'Anton Piller orders' (q.v.). An application must be supported by affidavit evidence: PD 25, para 3.1. For details concerning the supervising solicitor who carries out the search order, see PD 25, paras 7, 8. See *Gadget Shop Ltd* v *Bug Com Ltd* (2000) *The Times*, 28 June.

search, power of. Power to seek out, procure and preserve real evidence for the prosecution. There is no statutory power given to private individuals to search persons or property. Statutory power is given to, e.g., police officers, Department of Trade officials, customs officers. See, e.g., S.O.A. 1956, s 42; Firearms Act 1968, s 47; Th.A. 1968, s 26; Criminal Damage Act 1971, s 6; P.&C.E.A. 1984, ss 1, 2, 17, and revised Code B (1991) (introducing a standard Notice of Powers and Rights to be given to the subjects of searches); see *R* v *Sanghera* (2000) *The Times*, 26 October. Immigration Act 1971, s 28E, inserted by Immigration and Asylum Act 1999, s 132. For general power of special hospitals (e.g.

Broadmoor) to search mental detainees, see *R* v *Broadmoor Special Hospital Authority ex p S* [1998] COD 199. The police may search private premises without a warrant when, e.g., they are given permission by the occupiers to do so, or in order to make an arrest. See Proceeds of Crime Act 1995, s 12; P.C.C.(S.)A. 2000, s 142 (power of Crown Court to order search of persons before it); Terrorism Act 2000, s 42. *See* ARREST, SEARCH UPON.

search upon arrest. *See* ARREST, SEARCH UPON.

search warrant. Warrant (q.v.) issued by magistrates, e.g., for the entry and search of premises for stolen goods, or drugs or firearms. See, e.g., Th.A. 1968, s 26; Misuse of Drugs Act 1971, s 23; P.&C.E.A. 1984, Part III. 1984 Act, s 8, allows search warrants to be issued by magistrates for evidence of commission of a serious arrestable offence; this does not empower police to search persons found in the premises unless they are arrested or the warrant includes an appropriate power. The tort of 'maliciously procuring a search warrant' exists where a plaintiff is able to show that: defendant made or caused to be made a successful application for the warrant; defendant lacked reasonable and probable cause to make the application; defendant acted with malice; damage resulted from the issue or execution of the warrant: *Gibbs* v *Rea* [1998] AC 786. See *R* v *Chesterfield Justices ex p Bramley* [2000] QB 576 (taking goods away in exercising a search warrant); *R* v *Manchester Stipendiary Magistrate ex p Granada TV Ltd* (1999) *The Times*, 22 December (Scottish search warrant held valid in England). It was held, in *DPP* v *Meaden* [2003] EWHC 3005, that, for purposes of the Police and Criminal Evidence Act 1984, s 117, it is reasonable for police who are executing a search warrant to seek to restrict, by no more force than is necessary, the movement of occupiers of the premises while those premises are being searched.

search warrant, malicious procurement of. CA held in *Keegan* v *Chief Constable*

of Merseyside Police [2003] EWCA Civ 936, that the tort of malicious procurement of a search warrant necessitates proof of absence of any reasonable or probable cause by the police to seek such a warrant, and presence of an improper motive for procuring the warrant. Neither incompetence nor negligence will suffice. See also *Gibbs* v *Rea* [1998] AC 786.

search warrant, reasons for. Where justices were satisfied that an information from the police included all the material needed to establish that a search warrant ought to be issued, it was not necessary for a written record to be made showing the reason for grant of the warrant: *R (Cronin)* v *Sheffield Magistrates' Court* [2002] EWHC 2568.

seas, beyond the. *See* BEYOND THE SEAS.

sea, the. 'Includes any area submerged at mean high water springs, and also includes, so far as the tide flows at mean high water springs, an estuary or an arm of the sea and the waters of any channel, creek, bay or river': Offshore Petroleum Development (Scotland) Act 1975, s 20(2). See Territorial Sea Act 1987. *See* TERRITORIAL WATERS.

seaworthy. In the context of the Hague Rules, means that the ship, with her master and crew, is fit to encounter the perils of the voyage and fit to carry her cargo safely on that voyage: *Actis Co* v *Stanko Steamship Co* [1982] 1 WLR 119. See *The Benlawers* [1989] 2 Lloyd's Rep 51; *The Fjord Wind* [1998] CLC 1186.

seck rent. Dry rent (q.v.).

seclusion of patient. 'Seclusion' is defined (see para 19.16 of Code of Practice relating to Mental Health Act 1983) as the supervised confinement of a patient in a room which can be locked in order to protect other patients from significant harm. A lawfully-detained patient placed under seclusion has not been deprived of his liberty so as a result in the tort of false imprisonment, and the European Convention, art 5 (right to liberty) is not breached: *S* v *Airdale NHS Trust* [2002] EWHC 1780.

secondary action. Exists, in relation to a trade dispute (q.v.), only when a person induces another to break a contract of employment or interferes or induces another to interfere with its performance, or threatens that a contract of employment under which he or another is employed will be broken or its performance interfered with, or that he will induce another to break a contract of employment or to interfere with its performance, and the employer under the contract of employment is not the employer party to the dispute: T.U.L.R.(C.)A. 1992, s 224.

secondary evidence. *See* EVIDENCE, SECONDARY.

secondary legislation, ability of court to review. The legality of subordinate legislation, even where approved by affirmative resolution of each House of Parliament, can be reviewed by the court, in relation to questions of procedural impropriety, illegality or unreasonableness. See *R (Javed)* v *Home Secretary* (2001) *The Times*, 24 May, in which Court of Appeal reviewed legality of SI 96/2671 (Asylum (Designated Safe Third Countries) Order).

secondary party. One, other than the principal offender, who participates in the commission of a crime. See *R* v *Dunnington* [1984] QB 472; *R* v *Hyde* [1990] 3 All ER 892.

secondary use. Shifting use (q.v.).

second chamber, proposals for. *A House for the Future* (Royal Commission on Reform of House of Lords, 2000, Cm 4534) proposes a new 550-member second chamber, partly elected, partly nominated. There would be a minimum 20 per cent of independent cross-benchers and 30 per cent of women. Elections would be through the regions by proportional representation. An Appointments Commission would maintain a political balance of the chamber. Law Lords would be members of the chamber. All Christian denominations and non-Christian faiths would be represented.

second chamber, proposed powers of. The Wakeham Commission (see Cm 4534) suggests that the second chamber should retain its suspensory veto under the Parliament Acts, should have greater powers over voicing concerns and delay-

ing statutory instruments, should set up a constitutional committee to scrutinise the implications of legislation, and should establish a human rights committee to examine the content of all Bills.

second chamber, proposed roles of. The Wakeham Commission (see Cm 4534) suggests four leading roles for the reformed second chamber: bringing different perspectives to bear on the development of public policy; giving a Parliamentary voice to all parts of British society; playing a vital role as provider of constitutional checks and balances; providing a voice for the nations and regions of the UK in public affairs.

second marriage. Refers in O.P.A. 1861, s 57, to the second marriage charged in the indictment: *R* v *Taylor* [1950] 2 KB 368. See *R* v *Sagoo* [1975] QB 885. *See* BIGAMY.

second mortgage. *See* MORTGAGE, SECOND.

second serious offence leading to life sentence. *See* LIFE SENTENCE FOR SECOND SERIOUS OFFENCE.

secretary. *See* COMPANY SECRETARY.

Secretary of State. Member of the government in charge of a department. Appointed by the Crown and usually assisted by Parliamentary Under-Secretaries of State. See I.A. 1978, Sch 1.

secret profits. Profits made by an agent acting in that capacity and not accounted for to his principal. See *Hippisley* v *Knee Bros* [1905] 1 KB 1; *Boardman* v *Phipps* [1967] 2 AC 46; in relation to secret profit and theft, *A-G's Reference (No. 1 of 1985)* [1986] QB 491. *See* AGENT.

secret reserves. Reserves not disclosed in the balance sheet or accounts.

secret trust. A trust which exists where a will (q.v.) or other instrument discloses neither the existence of the trust nor its terms. Example: X bequeaths a legacy to Y and, during his (X's) lifetime Y promises that he will hold the subject matter of the legacy on trust for Z. See *Blackwell* v *Blackwell* [1929] AC 318; *Re Snowden* [1979] Ch 528. *See* HALF-SECRET TRUST.

sectioning. Colloquialism for procedures involved in the compulsory admission to a hospital of persons suffering from a mental disorder under an appropriate section of M.H.A. 1983 (see ss 2–6, 37). *See* HOSPITAL ORDER.

sections of an Act. Distinct, numbered sub-divisions of an Act of Parliament (q.v.). 'Every section of an Act takes effect as a substantive enactment without introductory words': I.A. 1978, s 1 (applying to Acts passed after commencement of 1978 Act and to existing Acts passed after 1850).

secure accommodation. Accommodation for the restriction of liberty of children in care who have a history of absconding and are likely to suffer harm if they abscond: Ch.A. 1989, s 25; Acc.J.A. 1999, Sch 4, para 45; C.&Y.P.A. 1969, s 23 (12), amended by Care Standards Act 2000, Sch 4, para 3; *Re K* (2000) *The Times*, 20 November.

secured creditor. *See* CREDITOR.

secure tenancy. Applied to a dwelling house let as a separate dwelling where the landlord was a local authority, housing association etc., and the tenant was an individual, occupying the dwelling house as his only or principal home, or, in the case of a joint tenancy, each tenant was an individual, and at least one of them occupied the dwelling house as his only or principal home: see H.A. 1985, ss 79–81. In general, a secure tenancy could not be brought to an end by the landlord except by obtaining an order for possession: s 82. Following H.A. 1988, a tenancy entered into after commencement of the Act cannot be a secure tenancy unless entered into under a contract made before commencement of the Act, or the landlord's interest belongs to, e.g., a local authority, new town corporation: s 35. For succession to a deceased tenant, see H.A. 1985, s 87; *Waltham Forest LBC* v *Thomas* [1992] 2 AC 198; *Kingston RLBC* v *Prince* [1998] EGCS 179 (minor could succeed to secure tenancy); *Burton* v *Camden LBC* (2000) *The Times*, 23 February. For repossession in relation to grounds of nuisance or annoyance to neighbours, see H.A. 1996, s 148. *See* ASSURED TENANCY.

securities. 1. Things deposited or pledged to ensure the fulfilling of an obligation. 2. Written evidence of ownership, e.g., certificates. 3. Under C.C.A. 1974, s 189(1), in relation to an actual or prospective consumer credit or hire agreement, a security is a mortgage, charge, pledge, bond, debenture, indemnity, guarantee, bill, note or other right provided by the debtor or hirer to secure the carrying out of obligations under the agreement. See, e.g., Transport Act 1985, s 137(1), under which 'securities', in relation to a body corporate, means any shares, stock, debentures, debenture stock, and any other security of a similar nature, of that body; I.C.T.A. 1988, ss 710, 729; T.C.G.A. 1992, Sch 9 'gilt-edged' securities (q.v.)). 'Convertible securities' means securities of a specified kind which can be converted into, or exchanged for, or which confer rights to acquire, other securities: F.S.M.A. 2000, Sch 11, para 17(2). *See* EURO-SECURITIES.

Securities and Investments Board. Agency set up under F.S.A. 1986, Sch 9, which authorises the carrying on of investment businesses (q.v.). See *SIB* v *Pantell SA* [1993] Ch 256; *Gordon* v *Wheatley & Co* (2000) *The Times*, 6 June.

securities, authorised. *See* AUTHORISED SECURITIES.

securities, listed. *See* LISTED SECURITIES.

securities, transfer of. The Secretary of State may make regulations for enabling title to securities to be evidenced and transferred without a written interest: Cos.A. 1989, s 207(1). 'Title' includes legal or equitable interest in securities. See SI 95/3272.

security consultants. Persons involved in the giving of advice about: the taking of security precautions in relation to any risk to property or to the person; or the acquisition of any services involving the activities of a security operative: P.S.I.A. 2001, Sch 2, para 5.

security for costs. *See* COSTS, SECURITY FOR.

Security Industry Authority. Set up under P.S.I.A. 2001, s 1, to keep under review provision of private security services, to carry out licensing functions and to set standards of conduct in relation to the industry. See Sch 1. It must establish and maintain a register of persons licensed under the Act: s 12.

security industry, licence requirement. Under P.S.I.A. 2001, s 3, it is an offence to engage in any licensable conduct, as defined under the Act, without a licence. Thus, it is an offence for a firm to use unlicensed security operatives or unlicensed wheel-clampers: ss 5, 6.

security industry services. Services provided under a contract for services and in the course of which the provider secures that the services of a security operative are carried out, or that a person is made available to carry out, under directions given by or on behalf of another person, any activities which will or are likely to consist of or include the activities of a security operative: P.S.I.A. 2001, s 25; Sch 2, Part I (outlining activities of security operatives).

security, national. *See* NATIONAL SECURITY.

security officers, court. Appointed under C.J.A. 1991, s 76, to search persons entering the courthouse, to exclude those who refuse to permit a search, or whose presence may interfere with the maintenance of order.

security of tenure. *See* TENURE, SECURITY OF.

Security Service. Operates under the authority of the Home Secretary. Its function is 'the protection of national security and, in particular, its protection against threats from espionage, terrorism and sabotage, from the activities of agents of foreign powers and from actions intended to overthrow or undermine parliamentary democracy by political, industrial or violent means': Security Service Act 1989, s 1. Under 1989 Act, s 1(4), added by Security Service Act 1996, s 1(1), it is also the function of the Service to act in support of the activities of the police forces and other law enforcement agencies in the prevention and detection of serious crime. Its operations are controlled by a Director-General appointed by the

Secretary of State: s 2(1). A tribunal investigates complaints about the Service: s 5(1), Schs 1, 2. See also Official Secrets Act 1989, s 1. F.I.A. 2000, s 23. *See* INTELLIGENCE SERVICE; NATIONAL SECURITY.

security, valuable. Includes any document creating, transferring, surrendering or releasing a right in or over property, or authorising the payment of money or delivery of any property, or the satisfaction of any obligation: see Th.A. 1968, s 20(3); *R v King* [1991] 3 WLR 246; *R v Kassim* [1992] 1 AC 9.

security, valuable, execution of. *See* PROCURING EXECUTION OF A VALUABLE SECURITY.

sedition. The publication, orally or in writing, of words intended 'to bring into hatred or contempt, or to excite disaffection against the person of Her Majesty, her heirs, or successors, or the government and constitution of the UK . . . or either House of Parliament . . . or to raise discontent or disaffection amongst Her Majesty's subjects, or to promote feelings of ill-will and hostility between different classes of such subjects': *R v Burns* (1886) 16 Cox CC 335.

seditious libel. Sedition (q.v.) in the form of printed words.

sed quaere. But question; enquire further.

seduction. Persuasion to disobedience, illicit sexual intercourse, desertion or other disloyalty. It is an offence under Incitement to Disaffection Act 1934 to endeavour to seduce a member of the Forces from his duty and allegiance to the Crown. See *R v Arrowsmith* [1975] QB 678.

segregation. Isolation, or setting apart, of individuals or groups. *See* RACIAL SEGREGATION.

seisin. (*Saisir* = to seize.) Feudal concept based on the physical occupation of land, so that an estate in freehold involved a right to seisin. Proof of seisin was required in actions for recovery of land. *Seisin in law:* seisin possessed by an heir whose ancestor had died seised of the land. *Seisin in deed:* actual possession of the freehold.

seized documents, disclosure of. CA held in *R (Kent Pharmaceuticals) v*

Director of Serious Fraud Office (2004) *The Times*, 18 November, that where SFO has expressed an intention to forward copies of seized documents to other government departments, it ought to give notice to document owners so that they might make appropriate representations.

seized goods. A person may attempt to invoke the discretionary procedure under the Customs and Excise Management Act 1979, Sch 3, aimed at the restoration of seized goods, imported without payment of appropriate duty. He may argue that the goods were bought for private use: *Commissioners of Customs and Excise* v *Dickinson* (2003) *The Times*, 15 October.

seized property, return of. CA held in *Gough* v *Chief Constable of West Midlands Police* (2004) *The Times*, 4 March, that where a police force retained material seized lawfully from an individual who had previously been in possession of it, they had the right to resist a civil claim by the former possessor for its return but only where it was possible to establish a statutory power allowing them a right to retain it in the circumstances.

seizure. Taking possession by force. For powers of seizure exercisable by a constable, see P.&C.E.A. 1984, ss 1(6), 19, 55(12). See also Th.A. 1968, s 26(3) (search in relation to stolen goods); *R* v *Chesterfield Justices ex p Bramley* [2000] 2 WLR 409.

seizure, powers of. C.J.P.A. 2002, s 50, where a person who is lawfully on premises finds something that he reasonably believes to be that for which he is authorised to search, and it is not reasonably practicable for it to be determined whether what he has found is something that he is entitled to seize, he may remove it from the premises. 'Seize' includes 'take a copy of': s 63.

select committee. *See* COMMITTEE, SELECT.

self-dealing. Transactions in which, e.g., a trustee, acting for himself and in his capacity as trustee, is placed in a position wherein his obligations are opposed to his self-interest. See *Re Thompson's Settlement* [1985] 2 All ER 720; *Kane* v *Radley Kane* [1998] 3 WLR 617.

self-defence. Acting so as to defend oneself, one's property or, possibly, some other person such as a parent, child, spouse, against violence or a reasonable apprehension of it. It may be an answer to a charge of, e.g., unlawful homicide (q.v.), where no more force is used than is necessary and there is an honest belief based on reasonable grounds that force is necessary. The plea is destroyed by a mistake of fact induced by voluntary intoxication: *R* v *O'Grady* [1987] 3 WLR 321. It is not the law that the accused should have retreated as far as possible before the attack: *R* v *McInnes* [1971] 3 All ER 295. See *R* v *Fisher* [1987] Crim LR 334; *DPP* v *Braun* (1998) *The Times*, 26 October; Law Com. No. 177, s 44. *See* REASONABLE FORCE.

self-defence, and conviction for murder, recommendations. The House of Lords Select Committee on Murder and Life Imprisonment (the Nathan Committee) recommended, in July 1989, that a new defence reducing murder to manslaughter be created to take effect where a person kills in self-defence or in the prevention of crime, but uses excessive force, if at the time of the act he honestly believed that the force used was reasonable in the circumstances. A further recommendation was that the mandatory life sentence for murder be abolished. *See* LIFE IMPRISONMENT.

self-defence in crime prevention. *See* REASONABLE FORCE.

self-defence in relation to burglary. Home Secretary announced (2005) *The Times*, 12 January, that the existing law allowing 'reasonable force' to be used against burglars was 'sound'. A publicity campaign would be mounted to help persons to understand the current law.

self-defence, right of nations. For relevant customary rule of international law, see *The Caroline Case* (1837) 2 Moore Digest 412. Under UN Charter, art 51, nations have the inherent right of individual or collective self-defence if an armed attack occurs against them, until the

Security Council has taken measures necessary to maintain international peace and security. See also NATO Treaty 1949, art 5.

self-employed. A person who is gainfully employed in Great Britain otherwise than in employed earner's employment: see, e.g., S.S.A. 1975, s 2(1)(*b*). See *Hall* v *Lorimer* [1992] STC 599; *Barnett* v *Brabyn* [1996] STC 716.

self-employment. CA held in *Mingeley* v *Pennock and Ivory* (2004) *The Times*, 4 March, that a self-employed taxi driver did not fall within the terms of the extended definition of 'employment' in the Race Relations Act 1976, s 78(1), relating to an obligation to personally execute any work or labour. See also *Mirror Group Newspapers* v *Gunning* [1986] 1 WLR 546.

self-help. An extra-judicial remedy whereby, e.g., in the case of trespass to land, the person in possession may eject the trespasser, using such force as is reasonable in the circumstances. See *Hemmings* v *Stoke Poges Golf Club* [1920] 1 KB 720; *R* v *Chapman* (1993) *The Times*, 29 June.

self-incriminating answers. It was held by the European Court of Human Rights, in *Kansal* v *UK (Application No. 21413/02)* (2004) *The Times*, 29 April, that where answers given under compulsion to the Official Receiver were utilised during a subsequent criminal trial, there existed a breach of the fair trial provisions of the European Convention on Human Rights, even though the trial was held prior to the incorporation of the Convention into English law under the Human Rights Act 1998.

self-incrimination, privilege against. The giving by a person of evidence or replies to questions, the result of which might lead that person to be prosecuted. 'When giving evidence, an accused person shall not be asked, and if asked shall not be required to answer, any question tending to show that he has committed or been convicted of or been charged with any offence other than that wherewith he is then charged or is of bad character',

unless, e.g., he has given evidence against some other person charged with the same offence: Criminal Evidence Act 1898, s 1(*f*) (as amended by Criminal Evidence Act 1979). See Criminal Evidence Act 1968, s 14(1); Criminal Damage Act 1971, s 9; S.C.A. 1981, s 72 (see *Istel Ltd* v *Tully* (1992) NLJ 88); C.J.P.O.A. 1994, s 36(1); *Bishopsgate Investment Management Ltd* v *Maxwell* [1993] Ch 1; *IJL* v *UK* (2000) *The Times*, 13 October; *Re Westminster Property Management Ltd* (2000) *The Times*, 19 January (self-incrimination is lawful in civil proceedings); Cos.A. 1985, s 434(5), as amended by Cos.A. 1989. *See* INCRIMINATE; SILENCE, RIGHT OF ACCUSED TO.

self-regulating organisation. A body, corporate or unincorporated, which regulates the carrying on of investment business of any kind by enforcing rules which are binding on persons carrying on business of that kind whether because they are members of that body or otherwise subject to its control: F.S.A. 1986, s 8(1).

self-serving statement. Statement, cautioned or uncautioned, in which defendant denies an offence, or admits an offence while offering an explanation. See *Leung Kam Kwok* v *R* (1985) 81 Cr App R 83.

sell, agreement to. Where under a contract of sale the transfer of the property in the goods is to take place at a future time or subject to some conditions later to be fulfilled, the contract is called an agreement to sell: S.G.A. 1979, s 2(4). It confers no title under s 21: *Shaw* v *CMP* [1987] 1 WLR 1332. See *Connell Estate Agents* v *Begej* (1993) 39 EG 125.

seller. Under S.G.A. 1979, s 61(1), one who sells or agrees to sell goods. It may include a person who is in the position of a seller, e.g., as agent (q.v.). See Sale and Supply of Goods Act 1994, Sch 2, para 5.

seller, unpaid. *See* UNPAID SELLER.

semble. It seems. Word used to suggest that a particular point may be doubtful.

sentence. Punishment or penalty imposed on a person found guilty by the court. (It does not include committal in default of payment: M.C.A. 1980, s 150(1); P.C.C.(S.)A. 2000, s 163.) Generally, save in case of murder or other offences for which penalty is fixed by law, the court has the discretion to select a sentence which it considers suitable in all the circumstances, e.g., the nature and gravity of offence, background and needs of the offender. Principles applied in sentencing were said, in *R v Sergeant* (1974) 118 SJ 753, to be retribution, deterrence, prevention and rehabilitation. See comments of Hilbery J on sentencing, in *R v Blake* (1961) 45 Cr App R 292; M.C.A. 1980, s 108(3). For review by A-G and Court of Appeal of apparently unduly lenient sentences, see C.J.A. 1988, s 36; SI 00/1924. See Crime (Sentences) Act 1997, for conditions relating to mandatory life sentences, etc. For exemplary sentences, see, e.g., *R v McMaster* [1998] 2 Cr App R (S) 300 (such sentences required to deter brutal attacks). For pre-sentence reports (q.v.), which are required, e.g., where a court is contemplating sentencing a defendant to prison for the first time (except for a very short period), see *R v Gillette* (1999) *The Times*, 3 December (and see, also, P.C.C.(S.)A. 2000, ss 156, 162). For relevance of defendant's old age to sentence, see *R v W* (2000) *The Times*, 26 September. *See* CONCURRENT AND CONSECUTIVE SENTENCES.

sentence appeals, prosecution and. CA noted in considering Practice Direction (Criminal proceedings: Sentences appeals) (2003) *The Times*, 4 October, that in future, the prosecution must be notified should defendant have been granted leave to appeal against sentence, or if his application, for leave to appeal against sentence had been referred to CA, in order that they might be represented at the hearing.

sentence, community. *See* COMMUNITY ORDERS AND SENTENCE.

sentence, custodial. Defined under P.C.C.(S.)A. 2000, s 76, as a sentence of imprisonment, detention, custody for life, detention in young offender institution, detention and training order. In the case of a discretionary custodial sentence

(e.g., one not fixed by law, and where the offence is violent or sexual) a custodial sentence may be passed if the offender fails to express his willingness to comply with the requirements of a probation or supervision order: s 70. Pre-sentence reports are required before the imposition of a discretionary custodial sentence: s 81. *See* IMPRISONMENT OF PERSONS UNDER 21.

sentence, deferring of. *See* DEFERRING OF SENTENCE.

sentence, discounting for valuable help. *R v A (Informer: Reduction of Sentence)* [1998] Crim LR 757 sets out principles under which a discount of sentence might be given where defendant pleads guilty and gives valuable information. Thus: sentence may be discounted to reflect an early plea of guilty; discount may be enhanced where defendant's statement leads to a co-defendant's plea of guilty or his conviction; extent of discount may reflect value of help given; information supplied after sentence will not ordinarily lead to a reduction of sentence.

sentence, procedure on. Defendant is asked if he has anything to say before sentence and pleas in mitigation are heard. Defendant's antecedents of the accused (character, etc.) are given. Defendant may be remanded for a medical or social enquiry report before sentence. He may ask for other offences to be taken into consideration. Sentence is then given orally by the trial judge. He is obliged to explain the practical effect of the sentence (including matters such as compensation, disqualification, costs, confiscation, etc.) so that it is understood by defendant, any victim and any member of the public who is present in court or reads a full report of the proceedings: *Practice Direction (Custodial Sentences: Explanation)* (1998) *The Times*, 24 January.

sentences, consecutive. In *R v Noble* (2002) *The Times*, 11 July (conviction following deaths of six persons by dangerous driving), the CA held that fact that multiple deaths were caused was not in itself a sufficient reason for imposing consecutive sentences; main focus of sentencing judge in a case of this nature should have been on the dangerous nature of the driving, and a consideration of all the circumstances and results of that driving. Note however, in *R v Greaves* (2003) *The Times*, 12 November, the CA held that where a weapon has been used in the process of robbery, a consecutive sentence ought to be imposed in relation to possession of the weapon.

sentences, extended. Where an extended sentence is being considered for defendants convicted of sex offences or offences of violence, under Powers of the Criminal Courts (Sentencing) Act 2000, s 85, defence counsel should be given advance warning. Sentencing necessitates: decision on sentence commensurate with gravity of offence; consideration of whether longer period in custody is essential for protection of public from offender; where sentence is four years or more (arising from sexual or violent offence), consideration of adequacy of sentence to prevent further offences by offender and to effect his rehabilitation. See *R v Nelson* (2001) *The Times*, 10 December. Where a prisoner is serving an extended sentence, imposed because it is considered that the public needs to be protected from serious harm he is likely to cause, he has no right under the European Convention, art 5.4, to an oral hearing by the Parole Board following the expiry of the punitive (tariff) element of his sentence. See *R (Giles) v Parole Board* [2003] UKHL 42.

sentences, guidelines. CA in *R v Lang & 12 Others* [2005] *The Times*, 10 November there are now a number of new sentences and factors under the Criminal Justice Act 2003, Sch 15, which need to be considered by the sentencers when sentencing offenders to life imprisonment, imprisonment for public protection and extended life sentences.

sentences, length of. CA held in *R v Barber* [2006] *The Times*, 4 April, where a judge departs from the usual practice direction of making a direction under s 240(3) of the Criminal Justice Act 2003, and does not take in to account the time an offender has spent

in remand as time served as part of the sentence, the defence council should be given an opportunity to address the judge on the matter.

sentences, life, review of. Where the Home Secretary had been obliged to make changes in the regime concerning the release of mandatory life prisoners, an interim procedure which had accelerated a prisoner's review of his sentence was not in breach of the European Convention, art 5.4. *Murray v Parole Board* (2003) *The Times*, 12 November.

sentences, longer, imposition of. A judge ought to inform counsel where he was considering the imposition on an offender of a sentence which was longer than that related to the seriousness of the offence, under Powers of Criminal Courts (Sentencing) Act 2000, s 80(2)(b), in order that counsel might be able to make a submission as to whether all the conditions necessary for such a sentence had been met. A sentence of this nature ought to be imposed only where it was shown that there was a need to protect the public from serious harm from the offender. See *R v Cameron* (2003) *The Times*, 12 February.

sentences, referral by Attorney General. CA held in *A-G's Reference (No. 10 of 2003) (R v Jutal* (2002)) *The Times*, 30 May, that where the AG seeks to refer a sentence which he considers too lenient, his reference must refer accurately to events at the trial, and the draft reference must be referred to counsel who acted for the prosecution at the trial so that he might make relevant comments while details of the trial were fresh in his mind.

sentences, suspended. A suspended sentence of 12 months' imprisonment for causing death by dangerous driving was referred by the AG as unduly lenient. The reference was allowed: there were situations where it might be possible to discover exceptional circumstances allowing the suspension of a sentence, but such circumstances would have to be 'truly exceptional', and none existed in this case. The sentence was, therefore, unduly lenient. See *AG's Reference (No. 85 of 2003)* [2004] EWCA Crim 386.

sentence, suspended. *See* SUSPENDED SENTENCE.

sentencing, determination of minimum term. CA held in *R v Peters; R v Palmer; R v Campbell* [2006] *The Times,* 29 March, when determining an appropriate sentence for a young offender for murder under the Criminal Justice Act 2003, Sch 21 the term should reflect the seriousness of the crime, and consider the offender's age and maturity.

sentencing for contempt. CA held in *Turnbull v Middlesbrough BC* (2003) *The Times,* 15 September, that a prison sentence of two years (the maximum) for contempt of court ought to be reserved for the most serious type of case. Where a young person was involved and no violence had taken place, the sentence was clearly excessive.

sentencing guidelines. The Sentencing Advisory Panel provides advice and information to the Court of Appeal (Criminal Division) concerning sentencing guidelines in relation to, e.g., need to promote consistency in sentencing: C.D.A. 1998, ss 80, 81.

sentencing, road rage. CA held in *R v Normanton* [2003] EWCA Crim 959, that in relation to assault involving bodily harm in a road rage incident, a custodial sentence will be almost inevitable, even though the offender is of good character. *See* ROAD RAGE.

sentencing, sex offenders. CA held in *AG's References (Nos 91, 119, 120 of 2002)* (2003) *The Times,* 7 February, that it was appropriate to apply rape sentencing guidelines, considerations to all cases involving an element of sexual interference, whether constituting the offence of rape or not. The necessity to deter sex offenders was important and had to be kept in mind. *See* SEX OFFENDERS.

sentencing, smuggling. CA held in *R v Czyzewski* (2003) *The Times,* 25 July, that the smuggling sentencing guidelines set out in *R v Dosanjh* [1999] 1 CrAppR(S) 107 had been modified, with the adoption of guidelines set out by the Sentencing Advisory Panel. The principal serious factors in smuggling offences include: level of duty evaded; sophistication of smuggling organisation; defendant's tasks within the organisation; level of profit he received. *See* SMUGGLING.

separate trials. *See* JOINDER OF OFFENDERS.

separation as ground for divorce. There is evidence that a marriage has broken down irretrievably if: the parties to the marriage have lived apart for a continuous period of at least two years immediately preceding the presentation of the petition and the respondent consents to the granting of a decree; the parties have lived apart for a continuous period of at least five years immediately preceding the presentation of the petition (consent of respondent is not required). See Mat.C.A. 1973, s 1. *See* BREAKDOWN OF MARRIAGE; DIVORCE; LIVING APART.

separation, judicial. *See* JUDICIAL SEPARATION.

separation of powers. The division of functions of government – legislative, executive, judicial – between independent, separate institutions (see Montesquieu's *L'Esprit des Lois* (1748)). 'It cannot be too strongly emphasised that the British Constitution, though largely unwritten, is firmly based on the separation of powers': *per* Lord Diplock in *Duport Steels v Sirs* [1980] 1 All ER 529. See *R v HM Treasury ex p Smedley* [1985] 1 All ER 589; *McGonnell v UK* (2000) *The Times,* 22 February (judge's impartiality and his legislative role).

sequestration. Order issued, e.g., where a person fails to perform an act or disobeys an injunction (q.v.), commanding persons ('sequestrators') to enter upon and take possession of his estate and keep it under sequestration (i.e., separated from the owner) until the judgment is complied with. Application for permission to issue the order must be made under CPR, Part 23 and must be heard by a judge. See *IRC v Hoogstraten* [1984] 3 All ER 245; *Richardson v Richardson* [1989] 3 WLR 865.

serious arrestable offence. *See* ARRESTABLE OFFENCE, SERIOUS.

Serious Fraud Office. Constituted under C.J.A 1987, s 1(1), headed by a Director (appointed by the A-G) who may investigate 'any suspected offence which appears to him on reasonable grounds to involve serious or complex fraud' (s. 1(3)). For procedure, see Sch 1.

SERPS. State Earnings Related Pension Scheme. To be replaced by a new state second pension (which will not be available, however, to the self-employed). See *A New Contract for Welfare Partnership in Pensions* (Cm 4170, 1998); W.R.P.A. 1999.

servant. One whose work is under the control and direction of another. 'Any person employed by another to do work for him on the terms that he, the servant, is to be subject to the control and direction of his employer in respect of the manner in which his work is to be done' (Salmond, approved in *Hewitt* v *Bonvin* [1940] 1 KB 188). See *Ready Mixed Concrete Ltd* v *Ministry of Pensions* [1968] 2 QB 497; *Russell* v *DPP* (1997) 161 JPN 184. *See* EMPLOYEE; EMPLOYER; INDEPENDENT CONTRACTOR.

servant, Crown. *See* CROWN SERVANT.

servant's duty of care. *See* CARE, SERVANT'S CONTRACTUAL DUTY OF.

service. 1. Duty owned by a tenant to his lord, or servant to his master. 2. 'Steps required by rules of court to bring documents used in court proceedings to a person's attention': CPR Glossary. 3. Delivery of claim (q.v.) by personal service or service on defendant's solicitor. See *Tadema Holdings Ltd* v *Ferguson* [1999] NPC 144. See CLAIM, SERVICE OF.

service by fax. *See* FAX, SERVICE BY.

service by post. *See* POST, SERVICE BY.

service charge. An amount payable by a tenant as part of or in addition to the rent, payable for services, repairs, maintenance or insurance or landlord's cost of management. See Landlord and Tenant Act 1985, s 31C, as substituted by H.A. 1996, s 83(3); *Scottish Mutual Assurance* v *Jardine PR Ltd* [1999] EGCS 43; *Aylesbond Estates* v *Macmillan* (2000) 3 HLR 1. See, for control of amount

chargeable: H.A. 1996, s 81(1); *Martin* v *Maryland Estates* [1999] ECGS 63.

service, endorsement of. *See* ENDORSEMENT OF SERVICE.

service of claim. *See* CLAIM, SERVICE OF.

service of claim, extending time. *See* CLAIM, SERVICE OF.

service out of the jurisdiction. *See* JURISDICTION, SERVICE OUT OF THE.

service, supply of a, contract for. 'A contract under which a person agrees to carry out a service': Supply of Goods and Services Act 1982, s 12(1). A contract of apprenticeship is excluded: s 12(2). For implied terms concerning care and skill, see ss 13–16. A contract for services will not, in general, be specifically enforced: *The Scaptrade* [1983] 2 AC 694. See *Hanson* v *Rapid Civil Engineering Ltd* (1987) 38 Build LR 106; *Eagle Star Life Assurance Co Ltd* v *Griggs* [1998] 1 Lloyd's Rep 256.

servient tenement. Land over which, e.g., an easement is exercisable. *See* DOMINANT TENEMENT; EASEMENT.

servitudes. Rights over another's property, i.e., easements (q.v.) and *profits à prendre* (q.v.).

sessions. Sittings of Parliament or the courts.

set aside. To annul, make void, overrule.

set-aside compensation. Policy under CAP (q.v.) aimed at minimising agricultural overproduction. In force since 1988, allowing farmers to be compensated for removing one-fifth of their land from productive use for a minimum period of five years. See *R* v *Ministry for Agriculture ex p Lower Bury Farms* [1999] Eu LR 129.

set of bills. *See* BILLS IN A SET.

set-off. Defence to the whole or part of a claim. Defendant (q.v.) acknowledges claimant's demand but sets up one which counterbalances it. Amount to be set off must have been due at the time of the issue of the claim: *Richards* v *James* (1848) 2 Exch 471. Nothing which is not a money claim may be set off. A defence of set-off may be included in the defence under CPR, r 16.6.

setting aside. 'Cancelling a judgment or order or a step taken by a party in the proceedings': CPR Glossary. See r 13.2 (court must set aside a judgment wrongly entered); r 27.11 (setting aside and re-hearing).

settled. 1. With reference to an account, means adjusted or paid. 2. With reference to a dispute, means adjusted or ended.

settled account. *See* ACCOUNT, SETTLED.

settled land. Land which is or is deemed to be the subject of a settlement (q.v.): S.L.A. 1925, s 2. See Trusts of Land and Appointment of Trustees Act 1996, Sch 1, para 6.

Settled Land Act trustees. Those persons competent under S.L.A. 1925, s 30, amended by Trusts of Land and Appointment of Trustees Act 1996, Sch 3, para 2, to act as trustees of the settle-ment, i.e., persons who under the settle-ment are trustees with the power of sale of the settled land; persons declared by settlement to be trustees; persons who under the settlement are trustees with the power of sale of any other land com-prised in the settlement subject to the same limitations as the land being dealt with; persons who under the settlement are trustees with a future power or duty to sell; persons appointed by deed by beneficiaries (who must be of full age and entitled to dispose of the entire settled estate). See Tr.A. 2000, Sch 2, paras 7–17.

settlement. 1. Limitation of property for persons usually by way of succession, e.g., 'to X for life, remainder to Y in fee simple'. The term includes 'strict settle-ments' and 'trusts for sale'. For purposes of S.L.A. 1925, a settlement is created when land stands: limited in trust for any persons by way of succession; limited in trust for any person in possession (e.g., for a base or determinable fee (q.v.)); limited in trust for any person for an estate in fee simple for a term of years absolute (q.v.) contingently on the happening of an event; charged for the benefit of persons. Under Trusts of Land and Appointment of Trustees Act 1996, no settlement created after the commencement of the Act is a settlement for purposes of S.L.A. 1925: s 2(1). Settlements relating to land are replaced by trusts. For duration of settlement created before 1997, see s 2(2). 2. The documents used to create a settlement. See I.C.T.A. 1988, s 681; T.C.G.A. 1992, s 68.

settlement, accumulation and mainte-nance. *See* ACCUMULATION AND MAIN-TENANCE SETTLEMENT.

settlement based on mistake. The court may, if it wishes, overturn a settlement of an action where it has been shown that a compromise was based on a mutual mistake relating to the law: *Brennan v Bolt Burdon* [2003] EWHC 2493 (QB).

settlement, compound. *See* COMPOUND SETTLEMENT.

settlement of claim before trial. Process whereby parties come to terms voluntarily. Where an offer to settle a claim is accepted, or a settlement is reached, or a claim is discontinued, which disposes of the whole of a claim for which a date has been fixed for the trial, the par-ties must ensure that the court listing officer is notified, and, if an order giving effect to the settlement or discontinuance is drawn up, a copy of the sealed order must be filed with him: PD 19, para 4.1. In *Hawley v Luminar plc and Others* [2006] *The Times*, 14 February, the CA held that it was an implied term of a Part 36 offer under the Civil Procedure Rules that an offer would not be available for acceptance after the hearing of proceed-ings had ended and the court reserved judgment.

settlements, *ad hoc*. Under S.L.A. 1925, s 21, the owner of land could execute a vesting deed (q.v.) stating that the legal estate was vested in him on trust to give effect to those equitable interests affecting the estate. The deed had to be executed by two or more trustees appointed by the court, or by a trust cor-poration (q.v.). Cannot be created after 1996.

settlements, post-nuptial. It was held in *C v C (Financial Provision)* [2004] EWCH 742, that the court possesses jurisdiction to vary a settlement which, at the time of its having been made was anti- or post-nuptial, even though prior to the date of the order the characteristics making it nuptial had been removed from it.

settlements, referential. Settlements (q.v.) which incorporate earlier settlements by reference: S.L.A. 1925, s 32.

settlor. One who makes a settlement of his property. See T.C.G.A. 1992, Sch 5, para 7.

several. 1. Separate (in contrast to 'joint'). 2. More than two: see *Clowes* v *Secretary for the Environment* [1996] EGCS 163.

several fishery. *See* FISHERY.

several tenancy. The separate holding of lands by a tenant (as contrasted with, e.g., joint tenancy (q.v.)).

severalty. Separate, distinct, and exclusive possession. Property is said to belong to X, Y and Z in severalty when the share of each is sole and exclusive (as contrasted with concurrent or joint ownership (q.v.)).

severance. 1. The conversion of a joint tenancy (q.v.) into a tenancy in common, e.g., by alienation, contract to sever, acquisition of another interest in the land. See L.P.A. 1925, s 36(2); *Hunter* v *Babbage* (1995) 69 P & CR 548; *Kinch* v *Bullard* [1998] Fam Law 738; *Grindal* v *Hooper* (2000) *The Times*, 8 February. 2. Retention of the good points of a contract and rejection of the bad (e.g., as in a partly-illegal contract). The promises must be separate and independent. See *Attwood* v *Lamont* [1920] 3 KB 571; *Barclays Bank* v *Caplan* [1998] 1 FLR 532. *See* BLUE PENCIL TEST.

severance pay. Payment to an employee whose contract of employment is terminated or whose contract of service has been cut short. See *Barry* v *Midland Bank plc* (1999) 149 NLJ 1253.

severance, words of. Words in a grant (q.v.) which served to show that tenants were to take a distinct share in the property, e.g., 'in equal shares', or 'to be divided between', or 'equally', or 'respectively'.

sex, change of. '. . . The biological sexual constitution of an individual is fixed at birth (at the latest) and cannot be changed, either by medical or surgical

means . . . The only cases where the term "change of sex" is appropriate are those in which a mistake as to sex is made at birth and subsequently revealed by further medical examination': *Corbett* v *Corbett (orse Ashley)* [1970] 2 All ER 33. See Mat.C.A. 1973, s 11(*c*); *Rees* v *UK* (1987) 17 Fam Law 157; *Cossey* v *UK* [1991] 2 FLR 492; *X* v *UK* [1997] 2 FLR 892. *See* GENDER REASSIGNMENT.

sex discrimination. *See* DISCRIMINATION, SEX.

sex education. A local education authority, governing body and head teacher are expected to take such steps as are reasonably practicable to secure that where sex education is given in school it is given in such a manner as to encourage pupils to have due regard to moral considerations and the value of family life: Education Act 1996, s 403(1).

sex establishments. Sex cinemas (i.e., premises used to a significant degree for the exhibition of moving pictures concerned principally with the portrayal of, or intended to stimulate, sexual activity) and sex shops (i.e., premises used to a significant degree for the selling or hiring of sex articles): see Local Government (Misc. Provs.) Act 1982, Sch 3, paras, 3, 4. See City of Westminster Act 1996, ss 3–6. For licensing requirements, see para 6; *R* v *Wandsworth LBC ex p Darker Enterprises Ltd* (1999) 1 LGLR 601.

sex offender. Means, for purposes of C.D.A. 1998, s 2 (sex offender orders (q.v.)), a person who has been convicted of a sexual offence to which Sex Offenders Act 1997 applies; has been found guilty of such an offence by reason of insanity, or found to be under a disability, and to have done the act charged against him in respect of such an offence; has been cautioned by a constable in respect of such an offence which he admitted; or has been punished overseas for an act which constituted an offence under overseas law and would have constituted a sexual offence if it had been done in the UK: s 3(1). *See* SENTENCING, SEX OFFENDERS.

sex offender order, relevant date. For purposes of an application for a sex offender order (see Crime and Disorder Act 1998, ss 2, 3) the relevant date is the date of the offender's latest conviction or the date of commencement of the statutory provision, if later: *Hopspn* v *Chief Constable of N Wales Police* (2002) *The Times*, 1 November.

sex offender orders. If it appears to a chief officer of police that, with respect to any person in his police area, that person is a sex offender (q.v.) and that the person has acted in such a way as to give reasonable cause to believe that an order is necessary to protect the public from serious harm from him, the chief officer may apply for an order to be made: C.D.A. 1998, s 2(1). A person who does anything which he is prohibited from doing by the order may be imprisoned, or fined, or both: s 2(8).

sex register record. The fair trial provisions guaranteed under European Convention, art 6, had been breached where a young person who had been accused of indecent assault had been given a formal warning without his having been informed that an admission of guilt and subsequent warning would result in his name being recorded on the register of sex offenders: *R (U)* v *Commissioner of Police of the Metropolis* (2002) *The Times*, 10 December.

sexual deviancy. The violation of conventional standards in the area of sexuality. 'Sexual deviancy' in M.H.A. 1983, s 1(3), means indulgence in deviation and not a tendency to deviation: *R* v *Mental Health Review Tribunal, ex p Clatworthy* [1985] 3 All ER 699.

sexual harassment. *See* HARASSMENT, SEXUAL.

sexual history of complainant, admissibility of. In *R* v *A (Complainant's Sexual History)* (2001) *The Times*, 24 May, the House of Lords held that, in some circumstances, the absence of evidential material relating to a prior consensual relationship between defendant and a complainant who alleged a sexual offence might be relevant to the question

of consent and the right to a fair trial under Convention on Human Rights, art 6. See also Y.J.C.E.A. 1999, s 41(3)(c). (The structure of S.O. (Amendment) A. 1976 was said to be 'flawed'.)

sexual immorality, contract for. An agreement to bring about, e.g., illicit intercourse: *Benyon* v *Nettlefield* (1850) 3 Mac & G 94. Generally it will be void, even if under seal.

sexual   intercourse,   proof   of. 'Intercourse shall be deemed complete upon proof of penetration only': S.O.A. 1956, s 44. Proof of rupture of the hymen is not necessary. See *R* v *Russen* (1777) 1 East PC 438; *R* v *Lines* (1844) 1 C & K 393.

sexual   intercourse,   unlawful. Illicit intercourse. The use of the word 'unlawful' in S.O.(Am.)A. 1976, s 1(1) (definition of rape), adds nothing and should be treated as mere surplusage in the enactment: *per* Lord Keith in *R* v *R* [1991] 3 WLR 767. *See* RAPE.

sexual misconduct. Defined under Employment Act 1996, s 11(6) (in relation to the restriction of publicity) as 'the commission of a sexual offence, sexual harassment or other adverse conduct (of whatever nature) related to sex, and conduct is related to sex whether the relationship with sex lies in the character of the conduct or its having reference to the sex or sexual orientation of the person at whom the conduct is directed.' See *Leicester University* v *A* [1999] IRLR 352. For comprehensive list of sexual offences, see P.C.C.(S.)A. 2000, s 161(2).

sexual offence outside UK, incitement to commit. Under S.O. (Conspiracy and Incitement) A. 1996, s 2, it is an offence to incite another person to commit a listed offence (see Schedule to 1996 Act) against children abroad. The section applies where the act done by a person in England and Wales would amount to the offence of incitement to commit a listed offence but for the fact that what he had in view would not be an offence triable in England and Wales, the whole or part of what he had in view was intended to take place outside the UK, and what he had in mind would involve the commission of an offence under the law in force in that country or territory: s 2(1).

sexual offences involving abuse of trust. It is an offence for a person aged 18 or over ('A') to have sexual intercourse with a person under that age ('B'), or to engage in any other sexual activity with or directed towards such a person if (in either case) he is in a position of trust in relation to that person: S.O.(Am.)A. 2000, s 3(1). 'Position of trust' means: A looks after persons under 18 detained in an institution by order of the court, and B is so detained; or, A looks after persons under 18 resident in a home or other place where accommodation and maintenance are provided under Ch.A. 1989, s 23(2), or s 59(1), and B is resident in that place; or, A looks after persons under 18 accommodated and cared for in a hospital or residential care home, community home, or home under Ch.A. 1989, s 82(5), and B is accommodated and cared for in that institution; or, A looks after persons receiving full-time education at an educational institution and B is receiving education there: s 4(1)–(5). A 'looks after' B for purposes of s 4 if he is regularly involved in caring for, training, supervising or being in sole charge of B: s 4(7). For defences, see s 3(2).

sexual offences, protected materials. 'Protected material', in relation to a sexual offence, means a copy, in whatever form, of: a victim's statement; a photograph or pseudo-photograph of a victim; medical examination report of a victim: S.O. (Protected Material) A. 1997, s 1(1). Disclosure of such material to defendant in a prosecution involving a sexual offence (see Schedule to the Act) is regulated under ss 3–5. See Y.J.C.E.A. 1999, s 38(7)(*b*).

sexual or violent offender, for purposes of C.J.C.S.A. 2000. One who is subject to notification requirement of Sex Offenders Act 1997, Part I; or is convicted of a sexual or violent offence within P.C.C.(S.)A. 2000, s 161; or dealt with under Criminal Procedure (Insanity) Act 1954; or convicted of an offence

against a child and sentenced to a custodial sentence of 12 months or more. See C.J.C.S.A. 2000, s 68.

shall. When used in drafting, the word suggests an imperative, a command, as compared with 'may', which involves permission (that which is allowed). 'Following a verdict of guilty, the judge *shall* pronounce sentence.' 'In the exercise of his discretion, the judge *may* imprison or fine the guilty person.' See *Storer* v *British Gas plc* (2000) *The Times*, 1 March.

sham. 'Acts done or documents executed by the parties to the "sham" which are intended by them to give to third parties or to the court the appearance of creating between the parties legal rights and obligations different from the actual legal rights and obligations (if any) which the parties intended to create': *per* Diplock LJ in *Snook* v *London & W Riding Investments* [1967] 2 QB 786. See *Hilton* v *Plustitle* [1989] 1 WLR 149 – sham company let (q.v.).

sham marriage. Known also as 'marriage of convenience'. A marriage, whether or not void, entered into between a person ('A') who is neither a British citizen nor a national of an EEA state (q.v.) other than the UK and another person (whether or not such a citizen or such a national); and entered into by A for the purpose of avoiding the effect of one or more provisions of UK immigration law or rules: Immigration and Asylum Act 1999, s 24(5). For duty on civil marriage registrars to report suspicious marriages, see s 24.

share. 'The interest of a shareholder in the company measured by a sum of money for the purpose of liability in the first place and of dividend in the second, but also consisting of a series of mutual covenants entered into by all the shareholders *inter se* in accordance with [the Companies Act]. The contract contained in the Articles of Association is one of the original incidents of the share': *Borland's Trustee* v *Steel Bros & Co Ltd* [1901] 1 Ch 279. A portion of the capital of a company giving shareholders the right to receive, in general, a proportion of the company's profits. Shares are legal choses in action (q.v.) (*Humble* v *Mitchell* (1839) 11 Add El 205), and are classed as personal estate: Cos.A. 1985, s 182(1). For the test in valuing shares, see *Holt* v *Holt* (1990) 134 SJ 1076. For issue of shares constituting a supply of services for VAT, see *Mirror Newspapers* v *Customs and Excise* (2000) *The Times*, 7 March. *See* COMPANY; SHARE, TYPES OF.

share acquisition, financial assistance for. It is illegal for a company to give direct or indirect financial assistance (e.g., by gift, loan, provision of guarantee) for this purpose: Cos.A. 1985, ss 151, 152. For exceptions, see ss 153–158. See *Belmont Finance* v *Williams Furniture* [1980] 1 All ER 393.

share and share alike. Phrase, often found in a will, creating a tenancy in common (q.v.); but where the context shows a joint tenancy (q.v.) to be intended, it is construed accordingly: *Armstrong* v *Eldridge* (1791) 3 Bro CC 215.

share capital. The total amount which a company's shareholders have contributed or are liable to contribute as payment for their shares. See Table A, art 2. References on a company's stationery or order forms to its 'share capital' must be to its paid-up share capital: Cos.A. 1985, s 351(2). See I.C.T.A. 1988, s 832(1); *Russell* v *Northern Bank Development Ltd* [1992] 1 WLR 588.

share capital, equity. The issued share capital of a company, excluding any part which, neither as respects dividend nor as respects capital, carries any right to participate beyond a specified amount in a distribution: Cos.A. 1985, s 744.

share certificate. *See* CERTIFICATE OF SHARES.

shared ownership lease. Lease granted on payment of a premium calculated by reference to a percentage of the value of demised premises or the cost of providing them, or under which the tenant (or his personal representatives) will or may be entitled to a sum calculated by reference, directly or indirectly, to the value of those premises: C.L.R.A. 2002, s 76.

share hawking. Also 'share pushing'. The personal offering of shares from house to house. Includes 'cold calling' and any unsolicited personal call or oral communication without express invitation, and is prohibited by F.S.A. 1986, s 56 (subject to exceptions under s 57).

share schemes, employee. The Employee Share Schemes Act 2002 has as its purpose the encouragement of wider employee share ownership through an extension of tax benefits for share schemes for companies intending to encourage such ownership. This involves an amendment to Finance Act 2000, Sch 8.

shareholder. One who owns shares as a member of a company (q.v.). See Cos.A. 1985, s 22. For liability of subsequent holders of allotted shares, see Cos.A. 1985, s 112. See also *Macaura* v *Northern Assurance Co* [1925] AC 619 (company assets are not owned by the shareholders); *Stein* v *Blake* [1998] 1 All ER 724 (shareholder's right to sue concerning wrongs done to company).

shareholders, foreign. Any issue relating to the rights of foreign resident stockholders must be decided by an English court because the corporation of the management was in England. See *Investments Ltd* v *Formula One Holdings Ltd (No. 2)* (2004) *The Times*, 18 November.

shareholders, protection of. Cos.A. 1985, Part XVII, allows a member of a company to petition the court for an order on the ground of the company's affairs being, or having been, conducted in a way unfairly prejudicial to the interests of some part of the membership, including himself, or that an actual or proposed act of the company is or would be unfairly prejudicial. See *Eastmanco* v *GLC* [1982] 1 WLR 2. For powers of FSA in relation to improperly acquired shares, see F.S.M.A. 2000, s 189.

shareholders, relief to. CA held, in *Citybranch Ltd* v *Rackind* [2004] EWCA (Cir) 815, that the court will be ready to consider the affairs of one company as the affairs of another where this will enable the grant of relief to a minority shareholder, in relation to Companies Act 1985, s 459.

share ownership, employee, plan. A plan established by a company, providing for shares to be appointed to employees without payment, or for shares to be acquired on behalf of employees out of sums deducted from their salary: Finance Act 2000, s 47, Sch 8, para 1(1).

share premium account. An account to which is transferred sums received from the issue of shares at a premium. The amount of the account appears in the balance sheet as part of the paid-up capital. See Cos.A. 1985, s 130.

share restriction order. *See* RESTRICTION ORDER, SHARE.

shares, acquisition by a company of its own. In general, a company may not acquire its own shares, whether by purchase, subscription or otherwise: Cos.A. 1985, s 143(1). For exceptions (e.g., in a reduction of capital duly made) see s 143(3).

shares at a premium. *See* PREMIUM, ISSUES OF SHARES AT A.

shares, bearer. *See* BEARER SHARES.

shares, bearer, and delivery. Under Cos.A. 1989, s 207(10), allowing the making of regulations whereby title to securities may be evidenced and transferred without a written instrument, e.g., by electronic transfer system (inserted by Bank of England Act 1999, s 35), bearer shares may be transferred without the need for delivery. See SI 95/3272. *See* BEARER SHARES.

shares, contracts for sale of. The contract need not be in any particular form. A 'short sale' refers to shares which the seller does not yet own at the time of the contract. The seller's duty is to deliver the share certificate and an executed transfer to the buyer and to assist his registration as a company member.

shares, forfeiture of. *See* FORFEITURE OF SHARES.

shares, lien on. A lien or other charge of a public company (q.v.) on its own shares (whether taken expressly or otherwise) is generally void: Cos.A. 1985, s 150(1). For the permitted charges, see s 150(2), (3).

shares, mortgage of. In a *legal mortgage*, the legal title passes from mortgagor to mortgagee and the transfer is entered in the company register. In an *equitable mortgage*, the mortgagor retains the legal title to the shares and deposits his share certificate with the mortgagee. See *Cuckmere Brick Co Ltd v Mutual Finance Ltd* [1971] Ch 949.

shares, payment for. Shares allotted by a company may be paid for in money or money's worth (e.g., know-how, goodwill (qq.v.)): Cos.A. 1985, s 99(1).

shares, placing of. Allocation of shares by a company to an issuing house which agrees to purchase and place them with clients.

shares, right to dividend from. A payment of dividends arising from the ownership of shares does not constitute a 'transaction in securities' in relation to the Income and Corporation Taxes Act 1988, s 703, so as to cancel relevant tax advantages. See *IRC v Laird Group plc* (2003) *The Times*, 23 October.

shares, surrender of. *See* SURRENDER OF SHARES.

shares, transfer of. *See* TRANSFER OF SHARES.

shares, transmission of. *See* TRANSMISSION OF SHARES.

share transfer. Document which must be prepared and furnished to a company when its shares are transferred, e.g., a stock transfer form, a brokers' transfer form. See, e.g., Stock Transfer Act 1963; Cos.A. 1985, s 182. *See* TRANSFER OF SHARES.

share, types of. Generally: ordinary; preference; deferred (qq.v.).

share warrant. *See* WARRANT, SHARE.

sheriff. Originally the 'shire-reeve'. He exercised civil and criminal jurisdiction as a judge of the sheriff's county court and sheriff's tourn. Today, he is the Crown's appointee and chief officer in the county. He is nominally in charge of, e.g., parliamentary elections, levying of forfeiture recognisances, and the execution of process issuing from criminal courts and the High Court. See L.G.A. 1972, s 219.

sheriff's interpleader. *See* INTERPLEADER SUMMONS.

shifting use. A use which cut short a preceding interest. Example: 'To X and his heirs to the use of Y and his heirs, but to the use of Z and his heirs as soon as Z shall become a doctor of medicine.' See L.P.A. 1925, ss 1, 39; and S.L.A. 1925, s 1(*ii*). *See* USE.

shift work. 'Any method of organising work in shifts whereby workers succeed each other at the same workstations according to a certain pattern, including a rotating pattern, and which may be continuous or discontinuous, entailing the need for workers to work at different times over a given period of days or weeks': SI 88/1833, reg 22.

ship. Any type of vessel used in navigation: Merchant Shipping Act 1995, s 313; *Lavery v MacLeod* [2000] STC 118. See C.P.A. 1987, s 45(1); Capital Allowances Act 1990, s 30; Finance Act 2000, Sch 22, para 142 ('ship' includes hovercraft). For 'British ship', see Merchant Shipping Act 1995, s 1. For qualifications for ownership, see s 3. An owner is liable for the unsafe operation of his ship: 1988 Act, s 31. See *The Derbyshire* [1987] 3 WLR 1181 (ship as 'equipment'); Shipping and Trading Interests (Protection) Act 1995.

ship, arrest of. *See* ARREST OF SHIP.

shipwreck. *See* WRECK.

shock, nervous. *See* NERVOUS SHOCK.

shop. Premises of which the sole and principal use is the carrying on there of retail trade or business; a building occupied by a wholesaler where goods are kept for sale, or part of a building so occupied; a building to which members of the public are invited to resort to deliver goods for repair or other treatment, or part of a building so used: Offices, Shops and Railway Premises Act 1963, s 1(3)(*a*). See also Shops Act 1950, s 4; Workplace (Health, Safety and Welfare) Regulations 1992; *Erewash BC v Ilkeston Co-op Society* (1989) 87 LGR 96; *Ritz Video v Tyneside MBC* [1996] COD 18. For consideration of meaning of 'shop window', see *Havering LBC v Networksites Ltd* (1998) 1 PLR 103.

shoplifters, sentencing of. CA held in *R v Page* (2004) *The Times*, 23 December, that different sentencing guidelines by the Court of Appeal applied in the cases of individual adult offenders and organised gangs employing violent methods.

shoplifting. Stealing goods from a shop. See Th.A. 1968, ss 1, 7. *See* THEFT.

shop steward. Elected, or appointed, union officer who represents members at a place of work.

shore. That ground between the ordinary high-water and low-water mark: Hale, *History of the Common Law* (1713).

short committal. *See* COMMITTAL, SHORT.

short title. *See* TITLE, SHORT.

SI. Statutory instrument(s) (q.v.).

sic. So; thus. Used so as to indicate that a word or statement is intended as written, in spite of an obvious error or absurdity.

sick pay, statutory. Scheme instituted by S.S. and Housing Benefits Act 1982 under which an employer became liable to pay to employees' sick pay in a stated amount for a stipulated period of interruption of employment by reason of incapacity. Replaced by 'incapacity benefit' from 1995.

sic utere tuo ut alienum non laedas. Common law maxim: So use your own property as not to interfere with that of your neighbour. But, 'a balance has to be maintained between the right of the occupier to do what he likes with his own, and the right of his neighbour not to be interfered with': *Sedleigh-Denfield v O'Callaghan* [1940] AC 880.

side notes. Marginal notes (q.v.).

sight, payable at. A bill payable on demand. See B.Ex.A. 1882, s 10. *See* BILL OF EXCHANGE.

signature. 1. A person's name written in his own hand. 2. Sign or other mark impressed on a document. 'The signature of the party serves to identify the writing as the very writing by which the party is to be bound . . . signature does not necessarily mean writing a person's Christian name and surname, but any mark which identifies it as the act of the party': *per* Maule J in *Morton v Copeland* (1855) 139 ER 861. For admissibility in evidence of electronic signatures (incorporated in an electronic communication (q.v.)), see Electronic Communications Act 2000, s 7; EU Electronic Signatures Directive (1999/93/EC).

signature of will. Under W.A. 1837, s 9 (as substituted by A.J.A. 1982, s 17), a will (q.v.) must be signed by the testator (or some person in his presence and at his direction) so that it appears that the testator intended by that signature to give effect to the will. The signature need not be written, so that a seal with the testator's initials affixed to the will has been held to suffice: *In b Emerson* (1882) 9 LR IR 443. See also *Re Adams* [1990] 2 All ER 97; *Wood* v *Smith* [1992] 3 All ER 556; A.J.A. 1982, ss 17 *et seq* (making new provision for wills generally).

silence in relation to contract. Silence is not generally deemed consent: *Felthouse* v *Bindley* (1862) 11 CB NS 869. Mere silence is not generally misrepresentation, save in cases where it distorts a representation, or there is a fiduciary relationship between parties, or where contracts are *uberrimae fidei* (q.v.). See *Dimmock* v *Hallett* (1866) 2 Ch App 21; *Way and Waller Ltd* v *Ryde* [1944] 1 All ER 9. *See* CONTRACT.

silence, right of accused to. 'Undoubtedly when persons are speaking on even terms, and a charge is made, and the person charged says nothing, and expresses no indignation, and does nothing to repel the charge, that is some evidence to show that he admits the charge to be true': *R* v *Mitchell* (1892) 17 Cox CC 503. Generally, a person commits no offence by refusing to answer questions put by one attempting to discover by whom an offence has been committed (but see, e.g., C.J.A. 1987, s 2). In determining the guilt of an accused person, a court or jury may now draw inferences as appear proper from evidence that he failed to mention, on being questioned under caution by the police, any fact relied on in his defence, or that on being charged, or officially informed that he might be prosecuted, he failed to mention any such fact, being a fact which, in the circumstances, he could reasonably have been expected to mention: C.J.P.O.A. 1994, s 35. Under Y.J.C.E.A. 1999, s 58, infer-

ences from accused's silence are not permissible where the accused was at an authorised place of detention at the time of his failure to mention facts and had no prior access to legal advice. See *R* v *X* (1999) *The Independent*, 8 December; *R* v *Rai* [2000] 1 Cr App R 242 (silence constituting deception); *Practice Direction: Right to Silence* (1995) 145 NLJ 885. HL held, in *R* v *Webber* [2004] UKHL 1, that a suggestion put to prosecution witness by or on behalf of defendant rejected by the witness and that had not been referred to by defendant in police during an interview can constitute a fact relied on by defendant during his defence, for purposes of Criminal Justice and Public Order Act 1994, s 34. In *R* v *Beckles* (2004) *The Times*, 17 November, the CA held that, where a jury is directed that they can draw adverse inferences from the fact that defendant was silent when interviewed by the police, there is an obligation on the trial judge to make clear that such inferences ought not to be drawn if they believed that defendant had remained silent, reasonably and genuinely, following advice from his solicitor. In *R* v *Hoare* [2004] EWCA Crim 784, the CA held that, in the final analysis, the question which is for the jury, is whether, regardless of advice, genuinely given and genuinely accepted, the accused had remained silent not because of that advice, but because he had no, or no satisfactory, explanation to give to the court. European Court of Human Rights held, in *Beckles* v *UK (Application no 44652/98)* (2002) *The Times*, 15 October, that, in relation to European Convention, art 6.1 (right to fair trial), the drawing of inferences from the silence of the accused does not necessarily infringe that right: what has to be taken into account is all the circumstances of the case, including right attached to inferences by national courts, degree of compulsion in such situations.

silk, to take. *See* QUEEN'S COUNSEL.

similar fact evidence. *See* EVIDENCE, SIMILAR FACT.

similarity of facts. '[There are] two meanings of the term "similarity". First, in the wider sense and the popular sense, a fact is similar to another whenever the two possess a common characteristic; but that common characteristic may be insufficient to render the first fact relevant in the legal sense as proof of the other. Secondly, in the narrower sense, a fact is similar to another only when the common characteristic is the significant one for the purpose of the inquiry at hand': *per* Gummow J in *DF Lyons Pty Ltd* v *Commonwealth Bank of Australia* (1991) 100 ALR 468. See EVIDENCE, SIMILAR FACT.

simple contract. Referred to also as 'parol contract'. Contract not under seal, and which requires consideration (q.v.) for its enforcement. May be oral or written. *See* CONTRACT.

simple trust. Bare trust (q.v.).

sine die. Without a day (or date), i.e., indefinitely.

Single European Market. Concept of a united market involving complete freedom of movement of persons, goods, capital and services, which was to be achieved by the end of 1992. See Single European Act, signed in 1986 and incorporated into UK law by European Communities (Amendment) Act 1986.

single private dwelling. In *Roberts* v *Howlett* [2002] 1 P & CR 19, it was held that property let to four students, each with his own study bedroom, sharing lounge and dining room, constituted a 'single private dwelling'; the students constituted a genuine social unit by their occupation of the premises.

single woman. Generally, an unmarried woman. See, however, the extended meaning given in (repealed) Affiliation Proceedings Act 1957, s 1. 'It seems to me that a woman whose husband has deserted her or cast her off can say to him, with as much force as she can say it to anyone else, that he has reduced her to living as a single woman': *per* Devlin J in *Kruhlak* v *Kruhlak* [1958] 2 QB 32.

site. A specific area of land set aside for operations such as building and general development. For use of the term in, e.g., Town and Country Planning (Control of Advertisements) Regulations 1989, r 8, see *Barking and Dagenham LBC* v *Mills & Allen Ltd* [1997] 2 CLY 4026.

sit-in. Occupation of premises as an act of protest. Normally trespassory; *Warwick University* v *De Graaf* [1975] 1 WLR 1126; C.L.A. 1977, s 9.

sittings of Court of Appeal and High Court. Michaelmas (1 Oct–21 December); Hilary (11 January–Wednesday before Easter Sunday); Easter (second Tuesday after Easter Sunday–Friday before Spring holiday (i.e., the bank holiday following on the last Monday in May or any other day appointed under Banking and Financial Dealings Act 1971, s 1(2))); Trinity (second Tuesday after the Spring holiday–31 July): PD 39B, para 1.1.

sittings of magistrates' courts. *See* MAGISTRATES' COURTS, SITTINGS OF.

skeleton arguments. Abbreviated notes of legal arguments, presented in the form of a succinct outline, compulsory, e.g., in all appeals to Court of Appeal (Civil Division), containing numbered list of points which the advocate proposes to argue, each stated in one or two sentences; references to supporting material, e.g., propositions of law, chronologies, glossaries. They should not normally exceed 10–15 pages. Four copies of appellant's and respondent's skeleton case are required to be lodged with the Court; they are intended to be read by the judge before the appeal. See *Practice Direction (Court of Appeal: Leave to Appeal and Skeleton Arguments)* [1999] 1 WLR 2; *St Alban's Court Ltd* v *Daldorch Estates* (1999) *The Times*, 24 May.

skin impression. In relation to any person, means any record (other than a fingerprint) which is a record (in any form and produced by any method) of the skin pattern and other physical characteristics or features of the whole or any part of his foot or of any other part of his body: C.J.P.A. 2002, s 8(5).

slander. Spoken words (or gestures) which amount to the tort of defamation (q.v.). Words are defined by Defamation Act 1952 to include pictures, visual images, broadcasting. It may be actionable *per se*, i.e., without proof of damage, in the case of, e.g., imputation of a crime, unfitness, incompetence. For time limitation for actions (one year), see Lim.A. 1980, s 4A, substituted by Defamation Act 1996, s 5.

slander of goods. Tort (q.v.) resulting from false and malicious comment on merchandise sold. See Defamation Act 1952, s 3(1); *White* v *Mellin* [1895] AC 154.

slander of title. Tort (q.v.) resulting from attacking a person's title to property. See Defamation Act 1952, s 3; Cable and Broadcasting Act 1984, s 28; *Riding* v *Smith* (1876) Ex D 91.

slander, unauthorised repetition of. Where a third party repeats a slander in unauthorised fashion, and this is a probable and natural outcome of the defendant's behaviour, it will be for the jury to decide, after consideration of the facts, whether the defendant was liable for any resulting additional damage: *McManus* v *Beckham* (2002) *The Times*, 11 July.

slavery. Condition of unfree persons who have no rights and who are in the ownership of their masters. 'The state of slavery is of such a nature . . . that nothing can be suffered to support it': *per* Lord Mansfield in *Sommersett's Case* (1772) 20 St Tr 1. 'No one shall be held in slavery or servitude': European Convention on Human Rights 1950, art 4. See UN Convention on Law of the Sea 1982, art 99.

sleeping partner. *See* DORMANT PARTNER.

sleeping rough. Colloquialism, referring to Vagrancy Act 1824 and C.J.A. 1982, s 70. Includes 'wandering abroad and lodging in any barn or outhouse, or in any deserted or unoccupied building, or in the open air or under a tent . . . and not giving a good account of himself'. Where, as a result of a decision by the Home Secretary, an asylum seeker is obliged to sleep rough, this may be considered as an inhuman or degrading treatment, it suffices to constitute a breach of rights under the Human Rights Convention, art 3.

sleepwalking. Known also as 'somnambulism'. A neurotic reaction of a sleeper who leaves his bed and, while asleep, walks or performs other motor actions. For relation to M'Naghten Rules, see *R* v *Burgess* [1991] 2 WLR 1206. 'Can anyone doubt that a man, who, though he might be perfectly sane, committed what would otherwise be a crime in a state of somnambulism, would be entitled to be acquitted? And why is this? Simply because he would not know what he was doing': *R* v *Tollson* (1889) 23 QBD 187. See *R* v *Parks* (1990) 56 CCC (3d) 449; *Finegan* v *Haywood* (2000) *The Times*, 10 May. *See* AUTOMATISM.

slip. Cover note (q.v.) used, e.g., in a marine insurance contract containing the essential details of the risk in outline form. See Marine Insurance Act 1906, ss 21, 89.

slip rule. Rule whereby a clerical error in an order or judgment, or an error based on an omission or accidental slip, may be corrected by the court. A party may apply for a correction without notice: CPR, r 40. 12. CPR, r 40.12(1), does allow the slip rule (q.v.) to be used so as to give effect to the original intention of the court: *Bristol-Myers Co* v *Baker Norton Inc* (2001) *The Times*, 26 April.

small agreements. Term used under C.C.A. 1974, s 17(1), to refer to agreements where the credit limit or payments under the agreement do not exceed a statutorily fixed amount and are not regulated by the Act and do not constitute a hire-purchase or conditional sale agreement (q.v.).

small claims track. The normal track for defended claims with value (currently) not exceeding £5,000: CPR, r 26.6(3). There will be no small claims track allocation: in personal injuries cases where value of claim exceeds £1,000; where tenants of residential premises claim repair orders to a value exceeding £1,000, or seek damages from landlords for harassment or unlawful eviction; in cases involving disputed allegations of dishonesty: see r 26; PD 26, para 8.1. *See* ALLOCATION TO TRACKS, CPR.

small claims track, final hearing. Takes place generally before a district judge (or a circuit judge). Parties may be represented by a lawyer or lay representative: PD 27, para 3.2. Hearing is in public; but, if parties agree, a private hearing may be held. See also r 29.2(3). If claimant does not attend or gives notice that he will not attend, claim may be struck out. If defendant does not attend or give notice, and claimant does attend, the court may decide the claim, taking into account only claimant's evidence. If neither party attends or gives notice, the court may strike out the claim. See r 22. There is a right of appeal where there was a serious irregularity in proceedings or the court has made a mistake in law: r 27.12(1). For costs, see r 44.11.

small claims track procedures after allocation. There are five alternatives. 1. Standard directions and fixed final hearing date: CPR, r 27.4(1)(a); 2. Special directions and further directions: r 27.4(1)(c); 3. Special directions and fixed final hearing date: r 27.4(1)(b); 4. Preliminary hearing (where it is necessary to ensure that a party understands what is involved in special directions; where it is claimed that one party has no real prospect of success; to enable the court to strike out a statement of case (q.v.) where there is no reasonable basis for a defence): r 27.4(1)(d); 5. Proceeding without a hearing (where all parties agree): r 27.10.

smuggling. Illegal export or import of merchandise, e.g., without payment of duties. See Customs and Excise Management Act 1979, s 50 (as amended by Forgery and Counterfeiting Act 1981, s 23). *See SENTENCING, SMUGGLING.*

socage tenure. *Soc* = ploughshare. A residual tenure, i.e., one which was neither military, spiritual nor servile. The name was derived from 'socmen', who sought the protection of a lord in return for fealty. Tenures Abolition Act 1660 transformed almost all tenures into free and common socage.

social care workers. Persons who engage in social work, or are employed at children's homes, residential family centres, fostering and voluntary adoption agencies, or manage such establishments, or are supplied by a domiciliary care agency to provide personal care in their own homes for persons unable to provide it for themselves without assistance: Care Standards Act 2000, s 55(2). They must be registered under s 56, and can be removed under s 59. It is an offence for an unregistered person to use the title 'social worker' with intent to deceive: s 61.

Social Chapter. Protocol on Social Policy, concluded between member states of EU (q.v.) as part of Treaty on European Union concerning, e.g., working conditions and environment, consultation with workers, sex equality with regard to labour market opportunities, etc. See, e.g., European Works Council Directive, 94/45/EC. The Treaty of Amsterdam 1997 incorporates the Social Protocol into EU Treaties. The UK 'opted out', but signed the Protocol in 1997.

social fund. 1. Fund operated by Secretary of State, payments from which may be made to those on low incomes to meet, in prescribed circumstances, maternity and funeral expenses, cold weather payments, community care grants, budget and crisis loans (qq.v.), and 'other needs in accordance with directions given or guidance issued by the Secretary of State': S.S.A. 1986, Part III. For social fund Commissioner, see S.S.A. 1998, s 37. See S.S. Contributions and Benefits Act 1992, Part VIII; S.S.A. 1998, s 70. See *R v Social Fund Inspector ex p Taylor* [1998] COD 152. 2. Fund established by EEC Treaty, art 123, intended to increase 'the geographical and occupational mobility of workers within the community'. See *R v Secretary of State for Social Services ex p Stitt* [1991] COD 68.

social landlord. *See* LANDLORD.

social policy rule. Interpretation of an Act (q.v.) by considering the social policy which gave rise to it. The courts do not generally favour the rule and it has been described as 'naked usurpation of the legislative function under the guise of interpretation': *Magor and St Mellors RDC v Newport Corporation* [1952] AC 189.

social security authorities, information from. Under Finance Act 1997, s 10, Department of Social Security is able to disclose information for use in the prevention, detection, investigation or prosecution of criminal offences to Inland Revenue and Customs and Excise. For social security investigation powers, see S.S. Administration Act 1992, Part VI, amended by C.S.P.S.S.A. 2000, Sch 6.

social security, categories of contributors. Classes of insured persons required to make contributions are: Class 1 – earnings related contributions paid by employed earners, employers and others; Class 2 – flat rate contributions payable weekly by self-employed earners; Class 3 – contributions paid voluntarily by earners, and others voluntarily; Class 4 – contributions payable in respect of profits, gains of a trade, profession or vocation, or in respect of equivalent earnings. See S.S. Contributions and Benefits Act 1992, s 1; S.S. Administration Act 1992.

Social Security Commissioners. A Chief Commissioner and Commissioners hear appeals on points of law from Social Security Appeal Tribunals. There is a right of appeal to the Court of Appeal. See S.S. Administration Act 1992, ss 22–24, 52; S.S.A. 1998, Sch 6, paras 3, 4.

social security functions, responsibility of Inland Revenue. Under S.S. Contributions (Transfer etc.) A. 1999, the day-to-day operational functions undertaken by the Contributions Agency (an executive agency of DSS) on behalf of Secretary of State for Social Security are transferred to Inland Revenue. Most of the functions set out in S.S. (Contributions) Regulations 1979 (SI 79/591) are transferred. See 1999 Act, s 1, Schs 1–3, Appendix.

Social Security Tribunals. Originally National Insurance Tribunals, they are the bodies which function under the S.S. Acts. See S.S. Administration Act 1992, s 22. Local tribunals, each comprising a chairman and two panel members, hear appeals relating to, e.g., disablement benefit claims. Appeal lies to a Social Security Appeal Tribunal. See S.S.A. 1980, s 14; S.S.A. 1986, s 52; S.S.A. 1998, s 4 (unified appeal tribunals).

social services, housing by. HL held in *R (G)* v *Barnet LBC* [2003] UKHL 57, that there was no duty for a local social services authority to provide residential accommodation for families so that children could be housed in circumstances considered appropriate to meet their assessed needs.

societas leonina. Leonine partnership. One in which a designated partner is liable for losses, but has no right to share in profits. Agreements to this end are usually void.

society, friendly. *See* FRIENDLY SOCIETY.

sodomy. Buggery (q.v.). See *Genesis* xiii: 13.

soit baillé aux seigneurs. Let it be handed to the Lords. Message used when a Bill (q.v.) is sent to the Lords from the Commons. When sent from the Lords to the Commons, it reads: '*Soit baillé aux communs*'.

soit fait comme il est désiré. Let it be as it is desired. Form of Royal Assent (q.v.).

solatium. An additional allowance awarded to a claimant for, e.g., injured feelings. See *McFarlane* v *Tayside Health Board* [1999] 3 WLR 1301.

soldier's will. *See* PRIVILEGED WILL.

sole. Unmarried; single; separate.

sole, corporation. *See* CORPORATION.

solemn form. *See* PROBATE.

sole trader. An individual business in which one person directs and bears the risks of a business, takes the profits and bears the losses. See CPR, Sch 2; CCR, O 5, r 10, enabling county court proceedings to be brought against a sole trader in defendant's trading title.

solicit. To importune (q.v.); to invite to a course of action.

soliciting, anti-social orders relating to. An anti-social order can be issued in relation to a prostitute where it had been proved that her conduct, taken on its own or in conjunction with other prostitutes, was likely to cause harassment, alarm or distress to other persons: *Chief Constable of Lancashire Constabulary* v

Potter (2003) *The Times*, 10 November. See Crime and Disorder Act 1998, s 1(1).

soliciting murder. X was sentenced to five years' imprisonment for soliciting the murder of her husband, after suspecting that he had hidden money overseas so as to avoid payments following a divorce. She had pleaded guilty after evidence was given of her having attempted to hire a 'hit man' to murder her husband. On appeal it was held that the sentence was not excessive, that she had pleaded guilty in the light of overwhelming evidence given against her, and that a strong deterrent element was necessary so as to warn persons who were prepared to solicit murder: *R* v *Molyneux* [2004] 1 CrAppR(S) 21.

soliciting to murder. It is an offence to 'solicit, encourage, persuade or endeavour to persuade or . . . propose to any person, to murder any other person': O.P.A. 1861, s 4 (as amended by C.L.A. 1977). See, e.g., *R* v *Most* (1881) 7 QBD 244; *R* v *Evans* [1986] Crim LR 470; *R* v *Kayani* [1997] 2 Cr App R (S) 313.

solicitor. A solicitor of the Supreme Court. One who may conduct legal proceedings or give advice on legal problems, having passed the examinations of The Law Society and possessing a certificate, which is in force, authorising him to practise. See C.L.S.A. 1990, s 86. 'Solicitors who act in litigation, whilst under a duty to do their best for their client, must never deceive or mislead the court': *Guide to Professional Conduct of Solicitors* (principle 21.07). A solicitor-advocate does not enjoy immunity from suit in respect of civil or criminal proceedings: *Hall & Co* v *Simons* (2000) 150 NLJ 1147. He may employ a member of another profession, but may not form a partnership with him: Solicitors' Practice Rules 1990, r 7(6). For conflict of duties, see *Re L (Minors) (Care Proceedings: Cohabiting Solicitors)* [2000] 3 FCR 71. See Solicitors Act 1974; CPR, Sch 1, O 106; A.J.A. 1985, Part I; *Ross* v *Caunters* [1980] Ch 297; *Citadel Management* v *Thompson* [1998] Fam Law 738.

solicitor, access of detained person to. A person arrested and held in custody at a police station or other premises is entitled to consult a solicitor privately at any time; permission must be given within 36 hours: P.&C.E.A. 1984, s 58(1), (5). In the case of a serious arrestable offence (q.v.), authorisation for delay may be given only by a police officer who believes that exercise of the right might, e.g., alert persons so that acts of terrorism become more difficult to prevent: s 56(8), (13)(*c*). See *Code C* (revised, April 1991), para 3.1. See *R* v *Chief Constable of S Wales ex p Merrick* [1994] 1 WLR 663; *Rixson* v *Chief Constable of Kent* (2000) *The Times*, 11 April.

solicitor and own client basis of costs. Basis of assessment of costs applicable between a party to an action and his solicitor. All costs incurred with the express or implied approval of the client are presumed to have been reasonably incurred and the amount to be reasonable if expressly or impliedly approved by the client. See r 48.8 (detailed assessment of costs).

solicitor, business of. CA held, in *J Coughlan Ltd* v *Ruparella* [2003] EWCA Civ 1057, that where the court is considering the liability of solicitors for acts performed by its partners, it is necessary to examine whether a general description of acts performed is contained within a solicitor's ordinary course of business.

solicitor, change of, notice. Where a party for whom a solicitor is acting wants to change his solicitor; or a party, after having conducted the claim in person, appoints a solicitor; or a party, after having conducted the claim by a solicitor, intends to act in person, notice of the change must be filed: CPR, r 42.2. A solicitor may apply for an order declaring that he has ceased to be a party's solicitor: r 42.3(1). Where a solicitor who has acted for a party has died, has become bankrupt, has ceased to practise, cannot be found, then any other party may apply for an order declaring that the solicitor has ceased to act in the case: r 42.4(1).

Solicitor-General. A law officer of the Crown, subordinate and deputy to the Attorney-General. He is usually a member of the House of Commons (q.v.) and holds office at the pleasure of the Crown.

solicitor, obligation of. In *Credit Lyonnais SA* v *Russell Jones & Walker* (2002) 152 NLJ 1071, it was held that there is no general obligation on a solicitor to devote time and energy to issues beyond those in his retainer, but where, in the courses of undertaking his retainer, he learns of a risk likely to affect his client, he has a clear duty to inform the client.

solicitor's clerk as informant. CA held in *R* v *Robinson* (2002) *The Times*, 13 November, that the use of a solicitor or solicitor's clerk as a police informant constitutes a breach of the solicitor-client relationship of confidentiality. See also *R (Daly)* v *Secretary of State for Home Department* [2001] 2 AC 532.

solicitors, costs in non-contentious business. CA held in *Jemma Trust Co* v *Liptrott* [2003] EWCA Civ 1476, that solicitors engaged in administering a large estate are entitled to charge for time spent on administration of the estate and also a scale fee based on the value of the estate.

Solicitors Disciplinary Tribunal. Formerly the Solicitors Disciplinary Committee. Composed of practising solicitors of not less than ten years' standing and lay members appointed by the Master of the Rolls (q.v.) to hear and determine complaints. The Tribunal may strike the name of a solicitor off the Roll and restore to the Roll the name of one formerly struck off. Appeal lies to the Master of the Rolls or High Court. See Solicitors Act 1974, ss 46–54, as amended by C.L.S.A. 1990, s 92. For redress for inadequate professional services, see Solicitors Act 1974, s 37A, inserted by C.L.S.A. 1990, s 93. *See* OSS.

solicitors duty. *See* DUTY SOLICITOR.

solicitor's duty of care. It was held by JCPC in *Pickersgill* v *Riley* (2004) *The Times*, 2 March, that, fundamentally, the scope and nature of a solicitor's duty of care depended on the instructions he had received and the particular circumstances of the case.

solicitor's lien. Method by which a solicitor may protect his right to recover his costs from a client by: passive or retaining lien (i.e., holding papers, deeds and other personal chattels); common law lien on personal property of the client preserved or recovered by his efforts in litigation; statutory lien enforceable by charging order under Solicitors Act 1974, s 73. *See* LIEN.

Solicitors' Practice Rules. Rules made by the Council of the Law Society under Solicitors Act 1974. The Council has power to waive in writing any of the provisions of the Rules.

solicitors, proceedings against. CA held in *R (On Application of Thompson)* v *Law Society* [2004] EWCA Civ 167, that proceedings against a solicitor before a panel of the Office for the Supervision of Solicitors, involving clients' complaints, were not to be considered as determining the solicitor's civil rights and obligations arising under the European Convention, art 6, so that an oral hearing was not necessary.

solicitor, striking off. CA held in *Law Society* v *Bultitude* (2005) *The Times*, 14 January, that it is inevitable that the committing of breaches of professional accounts rules will result in removal of the name from the roll of solicitors.

solicitor, suing of by fraudulent client. CA held in *Sweetman* v *Nathan and Others* (2003) *The Times*, 1 September, that a client who was involved jointly with his solicitor in a fraudulent enterprise was able to sue the solicitor for negligence in conveyancing.

solidary. As in 'solidary obligation', i.e., a 'joint and several' obligation, as where two or more creditors are entitled to the same obligation. See, e.g., *Ward* v *National Bank* (1883) 8 App Cas 755.

solitary confinement. Imprisonment during which a prisoner is not allowed to communicate with any other prisoner. See Prison Act 1952; s 14; Prison Rules 1964, r 43; *Williams* v *Home Office (No. 2)* [1981] 1 All ER 1211.

solus agreement. (*Solus* = alone.) Agreement whereby a retailer binds himself to buy a product from one source only. Example: garage proprietor agreeing to buy all his petrol from one oil company. See *Esso Petroleum Co Ltd* v *Harper's Garage Ltd* [1968] AC 269 (agreement held to be in restraint of trade); *Lobb Garages* v *Total Oil* [1983] 1 All ER 944. For effect of Treaty of Rome 1957, art 85, on this type of agreement, see *Brasserie* v *de Haecht SA (No. 1)* v *Wilkin* [1968] CMLR 26 (automatically void unless exempted). *See* RESTRAINT OF TRADE, CONTRACT IN.

solvency, declaration of. Where it is proposed to wind up a company voluntarily, the directors may make a statutory declaration that, after full enquiry, they believe the company will be able to pay its debts in full, plus interest, within a period not exceeding one year. See Ins.A. 1986, ss 89, 251.

solvent. Able to pay all debts or claims.

solvent abuse. It is an offence to supply or offer to supply a substance other than a controlled drug to a person under 18 or to one who is acting on behalf of a person of that age if the supplier knows that the fumes are likely to be inhaled by the person under 18 for the purpose of causing intoxication: Intoxicating Substances (Supply) Act 1985, s 1. Solvent sniffing is not drug abuse: *R* v *Southwark Coroner, ex p Kendall* [1989] 1 All ER 72.

somnambulism. *See* SLEEPWALKING.

Sovereign. The supreme ruler of the state, e.g., King, Queen. 'If a determinate human superior, not in a habit of obedience to a like superior, receive habitual obedience from the bulk of a given society, that determinate superior is sovereign in that society, and the society (including the superior) is a society political and independent': Austin. See I.A. 1978, s 10. *See* MONARCHY.

sovereign authority. 'The person (or body) to whose directions the law attributes legal force, the person in whom resides as of right the ultimate power either of laying down general rules or of issuing isolated rules or commands whose authority is that of the law itself': Bryce, *Studies in History and Jurisprudence* (1901).

sovereignty. 1. Political and legal concept relating to ultimate authority in a state. 2. Freedom of a state from external control.

sovereignty of Parliament. Doctrine stating that Parliament is the supreme power in the state and possessed, therefore, of unlimited legal power. 'What Parliament doth, no power on earth can undo': Blackstone. See *Macarthys Ltd* v *Smith* [1981] QB 180 (effect of EC legislation). *See* PARLIAMENT.

space, outer. 'Includes the moon and other celestial bodies': Outer Space Act 1986, s 13(1). Activities to which the Act applies, and which must be licensed, comprise launching or procuring the launch of, or operating, a space object, and 'any activity in outer space': s 1. For 'space objects', see s 19(1).

Speaker of the House of Commons. Presiding officer of the Commons, elected by members of the House, subject to the Sovereign's approbation. The Speaker neither speaks nor votes save in an official capacity; is the channel through which House communicates with the Crown; and gives a casting vote if the numbers in a division are equal. The first Speaker was Sir Peter de la Mare, 1376. *See* PARLIAMENT.

Speaker of the House of Lords. The Lord Chancellor. *See* CHANCELLOR.

special acceptance. Acceptance of a bill of exchange (q.v.) as payable at a special place.

special administration. Limited administration (q.v.).

special agent. *See* AGENT, SPECIAL.

special business. Business of a company that is transacted at an extraordinary general meeting (with the exception of declaring a dividend, the consideration of accounts, and the reports of the directors and auditors, the election of the directors in the place of those retiring and the appointment of, and the fixing of the remuneration of, the auditors).

special case. Procedure (now commonly called 'trial of a preliminary issue') whereby parties to an action, after the issue of a summons, agree on a statement of facts for submission to the court for an opinion on the law relating to those facts. See also M.C.A. 1980, s 111 (relating to the 'case stated' procedure); *Berry v Berry* [1987] Fam 1. See SI 96/3151.

special damages. *See* GENERAL AND SPECIAL DAMAGES.

special defence. A defence which was peculiar to one type of action and which had to be specifically pleaded. Example: defences of fair comment, justification, in an action for defamation (q.v.).

Special Forces. Those units of the armed forces of the Crown the maintenance of whose capabilities is the responsibility of the Director of Special Forces or which are for the time being subject to the operational command of that Director: F.I.A. 2000, s 84.

special hospital. Institution which received dangerous, violent or criminal persons requiring special security, e.g., Broadmoor (q.v.) See M.H.A. 1983, Part III; as modified by Health Act 1999, s 41. *See* PSYCHIATRIC SERVICES, HIGH SECURITY.

special jurisdiction, courts of. *See* COURTS OF SPECIAL JURISDICTION.

special manager. Appointed by the court where a company has gone into liquidation. He prepares accounts and exercises other powers entrusted to him by the court: Ins.A. 1986, s 177.

special plea. Plea in bar, e.g., plea of former acquittal. *See* AUTREFOIS ACQUIT.

special procedure for divorce. *See* DIVORCE AND JUDICIAL SEPARATION, SPECIAL PROCEDURE FOR.

special procedure material. Journalistic material, etc., other than items subject to legal privilege, and excluded material, held subject to some implied obligation to hold it in confidence: see P.&C.E.A. 1984, ss 11–14. An application for search is needed: s 9, Sch 1. See *R v Southampton Crown Court ex p J* [1993] COD 286. *See* PRODUCTION ORDER.

special relationship. 'It means no more than a relationship the nature of which is such that one party, for a variety of possible reasons, will be regarded by the law as under a duty of care to the other': *per* Ormrod J in *Esso Petroleum v Marden* [1976] QB 801.

special resolution. One passed by a majority of not less than three-quarters of those members who are entitled to, and do, vote in person, or where proxies are allowed, by proxy, at a general meeting of which at least 21 days' notice has been given. See Cos.A. 1985, s 378. Necessary, e.g., for altering the name, objects or articles of a company. See Cos.A. 1985, ss 4, 9, 135. *See* COMPANY.

specialty. A contract under seal (q.v.) ('specialty contract').

special verdict. A jury must not return a special verdict under the Trial of Lunatics Act 1883 (acquittal on ground of insanity) except on the written or oral evidence of two or more registered medical practitioners (at least one of whom is approved as having special experience in mental disorders): Criminal Procedure (Insanity and Unfitness to Plead) Act 1991, ss 1, 6(1). See also M.H.A. 1983, ss 37(2)(*a*), 54(2)(3); Criminal Cases Review (Insanity) Act 1999, enabling the obsolete verdict of 'guilty but insane' to be referred to and reviewed by the Court of Appeal, following reference by the Criminal Cases Review Commission; *A-G's Reference (No. 3 of 1998)* [1999] 3 All ER 40. *See* UNFITNESS TO PLEAD.

species, preservation of. CA held in *R (Newsum)* v *Welsh Assembly Government* (2004) *The Times*, 7 December, that the basis for the granting of a licence in relation to a protected species and its habitat, is not the preservation of the species itself.

specificatio. The making of a new article from the chattel of one person by the work of another.

specification. Form of information (relating to details of construction, operation, etc.) required in the application for a patent (q.v.). See Patents Act 1977; Copyright, Designs and Patents Act 1988.

specific delivery, writ of. *See* DELIVERY, WRIT OF.

specific devise. *See* DEVISE.

specific goods. *See* GOODS.

specific issue order. One of a range of 'section 8 orders', under Ch.A. 1989, whereby directions are given for the purpose of determining a specific question which has arisen, or may arise, in connection with any aspect of parental responsibility (q.v.) for a child: s 8(1). These orders may be made upon application or upon the court's own motion: s 10(1)(*a*), (*b*). See *Re J (A Minor) (Specific Issue Order)* [1995] 1 FLR 669; *Dawson* v *Wearmouth* [1999] 2 AC 308.

specific legacy. *See* LEGACY.

specific performance. Equitable, discretionary remedy *in personam* whereby a party to an agreement is ordered by the court to perform his obligations according to the terms of that agreement. Granted where the appropriate remedy at law is inadequate, and will not be granted if the court has no jurisdiction to do so: *Rushton* v *Smith* [1975] 2 All ER 905. Does not apply to contracts made for no consideration, or involving continuous supervision, or for personal services, etc. See L.P.A. 1925, s 49(2); S.G.A. 1979, s 52; S.C.A. 1981, ss 49, 50; PD 24, para 7; *Record* v *Bell* [1991] 1 WLR 853; *Cooperative Insurance Ltd* v *Argyll Stores Ltd* [1997] 2 WLR 898; *Rainbow Estates* v *Tokenhold Ltd* [1998] 3 WLR 980.

specimen charges. Procedure in criminal trials whereby evidence is presented relating to a series of incidents said to have taken place within the period specified in the indictment, where any one of those incidents might constitute the offence charged. See, e.g., *R* v *Evans* (1999) *The Times*, 8 June; *R* v *T* [1999] 1 Cr App R (S) 419.

specimen, driver's objection to providing. Where a police officer decides, without a reasonable basis for so doing, that a driver must provide a blood, rather than a urine, specimen, when the driver had made clear that he wished to provide a urine specimen, the decision of the officer was perverse; *Joseph* v *DPP* [2003] EWHC 3078.

speeding offence. 'A person who drives a motor vehicle on a road at a speed exceeding a limit imposed by or under any enactment to which this section applies shall be guilty of an offence': Road Traffic Regulation Act 1984, s 89(1). See also s 84, as amended by Road Traffic Act 1991, s 45. The evidence of more than one witness is generally required to establish liability: s 89(2). Fire brigade, ambulance and police vehicles may be exempted from observance of speed limits: s 87. See, generally, 1984 Act, Part VI; Road Traffic Offenders Act 1988, s 20, substituted by Road Traffic Act 1991, s 23. *See* RADAR TRAP.

spent convictions. Convictions which, under Rehabilitation of Offenders Act 1974, need not be disclosed, after a rehabilitation period (q.v.), and which are not proper grounds for dismissal from office, profession, occupation or employment: s 4. No one should refer in open court to a spent conviction without the judge's authority, which authority should not be given unless the interests of justice so require. See, e.g., F.S.A. 1986, s 189; Banking Act 1987, s 95; *R* v *Secretary of State for Home Department ex p Purcell* (1998) *The Times*, 5 March.

spes successionis. Hope or expectation of succeeding to some right in the property, e.g., as next of kin. It is not a title to property. See *Re Simpson* [1904] 1 Ch 1.

split-trial procedure. The court may order that the issue of liability be tried before any issue relating to the amount of damages to be awarded: see, e.g., PD 29, para 5.3(7).

sporting events, offences relating to. It is an offence to breach an exclusion order made by the court following offences connected with violence or the threat of violence on a journey to or from a football match or, where specified, any other sporting event: P.O.A. 1986, Part IV. See also Sporting Events (Control of Alcohol, etc.) Act 1985; Football (Offences) Act 1991, s 3.

sport referee's liability. A person who is refereeing an adult amateur rugby match is under a duty to members of the teams to take reasonable care for their safety during the game: *Vowles* v *Evans* [2002] EWHC 2612.

spot contract. *See* CONTRACT, SPOT.

spousal rights. Phrase used generally to signify the right of a spouse to occupy the matrimonial home (q.v.). The right may arise, e.g., at common law, under F.L.A. 1996, under Trusts of Land and Appointment of Trustees Act 1996 (where wife has a beneficial interest: s 12).

spouse. Husband or wife. See *Fraser* v *Haight* (1987) 36 DLR 459.

spouses, evidence of. The spouse of the accused is competent to give evidence for the prosecution and generally compellable to give evidence on behalf of the accused: P.&C.E.A. 1984, s 80, amended by Y.J.C.E.A. 1999, Sch 4, para 12. See *R* v *Director of the Serious Fraud Office ex p Johnson* [1993] COD 58. The spouse of the accused is competent to give evidence on behalf of the accused or any person charged with the accused: s 80(2A). Former spouses are compellable to give evidence as if they had never been married to each other: s 80(5). The failure of a wife or husband of a person charged in any proceedings to give evidence in the proceedings shall not be made the subject of any comment by the prosecution: s 80A, inserted by Y.J.C.E.A. 1999, Sch 4, para 14. For evidence of communications made during the period of marriage, see s 80(9).

springing use. A use intended to come into existence *in futuro*. Example: 'to X and his heirs to the use of Y when he shall marry'. See *Re Bird* [1927] 1 Ch 210. *See* USE.

spying. Secretly obtaining information for purposes hostile to the security of the state. See Official Secrets Act 1911, s 1(1); *AG* v *Blake* [1998] Ch 439.

squatter. One who is wrongfully in occupation of land and claiming the right or title to it. See CPR, Sch 1; O 113 (summary proceedings for possession of land); CPR, Sch 2; CCR, O 24; *Ellis* v *Lambeth LBC* [1999] EGCS 101 (squatter entitled to possession); *Pye* v *Graham* (2001) *The Times*, 13 February (discussion of meaning of 'clear intention to

process' and Lim.A. 1980). *See* ADVERSE POSSSESSION.

squatter and owner. CA held in *Topplan Estates* v *Townley* (2004) *The Times*, 15 November, that there is no general obligation to direct a landowner's attention to the fact that time has begun to run against him in relation to a squatter's occupation of his land.

squatter's intention to possess. HL held in *J A Pye Ltd* v *Graham* (2002) 3 WLR 221, that where a squatter asserts possessory title, he must show an intention to possess, and not to own, the relevant land and to exclude the paper title owner only so far as is reasonably possible. His expression of willingness to pay for occupation of the land, where asked to do so, is not inconsistent with his being in the meantime in possession of that land.

SR & O. Statutory rules and orders. *See* STATUTORY INSTRUMENTS.

stag. Speculator who subscribes to an issue of shares with no intention of keeping those allotted to him, but in the hope that he can sell out at a profit. See *R* v *Greenstein* [1975] 1 WLR 1353 (process of 'stagging').

stake. Sum of money risked for gain or loss on the outcome of some event attended by uncertainty.

stakeholder. One with whom a sum is deposited pending deciding of a wager or the outcome of some other event; the stakeholder undertakes to deliver the stake to the winner. See, e.g., *Hastingwood Property* v *Saunders Bearman Anselm* [1990] 3 WLR 623; *Rockeagle Ltd* v *Wilkinson* [1992] Ch 47.

stakeholder pension scheme. *See* PENSION SCHEME, STAKEHOLDER.

stakeholder's interpleader. *See* INTERPLEADER SUMMONS.

stale. Ineffective, usually because of lapse of time. *See* LACHES.

stale cheque. *See* CHEQUE, STALE.

stalking. A type of harassment (q.v.) involving a persistent course of conduct by one person aimed at another, and which is perceived by that other as threatening, often taking the form of unwanted and menacing communications, or the physical pursuit of that other person.

stamp duties. Taxes on certain types of instruments (rather than on the transactions represented), e.g., conveyances, first imposed by Stamp Act 1765 (now repealed). The stamps may be *ad valorem*, i.e., proportionate to the value of the property on which the instrument is based, or fixed in amount. See Finance Act 2000, Part IV; Sch 33.

standard form contracts. Known also as 'contracts of adhesion'. Contracts (1) which set out terms on which mercantile transactions of common occurrence are to be carried out, e.g., charterparties; (2) which are exemplified by the 'ticket cases' of the nineteenth century (see, e.g., *Parker* v *SE Rail Co* (1877) 2 CPD 416), the terms of which were not the subject of negotiations between the parties to them: *Schroeder Music Publishing Co* v *Macaulay* [1974] 1 WLR 1308. See Unfair Contract Terms Act 1977.

Standards Board for England. Body set up under L.G.A. 2000, s 57, comprising three members appointed by Secretary of State to enforce the ethical framework of the Act, e.g., appointment of ethical standards officers to investigate alleged breaches of codes of conduct. See Sch 4.

standards of proof. In *civil cases*, generally proof on a preponderance of probabilities. See, e.g., *Hornal* v *Neuberger Products Ltd* [1957] 1 QB 247. In *criminal cases*, where the burden of proof rests on the prosecution, proof beyond reasonable doubt (q.v.), but where the burden of proof is on the defence (see, e.g., *R* v *Podola* [1960] 1 QB 325) it is proof on a preponderance of probabilities. In *matrimonial cases*, it is, apparently, proof on a preponderance of probabilities (see *Blyth* v *Blyth* [1966] 1 All ER 524). If a crime is alleged in civil proceedings, the standard is the civil one. In the very unusual civil claim for damages for murder, it is the criminal standard: *Halford* v *Brookes and Another* [1991] 1 WLR 428. There can be no 'midway' standard of proof, between the civil and criminal

standards. See *Re H and R (Child Sexual Abuse: Standard of Proof)* [1996] 1 FLR 80: the standard of proof is 'the balance of probabilities on which there must be cogent evidence commensurate with the seriousness of the allegation'. In care proceedings the CA held in *Re (U) (a Child)* (2004), *The Times*, 27 May, that in care proceedings, the standard of proof which ought to be applied is the balance of probabilities. *See* BALANCE OF PROBABILITIES; PROOF.

standing by. Reference to the principle that where a person who knows what is happening is content to 'stand by and see others fighting his battle', he ought to be bound by the result. See *Nana Ofori Atta II* v *Nana Abu Bonsra II* [1958] AC 95.

standing civilian courts. Courts established under Armed Forces Act 1976, s 6, for the trial outside the UK of civilians to whom Part II of Army Act 1955 or Part II of Air Force Act 1955 (as amended by Armed Forces Act 1986, s 9), is applied by s 209 of either Act. Trial is before a magistrate, appointed from assistants to the Judge Advocate-General, and assessors selected from a panel: s 6(4)–(15). See 1976 Act, Sch 3; C.J.A. 1982, Sch 8, as amended by C.J.A. 1988, s 50.

standing committees. Committees appointed at the beginning of each parliamentary session by the Committee of Selection of the House of Commons (q.v.) to deal with public Bills at committee stage, or in the second reading and report stages. (A new committee may be chosen for each Bill considered.) Chairmen are appointed from the Chairmen's Panel by the Speaker. There are standing committees on, e.g., matters relating to Scotland, Wales, Northern Ireland. Special Public Bill Committees, which hear evidence from outside experts, were introduced in 1980, involving four sittings, three of which heard evidence.

standing mute. *See* MUTE.

standing orders. Orders formulated by a body, e.g., the House of Commons (q.v.), for the conduct in formal manner of its proceedings.

stare decisis. To stand by decided matters. (*Stare decisis et non quieta movere* = to stand by precedent and not to disturb settled points.) Doctrine according to which previous judicial decisions must be followed. *See* PRECEDENT.

state. 1. A politically organised community under a sovereign government. 'The organs of government of a national community': *per* Lord Devlin in *Chandler* v *DPP* [1964] AC 763. 2. Social position. 3. Estate (q.v.).

statehood. Criteria, according to Montevideo Convention 1933, are: permanent population; defined territory; government; capacity to enter into relations with other states.

state immunity. CA held in *Mitchell* v *Al-Dali* [2004] EWCA Civ 1394, that a foreign state cannot claim an absolute right to immunity in relation to civil claims against its officials for systematic torturing of suspects, even though this is alleged to have been committed outside to the borders of the country of suit. *See* IMMUNITY FROM JURISDICTION, STATE, SOVEREIGN.

stateless person. One who has no nationality. For provisions for reducing statelessness under B.N.A. 1981, see s 36, Sch 2.

statement. Includes any representation of fact, whether made in words or otherwise: Civil Evidence Act 1968, s 10(1). See Defamation Act 1996, ss 7, 17 ('statement' means words, pictures, visual images, gestures or any other method of signifying meaning). See *R* v *Derodra* [1999] Crim LR 978 (identification of 'maker of a statement').

statement of affairs. A statement required to be made by a bankrupt in certain cases, setting out details of his creditors, debts, liabilities, assets, etc., for the information of his official receiver: see the Ins.A. 1986, s 288. *See* BANKRUPTCY.

statement of case. *See* CASE, STATEMENT OF.

statement of truth. *See* TRUTH, STATEMENT OF.

statement of value. Statement to be made in claim form, where claimant is making a claim for money, based upon CPR, r 16.3 and PD 16. The statement does not limit the power of the court to give judgment for the amount which it finds the claimant is entitled to: r 16.3(7). *See* CLAIM FORM AND PARTICULARS OF CLAIM.

statements, liability for careless. Liability resulting from the failure to observe a duty to avoid making careless statements resulting in harm to some person. See *Hedley Byrne & Co Ltd* v *Heller & Partners Ltd* [1964] AC 465; *WB Anderson & Sons Ltd* v *Rhodes Ltd* [1967] 2 All ER 850.

statements, liability for false. *See* DECEIT.

state of emergency. *See* EMERGENCY POWERS.

station, railway. Any land or other property which consists of premises used for the purposes of a railway passenger station or terminal, including any approaches, forecourt, cycle store or car park: G.L.A.A. 1999, s 239(1).

status. 'The condition of belonging to a class in society to which the law ascribes peculiar rights and duties, capacities and incapacities': *per* Lord Simon in *The Ampthill Peerage* [1977] AC 547. For declarations of marital status, see F.L.A. 1986, s 55A, inserted by C.S.P.S.S.A. 2000, s 83; see Sch 8.

status quo ante. The same state as before.

statute. An Act of Parliament (q.v.). 'What the statute itself enacts cannot be unlawful, because what the statute says and provides is itself the law, and the highest form of law that is known to this country' *per* Ungoed-Thomas J in *Cheney* v *Conn* [1968] 1 All ER 779. For 'acts done in pursuance of statute', see *Hampson* v *DES* [1990] 3 WLR 42. A statute becomes law on a date specified therein, or on a date to be fixed by the Minister.

statute-barred debt. Debts in respect of which a creditor may not bring proceedings because the periods of time stated in the Limitation Acts have passed. In the winding-up of a company (q.v.), the liquidator (q.v.) must not pay statute-barred debts if shareholders object: *Re Fleetwood Syndicate* [1915] 1 Ch 486.

statute book. Collective title of those Acts of Parliament going back to 1235, which are currently in force.

statute, citation of. In early days statutes were cited by reference to the name of the place at which Parliament met, e.g., the Provisions of Oxford 1258. Later they were cited by reference to the regnal year and chapter; thus the Perjury Act 1911 was cited as 1 & 2 Geo. V, c. 6 (i.e., the sixth of the statutes passed in the parliamentary session of the first and second years of the reign of George V). Hence, the complete citation of a pre-1963 Act is, e.g., Homicide Act 1957 (5 & 6 Eliz. II, c. 11). Following Acts of Parliament Numbering and Citation Act 1962, an Act passed after January 1963 is cited by reference to the calendar year in which it was passed, e.g., Electronic Communications Act 2000 (c. 7). See also I.A. 1978, s 19.

statute, contempt of. *See* CONTEMPT OF STATUTE.

statute law. The body of law enacted by Parliament.

statutes, construction of. *See* INTERPRETATION OF STATUTES.

statutes, explanatory notes. Issued as an appendix to a statute to assist in understanding. They do not form part of the statute and have not been endorsed by Parliament. See, e.g., Road Traffic (NHS) Charges Act 1999, where the notes comprise an introduction, background, purpose of the Act, commentary on sections, Hansard references.

statutes, penal. *See* PENAL STATUTES.

statutes, presumptions relating to construction of. *See* PRESUMPTIONS RELATING TO CONSTRUCTION OF STATUTES.

statutes, revenue. *See* REVENUE STATUTES.

statutorily protected tenancy. A protected tenancy (q.v.) within the meaning of Rent Act 1977 or a tenancy to which Landlord and Tenant Act 1954, Part I, applied; a protected occupancy or statutory tenancy as defined in Rent (Agriculture) Act 1976; a tenancy to which Landlord and Tenant Act 1954, Part II, applied; a tenancy of an agricultural holding within Agricultural Holdings Act 1986 and Agricultural Tenancies Act 1995. Protection from Eviction Act 1977, s 8(1).

statutory authority, defence of. Defence in tort (q.v.), as where a statute authorises an action which interferes with some person's rights: see *Allen v Gulf Oil Refining Ltd* [1981] AC 1001 (in relation to Gulf (Oil Refining Act 1965, s 5(1) and suit for nuisance).

statutory books. Registers and other documents which a company must keep, i.e.: registers of members, directors and secretaries, directors' interests in debentures and shares, charges, interests in voting capital; minute books; directors' service contracts; records of receipts and expenditure; assets and liabilities, stock, sales and purchases. See, e.g., Cos.A. 1985, s 221; Cos.A. 1989, s 1.

statutory company. A company whose objects and powers are defined under a special private Act.

statutory corporation. Public corporation (q.v.).

statutory declaration. *See* DECLARATION.

statutory duty, breach of. Tort (q.v.) committed by one who injures another as the result of some breach of statute. The statutory duty must be owed to the plaintiff; the injury suffered must be of the nature which the statute was intended to prevent; the defendant must be guilty of a breach of his statutory obligation; the breach must have caused the damage. See *Wentworth v Wiltshire CC* (1992) 142 NLJ; *Murphy v Brentwood DC* [1990] 2 All ER 908.

statutory instrument, omission in. In *Confederation of Passenger Transport UK v Humber Bridge Board* (2003) *The Times*, 16 July, the CA held that where words in a Statutory Instrument had been omitted in error (see SI 97/1950, SI 2000/264, SI 2002/786), it was allowable to rectify the error by use of explanatory notes, and decision letters of secretary of state providing authority for the instrument to be drawn up.

statutory instruments. Documents by which power to make subordinate legislation has been exercised by the Queen in Council or a minister. Known formerly as 'statutory rules and orders' and usually cited by calendar year, number and occasionally the title, e.g., Social Security Benefits Up-rating Order 1999 (SI 1999/264). (A 'regulation' is a statutory instrument only where the parent Act declares the power to issue regulations is to be made by statutory instrument.) See Statutory Instruments Act 1946; Statutory Orders (Special Procedure) Acts 1945, 1965; European Communities Act 1972, s 2(2). Their validity may be challenged in the courts on grounds of *ultra vires* or failure to follow correct procedures in making the instrument (see, e.g., *Raymond* v *Honey* [1983] AC 1). *See* DELEGATED LEGISLATION.

statutory instruments, committees concerning. The *SI Reference Committee* decides questions concerning classification and numbering. The *Joint Select Committee on SI*, consisting of seven members of each House of Parliament (of whom two are a quorum) chaired by a Commons Member from the Opposition, considers SIs laid before each House. It must consider, in particular, the possibility of, e.g., defective drafting, unauthorised retrospective effect, unjustifiable delay in publication, imposition of a charge on the public revenues. See Commons Standing Order No. 124. The *Commons Select Committee on SI* considers instruments directed by statute to be laid before the Commons.

statutory interest on late payment of debts. Under Late Payment of Commercial Debts (Interest) Act 1998, it is an implied term in certain contracts that a debt created by such contracts carries simple interest: s 1(1). Contracts covered are those for sale of goods or services involving a transfer or agreement to transfer property in goods to another or agreeing to carry out a service: s 1(2), (3). Rate of statutory interest will be

prescribed by Secretary of State: s 6(1).

statutory interest, period for which it runs. Under Late Payment of Commercial Debts (Interest) Act 1998, statutory interest starts to run on day after relevant day for the debt: s 4(2). Where there is no agreement between supplier and purchaser for payment of the debt, relevant day is the last day of the period of 30 days beginning with day on which supplier's obligation to which debt relates is performed, or day on which purchaser has notice of amount of debt, whichever is the later: s 4(2), (5). Statutory interest ceases to run when interest would cease to run if it were carried under an express contract term: s 4(7).

statutory interpretation. *See* INTERPRETATION OF STATUTES.

statutory lives in being. Lives enumerated under P.&A.A. 1964, s 3(5), for purposes of the perpetuities rule (q.v.) as: (1) the person who made the disposition; (2) the person to whom, or in whose favour, the disposition was made; (3) parents and grandparents of the beneficiaries, in certain cases; (4) any person on the failure or determination of whose prior interest the disposition is limited to take effect. See *Re Thomas Meadows & Co Ltd* [1971] Ch 278.

statutory notice, accessibility of. CA held in *Jones and Others* v *T Mobile (UK) Ltd* (2003) *The Times*, 10 September, that where there is a requirement that a notice affixed to a telecommunications tower must be legible, this means that it has to be of a height, and unobstructed, so that it can be read with reasonable comfort; it did not mean, however, that it had to be capable of being read by a member of the public from land to which the public had no access.

statutory nuisance. *See* NUISANCE.

statutory owners. Term used in relation to a settlement to indicate those in whom, during a minority or where there is no tenant for life (q.v.), the legal estate is vested, i.e., persons of full age upon whom powers are conferred by the settlement and, in any other case, the trustees of the settlement: S.L.A. 1925, ss 23, 117. They have the powers of a tenant for life. See SETTLEMENT.

statutory provision, local. Means, under P.S.I.A. 2001, s 25: a provision of any local Act; a provision of any instrument in the nature of a local enactment; a provision of any instrument made under a local statutory provision.

statutory rules and orders. *See* STATUTORY INSTRUMENTS.

statutory tenancy. After the termination of a protected tenancy (q.v.) of a dwelling house, the person who, immediately before that termination, was the protected tenant, shall, if and so long as he occupies the dwelling house as his residence, be the statutory tenant of it and, when there is a statutory tenant of a dwelling house that house is referred to as subject to a statutory tenancy: Rent Act 1977, s 2(1)(*a*), (2). See H.A. 1988, s 39; *Killick* v *Roberts* [1991] 1 WLR 1146. *See* TENANT BY SUCCESSION, STATUTORY.

statutory trusts. 1. Trusts created or implied by statute, e.g., under L.P.A. 1925, ss 34, 36 or A.E.A. 1925, s 33. 2. Under A.E.A. 1925, s 49 ('statutory trusts in favour of issue and other classes of relatives of an intestate'), part of the property is held by a personal representative (q.v.) to be divided equally among children who are alive at the death of the intestate as soon as they attain 18, or marry. *See* TRUST.

statutory undertakers. Persons authorised by enactment to carry on specified activities, as in T.C.P.A. 1990, s 262(1), where phrase is used to refer to persons who are authorised to carry on 'any railway, light railway, tramway and transport, etc.'

stay of proceedings. 'A stay imposes a halt on proceedings, apart from taking any steps allowed by the Rules of the terms of the stay. Proceedings can be continued if a stay is lifted': CPR Glossary. See r 15.11; r 26.4; PD 26, para 3.1 (procedure for parties to extend stay order to allow for settlement).

stay of proceedings in relation to an offence. Prosecution of Offences Act

1985, s 22B (inserted by C.D.A. 1998, s 45) provides for re-institution of proceedings stayed under the 1985 Act, s 22(4) (amended by C.D.A. 1998, s 43) and 1985 Act, s 22A (inserted by C.D.A. 1998, s 44). Proceedings may be re-instituted by direction of, e.g., Chief Crown Prosecutor, within three months of date on which they were stayed (or a longer period if the court allows). See *PD (Crown Court: Abuse of Process)* (2000) *The Times*, 30 May.

stealing. Theft (q.v.).

stealing, going equipped for. *See* GOING EQUIPPED FOR STEALING.

stepchild. The child of one's husband or wife, born in a previous marriage. In relation to whether a stepchild who has never lived with nor been maintained by a step-parent may apply under Inheritance (Provision for Family and Dependants) Act 1975, s 15(1)(d), it is necessary to show that applicant had been treated as a child of the family (q.v.). See *R* v *Leach* [1985] 2 All ER 754.

sterilisation. Surgical removal of, or obstruction of the functions of, the reproductive organs so as to prevent reproduction. See *Re B* [1987] 2 WLR 1213 (House of Lords upheld order for sterilisation of a mentally retarded 17-year old female ward. *Per* Lord Hailsham, LC: The basic human right of a woman to reproduce is only such where reproduction is the result of informed choice); *Re E* [1991] 2 FLR 585; *Practice Note (Official Solicitor: Sterilisation)* [1996] 2 FLR 111; *Danns* v *Dept of Health* [1998] PIQR P226 (failure of DOH to warn of risk of pregnancy); *Re A (Mental Patient: Sterilisation)* (2000) *The Times*, 15 March (it is for the court to decide whether sterilisation is in the best interests of a mental patient); *Taylor* v *Shropshire HA (No. 2)* [2000] Lloyd's Rep Med 96 (negligence in sterilisation).

still-born child. 'A child which has issued forth from its mother after the 24th week of pregnancy and which did not at any time after being completely expelled from its mother breathe or show any other sign of life': Births and Deaths

Registration Act 1953, s 41, as amended by Still-Birth (Definition) Act 1992, s 1. See *Tan* v *East London HA* [1999] Lloyd's Rep Med 389.

stipendiary magistrates. Full-time, salaried magistrates who usually sit alone. Renamed 'District Judges (Magistrates' Courts)' (q.v.) (as from 31 August 2000: SI 00/1920), under Acc.J.A. 1999, s 28.

stipulation. Agreement, bond or undertaking. For 'stipulation to the contrary', see *Urban Manor Ltd* v *Sadiq* [1997] 1 WLR 1016.

stock. 1. Capital lent to the government or a local authority on which a fixed rate of interest is paid. 2. Fully paid shares which have been converted and combined into one unit, so that a company's capital, consisting formerly of, e.g., 100,000 separate shares of £1 each becomes stock worth £100,000. See Cos.A. 1985, s 121(2); *Re Home and Foreign Investment Agency Ltd* [1912] 1 Ch 72. 3. Goods available for sale. 4. A family or line of descent.

stock exchange. Recognised organisation of brokers and others who engage in the purchase and sale of stocks, shares and securities. See I.C.T.A. 1988, s 841(1).

stock, inscribed. *See* INSCRIBED STOCK.

stock lending. Practice allowing dealers in securities to borrow them from appropriate institutions when they require them for delivery on sales. The dealer agrees to replace them at a later date with the same type and amount of securities. See Finance Act 1991, s 57; SI 92/572.

stop and search powers. Police powers, under P.&C.E.A. 1984, Part I, to stop and search persons or vehicles in any place to which the public has access, for, e.g., stolen articles, offensive weapons. Reasonable force only may be used in exercise of the power: see s 117. See *Revised Code A* (1991) issued under 1984 Act, s 66; Sporting Events (Control of Alcohol, etc.) Act 1985, s 7(3); C.J.P.O.A. 1994, s 60 (anticipation of serious violence); Terrorism Act 2000, ss 44–47.

stop list relating to planning control. Notice served by a local planning authority after the serving of an enforcement notice (q.v.) requiring a breach of the planning order to be remedied, where the authority considers it expedient to prevent some activity alleged by the notice to constitute a breach. It is an offence for a person to contravene the stop notice. See T.C.P.A. 1990, s 183, amended by Planning and Compensation Act 1991, s 9.

stop list, trade. A list, usually drawn up by a trade association, of persons with whom members of the association are forbidden to deal. See *Hardie and Lane Ltd* v *Chilton* [1928] 2 KB 306.

stop notice. A notice which can be served on, e.g., a company ordering it not to register a transfer of shares without serving notice on the judgment creditors (q.v.). Issued so as to prevent a disposition of securities, by a judgment debtor. See CPR, Sch 1; O 50, relating to stop notices and orders prohibiting improper dealings with funds in the court, etc. For stop notices in relation to land planning, see T.C.P.A. 1990, ss 183–187, amended by Planning and Compensation Act 1991.

stoppage *in transitu*. *See* IN TRANSITU.

storm. 'Some sort of violent wind usually accompanied by rain or hail or snow. Storm does not mean persistent bad weather nor does it mean heavy rain or persistent rain by itself': *per* Veale J in *Oddy* v *Phoenix Assurance Co Ltd* [1966] 1 Lloyd's Rep 134.

stranger. One who is 'not privy or party to an act': Cowell.

Strategic Health Authorities. Under NHS Reform and Health Care Professions Act 2002, s 1, Health Authorities established for areas in England are to be known as Strategic Health Authorities. Their tasks include: creating a coherent strategic framework; agreeing annual performance agreements; considering appropriate building capacity.

Strategic Rail Authority. Body corporate, formed under Transport Act 2000, consisting of chairman and 7–14 other members, to promote use of rail network for carriage of passengers and goods, to secure development of the network, and to contribute to the development of an integrated system of transport of passengers and goods: ss 201(1), 202(1), 205. See Sch 14.

Strategic Rail Authority, exercise of functions. The Authority must act in the way best calculated: to protect interests of rail services' users; to contribute to achievement of sustainable development; to promote efficiency and economy on the part of persons providing rail services; to promote measures designed to facilitate making by passengers of journeys involving use of services of more than one passenger service operator; to enable rail service providers to plan future of their businesses with assurance: Transport Act 2000, s 207(2).

straw, man of. *See* MAN OF STRAW.

straying livestock. Where livestock belonging to any person strays on to land in the ownership or occupation of another and damages land or property thereon, or expenses are reasonably incurred by that other person in keeping the livestock (if, e.g., it cannot be restored at once to the owner), the person to whom the livestock belongs is liable for damage or expenses: Animals Act 1971, s 11. See also Highways Act 1980, s 155.

street. Public or private roadway running in front of houses or other buildings in a continuous line. It includes any highway, road, lane, footpath, square, court, alley or passage, whether a thoroughfare or not: Highways Act 1980, s 329(1). See New Roads and Street Works Act 1991, s 48(1); London Local Authorities Act 2000, s 32.

street offences. 1. Offences related to the obstruction of highways, disregard of police regulations. See, e.g., Metropolitan Police Act 1839, s 54; *Grant* v *Taylor* [1986] Crim LR 252. 2. Importuning and loitering. *See* IMPORTUNE; LOITER.

street trading. The selling or exposing or offering for sale of any article (including a living thing) in a street: Local Government (Misc. Provs.) Act 1982, Sch 4, para 1. See City of Westminster Act 1999; *Wandsworth LBC* v *Rosenthal* (1996) 160 JP Rep 734.

stress at work. *See* OCCUPATIONAL STRESS.

stress injury. Liability for a psychiatric injury resulting from stress at work was, in general terms, no different in principle from a general liability for any physical injury: *Hartman* v *S Essex Trust* (2005) *The Times*, 21 January.

stress, work-related damages for. An employee who wishes to recover damages for psychological stress resulting from stress at work must establish that he has shown sufficient signs for it to be reasonably foreseeable by his employer that the stress would cause injury to health: *Bonser* v *UK Coal Mining Ltd* (2003) *The Times*, 30 June. See *Hatton* v *Sutherland* [2002] ICR 613.

strict liability in criminal law. Term adopted in place of 'absolute liability'. 'If a matter is made a criminal offence, it is essential that there should be something in the nature of *mens rea* . . . But there are exceptions to this rule . . . and the reason for this is, that the legislature has thought it so important to prevent the particular act from being committed that it absolutely forbids it to be done; and if it is done the offender is liable to a penalty whether he has any *mens rea* or not, and whether or not he intended to commit a breach of the law': *Pearks, Gunston & Tee Ltd* v *Ward* [1902] 2 KB 1. See *Gammon* v *A-G of Hong Kong* [1985] AC 1; *R* v *Bradish* [1990] 2 WLR 223 (Firearms Act 1968, s 5, creating offence of strict liability); *R* v *Densu* [1998] 1 Cr App R 400. Where a statute is silent as to *mens rea*, the presumption that it is required may be rebutted, and in some cases (e.g., Food Safety Act 1990, ss 20, 21) a statute imposing strict liability may also provide a defence.

strict liability in tort. *See* DANGEROUS THINGS, LIABILITY RELATING TO.

strict liability offences in insolvency. Materially contributing to one's insolvency by gambling, contrary to Insolvency Act 1986, s 362 (1) (a), is an offence of strict liability, notwithstanding Human Rights Convention, art 7: *R* v *Muhamed* (2002) *The Times*, 16 August.

strict liability rule and contempt of court. *See* CONTEMPT OF COURT AND STRICT LIABILITY RULE.

strict settlement. Defined under S.L.A. 1925, s 1, as amended. It arises from a deed, will, etc. under which land is limited in trust by way of succession; it excludes land held on trust for sale and involves the use of a trust instrument and a vesting deed. Example: a settlement which was usually made on marriage whereby the husband received a life interest, the children of the marriage received entailed interests and the wife received pin money during her husband's life and an annual sum during widowhood. See *Ungarian* v *Lesnoff* [1990] Ch 206. See SETTLEMENT.

strike. The cessation of work by a body of employed persons acting in combination, or a concerted refusal, or a refusal under a common understanding, of any number of employed persons to continue to work for an employer in consequence of a dispute, done as a means of compelling their employer or any employed person or body of employed persons or to aid other employees in compelling their employer or employed persons to accept or not to accept terms or conditions of or affecting employment: E.R.A. 1996, s 235(5). For overtime ban considered as strike, see *Connex Ltd* v *NURMTW* [1999] IRLR 249. See BALLOT; INDUSTRIAL ACTION.

strike, official. A strike (q.v.) which is supported formally and financially by a recognised trade union (q.v.).

strike-out of claim. Although inordinate and inexcusable delay seems to characterize a case, the court should consider striking out a claim because of abuse of process only when there appears to be a real risk that it would be no longer possible to try the matter fairly and the interests of justice required a strike-out: *Fay* v *Chief Constable of Bedfordshire Police* (2003) 13 February.

striking off. Removal from a register, e.g., for professional misconduct. Under Medical Act 1983, Part V, the Professional Conduct Committee of the General Medical Council (GMC) may erase from the register a person convicted in the UK of a criminal offence, or who has been judged by the Committee to have been guilty of serious professional misconduct (q.v.). Appeal is to JCPC (q.v.). See Medical (Professional Performance) Act 1995, s 1, for suspension from register; *R* v *General Medical Council ex p Salvi* (1998) *The Times*, 24 February (GMC has no duty to give reasons for refusal to restore a name to the register). For striking off a company, see *R* v *Registrar of Companies ex p A-G* [1991] BCLC 746. *See* GENERAL MEDICAL COUNCIL.

striking out a statement of case. 'Striking out means the court ordering written material to be deleted so that it may no longer be relied on': CPR Glossary. The court may strike out a statement of case (q.v.) if it appears that it discloses no reasonable grounds for bringing or defending a claim, or that the statement of case is an abuse of the court's process or is otherwise likely to obstruct the just disposal of the proceedings, or there has been a failure to comply with a rule, PD or court order: r 3.4. The court may make any consequential order after striking out a statement of case. For judgment without trial after striking out, see r 3.5. See *Axia Insurance Co Ltd* v *Swire Fraser Ltd* (2000) *The Times*, 19 January.

structure fixed to a building. In T.C.P.A. 1971, s 54(9), means a structure which is ancillary and subordinate to the building itself and is either fixed to the main building or within its curtilage (q.v.): *Debenhams* v *Westminster CC* [1987] 1 All ER 51.

student loans, human rights and. Although art 2 of the First Protocol to the Human Rights Convention has application to tertiary education, arrangements relating to student loans do not fall within art 2. *R (on application of Douglas)* v *N. Tyneside MBC* [2003] EWCA Civ 1847.

subject. One who owes obedience to another (usually the Crown).

subject to contract. Generally, the use of this phrase prevents the document in which it is contained from being evidence of a concluded bargain. There may be a binding contract, however, if the court can conclude that all the terms of a bargain have been agreed and set down in writing and signed. See *Lyus* v *Prowsa Development* [1982] 1 WLR 1044; *Alpenstow Ltd* v *Regalian Properties* [1985] 1 WLR 721.

subject to survey. Use of this conditional phrase in contract for sale of property does not, apparently, prevent a binding contract from coming into existence. There is a duty on the purchaser, in such a case, to have a survey made. See *Ee* v *Kakar* (1979) 40 P & CR 223.

sub judice. Under judicial consideration; not yet decided.

sub judice **rule.** 1. Rule relating to contempt of court (q.v.) whereby the courts will act to prevent or punish the publishing of articles in the press which prejudice the fair trial of an action. See Contempt of Court Act 1981, s 1. 2. Principle of parliamentary procedure whereby a matter awaiting judicial decision is not generally referred to in debate nor as the subject of a question to a minister.

sub-lease. A lease emerging from, and shorter than, another leasehold interest. Known also as a 'sub-tenancy' or 'under-lease'. In effect, the sub-lessor has a reversionary interest in the land. The sub-lease will end if a head lease is forfeited; but under L.P.A. 1925, s 146(4) the sub-tenant may apply for relief in this case. See L.P. (Am.) A. 1929; *Barclays Bank plc* v *Prudential Assurance* [1998] BPIR 427; *Barrett* v *Morgan* [2000] 1 All ER 481.

sub-letting. Leasing by a tenant (q.v.) of premises leased to him. An agreement not to sub-let is not broken by sub-leasing part of the premises: *Cook* v *Shoesmith* [1951] 1 KB 752. See also H.A. 1985, s 94; Landlord and Tenant Act 1988.

sub modo. Under some restriction, modification or qualification.

sub-mortgage. The mortgage of a mortgage, e.g., as where a mortgagee borrows money on the security of the mortgage. Under L.P.A. 1925, s 86, where the mortgage has been created by a grant of a term of years a legal sub-mortgage can be made only by a grant of a sub-term or a legal charge. *See* MORTGAGE.

sub nom. Sub nomine. Under the name.

subordinate legislation. Delegated legislation (q.v.).

subornation. The influencing of a person to commit a criminal act. Thus, subornation of perjury is the offence of procuring another to commit perjury (q.v.): Perjury Act 1911, s 7(1). See *R* v *Ellahi* (1979) 1 Cr App R (S) 164.

subpoena. *Sub poena* = under a penalty. A writ which took the form of *subpoena duces tecum*, or *subpoena ad testificandum*, directing a person to give evidence and bring relevant documents.

subrogation. Substitution. Refers to a remedy intended to ensure that rights are transferred from one person to another by operation of law, e.g., an insurer's right to enforce a remedy which the assured could have enforced against a third party. See *Orakpo* v *Manson Investments* [1978] AC 95; *Faircharm Investments* v *Citibank International* [1998] Lloyd's Rep 127. For subrogation as a restitutionary, personal remedy, see *Banque Financière* v *Parc Ltd* [1998] 2 WLR 475.

subrogation, entitlement to. CA held in *C & G plc* v *Appleyard* (2004) *The Times*, 29 March, that claimants (the lenders) who were unable to register their mortgage as a legal charge (following opposition from a prior charge) had the right to be subrogated to a first lender whose mortgage had been paid off by the claimant's loan, although the claimants had some security, even though the amount was below that for which they had sought to bargain.

subscribing witness. One who signs a document as an attesting witness. *See* ATTESTATION.

subscription, minimum. *See* MINIMUM SUBSCRIPTION.

subsequent condition. *See* CONDITION.

subsidence. The sinking of ground to a lower level, often resulting in damage to land and buildings in the immediate area. See, e.g., Coal Mining Subsidence Act 1991; SI 96/593. For payments to houses rendered uninhabitable, see s 22. See *Holloway HA Ltd* v *Islington LBC* [1998] CLY 4052.

subsidiarity. Jurisprudential concept, concerned with the devolution of power, suggesting that the functions involved in the activities of a group, such as a society, should be carried out by the smallest group capable of so doing, in order that the autonomy of individuals within the group might be promoted. The concept has appeared in EU administrative doctrine (and is known also as the 'attained better' test), referring to the principle of devolving decision making and other activities as far down the power structure as is practicable and appropriate, e.g., at member state, rather than Commission, level. 'It is a principle for the allocation of power upwards and downwards; however it incorporates a presumption favouring a downwards allocation where there is a doubt': CEPR Report 1993.

subsidiary company. A company (S) is a subsidiary of another company (H) (its holding company) if H holds a majority of voting rights in S, or is a member of S and has the right to appoint or remove a majority of the board of directors of S, or is a member of S and controls alone, pursuant to an agreement with other shareholders or members, a majority of the voting rights in S, or if it is a subsidiary of a company which is itself a subsidiary of H: Cos.A. 1985, s 736, substituted by Cos.A. 1989, s 144. See *Michaels* v *Harley House* [1999] 1 All ER 356.

sub silentio. Under silence; without notice having been given to some matter. For use of the phrase, see *R* v *Gloucestershire CC* [1980] 2 All ER 746, referring to *Re DJMS* [1978] QB 120. For the rule that a precedent *sub silentio* is not authoritative, see, e.g., *Bradley-Hole* v *Cusen* [1953] 1 QB 305.

substantial damages. *See* DAMAGES.

substantive law. That part of the law concerned with the determination of rights, liabilities and duties, etc., as contrasted with adjective law (q.v.).

substantive offence. A definite, complete offence.

substitutional legacy. *See* LEGACY, SUBSTITUTIONAL.

substitutionary gift. Gift, e.g., to children in equal shares which provides that the children of a deceased child will take the share of that child. (In such a case, those who are substituted take, in general, as joint tenants.) See *Re Bourke's WT* [1980] 1 All ER 219.

substitution of parties. *See* PARTIES, PROCEDURE FOR ADDING AND SUBSTITUTING.

substratum rule. Where the main object or substratum of a company fails, it must not continue to operate the business under an ancillary power. Shareholders may petition for winding-up where the entire substratum (i.e., the basis of the business) has gone. See Ins.A. 1986, s 122(1)(*g*); *Re German Date Coffee Co* (1882) 20 Ch D 169.

sub-tenancy. Sub-lease (q.v.).

sub-tenant. An under-lessee of the original tenant.

sub-tenant, unlawful. Person occupying under a lease or tenancy granted by the head tenant, in breach of some covenant or agreement against sub-letting, assigning or parting with possession. Recovery of possession may be sought. See *Leith Properties* v *Byrne* [1983] QB 433.

sub tit. Sub titulo = under the title of.

sub-trust. Known also as a 'derivate trust'. Example: as where trustees A and B hold a fund in trust for C and D in equal shares, and C and D declare themselves trustees of their shares for their children. *See* TRUST.

subversion. Activities, often of a covert nature, directed to the undermining of the organs of government and their eventual overthrow. May consist of the written and spoken word, and, e.g., acts of a seditious nature.

sub voce. Under the title or heading.

succession. 1. The order in which persons succeed to property, or some title. 2. Term applied to the estate of a deceased person. 3. Process of becoming entitled to property of a deceased by operation of law or will. See A.E.A. 1925; *Re DWS* (2000) 150 NLJ 1788 (exclusion from benefit).

succession, public policy matters. Should a condition subsequent in a will act so as to deter a beneficiary from seeking to challenge it on the ground that he might thereby lose his benefit, the condition was not rendered void on grounds of public policy. The court would take the matter into account when considering an application: *Nathan v Leonard* (2002) *The Times*, 4 June.

sue. 1. To seek justice by the process of law. 2. To bring a claim against some person(s). See CPR 1998.

sufferance, tenancy at. Tenancy created where a tenant is in occupation 'by lawful demise and after his estate endeth continueth in possession and wrongfully holdeth over': Coke. In effect, mere possession, created only by construction of law, arising where a valid tenancy terminates but the tenant is holding over (q.v.) without the landlord's permission. See *Remon v City of London Real Property Co* [1921] 1 KB 49.

suffrage. Right or privilege to vote in an election.

suicide. The taking of one's own life intentionally and voluntarily. A crime until Suicide Act 1961. It is a crime, however, for a person to aid, abet, counsel or procure the suicide of another: s 2(1). See *R v McShane* (1977) 66 Cr App R 97; *R v McGranaghan* (1988) 9 Cr App R (S) 447. Suicide must be strictly proved at a coroner's inquest; it is not a verdict which ought to be reached as being the most likely cause of death: *R v City of London Coroner* [1975] 1 WLR 1310; *Kirkham v Chief Constable of Greater Manchester Police* [1990] 3 All ER 246.

suicide, assisted. In *R (on application of Pretty) v DPP* (2001) 151 NLJ 1819, it was held that DPP has no power to undertake not to prosecute any person before an offence (e.g., assisting in a suicide) has been committed); Suicide Act 1961, s 2(1), is not incompatible with Human Rights Convention; there is no right 'to die with dignity' under Convention, arts 2, 3, 8, 9. Court of Human Rights held (see (2002) 152 NLJ 707) that there had been no violation of art 8, and that arts 2, 3, 9 had not been engaged. (Mrs Pretty later died in a hospice

from motor neurone disease: *The Times*, 13 May 2002.)

suicide pact. An agreement between two or more persons having for its object the death of all of them, whether or not each is to take his own life: Homicide Act 1957, s 4(3). See also Suicide Act 1961, ss 2, 3; *Dunbar v Plant* [1998] Ch 412 (Forfeiture Act 1982 considered in relation to survivor of a suicide pact).

sui generis. Of its own right. Constituting a class of its own.

sui juris. Of one's own right. Having full legal capacity to act on one's own. See *ALIENI JURIS*.

suing of a ministry. MOD is under no duty to maintain a safe system of work for members of the armed forces who are engaged with an enemy in the course of combat. Further, 'course of combat' refers to all active operations against an enemy where service personnel are exposed, to the threat of attack or actual attack: *Multiple Claimants v MOD* (2003) *The Times*, 29 May.

suit. (*Suite* = act of following.) 1. Appeal to a superior (e.g., the King) for justice. 2. Action in court in pursuance of a right or claim. 3. Litigation in general.

summary. 1. An abridgment, digest, abstract. 2. When the term is applied to legal proceedings it refers to hearings which are often immediate and relatively concise in nature.

Summary Appeal Courts. See APPEAL COURTS, SUMMARY.

summary conviction. Conviction before magistrates.

summary dismissal. Dismissal of an employee without giving the notice to which the employee is entitled by virtue of the contract of employment. It is justified if the employee's conduct is such that it prevents 'further satisfactory continuance of the relationship': *Sinclair v Neighbour* [1967] 2 QB 279. See E.R.A. 1996, s 95.

summary judgment. Procedure whereby the court decides a claim or a particular issue against claimant or defendant without trial. See CPR, Part 24; PD 24. Grounds are: court considers that claimant has no real prospect of succeeding on claim or issue; or defendant has no real prospect of a successful defence; and there is no other reason why case or issue should be disposed of at a trial: r 24(2). Summary judgment may be given against a claimant in any type of proceedings, or against a defendant in any type of proceedings except proceedings for possession of essential premises against a mortgagor or tenant holding over (q.v.), or admiralty claim *in rem*: r 24.3. It is not available against the Crown: CPR, Schs 1, 2.

summary judgment procedure. Claimant applies only after defendant has filed acknowledgment of service or a defence (unless court gives permission or a PD provides otherwise): r 24.4. If claimant applies before defendant has filed a defence, defendant need not file his defence before a hearing. Where the hearing is fixed, 14 days' notice of date of hearing and issue to be decided must be given. Hearing normally takes place before a master or district judge; they may direct a hearing by a High Court or circuit judge: PD 24, para 4. When the court determines a summary judgment application it may give directions as to the filing and service of a defence, and give directions about the management of the case: r 24.6.

summary jurisdiction. Power of magistrates to try summary offences (q.v.). In general, the magistrates' court cannot try any information which was not laid within six months from the time of commission of the offence: M.C.A. 1980, s 127. See *Swan* v *Vehicle Inspectorate* [1997] RTR 187.

summary jurisdiction, court of. *See* COURT OF SUMMARY JURISDICTION.

summary offence. An offence which, if committed by an adult, is triable only summarily: C.L.A. 1977, s 64(1)(*b*). For general procedures, see M.C.A. 1980, ss 9–15. For procedure where summary trial of an offence triable either way appears more suitable, see M.C.A. 1980, s 21. For transfer of summary trials, see M.C.A. 1980, s 3B, inserted by Acc.J.A. 1999, s 80. See also I.A. 1978, Sch 1; C.J.A. 1988, ss 37, 39, 40, 41.

summary possession. *See* POSSESSION ACTION, FAST.

summary trial. The trial of petty offences and other offences triable summarily by magistrates. See M.C.A. 1980, ss 9–15.

summing-up. The judge's summary of a case, made following the closing speeches. It usually includes a direction on points of law, a review of the evidence (including, e.g., onus of proof, effect of presumptions of law, etc.). See *R* v *Briley* [1991] Crim LR 444; *R* v *Farr* [1999] Crim LR 506 (Court of Appeal guidance on content and length of summing-up); *R* v *Bowerman* [2000] 2 Cr App R 189 (judge's decision not to sum up).

summons. 1. 'A citation proceeding upon an information . . . laid before the magistrate who issues the summons, and conveying to the person cited the fact that the magistrate is satisfied that there is a prima facie case against him': *Dixon* v *Wells* (1890) 25 QBD 249. It must state the general matter of the information and the place and time the defendant is to appear and must be signed by the magistrate: *R* v *Brentford Justices, ex p Catlin* [1975] QB 455. See C.L.A. 1977, s 39; M.C.A. 1980, s 1. 2. Issue of a claim form (q.v.).

Sunday working. Restrictions on Sunday trading were removed under the Sunday Trading Act 1994. Protection for employees who do not wish to work on Sundays is governed by E.R.A. 1996, Part IV. Explanatory statements concerning Sunday work must be given to employees, under s 42.

superannuation scheme. Payment of annuities or lump sums to persons on their retirement at a certain age, or earlier incapacitation, or to their personal representatives, widows, relatives or dependants.

superficies solo cedit. That which is attached to the land forms a part of it. See L.P.A. 1925, s 62(1). *See* FIXTURES.

superior courts. Courts with a jurisdiction not limited, e.g., geographically or by value of the subject matter of an action. They include, e.g., House of Lords,

Court of Appeal, JCPC, High Court, Crown Court. *See* INFERIOR COURTS.

superior orders, obedience to. *See* OBEDIENCE TO SUPERIOR'S ORDERS, DEFENCE OF.

superstitious uses. A purported trust (q.v.) for celebrating or teaching doctrines and practices of a religion not generally tolerated by law, and, therefore, generally void. See, e.g., *Bourne v Keane* [1919] AC 815; *Gilmour v Coats* [1949] AC 427.

supervening cause. *See* CAUSA REMOTA.

supervening event. That which takes place as something extraneous or additional. See *Heil v Rankin* (2000) *The Times*, 20 June.

supervision and treatment orders. Orders by the court requiring the supervision of a person by a social worker or probation officer, made under Criminal Procedure (Insanity and Unfitness to Plead) Act 1991, s 5, and Sch 2, following evidence by two or more registered practitioners. For revocation of order, see Sch 2, Part III. *See* UNFITNESS TO PLEAD.

supervision order. A community sentence (q.v.) given by the court under P.C.C.(S.)A. 2000, s 63, placing a convicted child or young person (under 18) under the supervision of a local authority, probation officer, or member of a youth offending team (q.v.) for a period of up to three years. For requirements of order, see Sch 6; for breach and revocation, see Sch 7. See C.D.A. 1998, Sch 10.

supply. Includes: selling, hiring out, lending goods; entering a hire-purchase agreement to furnish the goods; the performance of any contract for work and materials to furnish the goods; providing the goods in exchange for any consideration (q.v.) other than money; providing the goods in connection with the performance of a statutory function; giving the goods as a prize or gift: C.P.A. 1987, s 46(1).

supply estimates. Basis of Parliament's consideration of the sanctioning of expenditure by legislation. The estimates are: ordinary annual main estimates; votes on account; supplementary estimates excess votes. *See* WAYS AND MEANS.

support, right of. *See* RIGHT OF SUPPORT.

suppression of documents, dishonest. Offence committed by a person who 'dishonestly with a view to gain for himself or another or with intent to cause loss to another, destroys, defaces or conceals any valuable security, any will or other testamentary document or any original document of or belonging to, or filed or deposited in, any court of justice or any government department . . .': Th.A. 1968, s 20(1). See Finance Act 1989, s 145 (falsification or destruction of documents relating to Inland Revenue).

supra protest. *See* ACCEPTANCE OF A BILL.

Supreme Court. This is a superior court of record of the United Kingdom, consisting of 12 judges appointed by Her Majesty by letters patent. The court has power to determine any question necessary to be determined for the purposes of doing justice in an appeal to it under any enactment. C.R.A 2005. It consists of Court of Appeal, High Court of Justice, and Crown Court; the Lord Chancellor is President: S.C.A. 1981, s 1.

Supreme Court, Justices of. The judges other than the President and Deputy President of the Supreme Court. C.R.A 2005.

Supreme Court, Masters of the. *See* MASTERS OF THE SUPREME COURT.

Supreme Court Rules. The President of the Supreme Court may make rules governing the practice and procedure to be followed in the Court. C.R.A 2005.

surcharge. The disallowing, following audits, of expenditure, enabling the recovery of financial losses. See, e.g., L.G.A. 2000, s 90.

surcharge and falsify. Phrase referring to an account in which there is an omission of a sum which ought to have been credited and of which proof of a wrongly-inserted item can be given. See CPR, r 25.1(1)(*n*) (order directing a party to prepare and file accounts relating to disputes of this nature); *Williamson v Barbour* (1877) 9 Ch D 529.

surety. A person who gives security for another. The procedure whereby magistrates bind over (q.v.) a person may involve his being ordered to find sureties for his keeping the peace. See M.C.A. 1980, s 115; Bail Act 1976; *R v Reading Crown Court, ex p Bello* (1991) 92 Cr App R 303 (principles to be applied to forfeiture of surety); *R v Clerkenwell Stipendiary Magistrate ex p Hooper* [1998] 1 WLR 800 (magistrate should hear surety representations).

surname. Family, as distinct from Christian, name. A child's surname is that of his father, and a wife is incompetent to change her child's surname by deed poll or registration of birth without the husband's consent or a court order: *D v B* [1977] Fam 145. The name of a woman conferred by marriage is not lost upon her divorce: *Fendall v Goldsmid* (1877) 2 PD 263. See Mat. Causes Rules 1977, r 92(8); *Re C (Minors) (Change of Name)* [1998] 1 FLR 549. *See* NAME, CHANGE OF.

surrender of shares. The yielding up, and acceptance by the directors of a company, of shares, for the purpose of being cancelled, exchanged, etc. If it involves a reduction of capital it is unlawful, except when sanctioned by the court. A voluntary share transfer to a trustee for the company does not constitute a surrender: *Kirby v Wilkins* [1929] 2 Ch 444. See Cos.A. 1985, s 146.

surrender of tenancy. A mode of determination of a tenancy (q.v.) whereby a tenant yields up his estate to the lessor. *Express surrender*, in the case of a lease exceeding three years, requires a deed: L.P.A. 1925, s 52. *Implied surrender* occurs, e.g., if the tenant delivers possession to the lessor who accepts it.

surrender value. The amount an insurance company will repay to a life policy holder who wishes to terminate that policy prior to the date of maturity.

surrogate. One appointed to act in place of another.

surrogate mother. A woman who carries a child in pursuance of an arrangement made before she began to carry the child, and made with a view to any child carried in pursuance of it being handed over to, and the parental rights being

exercised by, another person or persons: Surrogacy Arrangements Act 1985, s 1(1). The Act prohibits negotiation of surrogacy arrangements on a commercial basis, and relevant advertisements: ss 2, 3. See Human Fertilisation and Embryology Act 1990, s 36; Human Fertilisation and Embryology (Disclosure of Information) Act 1992; *Re W* [1991] 1 FLR 385; *Briody v St Helens HA* [2000] PIQR 165.

surveillance. Close observation. Classified under R.I.P.A. 2000, s 26 as: *directed*, i.e., covert but not intrusive, and undertaken for purposes of a specific investigation or operation; *intrusive*, i.e., covert, and carried out in relation to anything taking place on residential premises or in a private vehicle, involving the presence of an individual on the premises or in the vehicle, or is carried out by a surveillance device; *covert*, i.e., surveillance carried out in a manner calculated to ensure that persons who are subject to it are unaware that it is taking place. For authorisation of directed surveillance, see s 28. For authorisation of use of covert intelligence sources, see s 29. 'Includes covertly listening to or recording conversations or other sounds and any method of covertly obtaining information': P.S.I.A. 2001, s 25.

Surveillance Commissioners. The Chief Surveillance Commissioner keeps under review the exercise of powers and duties under R.I.P.A. 2000, Part II; s 62(1). He is appointed under Police Act 1997, s 91. Assistant Surveillance Commissioners (who hold or have held office as judges of the Crown Court or Circuit judges) are appointed under R.I.P.A. 2000, s 63, to assist the Chief Surveillance Commissioner.

survey. Skilled examination of land, dwellings, etc., in relation to apparent condition, generally undertaken in advance of the exchange of contracts. See *Bigg v Howard Son & Gooch* (1990) 12 EG 111 (measure of damages following negligent survey); *Swingcastle v Gibson* [1991] 2 WLR 1091; *Patel v Hooper* [1998] EGCS 160; *Platform Home Loans v Oyston Shipways* (1999) 149 NLJ 283.

survival of causes of action on death. *See* DEATH, SURVIVAL OF CAUSES OF ACTION ON.

survivors. 'A word which has caused perhaps more difficulty in the interpretation of wills than any other in the language': *Re Pickworth* [1899] 1 Ch 642. When property is bequeathed to 'the survivors' of individuals or members of a class, it is construed as meaning those who are living at the period of distribution: *Cripps* v *Wolcott* (1819) 4 Madd 11. See *Gilmour* v *MacPhillamy* [1930] 1 Ch 138.

survivorship, right of. The right of a survivor (e.g., of joint tenants (q.v.)) to the whole property. The death of a joint tenant vests the entire estate in the remaining joint tenants; his interest is extinguished. *See* JUS ACCRESCENDI.

suspect. Defined under Duty Solicitor Arrangements 1997, as amended, as a person who for the purposes of assisting with an investigation attends voluntarily at a police station or any other place where a constable is present or who accompanies a constable to a police station or any such other place without having been arrested or who has been arrested and is being held in a police station or other premises.

suspend. 1. To debar temporarily from the exercise of an office or occupation. 2. To revoke a law temporarily. See Bill of Rights 1688, which condemned the use of the power to suspend laws: 'The pretended power of dispensing with laws, or the execution of laws by regal authority . . . is illegal.'

suspended sentence. Sentence ordered not to take effect immediately. Under P.C.C.(S.)A. 2000, s 118, a court which passes a sentence of imprisonment for not more than two years may suspend the sentence unless, during a specified period, the offender commits in Great Britain another offence punishable with imprisonment. For power of court on conviction of further offence to deal with suspended sentence, see s 119. For suspended sentence supervision orders, see s 122.

suspicion. An opinion or belief derived from circumstances or facts that do not constitute proof. 'Suspicion in its ordinary meaning is a state of conjecture or surmise when proof is lacking': *per* Lord Devlin in *Hussein* v *Chong Fook Kam* [1970] AC 942.

swaps transactions. Essentially, gambling on movements in interest rates. Substantial transactions of this nature involving local authorities are *ultra vires* and, therefore, null and void: *Hazell* v *Hammersmith and Fulham LBC* [1992] 2 AC 1.

sweepstake. A wager based on the outcome of some event, e.g., result of a race. Held, in *Ellesmere* v *Wallace* [1929] 2 Ch 1, to be illegal as a lottery 'if the winner is determined by chance, but not if the winner is determined by skill'. See Lotteries and Amusements Act 1976, s 1. *See* GAMING; LOTTERY.

symbolic delivery. *See* DELIVERY.

synallagmatic contract. (*Synallagmatikos* = of a contract.) A reciprocal contract, i.e., one characterised by mutual duties and rights. 'Every synallagmatic contract contains in it the seeds of the problem: in what event will a party be relieved of his undertaking to do that which he has agreed to do but has not yet done?': *per* Diplock LJ in *Hong Kong Fir Shipping Co* v *Kawasaki Kisen Kaisha* [1962] 2 QB 26. See *United Dominions Trust* v *Eagle Services Ltd* [1968] 1 All ER 104; *Edmonds* v *Lawson* [2000] IRLR 18 (analysis of a contract of apprenticeship).

syndicate. Combination of business enterprises or individuals for the promotion of a common interest, generally the spreading of risk in a commercial transaction. A member is liable *pro rata* for the amount he has underwritten. The syndicate does not have legal personality (q.v.). See Finance Act 2000, s 107(7).

system, evidence of. Evidence given to show a propensity to commit a given crime by use of a certain technique. See, e.g., *Thompson* v *R* [1918] AC 221; *R* v *Straffen* [1952] 2 QB 911.

T

Table A. Specimen set of regulations for management of a company limited by shares. See the Companies (Tables A to F) Regulations 1985 (SI 85/805 as amended); Cos.A. 1985, s 8. Insofar as its contents are not excluded expressly, they are incorporated in the company's articles.

Table B. Form of memorandum of association (q.v.) for a private company limited by shares, set out in the 1985 Regulations.

Table C. Form of memorandum and articles of association (qq.v.) for a company limited by guarantee, and not having a share capital, set out in the 1985 Regulations.

Table D. Form of memorandum and articles of association (qq.v.) for a public company limited by guarantee, and having a share capital, set out in the 1985 Regulations.

Table E. Form of memorandum and articles of association (qq.v.) for an unlimited company having a share capital, set out in the 1985 Regulations.

Table F. Form of memorandum of association for a public company limited by shares, set out in the 1985 Regulations.

Table G. The Secretary of State may by regulations prescribe a Table G containing articles of association appropriate for a partnership company, that is, a company limited by shares whose shares are intended to be held to a substantial extent by or on behalf of its employees: Cos.A. 1985, chap I, inserted by Cos.A. 1989, s 128.

tabula in naufragio. Plank in a shipwreck. Doctrine, abolished by L.P.A. 1925, s 94, whereby if a legal mortgage to X was followed by an equitable mortgage to Y and then by an equitable mortgage to Z, then Z might obtain priority over Y by paying off X and acquiring the legal estate from him. The legal estate was considered as a 'plank in the shipwreck' by the use of which one mortgagee saved himself 'while the other was drowned'. (This applied only where Z did not know of an earlier mortgage to Y when he made the loan.) *See* MORTGAGE.

tachograph. Instrument used in goods vehicles, coaches, etc., for producing automatically a record of a driver's speeds and travel times. See Transport Act 1968, s 95; SI 98/2006; *Vehicle Inspectorate* v *Southern Coaches Ltd* (2000) *The Times*, 23 February. ('Driver' means any person who drives the vehicle even for a short period, or who is carried in the vehicle in order to be available for driving if necessary: Council Regulation EEC No. 3820/85, art 1); *R* v *Potter* [1999] 2 Cr. App R (S) 448; *A-G's Reference (No. 1 of 2000)* (2000) *The Times*, 28 November.

tacking. Prior to L.P.A. 1925, a legal mortgagee who had made a further loan to the mortgagor could tack together both loans and recover them prior to the intervening mortgagee, if he had received no notice of the intervener. Under the 1925 Act, s 94, legal or equitable mortgagees may tack where intervening mortgagees concur, where further advance was made with no notice at the time of the intervening mortgage and where the mortgage involved an obligation to make a further advance. See *Burnes* v *Trade Credits Ltd* [1981] 1 WLR 805. *See* MORTGAGE.

tail. *See* FEE TAIL.

tail general. Widest form of entailed interest. Example: land limited 'to X and the heirs of his body'. See now Trusts of Land and Appointment of Trustees Act 1996, Sch 1, para 5.

tail male general. Entailed interest which arises where land is limited 'to X and the heirs male of his body begotten'. Unlike the tail general (q.v.), only the *male heirs* of X may succeed. In case of *tail female general*, only *female heirs* take.

tail male special. Entailed interest arising by grant 'to X and Y and the heirs male of their two bodies begotten'. In case of *tail female special*, only *female heirs* take.

tainted gift. For purposes of determining recoverable amounts under Proceeds of Crime Act 2002, ss 7, 9, a gift is tainted if the court has declared that defendant has a criminal life style, or, if no such decision has been made, the gift has been made at any time during the six years ending on the day when relevant proceedings were started: s 77. Its value is ascertained by considering the value of the gift at the time it was made, with adjustments to take into account later changes in the value of money: s 81.

takeover offer. An offer to acquire shares in a body incorporated in UK which is a takeover offer within the meaning of Cos.A. 1985, Part XIIIA; an offer to acquire all or substantially all of the shares, or of the shares of a particular class, in a body incorporated outside UK; or an offer made to all the holders of shares, or of shares of a particular class, in a body corporate to acquire a specified portion of those shares: F.S.M.A. 2000, Sch 11, para 12.

talaq. Repudiation, in Islamic law, of a wife by her husband by means of a formal, triple declaration. See *Fatima v Home Secretary* [1986] AC 527; *El Fadl v El Fadl* [2000] 1 FLR 175.

tales. From the phrase *tales de circumstantibus* = so many of bystanders. Refers to the practice of making up the deficiency in the available number of jurors by commanding the sheriff (q.v.) to call others who can be found (known as *talesmen*). See now Juries Act 1974, ss 6, 11.

tangible property. Corporeal property, e.g., goods, as compared with intangible property, e.g., choses in action (q.v.).

tape recorders in court. It is a contempt of court to use tape recorders in court, except by leave, or to publish a recording of legal proceedings made by means of such an instrument: Contempt of Court Act 1981, s 9.

tape-recording. Record of sound imprinted on magnetic tape. See *Code E* (under which police record interrogations of suspects) issued under P.&C.E.A. 1984; *R v Riaz* [1992] Crim LR 336; P.&C.E.A. 1984; *R v Hagan* [1997] 1 Cr App R 464.

tariff. 1. A system of government-imposed duties on imports. 2. A scale of charges for a business or public utility. 3. The term 'whole life tariff' refers to a decision by the Home Secretary that there shall be no release from prison in the case of a particularly heinous crime: see *R v Secretary of State for Home Department ex p Doody* [1994] 1 AC 531; *R v Secretary of State for Home Department ex p Hindley* (2000) *The Times*, 31 March; *Practice Statement (Juveniles: Murder Tariffs)* (2000) *The Times*, 9 August. For circumstances in which a life sentence is not fixed by law, or the offender was under 18 at the time of the offence, see P.C.C.(S.)A. 2000, s 82A, inserted by C.J.C.S.A. 2000, s 60.

tariff, detention beyond. It was held in *R (on the application of Richards) v Secretary of State for Home Department* [2004] EWHC 93 (Admin) that following *Stafford v UK* [2002] 35 EHRR 1121, a person has a right under Human Rights Convention, art 5(5) to claim compensation for wrongful detention beyond tariff.

'tariff' in life sentences. See MINIMUM TERM.

tax. A compulsory contribution by individuals and companies to the state, levied on goods, services, income and wealth. See, e.g., I.C.T.A. 1988; T.C.G.A. 1992. See PD 7D (claims for the recovery of taxes). See INCOME TAX.

taxation, car fuel benefits. Income Tax (Cash Equivalents of Car Fuel Benefits)

Order 2002 (SI 02/706), provides for amended legislation, so that directors and employees earning £8,500 or more per year, for whom fuel is given for use in a company car, will be chargeable to income tax on an amount equal to the appropriate cash equivalent of that benefit.

taxation of costs. Examination by court of costs.

taxation, residence in UK. CA held, in *Agassi* v *Robinson* (2004) *The Times*, 27 November, that income tax could not be chargeable on payments arising from sports activities within the UK by non-resident sportsmen made by non-resident companies under control of the sportsmen but which had no tax presence in the UK.

tax avoidance. The arrangement of one's affairs so that liability to tax is reduced or disappears. Not, in itself, illegal. 'Every man is entitled to order his affairs so that the tax attaching under the appropriate Acts is less than it otherwise would be. If he succeeds in ordering them so as to secure this result, then, . . . he cannot be compelled to pay an increased tax': *Duke of Westminster* v *CIR* (1935) 19 TC 490. See *IRC* v *Willoughby* [1997] 1 WLR 1071 (consideration of I.C.T.A. 1988, s 739); *R* v *Dimsey & Allen* [1999] STC 846.

tax credits. Under Tax Credits Act 1999, family credit (q.v.) and disability working allowance are to be known as working families' tax credit and disabled person's tax credit: s 1(1). The Treasury is responsible for the prescribed schemes for tax credits, the determination and calculation of individual entitlement, and the uprating of benefits. Inland Revenue carries out other appropriate functions: see Sch 2. Employers are under an obligation to pay tax credits at the time of making payment of earnings subject to income tax under Schedule E: s 6. See SI 99/3219. *See* INCOME TAX.

taxes and crime. Under Finance Act 2000, s 68, when a business is computing its business profits, it is excluded from deducting any expenditure incurred in the making of payments outside the UK which, were they to have been made

within the UK, would have constituted a criminal offence. It is intended to cover corrupt payments and bribes.

taxes, recovery of. Under Finance Act 2002, s 134, no obligation of secrecy imposed by statute or otherwise precludes a tax authority in the UK from disclosing information to another tax authority in the UK in connection with a request for enforcement made by the competent authority of another EU member state from disclosing information that is required to be disclosed to the competent authority of another member State by virtue of the Mutual Assistance Recovery Directive (Council Directive 76/308/EEC, as amended by Council Directive 2001/44/EC); from disclosing information for the purposes of a request made by the tax authority under that Directive for the enforcement in another member State of an amount claimed by the authority in the UK.

tax evasion. The non-payment of taxes which one is under a duty to pay. Fraudulent evasion of income tax is an offence under Finance Act 2000, s 144. See *R* v *Dealy* [1995] 1 WLR 658 ('evasion' does not require the intention to default permanently on tax returns); *R* v *Charlton* [1996] STC 1418; *R* v *Latif* [1999] 1 Cr App R (S) 191.

tax evasion, penalties relating to. Under the Finance Act 2003, s 25, in any case where a person engages in any conduct for the purpose of evading any relevant tax or duty, and his conduct involves dishonesty (whether or not such as to give rise to any criminal liability) that person is liable to a penalty of an amount equal to the amount of the tax or duty evaded or, as the case may be, sought to be evaded.

tax haven. Nation or locality levying relatively low taxes, or none at all, on foreigners. Examples (at one time or another): Isle of Man, Channel Islands, Liechtenstein. See I.C.T.A. 1988, ss 739–741; OECD Report (2000), listing 35 tax havens.

taxing masters. Salaried officials of the Supreme Court Taxing Office who consider taxation of costs. They are appointed by the Lord Chancellor, with the agreement of the Treasury. See *Re Macro (Ipswich) Ltd* [1996] 1 WLR 145.

taxing officer. The person responsible for determining precisely what costs (q.v.) must be paid, after the judge has decided who is to pay and the basis for payment. His functions may be performed by a district judge in the county court, or in the High Court outside London, and a taxing master (q.v.). See, e.g., *Burrows* v *Vauxhall Motors* [1998] PIQR P48.

taxing statutes. Acts imposing taxation. They are construed as other statutes, but the tax must be imposed by plain words before persons will be held liable. 'The Crown does not tax by analogy but by statute': *Ormond Investment Co* v *Betts* [1928] AC 143. A construction which helps evasion will be avoided. See *IRC* v *Wolfson* [1949] 1 All ER 865.

tax inquiry, cautioning relating to. CA held, in *R* v *Gill* (2003) *The Times*, 29 August, that the role of an Inland Revenue special compliance officer investigating tax fraud necessitates the investigation of a criminal offence, so that Code C of the Police and Criminal Evidence Act 1984 Codes of Practice applies, a suspect must be cautioned, therefore, prior to his being questioned.

tax month. 'The period beginning with the 6th day of any calendar month and ending with the 5th day of the following calendar month': I.C.T.A. 1988, s 825(8).

tax underpayment. Where Inland Revenue becomes aware of an underpayment of tax, it has the right to raise an additional assessment on the basis of a 'discovery'. Such an assessment can be made only where the taxpayer has been negligent or where the tax inspector could not have been reasonably aware of the necessity for an assessment of this kind, given the relevant time limits. *Veltema* v *Langham* [2004] STC 544.

tax week. One of the successive periods in a tax year beginning with the first day of that year and every seventh day

thereafter; the last day of a tax year (or, in the case of a tax year ending in a leap year, the last two days) to be treated accordingly as a separate tax week: S.S.A. 1975, Sch 20.

tax year. *See* INCOME TAX, YEARLY ASSESSMENT.

Technology and Construction Court. Formerly the Official Referee's Department. It will hear, e.g., major construction litigation, disputes concerning hardware and software. Official Referees will be known as Judges of the Technology and Construction Court: statement of Lord Chancellor, 8 October 1998. See PD 49C, para 1.3.

telecommunication system. A system for the conveyance, through the agency of electric, magnetic, electro-magnetic, electro-chemical or electro-mechanical energy, of speech, music and other sounds, visual images, signals serving for the impartation of any matter otherwise than in the form of sounds or visual images, or signals serving for the actuation or control of machinery or apparatus: Tele-communications Act 1984, s 4(1).

telecommunication system, fraudulent use of. It is an offence under Tele-communications Act 1984, s 42, to dishonestly obtain a service provided by means of a licensed telecommunication system (q.v.) with intent to avoid payment of any charge applicable to the provision of that service. Telecommunications (Fraud) Act 1997, s 1, inserts s 42A in the 1984 Act, making it an offence to possess or supply anything for fraudulent purposes in connection with the use of a telecom-munication system.

telecommunication system, improper use of. The offence of sending a message or other matter that is grossly offensive, indecent, obscene or menacing by means of a public telecommunication system (defined in 1984 Act, ss 4(1), 9(1)): Tele-communications Act 1984, s 43, amended by C.J.P.O.A. 1994, s 92.

telephone, exchange of contracts by. Exchange can be effected in any manner recognised by the law as amounting to an exchange, and this includes telephone conversations: *Domb* v *Isoz* [1980] 2 WLR 565. See Law Society's General Conditions of Sale (1986).

telephone hearings. Where all parties consent and are legally represented, the court may order that an application or part of it be dealt with by telephone hearing: PD 23, para 6.1. (For video conferencing, see PD 23, para 7.)

telephone tapping. Form of electronic surveillance carried out by security services after authorisation by the Home Secretary. See *Malone* v *Commissioner for Metropolis* [1979] 2 All ER 620; *R* v *Aujla* (1998) 2 Cr App R 16; *R* v *P* (2000) *The Times*, 19 December (foreign telephone intercepts admissible). *See* INTERCEPTION OF COMMUNICATIONS.

television links, evidence through. A person other than the accused may give evidence through a live television link in a trial on indictment or on appeal to the Court of Appeal (Criminal Division) or the hearing of a reference under the Criminal Appeal Act 1968, s 17, if the witness is outside the UK or is under 14 and the offence charged is one stated in C.J.A. 1988, s 32(2), but such evidence does require leave of the court: C.J.A. 1988, s 32(1). A defendant may be treated as having been present at preliminary hearings (before the commencement of a trial) if in custody during those hearings and able to see and hear the court, through television, and be seen and heard by it: C.D.A. 1998, s 57(1). See *Garcin* v *Amerindo Investment Ltd* [1991] 1 WLR 1140. Criminal Justice Act 1988 (Commencement No. 14) Order 2004 (SI 04/2167) made under CJA 1988, s 171, allows, for purposes of trials on indictment, appeals to CA (Criminal Division), evidence to be given in these proceedings through a live TV link where a witness is outside the UK.

television reception, interfering with. The House of Lords held, in *Hunter* v *Canary Wharf* [1997] 2 WLR 684, that interference with television reception, caused by the mere presence of a building, was not actionable; licensees of the land affected could not succeed in a nuisance claim. *See* NUISANCE.

telex and contract. Instantaneous telex communication should follow the general rule that a contract is made when and where acceptance is received: *Brinkibon Ltd* v *Stahag Stahl* [1983] 2 AC 34.

temporary. That which lasts, or is intended to last, for a limited period only. See *R* v *Social Security Commissioner ex p Akbar* [1992] COD 335 (indefinite absence abroad may be construed as temporary).

tenancy. The relationship of a tenant (q.v.) to that land which he holds from another, and to that other. See *Street* v *Mountford* [1985] 2 All ER 289; *Family Housing* v *Jones* [1990] 1 All ER 385. *See* LEASE.

tenancy, assured. *See* ASSURED TENANCY.

tenancy, at sufferance. *See* SUFFERANCE, TENANCY AT.

tenancy at will. *See* TENANT AT WILL.

tenancy by entireties. Where land was granted to a husband and wife so that, had they not been married, they would have taken as joint tenants, they were tenants by entireties; each was tenant of the whole land; when one died the land passed absolutely to the survivor. Abolished as a doctrine under L.P.A. 1925, s 37. Tenancies by entireties existing at that date were converted into joint tenancies (q.v.).

tenancy by estoppel. Where, e.g., a mortgagor in possession grants a lease (q.v.) which does not satisfy the statutory provisions or the terms of the mortgage deed, the lease may bind the tenant and mortgagor (so that, e.g., he may sue for rent) under the doctrine of estoppel (q.v.). See *First National Bank* v *Thompson* [1996] Ch 231; *Bruton* v *London Quadrant Housing Trust* [1999] 3 WLR 150. *See* MORTGAGE.

tenancy, enfranchisement of. *See* ENFRANCHISEMENT OF TENANCY.

tenancy, housing association. *See* HOUSING ASSOCIATION TENANCY.

tenancy, implied. Tenancy presumed from the payment and acceptance of a sum in the nature of rent. See *Longrigg Burrough* v *Smith* (1979) 251 EG 847.

tenancy in common. *See* COMMON, TENANCY IN.

tenancy, long. *See* LONG TENANCY.

tenancy, periodic. *See* PERIODIC TENANCY.

tenancy, protected. *See* PROTECTED TENANCY.

tenancy, regulated. *See* REGULATED TENANCY.

tenancy, secure. *See* SECURE TENANCY.

tenancy, shorthold, assured. *See* ASSURED SHORTHOLD TENANCY.

tenancy, statutory. *See* STATUTORY TENANCY.

tenancy, succession of homosexual male partner to. In *Mendoza* v *Ghaidan* (2002) 152 NLJ 1715, CA held that the right of succession to a statutory tenancy extends to a surviving homosexual male partner, given an appropriate reading of Rent Act 1977, Sch 1, para 2, as amended by Housing Act 1998, in the light of European Convention, art 14 (prohibition of discrimination). *Fitzpatrick* v *Sterling House Association* [2001] 1 AC 27 was held to infringe art 14. The words of the Rent Act 1977, Sch 1, '. . . as his or her wife or husband . . .' were to be construed as meaning '. . . as if they were his or her wife or husband . . .'

tenancy, surrender of. *See* SURRENDER OF TENANCY.

tenancy, weekly. *See* WEEKLY TENANCY.

tenant. One who holds land of another. A lessee (q.v.). Includes, under Rent Act 1977, s 152(1), 'statutory tenant and also includes a sub-tenant and any person deriving title under the original tenant or sub-tenant'. See H.A. 1985, s 621(3).

tenantable repair. The quality of repair in a house rendering it fit for occupation by tenants. See, e.g., Landlord and Tenant Act 1985, s 11; H.A. 1988, s 116; *Irvine* v *Moran* [1991] 24 HLR 1.

tenant at sufferance. *See* SUFFERANCE, TENANCY AT.

tenant at will. One holding under a tenancy at will, which exists where the tenant (T) occupies L's land, with L's consent, on terms under which L or T may determine the tenancy at any time. 'In this case the lessee is called tenant at will because he hath no certain or sure estate, for the lessor may put him out at what time it pleaseth him': Littleton, *Tenures* (1481). It may be created by express agreement or implication and may be ended by L or T if, e.g., either should assign land, or die. See, e.g., *Manfield & Sons* v *Botchin* [1970] 2 QB 612; *Javad* v *Aquil* [1991] 1 All ER 243.

tenant by succession, statutory. After the termination of a protected tenancy (q.v.) of a dwelling house, the person who, immediately before the termination, was the protected tenant of the dwelling house is, so long as he occupied the house as his residence, the *statutory tenant* of it. One who, after the death of the statutory tenant, becomes the next statutory tenant is known as the 'statutory tenant by succession'. See Rent Act 1977, s 2, Sch 1; H.A. 1988, s 39.

tenant for life. 'The person of full age who is for the time being beneficially entitled under a settlement to possession of settled land for his life is for the purposes of this Act the tenant for life of that land and the tenant for life under that settlement': S.L.A. 1925, s 19(1). Two or more persons of full age so entitled as joint tenants together constitute the tenant for life for purposes of the Act: s 19(2). *See* SETTLEMENT.

tenant for life, powers of. These are conferred by S.L.A. 1925 and include power of sale and exchange, power to grant and accept leases, to borrow money and to apply capital money, to sell heirlooms and to compromise claims concerning settled land.

tenant for years. One who holds land for a term of years (q.v.).

tenant from year to year. One who holds a yearly tenancy, which may be created expressly ('to T from year to year') or by implication. It continues until ended by proper notice. See *Tickner* v *Buzzacott* [1965] Ch 426; *Prudential Assurance* v *LRB* [1992] 2 AC 386.

tenant, harassment of. *See* HARASSMENT OF OCCUPIER.

tenant-in-tail. One who holds an estate in fee tail (q.v.).

tenant in tail after possibility. If a gift of land is made 'to X and his heirs begotten by him on Y' and Y (X's wife) dies without leaving children, there exists no possibility of descendants of X and Y who could succeed. X (tenant in tail) is known as 'tenant in tail after possibility of issue extinct' (or 'tenant in tail after possibility'). X may not bar the entail in such a case, but he is given the statutory powers of a tenant for life (q.v.). See S.L.A. 1925, s 20(*l*)(i). *See* FEE TAIL.

tenant, occupying. *See* OCCUPYING TENANT.

tenant *pur autre vie*. *See* AUTRE VIE.

tenant's fixtures. In general, a landlord is entitled to fixtures which have been attached to the land by his tenant. There may be exceptions in the case of ornamental, domestic, agricultural and trade fixtures. See, e.g., Agricultural Holdings Act 1986, s 10. It is an offence under Th.A. 1968, s 4(2), for a person who is in possession of land under a tenancy to appropriate the whole or part of any fixture let to be used with the land. See *Elitestone Ltd v Morris* [1997] 1 WLR 687. *See* FIXTURES.

tenant, statutory. *See* TENANT BY SUCCESSION, STATUTORY.

tenant, sub-. *See* SUB-TENANT.

tender. 1. Attempted performance. 2. To offer for sale. 3. To offer money, etc. in payment or satisfaction of a debt or other obligation. 'Payment extinguishes the debt; tender does not.' There must be actual production of the exact sum of money, or a dispensation of such production, at an arranged, or otherwise appropriate, place. 4. An offer relating to the supply of goods. Thus, X requires 1,000 ingots and invites tenders. If he accepts Y's tender, there is a contract for the sale of 1,000 ingots by Y to X. See *Marston Construction Ltd v Kigass Ltd* (1989) 15 Con LR 116; *Blackpool Aero Club v Blackpool BC* [1993] 3 All ER 25. 5. Legal tender (q.v.).

tender before claim, defence of. 'A defence that, before the claimant started proceedings, defendant unconditionally offered to claimant the amount due, or, if no specified amount is claimed, an amount sufficient to satisfy the claim': CPR Glossary. Where defendant wishes to rely on this defence he must make payment into court of the amount which he says was tendered: CPR, r 37.2; PD 37, para 2.1.

tender of performance. Expressed readiness to perform an act in accordance with an obligation. May be equivalent to performance: *Startup v Macdonald* (1843) 6 Man & G 593. See *Farquharson v Pear Insurance Co Ltd* [1937] 3 All ER 124.

tenement. 1. Property held by tenure. 2. House in use as dwelling.

tenendum. To be held. Clause in a conveyance (q.v.) formerly used to indicate the mode of tenure.

tenor. 1. The substance of some matter. 2. An exact copy of writing.

tenor, executor according to. *See* EXECUTOR.

tenure. A relationship of lord and tenant which determined the terms upon which land was held. The old feudal tenures (free, lay, spiritual, unfree) were generally abolished by the land legislation of the 1920s, so that today there is one principal tenure only, i.e., freehold, which is the name now used for free and common socage (q.v.). See Tenures Abolition Act 1660; L.P.A. 1922 and 1925; Abolition of Feudal Tenure (Scotland) Act 2000.

tenure, security of. Statutory protection, e.g., under Rent Act 1977, or Protection from Eviction Act 1977, afforded to tenants, concerning rents and the landlord's right to recover possession.

term. (*Terminus* = limit or boundary.) 1. A part of the year in which business could be transacted in the courts. Terms were abolished under J.A. 1875; the year now comprises sittings (q.v.) and vacations (q.v.). 2. To 'keep term' is to dine in an Inn of Court (q.v.) on a specified number of formal occasions, as part of the qualification for call to the Bar (q.v.). 3. A fixed period of time. 4. Period for which an estate is granted. See *Brown v Gloucester CC* (1998) 1 EGLR 95. 5. Condition, provision or limitation. 6. Substantive part of a contract, creating a contractual obligation for whose breach an action lies.

term, customary. Term in a contract implied by a trade usage or the custom of a locality. Should be certain, notorious, reasonable and not contrary to the intention of any statute. May be excluded expressly or impliedly. See, e.g., *Hutton* v *Warren* (1836) 1 M & W 466.

Termes de la Ley. *Terms of the Law.* An early legal dictionary, written in law-French, with an English translation, by William Rastell, based upon his father's earlier *Exposition of the Terms of the Law* (1527).

term, express. *See* EXPRESS TERM.

term, fixed. *See* FIXED TERM.

term for years. Term of years (q.v.).

term, implied. *See* IMPLIED TERM.

term, innominate. *See* INNOMINATE.

term, intermediate. *See* INTERMEDIATE TERM.

term of years. Known also as 'term for years'. A lease. In essence, an estate or interest in land limited to a certain fixed period, e.g., a lease for 21 years. (A lease for more than three years must be created by deed: see L.P. (Misc. Provs.) A. 1989, s 1); it must be based on a definite period (see *Swift* v *Macbean* [1942] 1 KB 375); it must confer on the lessee a right to exclusive possession (see *Crane* v *Morris* [1965] 1 WLR 1104). See *EWP Ltd* v *Moore* [1992] QB 460. *See* LEASE.

term of years absolute. A term that is to last for a certain fixed period, although it may be liable to end before the expiration of that period by notice, re-entry, operation of law, etc. Includes a term for less than a year, or for a year or years and a fraction of a year or from year to year: L.P.A. 1925, s 205(1)(*xxvii*). See *Receiver for Metropolitan Police* v *Palacegate Properties* (2000) *The Times*, 21 March.

termor. One holding land for a term of years (q.v.).

territoriality, principle of. Concept in international law that a Sovereign ought not to engage in jurisdictional acts outside the limits of his territory. See *British Nylon Spinners* v *ICI Ltd* [1954] 3 All ER 88.

territorial waters. Sea area adjacent to a state's shores and subject to its exclusive jurisdiction; it extends for 12 nautical miles from the base lines drawn in relation to the Territorial Waters Order in Council 1964. See, e.g., Territorial Waters Jurisdiction Act 1878; Sea Fisheries Act 1968, s 6; Territorial Sea Act 1987; I.C.T.A. 1988, s 830; Water Resources Act 1991, s 104(1). 'United Kingdom waters' means the sea or other waters within the seaward limits of the territorial sea of the UK: Merchant Shipping Act 1995, s 313(2)(*a*). 'National waters', in relation to the UK, means UK waters landward of the baselines for measuring the breadth of its territorial sea: s 313(2)(*b*).

terrorism. The use or threat of action designed to influence the government or to intimidate the public, made for the purpose of advancing a political, religious or ideological cause, where that action involves serious violence against a person, serious damage to property, endangers a person's life, other than that of the person committing the action, creates a serious risk to the health or safety of the public or a section of it, or is designed seriously to interfere with or seriously disrupt an electronic system: Terrorism Act 2000, s 1(1). Fund-raising, money laundering for purposes of terrorism are offences: ss 14, 15. For incitement of terrorism overseas, see s 59.

terrorism, information concerning. It is an offence for a person to fail, without reasonable excuse, to disclose to a constable as soon as reasonably practicable any information, where he believes or suspects that another person has committed an offence under the Terrorism Act 2000, ss 15–18 and that his belief or suspicion has come to his attention in the course of a trade, profession, business or employment: s 19.

terrorist. A person who has committed an offence under the Terrorism Act 2000, under any of ss 11, 12, 15–18, 54, 56–63, or is or has been concerned in the commission, preparation or instigation of acts of terrorism: s 40(1). A constable may arrest without a warrant any person whom he reasonably suspects to be a terrorist: s 41(1).

terrorist, suspected international. Under Anti-terrorism, Crime and Security Act 2001, s 21, Secretary of State may issue a certificate if he reasonably believes that a person's presence in the UK is a risk to national security, and he suspects that the person is or has been concerned in the commission, preparation or instigation of acts of international terrorism or belongs to or has links with an international terrorist group. Detention, deportation and removal are covered in ss 22, 23.

testable. 1. Legally capable of making a will (q.v.) or bearing witness. 2. Disposable under a will.

testament. A will. 'The true declaration of our last will, of that we would be done after our death': *Termes de la Ley*. A distinction is sometimes drawn between a will (a disposition of *real property*) and a testament (relating to *personal property*). *See* WILL.

testamentary capacity. The ability in law to make a valid will, based on, e.g., the maker's being over 18, *animus testandi* (q.v.), and the ability to make a disposition of property 'with understanding and reason'. See *Re Simpson* (1977) 121 SJ 224. For delegation of testamentary power, see *Chichester Diocesan Fund* v *Simpson* [1944] 2 All ER 60; *Re Beatty's WT* [1990] 3 All ER 844. In *Clancy* v *Clancy* (2003) *The Times*, 9 September, it was held that a will could be executed validly even though the testatrix lacked testamentary capacity, where she had signed it but where it had been drawn up correctly according to her instructions and she had the capacity to understand that she was signing a will drawn up on the basis of those instructions.

testamentary expenses. Expenditure incurred in the proper performance of an executor's duties. See *Re Matthew's WT* [1961] 1 WLR 1415.

testamentary freedom. The right of a person to dispose of his property by will according to his wishes. Limited in practice by, e.g., Inheritance (Provision for Family and Dependants) Act 1975.

testamentary guardian. Guardian of a child under 18 appointed by will.

testamentary intention. Known also as *animus testandi* (q.v.). Essential for the validity of a will. Thus, a will executed in jest, or brought about by force, fear, fraud or undue influence will be set aside. See *Boyce* v *Rossborough* (1856) 6 HL Cas 2; *Killick* v *Pountney* (2000) 1 WLR 41.

testamentary script. In contentious probate proceedings (q.v.), claimant and every defendant who has acknowledged service of the claim form (q.v.) must, by affidavit or witness statement, describe any testamentary script of the deceased person whose estate is the subject of an action, of which he has knowledge, or state that he knows of no such script: PD 49, para 5.1(a). A testamentary script means a will or draft thereof, written instructions for a will made by or at the request, or under the instructions, of the testator, any document purporting to be evidence of the contents, or to be a copy, of a will which is alleged to have been lost or destroyed: PD 49, para 1.2(iii).

testamentary trust. An express trust intended to operate after death. It must be contained in an attested or duly executed will or codicil. *See* TRUST.

testate. Having made and left a valid will. *See* WILL.

testator. (*Fem: testatrix.*) A deceased person who had made a will (q.v.).

testator, presence of. Witnesses must attest and subscribe a will in the testator's presence: W.A. 1837, s 9 (as substituted by A.J.A. 1982, s 17). 'Presence' means that testator must be able to see witnesses subscribe and know what they are doing. See *Wyatt* v *Berry* [1893] P 5; *Re Colling* [1972] 3 All ER 729. *See* WILL; ATTESTATION.

testatum. The beginning of the operative part of a deed (q.v.): 'Now this deed witnesseth that . . .'.

test case. An action determining the legal position of many persons who are not parties to the action, as contrasted with, e.g., a representative action (q.v.).

testimonial evidence. *See* EVIDENCE, TESTIMONIAL.

testimonium. That final part of a deed stating that the parties have signed the deed 'in witness' of what it contains.

testimony. Statement of a competent witness in court, or by deposition, generally sworn, and offered as evidence of the truth of that which he asserts. In general, it must be based only on facts of which he has personal knowledge. The essence of judicial evidence (q.v.).

testimony, perpetuating. *See* PERPETU-ATING TESTIMONY.

textbooks, authority of. General rule is that books may be cited in court, if at all, by way of evidence as to the correct interpretation of the law, but not as independent sources from which the law can be derived. Exceptions are 'books of authority', e.g., Coke, Blackstone. Some very few living writers are occasionally cited, but rarely referred to directly as authorities. Example of modern reliance on Coke: *Reid* v *Police Commissioner of the Metropolis* [1973] QB 551; example of adoption of contemporary writers' definition: *Re Ellenborough Park* [1956] Ch 131 ('easements', from Cheshire's *Modern Law of Real Property*); *Haystead* v *DPP* (2000) 164 JP 396 (adoption of approach to *actus reus* of 'battery', set out in *Criminal Law* (9th edition) by Smith and Hogan).

theatre, obscenity in. It is an offence, under Theatres Act 1968, to present or direct an obscene performance unless the performance can be justified as being for the public good on grounds of literary or other artistic merit. For the stirring up of racial hatred in the theatre, see P.O.A. 1986, s 20.

theft. A person is guilty of theft 'if he dishonestly appropriates property belonging to another with the intention of permanently depriving the other of it; and "thief" and "steal" shall be construed accordingly': Th.A 1968, s 1(1). For 'property belonging to another', see *R* v *Klineberg* (1998) *The Times*, 19 November. *See* DISHONEST; PERMANENTLY DEPRIVING, INTENTION OF.

thing in action. Chose in action (q.v.).

thin-skull principle. *See* EGG-SHELL SKULL PRINCIPLE.

third party. A person other than the principals in any proceedings. See now CPR, Part 20 claim (q.v.); Contracts (Rights of Third Parties) Act 1999.

third-party rights in land. Rights over another's land are generally binding on its successive owners, e.g., easements, restrictive covenants (qq.v.).

third-party risks, insurance against. It is an offence to use, to cause or permit any other person to use, a motor vehicle on a road unless there is in force in relation to the use of the vehicle by that person a policy of insurance or some security in respect of third-party risks (i.e., risks to persons not parties to the policy). See Road Traffic Acts 1988, Part VI, 1991, s 20.

threat. The expression of an intention to inflict unlawful injury or damage of some kind 'so as to intimidate or overcome the will of the person to whom it is addressed'. 'An intimation by one to another that unless the latter does or does not do something, the former will do something which the latter will not like': *per* Peterson J in *Hodges* v *Webb* [1920] 2 Ch 70. 'Threatening' is to be taken in its ordinary meaning: *Brutus* v *Cozens* [1973] AC 854. For a threat to kill, see *R* v *Williams* (1986) 84 Cr App R 299; *R* v *Gidney* [1999] 1 Cr App R (S) 138. For use of threatening words or behaviour, see C.J.P.O.A. 1994, s 51. For 'threats at a distance', see *DPP* v *Mills* [1996] 3 WLR 1093. For threat by telephone to kill, see *R* v *McNally* [1992] 2 Cr App R (S) 30. See Y.J.C.E.A. 1999, Sch 4, para 22. *See* INTERFERING WITH WITNESSES; MURDER, THREATS TO.

threatening to destroy or damage another's property. Principal issues to be taken into account when considering ingredients of offence under Criminal Damage Act 1971, s 2, are: whether threat has objectively been made to another; whether the words and actions were objectively considered to be capable of constituting such a threat; whether defendant intended that person threatened would fear that the threat would be carried out: *R* v *Cakmak* (2002) *The Times*, 28 March.

three-tier system of Crown Court. Locations for sittings of the Crown Court (q.v.). The major centres (first-tier) have criminal and civil jurisdiction and are served by High Court judges, circuit judges and recorders. Second-tier centres have criminal jurisdiction only and are served as are first-tier centres. Third-tier centres have only criminal jurisdiction and are served by circuit judges and recorders.

tidal waters. Any part of the sea and any part of a river within the ebb and flow of the tide at ordinary spring tides, and not being a harbour: Merchant Shipping Act 1995, s 255.

tied cottage. Dwelling belonging to and maintained by an employer for occupancy by his employee. Common at one time among agricultural workers. A measure of security of tenure for agricultural workers housed by their employers and their successors was afforded under Rent (Agriculture) Act 1976, as amended by Rent Act 1977. ('Protected occupiers' (i.e., those who had worked whole-time in agriculture for a minimum of 91 out of the previous 104 weeks: 1976 Act, Sch 3) became statutory tenants following the ending of a protected occupancy.) See also Agricultural Holdings Act 1986; H.A. 1988, Sch 4, Part II (assured agricultural occupancies).

tied house. A public house, the lessee of which has covenanted with the lessor to buy all his supplies of beer, etc. only from that lessor.

timber. 'Oak, ash and elm are timber, provided they are of the age of 20 years and upwards, provided also they are not so old as not to have a reasonable quantity of usable wood in them, sufficient to make a good post. Timber, that is, the kind of tree which may be called timber, may be varied by local custom': *Honywood* v *Honywood* (1874) LR 18 Eq 306. (Birch in Yorkshire are considered by local custom as timber.) See also *Dashwood* v *Magniac* [1891] 3 Ch 306.

time as essence of a contract. Phrase referring to the common law principle that in the absence of contrary intention,

time is an essential condition in the performance of a contract if the nature of the subject matter of the contract or the surrounding circumstances indicate that it should be. Equitable doctrine was that time was not of the essence unless made so expressly or impliedly. Under L.P.A. 1925, s 41: 'Stipulations in a contract, as to time or otherwise, which according to rules of equity are not deemed to be or have become of the essence of the contract, are also construed and have effect at law in accordance with the same rules'. See *Behzadi* v *Shaftesbury Hotels* [1991] 2 WLR 1251; S.G.A. 1979, ss 10, 59, relating to stipulations as to time of payment (which are not generally of the essence of the contract in the absence of contrary intention); *United Scientific Holdings* v *Burnley BC* [1978] AC 904.

time charter. A charterparty (q.v.) for a specified period (compared with one for a particular voyage).

time for hearing. In AG's Reference (No 89/2004) (2005) *The Times*, 10 January, the CA held that accurate time estimates in relation to a hearing are vital if effective hearing is to be in the interests of all involved.

time for performance of service contract. Where, under a contract for the supply of a service (q.v.) by a supplier acting in the course of a business, the time for the service to be carried out is not fixed by the contract, left to be fixed in a manner agreed by the contract or determined by the course of dealing between the parties, there is an implied term that the supplier will carry out the service within a reasonable time: Supply of Goods and Services Act 1982, s 14(1). What is a 'reasonable time' is a question of fact: s 14(2).

time immemorial. Beyond legal memory, i.e., 'time whereof the memory of man runneth not to the contrary'. Fixed by Statute of Westminster I 1275, as the first year of the reign of Richard I (1189). See *Bryant* v *Foot* (1868) LR 3 QB 497.

time limits, disapplication of. The longer the delay the occurrence of matters giving rise to a claim (sexual abuse of children in this case), the more likely it was that the balance of prejudice would move against allowing the action to proceed by any disapplication of the period of limitation: *Various Claimants* v *Bryn Alyn Community Holdings Ltd* (2003) *The Times*, 17 February.

time off for dependants. An employee is entitled to be permitted by his employer to take a reasonable time off (unpaid) during working hours so as to take action necessary to provide assistance on an occasion when a dependant falls ill, gives birth, is injured, assaulted, or in consequence of the dependant's death. A 'dependant' is a spouse, child, parent, a person who lives in the same household as the employee, otherwise than by reason of being his employee, tenant, lodger or boarder. See E.R.A. 1996, s 57A, inserted by Employment Relations Act 1999, Sch 4, Part II.

time order. Order made by court under C.C.A. 1974, s 129, if it appears just to do so, allowing an extension of time on, e.g., an application for an enforcement order or an application made by a debtor or hirer after service on him of a default notice. See *Southern & District Finance* v *Barnes* (1995) 27 HLR 691, this has now been amended by Consumer Credit Act 2006 s 16 that inserts a new s 129A after s 129 CCA 1974. This allows a debtor or hirer to apply for time order after having received a notice of sums in arrears provided the debtor or hirer has given notice to the lender or owner and certain required information and a period of 14 days has passed since he gave notice to the creditor or owner.

time out of mind. Time immemorial (q.v.).

time policy. Policy of marine insurance where the contract is to insure for a fixed period of time.

time, reasonable. *See* REASONABLE TIME.

timeshare accommodation. Any living accommodation in the UK or elsewhere, used or intended to be used, wholly or partly for leisure purposes by 'timeshare users' all of whom have rights to use, or participate in arrangements under which they may use, that accommodation, or accommodation within a pool of accommodation to which that accommodation belongs, for intermittent periods of time: see Timeshare Act 1992, s 1. For rights to cancel timeshare agreements, see ss 2, 3. See Timeshare Regulations, SI 97/1081.

tipping-off. It is an offence for a person who knows, or suspects, that an investigation of money laundering (q.v.) is taking, or is about to take, place, to disclose that fact to some other person so that the investigation is prejudiced: C.J.A. 1988, s 93D, inserted by C.J.A. 1993, s 32. See *C* v *S* (1998) 148 NLJ 1723; *Bank of Scotland* v *A Ltd* (2001) *The Times*, 6 February.

tips, and employment contracts. The precise manner of dealing with waiters' tips (in relation to credit card payments, etc.) is to be determined by the contractual arrangements between the waiters and their employers: European Court of Human Rights in *Nerva* v *UK* (Application no 42295/98) (2002) The Times, 10 October.

tissue typing. The Administrative Court held, in *R (on application of Quintavalle)* v *Human Fertilisation and Embryology Authority* (2003) 153 NLJ 57, that the process of tissue typing, intended to establish whether an embryo could act as donor for an older sibling suffering from a genetic disorder, is prohibited under Human Fertilisation and Embryology Act 1990, s 3 (1)(b).

tithes. 'The tenth part of all fruits, praedial, personal, and mixt which are due to God, and consequently to his churches' ministers for their maintenance': Cowell, *Institutes of English Law* (1605). (*Praedial* = arising from the ground; *personal* = profits from labour; *mixt* = arising from things nourished from the ground, e.g., eggs.) Tithe Act 1936 replaced tithe rentcharges by redemption annuities. Finance Act 1962 provided for compulsory redemption of such annuities on the sale of land; their payment was ended under Finance Act 1977, s 56.

title. 1. Appellation of office or distinction. 2. Right to land or goods, or evidence of such right. 3. 'Good title' indicates that the land is free from incumbrances, and evidence of claim of title is conclusive. For 'defective title', see, e.g., *Rignall Developments* v *Halil* [1987] 3 WLR 394. For 'good holding (or marketable) title' (which is not to be construed as a title free from all encumbrances) see *Barclays Bank* v *Weeks* [1999] QB 309. For 'doubtful title', see *Rignall Developments* v *Halil* [1998] Ch 190. 4. Title of an Act of Parliament (q.v.) is its heading. It is legitimate to use the title for the interpretation of the Act as a whole and to discover its scope: *Johnson* v *Upham* (1859) 2 E & E 263.

title, abstract of. *See* ABSTRACT AND EPITOME OF TITLE.

title, chain of. *See* CHAIN OF TITLE.

title, conversion of. *See* CONVERSION OF TITLE.

title deeds. Those documents constituting evidence of legal ownership of land. See, e.g., L.P.A. 1925, s 45(9); *Clayton* v *Clayton* [1930] 2 Ch 12.

title, long. Formal title of an Act of Parliament (q.v.), e.g., 'An Act to consolidate the enactments relating to conveyancing and the law of property in England and Wales' (the long title of the Act, known generally by its short title of Law of Property Act 1925). See *Ward* v *Holman* [1964] 2 QB 580.

title, paramount. *See* PARAMOUNT.

title, root of. *See* ROOT OF TITLE.

title, short. Title by which an Act is usually and conveniently cited. See Short Titles Act 1896. Usually stated towards the end of the statute in a separate section, e.g., Th.A. 1968, s 36(1). It cannot be relied on for resolution of a doubt in construction; it can be examined in a case of ambiguity: *Manuel* v *A-G* [1982] 3 WLR 821. See *Re Boaler* [1915] 1 KB 21.

title to goods, documents of. *See* DOCUMENTS OF TITLE TO GOODS.

title to goods, transfer of. Where goods are sold by a person who is not their owner, and who does not sell them under the authority or with the consent of the owner, the buyer acquires no better title to the goods than the seller had, unless the owner of the goods is by his conduct precluded from denying the seller's authority to sell: S.G.A. 1979, s 21(1).

title, voidable, sale under. *See* VOIDABLE TITLE, SALE UNDER.

tobacco advertisement. Defined under Tobacco Advertisement and Promotion Act 2002, s 1, as an advertisement whose purpose is to promote a tobacco product, or whose effect is to do so. A person who in the course of a business publishes a tobacco advertisement, or causes one to be published, in the UK, is guilty of an offence: s 2(1). In *R (British American Tobacco Ltd)* v *Secretary of State for Health* (2004) *The Times*, 11 November, it was held that the very limited exception to the overall ban on tobacco products advertising (see S.I. 04/765) is not disproportionately restrictive, and is, therefore, lawful.

tobacco product. Defined under Tobacco Advertisement and Promotion Act 2002, s 1, as a product consisting wholly or partly of tobacco and intended to be smoked, sniffed, sucked or chewed.

tobacco, sales to children. It is an offence to sell any tobacco product to persons under 16: Protection of Children (Tobacco) Act 1986. See also C.&Y.P. (Protection from Tobacco) Act 1991; *St Helens MBC* v *Hill* [1992] 156 JP 602 (offence is one of strict liability). For 'tobacco', see C.&Y.P.A. 1933, s 7.

toll. 1. Tax paid for some privilege. 2. Compensation for service provided. See New Roads and Street Works Act 1991, s 6 (toll orders in relation to roads).

Tomlin Order. Order (originally drafted by Tomlin J) in which the court records the voluntary settlement of a claim and stays all further proceedings except for the purpose of carrying the agreed terms into effect. See *Horton Technologies* v *Lucky Wealth Ltd* [1992] 1 WLR 24; *Islam* v *Askar* (1994) 138 SJLB 215; *Wallace* v *Gale Associates* [1998] 1 FLR 1091. See CPR, r 40.6(3)(d).

tonnage tax. Tax on profits of a shipping company, calculated for the purposes of corporation tax by reference to the net tonnage of the company's seagoing ships of 100 tons or more used for carriage of cargo and passengers, towage and salvage: Finance Act 2000, s 82, Sch 22.

tontine. An insurance scheme whereby contributors pay into a fund which is divided, at the end of a specified period, among the survivors by way of payment of capital or an annuity.

tort. (*Tortus* = twisted, distorted.) A civil wrong independent of contract. Liability in tort arises from breach of a duty primarily fixed by law which is towards others generally, breach of which is redressable by a claim for unliquidated damages (q.v.), affording some measure of compensation. (Defined recently by Toulmin J, in *R* v *Secretary of State for Transport ex p Factortame (No. 7)* (2001) *The Times*, 10 January, and following an approach indicated by Lord Hoffmann, in *Banque Bruxelles* v *Eagle Star Insurance* [1997] AC 191, as 'a breach of non-contractual duty which gave a private law right to the party injured to recover damages at common law from the party causing the injury.') There is no actionable tort of procuring another to commit a tort: *Credit Lyonnais Bank* v *ECGD* [1999] 2 WLR 540. *See* MEASURE OF DAMAGES IN TORT.

tort, access to solicitor. HL held in *Cullen* v *Chief Constable of RUC* [2003] UKHL 39, that where there had been a breach of a statutory duty to provide reasons for delaying the exercise of an arrested persons' right of access to a solicitor, this did not give rise to a private law remedy in damages. Proof of a breach under Northern Ireland (Emergency Provisions) Act 1987 was not actionable in tort.

tortfeasor. One who commits a tort (q.v.).

tortious. Having the nature of a tort (q.v.).

tortious damages, apportioning liability. HL held in *Barker* v *Corus (UK) plc, Murray* v *British Shipbuilders (Hydrodynamics) Ltd and Others, Patterson* v *Smiths Dock Ltd and Another* [2006] *The Times*, 4 May, where a worker has contracted mesothelioma after being

exposed to asbestos, working for more than one employer then the amount of damages to be awarded should be apportioned between the employers according to the relative degree of risk or chance of causing such harm to the worker.

tort, off-duty police officier. In *Weir* v *Chief Constable of Merseyside Police* (2003) *The Times*, 4 February, the CA held that where an off-duty police officer apparently acting in his capacity as a constable, committed a tort after identifying himself as a police officer, the chief constable was vicariously liable in damages for the acts constituting the tort.

tort of interference with contractual rights. CA held in *Mainstream Properties Ltd* v *Young and Others* [2005] *The Times*, 28 July when looking at an action of tort of interference with contractual rights it is not sufficient to show that the defendant was reckless and that his conduct interfered with the claimant's contractual rights.

tort of misfeasance in public office. HL held in *Watkins* v *Secretary of State for the Home Department and Others* [2006] *The Times*, 3 April, for the purposes of bringing a tort of misfeasance action in public office, could only be brought where the claimant has suffered loss or damage by means of the tortious conduct of the public officer. The prime function of the law of tort is to provide financial compensation for damages suffered, not to punish the public officer.

tort, pure economic loss, and. No action in negligence can be brought by the owner or occupier of a defective building against persons involved in its construction, save where the building has caused damage to property, or personal injury. Any pure economic loss sustained by the owner or occupier is irrecoverable: *Murphy* v *Brentwood DC* [1990] 2 All ER 908.

torts, classification of. 1. Wrongs to the person, e.g., assault. 2. Wrongs to reputation, e.g., defamation. 3. Wrongs to property, e.g., trespass. 4. Wrongs to persons or property, e.g., nuisance. 5. Wrongs of interference in contractual

relations, e.g., inducing breach of contract.
6. Abuse of legal procedure, e.g., malicious prosecutions.

torture. An offence committed where a public official or person acting in an official capacity, intentionally inflicts severe pain or suffering on another in the performance of his official duties: C.J.A. 1988, s 134(1). It is immaterial whether the pain or suffering is physical or mental or whether it is caused by an act or omission: s 134(3). See European Convention on Human Rights 1950, art 3; *R v Special Adjudicator ex p Okonkwo* [1998] Imm AR 502 (consideration of rape as torture); *R v Bow Street Metropolitan Stipendiary Magistrate ex p Pinochet Ugarte (No. 3)* [1999] 2 WLR 827 (torture as extradition crime); *R v Secretary of State ex p Roszkowski* (2000) *The Times*, 29 November (racist attacks not torture).

tort, waiver of. *See* WAIVER OF TORT.

total loss. *See* LOSS, LIABILITY IN MARINE INSURANCE FOR.

totting up. Procedure of adding together penalty points based on convictions involving the endorsement of driving licences, and which may result in disqualification. See Road Traffic Act 1972; Road Traffic Act 1988, Sch 2; Road Traffic (New Drivers) Act 1995; *Jones v DPP* (2000) *The Times*, 20 October.

touching and concerning land. *See* COVENANT RUNNING WITH THE LAND.

town. At one time a group of dwellings that 'hath, or in time past hath had, a church and celebration of divine service, sacraments and burials': Coke, *Institutes* (1641). Now refers to a group of houses, etc., bigger than a village. A parish or community can resolve to adopt the status of a town: L.G.A. 1972, s 245.

town planning. Principles related to the improvement of land in the general interests of the community. See T.C.P.A. 1971, as variously amended; T.C.P.A. 1990; L.G.P.L.A. 1980, Part IX.

tracing money. Where property has been transferred under a contract which, because it has been obtained fraudulently, is voidable, such property is not to be considered as being held immediately on constructive trust for the transferor. A settlement will be held a sham when settlor and trustee share a common intention that the documents purporting to create the settlement were not intended in any way to create rights and obligations: *Shelson v Russo* [2003] EWHC 1637.

tracing trust property. Steps taken by beneficiaries to follow assets which have come into the hands of others. At common law right to trace will be lost if claimant's money has become mixed with another fund. In equity a charge can be imposed on the mixed fund to the full extent of the claimant's contribution. See *Re Hallett's Estate* (1879) 11 Ch D 772; *Re Diplock* [1948] Ch 495. For right to trace where there is no trust, but some other fiduciary element, see *Aluminium Industrie Vaassen BV v Romalpa Aluminium Ltd* [1976] 2 All ER 552; *Foskett v McKeown* [2000] 2 WLR 1299 (tracing through insurance policy).

trade. Business activity relating to the exchange of goods and services for money. 'Includes every trade, manufacture, adventure or concern in the nature of trade': I.C.T.A. 1988, s 832(1).

trade association. Phrase used, e.g., in Resale Prices Act 1976, s 24(1), to mean 'a body of persons (whether incorporated or not) which is formed for the purpose of furthering the trade interests of its members or the persons represented by its members'.

trade description. Under Trade Descriptions Act 1968, a description, direct or indirect, concerning goods, relating to: quantity, size, gauge; method of manufacture, production, etc; composition; fitness for purpose; other physical characteristics; testing and results; approval by any person; place or date of manufacture, production, etc.; person by whom manufactured or produced, etc.; other history. See *Southwark LBC v Time Computer Systems* (1997) *The Independent*, 14 July; *R v Bhad* [1999] 2 Cr App R (S) 139. In *R v Richards and Evans* [2004] 2 Cr App R(S) 51, the CA held that custodial sentences were not appropriate where neither appellant had participated in 'clocking vehicles' (winding back odometers); they were unaware that this had been done, but were merely trading in a negligent manner. See Trade Descriptions Act 1968. See FALSE TRADE DESCRIPTION.

trade dispute. Under T.U.L.R.(C.)A. 1992, s 218, a dispute between workers and their employers wholly or partly relating to: terms and conditions of employment, engagement or suspension of employment, allocation of work or other duties, discipline, union membership and non-membership, negotiating machinery and facilities for union officials. See T.U.R.E.R.A. 1993, ss 17–22; Employment Rights (Dispute Resolution) Act 1998; *P v NAS* (2001) *The Times*, 25 May.

trade dispute and tort. 'An act done by a person in contemplation or furtherance of a trade dispute is not actionable in tort on the ground only that it induces another person to break a contract or interferes or induces another person to interfere with its performance, or that it consists in his threatening that a contract (whether one to which he is a party or not) will be broken or its performance interfered with, or that he will induce another person to break a contract or interfere with its performance': T.U.L.R.(C.)A. 1992, s 219.

trade fixtures. A tenant may remove fixtures attached to the land for the purpose of conducting his trade. See *Smith v City Petroleum Co* [1940] 1 All ER 260. See FIXTURES.

trade mark. Any sign capable of being represented graphically which is capable of distinguishing goods or services of one undertaking from those of other undertakings. It may, in particular, consist of words (including personal names), designs, letters, numerals, or the shape of goods or their packaging: Trade Marks Act 1994, s 1(1). See also SI 00/136. A registered trade mark is a property right obtained by the registration of the trade mark under the Act and the proprietor of such a mark has the rights and remedies provided by the Act. No proceedings lie

to prevent or recover damages for the infringement of an unregistered trade mark as such, but the Act does not affect the laws concerning passing off (q.v.): s 2(1), (2). For 'Community trade mark' see s 51. See *Philips Electronics NV v Remington Ltd* [1998] RPC 283; *Premier Luggage Ltd v Premier Company Ltd* (2000) *The Times*, 19 October (law is reluctant to allow an ordinary descriptive word to be ringed round so that it becomes the personal property of one particular tradesman).

trade mark disputes, settlement of agreements. Where an intellectual property dispute has been settled by agreement, a defendant wishing to avoid the agreement has to show that circumstances exist justifying non-enforcement; but claimant need not show that the agreement is reasonable: *World Wide Fund for Nature v World Wrestling Federation* (2002) 152 NLJ 323.

trade mark, infringement of. Court of Justice of EC considered, in *Arsenal FC plc v Reed (Case C-206/01)* (2002) *The Times*, 18 November, the First Council Directive 89/104/EEC, art 5 (1) (a), and held that where a third party (a stallholder) used for trading purposes a sign identical to a registered trade mark on goods identical to those for which registration had been made, proprietors of the trade mark (Arsenal FC) could rely on art 5 to prevent the stallholder's actions in selling the goods.

trade mark, offences, in relation to. Under Trade Marks Act 1994, s 92(1), it is an offence for a person, with a view to gain for himself and another, to apply to goods or their packaging, a sign identical to or likely to be mistaken for, a registered trade mark, or to sell or offer for sale goods which bear such a sign. See *R v Keane* [2001] FSR7.

trade mark, sound as. Court of Justice of the European Communities held in *Shield Mark BV v Kist* (Case C-283/01) (2003) *The Times*, 4 December, that it is possible for a sound to constitute the subject of a trade mark if it could be represented graphically with precision.

Thus, a tune set out in complete musical notation would suffice.

trade, restraint of. *See* RESTRAINT OF TRADE.

trade secret. Some manufacturing or productive process, knowledge of which has economic value in that it is generally confined to a business which has a proprietary interest in it and utilisation of which provides an advantage over competitors. Disclosure of such information, as the result of a breach of confidence or where it has resulted from employment under contract, can be prevented by injunction. See *Initial Service Ltd* v *Putterill* [1968] 1 QB 396; *Faccenda Chicken Ltd* v *Fowler* [1986] 1 All ER 617; Law Commission Consultation Paper (1997), *Legislating the Criminal Code: Misuse of Trade Secrets*, F.I.A. 2000, s 43. *See* CONFIDENCE, BREACH OF; CONFIDENTIAL INFORMATION.

trade union. Under T.U.L.R.(C.)A. 1992, s 1, an organisation (whether permanent or temporary) which consists wholly or mainly of workers and is an organisation whose principal purposes include the regulation of relations between workers and employers or employers' associations, or consists wholly or mainly of constituent or affiliated organisations which fulfil the above conditions, or of representatives of such constituent or affiliated organisations. The Certification Officer (q.v.) keeps a list of unions: 1992 Act, s 2. They cannot be corporate bodies: 1992 Act, s 10 (but a union's property is vested in trustees). See European Convention on Human Rights 1950, art 11 (right to form and join trade unions). *See* BLACKLISTS RELATING TO TRADE UNIONS.

trade union activities. For purposes of Trade Union and Labour Relations (Consolidation) Act 1992, there appears to be no authority relating directly to the issue of what is and what is not a 'trade union activity', referring to s 146. A decision does not depend on whether or not the activity was carried out by a formal representative of the union: *Hamilton* v *Arriva Trains* (2004) NLJ 1691.

trade union duties and activities, time off for. An employer must permit an employee who is an official of an independent union recognised by the employer to take time off to carry out any duties of his, as such an official, concerned with negotiations with the employer that are related to or connected with matters within T.U.L.R.(C.)A. 1992, and in relation to which the union is recognised by the employer or any other duties concerned with the performance, on behalf of the employer's employees, of any functions related to matters falling within the 1992 Act, and that the employer has agreed may be so performed by the union: see E.R.A. 1996, s 61; SI 99/1925.

trade union funds, illegal use of. Use of funds for indemnifying unlawful conduct is illegal: T.U.L.R.(C.)A. 1992, s 15.

trade union, independent. Under E.R.A. 1996, s 235, a trade union which is not under the domination or control of an employer or group of employers or one or more employers' associations, and is not liable to interference by an employer or any such group or association (arising out of the provision of financial or material support or by any other means whatsoever) tending towards such control.

Trade unionists' rights, freedom of assembly and association. European Court of Human Rights has held in *Wilson* v *UK* *(Application* 30668/96) (2002) *The Times*, 5 July, that the right to freedom of assembly and association, guaranteed by Human Rights Convention, art 11, is violated by a financial inducement by employers to employees to surrender their right to union representation in the bargaining process.

trade union membership, detriment related to. An employee has the right not to be subjected to any detriment as an individual by any act, or any deliberate failure to act, by his employer if the act or failure takes place, for the purpose of preventing or deterring him from being or seeking to become a union member: T.U.L.R.(C.)A. 1992, s 146(1), amended by Employment Relations Act 1999, Sch 2. 'Detriment' is detriment short of dismissal: 1992 Act, s 146(6), inserted by 1999 Act, Sch 2.

trade union official. 'Any person who is an officer of the union or of a branch or section of the union or who is a person elected or appointed in accordance with the rules of the union to be a representative of its members or of some of them including any person so elected or appointed who is an employee of the same employer as the members or one or more of the members, whom he is to represent': T.U.L.R.(C.)A. 1992, s 119. For responsibility of unions for acts of officials, see 1992 Act, ss 20, 21.

trade union, recognition of. A union seeking recognition to be entitled to conduct collective bargaining on behalf of a group of workers, involving pay, hours and holidays, may make a request, under T.U.L.R.(C.)A. 1992, Sch A1, inserted by Employment Relations Act 1999, Sch 1, for recognition to the employer, followed, if necessary, by intervention of CAC (q.v.). If CAC is satisfied that the majority of workers in the bargaining unit are union members, a declaration of recognition is issued, unless CAC believes that a ballot should be held in the interests of good industrial relations. If a majority of those voting, constituting 40 per cent of the workers in the bargaining unit, support recognition, a declaration of recognition must be made. For ballot on derecognition, see Sch A1, para 133. For unfair dismissal connected with recognition, see E.R.A. 1996, s 128, amended by Employment Relations Act 1999, s 6.

trade union, resignation from. The contract of membership of a union contains an implied term allowing resignation on giving reasonable notice and complying with reasonable conditions: see T.U.L.R.(C.)A. 1992, s 69.

trade union, rights relating to training of workers. An employer must from time to time invite the trade union to send representatives to a meeting for the purpose of consulting on his policy for training workers within a bargaining unit and on his plans for training during the period of six months from the day of the meeting: T.U.L.R.(C.)A. 1992, s 70B, inserted by Employment Relations Act 1999, s 5. For complaints to employment tribunal on employer's failure to comply with s 70B, see s 70C.

trade unions, executive committee elections. The executive committee of a union must be elected, at intervals not exceeding five years, by ballot. For exemptions for certain unions, see T.U.L.R.(C.)A. 1992, s 57.

trade unions, industrial action ballots. Under T.U.L.R.(C.)A. 1992, s 226, immunity from legal action is removed where unions do not hold a ballot before authorising or endorsing a call for a strike (q.v.) or other form of industrial action which breaks a contract of employment of those called upon to participate in it. It must be held no later than four weeks before the action begins. For requirements to be satisfied, e.g., entitlement to vote, method of voting, conduct of ballot, see ss 228–231. See Employment Relations Act 1999, Sch 3, para 2.

trade union, unreasonable exclusion or expulsion from. An individual has a right not to be excluded or expelled from a trade union unless that is permitted by this section: T.U.L.R.(C.)A. 1992, s 174(1), substituted by T.U.R.E.R.A. 1993, s 14. Exclusion or expulsion is permitted if, and only if: entirely attributable to the individual's conduct; he does not satisfy an enforceable membership requirement of the union; he does not qualify for membership of the union because it operates only in a particular part or parts of Great Britain: s 174(2). Mere suspension from the privileges of union membership does not amount to constructive expulsion: *NACODS* v *Gluchowski* [1996] IRLR 252.

trading business. 'One which involves the purchase of goods and the selling of goods': *per* Lush J in *Higgins* v *Beauchamp* [1914] 3 KB 1192. For meaning of 'trading' for tax purposes, see *Ensign Tankers Ltd* v *Stokes* [1992], 2 WLR 469.

trading certificate. Certificate to commence business issued by the registrar to a public company (q.v.) under Cos.A. 1985, s 117, following a statutory declaration by the company, stating: that the nominal value of its allotted share capital is not less than the authorised minimum; amount of company's preliminary expenses and who paid them; amount paid up on company's allotted share capital, any amount paid or benefit given to a promoter and his consideration for it. (A private company (q.v.) can commence business on incorporation.)

trading, fraudulent. *See* FRAUDULENT TRADING.

trading interests, protection of. Under Protection of Trading Interests Act 1980, the Secretary of State may make orders prohibiting persons who carry on a business in the UK from complying with requirements or prohibitions which might damage the UK's trading interests, or infringe the UK's jurisdiction, or are otherwise prejudicial to the UK's sovereignty.

trading stamps. Stamps exchanged by a retailer's customer for free gifts from a stamp company. Under Trading Stamps Act 1964, as amended, the stamp must be clearly marked with a monetary value and the name of the issuing organisation.

trading stock. Trading stock is defined in Income and Corporation Taxes Act 1988, s 100(2) (and see also Taxation of Chargeable Gains Act 1992, s 288 (1)): the use of property-dealing subsidiaries to acquire properties to be held as investments for other companies constituting a group does not result in a transformation of those properties into trading stock: *New Angel Court Ltd* v *Adam* (2003) *The Times*, 8 August.

trading, wrongful. *See* WRONGFUL TRADING.

traffic calming works. Means, in relation to a highway, works affecting the movement of vehicular and other traffic for the purpose of promoting safety or preserving or improving the environment through which the highway runs: Highways Act 1980, s 329, inserted by Traffic Calming Act 1992, s 1. See Local Government

and Rating Act 1997, s 30; G.L.A.A. 1999, s 268.

traffic sign. Any object or device fixed or portable, for conveying, to traffic on roads or any specified class of traffic, authorised warnings, information, requirements, restrictions or prohibitions: Road Traffic Regulation Act 1984, ss 64, 74(*g*). For duty to comply with traffic signs and directions, see Road Traffic Act 1988, ss 35, 36.

traffic wardens. Persons appointed by police authorities to assist in control of road traffic. See Road Traffic Act 1972, Sch 7, as amended.

trailer, defective. It was held in *R (Newcastle upon Tyne CC)* v *Le Quelemec* (2005) *The Times*, 17 January, that a four-wheeled trailer with power brakes was not to be considered as unroadworthy when it was not carrying anything, even though its axle had broken, damaging a passing vehicle.

transaction. An act, or series of acts, involving business negotiations, e.g., buying, selling, and resulting in a change of legal rights and duties of the participants. See, e.g., S.L.A. 1925, s 64(2): 'transaction' includes sale, exchange, grant, lease, surrender, re-conveyance, etc. For 'artificial transactions', see *Curtain Dream* v *Churchill Merchandising* (1990) 5 BCC 341. *See* DEALINGS, COMMERCIAL.

transfer. The conveyance of title or other interest in property from one person to another, e.g., by sale or gift. See S.G.A. 1979, Part III.

transferable. 'The word "transferable" is of the widest possible import, and includes every means by which property may be passed from one person to another': *Gathercole* v *Smith* (1875) 17 Ch D 1.

transfer, blank. *See* BLANK TRANSFER.

transferee. 'In relation to a contract for the transfer of goods means (depending on the context) a person to whom the property in the goods is transferred under the contract, or a person to whom the property is to be so transferred, or a person to whom the rights under the contract of either of those persons have passed': Supply of Goods and Services Act 1982, s 18(1).

transfer of action. *See* CLAIM, TRANSFER OF.

transfer of shares. Shares are transferable subject to any restrictions in a company's articles (q.v.), and as a consequence of orders imposing restrictions (e.g., for failure to disclose individual interests in shares under s 210(5)): Cos.A. 1985, ss 182(1), 454. A transfer cannot be registered unless a proper instrument of transfer, correctly stamped, has been delivered to the company, executed by or on behalf of the transferor: s 183. See Stock Transfer Acts 1963, 1982; Cos.A. 1989, s 207; SI 95/3272. *See* SECURITIES, TRANSFER OF.

transfer of undertakings. Under Transfer of Undertakings (Protection of Employment) Regulations 1981 (SI 81/1794) (designed to implement EU Acquired Rights Directive), an employee acquires rights where his contract of employment is automatically transferred from one business to another when there is a change of ownership of the business. See Employment Relations Act 1999, s 38. See SI 99/1925; *Frankling* v *BPS Public Sector Ltd* [1999] ICR 347; SI 99/1925; *Whitehouse Leisure Ltd* v *Barnes* [2000] IRLR 456. See also *RCO Support Services* v *Unison* [2002] EWCA Civ 464. Under Directive 98/50/EC art 1, 'there is a transfer within the meaning of the Directive where there is a transfer of an economic entity which retains its identity, meaning an organised grouping of resources which has the objective of pursuing an economic activity, whether or not that activity is central or ancillary'.

transferor. 'In relation to a contract for the transfer of goods, means (depending on the context) a person who transfers the property in the goods under the contract, or a person who agrees to do so, or a person to whom the duties under the contract of either of those persons have passed': Supply of Goods and Services Act 1982, s 18(1).

transfer order. Court order, under C.C.A. 1974, s 133(1)(*b*)(*ii*), for the transfer to a debtor of a creditor's title to goods to which an agreement relates and the return to the creditor of the remainder of the goods.

transferred malice. *See* MALICE.

transformation, doctrine of. Doctrine under which rules of international law are not to be considered a part of English law unless made a part of law by an Act of Parliament (q.v.), judges' decisions or long established customs, as contrasted with the doctrine of incorporation (q.v.). See *Chung Chi Cheung* v *The King* [1939] AC 160.

transit passengers. In relation to Immigration and Asylum Act 1999, means persons of a description specified by order of the Secretary of State who, on arrival in UK, pass through to another country without entering UK; the order may specify persons by reference to nationality, citizenship, origin or other connection with a country, but not by reference to race, colour or religion: s 41(2). Such passengers may be required to hold a transit visa: s 41(1).

transitu, stoppage in. *See* IN TRANSITU.

transmission of shares. The vesting of shares in another, not by virtue of transfer, but by the operation of law, e.g., on the death or bankruptcy (q.v.) of a shareholder. See Cos.A. 1985, s 182.

transplant centre. A hospital or other institution, or department of it, which undertakes surgical operations for the transplantation of human organs: SI 91/408. For purposes of transplant, a 'donor' means a person who provides or offers to provide any of his organs, with a view to the organs being transplanted into another person, and includes a dead person from whom an organ is retrieved; a 'recipient' means a person who undergoes or is to undergo a surgical operation for the implantation of one or more organs removed from a living or dead person: SI 91/408. *See* ORGAN, HUMAN; UKTSSA.

transplants. *See* ORGAN, HUMAN; UKTSSA.

transport authority, local, plans. Each local transport authority must develop policies for promotion and encouragement of safe, integrated, efficient and economic transport facilities to, from and within their area, and must carry out their functions so as to implement those policies: Transport Act, 2000, s 108(1). Facilities and services mentioned in s 108(1) are those required to meet needs of persons living or working in the authority's area, or visiting or travelling through that area, and those required for freight transportation, and include pedestrian facilities and services: s 108(2).

transsexual, discrimination against. A male-to-female transsexual who had undergone gender reassignment, was to be regarded as female for purposes of employment, so as to meet the criteria of the rules derived from the jurisprudence of EC law: *Chief Constable of W Yorks Police* v *A* (2002) The Times, 14 November. See also *Goodwin* v *UK* (Application No. 19857/05) (2002) 35 EHRR 447.

transsexuals, human rights of. In *Goodwin* v *UK (Application No. 28957/ 95)* (2002) *The Times*, 12 July, the European Court of Human Rights held that arts 8, 12 of the Convention (rights to respect for private and family life, and to marry and found a family) had been violated, in relation to a post-operative male-to-female transsexual who complained of treatment concerning pensions, social security and the right to marry. In *Chief Constable of West Yorkshire Police* v *A* (2004) *The Times*, 7 May, that a transsexual who had undergone gender reassignment surgery and was living as a member of the reassigned gender was, for purposes related to employment, entitled to be treated on equal terms with ordinary persons belonging to that gender. HL also held that Matrimonial Causes Act 1973, s 11(c) was not compatible with the Convention on Human Rights, arts 8, 10.

travaux préparatoires. Preparatory work. Phrase used in discussions of statutory interpretation to refer to the background of legislation, e.g., reports of Royal Commissions, debates in Parliament. The judicial consideration of such matter has been generally forbidden in English law. See *Davis* v *Johnson* [1978] 1 All ER

1132. May now be used, apparently, with caution, in the interpretation of statutes: *Fothergill* v *Monarch Air Lines* [1981] AC 251: *Gatoil International* v *Arkwright-Boston Insurance Co* [1985] AC 255.

travel concessions. Under Travel Concessions (Eligibility) Act 2002, s 1, the age of entitlement for men and women to concessionary bus travel is equalised at 60. This is expected to be brought into force by April 2003. See SI 02/673; *Matthews* v *UK* (2002) *The Times*, 30 July.

travelling expenses. For purposes of income tax assessment, there may be deducted from an employee's emoluments to be taxed, those amounts necessarily expended on travel in performance of his duties or other expenses attributable to the necessary attendance at any place of the employee in the performance of those duties, excluding expenses of ordinary commuting or private travel: I.C.T.A. 1988, s 198(1), substituted by Finance Act 1998, s 61.

travel, private. Travel between the employee's home and a place that is not a workplace in relation to the employment, or between two places neither of which is a workplace in relation to the employment: I.C.T.A. 1988, Sch 12A, inserted by Finance Act 1998, Sch 10.

treason. The offence under the Statute of Treasons 1351, which is, in essence, a breach of allegiance to the Crown. It comprises, e.g., the levying of war against the King in his realm, being adherent to the King's enemies in his realm, giving them aid and comfort in the realm or elsewhere. See, e.g., *R* v *Casement* [1917] 1 KB 98; *Joyce* v *DPP* [1946] AC 347.

treason felony. Offence under Treason Felony Act 1848, committed by one within or without the realm, who compasses, imagines, devises or intends, to deprive or depose the Queen from the style or royal name of the imperial crown, to levy war against the Queen in the UK, to stir any foreigner to invade the UK. See C.D.A. 1998, Sch 10.

treason, misprision of. *See* MISPRISION.
treasure trove, common-law rule. 'When any money, gold, silver, plate or

bullion is found in any place and no man knoweth to whom the property is, then the property thereof belongeth to the King': *Termes de la Ley*. 'It is the hiding, and not the abandonment of the property that entitles the King to it': *A-G v Trustees of British Museum* [1903] 2 Ch 598.

treasure, under statute. Under the Treasure Act 1996, treasure is any object at least 300 years old when found which is not a coin, but has a metallic content at least ten per cent by weight of precious metal; when found, is one of at least two coins in the same find which are at least 300 years old at that time and have that percentage of precious metal; or when found, is one of at least ten coins in the same find which are at least 300 years old at the time. Any object at least 200 years old when found, which belongs to a class designated by the Secretary of State as of outstanding importance, is also included. See ss 1, 2. When treasure is found, it vests, subject to prior interests and rights, in the franchisee, if there is one, otherwise in the Crown: s 4(1).

Treasury. The government department, headed by the Chancellor of the Exchequer, concerned with the finances and economic and monetary policy of the nation. (The Prime Minister is nominally the First Lord of the Treasury.) It includes divisions concerned with domestic economy, overseas finance and public services.

Treasury Counsel. Barristers or solicitors nominated by A-G, who receive briefs from DPP relating to prosecutions at the Central Criminal Court (q.v.).

Treasury Solicitor. An official who acts for the Treasury. See Treasury Solicitor Act 1876. The office was separated from that of the DPP (q.v.) in 1908. He instructs parliamentary counsel (q.v.) on Bills, advises on the interpretation of the law, and directs the work of the Queen's Proctor (q.v.).

treat, invitation to. *See* INVITATION TO TREAT.

treaty. Written agreement, governed by international law, concluded between two or more states, or other subjects of international law, possessed of treaty-making capacity. In English law a treaty can be made only through the Crown. 'Treaties and declarations do not become part of our law until they are made law by Parliament': *per* Lord Denning in *R v Chief Immigration Officer ex p Bibi* [1976] 1 WLR 979. Thus, the EC Treaty was incorporated into English law by the European Communities Act 1972.

trespass. An unjustifiable interference with possession. A tort involving 'direct and forcible injury'. 'Every invasion of private property, be it ever so minute, is a trespass': *Entick v Carrington* (1765) 19 St Tr 1029. See, e.g., Security Service Act 1990, s 3, authorising entry on property by warrant. Known as 'the fertile mother of actions', since from the writ of trespass (which appeared *c*. 1250) there developed a large number of personal actions. For trespass as a crime, see, e.g., C.L.A. 1977, s 9, as amended. *See* PROPERTY, RIGHT TO SECURITY OF.

trespass, aggravated. A person commits the offence of aggravated trespass if he trespasses on land in the open air and, in relation to any lawful activity which persons are engaging in or are about to engage in on that or adjoining land in the open air, does there anything which is intended by him to have the effect: of intimidating those persons so as to deter them from engaging in that activity; of obstructing, or disrupting that activity: C.J.P.O.A. 1994, s 68. The senior police officer present has power to remove persons committing or participating in aggravated trespass: s 69. See *DPP v Barnard* (1999) 143 SJLB 256 (proving the elements of the offence).

trespass by relation. The fiction (q.v.) whereby a person being entitled to immediate possession, and entering upon the land, is deemed to have been in actual possession from the time that his right accrued. See *Dunlop v Macedo* (1891) 8 TLR 43.

trespasser ab initio. *See* AB INITIO.

trespasser, occupier's duty to. In general, a trespasser must take the land as he finds it. But the occupier owes the trespasser a duty to take such steps as common humanity or common sense would dictate, so as to exclude, warn, reduce or avert a danger: *British Rlwys Board* v *Herrington* [1972] AC 877. See *Harris* v *Birkenhead Corporation and Another* [1975] 1 WLR 379; Occupiers' Liability Act 1984. *See* OCCUPIERS' LIABILITY TO NON-VISITORS.

trespassers, power to remove. The police are empowered to direct persons to leave land and to remove their vehicles where they reasonably believe that two or more have entered as trespassers and are present there with the common purpose of residing there for any period, and that reasonable steps have been taken to ask them to leave, and that any of the persons has caused damage to property on the land or used threatening, abusive or insulting words and behaviour, or that they have brought six or more vehicles on the land: C.J.P.O.A. 1994, s 61. See C.R.W.A. 2000, Sch 6, para 17; *Krumpa* v *DPP* [1989] Crim LR 295. *See* ADVERSE POSSESSION OF RESIDENTIAL PREMISES.

trespassing on premises of foreign missions. An offence under C.L.A. 1977, s 9 (as amended by Diplomatic and Consular Premises Act 1987).

trespassing with weapon of offence. 'A person who is on any premises as a trespasser, after having entered as such, is guilty of an offence if, without lawful authority or reasonable excuse, he has with him on the premises any weapon of offence': C.L.A. 1977, s 8. See P.&C.E.A. 1984, s 17(1). *See* OFFENCE, WEAPON OF.

trespass on the case. Formerly, special writs of trespass based on indirect damage, e.g., trover and *assumpsit* (qq.v.).

trespassory assembly. *See* ASSEMBLY, TRESPASSORY.

trespass to goods. A wrongful, direct (and not consequential) or negligent interference with goods in claimant's possession at the time of the interference. Absence of intent is generally an excuse. See *Wilson* v *Lombank Ltd* [1963] 1 WLR 1294. See also Torts (Interference with Goods) Act 1977.

trespass to land. Unjustifiable, direct and immediate interference (of an intentional or negligent nature) with another's possession of land, e.g., by unauthorised walking on it, or improper use of a highway. It is actionable *per se*. See *Anchor Brewhouse Developments* v *Berkley House Development Ltd* [1987] 2 EGLR 173. For purposes of Th.A. 1968, s 9(1)(*b*), a person is a trespasser if he enters the premises of another knowing that he is entering in excess of the permission given him or being reckless whether he is so doing: *R* v *Jones* [1976] 1 WLR 672. For right of tolerated trespasser to bring action in nuisance, see *Pemberton* v *Southwark LBC* (2000) *The Times*, 26 April.

trespass to the person. Wrong suffered by a person, in the nature of assault, battery, false imprisonment, etc. An intent to injure is not an essential ingredient of the tort: *Wilson* v *Pringle* [1987] QB 237. For defences, see *Barnes* v *Nayer* (1986) *The Times*, 19 December.

trial. The formal investigation and determination of matters in issue between parties before a court. See European Convention on Human Rights 1950, art 6 (right to fair trial); *R* v *Francom* (2000) *The Times*, 24 October.

trial by battle. *See* BATTLE, TRIAL BY.

trial, integrity of, prejudice to. Privy Council held, in *Randall* v *The Queen* (2002) *The Times*, 24 April, that even though not every deviation from criminal proceedings conduct rules would make for an unfair trial, a point could be reached when deviations from good practice might be so gross, persistent, prejudicial, irremediable that the court would be obliged to condemn the trial as unfair and quash the conviction as unsafe, however strong the grounds were for believing defendant to be guilty.

trial, new. 1. In the case of a civil appeal, under CPR, Sch 1; O 59, r 11, the Court of Appeal (q.v.) may order a new trial on the ground of misdirection, or of the improper admission or rejection of evidence, or because the verdict of the jury was not taken upon a question which the judge at the trial was not asked to leave to them, but only where some substantial wrong or miscarriage has been thereby occasioned. See *Ladd* v *Marshall* [1954] 1 WLR 1489; *Langdale* v *Danby* [1982] 1 WLR 1123; *R* v *Henworth* (2001) *The Times*, 30 January (a third trial after prosecutions failed). 2. Under Criminal Appeal Act 1968, s 7, as amended by C.J.A. 1988, s 43, a new trial may be ordered if the interests of justice so require. See *R* v *Hemmings* [2000] 2 All ER 155; *R* v *Craven* (2001) *The Times*, 2 February. See CRIMINAL CASES REVIEW COMMISSION; *VENIRE DE NOVO*.

trial per pais. *See* IN PAIS.

tribunal, bias in. In *Lodwick* v *Southwark LBC* (2004) *The Times*, 9 April, the CA held that where the Employment Appeal Tribunal was considering allegations suggesting prejudice by tribunal chairman, who declined to stand down, they should not omit to take into account the question of whether or not a perception of bias had arisen.

Tribunal Financial Services and Markets. *See* FINANCIAL SERVICES AND MARKETS TRIBUNAL.

tribunal hearing of both sides. In *Logan* v *Customs and Excise Commissioners* [2003] EWCA Civ 1068, the CA held that the power of a tribunal to stop a hearing half way should be exercised cautiously, but there is no inflexible rule that both sides should be heard, although this should normally be done.

tribunals. Bodies outside the hierarchy of the courts with administrative or judicial functions, exercising an independent jurisdiction. ('Administrative' tribunals are established by the state; 'domestic tribunals' are set up by non-state bodies, e.g., professional associations.) Their members include lawyers and laymen with specialised knowledge. In some cases chairmen are selected from a panel and appointed by the Lord Chancellor. Appeal may lie (where statute provides) to Court of Appeal (see CPR, Sch 1; O 61), or, in some cases to the JCPC. See CPR, Sch 2; CCR, O 3, r 6 (appeals from tribunals to county court). See Tribunals and Inquiries

Act 1992; Employment Tribunals Act 1996. *See* COUNCIL ON TRIBUNALS.

tribunals, employment, procedural matters. In *Bache* v *Essex CC* (2000) *The Times*, 2 February, Mummery LJ stated: at the hearing the tribunal had to follow a procedure which was fair to both sides; tribunal was responsible for the fair conduct of the proceedings; procedural fairness applied to the conduct of all involved in the proceedings; response to the finding of an error in procedure should be proportionate. See *Storer* v *British Gas plc* (2000) *The Times*, 1 March (tribunal must sit in public).

trigger clause. Term in an agreement which, e.g., when broken, activates some other term. See, e.g., C.C.A. 1974, s 88(3); *Scotto* v *Petch* (2000) *The Times*, 16 February.

trover. An early type of action brought 'to recover the value of personal chattels wrongly converted by another to his use': *Cooper* v *Chitty* (1756) 1 Burr. The term was also applied to an action for conversion. See Torts (Interference with Goods) Act 1977, s 1. *See* CONVERSION, TORT OF.

truck system. Practice whereby wages were paid in goods or tokens, rather than money. Abolished by Truck Acts 1831–1940, which were repealed by Wages Act 1986, Sch 5. Deductions may now be made if required or authorised by statute or a contractual provision, or if the worker has previously given written consent: s 1(1). Complaints may be made to an employment tribunal (q.v.) in respect of unauthorised deductions: s 5. Methods of pay are now governed by the contract of employment. See E.R.A. 1996, ss 13, 23.

trust. In essence, an equitable obligation which imposes on a person described as a trustee certain duties of dealing with property held and controlled by him for the benefit of the persons described as the beneficiaries, or, if there are not such persons, for some purpose recognised and enforceable at law. See Tr.A. 1925, 2000. Example: A, the owner of Blackacre, conveys it to B in fee simple, directing B to hold it in trust for C; A is the *settlor*, B is the *trustee*, C is the *beneficiary* (or *cestui que trust* (q.v.)), Blackacre is the *trust property*. For the domicile of a trust, see C.J.J.A. 1982, s 45. See Recognition of Trusts Act 1987, Schedule, embodying Hague Conference Convention (1984), under which 'the term "trust" refers to the legal relationship created – inter vivos or on death – by a person, the settlor, when assets have been placed under the control of a trustee for the benefit of a beneficiary or for a specified purpose'. See *Burton* v *FX Music Ltd* [1999] EMLR 826 (inferring intention to create trust). *See* PRECATORY WORDS.

trust, blind. A trust characterised by, e.g., the settlor's placing of funds in the form of investments under the control of independent trustees, so that potential conflict of interests might be avoided.

trust, breach of. *See* BREACH OF TRUST.

trust, characteristics of. For purposes of the Hague Convention (1984): '(a) [The] assets constitute a separate fund and are not part of the trustee's own estate; (b) title to the trust assets stands in the name of the trustee or in the name of another person on behalf of the trustee; (c) the trustee has the power and the duty, in respect of which he is accountable, to manage, employ or dispose of the assets in accordance with the terms of the trust and the special duties imposed upon him by law. The reservation by the settlor of certain rights and powers, and the fact that the trustee may himself have rights as a beneficiary, are not necessarily inconsistent with the existence of a trust.' (The Convention applies only to trusts created voluntarily and evidenced in writing.) See Recognition of Trusts Act 1987, Schedule. See *Tinsley* v *Milligan* [1993] 3 All ER 65 (trust and the separation of legal and equitable interests in property).

trust, charitable. *See* CHARITABLE TRUST.

trust, completely constituted. *See* COMPLETELY CONSTITUTED TRUST.

trust, constructive. *See* CONSTRUCTIVE TRUST.

trust, controlled. *See* CONTROLLED TRUST.

trust corporation. A corporation constituted under the law of UK or any other member state of EU (q.v.), and empowered under its constitution to undertake trust business in England and Wales, having one or more places of business in UK, being a registered company with a capital of not less than the prescribed amount (or its equivalent in the currency of the state wherein it is registered) of which not less than a prescribed amount, or the equivalent, is paid up in cash. Treasury Solicitor, Official Solicitor and Public Trustee (qq.v.) are also included. See Tr.A. 1925, s 68; S.L.A. 1925, s 117(1); L.P. (Amendment) A. 1926, s 3; S.C.A. 1981, s 115; Tr.A. 2000, s 28.

trust deed, debenture. Document securing debentures (q.v) and debenture stock. The company offering debentures enters into a trust deed with trustees, e.g., a trust corporation; the trustees have a mortgage over the company's property so that those who subsequently make loans to the company do not gain priority over debenture holders or debenture stockholders.

trust documents. Documents in the possession of trustees *qua* trustees, containing trust information which beneficiaries are entitled to know, and in which they have a proprietary interest: see *Re Londonderry's ST* [1965] Ch 918.

trustee. One who holds property on trust for another, known as *cestui que trust* (q.v.) or beneficiary. Capacity to be a trustee exists where there is capacity to take or hold property. (A 'lay trustee' is one who is not a trust corporation, and does not act in a professional capacity: Tr.A. 2000, s 28(6).) Trustees may be appointed by the settlor, under express power conferred by a trust instrument, by court, under Tr.A. 1925, s 36. See *Adam Ltd* v *International Trustees Ltd* (2000) *The Times*, 17 March. See Trusts of Land and Appointment of Trustees Act 1996, s 20; Trustee Delegation Act 1999.

trustee, acceptance of office by. Acceptance may be express or presumed. In general, in absence of evidence to the contrary, acceptance is presumed. Conduct may operate as acceptance. There can be no renunciation after acceptance. See *Re Sharman's WT* [1942] Ch 311.

trustee *de son tort*. Where a person who is not a trustee and who has no authority from a trustee takes upon himself to intermeddle with trust matters or to carry out acts which are characteristic of the office of trustee, he makes himself a *trustee de son tort* ('of his own wrongdoing') and is held to be a constructive trustee. See *Re Barney* [1891] 2 Ch 265; *Re Bell's Indenture* [1980] 3 All ER 425.

trustee, duties of. Generally: to become acquainted with the terms of the trust; to ensure that the trust property is vested; to act gratuitously and not to profit from the trust; not to delegate (but see Tr.A. 2000, Part IV); to act impartially in the interests of all beneficiaries. See *Phipps v Boardman* [1967] 2 AC 44. See DELEGA-TUS NON POTEST DELEGARE.

trustee, general liability of. A trustee is liable for any loss he has caused directly or indirectly to the trust estate: see, e.g., *Bartlett* v *Barclays Trust Co* [1980] Ch 515. For effect of a clause in a settlement providing for a trustee's exemption from liability, see *Armitage v Nurse* [1997] 3 WLR 1046; *Wight v Olswang* [1998] NPC 111. *See* BREACH OF TRUST.

trustee in bankruptcy. *See* BANK-RUPTCY, TRUSTEE IN.

Trustee, Public. *See* PUBLIC TRUSTEE.

trustees' costs basis. A basis for taxation of costs whereby a party may recover his costs out of the fund of which he is trustee. The taxation is conducted on the same principles as for the indemnity basis for costs, but the costs are presumed to have been unreasonably incurred (and will therefore be disallowed) if they were incurred contrary to the duty of the trustee (or personal representative) as such. See *Holding and Management Ltd v Property Holding plc* [1989] 1 WLR 1373. *See* TAXATION OF COSTS.

trustee's duty of care. Under Tr.A. 2000, s 1(1), whenever the duty of care applies to a trustee, he must exercise such care and skill as is reasonable in the cir-

cumstances, having regard in particular to any special knowledge or experience that he has or holds himself out as having, and if he acts as trustee in the course of a business or profession, to any special knowledge or experience that it is reasonable to expect of a person acting in the course of that kind of business or profession. The duty applies, under Sch 1, to matters relating to: investment; acquisition of land; agents, nominees and custodians; compounding of liabilities; insurance; valuations and audits.

trustee's expenses. A trustee is entitled to be reimbursed from the trust funds, or may pay out of the trust funds, expenses properly incurred by him when acting on behalf of the trust: Tr.A. 2000, s 31(1).

trusteeship, termination of. A trustee can retire under any express power, by statutory power conferred by Tr.A. 1925, s 39, by the consent of all beneficiaries, or by order of the court. He can be removed from office under any express power, under statutory power (see Tr.A. 1925, ss 36, 41), or by the court. Trusteeship terminates on death: where there are two or more trustees and one dies, the rule of survivorship applies, so that the office devolves on the surviving trustees. On the death of the sole surviving trustee, the estate devolves on his personal representatives.

trustees of the settlement. *See* SET-TLED LAND ACT TRUSTEES.

trustee's power of acquiring land. A trustee may acquire freehold or leasehold land in UK as an investment, for occupation by a beneficiary, or for any other reason: Tr.A. 2000, s 8(1). A trustee who acquires land under this section has all the powers of an absolute owner in relation to the land: s 8(3). This does not apply to settled land: s 10(1).

trustee's power of appointing nominees and custodians. A trustee may appoint a person to act as nominee in relation to assets of the trust (other than settled land): Tr.A. 2000, s 16. A custodian may be appointed to undertake the safe custody of assets or relevant documents or records: s 17.

trustees' power of delegation. Trustees may authorise any person to exercise any or all of their delegable functions as their agent: Tr.A. 2000, s 11. Delegable functions in the case of a non-charitable trust, include any functions other than those concerning: distribution of trust assets; apportionment of fees and payments between income and capital; appointment of trustees; powers conferred by legislation and trust instrument; appointment of nominees and custodians. In the case of a charitable trust, delegable functions are: carrying out of trustees' decisions; functions relating to investment of assets; raising of funds otherwise than by means of profits of a trade essential for the charity's purpose: s 11(3).

trustee's power of insuring. A trustee may insure any property which is subject to the trust against risks of loss or damage due to any event, and pay the premiums out of trust funds: Tr.A. 1925, s 19, as substituted by Tr.A. 2000, s 34.

trustee's power of investment, advice relating to. Before exercising power of investment, a trustee must consider proper advice about exercise of the power in relation to standard investment criteria: Tr.A. 2000, s 5(1). (There is an exception where he reasonably concludes that it is unnecessary or inappropriate to seek advice: s 5(2).) 'Standard investment criteria' are: the suitability to the trust of investments of the same kind as any particular investment proposed to be made or retained and of that particular investment as an investment of that kind, and the need for diversification of trust investments insofar as appropriate to the circumstances of the trust: s 4(3). 'Proper advice' is the advice of a person who is reasonably believed by the trustee to be qualified to give it by his ability in and practical experience of financial and other matters relating to the proposed investments: s 5(4).

trustee's power of investment, general. A trustee may make any kind of investment that he could make if he were absolutely entitled to the trust assets: Tr.A. 2000, s 3(1). For investments relating to land, see ss 3(3), 8. The general power is in addi-

tion to powers conferred on trustees otherwise than by Tr.A. 2000, but subject to any restriction or exclusion imposed by the trust instrument or subordinate legislation: s 6(1).

trustees, protection of. The court may relieve a trustee either wholly or partly from personal liability for breach of trust if he has acted honestly and reasonably and ought fairly to be excused. The burden of establishing this is on the trustee. See Tr.A. 1925, s 61; Lim.A. 1980, s 21.

trustees, remuneration of. *See* RE-MUNERATION OF TRUSTEES.

trustees, Settled Land Act. *See* SET-TLED LAND ACT TRUSTEES.

trust, executed. See EXECUTED.

trust, executory. See EXECUTORY.

trust, express. See EXPRESS TRUST.

trust for sale. Means, in relation to land, 'an immediate trust for sale, whether or not exercisable at the request or with the consent of any person, "trustees for sale" means the persons (including a personal representative) holding land on trust for sale': L.P.A. 1925, s 205(1)(*xxix*), amended by Trusts of Land and Appointment of Trustees Act 1996, Sch 4. See *Re Inns* [1947] Ch 576; *Miller* v *Lakefield Estates* (1989) 19 EG 67. It may arise expressly or by operation of statute (e.g., A.E.A. 1925, s 31(1), where an estate owner dies intestate and the personal representative holds property 'as to the real estate upon trust to sell the same; and as to the personal estate upon trust to call in, sell and convert into money such part thereof as may not consist of money'). Trusts for sale, and strict settlements (q.v.), constitute 'settlements'. See L.R.A. 1925, ss 8, 9. Under Trusts of Land and Appointment of Trustees Act 1996, ss 2–5, it remains possible to create an express trust for sale but it will take effect as a trust of land; generally, however, existing trusts for sale become automatically trusts of land. *See* CONVERSION.

trust, housing. *See* HOUSING TRUST.

trust instrument. The document used in the creation of a settlement (q.v.), which appoints trustees, contains the power to appoint new trustees and declares trusts affecting the settlement, etc. See S.L.A. 1925, ss 4, 9, 117(1).

trust land, occupation by beneficiaries. A beneficiary who is beneficially entitled to an interest in possession of land subject to a trust is entitled by reason of his interest to occupy the land at any time, if, at that time, the purposes of the trust include making the land available for his occupation, or the land is held by trustees so as to be available: Trusts of Land and Appointment of Trustees Act 1996, s 12(1).

trust of land, creation of. 'A declaration of trust respecting any land or any interest therein must be manifested and proved by some writing signed by some person who is able to declare such trust or by his will': L.P.A. 1925, s 55(1)(*b*).

trust, power in nature of. Known also as 'trust-power'. Created where the donor has demonstrated a clear intention that property is to pass to the objects in any event. Whether it has been created or not is a matter of 'intention or presumed intention to be derived from the language of the instrument': *Re Scarisbrick's WT* [1951] 1 All ER 822. See *Re Brierley* (1984) 39 SJ 647. *See* POWER.

trust property. In general, all property, real or personal, legal or equitable, may be made the object of a trust. See *Lord Strathcona SS Co v Dominion SS Co* [1926] AC 108.

trust, public. *See* PUBLIC TRUST.

trust, purpose. Term applied to a trust not in favour of ascertainable individuals, e.g., a charitable trust. See *Re Astor's ST* [1952] Ch 534 (trust 'for the maintenance of good relations between nations'); *Re Grant's WT* [1979] 3 All ER 359.

trust purpose, discontinuance of. In *Fraser v Canterbury Diocesan Board of Finance* [2004] EWCA 15, the CA held that, following School Sites Act 1841 and Reverter of Sites Act 1987, where a trust purpose had come to an end (in this case education for 'children and adults of the labour, manufacturing and other poorer classes in the diocese . . .'), following a grant made in 1866, the funds would

revert to the grantor. The education of the qualifying persons, in the terms of the original grant, was no longer of practical significance.

trusts, classification of. 1. Imposed by statute. 2. Express. 3. Implied, or resulting and constructive. 4. Executed and executory. 5. Completely and incompletely constituted. 6. Private and public. 7. Simple and special. For an early classification by Lord Nottingham, see *Cook v Fountain* (1676) 3 Swan 585.

trusts for sale and power to postpone. In the case of a trust for land created by a disposition, there is implied a power for trustees to postpone sale of the land; trustees are not liable in any way for postponing sale, in the exercise of their discretion, for an indefinite period: Trusts of Land and Appointment of Trustees Act 1996, s 4(1).

trusts of land. Any trust of property which consists of or includes land. 'Trust' includes any description of trust (whether express, implied, resulting or constructive) including a trust for sale and a bare trust created before the commencement of the Trusts of Land and Appointment of Trustees Act 1996. ('Land' does not include land which is already settled land (under S.L.A. 1925).) See 1996 Act, s 1.

trust, sub-. *See* SUB-TRUST.

trusts, unenforceable. *See* UNENFORCEABLE TRUSTS.

trusts, unlawful. *See* UNLAWFUL TRUSTS.

trust, termination of by beneficiary. A beneficiary who is *sui juris* (q.v.) and absolutely entitled has the right to terminate a trust, irrespective of the wishes of the trustee or settlor. This applies also if there are several beneficiaries who are all *sui juris* and absolutely entitled: *Barton v Briscoe* (1822) Jac 603. Under these circumstances the trustees must convey the trust property, thus bringing the trust to an end. See *IRC v Executors of Hamilton-Russell* [1943] 1 All ER 474; Trusts of Land and Appointment of Trustees Act 1996, s 20.

trust, variation of. *See* VARIATION OF TRUST.

trust, void. A trust which, because it is illegal or contrary to public policy, will not be enforced. Examples: a trust which is to take effect on the future separation of a husband and wife (see *Westmeath* v *Westmeath* (1831) 1 Dow & Cl 519); a trust void for perpetuity (see *A-G of Cayman Islands* v *Wahr-Hansen* (2000) *The Times*, 27 July).

trust, voidable. A trust which, having been created as a result of, e.g., fraud, mistake, duress, may be set aside or rectified in certain circumstances. Example: T, apparently about to die, executed a voluntary settlement which he did not understand, which was not read to him, and from which a power of revocation had been purposely omitted (see *Forshaw* v *Welsby* (1860) 30 Beav 243).

truth, statement of. A statement ['I believe that the facts stated in this (document being verified) are true'] necessary to verify a document (e.g., statement of case). See CPR, r 22.1(*a*). A statement of case or response may be signed by the party or litigation friend (q.v.) or their legal representative. The statement may be contained in the document it verifies, or it may be in a separate document. See r 22, PD 22. *See* FALSE STATEMENTS, PROCEEDINGS IN RELATION TO.

truth, statement of, failure to provide. Where a party fails to verify his statement of case by a statement of truth (q.v.), statement of case remains effective unless struck out; but the party may not rely on the statement of case as evidence of any of the matters set out under it: CPR, r 22(1). The court may order verification: r 22.4(1). See PD 22, para 4.1.

truth tests. Evidence produced by the administration of mechanical, hypnotic or chemical 'truth tests' is not admissible: *Fennell* v *Jerome Property Maintenance* (1986) *The Times*, 26 November; *R* v *Browning* [1995] Crim LR 227 (referring to Home Office guidelines on truth tests). *See* LYING IN RELATION TO PROOF OF GUILT.

turbary, common of. Right to cut peat or turf on another's land, to be used as fuel.

Turnbull warning. Direction given by Court of Appeal in relation to evidence of identification, in *R* v *Turnbull* [1977] QB 224. Where the case against an accused depends wholly or very substantially upon the correctness of one or more identifications, and the correctness of the identification evidence is disputed by the defence, the trial judge must warn the jury in specific terms of the special need for the exercise of caution before convicting solely in reliance upon that identification. Where there is a failure to follow the judge's guideline, it is likely that any ensuing conviction will be quashed if, 'on all the evidence, the verdict is either unsatisfactory or unsafe'. See *Reid* v *R* [1990] 1 AC 363; *R* v *Grant* [1996] 2 Cr App R 272. *See* IDENTITY, EVIDENCE OF.

turning a blind eye. 'If a man, suspicious of the truth, turns a blind eye to it, and refrains from inquiry – so that he should not know it for certain – then he is to be regarded as knowing the truth. The "turning a blind eye" is far more blameworthy than mere negligence. Negligence in not knowing the truth is not equivalent to knowledge of it': *per* Lord Denning in *The Eurysthenes* [1976] 2 Lloyd's Rep 171. See *Manifest Shipping* Co v *Uni-Polaris Shipping* Co (2001) *The Times*, 23 January.

turning Queen's evidence. *See* QUEEN'S EVIDENCE.

two-counsel rule. Practice whereby the 'freedom by a QC to supply his services without being accompanied by or assisted by a junior' was restricted. Abolished as from October 1977. See now *Practice Direction (Crown Court: Counsel)* [1995] 1 WLR 261 (application for two-counsel order).

tying-in arrangements. The provision of residential property loans as part of a package including other services, such as conveyancing or removal services. Prohibited, under C.L.S.A. 1990, ss 104–107, unless certain conditions are complied with.

Tynwald, Court of. Governor, Legislative Council and Assembly (House of Keys) of the Isle of Man. See, for proof of Acts of Tynwald, Isle of Man Act 1979, s 12. *See* ISLE OF MAN.

tyre, liability relating to. In *Exel Logistics Ltd* v *Curran* [2004] *The Times*, 2 November, the CA held that the regulation which prohibits the use of a motor vehicle with an under-inflated tyre will not, in itself, render the driver liable in negligence for an accident caused by that defect.

U

uberrimae fidei. Of the utmost good faith. Applies to a contract in which the promisee must inform the promissor of all those facts and surrounding circumstances which could influence the promissor in deciding whether or not to enter the contract. See *Banque Financière* v *Westgate Insurance Co.* [1991] 2 AC 249; *HIH Casualty Insurance Ltd* v *Chase Manhattan Bank* (2000) *The Times*, 19 September.

ubi jus ibi remedium. Where there is a right there is a remedy. See *Ashby* v *White* (1703) 2 Ld Raym 938.

UKTSSA. UK Transplant Support Services Authority. A Special Health Authority which co-ordinates organ transplantations. Its functions include 'assisting in, and facilitating or promoting, the provision of a service for the transplantation of organs', and 'identifying persons who are potentially suitable recipients for organs, and notifying transplant centres of the availability of organs.' See UKTSSA Regulations 1991 (SI 91/408); Health Services and Public Health Act 1968. *See* ORGAN, HUMAN; TRANSPLANT CENTRE.

ultra vires. Beyond the powers. Term relating generally to the excess of legal powers or authority; specifically, the exercise by a corporation of powers beyond those conferred on it explicitly or implicitly. See *Ashbury Rail Carriage Co* v *Riche* (1875) LR 7 HL 653 (subject matter not included in the memorandum (q.v.) and on which the contract was based was held to be *ultra vires*); *Rolled Steel Products Ltd* v *British Steel Corp* [1986] Ch 246; *R* v *Secretary of State for the Environment ex p Spath Holme Ltd* [2001] 2 WLR 15 (SI 96/6 – maximum fair rents – made under Landlord and Tenant Act 1985, s 31, held *ultra vires* and invalid).

ultra vires rule and companies. The *ultra vires* doctrine (q.v.) was modified extensively in relation to the company and a third person by Cos.A. 1989, s 108, substituting a new s 35 in Cos.A. 1985. The validity of an act done by a company shall not be called into question on the ground of lack of capacity by reason of anything in the company's memorandum (q.v.). Section 35(2)(*a*) preserves the individual shareholder's personal right to seek an injunction (q.v.) to prevent a proposed act contrary to the memorandum. Under Cos.A. 1985, s 3A, inserted by Cos.A. 1989, s 110, a company's memorandum may state a single object (e.g., to carry on business as a general commercial company, with the power to do all such things as are incidental or conducive to the carrying on of its business).

ultra vires rule and public authority. Money paid by a citizen to a public authority in the form of taxes or other levies paid pursuant to an *ultra vires* demand by the authority is prima facie recoverable by the citizen as of right': *per* Lord Goff in *Woolwich Equitable BS* v *IRC* [1993] AC 70. See Taxes Management Act 1870, s 33; Finance Act 1989, s 29; Law Com. No. 227, 1994.

umpire. *See* ARBITRATION.

unascertained goods. Goods defined by description only, e.g., '1000 tonnes of coal'. Property in them does not pass until the goods are ascertained: S.G.A. 1979, s 16. See *Pignatarou* v *Gilroy* [1919] 1 KB 459; S.G. (Amendment) A. 1995, s 1 (unascertained goods forming part of an identified bulk), inserting S.G.A. 1979, s 20A.

unborn person, duty of care to. A doctor is under no legal obligation to a foetus (q.v.) to terminate its life; a child's claim for damages, having 'suffered entry into a life in which her injuries are highly debilitating', was considered contrary to public policy as being a violation of the sanctity of human life: *McKay v Essex Area Health Authority* [1982] QB 1166.

unborn persons, killing of. It is an offence to kill any child capable of being born alive (q.v.). See O.P.A. 1861, s 58; Infant Life Preservation Act 1929, s 1 (for the purposes of that Act evidence that a woman had been pregnant for 28 weeks was prima facie proof that she was pregnant of a child capable of being born alive); Abortion Act 1967. *See* ABORTION; CHILD DESTRUCTION.

uncalled capital. The amount remaining unpaid on the nominal value of a share.

uncertainty, void for. Term applied to a document (e.g., a will) so ambiguous or obscure that it cannot be understood.

unchastity, imputation of. Actionable as slander (q.v.) without proof of special damage. See Slander of Women Act 1891, s 1; *Kerr v Kennedy* [1942] 1 KB 409.

uncollected goods, disposal of. *See* DISPOSAL OF UNCOLLECTED GOODS.

unconscionable transaction. One 'such as no man in his senses and not under delusion could make on the one hand, and no honest and fair man would accept on the other; which are unequitable and unconscientious bargains': *Earl of Chesterfield v Jannsen* (1750) 2 Ves Sen 125. See *National Westminster Bank plc v Morgan* [1985] AC 686. 'Was the bargain fair? ... The test of fairness is, no doubt, whether the restrictions are both reasonably necessary for the protection of the legitimate interests of the promisee and commensurate with the benefits secured to the promisor under the contract. For the purposes of this test, all the provisions of the contract must be taken into consideration': *per* Lord Diplock. '[In considering] the test of unconscionability, I adhere to the concept of want of probity. In my

opinion, mere carelessness, neglect or oversight, which is not wilful or reckless, is not unconscionable': *per* Wylie J in *Equitcorp v Hawkins* [1991] 3 NZLR 700. See *Naeem v Bank of Credit and Commerce* (2000) 150 NLJ 650. *See* CATCHING BARGAIN.

unconstitutional. Not in accordance with a constitution or rules of procedure. 'It is often said that it would be unconstitutional for the United Kingdom Parliament to do certain things, meaning that moral, political and other reasons against doing them are so strong that most people would regard it as highly improper if Parliament did those things. But that does not mean that it is beyond the power of Parliament to do such things. If Parliament chose to do any of them the courts could not hold the Act of Parliament invalid': *per* Lord Reid in *Madzimbamuto v Lardner-Burke* [1969] 1 AC 645.

under-lease. A sub-lease (q.v.). See *Viscount Chelsea v Morris* (1997) 46 EG 159.

undertakers, statutory. *See* STATUTORY UNDERTAKERS.

undertaking. 1. Promise, usually resulting in an obligation. 2. A business or project. 'A body corporate or partnership, or an incorporated association carrying on a trade or business, with or without a view to profit': Cos.A. 1989, s 22. For 'associated undertaking', see Cos.A. 1989, Sch 2.

undervalue, transactions at an. A person enters into a transaction at an undervalue if he makes a gift on terms that provide for him to receive no consideration, or enters into a transaction in consideration of marriage, or enters into a transaction with another for a consideration the value of which is significantly less than the value of the consideration provided by that person: Ins.A. 1986, s 339(3).

underwater archaeology. Responsibility for underwater archeology is transferred to English Heritage: National Heritage Act 2002. Under s 6, 'protected wreck' is defined as any site which comprises the remains of a vessel protected by order under the Protection of Wrecks Act 1973, s 1, and is in, on or under the seabed within the seawards limits of UK territorial waters adjacent to England.

underwriter. One who subscribes his name to a policy of insurance against the sum for which he accepts liability. An underwriter of shares or debentures offers to take up shares and debentures not taken up by the public. A *sub-underwriting agreement* is a contract between an underwriter and another person which, in exchange for a commission, relieves the underwriter of liability. For the power of a company to pay underwriting commission, see Cos.A. 1985, s 97. See I.C.T.A. 1988, s 450; *Ludgate Insurance Ltd* v *Citibank NA* [1998] Lloyd's Rep IR 221.

underwriting contract. 'An agreement entered into before shares are brought before the public that in the event of the public not taking up the whole of them, or the number mentioned in the agreement, the underwriter will, for an agreed commission, take an allotment of such part of the shares as the public has not applied for': *Re Licensed Victuallers' Association* (1889) 42 Ch D 1.

undisclosed principal. *See* PRINCIPAL, UNDISCLOSED.

undivided share. Term relating to property held jointly or in common. See L.P.A. 1925, s 34, amended by Trusts of Land and Appointment of 1996, Sch 2, para 3; S.L.A. 1925, s 36. *See* JOINT TENANCY.

undue influence. 1. Improper pressure on a person resulting in his being at a manifest disadvantage in relation to some transaction. Such a transaction may be set aside by the court. 'The law requires that influence, however natural and however right, shall not be unduly exercised – that is, shall be exercised only in due proportion to the surrounding circumstances and the strength of the person submitting to it. The more powerful influence or the weaker patient alike evokes a stronger application of the safeguard': *Allcard* v *Skinner* (1887) 36 Ch D 145. It must be

shown that the transaction is to the manifest disadvantage of the person subjected to the dominating influence: *National Westminster Bank plc* v *Morgan* [1985] AC 686. See *Barclays Bank plc* v *Boulter* [1999] 1 WLR 1919 (requirement for wife to prove that bank had constructive notice of husband's undue influence); *Barclays Bank plc* v *Coleman* [2000] 1 All ER 385 (manifest disadvantage (i.e. clear and obvious disadvantage) remains a necessary ingredient in a case of undue influence, but the House of Lords had signalled that it might not continue to be an essential ingredient indefinitely: see *CIBC Mortgages plc* v *Pitt* [1994] 1 AC 200). 2. A corrupt practice in relation to an election, under Representation of the People Acts 1983–85. CA held in *Yorkshire Bank plc* v *Tinseley* [2004] EWCA Civ 816 that there where a mortgage is voidable for undue influence, a replacement mortgage from the same lending source will be considered voidable where the replacement mortgage is taken out so that it is conditional on discharging an earlier voidable mortgage, and this will be so even should it be demonstrated that the undue influence is not, in fact, operative at the time of the replacement. The CA held in *Pesticcio* v *Hunt* [2004] EWCA Civ 372, that the court may set aside a transaction as having been procured by undue influence, although the actions of the person who had derived benefit from it cannot be considered as wrongful, and claimant had taken advice from a solicitor at the appropriate time.

unemployment benefit. Benefit paid in respect of any day of unemployment which formed part of a period of interruption of employment: S.S.A. 1975, s 14(1)(*a*). Replaced by jobseeker's allowance (q.v.).

unenforceable contract. A contract (q.v.) which although valid cannot be enforced directly by action because of some technical defect, e.g., lapse of time.

unenforceable trusts. Trusts which cannot be enforced because, e.g., there is no *cestui que trust* to enforce them and they are not charitable. See *Pettingall* v *Pettingall* (1842) 11 LJ Ch 178; *Re Astor's ST* [1952] Ch 534. *See* TRUST.

unfair consumer practices. 'Contraventions of one or more enactments which impose duties, prohibitions or restrictions enforceable by criminal proceedings, whether any such duty, prohibition or restriction is imposed in relation to consumers as such or not and whether the person carrying on the business has or has not been convicted of any offence in respect of such contravention . . . or things done or omitted to be done in the course of that business in breach of contract or in breach of duty . . .': Fair Trading Act 1973, s 34. See Consumer Protection Act 1987; General Product Safety Regulations 1994.

unfair contract terms. Contractual terms, e.g., restricting or excluding liability for causing personal injury, or loss or damage resulting from negligence in manufacture of goods, and considered to be 'unreasonable' in the circumstances which were or ought reasonably to have been known by, or in contemplation of, the parties when the contract was made. See Unfair Contract Terms Act 1977; Occupiers' Liability Act 1984; SIs 94/3159, 99/2083; EU Directive 93/13; *Tudor Grange Holdings Ltd* v *Citibank NA* [1991] 4 All ER 1: *Director General of Fair Trading* v *First National Bank* (2000) *The Times*, 14 March.

unfair contract terms, regulations concerning. See Unfair Terms in Consumer Contracts Regulations 1999 (SI 99/2083), replacing the 1994 Regulations. The Regulations apply in general to unfair terms in a contract between a seller and consumer. 'Seller' (or 'supplier') is one who is acting for the purposes of his trade, business or profession (whether publicly or privately owned); 'consumer' is one who is acting for purposes outside his trade, business or profession. An 'unfair term' is one which has not been individually negotiated and which, contrary to the concept of good faith, creates a significant imbalance in the parties' rights and obligations under the contract, to the consumer's detriment.

unfair dismissal. *See* DISMISSAL, UNFAIR.

unfair dismissal compensation. Under Employment Rights (Increase of Limits) (No. 2) Order 2002 (SI 02/2927) maximum compensatory award in unfair dismissal cases where dismissal takes place after 1 February 2003, is increased from £52,600 to £53,500.

unfair relationships. Such relationships replace 'extrotionate credit bargains' under CCA 1974 ss 137–140 by CCA 2006 ss 19–22 which substitutes a new s 140A. The court may consider such a relationship arises out of the agreement between the creditor and the debtor because of the terms of the agreement, the way in which the agreement is operated by the creditor or any other thing done or not done by or on behalf of the creditor before or after the agreement was made. The court may take into account all matters it thinks relevant relating to the creditor or debtor in making its assessment. The court has a broad range of remedies under a new s 140B to address the unfairness.

unfavourable witness. One who, called by a party to prove a fact in issue (q.v.) or relevant to the issue, fails to prove that fact or proves an opposite fact. *See* HOSTILE WITNESS.

unfitness or incompetence, imputation of. Actionable as slander (q.v.) without proof of special damage. See Defamation Act 1952, s 2.

unfitness to plead. A finding of unfitness to plead requires evidence from two or more registered medical practitioners, including one who is experienced in mental disorder: Criminal Procedure (Insanity) Act 1964, ss 4, 4A, as substituted by Criminal Procedure (Insanity and Unfitness to Plead) Act 1991, s 2. The issue may be raised by defence, prosecution or judge; it must be determined by a jury and, where the accused is found unfit, the trial shall not proceed or proceed further: s 4A; nevertheless, on the basis of evidence adduced, a jury shall determine whether in respect of the counts charged, the accused was responsible for the offences: s 4A(2). See *R* v *Antoine* [2000] 2 All ER 208. For procedure after accused is found unfit to plead, see *R* v *O'Donnell* [1996] 1 Cr App R 286.

unfitness to plead, Court of Appeal and. Where the Court of Appeal substitutes a finding of insanity or unfitness to plead on appeal against conviction, or affirms disability of the accused on appeal against a verdict of not guilty because of insanity (under the Criminal Appeal Act 1968, s 12), the Court may make guardianship or supervision and treatment orders, etc.: see Criminal Appeal Act 1968, s 6, substituted by Criminal Procedure (Insanity and Unfitness to Plead) Act 1991, s 4. Where, having substituted a verdict of acquittal, but of the opinion (following the evidence of two or more medical practitioners) that the appellant should be admitted to a hospital for assessment, an appropriate admission order (see 1991 Act, Sch 1) will be made.

unfitness to plead, powers concerning. Where a special verdict (q.v.) is returned or a jury finds that the accused is under a disability and that he did the act or made the omission charged, the court may make an admission order (q.v.) without a restriction direction, a supervision and treatment order (q.v.), or an order for absolute discharge: Criminal Procedure (Insanity) Act, 1964, s 5, as substituted by Criminal Procedure (Insanity and Unfitness to Plead) Act 1991, s 3. Where the sentence is fixed by law (as in murder), the court must make an admission order with a restriction direction unlimited in time. See *R* v *Maidstone Crown Court ex p Harrow LBC* [2000] 2 WLR 237.

unilateral contract. A contract (q.v.) arising where an offer is made in the form of a promise to pay in return for the performance of an act, so that the performance of the act is taken to imply assent. See, e.g., *Carlill* v *Carbolic Smoke Ball Co* [1893] 1 QB 256; *NZ Shipping Co* v *Satterthwaite & Co* [1975] AC 154.

unilateral discharge. In a contract, the terms of which are carried out by X, but not by Y (the other party), the release of Y from his obligations by X.

unilateral mistake. *See* MISTAKE.

unincorporated bodies. *See* INCORPORATE.

union learning representatives. Trade Union and Labour Relations (Consolidation) Act 1992, s 168A, inserted by Employment Act 2002, s 43 (2), gives the right to take time off during working hours to a member of a recognised union who is a learning representative, so as to analyse learning or training needs, arranging and promoting the value of learning or training.

union, trade. *See* TRADE UNION.

unitary authority. This means (a) the council of a county so far as it is the council for an area for which there are no district councils; (b) the council of any district comprised in an area for which there is no county council. See Charities Act 2006 s 47.

United Kingdom. 'The United Kingdom of Great Britain and Northern Ireland.' It comprises England, Wales and Scotland (which make up Great Britain) plus Northern Ireland. See I.A. 1978, Sch 1; and BNA 1981, s 50(1).

United Nations. International organisation established on 24 October 1945, so as to maintain international peace and security, develop general welfare and relations among nations and encourage international co-operation in the solution of economic, social and humanitarian problems.

unities, four. *See* JOINT TENANCY.

unit trust schemes, authorised. Approved schemes authorised by FSA (q.v.), enabling investors to purchase a spread of interests in a number of companies by membership of a collective investment scheme (q.v.), allowing property to be held in trust for participants. See F.S.A. 1986, s 75(8); F.S.M.A. 2000, ss 140, 242. For revocation of authorisation, see 2000 Act, s 254; for investigation, see s 284.

unity of possession. Holding of one estate in undivided shares by two or more persons, or possession by one person of two or more rights based on separate titles.

universal agent. *See* AGENT, UNIVERSAL.

university. Includes a university college and any college, or institution in the nature of a college, in a university: Further and Higher Education Act 1992, s 90(3). For power of institutions to award degrees, see 1992 Act, s 76. For use of 'university' in title of an institution, see s 77; Teaching and Higher Education Act 1998, ss 39, 40.

unjust enrichment. The unjust obtaining of money benefits at the expense of the claimant: see *Lipkin Gorman v Karpnale Ltd* [1991] AC 548. See *Barclays Bank plc v Hammersmith and Fulham LBC* (1991) *The Times*, 27 November. For principles of restitution, see *Boissevain v Weil* [1950] AC 327. See *Brennan v Brighton BC* [1997] EGCS 76; *Grantham Cricket Club (No. 3) v Customs and Excise Commissioners* [1998] BVC 2272; *Banque Financière v Parc Ltd* [1998] 2 WLR 475. *See* QUASI-CONTRACTS; RESTITUTION.

unlawful. Contrary to law. 'In defining a criminal offence the word "unlawful" is surely tautologous and can add nothing to its essential ingredients': *per* Hodgson J in *Albert v Lavin* [1981] 1 All ER 628.

unlawfully at large. Term applied to one who has escaped from lawful arrest, prison, detention centre, etc. See Prison Act 1952, s 49(2) (as modified by C.J.A. 1982, C.D.A. 1998, Sch 8, para 7); M.H.A. 1983, s 50(4); P.&C.E.A. 1984, s 17(1); Prisoners (Return to Custody) Act 1995; Crime (Sentences) Act 1997, Sch 4, para 12.

unlawful sexual intercourse. *See* SEXUAL INTERCOURSE, UNLAWFUL.

unlawful trusts. Trusts (q.v.) which are liable to be declared void, e.g., as offending the rule against perpetuities (q.v.) or as preventing the carrying out of parental duties (see *Re Sandbrook* [1912] 2 Ch 471) or in restraint of marriage (see *Leong v Chye* [1955] AC 648).

unlawful wounding. It is an offence to unlawfully and maliciously wound a person with intent to do grievous bodily harm: O.P.A. 1861, s 18. See also s 20. Provocation is no defence: *R v Cunningham* [1959] 1 QB 288; *R v Derby Magistrates' Court ex p DPP* (1999) *The Times*, 17 August (victim's head was struck against a glass door – the

use of the door did not amount to the use of a weapon, an aggravating factor in sentencing under s 20). *See* WOUNDING; WOUNDING WITH INTENT.

unless order. Order by the court, stating, e.g., that 'unless an order is complied with', certain sanctions may follow. See, for appropriate penal notice, PD 40B, para 9.1. See *Beeforth v Beeforth* (1998) *The Times*, 17 September (need for proportionality in imposing sanction); *OPS Consultants Ltd v Kruger Tissue Ltd* [1999] BLR 366. For drafting order, see PD 40B, para 8.2.

unlimited company. Private company (q.v.) in which the liability of members is not limited. It need not have a share capital; it must have articles (q.v.). See Cos.A. 1985, ss 1, 24(4). *See* LIMITED COMPANY.

unliquidated damages. *See* DAMAGES.

unopposed proceedings. Proceedings where a person who is entitled to oppose has been given the opportunity of doing so and has not done so.

unpaid seller. A seller in circumstances in which any portion of the price remains unpaid or where a negotiable instrument (q.v.) received as conditional payment has been dishonoured.

unpaid seller's rights. Even though the property in goods has passed to the buyer, the unpaid seller has a lien (q.v.) for the price, a right of stoppage in transitu (q.v.) if the buyer is insolvent and a right of resale (e.g., where the goods are of a perishable nature: S.G.A. 1979, s 39). For loss of lien, see s 43.

unread terms. In general, in the absence of fraud or misrepresentation (q.v.), a person who has not read the contents of a document or has chosen that they remain unread may be bound by his signature to that document.

unreasonable. 'No one can properly be labelled as unreasonable unless he is not only wrong but unreasonably wrong, so wrong that no reasonable person could sensibly take that view': *per* Lord Denning in *Secretary of State for Education and Science v Tameside Metropolitan BC* [1976] 3 All ER 665.

unreasonable conduct. Under Mat.C.A. 1973, s 1(2)(*b*), conduct by respondent of such a type that the petitioner cannot reasonably be expected to live with respondent. Examples: physical violence, persistent drunkenness. It may justify the conclusion that the marriage has broken down irretrievably: *Stringfellow* v *Stringfellow* [1976] 1 WLR 645. See *Bergin* v *Bergin* [1983] 1 WLR 279. See F.L.A. 1996, s 5 (not yet in force). *See* BREAKDOWN OF MARRIAGE.

unregistered company. A company not registered under the provisions of Companies Acts. See Cos.A. 1985, ss 665, 718. For winding-up, see s 666.

unregistered land. Land, title to which has not been registered under L.R.A. 1925–86 and Land Registration Rules 1925. *See* LAND REGISTRATION.

unreported cases. Transcripts of cases that do not appear in the published law reports. For leave to cite unreported cases, see *Practice Note* [1996] 1 WLR 854. *See* CITATION; LAW REPORTS.

unrestricted-use credit. Any form of credit which is not restricted-use credit (q.v.): C.C.A. 1974, s 11. Example: a bank overdraft. See *National Westminster Bank* v *Story* [1999] CCLR 70.

unsecured creditor. *See* CREDITOR.

unsightly land. If it appears to the local planning authority that the amenity of a part of their area, or of an adjoining area, is adversely affected by the condition of land in their area, they may serve notice on the owner or occupier ordering steps to be taken for the remedying of that condition of land: T.C.P.A. 1990, s 215.

unsigned form, validity of. In a case in which a form requiring details concerning a driver's identity where a vehicle has been involved in a traffic offence, it is not sufficient for the driver's name to be inserted without his actual signature: *Mawdesley* v *Chief Constable of Cheshire Constabulary* (2003) *The Times*, 11 September.

unsolicited goods. Goods sent to persons who had not asked for them. Under Unsolicited Goods and Services

Act 1971, as amended under SI 00/2334, such goods will become the property of the recipient immediately they have been received. It is an offence to demand payment for unsolicited goods where the person making the demand has no cause to believe there is a right to payment. See also Unsolicited Goods and Services (Amendment) Act 1975.

unsound mind, persons of. Referred to, since M.H.A. 1959, as persons suffering from mental disorder (q.v.). 'It is impossible to distinguish between unsoundness of mind and insanity': *per* Merriman P in *Smith* v *Smith* [1940] P 179.

unsworn evidence. *See* EVIDENCE, UNSWORN.

unvalued policy. Policy of insurance (q.v.) where the value of the subject matter is left to be ascertained later, subject to the limit of the amount insured.

urban development areas. Areas designated by the Secretary of State with the object of their regeneration through, e.g., bringing land and buildings into effective use, creating an attractive environment. See L.G.P.L.A. 1980, ss 134–143. (The London Docklands and Merseyside have been designated.) See New Towns and Urban Development Corporations Act 1985; T.C.P.A. 1990, s 7.

urine test. A laboratory test carried out on the urine of a person arrested under Road Traffic Act 1972. Used as an alternative to breath test (q.v.). See *DPP* v *Baldwin* (2000) 164 JP 606.

usage. A practice which has continued over a long period. '"Usage" as a practice which the court will recognise is a mixed question of fact and law. For the practice to amount to such a recognised usage it must be certain, in the sense that the practice is clearly established; it must be notorious, in the sense that it is so well known in the market in which it is alleged to exist that those who conduct business in that market contract with usage as an implied term; and it must be reasonable. The burden lies on those alleging usage to establish it': *per* Ungoed-Thomas J in *Cunliffe-Owen* v *Teather* [1967] 3 All ER 561. 'Usage is only admissible to explain what is doubtful, never to contradict what is plain': *per* Lord Lyndhurst in *Blackett* v *Royal Exchange Assurance Corp* (1832) 3 C & J 244.

use. Term which may have originated in *opus* (*X tenet ad opus Y* – X holds for the benefit of Y). Example: Tenant, A, transferred land by common-law conveyance to the transferee, B, who undertook to hold it 'to the use of' (i.e., on behalf of) C. A was known as the *feoffor*, B was the *feoffee to uses* (i.e., party to whom feoffment of land had been made), C was *cestui que use* (shortened version of *cestui à que use le feoffment fuit fait* – to whom feoffment had been made). Before Statute of Uses 1535 (repealed by L.P.A. 1925, Sch 7), B would have had the legal estate, C would have had the equitable estate. Following the Statute, C had the legal estate.

use and occupation. A claim which exists where one has used and occupied another's lands with his permission, but in the absence of a lease (q.v.) or agreement for a lease.

use classes. *See* DEVELOPMENT.

user. 1. Use or enjoyment of a right. See, e.g., Landlord and Tenant Act 1954, s 53. 2. One who makes use of property or services. See *Trasimex Holdings* v *Addax BV* [1997] 1 Lloyd's Rep 610.

user as of right. *See* NEC VI, NEC CLAM, NEC PRECARIO.

user, continuous and apparent. Phrase used, in relation to implied grant of quasi-easements (q.v.), by Thesiger LJ in *Wheeldon* v *Burrows* (1879) 12 Ch D 31, to express a limiting condition of implication. 'Continuous' has been held to refer to enjoyment of user over a considerable period of time; 'apparent' refers to user which may be discovered 'on careful inspection by a person ordinarily conversant with the subject': *Pyer* v *Carter* (1857) 1 H & N 916; *Hansford* v *Jago* [1921] 1 Ch 322.

user, evidence of. Evidence of the way in which parties to a document have acted before or after its execution. May be received by the court: to show alterations by consent in a partnership deed; to remove uncertainty in a patent or latent ambiguity (q.v.); where there has been a change in the meaning of words used in an ancient document (see *NE Rlwy* v *Lord Hastings* [1900] AC 260). *See* EVIDENCE.

use upon a use. Conveyance 'to X and his heirs to the use of Y and his heirs to the use of Z and his heirs'. Void under *Tyrrel's Case* (1557) 2 Dy 115a, so that the entire legal and equitable interest was given to Y. Later, the second use was enforced in equity. See *Sambach* v *Dalston* (under *Morris* v *Darston* (1635) Nels 30). *See* USE.

usque ad medium filum aquae (viae). As far as the middle of the stream (or road). Refers to boundaries which are rivers or roads. In the absence of evidence to the contrary, each owner is presumed to own the river or road up to an imaginary line drawn through the centre of the river or road.

usucapion. Mode of acquiring title by uninterrupted possession. *See* PRESCRIPTION.

usurpation. Unauthorised or illegal assumption of rights, e.g., by dispossession.

usury. An exorbitant or illegal amount or rate of interest. Statutes relating to usury were largely repealed in 1854. See now C.C.A. 1974, ss 137–140.

uti possidetis. As you possess. Doctrine of international law, whereby, e.g., parties to a treaty ending war retain possession of what they have when hostilities cease. See *Burkina Faso* v *Mali* (1996) ICJ Rep 554; *El Salvador* v *Honduras* (1992) *The Times*, 8 October.

utmost good faith. *See* UBERRIMAE FIDEI.

V

v. Versus (q.v.).

vacant possession. Term applied to premises sold or offered for sale and not subject to a lease. The vendor must give vacant possession on completion, subject to an express agreement to the contrary. Means more than 'empty and unoccupied; property conveyed must be capable of occupation by a purchaser': *Topfell* v *Galley Properties* [1979] 1 WLR 446. See *Standard Conditions of Sale*, condition 5.

vacation of register. The removal by court order of an entry from, e.g., the registers in the Land Registry: see L.C.A. 1972, s 1(6); *Northern Developments* v *UDT Securities* [1976] 1 WLR 1230. (To 'vacate' is to empty, cancel, remove.) *See* LAND CHARGES, REGISTER OF.

vacations. See Court of Appeal Practice Direction, para 11.2. In the High Court one or more judges of each Division will sit on such days as the senior judge of that Division may direct, to hear cases, claims, matters or applications such as require to be immediately or promptly heard: PD 39B, para 3.1(1). There is no distinction between term time and vacation so far as business before Chancery Masters is concerned: PD 39B, para 3.4.

vagabonds. *See* ROGUES AND VAGABONDS.

vagrant. One who, under the Vagrancy Act 1824, as amended, was found to be a rogue or vagabond, or an idle or disorderly person. See C.J.A. 1982, s 70; *Gapper* v *Chief Constable of Avon* [2000] QB 29.

valuable consideration. *See* GOOD CONSIDERATION.

valuation. The act of ascertaining, or estimating, the value or price of some object. See S.G.A. 1979, s 9 (sale of goods at a price to be fixed by valuation);

Swingcastle Ltd v *Alastair Gibson* [1991] 2 WLR 1091 (damages for negligent valuation); *Australia Asset Corporation* v *Eagle Star Insurance Co* [1996] 3 WLR 87.

value. Generally, valuable consideration, as in 'purchaser for value' (q.v.).

value-added tax. Tax introduced into the UK in 1973, under Finance Act 1972. A broad, indirect tax falling on goods and services, with specified exemptions, levied at every stage of production and distribution on the value added at every point of sale. The rate is fixed in the annual Finance Acts. Local VAT tribunals hear disputes and appeal lies, on points of law only, to the High Court (q.v.). See Value Added Tax Acts 1983, 1994; Finance Acts 1988, Part II; 1989, chap II; 1992, chap II; 1997, Part III. The standard rate is currently 17.5 per cent; the lower rate (applied, e.g., to fuel and power) is 5 per cent; the registration threshold after 31 March 2000 is £52,000. See *R* v *Customs and Excise ex p F and I Services* (2000) *The Times*, 26 April (Customs and Excise might owe duty of care concerning VAT advice). *See* ZERO RATING.

value received. Phrase referring to acceptance for value of a bill of exchange (q.v.).

vandalism. Malicious, mindless injury to, or destruction of, property. See *Smith* v *Littlewoods Ltd* [1987] AC 241.

variation of contract. *See* CONTRACT, VARIATION OF.

variation of trust. Under Variation of Trusts Act 1958, the court may, if it thinks fit, approve any arrangement varying a trust, on behalf of persons unborn, persons having an interest in the trust but who are incapable of assenting, persons who may become entitled to an interest in the trust at some future date. 'It is the agreement which has to be approved, not just the limited interest of the person on whose behalf the court's duty is to consider it'. See *Re Steed's WT* [1960] Ch 407; Tr.A. 1925, ss 53, 57(1); S.L.A. 1925, s 64(1); Charities Act 1985; *Goulding* v *James* [1997] 2 All ER 239. See TRUST.

VAT. Value-added tax (q.v.).

VAT, postage and. In *Commissioners of Customs and Excise* v *Plantiflor Ltd* (2002) *The Times*, 31 July, the HL held that, in relation to the business dealings of a mail order firm, there was a liability for output VAT on the postage element of the firm's 'postage and packing' charge to its customers. See VAT Act 1994, s 19 (2); Council Directive 77/338 EEC, art 11; *Commissioners of Customs and Excise* v *BT plc* [1999] 1 WLR 1376.

VC. Vice-Chancellor (q.v.).

vehicle. That which can be, or is, used for the carriage of persons or things. For tests of vehicles, see Road Traffic Act 1988, ss 45–47, 67, as amended by Road Traffic (Vehicle Testing) Act 1999. For offence of keeping an unlicensed vehicle, see Vehicle Excise and Registration Act 1994, s 29. A 'private hired vehicle' is one constructed or adapted to seat fewer than nine passengers, made available with a driver to the public for hire, other than a licensed taxi or public service vehicle: Private Hire Vehicles (London) Act 1998, s 1(1).

vehicle, goods. A motor vehicle constructed or adapted for use for the carriage of goods, or a trailer so constructed or adapted: Goods Vehicles (Licensing of Operators) Act 1995, s 58(1). 'Goods' include goods or burden of any description. See *National Trailer and Towing Association* v *DPP* (1997) *The Times*, 11 December.

vehicle, immobilisation of parked. A constable may fix an immobilisation device to an illegally parked vehicle and affix a notice specifying the steps to be taken to secure its release: Road Traffic Regulation Act 1984, s 104, amended by Road Traffic Act 1991, Sch 4. See *Lloyd*

v *DPP* [1992] 1 All ER 982 (motorist who parked his vehicle in a private car park, without permission, aware of risk of wheel clamping, had no legal excuse to damage or destroy the clamp).

vehicle, interference with. Offence, under Criminal Attempts Act 1981, s 9, of interfering with a motor vehicle or trailer or with anything carried therein with the intention of theft of the vehicle or trailer or part of it, or its contents or taking and driving away without the consent of the owner. A constable may arrest without warrant anyone who is or whom he with reasonable cause suspects to be guilty of an offence under s 9: s 9(4). See *C (A Minor)* v *DPP* [1995] 2 WLR 383.

vehicle, public services. A motor vehicle (other than a tramcar) which is adapted to carry more than eight passengers, is used for carrying passengers for hire or reward; or being a vehicle not so adapted, is used for carrying passengers for hire or reward; or being a vehicle not so adapted, is used for carrying passengers for hire or reward at separate fares in the course of a business of carrying passengers: Public Passenger Vehicle Act 1981, s 1(1).

vehicle registration plates, counterfeit. A person who sells a counterfeit registration plate is guilty of an offence. A person who supplies plates to one whose business involves the sale of such plates is guilty of an offence: V.(C.)A. 2001 ss 28, 29.

vehicle-taking, aggravated. It is an offence under Th.A. 1968, s 12A, inserted by Aggravated Vehicle-Taking Act 1992, s 1, for a person to commit an offence under the 1968 Act, s 12(1) and it is established that before recovery of the vehicle it was driven dangerously or was damaged or was driven in a way which led to personal injury or damage to other property. For defences, see 1968 Act, s 12A(3). See *R* v *Hall* [1997] 1 Cr App R (S) 62; *R* v *Frastick* [1998] 1 Cr App R (S) 257. *See* DRIVING, DANGEROUS; JOY RIDING; MOTOR VEHICLE, TAKING OF.

vehicle under the owner's control. Means a vehicle which is being driven by the owner or a servant of the owner in the course of his employment or is otherwise subject to the control of the owner: Road Traffic Act 1988, s 161(1).

veil, lifting the. *See* LIFTING THE CORPORATE VEIL.

vendee. A buyer (of goods, or, more usually, land).

vendor. A seller (usually, of land).

vendor and purchaser summons. Procedure, introduced by Vendor and Purchaser Act 1874, now governed by L.P.A. 1925, s 49(1), whereby parties to a contract for the sale of land who disagree on a matter which prevents completion of contract, e.g., construction of terms, may apply to a judge in chambers for an order. The court may grant an order and any consequential reliefs, e.g., the return of any deposit. See, e.g., *Faraqui* v *English Real Estate Ltd* [1979] 1 WLR 963; *Safehaven Investments* v *Springbok Ltd* (1996) 71 P & CR 59.

vendor's duty. In *Englewood Properties Ltd* v *Patel and Another* [2005] *The Times*, 9 March it was held that after contract, and until completion the vendor was a trustee for the purchaser and equity placed obligations on the vendor to keep reasonable care to preserve the property in question.

vendor's lien. *See* VENDOR'S RIGHTS.

vendor's rights. Pending the completion of the sale of land, the vendor possesses an equitable lien (q.v.) on the property for the full amount of the purchase money, and that lien arises at the date of the contract. He has a right to remain in possession until the purchase price is paid, and to rents and profits until the time fixed for completion. See *Re Birmingham* [1959] Ch 523; L.C.A. 1972, s 2(4)(*iii*).

venereal disease. Disease (e.g., syphilis, gonorrhea) acquired as the result of sexual intercourse. It may be prima facie evidence of adultery (q.v.), the onus being on the respondent (q.v.) to rebut the presumption of its contraction as a result of intercourse with a person other than the petitioner: *Anthony* v *Anthony* (1919) 35 TLR 559. A marriage may be voidable on the grounds that at the time of the

marriage the respondent was suffering from a venereal disease in a communicable form: Mat.C.A. 1973, s 12(*e*).

venia aetatis. Privilege of age. Privilege allowed an infant (q.v.) whereby he may act in some circumstances as though of full age.

venire de novo. Order directing a new trial after a mistrial involving a fundamental irregularity (e.g., as where the judge was not qualified to act in the proceedings). The first trial is regarded as a nullity. See *R v Rose* [1982] AC 822; *R v Tarrant* [1998] Crim LR 342; *Mario v Home Secretary* [1998] Imm AR 28. *See* TRIAL, NEW.

venue. Place where a case is to be tried. (See, e.g., CPR, Sch 2; CCR, O 4, r 3: proceedings for the recovery of land or foreclosure or redemption of a mortgage may be commenced only in the court for the district in which the land is situated.) Originally it signified 'a place next to that where any thing that comes to be tried is supposed to be done': *Termes de la Ley*.

verba chartarum fortius accipiuntur contra proferentem. The words of deeds should be interpreted most strongly against the person who uses them [provided that this works no wrong]. See *GA Estates* v *Caviapen Trustees Ltd* (1991) *The Times*, 22 October; *Tan Wing Chuen* v *Bank of Credit and Commerce* [1996] 2 BCLC 69.

verbatim. Word for word; exactly; precisely.

verdict. (*Vere dictum* = truly said.) Answer of a jury to a question committed to their examination and for their decision. Verdict is usually announced by the *foreman* (chosen by jury members to speak for them). The judge may not enquire into proceedings whereby the verdict was reached. Where the jury fail to agree they will be discharged and a new jury called to try the case. See *R v Watson* [1988] 1 All ER 897; *R v Buono* (1992) 95 Cr App R 338. If there is yet another disagreement it is usual for the prosecution not to offer evidence in a third trial and the accused is then acquitted. See C.J.A. 1967; Juries Act 1974, s 17; *R v Andrews* (1986) 82 Cr App R 148; *R v Diedrich* [1997] 1 Cr App R 361 (appeal on inconsistency of verdict); *R v Bills* [1995] (1995) *The Times*, 1 March (attempt by jury to change verdict after hearing defendant's record).

verdict, alternative. Verdict under C.L.A. 1967, s 6(3), whereby a jury is enabled to return a verdict of not guilty of the offence specifically charged in the indictment, but guilty of another offence, provided that the allegations in the indictment amount to or include (expressly or by implication) an allegation of another offence. Where defendant is convicted of an offence and the jury, on that same indictment, could have found him guilty of another offence, the court may substitute a verdict of guilty of that other offence and pass sentence for it: Criminal Appeal Act 1968, s 3(1). See, e.g., *R v Maxwell* [1990] 1 All ER 801; *R v Peterson* [1997] Crim LR 339; *R v Weekes* [1999] 2 Cr App R 520.

verdict, finality of. A jury's verdict is considered complete as soon as it is announced. Evidence to show what has occurred in the jury room will not be considered by the Court of Appeal (q.v.): *R v Roads* [1967] 2 QB 108; *R v Froude* [1990] Crim LR 197 (judge was entitled to accept a verdict which the foreman of the jury had announced incorrectly, but rectified immediately). See also Contempt of Court Act 1981, s 8(1).

verdict, majority. Introduced under C.J.A. 1967. The verdict need not be unanimous if, in a case where there are not less than 11 jurors, ten of them agree on the verdict, or in a case where there are ten jurors, nine of them agree on the verdict. A majority verdict is not accepted unless it appears to the court that the jury have had not less than two hours for deliberation (or longer where considered appropriate) and unless the foreman states the numbers agreeing and disagreeing with the verdict: Juries Act 1974, s 17. In civil cases majority verdicts were introduced by the Courts Act 1971, s 39 (now repealed and replaced by Juries Act 1974, s 17). For the general directions required as to unanimity, before a majority verdict is contemplated, see *R v Watson* (1988)

The Times, 10 March. See *R v Millward* [1999] 1 Cr App R 61.

verdict, open. *See* OPEN VERDICT.

verdict, perverse. *See* PERVERSE VERDICT.

verdict, special. *See* SPECIAL VERDICT.

versus. Against. Abbreviated to 'v', as in *R v Jones* ('v' is read as 'against' in criminal cases, and as 'and' in civil cases).

vessel. A ship or boat, rig, raft or floating platform, seaplane, hovercraft or any other amphibious vehicle: Dangerous Vessels Act 1985, s 7. A 'fishing vessel' is one which is used in connection with sea fishing other than a vessel used for fishing other than for profit: Merchant Shipping Act 1988, s 12. See *Whistler International Ltd v Kawasaki Kisen Ltd* [1998] 3 WLR 184 (master's discretion to decide route of vessel).

vest. 1. To put a person in possession of land. 2. To give legal rights to a person. See *Richardson v Robertson* (1826) 6 LT 75.

vested in interest. Term indicating a present right to future enjoyment, e.g., 'to X for life, remainder to Y for life, remainder to Z in fee simple should he survive Y'. Y's interest is said to be 'vested in interest'. It is, in effect, a 'vested remainder'. See *Barclays Trust Co v McDougall* (2000) *The Times*, 3 August (conversion of vested into contingent interest).

vested in possession. Term indicating an interest which gives a right of present enjoyment, e.g., 'to X for life, remainder to Y for life . . .' X's interest is vested in possession.

vested remainder. *See* VESTED IN INTEREST.

vested rights. Rights secured to their possessor. 'The well-established presumption is that the legislature does not intend to limit vested rights further than clearly appears from the enactment': *Metropolitan Film Studios v Twickenham Film Studios* [1962] 3 All ER 508.

vesting assent. An assent in writing, but not under seal, whereby a personal representative (q.v.) vests settled land in the person entitled as tenant for life (q.v.) or statutory owner. See S.L.A. 1925, ss 8,

117(1)(*xxx*), as amended. *See* SETTLED LAND.

vesting, conditions of. A remainder (q.v.) is vested where the person entitled is ascertained and it is ready to take effect in possession at once. Where conditions are not satisfied the remainder is contingent only.

vesting declaration. Declaration under Tr.A. 1925 during the appointment of new trustees (q.v.), that the property is to vest in the trustees. In the case of an appointment of new trustees by deed executed after 1925, such a declaration is implied in the absence of a statement to the contrary. Trust property (q.v.) cannot be transferred by vesting declaration where, e.g., it consists of land held by trustees by way of a mortgage (q.v.) for securing trust property.

vesting deed. 'Every settlement of a legal estate in land *inter vivos* shall, save as in this Act otherwise provided, be effected by two deeds, namely, a vesting deed and a trust instrument and if effected in any other way shall not operate to transfer or create a legal estate': S.L.A. 1925, s 4(1). A vesting deed must contain, under s 5(1): a description of settled land, the names of trustees of settlement, any additional powers conferred by the trust instrument, the name of any person entitled under trust instrument to appoint new trustees, and a statement that the settled land is vested in the person(s) to whom it is conveyed or in whom it is declared to be vested upon trusts from time to time affecting the settled land. It is known as the 'principal vesting deed'.

vesting deed, subsidiary. When other land is brought into a settlement (q.v.) which is in existence, a subsidiary vesting deed is needed, under S.L.A. 1925, s 10. It contains: particulars of principal vesting instrument, names of trustees of settlement and of those entitled to appoint new trustees, and a statement that the land conveyed is to be held subject to the same trusts as the land comprised in the principal vesting instrument.

vesting order. A court order having the effect of vesting, conveying or creating a

legal estate (q.v.) as if the legal estate owner had executed a conveyance. See L.P.A. 1925, s 9; Tr.A. 1925, ss 44–56; S.L.A. 1925, ss 12, 16; A.E.A. 1925, s 38; Trusts of Land and Appointment of Trustees Act 1996, Sch 3, para 12.

veto. 1. Power to prohibit or refuse. 2. Refusal to assent to a Parliamentary Bill. 3. Power of, e.g., any permanent members of the Security Council of the United Nations (q.v.) to refuse to agree to a proposed course of action.

vetting. Thorough, formal investigation of a person's activities and antecedents prior to grant of 'security clearance' allowing employment in certain enterprises and government employment. See, e.g., Cmnd 8540 (May 1982) (criteria for clearance include references to 'obvious indications of untrustworthiness', such as involvement with seditious activities; membership of or sympathy with subversive organisations; character defects); *Vetting Guidelines* (HC Deb vol 177, 24 July 1990); Security Service Act 1989, s 2(3); *R* v *Director of GCHQ, ex p Hodges* (1988) *The Times*, 26 July. *See* JURY VETTING; NATIONAL SECURITY.

vexatious litigant. CA held in *R (Mahajan)* v *Central London County Court* (2004) *The Times*, 13 July, that it is empowered when it has made a general civil restraint order, to prevent litigant against whom the order was made from instituting proceedings in the county court and, additionally, the High Court and Court of Appeal.

vexatious litigant, injunction. The court's supervisory role includes regulation of the mode in which the court process is utilised; hence the court is empowered to prevent litigants wasting the time of court staff by obsessively attempting litigation which has no merit. An injunction was granted in *AG* v *Ebert* [2002] 2 All ER 789, prohibiting a person from entering any part of the Royal Courts of Justice except in relation to specified circumstances.

vexatious proceeding. A proceeding which has little or no basis in law; the effect of which (whatever its intention) is to subject defendant to inconvenience, harassment and expense out of all proportion to any likely gain to the claimant; which involves an abuse of the court's process, i.e., using that process for a purpose or in a manner significantly different from its ordinary and proper use: *per* Lord Bingham in *A-G v Barker* (2000) *The Times*, 7 March. For restriction of vexatious prosecutions, see S.C.A. 1981, s 42, amended by Prosecution of Offenders Act 1985, s 24. See also PD 3, para 7.

vicarious. Performed by one person as a substitute for, or for the benefit of, another.

vicarious immunity. *See* IMMUNITY, VICARIOUS.

vicarious liability. *See* LIABILITY, VICARIOUS.

vicarious performance of contract. Performance of a contract (q.v.) based on the delegation of work to a third person. Vicarious performance does not release the contracting party; obligations 'cannot be shifted off the shoulders of a contractor or on to those of another without the consent of the contractee': *Tolhurst v Associated Portland Cement Manufacturers* [1902] 2 KB 660. Vicarious performance of a personal contract is generally no performance if personal performance is of the essence of the contract: *Davies v Collins* [1945] 1 All ER 247.

vicarious responsibility. *See* LIABILITY, VICARIOUS.

Vice-Chancellor. Judge, first appointed in 1813 to assist the Lord Chancellor in the Court of Chancery (q.v.). They were transferred to the High Court in 1873 as judges of the Chancery Division. A Vice-Chancellor is appointed, with responsibility to the Lord Chancellor, for the organisation and management of Chancery Division business. See S.C.A. 1981, s 10.

vice, inherent. *See* INHERENT VICE.

vicious propensity. Tendency of animals to act so as to endanger persons or property. See, e.g., Animals Act 1971, s 2(2); Dangerous Dogs Act 1991; *Wallace v Newton* [1982] 1 WLR 375; *Jaundrill v Gillett* (1996) *The Times*, 30 January.

victim impact statement. Statement by victim or friend or relative, made before sentence is pronounced. 'An increasingly common feature of the sentencing process': *per* Garland J in *R v Perks* (2000) *The Times*, 5 May, stating guidelines to be followed: a sentencer must not make assumptions unsupported by evidence, concerning effects of offence on victim; court should take into account particularly damaging or distressing effects upon victim; evidence of effects on victim must follow proper form (see C.D.A. 1967, s 9; *R v Hobstaff* (1993) 14 Cr App R (S) 605); opinions of victim and relatives concerning appropriate level of sentence should not be taken into account. *See* FORGIVENESS OF VICTIM.

victimisation. 1. Subjection of a person to some exploitation, crime or tort. 2. The unwarranted singling out of a person or group for subjection to unfair treatment: see, e.g., *TNT Express Ltd v Brown* (2000) *The Times*, 18 April. *See* DISCRIMINATION, RACIAL.

victim, personal statement by. Lord Woolf LCJ has issued a practice statement [2001] All ER (D) 216 (1 October)) concerning personal statements by victims in relation to sentencing: statement and supporting evidence should be taken into account prior to passing sentence; evidence of effects of offence should be in proper form and served on defendant prior to sentencing; opinions of victim concerning sentence are not relevant.

victim's distress, weight to be given to. CA held in *R v Romeo* (2003) *The Times*, 2 October, that, in a case involving indecent assault, the weight which should be given to the distress caused to the victim would vary in many ways. A jury should be warned by the judge that they must be aware of the possibility of the distress having been feigned, and that this must be considered carefully in appropriate cases.

video conference link. In *Polonski v Conde-Nast Publications* (2005) *The Times*, 11 February, the HL held that where claimant was not willing to come to UK so as to give evidence in a libel action, given his fear of extradition to USA, permission will be granted to offer evidence by video conference link.

video recording. Any disc or magnetic tape containing information by the use of which the whole or part of a video work (i.e., a series of visual images produced electronically and shown as a moving picture) may be produced: Video Recordings Act 1984, s 1. (The term 'video recording' may include the accompanying sound-track: Y.J.C.E.A. 1999, s 63(1).) It is an offence to supply a video recording for which no classification certificate has been issued unless the supply is exempted under the Act: s 9. For video recordings as evidence, see *R v Z* [1990] 2 All ER 971. See C.J.A. 1988, s 162. For use of video recordings of testimony, see Y.J.C.E.A. 1999, s 27(1); PD 23, para 7 (video conferencing in relation to a hearing). See Video Recordings Act 1993. For use of video camera amounting to an offence under P.O.A. 1986, s 5, see *Vigon v DPP* [1998] Crim LR 289.

video recording, covert, use of. The European Court of Human Rights held, in *Perry v UK* (Application No. 63737/00) (2003) *The Times*, 26 August, that covert videotaping by the police, which, breached the Codes of Practice based upon the Police and Criminal Evidence Act 1984, s 66, constituted an unjustified interference with the private life of the applicant. See European Convention, art 8.

vi et armis. With force and arms. Words used to describe trespass resulting from the use of actual violence.

view. An inspection by a judge of some object or place outside the court where the characteristics of the object or place constitute facts from which facts in issue (q.v.) may be inferred. *See* INSPECTION BY JUDGE.

vigilantibus non dormientibus jura subveniunt. The laws give help to those who are watchful, not to those who sleep. Principle of the doctrine of laches (q.v.).

village. Self-contained, relatively small community of dwelling houses, shops, etc., with defined boundaries. See *R v*

Oxfordshire CC ex p Sunningwell Parish Council [1999] 3 WLR 160 (village green user 'as of right' within Commons Registration Act 1965, s 22); C.R.W.A. 2000, s 28.

vindictive damages. *See* DAMAGES.

violence. Defined, for purposes of P.O.A. 1986, as any violent conduct so that it includes violent conduct towards property as well as towards persons, and it is not restricted to conduct causing or intended to cause injury or damage, but includes any other violent conduct (e.g., throwing at or towards a person a missile of a kind capable of causing injury which does not hit or falls short): s 8. See *Atkin v DPP* [1989] Crim LR 581. For 'violent offence', see P.C.C.(S.)A. 2000, s 161(3): an offence which leads, or is intended or likely to lead to a person's death or to physical injury to a person and includes an offence which is required to be charged as arson (q.v.) (whether or not it would otherwise fall within this definition). For 'sexual or violent offender', see C.J.C.S.A. 2000, s 68.

violence, domestic. *See* DOMESTIC VIOLENCE.

violence for securing entry. *See* ENTRY, VIOLENCE FOR SECURING.

violent disorder. *See* DISORDER, VIOLENT.

virtute officii. By virtue of office.

visa. Endorsement on a passport indicating that it has been examined and found correct. Usually made by a foreign authority for the purpose of allowing entry.

visitor. 1. A person appointed to visit other persons and inspect institutions. See, e.g., Education Reform Act 1988, s 206; *Pearce v University of Aston* [1991] 2 All ER 461. See also S.C.A. 1981, s 44; M.H.A. 1983, s 103. 2. In relation to premises, a visitor is one who would at common law have been treated as an invitee (q.v.) or licensee (q.v.): see Occupiers' Liability Acts 1957, 1984; *Greenhalgh v British Railways Board* [1969] 2 QB 286. *See* CARE, COMMON DUTY TOWARDS VISITORS; PRISON.

vis major. Greater force; irresistible force, e.g., a storm which, because it cannot be prevented, may relieve parties to a contract from some obligations. Often used synonymously with 'Act of God' (q.v.).

vocation. One's regular occupation. The way in which a person passes his life': *per* Denman J in *Partridge* v *Mallandaine* (1886) 18 QBD 276. See also *Nagle* v *Fielden* [1966] 2 QB 633.

voice identification. Where an issue relating to evidence is voice identification, there must be expert evidence of acoustic and auditory analysis; but there is an exception where the speaker is identifiable because of rare characteristics, or where the issue concerns the speaker's accent or dialect: *R* v *O'Doherty* [2003] 1 Cr App R 5.

void. Empty; without force; of no legal effect. 'A void contract is a paradox; in truth there is no contract at all': *Fawcett* v *Star Car Sales Ltd* [1960] NZLR 406. It is a nullity from its beginning. For void and voidable orders made by a court, see *Isaacs* v *Robertson* [1985] AC 97.

voidable. Capable of being voided, i.e., set aside. A voidable contract has legal effect until avoided at the option of one of the parties (e.g., where the contract has been induced by misrepresentation). See S.G.A. 1979, s 23.

voidable marriage. *See* NULLITY OF MARRIAGE.

voidable title, sale under. When the seller of goods has a voidable title to them, but his title has not been avoided at the time of the sale, the buyer acquires a good title to the goods, provided he buys them in good faith and without notice of the seller's defect of title: S.G.A. 1979, s 23.

voidable trust. *See* TRUST, VOIDABLE.

void marriage. *See* NULLITY OF MARRIAGE.

void trust. *See* TRUST, VOID.

voir dire. (Also *voire dire.*) *Vrai dire* = to speak the truth. Preliminary examination of a witness by the judge, e.g., to determine whether a confession was voluntary; i.e., the trial of incidental issues ('trial within a trial'). See *Wong Kam Ming* v *R* [1980] AC 247; P.&C.E.A. 1984, s 76(5); *R* v *Davis* [1990] Crim LR 860; *Mitchell*

v *R* [1998] AC 695 (it is not proper for a trial judge to reveal to the jury his decision after a *voir dire* (*per* Lord Steyn)); *R* v *Honeyghon and Sayles* [1999] Crim LR 221 (the decision whether or not to hold a *voir dire* is a matter for the judge's discretion).

volenti non fit injuria. That to which a person consents cannot be considered an injury. Term referring to the harm suffered with the plaintiff's freely given assent and with his prior knowledge of the risk involved, and, hence, a general defence in tort. Knowledge is not assent, but merely evidence of assent: *Dann* v *Hamilton* [1939] 1 KB 509. A person does not necessarily assent to a situation because he has knowledge of its potential danger: *Baker* v *James* [1921] 2 KB 674. 'Knowledge of the risk of injury is not enough. Nor is a willingness to take the risk of injury. Nothing will suffice short of an agreement to waive any claim for negligence': *Nettleship* v *Weston* [1971] 3 All ER 581. See *Friend* v *Civil Aviation Authority* [1998] IRLR 253; *Reeves* v *CPM* [1999] 3 WLR 363 (defence rejected).

voluntary. 1. Proceeding from some exercise of the will and involving an act of choice. 2. Without valuable consideration (q.v.).

voluntary bill procedure. *See* BILL PROCEDURE, VOLUNTARY.

voluntary conduct. Conduct resulting from the exercise of one's will. In general, a person will not be held liable for any harmful result produced by conduct which was not voluntary.

voluntary confession. *See* CONFESSION.

voluntary conveyance. *See* VOLUNTARY DISPOSITION.

voluntary disposition. A disposition of land not founded upon valuable consideration (q.v.). 'Every voluntary disposition of land made with intent to defraud a subsequent purchaser is voidable at the instance of that purchaser': L.P.A. 1925, s 173(1).

voluntary liquidation. *See* VOLUNTARY WINDING-UP.

voluntary settlement. A settlement (q.v.) made without valuable consideration.

voluntary waste. Waste (q.v.) arising from an injury to land actively caused by the tenant (q.v.), e.g., cutting timber. See *Honywood* v *Honywood* (1874) LR 18 Eq 306. A tenant for years, yearly tenant, tenant at sufferance, will be liable for voluntary waste.

voluntary winding-up. The winding-up of a company (q.v.) so that company and creditors may settle their affairs before coming to court. It may be carried out when: the period fixed for the duration of the company has ended; the company has passed a special resolution to wind up voluntarily; the company has passed an extraordinary resolution that it is expedient that the company be wound up. Voluntary winding-up dates from the passing of a resolution authorising it. The resolution must be advertised in the *London Gazette* within 14 days. See, e.g., Ins.A. 1986, s 85.

volunteer. One who takes under a disposition for which neither he nor anyone on his behalf has given valuable consideration (q.v.). Equity will not aid a volunteer. See, e.g., *Plumptre's Marriage Settlement* [1910] 1 Ch 609.

vote. 1. To express one's opinion formally, as at an election: see Representation of the People Acts 1985–2000. 2. That which is voted, e.g., a grant of money. *See* PARLIAMENTARY ELECTORS.

voting at meetings. Generally by show of hands. In the case of a registered company a resolution (q.v.) is decided on by show of hands, unless a poll (q.v.) is demanded. See Cos.A. 1985, s 370; Table A, arts 55–58. *See* MEETINGS, COMPANY.

voting shares, disclosure of interests in. Where a person, to his knowledge,

acquires an interest in, or ceases to be interested in, a public company's relevant share capital, he must notify this to the company: Cos.A. 1985, s 198(1). For 'relevant share capital', see s 198(2). See also Cos.A. 1989, s 134(2).

vouch. 1. To summon. 2. To bear witness. 3. To answer for.

voucher. 1. Receipt. 2. Process of vouching to warranty, i.e., calling to court a person who has warranted land to another. A process used in the old common recovery (q.v.).

voyage charter. A charterparty (q.v.) under which a ship is hired for one or more voyages (as compared with a time charter (q.v.)).

voyeurism. A person commits an offence under the Sexual Offences Act 2003, s 67 if, for the purpose of obtaining sexual gratification, he observes another person doing a private act, and he knows that the other person does not consent to his being observed for his sexual gratification.

vulnerable. Susceptible of injury. Less able to fend for oneself so that injury or detriment might result: *R* v *Waveney DC ex p Bowers* [1983] QB 238; *R* v *Lambeth LBC ex p Carroll* (1988) 20 HLR 142. 'Vulnerable adults' are those to whom accommodation and nursing or personal care are provided in a care home; those to whom personal care is provided by a domiciliary care agency in their own home; those to whom prescribed services are provided by independent hospitals or NHS agencies: Care Standards Act 2000, s 80. The names of persons considered unsuitable to work with them are listed by the Secretary of State: see ss 81, 95; Protection of Children Act 1999, s 2.

W

wage, national minimum. A person who qualifies for the national minimum wage shall be paid at a rate not less than that wage: National Minimum Wage Act 1998, s 1(1). (Rate is, currently: £3.70 per hour for workers over 21; £3.20 per hour for workers aged 18–20.) A worker qualifies if he is working or ordinarily works in the UK under his contract, and has ceased to be of compulsory school age: s 1(2). Hourly rate is determined by Secretary of State: s 2(1). There are financial penalties for non-compliance: s 21. See Employment Relations Act 1999, s 39; SI 00/1411, 1989. *See* LOW PAY COMMISSION.

wager. The risking of a sum of money on an uncertain, eventual outcome. See *Ellesmere* v *Wallace* [1929] 2 Ch 1. *See* BET.

wagering contract. 'One by which two persons, professing to hold opposite views touching the issue of a future, uncertain event, mutually agree that, dependent upon the determination of that event, one shall win from the other, and the other shall pay or hand over to him, a sum of money or other stake; neither of the contracting parties having any other interest in that contract than the sum or stake he will so win or lose, there being no other real consideration for the making of such contract by either of the parties': *Carlill* v *Carbolic Smoke Ball Co* [1892] 2 QB 484. Null and void under, e.g., Gaming Act 1845, s 18. See *Hill* v *William Hill Ltd* [1949] AC 530. *See* BET; GAMING.

wagering policy. A policy of assurance in the subject matter of which the assured person does not have an interest, or for purposes of gambling. Example: insuring of a stranger's life.

wager of battle. *See* BATTLE, TRIAL BY.

wages. Any sums payable to the worker (q.v.) by his employer in connection with his employment, including any fee, bonus, commission, holiday pay or other emolument referable to his employment, whether payable under his contract or otherwise: E.R.A. 1996, s 27. For the purposes of the subsection, the definition includes, e.g., maternity pay, statutory sick pay, etc. *See* DEDUCTIONS FROM WAGES.

wait and see principle. Rule relating to perpetuities. Under common law there was no 'wait and see', so that a limitation was void if it could *possibly* fail to vest during the perpetuity period. Under P.&A.A. 1964, s 3, the principle applies to instruments which became effective after July 1964 in the following cases: an interest capable of vesting after the perpetuity period will not be treated as void under the perpetuity rule until it is established that it will vest, if at all, after the end of the perpetuity period; in the case of a general power of appointment (q.v.) which could possibly be exercised after the end of the perpetuity period, the power will be treated as valid until such time (if any) as it becomes established that the power will not be exercised in the perpetuity period; in the case of a disposition consisting of the conferring of power, option or other right which might be exercised after the end of the perpetuity period, such disposition will be void only if, and so far as, the right is not fully exercised within that period. *See* PERPETUITIES, RULE AGAINST.

waiver. 1. Relinquishing of a claim freely. 'The abandonment of a right in such a way that the other party is entitled

613

to plead the abandonment by way of confession and avoidance if the right is thereafter asserted': *Banning* v *Wright* [1972] 2 All ER 987. 'A waiver must be an intentional act with knowledge': *Darnley* v *London, Chatham and Dover Rwy* (1867) 16 LT 217. 2. The instrument which declares an act of waiving. 3. Surrender by operation of law. 4. Variation of a contract (see *Hickman* v *Haynes* (1875) LR 10 CP 598).

waiver of tort. The foregoing by a person of a remedy in tort in favour of some other remedy (e.g., an action based on a quasi-contract). The waiver extinguishes the right of action in tort. See *Re Simmons* [1934] Ch 24. *See* TORT.

walking possession. A procedure involving agreement by a debtor that goods will remain on his premises, subject to the right of the bailiff to return to those premises and remove the goods for sale. See *Abingdon RDC* v *O'Gorman* [1968] 2 QB 811; Finance Act 2000, Sch 6, para 90. *See* IMPOUND.

wall, party. *See* PARTY WALL.

war. Military operations and armed conflict between opposing forces of nations or states. In an insurance policy the word 'war' includes 'civil war' (see *Spinney's Ltd* v *Royal Insurance Co Ltd* [1980] 1 Lloyd's Rep 406) unless the context indicates different intentions: see *Pesquerias* v *Beer* (1949) 82 Ll LR 501. Whether a state of hostilities (q.v.) amounts to 'war' is a question of fact in each case: *Kawasaki Kisen* v *Bantham Steamships (No. 2)* [1939] 2 KB 544. 'With certain exceptions the outbreak of war prevents the further performance of contracts between persons in this country and persons in enemy territory': *per* Lord Reid in *Arab Bank Ltd* v *Barclays Bank* [1954] AC 495. *See* INSURRECTION; REBELLION.

war crimes. Murder, manslaughter or culpable homicide committed by a person during 15 September 1939–5 June 1945 in a place which at the time was part of Germany or under German occupation and which constituted a violation of the laws and customs of war: see War Crimes Act

1991, s 1(1); *R* v *Sawoniuk* [2000] 2 Cr App R 220. See also Nuremberg Trial Indictment 1945; *Prosecutor* v *Rajic* (1997) 1 BHRC (in relation to statute of the International Tribunal, arts 2, 3); C.P.I.A. 1996, s 46, Sch 4, para 19. *See* CRIMES AGAINST HUMANITY.

ward. One under the protection or care of another. See S.C.A. 1981, s 41; Ch.A. 1989, s 100, for restrictions on powers of the High Court, e.g., to make a child who is the subject of a care order a ward of court. See, e.g., *Re E* [1991] 1 FLR 420; *Re K* (2000) 150 NLJ 153B (media interview with ward not contempt).

wardship. 1. The exercise of care and protection of a ward (q.v.). See *Re T (A Minor)* [1997] 1 WLR 242. 2. Right, exercised in feudal times, to the custody of a ward and the ward's property.

warrant. 1. Document authorising some action, e.g., payment of money. 2. Document issued by a magistrate (q.v.) ordering that a person be arrested and brought before the court. The person must be mentioned by name, or described otherwise. It must contain a statement of the offence charged and it should be signed by the issuing magistrate. See C.L.A. 1977, s 38; M.C.A. 1980, s 1. 3. An instrument which entitles the holder to subscribe for shares in a company or assets representing a loan relationship of a company; and for these purposes it is immaterial whether the shares or assets to which the warrant relates exist or are identifiable: Finance Act 2000, Sch 26, para 12(9).

warrant, arrest with and without. *See* ARREST AND WARRANT.

warrant endorsed for bail. *See* BAIL, WARRANT ENDORSED FOR.

warrant, entry without. Right, under common law or statute, of a constable to enter a dwelling house or other premises without warrant. See P.&C.E.A. 1984, s 17; Planning and Compensation Act 1991, s 11; *McLorie* v *Oxford* [1982] QB 1290; *O'Loughlin* v *Chief Constable of Essex* [1998] 1 WLR 374.

warrant, general. *See* GENERAL WARRANT.

warrant, Royal. *See* ROYAL WARRANT.

warrant, search. *See* SEARCH WARRANT.

warrant, share. Document under seal stating that the bearer is entitled to shares specified therein. A warrant is a negotiable instrument (q.v.). See Cos.A. 1985, s 188, as amended by Cos.A. 1989, s 130.

warranty. An agreement with reference to goods which are the subject of a contract of sale, but collateral to the main purpose of such contract, the breach of which gives rise to a claim for damages, but not to a right to reject the goods and treat the contract as repudiated: S.G.A. 1979, s 61(1). It may be express or implied. See S.G.A. 1979, s 11(1); Sale and Supply of Goods Act 1994, Sch 2, para 5. For remedy for breach of warranty, see S.G.A. 1979, s 53; *Bence Graphics v Fasson Ltd* [1998] QB 87. For special meaning in contracts of marine insurance, see Marine Insurance Act 1906. *See* CONDITION.

waste. 1. Acts or omissions by a tenant which alter (often negatively) the nature of land or houses. They may be voluntary; permissive; ameliorating; equitable (qq.v.). See *Mancetter Developments Ltd* v *Garmanson Ltd* [1986] 1 All ER 449; *Dayani v Bromley LBC* [1999] 3 EGLR 144. Remedies for waste include damages (i.e., loss of value to the reversion) and injunction. 2. Includes any substance which constitutes a scrap material or an effluent or other unwanted surplus substance arising from the application of any process and any substance or article which requires to be disposed of as being broken, worn out, contaminated or otherwise spoiled: En.P.A. 1990, s 75. See Controlled Waste Regulations 1992; Waste Minimisation Act 1998, allowing certain local authorities to take steps to minimise generation of waste in their areas: Pollution Prevention and Control Act 1999, s 4; *Mayer Parry Recycling Ltd* v *Environment Agency* (1999) *The Times*, 3 December (meaning of 'discarding' waste). It was held by the European Court of Justice in *Commission of European Communities* v *UK* (Case C-62/83) (2005) *The Times*, 6 January, that

a general exclusion of agricultural and mining waste from UK legislation on waste control is contrary to EC law.

wasted costs order. In *Medcalf* v *Mardell* (2002) The *Times*, 28 June, the HL held that where a wasted costs order is requested against a practitioner unable, because of legal professional privilege, to give a full answer to an application, an order ought not to be made unless the court is satisfied that there was nothing the practitioner might have been able to say, if unconstrained, so as to resist the order, and in all the existing circumstances it would be fair to grant the order. See also *R* v *Pendlebury* (2002) 152 NLJ 1072.

waste, defences to claim for. Proof that the damage resulted from the reasonable and ordinary use of premises or that it was caused by an Act of God (q.v.) or that it resulted from the exercise of common law rights (e.g., to estovers (q.v.)). See, e.g., *Manchester Bonded Warehouse Co* v *Carr* (1880) 5 CPD 507.

waste land of a manor. 'The open, uncultivated and unoccupied lands parcel of the manor, or open lands parcel of the manor other than the demesne lands of the manor': *A-G* v *Hammer* (1858) 27 LJ Ch 837, applied in *Re Britford Common* [1977] 1 WLR 39. See *Hampshire CC* v *Milburn* [1990] 2 WLR 1240.

waste, unlicensed disposal of. Except in prescribed cases, a person must not deposit on any land controlled waste (i.e., household, industrial and commercial waste): En.P.A. 1990, s 33. See SI 96/1279; *Environmental Agency* v *Singer* [1998] Env LR 380.

wasting assets. Assets or securities which are subject to depletion, or which have a terminating nature, e.g., leaseholds. See T.C.G.A. 1992, s 44(1); *Lewis* v *Walters* [1992] STC 97.

water, classification of. At common law: tidal rivers and the sea; non-tidal (rivers, streams, lakes, ponds, water in artificial channels, etc.). See Water Resources Act 1991.

watercourse. Includes all rivers, streams, ditches, drains, cuts, culverts, dykes, sluices, sewers and passages through which water flows except mains and pipes used by the Water Authority or a water undertaker or any other person for the purpose of supplying water to premises: Water Act 1989, s 189(1). See Public Health Act 1936, s 259(1); Land Drainage Act 1991, s 72; British Waterways Act 1995; *National Rivers Authority* v *Yorks Water Service* [1995] 1 AC 444; *R* v *Falmouth HA ex p SW Water Ltd* (2000) *The Times*, 24 April (the term 'watercourse', for purposes of the 1936 Act, did not include a river or estuary).

water ordeal. *See* ORDEAL, TRIAL BY.

waters, coastal. *See* COASTAL WATERS.

waters, inland. *See* INLAND WATERS.

waters, marine. *See* MARINE WATERS.

waters, territorial. *See* TERRITORIAL WATERS.

waters, tidal. *See* TIDAL WATERS.

water supply, right to. CA held, in *Mitchell* v *Potter* (2005) *The Times*, 24 January, that in the case of a grant to a conveyance of right of water from a reservoir on vendor's land fed by a spring on his land to affirm purchase, was in the nature of a *profit à prendre*; it was neither an easement nor a residual right.

wayleave. A right of way over or through land for purposes connected with telegraphic, electric and telephone wires, cableways, etc. See Taxes Act 1988, s 120, amended by Finance Act 1997, s 60.

way, right of. *See* RIGHT OF WAY.

ways and means. Parliamentary expression relating to the provision of revenue to meet national expenditure and the demands of general economic policy. Ways and means are taken to involve imposition of taxes, raising of loans, payments under the Consolidated Fund or the National Loans Fund. The former Committee of Ways and Means was abolished in 1967. *See* SUPPLY ESTIMATES.

weapon, offensive. *See* OFFENSIVE WEAPON.

weapon of offence. *See* OFFENCE, WEAPON OF.

weapon, prohibited. *See* PROHIBITED ARTICLE.

wear and tear. Deterioration or depreciation of a thing resulting from its ordinary reasonable use. *See* FAIR WEAR AND TEAR.

Wednesbury principles. Stated by Lord Greene, in *Assoc'd Provincial Picture Houses* v *Wednesbury* [1948] 1 KB 123, relating to purported exercise by an executive authority of its discretion. 'The exercise of such a discretion must be a *real* exercise of the discretion.' Irrelevant collateral matters must be disregarded. The court will interfere only when the authority's conclusion is 'so unreasonable that no reasonable authority could ever have come to it'. See, e.g., *R* v *University for Central England ex p Sandhu* [1999] Ed CR 594. The principles were criticised by Lord Cooke in *R (Daly)* v *Secretary of State for Home Department* (2001) *The Times*, 25 May.

week. A period of seven days, beginning with midnight between Saturday and Sunday (except where otherwise defined): see, e.g., S.S.A. 1975, Sch 20. See *Omoregei* v *Secretary for the Environment* [1997] 4 CL 185.

weekly tenancy. A tenancy from week to week, which can be created similarly to a yearly tenancy, e.g., by express agreement, or by inference. *See* TENANCY.

weight, gross. *See* GROSS WEIGHT.

weights and measures. Units and standards of measurement referred to in Weights and Measures Act 1985, Part I, under which customers must be properly informed as to the weight and quantity of goods on sale.

welfare law. The area of law concerned with social security legislation, factory safety and welfare of workers, public health, housing, consumer protection, security of employment, preservation of amenities, legal aid, etc.

welfare of a child. 'Includes material welfare . . . More important are the stability and security, the loving and understanding care and guidance, the warm and compassionate relationship, that are essential for the full development of the child's own character, personality and talents': *per* Hardie Boyce J in *Walker v Harrison* (1981) NZLR 257. The paramount consideration for a court determining a question of a child's upbringing: Ch.A. 1989, s 1(1). The court will have particular regard to, e.g., the child's wishes, his age, any harm he has suffered or is at risk of suffering, capability of each of his parents: s 1(3). For welfare reports ordered by the court, see s 7, amended by C.J.C.S.A. 2000, Sch 7, para 88. See *Re P* [1992] 1 FLR 316 (court's duty to listen to expression of child's wishes). For welfare of children in boarding schools, see Ch.A. 1989, s 87, amended by Care Standards Act 2000, s 105; 2000 Act, ss 107–109.

Welsh language, use in proceedings. Under Welsh Language Act 1993, s 22, the Welsh language may be used in any legal proceedings in Wales or Monmouthshire by any party desiring to use it. See *Collector of Taxes v Morgan* [1977] CLY 2537; *Practice Direction (Welsh Language)* [1998] 1 WLR 1677. For equal treatment of English and Welsh languages in the National Assembly for Wales (q.v.), see Government of Wales Act 1998, s 47. See *Williams v Cowell* [2000] 1 WLR 187 ('legal proceedings in Wales' in s 22 refers to the geographical location of the proceedings).

Welsh mortgage. A mortgage (q.v.) in which there was no covenant for repayment of the loan and the mortgagee could not compel redemption or foreclosure (qq.v.). See now L.P.A. 1925, s 85.

WEU. Western European Union. Organisation founded in May 1955, based on a grouping of Belgium, Germany, Italy, Netherlands, Portugal, UK. Viewed under the Maastricht Treaty as a defence component of EU, responsible for the formulation of a common European Defence policy.

wheel-clamping, trespass, in relation to. Where a clamper cannot establish that the car owner saw and understood the significance of a warning notice, the act of clamping is an act of trespass to the car owner's property, and the clamper might

be liable in damages: *Vince v Waltham Forest LBC* [2000] 4 All ER 169.

whip. 1. Government or Opposition official responsible for controlling the presence of MPs at debates and votes, arranging pairs, etc. 2. A command by his party to an MP to attend a House of Commons (q.v.) vote. A 'three-line whip' is an urgent command (underlined three times) to attend a vote. See PARLIAMENT.

whistleblowers, statutory protection of. In the case of an employee who complains of dismissal following his having made a protected disclosure (under Employment Rights Act 1996, s 47B) as a whistleblower, an employment tribunal must also hold a directions hearing so as to note what evidence is to be called, and to ensure that the statutory protection requirements have been satisfied. See *ALM Medical Services v Bladon* [2002] EWCA Civ 1085.

whistleblowing. Term used in relation to acts by employees who raise genuine concerns about, e.g., apparent negligence, dangers to health and safety. See E.R.A. 1996, ss 43A, 43B, inserted by Public Interest Disclosure Act 1998, s 1; Pensions Act 1995, s 48. *See* DISCLOSURE, PROTECTED.

white paper. *See* PARLIAMENTARY PAPERS.

whole blood. *See* BLOOD RELATIONSHIP.

widowed parent's allowance. Where a parent whose spouse dies on or after the appointed day is under pensionable age at the time of the spouse's death, or a man whose wife died before the appointed day has not remarried before that day and is under pensionable age on that day, the surviving spouse shall be entitled to a widowed parent's allowance: Social Security Contributions and Benefits Act 1992 s 39A, inserted by W.R.P.A. 1999, s 55(2). For case of pregnant widow, see s 39A(2)(b).

widow's and widower's payment. *See* BEREAVEMENT PAYMENT.

wife, provision for. Under Inheritance (Provision for Family and Dependants) Act 1975, the wife or former wife of the deceased may apply for financial provision from the deceased's estate if the disposition of that estate effected by his will or the law relating to intestacy (q.v.) is not such as to make reasonable financial provision for the applicant: ss 1, 2. See Law Reform (Succession) Act 1995, s 2. See DEPENDANT.

wild creatures, theft of. A person cannot steal a wild creature not tamed nor ordinarily kept in captivity unless it has been reduced into possession by or on behalf of another person and possession has not since been lost or abandoned: Th.A. 1968, s 4(4). See ANIMAL, WILD.

wild mammals, cruelty to. It is an offence for a person to mutilate, kick, beat, nail or otherwise impale, stab, burn, stone, crush, drown, drag or asphyxiate any wild mammal with intent to inflict any suffering: Wild Mammals (Protection) Act 1996, s 1. For exceptions (as doing anything authorised by any enactment), see s 2.

wilful. Refers to the deliberate conduct of a person who is a free agent, knows what he is doing and intends to do what he is doing. 'If a man permits a thing to be done, it means that he gives permission for it to be done, he knows what is to be done or is being done, and, if he knows that, it follows that it is wilful': *Lomas* v *Peck* [1947] 2 All ER 574. Used synonymously with 'intentional' in *Wheeler* v *New Merton Mills* [1933] 2 KB 669. 'Wilfully' means 'that the act is done deliberately and intentionally, not by accident or inadvertence, but so that the mind of the person who does the act goes with it': *per* Lord Russell in *R* v *Senior* [1899] 1 QB 480. See *Dibble* v *Ingleton* [1972] 1 QB 480; *Kent CC* v *Upchurch River Valley Golf Course Ltd* [1998] CLY 979.

wilful default. 'Either a consciousness of negligence or breach of duty, or a recklessness in the performance of a duty': *Re City Equitable Fire Insurance Co* [1925] Ch 407.

wilful misconduct. 'To be guilty of wilful misconduct the person concerned must appreciate that he is acting wrongfully, or is wrongfully omitting to act, and

yet persists in so acting or omitting to act regardless of the consequences, or acts or omits to act with reckless indifference as to what the results may be': *Horabin* v *BOAC* [1952] 2 All ER 1016.

wilful neglect. Intentional or purposeful (i.e., deliberate) omission to carry out some action.

wilful refusal. A refusal without adequate cause. For the imposition of imprisonment upon wilful refusal to pay a fine, see M.C.A. 1980, ss 76 *et seq.*

wilful refusal to consummate. 'A wilful, determined and steadfast refusal to perform the obligations and to carry out the duties which the matrimonial contract involves': *Dickinson* v *Dickinson* [1913] P 198. 'A settled and definite decision come to without just excuse not to consummate': *Horton* v *Horton* [1947] 2 All ER 871. See also *Jodla* v *Jodla* [1960] 1 All ER 625; Mat.C.A. 1973, s 12; F.L.A. 1996. See CONSUMMATION OF A MARRIAGE.

will. A declaration, which is revocable and ambulatory (q.v.), made in the prescribed form, of the intentions of the maker concerning the disposition and devolution of his property, and other matters, which he desires should become effective on and after the event of his death. 'The word "will" shall extend to a testament, and to a codicil (q.v.), and to an appointment by will or by writing in the nature of a will in exercise of a power . . . and to any other testamentary disposition': W.A. 1837, s 1. See, e.g., *Re White* [1990] 3 WLR 187 (alteration of will). For duty of care of lay will writers to intended beneficiaries under proposed will, see *Esterhuizen* v *Allied Dunbar Assurance plc* [1998] 2 FLR 668. See also *Carr-Glynn* v *Frearsons* [1998] 4 All ER 225; *Gibbons* v *Nelsons* (2000) *The Times*, 21 April. See DEPENDANT; PROBATE TESTAMENTARY SCRIPT.

will, conditional. See CONDITIONAL WILL

will, destruction of. The revocation of a will (q.v.) by destruction involves 'the burning, tearing or otherwise destroying the same by the testator, or by some person in his presence, and by his direction with the intention of revoking the same': W.A. 1837, s 20. A symbolic destruction will not suffice. See *Cheese* v *Lovejoy* (1877) 37 LT 295; *Gill* v *Gill* [1909] P 157.

will, divorce and. In relation to a will made by a person dying on or after 1 January 1995, any property which, or an interest in which, is devised or bequeathed to the former spouse, will pass as if the former spouse had died on the date on which the marriage was dissolved or annulled: Law Reform (Succession) Act 1995, s 3. (As a result, only the former spouse, and not any other beneficiary, is deprived of a benefit.)

will, forfeiture of benefit under. *See* FORFEITURE OF BENEFIT UNDER WILL.

will in contemplation of marriage. *See* MARRIAGE, WILL IN CONTEMPLATION OF.

willing. Ready to act as the result of choice. 'A man cannot be said to be truly "willing" unless he is in a position to choose freely, and freedom of choice predicates, not only full knowledge of the circumstances on which the exercise of choice is conditional, so that he may be able to choose wisely, but the absence of any feeling of constraint so that nothing shall interfere with the freedom of his will': *per* Scott LJ in *Bowater* v *Rowley Regis Corporation* [1944] KB 476. *See* CONSENT.

will, international. Will made in accordance with Annex to Convention on International Wills as set out in A.J.A. 1982, Sch 2. It is valid as regards form, irrespective particularly of the place where it is made, of the location of the assets and of the testator's nationality, domicile or residence.

will, living. *See* LIVING WILL.

will, mutual. *See* MUTUAL WILLS.

will, nuncupative. *See* NUNCUPATIVE WILL.

will, partnership at. *See* PARTNERSHIP AT WILL.

will, privileged. *See* PRIVILEGED WILL.

will, rectification of. *See* RECTIFICATION OF WILL.

will, republication of. *See* REPUBLICATION OF WILL.

will, revival of. *See* REVIVAL OF WILL.

will, revocation of. *See* REVOCATION OF WILL.

will, solicitors' duty. Where appropriate instructions had been given to a firm of solicitors in relation to the drafting of a will, and the execution of that will had not been supervised by members of the firm, it was held that they had a duty to make appropriate checks so as to ensure that the principles of execution had been observed thoroughly when it had been returned to them to be held in safe custody. See *Humblestone* v *Martin Tolhurst Partnership* (2004) *The Times*, 27 February.

will, tenant at. *See* TENANT AT WILL.

will, validity of. 'No will shall be valid unless (*a*) it is in writing, and signed by the testator, or by some other person in his presence and by his direction; and (*b*) it appears that the testator intended by his signature to give effect to the will; and (*c*) the signature is made or acknowledged by the testator in the presence of two or more witnesses present at the same time; and (*d*) each witness either (i) attests and signs the will; or (ii) acknowledges his signature, in the presence of the testator (but not necessarily in the presence of any other witness), but no form of attestation shall be necessary': W.A. 1837, s 9 (as substituted by A.J.A. 1982, s 17); *Couser* v *Couser* [1996] 1 WLR 1301. *See* SIGNATURE OF WILL.

will, witness, benefits for. The attestation of a will by a person to whom or to whose spouse there is given or made a disposition is disregarded if the will is duly executed without his attestation and without that of any other such person: W.A. 1968, s 1(1), modifying W.A. 1837, s 15. Hence, if a will is attested by X, Y and Z, and X and Y are not beneficiaries, but Z is, then Z will not lose a gift made to him.

windfalls. Trees and their fruit blown down by the wind. They belong, in general, to the owner of the inheritance; but dotards (q.v.) may be taken by the tenant (q.v.). See *Re Harrison's Trusts* (1885) 28 Ch D 220.

winding-up. Process whereby a company is brought to an end, e.g., following insolvency. It may be: compulsory winding-up by the court (q.v.); winding-up under the court's supervision; voluntary winding-up (q.v.). Thus, a company may be wound up: when the period fixed in the articles for the company's duration expires; if the company resolves by extraordinary resolution to wind up because of liabilities; for any cause if a sufficient number of members pass a special resolution to that end. Petitions for winding-up may be presented by Secretary of State, Official Receiver, A-G (if company is a charity), creditors, contributories. See Ins.A. 1986, s 84 (voluntary winding-up) and s 122 (winding-up by the court); *Re McBacon Ltd (No. 2)* [1990] BCLC 607 (winding-up costs); F.S.M.A. 2000, s 365. The HL held, in *Buchler* v *Talbot* [2004] UKHL 9, that the costs and expenses of winding up a company may not be paid out of assets subject to a floating charge until the entirety of the principal and interest charged thereon has been paid, compensation.

winding-up, compulsory. *See* COMPULSORY WINDING-UP BY THE COURT.

winding-up, voluntary. *See* VOLUNTARY WINDING-UP.

witchcraft. Prior to Witchcraft Act 1735, a capital offence. Fraudulent Mediums Act 1951 repealed the 1735 Act and provided that it is an offence for a person with intent to deceive and for reward to purport to act as a medium and in so purporting to act, to use a fraudulent device. See *R* v *Duncan and Others* [1944] KB 713.

withdrawal of issue from jury. Procedure whereby a judge, who is not satisfied that there is sufficient evidence in support of a proponent's contention, discharges the jury and enters judgment for the opponent, or directs the jury to return a verdict in the opponent's favour. See *Ryder* v *Wombwell* (1868) LR 4 Ex 32; *R* v *Abbott* [1955] 2 QB 497.

within. When used in the context of a period of time is capable of meaning 'during' or 'before or at the expiry of' that period: *Manorlike* v *Le Vitas Travel Agency* [1986] 1 All ER 573.

with intent to. In *R* v *Zaman* (2002) *The Times*, 22 July, the CA considered whether the phrases 'with intent to' and 'with a view to' were synonymous, and held that Parliament had intended to differentiate them in Trade Marks Act 1994, s 92 (1).

without prejudice. *See* PREJUDICE.

without reserve. Phrase used in a sale by auction (q.v.), showing that no price has been reserved. See *Barry* v *Davies* [2000] 1 WLR 1962.

with profits. Title of insurance policy under which bonuses from profits of insurance company are used to increase policy value.

witness. 1. To give evidence or proof. 2. To attest by signature. 3. One who gives formal or sworn evidence at a hearing. 4. In relation to criminal proceedings, any person called, or proposed to be called, to give evidence in the proceedings: Y.J.C.E.A. 1999, s 63(1).

witness, counselling of. In *R* v *Momodov* (2005) *The Times*, 9 February, the CA held that to coach or train a witness for purposes of criminal proceedings, is not allowed.

witness, credibility of. In *EPI Environmental Technologies* v *Symphony Plastics* (2005) *The Times*, 14 January, it was held that when a court attends to expert or non-expert evidence, the performance of the witness must be enlisted in the light of the totality of his evidence.

witnesses, adverse. *See* ADVERSE WITNESSES.

witnesses, child, special provisions in criminal trials. Under Y.J.C.E.A. 1999, s 21, there are special provisions relating to child witnesses, allowing, e.g., the giving of evidence in chief by video recordings or live link where available (see s 18(2)), although this may not be used where the interests of justice so require (s 27(2)). In the case of a child witness 'in need of special protection' (i.e., in cases relating to sexual offences, assault, kidnapping) video recorded cross examination and re-examination may be facilitated. See also ss 16, 19.

witnesses, compellable. Those who are obliged to give evidence. A witness is not generally compellable to answer a question which might expose him to a criminal charge: *R v Boyes* (1861) 30 LJ QB 301. *See* SPOUSES, EVIDENCE OF.

witnesses, competence of. In general, any person is competent to give evidence at every stage in criminal proceedings, unless it appears to the court that he is not a person who is able to understand questions put to him as a witness, and give answers to them which can be understood: Y.J.C.E.A. 1999, s 53(1), (3). A person charged in criminal proceedings is not competent to give evidence for the prosecution: s 53(4). Competence of witnesses is to be determined by the court: s 54.

witnesses, intimidation, harming and threatening of. C.J.P.A. 2002, s 39, creates an offence involving an act by a person which intimidates, and is intended to intimidate, the victim, and who does the act knowing or believing that the victim is or may be a witness in any relevant proceedings, and intending by his act to cause the course of justice to be obstructed, perverted, or interfered with, and the act is done after the commencement of those proceedings. Harming a witness or threatening him are covered in s 40.

witnesses, order of calling. Generally an advocate is entitled to call witnesses in order of his choice. '[This is] solely a matter for counsel. It is a grave responsibility and it rests on him and him alone': *Briscoe v Briscoe* [1966] 1 All ER 465. See also *Barnes v BPC Ltd* [1975] 1 WLR 1565.

witnesses, protection of. CA held in *R (Bloggs) v Secretary of State for Home Department* (2003) *The Times*, 4 July, that the police lack authority to bind the prison service following a promise to a prisoner that he will be allowed to serve his sentence in a protected witness unit.

witnesses, securing attendance of. *See* WITNESS ORDER.

witnesses, vulnerable and intimidated, special measures directions. Under Y.J.C.E.A. 1999, Part II, assistance may be given by the court to witnesses (but not generally to the accused) in certain categories, in criminal proceedings. Such categories include: witnesses eligible on grounds of age (under 17 at time of the hearing) or incapacity (physical or mental) affecting ability to give complete, coherent and accurate evidence (s 16); witnesses eligible on grounds of fear or distress about testifying (s 17). Special measures directions may provide for screening witness from accused, giving evidence by live link or by video, giving evidence in private (but not in absence of accused), examination of witness through intermediary. See ss 23–30. *See* SCREENS IN COURT.

witness, eye. *See* EYE WITNESS.

witness, failure to call. CA held, in *R v Hampton* [2004] EWCA Crim 2139, that where defendant who was able to call a witness, took a deliberate decision not to do so, he should not expect an appeal which relies on fresh evidence to succeed.

witness, hostile. *See* HOSTILE WITNESS.

witness, interfering with. *See* INTERFERING WITH WITNESSES.

witness, intimidation of. *See* INTIMIDATION.

witness order. Procedure for the compelling of attendance by witnesses in criminal trials at the court, failure to comply with which was a contempt of court (q.v.): Criminal Procedure (Attendance of Witnesses) Act 1965. A 'conditional witness order' required him to attend only if given notice. (Abolished under C.P.I.A. 1996, s 65.) *See* WITNESS SUMMONS IN CRIMINAL PROCEEDINGS.

witness, privilege of. *See* PRIVILEGE OF WITNESS.

witness, recall of. The judge has a discretionary power to allow the recall of a witness after the close of a party's case to allow evidence in rebuttal. See, e.g., *R v Flynn* (1957) 42 Cr App R 15.

witness's notes. Notes used by a witness to refresh his memory. Cross-examining counsel is entitled to inspect them so as to check their content: *R* v *Britton* [1987] 1 WLR 539.

witness's oath. *See* OATH.

witness statement. A written statement signed by a person, which contains the evidence which that person would be allowed to give orally: CPR, r 32.4(1). Its form must comply with requirements as set out in relevant PD, and must be verified by a statement of truth (q.v.): r 32.8. See PD 32, para 19.1 (format of statement); r 32.11 (cross-examination on a witness statement). A witness statement which stands as evidence in chief is open to inspection unless the court directs otherwise during the trial: r 32(13).

witness statements for use at trial, requirement to serve. The court will order a party to serve on the other parties any witness statement of the oral evidence which the party serving the statement intends to rely on in relation to any issues of fact to be decided at the trial: CPR, r 32.4(2). For late service, see *Mealey Horgan plc* v *Horgan* (1999) *The Times*, 6 July.

witness statements which have been served, use at trial. Where a party has served a witness statement and wishes to rely on the evidence of the person who made the statement, he must call that person to give oral evidence unless the court orders otherwise or he puts the statement in as hearsay evidence (q.v.): CPR, r 32.5(1); the witness statement stands as his evidence in chief: r 32.5(2). The witness may amplify his witness statement at trial: r 32.5(3). See *McPhilemy* v *Times Newspapers* [2000] 1 WLR 1732.

witness summary. A summary of the evidence, if known, which would otherwise be included in a witness statement (q.v.); or, if the evidence is not known, the matters about which the party serving the summary proposes to question the witness. A party who is required to serve a witness statement for use at trial, but is unable to obtain one, may apply, without notice, for permission to serve a witness summary: CPR, r 32.9.

witness summons in criminal proceedings. Where the Crown Court is satisfied that a person is likely to be able to give evidence likely to be material, or produce any document or thing likely to be material, for the purpose of proceedings before the Crown Court, and that person will not voluntarily attend as a witness, or will not voluntarily produce the document or thing, the Crown Court may issue a summons: Criminal Procedure (Attendance of Witnesses) Act 1965, s 2, substituted by C.P.I.A. 1996, s 66. Failure to attend is a contempt. A warrant to arrest a witness who fails to comply with the summons may be issued by the Crown Court: 1965 Act, s 4(1), amended by C.P.I.A. 1996, s 67. See C.P.I.A. 1996 (Commencement) Section 67 Order 1999 (SI 99/716); Crown Court (Misc. Amendment) Rules 1999 (SI 99/598). The obtaining of involuntary disclosure of material from a third party involves a written application by defence, affidavit in support, service of application and affidavit on the court and the relevant third party, a period of seven days from service to notify the court of any opposition to the application hearing.

witness summons under CPR. A document issued by the court, requiring a witness to attend court to give evidence or produce documents to the court. There must be a separate summons for each witness. See r 34.2. Two copies must be filed with the court for sealing: PD 34, para 1.2. Date of issue is that entered on the summons by the court. The court's permission is needed where a party wishes to have a summons issued less than seven days before trial date: r 34.3(2). The court may issue a witness summons in aid of an inferior court or tribunal: r 34.4. A witness summons may be issued by the party himself where he has indicated to the court in writing that he wishes to do so: r 34.6(2).

witness, unfavourable. *See* UNFAVOURABLE WITNESS.

witness warrant. A notice ordering a witness who is required to attend before the Crown Court (q.v.) to attend forthwith or at a time specified in the future. See Criminal Procedure (Attendance of

Witnesses) Act 1965; M.C.A. 1980, s 97 (procuring attendance of witnesses at magistrates' courts), amended by C.P.I.A. 1996, s 51.

witness, zealous. *See* ZEALOUS WITNESS.

woman. A female adult person. In Sex Discrimination Act 1975, s 81(1), the term is used to include a female 'of any age'.

women, abduction of. *See* ABDUCTION.

women, indecent assault on. *See* INDECENT ASSAULT ON WOMEN.

women, procurement of. *See* PROCUREMENT.

words of art. Words which have a particular, fixed legal meaning not generally modified by their context. The phrase describes an expression used by persons skilled in some particular profession, art or science, and which the practitioners clearly understood even if the uninitiated did not: *per* Walker LJ in *Skerrits Ltd v Secretary of State for the Environment* (2000) *The Times*, 8 March (doubt as to whether 'curtilage' (q.v.) could usefully be called a 'term of art'). See, e.g., *Barclays Bank v Cole* [1967] 2 QB 738 (meaning of 'fraud').

words of limitation. *See* LIMITATION, WORDS OF.

words of procreation. *See* PROCREATION, WORDS OF.

words of purchase. *See* PURCHASE, WORDS OF.

words of severance. *See* SEVERANCE, WORDS OF.

words, operative. *See* OPERATIVE WORDS.

words, precatory. *See* PRECATORY WORDS.

words, primary and secondary meanings of. Phrase used in reference to the ordinary and extended meanings of words. 'The first question to ask always is what is the ordinary meaning of [a] word or phrase in its context in the statute. It is only when that meaning leads to some result which cannot reasonably be supposed to have been the intention of the legislature that it is proper to look for some other permissible meaning of the word or phrase': *Pinner v Everett* [1962] 3 All ER 257 ('There is no word the primary meaning of which may not be modified by the context': *per* Griffith CJ in *Nicol v Chant* (1909) 7 CLR 69.) See also *IRC v Hinchy* [1960] AC 748; *Wiltshire v Barrett* [1966] 1 QB 312. 'We have been warned time and again not to substitute other words for the words of a statute. And there is very good reason for that. Few words have exact synonyms. The overtones are almost always different': *per* Denning LJ in *British Launderers' Association v Borough of Hendon* [1949] 1 KB 462.

work. 'Either the labour which a man bestows upon a thing, or the thing upon which the labour is bestowed': *Atkinson v Lumb* [1903] 1 KB 861. 'An employee is "at work" throughout the time when he is in the course of his employment but not otherwise; and the self-employed person is at work throughout such time as he devotes to work as a self-employed person': H.S.W.A. 1974, s 52. See Police (Health and Safety) Act 1997, s 2. See *Manor Bakeries v Nazir* [1996] IRLR 604; *Kazantzis v Chief Adjudication Officer* (1999) 96 (26) LSG 28. 'Working place' means every place at which men are working or may be expected to work: *Hammond v NCB* [1984] 1 WLR 1218.

work done and materials supplied, contracts for. Contracts in which there is an implied condition that work is to be properly done in the manner contemplated and that materials supplied are to be reasonably fit for the purpose contemplated. Example: it was an implied condition that dentures would fit the person for whom they were made (*Samuels v Davis* [1943] 1 KB 526).

worker. An individual who has entered into or works (or has worked) under a contract of employment or any other contract whereby the individual undertakes to do or perform personally any work or services for another party to the contract whose status is not by virtue of the contract that of a client or customer of any profession or business carried on by the individual: E.R.A. 1996, s 230. See also s 43K, inserted by Public Interest Disclosure Act 1998, s 1; *Express and*

Echo Publications v *Tanton* [1999] IRLR 367; SI 00/1551, Part I, para 1. *See* EMPLOYEE; SERVANT.

worker, adult. A worker who has attained the age of 18: SI 98/1833.

worker, part-time. *See* PART-TIME WORKER.

worker, piece and time. A piece worker is one whose contract provides for the remuneration payable to him in respect of work executed by him to be calculated only by reference to piece rates; a time worker is 'a worker other than a piece worker (whether the worker's remuneration is determined by reference to the actual number of hours worked by him or not)': Wages Act 1986, s 26(1).

workers, fixed-term, discrimination against. It was held in *Cure* v *Coutts plc* (2004) *The Times*, 25 October, that the time limit relating to a complaint by a fixed-term employee of less favourable treatment, i.e., non-payment of a non-contractual bonus which was given to permanent employees began to run from the date of the act which was the basis of the complaint.

workers, freedom of movement for. Under the Treaty of Rome 1957, art 48, there is a right to work freely within the territory of member states and this involves 'the abolition of any discrimination based on nationality between the workers of member states [of the EU] as regards employment, remuneration and other conditions of work and employment'. This does not apply to employment in the public service. See *R* v *Pieck* [1981] QB 571.

worker, young. A worker who has attained the age of 15 but not the age of 18 and who is over compulsory school age (construed by reference to Education Act 1996, s 8): SI 98/1833.

work-focused interview. An interview conducted for such purposes connected with employment or training in the case of a person as may be specified, including purposes connected with that person's existing or future employment or training prospects or needs, and (in particular) assisting or encouraging a person

to enhance his employment prospects: S.S. Administration A. 1992, s 2A(8), inserted by W.R.P.A. 1999, s 57. It is intended that the interview shall be a pre-condition to making claims for benefits such as income support, incapacity benefit, housing benefits. See SI 00/1926 (lone parents required to take part in such interviews).

workforce agreement. A written agreement, having effect for a specified period not exceeding five years, applying to all the relevant members of a workforce, or those who belong to a particular group (who undertake a particular function) or belong to a particular department within the employer's business: SI 98/1833, Sch 1.

work-in. A type of industrial action, in which employees occupy their place of work and continue production. Normally trespassory. Injunctions (q.v.) to restrain this type of action can be given.

working families tax credit. Formerly 'family credit'. Benefit under S.S. Contributions and Benefits Act 1992, s 128, substituted by Tax Credits Act 1999, s 1(2). Paid for 26 weeks to a person who is (or whose partner is) engaged and normally engaged in remunerative work, whose income does not exceed the applicable amount, and who is responsible for a child of the same household of which he is a member. *See* TAX CREDITS.

working, flexible. Under Employment Rights Act 1996, s 80F, inserted by Employment Act 2002, s 47 (2), an employee may apply for a change to his terms and conditions of employment where the change relates to hours and times and place where he is required to work, and where his application is intended to enable him to care for a child.

working hours. Under EU Directive 93/104 and SI 98/1833, Part II, reg 4, a worker's maximum working time, including overtime, must not exceed an average of 48 hours for each seven days. Individuals can agree voluntarily to work in excess of this period. See *Gibson* v *E Riding of Yorks DC* [2000] IRLR 598.

working life. The period between (inclusive) the year in which a person attained the age of 16 and (exclusive) the year in which he attained pensionable age or died under that age: S.S.A. 1975, s 27(2).

working time. In relation to a worker, means any period during which he is working, at his employer's disposal and carrying out his activity or duties, any period during which he is receiving relevant training, and any additional period to be treated as working time for purposes of the Working-Time Regulations 1988, under a relevant agreement: SI 98/1833, reg 2. From October 2001, Working Time Regulations (SI 1998/1833) are amended so as to remove qualifying period necessary to receive entitlement to paid annual leave; a worker now has a right to paid annual leave from the first day of his employment.

work in progress. Any services performed in the ordinary course of a trade, the performance of which was partly completed at a material time and for which it would be reasonable to expect that a charge will subsequently be made, and any article produced, and any such material as is used, in the performance of any such services: Finance Act 1981, Sch 9, Part V.

work, stress at. *See* STRESS AT WORK.

work, system of. 'It is the distinction between what is permanent or continuous on the one hand, and what is merely casual . . . It may include the physical lay-out of the job, the setting . . . the sequence in which the work is to be carried out . . . and the issue of special instructions': *per* Lord Greene in *Speed* v *Thomas Swift & Co Ltd* [1943] KB 557. For liability for safety of work equipment, see SI 92/2932; *Stark* v *Post Office* [2000] ICR 1013.

work to rule. *See* GO-SLOW.

World Court. International Court of Justice (q.v.).

worship. 'Worship I take to be something which must have some, at least, of the following characteristics: submission to the object worshipped, veneration of that object, praise, thanksgiving, prayer or intercession': *per* Buckley LJ in *R* v *Registrar General ex p Segerdal* [1970] 3 All ER 886. For 'collective worship' in relation to schools, see Schools Standards and Framework Act 1998, s 70, Sch 20.

wounding. The infliction of an injury which breaks the continuity of the whole skin, internal or external. A scratch or burn is not a wound. See *R* v *Wood* (1830) 4 C & P 381; *C* v *Eisenhower* [1984] QB 331.

wounding, malicious. *See* MALICIOUS WOUNDING.

wounding with intent. It is an offence under O.P.A. 1861, s 18, as amended by C.L.A. 1967, Sch 3, Part III, unlawfully and maliciously by any means whatsoever to wound or cause any grievous bodily harm to any person, with intent to do some grievous bodily harm to any person, or with intent to resist or prevent the lawful apprehension or detainer of any person. See *R* v *Belfon* [1976] 1 WLR 741; *R* v *Pearman* [1985] RTR 39; *A-G's Reference (No. 23 of 1990)* (1990) 12 Cr App R (S) 575; *A-G's Reference (No. 24 of 1998)* [1999] 1 Cr App R (S) 278. *See* MALICIOUS WOUNDING.

wreck. 1. The damage of a ship so that she ceases to be of service. 2. Boats and gear lost or abandoned at sea: Merchant Shipping Act 1995, s 255. 3. 'Jetsam, flotsam, lagan (goods on the sea bed) and derelict found in or on the shores of the sea or any tidal water': s 255.

writ. 1. Instrument under seal issued in the name of the Sovereign, declaring some command. See, e.g., the summons to Parliament by the Queen's writ (by advice of the Privy Council (q.v.)). 2. Order in the name of the Sovereign or court, ordering some action or forbearance from some action. 3. A *judicial writ* was issued by a court to originate some actions. See now 'claim form' (q.v.), in relation to civil procedure.

writing. Term includes printing, lithography, photography and other modes of representation or reproduction of words in a variable form: I.A. 1978, Sch 1. 'Includes any form of notation or code, whether by hand or otherwise and regardless of the method by which, or medium in which, it is recorded': Copyright, Designs and Patents Act 1988, s 178.

wrong. 1. An act contrary to the rules of natural or legal justice. 'Every wrong is an act which is malicious in the eye of the law – an act to which the law attributes harmful consequences': Salmond, *Law of Torts* (1907). 2. To violate the rights of persons. 3. A tort (q.v.) involving the infringement of a right. 4. In the M'Naghten Rules (q.v.) 'wrong means contrary to law and not "wrong" according to the opinion of one man or of a number of people on the question whether a particular act might or might not be justified': *R v Windle* [1952] 2 QB 826.

wrongful credit, dishonestly retaining. A person is guilty of an offence if: a wrongful credit has been made to an account kept by him or in respect of which he has any right or interest; he knows or believes that the credit is wrongful; and he dishonestly fails to take such steps as are reasonable in the circumstances

to secure that the credit is cancelled: Th.A. 1968, s 24A, inserted by Th. (Amendment) A. 1996, s 2(1).

wrongful dismissal. Dismissal of an employee without justification, which is, in effect, a repudiation of the contract. *See* DISMISSAL, UNFAIR.

wrongful interference with goods. *See* INTERFERENCE WITH GOODS, WRONGFUL.

wrongful trading. Under Ins.A. 1986, s 214, a director may be made personally liable by court order for a company's debts if he allows the company to continue trading when he knew or should have known that there was no reasonable prospect of the company being able to avoid liquidation. See *Re Pierson Contractors Ltd* [1999] BCC 26.

WTO. World Trade Organisation. Founded in 1995 as successor to GATT (General Agreement on Tariffs and Trade). It seeks to obtain agreement on a common code of conduct in international trade, to provide a forum for the examination of problems of trade, and to reduce trade barriers. A ministerial conference held every two years controls the organisation.

X

xc. Stock Exchange abbreviation for ex capitalisation.

xd. Stock Exchange abbreviation for ex dividend. *See EX DIV.*

xr. Stock Exchange abbreviation for ex rights (q.v.).

Y

year. A period of 12 calendar months calculated either from 1 January or some other stated day and consisting of 365 days (or 366 in a leap year). See *Gibson* v *Barton* (1875) LR 10 QB 329; *IRC* v *Hobhouse* [1956] 1 WLR 1393; L.G.P.L.A. 1980, s 68(1).

year and day rule. Common-law rule that no person could be convicted of murder or manslaughter 'where the death does not occur within a year and a day after the injury was inflicted, for in that event it must be attributed to some other cause': *per* Lord Alverstone in *R* v *Dyson* [1908] 2 KB 454. Abolished under Law Reform (Year and A Day Rule) Act 1996.

year and thereafter. The expression 'to T for a year and thereafter from year to year' confers a minimum tenancy of two years upon T, i.e., an express term of one year plus a yearly tenancy which may be terminated not earlier than the end of the second year. See *Re Searle* [1912] 1 Ch 610.

Year Books. A series of reports, authors unknown, running from 1282–1536, spanning the reigns of Edward I and Henry VIII. The title is derived from their being grouped under the regnal years of the Sovereigns in whose reigns the cases reported were decided.

year, executor's. *See* EXECUTOR'S YEAR.

year, financial. *See* FINANCIAL YEAR.

year, legal. *See* LEGAL YEAR.

yearly tenancy. *See* TENANT FROM YEAR TO YEAR.

years, estate for. An estate (q.v.) granted for a term of years (q.v.).

year to year. *See* TENANT FROM YEAR TO YEAR.

York–Antwerp rules. Shipping code, formulated in 1877, referring to rules of general average (q.v.) etc., which is usually incorporated in contracts of affreightment (q.v.).

young defendants in Crown Court, trial of. See *Practice Direction (Crown Court: Trial of Children and Young Persons)* (2000) *The Times*, 17 February (published in response to judgment of ECHR in *V* v *UK*; *T* v *UK* (1999) *The Times*, 17 December), under which, e.g., the trial process should not expose a young defendant to avoidable intimidation, humiliation or distress, and all possible steps must be taken to assist defendant to understand and participate in the proceedings.

young man's defence. Defence Under Sexual Offences Act 1956, s 6 (3), in relation to allegation of unlawful sexual intercouse with girl under 16, where defendant is under 24 and has not previously been charged with a like offence and believed her to be 16 or over and had reasonable cause for that belief, is neither discriminatory nor disproportionate nor incompatible with Human Rights Convention, arts 6, 14: *R* v *Kirk* (2002) *The Times*, 26 June.

young offenders, power to detain for specified periods. Under P.C.C.(S.)C.A. 2000, s 91, in the case of persons under 18, convicted on indictment of an offence punishable in the case of a person over 21 with 14 years' imprisonment, or under S.O.A. 1956, ss 14, 15, the court may sentence the offender to detention for a period not exceeding the maximum term of imprisonment with which the offence is punishable in the case of a person aged 21 or over. See also 2000 Act, ss 100–192.

young offenders, referral orders. The court has a duty to refer to a youth offender panel, a person under 18, where neither the offence nor any connected one involves a sentence fixed by law, and where the court is not proposing to impose a custodial offence or make a hospital order or to discharge him absolutely, and the compulsory referral conditions are satisfied: P.C.C.(S.)A. 2000, s 16(1), (2). For discretionary referral, see s 16(3). Compulsory referral conditions are: offender has pleaded guilty, has never been convicted by a court in UK of any offence other than the one under consideration, and has never been bound over to keep the peace: s 17(1).

young offenders, remission for sentence. Where a child or young person (aged under 18) is convicted of an offence other than homicide, the court may (or, if not a youth court, must) remit the case to a youth court for sentence: P.C.C.(S.)A. 2000, s 8. When the offender attains the age of 18, the case must be remitted by a youth court to a magistrates' court for sentence: s 9.

young person. One who has reached 14 and is under 18: P.C.C.(S.)A. 2000, s 163. Under Factories Act 1961, one over compulsory school age, but not yet 18. *See* CHILD.

youth courts. Formerly 'juvenile courts'. They are, in general, magistrates' courts exercising jurisdiction over offences committed by, and other matters related to, children and young persons. They consist of a chairman and other justices. See C.D.A. 1998, s 48 (power of district judges (magistrates' courts) to sit alone in a youth court sitting in the Inner London area); s 47 (power of youth courts to remit cases to other courts). See also C.&Y.P.A. 1933, Sch, amended by Acc.J.A. 1999, Sch 11, para 12. See *R v Birmingham Justices ex p F* (2000) 164 JP 523.

youth justice. SI 04/299, made under the Youth Justice and Criminal Evidence Act 1999, ss 64, 68, has brought into force a number of provisions of the 1999 Act, in particular s 29, which involves applications for a Special Measures Direction for an intermediary.

Youth Justice Board. Body corporate set up under C.D.A. 1998, s 41, comprising 10–12 members appointed by Secretary of State, and including persons 'who have extensive recent experience of the youth justice system'. Functions include the monitoring of the youth justice system and provision of youth justice services, identifying and promoting good practice in the youth justice system and commissioning appropriate research. See Sch 2.

youth justice system, aim and organisation of. The youth justice system is 'the system of criminal justice in so far as it relates to children and young persons': C.D.A. 1998, s 37. The principal aim of the system is to prevent offending by children and young persons: s 37. Local authorities have the duty to ensure that all youth justice services (see s 38(4)) are available in their areas. The chief officer of police, police authority, health authority, and probation committee have the duty to work together in the discharge by the local authority of its duty: s 38(1), (2).

youth offender contract. Agreement by offender (under 18) with youth offender panel (q.v.) on a programme of behaviour, the aim of which is the prevention of reoffending by the offender. It may include provision for reparations, mediation sessions with victim, unpaid community service, curfew, rehabilitation programme related to alcohol or drugs. See P.C.C.(S.)A. 2000, s 23.

youth offender panels. Where an offender under 18 is made the subject of a referral order, it becomes the duty of the youth offending team (q.v.) to establish a panel, consisting of at least one member of the team and two non-members, which will seek to agree a youth offender contract (q.v.) with the offender. Where the panel decides that the offender has complied satisfactorily with the contract, the referral order is effectively discharged, otherwise the offender is referred back to the appropriate court: P.C.C.(S.)A. 2000, s 21.

youth offending teams. Groups responsible for implementing referral orders and for arranging for provision of administrative staff, accommodation, required by youth offender panels (q.v.). They arrange for supervision of offenders' compliance with the terms of the youth offender contracts (q.v.): P.C.C.(S.)A. 2000, s 29.

Z

zealous witness. A witness who attempts to give evidence in a manner which makes it as partial and favourable as possible for a party to the proceedings. *See* WITNESS.

zebra crossing. A road crossing, the presence and limits of which are indicated in accordance with the provisions of SI 97/2400 (Zebra, Pelican and Puffin Pedestrian Crossings Regulations and General Directions). See SI 99/1750. An 'uncontrolled zebra crossing' is a zebra crossing at which traffic is not for the time being controlled by a police constable in uniform or by a traffic warden. See *Connor* v *Paterson* [1977] 1 All ER 516.

zero rating. Term used in the administration of value-added tax (q.v.) to indicate that no tax is levied on certain goods sold to final customers and that any tax charged on an input used to produce those goods can be recovered. Principal zero-rated categories include exports, books (see *Customs and Excise* v *Colour Offset* [1995] STC 85) and newspapers. See Value Added Tax Acts 1983, 1994; SI 97/1836; Finance Act 1997, ss 33, 34. In *Customs and Excise Commissioners v Zelinski Baker and Partners* [2004] 1 WLR 707, the HL held that where listed buildings are involved, the benefit of a zero rating for purpose of VAT Act 1994, Sch 8, Group 6, Item 2, will be available only in relation to buildings which are intended to be used for residential purposes. See also Planning (Listed Buildings and Conservation Areas) Act 1990, s 1(5).

zero tolerance. Colloquialism referring to the essential feature of a law-enforcement regime characterised by a policy of strict policing and intensive and methodical application of the law.

zone, Scottish. The sea within British fishery limits (that is, the limits set by or under the Fishing Limits Act 1976, s 1) which is adjacent to Scotland: Scotland Act 1998, s 126.

zones, education action. *See* EDUCATION ACTION ZONES.

zones, enterprise. *See* ENTERPRISE ZONES.

zones, exclusion, shipping, temporary. *See* EXCLUSION ZONES, SHIPPING, TEMPORARY.

zones, simplified planning. Introduced under H.&P.A. 1986, Part III and Sch 6. Local planning authorities may grant general planning permission for an SPZ, and developers may then undertake development up to the parameters of the scheme without need for further planning permission. See T.C.P.A. 1990, s 82; Planning and Compensation Act 1991, Sch 5. Land in a National Park (q.v.) or conservation area may not be included in an SPZ: 1990 Act, s 87.

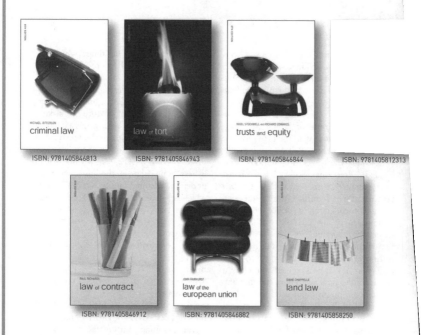